Lecture Notes in Computer Science 8691

Commenced Publication in 1973
Founding and Former Series Editors:
Gerhard Goos, Juris Hartmanis, and Jan van Leeuwen

David Fleet   Tomas Pajdla   Bernt Schiele
Tinne Tuytelaars (Eds.)

Computer Vision – ECCV 2014

13th European Conference
Zurich, Switzerland, September 6-12, 2014
Proceedings, Part III

 Springer

Volume Editors

David Fleet
University of Toronto, Department of Computer Science
6 King's College Road, Toronto, ON M5H 3S5, Canada
E-mail: fleet@cs.toronto.edu

Tomas Pajdla
Czech Technical University in Prague, Department of Cybernetics
Technicka 2, 166 27 Prague 6, Czech Republic
E-mail: pajdla@cmp.felk.cvut.cz

Bernt Schiele
Max-Planck-Institut für Informatik
Campus E1 4, 66123 Saarbrücken, Germany
E-mail: schiele@mpi-inf.mpg.de

Tinne Tuytelaars
KU Leuven, ESAT - PSI, iMinds
Kasteelpark Arenberg 10, Bus 2441, 3001 Leuven, Belgium
E-mail: tinne.tuytelaars@esat.kuleuven.be

ISSN 0302-9743   e-ISSN 1611-3349
ISBN 978-3-319-10577-2   e-ISBN 978-3-319-10578-9
DOI 10.1007/978-3-319-10578-9
Springer Cham Heidelberg New York Dordrecht London

Library of Congress Control Number: 2014946360

LNCS Sublibrary: SL 6 – Image Processing, Computer Vision, Pattern Recognition,
and Graphics

Typesetting: Camera-ready by author, data conversion by Scientific Publishing Services, Chennai, India

Printed on acid-free paper

Springer is part of Springer Science+Business Media (www.springer.com)

Foreword

The European Conference on Computer Vision is one of the top conferences in computer vision. It was first held in 1990 in Antibes (France) with subsequent conferences in Santa Margherita Ligure (Italy) in 1992, Stockholm (Sweden) in 1994, Cambridge (UK) in 1996, Freiburg (Germany) in 1998, Dublin (Ireland) in 2000, Copenhagen (Denmark) in 2002, Prague (Czech Republic) in 2004, Graz (Austria) in 2006, Marseille (France) in 2008, Heraklion (Greece) in 2010, and Florence (Italy) in 2012. Many people have worked hard to turn the 2014 edition into as great a success. We hope you will find this a mission accomplished.

The chairs decided to adhere to the classic single-track scheme. In terms of the time ordering, we decided to largely follow the Florence example (typically starting with poster sessions, followed by oral sessions), which offers a lot of flexibility to network and is more forgiving for the not-so-early-birds and hard-core gourmets.

A large conference like ECCV requires the help of many. They made sure there was a full program including the main conference, tutorials, workshops, exhibits, demos, proceedings, video streaming/archive, and Web descriptions. We want to cordially thank all those volunteers! Please have a look at the conference website to see their names (http://eccv2014.org/people/). We also thank our generous sponsors. Their support was vital for keeping prices low and enriching the program. And it is good to see such a level of industrial interest in what our community is doing!

We hope you will enjoy the proceedings ECCV 2014.

Also, willkommen in Zürich!

September 2014   Marc Pollefeys
                                                                            Luc Van Gool
                                                                          General Chairs

Preface

Welcome to the proceedings of the 2014 European Conference on Computer Vision (ECCV 2014) that was in Zurich, Switzerland. We are delighted to present this volume reflecting a strong and exciting program, the result of an extensive review process. In total, we received 1,444 paper submissions. Of these, 85 violated the ECCV submission guidelines and were rejected without review. Of the remainder, 363 were accepted (26,7%): 325 as posters (23,9%) and 38 as oral presentations (2,8%). This selection process was a combined effort of four program co-chairs (PCs), 53 area chairs (ACs), 803 Program Committee members and 247 additional reviewers.

As PCs we were primarily responsible for the design and execution of the review process. Beyond administrative rejections, we were not directly involved in acceptance decisions. Because the general co-chairs were permitted to submit papers, they played no role in the review process and were treated as any other author.

Acceptance decisions were made by the AC Committee. There were 53 ACs in total, selected by the PCs to provide sufficient technical expertise, geographical diversity (21 from Europe, 7 from Asia, and 25 from North America) and a mix of AC experience (7 had no previous AC experience, 18 had served as AC of a major international vision conference once since 2010, 8 had served twice, 13 had served three times, and 7 had served 4 times).

ACs were aided by 803 Program Committee members to whom papers were assigned for reviewing. There were 247 additional reviewers, each supervised by a Program Committee member. The Program Committee was based on suggestions from ACs, and committees from previous conferences. Google Scholar profiles were collected for all candidate Program Committee members and vetted by PCs. Having a large pool of Program Committee members for reviewing allowed us to match expertise while bounding reviewer loads. No more than nine papers were assigned to any one Program Committee member, with a maximum of six to graduate students.

The ECCV 2014 review process was double blind. Authors did not know the reviewers' identities, nor the ACs handling their paper(s). We did our utmost to ensure that ACs and reviewers did not know authors' identities, even though anonymity becomes difficult to maintain as more and more submissions appear concurrently on arXiv.org.

Particular attention was paid to minimizing potential conflicts of interest. Conflicts of interest between ACs, Program Committee members, and papers were based on authorship of ECCV 2014 submissions, on their home institutions, and on previous collaborations. To find institutional conflicts, all authors,

Program Committee members, and ACs were asked to list the Internet domains of their current institutions. To find collaborators, the DBLP (www.dblp.org) database was used to find any co-authored papers in the period 2010–2014.

We initially assigned approximately 100 papers to each AC, based on affinity scores from the Toronto Paper Matching System and authors' AC suggestions. ACs then bid on these, indicating their level of expertise. Based on these bids, and conflicts of interest, approximately 27 papers were assigned to each AC, for which they would act as the primary AC. The primary AC then suggested seven reviewers from the pool of Program Committee members (in rank order) for each paper, from which three were chosen per paper, taking load balancing and conflicts of interest into account.

Many papers were also assigned a secondary AC, either directly by the PCs, or as a consequence of the primary AC requesting the aid of an AC with complementary expertise. Secondary ACs could be assigned at any stage in the process, but in most cases this occurred about two weeks before the final AC meeting. Hence, in addition to their initial load of approximately 27 papers, each AC was asked to handle three to five more papers as a secondary AC; they were expected to read and write a short assessment of such papers. In addition, two of the 53 ACs were not directly assigned papers. Rather, they were available throughout the process to aid other ACs at any stage (e.g., with decisions, evaluating technical issues, additional reviews, etc.).

The initial reviewing period was three weeks long, after which reviewers provided reviews with preliminary recommendations. Three weeks is somewhat shorter than normal, but this did not seem to cause any unusual problems. With the generous help of several last-minute reviewers, each paper received three reviews.

Authors were then given the opportunity to rebut the reviews, primarily to identify any factual errors. Following this, reviewers and ACs discussed papers at length, after which reviewers finalized their reviews and gave a final recommendation to the ACs. Many ACs requested help from secondary ACs at this time.

Papers, for which rejection was clear and certain, based on the reviews and the AC's assessment, were identified by their primary ACs and vetted by a shadow AC prior to rejection. (These shadow ACs were assigned by the PCs.) All papers with any chance of acceptance were further discussed at the AC meeting. Those deemed "strong" by primary ACs (about 140 in total) were also assigned a secondary AC.

The AC meeting, with all but two of the primary ACs present, took place in Zurich. ACs were divided into 17 triplets for each morning, and a different set of triplets for each afternoon. Given the content of the three (or more) reviews along with reviewer recommendations, rebuttals, online discussions among reviewers and primary ACs, written input from and discussions with secondary ACs, the

AC triplets then worked together to resolve questions, calibrate assessments, and make acceptance decisions.

To select oral presentations, all strong papers, along with any others put forward by triplets (about 155 in total), were then discussed in four panels, each comprising four or five triplets. Each panel ranked these oral candidates, using four categories. Papers in the two top categories provided the final set of 38 oral presentations.

We want to thank everyone involved in making the ECCV 2014 Program possible. First and foremost, the success of ECCV 2014 depended on the quality of papers submitted by authors, and on the very hard work of the reviewers, the Program Committee members and the ACs. We are particularly grateful to Kyros Kutulakos for his enormous software support before and during the AC meeting, to Laurent Charlin for the use of the Toronto Paper Matching System, and Chaohui Wang for help optimizing the assignment of papers to ACs. We also owe a debt of gratitude for the great support of Zurich local organizers, especially Susanne Keller and her team.

September 2014   David Fleet
                                                       Tomas Pajdla
                                                      Bernt Schiele
                                                    Tinne Tuytelaars

Organization

General Chairs

Luc Van Gool   ETH Zurich, Switzerland
Marc Pollefeys   ETH Zurich, Switzerland

Program Chairs

Tinne Tuytelaars   KU Leuven, Belgium
Bernt Schiele   MPI Informatics, Saarbrücken, Germany
Tomas Pajdla   CTU Prague, Czech Republic
David Fleet   University of Toronto, Canada

Local Arrangements Chairs

Konrad Schindler   ETH Zurich, Switzerland
Vittorio Ferrari   University of Edinburgh, UK

Workshop Chairs

Lourdes Agapito   University College London, UK
Carsten Rother   TU Dresden, Germany
Michael Bronstein   University of Lugano, Switzerland

Tutorial Chairs

Bastian Leibe   RWTH Aachen, Germany
Paolo Favaro   University of Bern, Switzerland
Christoph Lampert   IST Austria

Poster Chair

Helmut Grabner   ETH Zurich, Switzerland

Publication Chairs

Mario Fritz   MPI Informatics, Saarbrücken, Germany
Michael Stark   MPI Informatics, Saarbrücken, Germany

Demo Chairs

Davide Scaramuzza   University of Zurich, Switzerland
Jan-Michael Frahm   University of North Carolina at Chapel Hill,
                         USA

Exhibition Chair

Tamar Tolcachier   University of Zurich, Switzerland

Industrial Liaison Chairs

Alexander Sorkine-Hornung   Disney Research Zurich, Switzerland
Fatih Porikli   ANU, Australia

Student Grant Chair

Seon Joo Kim   Yonsei University, Korea

Air Shelters Accommodation Chair

Maros Blaha   ETH Zurich, Switzerland

Website Chairs

Lorenz Meier   ETH Zurich, Switzerland
Bastien Jacquet   ETH Zurich, Switzerland

Internet Chair

Thorsten Steenbock   ETH Zurich, Switzerland

Student Volunteer Chairs

Andrea Cohen   ETH Zurich, Switzerland
Ralf Dragon   ETH Zurich, Switzerland
Laura Leal-Taixé   ETH Zurich, Switzerland

Finance Chair

Amael Delaunoy   ETH Zurich, Switzerland

Conference Coordinator

Susanne H. Keller   ETH Zurich, Switzerland

Area Chairs

Lourdes Agapito	University College London, UK
Sameer Agarwal	Google Research, USA
Shai Avidan	Tel Aviv University, Israel
Alex Berg	UNC Chapel Hill, USA
Yuri Boykov	University of Western Ontario, Canada
Thomas Brox	University of Freiburg, Germany
Jason Corso	SUNY at Buffalo, USA
Trevor Darrell	UC Berkeley, USA
Fernando de la Torre	Carnegie Mellon University, USA
Frank Dellaert	Georgia Tech, USA
Alexei Efros	UC Berkeley, USA
Vittorio Ferrari	University of Edinburgh, UK
Andrew Fitzgibbon	Microsoft Research, Cambridge, UK
JanMichael Frahm	UNC Chapel Hill, USA
Bill Freeman	Massachusetts Institute of Technology, USA
Peter Gehler	Max Planck Institute for Intelligent Systems, Germany
Kristen Graumann	University of Texas at Austin, USA
Wolfgang Heidrich	University of British Columbia, Canada
Herve Jegou	Inria Rennes, France
Fredrik Kahl	Lund University, Sweden
Kyros Kutulakos	University of Toronto, Canada
Christoph Lampert	IST Austria
Ivan Laptev	Inria Paris, France
Kyuong Mu Lee	Seoul National University, South Korea
Bastian Leibe	RWTH Aachen, Germany
Vincent Lepetit	TU Graz, Austria
Hongdong Li	Australian National University
David Lowe	University of British Columbia, Canada
Greg Mori	Simon Fraser University, Canada
Srinivas Narasimhan	Carnegie Mellon University, PA, USA
Nassir Navab	TU Munich, Germany
Ko Nishino	Drexel University, USA
Maja Pantic	Imperial College London, UK
Patrick Perez	Technicolor Research, Rennes, France
Pietro Perona	California Institute of Technology, USA
Ian Reid	University of Adelaide, Australia
Stefan Roth	TU Darmstadt, Germany
Carsten Rother	TU Dresden, Germany
Sudeep Sarkar	University of South Florida, USA
Silvio Savarese	Stanford University, USA
Christoph Schnoerr	Heidelberg University, Germany
Jamie Shotton	Microsoft Research, Cambridge, UK

Kaleem Siddiqi	McGill, Canada
Leonid Sigal	Disney Research, Pittsburgh, PA, USA
Noah Snavely	Cornell, USA
Raquel Urtasun	University of Toronto, Canada
Andrea Vedaldi	University of Oxford, UK
Jakob Verbeek	Inria Rhone-Alpes, France
Xiaogang Wang	Chinese University of Hong Kong, SAR China
Ming-Hsuan Yang	UC Merced, CA, USA
Lihi Zelnik-Manor	Technion, Israel
Song-Chun Zhu	UCLA, USA
Todd Zickler	Harvard, USA

Program Committee

Gaurav Aggarwal	Joao Barreto	Kristin Branson
Amit Agrawal	Jonathan Barron	Steven Branson
Haizhou Ai	Adrien Bartoli	Francois Bremond
Ijaz Akhter	Arslan Basharat	Michael Bronstein
Karteek Alahari	Dhruv Batra	Gabriel Brostow
Alexandre Alahi	Luis Baumela	Michael Brown
Andrea Albarelli	Maximilian Baust	Matthew Brown
Saad Ali	Jean-Charles Bazin	Marcus Brubaker
Jose M. Alvarez	Loris Bazzani	Andres Bruhn
Juan Andrade-Cetto	Chris Beall	Joan Bruna
Bjoern Andres	Vasileios Belagiannis	Aurelie Bugeau
Mykhaylo Andriluka	Csaba Beleznai	Darius Burschka
Elli Angelopoulou	Moshe Ben-ezra	Ricardo Cabral
Roland Angst	Ohad Ben-Shahar	Jian-Feng Cai
Relja Arandjelovic	Ismail Ben Ayed	Neill D.F. Campbell
Ognjen Arandjelovic	Rodrigo Benenson	Yong Cao
Helder Araujo	Ryad Benosman	Barbara Caputo
Pablo Arbelez	Tamara Berg	Joao Carreira
Vasileios Argyriou	Margrit Betke	Jan Cech
Antonis Argyros	Ross Beveridge	Jinxiang Chai
Kalle Astroem	Bir Bhanu	Ayan Chakrabarti
Vassilis Athitsos	Horst Bischof	Tat-Jen Cham
Yannis Avrithis	Arijit Biswas	Antoni Chan
Yusuf Aytar	Andrew Blake	Manmohan Chandraker
Xiang Bai	Aaron Bobick	Vijay Chandrasekhar
Luca Ballan	Piotr Bojanowski	Hong Chang
Yingze Bao	Ali Borji	Ming-Ching Chang
Richard Baraniuk	Terrance Boult	Rama Chellappa
Adrian Barbu	Lubomir Bourdev	Chao-Yeh Chen
Kobus Barnard	Patrick Bouthemy	David Chen
Connelly Barnes	Edmond Boyer	Hwann-Tzong Chen

Tsuhan Chen	Anthony Dick	David Fofi
Xilin Chen	Ajay Divakaran	Wolfgang Foerstner
Chao Chen	Santosh Kumar Divvala	David Forsyth
Longbin Chen	Minh Do	Katerina Fragkiadaki
Minhua Chen	Carl Doersch	Jean-Sebastien Franco
Anoop Cherian	Piotr Dollar	Friedrich Fraundorfer
Liang-Tien Chia	Bin Dong	Mario Fritz
Tat-Jun Chin	Weisheng Dong	Yun Fu
Sunghyun Cho	Michael Donoser	Pascal Fua
Minsu Cho	Gianfranco Doretto	Hironobu Fujiyoshi
Nam Ik Cho	Matthijs Douze	Yasutaka Furukawa
Wongun Choi	Bruce Draper	Ryo Furukawa
Mario Christoudias	Mark Drew	Andrea Fusiello
Wen-Sheng Chu	Bertram Drost	Fabio Galasso
Yung-Yu Chuang	Lixin Duan	Juergen Gall
Ondrej Chum	Jean-Luc Dugelay	Andrew Gallagher
James Clark	Enrique Dunn	David Gallup
Brian Clipp	Pinar Duygulu	Arvind Ganesh
Isaac Cohen	Jan-Olof Eklundh	Dashan Gao
John Collomosse	James H. Elder	Shenghua Gao
Bob Collins	Ian Endres	James Gee
Tim Cootes	Olof Enqvist	Andreas Geiger
David Crandall	Markus Enzweiler	Yakup Genc
Antonio Criminisi	Aykut Erdem	Bogdan Georgescu
Naresh Cuntoor	Anders Eriksson	Guido Gerig
Qieyun Dai	Ali Eslami	David Geronimo
Jifeng Dai	Irfan Essa	Theo Gevers
Kristin Dana	Francisco Estrada	Bernard Ghanem
Kostas Daniilidis	Bin Fan	Andrew Gilbert
Larry Davis	Quanfu Fan	Ross Girshick
Andrew Davison	Jialue Fan	Martin Godec
Goksel Dedeoglu	Sean Fanello	Guy Godin
Koichiro Deguchi	Ali Farhadi	Roland Goecke
Alberto Del Bimbo	Giovanni Farinella	Michael Goesele
Alessio Del Bue	Ryan Farrell	Alvina Goh
Hervé Delingette	Alireza Fathi	Bastian Goldluecke
Andrew Delong	Paolo Favaro	Boqing Gong
Stefanie Demirci	Michael Felsberg	Yunchao Gong
David Demirdjian	Pedro Felzenszwalb	Raghuraman Gopalan
Jia Deng	Rob Fergus	Albert Gordo
Joachim Denzler	Basura Fernando	Lena Gorelick
Konstantinos Derpanis	Frank Ferrie	Paulo Gotardo
Thomas Deselaers	Sanja Fidler	Stephen Gould
Frederic Devernay	Boris Flach	Venu Madhav Govindu
Michel Dhome	Francois Fleuret	Helmut Grabner

Roger Grosse
Matthias Grundmann
Chunhui Gu
Xianfeng Gu
Jinwei Gu
Sergio Guadarrama
Matthieu Guillaumin
Jean-Yves Guillemaut
Hatice Gunes
Ruiqi Guo
Guodong Guo
Abhinav Gupta
Abner Guzman Rivera
Gregory Hager
Ghassan Hamarneh
Bohyung Han
Tony Han
Jari Hannuksela
Tatsuya Harada
Mehrtash Harandi
Bharath Hariharan
Stefan Harmeling
Tal Hassner
Daniel Hauagge
Søren Hauberg
Michal Havlena
James Hays
Kaiming He
Xuming He
Martial Hebert
Felix Heide
Jared Heinly
Hagit Hel-Or
Lionel Heng
Philipp Hennig
Carlos Hernandez
Aaron Hertzmann
Adrian Hilton
David Hogg
Derek Hoiem
Byung-Woo Hong
Anthony Hoogs
Joachim Hornegger
Timothy Hospedales
Wenze Hu

Zhe Hu
Gang Hua
Xian-Sheng Hua
Dong Huang
Gary Huang
Heng Huang
Sung Ju Hwang
Wonjun Hwang
Ivo Ihrke
Nazli Ikizler-Cinbis
Slobodan Ilic
Horace Ip
Michal Irani
Hiroshi Ishikawa
Laurent Itti
Nathan Jacobs
Max Jaderberg
Omar Javed
C.V. Jawahar
Bruno Jedynak
Hueihan Jhuang
Qiang Ji
Hui Ji
Kui Jia
Yangqing Jia
Jiaya Jia
Hao Jiang
Zhuolin Jiang
Sam Johnson
Neel Joshi
Armand Joulin
Frederic Jurie
Ioannis Kakadiaris
Zdenek Kalal
Amit Kale
Joni-Kristian
  Kamarainen
George Kamberov
Kenichi Kanatani
Sing Bing Kang
Vadim Kantorov
Jörg Hendrik Kappes
Leonid Karlinsky
Zoltan Kato
Hiroshi Kawasaki

Verena Kaynig
Cem Keskin
Margret Keuper
Daniel Keysers
Sameh Khamis
Fahad Khan
Saad Khan
Aditya Khosla
Martin Kiefel
Gunhee Kim
Jaechul Kim
Seon Joo Kim
Tae-Kyun Kim
Byungsoo Kim
Benjamin Kimia
Kris Kitani
Hedvig Kjellstrom
Laurent Kneip
Reinhard Koch
Kevin Koeser
Ullrich Koethe
Effrosyni Kokiopoulou
Iasonas Kokkinos
Kalin Kolev
Vladimir Kolmogorov
Vladlen Koltun
Nikos Komodakis
Piotr Koniusz
Peter Kontschieder
Ender Konukoglu
Sanjeev Koppal
Hema Koppula
Andreas Koschan
Jana Kosecka
Adriana Kovashka
Adarsh Kowdle
Josip Krapac
Dilip Krishnan
Zuzana Kukelova
Brian Kulis
Neeraj Kumar
M. Pawan Kumar
Cheng-Hao Kuo
In So Kweon
Junghyun Kwon

Junseok Kwon
Simon Lacoste-Julien
Shang-Hong Lai
Jean-François Lalonde
Tian Lan
Michael Langer
Doug Lanman
Diane Larlus
Longin Jan Latecki
Svetlana Lazebnik
Laura Leal-Taixé
Erik Learned-Miller
Honglak Lee
Yong Jae Lee
Ido Leichter
Victor Lempitsky
Frank Lenzen
Marius Leordeanu
Thomas Leung
Maxime Lhuillier
Chunming Li
Fei-Fei Li
Fuxin Li
Rui Li
Li-Jia Li
Chia-Kai Liang
Shengcai Liao
Joerg Liebelt
Jongwoo Lim
Joseph Lim
Ruei-Sung Lin
Yen-Yu Lin
Zhouchen Lin
Liang Lin
Haibin Ling
James Little
Baiyang Liu
Ce Liu
Feng Liu
Guangcan Liu
Jingen Liu
Wei Liu
Zicheng Liu
Zongyi Liu
Tyng-Luh Liu

Xiaoming Liu
Xiaobai Liu
Ming-Yu Liu
Marcus Liwicki
Stephen Lombardi
Roberto Lopez-Sastre
Manolis Lourakis
Brian Lovell
Chen Change Loy
Jiangbo Lu
Jiwen Lu
Simon Lucey
Jiebo Luo
Ping Luo
Marcus Magnor
Vijay Mahadevan
Julien Mairal
Michael Maire
Subhransu Maji
Atsuto Maki
Yasushi Makihara
Roberto Manduchi
Luca Marchesotti
Aleix Martinez
Bogdan Matei
Diana Mateus
Stefan Mathe
Yasuyuki Matsushita
Iain Matthews
Kevin Matzen
Bruce Maxwell
Stephen Maybank
Walterio Mayol-Cuevas
David McAllester
Gerard Medioni
Christopher Mei
Paulo Mendonca
Thomas Mensink
Domingo Mery
Ajmal Mian
Branislav Micusik
Ondrej Miksik
Anton Milan
Majid Mirmehdi
Anurag Mittal

Hossein Mobahi
Pranab Mohanty
Pascal Monasse
Vlad Morariu
Philippos Mordohai
Francesc Moreno-Noguer
Luce Morin
Nigel Morris
Bryan Morse
Eric Mortensen
Yasuhiro Mukaigawa
Lopamudra Mukherjee
Vittorio Murino
David Murray
Sobhan Naderi Parizi
Hajime Nagahara
Laurent Najman
Karthik Nandakumar
Fabian Nater
Jan Neumann
Lukas Neumann
Ram Nevatia
Richard Newcombe
Minh Hoai Nguyen
Bingbing Ni
Feiping Nie
Juan Carlos Niebles
Marc Niethammer
Claudia Nieuwenhuis
Mark Nixon
Mohammad Norouzi
Sebastian Nowozin
Matthew O'Toole
Peter Ochs
Jean-Marc Odobez
Francesca Odone
Eyal Ofek
Sangmin Oh
Takahiro Okabe
Takayuki Okatani
Aude Oliva
Carl Olsson
Bjorn Ommer
Magnus Oskarsson
Wanli Ouyang

Geoffrey Oxholm
Mustafa Ozuysal
Nicolas Padoy
Caroline Pantofaru
Nicolas Papadakis
George Papandreou
Nikolaos
    Papanikolopoulos
Nikos Paragios
Devi Parikh
Dennis Park
Vishal Patel
Ioannis Patras
Vladimir Pavlovic
Kim Pedersen
Marco Pedersoli
Shmuel Peleg
Marcello Pelillo
Tingying Peng
A.G. Amitha Perera
Alessandro Perina
Federico Pernici
Florent Perronnin
Vladimir Petrovic
Tomas Pfister
Jonathon Phillips
Justus Piater
Massimo Piccardi
Hamed Pirsiavash
Leonid Pishchulin
Robert Pless
Thomas Pock
Jean Ponce
Gerard Pons-Moll
Ronald Poppe
Andrea Prati
Victor Prisacariu
Kari Pulli
Yu Qiao
Lei Qin
Novi Quadrianto
Rahul Raguram
Varun Ramakrishna
Srikumar Ramalingam
Narayanan Ramanathan

Konstantinos
    Rapantzikos
Michalis Raptis
Nalini Ratha
Avinash Ravichandran
Michael Reale
Dikpal Reddy
James Rehg
Jan Reininghaus
Xiaofeng Ren
Jerome Revaud
Morteza Rezanejad
Hayko Riemenschneider
Tammy Riklin Raviv
Antonio Robles-Kelly
Erik Rodner
Emanuele Rodola
Mikel Rodriguez
Marcus Rohrbach
Javier Romero
Charles Rosenberg
Bodo Rosenhahn
Arun Ross
Samuel Rota Bul
Peter Roth
Volker Roth
Anastasios Roussos
Sebastien Roy
Michael Rubinstein
Olga Russakovsky
Bryan Russell
Michael S. Ryoo
Mohammad Amin
    Sadeghi
Kate Saenko
Albert Ali Salah
Imran Saleemi
Mathieu Salzmann
Conrad Sanderson
Aswin
    Sankaranarayanan
Benjamin Sapp
Radim Sara
Scott Satkin
Imari Sato

Yoichi Sato
Bogdan Savchynskyy
Hanno Scharr
Daniel Scharstein
Yoav Y. Schechner
Walter Scheirer
Kevin Schelten
Frank Schmidt
Uwe Schmidt
Julia Schnabel
Alexander Schwing
Nicu Sebe
Shishir Shah
Mubarak Shah
Shiguang Shan
Qi Shan
Ling Shao
Abhishek Sharma
Viktoriia Sharmanska
Eli Shechtman
Yaser Sheikh
Alexander Shekhovtsov
Chunhua Shen
Li Shen
Yonggang Shi
Qinfeng Shi
Ilan Shimshoni
Takaaki Shiratori
Abhinav Shrivastava
Behjat Siddiquie
Nathan Silberman
Karen Simonyan
Richa Singh
Vikas Singh
Sudipta Sinha
Josef Sivic
Dirk Smeets
Arnold Smeulders
William Smith
Cees Snoek
Eric Sommerlade
Alexander
    Sorkine-Hornung
Alvaro Soto
Richard Souvenir

Anuj Srivastava
Ioannis Stamos
Michael Stark
Chris Stauffer
Bjorn Stenger
Charles Stewart
Rainer Stiefelhagen
Juergen Sturm
Yusuke Sugano
Josephine Sullivan
Deqing Sun
Min Sun
Hari Sundar
Ganesh Sundaramoorthi
Kalyan Sunkavalli
Sabine Süsstrunk
David Suter
Tomas Svoboda
Rahul Swaminathan
Tanveer
  Syeda-Mahmood
Rick Szeliski
Raphael Sznitman
Yuichi Taguchi
Yu-Wing Tai
Jun Takamatsu
Hugues Talbot
Ping Tan
Robby Tan
Kevin Tang
Huixuan Tang
Danhang Tang
Marshall Tappen
Jean-Philippe Tarel
Danny Tarlow
Gabriel Taubin
Camillo Taylor
Demetri Terzopoulos
Christian Theobalt
Yuandong Tian
Joseph Tighe
Radu Timofte
Massimo Tistarelli
George Toderici
Sinisa Todorovic

Giorgos Tolias
Federico Tombari
Tatiana Tommasi
Yan Tong
Akihiko Torii
Antonio Torralba
Lorenzo Torresani
Andrea Torsello
Tali Treibitz
Rudolph Triebel
Bill Triggs
Roberto Tron
Tomasz Trzcinski
Ivor Tsang
Yanghai Tsin
Zhuowen Tu
Tony Tung
Pavan Turaga
Engin Türetken
Oncel Tuzel
Georgios Tzimiropoulos
Norimichi Ukita
Martin Urschler
Arash Vahdat
Julien Valentin
Michel Valstar
Koen van de Sande
Joost van de Weijer
Anton van den Hengel
Jan van Gemert
Daniel Vaquero
Kiran Varanasi
Mayank Vatsa
Ashok Veeraraghavan
Olga Veksler
Alexander Vezhnevets
Rene Vidal
Sudheendra
  Vijayanarasimhan
Jordi Vitria
Christian Vogler
Carl Vondrick
Sven Wachsmuth
Stefan Walk
Chaohui Wang

Jingdong Wang
Jue Wang
Ruiping Wang
Kai Wang
Liang Wang
Xinggang Wang
Xin-Jing Wang
Yang Wang
Heng Wang
Yu-Chiang Frank Wang
Simon Warfield
Yichen Wei
Yair Weiss
Gordon Wetzstein
Oliver Whyte
Richard Wildes
Christopher Williams
Lior Wolf
Kwan-Yee Kenneth
  Wong
Oliver Woodford
John Wright
Changchang Wu
Xinxiao Wu
Ying Wu
Tianfu Wu
Yang Wu
Yingnian Wu
Jonas Wulff
Yu Xiang
Tao Xiang
Jianxiong Xiao
Dong Xu
Li Xu
Yong Xu
Kota Yamaguchi
Takayoshi Yamashita
Shuicheng Yan
Jie Yang
Qingxiong Yang
Ruigang Yang
Meng Yang
Yi Yang
Chih-Yuan Yang
Jimei Yang

Bangpeng Yao
Angela Yao
Dit-Yan Yeung
Alper Yilmaz
Lijun Yin
Xianghua Ying
Kuk-Jin Yoon
Shiqi Yu
Stella Yu
Jingyi Yu
Junsong Yuan
Lu Yuan
Alan Yuille
Ramin Zabih
Christopher Zach

Stefanos Zafeiriou
Hongbin Zha
Lei Zhang
Junping Zhang
Shaoting Zhang
Xiaoqin Zhang
Guofeng Zhang
Tianzhu Zhang
Ning Zhang
Lei Zhang
Li Zhang
Bin Zhao
Guoying Zhao
Ming Zhao
Yibiao Zhao

Weishi Zheng
Bo Zheng
Changyin Zhou
Huiyu Zhou
Kevin Zhou
Bolei Zhou
Feng Zhou
Jun Zhu
Xiangxin Zhu
Henning Zimmer
Karel Zimmermann
Andrew Zisserman
Larry Zitnick
Daniel Zoran

Additional Reviewers

Austin Abrams
Hanno Ackermann
Daniel Adler
Muhammed Zeshan
   Afzal
Pulkit Agrawal
Edilson de Aguiar
Unaiza Ahsan
Amit Aides
Zeynep Akata
Jon Almazan
David Altamar
Marina Alterman
Mohamed Rabie Amer
Manuel Amthor
Shawn Andrews
Oisin Mac Aodha
Federica Arrigoni
Yuval Bahat
Luis Barrios
John Bastian
Florian Becker
C. Fabian
   Benitez-Quiroz
Vinay Bettadapura
Brian G. Booth

Lukas Bossard
Katie Bouman
Hilton Bristow
Daniel Canelhas
Olivier Canevet
Spencer Cappallo
Ivan Huerta Casado
Daniel Castro
Ishani Chakraborty
Chenyi Chen
Sheng Chen
Xinlei Chen
Wei-Chen Chiu
Hang Chu
Yang Cong
Sam Corbett-Davies
Zhen Cui
Maria A. Davila
Oliver Demetz
Meltem Demirkus
Chaitanya Desai
Pengfei Dou
Ralf Dragon
Liang Du
David Eigen
Jakob Engel

Victor Escorcia
Sandro Esquivel
Nicola Fioraio
Michael Firman
Alex Fix
Oliver Fleischmann
Marco Fornoni
David Fouhey
Vojtech Franc
Jorge Martinez G.
Silvano Galliani
Pablo Garrido
Efstratios Gavves
Timnit Gebru
Georgios Giannoulis
Clement Godard
Ankur Gupta
Saurabh Gupta
Amirhossein Habibian
David Hafner
Tom S.F. Haines
Vladimir Haltakov
Christopher Ham
Xufeng Han
Stefan Heber
Yacov Hel-Or

David Held
Benjamin Hell
Jan Heller
Anton van den Hengel
Robert Henschel
Steven Hickson
Michael Hirsch
Jan Hosang
Shell Hu
Zhiwu Huang
Daniel Huber
Ahmad Humayun
Corneliu Ilisescu
Zahra Iman
Thanapong Intharah
Phillip Isola
Hamid Izadinia
Edward Johns
Justin Johnson
Andreas Jordt
Anne Jordt
Cijo Jose
Daniel Jung
Meina Kan
Ben Kandel
Vasiliy Karasev
Andrej Karpathy
Jan Kautz
Changil Kim
Hyeongwoo Kim
Rolf Koehler
Daniel Kohlsdorf
Svetlana Kordumova
Jonathan Krause
Till Kroeger
Malte Kuhlmann
Ilja Kuzborskij
Alina Kuznetsova
Sam Kwak
Peihua Li
Michael Lam
Maksim Lapin
Gil Levi
Aviad Levis
Yan Li

Wenbin Li
Yin Li
Zhenyang Li
Pengpeng Liang
Jinna Lie
Qiguang Liu
Tianliang Liu
Alexander Loktyushin
Steven Lovegrove
Feng Lu
Jake Lussier
Xutao Lv
Luca Magri
Behrooz Mahasseni
Aravindh Mahendran
Siddharth Mahendran
Francesco Malapelle
Mateusz Malinowski
Santiago Manen
Timo von Marcard
Ricardo Martin-Brualla
Iacopo Masi
Roberto Mecca
Tomer Michaeli
Hengameh Mirzaalian
Kylia Miskell
Ishan Misra
Javier Montoya
Roozbeh Mottaghi
Panagiotis Moutafis
Oliver Mueller
Daniel Munoz
Rajitha Navarathna
James Newling
Mohamed Omran
Vicente Ordonez
Sobhan Naderi Parizi
Omkar Parkhi
Novi Patricia
Kuan-Chuan Peng
Bojan Pepikj
Federico Perazzi
Loic Peter
Alioscia Petrelli
Sebastian Polsterl

Alison Pouch
Vittal Premanchandran
James Pritts
Luis Puig
Julian Quiroga
Vignesh Ramanathan
Rene Ranftl
Mohammad Rastegari
S. Hussain Raza
Michael Reale
Malcolm Reynolds
Alimoor Reza
Christian Richardt
Marko Ristin
Beatrice Rossi
Rasmus Rothe
Nasa Rouf
Anirban Roy
Fereshteh Sadeghi
Zahra Sadeghipoor
Faraz Saedaar
Tanner Schmidt
Anna Senina
Lee Seversky
Yachna Sharma
Chen Shen
Javen Shi
Tomas Simon
Gautam Singh
Brandon M. Smith
Shuran Song
Mohamed Souiai
Srinath Sridhar
Abhilash Srikantha
Michael Stoll
Aparna Taneja
Lisa Tang
Moria Tau
J. Rafael Tena
Roberto Toldo
Manolis Tsakiris
Dimitrios Tzionas
Vladyslav Usenko
Danny Veikherman
Fabio Viola

Minh Vo
Christoph Vogel
Sebastian Volz
Jacob Walker
Li Wan
Chen Wang
Jiang Wang
Oliver Wang
Peng Wang
Jan Dirk Wegner
Stephan Wenger
Scott Workman
Chenglei Wu

Yuhang Wu
Fan Yang
Mark Yatskar
Bulent Yener
Serena Yeung
Kwang M. Yi
Gokhan Yildirim
Ryo Yonetani
Stanislav Yotov
Chong You
Quanzeng You
Fisher Yu
Pei Yu

Kaan Yucer
Clausius Zelenka
Xing Zhang
Xinhua Zhang
Yinda Zhang
Jiejie Zhu
Shengqi Zhu
Yingying Zhu
Yuke Zhu
Andrew Ziegler

Table of Contents

Computational Photography and Low-Level Vision

Poster Session 4

The 3D Jigsaw Puzzle:
Mapping Large Indoor Spaces

Ricardo Martin-Brualla[1], Yanling He[1], Bryan C. Russell[2], and Steven M. Seitz[1]

[1] University of Washington, USA
[2] Intel, USA

Abstract. We introduce an approach for analyzing annotated maps of a site, together with Internet photos, to reconstruct large indoor spaces of famous tourist sites. While current 3D reconstruction algorithms often produce a set of disconnected components (3D pieces) for indoor scenes due to scene coverage or matching failures, we make use of a provided map to lay out the 3D pieces in a global coordinate system. Our approach leverages position, orientation, and shape cues extracted from the map and 3D pieces and optimizes a global objective to recover the global layout of the pieces. We introduce a novel crowd flow cue that measures how people move across the site to recover 3D geometry orientation. We show compelling results on major tourist sites.

Keywords: Indoor scene reconstruction, maps, 3D jigsaw puzzle.

1 Introduction

Recent breakthroughs in computer vision now allow us to model our world in 3D with extraordinary accuracy and visual fidelity from just about any set of overlapping photos [1,2,3]. However, a limitation of state-of-the-art 3D reconstruction techniques from Internet photos is that large scenes tend to break up into a collection of disconnected pieces due to gaps in the depicted scene coverage or matching failures. Rather than a single, fully-connected Vatican model, for instance, we get a collection of smaller 3D pieces for different rooms, such as the Sistine Chapel, the Raphael Rooms, and the Hall of Maps, each having their own 3D coordinate system. A major challenge is to automatically put these 3D pieces together correctly into a global coordinate frame. This is akin to solving a *3D jigsaw puzzle*, where the scale, rotation, and translation of the 3D pieces must be recovered with respect to the global coordinate frame.

Solving the 3D jigsaw puzzle is extremely difficult using image information alone due to the aforementioned coverage and matching failures. Instead, we seek to leverage readily available map data to solve the 3D jigsaw puzzle. Such data provides additional information that helps constrain the spatial layout of the 3D pieces. For example, a map of the Vatican shows an annotated floorplan of the different rooms, with a legend providing the names of the rooms and any objects located inside the rooms. Such maps are plentiful and widely available,

D. Fleet et al. (Eds.): ECCV 2014, Part III, LNCS 8691, pp. 1–16, 2014.

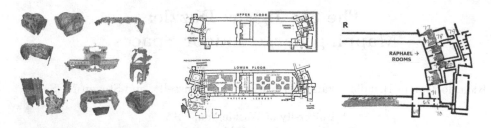

Fig. 1. Given a set of disconnected reconstructed 3D models of a large indoor scene, for example the Vatican (left), we jointly reason about a map of the site (middle) and the 3D pieces to produce a globally consistent reconstruction of the entire space (blow up at right)

for example in tourist guidebooks (e.g. Rick Steves, Lonely Planet, Baedeker) and online (e.g. planetware.com).

Automatically leveraging map data for the 3D jigsaw puzzle is challenging as the pieces are unlabeled and lack absolute position, orientation, and scale. The 3D Wikipedia system provided one approach to automatically link objects described in text to their spatial location in a 3D model [4]. While [4] can be used to link the 3D pieces to text on an annotated map, it does not provide information on how to *place* the pieces in a global coordinate system. Moreover, most maps provide only 2D cues (e.g., via a floorplan), with objects and dimensions placed only approximately. Finally, we must cope with rooms having orientation ambiguities (e.g. square or rectangular rooms), which the map and 3D piece geometry alone cannot disambiguate.

The key to our approach is to extract and integrate position, orientation, and scale cues from the 3D pieces and the map. These include the room shape, map annotations, cardinal direction (available as compass measurements provided in the image EXIF data used to reconstruct the 3D pieces), and crowd flow through the different rooms of the site. The latter crowd flow cue, which measures the dominant direction of travel through the 3D pieces, provides information on the orientation of the pieces. For example, in the Vatican Museum tourists tend to go from the entrance toward the Sistine Chapel, passing through the Gallery of Candelabra, Gallery of Tapestries, and Hall of Maps along the way. We formulate the 3D jigsaw puzzle problem as an integer quadratic program with linear constraints to globally solve for the 3D layout of the pieces. Ours is the first system to reconstruct large indoor spaces of famous tourist sites from Internet photos via joint reasoning with map data and disconnected 3D pieces returned by structure-from-motion.

We show compelling results on four major sites. Our system reliably assigns and orients many of the 3D pieces relative to the input maps (we provide a detailed analysis of assignment precision/recall and orientation accuracy). Moreover, we show an integrated visualization of the map and reconstructed 3D geometry, where a user can interactively browse and fly to different rooms of the site (please see the video [5]).

2   Related Work

Our work is related to prior research leveraging auxiliary information, such as geographic data, human path of travel, and text, to augment 3D reconstruction and image localization. Geographic data, such as Google Street View and Google Earth 3D models, has been used to georegister point clouds generated from Internet images [6]. Maps have been used in conjunction with visual odometry for self localization [7,8]. Human path of travel has been used for image geolocalization [9] and predicting tourists' path of travel [10]. Note that in this work we use human path of travel to recover 3D piece orientation. Finally, text has been used to automatically label objects in reconstructed geometry [4].

Most related is prior work that matched free space from a 3D reconstruction to white space in a map [11]. However, [11] addressed a particularly simple case where the 3D jigsaw puzzle has only one large piece (the 3D model), and the floor plan is accurate. While aligning 3D geometry shards has been explored by other authors (e.g., Stanford's Forma Urbis project [12]), our problem is more challenging as the scale of each piece is unknown and we do not have access to complete scans. Also related are approaches for solving 2D jigsaw puzzles [13,14,15], which operate entirely on 2D rectangular puzzle pieces and determine puzzle piece locations through absolute position cues (e.g. corners, edges, color) and adjacency cues (e.g. shape). The analogy in our case is that label correspondences provide absolute cues and tourist flow provides adjacency.

Reconstructing large indoor spaces is a challenging problem due to lack of texture on many surfaces and the difficulty of systematically scanning every surface of a site. Major efforts to scan and reconstruct large indoor scenes include the Google art project [16], museum reconstruction via constructive solid geometry [17], and human-operated systems to scan a large site [18,19].

3   System Overview

In this paper we present a system to solve the 3D jigsaw puzzle via joint reasoning over 3D geometry and annotated map data. Our system takes as inputs: (i) one or more reconstructed 3D pieces for a site and (ii) an annotated map corresponding to a set of 2D map points of interest (associated with rooms and named objects), with corresponding 2D map regions (the extent of rooms and objects in the map) and text annotations (the legend).

Our system begins by generating a discrete set of candidate placements of the 3D pieces to the map points of interest (Section 4.2). 3D pieces are assigned to the map by querying Google Image Search using the extracted text annotations from the map and linking the returned images to the 3D pieces via camera resectioning. This provides links between a given map point of interest to candidate 3D locations on the 3D pieces. Note that the links are noisy as the returned images may depict incorrect locations of the site. Given the links, a discrete set of candidate 3D transformations to the global coordinate system are generated for each 3D piece.

Given the candidate placements, we optimize an objective function that seeks a globally consistent layout of the 3D pieces by integrating cues extracted over the points of interest, their 2D map regions, and the 3D pieces, described in Section 4. The objective integrates cues about the shape of the rooms, cardinal direction, crowd flow through the site, and mutual exclusion of the 3D pieces. We show results of our system in Section 5.

4   Model for the 3D Jigsaw Puzzle

Given a discrete set of candidate placements of 3D pieces to map points of interest, we seek a globally consistent layout of the 3D pieces. Let $p \in \{1, \ldots, P\}$ index the map points of interest, $m \in \{1, \ldots, M\}$ the 3D models, $q_m \in \{1, \ldots, Q_m\}$ 3D locations on 3D model m, and $t_m \in \{1, \ldots, T_m\}$ candidate 3D transformations of 3D model m to the global coordinate system. A candidate placement is the tuple (p, m, q, t), where we omit the subindices for brevity.

A solution to the 3D jigsaw puzzle is a selection of 3D piece placements from the candidate set. We define binary variables $x_{p,m,q,t} \in \{0,1\}$ to indicate whether the candidate placement appears in the solution set and auxiliary binary variables $y_{m,t} \in \{0,1\}$ to indicate that 3D model m is placed in the global coordinate system under 3D transformation t. We formulate the 3D jigsaw puzzle as an integer quadratic program with linear constraints where vector b and matrix A encode unary and pairwise cues over the position, scale, and orientation of the candidate placements (described in Section 4.1):

$$\max_{x,y} \quad x^T A x + b^T x \tag{1}$$

$$\text{s.t.} \quad \forall p \quad \sum_{m,q,t} x_{p,m,q,t} \leq 1 \qquad \forall q \quad \sum_{p,m,t} x_{p,m,q,t} \leq 1 \tag{2}$$

$$\forall m \quad \sum_{t} y_{m,t} \leq 1 \qquad \forall p, m, q, t \quad x_{p,m,q,t} \leq y_{m,t} \tag{3}$$

Constraints (2) enforce mutual exclusion of the 3D puzzle pieces. We require each point of interest p to be assigned to at most one 3D location q on a model, and vice versa. We find that enforcing mutual exclusion is critical for our problem since we are reconstructing unique object instances of a site. Constraints (3) enforce each model m to be placed in the global coordinate system under a single 3D transformation t.

Given pairwise and unary coefficients A and b, we optimize Objective (1) using mixed-integer quadratic programming [20]. Note that while it has been shown that solving jigsaw puzzles with uncertainty in the piece compatibility is NP-hard [21], the small size of our datasets, of up to a few dozen pieces, enables us to express the mutual exclusion constraints exactly. This is in contrast to recent work in modeling 2D jigsaw puzzles that have formulated the problem as a Markov Random Field with mutual exclusion constraints approximated by a set of local pairwise terms due to large problem size [13,14].

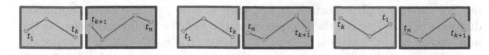

Fig. 2. Illustration of the crowd flow cue for two adjacent rooms on the map. For a sequence of photos captured by a particular user, green points show the location where the images where taken and $t_1, \ldots, t_n$ their ordered time stamps. Here, the user moved from the blue to the red room from left to right. Our goal is to orient the rooms to be consistent with the direction of travel. Left: room orientations are consistent with the user path through both rooms. Middle: the red room is inconsistent with the user path. Right: both rooms are inconsistent with the user path.

4.1 Cues for Position, Scale, and Orientation

In this section we describe the cues that are used to pose the 3D pieces relative to the map. These cues encode the crowd flow through the space, number of registered image search results to 3D pieces, cardinal direction of the pieces, and room shape.

Crowd Flow Potential. As previously noted [10], for many popular places people tend to visit different parts of the scene in a consistent order. For example, in the Vatican Museum, most tourists walk from the entrance toward the Sistine Chapel, passing through the Gallery of Candelabra, Gallery of Tapestries, and Hall of Maps along the way. We seek to harness the "flow of the crowd" to help disambiguate the orientation of the 3D pieces.

We wish to characterize the crowd flow within each 3D piece m and between 3D pieces m and m'. We start by considering the sets of photos taken by individual Flickr users that were aligned to the 3D pieces and sort the photos based on their timestamps. These aligned images indicate the users' direction of travel within the 3D pieces (e.g., tourists move from right to left of the main painting inside the Hall of the Immaculate Conception) and across the 3D pieces (e.g., tourists visit the Galeria of Candelabra before the Gallery of Maps). We say that the candidate placements of two 3D pieces agree with the crowd flow if the dominant direction of travel *across* the two pieces is oriented in the same direction as *within* the pieces after placing them onto the global coordinate system. We illustrate the crowd flow cue in Figure 2.

More concretely, given the camera locations for the images for a particular user i in model m, let $d_{i,k}^m$ be a unit vector in the direction of travel between consecutive images k and $k+1$ in the sequence, which corresponds to how the user moved between shots. For candidate placement $\alpha = (p, m, q, t)$, we define the dominant direction of travel within 3D piece m as $\delta_\alpha = H_t(norm(\sum_{i,k} d_{i,k}^m))$ where $H_t(\cdot)$ is the 3D transformation for t and $norm(\cdot)$ normalizes the input vector to unit length.

To estimate the dominant direction of travel across 3D pieces m and m', we count the number of users $u_{m,m'}$ that took a picture first in m and later in

m'. For candidate placements α and α' with $m \neq m'$, we denote the dominant direction of travel across the two pieces in the global coordinate system as the unit vector $\delta_{\alpha,\alpha'} = sign(u_{m,m'} - u_{m',m}) \cdot norm(H_{t'}(c_{m'}) - H_t(c_m))$ where c_m is the 3D centroid of 3D piece m. Note that if most users travel from m to m', $\delta_{\alpha,\alpha'}$ will point in the direction from 3D piece m to m' in the global coordinate system. We define the crowd flow cue for candidate placements α and α' as the sum of inner products:

$$A_{\alpha,\alpha'} = \; < \delta_{\alpha,\alpha'}, \delta_\alpha > + < \delta_{\alpha,\alpha'}, \delta_{\alpha'} > \tag{4}$$

Unary Potentials. For each candidate placement we extract unary potentials for assignment $\phi^{assign}(\alpha)$, cardinal direction $\phi^{card}(\alpha)$, and room shape $\phi^{shape}(\alpha)$. We concatenate these potentials into vector $\Phi(\alpha)$ and, given weights w, define the unary coefficients b as:

$$b_\alpha = w^T \Phi(\alpha) \tag{5}$$

We wish to leverage the vast amounts of labeled imagery online to connect the map points of interest to their locations in the 3D pieces. Using the text annotation for each point of interest in the map, we issue a query to Google Image Search concatenating the annotation text with the site name, followed by registering the returned images to the 3D pieces. We define $\phi^{assign}(\alpha) = count(p, m, q)$ as the number of images retrieved by querying for the text associated with map point of interest p that are registered to the 3D location q in model m.

A small fraction of Flickr images contain heading information in EXIF tags (e.g., via compass). Although we have found such data to be sparse and not always reliable, we can exploit it when available. The cardinal direction potential $\phi^{card}(\alpha)$ measures the compatibility of compass measurements corresponding to images used to reconstruct a 3D piece to a cardinal direction given on the map (e.g. "north"). Let $C_m > 0$ be the number of images used to reconstruct 3D piece m having a heading and $C_{m,t}$ be the number of such images that agree on the orientation of the provided cardinal direction within τ degrees after applying 3D transformation t into the global coordinate system. We define the potential to be $\phi^{card}(\alpha) = C_{m,t}/C_m$.

Next we wish to encode how well the 3D piece matches the shape of a given 2D region on the map. We encode the shape by projecting the structure-from-motion points of model m onto the map via transformation t and rasterize the points into a grid of cells. The shape potential $\phi^{shape}(\alpha)$ is a weighted sum of three terms: (i) the ratio of intersection area over union between the 2D region and occupied grid cells, (ii) average truncated distance of each grid cell to the 2D map region edge, and (iii) fraction of grid cells that lie outside of the region.

4.2   Generating Candidate Placements

In this section we describe how to generate the set of candidate placements of 3D pieces to map points of interest. First, we parse the map into a set of regions

Fig. 3. Left: A 3D piece of our system corresponding to the Hall of the Immaculate Conception. Middle: Colored 2D regions extracted from the floorplan. Number 72 in purple corresponds to the ground truth location of the 3D piece. Right: Candidate placements of the 3D piece to the 2D region.

and points of interest with accompanying text, described in Appendix A. Then we describe how we assign and align the 3D pieces to the map regions and points of interest.

Given the extracted text annotations from the map, we align images downloaded from Google image search to the 3D pieces. We cluster the set of inlier 3D points across all queries and set the 3D locations q as the centers of mass of the clusters. We orient the vertical direction of each 3D piece by aligning its z-axis with its up vector and setting the ground plane ($z = 0$) at the bottom of the piece. The up vector is the normal direction of a plane fitted to the inlier camera centers of the piece, oriented towards the cameras' up vectors.

A map may provide labels for only the room and/or for multiple objects in a room. For example, the Vatican Museums have only the rooms labeled, whereas the Pantheon has objects labeled within the main room. We wish to account for both cases when generating candidate placements. When only the room is labeled, we generate multiple candidate placements by finding local maxima of the unary shape potential $\phi^{shape}(\alpha)$. When multiple objects are labeled, we use the candidate assignments between the 3D locations on the models and the 2D points of interest on the map as putative matches. We then estimate a similarity transformation given the matches to yield the candidate placements. Example candidate placements are shown in Figure 3.

5   Results

We evaluated our system on four major tourist sites: the Vatican Museums, St. Peter's Basilica in Rome, Pantheon in Rome, and the Hearst Castle. We collected maps for each site and reconstructed 3D models for the sites by downloading images from Flickr by querying for the site name and running VisualSFM [22,23]. In addition, for each reconstructed Flickr photo, we downloaded all photos taken by the same user within 2 hours and match them to the reconstructed pieces, yielding a much larger image set (factor of 5-10). For visualization purposes we use PMVS for multi-view stereo [24] and Poisson Surface Reconstruction [25] to generate colored meshes. Note that all these packages are freely available online.

Table 1. Site statistics: # POIs – number of points of interest in the map, # GT POIs – number of points of interest in the map with ground truth 3D model assignments, # GT Orientations – number of points of interest in the map with ground truth 3D model orientation assignments, # Images – number of images used in the 3D reconstruction, # 3D Pieces – number of reconstructed 3D pieces

Site	# POIs	# GT POIs	# GT Orientations	# Images	# 3D Pieces
Vatican Museums	75	30	11	11K	68
Hearst Castle	22	5	5	3K	30
Pantheon	9	8	8	705	11
St. Peter's	34	13	11	3K	55

We collected ground truth assignments between the pieces and the map legends by finding information in authoritative sites, such as Wikipedia articles and specialized sites about the landmarks, like the official website of the Vatican Museums or saintpetersbasilica.org. Collecting ground truth orientations of the 3D pieces is challenging given that images alone do not disambiguate between orientations. Fortunately some authoritative sites contain more detailed maps for a small section of a landmark that place different objects inside the rooms or enumerate the views with their cardinal orientations. We can also infer the orientation of some rooms from official museum itineraries by correlating the direction of travel of the 3D pieces with the observed direction of travel from the Flickr users. We summarize the ground truth dataset statistics in Table 1.

The Vatican Museums and the Hearst Castle datasets are examples of very large multiroom scenes where most pieces correspond to complete rooms in the site, like the Sistine Chapel or the Raphael Rooms in the Vatican Museums. Figures 4 and 5 show the recovered layout of the different 3D pieces using the annotated maps for the Vatican Museums and Hearst Castle, respectively. Notice that we are able to correctly position and scale/orient many of the 3D pieces. While our 3D model coverage appears sparse in some regions, particularly the lower floor of the Vatican and 2nd floor of Hearst Castle, we correctly place most of the most visited and well-photographed rooms, such as the Raphael Rooms and the 2nd floor galleries of the Vatican Museums. Indeed, the correctly aligned pieces account for 75% and 73% of all reconstructed images for the Vatican Museums and Hearst Castle respectively. Note that some pieces are incorrectly scaled, like the Pigna Courtyard, due to the lack of a complete model of the room, as well as errors in the map parsing.

The Pantheon and St. Peter's Basilica are examples of single large rooms, where the annotated maps detail the specific objects names present in the site. Both sites contain large open spaces that enable the 3D reconstruction process to create a mostly complete 3D model of the entire site. Figures 6 and 7 show the recovered layout for both sites. The Pantheon model was aligned to the map by the assignment of 7 of its objects to points of interest in the map. In the St. Peter's case, three objects contained in the large 3D model were assigned to

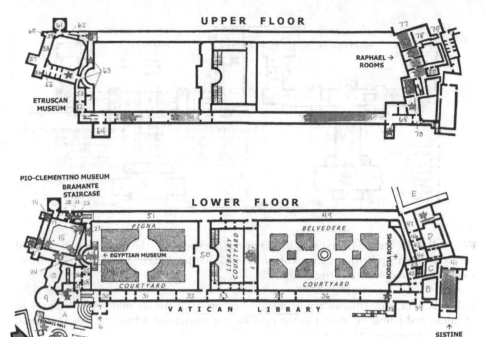

Fig. 4. Results for the Vatican Museums. 3D pieces are shown as the projection of the SfM points on the map, with different colors for each model. Green stars represent correct assignments, red stars incorrect ones. Please zoom in on the electronic version to see the details.

points of interest as well as other smaller models, such as Michelangelo's Pieta and the Chapel of Presentation.

We quantitatively evaluate the assignments of 3D pieces to the points of interest in the map and the orientation of those assignments in Table 2. As a baseline we use only the assignment potential score $\phi^{assign}(\alpha)$ described in Section 4.1, which ignores the mutual exclusion constraint. Our system consistently improves the precision of the assignment over the baseline. The orientations proposed by our system for the correctly assigned points of interest are correct in 25 out of 33 cases across all sites.

We perform an ablative study over the orientation cues for the sites with multiple rooms (Vatican Museums and Hearst Castle). Note that the Pantheon is a single large room and St. Peter's has stand-alone objects (e.g. the Pieta, the Altar of St. Jerome), plus one central room. In Table 3 we show statistics of the data collected for the cues and orientation accuracy values using the crowd flow cue, the cardinal direction cue and the joint model. The crowd flow cue disambiguates cases such as the galleries in the second floor of the Vatican, but

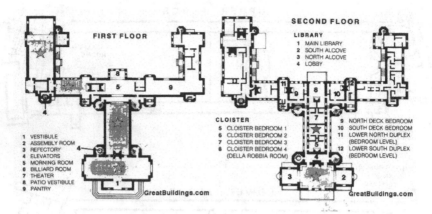

Fig. 5. Results for the Hearst Castle. 3D pieces are shown as the projection of the SfM points on the map, with different colors for each model. Green stars represent correct assignments, red stars incorrect ones.

Table 2. For each site, we report assignment precision/recall values with respect to all annotated points of interest in the map for our model and a baseline (see text), and orientation accuracy of our model

Site	Assignment				Orientation
	Baseline		Model		Model
	Precision	Recall	Precision	Recall	Accuracy
Vatican Museums	53%	57%	73%	43%	91%
Hearst Castle	83%	27%	83%	27%	60%
Pantheon	67%	89%	100%	78%	100%
St. Peter's	45%	59%	70%	29%	50%

Table 3. For each site, we report orientation accuracy using the crowd flow cue, the cardinal direction cue and the joint model

Site	Crowd flow	Cardinal Direction	Joint Model
Vatican Museums	27%	72%	91%
Hearst Castle	40%	40%	60%

fails on 3D pieces representing objects, such as statues or paintings, since users don't move in a predetermined path of travel when photographing them. The compass cue is powerful when enough data is available, but is ineffective for datasets with fewer photos, like the Hearst Castle, where we only match 3 out of the 16 photos with compass heading to the assigned 3D pieces. Augmenting the image dataset by downloading more photos for the set of users is critical for the crowd flow and cardinal direction cues, as it vastly increases the number of reconstructed photos and also the number of reconstructed photos per user. In Table 4 we report statistics of the dataset expansion.

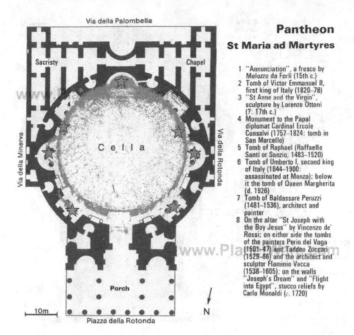

Fig. 6. Results for the Pantheon. 3D pieces are shown as the projection of the SfM points on the map, with different colors for each model. Green stars represent correct assignments, red stars incorrect ones.

For each dataset, the integer quadratic program contained up to a thousand variables and was solved within 5 seconds on a single workstation with 12 cores.

5.1 Failure Cases

We have observed different failure cases of our system, showcasing the challenges of reconstructing indoor spaces from 3D pieces.

In some cases, the annotated text in the map may yield noisy image search results, leading to incorrect assignments. For example, in Figure 8(a), we show the model recovered for the point of interest labeled as "Round Vestibule" in the Vatican Museums that is actually the "Circular Hall", which is located in the same Pio Clementino Museum.

Table 4. For each site, we report the number of Flickr users, number of photos before and after the dataset expansion and number of reconstructed photos before and after dataset expansion

Site	Users	Photos		Recons. Photos	
		Before	After	Before	After
Vatican Museums	2112	11K	99K	4K	11K
Hearst Castle	367	3K	16K	828	3K

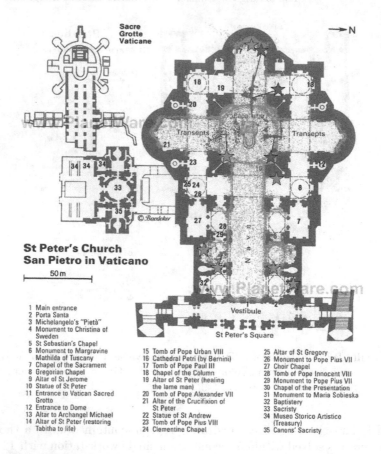

Fig. 7. Results for the St. Peter's Basilica. 3D pieces are shown as the projection of the SfM points on the map, with different colors for each model. Green stars represent correct assignments, red stars incorrect ones.

Another interesting case are the recovered 3D pieces corresponding to individual objects, such as the painting in the "Sobieski Room", shown in Figure 8(b). The room that contains the painting is rectangular and provides no cues for precise alignment of the object, even when the orientation is recovered from heading measurements. Our system can still provide a plausible alignment of the object along one of the walls, but the object might be scaled incorrectly.

Our system also fails to produce precise alignments to the walls of the rooms, such as the "Raphael Rooms" shown in Figure 8(c), due to inacurracies of the map. In the annotated map of the Vatican Museum dataset, the first three Raphael Rooms appear to have a 2:1 aspect ratio, although our 3D models indicate an aspect ratio closer to 1:1. By consulting other maps from different sources, we are able to determine that the aspect ratio of our models is actually correct, i.e., the map is wrong. Being able to register multiple maps together and detect these map inaccuracies is a promising direction for future work.

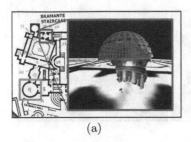
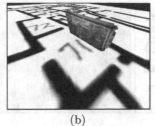
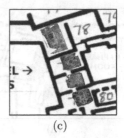

(a)   (b)   (c)

Fig. 8. Failure modes: (a) Incorrectly placed 3D model of the "Round Hall"; assigned point of interest marked in red, correct one in green, (b) ambiguous placement of object due to lack of scale and orientation information, (c) inaccurate map with incorrect aspect ratio for the rooms

5.2   Navigation

We showcase the results of our indoor reconstructions via an interactive web visualization tool. We illustrate the interactions of the visualization tool in Figure 9, but we refer the reader to the video available at the project website [5]. We feature two navigation modes to explore the map and reconstructed geometry. In map navigation mode, we allow common panning and zooming capabilities of the map. When you click on a room that has been assigned a 3D piece, the visualization automatically flies into the aligned 3D piece. You can navigate through the piece via an image-based rendering visualization, similar to the one in PhotoTourism [26]. When you look towards a neighbouring room, an arrow appears on the bottom of the screen pointing towards it. When you click on the arrow, the visualization transitions between the two rooms, recreating the experience of moving from one room to another.

6   Conclusion

This paper introduced the first system to reconstruct large indoor spaces of famous tourist sites from Internet photos via joint reasoning with map data and disconnected 3D pieces returned by structure-from-motion. We framed the problem as a 3D jigsaw puzzle and formulated an integer quadratic program with linear constraints that integrate cues over the pieces' position, scale, and orientation. We also introduced a novel crowd flow cue that measures how people travel through a site. Experiments on multiple sites showed consistently high precision for 3D model assignment and orientation relative to the input map, which allows for high quality interactions in the visualization tool. Our system works on popular tourist sites as it requires lots of images, text, and image metadata.

Acknowledgements. The research was supported in part by the National Science Foundation (IIS-1250793), the Intel Science and Technology Center for Visual Computing (ISTC-VC), the Animation Research Labs, and Google.

(a)   (b)   (c)

Fig. 9. Screenshots of our interactive visualization: (a) The annotated map is shown with the aligned 3D models rendered on top. When the user clicks on the model of the Hall of Immaculate Conception, the visualization flies into the room showing a photo taken in it (b). An arrow points to the location of the next room, the Incencio Room, and when clicked, the visualization flies the user to that room (c).

A   Map Parsing

Given an annotated map of a site, we seek to extract the spatial layout of the different rooms and objects depicted on the map. Automatically parsing a map is an interesting problem, but not strictly necessary for our task, as it would be straightforward to have manual workers parse maps for all leading tourist sites, or have future map-makers generate maps with the requisite annotations. For completeness, we describe a semi-automatic method of extracting the spatial layout and the object labels. We have restricted ourselves to annotated maps depicting the floorplan of a space, with referenced rooms and objects in the map appearing as text in a legend, as illustrated in Figure 6.

Our map parsing procedure begins by recovering a set of 2D regions from the floorplan corresponding to rooms, hallways, courtyards and other features of the site. We extract the floor plan of the map by clustering the pixel values found in the map image by K-means. We generate 2-4 clusters and manually select the cluster corresponding to the floorplan to form a binary image. To extract regions corresponding to the rooms we must close small gaps in the floor plan corresponding to doors and passages, which we achieve by simple morphological operations. We recover a segment for the room region by flood filling seeded by the room annotation marker on the map.

While OCR systems (e.g. Tesseract [27]) have shown much success in reading text in images, automatically recognizing text labels and markers in maps is still very difficult since the text is not generally structured into lines and may appear in different orientations, thus violating critical assumptions made by these systems. Moreover, markers and other visual elements appearing on the floorplan confuse the text line detection algorithms. The application of recently developed scene text recognition systems [28,29,30] to annotated maps remains outside the scope of this work and an interesting topic for future work. For our purposes we have manually annotated the map using LabelMe [31] by marking each text label or marker with the appropriate text label.

References

1. Agarwal, S., Snavely, N., Simon, I., Seitz, S.M., Szeliski, R.: Building rome in a day. In: International Conference on Computer Vision (2009)
2. Agarwal, S., Furukawa, Y., Snavely, N., Simon, I., Curless, B., Seitz, S.M., Szeliski, R.: Building rome in a day. Commun. ACM 54(10), 105–112 (2011)
3. Shan, Q., Adams, R., Curless, B., Furukawa, Y., Seitz, S.M.: The visual Turing test for scene reconstruction. In: Joint 3DIM/3DPVT Conference (3DV) (2013)
4. Russell, B.C., Martin-Brualla, R., Butler, D.J., Seitz, S.M., Zettlemoyer, L.: 3D Wikipedia: Using online text to automatically label and navigate reconstructed geometry. ACM Transactions on Graphics (SIGGRAPH Asia 2013) 32(6) (November 2013)
5. http://grail.cs.washington.edu/projects/jigsaw3d
6. Wang, C.P., Wilson, K., Snavely, N.: Accurate georegistration of point clouds using geographic data. In: 3DV (2013)
7. Levin, A., Szeliski, R.: Visual odometry and map correlation. In: IEEE Computer Vision and Pattern Recognition or CVPR (2004)
8. Brubaker, M., Geiger, A., Urtasun, R.: Lost! Leveraging the crowd for probabilistic visual self-localization. In: IEEE Computer Vision and Pattern Recognition or CVPR (2013)
9. Kalogerakis, E., Vesselova, O., Hays, J., Efros, A.A., Hertzmann, A.: Image sequence geolocation with human travel priors. In: Proceedings of the IEEE International Conference on Computer Vision, ICCV 2009 (2009)
10. Simon, I.: Scene Understanding Using Internet Photo Collections. PhD thesis, University of Washington (2010)
11. Kaminsky, R., Snavely, N., Seitz, S.M., Szeliski, R.: Alignment of 3D point clouds to overhead images. In: Workshop on Internet Vision (2009)
12. Koller, D., Trimble, J., Najbjerg, T., Gelfand, N., Levoy, M.: Fragments of the city: Stanford's digital forma urbis romae project. J. Roman Archaeol. 61(suppl.3), 237–252 (2006)
13. Cho, T.S., Avidan, S., Freeman, W.T.: The patch transform. IEEE Transactions on Pattern Analysis and Machine Intelligence 32(8), 1489–1501 (2010)
14. Cho, T.S., Avidan, S., Freeman, W.T.: A probabilistic image jigsaw puzzle solver. In: IEEE Conference on Computer Vision and Pattern Recognition, CVPR (2010)
15. Gallagher, A.: Jigsaw puzzles with pieces of unknown orientation. In: IEEE Conference on Computer Vision and Pattern Recognition, CVPR (2012)
16. Google art project, http://www.google.com/culturalinstitute/project/art-project
17. Xiao, J., Furukawa, Y.: Reconstructing the world's museums. In: Proceedings of the 12th European Conference on Computer Vision (2012)
18. Liu, T., Carlberg, M., Chen, G., Chen, J., Kua, J., Zakhor, A.: Indoor localization and visualization using a human-operated backpack system. In: 2010 International Conference on Indoor Positioning and Indoor Navigation, IPIN (2010)
19. Xiao, J., Owens, A., Torralba, A.: SUN3D: A database of big spaces reconstructed using SfM and object labels. In: International Conference on Computer Vision (2013)
20. Bemporad, A.: Hybrid Toolbox - User's Guide (2004), http://cse.lab.imtlucca.it/~bemporad/hybrid/toolbox
21. Demaine, E., Demaine, M.: Jigsaw puzzles, edge matching, and polyomino packing: Connections and complexity. Graphs and Combinatorics 23 (2007)

22. Wu, C., Agarwal, S., Curless, B., Seitz, S.M.: Multicore bundle adjustment. In: IEEE Conference on Computer Vision and Pattern Recognition (CVPR), pp. 3057–3064. IEEE (2011)
23. Wu, C.: VisualSFM - a visual structure from motion system (2011), http://ccwu.me/vsfm/
24. Furukawa, Y., Ponce, J.: Accurate, dense, and robust multi-view stereopsis. IEEE Trans. Pattern Analysis and Machine Intelligence 32(8), 1362–1376 (2010)
25. Kazhdan, M., Bolitho, M., Hoppe, H.: Poisson surface reconstruction. In: Proceedings of the 4th Eurographics Symposium on Geometry Processing (SGP), pp. 61–70 (2006)
26. Snavely, N., Seitz, S.M., Szeliski, R.: Photo tourism: Exploring photo collections in 3d. ACM Trans. Graph. 25(3), 835–846 (2006)
27. tesseract-ocr, https://code.google.com/p/tesseract-ocr/
28. Epshtein, B., Ofek, E., Wexler, Y.: Detecting text in natural scenes with stroke width transform. In: 2013 IEEE Conference on Computer Vision and Pattern Recognition, pp. 2963–2970 (2010)
29. Goodfellow, I.J., Bulatov, Y., Ibarz, J., Arnoud, S., Shet, V.: Multi-digit number recognition from street view imagery using deep convolutional neural networks. CoRR abs/1312.6082 (2013)
30. Bissacco, A., Cummins, M., Netzer, Y., Neven, H.: Photoocr: Reading text in uncontrolled conditions. In: The IEEE International Conference on Computer Vision (ICCV) (December 2013)
31. Russell, B.C., Torralba, A., Murphy, K.P., Freeman, W.T.: Labelme: A database and web-based tool for image annotation. Int. J. Comput. Vision 77(1-3), 157–173 (2008)

Pipe-Run Extraction and Reconstruction
from Point Clouds

Rongqi Qiu[1], Qian-Yi Zhou[2], and Ulrich Neumann[1,*]

[1] University of Southern California, USA
[2] Stanford University, USA

Abstract. This paper presents automatic methods to extract and reconstruct industrial site pipe-runs from large-scale point clouds. We observe
three key characteristics in this modeling problem, namely, primitives,
similarities, and joints. While *primitives* capture the dominant cylindric shapes, *similarities* reveal the inter-primitive relations intrinsic to
industrial structures because of human design and construction. Statistical analysis over point normals discovers primitive similarities from raw
data to guide primitive fitting, increasing robustness to data noise and
incompleteness. Finally, *joints* are automatically detected to close gaps
and propagate connectivity information. The resulting model is more
than a collection of 3D triangles, as it contains semantic labels for pipes
as well as their connectivity.

1 Introduction

3D digital models for industrial sites are crucial in many applications, including
operator training, disaster simulations and response planning. As a dominant
feature of industrial sites, pipe-runs are an important part of operations and
maintenance. In older facilities, initial CAD models may not exist or are out of
date, prompting the need for creating new models. While modern laser scanners
can produce dense point clouds capturing the surface geometry, the automated
transformation of point clouds to pipe-run models including cylinder geometry
and accurate connectivity remains an open problem.

A popular strategy of 3D reconstruction from point scans is to simplify a triangular mesh that minimizes the geometric fitting error with respect to the input
points (*e.g.*, [2,5,14]). However, pure data-driven methods (*e.g.*, Ball-Pivoting Algorithm [2]) have no capability to simplify or filter noisy input data and generate
3D meshes with rough surfaces and cracks that are faithful to the point scans
(*e.g.*, Figure 2(d)). What is more, the resulting triangles contain no structural
semantic or connectivity data.

Another strategy of reconstruction attempts to fit *primitives* (*e.g.*, cylinders,
spheres and planes) to the raw data, capturing geometric information conveyed

* The authors thank Suya You and anonymous reviewers for their valuable comments.
This work is supported by Chevron, USA under the joint project, Center for In-
teractive Smart Oilfield Technologies and an Annenberg Graduate Fellowship from
USC.

D. Fleet et al. (Eds.): ECCV 2014, Part III, LNCS 8691, pp. 17–30, 2014.

in the input points (*e.g.*, [11,24,23]). This strategy is well-suited to industrial sites since most parts of them are composed of primitive shapes ([12,20,21]). However, such methods rarely extract complete pipe-runs with accurate connectivity. Moreover, bottom-up primitive fitting adopted in these methods is non-robust due to sensitivity to noise and outliers (Figure 2(e)).

We present an automatic robust method to reconstruct pipe-runs in 3D point clouds (*e.g.*, Figure 1). As cylindric shapes are often the dominant geometry of interest in such sites, we focus on methods to reconstruct pipes and joints. In addition, we make use of global similarities because they are more stable than local features in the noisy and complex input data. Our method differs from prior uses of global regularities enforced as a post-process (*e.g.*, [18]). The effectiveness of post processing is bounded by the unreliable initial primitive detection (*e.g.*, Figure 2(f)). Instead, we introduce global similarities in the early detection stage to improve the primitive detection and fitting processes. Finally, to reliably capture primitive junctions and propagate connectivity between primitives, we detect *joints* between adjacent pipes. Our combined methods robustly reconstruct complete pipe networks from point clouds of industrial structures (*e.g.*, Figure 2(b)(c)).

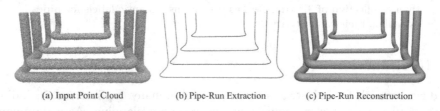

(a) Input Point Cloud   (b) Pipe-Run Extraction   (c) Pipe-Run Reconstruction

Fig. 1. Given a point cloud of industrial structures (a), our method automatically extracts a pipe axis network (b) and reconstructs pipe-runs (c)

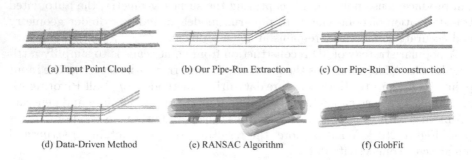

(a) Input Point Cloud   (b) Our Pipe-Run Extraction   (c) Our Pipe-Run Reconstruction

(d) Data-Driven Method   (e) RANSAC Algorithm   (f) GlobFit

Fig. 2. Given a real-world scan of industrial structures (a), we show 3D reconstruction results from different approaches: (b) extracted pipe axis network by our approach, (c) reconstructed pipe-runs by our approach, (d) Ball-Pivoting Algorithm [2], (e) RANSAC algorithm [23], and (f) GlobFit [18]

2 Related Work

2.1 Modeling from Point Clouds

A general strategy of 3D reconstruction from point clouds is to simplify a triangular mesh model that minimizes the distance between the input points and the mesh surface. Research efforts following this strategy are usually known as *data-driven* reconstruction because they take the input data as *truth* and make a trade-off between the size of the mesh and the geometry fitting error [2,14]. Different heuristics are introduced to produce modeling preferences such as smoothness [3,17] and sharp feature [9]. Data-driven reconstruction has the advantage of generality and adaptation to a variety of input point clouds. However, none of these methods can produce semantic or connectivity information, which limits their application.

Introducing prior knowledge of object shapes can significantly reduce the solution space and thus simplifies the reconstruction problem. For instance, Schnabel *et al.*[23] present an efficient RANSAC approach to detect primitive shapes from point clouds. Hofer *et al.*[13] adopt line geometry for the recognition and reconstruction of 3D surfaces. Many methods of fitting primitives are designed for reverse engineering such as [1]. Another existing method employs Hough transform [15]. Even though efforts have been made to reduce their space and time complexity [21], memory size limits still make these methods impractical for large-scale input.

2.2 Global Similarity in Reconstruction

In addition to the prior knowledge of primitive shapes, higher level of knowledge representing the similarities and relations between primitive elements are also introduced and explored by Li *et al.*[18]. This work deals with small scale objects and produces primitives exhibiting global relations. However, as stated in Section 1, it relies heavily on fitting quality of primitives, thus loses accuracy when dealing with complicated industrial structures. Our approach, on the other hand, overcomes this drawback by introducing similarities among primitives in an early stage, thus it is more successful at handling large-scale industrial sites.

Top-down geometry reconstruction is studied by Chen and Chen [4]. It employs statistical models on point normals to detect planar regions. A similar strategy in our approach focuses on reconstructing the cylinders and joints dominating in industrial sites.

2.3 Pipe-Run Reconstruction

The problem of pipe-run reconstruction has drawn much attention in both academia and industry. For instance, Liu *et al.*[19] attempt to reconstruct pipeline plants by reducing the reconstruction problem into a set of circle detections. However, their work uses prior knowledge of specific scenes such as the ground plane. Their assumption that pipes are either orthogonal or parallel to the ground is not general (*e.g.*, Figure 2). Fu *et al.*[10] adopt local RANSAC detection of pipes and uses standard elbow pieces to connect pipes. This method produces connected pipe-runs but only handles joints of some pre-defined size and shape. Commercial software (*e.g.*, [6]) is also available to interactively reconstruct pipe-runs. However, these products usually require substantial manual work. Our method, on the other hand, is fully automatic without any user intervention.

3   Overview

Our processing pipeline accepts point clouds as input and models pipe-runs in the scene. It is composed of the following steps (Figure 3).

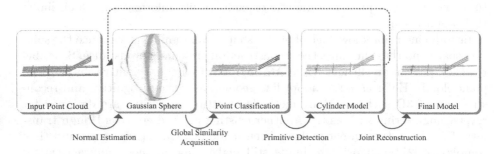

Fig. 3. Our modeling pipeline. Normals of input points are estimated and projected onto a Gaussian sphere, where patterns of great circles are detected to determine orientations of cylinders. Points within the same orientation are further separated to decide placement of different primitives. Orientation detection and placement extraction are iteratively performed until all primitives are detected. Joints between cylinders are then detected and generated to connect pipes into complete pipe-runs in the final models.

- **Global Similarity Acquisition:** We make a key observation that discovering global similarities is more robust than fitting primitives as the first stage. The reason is that global similarities appear more stable than local features in the noisy input point clouds. Thus, the first step of our approach analyzes the orientations of cylinders since they often exhibit similarities due to common design and construction practices. Statistical analysis on point normals is applied for extracting orientations of primitives.
- **Primitive Detection:** We use the global similarity information extracted from the last step to reduce the degrees of freedom of primitive fitting. This sequence significantly increases the robustness of primitive detection relative to the use of only local data for fitting. Points with the same orientation are projected onto an orthogonal plane used to detect 2D circles. Cylinders are detected within points contributing to the circle projections.
- **Joint Reconstruction:** The preceding stage typically extracts a large number of disconnected pieces of pipes. The next stage links them into a fully-connected pipe network. Three kinds of joints (*i.e.*, T-junctions, curved joints and boundary joints) are constructed to connect pipes smoothly.

4   Global Similarity Acquisition

While global similarities exist in any portions of an industrial scene point cloud, we observe that local sub-regions usually exhibit more consistent similarities than that in the whole scene. Therefore, we divide the whole scene into uniform cubic sub-volumes to process separately, and then seamlessly merge the results together in a later stage. This divide-and-conquer strategy is efficient for discovering global similarities. It also enables our system to handle arbitrary-sized input without encountering memory size limitations.

The most significant global similarities are orientations of cylinders. In a local region, cylinders tend to group into a few directions, denoted as *principal directions* in this paper. We detect these principal directions by adopting the following fact: if a point lies on a cylinder, its normal is perpendicular to the cylinder axis. Therefore, the point normals from cylinders of the same direction $\mathbf{d}$ will all be perpendicular to $\mathbf{d}$. When mapped onto a Gaussian sphere, they will distribute as the great circle that is perpendicular to $\mathbf{d}$, as illustrated in Figure 4(a). Therefore, we detect principal directions by mapping all the point normals onto the Gaussian sphere and detect great circle patterns. In the ideal case without noise, RANSAC [8] will reliably detect great circles. In particular, we randomly choose a pair of normals $(\mathbf{n}_i, \mathbf{n}_j)$, compute a perpendicular direction

$$\mathbf{d} = \mathbf{n}_i \times \mathbf{n}_j, \tag{1}$$

and validate the direction $\mathbf{d}$ with the number of points on the corresponding great circle, i.e., the size of set $\{\mathbf{p} | 1 - |\mathbf{n_p} \cdot \mathbf{d}| < \epsilon\}$. Once a principal direction is detected, we remove the points that contribute to that direction, then iteratively perform the detection process until all the principal directions have been found in this local region. In practice, however, the data is noisy and the points form thick rings around a great circle (e.g., green samples in Figure 4(a)). Thus a simple RANSAC becomes unstable and hard to converge. We adopt unsupervised clustering in the space of cylinder directions to solve this problem. In particular, we choose many random point pairs and compute cylinder direction candidates

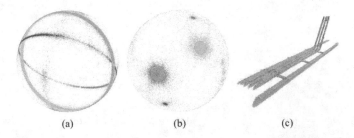

(a)   (b)   (c)

Fig. 4. The process of global similarity acquisition: point normals are projected onto a Gaussian sphere (a) where great circles are detected by transforming to a cylinder detection sphere (b); points are then segmented based on cylinder orientation (c)

that lie on a spherical map of potential cylinder direction (Figure 4(b)). The intuition is that even with noisy normal directions, the computed cylinder directions will lie close to the true principal direction. Therefore, we use Mean-shift [7] to detect modes on the spherical map of potential cylinder directions. In particular, starting from a random sample $\mathbf{x}$, it is iteratively updated with:

$$\mathbf{x} \leftarrow \frac{\sum_{\mathbf{x}_i \in N(\mathbf{x})} K(\| \mathbf{x} - \mathbf{x}_i \|) \mathbf{x}_i}{\sum_{\mathbf{x}_i \in N(\mathbf{x})} K(\| \mathbf{x} - \mathbf{x}_i \|)}, \tag{2}$$

where $K(\cdot)$ is Gaussian kernel function. After each iteration, the sample center $\mathbf{x}$ is not guaranteed to stay on the sphere. Therefore, we coerce it back onto the sphere. The centers of the modes are adopted as the principal directions in this local region.

Segmentation: A by-product of global similarity acquisition is the point segmentation based on cylinder orientations (Figure 4(c)). In particular, we identify points within a thick stripe on the Gaussian sphere as a category with the same cylinder orientation.

5   Primitive Detection

So far we have extracted principal directions of cylinders. In this section we show how global information helps extracting cylinder primitives. This task is accomplished in two steps: first, cylinder positions are discovered by mapping associated points on a plane and detecting circles; second, cylinder boundaries are determined.

5.1   Cylinder Position Calculation

We take points belonging to cylinders of the same direction $\mathbf{d}$. Intuitively, by mapping these points onto a plane that is perpendicular to the cylinder direction $\mathbf{d}$ (*e.g.*, Figure 5(a)), the projected points exhibit circular patterns (*e.g.*, Figure 5(b)). Therefore, instead of fitting 3D cylinders, we detect circles on a 2D projection plane of direction $\mathbf{d}$.

(a)   (b)   (c)

Fig. 5. The process of calculating cylinder positions: segmented points are projected to an orthogonal plane (a), where circular patterns are detected (b) by transforming to a circle-center map (c)

We also note that the normals of points can be projected onto the projection plane as 2D directions pointing either towards or outwards the cylinder center $\tilde{\mathbf{c}}$. Therefore, two projected points and normals are enough to determine a circle on the projection plane. Specifically, given two 2D points as $\tilde{\mathbf{p}}$, $\tilde{\mathbf{q}}$ and their 2D normals as $\tilde{\mathbf{n}}_{\mathbf{p}}$, $\tilde{\mathbf{n}}_{\mathbf{q}}$, the circle center $\tilde{\mathbf{c}}$ is determined by the intersection of two lines $L_1(u) = \tilde{\mathbf{p}} + u\tilde{\mathbf{n}}_{\mathbf{p}}$ and $L_2(v) = \tilde{\mathbf{q}} + v\tilde{\mathbf{n}}_{\mathbf{q}}$. The radius r is then calculated by $r = \frac{|\tilde{\mathbf{c}}\tilde{\mathbf{p}}| + |\tilde{\mathbf{c}}\tilde{\mathbf{q}}|}{2}$, if $|\tilde{\mathbf{c}}\tilde{\mathbf{p}}| \approx |\tilde{\mathbf{c}}\tilde{\mathbf{q}}|$.

However, in the presence of noise, projected cylinder points are distributed near circles (*e.g.*, Figure 5(b)). To address this issue, we choose many point pairs to get a collection of candidate circles. Our observation is that these candidate circles tend to form clusters (*e.g.*, Figure 5(c)) and the centers of clusters approximate cross-sections of cylinders. Mean-Shift algorithm [7] is adopted to detect these clusters, corresponding to cylinders and their associated points.

5.2   Cylinder Boundary Extraction

Given the positions of cylinders, the remaining parameters to be determined are the boundaries (*i.e.*, the start and end of the cylinder axis). End points are determined by the point coverage along cylinder surfaces. To be specific, we discretize the maximum discovered cylinder extents into small axial sections. The existence of each section is examined and the verified ones are reconstructed into contiguous cylinder pieces (*e.g.*, Figure 6(b)).

Pipe segment existence is based on two coverage tests. Axis coverage is a simple measure of point density per linear length of pipe. We set a minimum threshold for the total number of points along a valid pipe segment. Cross section coverage is a measure of the distribution of points around a pipe axis. We observe that plane normals can easily be mistaken for sides of cylinders by our algorithm. To avoid this, we require cylinders to exhibit more than 180-degrees of cross-section coverage.

In real-world scans, the gaps along pipes (*e.g.*, Figure 6(a)) are usually created with data incompleteness due to occlusions, data loss, and noise. To avoid over-segmenting a continuous pipe, we apply morphological operations of opening and closing to smooth the result. (*e.g.*, Figure 6(c)).

(a)
(b)
(c)

Fig. 6. Given incomplete scans of pipes (a), cylinder boundaries are determined by the point coverage along cylinder surfaces (b) and smoothed using morphological operations (c)

6 Joint Reconstruction

So far we have detected all the cylinder primitives in the scene. To reconstruct complete and fully-connected pipe-runs, we also need to link these cylinders together. We achieve this by introducing joints. Three categories of joints (*i.e.*, T-junctions, curved joints and boundary joints) are detected in our system (*e.g.*, Figure 7). T-junctions are extensions of one cylinder merging into another cylinder. Curved joints are elbows connecting two cylinders to allow a change of direction. Boundary joints are cylinder segments that fill small gaps between two cylinders. The gaps usually appear at the boundary of dividing sub-volumes.

6.1 Positions and Types of Joints

Our first thought was to detect joints as primitives like cylinders. However, it is not a trivial problem since joints are either two small (T-junctions and boundary joints) or have a complicated shape far from a simple primitive with a few parameters (curved joints). We observe that joints must connect two nearby cylinders. Therefore, we hypothesize all the possible joint locations and shapes and then select the most likely cases based on agreement with the point cloud data. Given the huge number of cylinders detected in the preceding stages, enumerating all candidate cylinder pairs would be impractical. Thus we employ several important heuristic criteria for joint positions (Figure 8(a)). Joint radius, gap distance (defined as the nearest distance between central lines), skew and angle are limited to reasonable ranges that are functions of the connecting pipe diameters. We thereby ensure that the connecting cylinders are nearby, similar-sized, co-planar and non-parallel for T-junctions and curved joints (or parallel for boundary joints).

To decide types of hypothetic joints, noting that all joints include at least one cylinder end, we examine extensions of cylinder ends. If an extension intersects with another cylinder, our hypothesis is a T-junction. If an extension intersects the extension of another cylinder, our hypothesis is a curved joint. If an extension coincides with another cylinder, our hypothesis is a boundary joint.

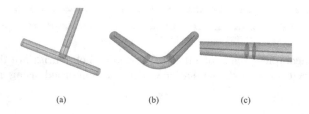

(a)   (b)   (c)

Fig. 7. Three types of joints included in our system: (a) T-junctions, (b) curved joints, and (c) boundary joints

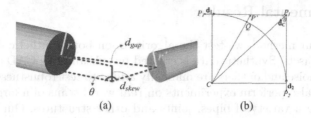

Fig. 8. (a) Four criteria of joint positions. (b) The process of calculating major radius of curved joints.

6.2   Reconstruction of Joints

The reconstruction of T-junctions and boundary joints is straight-forward, because all of their parameters has been determined. For T-junctions, the joint can be modeled by extending the end point of one cylinder into the axis of another cylinder. For boundary joints, we reconstruct a cylinder connecting two adjacent ones.

If two cylinders are connected with a curved joint, the only free parameter is the major radius. We determine the major radius of the optimal curved joint as the one with the most points lying on its surface among the range of possible major radius options. The intuition is that if we make every data point in the hypothetical joint volume vote for radius values such that the joint surfaces touch it, the value with most votes would be the optimal radius. The following portion shows how to calculate the major radius for a given data point.

As shown in Figure 8(b), assume the end points of two cylinders are P_1 and P_2 with corresponding direction $\mathbf{d_1}$ and $\mathbf{d_2}$. Since the two cylinders are near co-planar, we first force them onto the same plane, and then calculate the intersection of their axes as P_I. The goal is to find the circle center C and major radius R, so that the circle is tangent to both P_1P_I and P_2P_I. It can be shown that C must lie on the interior bisector of $\angle P_1P_IP_2$ (denoted as θ). If $\mathbf{d_C}$ is the unit direction of this bisector, then C and R can be expressed as:

$$C = P_I + |CP_I| \cdot \mathbf{d_C},$$
$$R = |CP_I| \cdot \sin\frac{\theta}{2}. \tag{3}$$

For every data point P, we first need to decide which point (denoted as Q) on circle C is the circle center of the cross section that contains P. It can be shown that the line connecting projected point P' and C intersects circle C at Q. Since $|P'Q|$ is known ($|P'Q| = \sqrt{r^2 - d^2}$, where r is cylinder radius and d is projection distance of P), $|CP'|$ can be expressed by:

$$|CP'| = R \pm |P'Q|. \tag{4}$$

Bringing Equation 3 into Equation 4 gives a quadratic equation of R, where R can be solved.

7   Experimental Results

To evaluate our method, we test the algorithm on both synthetic datasets and
real-world datasets. Synthetic data is created by subsampling CAD models. Various levels of noise and outliers are manually added to test robustness of different
methods. We also perform experiments on real-world scans of a large industrial
site containing a variety of pipes, joints and other structures. Our approach is
compared to both sequential RANSAC [23] and GlobFit [18] as post-application
of global similarities. For fair comparisons, we use the same set of parameters
throughout all experiments within each method.

7.1   Synthetic Dataset Experiments

Figure 9 shows that the RANSAC method [23] neglects global relationships of
primitives and gets lost in local errors. GlobFit [18] takes global similarities
into consideration, but is still bounded by the effects of initial RANSAC. Our
method, on the other hand, discovers global similarities before fitting primitives
and produces clean and accurate models.

Noise Experiments. To test the robustness of our algorithm, we add various
levels of noise to the input. Two types of noise are tested, *i.e.*, surface noise
and background noise. Surface noise (K_S in Figure 10) is random Gaussian

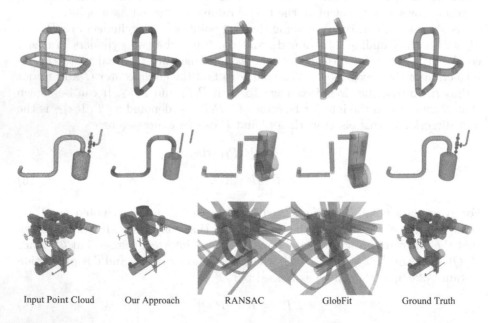

Input Point Cloud   Our Approach   RANSAC   GlobFit   Ground Truth

Fig. 9. Experiments on synthetic datasets. From left to right: input point cloud, our
result, RANSAC [23] result, GlobFit [18] result and ground truth.

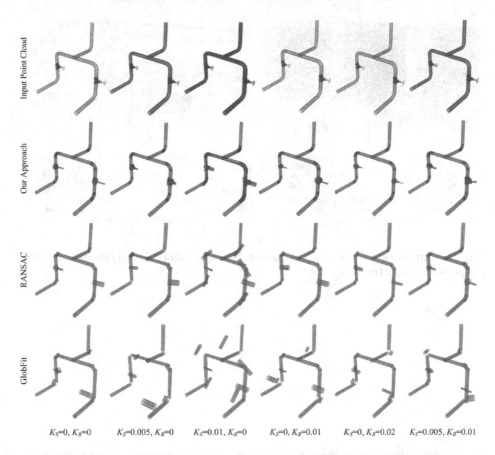

Input Point Cloud

Our Approach

RANSAC

GlobFit

$K_S{=}0, K_B{=}0$ $K_S{=}0.005, K_B{=}0$ $K_S{=}0.01, K_B{=}0$ $K_S{=}0, K_B{=}0.01$ $K_S{=}0, K_B{=}0.02$ $K_S{=}0.005, K_B{=}0.01$

Fig. 10. Reconstruction under various noise levels. From top to bottom: input point cloud, our result, RANSAC [23] result and GlobFit [18] result. K_S stands for surface noise and K_B stands for background noise.

noise in the direction of surface normals. Background noise (K_B in Figure 10) is uniformly random noise in 3D space. Both types of noise are to simulate data problems encountered in real world scans such as scanner hardware noise or registration error. As shown in Figure 10, our results remain stable as the noise level increases, while RANSAC [23] results are dramatically affected by noise, even if global similarities are enforced as a post-process using GlobFit [18].

7.2   Real-World Dataset Experiments

Figure 11(b) shows models reconstructed from 381M LiDAR points (Figure 11(a)) in a 25 meters × 25 meters × 10 meters scene. In pre-processing, we employ a voxel-grid method [22] to make the surface point density more uniform. We observe that planar objects may cause problems for our method, so we pre-filter points in planar areas (occupy 49.5% of points) using a method presented in [16]. Our method suc-

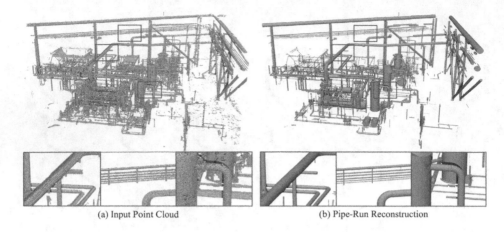

(a) Input Point Cloud   (b) Pipe-Run Reconstruction

Fig. 11. Experiments on a real-world dataset: (a) input point cloud (1/40 subsampled); (b) pipe-run reconstruction

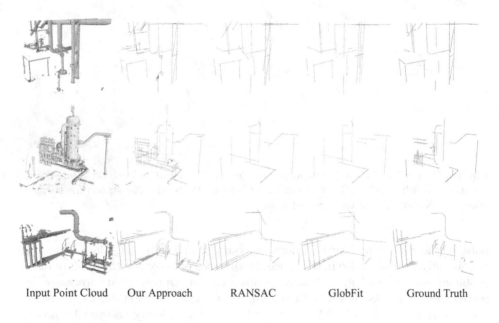

Input Point Cloud   Our Approach   RANSAC   GlobFit   Ground Truth

Fig. 12. Extracted pipe axis networks on real-world datasets. From left to right: input point cloud, our result, RANSAC [23] result, GlobFit [18] result and ground truth.

cessfully extracts pipe-run networks within 24 hours on a consumer-level desktop (Intel Core i7-3610QM 2.30GHz CPU with 6GB RAM). A detailed comparison with commercial software [6] is included in the supplementary material.

To quantitatively evaluate pipe-run extraction, we manually mark pipe networks of three sub-volumes to be compared with automatically extracted pipe-runs

Table 1. Quantitative evaluation of results shown in Figure 12

Models in Figure 12	First row			Second row			Third row		
	RANSAC [23]	GlobFit [18]	Our approach	RANSAC [23]	GlobFit [18]	Our approach	RANSAC [23]	GlobFit [18]	Our approach
Precision	0.804	0.603	0.603	0.745	0.714	0.481	0.629	0.594	0.402
Recall	0.938	0.748	0.953	0.486	0.476	0.986	0.630	0.625	0.915

(Figure 12). The pipe axes are sampled by an interval of 1cm so that each sample represents 1cm of pipe. These sampled points are compared based on proximity to calculate precision and recall for our method, RANSAC [23] and GlobFit [18] (Table 1). Our method achieves scalability by fully utilizing global similarities. Small cylinders are successfully captured (*e.g.*, the handrails and ladders in Figure 12, third row) because their orientations fall into principal directions in the scene and the detected orientations become a strong constraint in cylinder fitting.

8 Conclusion

We describe a novel robust processing pipeline to automatically extract pipe-runs from large-scale 3D point clouds. Our approach introduces the global information in an early stage by applying unsupervised analysis on point normals, and treats orientation detection and placement extraction as two separate sub-problems, thus avoiding degradation by local data errors. Joints are detected and modeled to recover connectivity information and smoothly connect cylinders.

References

1. Benkö, P., Martin, R.R., Várady, T.: Algorithms for reverse engineering boundary representation models. CAD (2001)
2. Bernardini, F., Mittleman, J., Rushmeier, H., Silva, C., Taubin, G.: The ball-pivoting algorithm for surface reconstruction. IEEE Transactions on Visualization and Computer Graphics 5(4), 349–359 (1999)
3. Carr, J.C., Beatson, R.K., Cherrie, J.B., Mitchell, T.J., Fright, W.R., McCallum, B.C., Evans, T.R.: Reconstruction and representation of 3d objects with radial basis functions. In: ACM SIGGRAPH (2001)
4. Chen, J., Chen, B.: Architectural modeling from sparsely scanned range data. International Journal of Computer Vision 78(2-3), 223–236 (2008)
5. Cignoni, P., Callieri, M., Corsini, M., Dellepiane, M., Ganovelli, F., Ranzuglia, G.: Meshlab: An open-source mesh processing tool. In: Eurographics Italian Chapter Conference (2008)
6. ClearEdge3D: Edgewise plant (December 2012), http://www.clearedge3d.com/, http://www.clearedge3d.com/Products.aspx?show=EdgeWisePlant
7. Comaniciu, D., Meer, P.: Mean shift: A robust approach toward feature space analysis. IEEE Transactions on Pattern Analysis and Machine Intelligence 24(5), 603–619 (2002)

8. Fischler, M., Bolles, R.: Random sample consensus: A paradigm for model fitting with applications to image analysis and automated cartography. Communications of the ACM 24(6), 381–395 (1981)
9. Fleishman, S., Cohen-Or, D., Silva, C.: Robust moving least-squares fitting with sharp features. ACM Transactions on Graphics (TOG) 24, 544–552 (2005)
10. Fu, Y., Zhu, X., Yang, J., Yuan, Z.: Pipe reconstruction from unorganized point cloud data. U.S. Patent Application 12/849, 647 (2010)
11. Gal, R., Shamir, A., Hassner, T., Pauly, M., Cohen-Or, D.: Surface reconstruction using local shape priors. In: Symposium on Geometry Processing (2007)
12. Hakala, D., Hillyard, R., Malraison, P., Nource, B.: Natural quadrics in mechanical design. Proc-AUTOFACT West 1, 17–20 (1981)
13. Hofer, M., Odehnal, B., Pottmann, H., Steiner, T., Wallner, J.: 3d shape recognition and reconstruction based on line element geometry. In: ICCV (2005)
14. Hoppe, H., DeRose, T., Duchamp, T., McDonald, J., Stuetzle, W.: Surface reconstruction from unorganized points. In: ACM SIGGRAPH (1992)
15. Hough, P.: Method and means for recognizing complex patterns. U.S. Patent No. 3,069, 654 (1962)
16. Huang, J., You, S.: Detecting objects in scene point cloud: A combinational approach. In: 2013 International Conference on 3DTV-Conference (2013)
17. Kazhdan, M., Bolitho, M., Hoppe, H.: Poisson surface reconstruction. In: Symposium on Geometry Processing (2006)
18. Li, Y., Wu, X., Chrysathou, Y., Sharf, A., Cohen-Or, D., Mitra, N.: Globfit: Consistently fitting primitives by discovering global relations. ACM Transactions on Graphics (TOG) 30, 52 (2011)
19. Liu, Y.J., Zhang, J.B., Hou, J.C., Ren, J.C., Tang, W.Q.: Cylinder Detection in Large-Scale Point Cloud of Pipeline Plant. IEEE Transactions on Visualization and Computer Graphics, 1–8 (April 2013)
20. Petitjean, S.: A survey of methods for recovering quadrics in triangle meshes. ACM Computing Surveys (CSUR) 34(2), 211–262 (2002)
21. Rabbani, T., Van Den Heuvel, F.: Efficient hough transform for automatic detection of cylinders in point clouds. ISPRS WG III/3, III/4 3, 60–65 (2005)
22. Rusu, R., Cousins, S.: 3d is here: Point cloud library (pcl). In: 2011 IEEE International Conference on Robotics and Automation (ICRA), pp. 1–4. IEEE (2011)
23. Schnabel, R., Wahl, R., Klein, R.: Efficient ransac for point-cloud shape detection. In: Computer Graphics Forum, vol. 26, pp. 214–226. Wiley Online Library (2007)
24. Schnabel, R., Degener, P., Klein, R.: Completion and reconstruction with primitive shapes. Computer Graphics Forum (2009)

Image-Based 4-d Reconstruction
Using 3-d Change Detection

Ali Osman Ulusoy and Joseph L. Mundy

School of Engineering, Brown University
Providence RI, USA

Abstract. This paper describes an approach to reconstruct the complete history of a 3-d scene over time from imagery. The proposed approach avoids rebuilding 3-d models of the scene at each time instant. Instead, the approach employs an initial 3-d model which is continuously updated with changes in the environment to form a full 4-d representation. This updating scheme is enabled by a novel algorithm that infers 3-d changes with respect to the model at one time step from images taken at a subsequent time step. This algorithm can effectively detect changes even when the illumination conditions between image collections are significantly different. The performance of the proposed framework is demonstrated on four challenging datasets in terms of 4-d modeling accuracy as well as quantitative evaluation of 3-d change detection.

1 Introduction

This paper proposes a new approach to reconstruct the evolution of a 3-d scene over time from imagery, *i.e.* image-based 4-d reconstruction. This work is targeted towards modeling of complex and ever-changing urban or natural environments. 4-d modeling of such scenes has various applications including urban growth analysis [1,2], construction site monitoring [3], natural resource management, surveillance and event analysis [4].

A naive approach to 4-d modeling is to reconstruct independent 3-d models for every time instant. This naive approach is motivated by the recent success of multi-view stereo (MVS) algorithms [5,6]. Nevertheless, 3-d reconstruction from images is an inherently ill-posed problem and reconstructing *dense* and *accurate* models of realistic urban or natural environments is still very challenging. Difficulties include areas of uniform appearance, transient objects, reflective surfaces, and self-occlusions. Model structure is highly dependent on illumination conditions, image resolution, and camera placement, which typically vary between data collections. Therefore, reconstructions of the same structures at different times typically contain many inconsistencies [4,7,8]. For instance, a building may be accurately reconstructed on an overcast day but not on a bright day with shadows and specular reflections that cause building surfaces to be fragmented in the model. These inconsistencies also complicate differentiating between actual changes in the scene from false alarms caused by inconsistent reconstructions, and therefore hinder 4-d analysis.

D. Fleet et al. (Eds.): ECCV 2014, Part III, LNCS 8691, pp. 31–45, 2014.

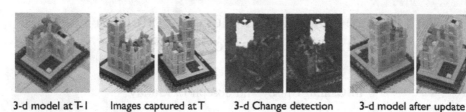

3-d model at T-1   Images captured at T   3-d Change detection   3-d model after update

Fig. 1. Overview of the proposed 4-d modeling algorithm. The 3-d model at time T-1 is updated using the images captured at T. The algorithm first detects the 3-d changes in the scene by fusing change evidence from multiple views. Subsequently, surface geometry and appearance are estimated to update the evolving 4-d model.

Most importantly, this naive approach does not exploit the fact that in realistic scenes, many objects, such as buildings and roads, persist through long periods of time and need not be repeatedly estimated. Once a 3-d model of the scene is obtained, no further processing is necessary until a change occurs.

Motivated by these observations, this paper proposes a 4-d reconstruction algorithm based on change detection. The algorithm utilizes an initial accurate 3-d model of the scene. In subsequent frames, images from multiple (arbitrary) viewpoints are used to detect 3-d changes in the environment. This scheme circumvents reconstruction of the entire scene and can be achieved from only a sparse set of views. The image regions corresponding to unchanged parts of the scene can be safely discarded and model update is targeted only on the changed volumes. The steps of the proposed algorithm are depicted in Figure 1.

The algorithm continuously detects and incorporates changes in a scene over time to produce a complete 4-d representation. Such changes could include variations in both geometry and surface reflectance. However, if there exist vast illumination differences between data collections, the algorithm can effectively discard the effects of illumination and detect changes only in geometry.

The framework employs a probabilistic representation of 4-d surface geometry and appearance. Appearance is defined as the combination of surface reflectance and illumination giving rise to the pixel intensity or color seen in observations of the surface. This 4-d representation allows modeling the evolution of arbitrary and complex 3-d shapes, with no constraints on changing scene topology. The resulting 4-d models allow visualization of the full history of the scene from novel viewpoints as shown in Figure 2, as well as spatio-temporal analysis for applications such as tracking and event detection.

This paper makes three main contributions. The first contribution is a probabilistic formulation to detect 3-d changes at each time step without reconstructing a 3-d model for the entire scene. This inference process generates 3-d change volumes rather than pixel-level image change probabilities as in earlier applications of probabilistic volumetric representations [9]. The second contribution is an algorithm to discard the effects of varying illumination to detect structural 3-d changes. The final contribution is the 4-d modeling pipeline which utilizes this change detection algorithm to continuously incorporate changes in a 4-d

Fig. 2. Renderings of a 4-d model reconstructed using the proposed algorithm. The model captures the step-by-step construction of a toy Lego tower. The framework allows visualizing the 4-d model at any time instant from novel views.

time-varying model. To the best of our knowledge, no other work has demonstrated such continuous operation in realistic and challenging urban scenes.

2 Related Work

The proposed 4-d reconstruction pipeline performs 3-d change detection using the current set of images and the 3-d model from the previous time step. This 3-d change detection expands on the probabilistic and volumetric modeling (PVM) framework of Pollard and Mundy [9]. Their model encodes occupancy (surface) probability and an appearance distribution of each voxel in a volumetric grid, which is similar to other probabilistic voxel-based algorithms [10,11]. The surface and appearance distributions are jointly estimated using online Bayesian learning. The resulting 3-d model allows computing the probability of observing a given intensity or color, from an arbitrary (but known) viewpoint and without reference to training imagery. This probability can be used to compute the probability of change of each pixel in the image. Inspired by the PVM, the proposed framework encodes probabilistic surface and appearance information in 4-d.

The first contribution of this paper is a 3-d change detection algorithm based on combining pixel-wise change evidence from different viewpoints to compute the probability of change in each 3-d cell. Note that the algorithm of [9] detects changes *on the image domain*, whereas the proposed formulation estimates the volumetric structure of change *in the 3-d domain*.

The second contribution of this paper is an algorithm to detect changes only in 3-d geometry, *i.e.* structural change detection. Earlier algorithms that utilize the PVM for change detection assume either that illumination conditions vary slowly with respect to the model update rate or that illumination variations can be removed through global normalization [12]. However, in real outdoor settings, the variations in illumination and shadows are too complex to allow such normalization schemes. The proposed algorithm estimates a new appearance model for the PVM so as to match the appearance of the current image collection. Once the illumination conditions in the PVM and the corresponding appearance of surfaces as seen in the images are consistent, the 3-d change detection algorithm can be directly utilized to detect the structural differences.

The proposed approach is motivated by "appearance transfer"-based change detection methods [13] but at the same time, it extends them. Such methods exploit the prior 3-d scene geometry as a proxy to transfer pixels of one image onto the view of the other image and then compare the corresponding pixels. Matching pixels indicate where the geometry is still valid, *i.e.* background. Non-matching pixels indicate a foreground object. Kosecka exploit the appearance transfer concept for change detection in urban environments using StreetView images [14]. Deguchi *et al.* present a similar method where the uncertainty during depth estimation is also utilized [4]. Taneja *et al.* employs a surface mesh for appearance transfer between pairs of wide-baseline images [15,8]. Their approach also fuses the foreground maps in 3-d, using a similar approach to multi-view silhouette fusion [16]. The foreground estimate is then used as a coarse update to the initial mesh. Such methods compare pairs of images *on the image domain*. In contrast, the proposed method incorporates all image evidence simultaneously in 3-d using a probabilistic representation of surface geometry.

The third contribution of this paper is the 4-d modeling pipeline suitable for realistic urban or natural scenes. Another approach which utilizes the PVM in modeling 4-d scenes is by Ulusoy *et al.* [17], which generates 4-d models by reconstructing full 3-d models (PVMs) at each time step. Their results are limited to indoor studio data, which has static cameras as well as foreground segregation, that allows producing high-quality independent reconstructions. Such independent reconstruction is highly undesirable in realistic urban scenes for two reasons. First, such scenes contain many static or slowly varying structures which need not be repeatedly estimated at every frame. Second, 3-d reconstruction from images is an ill-posed problem and variations in imaging conditions typically result in significantly different reconstructions of the same structures. In contrast, the proposed pipeline estimates updates to the previous time step's PVM from subsequent imagery in two phases. In the first phase, the 3-d change detection algorithm is used to compute the probability of change in each 3-d cell. Then, reconstruction is targeted at cells with significant change probability so as to estimate only their changed surface and appearance distributions.

Ulusoy *et al.* define an efficient representation for 4-d volumetric scenes, which is also used in the algorithms proposed here. The representation,based on shallow octrees with binary time trees at each leaf is well-matched to highly parallel GPU processing. It is emphasized that the change-driven 4-d modeling algorithms proposed here represent a significant departure from their approach of reconstructing a full 3-d model at each time step.

3   4-d Reconstruction Pipeline Overview

The proposed framework encodes a occupancy (surface) probability and an appearance distribution of each cell in 4-d. These quantities are stored in the 4-d data structure proposed by Ulusoy *et al.* [17]. In brief, a volume is decomposed as an octree and the temporal variation in each cell is modeled by a binary tree. This 4-d representation is initialized with a PVM (3-d model) that represents the initial state of the scene. At subsequent times, imagery taken roughly simultaneously from arbitrary viewpoints are input to the 3-d change detection algorithm. The images are registered to the 3-d model using standard tools. The details of registration can be found in the experiments section. The proposed change detection algorithm and its extension to varying illumination conditions are explained in Sections 4 and 5 respectively. These algorithms compute the probability of change in each 3-d cell. Subsequently, the new surface and appearance distributions of cells with significant change probability estimated from the current set of images to update the current 3-d model. Namely, the binary time trees of the changed cells in the 4-d representation are sub-divided to allocate new memory for the update. The cells to be updated are initialized as empty (low surface probability) and the online learning algorithm of [9] is used to estimate the surface probabilities and appearance distributions. It should be noted that this process does not estimate the changed parts of the model in isolation, but uses the entire PVM for visibility and occlusion reasoning. This 3-d context supports change analysis in cases where objects are heavily occluded by background surfaces. These steps of 3-d change detection and model update are repeated for each time instant to achieve a complete 4-d model.

4   3-d Change Detection

This section describes 3-d change detection in the PVM from subsequent images captured from multiple viewpoints. The simplest situation is where illumination conditions are assumed to vary slowly such that the appearance encoded in the PVM at frame $T - 1$ is similar to that of the images captured at T. Note that this assumption does not require the appearance of the initial PVM and all subsequent frames to be similar; it only requires the appearance of neighboring times to be similar. The assumption of slowly varying illumination will later be relaxed but enables a straightforward description of the algorithm. Based on this assumption, events that vary the appearance of the scene qualify as change. Such events include structural changes, *e.g.* a new building, as well as changes in surface colors, *e.g.* new paint on a wall.

The PVM is represented in a grid of cells, where each cell X contains a surface probability, $p(X_S)$, and an appearance distribution, $p(X_I)$. Appearance is defined as the intensity or color of surface voxels as seen in the image pixels. The problem is to compute the presence or absence of change in each cell given subsequent images $\{I_i\}_{i=1}^N$. A binary random variable, X_C is defined for each cell, where $X_C = 1$ denotes the presence of change and $X_C = 0$ denotes no change. The problem can be posed as maximum a-posteriori estimation,

$$\{X_C\}^* = \underset{\{X_C\}}{\operatorname{argmax}} p(\{X_C\}|\{I\}) \propto p(\{I\}|\{X_C\}) p(\{X_C\}) \tag{1}$$

The likelihood term, $p(\{I\}|\{X_C\})$, models evidence from the images. The prior term, $p(\{X_C\})$, represents all previous knowledge regarding which parts of scene may contain changes. Such information can be obtained from various sources including semantic cues, $e.g.$ a construction site is likely to contain many changes, whereas the Eiffel tower is almost surely static. However in the work here, a uniform prior is assumed, $i.e.$ each voxel is equally likely to change.

For tractability, the change probability of each cell is considered conditionally independent given the images. This assumption leads to a simple solution to eq. (1) where a cell is labeled as containing change if,

$$\frac{p(\{I\}|X_C = 1)}{p(\{I\}|X_C = 0)} > \frac{p(X_C = 0)}{p(X_C = 1)} \tag{2}$$

Note that this solution is the likelihood ratio test arising from Bayesian decision theory. The terms $p(\{I\}|X_C = 1)$ and $p(\{I\}|X_C = 0)$ model image evidence in the presence and absence of change respectively. Assuming conditional independence, the terms are simplified as follows,

$$p(\{I\}|X_C) = \prod_{i=1}^{N} p(I_i|X_C) \tag{3}$$

The image intensities (or color) observed at a pixel are either due to background (PVM) or foreground (change). In general, no a-priori information is available about the appearance of a "change" and therefore, the intensities are assumed to be uniformly distributed. On the other hand, if the pixel is generated by the background, the PVM allows computing the probability of observing intensity I along ray R as follows:

$$p(I) = \sum_{X \in R} p(I|V = X) p(V = X) \tag{4}$$

$$p(V = X) = p(X_S) p(X \text{ is visible}) \tag{5}$$

$$p(X \text{ is visible}) = \prod_{X' < X} (1 - p(X'_S)) \tag{6}$$

where V denotes the cell along the ray that is responsible for producing the pixel intensity and $p(I|V = X)$ is the appearance distribution of the cell.

Assuming the cell X back-projects into a single pixel in image I_i, predicates B_X^i and F_X^i can be defined for each pixel, indicating whether the pixel was generated by background or change respectively. The term $p(I_i|X_C = 1)$ can be expressed using these predicates as follows,

$$p(I_i|X_C = 1) = p(I_i|F_X^i) p(F_X^i|X_C = 1) + p(I_i|B_X^i) p(B_X^i|X_C = 1) \tag{7}$$

where $p(I_i|F_X^i)$ is the uniform distribution and $p(I_i|B_X^i)$ is computed as in eq. (4). The term $p(B_X^i|X_C = 1)$ is the probability of observing background in the pixel when cell X along the ray contains change. It is expanded by applying the Bayes rule,

$$p(B_X^i|X_C) = \frac{p(X_C|B_X^i)\,p(B_X^i)}{p(X_C|B_X^i)\,p(B_X^i) + p(X_C|F_X^i)\,p(F_X^i)} \tag{8}$$

where $p(F_X^i)$ and $p(B_X^i)$ can be set to 0.5 in the absence of prior knowledge. The likelihood term $p(X_C = 1|B_X^i)$ can be expressed based on the following intuition. Given the pixel is background, the voxels between the camera and the surface voxel, $i.e.$ visible voxels, can be labeled as containing no change. However, nothing can be said about the voxels after the surface voxel along the ray, $i.e.$ occluded voxels. Thus, the term can be expanded as follows,

$$p(X_C|B_X^i) = p(X_C|vis, B_X^i)\,p(vis|B_X^i) + p(X_C|\neg vis, B_X^i)\,p(\neg vis|B_X^i) \tag{9}$$

where $vis|B_X^i$ is shorthand for "X is visible" given the pixel is generated by background. Note that $p(X_C = 1|vis, B_X^i) = 0$, since a visible voxel that backprojects into a background pixel cannot contain change. However, when the voxel is not visible, the term $p(X_C = 1|\neg vis, B_X^i)$ is set to 0.5 to denote the uncertainty. The probability of visibility, $p(vis|B_X^i)$, can be computed exactly as in eq. (6). However, note that this computation is only possible because the pixel is known to be background, $i.e.$ the PVM geometry along the ray is still accurate. In general, visibility or other measurements in the PVM may no longer be correct due to the changes in the scene. The likelihood is simplified as,

$$p(X_C|B_X^i) = 0.5\,p(X \text{ is not visible}) \tag{10}$$

Finally, $p(X_C = 1|F_X^i)$ is set to 1. Since the pixel is foreground, the geometry in the PVM is no longer accurate and therefore, nothing can be said regarding visibility of change. In the absence of such information, it is best to assume change may be present in any cell along the ray.

Overall, this formulation incorporates change evidence from all viewpoints while reasoning about visibility and occlusions. The solution, eq. (2), allows processing each image separately and then making a decision locally at each 3-d cell. Note that this framework can be augmented with spatial priors. However, such priors typically require large scale global inference algorithms. Moreover, traditional priors such as smoothness or planarity are often not valid in complex urban settings with changes due to construction or transportation.

5 Structural 3-d Change Detection

The change detection algorithm described in the previous section utilizes 3-d appearance in the PVM to detect 3-d changes in the model. When the illumination conditions of a new image collection are significantly different from that of an existing PVM, this algorithm can no longer be used. In such cases, the entire scene might have changed in appearance and therefore, changes only in geometry are considered. This section describes a method to effectively discard the effects of illumination change between collections to detect changes only in geometry.

In such cases, the appearance distributions stored in the PVM do not directly relate to the new appearance of the scene. Therefore, the proposed algorithm discards these distributions and retains only the probabilistic 3-d geometry. Then, the algorithm estimates the current appearance probability distributions in the PVM from the input images. Once the illumination conditions in the PVM match to that of the images, the change detection algorithm of Section 4 can be applied to detect the changes in geometry.

First, assume that the 3-d geometry represented by the PVM is unchanged. Under this assumption, the appearance of a surface voxel can be estimated from the images it is visible in. Each image provides an intensity or color observation, as well as a weight (see eq. 5) for each voxel in its field of view. An appearance distribution is fit to the set of weighted samples. The weight prevents occluded voxels from being trained with occluding surfaces' color. Under the Lambertian reflectance assumption, a Gaussian distribution is sufficient to explain the intensities observed from different viewpoints.

In general, the scene will contain geometric changes (additions or removals) that are currently not modeled in the PVM. The changes will cause the appearance models of some voxels to be trained with erroneous observations. This situation can be analyzed in Figure 3, where the addition and removal of a blue object are shown in Figures 3a and 3b respectively. In the case of addition, the appearance model of the occluded voxel X_1 is incorrectly trained with the object color. When the object is removed voxel X_2, which no longer contains a surface, is trained with colors from different parts of the surface behind. Also, X_1 is no longer occluded in the middle camera but the pixel observation is still weighted with an incorrect low visibility probability.

The challenge of appearance estimation is then to segregate in each voxel, the actual color of the surface from the pixel observations caused by changes. Note that this problem is very similar to background modeling in the image domain. Inspired by Stauffer and Grimson's approach [18], the appearance of each voxel

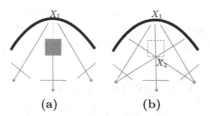

(a)   (b)

Fig. 3. A simple scene to study the effects of appearance estimation when new object (blue square) is added (a) or removed (b) from the scene

is modeled using a mixture of Gaussians distribution. The training follows the online EM based algorithm of [18]. The "background" mixture modes, which correspond to the actual surface color, are chosen to be those with high mixture weight and low variance. The rest of the modes, caused by changes in the scene, can be discarded for the purposes of this algorithm.

This scheme relies on being able to classify the actual color modes of surfaces, which depends on the scene and camera poses. In general, multiple observations of the surface are needed to form "background" modes such that any other mode created by the changes can be classified as otherwise. Consider voxel X_1 in Figure 3a, which receives one incorrect and two correct observations, resulting in a low variance mode for the actual color and a higher variance mode for the occluding object color. Hence, the appearance of X_1 can be correctly computed.

A demonstration of appearance estimation is provided in Figure 4 on a street scene. A rendering of the initial PVM is presented in Figure 4a. Subsequent images (see Figure 4b) were captured under significantly different illumination

| (a) | (b) | (c) |
| (d) | (e) | (f) |

Fig. 4. Demonstration of estimating the new appearance of the PVM from subsequent images. (a) The rendering of the initial PVM. (b) One of eight subsequent images captured under different illumination conditions than that of the PVM. Note the additional object (speed camera) next to the tree. (c-e) The rendering of the PVM after having discarded the old appearance model and estimated the new appearance with a single image (c), two images (d) and eight images (e). (f) Rendering of the PVM after 3-d model update.

and reveal the addition of a speed camera next to the tree. Note that this object is not present in the initial PVM. Figure 4c displays the PVM after having discarded the old appearance models and using a single image to estimate the new appearance. The image pixels corresponding to the speed camera get projected onto the wall since the speed camera's 3-d geometry is not yet modeled in the PVM. Figures 4d and 4e display renderings of the PVM after using two and eight images respectively. As more images are used, the ghosting effects of the speed camera fade away and the correct (current) color of the wall can be estimated. Once the new appearance distributions are estimated, the change detection algorithm of Section 4 can applied directly to detect changes in geometry, such as the shape of the speed camera.

6   Experiments

The framework is evaluated on four different datasets. Each dataset consists of imagery captured from multiple arbitrary viewpoints at each time instant. All datasets except the last one contain multiple time steps to demonstrate continuous operation of the 4-d reconstruction framework.

The images for the first three datasets were captured using a handheld camera with 1 megapixel resolution. The images were calibrated with incremental Structure-from-Motion using the VisualSFM software [19]. The initial set of images were calibrated using the standard SfM pipeline. The resulting image matches and point cloud are used to register subsequent images. In all three datasets, this procedure achieved sub-pixel reprojection error. These datasets are available at http://www.lems.brown.edu/~au/4d_datasets.

For the first two datasets, the illumination conditions vary slowly with respect to the time step such that the appearance of the scene does not change much between collections. Both datasets contain small-scale objects so that changes can be easily produced, but were captured *outdoors under natural illumination*. The 3-d change detection algorithm of Section 4 is employed here to reconstruct the 4-d model. The final two datasets contain image sets captured under significantly different illumination in real ground-level urban scenes and are used to evaluate the framework with the structural change detection algorithm. The choice of which change detection algorithm to use is decided manually for now. The last dataset, which consists of two time steps, was taken from Taneja *et al.* [8] where they used it to demonstrate their structural change detection approach. This dataset is used to compare the proposed algorithm to this previous work.

The first dataset captures the step by step construction of a Lego Big Ben tower. The scene initially contains the base plate and the tower is erected in a total of six time steps. Each time step is modeled from roughly forty images taken around the object in two circles. Renderings from the resulting 4-d model is displayed in Figure 2. The proposed algorithm effectively captures the evolution of the scene with high resolution.

Example 3-d change detection and model update results are displayed in Figure 1. It can be observed that the detections are correctly localized on the two

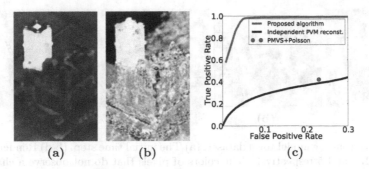

(a)   (b)   (c)

Fig. 5. Comparison of 3-d change detection results for the first dataset. Volume rendering of changes predicted by the proposed approach (a) and the approach of independently reconstructing PVMs (b). The ROC curve is displayed in (c).

new blocks added to the tower. The change detection results are compared to the approach of reconstructing 3-d models for each time step in Figure 5. Separate PVM models are reconstructed for $T-1$ and T and the models are compared in 3-d, where the change probability of a cell is computed as the difference between the corresponding surface probabilities at $T-1$ and T. The resulting change probabilities are displayed using volume rendering in Figure 5b, where the inconsistencies between the models can be observed. The comparison is quantified using an ROC curve shown in Figure 5c. The ground truth 3-d changes are delineated manually and the detection threshold in eq. (2) is varied to construct the curves. The significant inconsistency between individually reconstructed PVM models results in a high number of false positives. This comparison was also repeated using PMVS[20]+Poisson[21] reconstruction instead of the PVM approach. The resulting meshes were voxelized for 3-d binary change detection, which yields a single point on the ROC curve. The PMVS+Poisson result is similar to that of the PVM. These results demonstrate the inherent ill-posed nature of inferring 3-d geometry from images. Small imaging differences (slight variations in illumination and camera poses) produce larger 3-d model surface variations which lead to dissimilarities in the reconstructions of unchanged regions. These dissimilarities complicate distinguishing between actual changes in the scene from false alarms. In contrast, the proposed algorithm is robust to these imaging differences due to its probabilistic multi-view change reasoning.

This dataset was also used to assess the computation time of the proposed algorithm with respect to reconstructing 3-d models from scratch. Both methods were implemented based on the code made available in [17], which provides an implementation of the 4-d representation optimized for computation in the GPU. The change detection algorithms and the model update algorithm were implemented to exploit this parallelism. All algorithms process images in an online fashion. On average, reconstructing 3-d models from scratch takes roughly 7 minutes while the proposed pipeline takes 5 minutes. The computation time is improved because during model update, only the changed pixels are used to

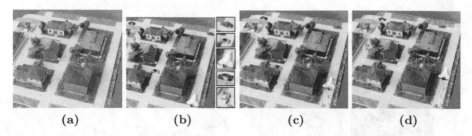

(a) (b) (c) (d)

Fig. 6. Results from the model town dataset. (a) The initial time step. (b-d) Renderings from frames 1, 3 and 5 respectively. The colors of pixels that do not observe a change are converted to grey to highlight the dynamic objects. The column to the right of (b) shows a close up view of the changes for that time step. Please zoom in the images to appreciate the reconstruction quality.

cast rays to update the volume. Moreover, since many structures in the scene are already reconstructed, the update algorithm converges much faster.

The second dataset contains toy cars moving on a lifelike miniature model town. The initial time step consists of only the model town and is modeled from roughly fifty images. The initial PVM is presented in Figure 6a. For each of the rest of the time steps, only ten images are available. In the second time step, the cars are placed on the model town. Then, in each subsequent frame, the cars are moved gradually along the road. This dataset poses additional challenges due to the limited number of views at each time step. Moreover, the scene contains many complex structures, such as the buildings and trees, that frequently occlude the cars. The resulting 4-d model is displayed from a novel viewpoint for three time steps in Figures 6b-6d. The detected 3-d changes are used to grey out the pixels that do not observe a change. It can be seen that the moving cars are accurately detected and reconstructed.

Static structures in the model town, that were reconstructed accurately in the initial time step, are detected as unchanging, which allows their reconstructions to persist from the initial time step to future time steps. In contrast, the method of reconstructing individual models at each time step attempts to reconstruct the *entire scene structure* from the sparse set of images. Experiments show both PVM and PMVS+Poisson fail to produce acceptable 3-d models in this setting. Please see the supplementary document for the comparisons.

The third dataset was captured in an urban environment. The initial five time steps involve the process of taking two trash cans outside and then removing them, one by one. The first time step was modeled from fifteen images and the next four time steps from six images on average. The resulting 4-d model is rendered in Figure 7, where the appearance and disappearance of the trash cans are modeled accurately ($T2 - T4$). Next, the scene was imaged during a construction several months later ($T = 5$), where no major structural changes are present. The structural change detection algorithm correctly detects no significant changes in the scene even though the illumination has changed drastically.

Fig. 7. Renderings of the 4-d model of the third dataset

The rendering of the scene after the new appearance can be seen in the image labeled $T = 5$. Note the presence of direct sunlight and shadows. Finally, the next day ($T = 6$), images were taken under new illumination conditions, when a construction cone was placed on the sidewalk. The geometry of the cone is modeled accurately as seen in the figure. Similarly to the previous dataset, the small number of images in some time steps does not allow independent 3-d reconstruction of each time step.

The final dataset consist of two sets of eight images of an urban environment with (see Figure 4b) and without a speed camera, as well as a mesh model of the scene without it. Taneja *et al.* exploit this mesh model as a proxy to compare pairs of images and integrate image inconsistencies in the volume [8]. Their approach assumes spatial smoothness of changed regions and exploits the output of object (vegetation, human, and car) detectors to suppress false positives. In contrast, the proposed approach employs all image evidence (not just image pairs) simultaneously in an entirely probabilistic representation of surface geometry, appearance and change. Moreover, the proposed approach does not assume

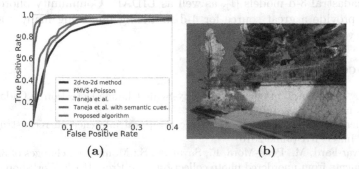

(a)   (b)

Fig. 8. (a) Change detection ROC curve for the fourth dataset. (b) The rendering of the PVM after the reverse experiment of removing the object.

a smoothness prior or assume such semantic cues are available. The comparison is carried out using the ground truth change masks provided in the dataset. The 3-d changes are projected onto the ground truth masks to compute true and false positive rates. The resulting ROC curve is displayed in Figure 8a, where rest of the curves were taken from [8]. The proposed approach performs better than Taneja *et al.*'s approach (green curve), which uses a spatial smoothness prior to regularize the detections, as well as when their approach additionally exploits semantic cues (blue curve). However, it can be observed that the proposed approach does not reach a full detection rate. The missed detections occur at the bottom of the speed camera, where the camera (changed region) borders the pavement (original geometry). Taneja *et al.*'s approach is able to detect this region due to the spatial smoothness term in the formulation.

Figure 4f displays the updated model which includes the speed camera. The reverse experiment was also performed, where this updated model was used together with the images excluding the object to detect the disappearance of the object. The resulting model is presented in Figure 8b.

7   Conclusion

This paper presented a novel image-based 4-d reconstruction algorithm suited for capturing the evolution of ever-changing urban or natural environments. The proposed algorithm avoids rebuilding 3-d models of the scene at each time instant through detection of changes and reconstructing only the changed surfaces. Through accurate change detection and model update, the algorithm is able to achieve continuous operation in challenging datasets. Experiments confirm that this approach yields higher quality 4-d models, better change detection accuracy and running time compared to the baseline approach of independent 3-d reconstruction of each time step. The reconstruction algorithm is based on a novel 3-d change detection algorithm which can detect changes in geometry and appearance, or only in geometry in case of significant illumination difference between collections. The algorithm performs favorably compared to previous works.

Future work includes city-wide large scale 4-d reconstruction, where various sources of information can be exploited, *e.g.* aerial, ground level and satellite imagery, cadastral 3-d models [1], as well as LIDAR. Community photo collections also provide a great source for 4-d modeling but bring many additional challenges yet to be addressed [22].

References

1. Taneja, A., Ballan, L., Pollefeys, M.: City-Scale Change Detection in Cadastral 3D Models using Images. In: CVPR (2013)
2. Schindler, G., Dellaert, F.: Probabilistic temporal inference on reconstructed 3D scenes. In: CVPR (June 2010)
3. Golparvar-Fard, M., Pena-Mora, F., Savarese, S.: Monitoring changes of 3D building elements from unordered photo collections. In: Proc. IEEE Workshop on Computer Vision for Remote Sensing of the Environment (in conjunction with ICCV 2011) (2011)

4. Sakurada, K., Takayuki, O., Deguchi, K.: Detecting Changes in 3D Structure of a Scene from Multi-view Images Captured by a Vehicle-mounted Camera. In: CVPR (2013)

5. Pons, J.P., Labatut, P., Vu, H.H., Keriven, R.: High Accuracy and Visibility-Consistent Dense Multiview Stereo. PAMI (2012)

6. Tola, E., Strecha, C., Fua, P.: Efficient large-scale multi-view stereo for ultra high-resolution image sets. Machine Vision and Applications 27(5), 1–18 (2011)

7. Restrepo, I.M.: Characterization of Probabilistic Volumetric Models for 3-d Computer Vision. PhD thesis, Brown University (2013)

8. Taneja, A., Ballan, L., Pollefeys, M.: Image based detection of geometric changes in urban environments. In: ICCV (November 2011)

9. Pollard, T., Mundy, J.L.: Change Detection in a 3-d World. In: CVPR (June 2007)

10. Bonet, J.D., Viola, P.: Poxels: Probabilistic voxelized volume reconstruction. In: ICCV (1999)

11. Broadhurst, A., Drummond, T.W., Cipolla, R.: A Probabilistic Framework for Space Carving. In: ICCV (2001)

12. Pollard, T.B.: Comprehensive 3-d Change Detection Using Volumetric Appearance Modeling. PhD thesis, Brown University (2009)

13. Ivanov, Y., Bobick, A., Liu, J.: Fast lighting independent background subtraction. IJCV, 1–14 (2000)

14. Košecka, J.: Detecting changes in images of street scenes. In: Lee, K.M., Matsushita, Y., Rehg, J.M., Hu, Z. (eds.) ACCV 2012, Part IV. LNCS, vol. 7727, pp. 590–601. Springer, Heidelberg (2013)

15. Taneja, A., Ballan, L., Pollefeys, M.: Modeling dynamic scenes recorded with freely moving cameras. In: Kimmel, R., Klette, R., Sugimoto, A. (eds.) ACCV 2010, Part III. LNCS, vol. 6494, pp. 613–626. Springer, Heidelberg (2011)

16. Franco, J.S., Boyer, E.: Fusion of multiview silhouette cues using a space occupancy grid. In: ICCV (2005)

17. Ulusoy, A.O., Biris, O., Mundy, J.L.: Dynamic Probabilistic Volumetric Models. In: ICCV (2013)

18. Stauffer, C., Grimson, W.: Adaptive background mixture models for real-time tracking. In: CVPR (1998)

19. Wu, C.: Towards Linear-time Incremental Structure from Motion. 3DV (June 2013)

20. Furukawa, Y., Ponce, J.: Accurate, dense, and robust multiview stereopsis. PAMI (August 2010)

21. Kazhdan, M., Bolitho, M., Hoppe, H.: Poisson surface reconstruction. Eurographics (2006)

22. Snavely, N., Seitz, S.M., Szeliski, R.: Modeling the World from Internet Photo Collections. IJCV (December 2007)

VocMatch: Efficient Multiview Correspondence for Structure from Motion

Michal Havlena and Konrad Schindler

Institute of Geodesy and Photogrammetry, ETH Zürich, Switzerland
{michal.havlena,schindler}@geod.baug.ethz.ch

Abstract. Feature matching between pairs of images is a main bottle-neck of structure-from-motion computation from large, unordered image sets. We propose an efficient way to establish point correspondences between *all* pairs of images in a dataset, without having to test each individual pair. The principal message of this paper is that, given a sufficiently large visual vocabulary, *feature matching can be cast as image indexing*, subject to the additional constraints that index words must be rare in the database and unique in each image. We demonstrate that the proposed matching method, in conjunction with a standard inverted file, is 2-3 orders of magnitude faster than conventional pairwise matching. The proposed vocabulary-based matching has been integrated into a standard SfM pipeline, and delivers results similar to those of the conventional method in much less time.

Keywords: Feature matching, Image clustering, Structure from motion.

1 Introduction

Recent developments in large-scale structure-from-motion (SfM) from unordered datasets make it possible to automatically construct 3D models from tens or even hundreds of thousands of photos downloaded from Internet photo-sharing sites [1,4]. The two most expensive subtasks in unordered SfM are *(i)* feature matching between images and *(ii)* bundle adjustment. The efficiency required to process such large image sets is achieved mainly by limiting those two tasks to cleverly selected subsets of images, and massively parallelizing them. Specifically, even with parallelization it would be prohibitive (quadratic in the size of the image set) to match all pairs of images, hence the set of candidate pairs to be matched is first pruned to only those pairs for which it is likely that enough correspondences can be found. There are two popular ways of reducing the number of candidate image pairs: either image indexing via shared visual words [20,14], or clustering with global image descriptors such as GIST [15] to select a subset of "iconic" images. Both methods bring a significant speed-up, but also tend to miss some image pairs that could in fact be matched, leading to unnecessary fragmentation of the resulting models.

Here, we propose an efficient way to match *all* pairs of images in a database *without* the need to exhaustively test each individual image pair. The method

D. Fleet et al. (Eds.): ECCV 2014, Part III, LNCS 8691, pp. 46–60, 2014.

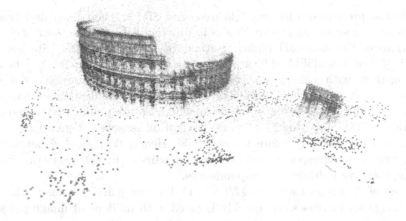

Fig. 1. Colosseum and Arch of Constantine, one of 13 models in the ROME dataset computed with Bundler from feature point matches of the proposed *VocMatch* method. Finding matches between all 13,049 images of Rome took ≈ 2 hours on a single CPU core. Red pyramids denote camera poses, the 3D point cloud is visualized by small dots colored from the respective images.

builds upon a simple observation: if we employ a visual vocabulary to quantize the feature descriptors from an image, then similar features will be mapped to the same visual word. As we increase the size of the vocabulary, fewer features will map to each word, until eventually most visual words will only be found *once in a given image*. We show that with a huge vocabulary the quantization is fine enough to directly define the multi-view matching: many visual words appear in multiple images, but are unique in every one of them, hence no subsequent matching step is required to establish correspondence. By construction, the approach directly finds a list of matches for the same point across multiple images. Following [12] we call such a list a "track", borrowing the term from sequential SfM. The set of all discovered tracks can be fed into a standard SfM pipeline to reconstruct camera poses and a sparse 3D reconstruction. Although the clustering and export steps required for this integration are still quadratic in the size of the image set, they only require simple operations and are orders of magnitude faster than full matching.

We make the following contributions: *(i)* we show that, with a sufficiently large vocabulary, exhaustive feature matching in large image sets can be cast as image indexing, subject to the additional constraints that index words must be rare in the database and unique in each image; *(ii)* we demonstrate that the proposed matching method, in conjunction with a standard inverted file, yields a speed-up by three orders of magnitude, and along the way delivers the clustering of the image set into independent 3D models for free; *(iii)* we integrate the proposed matching scheme into a standard SfM pipeline, and obtain results comparable with the conventional approach in much less time, see Figure 1.

2   Related Work

An essential prerequisite for any feature-based SfM method is to find tracks, *i.e.* lists of corresponding feature points in different images that tentatively are projections of the same 3D point. A standard incremental SfM pipeline like Bundler [21] or VisualSFM [22], starts by detecting salient image points and encoding them with a descriptor, typically SIFT [11]. For unordered datasets no assumptions about the ordering of images can be made to constrain the matching problem—unlike SfM from video, where feature points are tracked over time [18], or SfM supported by external navigation sensors, where approximate camera poses are known before matching [8]. Hence, tracks are generated by finding two-view correspondences between all pairs of images and transitively chaining them to multiview correspondences.

In a set of N images there are $\frac{1}{2}N(N-1)$ different pairings, thus as the size of the image set increases one quickly is faced with millions of image pairs. It thus becomes necessary to prefilter the possible pairs with some proxy that is much faster than feature matching. A popular method is to represent images as *tf-idf* vectors (weighted bags-of-words [20]) and compute the scalar product between those vectors [6,1]. That scalar product (*i.e.* the cosine between the two high-dimensional *tf-idf* signatures) is often a good proxy for the the amount of overlap between the images' fields of view, and thus an indication how likely it is to find corresponding scene points. Pairwise feature matching still needs to be done, but only for the smaller set of image pairs that have similar *tf-idf* signatures. Since the proxy is not perfect it can (and often does) happen that some matchable image pairs are discarded, too. In some cases this will disconnect image blocks that show the same scene and lead to unwanted fragmentation of the 3D model.

Another group of methods aims at reducing the size of the image set, and as a consequence also the set of possible pairs. Data from Internet photo-sharing sites such as Flickr [23] often contain many similar views of the same scene. For the purpose of reconstruction these are redundant (3D reconstruction can reliably be performed using only one of them), therefore it has been proposed to cluster images based on a cheap signature such as the GIST descriptor [15] and only retain one best representative per cluster [9,4]. Alternatively, one can construct a camera graph in which edges connect images with high *tf-idf* similarities, and search for the minimum dominating set of that graph, *i.e.* the smallest subset of images that adequately covers the entire camera network [7]. When pruning images rather than image pairs there is an even greater risk of fragmentation, because in most cases removing an image disconnects several possible pairs.

Our proposed method is orthogonal to the two approaches described above. We neither reduce the number of images nor restrict the set of possible pairings, but rather present a way to greatly speed up the multiview matching itself. In particular, our method naturally fits with most works described above, since it also starts with quantizing descriptors into visual words, which existing methods [6,1,7] do anyway. Given the quantization we then generate an inverted file, in time linear in the number N of images. The trick in our method is to make the quantization so fine that the file entries directly correspond to feature tracks.

Our way of generating tracks can be seen as a limiting case of [19], where conventional matching is performed, but only between those features that map to the same visual word of a smaller vocabulary. Instead, we make sure that every image contains at most one instance of every relevant word, such that the matching becomes trivial.

Another view of the proposed method is as an extreme representative of a class of image retrieval methods which, given a large image database, aim to find images showing the same location [17,3]. These methods also index and query the database with *tf-idf* vectors w.r.t. a large visual vocabulary, verify the retrieved images using the spatial layout of feature points, and optionally expand the retrieved set by resubmitting the results as further query images. The verification step amounts to robustly fitting a geometric transformation which aligns corresponding feature points. Our method could be seen as a retrieval system that submits every image of the database as query so as to directly get maximally expanded sets of spatially related images, and then runs full SfM on these sets as geometric verification.

3   Method

The method builds on a huge, publicly available visual vocabulary that allows for a fine quantization into 16 million visual words [12]. The vocabulary has 2 layers ($4{,}096{\times}4{,}096$ words) and was trained on a database of 11 billion SIFT descriptors computed at Hessian-Affine interest points [16]. To use the vocabulary we resample all images in the database to a common resolution, extract the same features, and quantize them with two rounds of approximate nearest-neighbor search (FLANN, [13]). Note that all these operations are linear in the number of images and can be massively parallelized.

Next, a simple loop through all processed images generates an inverted file, *i.e.* for each visual word a list of all images in which that word appears, see Figure 2. For our purposes two additional conditions must be fulfilled to include an image in the list: *(i)* the word must be *unique* (appear only once) in the respective image; and *(ii)* the word must be *rare* (appear in $\leq 1\%$ of all images of the database). Condition *(i)* is used for technical reasons: it avoids having to resolve ambiguous correspondences, which would mean to again revert to some form of explicit matching. Due to the fine quantization the condition rejects only a negligible fraction of feature points—in our experiments on average 2.5% of the detected features in an image, which corresponds to what was observed in [2]. Condition *(ii)* on the other hand improves both the quality and the efficiency of the method. The idea behind this condition is similar to the one behind *tf-idf* weighting: words that appear rarely are more informative and/or more discriminative than those which are present in too many images. If a word appears in, say, 10% of all images then it is unlikely that the hundreds of image points are projections of the same 3D feature, even if the word is unique in each

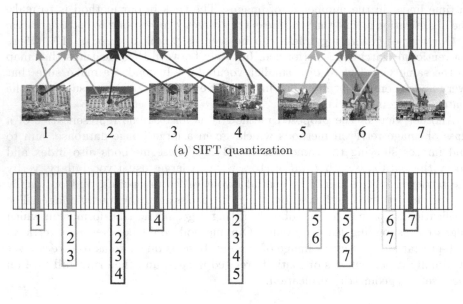

(a) SIFT quantization

(b) inverted file generation

Fig. 2. Records of the inverted file correspond to feature tracks. Every record stores all instances of a visual word that were found in the database. If each instance is from a different image then this implies that their associated feature points are in correspondence (assuming the quantization were perfect).

image. Moreover, for later steps one needs to restore matches between image pairs.[1] Since the number of pairwise matches is combinatorial in the length of the inverted file records, limiting that length also improves efficiency. Again, the large vocabulary size ensures that only few words are affected—in our experiments $\approx 3{,}500$ out of 16M words were eliminated because they appeared too frequently, whereas more than 600,000 words did not form a track because they were not detected in any of the database images. For simplicity, whenever we talk about "visual words" or the "vocabulary" in the following, we only mean those visual words which fulfill both conditions.

3.1 Clustering

Even though our method in principle generates matches between all images, most crowd-sourced image collections naturally decompose into several smaller clusters that are disconnected (*i.e.* there are no matches between different clusters, or so few matches that there is no point in reconstructing them together).

---

[1] The step back to two-view or three-view correspondences is necessary anyway, because incremental SfM pipelines work by chaining epipolar or trifocal geometries.

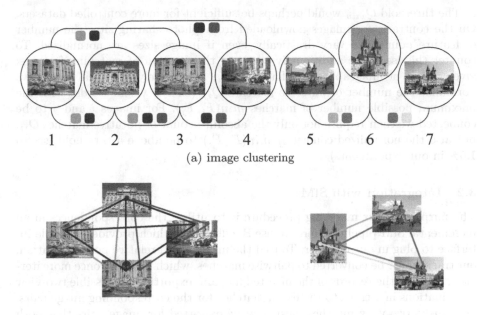

(a) image clustering

(b) export of matches

Fig. 3. Extracting clusters and pairwise matches from the inverted file. *(a)* Images belong to a cluster if they share a sufficient number of unique visual words (*i.e.* matches) with at least one of its members. *(b)* Finding two-view correspondences amounts to enumerating, in each record of the inverted file, all 2-element subsets that fall in the same cluster.

A sensible, and widely used strategy for SfM is to reconstruct each cluster separately. The clustering into independent models can be done using only information present in the inverted file, therefore the *clusters fall out naturally* in the proposed vocabulary-based matching framework. It is easy to count the number of putative matches for each pair of images (words detected in both images) and record them in a symmetric $N \times N$ matrix $\mathbf{Q}$, by iterating through all records in the inverted file. To find clusters that are only weakly connected to each other, all one has to do is threshold the matrix with a minimum desired number of matches Q_{min}. The resulting binary adjacency matrix $\mathbf{B}$ indicates which images have enough matches to be part of the same cluster, and connected component search on $\mathbf{B}$ yields the independent clusters. Note, if Q_{min} is set to the minimum number of correspondences that the SfM pipeline demands for epipolar geometry estimation, then no two-view connections are lost. In practice we set the threshold slightly higher, $Q_{min} = 50$, since very weak connections in the camera network are a potential source of drift and gross pose errors. Clusters with < 100 images are discarded and not considered further. This weeds out small sets of isolated or unrelated images, which are invariably present in crowd-sourced datasets.

The threshold Q_{min} would perhaps be sufficient for more controlled datasets. On the contrary, for images downloaded from photo-sharing sites the number of feature points can vary drastically, even if image sizes are normalized. To counter this issue, we additionally compute the fraction of matching features: given a pair of images i and j that have F_i, respectively F_j visual words, we normalize the number of putative matches Q_{ij} (shared visual words) with the maximum possible number of matches $min(F_i, F_j)$. For images i and j to be connected we then require not only the absolute count of putative matches Q_{ij}, but also the normalized count $Q_{ij}/min(F_i, F_j)$ to be above a threshold (set to 1.5% in our experiments).

3.2   Integration with SfM

The purpose of our matching procedure is to utilize the correspondences in an incremental SfM pipeline. Here we use Bundler [21], which provides a simple interface to plug in our matcher. To feed the incremental relative pose estimation, our tracks must be converted to pairwise matches, which we do by once more iterating through the records of the inverted file, and exporting all possible two-view combinations in a track to the list of matches for the corresponding image pairs. Obviously, two-view matches must only be exported for image pairs that both fall into the same cluster, see Figure 3. Note that some tracks may extend across more than one cluster. In that case (and assuming that the clusters are correct), clustering also helps to break down incorrectly merged tracks into correct ones, see Online Resource 1. Following the default setting of Bundler, we only export two-view matches if an image pair has at least 16 putative matches, otherwise no relative pose is computed. Having generated all two-view correspondences we run Bundler with the default settings, using the focal length specified in the EXIF tag as approximation whenever there is one available.

As an obvious baseline we also run Bundler with conventional matching. Corresponding SIFT descriptors from two images are found in the standard way with approximate nearest-neighbor (ANN) search in KD-trees. This two-view matching is run exhaustively over all pairs of images within a cluster. Note that pairwise matching only within clusters is already vastly more efficient than exhaustively checking all pairs of images in the dataset. On the contrary, in our method the complete set of tracks is inherently available, and independent clusters only afford small savings during the export of two-view matches. Nevertheless, the proposed vocabulary-based matching is three orders of magnitude faster than full ANN matching on our datasets, whereas the quality of the obtained 3D models is nearly on par. We could not test ANN matching without the preceding clustering step, because it turned out to be intractable for our datasets.

4   Experiments

The proposed method is validated using two datasets sourced from Flickr [23]. The first one, MERGED, was kindly provided by the authors of [5]. It consists

Table 1. Time spent for different steps of the method. Note, SIFT extraction would need to be performed by any feature-based SfM method, and feature quantization is needed by any methods that involves bag-of-words signatures [6,1]. The actual time needed to generate tracks is less than 1 hour for both datasets. Exporting two-view matches takes about as long as track generation.

	MERGED [5]	ROME [10]
number of images	9,469	13,049
SIFT extraction [16] (6 threads)	8h 40min	11h 30min
feature quantization [13]	5h 20min	6h 50min
inverted file generation	**35min**	**41min**
counting number of shared VWs	**10min**	**17min**
number of discovered clusters	3	13
export of matches	**30min**	**1h 15min**

of 9,469 images from three different landmarks: roughly one third of them depicts the Fontana di Trevi in Rome, another third the Duomo in Milan, and the last third the Old Town Square in Prague. All images are resampled to a size of ≈ 3 Mpix for further processing, a standard practice for SfM with uncontrolled data. The second dataset, ROME, is very similar to the one of [10]. The small difference is caused by the fact that the authors only provide feature descriptors on the project website. Since their interest point detector and SIFT implementation are incompatible with the pretrained vocabulary we use, we had to download the original images again from Flickr. A small number of images were no longer available, which causes the difference. In total our version consists of 13,049 images depicting several famous landmarks of Rome (Colosseum, St. Peter's Basilica, Fontana di Trevi, Pantheon, *etc.*). Again all images are resized to ≈ 3 Mpix.

We point out an important difference between the two datasets. MERGED is the raw result of searching Flickr with text tags, whereas ROME contains only images that were connected to a 3D model in [10], *i.e.* for these images SfM computation already succeeded once. The more realistic situation is the one without pre-filtering, where the matching and clustering must also cope with unusable and unrelated images, as in the MERGED set. Still we also test on the ROME data, which it is more widely known and used, in order to better put our method into context.

4.1 Feature Extraction and Clustering

As described in Section 3, we extract Hessian-affine interest points in all input images, convert them to SIFT descriptors, and quantize them against the 2-layer $(4,096 \times 4,096)$ visual vocabulary of [12] with ANN search using FLANN [13]. One can exploit the hierarchical nature of the vocabulary to gain some efficiency, by grouping the features from several images together in order to lower the number

Table 2. Clustering results for MERGED. The dataset contains a significant number of clutter images not directly related to the query. The recovered clusters cover the large majority of relevant images. The wrongly included images in M_3 are mostly caused by similarly decorated Christmas trees that were present at different sites.

	# img	M_1	M_2	M_3
DITREVI	3,110	1,973	0	1
DUOMO	3,104	0	580	11
OLDTOWN	3,255	0	0	1,402

Table 3. Clustering results for ROME. The dataset mainly contains related images because they were connected to a 3D model in [10]. With few exceptions (one of which is a mistake in the ground truth) the recovered clusters are clean. See text for details.

	# img	R_1	R_2	R_3	R_4	R_5	R_6	R_7	R_8	R_9	R_{10}	R_{11}	R_{12}	R_{13}
COLOSS.	1,664	1,392	0	0	0	0	0	0	0	0	0	0	0	0
DITREVI	1,518	0	1,381	0	0	0	0	0	0	0	0	0	0	0
ST.PET.	1,129	0	0	967	0	0	0	0	0	0	0	0	0	0
COL_IN	1,089	0	0	0	774	0	0	0	0	0	0	0	0	0
ST.P_IN	952	0	0	0	0	728	0	0	0	0	0	0	0	0
PANTH.	775	0	0	721	0	0	0	0	0	0	0	0	0	0
PAN_IN	672	0	0	0	0	0	512	0	0	0	0	0	0	0
ALTPAT	604	0	0	498	0	0	0	0	0	0	0	0	0	0
ANGELO	304	0	0	0	0	0	0	251	0	0	0	0	0	0
SPAN_DN	220	0	0	0	0	0	0	0	0	0	0	0	0	0
SPAN_UP	212	0	0	0	0	0	0	0	136	0	0	0	0	0
ARCH	211	166	0	0	0	0	0	0	0	0	0	0	0	0
FORUM	208	0	0	0	0	0	0	0	0	138	0	0	0	0
SENAT	206	0	0	0	0	0	0	0	0	0	156	0	0	0
COLON.	206	0	0	0	0	0	0	0	0	0	0	158	0	0
SISTINE	195	0	0	0	0	0	0	0	0	0	0	0	108	0
ST.P_TV	182	0	0	0	0	0	0	0	0	0	0	0	0	152
other	2,702	0	0	225	0	0	0	0	0	0	0	0	0	0

of FLANN calls in the second layer. Note that in the following only the visual word index is needed for our method, so in principle one need not store the original descriptors after they have been quantized.

Table 1 shows computation times measured on a standard desktop machine (Intel(R) Core(TM) i7-3930K with 24 GB of RAM) running 64bit Linux. Apart from SIFT extraction running in 6 threads, all steps are currently single-threaded and implemented in MATLAB. In particular, due to format and implementation details of the pretrained vocabulary, an older, single-threaded version of FLANN had to be used for the quantization, so our timings are a conservative upper bound for the potential of the method.

(a) MERGED   (b) ROME

Fig. 4. *(a)* The only inaccuracies in the clustering of MERGED. *(b)* The sole failure of vocabulary-based clustering for ROME. See text for details.

After generating the inverted file the absolute and relative numbers of shared visual words are counted for all pairs of images. Note that this step is only needed for incremental SfM—if approximate pose information is available from external sources, then one might be able to filter outliers based on the full tracks and directly proceed to bundle adjustment. Constructing the adjacency graph and searching connected components takes less than 10 seconds. The resulting clusters nicely match the structure of the data, see Tables 2 and 3. For MERGED the three ground truth clusters are given explicitly, because the images were found with three different queries. We point out that the "ground truth" clusters each contain a significant amount of unrelated images, so one should not expect the estimated clusters to include all images. The clusters are very clean: we verified by visual inspection that the overwhelming majority of unrelated images was correctly rejected and very few unrelated images are contained in any of the three retained clusters. Regarding confusions between clusters, only 12 images are assigned to the wrong cluster. None of these mistakes are specific to the proposed vocabulary-based matching: the 11 images from DUOMO are due to similarly decorated Christmas trees present at both locations. The 1 failure image from DITREVI is due to a dotted dress, which also matches the Christmas trees, see Figure 4a. All 12 images are later removed during SfM computation. The reason for the low number of images in M_2 is a technical issue: the relevant DUOMO images are actually made up of three only weakly connected sub-clusters for the front facade, the inside and the roof. These are indeed recovered separately, but only the one for the front facade is large enough to be exported (≥ 100 images).

For ROME we consider the division into individual 3D models (which is provided together with the data) as the ground truth clustering. Also in this case the recovered clusters are clean w.r.t. the ground truth grouping, with two exceptions. In R_1 our clustering corrects the ground truth: the Constantine ARCH and the outside of COLOSSEUM are located near each other and can in fact be reconstructed into a connected 3D model. R_3 is an actual failure case, where multiple sites (the front of St. Peter's Basilica, the front of the Pantheon, and the Altare della Patria) are mixed, because the images are dominated by similar column structures, see Figure 4b. Nevertheless, all the sub-models could be reconstructed. The recovered cluster for SPANISH STEPS DOWN had less than

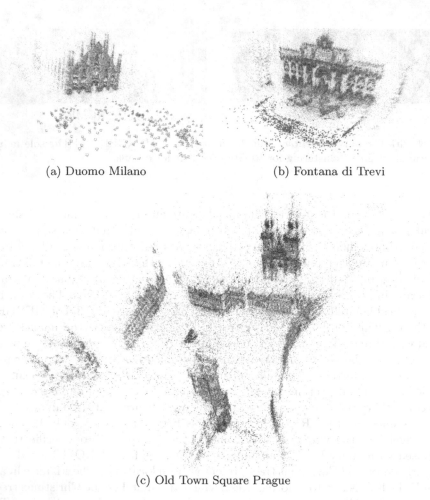

(a) Duomo Milano   (b) Fontana di Trevi

(c) Old Town Square Prague

Fig. 5. SfM results for the MERGED dataset (matches created by the proposed method). Estimated camera poses are denoted by red pyramids.

100 images and thus was removed. Since for the ROME dataset clean ground truth clusters without unrelated clutter are given we could also check the completeness of our clustering. On average, $> 77\%$ of all images were found for a given landmark.

Overall, the quality of clustering is more than satisfactory, considering the fact that it was performed without any geometric verification.

4.2   Export of Matches and 3D Reconstruction

After exporting the matches for each cluster, Bundler was called with the default settings to perform sparse 3D reconstruction, see Figures 5, 1, and 6. In most cases, all or almost all relevant images from a cluster could be oriented.

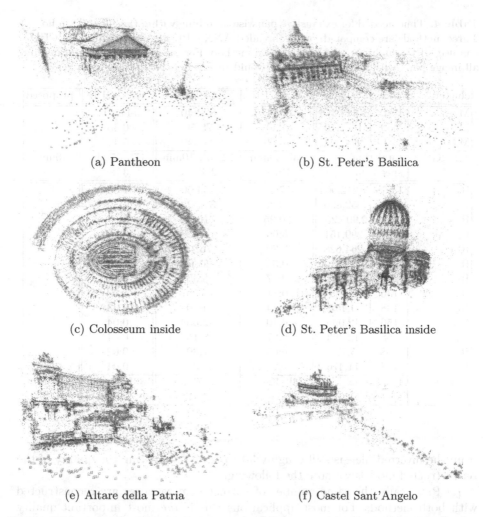

(a) Pantheon   (b) St. Peter's Basilica

(c) Colosseum inside   (d) St. Peter's Basilica inside

(e) Altare della Patria   (f) Castel Sant'Angelo

Fig. 6. SfM results for the ROME dataset (matches created by the proposed method). Estimated camera poses are denoted by red pyramids.

This demonstrates that for practically all images the inlier fraction of the proposed vocabulary-based matching is high enough to successfully RANSAC correct epipolar geometries. The worst failure is that for PANTHEON 20% of the images, which show the inside of the building, could not be connected.

As baseline we also perform standard pairwise ANN matching (Bundler default) in each image cluster. As expected, the running time is orders of magnitude longer, even if the matching is parallelized in 24 threads, see Table 4. Note that state-of-the-art CUDA-enabled SiftGPU matching from VisualSFM for a slightly smaller number of SIFT features was not much faster than the multi-threaded CPU matching either, the proposed method—export of matches

Table 4. Time needed for exhaustive pairwise matching within the clusters (in hours). Three methods are compared: multi-threaded ANN CPU matching, SiftGPU (CUDA-enabled GPU matching), and the proposed method. For the first two methods matching all image pairs without prior clustering would take orders of magnitude longer.

cluster	# img	# pair	24× CPU	$\sum$ CPU time	448× GPU	proposed
M_1	1,973	1,945,378	35:00	822:40	11:10	
M_2	580	167,910	3:30	75:50	0:55	
M_3	1,414	998,991	15:00	341:40	5:40	
MERGED	total time		53h 30min	1,240h 10min	17h 45min	30min
	speed-up		107×	2,480×	35×	
R_1	1,558	1,212,903	17:25	404:00	7:00	
R_2	1,381	952,890	13:35	314:20	5:30	
R_3	2,411	2,905,255	30:25	716:30	16:45	
R_4	774	299,151	6:06	138:50	1:45	
R_5	728	264,628	3:20	76:10	1:30	
R_6	512	130,816	0:55	20:15	0:45	
R_7	251	31,375	0:27	8:30	0:10	
R_8	136	9,180	0:11	3:20	0:03	
R_9	138	9,453	0:14	4:00	0:03	
R_{10}	156	12,090	0:10	2:50	0:04	
R_{11}	158	12,403	0:27	8:15	0:04	
R_{12}	108	5,778	0:05	1:30	0:02	
R_{13}	152	11,476	0:20	6:30	0:04	
ROME	total time		73h 40min	1,705h	33h 45min	1h 15min
	speed-up		59×	1,364×	27×	

from the inverted file—is still roughly 30× faster. Comparing the quality of the reconstructed models we note the following:

(*i*) Practically the same number of correct camera poses are reconstructed with both methods. For most applications this is *the* most important quality criterion. In localization/navigation-type applications the camera pose is the immediate goal. If the goal is 3D object modeling then SfM also serves mainly to recover the camera poses, since the final model is constructed in a subsequent step with some form of dense matching or 3D surface reconstruction.

(*ii*) Full pairwise matching on average generates about twice as many matches as the vocabulary-based method, whereas both yield approximately the same number of 3D structure points. It seems that vocabulary-based matching is in fact stricter and cannot always find the complete track for an object point. This is in all likelihood also the reason why Bundler took significantly longer to construct the 3D models from conventional pairwise matches.

(*iii*) The vocabulary-based point clouds are a bit noisier, which means that the correspondences detected with the proposed method are either not quite as accurate, or that they contain more epipolar-consistent miss-matches. The lower accuracy is somewhat expected, since shorter tracks mean fewer rays per point and thus higher uncertainty of the triangulation. While the issue still needs to be investigated in more detail, we believe that also miss-matches play a role: in Internet photo collections many images are typically taken from the same height with similar viewing direction, *e.g.* viewing the front side of a monument from street level. Under that viewing geometry repetitive or diffuse appearance along the (horizontal) epipolar lines can lead to miss-matches. Such matches will be rejected by the 2nd-best ratio test in standard SIFT matching, but the vocabulary-based approach includes no such test.

5   Conclusions

We have shown that multiview correspondence can be efficiently established even for large datasets, if one replaces pairwise image feature matching with image indexing, using only visual words that appear at most once in every image. What makes the proposed method practical is the realization that today's visual vocabularies are large enough to ensure that, even in datasets $> 10,000$ images, the overwhelming majority of all words are in fact unique in all images they appear in.

Formally speaking, the steps required for *feature track generation* with the proposed *VocMatch* method, namely *(i)* interest point extraction, *(ii)* feature quantization against a fixed vocabulary, and *(iii)* inverted file generation are all linear in the size of the image set. The additional steps needed to *integrate* the method with incremental SfM, namely *(iv)* clustering based on match counts and *(v)* export of two-view matches are still quadratic. But they involve only very simple operations and in practice are orders of magnitude faster than full ANN matching.

Regarding scalability of the proposed approach, for 100,000 images with 10,000 features per image, the inverted file would take 6 GB of RAM (6 bytes per feature) and the clustering matrix $\mathbf{Q}$ would take 10 GB (2 bytes per image pair). Extrapolating the measured times, inverted file generation would take 6 hours (linear in the total number of features) and generation of $\mathbf{Q}$ 16 hours (quadratic in the track length) using a single thread, which are still very competitive times. For 1,000,000 images the method is currently not feasible, storing matrix $\mathbf{Q}$ in RAM would be impossible (1 TB).

An open question is when a vocabulary becomes *too large* to be useful for matching. It seems clear that a too fine quantization will cause tracks to become fragmented, or lost altogether. We did not experience problems in our experiments, but note that the critical size is also dependent on the dataset: image sets with few interest points or weak connectivity are more vulnerable to a loss of correspondences. To counter the problem it might be possible to exploit the similarity between different visual words, either by direct comparison or by analyzing the descriptors they were trained on, and augment the vocabulary with neighborhood information. This could potentially allow one to also match descriptors if they do not quantize to the exact same visual word.

References

1. Agarwal, S., Snavely, N., Simon, I., Seitz, S., Szeliski, R.: Building Rome in a day. In: ICCV (2009)
2. Chum, O., Perdoch, M., Matas, J.: Geometric min-Hashing: Finding a (thick) needle in a haystack. In: CVPR (2009)
3. Chum, O., Philbin, J., Sivic, J., Isard, M., Zisserman, A.: Total recall: Automatic query expansion with a generative feature model for object retrieval. In: ICCV (2007)
4. Frahm, J.-M., et al.: Building Rome on a cloudless day. In: Daniilidis, K., Maragos, P., Paragios, N. (eds.) ECCV 2010, Part IV. LNCS, vol. 6314, pp. 368–381. Springer, Heidelberg (2010)
5. Havlena, M., Hartmann, W., Schindler, K.: Optimal reduction of large image databases for location recognition. In: BD3DCV (2013)
6. Havlena, M., Torii, A., Knopp, J., Pajdla, T.: Randomized structure from motion based on atomic 3D models from camera triplets. In: CVPR (2009)
7. Havlena, M., Torii, A., Pajdla, T.: Efficient structure from motion by graph optimization. In: Daniilidis, K., Maragos, P., Paragios, N. (eds.) ECCV 2010, Part II. LNCS, vol. 6312, pp. 100–113. Springer, Heidelberg (2010)
8. Klingner, B., Martin, D., Roseborough, J.: Street view motion-from-structure-from-motion. In: ICCV (2013)
9. Li, X., Wu, C., Zach, C., Lazebnik, S., Frahm, J.-M.: Modeling and recognition of landmark image collections using iconic scene graphs. In: Forsyth, D., Torr, P., Zisserman, A. (eds.) ECCV 2008, Part I. LNCS, vol. 5302, pp. 427–440. Springer, Heidelberg (2008)
10. Li, Y., Snavely, N., Huttenlocher, D.P.: Location recognition using prioritized feature matching. In: Daniilidis, K., Maragos, P., Paragios, N. (eds.) ECCV 2010, Part II. LNCS, vol. 6312, pp. 791–804. Springer, Heidelberg (2010)
11. Lowe, D.: Distinctive image features from scale-invariant keypoints. IJCV 60(2), 91–110 (2004)
12. Mikulik, A., Perdoch, M., Chum, O., Matas, J.: Learning vocabularies over a fine quantization. IJCV 103(1), 163–175 (2013)
13. Muja, M., Lowe, D.: Fast approximate nearest neighbors with automatic algorithm configuration. In: VISAPP (2009)
14. Nistér, D., Stewénius, H.: Scalable recognition with a vocabulary tree. In: CVPR (2006)
15. Oliva, A., Torralba, A.: Modeling the shape of the scene: A holistic representation of the spatial envelope. IJCV 42(3), 145–175 (2001)
16. Perdoch, M., Chum, O., Matas, J.: Efficient representation of local geometry for large scale object retrieval. In: CVPR (2009)
17. Philbin, J., Chum, O., Isard, M., Šivic, J., Zisserman, A.: Object retrieval with large vocabularies and fast spatial matching. In: CVPR (2007)
18. Pollefeys, M., Van Gool, L., Vergauwen, M., Verbiest, F., Cornelis, K., Tops, J., Koch, R.: Visual modeling with a hand-held camera. IJCV 59(3), 207–232 (2004)
19. Sattler, T., Leibe, B., Kobbelt, L.: Fast image-based localization using direct 2D-to-3D matching. In: ICCV (2011)
20. Šivic, J., Zisserman, A.: Video Google: Efficient visual search of videos. In: Toward Category-Level Object Recognition, CLOR (2006)
21. Snavely, N., Seitz, S., Szeliski, R.: Modeling the world from internet photo collections. IJCV 80(2), 189–210 (2008)
22. Wu, C.: VisualSFM: A visual structure from motion system (2013), http://ccwu.me/vsfm
23. Yahoo!: Flickr: Online photo management and photo sharing application (2005), http://www.flickr.com

Robust Global Translations with 1DSfM

Kyle Wilson and Noah Snavely

Cornell University, Ithaca, NY, USA
{wilsonkl,snavely}@cs.cornell.edu

Abstract. We present a simple, effective method for solving structure from motion problems by averaging epipolar geometries. Based on recent successes in solving for global camera rotations using averaging schemes, we focus on the problem of solving for 3D camera translations given a network of noisy pairwise camera translation directions (or 3D point observations). To do this well, we have two main insights. First, we propose a method for removing outliers from problem instances by solving simpler low-dimensional subproblems, which we refer to as 1DSfM problems. Second, we present a simple, principled averaging scheme. We demonstrate this new method in the wild on Internet photo collections.

Keywords: Structure from Motion, translations problem, robust estimation.

1 Introduction

Recent work on the unstructured Structure from Motion (SfM) problem has had renewed interest in global methods. Unlike sequential approaches which build 3D models from photo collections by iteratively growing a small seed model, global (or batch) methods for SfM consider the entire problem at once. By doing this they avoid several disadvantages of sequential methods, which have tended to be costly, requiring a repeated nonlinear model refinement (bundle adjustment) to avoid errors. Also, unlike global methods, sequential SfM necessarily treats images unequally, where those considered first can have a disproportionate effect on the final model. In practice, this behavior can sometimes lead to cascading mistakes and can exacerbate the problem of drift.

However, global methods have difficulties of their own. A key problem is that reasoning about outliers is challenging. Techniques from sequential methods, such as filtering out measurements inconsistent with the current model at each step, are not directly applicable in a global setting. It is harder to reason *a priori* about which measurements are unreliable.

In this work, we present a new global SfM method; like other methods, we solve first for global camera rotations, then translations, given a set of pairwise epipolar geometries. As there has been significant progress on the rotations problem, we focus on translations, and offer two key insights. The first, which we call **1DSfM**, is a simple way to preprocess a problem instance to remove outlier measurements. 1DSfM is based on reducing a difficult problem to single-dimensional subproblems where inference becomes a more straightforward combinatorial computation. Under this 1D projection, a

D. Fleet et al. (Eds.): ECCV 2014, Part III, LNCS 8691, pp. 61–75, 2014.
© Springer International Publishing Switzerland 2014

translations problem becomes an instance of MINIMUM FEEDBACK ARC SET, a well studied graph problem. By solving for a 1D ordering, we recover information about which 3D measurements are likely inconsistent. Second, we describe a new, very simple solver for the translations problem. Surprisingly, we find that non-linear optimization with this solver—even with random initialization—works remarkably well, especially once outliers have been removed. Hence, our 1DSfM-based outlier removal technique goes hand in hand with our simple translations solver to achieve high-quality results.

We show the effectiveness of our two methods on a variety of landmark-scale Internet community photo collections, covering a range of sizes and scene types. Our code and data are available at http://www.cs.cornell.edu/projects/1dsfm.

2   Related Work

While some earlier SfM methods were global, such as factorization [20], most current large-scale SfM systems involve sequential reconstruction [19,2,9]. Sequential methods build models a few images at a time, often with bundle adjustment in between steps. However, there has been significant recent interest in revisiting global methods because of their potential for improved speed and decreased dependence on local decisions or image ordering. These methods often work by first estimating an initial set of camera poses (typically through use of estimated relative poses between pairs or triplets), followed by a global bundle adjustment to refine this initial solution. With a few exceptions (e.g. [12]), these methods first solve for camera rotations, and then camera translations.

Rotations. A number of methods have been proposed for solving for global rotations from pairwise estimates of relative rotations. Some methods formulate the problem as a linear system by relaxing constraints on rotation parameterizations [11,17,3]. Enqvist et al. [8] look for a best spanning tree of pairwise rotations to filter outliers in advance. Sinha et al. [18] use vanishing point estimates as an additional cue. More recently, Hartley et al. [13] as well as Chatterjee and Govindu [5] have presented robust l_1 methods based on the Lie algebraic structure of the manifold of rotations. Finally, Fredriksson and Olsson [10] present an approach based on primal and dual problems which can certify if a solution is globally optimal. We have found the method of Chatterjee and Govindu [5] particularly effective, and use it to produce input for our method.

Translations. Like the rotations problem, the translations problem is often formulated as computing global camera translations from pairwise ones. Some approaches to solving this problem are based on a linear system of cross product constraints [11,3]. Others use Second Order Cone Programming, based on the l_∞ norm [16,17]. Such methods require very careful attention to outliers. Brand et al. [4] use a spectral approach, but do not address outlier noise. Sinha et al. [18] robustly compute similarity transformations that align pairs of reconstructions, and then average over these transformations. Recently Jiang et al. [14] have formulated a linear constraint with geometric, rather than algebraic meaning, based on co-planarity in triplets of cameras. Finally, Crandall et al. [6] take a different approach to optimization, using a complex scheme involving a discrete Markov Random Field search and a continuous Levenberg-Marquardt refinement to robustly explore the solution space. Our translations solver optimizes an objective function that depends only on comparing measurement directions to model directions, as opposed to other methods [11,3] where the objective function is also a function of the distance between images. To avoid the resulting bias, Govindu proposes an iterative reweighting scheme [11], which is unnecessary in our approach. Jiang et al. discuss the importance of geometric vs. algebraic cost functions, as they minimize a value that has physical significance. In this sense our cost function is also geometric (but in the space of measurements, rather than in the solution space).

Handling Outliers. A key contribution of our work is a simple algorithm for removing outliers in a translations problem. Zach et al. [23] detect outlier epipolar geometries by looking at loop closure in graph cycles. Our method for outlier removal is similar in motivation, but by projecting into a single dimension we solve tractable subproblems that reduce to a simple combinatorial graph problem.

3 Problem Formulation

The gold standard method for structure from motion is bundle adjustment—the joint nonlinear refinement of camera and structure parameters [21]. However, bundle adjustment is a largely local search, and its success depends critically on initialization. Given a good initial guess, bundle adjustment can produce high quality solutions, but if the guess is bad, the optimization may fall into local minima far from the optimal solution. For this reason most SfM methods focus on creating a close-enough initialization which can then be refined with bundle adjustment; sequential (or incremental) SfM methods are one such approach that use repeated bundle adjustment on increasingly large problems to reach a good solution.

Initializing bundle adjustment involves estimating a rotation matrix and a position for each camera. In our notation, a rotation matrix R_i represents a mapping from world coordinates to camera coordinates, and a translation t_i represents a location in the world coordinate frame (in our work, we use "location" and "translation" interchangeably, in a slight abuse of terminology). As with other recent global methods, our input is a set of images V, and a network of computed epipolar geometries $(\hat{R}_{ij}, \hat{t}^l_{ij})$ between pairs (i, j) of overlapping images. (We will use a hat for epipolar geometries, to emphasize that they are our input measurements. We use a superscript l for relative translations between two cameras, which are defined in a local coordinate system.) These epipolar geometries are not available for all camera pairs, because not all pairs of images visually overlap. These inputs define a graph we call the epipolar geometry (EG) graph $G = (V, E)$ on a set of images V, where for every edge $(i, j) \in E$ we have a measurement $(\hat{R}_{ij}, \hat{t}^l_{ij})$. Given perfect measurements, global camera poses (R_i, t_i) would satisfy

$$\hat{R}_{ij} = R_i^\top R_j \tag{1}$$
$$\lambda_{ij} \hat{t}^l_{ij} = R_i^\top (t_j - t_i) \tag{2}$$

where λ_{ij}'s are unknown scaling factors (unique up to global gauge ambiguity).

Following a now-common approach [11,16,17,6,3,14], we separate the initialization into two stages: a rotations problem and a translations problem. These two together produce an initialization to a final bundle adjustment. Recent work has been successful in solving the rotations problem robustly [13,10,5]; we build on this work and focus on the translations problem. Given estimates $\mathbf{R}_i$ of camera rotation matrices, we can write our measurement of the direction from camera i to camera j as $\hat{\mathbf{t}}_{ij} = \mathbf{R}_i \hat{\mathbf{t}}^l_{ij}$, where $\hat{\mathbf{t}}_{ij}$ is a unit 3-vector (i.e., a point on the unit sphere) in the global coordinate system. Hence, the translations problem reduces to the following graph embedding problem:

$$
\begin{aligned}
\text{Given:} \quad & \text{Graph } G = (V, E) \\
& \text{Measurements } \hat{\mathbf{t}}_{ij} : E \to S^2 \\
& \text{Metric } d : S^2 \times S^2 \to \mathbb{R} \\
\text{Minimize:} \quad & \sum_{(i,j) \in E} d\left(\hat{\mathbf{t}}_{ij}, \frac{\mathbf{t}_j - \mathbf{t}_i}{\|\mathbf{t}_j - \mathbf{t}_i\|} \right) \\
\text{over embeddings:} \quad & \mathcal{T} : V \to \mathbb{R}^3 \qquad \text{i.e. } \mathcal{T} = \{\mathbf{t}_i | i \in V\}
\end{aligned}
$$

Note that in this framework, the second endpoint j of an edge may be a point or a camera. Camera-point constraints can be important for achieving full scene coverage, and for avoiding degeneracies arising from collinear motion, an issue discussed in [14].

The formulation above does not specify the exact form of our objective function. It also excludes objective functions that depend on the distance between $\mathbf{t}_i$ and $\mathbf{t}_j$, rather than only the direction. These issues will both be discussed in Section 5.

Finally, this problem is made greatly more difficult by noise. We hope that most EGs will be approximately correct, but sometimes calculating EGs returns a wildly incorrect solution. For the translations problem we assume a mixed model of small variance inlier noise with a smaller fraction of outlier noise distributed uniformly over S^2.

4   Outlier Removal Using 1DSfM

By removing bad measurements in advance we can solve problems more accurately and reliably. In this section, we present a new method for identifying outlier measurements by projecting translations problems to 1-dimensional subproblems which we can solve more easily. Our approach is related to previous work [23] which detects outliers as measurements that cannot be consistently chained along cycles. However, there are usually many cycles to enumerate, and inferring erroneous measurements from bad cycles is difficult for large problems. Our method is based on many smaller, simpler inferences that are then aggregated. This makes outlier detection tractable even for large problems where [23] has difficulty.

The translations problem described above is a 3-dimensional embedding. One way to approach outlier detection is to try to first simplify this underlying problem. For instance, we could project the 3D problem onto a ground plane, resulting in a 2D graph embedding problem. In other words, we could ignore the z component of each measurement, and consider only the 2D projections: $\hat{\mathbf{t}}_{ij} \mapsto \hat{\mathbf{t}}_{ij} - \text{proj}_{\hat{\mathbf{k}}} \hat{\mathbf{t}}_{ij}$, where $\hat{\mathbf{k}} = \langle 0, 0, 1 \rangle$. In this projected problem, we would need to assign an (x, y) pair to each vertex.

In our work, we take this idea a step further and project onto a *single* dimensional subspace. Consider projecting a translations problem onto the x-axis, as in the blue problem in Figure 1. Only the x component of each translations measurement is now

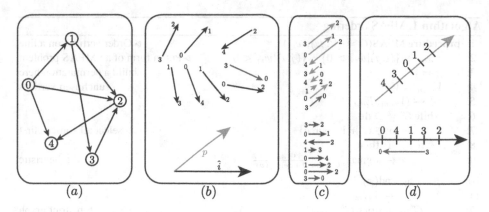

Fig. 1. A toy illustration of 1DSfM. Panel (a) is a good solution to a translations problem for reference. Panel (b) shows the translations problem input—a set of edges with orientations. One outlier edge has been added in red. We also show two directions for projection: $\hat{i}$ and p. Panel (c) contains only the projected translations problems, one for each projection direction. These problems are instances of MINIMUM FEEDBACK ARC SET. Finally, (d) contains good solutions to the 1D problems in (c). In the lower case, not all ordering constraints can be satisfied, due to the outlier edge. Note that outlier edges may be consistent in some subproblems but not in others.

relevant to the problem: $\hat{t}_{ij} \cdot \langle 1, 0, 0 \rangle = x_{ij}$, and we need to assign an x-coordinate to each vertex. Recall that our pairwise translation measurements represent directions, but not distances. On the x-axis there are only two directions: left and right. Hence, an embedding is consistent with edge (i, j) if $x_{ij} > 0$ and i embeds to the left of j, and vice versa for $x_{ij} < 0$. Figure 1 panel (d) shows such an embedding. Note that in 1D, edge directions have become *ordering constraints*: all embeddings with the same ordering are equally consistent with our problem. Hence, this 1D problem is a combinatorial ordering problem, rather than a continuous optimization problem: we want to find a global ordering of the vertices that satisfies the pairwise orderings as well as possible. We can formulate this problem on a directed version of our graph G, as described below.

Figure 1 also illustrates projecting the same problem in a different direction (in green). Notice that the outlier shown in red is inconsistent in one projection direction, but not in another. To catch as many outliers as possible, we embed a graph in many 1D subspaces, each defined by a unit vector p. For each subproblem only the component of translations measurements $\hat{t}_{ij}$ in the direction of p is relevant to the optimization: $\hat{t}_{ij} \mapsto p \cdot \hat{t}_{ij} = w_{ij}$. By regarding the pair $(i, j), w_{ij}$ as equivalent to $(j, i), -w_{ij}$, we can form a problem with directed edges with positive edge weights. Given a directed graph formed in this way, we try to find an ordering that satisfies as many of these pairwise constraints as possible; the edges that are inconsistent with this ordering are potential outliers. This is a well-studied problem in optimization called MINIMUM FEEDBACK ARC SET (MFAS). Unfortunately it is NP-complete, but there is a rich literature of approximation algorithms. We found that a variant of [7], as detailed in Algorithm 1, worked very well on our problems. This algorithm greedily builds an order from left to right. It always selects a next node that breaks no order constraints if possible. If not, it selects the next node to maximize a heuristic: $(1 + \deg_{out}(v))/(1 + \deg_{in}(v))$,

---

Algorithm 1. MFAS ordering

1: **procedure** MFAS($G = (V, E), w_{ij}$)   ▷ Order vertices on a line
2:     $E_{dir} \leftarrow \{(i,j)|w_{ij} > 0\} \cup \{(j,i)|w_{ij} < 0\}$ ▷ Put in form of an MFAS problem
3:     $\pi = [\,]$ ▷ build a permutation here
4:     $V_{rem} = V$ ▷ unchosen vertices
5:     $G' \leftarrow (V_{rem}, E_{dir})$
6:     **while** $G' \neq \varnothing$ **do**
7:         $x \leftarrow \{v \in G'|v \text{ is source}\}$ ▷ select all sources first
8:         **if** $x = \varnothing$ **then**
9:             $x \leftarrow \text{argmax}_{v \in V_{rem}} \frac{1 + \deg_{out}(v)}{1 + \deg_{in}(v)}$ ▷ heuristic
10:        $\pi.\text{append}(x)$
11:        $V_{rem} \leftarrow V_{rem} - x$
12:        $G' \leftarrow \text{restrict}(G', V_{rem})$ ▷ restrict graph

---

Algorithm 2. Combinatorial Cleaning

1: **procedure** CLEAN($G = (V, E), \hat{t}, N, \tau$)   ▷ Remove outlier measurements from E
2:     $x_{ij} \leftarrow 0 \quad \forall (i,j) \in E$ ▷ Accumulator for broken edge weight
3:     **for** $k \leftarrow 1, N$ **do**
4:         $\hat{p} \leftarrow \text{RAND}(\hat{t})$ ▷ Sample $\hat{p}$ proportional to density of $\hat{t}$ on S^2
5:         $w_{ij} \leftarrow \hat{p} \cdot \hat{t}_{ij} \quad \forall (i,j) \in E$
6:         $\pi \leftarrow \text{MFAS}((V, E), w_{ij})$ ▷ Order vertices along direction $\hat{p}$
7:         **for** $(i,j) \in E$ **do**
8:             **if** $\text{sgn}(\pi(j) - \pi(i)) \neq \text{sgn}(w_{ij})$ **then**
9:                 $x_{ij} \leftarrow x_{ij} + |w_{ij}|$
10:    $E \leftarrow \{(i,j)\,|x_{ij}/N < \tau\}$

---

where $\deg_{in}(v)$ and $\deg_{out}(v)$ are the sum of weights of outgoing and incoming edges of node v, respectively. We found that this ratio heuristic performs much better on our problems than the heuristic used in [7] (namely, $\deg_{out}(v) - \deg_{in}(v)$).

Projection from 3D to 1D necessarily loses information. Bad measurements could be missed entirely by some choices of projection direction p. To identify outliers reliably we aggregate the results of solving 1D subproblems projected in many different directions. We use a kernel density estimator to sample these projection directions randomly, proportional to the density of directions of measurements in the input problem. We sample this way because outliers stand out most clearly in directions where many edges project with high weight; picking uncommon directions (like straight up) tends to have poor signal-to-noise ratio. For each direction, if an edge (i, j) is inconsistent with the ordering we compute, we accumulate the weight $|w_{ij}|$ on that edge. Edges that accumulate weight in many subproblems are inconsistent and probably bad. After running in N sampled directions we reject edges (i, j) which have accumulated more than a threshold $\tau \cdot N$ of weighted inconsistency. This process is summarized in Algorithm 2.

5   Solving the Translations Problem

Now that we have a cleaner set of pairwise relative translations, we use them to solve for a global set of translations. In order to make our translations problem concrete, we must

Table 1. Common distances on S^2

Name	Formula	Equivalent
Geodesic	$\angle(\mathbf{u}, \mathbf{v})$	θ
Cross Product	$\mathbf{u} \times \mathbf{v}$	$\sin \theta$
Inner Product	$1 - \mathbf{u} \cdot \mathbf{v}$	$2\sin^2 \frac{\theta}{2}$
Squared Chordal Distance	$\|\mathbf{u} - \mathbf{v}\|^2$	$4\sin^2 \frac{\theta}{2}$

first choose an objective function to minimize. After evaluating a number of metrics, we opted to use the sum of squared chordal distance:

$$err_{ch}(\mathcal{T}) = \sum_{(i,j) \in E} d_{ch}\left(\hat{\mathbf{t}}_{ij}, \frac{\mathbf{t}_j - \mathbf{t}_i}{\|\mathbf{t}_j - \mathbf{t}_i\|}\right)^2 \tag{3}$$

$$d_{ch}(\mathbf{u}, \mathbf{v}) = \|\mathbf{u} - \mathbf{v}\|_2 \tag{4}$$

This is a nonlinear least squares problem, with the nonlinearity coming from the division mapping vectors to directions. We minimize it using Levenberg-Marquardt, as implemented in the Ceres software package [1]. In general, nonlinear least squares problems are not guaranteed to have a single local minimum, so a good initialization is critical. Surprisingly, we find that with this distance metric, our problems generally converged well for our test datasets even from random initialization. Although the node orderings from 1DSfM could provide an initialization, we found this no more effective than randomization.[1]

Comparative Discussion. The SfM translations problem recovers coordinates in $\mathbb{R}^3$ from measurements on the sphere S^2. Previous work has proposed objective functions based on different combinations of these two spaces. For example, the cross product used in [11] maps $S^2 \times \mathbb{R}^3 \to \mathbb{R}$. This biases the problem as error is proportional to the length of the edges in a solution. To compensate, they use an iterative reweighting framework to divide out edge length. This framework approximates a cross product map $S^2 \times S^2 \to [-1, 1]$.

We avoid this bias by comparing measurements (on S^2) directly to edge directions for a solution (also on S^2). Table 1 shows several ways to measure the distance between two directions. A natural distance on a sphere is the geodesic (great circle) distance, so each distance is also given in terms of this angle θ. Note that the cross product has both parallel and antiparallel minima, which is undesirable. The inner product and the squared chordal distance are equivalent up to a constant, but the latter is a preferable formulation because it is a sum of squares.

While our 1DSfM method seeks to remove outlier measurements, we note that one could also handle outliers using robust cost functions. Crandall et al. [6] demonstrate the utility of robust cost functions for global SfM problems, but operated within a complex discrete optimization algorithm. In our case, within an continuous optimization framework, we have found that the choice of robust function is very important—Cauchy and

---

[1] Formally, Eq. 5 is undefined if ever $\mathbf{t}_j = \mathbf{t}_i$ for any edge. With a random initialization and natural problems this is exceedingly unlikely. However, in this case a random perturbation could allow the algorithm to continue.

threshold-based robust costs lead to poor convergence, but we find that a Huber loss to be very effective. Our results will show that a Huber loss can improve solution quality while retaining good convergence, and that the benefit is largely orthogonal to 1DSfM.

Convergence Properties. We now give a basis for confidence in minimizing our objective function. Consider two vectors x_0 and x_1 in $\mathbb{R}^3$, and a convex combination of them, $x_\lambda = (1 - \lambda)x_0 + \lambda x_1$. The chordal distance is not convex here (nor quasi-convex), but a related (weaker) inequality holds: [2]

$$d_{ch}\left(\frac{x_\lambda}{\|x_\lambda\|}, \hat{t}\right)^2 \leq \max\left\{d_{ch}\left(\frac{x_0}{\|x_0\|}, \hat{t}\right)^2, d_{ch}\left(\frac{x_1}{\|x_1\|}, \hat{t}\right)^2\right\} \quad (5)$$

(In fact, this also holds without squares, so these results also apply to a robust L_1 cost.)

So if $\mathcal{T}_0$ and $\mathcal{T}_1$ are embeddings (maps taking each vertex to $\mathbb{R}^3$), and $\mathcal{T}_\lambda$ is a convex combination of them, then we can bound the objective function at $\mathcal{T}_\lambda$:

$$err_{ch}(\mathcal{T}_\lambda) = \sum_{(i,j)\in E} d_{ch}\left(\frac{\mathcal{T}_\lambda(j) - \mathcal{T}_\lambda(i)}{\|\mathcal{T}_\lambda(j) - \mathcal{T}_\lambda(i)\|}, \hat{t}_{ij}\right)^2 \leq err_{ch}(\mathcal{T}_0) + err_{ch}(\mathcal{T}_1) \quad (6)$$

This means that in a noise-free problem ($err_{ch}(\mathcal{T}_0) = 0$) the error surface would be perfectly non-decreasing away from a global minimum $\mathcal{T}_0$ (though note that all solutions are only unique up to a global gauge, and ill-posed problems may have an even larger space of global minima). With small noise we are still guaranteed that the barrier between any solution and an optimum is no higher than the optimal value of the objective function. This bound is not necessarily tight, and is not achieved in natural problems. In practice, once most outliers have been removed (by 1DSfM) we consistently find good solutions.

6   Implementation

Solving for Rotations. To compute global rotations, we run Chatterjee and Govindu's rotations averaging method [5], with the parameters suggested in their paper.

Forming a Translations Problem. Given rotations, we form a translations problem with both camera-to-camera and camera-to-point edges. We find camera-to-camera edges to be crucial for accuracy and compute them from EGs. However, these camera-to-camera edges often have areas of sparse coverage—we find that popular parts of the scene are well represented, but less photographed areas can have many fewer measurements, resulting in reconstructions that can break apart into disconnected submodels.

To address this problem, we augment the translations problem with camera-to-point edges. We find that on their own these yield a noisy solution, but they increase scene coverage and connectedness. In addition, these edges are crucial for avoiding degeneracies when cameras are nearly collinear, as discussed in [14].

---

[2] To be precise, this follows if we assume that $\hat{t}$ and the geodesic from x_0 to x_1 lie in open hemisphere. Since we think of $err_{ch}(\mathcal{T}_0)$ as small, this constraint is easy to satisfy.

We use only some of all possible camera-to-point edges, as they increase problem size, with diminishing returns. Similar to [6], to choose a subset of points to add to our problem we solve a simple graph covering problem: we greedily choose points that are visible to the most (as-yet-uncovered) cameras, until all cameras see k points. (We use $k = 6$ in our experiments.) Every camera-to-point edge in with this subset of points is included in our translations problem.

Cleaning with 1DSfM. We run 1DSfM on $N = 48$ random subproblems. We then remove all edges with accumulated inconsistency scores $\geq \tau \cdot N$ from the translations problem. We use $\tau = 0.10$ in our experiments.

Solving a Translations Problem. We minimize our sum of squared chordal distance objective function using Ceres Solver [1], a state-of-the-art nonlinear least squares package. We use default solver settings, except that we set the linear solver to be an iterative Schur method with Jacobi preconditioning. Additionally, we weight each constraint to prevent camera-to-point edges from dominating the problem, since there are many more of these than camera-to-camera edges. We set camera-to-camera (cc) edge weights to 1.0 and camera-to-point (cp) edges weights to $\alpha \cdot |cc \text{ edges}| / |cp \text{ edges}|$. In our experiments we use $\alpha = 0.5$, so cc edges contribute twice as much to the objective function as cp edges. For runs using a robust cost function, we use a Huber loss with width 0.1, implemented in Ceres. After solving the translations problem, we use this initialization, along with the camera rotations, to triangulate all points, and run a final bundle adjustment using the standard reprojection error.

7   Results

We evaluated our algorithm on realistic synthetic scenes, as well as a number of medium- to large-scale Internet datasets downloaded by geotag search from Flickr, as summarized in Table 2, and shown as point clouds in Figure 3. The **Notre Dame** dataset is publicly available online with Bundler [19].

1DSfM. We demonstrate that 1DSfM accurately identifies outliers in two ways. First, we tested on synthetic problems where the error on each edge (and its inlier/outlier status) is known. We observed that synthetic problems created with some common random graph models are easier than real problems, so we form our synthetic problems by using an existing reconstruction as a problem instance (reusing the epipolar graph structure and computing pairwise translations from the sequential SfM camera positions), and then adding known perturbations to every translation direction. We sampled a random 15% of edges, replacing them with translation directions sampled uniformly at random, and perturbed the rest of the translation directions with Gaussian noise with standard deviation 11.4 degrees. (We chose these numbers as representative of real problems we have observed.) Edges with error greater than 30 degrees were deemed to be the ground truth outliers for the purposes of analysis. We ran our 1DSfM algorithm on problem instances generated from four scenes—**Roman Forum**, **Tower of London**, **Ellis Island**, and **Notre Dame**. At our threshold of $\tau = 0.1$, we found that 1DSfM classified edges with a precision of 0.96 and an recall of 0.92 (averaged across the four datasets). This high classification accuracy gives us confidence in the method.

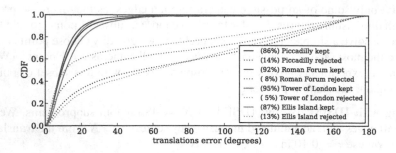

Fig. 2. Performance of 1DSfM at identifying outliers in real data. The x-axis is the error for each input translation direction. 1DSfM classifies each of these as accepted or rejected. The lines are cumulative distribution functions for both accepted edges (solid lines) and rejected edges (dotted lines) for four datasets. We see that the accepted edges have many more low residual edges, and the rejected edges contain many edges with much higher residuals.

We also demonstrate 1DSfM on real problems where ground truth is not known, but for which we can still compare translation directions from pairwise EGs to a reference reconstruction. Figure 2 shows cumulative distributions of errors in pairwise translation estimates, for edges deemed inliers and outliers by 1DSfM on four of our datasets. To approximate the inherent noisiness of the input epipolar geometries, we see how well they agree with a good sequential SfM model built using [19]. The residuals in each edge (the distance between the epipolar geometry translations direction and the translation direction computed from the reference sequential SfM model, measured with the geodesic distance) is closely tied to the noise in the input measurements. Our 1DSfM algorithm divides these input translation edges into a set to keep, and a set to discard. Figure 2 shows the distribution of residuals in these two sets. Notice that while most inlier edges have low residual (are not very noisy) the edges selected to be removed are much noisier. For example, we can see that the median error for rejected edges is around 80° for several datasets. 1DSfM removes a relatively small number of correct edges, but helps significantly by getting rid of most outlier edges.

Comparison to Sequential SfM. Because ground truth positions are usually unavailable for large-scale SfM problems, we show our method gives similar results to a sequential SfM system based on Bundler [19], but in much less time. Table 2 shows the similarity between these sequential SfM solutions and the results of several global algorithms, computed as mean and median distances between corresponding cameras between the two SfM models, across all of our datasets. The units in Table 2 are approximately in meters, as we use geotags associated with images in the collection to place each sequential SfM reconstruction in an approximate world coordinate frame, and use a RANSAC approach to compute the absolute orientation between a candidate reconstruction and the sequential SfM solution (using correspondences between camera centers).

In Table 2, we compare several variants of our method: with and without a final bundle adjustment (BA), and with four combinations of outlier treatments. We see that in all cases, we return a result with a median within several meters of the sequential SfM

Table 2. Comparison of several methods to a reference sequential SfM method based on [19]. Units are approximately in meters; sizes are the number of cameras in the largest component of the input EG graph. The methods are our translations solver combined with all four permutations of using 1DSfM and robust cost functions. The fifth column is a baseline method [11]. Results are given as N_c, the number of cameras reconstructed, $\bar{x}$, the average error, and $\tilde{x}$, the median error, where by errors are the distances to corresponding cameras in [19]. Lower error is closer to the reference method. The lowest mean and median in each row are bolded, as well as two-way ties.

| | | | without 1DSfM | | with 1DSfM | | Robust Loss | | [11] |
| | | | no BA | BA | no BA | BA | BA | 1DSfM+BA | BA |
Name	Size	N_c	$\tilde{x}$	N_c $\tilde{x}$ $\bar{x}$	$\tilde{x}$	N_c $\tilde{x}$ $\bar{x}$	N_c $\tilde{x}$ $\bar{x}$	N_c $\tilde{x}$ $\bar{x}$	N_c $\tilde{x}$
Piccadilly	80	2152	3.2	1905 1.0 9e3	4.1	1932 0.6 **5e1**	1965 **0.3** 9e3	1956 0.7 7e2	1638 10
Union Square	300	789	9.9	700 3.3 3e3	5.6	702 3.5 5e2	699 3.2 2e2	710 3.4 **9e1**	521 10
Roman Forum	200	1084	6.9	973 1.5 3e4	6.1	981 0.3 4e1	1000 2.7 9e5	989 **0.2 3e0**	840 37
Vienna Cathedral	120	836	5.5	758 0.9 9e3	6.6	757 0.5 **8e3**	770 0.7 7e4	770 **0.4** 2e4	652 12
Piazza del Popolo	60	328	1.8	311 **1.2** 2e1	3.1	303 2.6 **4e0**	317 1.6 9e1	308 2.2 2e2	93 16
NYC Library	130	332	1.7	297 1.5 7e2	2.5	292 0.9 2e1	307 **0.2** 8e1	295 0.4 **1e0**	271 1.4
Alamo	70	577	1.0	528 0.2 7e3	1.1	521 0.3 **7e0**	541 0.2 7e5	529 0.3 2e7	422 2.4
Metropolis	200	341	6.0	282 0.5 1e3	9.9	288 1.2 **9e0**	292 0.6 3e1	291 0.5 7e1	240 18
Yorkminster	150	437	7.0	405 0.2 3e3	3.4	395 0.2 1e4	416 0.4 9e3	401 0.1 **5e2**	345 6.7
Montreal N.D.	30	450	0.9	431 0.2 4e3	2.5	425 0.9 1e0	431 **0.1 4e-1**	427 0.4 1e0	357 9.8
Tower of London	300	572	9.4	417 1.1 2e3	11	414 0.4 3e3	427 **0.2** 3e4	414 1.0 **4e1**	306 44
Ellis Island	180	227	4.1	211 0.4 4e0	3.7	213 0.4 4e1	213 0.3 3e0	214 0.3 3e0	203 8.0
Notre Dame	300	553	19	524 **0.7** 2e4	10	500 2.1 **7e0**	530 0.8 7e4	507 1.9 **7e0**	473 2.1

solution, and often a much smaller distance. In general, bundle adjustment significantly reduces error. The effect of 1DSfM shows up clearly in the average error, which usually is reduced by orders of magnitude. While we see that both robust cost functions and 1DSfM improve reconstructions, they are not interchangeable—rather, 1DSfM is able to greatly reduce average error, while robust cost functions usually increase it, while decreasing median error. These two approaches cope with outliers in complementary ways, and so we advocate using both 1DSfM and a Huber loss function (as mentioned earlier, we found that other, non-convex loss functions performed poorly).

Qualitatively, our reconstructions have high quality; visualizations of many of the results are shown in Figure 3. Finally, Figure 4 shows our largest reconstruction, **Trafalgar**, with 4591 images. This model was computed with 1DSfM and bundle adjustment. The cameras have a median error of about 0.60 meters compared to sequential SfM, and it took about 3.4 hours to run, compared to 8.1 hours for sequential SfM.

Table 3 shows timing information for the experiments in Table 2, comparing our method especially with sequential SfM. All experiments were run on a machine with two 2.53 GHz Intel Xeon E5540 quad core processors. Our method is always faster than sequential SfM, usually 2-4 times faster, with even bigger improvements on larger datasets such as **Piccadilly**. The majority of our time in each dataset is spent on bundle adjustment, although unlike sequential SfM we only need to do a single large bundle adjustment, rather than many repeated ones.

Comparison to [11]. We also compared our results to [11], which solves the translations problem by minimizing the cross product of solution translations with input pairwise translations. To avoid bias from the cross product, this linear method is wrapped in an iterative reweighting framework. We used our own SciPy implementation, on the same machine as the other trials. In a slight departure, we use only three rounds of reweighting rather than four, since with each round of reweighting the underlying linear system

Table 3. Timing information, in seconds for the results in Table 2. Times are listed for solving for rotations with [5] (T_R), removing outliers with 1DSfM (T_O), running a translations problem solver (T_S), and for bundle adjustment (T_{BA}).

| Name | T_R | without 1DSfM | | | with 1DSfM | | | | using [11] | | | using [19] |
		T_S	T_{BA}	Σ	T_O	T_S	T_{BA}	Σ	T_S	T_{BA}	Σ	T
Piccadilly	570	177	3252	3999	122	366	2425	3483	9497	1046	11113	44369
Union Square	17	71	401	489	20	75	340	452	277	150	444	1244
Roman Forum	37	104	1733	1874	40	135	1245	1457	290	694	1021	4533
Vienna Cathedral	98	225	3611	3934	60	144	2837	3139	1282	893	2273	10276
Piazza del Popolo	14	28	213	255	9	35	191	249	98	26	138	1287
NYC Library	9	38	382	429	13	54	392	468	21	190	220	3807
Alamo	56	96	646	798	29	73	752	910	1039	308	1403	1654
Madrid Metropolis	15	32	224	271	8	20	201	244	57	67	139	1315
Yorkminster	11	60	955	1026	18	93	777	899	81	302	394	3225
Montreal Notre Dame	17	76	1043	1136	22	75	1135	1249	25	382	424	2710
Tower of London	9	52	750	811	14	55	606	648	17	238	264	1900
Ellis Island	12	17	276	305	7	13	139	171	7	108	127	1191
Notre Dame	53	152	2139	2344	42	59	1445	1599	299	841	1193	6154

becomes increasingly poorly conditioned. We evaluated [11] on translations problems produced by 1DSfM, reporting the results after bundle adjustment, since this combination gave the best results. Median error is reported in Table 2 and timing information in Table 3. While [11] is usually faster than our method (especially on smaller problems), the accuracy (and number of reconstructed cameras) greatly suffers.

Discussion. Our method has at its core a nonlinear optimization framework that we have found to be particularly effective, even with random initialization (once outliers are removed). Our analysis of convergence in Section 5 suggests reasons for this, but understanding fully the convergence properties of translations problems is still an interesting avenue for future work. As we noted previously, the same analysis extends to L_1 style robust cost functions as well. We believe our work points to nonlinear optimization being reconsidered as a tool for structure-from-motion beyond bundle adjusting a good solution. It is also instructive to contrast ours with other global methods. In particular, the recent linear method by Jiang et al. works on very different principles to ours, both in addressing outliers and in its efficient linear optimization framework built on triplets. Other recent methods use more sophisticated optimization methods (including discrete optimization) [6]. We believe a strength of our method is its simplicity—it relies on a well-studied combinatorial optimization problem, and a simple non-linear solver.

Limitations. Our method is based on averaging epipolar geometries to compute an accurate initialization. This works well when there are many EGs to reason about. However, sometimes EGs are sparse, such as when scenes are poorly connected. Averaging very few measurements may not be accurate. Figure 5 shows a failure case of our method. A correct reconstruction from [19] is on the left, and our broken solution is on the right. The scene has a central building with smaller domed buildings on each side. This scene is challenging because of the wide baseline between the buildings, and the similar appearance of the domes. There are few EGs that connect cameras which view different buildings. A second limitation is that our method does not reason about self-

Fig. 3. Selected renders of models produced by our method

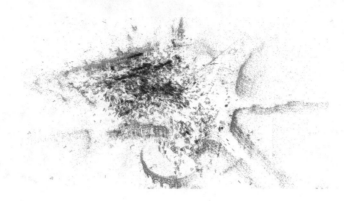

Fig. 4. A large reconstruction of Trafalgar Square containing 4597 images

Fig. 5. (a) A correct model of **Gendarmenmarkt** from [19]. (b) A broken model by our method.

consistent outliers, such as those arising from ambiguous structures in the scene. To deal with these cases, SfM disambiguation methods could be used [23,15,22].

8   Conclusion

We presented a new method for solving the global SfM translations problem. Our method has two pieces: 1DSfM, a a method for removing outliers by solving 1-dimension ordering problems, and a simple translations solver based on squared chordal distance. Like other global methods, it treats images equally and runs faster than common sequential methods. Our method stands out by being particularly simple, and represents a different take on the problem from previous methods which focus on linear formulations.

We have demonstrated the effectiveness of our method on a range of datasets in the wild; these are available, along with code, at http://www.cs.cornell.edu/projects/1dsfm. We produce models comparable to existing sequential methods in much less time. In the future we hope to explore further ways of aggregating 1DSfM subproblems than simple summation, which could shed light on more complicated outliers, such as those arising from ambiguous scene structures.

Acknowledgements. This work was funded in part by NSF grants IIS-1149393 and IIS-0964027, and by support from the Intel Science and Technology Center for Visual Computing. We would also like to thank David Williamson and Robert Kleinberg for their valuable help.

References

1. Agarwal, S., Mierle, K., et al.: Ceres solver, https://code.google.com/p/ceres-solver/
2. Agarwal, S., Snavely, N., Simon, I., Seitz, S.M., Szeliski, R.: Building Rome in a day. In: ICCV (2009)
3. Arie-Nachimson, M., Shahar, S.Z., Kemelmacher-Shlizerman, I., Singer, A., Basri, R.: Global motion estimation from point matches. In: 3DIMPVT (2012)
4. Brand, M., Antone, M., Teller, S.: Spectral solution of large-scale extrinsic camera calibration as a graph embedding problem. In: Pajdla, T., Matas, J(G.) (eds.) ECCV 2004. LNCS, vol. 3022, pp. 262–273. Springer, Heidelberg (2004)
5. Chatterjee, A., Govindu, V.M.: Efficient and robust large-scale rotation averaging. In: ICCV (2013)
6. Crandall, D., Owens, A., Snavely, N., Huttenlocher, D.: Discrete-continuous optimization for large-scale structure from motion. In: CVPR (2011)
7. Eades, P., Lin, X., Smyth, W.F.: A fast and effective heuristic for the feedback arc set problem. In: Information Processing Letters (1993)
8. Enqvist, O., Kahl, F., Olsson, C.: Nonsequential structure from motion. In: OMNIVIS (2011)
9. Frahm, J.-M., et al.: Building Rome on a cloudless day. In: Daniilidis, K., Maragos, P., Paragios, N. (eds.) ECCV 2010, Part IV. LNCS, vol. 6314, pp. 368–381. Springer, Heidelberg (2010)
10. Fredriksson, J., Olsson, C.: Simultaneous multiple rotation averaging using Lagrangian duality. In: Lee, K.M., Matsushita, Y., Rehg, J.M., Hu, Z. (eds.) ACCV 2012, Part III. LNCS, vol. 7726, pp. 245–258. Springer, Heidelberg (2013)
11. Govindu, V.M.: Combining two-view constraints for motion estimation. In: CVPR (2001)
12. Govindu, V.M.: Lie-algebraic averaging for globally consistent motion estimation. In: CVPR (2004)
13. Hartley, R., Aftab, K., Trumpf, J.: L_1 rotation averaging using the Weiszfeld algorithm. In: CVPR (2011)
14. Jiang, N., Cui, Z., Tan, P.: A global linear method for camera pose registration. In: ICCV (2013)
15. Jiang, N., Tan, P., Cheong, L.: Seeing double without confusion: Structure-from-motion in highly ambiguous scenes. In: CVPR (2012)
16. Kahl, F.: Multiple view geometry and the L_∞-norm. In: ICCV (2005)
17. Martinec, D., Pajdla, T.: Robust rotation and translation estimation in multiview reconstruction. In: CVPR (2007)
18. Sinha, S.N., Steedly, D., Szeliski, R.: A multi-stage linear approach to structure from motion. In: Kutulakos, K.N. (ed.) ECCV 2010 Workshops, Part II. LNCS, vol. 6554, pp. 267–281. Springer, Heidelberg (2012)
19. Snavely, N., Seitz, S., Szeliski, R.: Photo tourism: Exploring photo collections in 3D. In: SIGGRAPH (2006)
20. Tomasi, C., Kanade, T.: Shape and motion from image streams under orthography: A factorization method. In: IJCV (1992)
21. Triggs, B., McLauchlan, P.F., Hartley, R.I., Fitzgibbon, A.W.: Bundle adjustment—a modern synthesis. In: Triggs, B., Zisserman, A., Szeliski, R. (eds.) Vision Algorithms 1999. LNCS, vol. 1883, pp. 298–372. Springer, Heidelberg (2000)
22. Wilson, K., Snavely, N.: Network principles for SfM: Disambiguating repeated structures with local context. In: ICCV (2013)
23. Zach, C., Klopschitz, M., Pollefeys, M.: Disambiguating visual relationships using loop constraints. In: CVPR (2010)

Comparing Salient Object Detection Results without Ground Truth

Long Mai and Feng Liu

Department of Computer Science, Portland State University, USA

Abstract. A wide variety of methods have been developed to approach the problem of salient object detection. The performance of these methods is often image-dependent. This paper aims to develop a method that is able to select for an input image the best salient object detection result from many results produced by different methods. This is a challenging task as different salient object detection results need to be compared without any ground truth. This paper addresses this challenge by designing a range of features to measure the quality of salient object detection results. These features are then used in various machine learning algorithms to rank different salient object detection results. Our experiments show that our method is promising for ranking salient object detection results and our method is also able to pick the best salient object detection result such that the overall salient object detection performance is better than each individual method.

1 Introduction

Visual saliency measures the low-level stimuli that grabs viewers' attention in the early stage of human vision [21]. It has been used as an alternative to semantic image understanding in a range of applications in computer vision, computer graphics, and multimedia, such as object detection [22], adaptive image compression [9], and content-aware image manipulation [35,42]. There is now a rich literature on visual saliency analysis [1,4,8,10,13–16,18,19,22,23,26,30,31,33,34, 36–41,43,44,50–54,56,57]. Many of these methods aim to detect salient objects from an input image as recently surveyed in [2], which is also the focus of this paper.

While the research on salient object detection has been progressing quickly and has achieved good results statistically on public benchmarks [7,24,25,28, 29,33,37,40,50,53,54], each individual method has its own advantages and disadvantages. As shown in Fig. 1, each method can produce good results for some images but none of them can outperform the other methods for all the images. For a specific input image, it is often useful to select the best salient object detection result from many results created by different methods. This is a challenging task as the quality of different salient object detection results need to be compared without knowing the ground truth.

Our problem is relevant to the research on non-reference image quality assessment, which estimates the quality of an image without a ground-truth one [45,49].

D. Fleet et al. (Eds.): ECCV 2014, Part III, LNCS 8691, pp. 76–91, 2014.

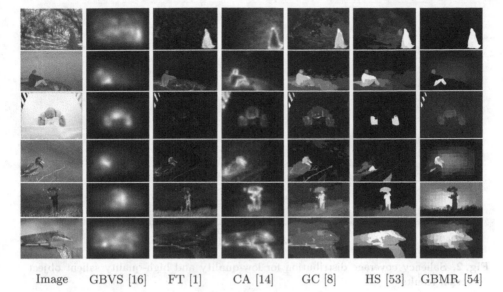

| Image | GBVS [16] | FT [1] | CA [14] | GC [8] | HS [53] | GBMR [54] |

Fig. 1. Saliency detection examples. Different saliency detection methods have their own advantages and disadvantages. Each method can produce good results on some images but none of them can outperform the others on all the cases.

The non-reference image quality assessment methods mostly detect and measure image artifacts, such as those from compression. They cannot be used in our problem.

This paper addresses the problem of comparing salient object detection results without ground truth using a data-driven approach. We study what makes a good salient object detection result and design a range of features to measure the quality of salient object detection. We then use a learning-to-rank method to rank salient object detection results of the same input image. Specifically, we first train a binary classifier to compare the quality between every two detection results and then aggregate these pair-wise comparison results to rank all the detection results.

To the best of our knowledge, this paper provides the first method that is able to rank the quality of salient object detection results without any ground truth. While this paper does not provide a new salient object detection method per se, we provide a way to better leverage the vast amount of detection methods provided by the community. As shown in our experiments, our method can reliably select for each input image the best detection result or the good results from a range of different methods.

2   Feature Design

In this section, we discuss what makes a good salient object detection result. According to previous research as well as our observation, we measure the quality

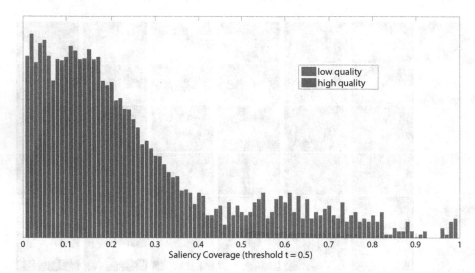

Fig. 2. Saliency coverage distribution for low-quality and high-quality salient object detection results

of salient object detection through the analysis of the saliency map itself as well as the interaction between the saliency map and the original image. Below we describe how we design features to capture the aspects of a good saliency map in detail.

Saliency Coverage. The sizes of salient objects in natural images often fall into a certain range. Therefore, when a saliency map has its salient pixels covering an abnormally large or small area in the image, it is unlikely to be a good map. We design the saliency coverage feature f_C to encode this knowledge.

Given a saliency map M (whose value is scaled to the range $[0, 1]$), we binarize it using a threshold value $t \in [0, 1]$ and compute the saliency coverage value as

$$f_C(M) = \frac{1}{n} \sum_{i \in M} \delta\{M(i) > t\} \tag{1}$$

where n denotes the number of pixels in M. $\delta\{.\}$ is an indicator function whose value is 1 if its argument is true and 0 otherwise.

To examine the ability of this feature in discriminating between high- and low-quality saliency maps, we conduct a small experiment. We randomly collect 3,000 images from the salient object detection benchmark THUS-10000 [7]. For each image, we apply five different saliency detection methods GC [8], HC [8], LC [55], GBMR [54], and HS [53] and create 15,000 saliency maps in total. We then form two groups of images out of those saliency maps according to their AUC score computed using the ground truth. The high-quality group contains only good saliency maps with AUC score at least 0.9. The low-quality group contains only the results with AUC score below 0.6.

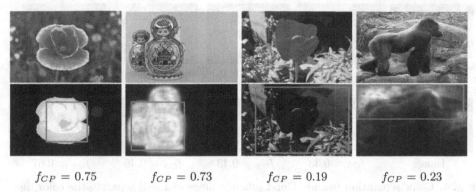

$$f_{CP} = 0.75 \qquad f_{CP} = 0.73 \qquad f_{CP} = 0.19 \qquad f_{CP} = 0.23$$

Fig. 3. Saliency map compactness feature. The green windows contain 75 % of total saliency values. A good saliency map tends to have a high average saliency value inside the enclosing window.

For each map from these two groups, we compute the saliency coverage value (with threshold $t = 0.5$). We show the normalized histograms on the saliency coverage value over each of these two groups in Fig. 2. This figure demonstrates that the high-quality and low-quality saliency maps have clearly different distributions, which shows the capability of the saliency coverage feature in discriminating the high- and low-quality saliency maps.

To make our system robust against the choice of the threshold t, we use 10 different threshold values in the range between 0 and 1. For each threshold value, we compute a corresponding saliency coverage value. Finally, we concatenate the 10 saliency coverage values into a feature vector.

Saliency Map Compactness. Previous research on saliency analysis shows that a good saliency map should concentrate its salient pixels in a compact region in the image [7, 16, 26]. To encode this observation, we estimate how dense the salient pixel distribution is in the most salient area predicted by the saliency map. Specifically, we first compute the minimal image window W_p covering the proportion p of the total saliency in the saliency map M. We then compute the compactness value f_{CP} as the average saliency value inside W_p. In computing W_p, we resize the saliency map to 100 x 100 to reduce the search space. We then use the integral image method [48] to speed up the computation of the total saliency in a candidate window in each search step, which involves only 3 additions and subtractions in total. For $p = 0.5$, W_p can typically be found in 0.02 seconds on a desktop machine with an i7 3.40 GHz CPU.

As demonstrated in Fig. 3, good saliency maps tend to have a high average enclosed saliency value. To make our method robust against the selection of the parameter value for p, we compute the compactness values using multiple values for p and concatenate them all into a single feature vector. In this paper, we use three p values, namely 0.25, 0.5, and 0.75.

| Image | $f_{CS} = 0.28$ | $f_{CS} = 0.45$ | $f_{CS} = 0.56$ | $f_{CS} = 0.63$ |
| Image | $f_{CS} = 0.33$ | $f_{CS} = 0.43$ | $f_{CS} = 0.46$ | $f_{CS} = 0.67$ |

Fig. 4. Color separation feature. Good saliency maps can well separate the color distributions of salient regions and background regions. They thus give small f_{CS} values.

Saliency Histogram. The distribution of saliency values in the saliency map can also be an indicator of its quality. For example, in salient object detection, a good saliency map should well separate salient objects from the image background. This favors saliency histograms with concentrated peaks at two ends. On the other hand, a saliency map where most of the pixels have middle-range saliency values is unlikely to be a good map as it is mostly fuzzy. To capture this observation, we compute the normalized 20-bin histogram over saliency values in the saliency map and use it as our feature f_H.

Color Separation. Many of the previous saliency analysis methods use a global contrast assumption [1,8,14]. This assumption suggests that salient regions and background regions tend to be different from each other. We design the feature f_{CS} to score a saliency map according to the separation between the color distributions of salient regions and non-salient regions based on the saliency map.

We use color histograms to model the color distributions. As saliency often provides a soft assignment of image pixels into salient and background regions, we adopt a weighting-based technique to incorporate the saliency values into the computation of the color histograms. In this paper, we use the histograms with 16 bins per-channel in the RGB color space.

Let b_i denote the color range of the ith bin, the salient region's normalized color histogram h_s can be computed as

$$h_s(i) = \frac{\sum_{p \in I} M(p)\delta\{I(p) \in b_i\}}{\sum_{p \in I} M(p)} \tag{2}$$

where $M(p)$ and $I(p)$ denote the saliency value and color at pixel p. δ is the indicator function defined previously. Similarly, we compute the normalized background color histogram h_g as

$$h_g(i) = \frac{\sum_{p \in I}(1 - M(p))\delta\{I_p \in b_i\}}{\sum_{p \in I}(1 - M(p))} \tag{3}$$

We estimate the color separation feature f_{CS} as the intersection between the histograms for the salient and background region as follows,

$$f_{CS}(M) = \frac{1}{n_h} \sum_{i=1}^{n_h} \min(h_s(i), h_g(i)) \tag{4}$$

where n_h denotes the number of bins in the histograms. Fig. 4 compares different saliency maps generated from the same images. The examples show that good saliency maps tend to have smaller feature values (i.e. the salient and background color distributions are better separated) than those less accurate ones.

Segmentation Quality. Salient object detection should give a good object segmentation result. We design the feature f_{NC} to measure the quality of a saliency map by assessing the segmentation result it induces.

We first obtain the induced segmentation by binarizing the saliency map with a threshold value t, which partitions an image into the salient region S_t and background region B_t. According to the normalized-cut image segmentation method [46], a good segmentation result should maximize the intra-region similarity while minimizing the inter-region similarity. The estimation for the segmentation quality can then be computed using the normalized-cut energy function.

$$f_{NC}(S_t, B_t) = \frac{\sum_{i \in S_t, j \in B_t, j \in N(i)} w_{ij}}{\sum_{i \in S_t, j \in N(i)} w_{ij}} + \frac{\sum_{i \in S_t, j \in B_t, j \in N(i)} w_{ij}}{\sum_{i \in B_t, j \in N(i)} w_{ij}} \tag{5}$$

where $N(i)$ denotes the set of pixels neighboring to i. w_{ij} represents the color similarity between the neighboring pixels i and j. Following [31], we compute w_{ij} as

$$w_{ij} = exp(-\eta \|I_i - I_j\|) \tag{6}$$

where I_i and I_j represent the RGB color values at the pixels i and j, respectively. $\|.\|$ denotes the L_2 norm. η is set as $\eta = 2 < \|I_i - I_j\|^2 >^{-1}$ [31], where $< . >$ denotes the expectation operator. For the sake of robustness, we compute the feature values using three different values for the threshold t, namely 0.5, 0.75, and 0.95, and concatenate them into the feature vector.

Boundary Quality. Good saliency maps should provide accurate and well-defined object boundaries. Therefore, the object boundary reflected in the saliency map M should align well with strong edges in the input image I. We design the boundary quality feature f_B to encode this observation. Specifically, given the input image I and its saliency map M, we compute the boundary map B_M from M and measure how well it correlates with the strong edge map E_I of the image I.

We generate E_I using the structured-forests edge detection method [11]. We then compute the saliency boundary map B_M from M as

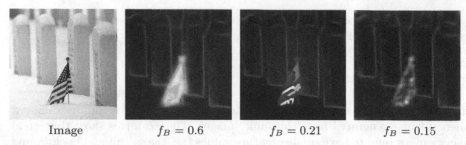

| Image | $f_B = 0.6$ | $f_B = 0.21$ | $f_B = 0.15$ |

Fig. 5. Boundary-quality feature. The strong edge maps have been overlayed in red onto the saliency maps. The middle saliency map has low f_B value because its boundary does not correlate well with strong image edges, while the right-most saliency map has low f_B value because it fails to provide a well-defined boundary.

$$B_M(p) = \frac{w_p |M(p_1) - M(p_2)|}{\sum_{p \in M} w_p} \quad (7)$$
$$w_p = M(p) \max(|M(p) - M(p_1)|, |M(p) - M(p_2)|)$$

where p_1 and p_2 denote two neighboring pixels of p. Those two neighboring pixels are taken orthogonal to edge direction at p. w_p computes the saliency-weighted edge magnitude in the saliency map.

The factor $|M(p_1) - M(p_2)|$ in Equation 7 weighs the boundary map computation based on how well the edge point separates the salient region and the background region. A large value of the factor indicates that the boundary is well defined.

The boundary-quality feature f_B measures the correlation between B_M and E_I using the dot product between two edge maps.

$$f_B(M, I) = \sum_{p \in I} B_M(p) E_I(p) \quad (8)$$

As shown in Fig. 5, better saliency maps tend to have higher boundary-quality values. The saliency map in the third column fails because a portion of its predicted boundary has a low edge value, which results in the low correlation between B_M and E_I. In the right most saliency map, as most of the edge points do not separate salient region and background region, the boundary map B_M was suppressed, which suggests the low-quality boundary and thus leads to a small boundary-quality value.

As edge detection often depends on image scale, we compute the above boundary-quality value at each of four different image scales, namely 0.25, 0.5, 0.75, and 1.0 and concatenate them into the feature vector.

3   Salient Object Detection Ranking

Given an image I and its k saliency maps $\{M_i\}_{i=1..k}$, our goal is to rank these maps according to their quality without any ground truth. In this paper, we adopt the pairwise-based learning-to-rank methodology [5, 12, 20]. Specifically, we compare every pairs among the k saliency maps and then aggregate these pairwise comparison results to produce the final overall ranking.

Before describing our method, let us describe how we obtain the labeled training data. For each image in the dataset, we use k different salient object detection methods to generate k saliency maps. We then use the salient object mask provided with each image to measure the quality of each saliency map. In this paper, we use the popular Area Under the ROC Curve (AUC score) as the objective quality measurement for saliency maps. We obtain the ground-truth ranking for each image by ranking its k saliency maps according to their AUC scores.

We now elaborate our pairwise-based ranking method. Given two saliency maps M_i and M_j generated for the same image, we model the pairwise preference (quality comparison) as the probability that M_i has higher quality than M_j

$$P_{M_i, M_j} = P(M_i \succ M_j | f_{M_i}, f_{M_j}) \tag{9}$$

where $M_i \succ M_j$ means that M_i has higher quality than M_j. f_M denotes the feature vector extracted from the map M using the feature extraction method described in Section 2.

To obtain the pairwise preference model P_{M_i, M_j}, we consider it as a binary classifier. For a given pair of saliency maps M_i and M_j, the feature vector $f_{M_i M_j}$ is created by concatenating f_{M_i} and f_{M_j}. We train a binary classifier C that takes $f_{M_i M_j}$ as input and outputs the preference label 1 if $M_i \succ M_j$, and 0 otherwise. The output of C can be used as an estimation for P_{M_i, M_j}. To train the classifier, we obtain the preference labels for every pairs of saliency maps from each image in the dataset using its ground-truth map ranking computed previously.

In this paper, we experimented with three binary classification methods, including Random Forest Classifier (RFC) [3], Support Vector Machine (SVM) [47], and Multi-Layer Perceptron (MLP) [17]. Specifically, for SVM, we use the RBF-kernel probabilistic SVM implemented in the LIBSVM package [6]. For RFC, we use the Random Forest implementation for MATLAB from Jaiantilal et al.[1]. For MLP, we use the MATLAB Neural Network Toolbox implementation[2] to train an MLP network with one hidden layer. All the models' hyperparameters are selected automatically via cross validation.

Ranking Prediction. Once the pairwise preference model has been trained, it can be used for ranking salient object detection results on new images. Specifically, given an image I and a set $\{M_i\}_{i=1..k}$ of k saliency maps generated from I, we compute a relative score for each saliency map M_i as

$$r(M_i) = \sum_{j=1..k, j \neq i} P_{M_i, M_j} \tag{10}$$

---

[1] https://code.google.com/p/randomforest-matlab/
[2] http://www.mathworks.com/help/nnet/index.html

The overall ranking for every M_i's can then be obtained by sorting to their scores.

4 Experiments

We experiment with our method on the public salient object detection benchmark THUS-10000 [7]. This dataset contains 10,000 images. Each image is associated with a manually segmented salient object mask. For each of the experiments in this section, we randomly select from the dataset 2,000 images for training our ranking model, and use the remaining 8,000 images for testing. For all experiments, we repeat this random partition 10 times and report the average results.

In our experiments, we use ten state-of-the-art salient object detection methods, including GBVS [16], IT [23], FT [1], GC [8], HC [8], LC [55], SR [19], CA [14], GBMR [54], HS [53]. For each image in the dataset, we use the codes published by the authors of those methods to generate ten saliency maps. We then perform the ranking on the resulting saliency maps for each image.

4.1 Ranking Accuracy

We examine the quality of the our ranking results by assessing how well they correlate with the ground-truth ranking. To the best of our knowledge, our work is the first to approach the problem of ranking salient object detection results. To serve as the baseline for our comparison, we consider the ranking strategy that assigns a fix ranking to every input image. That fix ranking is computed based on the performance of each salient object detection method over the whole training set. In particular, we compare our method against the following two baseline ranking methods.

Mean-AUC-Based Ranking (MAR) : In this baseline ranking method, the mean AUC score over the whole training set is computed for each method. The MAR ranking is obtained by sorting the methods according to their mean AUC scores. The resulted ranking is applied for all testing images.

Voting-Based Ranking (VBR) : In this method, each image in the training set casts a vote for the saliency method that works best for it (according to the AUC score). The resulted ranking is then obtained by sorting the methods according to their number of votes over the whole training set.

We implement both methods and compare their performance to that from our image-specific ranking method.

Correlation with Ground-Truth Ranking. To evaluate how well our ranking results agree with the ground-truth ranking, we compute their rank correlation. In particular, we experiment with two rank correlation metrics.

Table 1. Rank correlation

	Kendall τ correlation	Weighted Kendall τ correlation
MAR Baseline Ranking	0.49	0.74
VBR Baseline Ranking	0.48	0.73
Our Method (RFC)	0.62	0.81
Our Method (MLP)	0.64	0.83
Our Method (SVM)	**0.65**	**0.83**

Kendall τ Rank Correlation : The Kendall τ rank correlation [27] is one of the most well known method for comparing ranking results [32]. Given a set of elements $S = \{s_i, i = 1..n\}$ and two ranking functions r_1 and r_2, the Kendall τ rank correlation is computed as

$$\tau(r_1, r_2) = 1 - \frac{2\sum_{i,j} \delta\{r_1(i,j) \neq r_2(i,j)\}}{n(n-1)} \qquad (11)$$

where δ denotes the indicator function. $r(i,j)$ outputs 1 if the ranking function r gives i the higher rank than j, and 0 otherwise. This metric penalizes a pair of elements if their relative orders given by the two ranking functions disagree.

Weighted Kendall τ Rank Correlation : Inspired by [32], we also experiment with the weighted Kendall τ rank correlation metric

$$\tau(r_1, r_2) = 1 - \frac{2\sum_{i,j} w_{ij}\delta\{r_1(i,j) \neq r_2(i,j)\}}{n(n-1)} \qquad (12)$$

where the weight w_{ij} is defined as

$$w_{ij} = max\{AUC(i), AUC(j)\}|AUC(i) - AUC(j)| \qquad (13)$$

Intuitively, the weighted Kendall τ rank correlation reduces the penalty on the discordant pairs of maps when their AUC scores are close to each other. At the same time, it emphasizes the penalty on the pairs containing high-quality maps.

Table 1 shows the average rank correlation on the test data. The results show that the saliency map ranking from our method has significantly higher correlation with the ground-truth ranking than those from the baseline methods.

Rank-n Accuracy. In this experiment, we examine the effectiveness of our ranking results for the task of retrieving the best saliency map for a given image. For evaluation, we measure the rank-n accuracy.

Given the ranking results for all testing images, the rank-n accuracy is computed as the percentage of the test data for which the actual best method is ranked within the top n positions.

Fig. 6 shows rank-1, rank-2, rank-3, and rank-4 accuracy from our methods, as well as those from the baseline ranking methods. From the figure, we can see

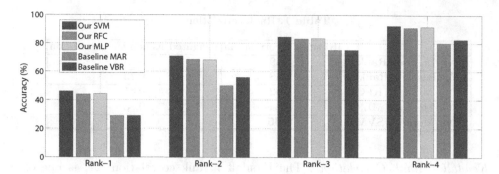

Fig. 6. Rank-n accuracy. The ranking predicted by our model is significantly better than the baseline ranking in selecting the best salient object detection results.

that the ranking results from our methods can provide significantly better best map prediction accuracy than those from the baseline ranking methods.

Discussion. To further evaluate the robustness of our saliency map ranking method, we perform an additional test. For each image in the dataset, we randomly select the ground-truth mask from another image to use as its additional saliency map. This map can be considered a "noisy" individual map as it is a good map on its own but is likely inaccurate with respect to the input image. With the resulting new set of individual maps, we redo all the experiments described previously in this section.

Examining the results, we observe that the ranking accuracy is almost unaffected by the inclusion of the additional map. Specifically, we obtain the rank-1 accuracy of 44.8%, the average Kendall τ rank correlation of 0.66, and the weighted Kendall τ rank correlation of 0.83. This result shows that our method is robust against the inclusion of such a "noisy" individual map.

4.2 Saliency Map Selection Quality

We now further evaluate the ability of our method in selecting the best saliency map given an input image. While rank-1 assessment can give the absolute accuracy, it gives little insight for the cases where the system fails to predict the true best map. In practice, there are scenarios where an incorrectly selected saliency map is still useful as long as its quality is close to that of the true best map.

To take that into account, we consider an alternative method to evaluate the best-map selection quality. In particular, a best map selection result is considered correct if the AUC score of the selected saliency map differs from that of the true best map by no more than a tolerance value ϵ. The accuracy of a saliency map selection method can then be measured as the percentage of all testing images for which the map selection are correct according to this condition. We call this the tolerance-based accuracy. For comparison, we consider the baseline best-map selection methods that always pick a single saliency detection algorithm to use for all images. In particular, we experiment with three methods that always

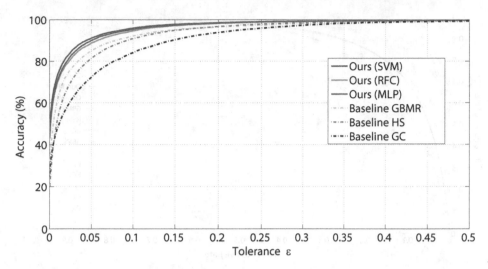

Fig. 7. Tolerance-based best map selection accuracy. At the high tolerance values, our results produce noticeably smaller number of errors than selecting any single method to use for all images. Note that the larger the tolerance value is, the more severe an error would be.

select the GBMR, HS, and GC saliency map, respectively. We choose those three methods for our comparison as they have the highest mean AUC scores over the whole dataset.

Table 2 shows the tolerance-based accuracy at $\epsilon = 0.02$ (i.e. two percent of the AUC range). This result shows that for 82% of all testing images our method can select the good saliency maps that are close to the ground-truth best maps.

Table 2. Tolerance-based accuracy at $\epsilon = 0.02$

	Our SVM	Our RF	Our MLP	Baseline GBMR
Accuracy (%)	**82**	79.5	80	72

We note that the higher the tolerance threshold is, the more severe an incorrect map selection would be. We provide in Fig. 7 the curve representing the tolerance-based best-map selection accuracy measured over the wide range of tolerance values ϵ. The curves show that our methods make noticeably smaller number of errors with small values of ϵ compared to the baseline methods.

4.3 Salient Object Detection Performance

Although our main goal in this paper is not to develop a new salient object detection method, it is interesting to investigate how our method can be used to improve the overall performance of individual methods. For each testing image,

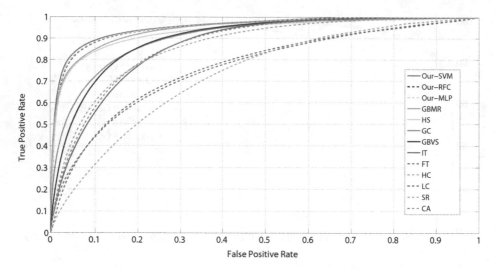

Fig. 8. ROC curves for different salient object detection methods

we use the saliency map ranking obtained for that image to select the best saliency map and use it as our final salient object detection result.

Fig. 8 shows the ROC curves measured from the saliency maps generated using different methods. The figure shows that using the saliency maps selected by our methods, we can improve the ROC curves over each individual method. This confirms the observation that although some methods clearly dominate the others over a large number of images, selecting the image-dependent best saliency map for each specific image is promising in pushing forward the salient object detection performance.

Limitation. One limitation of our method is that it requires to run all the individual salient object detectors for each input image. Some of the individual detectors are slow, which makes our method computationally expensive in terms of running time. This limits the applicability of our method compared to some fast individual methods. However, we note that in practice we can pick the best one from only a few fast and statistically best-performed detectors instead of using all available detectors. This will significantly speed up our method as our method typically takes only 20 seconds to execute both the feature extraction step and the saliency map ranking step.

5   Conclusion

In this paper, we develop a data-driven approach for comparing salient object detection results without knowing the ground truth. We designed a wide range of dedicated features to capture the saliency map quality. Those features are used in our learning-to-rank framework to produce the saliency map ranking for each input image. Experiments on the large salient object detection benchmark show that our method can produce ranking results that correlate well with the ground-truth ranking. Our method can be used to adaptively select good saliency maps for each input image, which can improve the overall salient object detection performance.

Acknowledgement. This work was supported in part by NSF grants IIS-1321119, CNS-1205746, and CNS-1218589.

References

1. Achanta, R., Hemami, S., Estrada, F., Süsstrunk, S.: Frequency-tuned salient region detection. In: IEEE Conference on Computer Vision and Pattern Recognition (2009)
2. Borji, A., Sihite, D.N., Itti, L.: Salient object detection: A benchmark. In: Fitzgibbon, A., Lazebnik, S., Perona, P., Sato, Y., Schmid, C. (eds.) ECCV 2012, Part II. LNCS, vol. 7573, pp. 414–429. Springer, Heidelberg (2012)
3. Breiman, L.: Random forests. Machine Learning 45(1), 5–32 (2001)
4. Bulling, A., Alt, F., Schmidt, A.: Increasing the security of gaze-based cued-recall graphical passwords using saliency masks. In: SIGCHI International Conference on Human Factors in Computing Systems (2012)
5. Cao, Z., Qin, T., Liu, T.Y., Tsai, M.F., Li, H.: Learning to rank: From pairwise approach to listwise approach. In: International Conference on Machine Learning (2007)
6. Chang, C.C., Lin, C.J.: Libsvm: A library for support vector machines. ACM Trans. Intell. Syst. Technol. 2, 27:1–27:27 (2011)
7. Cheng, M.M., Warrell, J., Lin, W.Y., Zheng, S., Vineet, V., Crook, N.: Efficient salient region detection with soft image abstraction. In: IEEE International Conference on Computer Vision (2013)
8. Cheng, M., Zhang, G., Mitra, N.J., Huang, X., Hu, S.: Global contrast based salient region detection. In: IEEE CVPR (2011)
9. Christopoulos, C., Skodras, A., Ebrahimi, T.: The jpeg2000 still image coding system: An overview. IEEE Trans. on Consumer Electronics 46(4), 1103–1127 (2000)
10. Cohen, Y., Basri, R.: Inferring region salience from binary and gray-level images. Pattern Recognition 36, 2349–2362 (2003)
11. Dollár, P., Zitnick, C.L.: Structured forests for fast edge detection. In: IEEE International Conference on Computer Vision (2013)
12. Fürnkranz, J., Hüllermeier, E.: Pairwise preference learning and ranking. In: Lavrač, N., Gamberger, D., Todorovski, L., Blockeel, H. (eds.) ECML 2003. LNCS (LNAI), vol. 2837, pp. 145–156. Springer, Heidelberg (2003)
13. Gao, D., Vasconcelos, N.: Bottom-up saliency is a discriminant process. In: IEEE International Conference on Computer Vision (2007)
14. Goferman, S., Zelnik-manor, L., Tal, A.: Context-aware saliency detection. In: IEEE Conference on Computer Vision and Pattern Recognition (2010)
15. Hall, D., Leibe, B., Schiele, B.: Saliency of interest points under scale changes. In: British Machine Vision Conference (2002)
16. Harel, J., Koch, C., Perona, P.: Graph-based visual saliency. In: NIPS, pp. 545–552 (2006)

17. Haykin, S.: Neural Networks: A Comprehensive Foundation, 2nd edn. Prentice Hall PTR, Upper Saddle River (1998)
18. Holtzman-gazit, M., Zelnik-manor, L., Yavneh, I.: Salient edges: A multi scale approach. In: European Conference on Computer Vision Workshop on Vision for Cognitive Tasks (2010)
19. Hou, X., Zhang, L.: Saliency detection: A spectral residual approach. In: IEEE Conference on Computer Vision and Pattern Recognition (2007)
20. Hüllermeier, E., Fürnkranz, J., Cheng, W., Brinker, K.: Label ranking by learning pairwise preferences. Artificial Intelligence 172(16-17), 1897–1916 (2008)
21. Itti, L., Koch, C.: Computational modeling of visual attention. Nature Reviews Neuroscience 2, 194–203 (2001)
22. Itti, L., Koch, C.: A saliency-based search mechanism for overt and covert shifts of visual attention. Vision Research 40, 1489–1506 (2000)
23. Itti, L., Koch, C., Niebur, E.: A model of saliency-based visual attention for rapid scene analysis. IEEE Trans. Pattern Anal. Mach. Intell. 20, 1254–1259 (1998)
24. Jiang, B., Zhang, L., Lu, H., Yang, C., Yang, M.H.: Saliency detection via absorbing markov chain. In: IEEE International Conference on Computer Vision (2013)
25. Jiang, Z., Davis, L.S.: Submodular Salient Region Detection. In: IEEE Conference on Computer Vision and Pattern Recognition (2013)
26. Judd, T., Ehinger, K., Durand, F., Torralba, A.: Learning to predict where humans look. In: IEEE International Conference on Computer Vision (2009)
27. Kendall, M.G.: A new measure of rank correlation. Biometrika 30(1/2), 81–93 (1938)
28. Li, X., Li, Y., Shen, C., Dick, A., Hengel, A.V.D.: Contextual hypergraph modeling for salient object detection. In: IEEE International Conference on Computer Vision (2013)
29. Li, X., Lu, H., Zhang, L., Ruan, X., Yang, M.H.: Saliency detection via dense and sparse reconstruction. In: IEEE International Conference on Computer Vision (2013)
30. Liu, F., Gleicher, M.: Region enhanced scale-invariant saliency detection. In: 2006 IEEE International Conference on Multimedia and Expo (2006)
31. Liu, T., Sun, J., Zheng, N.N., Tang, X., Shum, H.Y.: Learning to detect a salient object. In: IEEE Conference on Computer Vision and Pattern Recognition (2007)
32. Liu, Y., Wang, J., Cho, S., Finkelstein, A., Rusinkiewicz, S.: A no-reference metric for evaluating the quality of motion deblurring. ACM Trans. Graph. 32(6), 175:1–175:12 (2013), http://doi.acm.org/10.1145/2508363.2508391
33. Mai, L., Niu, Y., Liu, F.: Saliency aggregation: A data-driven approach. In: IEEE Conference on Computer Vision and Pattern Recognition (2013)
34. Marchesotti, L., Cifarelli, C., Csurka, G.: A framework for visual saliency detection with applications to image thumbnailing. In: IEEE International Conference on Computer Vision (2009)
35. Margolin, R., Zelnik-Manor, L., Tal, A.: Saliency for image manipulation. The Visual Computer, 1–12 (2012)
36. Ming, Y., Li, H., He, X.: Winding number for region-boundary consistent salient contour extraction. In: IEEE Conference on Computer Vision and Pattern Recognition (2013)
37. Niu, Y., Geng, Y., Li, X., Liu, F.: Leveraging stereopsis for saliency analysis. In: IEEE Conference on Computer Vision and Pattern Recognition (2012)
38. Oikonomopoulos, A., Patras, I., Pantic, M.: Spatiotemporal salient points for visual recognition of human actions. IEEE Transactions on Systems, Man, and Cybernetics, Part B: Cybernetics 36(3), 710–719 (2005)

39. Parikh, D., Zitnick, C.L., Chen, T.: Determining patch saliency using low-level context. In: Forsyth, D., Torr, P., Zisserman, A. (eds.) ECCV 2008, Part II. LNCS, vol. 5303, pp. 446–459. Springer, Heidelberg (2008)
40. Perazzi, F., Krhenbl, P., Pritch, Y., Hornung, A.: Saliency filters: Contrast based filtering for salient region detection. In: IEEE Conference on Computer Vision and Pattern Recognition (2012)
41. Ramanathan, S., Katti, H., Sebe, N., Kankanhalli, M., Chua, T.-S.: An eye fixation database for saliency detection in images. In: Daniilidis, K., Maragos, P., Paragios, N. (eds.) ECCV 2010, Part IV. LNCS, vol. 6314, pp. 30–43. Springer, Heidelberg (2010)
42. Rubinstein, M., Gutierrez, D., Sorkine, O., Shamir, A.: A comparative study of image retargeting. ACM Trans. Graph. 29, 160:1–160:10 (2010)
43. Rudoy, D., Goldman, D.B., Shechtman, E., Zelnik-Manor, L.: Learning video saliency from human gaze using candidate selection. In: IEEE Conference on Computer Vision and Pattern Recognition (2013)
44. Rutishauser, U., Walther, D., Koch, C., Perona, P.: Is bottom-up attention useful for object recognition (2004)
45. Sheikh, H., Bovik, A., Cormack, L.: No-reference quality assessment using natural scene statistics: Jpeg2000. IEEE Transactions on Image Processing 14(11), 1918–1927 (2005)
46. Shi, J., Malik, J.: Normalized cuts and image segmentation. In: IEEE Conference on Computer Vision and Pattern Recognition (1997)
47. Vapnik, V.N.: The nature of statistical learning theory. Springer-Verlag New York, Inc., New York (1995)
48. Viola, P.A., Jones, M.J.: Rapid object detection using a boosted cascade of simple features. In: CVPR, vol. (1), pp. 511–518 (2001)
49. Wang, Z., Bovik, A., Sheikh, H., Simoncelli, E.: Image quality assessment: From error visibility to structural similarity. IEEE Transactions on Image Processing 13(4), 600–612 (2004)
50. Wei, Y., Wen, F., Zhu, W., Sun, J.: Geodesic saliency using background priors. In: Fitzgibbon, A., Lazebnik, S., Perona, P., Sato, Y., Schmid, C. (eds.) ECCV 2012, Part III. LNCS, vol. 7574, pp. 29–42. Springer, Heidelberg (2012)
51. Wu, C., Frahm, J.-M., Pollefeys, M.: Detecting large repetitive structures with salient boundaries. In: Daniilidis, K., Maragos, P., Paragios, N. (eds.) ECCV 2010, Part II. LNCS, vol. 6312, pp. 142–155. Springer, Heidelberg (2010)
52. Xie, Y., Lu, H., Yang, M.H.: Bayesian saliency via low and mid level cues. IEEE Transactions on Image Processing 22(5), 1689–1698 (2013)
53. Yan, Q., Xu, L., Shi, J., Jia, J.: Hierarchical saliency detection. In: IEEE Conference on Computer Vision and Pattern Recognition (2013)
54. Yang, C., Zhang, L., Lu, H., Ruan, X., Yang, M.H.: Saliency detection via graph-based manifold ranking. In: IEEE Conference on Computer Vision and Pattern Recognition (2013)
55. Zhai, Y., Shah, M.: Visual attention detection in video sequences using spatiotemporal cues. In: ACM Multimedia (2006)
56. Zhao, R., Ouyang, W., Wang, X.: Person re-identification by salience matching. In: IEEE International Conference on Computer Vision (2013)
57. Zhao, R., Ouyang, W., Wang, X.: Unsupervised salience learning for person re-identification. In: IEEE Conference on Computer Vision and Pattern Recognition (2013)

RGBD Salient Object Detection:
A Benchmark and Algorithms

Houwen Peng[1], Bing Li[1], Weihua Xiong[1], Weiming Hu[1], and Rongrong Ji[2]

[1] Institute of Automation, Chinese Academy of Sciences, China
[2] Department of Cognitive Science, Xiamen University, China
http://sites.google.com/site/rgbdsaliency

Abstract. Although depth information plays an important role in the human vision system, it is not yet well-explored in existing visual saliency computational models. In this work, we first introduce a large scale RGBD image dataset to address the problem of data deficiency in current research of RGBD salient object detection. To make sure that most existing RGB saliency models can still be adequate in RGBD scenarios, we continue to provide a simple fusion framework that combines existing RGB-produced saliency with new depth-induced saliency, the former one is estimated from existing RGB models while the latter one is based on the proposed multi-contextual contrast model. Moreover, a specialized multi-stage RGBD model is also proposed which takes account of both depth and appearance cues derived from low-level feature contrast, mid-level region grouping and high-level priors enhancement. Extensive experiments show the effectiveness and superiority of our model which can accurately locate the salient objects from RGBD images, and also assign consistent saliency values for the target objects.

1 Introduction

Visual saliency has been a fundamental problem in neuroscience, psychology, and vision perception for a long time. It refers to the measurement of low-level stimuli that grab human attention in the early stage of visual processing [17]. We witness that the computation of saliency is originally a task of predicting where people look at an image, and recently has been extended to object-level saliency detection that involves separating the most conspicuous object from the background. This work focuses on the object-level saliency modeling, which benefits various applications including object detection and recognition [36], content based image retrieval [41][39], object aware image thumbnailing [31][14], etc.

Recently, detecting salient objects from RGBD images attracts lots of interest due to the birth of a new generation of sensing technologies, such as the *Microsoft Kinect* [1]. Although a small number of prior works aim to explore the role of depth in saliency analysis [25][13] and leverage depth to facilitate the saliency estimation [12][33], they are still at the initial stage of exploration and share common limitations: (1) Current studies on RGBD salient object detection are lack of a benchmark dataset that covers sufficient images with corresponding

D. Fleet et al. (Eds.): ECCV 2014, Part III, LNCS 8691, pp. 92–109, 2014.

accurate depth data and unified evaluation metrics. (2) The effective strategy that makes existing RGB-based saliency computation models work well in RGBD scenarios is not well explored. (3) Depth cues always work as an independent image channel for saliency detection in existing RGBD models [13][25], which inevitably ignores the strong complementarities between appearance and depth correspondence cues.

To address these problems, we first build up a large scale RGBD salient object benchmark with unified evaluation metrics, aiming at avoiding overfitting and biases. The benchmark contains 1,000 natural RGBD images captured by *Microsoft Kinect* together with the corresponding human-marked ground truth. To the best of our knowledge, it is the first large scale RGBD benchmark specially dedicated to the task of salient object detection. Second, to hold existing RGB-based saliency models still adequate in RGBD scenarios, we introduce a simple fusion strategy which extends RGB-based saliency models by incorporating depth-induced saliency. Specifically, the depth-induced saliency is produced by the proposed multi-contextual contrast method which computes depth rarity of a segmented patch from its local, global and background contexts. Finally, by considering low-level feature contrast, mid-level region grouping and high-level object-ware priors, we propose a novel multi-stage RGBD saliency estimation algorithm which combines depth information and appearance cues in a coupled manner. Experimental results on the benchmark show that our method can successfully identify salient content from RGBD images, which are difficult for existing visual saliency methods.

2 Related Work

2D Saliency: For saliency detection on 2D RGB image, most existing algorithms can be roughly divided into two categories, *i.e.*, local and global. Local approaches detect salient objects by measuring the rarity of a particular image region with respect to its neighborhoods. Itti *et al.* [17] first propose an influential saliency computational model, which performs center-surrounding differences on feature maps to obtain the local maxima of stimuli [24]. Harel *et al.* [15] define a graph on image and adopt random walks to compute saliency. To highlight the whole salient object, multi-scale contrast [29][44][27] and multi-cues integration [20,21] techniques are used. Due to lacking of global relations and structure, local contrast methods are sensitive to high frequency content or noises.

Global methods estimate saliency of a region based on its holistic rarity from an image. In [2], the authors define saliency by computing color difference from the mean image color on pixel level. Yet, this definition only accounts for first order average color and easily results in degraded performance on cluttered scenes. Goferman *et al.* [14] propose an improved method that highlights salient objects with their contexts in terms of low-level clues and global relationships. Cheng *et al.* [10] design a global contrast model that computes dissimilarities between 3D color histogram bins of all image regions. Perazzi *et al.* [34] formulate saliency estimation as two Gaussian filters performing on region uniqueness and distribution respectively. Other global models such as appearance reconstruction [28] and the fully connected MRF [18] are recently proposed to identify salient objects uniformly. Although global methods present superior results in some cases, they face challenges when an image contains similar foreground and background.

In addition, high-level priors are also incorporated into recent proposed methods to enhance the detection. Wei *et al.* [42] turn to background priors to guide the saliency detection, while Yang *et al.* [45] and Jiang *et al.* [19] integrate the background cues into the designed manifold ranking model and absorbing Markov chain, respectively. Shen and Wu [40] unify the high-level center, color and semantic priors into a low-rank matrix recovery framework. The prior from general object detector [4] is also considered in recent works [9][22][18].

3D Saliency: Contrary to the significant progress in 2D saliency research, the work leveraging depth information for saliency analysis is a bit limited. Niu *et al.* [33] exploit binocular images to estimate a disparity map and only use depth data to identify salient objects. So the performance is highly dependent on the quality of disparity map estimation which is another classical and challenging computer vision problem. Later, Lang *et al.* [25] conduct a comparative study of eye fixation prediction, rather than salient object detection, in 2D and 3D scenes after collecting a pool of 600 2D-vs-3D image pairs. Most recently, two related works [13][12] focus the task of detecting salient regions (other than salient objects) from RGBD images: Desingh *et al.* [13] verify that depth really matters on a small datasets with 80 images and propose to fuse saliency maps, produced by appearance and depth cues independently, through non-linear support vector regression. Ciptadi *et al.* [12] demonstrate the effectiveness of 3D layout and shape features from depth images in computing more informative saliency maps.

Compared with previous works, this paper has three fundamental differences: (1) Our RGBD salient object detection benchmark contains 1,000 images with accurate depth data captured from various scenarios, while the existing 3D datasets, *i.e.*, SSB [33], GIT [12] and NTU [13], are comparatively much smaller and simpler as shown in Table 1. (2) Rather than directly combining depth-induced saliency with color-produced saliency via simple fusion strategies [25][13], the proposed RGBD saliency model simultaneously takes account of depth and appearance information from multiple layers. (3) Last but not the least, a detailed quantitative analysis is given out about under what circumstance depth is indeed helpful, which is not explored in previous studies.

Table 1. Comparison of the benchmark and existing 3D datasets in terms of dataset size, number of objects contained within the images, type of scene and object, center bias, depth data, and publicity

3D Salient Object Detection Datasets							
Name	Size	Object No.	Scene Types	Object Types	Center Bias	Depth	Publicly Available
SSB [33]	1000	one (mostly)	>10	>400	Yes	No	Yes
NTU [13]	33	– –	– –	– –	– –	Yes	No
GIT [12]	80	multiple	<5	<20	No	Yes	Yes
Ours	1000	one (mostly)	>10	>400	Yes	Yes	Yes

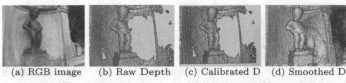

(a) RGB image   (b) Raw Depth   (c) Calibrated D   (d) Smoothed D

Fig. 1. Depth image calibration and filling

Fig. 2. A sample of image annotation. The image (b) is consistently labeled by five participants and included into our benchmark. (c) shows the final annotated salient object.

(a) Input image   (b) Labelled image   (c) Ground truth

3   RGBD Salient Object Benchmark

3.1   Dataset Construction

To remedy the data deficiency in current works and stimulate the research of detecting salient objects from RGBD images, we capture 5,000 images and their corresponding depth maps in diverse scenes. After preprocessing and annotation, we pick up 1,000 out of them to compose the final benchmark.

Hardware Setup: The reference depth map of our dataset is constructed using a standard *Microsoft Kinect*. The original *Kinect* device is not portable enough since it requires a mains power adapter with 110V or 220V AC. To solve the issue, we replace the adapter with a lithium battery (4400mAh 12V DC) that can power the *Kinect* for 4 hours of operation. To avoid camera shake and blur when capturing data, we strap the *Kinect* to a sturdy tripod. The output data of the *Kinect* is recorded by a connected laptop synchronously.

Data Capture: We visit a series of indoor and outdoor locations, *e.g.*, offices, supermarkets, campuses, streets and so on, and use the remoulded *Kinect* device to capture images of those scenes. Specifically, outdoor scenes are always captured in cloudy days or sunny dusks to avoid direct sunshine which may impair the precision of the infrared depth camera. To reduce imbalance due to human's preference, each scene is captured by a pair of collectors, and each object is photographed from at least four directions with different depth ranging from 0.5 to 10 meters.

Data Preprocessing: Because the color and infrared depth cameras on *Kinect* are a few centimeters apart horizontally, the captured color and depth images are not aligned as shown in Fig. 1(a) and (b). Thus, we calibrate each pair of color and depth images using the correction toolkit provided by *Microsoft Kinect SDK* to obtain more precise matching results (see Fig. 1(c)). It is worth noting that some regions in the aligned depth map are missing (see Fig. 1(c)) since they cannot be reached by the infrared laser projector. To obtain a filled and smoothed depth image, we adopt a colorization scheme [26] to repair the calibrated depth map. The processed depth image is shown in Fig. 1(d).

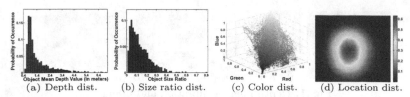

(a) Depth dist.   (b) Size ratio dist.   (c) Color dist.   (d) Location dist.

Fig. 3. Bias statistics over object depth, color, size and location

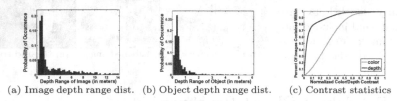

(a) Image depth range dist.   (b) Object depth range dist.   (c) Contrast statistics

Fig. 4. Complexity statistics of the benchmark

Salient Object Annotation: After collecting 5,000 natural images and their depth maps, we first manually selected 2,000 images, each of which contains one or more distinctive foreground objects. Then, for each selected image, five participants are asked to draw a rectangle according to their first glance at the most attention-grabbing object. Since different people may have different opinions on what a salient object is in the same image, we exclude those images with low labeling consistency [29] and choose the top 1,000 satisfactory images. Finally, two participants use *Adobe Photoshop* to segment the salient object manually from each image. Fig. 2 shows a typical example.

3.2   Dataset Statistics and Analysis

We present the statistical characteristics of our dataset and show that it is suitable for evaluating different salient object detection algorithms.

Diversity: The resulting dataset contains more than 400 kinds of common objects captured in 11 types of scenes under different illumination conditions. The indoor scenes include offices, apartments, supermarkets, museums, etc., while the outdoor locations cover parks, campuses, streets, etc. Most images contain single salient object, while the others include multiple objects. Each object only appears once in the dataset after manually selection.

Bias: Besides high diversity, low bias is another important characteristic for a benchmark dataset. Fig. 3 shows the color, depth, size and location distributions of salient objects across all images in the dataset. We can see that the color and depth of patches in salient objects distribute across a widespread range in RGB and D(depth) space (see Fig. 3(a) and (c)). The size ratio between a salient object and its corresponding image varies from 0.16% to 80%, and most objects occupy less than half area of the images. The locations of salient objects correlate strongly with a centered Gaussian distribution as show in Fig. 3(d). It is caused by the fact that human naturally frame an object of interest near the center of

Fig. 5. The extension framework: depth saliency is produced by the multi-contextual contrast method, while RGB saliency is estimated by any existing 2D saliency methods

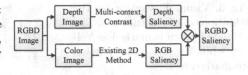

the image when taking pictures. We can also find such type of center bias in other public datasets such as MSRA [29] and SSB [12] (see Table 1).

Difficulty: To avoid that the salient objects can be easily extracted by a simple thresholding on depth maps, both the objects and depth images in the benchmark dataset share variable depth ranges as show in Fig. 4(a) and (b). We calculate the color and depth contrast between the foreground objects and background within a single image. Fig. 4(c) shows the cumulative histograms of the normalized contrast. It tells us that almost all the images in our benchmark have relatively low contrast between the background and salient objects. For example, 90% images have depth contrast within a distance of 0.3, while nearly 50% images have color contrast within this distance. The benchmark with low contrast inevitably brings up more challenges for detecting salient objects.

3.3 Evaluation Metrics

We introduce two types of measures to evaluate algorithm performance on the benchmark. The first one is the gold standard: Precision-Recall (PR) curve and F-measure. Precision corresponds to the percentage of salient pixels correctly assigned to all the pixels of extracted regions, and recall is the fraction of detected salient pixels belonging to the salient object in the ground truth. The PR curve is created by varying the saliency threshold from 0 to 255 that determines if a pixel is on the salient object. F-measure indicates the weighted harmonic of precision and recall: $F_\beta = \frac{(1+\beta^2) \times Precision \times Recall}{(\beta^2 \times Precision + Recall)}$, where β^2 is set to be 0.3 to stress precision more than recall. The F-measure is computed with an adaptive saliency threshold that is defined as twice the mean saliency of the image [2].

The second is Receiver Operating Characteristic curve (ROC) and the Area Under the ROC Curve (AUC). By thresholding over the saliency maps and plotting true positive rate vs. false positive rate, an ROC curve is acquired. The AUC score is calculated as the area underneath the ROC. Perfect performance corresponds to an AUC score of 1 while a score of 0.5 indicates chance level.

4   Extending 2D Saliency Models for RGBD Images

To make existing RGB salient object detection models still adequate in RGBD scenarios, this section proposes a framework that extends 2D saliency models for RGBD images.

Fig. 6. Visual illustration for the definitions of contextual sets. The estimated patch is marked as Yellow, while its contextual patches are marked as Red.

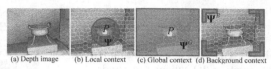

(a) Depth image   (b) Local context   (c) Global context   (d) Background context

4.1   Extension Framework

The proposed extension framework is a fusion process which includes three major steps as shown in Fig. 5: (1) separate the input RGBD image into two independent components: a RGB image and a depth map, (2) calculate their own saliency maps and (3) fuse these two saliency maps into a final one through the standard pixel-wise multiplication [6]. Specifically, to produce depth-induced saliency maps, we propose a multi-contextual contrast-based saliency estimation method. RGB saliency maps are obtained by any existing saliency detection algorithm on RGB images.

4.2   Depth Saliency from Multi-contextual Contrast

From the observation that an object lying at a different depth level from the others will noticeably attract our attention, thus we define our depth saliency computation based on the contrast analysis. To take advantage of local center-surrounding relationship, global distinctiveness and background information of the depth image, we introduce three types of contextual contrast, *i.e.*, local, global and background. Specifically, we first divide the depth image into N non-overlapping patches using SLIC algorithm [3]. For any patch P, we define its saliency $S(P)$ as the multiplication of these three types contextual contrast

$$S(P) = \prod_{k \in \{L,G,B\}} C(P, \Psi^k), \tag{1}$$

where $C(\cdot)$ is a typical contrast computation function, $\Psi^L = \{P_1^L, ..., P_{n_L}^L\}$ represents the local contextual set which consists of n_L nearest neighbor patches to P, $\Psi^G = \{P_1^G, ..., P_{n_G}^G\}$ indicates the global contextual set including all patches of the depth image except for P, and $\Psi^B = \{P_1^B, ..., P_{n_B}^B\}$ represents the pseudo-background context which consists of n_B patches from the four corners of the depth image as shown in Fig. 6. The definition of pseudo-background is inspired by the observation that the patches from corners of images are more likely to be background and contain lots of scene information which contributes to distinguish salient objects. Background context from image corners is more robust than that from image boundaries [42] in practice, because the salient objects have lower probabilities to touch corners of image.

Different from the traditional definition of contrast computation function that is the difference between P and the patches in Ψ^k ($k \in \{L, G, B\}$) with respect to visual features [10][20][34], we exploit Shannon's self-information, *i.e.*, $-\log(p(\cdot))$, as the measure of visual saliency. Self-information is a plausible biological metric [7], implying that an image patch will contain more distinctive information when it occurs in feature space with less probability. Thus, $C(\cdot)$ is defined as

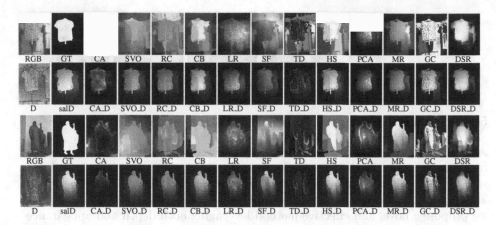

Fig. 7. Visual comparisons of saliency maps before and after fusing depth saliency. The odd rows are the results of existing 12 RGB saliency models, while the even rows show the maps after fusing depth saliency. Here, "salD" is the saliency map produced by our multi-contextual contrast method.

$$C(P, \Psi^k) = -\log(p(P|\Psi^k)). \tag{2}$$

Here, the conditional probability $p(P|\Psi^k)$ represents the underlying density of P with the given context Ψ^k. Specially, let $\mathbf{d}$ represent the average depth of P, and $D^k = \{\mathbf{d}_1^k, \mathbf{d}_2^k, ..., \mathbf{d}_{n_k}^k\}$ be the depth value set corresponding to the average depth of all patches in Ψ^k, then we have

$$p(P|\Psi^k) = \hat{p}(\mathbf{d}|D^k). \tag{3}$$

To model the depth distribution of salient objects with mixture of depth values, we adopt Gaussian kernel density estimator [38] to compute the probability density of $\hat{p}(\mathbf{d}|D^k)$ in Eq.(3) as

$$\hat{p}(\mathbf{d}|D^k) = \frac{1}{n_k} \sum_{j=1}^{n_k} e^{-\frac{\|\mathbf{d}-\mathbf{d}_j^k\|^2}{2(\sigma_d^k)^2}}, \tag{4}$$

where σ_d^k is the bandwidth of Gaussian kernel that controls the influence of depth difference. The kernel density of this type does not assume any specific underlying distribution and, theoretically, the estimation can converge to any density function with enough samples [38].

The above procedure works on each patch and results in patch-level saliency. The final pixel-wise depth-induced saliency map is obtained through assigning the saliency value of each patch to every pixel belonging to it.

Examples of depth-induced saliency map derived from multi-contextual contrast are shown in Fig. 7. We can see that when the depth level of foreground object is distinct from background, our method is able to roughly locate the salient regions and approximately highlight the object. Through fusing the depth saliency with RGB saliency produced by existing 2D saliency algorithms, we obtain more visually feasible results.

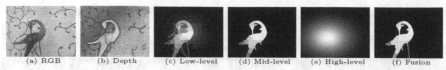

Fig. 8. Saliency maps produced by the key three stages in our approach

5   A Novel Saliency Model for RGBD Images

Although the simple late fusion strategy achieves improvements, it still suffers from inconsistency in the homogeneous foreground regions and is lack of precision around object boundaries. It may be ascribed to treating the appearance and depth correspondence cues in an independent manner. To resolve the issue, we propose a novel and effective method leveraging both depth and appearance cues from multiple levels. Our approach consists of three stages. First, we extend the low-level multi-contextual contrast method proposed in the previous section to RGBD cases and produce an initial saliency map. Next, we exploit thresholding on the initial saliency map to yield saliency seeds which are diverse regions with high saliency values. Starting with any one of saliency seeds, region grouping is performed on a weighted graph by using Prim's algorithm [35] to select candidate regions which have high probabilities belonging to the foreground object. This procedure is repeated until all the seeds are traversed. A visual consistent saliency map is generated at the end of this stage. Finally, saliency maps generated by previous two stages are combined through a Bayesian fusion strategy [28]. Besides, a high-level object-aware prior is also integrated to boost the performance. We illustrate this process on an example image in Fig. 8.

5.1   Low-Level Feature Contrast

For RGBD saliency detection, the classical low-level center-surrounding contrast can still work as a fundamental and support principle. Thus we extend the multi-contextual contrast model presented in Sec. 4.2 from depth space to RGBD scenarios by simply altering the feature and the technique of density estimation.

Feature Selection: Based on the verified conclusions that color, size and spatial position are undoubted attributes for guiding visual attention [43], we define the feature representation of RGBD images as the stack of these low-level features and depth value. Formally, for any patch P, its feature vector is defined as $\mathbf{f} = [\mathbf{c}, \mathbf{l}, \mathbf{r}, \mathbf{d}]^T$, where $\mathbf{c}$ is the average CIELab color value of pixels in P since CIELab can better approximate human color perception [5], $\mathbf{l}$ represents center location of pixels in P on the image plane, $\mathbf{r}$ is the region size defined by the number of contained pixels, and $\mathbf{d}$ is the average depth value of pixels in P.

Density Estimation: With the above constructed features and multiple contexts, we estimate the probability $p(P|\Psi^k)$ in Eq. (3) by a weighted version of Gaussian kernel density technique formulated as

$$p(P|\Psi^k) = \hat{p}(\mathbf{f}|F^k) = \frac{1}{n_k}\sum_{j=1}^{n_k}\alpha_j^k e^{-\frac{\|\mathbf{c}-\mathbf{c}_j^k\|^2}{2(\sigma_c^k)^2}}e^{-\frac{\|\mathbf{l}-\mathbf{l}_j^k\|^2}{2(\sigma_l^k)^2}}e^{-\frac{\|\mathbf{d}-\mathbf{d}_j^k\|^2}{2(\sigma_d^k)^2}}, \qquad (5)$$

where $F^k = \{\mathbf{f}_1^k, ..., \mathbf{f}_{n_k}^k\}$ is the feature representation corresponding to the surrounding patch set Ψ^k, and $\alpha_j^k = \mathbf{r}_j^k/\mathbf{r}$ is the weight coefficient defined by the size ratio between the target patch P and the contextual patch P_j^k. Here, the use of different bandwidths for different features is desirable since the variances are inconsistent in each feature dimension. For example, the color usually has more variance than the location and therefore should be assigned wider range. Through computing the probability density for each patch and merging all together, we obtain the initial patch-level saliency map (see Fig. 8(c)).

5.2   Mid-Level Region Grouping

To completely extract salient objects with precise boundaries, we perform mid-level salient region grouping with the help of the initial results obtained from low-level stage. Following the general object detection methods [8][30], the proposed region grouping is based on Prim's algorithm which greedily computes the maximum spanning tree of a weighted graph.

Graph Construction: Let $\mathcal{G} = (\mathcal{V}, \mathcal{E}, \rho)$ be the weighted connective graph of the superpixel segmentation [3] of an RGBD image, where the vertices $\mathcal{V}$ are the patches and the edges $(P, Q) \in \mathcal{E}$ connect the neighbor patches P and Q. The weight function $\rho : \mathcal{E} \to [0, 1]$ assigns weights $\rho(P, Q) = \rho_{P,Q}$ to edges. Following [30], we model the weight ρ with a logistic function:

$$\rho_{P,Q} = \sigma(\mathbf{w}^T \mathbf{x}_{P,Q} + b), \qquad \sigma(x) = (1 + \exp(-x))^{-1}, \tag{6}$$

where $\mathbf{x}_{P,Q}$ is a feature vector containing efficient features that measure the similarity and compactness of patches P and Q. The computation of the weight parameter $\mathbf{w}$ and bias b is resort to learning on the training data. Towards this end, we first assign a patch to a foreground object if over 80% of the number of pixels in the patch belongs to the object. Then we mine for pairs of patches which are involved in the same object and label them as the positive samples ($y_{P,Q} = 1$), otherwise, as the negative samples ($y_{P,Q} = 0$). The estimation of optimal parameters are computed by maximizing the log likelihood:

$$\{\mathbf{w}^*, b\} = \arg\max_{\mathbf{w}, b} \sum_{\forall (P,Q) \in \mathcal{E}} y_{P,Q} \log \rho_{P,Q} + (1 - y_{P,Q}) \log(1 - \rho_{P,Q}). \tag{7}$$

The features defined in $\mathbf{x}$ consist: (1) Color similarity x_c: color consistency is a important cue for objectness. With the CIELab color values $\mathbf{c}_P$ and $\mathbf{c}_Q$ of patches P and Q, we define the color similarity $x_c \in [0, 1]$ of patches as $x_c = \exp(-\|\mathbf{c}_P - \mathbf{c}_Q\|^2)$. (2) Surface normal consistency x_d: patches in the same plane have high probability belonging to one semantic region. To determine whether patches come from one plane, we compare their surface normals following the procedure proposed in [16]. The surface normal $\mathbf{s}_P$ of patch P is calculated as the cross product of two principle tangential vectors to local surface at the center location of P. Similar to color similarity, surface normal consistency is computed by $x_d = \exp(-\|\mathbf{s}_P - \mathbf{s}_Q\|^2)$. This cue is favor of combining patches from the same plane. (3) Border overlapping x_b: patches share common borders are likely to be grouped into one same region. Let l_P and l_Q be

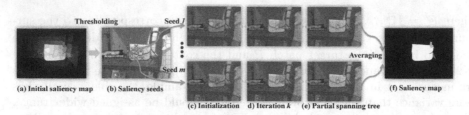

Fig. 9. Illustration of mid-level salient region grouping. The image patches existing in the partial spanning tree are marked as Green, while the patches to be added into the tree are marked as Red.

the perimeters of patches P and Q, then the border overlapping is defined as $x_b = (l_P \cap l_Q)/\min(l_P, l_Q)$ which represents the maximum ratio between their common border and each of their perimeters. This feature favors the merging of patches with longer overlapping border. Through learning on the training data, the weight $\mathbf{w}^*$ for these features is obtained.

Salient Region Grouping: Given the constructed graph, we perform region grouping using Prim's algorithm which generates a partial spanning tree with high sum of edge weights starting from a salient seed. The key procedure of our region grouping for an RGBD image is summarized as follows (see Fig. 9):

1. Generate a salient seed set $\{s_1, ..., s_m\}$, which is consisted by m image patches with high saliency values, through thresholding on the initial saliency map.
2. For each seed s_i in the set, repeat following procedure:
   - Initialize a spanning tree $T_1^{(i)}$ with the seed s_i.
   - Perform an iterative tree-grouping procedure based on Prim's algorithm which greedily selects the connected edge $(P, Q) \in \mathcal{E}$ with the maximum weight $\rho_{P,Q}$ and adds into the spanning tree $T_k^{(i)}$
   - Output the partial spanning tree $T^{(i)}$ when Prim's algorithm meets the terminal condition.
3. Generate a saliency map by computing the frequency of each patch appeared in all the spanning trees $\{T^{(1)}, ..., T^{(m)}\}$.

Specifically, to generate the salient seed set in Step 1, we experimentally set a threshold T to partition the patches embedded in the initial saliency map into a high-confidence group and a low-confidence group according to their saliency values. The members in the high-confidence group server as the seminal patches and constitute the salient seed set. In the iteration of Prim's algorithm, an effective stopping criterion is necessary in order to yield desirable partial spanning trees that firmly cover the nodes within the object, rather than the full nodes on the graph. To the end, we design a termination function which includes two terms: (1) The probability $1 - \Omega_{P,Q}$ that the candidate edge (P, Q) does not connect patches of the same object. (2) The difference of saliency value $S(P) - S(Q)$, which is estimated in the low-level computation stage, reflects the low-level saliency contrast. In practice, the termination function defined as the mean of these two terms works well:

$$f_{P,Q} = (1 - \Omega_{P,Q} + S(P) - S(Q))/2. \tag{8}$$

With this function, Prim's algorithm checks the terminal condition $f_{P,Q} > f_0$ at each iteration to decide whether the edge (P, Q) is added to the tree. Here, f_0 is a parameter set at the initialization step of the algorithm. An illustration example of the whole procedure of mid-level region grouping is shown in Fig. 9.

5.3 High-Level Priors Enhancement

In the final stage, we fuse the saliency maps produced by previous two stages, and further incorporate high-level priors to boost the performance. To combine the saliency maps from low-level and mid-level, we adopt the Bayesian integration method proposed in [28] which sums two posterior probabilities computed by one saliency map serves as the prior while the other works as the likelihood. Different from the high-level priors adopted in previous work [23][40][44][28], we propose an object-aware prior which take account of both location and size of salient objects. The prior is formulated as a Gaussian model:

$$G(a) = \exp[-(\frac{(x_a - \mu_x)^2}{2\sigma_x^2} + \frac{(y_a - \mu_y)^2}{2\sigma_y^2} + \frac{(z_a - \mu_z)^2}{2\sigma_z^2})], \tag{9}$$

where (x_a, y_a, z_a) are the coordinates of pixel a in the normalized image plan $X - Y$ and the depth range Z, (μ_x, μ_y, μ_z) are the coordinates of object center derived from the average values of patches within the salient seed set. Considering the impact of object size, we set the variance $(\sigma_x^2, \sigma_y^2, \sigma_z^2)$ to be $(2o_x, 2o_y, 2o_z)$, where o_x is the range of all saliency seeds on X-coordinate, while o_y and o_z are ranges on Y and Z coordinates respectively. Finally, the pixel-wise saliency map induced by the object-aware prior is integrated with the resulting map of Bayesian fusion by simple multiplication, as shown in Fig. 8, which generates the final result of our RGBD saliency model.

6   Experiments and Comparisons

6.1   Experimental Setup

Depth Model: In the implementation of the multi-contextual contrast model for depth images, we first use the SLIC superpixels [3] to partition the input depth image into $N = 200$ non-overlapping patches. For each patch P, we select $n_L = 32$ spatial nearest neighbor patches on the image plane as its local context Ψ^L, while all patches of the depth image except for P as the global context Ψ^G. To get the pseudo-background context Ψ^B, we pick out $n_B = 36$ boundary patches that are closest to the four corners of the image. The bandwidths of Gaussian kernel are empirically set as $(\sigma_d^L)^2 = 0.1$, $(\sigma_d^G)^2 = 0.05$, and $(\sigma_d^B)^2 = 0.25$.

RGBD Model: For low-level feature contrast computation in the RGBD model, we set N and $n_k(k \in L, G, B)$ to the same values as in the depth model. For the multivariable extension of kernel density estimation, we adopt the applicable Sheather-Jones plug-in approach [38] which minimizes an estimate of mean integrated squared error to estimate the kernel bandwidth σ_ξ^k ($\xi \in \{c, l, d\}$). To obtain the parameters $\mathbf{w}$ and b, we first divide the benchmark into two equal

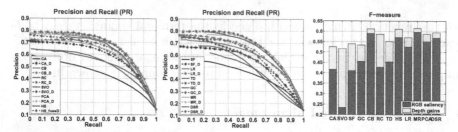

Fig. 10. The quantitative comparisons of the performance of existing saliency detection methods before and after fusing depth saliency by the proposed extension framework

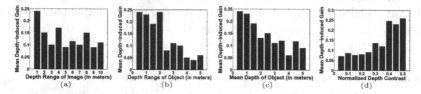

Fig. 11. Depth-induced gains analysis with respect to (a) depth range of images (DRI), (b) depth range of objects (DRO), (c) average depth of objects (ADO), and (d) normalized depth contrast between foreground and background (DC)

subsets and then choose one subsect for training and the other for testing. The optimal $\mathbf{w}^*$ and b^* are computed through 5-fold cross validation on the training subset according to Eq. (7), which is solved by gradient ascent. The threshold T and terminal parameter f_0 are empirically set to 0.8 and 0.45 respectively.

6.2   Experimental Results and Comparisons

In this section, we perform two sets of experiments: (1) evaluations of 12 prevailing RGB saliency methods before and after the fusion of depth saliency, (2) comparisons between our RGBD model and existing 3D models, and analysis of performance contributions of each individual component in the RGBD model.

Evaluations of 2D Models: We first compare the performances of existing RGB saliency models before and after fusing depth saliency produced by our multi-contextual contrast model. We select 12 state-of-the-art RGB saliency detection approaches, including the top 4 models ranked in the survey[6]: SVO[9], CA[14], CB[20], and RC[10], and 8 recently developed prominent methods: SF[34], LR[40], HS[44], MR[45], PCA[32], TD[37], GC[11], and DSR[28]. Fig. 10 presents the experimental results, in which the postfix '_D' denotes the method after fusing the depth saliency. We can see that both the PR curves and F-measure values of all the RGB salient object detection algorithms are improved by extra depth-produced saliency. It indicates that (1) the additional depth information is beneficial for salient object detection, (2) our multi-contextual contrast method performed on depth images are effective, (3) existing 2D saliency models are able to hold availability in RGBD scenarios through the proposed extension framework. Furthermore, let's review the examples shown in Fig 7 and investigate the

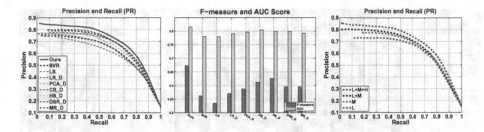

Fig. 12. Left and Middle: Quantitative comparisons of our approach with 8 competing RGBD methods. Right: Evaluation of performance contributions of each individual component in the RGBD model. The uppercase 'L', 'M', and 'H' represent the results of low-, mid- and high-level saliency respectively.

underlying reason why depth brings in improved performance. It is obviously that most existing saliency detection methods will fail when the object has similar appearance to the background. However, the introduction of depth contrast helps to extract the salient objects successfully.

We further analyze the situations in which depth is more helpful. To the end, we quantify the depth-induced gains for existing RGB saliency computational models against four aspects: depth range of images (DRI), depth range of objects (DRO), average depth of objects (ADO), and depth contrast between foreground and background (DC). The statistical diagrams are shown in Fig. 11. It is observed that (1) DRI nearly has no direct effect on depth effectiveness, but objects with lower depth ranges are more possible to be identified by depth saliency (see Fig. 11(a, b)). (2) If objects lie at close depth levels, *i.e.*, near to the camera, depth-induced gains are relatively high (Fig. 11(c)). (3) The higher depth contrast (DC) between foreground and background is, the more improvements from depth in identifying salient objects can be achieved (Fig. 11(d)). In conclusion, depth is more helpful when objects have relatively lower depth range, lie closer to the camera, or have high depth contrast with background.

Comparisons and Analysis of RGBD Models: We choose the top 6 2D saliency approaches after fusing depth saliency: DSR_D, MR_D, HS_D, CB_D, PCA_D and LR_D, and 2 recent proposed RGBD salient region detection methods: SVR [13] and LS [12] as baselines to compare their performances with our RGBD model. Fig. 12 shows the quantitative comparisons among these method on the constructed RGBD datasets in terms of PR curves, F-measure and AUC scores. It is observed that the proposed RGBD method is superior to baselines in terms of all the evaluation metrics. Interestingly, the method SVR, which uses non-linear support vector regression to fuse depth and RGB saliency, has lower performance compared to methods which uses the simple multiplication as fusion strategy. The underlying reasons are (1) SVR selects RC [10] to serve as the RGB method which is not the best one in 2D models, (2) SVR is designed for salient region detection, which is a little different from object-level saliency. Fig. 13 shows the qualitative comparisons on several RGBD images. We can see that the proposed method can accurately locate the salient objects, and also produce

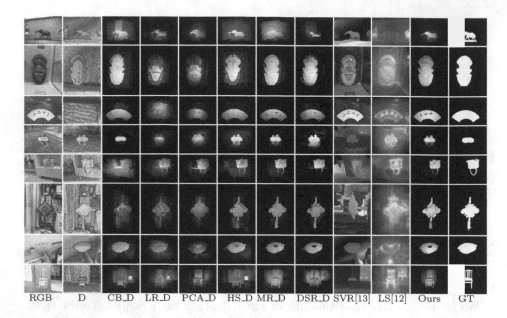

RGB   D   CB_D LR_D PCA_D HS_D MR_D DSR_D SVR[13] LS[12] Ours   GT

Fig. 13. Visual comparison of saliency maps

nearly equal saliency values of the pixels within the target objects. It confirms the effectiveness of our RGBD model which takes advantage of both depth and appearance cues from low-, mid-, and high-level.

We are also interested on the contributions of each component in our RGBD model. So we quantify the three key stages respectively. Fig. 12 (Right) illustrates the PR curves resulting from the accumulation of each component. It is seen that every stage in the RGBD model helps to improve the final performance. Particularly, the second stage brings lots of contributions on promoting the precision, this is mainly because the mid-level salient region grouping enhances the consistency and compactness of salient patches.

7 Conclusion

In this paper, we provide a comprehensive study on RGBD salient object detection including building up a benchmark, introducing an extension framework for 2D saliency models, and proposing a novel multi-stage RGBD model. Experiments verify that the depth-produced saliency can work as a helpful complement to existing color-based saliency models, especially when objects stay closer to the camera, have high depth contrast with background, or experience relatively low depth range. Compared with other competing 3D models, our proposed RGBD model achieves superior performance and produces more robust and visual favorable results. We believe that the constructed benchmark and our work are helpful to stimulate further research in the area.

Acknowledgements. This work is partly supported by the 973 Basic Research Program of China (No. 2014CB349303), the National 863 High-Tech R&D Program of China (No. 2012AA012503, 2012AA012504), the National Nature Science Foundation of China (No. 61370038, 61202327, 61303086), the Natural Science Foundation of Beijing (No. 4121003), the Fundamental Research Funds for the Central Universities (No. 2013121026), and the Guangdong Natural Science Foundation (No. S2012020011081).

References

1. Microsoft Corp. Redmond WA. Kinect for Xbox 360
2. Achanta, R., Hemami, S., Estrada, F., Süsstrunk, S.: Frequency-tuned salient region detection. In: CVPR, pp. 1597–1604 (2009)
3. Achanta, R., Shaji, A., Smith, K., Lucchi, A., Fua, P., Süsstrunk, S.: Slic superpixels compared to state-of-the-art superpixel methods. IEEE TPAMI 34(11), 2274–2282 (2012)
4. Alexe, B., Deselaers, T., Ferrari, V.: What is an object? In: CVPR, pp. 73–80 (2010)
5. Borji, A., Itti, L.: Exploiting local and global patch rarities for saliency detection. In: CVPR, pp. 478–485 (2012)
6. Borji, A., Sihite, D.N., Itti, L.: Salient object detection: A benchmark. In: Fitzgibbon, A., Lazebnik, S., Perona, P., Sato, Y., Schmid, C. (eds.) ECCV 2012, Part II. LNCS, vol. 7573, pp. 414–429. Springer, Heidelberg (2012)
7. Bruce, N.D.B., Tsotsos, J.K.: Saliency based on information maximization. In: NIPS (2005)
8. Carreira, J., Sminchisescu, C.: Cpmc: Automatic object segmentation using constrained parametric min-cuts. PAMI 34(7), 1312–1328 (2012)
9. Chang, K.Y., Liu, T.L., Chen, H.T., Lai, S.H.: Fusing generic objectness and visual saliency for salient object detection. In: ICCV, pp. 914–921 (2011)
10. Cheng, M., Zhang, G., Mitra, N.J., Huang, X., Hu, S.: Global contrast based salient region detection. In: CVPR, pp. 409–416 (2011)
11. Cheng, M.M., Warrell, J., Lin, W.Y., Zheng, S., Vineet, V., Crook, N.: Efficient salient region detection with soft image abstraction. In: ICCV, pp. 1–8 (2013)
12. Ciptadi, A., Hermans, T., Rehg, J.M.: An in Depth View of Saliency. In: BMVC, pp. 1–11 (2013)
13. Desingh, K., Krishna, K.M., Jawahar, C.V., Rajan, D.: Depth really matters: Improving visual salient region detection with depth. In: BMVC, pp. 1–11 (2013)
14. Goferman, S., Manor, L.Z., Tal, A.: Context-aware saliency detection. In: CVPR, pp. 1915–1926 (2010)
15. Harel, J., Koch, C., Perona, P.: Graph-based visual saliency. In: NIPS, pp. 545–552 (2006)
16. Holz, D., Holzer, S., Rusu, R.B., Behnke, S.: Real-time plane segmentation using rgb-d cameras. In: RoboCup, pp. 306–317 (2011)
17. Itti, L., Koch, C., Niebur, E.: A model of saliency-based visual attention for rapid scene analysis. IEEE TPAMI 20(11), 1254–1259 (1998)
18. Jia, Y., Han, M.: Category-independent object-level saliency detection. In: ICCV, pp. 1761–1768 (2013)
19. Jiang, B., Zhang, L., Lu, H., Yang, C., Yang, M.H.: Saliency detection via absorbing markov chain. In: ICCV, pp. 1665–1672 (2013)

20. Jiang, H., Wang, J., Yuan, Z., Liu, T., Zheng, N., Li, S.: Automatic salient object segmentation based on context and shape prior. In: BMVC, pp. 1–12 (2011)
21. Jiang, H., Wang, J., Yuan, Z., Wu, Y., Zheng, N., Li, S.: Salient object detection: A discriminative regional feature integration approach. In: CVPR, pp. 1–8 (2013)
22. Jiang, P., Ling, H., Yu, J., Peng, J.: Salient region detection by UFO: Uniqueness, focusness and objectness. In: ICCV, pp. 1976–1983 (2013)
23. Judd, T., Ehinger, K.A., Durand, F., Torralba, A.: Learning to predict where humans look. In: ICCV, pp. 2106–2113 (2009)
24. Koch, C., Ullman, S.: Shifts in selective visual attention: Towards the underlying neural circuitry. Human Neurobiology 4(4), 219–227 (1985)
25. Lang, C., Nguyen, T.V., Katti, H., Yadati, K., Kankanhalli, M., Yan, S.: Depth matters: Influence of depth cues on visual saliency. In: Fitzgibbon, A., Lazebnik, S., Perona, P., Sato, Y., Schmid, C. (eds.) ECCV 2012, Part II. LNCS, vol. 7573, pp. 101–115. Springer, Heidelberg (2012)
26. Levin, A., Lischinski, D., Weiss, Y.: Colorization using optimization. ACM Trans. Graph. 23(3), 689–694 (2004)
27. Li, X., Li, Y., Shen, C., Dick, A.R., van den Hengel, A.: Contextual hypergraph modeling for salient object detection. In: ICCV, pp. 3328–3335 (2013)
28. Li, X., Lu, H., Zhang, L., Ruan, X., Yang, M.H.: Saliency detection via dense and sparse reconstruction. In: ICCV, pp. 2976–2983 (2013)
29. Liu, T., Sun, J., Zheng, N., Tang, X., Shum, H.Y.: Learning to detect a salient object. In: CVPR, pp. 1–8 (2007)
30. Manen, S., Guillaumin, M., Gool, L.J.V.: Prime object proposals with randomized prim's algorithm. In: ICCV, pp. 2536–2543 (2013)
31. Marchesotti, L., Cifarelli, C., Csurka, G.: A framework for visual saliency detection with applications to image thumbnailing. In: ICCV, pp. 2232–2239 (2009)
32. Margolin, R., Tal, A., Zelnik-Manor, L.: What makes a patch distinct? In: CVPR, pp. 1139–1146 (2013)
33. Niu, Y., Geng, Y., Li, X., Liu, F.: Leveraging stereopsis for saliency analysis. In: CVPR, pp. 454–461 (2012)
34. Perazzi, F., Krähenbühl, P., Pritch, Y., Hornung, A.: Saliency filters: Contrast based filtering for salient region detection. In: CVPR, pp. 733–740 (2012)
35. Prim, R.: Shortest connection networks and some generalizations. Bell System Tech. J., 1389–1401 (1957)
36. Rutishauser, U., Walther, D., Koch, C., Perona, P.: Is bottom-up attention useful for object recognition? In: CVPR, pp. 37–44 (2004)
37. Scharfenberger, C., Wong, A., Fergani, K., Zelek, J.S., Clausi, D.A.: Statistical textural distinctiveness for salient region detection in natural images. In: CVPR, pp. 979–986 (2013)
38. Scott, D.W.: Multivariate Density Estimation: Theory, Practice, and Visualization. Wiley (1992)
39. Sharma, G., Jurie, F., Schmid, C.: Discriminative spatial saliency for image classification. In: CVPR, pp. 3506–3513 (2012)
40. Shen, X., Wu, Y.: A unified approach to salient object detection via low rank matrix recovery. In: CVPR, pp. 2296–2303 (2012)
41. Wang, P., Wang, J., Zeng, G., Feng, J., Zha, H., Li, S.: Salient object detection for searched web images via global saliency. In: CVPR, pp. 1–8 (2012)
42. Wei, Y., Wen, F., Zhu, W., Sun, J.: Geodesic saliency using background priors. In: Fitzgibbon, A., Lazebnik, S., Perona, P., Sato, Y., Schmid, C. (eds.) ECCV 2012, Part III. LNCS, vol. 7574, pp. 29–42. Springer, Heidelberg (2012)

43. Wolfe, J.M., Horowitz, T.S.: Opinion: What attributes guide the deployment of visual attention and how do they do it? Nature Reviews Neuroscience 5(6), 495–501 (2004)
44. Yan, Q., Xu, L., Shi, J., Jia, J.: Hierarchical saliency detection. In: CVPR, pp. 1155–1162 (2013)
45. Yang, C., Zhang, L., Lu, H., Ruan, X., Yang, M.H.: Saliency detection via graph-based manifold ranking. In: CVPR, pp. 3166–3173 (2013)

Saliency Detection with Flash and No-flash Image Pairs

Shengfeng He and Rynson W.H. Lau

Department of Computer Science
City University of Hong Kong, Hong Kong, China
shengfeng_he@yahoo.com, rynson.lau@cityu.edu.hk

Abstract. In this paper, we propose a new saliency detection method using a pair of flash and no-flash images. Our approach is inspired by two observations. First, only the foreground objects are significantly brightened by the flash as they are relatively nearer to the camera than the background. Second, the brightness variations introduced by the flash provide hints to surface orientation changes. Accordingly, the first observation is explored to form the background prior to eliminate background distraction. The second observation provides a new orientation cue to compute surface orientation contrast. These photometric cues from the two observations are independent of visual attributes like color, and they provide new and robust distinctiveness to support salient object detection. The second observation further leads to the introduction of new spatial priors to constrain the regions rendered salient to be compact both in the image plane and in 3D space. We have constructed a new flash/no-flash image dataset. Experiments on this dataset show that the proposed method successfully identifies salient objects from various challenging scenes that the state-of-the-art methods usually fail.

Keywords: Saliency detection, Flash photography, Background elimination, Surface orientation.

1 Introduction

The underlying goal of saliency detection is to locate regions or objects in an image that gain the viewer's visual attention. There is a wide range of computer vision, graphics and multimedia applications of saliency detection, including classification [31], image segmentation [10], image retrieval [6], and content-aware image/video resizing [23].

Numerous studies in psychological science [29,13,25] have shown that the most influential factor to visual saliency in the human visual system is *contrast*. As such, a lot of algorithms that are based on some kind of contrast priors have been proposed to detect salient objects from images. The most widely adopted visual attribute is color contrast [7,26,40]. However, contrast based methods are usually limited to scenes with simple background or with high contrast between foreground and background. In the case where salient objects cannot be clearly distinguished from a complex background or the background has a similar color as the foreground, detecting salient objects become very challenging with existing methods, as shown in Figures 1b to 1e. Background priors [37,41] have been used to tackle this limitation by considering both foreground and background cues in a different way with assumptions. However, these methods fail

D. Fleet et al. (Eds.): ECCV 2014, Part III, LNCS 8691, pp. 110–124, 2014.

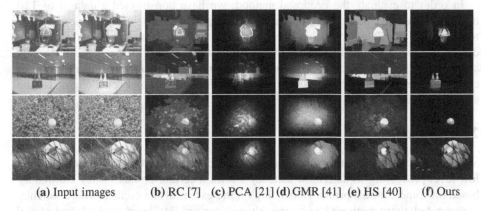

(a) Input images   (b) RC [7]   (c) PCA [21] (d) GMR [41]   (e) HS [40]   (f) Ours

Fig. 1. Comparison with the state-of-the-art methods [7,21,41,40] on the output saliency maps. (a) are the input flash and no-flash images. These scenarios contain challenging factors, including similar colors between the salient object and its surrounding, and complex background. All the state-of-the-art methods (b-e) fail in these scenarios. (f) Our method considers the rough depth, surface orientation contrast, color contrast and compactness together to detect salient objects from the foreground (rows 1 and 2) as well as from the background (rows 3 and 4).

when one of the assumptions is invalid, as illustrated in Figure 1d. Orientation contrast [24,30] has also been shown to play an important role in the human visual system. However, this principle is not appropriate for detecting salient objects in practice. This is because orientation contrast (as well as other related cues such as curvedness [36] and pattern [21]) focuses on object boundaries, leading to attenuated object interior when detecting homogeneous regions, as shown in Figure 1c.

In this paper, we propose a new approach to saliency detection using a flash/no-flash image pair. Our approach is based on two observations. First, only the foreground objects are significantly brightened by the flash, as they are nearer to the camera, while the background is less affected by the flash. Second, the brightness variations on object surfaces due to the flash provide hints on surface orientation. These two observations suggest additional cues for saliency detection. First, we can make use of the difference between the flash and no-flash images from the first observation to extract the foreground layer from the image pair. However, background near to the foreground objects (in terms of depth) may not be trivially separated, and not all objects in the foreground layer are necessarily salient. As a complement to the first observation, we estimate the surface orientation contrast and spatial priors from the second observation. These surface orientation contrast and spatial priors help detect and recover salient regions when background prior is invalid. As demonstrated in [9], surface orientation contrast is as effective as 2D orientation contrast in attracting visual attention in the human visual system. However, unlike 2D orientation contrast which focuses on object boundaries, our surface orientation contrast identifies homogeneous salient regions. The spatial priors focus on three types of compactness of the salient objects – regions that are compact in both the image plane and the 3D space tend to be salient.

In order to evaluate the proposed method, we have constructed a dataset of 120 flash/no-flash image pairs. Flash/no-flash photography has been studied for decades, but to the best of our knowledge, this is the first flash/no-flash dataset created for saliency detection. Our experimental results from this dataset show that the proposed method is able to detect salient objects even when a salient object and its surrounding have similar colors or when the background is very complex, which is extremely challenging for the state-of-the-art methods.

2   Related Work

Saliency Detection. Existing bottom-up saliency detection methods commonly utilize low-level processing to determine saliency within a certain context. They are mainly based on some contrast priors. Depending on the extent of the context where saliency is computed, these methods can be roughly categorized into *local methods* and *global methods*. Comprehensive literature review on these saliency detection methods can be found in [4,35]. Here, we briefly review the representative ones.

Local methods compute saliency of an image region with respect to a small neighborhood. An earlier local saliency detection method [14] is based on a biologically-plausible architecture [16]. It uses an image pyramid to compute color and orientation contrasts. Ma and Zhang [20] combine local contrast analysis with a fuzzy growth model. Harel et al. [11] propose a graph-based random walk method using multiple features. As these methods are based on computing local contrast, they are only sensitive to high frequency content like image edges or noise, and they attenuate any homogenous interior regions.

Global methods estimate saliency by considering contrast relations over the entire image. Achanta et al. [1] detect salient regions by computing color deviation from the mean image color on a per-pixel basis. Cheng et al. [7] propose a fast color histogram based method, and compute saliency based on dissimilarity among the histogram bins. To take into account spatial relationships, Perazzi et al. [26] apply two contrast measures based on the uniqueness and spatial distribution of elements. Yan et al. [40] propose a hierarchical framework to reduce the effect of small-scale structures on saliency detection. Despite the demonstrated success, it is still difficult to distinguish salient objects from clustered and textured background by using global contrast alone.

Recently, other than contrast priors, background priors are also used to reduce the distraction from the background. These methods are generally based on assumptions such as having a large and homogeneous background [37] or image boundaries mostly belonging to the background [41]. They become unreliable when these assumptions are not valid. Another method proposes to detect salient objects with the depth cue from stereo images [22]. Although background distraction can be mitigated, its performance strongly depends on the quality of the disparity map. In addition, it fails if the salient object cannot be distinguished in the depth level. Despite many recent improvements, the saliency detection problem on complex background is still highly ill-posed. Our method introduces additional cues from the flash image, and integrates the background, contrast and spatial priors together to address this problem. Our results show that it is able to detect saliency robustly.

Flash Photography. Many applications have adopted flash-based techniques to address different problems in recent years. Eisemann and Durand [8] use joint-bilateral filtering for flash image enhancement. Agrawal et al. [3] propose a gradient projection scheme to remove photographic artifacts introduced by the flash. Petshnigg et al. [27] show that additional information from the flash image can benefit many applications, such as denoising, detail transfer, white balancing, continuous flash, and red-eye correction. Some other applications extract cues by changing the light source position. In multiple flash imaging [28], the shadows casted by the flash are used to extract depth edges for non-photorealistic rendering. Active illumination [18] has also been used for depth recovery by adjusting the light source position. In this paper, we use flash/no-flash images for a different application - saliency detection.

The flash/no-flash idea has also been used for matting [33], foreground extraction [34] and stereo matching [42]. The work most related to ours is foreground extraction [34], in which the rough depth information and a motion compensation model are used to extract foreground objects with some amount of motion. However, this method is limited to very distant background, and the whole foreground layer will be segmented as long as it receives the flash light (even though some of the foreground objects may not necessary be salient). The proposed saliency detection method may extract salient objects from the foreground as well as from close background by taking four complementary cues into account.

3 Flash/No-flash Saliency Detection

The proposed method consists of three complementary priors: background, contrast and spatial priors. The difference between the flash and no-flash images provides reliable information for foreground-background separation. We treat this rough depth information as the background prior. We also use two contrast priors in our approach: surface orientation and color contrasts. Surface orientation contrast is used to differentiate objects with different orientations. Finally, we use the spatial priors to constraint the rendered salient pixels to be compact in both the image plane and the 3D space. These three priors are combined to form the final saliency map.

We first model the flash and no-flash images as follows. Considering Lambertian surfaces, the intensity I_n of a pixel p in the no-flash image is determined according to ambient illumination, surface shape, and reflectivity as:

$$I_n(p) = \eta \cdot L_a \cdot U, \tag{1}$$

where η is a proportionality constant between scene radiance and irradiance. L_a is the intensity of the ambient illumination at p, while U is the surface reflectivity at p. The intensity I_f of a pixel p in the flash image is modeled as:

$$I_f(p) = \eta \cdot L_a \cdot U + \eta \cdot L_f \cdot \frac{\cos\theta}{r^2} \cdot U, \tag{2}$$

where L_f is the flash intensity, θ is the angle between the direction of the flash and the surface normal at p. r is the distance from the flash unit to p. The following subsections introduce our difference image, ratio image and three proposed priors.

(a) Input images   (b) Diff. image (c) Ratio image (d)Rough depth(e) Surf. orien.
                                                         saliency   contrast

Fig. 2. The saliency maps produced by the difference and ratio images: (a) the input images; (b) the difference images; (c) the background-eleminated ratio images, mapped to a color space so that surfaces of similar orientations can be easily seen; (d) the rough depth saliency. Although the result in the first row is good, the other two are not as the salient objects cannot be distinguished in depth level; (e) the surface orientation contrast saliency.

3.1 Saliency from the Difference Image

To cope with the difficulties in detecting saliency in complex scenarios, existing methods usually assume that salient objects are placed in the foreground [37,41]. Although the role of depth cues in the human visual system is still under debate [39], this assumption is practical since people tend to arrange the target object in a photo at a different depth level from the background. Hence, we extract the foreground layer based on this assumption. Our idea to achieve this is by computing a difference image, D, from Eq. (1) and (2) as:

$$D(p) = I_f(p) - I_n(p) = \eta \cdot L_f \cdot \frac{\cos\theta}{r^2} \cdot U. \tag{3}$$

We can see that D is only related to a single light source, the flashlight, and the flash intensity L_f falls off quickly with distance r, due to the inverse square law.

Since we assume that the background scene is further away from the camera than the foreground objects, the appearance change of the background in the flash and no-flash images is expected to be much smaller. The first row of Figure 2 shows such an example. Consequently, the difference image D provides us a very robust cue for foreground extraction. We consider the difference image D as a rough depth map to obtain rough depth saliency.

Similar to previous approaches [21,41], we first employ SLIC super-pixels [2] to segment the input image, and then determine the salient regions. In order to obtain better foreground-background separation, we combine the flash image, the no-flash image and the ratio image (see Section 3.2) into a three-channel image for segmentation. A rough depth saliency value for a region R_i is computed based on its contrast with all other regions in the image as:

$$S_d(R_i) = \sum_{j=1}^{M} w(R_j)\phi(i,j)\|d_i - d_j\|, \tag{4}$$

where M is the total number of regions. d_i and d_j are the mean rough depth values of regions R_i and R_j, respectively. $w(R_j)$ is the number of pixels in R_j. We consider that a larger region contributes higher to saliency than a smaller one. $\phi(i,j)$ is defined as $\exp(-\frac{\|R_i - R_j\|^2}{2\sigma_r^2})$ to control the influenced distance, where $\|R_i - R_j\|^2$ is the L_2 distance between the centers of R_i and R_j, and σ_r is set to 0.45 in this paper. With $\phi(i,j)$, regions that are closer to R_i have higher influence on the computed saliency.

The rough depth can be used to identify foreground objects. However, it only considers the distance and is not sufficient for all cases. The second and the third rows of Figures 2b and 2d show two failure examples – the background is not sufficiently distant or the salient object is placed in close background. We alleviate this limitation by considering contrast and spatial priors.

3.2 Saliency from the Ratio Image

The effectiveness of orientation cues in the image plane has been demonstrated both in psychological science [39] and computer vision [14]. It is natural to ask if the same conclusion holds for surface orientation in a 3D scene. Experiments have been conducted on surface orientation in psychological science [9,12,38], showing that surface orientation is more important than other 3D factors such as depth and shading to visual attention. However, traditional techniques based on analysing a single image are not able to recover surface orientation. We notice that the ratio value obtained from the flash/no-flash images provides cues on surface orientations.

We divide Eq. (2) by Eq. (1) and take the logarithm to obtain the ratio image T as:

$$T(p) = \log \frac{I_f(p)}{I_n(p)} = \log(1 + \frac{L_f}{L_a} \cdot \frac{\cos\theta}{r^2}). \tag{5}$$

To avoid division-by-zero, the ratio image is defined as $T = \log(I_f + \epsilon) - \log(I_n + \epsilon)$ in our implementation, where ϵ is a small positive value. We can see that $T(p)$ is essentially independent of surface reflectivity. Instead, it varies according to depth and surface orientation. Our key finding here is that two neighboring regions with different ratio values indicate that they either have different surface orientations or are at different depth levels, while two neighboring regions with similar ratio values likely belong to the same surface. We note that Eq. (5) may not be accurate for non-Lambertian surfaces, and given two neighboring regions with different ratio values, we are not able to tell if they have different surface orientations or are at different depth levels. Nevertheless, the ratio values can be used to differentiate different surfaces. By considering also the information from the difference image, we may obtain the surface orientation contrast.

Although the properties of the ratio image hold whether the background is distant or not, removing distant background may improve detection performance. Here, we aim at eliminating the influence of distant background, while making sure that the computation of surface orientation saliency would not be affected by close background. To do this, we determine the first local minimum β of a 128-bin histogram of the difference image D. The histogram is smoothed using a Gaussian kernel. We then apply a threshold of 0.6β to remove pixels that are highly likely belonging to the distant background. Finally, we obtain a new background-eliminated ratio image $\hat{T}$ as:

$$\hat{T}(p) = \begin{cases} T(p) & \text{if } D(p) > 0.6\beta \\ 0 & \text{otherwise} \end{cases}.$$ (6)

Based on $\hat{T}$, we may compute the surface orientation contrast between R_i and all other regions in the image as:

$$S_s(R_i) = \sum_{j=1}^{M} w(R_j)\phi(i,j)\|\hat{t}_i - \hat{t}_j\|,$$ (7)

where $\hat{t}_i$ and $\hat{t}_j$ are the mean background-eliminated ratio values of R_i and R_j, respectively. As shown in Figure 2e, our surface orientation contrast produces much better salient maps than the rough depth in the scenes with close background or with salient objects that cannot be differentiated in depth level. Note that this background-eliminated ratio image is only used in here. When computing the spatial priors in Section 3.4, we use the original ratio image T instead.

3.3 Color Saliency

Although the above background prior and the surface orientation contrast can detect foreground and distinct surfaces, it is not sufficient for all cases. We further consider color contrast as another contrast prior. We note that the flash image and the no-flash image may each have different color contrast. Hence, for each region in the two images, we compute its color contrast with each of the other regions in both two images in order to reduce the background contribution, since the background changes relatively small in both images. In other words, we compute two inter-color contrasts as the sum of L_2 distances in CIE LAB color-space for each pair of regions in the two images:

$$S_n(R_i) = \sum_{j=1}^{M} w(R_j)\phi(i,j)(\|n_i - n_j\|^2 + \|n_i - f_j\|^2),$$ (8)

$$S_f(R_i) = \sum_{j=1}^{M} w(R_j)\phi(i,j)(\|f_i - f_j\|^2 + \|f_i - n_j\|^2),$$ (9)

where f_i and n_i are the mean color values of R_i in the flash and no-flash images, respectively. Likewise, f_j and n_j are the mean color values of R_j in the flash and no-flash images. The final color contrast is the average of the two inter-color contrasts, i.e., $S_c(R_i) = \frac{S_n(R_i)+S_f(R_i)}{2}$.

3.4 Spatial Priors

Compactness is the main guiding principle used in spatial priors. Previous approaches consider color-spatial compactness [26,32]: generally, colors belonging to the background have high spatial variance, while salient objects are typically more compact.

To extend this idea further, we consider two more types of compactness to describe salient objects. A salient object should be compact both in the image plane and in the 3D space. (As mentioned in Section 3.2, the ratio image T is used to separate different surfaces.) Hence, three types of compactness are used in our approach:

- *Color-spatial compactness.* A region with a low spatially distributed color is considered as more salient than one with high spatially distributed colors.
- *Color-surface compactness.* A region with an average color that mainly appears in the surface that the region belongs to should be considered as salient.
- *Surface-spatial compactness.* A region with low spatially distributed ratio values is considered as more salient than one with high spatially distributed ratio values.

Here, we may treat the ratio value as Z dimension information to compute 3D compactness. Although this may not be accurate, regions belonging to the same surface usually have similar ratio values. Hence, we compute the color-spatial compactness as:

$$S_{cs}(R_i) = \sum_{j=1}^{M} \phi(c_i, c_j) \| x_j - \mu_i^{cs} \|^2, \tag{10}$$

where x_j is the center of region R_j. $\phi(c_i, c_j) = \exp(-\frac{\|c_i - c_j\|^2}{2\sigma_c^2})$ describes the similarity of two colors. Note that the color used here is the average color of the flash/no-flash images. We define $\mu_i^{cs} = \sum_{j=1}^{M} \phi(c_i, c_j) x_j$ as the weighted mean position of color c_i to take into account all color contributions. In our implementation, σ_c is set to 20.

The color-surface compactness can be computed by substituting the mean position μ_i^{cs} of Eq. (10) by the mean ratio $\mu_i^{cp} = \sum_{j=1}^{M} \phi(c_i, c_j) t_j$ as:

$$S_{cp}(R_i) = \sum_{j=1}^{M} \phi(c_i, c_j) \| t_j - \mu_i^{cp} \|^2. \tag{11}$$

The surface-spatial compactness is defined similarly as:

$$S_{ps}(R_i) = \sum_{j=1}^{M} \phi(t_i, t_j) \| x_j - \mu_i^{ps} \|^2, \tag{12}$$

where $\mu_i^{ps} = \sum_{j=1}^{M} \phi(t_i, t_j) x_j$ is the weighted mean position of ratio t_i. $\phi(t_i, t_j) = \exp(-\frac{\|t_i - t_j\|^2}{2\sigma_t^2})$ is the similarity between ratio values t_i and t_j. σ_t is set to 0.2 in all our experiments.

Note that in Eq. (10)-(12), a lower value indicates a higher compactness and hence higher saliency. We use an exponential function to emphasize on small values. The final compactness is obtained by combining the three normalized compactness values as:

$$S_m(R_i) = \exp(-k(S_{cs} + S_{cp} + S_{ps})), \tag{13}$$

where k is set to 0.15 in all the experiments.

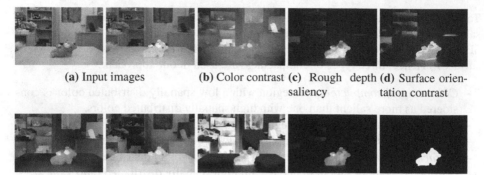

(a) Input images   (b) Color contrast (c) Rough depth (d) Surface orien-
                                            saliency   tation contrast

(e) Color-spatial (f) Color-surface (g) Surface-spatial (h) Final saliency (i) Ground Truth
compactness   compactness   compactness

Fig. 3. Outputs of various components used in our approach

3.5 Final Saliency Map

We have now introduced four cues used in our approach, i.e., rough depth, surface orientation, color contrast and spatial compactness. Although each of them has its own
advantages and limitations, their advantages largely compliment each other's limitations. As we seek to obtain objects that are salient in all four cues, we multiple the
normalized saliency maps as:

$$S_f(R_i) = S_d(R_i) \cdot S_s(R_i) \cdot S_c(R_i) \cdot S_m(R_i). \tag{14}$$

The final saliency map is again normalized to $[0, 1]$.

In order to robustly detect salient regions of different sizes, we use a multi-scale
approach to saliency detection. All the saliency maps are computed using four different
numbers of super-pixels: 100%, 75%, 50% and 25%. The final saliency map is the
average of these four scales.

Figure 3 shows the outputs of individual components of our saliency detection method.
Note that none of the fours cues alone suffices to achieve good results.

4 Experiments and Results

This section evaluates the proposed saliency detection method on a new flash/no-flash
database of 120 image pairs with manually labeled binary ground truth. We have implemented the proposed method in Matlab using a single core and tested it on a PC with an
Intel i5 3.3GHz CPU and 8GB RAM. Our algorithm takes on average 2.1s to process
one pair of images of resolution 400×300.

4.1 The Flash/No-flash Image Database

Although flash photography has been studied for decades, there is not a standard dataset
for this purpose. In order to evaluate the proposed method, we have constructed a

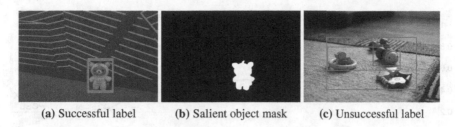

(a) Successful label   (b) Salient object mask   (c) Unsuccessful label

Fig. 4. Two example images of our dataset. (a) is consistently labeled by all users and included in our database. (b) is the ground truth manually segmented by a user. (c) is a failure example. The users have different opinions on what should be the salient objects.

flash/no-flash dataset with ground truth, following the benchmark dataset building procedure [19].

We took 170 photo pairs with a tripod, and asked three separate users to mark the most salient object in each image pair using a rectangle. For images with inconsistent users selections, we remove them from consideration. The most consistent 120 image pairs, according to the overlapping ratio of the rectangles, were chosen to form the database. One user was asked to manually segment the salient object(s) using *Adobe Photoshop* to serve as the ground truth. Figure 4 shows a successful example and an inconsistent labeled example while constructing our database. The flash/no-flash dataset with ground truth can be downloaded from our project website [1].

4.2 Evaluation on the Benchmark

We have compared the proposed method with seven state-of-the-art methods, the top four algorithms (RC [7], SVO [5], CNTX [10], CBS [15]) according to [4], plus three latest algorithms (GMR [41], HS [40], PCA [21]). The implementations provided by the authors were used for fair comparison. Similar to previous work [26,40], we quantitatively evaluate the performances of these methods by measuring the *precision-recall* values. Precision indicates the percentage of the output salient pixels that are correct, while recall indicates the percentage of the ground truth pixels detected. Since we have a pair of two input images in each test, the performances of the seven state-of-the-art methods on these two images may not be consistent. We use the average score obtained from each pair of images.

We evaluate all the methods using the Precision-Recall curves and the F-measure metrics, which is defined as:

$$F_\beta = \frac{(1+\beta^2) \cdot precision \cdot recall}{\beta^2 \cdot precision + recall},\tag{15}$$

where β^2 is set to 0.3 to emphasize on precision [1].

---

[1] http://www.cs.cityu.edu.hk/~shengfehe2/saliency-detection-with-flash-and-no-flash-image-pairs.html

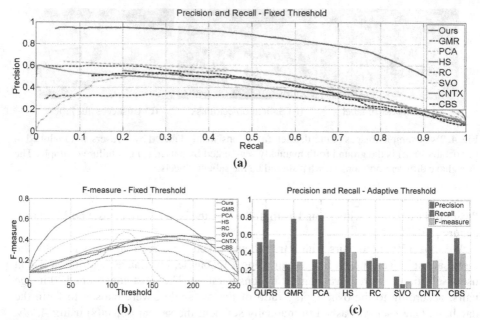

Fig. 5. Comparison with the state-of-the-art methods. (a-b) are the precision-recall curves and F-measure curves using 255 fixed thresholds. (c) shows the precision, recall and F-measure using an adaptive threshold.

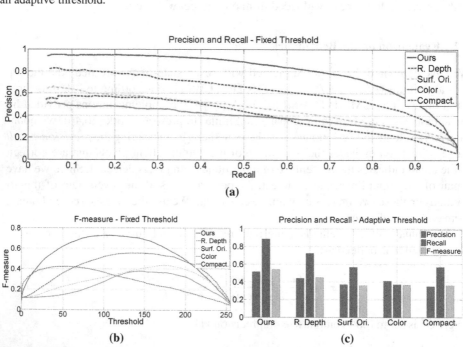

Fig. 6. Performance of each component of the proposed method. (a-b) are the precision-recall curves and F-measure curves using 255 fixed thresholds. (c) shows the precision, recall and F-measure using an adaptive threshold.

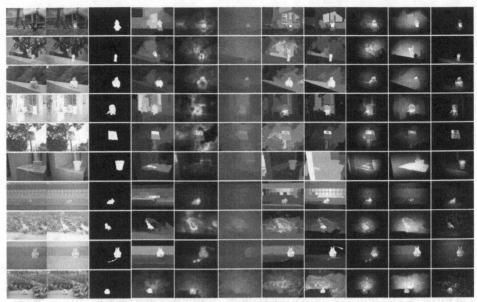

(a)Input images   (b)GT   (c)CBS (d)CNTX(e) SVO   (f) RC   (g) HS   (h) PCA (i) GMR (j) Ours

Fig. 7. Comparison with the state-of-the-art methods. The proposed method consistently produces better saliency results in distant as well as close backgrounds.

We conduct two experiments using different threshold criteria. In the first experiment, we binarize the saliency map for every threshold in the range of [0, 255]. Figures 5a and 5b show that the proposed method achieves the best performance in most of the recall rates and thresholds. In the second experiment, we use an image dependent adaptive threshold [1], which is computed as twice the mean value of the saliency map. Figure 5c shows that the proposed method outperforms the state-of-the-art methods in all three aspects. We further analyze the effectiveness of each component. Figure 6 shows that these components complement each other. Thus, the final saliency outperforms individual ones.

Figure 7 shows the qualitative comparison of all the methods. As the seven existing methods produce two results from each input image pair, we choose the result with higher F-measure value using the adaptive threshold. We can see that the proposed method can detect salient objects properly from complex background and in scenes with similar color between salient objects and surrounding regions. Benefiting from four complementary cues, the proposed method still works while the background prior is invalid to certain extent, e.g., the background is not distant enough or the salient objects are not distinct in depth level (rows 6 to 10 in Figure 7).

4.3   Limitations and Discussion

In general, the proposed method suffers from similar limitations as flash/no-flash photography. First, the difference image and the ratio image benefit saliency detection only when the salient objects are reachable by the flash. Second, the proposed method is only suitable for static scenes. Extending it to cover non-static scenes may be a possible topic for future work. Third, the proposed method may not produce reliable results when applied to scenes with strong specular surfaces.

Despite these limitations, the proposed method can be applied in mobile phones, where the shutter speed is typically fast. We can easily take two consecutive (no-flash followed by flash) images, without the user being aware that two images are taken instead of one. The proposed method may benefit a lot of existing mobile applications that require automatic detection / extraction of salient objects, such as cloud-based object detection/retrieval and object level image manipulation. On the other hand, integrating with the dark flash [17] is another possible topic for future work, which is able to extract salient objects without revealing the detectors.

5   Conclusion

In this paper, we have proposed a new saliency detection approach using flash/no-flash image pairs. The proposed method takes advantages of the additional information obtained from the two image pair to discriminate the salient object from the background and surfaces with different surface orientations. We further introduce the spatial priors to ensure that salient objects are compact in both the image space and the 3D space. We have evaluated the proposed method on a newly constructed flash/no-flash dataset and compared its performance with those of the state-of-the-art methods. Experimental results show that the proposed method outperforms those methods consistently, even in challenging scenarios.

Acknowledgement. We thank Zhe Huang, Chengcheng Dai and Xufang Pang for their help with flash/no-flash data collection. This work was partially supported by a SRG grant from City University of Hong Kong (Project Number: 7002768).

References

1. Achanta, R., Hemami, S., Estrada, F., Susstrunk, S.: Frequency-tuned salient region detection. In: CVPR, pp. 1597–1604 (2009)
2. Achanta, R., Shaji, A., Smith, K., Lucchi, A., Fua, P., Susstrunk, S.: SLIC superpixels compared to state-of-the-art superpixel methods. IEEE TPAMI, 2274–2282 (2012)
3. Agrawal, A., Raskar, R., Nayar, S., Li, Y.: Removing photography artifacts using gradient projection and flash-exposure sampling. ACM TOG 24(3), 828–835 (2005)
4. Borji, A., Sihite, D.N., Itti, L.: Salient object detection: A benchmark. In: Fitzgibbon, A., Lazebnik, S., Perona, P., Sato, Y., Schmid, C. (eds.) ECCV 2012, Part II. LNCS, vol. 7573, pp. 414–429. Springer, Heidelberg (2012)
5. Chang, K., Liu, T., Chen, H., Lai, S.: Fusing generic objectness and visual saliency for salient object detection. In: ICCV (2011)
6. Chen, T., Cheng, M., Tan, P., Shamir, A., Hu, S.: Sketch2photo: Internet image montage. ACM TOG 28(5), 124:1–124:10 (2009)
7. Cheng, M., Zhang, G., Mitra, N., Huang, X., Hu, S.: Global contrast based salient region detection. In: CVPR, pp. 409–416 (2011)

8. Eisemann, E., Durand, F.: Flash photography enhancement via intrinsic relighting. ACM TOG 23(3), 673–678 (2004)
9. Enns, J., Rensink, R.: Sensitivity to three-dimensional orientation in visual search. Psychological Science 1, 323–326 (1990)
10. Goferman, S., Zelnik-Manor, L., Tal, A.: Context-aware saliency detection. In: CVPR (2010)
11. Harel, J., Koch, C., Perona, P.: Graph-based visual saliency. In: NIPS, pp. 545–552 (2007)
12. He, Z., Nakayama, K.: Visual attention to surfaces in 3-d space. Proc. National Academy of Sciences 92, 11155–11159 (1995)
13. Itti, L., Koch, C.: Computational modelling of visual attention. Nature Reviews Neuroscience 2(3), 194–203 (2001)
14. Itti, L., Koch, C., Niebur, E.: A model of saliency-based visual attention for rapid scene analysis. IEEE TPAMI 20(11), 1254–1259 (1998)
15. Jiang, H., Wang, J., Yuan, Z., Liu, T., Zheng, N.: Automatic salient object segmentation based on context and shape prior. In: BMVC (2011)
16. Koch, C., Ullman, S.: Shifts in Selective Visual Attention: Towards the Underlying Neural Circuitry. Human Neurobiology 4, 219–227 (1985)
17. Krishnan, D., Fergus, R.: Dark flash photography. ACM TOG 28(3), 96:1–96:11 (2009)
18. Liao, M., Wang, L., Yang, R., Gong, M.: Light fall-off stereo. In: CVPR, pp. 1–8 (2007)
19. Liu, T., Yuan, Z., Sun, J., Wang, J., Zheng, N., Tang, X., Shum, H.: Learning to detect a salient object. IEEE TPAMI 33(2), 353–367 (2011)
20. Ma, Y., Zhang, H.: Contrast-based image attention analysis by using fuzzy growing. ACM Multimedia, 374–381 (2003)
21. Margolin, R., Tal, A., Zelnik-Manor, L.: What makes a patch distinct? In: CVPR (2013)
22. Niu, Y., Geng, Y., Li, X., Liu, F.: Leveraging stereopsis for saliency analysis. In: CVPR (2012)
23. Niu, Y., Liu, F., Li, X., Gleicher, M.: Warp propagation for video resizing. In: CVPR (2010)
24. Nothdurft, H.: Salience from feature contrast: additivity across dimensions. Vision Research 40(10), 1183–1201 (2000)
25. Parkhurst, D., Law, K., Niebur, E.: Modeling the role of salience in the allocation of overt visual attention. Vision Research 42(1), 107–123 (2002)
26. Perazzi, F., Krähenbühl, P., Pritch, Y., Hornung, A.: Saliency filters: Contrast based filtering for salient region detection. In: CVPR, pp. 733–740 (2012)
27. Petschnigg, G., Szeliski, R., Agrawala, M., Cohen, M., Hoppe, H., Toyama, K.: Digital photography with flash and no-flash image pairs. ACM TOG 23(3), 664–672 (2004)
28. Raskar, R., Tan, K., Feris, R., Yu, J., Turk, M.: Non-photorealistic camera: depth edge detection and stylized rendering using multi-flash imaging. ACM TOG 23(3), 679–688 (2004)
29. Reinagel, P., Zador, A.: Natural scene statistics at the centre of gaze. In: Network: Computation in Neural Systems, pp. 341–350 (1999)
30. Reynolds, J., Desimone, R.: Interacting roles of attention and visual salience in V4. Neuron 37(5), 853–863 (2003)
31. Sharma, G., Jurie, F., Schmid, C.: Discriminative spatial saliency for image classification. In: CVPR (2012)
32. Shi, K., Wang, K., Lu, J., Lin, L.: PISA: Pixelwise image saliency by aggregating complementary appearance contrast measures with spatial priors. In: CVPR (2013)
33. Sun, J., Li, Y., Kang, S., Shum, H.: Flash matting. ACM TOG 25(3), 772–778 (2006)
34. Sun, J., Sun, J., Kang, S., Xu, Z., Tang, X., Shum, H.: Flash cut: Foreground extraction with flash and no-flash image pairs. In: CVPR (2007)
35. Toet, A.: Computational versus psychophysical bottom-up image saliency: A comparative evaluation study. IEEE TPAMI 33(11), 2131–2146 (2011)
36. Valenti, R., Sebe, N., Gevers, T.: Image saliency by isocentric curvedness and color. In: ICCV (2009)

37. Wei, Y., Wen, F., Zhu, W., Sun, J.: Geodesic saliency using background priors. In: Fitzgibbon, A., Lazebnik, S., Perona, P., Sato, Y., Schmid, C. (eds.) ECCV 2012, Part III. LNCS, vol. 7574, pp. 29–42. Springer, Heidelberg (2012)
38. Wexler, M., Ouarti, N.: Depth affects where we look. Current Biology 18(23), 1872–1876 (2008)
39. Wolfe, J., Horowitz, T.: What attributes guide the deployment of visual attention and how do they do it? Nature Reviews Neuroscience 5(6), 495–501 (2004)
40. Yan, Q., Xu, L., Shi, J., Jia, J.: Hierachical saliency detection. In: CVPR (2013)
41. Yang, C., Zhang, L., Lu, H., Ruan, X., Yang, M.H.: Saliency detection via graph-based manifold ranking. In: CVPR (2013)
42. Zhou, C., Troccoli, A., Pulli, K.: Robust stereo with flash and no-flash image pairs. In: CVPR, pp. 342–349 (2012)

Alpha Matting of Motion-Blurred Objects in Bracket Sequence Images

Heesoo Myeong[1,*], Stephen Lin[2], and Kyoung Mu Lee[1]

[1] Department of ECE, ASRI, Seoul National University, Korea
[2] Microsoft Research, China

Abstract. We present a method that utilizes bracket sequence images to automatically extract the alpha matte of a motion-blurred object. This method makes use of a sharp, short-exposure snapshot in the sequence to help overcome major challenges in this task, including blurred object detection, spatially-variant object motion, and foreground/background color ambiguity. A key component of our matte estimation is the inference of approximate, spatially-varying motion of the blurred object with the help of the sharp snapshot, as this motion information provides important constraints on the aforementioned issues. In addition, we take advantage of other relationships that exist between a pair of consecutive short-exposure and long-exposure frames, such as common background areas and consistencies in foreground appearance. With this technique, we demonstrate successful alpha matting results on a variety of moving objects including non-rigid human motion.

Keywords: Alpha matting, motion blur, exposure bracketing.

1 Introduction

Matting aims to extract a foreground object from an image while accounting for fractional opacity values of foreground pixels. In most previous works on matting, the foreground object is assumed to be static, and fractional opacity arises from partial pixel coverage by the object, such that the pixel color is formed from a combination of foreground and background colors. A common example is a strand of hair, which is often too thin to fully occupy pixels, so that the pixels it appears in are shared with the background behind it. Another source of fractional opacity is object motion, in which a pixel is occupied by the foreground object for only part of the camera exposure period, and occupied by the background for the rest of the snapshot. We deal in this paper with matting of motion-blurred objects, which is a needed step in compositing such objects into other images, and for deblurring of moving objects as well. Important practical applications of matting motion-blurred objects also include video editing and post-production.

While matting techniques designed for static foregrounds can be applied to motion-blurred objects, this can lead to inadequate results as observed in previous works on motion deblurring [9,16]. This problem can be attributed in part

---

* This work was done while Heesoo Myeong was an intern at Microsoft Research.

D. Fleet et al. (Eds.): ECCV 2014, Part III, LNCS 8691, pp. 125–139, 2014.
© Springer International Publishing Switzerland 2014

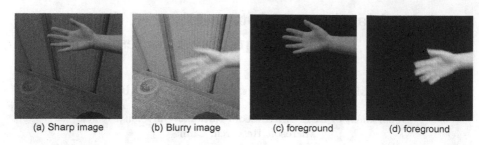

(a) Sharp image   (b) Blurry image   (c) foreground   (d) foreground

Fig. 1. (a) and (b) are taken sequentially using the auto-bracket mode of a digital camera. (c) is the binary segmentation of the sharp foreground in (a). (d) is the alpha matte extracted by our method for the motion-blurred object in (b). The matte is computed automatically without any user guidance.

to blurred colors in the foreground region and broad areas of fractional opacity along the motion direction. Recently, a few matting methods have been proposed to specifically deal with motion-blurred objects. To help solve this problem, some of these methods require some form of external input, such as a user-supplied trimap indicating which regions are fully foreground and which are fully background [13], user-drawn scribbles that indicate motion paths of the foreground [22], or known blur kernels [10]. Obtaining this information, however, can itself be challenging or require much user assistance. Alternatively, other methods employ special hardware that obtains motion information to aid in motion-blurred object matting [14,20,21].

In this work, we propose a fully automatic technique for alpha matting of motion-blurred objects that does not require special equipment. We instead utilize bracket sequence imaging, a standard function in digital cameras where photos are taken consecutively at different exposure levels. Exposure bracketing yields images with blurred object motion at longer exposures, and also a short-exposure image in which moving foreground objects typically appear sharp. From computed blur-aware correspondences between a short and a long exposure image, as well as consistencies in their foreground and background, we derive approximate information on both the trimap for the blurred object and spatially variant blur kernels over the foreground region. Constraints formulated from this information are incorporated into a conventional alpha matting framework to more accurately extract the alpha mattes of motion-blurred objects.

Assumptions made in this work are that blurs from hand shake are negligible in the images, that the scale of the moving object changes little between the consecutively captured images, that the background is static, and that moving objects are opaque and contain no saturated pixels. With bracketed images captured under these conditions, our method is shown to generate alpha mattes comparable to those estimated with the help of considerable user interaction. In addition, reasonable performance is obtained in challenging cases such as non-rigid human motion and highly textured backgrounds, as demonstrated in Figure 1.

2 Related Work

A comprehensive survey of general matting techniques was presented in [24]. Here we review matting algorithms most closely related to our method, as well as relevant work on motion deblurring.

Motion-Blurred Object Matting. A few matting techniques explicitly account for the motion blur of a foreground object. In [13], a solution is computed by adding a regularization constraint to existing matting formulations [12,23] that suppresses the matte gradient along the local motion direction. Local motions are estimated from local gradient statistics, based on an assumption that image patches without motion blur have a uniform distribution of image gradients. The method does not detect blurred regions but instead requires a trimap to be provided by the user. By making use of a short-exposure image, our technique avoids the need for a user-supplied trimap, and estimates motion blur information without strong assumptions on local gradient statistics.

In [10], a known blur kernel is incorporated into closed-form matting [12] by modeling the alpha matte as the convolution of a foreground mask and the blur kernel. A trimap also needs to be provided by the user. Our work by contrast infers trimap and blur kernel information from a companion bracket sequence image, and also addresses spatially-variant blur for which blur kernels are difficult to obtain by existing automatic deblurring methods.

A different approach to this problem is to employ a hardware solution for recovering object motion. In [14,20,21], hybrid camera systems are used for this purpose, where one of the cameras captures multiple, unblurred, high-speed images of the scene while at the same time the other camera records a longer-exposure image with object motion blur. Optical flow in the high-speed sequence is used to recover motion trajectories in the longer-exposure image.

A coded exposure camera is utilized in [22] together with scribbles drawn by the user along motion paths of the foreground object. From the motion paths and coded-exposure image, blur kernels are estimated and then used with a sparsity constraint to deblur the matte obtained from closed-form matting [12]. This result is then re-blurred to obtain the alpha matte. Unlike coded exposure imaging, the exposure bracketing used in our work is widely available on digital cameras and does not introduce unsightly discontinuities into the motion blur.

Image Pairs. Previous techniques have utilized image pairs for unsupervised extraction of mattes. In [18], an image with flash and another without flash are taken, and a matte is computed based on the property that only the foreground is significantly brightened by flash, while the background is not if it is sufficiently distant. As this method requires accurate pixel alignment between the two images, the scene is assumed to be static. This approach was later extended to handle some misalignment due to hand shake and scene motion through an analysis of color histograms [19]. This extension deals with foreground segmentation instead of matting, which would be difficult to handle in this color histogram approach because of the changing color blends of moving foreground points with fractional opacity. Like exposure bracketing, flash/no-flash image pairs can be captured by ordinary cameras, but a flash has a limited effect in daylight settings and for distant foreground objects.

In [25], a method is presented for co-matting, which is the joint matting of two images with the same foreground, different backgrounds, and similar matte properties. This method for static scenes would be difficult to extend to motion-blurred objects since the algorithm requires foreground alignment and assumes consistency between the mattes of the two images.

Similar to our work, a long-exposure and short-exposure image pair is captured as input in [26], which uses this data to estimate a spatially-invariant blur kernel to deblur the long-exposure image. The method deals with camera shake rather than object motion, and focuses mainly on using the short-exposure image to reduce deconvolution artifacts. The blur kernel is estimated using large-scale, sharp image features in the short-exposure image, which may not be sufficiently dense to recover spatially-varying blur.

A blurry photo is deblurred with the help of a sharp reference example in [8], which alternately computes locally aggregated correspondences between the two images, estimates blur kernels, and solves for the sharp image. In contrast to their work on deblurring of camera shake, ours deals with matting of motion-blurred objects, for which we compute globally optimized dense correspondences that cover the boundary of the object. Such an approach often yields a denser set of correspondences needed in our work to constrain the alpha matte.

Motion Deblurring. Given the alpha matte of a blurred object, the method in [4] estimates local motions of the object using a motion blur constraint in which the image gradient at a blurred point is equal to the difference between two non-blurred points along a linear blur direction. With the help of a short-exposure image, our method does not require a greatly simplified motion blur model.

Motion-blurred regions have been segmented from a single image based on their differences in intensity gradient distributions from the background [11] and additionally using a prior model on the local frequency components of sharp images [2]. These methods compute a hard segmentation of motion-blurred objects rather than a blur matte, and they obtain promising results for this challenging problem. In our work, we take advantage of an image that contains the foreground object without blur to more robustly detect and matte motion-blurred foreground objects.

3   Proposed Method

In this section, we present the proposed method for automatic alpha matting of a motion-blurred object in a bracket sequence image pair. Our approach consists of four main steps: (1) estimating a binary segmentation through integrating a foreground/background color model and a background probability model computed from sparse correspondences between the two images; (2) establishing dense correspondence between the moving object in both images while considering potential motion blur; (3) estimating spatially varying blur kernels for the motion-blurred foreground object in the longer-exposure image with the help of the corresponding sharp object in the shorter-exposure image; (4) extracting an alpha matte of the motion-blurred object through an optimization that accounts for the binary segmentation, dense correspondences, and motion blur information. To improve the estimation of dense correspondences and blur kernels, the second and third steps are iterated until there is convergence in the correspondences. Each of the four steps is presented in the following.

3.1 Binary Segmentation

We start by computing a binary segmentation of the moving object in both of the images. After matching the exposure levels of the two images via the relative response function [5], the appearance of the background should be similar, as the two images are captured in rapid succession. We utilize this as a cue for segmenting the moving object.

We formulate foreground/background segmentation as a binary labeling problem. Given the two images, where the short-exposure image with a sharp foreground is denoted as I^{sharp} and the longer-exposure image as I^{blurry}, we define an energy function measuring the quality of binary segmentation of each image as

$$E(\mathbf{x}) = \sum_{i \in \mathcal{P}} D_i(x_i) + \sum_{(i,j) \in \mathcal{N}} V_{ij}(x_i, x_j), \tag{1}$$

where x_i is the binary label of pixel i, $\mathcal{P}$ denotes the set of all pixels, $\mathcal{N}$ denotes pairs of adjacent pixels, D_i is a data term for i, and V_{ij} is a pairwise term defined between two adjacent pixels i and j.

Data Term: The data term for each pixel consists of two parts:

$$D_i(x_i) = \gamma D_i^b(x_i) + D_i^c(x_i), \tag{2}$$

where $D_i^b(x_i)$ is the background likelihood term, $D_i^c(x_i)$ is the foreground/background color likelihood term, and γ is a weighting parameter set to 5 in our implementation. To compute the background likelihood term, we first obtain sparse correspondences between the two images using the SURF matching algorithm. The matches should primarily be of background points, since the colors and gradients of the foreground object become distorted by motion blur in I^{blurry}. The matched background points should be similar in appearance, and we model this similarity in terms of the intensity difference of pixel i between I^{sharp} and I^{blurry}:

$$\triangle I_i = \frac{h(I_i^{sharp}) - h(I_i^{blurry})}{h(I_i^{sharp}) + h(I_i^{blurry})}, \tag{3}$$

where $h(I_i)$ denotes the exposure normalized pixel value of I_i. Similar to [19], we model the distribution of these background pixel differences as a Gaussian $N(\triangle I_i | \mu, \sigma^2)$ with mean μ and standard deviation σ.

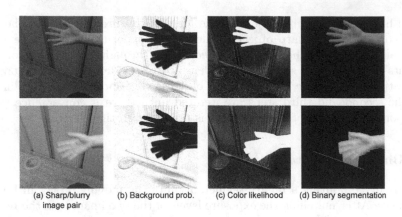

(a) Sharp/blurry image pair   (b) Background prob.   (c) Color likelihood   (d) Binary segmentation

Fig. 2. Binary segmentation results of a short/long exposure image pair. (a) input image pair, (b) background probability, (c) foreground color likelihood, and (d) binary segmentation.

Then, we can define the probability $f_b(i)$ of a pixel i belonging to the background as

$$f_b(i) = exp(-\|\triangle I_i - \mu\|/\sigma). \tag{4}$$

Note that $f_b(i)$ lies within the range of [0,1]. If the difference of a certain pixel is far from μ, then we assign low background probability to that pixel. This probability is computed for every image pixel, using correspondences obtained by registering the two images via a homography computed from the sparse SURF matches. Figure 2 shows an example of the calculated background probability.

Finally, the background likelihood term $D_i^b(x_i)$ is defined as

$$D_i^b(x_i) = \begin{cases} 2\max\{f_b(i), 0.5\} - 1 & \text{if } x_i = 1 \\ 0 & \text{if } x_i = 0 \end{cases}. \tag{5}$$

This energy term assigns a penalty if the pixel i is labeled as foreground ($= 1$) and the background probability $f_b(i)$ is higher than 0.5. From this, the labels are determined using only the color and regularization terms when $f_b(i) < 0.5$.

The foreground/background color likelihood term $D_i^c(x_i)$ is calculated using the negative log likelihood of Gaussian mixture models, which are constructed from all pixels with $f_b(i) > 0.6$ and $f_b(i) < 0.4$, respectively.

Pairwise Term: The pairwise term is defined as the usual contrast dependent energy $V_{ij}(x_i, x_j) = |x_i - x_j|exp(-\beta\|I_i - I_j\|^2)$, with β is set to the inverse of the standard deviation of I.

Binary graph cut [1] is applied to minimize the objective function in Eq. (1). This is a standard formulation for using motion information to extract a foreground object [3,17].

The results of binary segmentation are shown for an example image pair in Figure 2. Since the boundary of the motion-blurred object is less distinct and has inconsistent color likelihoods, the binary segmentation result is not as accurate for the blurred foreground as it is for the sharp object. It nevertheless provides a useful cue for matting, and we use it in conjunction with other cues soon to be described.

3.2 Blur-Aware Dense Correspondence Estimation

After binary segmentation of the foreground object in both images, we establish a dense correspondence between the two segmented regions. The blurred/sharp object regions are represented as graphs $\mathcal{G}$ and $\mathcal{G}'$, respectively, whose nodes represent image patches defined by a coarse image grid in each segment. For the patch I_p of node p in $\mathcal{G}$, we denote its associated local motion blur kernel as b_p. Similar to [6], we represent correspondences between $\mathcal{G}$ and $\mathcal{G}'$ as displacements within the graph grid, such that for a node p in $\mathcal{G}$ matched to a node p' in $\mathcal{G}'$, its correspondence is represented as displacement d_p, where $I_{p'} = I_{p+d_p}$.

We define an energy function that measures the quality of displacements as

$$E(d) = \sum_p^N D_p(d_p) + \sum_{p,q \in \mathcal{E}} P_{pq}(d_p, d_q), \qquad (6)$$

where D and P denote unary and binary potentials, N is the number of nodes, and $\mathcal{E}$ is the set of neighboring node pairs. For computational considerations, we set a maximum displacement of K in each direction, which leads to a total of K^2 possible displacements d_p for each node n. We empirically set K to 30 and the patch size to 50.

The unary term D_p is defined as

$$D_p(d_p) = ||A_{(p+d_p)} * b_p - I_p^b||_2, \qquad (7)$$

where $A_{(p+d_p)}$ denotes the patch in the sharp object graph $\mathcal{G}'$ with a displacement d_p from the patch of node p in $\mathcal{G}$. Note that this term accounts for the motion blur b_p of p's patch in measuring this match cost. The pairwise term is used to enforce spatial consistency, and is formulated as done in [6]:

$$P_{pq}(d_p, d_q) = P_{pq}^s(d_p, d_q) + P_{pq}^c(d_p, d_q). \qquad (8)$$

The first term penalizes the L1 distance between two neighboring displacements:

$$P_{pq}^s(d_p, d_q) = -\lambda ||d_p - d_q||_1, \qquad (9)$$

where λ is a positive constant set to 5 in our implementation. The second term penalizes instances where two neighboring displacements indicate a switch in the order of the two patches:

$$P_{pq}^c(d_p, d_q) = \begin{cases} -\mu[dx_q - dx_p]_+ & \text{if } x_q = x_p + 1 \text{ and } y_q = y_p \\ -\mu[dy_q - dy_p]_+ & \text{if } y_q = y_p + 1 \text{ and } x_q = x_p , \\ 0 \text{ } otherwise \end{cases} \qquad (10)$$

(a) Sharp matte   (b) Dense correspondence   (c) Transferred matte

Fig. 3. Dense correspondence of patches and the transferred matte, which is transformed from the binary segmentation of the sharp object. (a) Binary segmentation of the sharp foreground object. (b) Blur-aware dense correspondence. (c) Transferred matte from the sharp object to the blurry object.

where μ is a positive constant set to 10 in our implementation, (x_p, y_p) are the grid coordinates of p's patch, and $[z]_+ = \max\{0, z\}$. Equation (6) is optimized using the curve-expansion method for solving dense graph matching problems.

This optimization can be time-consuming since the unary term in Equation (7) requires K^2 convolutions per patch in the motion-blurred object region. To reduce computation, instead of estimating correspondences for the blurred region patches, we first solve for correspondences from the sharp region patches, which need only one convolution to be computed per patch. Negative values of the computed displacements are then used as initial displacement estimates for the blurred region patches, and the displacement range is reduced from $K \times K$ to a small 5×5 neighborhood around the initial displacement estimate.

The first time that dense correspondence is computed, no blur kernel information is available, so we simply use uniform kernels as the initial kernels. After estimating blur kernels in the next step, this step is repeated with the updated kernels.

An example of dense patch correspondence is shown in Figure 3(b), where the red lines link corresponding patches in the two regions. With this correspondence, the binary segmentation of the sharp object (a) can be transformed into a transferred matte of the blurred object (c), by mapping the sharp patches using their corresponding displacements and applying the associated local motion blur kernels. We utilize this transferred matte as another cue in computing the final matte solution.

3.3 Spatially Varying Blur Kernel Estimation

For each blurred patch I_p^b, we now have its corresponding sharp reference patch $A_{(p+\hat{d}_p)}$. With each patch pair, the local blur kernel $\hat{b}_p$ for I_p^b is solved as follows:

$$\hat{b}_p = \mathrm{argmin}_{b_p \geq 0} \|A_{(p+\hat{d}_p)} * b_p - I_p^b\|^2, \tag{11}$$

where $\hat{d}_p$ denotes the optimized displacement vector from the dense correspondence estimation in Section 3.2. After obtaining the blur kernels $\hat{b}_p$ for all the patches, we replace each local blur kernel $\hat{b}_p$ by a weighted average of computed blur kernels from neighboring patches to impose local smoothness among the blur kernels. The blur kernel estimation of Equation (11) and weighted averaging of neighboring blur kernels are iteratively repeated ten times. In our implementation, we used a kernel size of 31×31. In the iterative process, a weighted average of neighboring kernels is computed using equal weights among the ten nearest neighbor patches. We empirically found the iterative method to converge. The kernels of nearby points on a moving object tend to be similar, and we use this averaging as an easy way to apply this constraint. This regularization could alternatively be imposed in the objective, but would result in a large and complex optimization problem.

The converged blur kernels are used to re-estimate the dense correspondence in the previous step. The correspondence and blur kernel steps are iterated until the correspondences do not change.

3.4 Motion-Blurred Matte Estimation

Conventional image matting algorithms need user guidance to estimate accurate mattes. In our formulation, instead of user guidance we use the binary segmentation, blur-aware dense correspondence, and motion blur kernels computed in the previous steps to automatically guide our matte extraction of motion-blurred objects. Our method is built upon closed-form matting [12], whose energy function is defined as

$$\alpha = \mathrm{argmin} \alpha^T L \alpha + \lambda (\alpha - \tilde{\alpha})^T D_S (\alpha - \tilde{\alpha}) \tag{12}$$

where $\tilde{\alpha}$ is a vector of specified alpha values (e.g., foreground and background pixels in a trimap); D_S is a diagonal matrix whose diagonal elements are set to 1 for pixels with alpha value constraints and set to 0 for unconstrained pixels; λ is a weight typically set to a large value; and L is the matting Laplacian matrix, whose (i,j)-th element is

$$\sum_{k|(i,j)\in w_k} (\delta_{ij} - \frac{1}{|w_k|}(1 + (I_i - \mu_k)(\sum_k + \frac{\epsilon}{w_k} I_3)^{-1}(I_j - \mu_k))) \tag{13}$$

where $\sum_k$ is a 3×3 covariance matrix, μ_k is a 3×1 mean vector of the colors in a window w_k, and I_3 is the 3×3 identity matrix.

The binary segmentation provides information on a potential trimap for the motion-blurred object, by using morphological operations on the binary segmentation to determine the unknown region of the trimap. Our morphological kernel is set to half the blur kernel size. We specifically use the binary segmentation to obtain a partial trimap that only indicates definite foreground pixels through erosion of the segment. However, as shown in Figure 2, a binary segmentation may fail to accurately capture the boundary of the motion blurred object. The blur-aware dense correspondences and motion blur kernels can also provide a constraint on alpha values in the form of the transferred matte, computed by mapping the patches of the sharp region to the blurred region via the correspondences and then applying the associated blurs to the patches to obtain an alpha

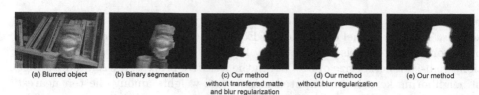

| (a) Blurred object | (b) Binary segmentation | (c) Our method without transferred matte and blur regularization | (d) Our method without blur regularization | (e) Our method |

Fig. 4. Effect of each matting component on the alpha matte result. (a) Original image. (b) Binary segmentation. (c) Alpha matting without the transferred matte and motion blur regularization. (d) Alpha matting without motion blur regularization. (e) Proposed method.

map. In addition, the alpha gradients can be constrained as in [13] according to the local motion direction and strength indicated by the blur kernels. Incorporating all of this information into closed-form matting gives us the following energy function:

$$\alpha = \operatorname{argmin} \alpha^T L \alpha + \lambda (\alpha - \tilde{\alpha})^T D_S (\alpha - \tilde{\alpha}) + \mu (\alpha - \hat{\alpha})^T D_T (\alpha - \hat{\alpha}) + \sum_d w_d \nabla_d \alpha^T \nabla_d \alpha$$

(14)

where the second, third and fourth terms account for the partial trimap obtained from the binary segmentation, the transferred matte $\hat{\alpha}$ from dense correspondences and blur kernels, and the alpha gradient constraints, respectively. Denoting the partial trimap constraints from the binary segmentation as D_S and $\tilde{\alpha}$ as in Equation (12), we define D_T as a diagonal matrix whose diagonal elements are the intersection of D_S and all pixels with $\hat{\alpha} > 0.99$. $\nabla_d \alpha$ is the α-gradient in direction d, and w_d is the weight of regularization for direction d, where d is sampled in the eight directions of the eight-connected pixel neighbors. The motion strength w_d is obtained by convolving the local blur kernel with a linear motion in direction d.

The impact of each of these components on the alpha matting result is illustrated in Figure 4, which shows the original binary segmentation (b), the result using only the partial trimap computed from the binary segmentation (c), the result using the partial trimap and transferred matte (d), and the result using all the components (e). Improvements are obtained by adding each component into the optimization.

4   Results

We evaluated our method on both synthetic and real bracket sequence pairs. The real bracket sequences were acquired using a Panasonic DMC-LX5 camera, and the synthetic pairs were produced using imagery from this camera as well. We determined the parameters of our algorithm empirically and fixed all of them throughout the experiments.

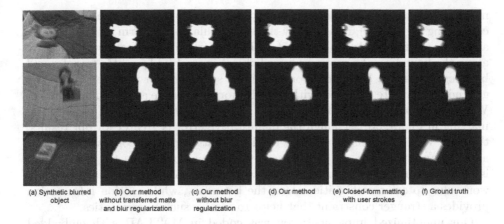

(a) Synthetic blurred object (b) Our method without transferred matte and blur regularization (c) Our method without blur regularization (d) Our method (e) Closed-form matting with user strokes (f) Ground truth

Fig. 5. Alpha matting results on synthetic data. (a) Synthesized image with motion-blurred object. (b) Motion matting without matte transfer and motion blur regularization. (c) Motion matting without motion blur regularization. (d) The proposed motion matting method combining all cues. (e) Closed-form matting with user strokes. (f) Ground truth alpha matte.

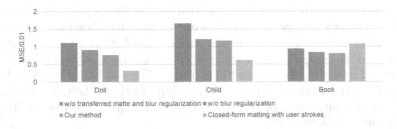

Fig. 6. Quantitative error comparisons. Doll, Child and Book sequences correspond to the first, second and third rows of Figure 5.

4.1   Synthetic Images

We first validate our method on synthetic data, from which ground truth is available for quantitative evaluation. To generate a bracket pair, we first capture two sharp images with the same short-exposure setting: one of a static foreground object in front of a background, and another of just the background. The first image is used as the short-exposure image in the bracket pair. We also apply GrabCut [15] with user strokes to it to extract the foreground object from the background, and apply a known motion blur to this foreground object region. The motion-blurred object is then composited on the second image using the corresponding alpha matte, and a gain is added to the resulting image to synthesize the long-exposure image.

The performance of our proposed approach is exhibited with three such image pairs in Figure 5. To show the contribution of each term in motion-blurred object matting, we remove the transferred matte term and blur regularization term in computing Figure 5(b), remove only the blur regularization term for Figure 5(c), and show our full results in Figure 5(d). The uncertainty in binary segmentation along the boundary of a motion-blurred object is resolved by matte transfer and blur regularization. The corresponding mean squared error with respect to the ground-truth matte decreases with the addition of each cue as shown in Figure 6. We also compare our automatic image matting to human-guided closed-form matting in Figure 5(e). Though the quantitative error is greater for our results, they are visually similar to the user-guided matte and are computed without any human interaction. In cases like the book example where the background is highly textured, closed-form matting with user strokes may actually perform worse due to color ambiguities along the boundary, while motion information provides a stronger constraint that helps to resolve such uncertainties.

Our unoptimized implementation was coded in MATLAB with embedded C++ functions on a PC with a 3.3GHz Intel quadcore i5 CPU and 16GB RAM. We resize images to 1024×577 for efficiency. For the Doll sequence, the overall run time was about 12 minutes, and peak memory usage was 1 GB.

4.2 Real Images

We also tested our method on a variety of real bracket image pairs. Similar to the results for synthetic images, we compare our method to a version of it without matte transfer and motion blur regularization. The first two rows of Figure 7 contain non-rigid human motion, which is effectively handled by our approach. In the second example, the detailed blur of each finger is better extracted with the help of matte transfer and motion blur regularization. The third and fourth rows are challenging cases of textured foreground objects moving in front of highly textured backgrounds.

5   Discussion

The method of HaCohen et al. [8] also computes non-rigid dense correspondences between a blurred and sharp image, using the method of [7] interleaved with kernel estimation and deconvolution. Correspondences computed using only [7] (without iterations of kernel estimation and deconvolution) are shown in Figure 8. The correspondences are less dense than ours, perhaps because their bottom-up aggregation of consistent patches may fail in textured areas. The correspondence density is nevertheless sufficient for the purpose of non-uniform deblurring of camera shake, and would likely be increased by interleaving kernel estimation and deconvolution as done in [8]. By contrast, our alpha matting approach requires denser correspondences for computing the transferred matte and the motion blur regularization constraint along the matte boundary, so the proposed method is designed to compute a much denser correspondence that better serves our purpose.

A limitation of the proposed method is that its performance largely depends on the accuracy of binary segmentation for the sharp foreground object. Errors

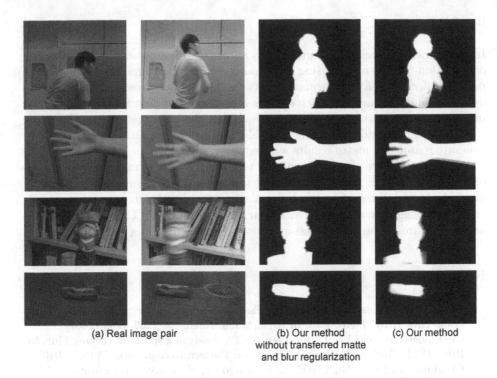

(a) Real image pair   (b) Our method   (c) Our method
                        without transferred matte
                        and blur regularization

Fig. 7. Alpha matting results of our method on real bracket pairs

in that binary segmentation will degrade the quality of the transferred matte, and may affect the amount of blur kernel information computed. This binary segmentation could potentially be refined in future work by re-estimating it in the matting pipeline using inter-image information. Another limitation is that our current method cannot be applied if the foreground in the short-exposure image is also motion-blurred.

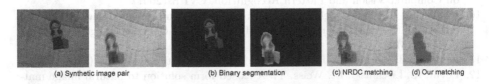

(a) Synthetic image pair   (b) Binary segmentation   (c) NRDC matching   (d) Our matching

Fig. 8. Differences in correspondence density between our method and NRDC [7]. Our method establishes non-rigid dense correspondence between two segmented region pairs (b). For the motion-blurred object region, (c) shows the matched patches with NRDC, and (d) shows a thresholded version of our transferred matte.

6   Conclusion

In this paper, we presented a method to automatically extract the alpha matte of a motion-blurred object using inter-image information in a bracket sequence pair. To effectively share information between images, we presented a blur-aware dense matching technique, which enables our method to determine a transferred matte and infer dense local blur kernels. Using this information together with a binary segmentation of the motion-blurred object region, our method can generate reasonable matte results without user guidance.

In future work, we plan to extend our technique to matte multiple foreground objects in a dynamic scene. Our current implementation assumes that only one moving object is present in the bracket sequence. Furthermore, scale and orientation change is not considered in our current pipeline. This issue could be addressed through an orientation-aware scale-space matching scheme.

References

1. Boykov, Y., Veksler, O., Zabih, R.: Fast approximate energy minimization via graph cuts. IEEE Trans. Pattern Anal. Mach. Intell. 23, 1222–1239 (2001)
2. Chakrabarti, A., Zickler, T., Freeman, W.T.: Analyzing spatially-varying blur. In: Proc. IEEE Conf. on Computer Vision and Pattern Recognition, CVPR (2010)
3. Criminisi, A., Cross, G., Blake, A., Kolmogorov, V.: Bilayer segmentation of live video. In: Proc. IEEE Conf. on Computer Vision and Pattern Recognition (CVPR) (2006)
4. Dai, S., Wu, Y.: Motion from blur. In: Proc. IEEE Conf. on Computer Vision and Pattern Recognition, CVPR (2008)
5. Debevec, P.E., Malik, J.: Recovering high dynamic range radiance maps from photographs. In: ACM SIGGRAPH (1997)
6. Duchenne, O., Joulin, A., Ponce, J.: A graph-matching kernel for object categorization. In: Proc. Int'l Conf. on Computer Vision, ICCV (2011)
7. HaCohen, Y., Shechtman, E., Goldman, D.B., Lischinski, D.: Nrdc: Non-rigid dense correspondence with applications for image enhancement. In: ACM Trans. Graph (2011)
8. HaCohen, Y., Shechtman, E., Lischinski, D.: Deblurring by example using dense correspondence. In: Proc. Int'l Conf. on Computer Vision, ICCV (2013)
9. Jia, J.: Single image motion deblurring using transparency. In: Proc. IEEE Conf. on Computer Vision and Pattern Recognition, CVPR (2007)
10. Köhler, R., Hirsch, M., Schölkopf, B., Harmeling, S.: Improving alpha matting and motion blurred foreground estimation. In: Proc. Int'l Conf. on Image Processing, ICIP (2013)
11. Levin, A.: Blind motion deblurring using image statistics. In: NIPS (2006)
12. Levin, A., Lischinski, D., Weiss, Y.: A closed-form solution to natural image matting. IEEE Trans. Pattern Anal. Mach. Intell. 30(2), 228–242 (2008)
13. Lin, H.T., Tai, Y.W., Brown, M.S.: Motion regularization for matting motion blurred objects. IEEE Trans. Pattern Anal. Mach. Intell. 33(11), 2329–2336 (2011)
14. Nayar, S.K., Ben-Ezra, M.: Motion-based motion deblurring. IEEE Trans. Pattern Anal. Mach. Intell. 26(6), 689–698 (2004)

15. Rother, C., Kolmogorov, V., Blake, A.: Grabcut: Interactive foreground extraction using iterated graph cuts. ACM Trans. Graph. 23(3), 309–314 (2004)
16. Shan, Q., Xiong, W., Jia, J.: Rotational motion deblurring of a rigid object from a single image. In: Proc. Int'l Conf. on Computer Vision, ICCV (2007)
17. Sheikh, Y., Javed, O., Kanade, T.: Background subtraction for freely moving cameras. In: Proc. Int'l Conf. on Computer Vision, ICCV (2009)
18. Sun, J., Lin, Y., Kang, S.B., Shum, H.Y.: Flash matting. ACM Trans. Graph. 25(3), 772–778 (2006)
19. Sun, J., Sun, J., Kang, S.B., Xu, Z.B., Tang, X., Shum, H.Y.: Flash cut: Foreground extraction with flash and no-flash image pairs. In: Proc. IEEE Conf. on Computer Vision and Pattern Recognition, CVPR (2007)
20. Tai, Y.W., Du, H., Brown, M.S., Lin, S.: Image/video deblurring using a hybrid camera. In: Proc. IEEE Conf. on Computer Vision and Pattern Recognition, CVPR (2008)
21. Tai, Y.W., Du, H., Brown, M.S., Lin, S.: Correction of spatially varying image and video motion blur using a hybrid camera. IEEE Trans. Pattern Anal. Mach. Intell. 32(6), 1012–1028 (2010)
22. Tai, Y.W., Kong, N., Lin, S., Shin, S.Y.: Coded exposure imaging for projective motion deblurring. In: Proc. IEEE Conf. on Computer Vision and Pattern Recognition (CVPR) (2010)
23. Wang, J., Cohen, M.F.: Optimized color sampling for robust matting. In: Proc. IEEE Conf. on Computer Vision and Pattern Recognition, CVPR (2007)
24. Wang, J., Cohen, M.F.: Image and Video Matting. NOW Publishers Inc. (2008)
25. Wang, L., Xia, T., Guo, Y., Liu, L., Wang, J.: Confidence-driven image co-matting. Computers & Graphics 38(2), 131–139 (2013)
26. Yuan, L., Sun, J., Quan, L., Shum, H.Y.: Image deblurring with blurred/noisy image pairs. ACM Trans. Graph. 26(3) (2007)

An Active Patch Model for Real World Texture and Appearance Classification

Junhua Mao, Jun Zhu, and Alan L. Yuille

University of California, Los Angeles, USA
{mjhustc@,jzh@,yuille@stat.}ucla.edu

Abstract. This paper addresses the task of natural texture and appearance classification. Our goal is to develop a simple and intuitive method that performs at state of the art on datasets ranging from homogeneous texture (e.g., material texture), to less homogeneous texture (e.g., the fur of animals), and to inhomogeneous texture (the appearance patterns of vehicles). Our method uses a bag-of-words model where the features are based on a dictionary of active patches. Active patches are raw intensity patches which can undergo spatial transformations (e.g., rotation and scaling) and adjust themselves to best match the image regions. The dictionary of active patches is required to be compact and representative, in the sense that we can use it to approximately reconstruct the images that we want to classify. We propose a probabilistic model to quantify the quality of image reconstruction and design a greedy learning algorithm to obtain the dictionary. We classify images using the occurrence frequency of the active patches. Feature extraction is fast (about 100 ms per image) using the GPU. The experimental results show that our method improves the state of the art on a challenging material texture benchmark dataset (KTH-TIPS2). To test our method on less homogeneous or inhomogeneous images, we construct two new datasets consisting of appearance image patches of animals and vehicles cropped from the PASCAL VOC dataset. Our method outperforms competing methods on these datasets.

Keywords: Active Patch, Texture Classification, Appearance Recognition.

1 Introduction

Visual appearance is one of the most essential cues for human vision cognition. In particular, analysis and recognition of the appearance on real-world textured surfaces/ materials has been an increasingly important research topic in computer vision. It also has great significance in many applications such as remote sensing, biomedical image processing, object recognition and image segmentation. Previous texture analysis works have mainly concentrated on the recognition of material categories from a wide range of pose, viewpoint, scale and illumination variations. Accordingly, much effort has been devoted to building benchmark material datasets for texture classification, such as CuRET [8], Outex [22], Brodatz [32], KTH-TIPS [14] and KTH-TIPS2 [3]. In the left panel of Fig. 1, some example images are shown from the KTH-TIPS2 dataset [3]. As we can see, the material texture images tend to be roughly homogeneous and have frequently repeated local patterns. Although recent methods [13,27,28] show satisfactory results on those material datasets, these methods have not been systemically

D. Fleet et al. (Eds.): ECCV 2014, Part III, LNCS 8691, pp. 140–155, 2014.

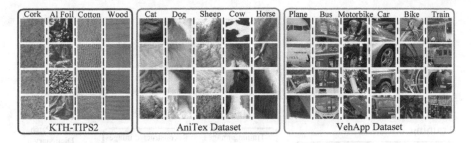

Fig. 1. Sample images from the three types of appearance datasets studied in this paper. Left panel: material texture dataset (KTH-TIPS2); Middle panel: animal texture dataset (AniTex); Right panel: vehicle appearance dataset (VehApp). The images range from roughly homogeneous (KTH-TIPS2) to partially homogeneous (AniTex), and to inhomogeneous (VehApp). (Best viewed in color).

explored for the related tasks of recognizing the less homogeneous or inhomogeneous visual appearance of general object categories (e.g., animals and vehicles).

In order to explore less homogeneous texture and appearance, in this paper, we construct two new real-world appearance datasets (called "AniTex" and "VehApp")[1]. They include more complex and less homogeneous visual patterns than previous material datasets as shown in Fig. 1. More precisely, our AniTex and VehApp datasets include a variety of animal texture patches and vehicle appearance regions respectively, all of which are taken from the PASCAL VOC dataset [11]. From the middle panel of Fig. 1, we can see that the image patches from AniTex possess less homogeneous texture patterns compared to traditional material images. This results in larger intra-class variations and inter-class ambiguities, hindering discrimination of appearance between different categories. As shown in the right panel of Fig. 1, the inhomogeneity of appearance increases further for man-made vehicle objects, which exhibit larger visual variations spatially.

In the literature, there are different approaches for addressing the appearance classification problem. For material textures, the filter-bank-based methods [8,16,39] are the most widely used methods in the early stage. They typically exploit a variety of filter response features at multiple scales and orientations, to capture summary statistics for representing the texture images. Winn *et. al* [35] learned a universal dictionary based on these features to categorize objects. Recently, Varma *et. al* [33] demonstrated that local image patches can obtain better results than filter banks. They also provided theoretical arguments which justify the use of raw intensity image patches. Their approach, however, has several limitations such as some sensitivity to image rotations. For more complex and less homogeneous appearance of structural objects (e.g., animals and vehicles), some other descriptors such as SIFT [18] and HOG [7] are commonly adopted in literature, and traditional texture descriptors tend to be less investigated in these cases.

---

[1] Both datasets are available at http://www.stat.ucla.edu/~junhua.mao/texture.html

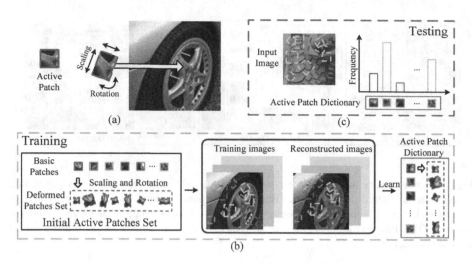

Fig. 2. Illustration of our approach. (a). An active patch will take actions to best fit the image region near a target position (the green rectangle region in the image) in the best way. The actions consist of the combination of scaling and rotation. (b). To implement these actions efficiently, each active patch consists of a basic patch (e.g. the patch in the solid red rectangle in the left panel of (b)) and a deformed patches set (e.g. the patches in the dashed red rectangle). Given an image position, the active patch will find one of its deformed patches that has the maximum matching score with the image region near this position. If the score is larger than a threshold, the active patch is "fired" at the image region. In this way, the images can be reconstructed and represented by a set of firing active patches. We learn the active patch dictionary in a greedy manner using criteria based on the reconstruction of the training images. (c). The histogram of firing frequencies of the active patches in the dictionary will be treated as the feature for appearance classification. (Best viewed in color).

In this paper, we present a unified appearance classification method and apply it to all of the three types of datasets with different granularities of visual complexity and homogeneity. We develop a new image representation for appearance modeling and classification based on *Active Patches*. They are raw intensity patches which can undergo spatial transformations (e.g., rotation and scaling) and adjust themselves to fit the target image region (see Fig. 2). We use normalized cross-correlation to calculate the matching score. If the matching score is larger than a threshold, we treat it as a firing active patch for that region. Images can be reconstructed by a set of firing active patches in this way and we allow patches to overlap with each other. Compared with traditional filter-bank-based texture analysis approaches, our method, which utilizes raw intensity patches, has the advantages of being simple and intuitive. We introduce a probabilistic model based on our active patches to quantify the reconstruction quality. On the basis of this model, we propose a novel greedy learning algorithm to establish a compact yet representative active patch dictionary. Starting from a large candidate pool of active patches, our learning algorithm greedily selects the ones with high firing frequency, taking into account the criteria such as small reconstruction error and small overlapping area with other patches in the reconstructed image. For appearance classification task, we simply use the histogram of the firing frequency of the active patches in the dictionary as the image feature descriptor. In our experiments, we evaluate the proposed method on three challenging appearance/texture datasets (i.e., KTH-TIPS2 [3], AniTex and VehTex), which are illustrated in Fig. 1. The experimental results validate the effectiveness of our approach in real-world appearance classification, and show consistent performance improvement w.r.t. the previous texture classification approaches on all of the three datasets.

The main contributions of this paper are summarized as follows: (1) We present an active patch model and a probabilistic formulation to quantify the quality of images reconstructed using a set of active patches. (2) We propose a novel greedy forward feature selection algorithm to learn a compact and representative active patch dictionary based on the representation-by-reconstruction principle. (3) We build two new datasets (AniTex and VehApp) for real-world appearance recognition, which provide a comprehensive evaluation scenario for less homogeneous or inhomogeneous visual patterns than traditional material textures. Using image features based on the learned dictionary, our method consistently outperforms the previous approaches on these two datasets as well as a challenging material texture benchmark dataset (KTH-TIPS2).

2   Related Work

Traditional filter-bank-based approaches [8,16,39] have been dominant in texture analysis literature in early years. The filter banks extract salient statistical characteristics from a large support of image patch around the central pixel, and their responses can be used to represent the repeated visual patterns in texture images. Recently, the necessity of the use of filter bank was argued by many methods based on the local pixel neighborhood statistics [27,4,23,30], which can capture the repeated micro-structure from relatively smaller texture patches (e.g., 3×3). This sort of approaches includes local binary patterns (LBP) [13,12,23], local ternary patterns (LTP) [30], Weber local descriptor (WLD) [4], local higher statistics (LHS) [27], etc. In particular, the LHS method extends the original LBP by considering the second order statistics in local pixel intensities of a small patch using gaussian mixture model and fisher vector encoding [26]. It achieves the state-of-the-art results on several texture benchmark datasets such as KTH-TIPS2. Besides, there are some very recent works which utilize deep convolutional network [28] and semantic attributes [21] for texture analysis. However, the descriptors generated from above methods cannot be used to reconstruct the images and not very interpretable. On the other hand, Varma *et. al* [33] proposed a method based on intensity patches for material texture classification and demonstrated the power of using intensity patches both experimentally and theoretically.

Intensity patches have been increasingly used in the field of computer vision in recent years. In particular, patch-based methods have dominated the field of texture synthesis [9,17]. Wolf *et. al* [36] used patches as an alternative to traditional filter-bank-based methods for edge detection and segmentation, but they did not use a large patch dictionary. In addition, Ullman and his collaborators used patches for object classification [10,31] and image segmentation [2]. Coates *et. al* [6] exploited a single-layer network

Table 1. Summary of important notations in section 3

Notation	Description	Notation	Description
$\mathbb{A}$	Active patch	$I_R(I)$	Reconstructed image of I
S_B	Basic patch	Ω	Training image set
$\mathbb{S}_D$	Deformed patches set	λ_e, λ_{ov}	Non-zero weights for energy terms
S_{d_t}	Deformed patch in $\mathbb{S}_D$	$M(\mathbb{A}, I, pos)$	Matching score between $\mathbb{A}$ & image I at pos
$\mathcal{D}$	Active patch dictionary	$M^{best}(I, pos)$	Best matching score for image I at pos
$\mathcal{D}_o$	Over-completed dictionary	$S_{d_t}^{best}$	Best fitted deformed patch in $\mathbb{S}_D$
$\mathcal{D}_f$	Final dictionary	$F(\mathbb{A}, I)$	Firing frequency of $\mathbb{A}$ for image I

with optimal parameter settings using patches as features. Singh *et. al* [29] presented a mid-level patch work based on HOG descriptors to sparsely detect discriminative image regions. However, the patches used in the works mentioned above are not active and thus may not deal well with the scaling and rotation transformations of real-world appearance/ texture. In [15], an epitome framework was proposed for image representation, and was recently developed by [24,5]. For an epitome, the basis patches spatially overlap in a single image (the epitome), which is not a constraint in this paper. Another related work is from Ye *et. al* [38]. It presented a deformable patch method for handwritten digit recognition. In addition, Wu *et. al* [37] propose a generative model for object detection based on active basis. Their active basis model consists of a small number of handcrafted Gabor wavelet filters at selected locations and orientations, which is different from our learned dictionary of raw pixel intensity active patches. Besides, their model concentrates on recognizing shape of objects and not modeling their appearance.

3   The Active Patch Model For Appearance Modeling

In Section 3.1, we introduce our active patch model and describe how to use a set of active patches to reconstruct and represent images. Then we present a probabilistic model to quantify the quality of the reconstruction in Section 3.2. A simple but effective greedy learning algorithm based on this probabilistic model will be introduced in Section 3.3 to build the active patch dictionary. Image features for classification can be generated using the dictionary. We show the implementation details in Section 3.4. Some important notations are summarized in Table 1.

3.1   The Active Patch Model

An active patch (denoted as $\mathbb{A}$) consists of two parts: a basic patch S_B and a deformed patches set $\mathbb{S}_D$ (see Fig. 2(b)). The deformed patches (denoted as $S_{d_t}, t = 1, 2, \ldots, n_T$) in $\mathbb{S}_D$ are generated by applying various spatial transformations on the basic patch S_B. n_T is the number of the allowed transformations. The transformation, represented by $T = (s^x, s^y, \theta)$, involves combination of rotation and scaling. (s^x, s^y) denotes the width and height of the patch in its upright form after scaling. θ represents the rotation angle. Our active patches use the raw intensity pixels as basic features for its basic patch and deformed patches.

Given an input image I and a position pos, an active patch will automatically select one of its deformed patches which best fits the input image region near the position. To make the fitting robust and get rid of the redundancy for duplicate matches in the nearby positions, we apply a spatial max-pooling operation to the neighborhood positions $\mathcal{N}(pos)$ of pos. $\mathcal{N}(pos)$ is set as a 3×3 region centering at pos. Normalized Cross-Correlation (NCC) is adopted to calculate the matching score $M(\mathbb{A}, I, pos)$:

$$M(\mathbb{A}, I, pos) = \max_{pos' \in \mathcal{N}(pos)} \max_{S_{d_t} \in \mathbb{S}_D} \{\text{NCC}(S_{d_t}, I(pos'))\} \tag{1}$$

$I(pos')$ denotes the image region near pos', which has the same dimension as S_{d_t}. If the matching score is larger than a threshold (we use 0.8 to ensure perceptual similarity and high performance in this paper, please see supplementary material for detailed justification.), the active patch will be treated as a firing one for image I at pos. Otherwise, we will treat the position as "not fired" by this active patch.

We can learn a dictionary of active patches $\{\mathbb{A}^{(1)}, \mathbb{A}^{(2)}, \ldots, \mathbb{A}^{(n)}\}$ from the training set of a dataset (e.g. KTH-TIPS2, AniTex or VehApp). The dictionary size n equals to the number of different active patches. We will introduce the learning process later. Given the dictionary $\mathcal{D}$, we can reconstruct the images using $\mathcal{D}$. The reconstructed image $I_R(I)$ is generated by copying the pixel value of the best fitted deformed patch of a fired active patch to the corresponding image position. Some of the image regions might not be covered by any active patches in the dictionary. We will treat the pixels in these regions as unreconstructed pixels and set the corresponding pixels in $I_R(I)$ as void. If several fired active patches overlap over one pixel, that pixel will be set as the corresponding pixel value of the active patch with the largest matching score. We will use the quality of the reconstructed image and the compactness of the dictionary as the measurements for choosing the optimal active patch dictionary.

3.2 The Probabilistic Model as Criterion for Image Reconstruction

We model the probability of reconstructing and representing an image I by the active patch dictionary $\mathcal{D}$ as an exponential distribution with energy term $E(I|\mathcal{D})$:

$$P(I|\mathcal{D}) = \frac{1}{|Z|} e^{-E(I|\mathcal{D})}. \tag{2}$$

$$\mathcal{D}^* = \arg\min_{\mathcal{D}} \sum_{I \in \Omega} E(I|\mathcal{D}). \tag{3}$$

We incorporate the reconstruction quality and the compactness of $\mathcal{D}$ into the energy function (Equ. 4). It consists of three terms, where λ_e and λ_{ov} are non-zero weights for the energy terms, $\#(I)$ denotes the number of pixels in I, p denotes the pixel value in the original image I, which is normalized to [0 1], and p_r denotes the corresponding reconstructed pixel in $I_R(I)$.

$$E(I|\mathcal{D}) = \frac{1}{\#(I)}[\sum_{p_r \in I_R(I)} E_c(p_r) + \lambda_e \cdot \sum_{p \in I} E_e(p|p_r) + \lambda_{ov} \cdot \sum_{p \in I} E_{ov}(p|\mathcal{D})] \tag{4}$$

The first term is $\sum_{p_r \in I_R(I)} E_c(p_r)$, where $E_c(p_r) = 1$ if $p_r = void$ (i.e. p_r is unreconstructed), otherwise $E_c(p_r) = 0$. This term encourages more reconstructed pixels.

The second term is $\sum_{p \in I} E_e(p|p_r)$, where $E_e(p|p_r) = |p - p_r|$ if $p_r \neq void$, otherwise $E_e(p|p_r) = 0$. This term encourages a small difference of intensity value between the original image pixel and the corresponding reconstructed pixel.

The third term is $\sum_{p \in I} E_{ov}(p|\mathcal{D})$, where $E_{ov}(p|\mathcal{D})$ is set as the number of firing active patches overlapped on pixel p. This term encourages a small overlapping area for different active patches. If most of the reconstructed regions of an active patch $\mathbb{A}$ overlap with those of other patches in $\mathcal{D}$, it is highly possible that $\mathbb{A}$ can be replaced. This term will reduce the redundancy in the dictionary and restrict the dictionary size.

The energy function of the whole training images can be calculated by Equ. 5, where $\#(\Omega)$ represents the number of images in Ω.

$$E(\Omega|\mathcal{D}) = \frac{1}{\#(\Omega)} \sum_{I \in \Omega} E(I|\mathcal{D}) \tag{5}$$

We set λ_e and λ_{ov} to get a relatively small dictionary that can reconstruct more than 90% pixels with the root-mean-square error of pixel intensity less than 0.1. In this paper, we set $\lambda_e = 1$, $\lambda_{ov} = 0.5$ by cross validation on KTH-TIPS2. With these settings, we can acquire appropriate dictionaries for all the three datasets (i.e. KTH-TIPS2, AniTex and VehApp) in our experiments. Please refer to Section 4.5 to understand how performance varies with the dictionary size.

3.3   Greedy Learning of the Active Patch Dictionary

It is hard to learn the model directly because the parameter space of $\mathcal{D}$ is very large. Instead, we first acquire an over-complete active patch dictionary $\mathcal{D}_o$ by unsupervised clustering (e.g. Kmeans) randomly sampled patches in dataset images to get the basic patches. Then we select active patches from $\mathcal{D}_o$ as the final dictionary $\mathcal{D}_f$.

If we want to exhaustively search for the optimal $\mathcal{D}_f$, we have to run the reconstruction process 2^m times, where m is the size of the $\mathcal{D}_o$. This is impractical. To efficiently get the results, we adopt a fast greedy forward feature selection strategy to learn $\mathcal{D}_f$ and reconstruct training images at the same time (some reconstructed samples are shown in Fig. 3). This greedy algorithm sequentially selects the active patches that provide the highest reconstruction quality with the minimal redundancy. More specifically, we first

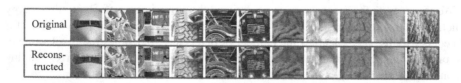

Fig. 3. Sample reconstructed and the original images from VehApp and AniTex using the learned dictionaries from the two datasets respectively

---

Algorithm 1. Our learning method for active patch dictionary

Initialization:
1. Get $\mathcal{D}_o$ from clustering algorithm;
2. $\mathcal{D}_f \leftarrow \emptyset$; $\forall M^{best}(I, pos) \leftarrow 0$; $\forall p_r \leftarrow void, p_r \in \forall I_R(I)$;

Process:
3. Sort $\mathbb{A}^{(k)} \in \mathcal{D}_o$ w.r.t. $F(\mathbb{A}^{(k)})$ in descending order;
4. **for** each $\mathbb{A}^{(k)} \in \mathcal{D}_o$ **do**
5. $\quad \forall I \in \Omega$, record current $I_R(I)$ and $M^{best}(I, pos)$; $\Delta E \leftarrow 0$;
6. $\quad$ **for** each position pos of each image $I \in \Omega$ where $\mathbb{A}^{(k)}$ is firing **do**
7. $\quad\quad$ **for** each pixel $p_d \in S_{d_t}^{best}$, $S_{d_t}^{best} \in \mathbb{S}_D^{(k)}$ **do**
8. $\quad\quad\quad$ Calculate ΔE according to Equ. 4;
9. $\quad\quad\quad$ **if** the corresponding $p_r = void$ or $M(\mathbb{A}^{(k)}, I, pos) > M^{best}(I, pos)$ **then**
10. $\quad\quad\quad\quad p_r \leftarrow p_d$; $M^{best}(I, pos) \leftarrow M(\mathbb{A}^{(k)}, I, pos)$;
11. $\quad\quad\quad$ **end if**
12. $\quad\quad$ **end for**
13. $\quad$ **end for**
14. $\quad$ **if** $\Delta E < 0$ **then**
15. $\quad\quad$ Add $\mathbb{A}^{(k)}$ to $\mathcal{D}_f$
16. $\quad$ **else**
17. $\quad\quad \forall I \in \Omega$, restore $I_R(I)$ and $M^{best}(I, pos)$ to previous value;
18. $\quad$ **end if**
19. **end for**

---

sort the active patches $\mathbb{A}^{(k)}$ in $\mathcal{D}_o$ in the descending order of their firing frequency $F(\mathbb{A}^{(k)})$ for all the training images. $F(\mathbb{A}^{(k)}) = \sum_{I \in \Omega} F(\mathbb{A}^{(k)}, I)$ where $F(\mathbb{A}^{(k)}, I)$ denotes the firing frequency of an active patch $\mathbb{A}^{(k)}$ for image I. We then check the active patches one by one. If the energy function decreases when adding $\mathbb{A}^{(k)}$ to $\mathcal{D}_f$ (i.e. $\Delta E < 0$), $\mathbb{A}^{(k)}$ will be selected and its firing image regions will be reconstructed.

The detailed algorithm is shown in Algorithm 1. $M^{best}(I, pos)$ records the current best matching score for image I at position pos for all the previously selected active patches in $\mathcal{D}_f$. $S_{d_t}^{best} \in \mathbb{S}_D^{(k)}$ is the deformed patch of an active patch $\mathbb{A}^{(k)}$ that best matches the target image region. Before each iteration of the greedy algorithm, we record the previous reconstruction state (line 5) in order to restore if the candidate active patch is not selected (line 17).

The learning algorithm is unsupervised and does not need the labels of the training images. This is an advantage because we can readily apply the algorithm to a large dataset without too much human labor.

Assuming that the learned dictionary is $\mathcal{D}_f = \{\mathbb{A}_f^{(1)}, \mathbb{A}_f^{(2)}, \ldots, \mathbb{A}_f^{(n)}\}$, the corresponding feature descriptor of an image I is set as the histogram of the firing frequencies of the active patches in $\mathcal{D}_f$ for I:

$$[F(\mathbb{A}_f^{(1)}, I), F(\mathbb{A}_f^{(2)}, I), \ldots, F(\mathbb{A}_f^{(n)}, I)] \qquad (6)$$

We apply L1 normalization and power normalization (square root) [25] to this feature descriptor for classification tasks.

3.4 Implementation Details

The possible transformations $\{T\}$ applied on the basic patch S_B are described as follows. For rotation, the direction of the patches ranges from $-45°$ to $45°$ with a step size of $15°$. For scaling, the maximum and minimum heights of the deformed patches are $1.2\times$ and $0.8\times$ the height of the basic patch respectively. We adopt the same scaling setting for the width of the deformed patches. The step size for scaling is 2 pixels.

We use the Kmeans algorithm to initialize the greedy forward feature selection algorithm. The seed patches are randomly sampled from the training images. Their sizes are 10×10, 7×7, and 5×5. We also experimented with seed patches of larger sizes. However, it does not improve the performance. On the other hand, using larger patches requires much larger dictionaries if we want to achieve the same reconstruction ability as the small patch dictionary. We conduct zero-mean whitening [1] on seed patches before clustering them. The number of seed patches is about 500,000.

The normalized cross-correlation operation can be treated as a matrix multiplication operation if we normalize the patches and target image regions beforehand. We utilize highly optimized matrix operation packages (i.e. Matlab Distributed Computing Tool Box and CUDA with cudablas library) to efficiently calculate the matching statistics of a set of active patches. The speed of our algorithm is very fast. It takes 100 ms on average to extract the proposed feature descriptors for a KTH-TIPS2 image with a computer using one Tesla C1060 GPU.

4   Experiments

To validate the effectiveness of the active patch model, we test it on a range of real world appearance images from a roughly homogeneous dataset (KTH-TIPS2), to a partially homogeneous dataset (AniTex), and to a inhomogeneous dataset (VehApp). Some sample images of these datasets are shown in Fig. 1. The AniTex and VehApp datasets contain color images cropped from the PASCAL VOC dataset [11]. We will first introduce the details of these two datasets then compare the classification performance on all the three datasets with previous methods. Finally, the effect of the transformations and the dictionary size will be analyzed.

For a fair comparison, we use a SVM classifier with histogram intersection kernel [19] for all the methods. It is a very efficient kernel and has no hyperparameters. As most of the existing state-of-the-art texture analysis methods ([23,12,13,27]), we focus on the analysis of gray scale texture information in the dataset images. We discuss the role of color in the supplementary material, and show that color will provide additional information and further improve the results.

4.1 The Two New Texture Datasets

The Animal Texture Dataset (AniTex). This dataset contains a main image set and a supplementary image set. The main image set contains 3120 texture patch images extracted randomly (i.e. cropped) from the torso region inside the silhouette of different animals in the PASCAL VOC 2012 database. Only one image will be cropped from the same object in an image. We do not re-scale or rotate the original PASCAL images before extraction. No object contour information is included. There are no background pixels and no easily identifiable features, such as the face of animals in these patch images. There are five classes of animals: cat, dog, sheep, cow and horse. Each class consists of 624 images. The size of the images in the dataset ranges from 64×64 to 100×100 pixels. The images in this database are under a range of harsh image conditions, such as scaling, rotation, viewing angle variations and lighting condition change. Some images suffer from low resolution. Occlusion sometimes occurs, such as the dog collars in some dog images and the sheepfold in some sheep images. We denote this dataset as the **3120 animal texture dataset (3120AniTex)**.

The supplementary image set contains 250 images of animals from the same five classes, with 50 images for each class. This dataset is built to meet the requirement of some psychophysics experiments for testing human's performance on the classification of animals' fur texture. We briefly discuss these experiments in section 5. The size of the images is 100×100 pixels. They are sampled using the same strategy as the 3120AniTex. But care was taken to select cropped regions which contained consistent textural information and no tell-tale signs of category membership (e.g., dog collars or sheepfold). There are no overlapping images between this set and the 3120AniTex set. Although the images in general are clearer than those in the 3120AniTex set, this dataset is also very challenging. The experiment shows that humans also do not perform very well in this task (see Section 5). We denote this image set as the **250 animal texture dataset (250AniTex)**.

For the 3120AniTex dataset, we separate it into training set and testing set randomly. There are 2496 training images and 624 testing images. We treat the 250AniTex dataset only as a *testing dataset*. Neither dictionary nor classifier is trained, or retrained, on this image set for any of the methods we compared in the experiments. Only the training set of 3120AniTex is available for learning the dictionary and the classifier. So the 250An-iTex set can also be used to evaluate the effectiveness of algorithms on the learning transfer test. This is similar to the intuition behind the development of the KTH-TIPS2 dataset from the original KTH-TIPS dataset [3].

The Vehicle Appearance Dataset (VehApp). This dataset also contains a main image set and a supplementary image set. The main image set contains 13723 images cropped from the PASCAL VOC dataset. They consist of 6 kinds of vehicles: aeroplane, bicycle, car, bus, motorbike, and train. The image size is 100×100. The sampling strategy is similar to 3120AniTex and 250Anitex except that we allow the images to contain a small portion of background pixels ($\leq 20\%$). The reason is that the contour of the vehicles (bicycle and motorbike in particular) is much more irregular than animals. Sometimes it is impossible to crop a 100×100 image patch that is totally inside the silhouette region. The large variance of the background pixels also makes this dataset challenging. We separate this image set into a training set (80%) and a testing set (20%) randomly. We denote this dataset as $\text{VehApp}_{\text{crop}}$.

To further evaluate the performance of existing method on long-range appearance patterns, we also build a supplementary image set consisting of the silhouette regions of the same kinds of vehicles. There are 2408 images in the dataset. All the images

Table 2. Performance comparison on AniTex and VehApp

	LBP [23]	HOG [7]	SIFT [18]	LCP [12]	disCLBP [13]	LHS [27]	Ours
3120AniTex	35.6	39.2	31.7	35.5	40.8	48.1	**50.8**
250AniTex	30.4	53.2	33.6	29.6	36.8	50.0	**56.8**
VehApp$_{crop}$	42.9	55.6	44.0	49.8	47.8	53.3	**63.4**
VehApp$_{sih}$	53.4	65.9	45.8	62.1	62.1	69.1	**76.6**

are rescaled to ensure that their height and width are both no larger than 100 pixels. We generate a foreground mask for each image and the background pixels are set to 0. All the methods are only allowed to extract features within the mask in order to insure that they only utilize the appearance information. We also separate this image set into a training set (80%) and a testing set (20%) randomly. Training and testing on this image set are independent of VehApp$_{crop}$. We denote this image set as **VehApp$_{sih}$**.

4.2   Performance Evaluation on AniTex and VehApp

To validate the effectiveness of our algorithm on the AniTex and VehApp datasets, we compare it with four state-of-the-art texture descriptors and report their performance. They are the Local High-order Statistics (LHS) [27], the general Local Binary Patterns (LBP) [23] and two of its most recent extensions, the Discriminative Features of LBP Variants (disCLBP [13]) and the Local Configuration Pattern (LCP [12]). For LBP and disCLBP, we use the code released by the authors. For LHS, we implement the algorithm exactly according to the paper and the suggestions from the authors. We achieve similar classification accuracy of 71.1 ± 4.9 (rectangular sampling) on KTH-TIPS2 compared to 71.7 ± 5.7 reported by the original paper. The small difference might be due to the different settings of whitening or other implementation details. The feature dimension of LHS is 2048. In [27], it shows that LHS feature with larger dimension (e.g. 4096) does not improve the performance. HOG and SIFT features are extracted as the baselines in these two datasets. These two features have been successfully applied in the field of object detection and classification [7,18,20]. We use VLFeat [34] implementation of HOG and SIFT. For HOG, the cell size is set to 10 pixels. For dense SIFT, the scale and step is set to 10 pixels and 5 pixels respectively. The bag-of-visual-word algorithm is applied to improve their performances. The number of visual words is set to 3000 for both HOG and SIFT.

The results are summarized in Table 2 and the detailed comparisons for different categories are given in Fig. 4. For our method, we learned the dictionaries of size 2799, 2981 and 2958 for AniTex, VehApp$_{crop}$ and VehApp$_{sih}$ respectively. Our method outperforms all the competing methods. For AniTex datasets, the performance gains are 2.7% and 6.8% on 3120AniTex and 250AniTex respectively compared to LHS (the second best performed method on 3120AniTex). The performance gains are 11.6% and 3.6% on 3120AniTex and 250AniTex respectively compared to HOG (the second best performed method on 250AniTex). In addition, for most of the categories, our algorithm is the best or the second best method. Some comparing methods might be more effective on some specific categories, such as LBP for sheep and HOG for horse.

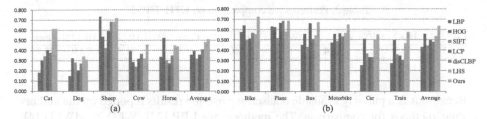

Fig. 4. Performance comparisons on (a) 3120AniTex for the five animal categories, and (b) VehApp$_{crop}$ for the six vehicle categories. (Best viewed in color)

But their overall performances are much lower than our method. Since the AniTex dataset contains images under harsh real image conditions, the results show that our algorithm can handle the classification task of real world partially homogeneous texture. It is a little surprising that SIFT does not perform well in these datasets. It is perhaps because the small image size is not suitable for SIFT as discussed in [4].

It is also interesting to compare the results between 3120AniTex and 250AniTex. As stated in Section 4.1, the images in 250AniTex are clearer visually than those in 3120AniTex, which makes 250AniTex easier than 3120AniTex. We should expect the performance increase on 250AniTex even using the dictionary and the classifier trained by the training set of 3120AniTex. Our algorithm indeed performs better on 250AniTex than 3120AniTex with a margin of 6.0% in this training transfer experiment.

For VehApp$_{crop}$ and VehApp$_{sih}$ datasets, the performance gains of our method are 7.8% and 7.5% respectively compared to the second best methods. In addition, our algorithm is the best method for all the categories on VehApp$_{crop}$ and four categories out of six on VehApp$_{sih}$. All the methods generally perform better on VehApp$_{sih}$ than VehApp$_{crop}$ because the former one provides more spatial structure information. These two datasets contain inhomogeneous appearance with more variance spatially. The high accuracy on these datasets demonstrates the capability of our algorithm to capture long-range appearance patterns.

4.3 Performance Evaluation on KTH-TIPS2

We also test our algorithm on a benchmark material texture dataset (i.e., KTH-TIPS2). It is developed based on the CUReT and KTH-TIPS, and contains more variations of scale, pose and illumination. There are 11 material categories in this dataset and each category is separated into 4 groups of samples. The samples are photographed under 9 scales, 3 poses and 4 different illumination conditions. The motivation of building this dataset is to evaluate the capability of the algorithm on previous unseen instances of materials [3]. All these settings make it an extremely challenging texture dataset. The best published result so far is 73% [27] to our best of knowledge while the highest accuracies of other traditional texture datasets are over 90%. We adopt the standard testing protocol [3,4,27] for this dataset: We run the classification four times and report the average accuracy. One group of samples will be treated as the testing set while the other three groups are treated as the training set at each time.

Table 3. Performance comparison on KTH-TIPS2

LBP [23]	HOG	SIFT	WLD [4]	MWLD [4]	LCP [12]	Caputo [3]	LTP [30]	LHS [27]	Ours
53.6	63.5	52.7	56.4	64.7	60.8	71.0	71.3	73.0	**75.7**

Because it is a publicly available dataset, we use the results reported by the authors of their methods for comparison. The methods are LBP [23], WLD & MWLD [4], LCP [12], Caputo et. al [3], LTP [30], and LHS [27]. We also try SIFT and HOG for this dataset. The results are shown in Table 3. Our algorithm achieves a better result than the previous best published result of LHS. Since KTH-TIPS2 is a very challenging benchmark dataset taken under the settings of the traditional material texture task, this demonstrates the effectiveness of our active patch model on homogeneous and densely repeated texture patterns with large variations of scale, pose and illumination.

4.4 Active vs. Non-active

To evaluate the importance of our active patch model, we conduct experiments on a non-active dictionary that allows no transformations on basic patches. The results are shown in Fig. 5(a). We can see that the active patch dictionary performs better than the non-active counterpart on all the datasets. The performance gains are 7.9%, 7.2%, 5.2%, 4.8% and 3.2% respectively on KTH-TIPS2, 3120AniTex, 250AniTex, VehApp$_{crop}$ and VehApp$_{sih}$, demonstrating the advantage and importance of applying rich transformations on the active patch dictionary. It has superior discriminability on handling scale, rotation and pose variations of real world appearance than the non-active one.

4.5 The Effect of Dictionary Size

To investigate the effect of the dictionary size, we train several dictionaries with different sizes on KTH-TIPS2 by changing the value of λ_{ov} in Equ. 4. λ_{ov} is the weight for the energy term $E_{ov}(p|\mathcal{D})$. A Larger value of λ_{ov} means that there is a larger penalty

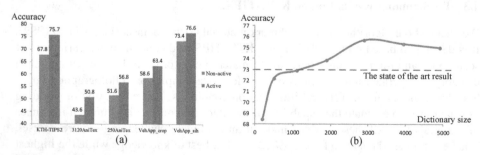

Fig. 5. (a). Performance comparison between the non-active dictionary and the active patch dictionary. (b) Performance comparison with different sizes of dictionaries on KTH-TIPS2 (Best viewed in color).

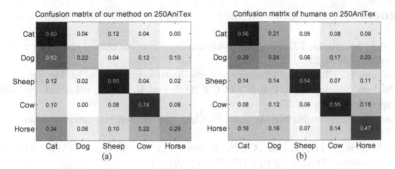

Fig. 6. The confusion matrice for (a) our algorithm and (b) humans on the 250AniTex dataset

when patches in the dictionary overlap with others in the reconstruction process, and will lead to a smaller dictionary size. The results are shown in Fig. 5(b).

From Fig. 5(b), we can see that the performance improves with the increase of dictionary size initially and reaches the maximum at a dictionary size of 2951. When the dictionary size increases further, the performance even deteriorates. The reason might be that a dictionary with 2951 active patches is large enough to model appearance patterns for KTH-TIPS2 images. Adding redundant patches is not useful and may lead to over-learning. We also show that an active dictionary of size 1100 can produce the same result as the state-of-the-art algorithm (LHS) which uses a feature of dimension 2096.

5   Discussion

We propose a probabilistic Active Patch Model for real world texture/appearance classification. A simple but effective greedy learning method is presented to obtain the active patch dictionary. Image features are generated using this dictionary, which are interpretable enough to reconstruct the images and have strong discriminability for the classification task. We validate our method on one published benchmark texture dataset (KTH-TIPS2) and two newly constructed datasets (AniTex and VehApp). Our algorithm performs better than previous methods in all of the three datasets. In the future work, we will explore the potential of this method on other tasks such as image labeling and object segmentation.

To study the difficulty of these classification tasks, in related work with C. Wallraven, we also performed psychophysics experiments on the 250AniTex dataset. The experimental results show that humans do not perform very well in this task. The accuracy is 46.8% on average. Our method shows similar error patterns with humans (e.g., the tendency of confusing dog textures with cats or horses, see Fig. 6). We put the details of psychophysics experiments in the supplementary material.

Acknowledgment. We gratefully acknowledge funding support from the National Science Foundation (NSF) with award CCF-1317376, and from the National Institute of Health NIH Grant 5R01EY022247-03.

References

1. Bell, A.J., Sejnowski, T.J.: The "independent components" of natural scenes are edge filters. Vision research 37(23), 3327–3338 (1997)
2. Borenstein, E., Ullman, S.: Class-specific, top-down segmentation. In: Heyden, A., Sparr, G., Nielsen, M., Johansen, P. (eds.) ECCV 2002, Part II. LNCS, vol. 2351, pp. 109–122. Springer, Heidelberg (2002)
3. Caputo, B., Hayman, E., Mallikarjuna, P.: Class-specific material categorisation. In: ICCV (2005)
4. Chen, J., Shan, S., He, C., Zhao, G., Pietikainen, M., Chen, X., Gao, W.: Wld: A robust local image descriptor. TPAMI 32(9), 1705–1720 (2010)
5. Chen, L.C., Papandreou, G., Yuille, A.L.: Learning a dictionary of shape epitomes with applications to image labeling: Supplementary material (2013)
6. Coates, A., Ng, A.Y., Lee, H.: An analysis of single-layer networks in unsupervised feature learning. In: ICAIS (2011)
7. Dalal, N., Triggs, B.: Histograms of oriented gradients for human detection. In: CVPR (2005)
8. Dana, K.J., Van Ginneken, B., Nayar, S.K., Koenderink, J.J.: Reflectance and texture of real-world surfaces. TOG 18(1), 1–34 (1999)
9. Efros, A.A., Freeman, W.T.: Image quilting for texture synthesis and transfer. In: SIGGRAPH (2001)
10. Epshtein, B., Uliman, S.: Feature hierarchies for object classification. In: ICCV (2005)
11. Everingham, M., Van Gool, L., Williams, C.K., Winn, J., Zisserman, A.: The pascal visual object classes (voc) challenge. IJCV 88(2), 303–338 (2010)
12. Guo, Y., Zhao, G., Pietikäinen, M.: Texture classification using a linear configuration model based descriptor. In: BMVC (2011)
13. Guo, Y., Zhao, G., Pietikäinen, M.: Discriminative features for texture description. PR 45(10), 3834–3843 (2012)
14. Hayman, E., Caputo, B., Fritz, M., Eklundh, J.-O.: On the significance of real-world conditions for material classification. In: Pajdla, T., Matas, J(G.) (eds.) ECCV 2004. LNCS, vol. 3024, pp. 253–266. Springer, Heidelberg (2004)
15. Jojic, N., Frey, B.J., Kannan, A.: Epitomic analysis of appearance and shape. In: CVPR (2003)
16. Leung, T., Malik, J.: Representing and recognizing the visual appearance of materials using three-dimensional textons. IJCV 43(1), 29–44 (2001)
17. Liang, L., Liu, C., Xu, Y.Q., Guo, B., Shum, H.Y.: Real-time texture synthesis by patch-based sampling. TOG 20(3), 127–150 (2001)
18. Lowe, D.: Distinctive image features from scale-invariant keypoints. IJCV 60(2), 91–110 (2004)
19. Maji, S., Berg, A.C., Malik, J.: Classification using intersection kernel support vector machines is efficient. In: CVPR (2008)
20. Mao, J., Li, H., Zhou, W., Yan, S., Tian, Q.: Scale based region growing for scene text detection. ACM Multimedia, 1007–1016 (2013)
21. Matthews, T., Nixon, M.S., Niranjan, M.: Enriching texture analysis with semantic data. In: CVPR (2013)
22. Ojala, T., Maenpaa, T., Pietikainen, M., Viertola, J., Kyllonen, J., Huovinen, S.: Outex-new framework for empirical evaluation of texture analysis algorithms. In: ICPR (2002)
23. Ojala, T., Pietikainen, M., Maenpaa, T.: Multiresolution gray-scale and rotation invariant texture classification with local binary patterns. TPAMI 24(7), 971–987 (2002)
24. Papandreou, G., Chen, L.C., Yuille, A.L.: Modeling image patches with a generic dictionary of mini-epitomes. In: CVPR (2014)

25. Pele, O., Werman, M.: The quadratic-chi histogram distance family. In: Daniilidis, K., Maragos, P., Paragios, N. (eds.) ECCV 2010, Part II. LNCS, vol. 6312, pp. 749–762. Springer, Heidelberg (2010)

26. Perronnin, F., Sánchez, J., Mensink, T.: Improving the fisher kernel for large-scale image classification. In: Daniilidis, K., Maragos, P., Paragios, N. (eds.) ECCV 2010, Part IV. LNCS, vol. 6314, pp. 143–156. Springer, Heidelberg (2010)

27. Sharma, G., ul Hussain, S., Jurie, F.: Local higher-order statistics (lhs) for texture categorization and facial analysis. In: Fitzgibbon, A., Lazebnik, S., Perona, P., Sato, Y., Schmid, C. (eds.) ECCV 2012, Part VII. LNCS, vol. 7578, pp. 1–12. Springer, Heidelberg (2012)

28. Sifre, L., Mallat, S., DI, E.N.S.: Rotation, scaling and deformation invariant scattering for texture discrimination. In: CVPR (2013)

29. Singh, S., Gupta, A., Efros, A.A.: Unsupervised discovery of mid-level discriminative patches. In: Fitzgibbon, A., Lazebnik, S., Perona, P., Sato, Y., Schmid, C. (eds.) ECCV 2012, Part II. LNCS, vol. 7573, pp. 73–86. Springer, Heidelberg (2012)

30. Tan, X., Triggs, B.: Enhanced local texture feature sets for face recognition under difficult lighting conditions. TIP 19(6), 1635–1650 (2010)

31. Ullman, S., Sali, E.: Object classification using a fragment-based representation. In: BMCV (2000)

32. Valkealahti, K., Oja, E.: Reduced multidimensional co-occurrence histograms in texture classification. TPAMI 20(1), 90–94 (1998)

33. Varma, M., Zisserman, A.: A statistical approach to material classification using image patch exemplars. TPAMI 31(11), 2032–2047 (2009)

34. Vedaldi, A., Fulkerson, B.: VLFeat: An open and portable library of computer vision algorithms (2008), http://www.vlfeat.org/

35. Winn, J., Criminisi, A., Minka, T.: Object categorization by learned universal visual dictionary. In: Tenth IEEE International Conference on Computer Vision, ICCV 2005, vol. 2, pp. 1800–1807. IEEE (2005)

36. Wolf, L., Huang, X., Martin, I., Metaxas, D.: Patch-based texture edges and segmentation. In: Leonardis, A., Bischof, H., Pinz, A. (eds.) ECCV 2006. LNCS, vol. 3952, pp. 481–493. Springer, Heidelberg (2006)

37. Wu, Y.N., Si, Z., Gong, H., Zhu, S.C.: Learning active basis model for object detection and recognition. IJCV 90(2), 198–235 (2010)

38. Ye, X., Yuille, A.: Learning a dictionary of deformable patches using gpus. In: Workshop on GPU's in Computer Vision Applications, ICCV (2011)

39. Zhu, S.C., Wu, Y., Mumford, D.: Filters, random fields and maximum entropy (frame): Towards a unified theory for texture modeling. IJCV 27(2), 107–126 (1998)

Material Classification Based on Training Data Synthesized Using a BTF Database

Michael Weinmann, Juergen Gall, and Reinhard Klein

Institute of Computer Science, University of Bonn, Germany

Abstract. To cope with the richness in appearance variation found in real-world data under natural illumination, we propose to synthesize training data capturing these variations for material classification. Using synthetic training data created from separately acquired material and illumination characteristics allows to overcome the problems of existing material databases which only include a tiny fraction of the possible real-world conditions under controlled laboratory environments. However, it is essential to utilize a representation for material appearance which preserves fine details in the reflectance behavior of the digitized materials. As BRDFs are not sufficient for many materials due to the lack of modeling mesoscopic effects, we present a high-quality BTF database with 22,801 densely measured view-light configurations including surface geometry measurements for each of the 84 measured material samples. This representation is used to generate a database of synthesized images depicting the materials under different view-light conditions with their characteristic surface geometry using image-based lighting to simulate the complexity of real-world scenarios. We demonstrate that our synthesized data allows classifying materials under complex real-world scenarios.

Keywords: Material classification, material database, reflectance, texture synthesis.

1 Introduction

Image-based scene understanding depends on different aspects such as the detection, localization and classification of objects. For these tasks, it is essential to consider characteristic object properties like shape or appearance. While its shape tells us how to grasp a particular object, its material tells us how fragile, deformable, heavy, etc. it might be and hence, how we have to handle it. The understanding of the recognized surface material thus guides the interaction of humans with the corresponding object in daily life, and it also represents a key component regarding industrial applications. However, image-based classification of materials in real-world environments is a challenging problem due to the huge impact of viewing and illumination conditions on material appearance. Therefore, training an appropriate classifier requires a training set which covers all these conditions as well as the intra-class variance of the materials.

D. Fleet et al. (Eds.): ECCV 2014, Part III, LNCS 8691, pp. 156–171, 2014.

So far, there have been two main approaches to generate suitable training sets. One approach is to capture a single representative per material category under a multitude of different conditions, such as scale, illumination and viewpoint, in a controlled setting [8,13,7,18] (see Table 1). However, the measured viewing and illumination configurations are rather coarse and hence not descriptive enough to capture the mesoscopic effects in material appearance, which consider the light interaction with material surface regions mapped to approximately one pixel, in an accurate way. In addition, the material samples are only measured under controlled illumination or lab environments which does not generalize to material appearance under complex real-world scenarios. As an alternative, the second category of methods uses images acquired under uncontrolled conditions. In [25], images from an internet image database (Flickr) have been used. This has the advantage that both the intra-class variance of materials and the environment conditions are sampled in a representative way. Unfortunately, the images have to be collected manually, and the materials appearing in the images have to be segmented and annotated. The necessary effort again severely limits the number of configurations that can be generated this way (see Table 1).

In this paper, we instead make use of synthesized data which has already been explored for different applications (e.g. [11,21,29,28,27,19,2,3]). In particular, separately acquired material characteristics and illumination conditions offer the possibility to create synthetic training data for material classification that capture the variations of real-world data. This decoupling of the sampling of material from environment conditions allows us to overcome the limitations of existing material databases that contain only a few hundred configurations of viewing and lighting conditions per material category. For these synthetic images, perfect segmentations are directly available without the need for manual segmentation, and a huge number of them can be obtained easily and fully automatically. This approach requires creating realistic renderings, which accurately simulate the appearance of a material in a real-world scenario. In particular, the appearance of many daily life materials like cloth, skin, etc. is determined by effects taking place on surface structures mapped to a size of approximately 1 pixel (e.g. scratches or fibers) such as subsurface scattering, interreflections, self-shadowing and self-occlusion. These effects cannot be modeled by standard Bidirectional Reflectance Distribution Function (BRDF) models, which are suitable especially for locally smooth surfaces like plastic or metal as these fulfill the assumption of a homogeneous surface reflectance behavior. This was pointed out in [35], where the concept of Apparent BRDFs (ABRDFs) has been introduced to take the above-mentioned effects into account. Bidirectional Texture Functions (BTFs) [9] are a data-driven approach to efficiently capture and store ABRDFs and represent these mesoscopic effects. The results in [16], where training data has been synthesized based on BRDFs, support exactly this claim by showing that using BRDF materials for synthetic training data alone is not sufficient and leads to classification results significantly worse than using real-world images. In contrast, our experiments indicate that using an appropriate representation of the reflectance behavior like the BTF opens the possibility for using solely synthesized training data for classification tasks. We demonstrate that the classification of real-world test data can be boosted significantly by using image-based lighting via environment maps [10] instead of simple directional light sources. To achieve this, we generate synthesized training samples under a vast amount of different lighting conditions simulated by arbitrary HDR environment maps which adequately represent the complexity of real-world materials and lighting.

For this purpose, we have acquired a database containing dense BTF measurements of 84 material samples. The samples can be grouped into 7 categories (i.e. 12 samples per class). Per BTF, all combinations of 151 view and 151 light directions have been measured which results in 22,801 images per sample or a total of $7 \cdot 12 \cdot 22,801 > 1.9M$ images respectively. The data of our measured database with directional illumination is used as input for generating the synthesized data. By acquiring a height map of each material sample via structured light, we also include the complexity of the geometric structure of the different materials in the process of generating synthetic training images. While in fact an arbitrary number of configurations could be easily included in the synthesized database, we so far used 42 different viewpoints and 30 different illumination conditions per material sample.

In summary, the key contributions of our paper are:

- a technique for decoupling the acquisition of material samples from the environment conditions by generating synthetic training samples
- a publicly available novel BTF database of 7 material categories, each consisting of measurements of 12 different material samples, measured in a darkened lab environment with controlled illumination
- a second, novel database containing data synthesized under natural illumination which is a clear difference to other datasets which only use directional illumination or an additional single ambient illumination
- an evaluation which shows that these synthetic training samples can be used to classify materials in photographs under natural illumination conditions

2   Previous Work

In this section, we briefly review commonly used databases for material recognition and discuss their limitations. Subsequently, we discuss approaches that follow the recent trend of using synthetic training data in various applications.

Databases. Table 1 gives an overview of several different material databases. The CUReT database [8] has been extended in the scope of the KTH-TIPS database [13] in terms of varying the distance of the acquired sample to the camera, i.e. the scale of the considered textures, in addition to changing viewpoint and illumination angle. In both databases, however, only a single material instance is provided per class, and thus the intra-class variation is not represented. Aiming for a generalization to classifying object categories, the KTH-TIPS database was further extended by adding measurements of different samples of the same material category and also considering ambient lighting in the

Table 1. Overview of different databases. Please note that the FMD considers different configurations of viewing and lighting conditions as well as different material samples for each individual image. Our databases are highlighted in red (*: in principle, an arbitrary number of configurations could be considered in the synthesis).

	CUReT [8]	KTH-TIPS [13]	KTH-TIPS2 [7]	MPI-VIPS [16]	spectral database [18]	measured database	FMD [25]	synthesized database
material samples	61	10	44	11	90	84	1,000	84
categories	61	10	11	11	8	7	10	7
samples per category	1	1	4	1	N.N.	12	100	12
illuminations	4 ... 55	3	4	4	150	151	100	30*
illumination type	controlled	controlled	controlled & ambient	controlled & ambient	controlled	controlled	natural	natural
viewpoints	7	27	27	27	1	151	100	42*
images per sample	205	81	108	108	150	22,801	1	1,260*
total image number	12,505	810	4,752	1,188	13,500	1,915,284	1,000	105,840*

KTH-TIPS2 database [7]. However, taking only four samples per category still limits the representation of the intra-class variance of materials observed in real-world scenarios. More recently, a spectral material database was used in [18]. However, the samples are imaged from only one single viewpoint. A common limitation of all these databases is the rather limited number of measurements, which are furthermore acquired in a lab environment. Hence, the influence of the complexity of real-world environment conditions is not taken into account.

The Flickr Material Database (FMD) [25] is designed to capture the large intra-class variation in appearance of materials in complex real-world scenarios. Images downloaded from Flickr.com show different associated material samples under uncontrolled viewing and illumination conditions and compositions. While manual segmentations are available, these masks are not always accurate, leading to the inclusion of background appearance and problematic artifacts for material classification. Since the manual annotation is time-consuming, the number of images is very small in comparison to the other databases. While standard classification schemes such as [32] reach excellent results on the above-mentioned databases, there is a significant decrease in the performance on the FMD [17]. This is a hint on the fact, that the CUReT and KTH-TIPS databases are not sufficient to represent the complexity of real-world materials.

Synthetic Training Data. Recombination methods focus on some specific aspects present in real-world examples and recompose them to new examples as done in [11,21] to enlarge the available training data by recombining shape, appearance and background information for pedestrian detection. In [29], new virtual training images are synthesized via photometric stereo for texture classification. This way, less training images need to be acquired. In contrast, rendering techniques can be used to produce new examples based on an underlying model, e.g. pose estimation was facilitated using synthesized depth maps in [27]. In [28], object detection based on 3D CAD models is investigated using viewpoint-dependent, non-photorealistic renderings of the object contours for learning shape models in 3D, which then can be matched to 2D images showing the corresponding object. Furthermore, an evaluation of the commonly used image descriptors based on a photorealistic virtual world has been carried out in [15]. This virtual scenario represents a well-suited setting for analyzing the effect of illumination and viewpoint changes. The methods in [2] and [3] use a renderer to synthesize shading images based on given depth maps and a spherical harmonic model of illumination for estimating shape, illumination and reflectance from input images. This way, a decoupling of albedo and illumination is reached. The decoupling of measured surface material and environmental lighting has also been addressed in [19], where shape and BRDF of objects have been jointly estimated under known illumination from synthetic data, generated from different combinations of shapes, environment illuminations and BRDFs. In [33], geometric textons are rendered under different view-light configurations for estimating geometric texton labels used in a hybrid model for geometry and reflectance.

Recently, this trend has resulted in the development of the virtual MPI-VIPS database introduced in [16] (see Table 1). This database is based on using BRDFs for representing the light exchange on the surface of an object and does not rely on physical measurements but uses a texture map and material shaders of available rendering packages. Bump maps are used to simulate the local mesostructure of the material surface for improving the shading effects. The selection of shaders, viewpoints and illuminations for rendering the materials are closely oriented on the KTH-TIPS2 database. The texture map does not capture intraclass variance and the approximate rendering models result in a loss concerning the realistic depiction of some materials such as aluminum foil, which appear rather artificial, especially in complex light situations. The reason for this is that mesoscopic effects contributing to the appearance of many materials are not modeled. The investigations in [16] therefore indicate that a training set based on the utilized virtual samples alone performs poorly for material classification and a mixture of real and rendered samples is necessary to get acceptable results. In contrast to these studies, we show that the approach for synthesizing virtual samples matters. Our measured database better covers intra-class variances and includes significantly more viewing and lighting configurations than any of the other databases. These dense measurements are required for the realistic depiction of many materials with their characteristic traits in a virtual scene via BTFs to preserve the mesoscopic effects in the synthesized data.

3   Generation of Synthetic Training Data

In this section, we discuss the details of our database of measured BTF material samples and how it is used to produce synthetic training images of these samples under a range of different viewing and illumination conditions.

3.1   BTF Material Database

Since we intend to create synthetic training images, it is necessary to digitize the material samples in such a way that it becomes possible to reproduce the material appearance under nearly arbitrary viewing and lighting conditions. Though a wide range of material descriptions exists, image-based BTFs have proven to be a representation which is suitable for a wide range of materials as already discussed in Section 1. Since their introduction in [8], the technology has advanced considerably, and today devices for the practical acquisition of BTFs at high angular and spatial resolutions are available (e.g. [24]). In contrast to the small number of representative images acquired for the other databases listed in Table 1, these setups allow to acquire tens of thousands of images. Those images are taken in a lab environment and, hence, not directly applicable for typical real-world scenarios. However, this much larger number of viewing and lighting conditions offers the possibility to render high-quality images of the materials under nearly arbitrary viewing and lighting conditions, where material traits are still accurately preserved. For a recent survey on BTFs, we refer to [12].

Our measured database is formed by 7 semantic classes which are relevant for analyzing indoor scenarios (see Fig. 1). To sample the intra-class variances, each of these 7 material categories of our database contains measurements of 12 different material instances. These instances share some common characteristics of the corresponding category but also cover a large variability. With a total of 84 measured material instances, we provide more than CUReT, KTH-TIPS and KTH-TIPS2 (see Table 1). For each of the materials, we have measured a full BTF with 22,801 HDR images (bidirectional sampling of 151 viewing and 151 lighting directions) of a 5cm × 5cm patch with a spatial resolution of 512 × 512 texels. Thus, our database contains more than 1.9 million images. Additionally, for each sample, a height map has been acquired via structured light. This helps to reduce compression artifacts and allows to render realistic silhouettes. We employed a reference geometry to evaluate the RMS error between the reconstruction and the ground truth geometry which was approx. 25μm. The acquisition of both geometry and BTF of a material sample was achieved fully automatically in approximately 3 hours, and up to 4 samples can be acquired simultaneously. In particular, there is no need for manual annotation which is not feasible for large image collections. Our database is available at http://cg.cs.uni-bonn.de/en/projects/btfdbb/download/ubo2014/.

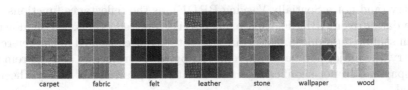

carpet   fabric   felt   leather   stone   wallpaper   wood

Fig. 1. Representative images for the material samples in the 7 categories

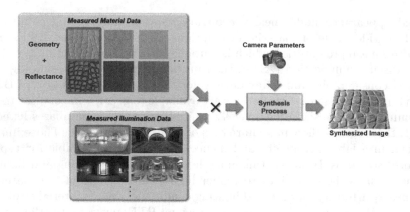

Fig. 2. Synthesis of representative training data: The full Cartesian product of material data (corresponding geometry and reflectance) and environment lighting (environments taken from [1]) can easily be rendered by using a virtual camera with specified extrinsic and intrinsic parameters. The illustrated output image is generated using the material and illumination configuration highlighted in red.

3.2   Synthesizing Novel Training Images

Once the materials have been measured, it is in principle possible to render images showing the materials under nearly arbitrary viewing and lighting conditions. For training a material classifier, we have to decide for which conditions we synthesize the training images, and we need a technique to synthesize a sufficiently large number of images efficiently. Additionally, the material representation used for producing the renderings needs to be capable of accurately depicting the traits in material appearance. In the synthesis process (see Fig. 2), the measured geometry and BTF of a considered material sample are rendered under different illumination conditions simulated by environment maps which is a standard in computer graphics (e.g. [10]). Furthermore, utilizing the measured geometry allows compensating parallax effects. The latter would otherwise be induced by surface regions which significantly protrude from the modeled reference surface and result in a blurring of the surface details. We followed the technique in [23] which is based on the reprojection of the BTF onto the geometry. The result remains a BTF parameterized over the respective (non-planar) reference geometry (and not a Spatially Varying BRDF), as the reflectance functions still remain data-driven ABRDFs. Hence, effects like interreflections, self-shadowing, etc. can still be reproduced. For geometric details not contained in the reference geometry, the major parallaxes are removed by the reprojection and the remaining disparities do not significantly influence the appearance of the synthesized material.

In the rendering process, the exitant radiance $L_r(\mathbf{x}, \omega_o)$ is calculated for each surface point $\mathbf{x}$ via the image-based relighting equation

$$L_r(\mathbf{x}, \omega_o) = \int_\Omega \mathrm{BTF}(\mathbf{x}, \omega_i, \omega_o) \, L_i(\omega_i) \, V(\mathbf{x}, \omega_i) \, d\omega_i, \tag{1}$$

Fig. 3. Examples for synthesized images of the same material sample demonstrating the large variation under different viewing and illumination conditions

where ω_i and ω_o represent the incoming and outgoing light direction. $L_i(\omega_i)$ denotes the radiance distribution in the environment map over the spherical domain Ω. The visibility function $V(\mathbf{x}, \omega_i)$ represents a binary indicator function considering if the environment map is visible from surface point $\mathbf{x}$ in the direction ω_i. To solve the integral, the Mitsuba pathtracer [34] can be used. Due to the enormous number of images we want to synthesize, the use of an efficient rendering technique is mandatory. Therefore, we decided to additionally use an OpenGL-based renderer for generating our database. To simulate the HDR environment in this renderer, we approximated it in a similar way to the work in [4] with 128 directional light sources, distributed representatively over the environment via a relaxation algorithm. In this case, the equation for evaluating the exitant radiance $L_r(\mathbf{x}, \omega_o)$ reduces to

$$L_r(\mathbf{x}, \omega_o) = \sum_{\omega_i \in \mathcal{L}} \mathrm{BTF}(\mathbf{x}, \omega_i, \omega_o) \, L_i(\mathbf{x}, \omega_i) \, V(\mathbf{x}, \omega_i) \qquad (2)$$

where $V(\mathbf{x}, \omega_i)$ represents a shadowing term computed via shadow mapping [22] and $\mathcal{L}$ denotes the set of light source directions, i.e. the ω_i represent the directions to the utilized directional light sources. That way, it becomes possible to render the images with a double resolution full-scene anti-aliasing at a resolution of $1{,}280 \times 960$ pixels in about 2s on a GPU, including the computation of the 128 shadow-maps necessary to compute $V(\mathbf{x}, \omega_i)$. Fig. 3 illustrates the considerable variations in material appearance captured in the synthesized data due to changes in the illumination and viewing conditions.

For every combination of material sample and environment map, we then generated training images, depicting a planar material sample under a range of 21 different rotations of the material sample ($\theta \in \{0.0°, 22.5°, 45.0°\} \times \varphi \in \{-67.5°, -45.0°, -22.5°, 0.0°, 22.5°, 45.0°, 67.5°\}$) and in two different distances to also consider the scale-induced variations in appearance of the materials. To further increase the variance captured by our dataset, we also use 6 rotated versions of each of the 5 environment maps available at [1]. As a consequence, we obtain 1,260 images per material sample (see Table 1). Though we only used planar samples for this paper, the BTFs could in principle also be rendered on arbitrary geometry to further increase the space of sampled conditions.

4 Classification Scheme

Fig. 4 illustrates our classification scheme. For capturing different aspects of material appearance, we use densely sampled 3×3 color patches and SIFT features which represent standard descriptors (e.g. [17]). Although the color of a material varies depending on the environmental conditions and the viewpoint, it still contains valuable information as the variance of the color of a certain material sample under natural illumination is typically limited. Furthermore, we extract dense SIFT features which has become a popular choice in scene, object and material recognition [5,36,17,16]. These features capture the local spatial and directional distribution of image gradients and provide robustness to variations in illumination and viewpoint. In our system, these features are extracted on multiple scales ($s \in \{1, 2, 4, 6, 8\}$). Both descriptor types are extracted on a regular grid with a spacing of 5 pixels as in [17].

Once features have been extracted, an appropriate representation for the content of the masked image regions has to be computed for each type of descriptor. For this purpose, we first generate a dictionary of visual words for the individual feature types by k-means clustering of the respective descriptors extracted from the images in the training set. This allows us to represent the single images either by histograms as used in standard bag-of-words (BOW) approaches or by more sophisticated representations such as Fisher vectors [20] or vectors of locally aggregated descriptors (VLADs) [14] which have shown to yield superior performance when compared to standard BOW. Hence, we choose VLADs for describing the content of the masked regions. This means that all the local descriptors $\mathbf{x}_i$ in an image are first assigned to their nearest neighbor $\mathbf{c}_j$ with $j = 1, \ldots, k$ in the corresponding dictionary with k visual words for each feature type. Subsequently, the entries in the VLAD descriptor are formed by accumulating the differences $\mathbf{x}_i - \mathbf{c}_j$ of the local descriptors and their assigned visual words according to

$$\mathbf{v}_j = \sum_{\{\mathbf{x}_i | \mathrm{NN}(\mathbf{x}_i) = \mathbf{c}_j\}} \mathbf{x}_i - \mathbf{c}_j. \tag{3}$$

The final descriptor is built via the concatenation $\mathbf{v} = \left[\mathbf{v}_1^T, \ldots, \mathbf{v}_k^T \right]^T$. However, the dimensionality of this representation is rather high-dimensional ($d \cdot k$). Here, d represents the dimensionality of the local descriptors (e.g. $d = 128$ for SIFT) and k the number of words in the dictionary. We utilize PCA and take the 250 most relevant components of the PCA space per descriptor type for the training data. The VLAD representations of the test set are projected into this space.

The final classification task can be performed using standard classifiers such as the nearest neighbor classifier, random forests [6] or support vector machines [31]. The latter have already been successfully applied in the domain of material recognition [32,7,26]. Since an SVM with RBF kernel outperformed the nearest neighbor classifier or random forests in our experiments, we only report the numbers for the SVM, where the regularization parameter and the kernel parameter are estimated based on the training data using grid search.

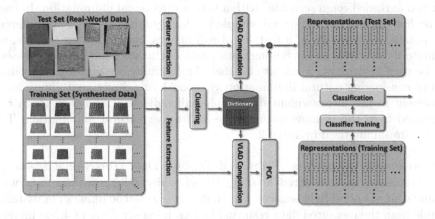

Fig. 4. Classification scheme: Based on the descriptors extracted from the synthetic training data (where the masks for the presence of materials are automatically given) we calculate a dictionary via k-means clustering. This dictionary is used to encode the descriptors per masked region via VLADs. Then, a dimensionality reduction of these VLADs is performed via PCA which is followed by an SVM-based classification.

5 Experimental Results

In the scope of our experiments, we focus on whether real-world materials can be classified using synthesized training data. For this purpose, we first validate our classification scheme on standard material databases. In the next step, we perform a detailed evaluation of using our synthesized training data for material classification which is followed by a comparison to using other datasets. After this, we analyze the potential of our synthesized training data for classifying materials in internet photos. For obtaining the VLAD representation of the individual feature types, we use dictionaries with 150 visual words for the color descriptor and 250 visual words for the SIFT descriptor in our experiments.

Validation of Classification Scheme on Commonly Used Material Databases. With accuracies of 99.11% and 99.25% on the CUReT database and the KTH-TIPS database respectively, our system is on par with recent state-of-the-art approaches as listed in [30] which achieve accuracies of around 99%.

Analysis of Using Synthetic Training Data. Our main experiments target material classification under everyday illumination conditions. For this reason, we acquired photographs of the samples of the 7 classes considering arbitrarily chosen poses of the camera w.r.t. the material samples for the test set $\mathcal{T}_{te,1}$. Different illumination conditions are taken into account by placing the material samples into different environments: a room with natural illumination, a room with a mix of natural illumination and neon lamps, a room with neon lamps and two darkened room scenarios with a rather directional illumination. In each of the 5 scenarios, each material sample is photographed twice using different viewpoints which results in a test set of 840 images. Based on this test set, we evaluate if our synthesized training data (both pathtraced and OpenGL-based) can be used for training a robust classifier. Additionally, we perform an evaluation of considering natural illumination vs. considering directional illumination as present in the measurement data. This will indicate if and how much can be gained from the training data synthesized under natural illumination. The results are summarized in Table 2.

Comparison of Measured vs. Pathtraced Training Data (Directional Lighting). In a first step, we considered learning the classifier using training data with illumination via point light sources. We randomly selected 50 images per material sample from the measured data resulting in a training set $\mathcal{T}_{tr,m}$ of 4,200 images. Using this training data, we obtain a classification accuracy of 58.92% on $\mathcal{T}_{te,1}$. To support our assumption that virtual images are of a similar quality as their real-world counterparts, we generated a virtual duplicate of the utilized measurement device using the pathtracer implementation in [34]. Using this virtual setup, we produce synthetic training data following Fig. 2 for exactly the same viewing and illumination configurations as present in $\mathcal{T}_{tr,m}$. In this case, we use illumination by point light sources as present in the real device instead of environment maps. The resulting classification accuracy of 60.48% closely matches to the accuracy obtained for the real-world measurement data.

Comparison of Measured vs. Pathtraced Training Data (Natural Lighting). Here, we analyzed the effect of considering more complex illumination as encountered in typical real-world scenarios for the training. We captured all the 84 material samples under two representative room environments and an outside environment in a courtyard, and from two different viewpoints which results in a training set of 504 images. Based on this training set, where we expect the camera settings (viewpoints w.r.t. material samples, white-balancing, . . .) to be close to the ones used for the test set, we obtain a classification accuracy of 75.83%. For synthetically simulating this scenario, we captured light probes of the three environments and used them for generating training data under more typical real-world lighting but under the same viewpoints as present in $\mathcal{T}_{tr,m}$. This results in a training set of 12,600 images for which we obtain an accuracy of 68.21%.

Obviously, there is a clear benefit of using representative environments in the generation of the easy-to-produce synthetic training data in comparison to the illumination via point light sources as present in $\mathcal{T}_{tr,m}$. In addition, the characteristic material traits seem to be preserved sufficiently within our synthesized data. However, we recognize a difference in performance between using the training set of 12,600 images synthesized under environment lighting and the use of the 504 photos taken in the respective environments. This might be due to the noise introduced by the pathtracer with only 32*spp* (samples per pixel) which influences the descriptors as well as not perfectly matching the assumptions of far field illumination and the neglection of emitting surfaces. The reason for only taking $32spp$ is that data generation using a pathtracer takes a lot of time, especially if different environmental lighting and different scales are desired. Rendering the 4,200 images for the virtual measurement device (under one single environment map) for instance already takes about two days using $32spp$ with our implementation based on Mitsuba on a Intel Xeon CPU $E5-2690v2$ workstation (32 cores, 3 GHz). We also did not perform a white balancing of the data under the environmental lighting which might influence both descriptor types. Furthermore, the acquisition conditions (view conditions, camera characteristics) of both $\mathcal{T}_{te,1}$ and the 504 real-world training images were similar.

Comparison of Measured vs. Rasterized Training Data (Natural Lighting). As a consequence of the slow rendering via a pathtracer, we used our OpenGL-based synthesis procedure for generating the huge amount of images in our synthesized database. As training set, we consider a random subset of 600 different viewing and illumination conditions from this synthesized data for each of the classes resulting in 4,200 images. In this scenario, our classifier yields a classification accuracy of 72.74% which again significantly outperforms the accuracy of 58.92% obtained when using 4,200 photos acquired during the measurement of the samples in a lab with controlled illumination for the training. It even almost reaches the accuracy of 75.83% from the experiment mentioned before. This might be due to the fact, that we do not encounter the problem of noise induced by the pathtracing approach when using the OpenGL-based synthesis as well as better matching the viewpoint conditions in $\mathcal{T}_{te,1}$ by accounting for multiple scales.

Furthermore, we analyzed the impact of using different numbers of the OpenGL-synthesized images for the training. The accuracy increases with an increasing size of the training data, which is to be expected, as larger training sets cover a larger variance of the utilized viewing and illumination conditions (Table 2).

Comparison of Per-class Accuracies. There seems to be a trend that in particular the samples of the categories fabric, felt, leather and stone can be categorized more reliably when using the synthesized training data (OpenGL-based) with natural illumination in comparison to measurement data with directional illumination (improvements of around 22% (fabric), 10% (felt), 30% (leather), 35% (stone) and less overfitting to the remaining categories). This agrees with our motivation for this study as we expect the samples of these classes to have more variance in appearance under the different illumination conditions due to their deeper meso-structure and their surface reflectance behavior.

Classifier Generalization to Unseen Material Samples in Different Environments Based on Synthesized Data. For each of the classes, we draw a random subset of 600 images with different viewing and illumination conditions from the complete synthetic training data. We split the material samples of the 7 classes into disjoint training and test sets by using 8 material samples observed under 4 different environments for the training set and the remaining 4 samples rendered under

Table 2. Classification on the manually acquired photos in $\mathcal{T}_{te,1}$ using different training sets (*: pathtraced using Mitsuba renderer [34]; **: OpenGL-based synthesis using 5 environment maps available from [1])

training set	illumination type	type of training data	performance on $\mathcal{T}_{te,1}$
4,200 images from measurement	directional	real-world	58.92%
4,200 synthesized images (pathtraced*) using the same viewing and lighting conditions as present in measurement	directional	synthetic	60.48%
12,600 synthesized images (pathtraced*) using the same viewing conditions as present in the measurement data but under 3 measured environments	natural	synthetic	68.21%
504 photos acquired in 3 measured environments	natural	real-world	75.83%
525 synthesized images (OpenGL-based**)	natural	synthetic	62.74%
1,050 synthesized images (OpenGL-based**)	natural	synthetic	65.71%
2,100 synthesized images (OpenGL-based**)	natural	synthetic	68.69%
4,200 synthesized images (OpenGL-based**)	natural	synthetic	72.74%

the fifth environment map as the test set. The resulting accuracy of 62.29% indicates the ability of our classifier to generalize to unseen material samples and illumination conditions. Using more material samples per category and more environment maps would probably lead to an increasing accuracy.

Using Our Synthesized Database vs. Using Previous Synthesized Training Data for Classifier Training. A comparison to other approaches using synthesized data, such as [16], is not directly possible. We focus on different material categories that might be more relevant for analyzing offices, buildings or streets and our synthesized data differs significantly from the data in [16] as we utilize natural lighting conditions which allows material classification outside a controlled lab environment. We show the benefit of using more realistic data for the overlapping material category wood in the supplementary material.

Classifying Materials in Internet Photos. We downloaded for each of our 7 material categories 20 images and performed a manual segmentation on each image. Then, the masked material regions form $\mathcal{T}_{te,20}$. Taking a subset of 15 images per class from $\mathcal{T}_{te,20}$ gives another test set $\mathcal{T}_{te,15}$. Using our aforementioned training data of 4,200 images synthesized using OpenGL and under consideration of environmental illumination gives accuracies of 65.71% ($\mathcal{T}_{te,15}$) and 62.86% ($\mathcal{T}_{te,20}$). In comparison, using $\mathcal{T}_{tr,m}$ for the training results in an accuracy of only 56.19% for $\mathcal{T}_{te,15}$ and 56.43% for $\mathcal{T}_{te,20}$.

In addition, training the classifier on 5 of the images per class not included in $\mathcal{T}_{te,15}$ gives an accuracy of 41.90% on $\mathcal{T}_{te,15}$. The influence of adding synthesized data to this training set on the accuracy obtained for $\mathcal{T}_{te,15}$ as well as a summary of the other results in this paragraph are shown in Table 3. Taking more training data with a larger variance of the utilized illumination conditions and the utilized viewpoints leads to an increasing performance. This clearly demonstrates the power of using synthesized materials for practical applications.

Table 3. Classification of internet images ($\mathcal{T}_{te,15}$ and $\mathcal{T}_{te,20}$) using different training sets (*: OpenGL based synthesis using 5 environment maps available from [1]; †: category leather is not covered in the CUReT database)

training set	illumination type	type of training data	$\mathcal{T}_{te,15}$ 15 internet images	$\mathcal{T}_{te,20}$ 20 internet images
CUReT images †	directional	real-world	41.11%	36.67%
4,200 images from measurement	directional	real-world	56.19%	56.43%
4,200 synthesized images*	natural	synthetic	65.71%	62.86%
internet images	natural	real-world	41.90%	–
internet images+ 4,200 synthesized images*	natural	mixed	66.67%	–
internet images+ 16,800 synthesized images*	natural	mixed	72.38%	–

Except for the category leather, we also used the samples present in the CUReT database to represent the categories. For each category, we selected 92 images equally distributed over the material samples contributing to the classes (carpet: samples 18,19; fabric: samples 2,3,7,22,29,42,44,46; felt: sample 1; stone: samples 10,11,17,30,33,34,36,37,41,49,50; wallpaper: samples 12,31,38; wood: samples 54,56). In this experiment, we obtained accuracies of 41.11% ($\mathcal{T}_{te,15}$) and 36.67% ($\mathcal{T}_{te,20}$) hinting on a bad generalization of the CUReT database to natural illumination, varying viewing conditions and intra-class variances. Furthermore, the image quality is rather low for the CUReT database.

6 Conclusion

In this paper, we have presented an approach for creating synthetic training samples for material classification. This way, it is possible to decouple the acquisition of the material samples from the acquisition of the illumination conditions under which the material is observed. In addition, using synthesized data overcomes the need for time-consuming manual acquisition, annotation and segmentation of images. To evaluate our approach, we acquired a database of BTFs, containing 7 classes with 12 samples each, from which the training data is generated. Our evaluation demonstrates that our approach represents a significant step towards classifying materials in everyday environments and clearly outperforms the alternative of taking images from the measurement of the material samples under controlled illumination conditions as training data. This makes our approach valuable for many applications in the area of texture classification and automatic segmentation of images. We intend to extend the database by additional material classes. In addition, the number of viewing and lighting conditions could also be increased for the synthesized database.

Acknowledgements. The research leading to these results was funded by the European Community's Seventh Framework Programme (FP7/2007-2013) under grant agreement no. 323567 (Harvest4D), 2013-2016 and by the DFG Emmy

Noether program (GA 1927/1-1). The authors also thank Welf Warnecke for helping with the measurements.

References

1. (November 2013), http://www.pauldebevec.com/
2. Barron, J.T., Malik, J.: Shape, albedo, and illumination from a single image of an unknown object. In: CVPR, pp. 334–341 (2012)
3. Barron, J., Malik, J.: Intrinsic scene properties from a single rgb-d image. In: CVPR, pp. 17–24 (2013)
4. Ben-Artzi, A., Ramamoorthi, R., Agrawala, M.: Efficient shadows for sampled environment maps. J. Graphics Tools 11(1), 13–36 (2006)
5. Bosch, A., Zisserman, A., Muñoz, X.: Scene classification via pLSA. In: Leonardis, A., Bischof, H., Pinz, A. (eds.) ECCV 2006. LNCS, vol. 3954, pp. 517–530. Springer, Heidelberg (2006)
6. Breiman, L.: Random forests. Mach. Learn. 45(1), 5–32 (2001)
7. Caputo, B., Hayman, E., Mallikarjuna, P.: Class-specific material categorisation. In: ICCV, vol. 2, pp. 1597–1604 (2005)
8. Dana, K.J., van Ginneken, B., Nayar, S.K., Koenderink, J.J.: Reflectance and texture of real world surfaces. Tech. rep. (1996)
9. Dana, K.J., Nayar, S.K., Ginneken, B.V., Koenderink, J.J.: Reflectance and texture of real-world surfaces. In: CVPR, pp. 151–157 (1997)
10. Debevec, P.: Rendering synthetic objects into real scenes: bridging traditional and image-based graphics with global illumination and high dynamic range photography. In: SIGGRAPH, pp. 189–198 (1998)
11. Enzweiler, M., Gavrila, D.M.: A mixed generative-discriminative framework for pedestrian classification. In: CVPR, pp. 1–8 (2008)
12. Filip, J., Haindl, M.: Bidirectional texture function modeling: A state of the art survey. IEEE Trans. Pattern Anal. Mach. Intell. 31, 1921–1940 (2009)
13. Hayman, E., Caputo, B., Fritz, M., Eklundh, J.-O.: On the significance of real-world conditions for material classification. In: Pajdla, T., Matas, J(G.) (eds.) ECCV 2004. LNCS, vol. 3024, pp. 253–266. Springer, Heidelberg (2004)
14. Jegou, H., Douze, M., Schmid, C., Pérez, P.: Aggregating local descriptors into a compact image representation. In: CVPR, pp. 3304–3311 (2010)
15. Kaneva, B., Torralba, A., Freeman, W.T.: Evaluation of image features using a photorealistic virtual world. In: ICCV, pp. 2282–2289 (2011)
16. Li, W., Fritz, M.: Recognizing materials from virtual examples. In: Fitzgibbon, A., Lazebnik, S., Perona, P., Sato, Y., Schmid, C. (eds.) ECCV 2012, Part IV. LNCS, vol. 7575, pp. 345–358. Springer, Heidelberg (2012)
17. Liu, C., Sharan, L., Adelson, E.H., Rosenholtz, R.: Exploring features in a bayesian framework for material recognition. In: CVPR, pp. 239–246 (2010)
18. Liu, C., Yang, G., Gu, J.: Learning discriminative illumination and filters for raw material classification with optimal projections of bidirectional texture functions. In: CVPR, pp. 1430–1437 (2013)
19. Oxholm, G., Nishino, K.: Shape and reflectance from natural illumination. In: Fitzgibbon, A., Lazebnik, S., Perona, P., Sato, Y., Schmid, C. (eds.) ECCV 2012, Part I. LNCS, vol. 7572, pp. 528–541. Springer, Heidelberg (2012)
20. Perronnin, F., Dance, C.R.: Fisher kernels on visual vocabularies for image categorization. In: CVPR (2007)

21. Pishchulin, L., Jain, A., Wojek, C., Andriluka, M., Thormählen, T., Schiele, B.: Learning people detection models from few training samples. In: CVPR, pp. 1473–1480 (2011)
22. Reeves, W.T., Salesin, D.H., Cook, R.L.: Rendering antialiased shadows with depth maps. SIGGRAPH Comput. Graph. 21(4), 283–291 (1987)
23. Ruiters, R., Schwartz, C., Klein, R.: Example-based interpolation and synthesis of bidirectional texture functions. Computer Graphics Forum (Proceedings of the Eurographics 2013) 32(2), 361–370 (2013)
24. Schwartz, C., Weinmann, M., Ruiters, R., Klein, R.: Integrated high-quality acquisition of geometry and appearance for cultural heritage. In: The 12th International Symposium on Virtual Reality, Archeology and Cultural Heritage VAST 2011, pp. 25–32 (2011)
25. Sharan, L., Rosenholtz, R., Adelson, E.H.: Material perception: What can you see in a brief glance? Journal of Vision 8 (2009)
26. Sharan, L., Liu, C., Rosenholtz, R., Adelson, E.H.: Recognizing materials using perceptually inspired features. IJCV 103(3), 348–371 (2013)
27. Shotton, J., Fitzgibbon, A.W., Cook, M., Sharp, T., Finocchio, M., Moore, R., Kipman, A., Blake, A.: Real-time human pose recognition in parts from single depth images. In: CVPR, pp. 1297–1304 (2011)
28. Stark, M., Goesele, M., Schiele, B.: Back to the future: Learning shape models from 3d cad data. In: BMVC. pp. 106.1–106.11 (2010)
29. Targhi, A.T., Geusebroek, J.-M., Zisserman, A.: Texture classification with minimal training images. In: International Conference on Pattern Recognition, pp. 1–4 (2008)
30. Timofte, R., Van Gool, L.: A training-free classification framework for textures, writers, and materials. In: BMVC, pp. 1–12 (2012)
31. Vapnik, V.N.: The nature of statistical learning theory. Springer-Verlag New York, Inc., New York (1995)
32. Varma, M., Zisserman, A.: A statistical approach to material classification using image patch exemplars. IEEE Trans. Pattern Anal. Mach. Intell. 31(11), 2032–2047 (2009)
33. Wang, J., Dana, K.J.: Hybrid textons: Modeling surfaces with reflectance and geometry. In: CVPR, vol. 1, pp. 372–378.
34. Wenzel, J.: Mitsuba renderer (2010), http://www.mitsuba-renderer.org
35. Wong, T.-T., Heng, P.-A., Or, S.-H., Ng, W.-Y.: Image-based rendering with controllable illumination. In: EGWR, pp. 13–22 (1997)
36. Zhang, J., Marszalek, M., Lazebnik, S., Schmid, C.: Local features and kernels for classification of texture and object categories: A comprehensive study. IJCV 73(2), 213–238 (2007)

Déjà Vu:
Motion Prediction in Static Images

Silvia L. Pintea, Jan C. van Gemert, and Arnold W.M. Smeulders

Intelligent Systems Lab Amsterdam (ISLA), University of Amsterdam
Science Park 904, 1098 HX, Amsterdam, The Netherlands

Abstract. This paper proposes motion prediction in single still images by learning it from a set of videos. The building assumption is that similar motion is characterized by similar appearance. The proposed method learns local motion patterns given a specific appearance and adds the predicted motion in a number of applications. This work (i) introduces a novel method to predict motion from appearance in a single static image, (ii) to that end, extends of the Structured Random Forest with regression derived from first principles, and (iii) shows the value of adding motion predictions in different tasks such as: weak frame-proposals containing unexpected events, action recognition, motion saliency. Illustrative results indicate that motion prediction is not only feasible, but also provides valuable information for a number of applications.

1 Introduction

In human visual perception, expectation of what is going to happen next is essential for the on time interpretation of the scene and preparing for reaction when needed. The underlying idea in estimating motion patterns from a single image is illustrated by the walking person in figure 1. This figure is obtained from the proposed method by warping the static image with the predicted motion at different magnitude steps. For a human observer it is obvious what to expect in figure 1: motion in the legs and arms, while the torso moves to the right. From these clues we build our expectation. (That is the reason why the moonwalk by Michael Jackson is so salient as it refutes the expectation.) Closer inspection of figure 1 reveals that only the face, the legs and hands expose the expected motion

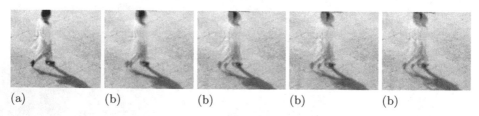

(a)   (b)   (b)   (b)   (b)

Fig. 1. (a) Original still image. (b) Warps with different motion magnitude steps — obtained from predicted motion — overlaid over original image.

D. Fleet et al. (Eds.): ECCV 2014, Part III, LNCS 8691, pp. 172–187, 2014.

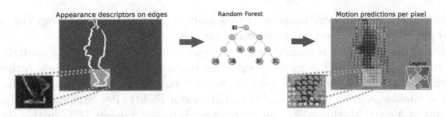

Fig. 2. The Random Forest receives as input pairs of appearance-motion patches and learns the correlation from the part-based appearance to its corresponding motion

direction, whereas the torso cannot reveal the difference to left or to the right. This indicates that motion is locally predictable. Therefore, for building motion expectation we start with local parts rather than the complete silhouette.

The paper shows that motion prediction in static images is possible by learning it from videos and transferring this knowledge to unseen static images. The proposed method does not use any localized object-class labels or frame-level annotations; it only requires suitable training videos. We consider a few applications of predicted motion: weak proposals of frames containing unexpected events, action recognition, motion saliency. This work has three main contributions: (i) a method for learning to predict motion in single static images from a training set of videos; (ii) to that end, extension of Structured Random Forests (SRF) with regression; (iii) a set of proposed possible applications for the motion prediction in single static images. Figure 2 illustrates the submitted approach.

2   Related Work

Adding motion to still images is also considered in SIFT flow [22], albeit with a different goal in mind — global image aligning for scene matching. As opposed to this work, in [22] two images are first aligned by matching local information and, subsequently, the motion from the training frame is transferred to the test frame. Other work visualizes motion in a static image by locally blurring along a vector field [3] or creates a motion sensation illusion by varying oriented image filters [12]. In [6] the authors learn affine motion models from the blurring information in the α-channel, while [4] proposes a grouping of point trajectories based on different types of estimated camera motion. The authors of [16] focus on trajectory prediction by using scene information. Unlike these works, the proposed method predicts local motion by learning it from videos.

Local methods in video-based action recognition only depend on a pair of consecutive frames to compute the temporal derivative [10,17] or optical flow [20,31]. Because the temporal derivative lacks the motion direction and magnitude, this work focuses on predicting the more informative optical flow. Next to optical flow we also consider representing the motion as flow derivatives. These have been used in [7] for MBH (Motion Boundary Histograms) computation.

Cross-modal approaches use static images to recognize actions in videos [15] and appearance variations in videos to predict and localize objects in static images [24]. Similarly, we propose a cross-modal approach: learning from videos and applying the learned model to static images.

Structured learning is suitable for this approach because motion is spatially correlated. Therefore, it is more appropriate to consider motion-patches, rather than look at pixel-wise motion vectors. Several structured learning approaches are available, such as CRF (Conditional Random Field) [19], Structured SVM (Support Vector Machines) [28] or Structured Random Forests [18]. In this paper we use an SRF (Structured Random Forest) because it has innate feature selection and allows for easy parallelization.

In [18], the authors use SRF for semantic segmentation. Here, each feature-patch has a corresponding patch of semantic labels instead of a single pixel label. In contrast to Kontschieder et al. [18], we predict motion in static images. Thus, we work with continuous data (regression) where the labels are patches of measured motion vectors, not discrete classes. Apart from solving different problems: motion prediction versus image segmentation, we also perform different learning tasks: regression (continuous motion vectors) versus classification (pixel-level class labels). The more recent work of Dollár et al. [9] proposes the use of SRF for edge detection. Rather than estimating joint probabilities for the edge-pixels — which would be prohibitively expensive — they map their structured space to a discrete unidimensional space on which they evaluate the goodness of each split. Contrary to [9], in this work the outputs are continuous motion vectors, thus mapping from patches of continuous vectors to a discrete space is not straight-forwardly done and not without discarding useful information.

3   Motion Prediction — Formalism

Closer inspection of figure 2 reveals that the motion magnitude and direction are correlated with the appearance and they are consistent in a given neighborhood, therefore the problem requires structured output rather than single pixel-wise predictions. Thus, to learn motion from local appearance, this method uses a structured learning approach — SRF — which is fine tuned for regression.

A random forest is composed out of a number of trees. Each tree receives as input a set of training patches, $\mathcal{D}$, and their associated continuous motion patches — spatial derivatives of optical flow or optical flow, as in figure 3.a.

Node Splitting. For each node in the tree, a number of splits Ψ, are generated by sampling: two random dimensions of the training features — $\mathbf{F}$, denoted by p_1 and p_2, a random threshold t and a split type that is randomly picked out of the following four split types:

$$\Psi_1 = \mathbf{F}(p_1) \geq t \qquad\qquad \Psi_3 = \mathbf{F}(p_1) - \mathbf{F}(p_2) \geq t \qquad (1)$$
$$\Psi_2 = \mathbf{F}(p_1) + \mathbf{F}(p_2) \geq t \qquad\qquad \Psi_4 = \mid \mathbf{F}(p_1) - \mathbf{F}(p_2) \mid \geq t. \qquad (2)$$

Each generated split, Ψ, is evaluated at every training sample in the set $\mathcal{D}$. This decides if the sample goes to the left child, containing the values larger than t or to the right child with values lower than t.

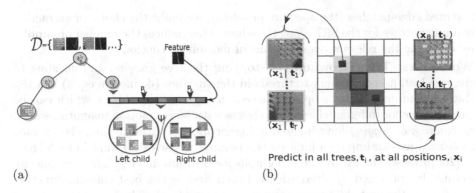

(a)   (b)

Fig. 3. (a) Random Forest splitting: pixel-wise variance over the continuous motion vectors is estimated for all the training samples and all the splits. (b) Motion prediction in neighborhood: the neighbors of the current patch contribute to the final prediction at the current location due to overlap.

Split Optimization. At each node, the best split — Ψ^* — is retained. The quality of a split is often evaluated by an information gain criterion [1,18]. Alternatively, [11] optimizes the splits by minimizing a problem-specific energy formulation. Unlike in the common RF problems, here the predictions are continuous optical flow/flow derivative. This entails an SRF regression — which is based on a motion similarity measure.

In [14], continuous predictions in the RF are approached by estimating the best split as the one corresponding to the smallest squared distance to the mean in each node. Despite its simplistic nature, the use of variance for regression in RF is also indicated as effective in practice in [5,9]. In this case, the predictions are motion patches rather than single labels, which requires a measure of diversity of patterns inside these patches. For this purpose, we use pixel-wise variance:

$$\mathcal{V}_{\mathcal{S}_\Psi} = \sum_{\mathbf{x} \in \mathcal{S}_\Psi} \frac{1}{|P|} \sum_{i \in P} \frac{\sum_j^D (x_i^j - \mu_i^j)^2}{|\mathcal{S}_\Psi| - 1}, \tag{3}$$

where $\mathcal{S}_\Psi \in \{\mathcal{L}_\Psi, \mathcal{R}_\Psi\}$ is the left/right child node, P is the set of pixels in a patch — $\mathbf{x}$, D is the number of dimensions (i.e. the 2 flow components) and μ_i^j is the mean motion at pixel i and dimension j.

Consequently, the best split is the one characterized by minimum variance of patch patterns inside the two generated children:

$$\Psi^* = \mathrm{argmin}_\Psi \frac{\mathcal{V}_{\mathcal{L}_\Psi} |\mathcal{L}_\Psi| + \mathcal{V}_{\mathcal{R}_\Psi} |\mathcal{R}_\Psi|}{|\mathcal{L}_\Psi| + |\mathcal{R}_\Psi|}, \tag{4}$$

where $\mathcal{V}_{\mathcal{L}_\Psi / \mathcal{R}_\Psi}$ are the variances of the two child nodes (eq. 3). The weighting by the node sizes is regularly used in RF to encourage more balanced splits [18].

Edge Features. The features used are patch-based HOG descriptors extracted over the opponent color space [29]. Given that motion can only be perceived at textured edge-patches (the aperture problem), we make the choice of extracting training patches for the SRF along the edges. This reduces the number of samples by retaining the relevant ones in terms of motion perception.

Worst-First Tree Growing. For stopping the tree growing and deciding to create a leaf, it is customary to threshold the variance (defined in eq. 3) [1,5,18]. Rather than deciding to stop only based on variance thresholds, which can be cumbersome for different classes: i.e. classes with larger motion magnitudes such as *running* or *jogging* have inherently higher motion variance than classes such as *boxing*, we can impose a limit on the number of leaves we want in each tree.

[26] proposes the use of directed graphs for decision making. These graphs are iteratively optimized by alternating between finding the best splitting function and finding the best child assignment to parent nodes. Unlike here, the proposed "worst-first" tree growing changes the order in which the nodes are visited, but not the topology of the trees. At each timestep the worst node — with the highest variance as defined in equation 3 — is chosen to be split next. Finally, when the number of terminal nodes reaches the number of desired leaves, the splitting process ends and all terminal nodes are transformed into leaves.

By following this procedure we ensure that the more diverse nodes are split first, thus allowing for a fairly balanced tree at stopping time — when the desired number of leaves is reached. Given that the data is more evenly split, this can be seen as a measure against overfitting as well as a speedup.

Leaf Patch. A leaf is created when all the patches in one node have a similar pattern. To enforce this, one can threshold the variance measure defined in equation 3 or additionally, as discussed above, grow the trees in a worst-first manner and select a desired number of leaves. At the point when a leaf node is created, it contains a set of patches, that are assumed to have a uniform appearance. Thus, we define the leaf prediction as the average over the patches in the node. This is a common approach for regression RF [5,14] and, despite its simplicity, proves effective in practice.

Motion Prediction. Given an input test appearance patch, the goal is to obtain a motion prediction, $\mathbf{x}^*$, from the trained SRF. For this, the method first evaluates at each edge-pixel in the image the most likely prediction over the trees of the SRF. Following the approach of [5,14] we define the prediction over trees as the average patch: $\mathbf{x}^* = \frac{1}{|\mathcal{T}|} \sum_{\mathbf{x} \in \mathcal{T}} \mathbf{x}$, where $\mathcal{T}$ is the set of tree predictions at the current position. At last, because the patches overlap as shown in figure 3.b, the final prediction at each pixel position is the average over all overlapping predictions at that position.

4   Motion Prediction — Learning and Features

SRF Patch Size Selection. All experiments use the same patch size for features and for motion. Figures 4.a and 4.b show that a small patch size would fail to provide an indication for the expected motion direction. On the other hand, large patch sizes would be prone to prediction mistakes since full-body poses are characterized by larger motion diversity, thus, harder to learn than local patches.

(a) Patch 11 × 11   (b) Patch 32 × 32   (c) Original flow   (d) Corrected flow

Fig. 4. (a) & (b) Patch size selection: small patch sizes fail to capture motion direction, while large ones are more error prone. (c) & (d) Camera motion correction — section 6.3: (c) original Farnebäck flow estimation, (d) affine corrected flow estimation.

We have experimented with different patch sizes, and found a patch size approximately 5 times smaller than the maximum image size to be reasonable.

Training Features and Labels. The model learns motion from static appearance features at Canny edges to avoid the aperture problem. Motion is represented by dense optical flow, and optical flow derivatives respectively, measured at every pixel in the patch. For flow estimation we use the *OpenCV* library[1]. One opponent-HOG descriptor is extracted over each training patch. Each HOG computation uses 2×2 spatial bins, 9 orientations and has 3 color-channels.

SRF Parameter Settings. The SRF uses 50 iterations per node during training and another 10 for finding the optimal threshold (eq. 2). Given that the patch-features have 108 dimensions, the number of iterations — usually set to the square root of the number of feature dimensions — is sufficient. All trees are grown in the "worst-first" manner until a number of 1,000 leaves is reached, additionally leaves are created when the variance (eq. 3) goes below a 0.1 threshold. Each tree in the SRF is trained on 20 random pairs of sequential frames.

5 Evaluating Motion Prediction

This section focuses on evaluating the SRF motion predictions with respect to measured and ground truth video motion. The goal of this experiment is to test the ability to learn motion from appearance. For evaluation, we use both KTH [25] and Sintel [2] datasets. The choice for the simplistic KTH dataset is motivated by its laboratory setting providing limited appearance variations and reliable optical flow measurements — limited to no camera motion.

Setup. We use the KTH dataset where the data is split in the standard manner [25]. From each video we retain only a set of 20 sequential frames. We compare the motion predictions against measured flow on the complete data — trainval and test. For each one of the 6 classes we train an SRF regressor containing 11 trees. We train SRFs on the training set and use them to predict on the validation set and vice versa. Finally, we merge the SRFs of the two sets and use them for predicting on the test. Given that we extract motion patches along the

---

[1] http://opencv.org

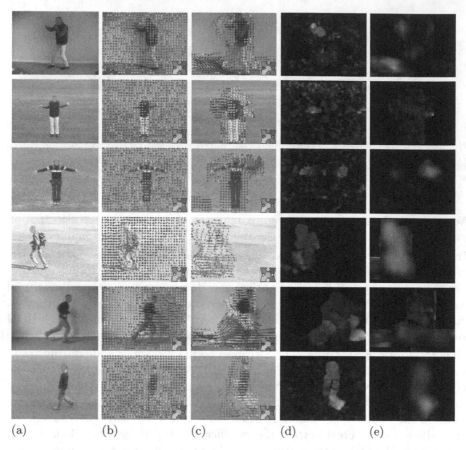

Fig. 5. (a) Original image. (b) Measured optical flow vectors. (c) Predicted optical flow vectors. (d) Measured flow map. (e) Flow map of the predictions (colors as in [23]).

Canny edges, we evaluate the motion predictions at the edge points. We use the standard optical flow error estimation — EPE (End-Point-Error) — which computes the Euclidian distance between the end point of the measured OF and the predicted one. We also evaluate the direction of predicted flow by computing the cosine similarity between the prediction and the measurement: $\frac{x_1 x_2 + y_1 y_2}{\sqrt{x_1^2 + y_1^2}\sqrt{x_2^2 + y_2^2}}$. The orientation of the flow is estimated as the angle between the prediction and the measured OF on the half-circle: $\frac{|x_1 x_2 + y_1 y_2|}{\sqrt{x_1^2 + y_1^2}\sqrt{x_2^2 + y_2^2}}$.

Evaluation. Figure 5 depicts a few examples of measured motion comparative to predicted motion and their corresponding flow maps. Noteworthy here is that the predicted motion is realistic and in agreement with the expectation of the observer. Moreover, the flow maps for the measured flow are similar to the flow maps of the predicted motion. Table 1 shows that for *jogging*, *running* and *walking* the EPEs are lower than the 0-prediction and also on average the predicted

Table 1. Predicted EPE (End-Point-Error) at the Canny edges compared to the EPE of the zero prediction. Cosine similarity at edge-points for direction estimation. Cosine similarity at edge-points using the angle on the half-circle for orientation estimation. The direction and orientation should be as close as possible to 100%.

	Edge EPE	0-Edge EPE	Edge direction	Edge orientation
Boxing	1.23 px	**1.21** px	3.86 %	66.60 %
Clapping	1.13 px	**1.08** px	1.18 %	65.80 %
Waving	1.65 px	**1.59** px	-0.49 %	67.52 %
Jogging	**4.51** px	4.61 px	14.39 %	76.52 %
Running	**8.41** px	8.62 px	26.68 %	77.02 %
Walking	**3.90** px	3.92 px	10.80 %	72.17 %
Avg.	**3.47** px	3.50 px	9.40 %	70.94 %

motion is better than the 0-EPE. While looking at the direction estimation, one can see that the first 3 classes are quite often wrong — due to the characteristic bidirectional motion. On the other hand, the orientation of the flow is considerably better (closer to 100%) especially for the last 3 classes that involve larger motion magnitudes — *jogging, running* and *walking*.

Impact of Flow Algorithm. Table 2 shows the average scores over the classes when the training of the SRFs is based on different existing flow algorithms. Farnebäck and Simple Flow are characterized by smaller errors in both flow magnitude as well as flow direction and orientation — Simple Flow has a 10% relative gain over the 0-baseline in magnitude while Farnebäck gains a 3% over the 0-baseline. Yet the direction of the prediction is more often correct when training on Farnebäck flow.

We run an additional experiment on the Sintel dataset [2] for which ground truth flow is provided. We have retained 10 frames out each training video for learning the SRF and used the rest for testing. We have trained only one SRF containing 11 trees where each tree was trained on maximum 20 randomly sampled frame pairs. We have compared the predictions of the SRF when using the ground truth flow with the measured flow for both Simple Flow and Farnebäck.

Table 2. Average scores over classes at the Canny edges compared to the scores of the zero prediction when the training of the SRFs uses different flow algorithms: Farnebäck, Horn-Schunck, Lucas-Kanade, Simple Flow

	Edge EPE	0-Edge EPE	Edge direction	Edge orientation
Horn-Schunck	4.25 px	4.21 px	02.72 %	65.69 %
Lucas-Kanade	3.18 px	3.22 px	08.30 %	70.03 %
Farnebäck	3.47 px	3.50 px	09.40 %	**70.94** %
Simple Flow	**0.91** px	1.01 px	**18.30** %	70.08 %

Table 3. Average scores over classes on Sintel data estimated at Canny edges. The measured Farnebäck and Simple Flow are compared to the SRF predictions.

	SRF prediction	Simple Flow	Farnebäck
Edge EPE	11.46 px	**09.26** px	14.42 px
Edge direction	38.64 %	71.18 %	**71.26** %
Edge orientation	73.45 %	80.88 %	**84.63** %

Table 4. Average EPE over classes on KTH data estimated at Canny edges when all methods are trained on Farnebäck flow

	0-prediction	SRF	SVR	Least squares
Edge EPE	3.50 px	**3.47** px	5.02 px	6.09 px

The scores are computed with respect to the ground truth flow. Table 3 displays the results. Predicted flow outperforms Farnebäck measurements in terms of edge EPE, while the direction of the predicted flow is often correct.

Comparison with Other Learning Methods. Table 4 compares the SRF motion predictions on the KTH data with motion predictions obtained by training a pixel-wise SVR (Support Vector Regressor) with linear kernel and pixel-wise least squares regression. We train a separate regressor for the x and y coordinates of the flow. The SRF obtains the smallest error — 3% relative gain over the 0 baseline while the other two methods perform worse than the 0-baseline. This experiment ascertains the need for a structured learning regression method.

6   Applications of Motion Prediction

In this section, we bring forth a few possible uses of the predicted motion. One could consider other applications, as this is not a complete list of tasks that could benefit from motion prediction. **Application 1** gives an illustration of weakly detecting unexpected events in videos. **Application 2** evaluates how far off is the predicted motion from the measured motion in the context of action recognition. **Application 3** focuses on the gain of adding motion prediction to action recognition in still images, while **application 4** proposes a method for motion saliency in static images.

6.1   Application 1 — Illustration of Finding Unexpected Events

This application shows a possible use of the motion prediction — finding unexpected events. We do not present this as an end goal of the proposed motion prediction method, but rather as an illustration of its usefulness. Given an SRF trained on a set of videos, one could use the SRF to obtain motion predictions

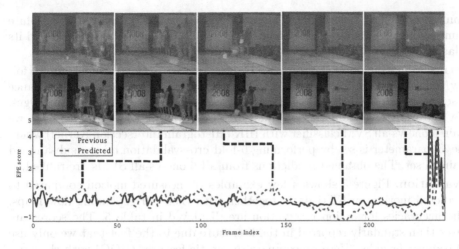

Fig. 6. EPE between measured flow at previous frame and current frame in blue. EPE between measured flow at current frame and predicted flow at current frame in red. The two graphs are centered on 0 for illustration purpose. Images containing unexpected motion together with their associated EPE heatmaps are displayed on top.

at each frame in a given unseen video. If the EPE between the measured motion vectors and the predicted ones is large, it can be assumed that a motion that has not been seen before in the training data occurs at some point in the video. **Setup.** For speed considerations, the SRF uses 3 trees. The training videos are queried from the TRECVid (TREC Video Retrieval Evaluation) [27,30] development set. The frames are resized to maximum 300 px. We obtain motion predictions at each frame in the test video and compute the EPE score between the measured Farnebäck optical flow and the predicted flow. We retain the frames whose EPE scores are over one standard deviation from the mean. The same procedure is repeated for the baseline comparison, but this time by computing the EPE between the motion at the previous frame and the current frame.

Evaluation. Figure 6 displays the EPE error over the video frames, with respect to both previous frame and predicted motion. Frames containing interesting motion are displayed together with their corresponding EPE heatmaps. The video contains a catwalk show during which one person falls through the floor — unexpected event. Noteworthy is that the predicted motion graph is reasonably similar to the one based on the errors to the previous frame, while better emphasizing the interesting moments — when the person falls or is no longer visible in the frame — through the graph peaks.

6.2   Application 2 — Predicted vs. Measured Motion for AR

Being able to predict motion can provide useful information in the action recognition context. The predictions obtained from appearance can be combined with appearance features in an action recognition pipeline. We present this application from a compelling theoretical perspective as we are not interested in absolute numbers but in gaining insight about the feasibility of motion prediction and its relative usefulness when compared to measured motion.

Setup. We evaluate on the same KTH datatset. For action recognition, we follow the setting of Laptev et al. [20]. We extract HOG features for appearance description, and HOF, MBH respectively for motion description at Canny edges. We also use a level-2 spatial pyramid for all descriptors [21]. For each class we train a one-vs-all SVM classifier with HIK (Histogram Intersection Kernel) where the C parameter is set by performing 5-fold crossvalidation on the subsampled trainval set. The obtained predictions from all 6 one-vs-all SVMs are ranked.

Evaluation. Figure 5 shows a few examples of measured motion compared to predicted motion on KTH data, together with their corresponding flow maps. The accuracies for action recognition are displayed in table 5. The scores are lower than standarly reported in the literature due to the fact that we only use 20 frames per video. Here we compare the static features (HOG) with the combination of HOG and predicted motion (HOF and MBH). The measured motion exceeds the predicted motion in itself, but in combination with the appearance, the predicted motion can actually reach the scores of the measured motion. As expected, adding the motion information improves for categories that involve a larger amount of motion such as: *running, jogging* and *walking* and less so for *boxing, handclapping* and *handwaving*. It is worth noting that the combination of predicted HOF and HOG equals the measured HOF for this dataset. This proves that motion, even imperfect, brings useful information.

6.3   Application 3 — Predicted Motion for AR in Still Images

While application 2 estimates how far apart are the predicted motion and the measured motion in the context of action recognition, here we predict motion

Table 5. Action Recognition accuracy on the KTH dataset for HOG only, predicted/ measured HOF — pHOF/mHOF — and predicted/measured MBH — pMBH/mMBH. The underlined text shows where the prediction results are better than static (HOG) while the bold shows the best.

	HOG	Predicted Motion				Measured motion	
		pHOF	HOG+ pHOF	pMBH	HOG+ pMBH	mHOF	mMBH
Boxing	0.58	0.56	0.58	0.61	**0.70**	0.75	0.78
Clapping	0.83	0.64	0.89	0.87	**0.92**	0.89	0.89
Waving	0.97	0.89	**0.97**	0.86	0.94	1.00	0.94
Jogging	0.72	0.61	**0.78**	0.56	0.70	0.78	0.81
Running	0.83	0.83	**0.89**	0.86	0.89	0.81	0.86
Walking	0.97	0.97	**1.00**	0.80	0.91	0.89	0.97
Avg.	0.82	0.75	**0.85**	0.76	0.84	0.85	0.88

(a)   (b)   (c)   (d)

Fig. 7. (a) Examples of images from the static Willow dataset [8]. (b) Warped image using the predicted motion, overlaid over the original image. (c) Predicted flow vectors. (c) The training appearance associated in the SRF with the predictions. More examples of static images animated with predicted motion can be found at: https://staff.fnwi.uva.nl/s.l.pintea/dejavu.

over inherently static images which lack the video compression artifacts or motion blurring. The models are trained on realistic video-data and this application analyzes if the learned motion can, indeed, be transferred to still images. We measure the value of the static motion predictions in the context of image-based action recognition. Again, the goal here is to test the ability of predicting motion and its added value, and less so to improve over state-of-the-art.

Setup. We apply the motion predictions on a static action recognition dataset — Willow [8]. For each class we train a separate SRF on TRECVid data as in application 1. For each image we obtain seven flow/flow derivative predictions — one per class, subsequently used for HOF/MBH descriptor extraction. In the action recognition part we use the same setting as in application 2, except that we extract descriptors densely over the images.

Affine Camera Motion Correction. The videos used for training SRFs are realistic videos characterized by large camera motion which drastically affects the Farnebäck measurements. To correct for camera motion we assume an affine motion model whose parameters we determine by first selecting a set of interest points in the two sequential frames. These interest points are matched between frames and the consistent matches are retained by employing RANSAC. From the kept point-matches we estimated the parameters of the affine model. Given the affine camera motion estimation, we then correct the second frame for this motion and subsequently perform flow estimation. Figures 4.c and 4.d show an example of original flow estimation and camera-motion corrected flow.

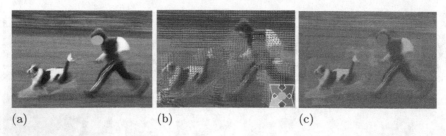

(a)   (b)   (c)

Fig. 8. (a) Original still image. (b) Predicted flow vectors in the still image. (c) Grouping descriptors based on their predicted motion — each color represents a pool in the flow-based spatial pyramid.

Evaluation. Figure 7 displays a few examples from the static dataset together with their predicted motion vectors, the appearance associated in the SRF with that motion and the static image warped with the predicted motion overlaid on top of the original image. Interesting to notice in figure 7 is that the SRF manages to distinguish the foreground motion from the background motion. We notice here, that unlike in the case of KTH predictions (figure 5), there is predicted background flow, but this flow has at all times a different direction from the foreground motion.

The results of Delaitre et al. [8] (0.63 MAP) exceed the proposed motion prediction results due to the more sophisticated model and more fine-tuned features. Provided that we would process our features — HOG and HOF/MBH descriptors — in the manner described in [8], the relative improvement should remain. Despite the drawbacks of noisy motion estimations (i.e. figures 4.c and 4.d), low video quality as well as large camera motion, the SRFs are capable of learning the motion patterns characteristic for each class. By adding predicted HOF to the static HOG descriptors we obtain a relative gain of 1% in MAP – from 50% to 51% — and a 2% relative gain in accuracy.

6.4   Application 4 — Motion Saliency

Motion saliency is yet another possible use for the predicted motion. Objects that move differently from their background are salient and capture the viewer's attention. Being able to predict motion in static images provides the advantage of finding pixels that can be distinguished from their surrounding pixels through their motion. Inspired by [13], we propose descriptor pooling based on predicted flow. Rather than pooling image descriptors on spatial location only, here we also pool them on their predicted motion.

Setup. This application uses the same experimental setup as application 3. We add to the spatial pyramid 10 more pools based on the predicted motion: 4 pools for the quadrants of the flow angles, 1 pool for the 0 prediction times 2 pools for flow magnitude larger/equal to 0.

Evaluation. Figure 8 displays an example of a static image together with its associated predicted motion vectors from the SRF and the corresponding motion grouping in the motion-based pooling framework. We notice that the background is grouped into a different pool than the foreground and also the pixels associated with the dog are grouped together while the ones corresponding to the boy are organized into a separate group.

By adding motion based pooling to static images, we obtain a 1% relative improvement in both MAP and accuracy over the results in application 3. Thus, overall we have a relative gain on 2% in MAP and 3% in accuracy over static HOG features by adding motion — predicted HOF features and flow-based pooling. Adding the flow-based pooling leads to improvements especially for the classes that involve a larger amount of motion: *riding bike*, *riding horse* and *walking*. The outcome of this application ascertains that grouping pixels that have similar motion brings conclusive information.

7 Discussion

The experimental evaluation tests the ability of the proposed method to learn motion given appearance features. One limitation of the method is data dependency — the learned motion depends on the quality of the training data and its similarity to the test data. This can be observed in application 3 where motion is learned from complex realistic videos characterized by noise, motion blur and camera motion, yet the predictions are tested on high quality static images. Another drawback is the class dependency — each action class is characterized by a certain direction and magnitude in the motion of the part (i.e. arms, legs) and the SRFs learn class specific motion (figure 5). Nonetheless, the considered applications show that learning motion from appearance is possible. Finally, the SRF code is made available online at: https://staff.fnwi.uva.nl/s.l.pintea/dejavu.

8 Conclusions

This paper proposes a method for motion prediction based on structured regression with RF. The undertaken task of performing structured regression in Random Forest is novel, as well as the problem of learning to predict motion in still images. We experimentally provide an answer to our first research question: can we learn to predict motion from appearance only? And we prove that this is possible provided proper training data and reliable optical flow estimates. Furthermore, for illustrative purposes, we apply the proposed motion prediction method to a set of tasks and validate that the predicted, imperfect, motion adds novel and useful information over the static appearance features only, which answers our second research question. Finally, motion prediction can be employed in a multitude of topics such as: action anticipation or conflict detection. Another possible use for motion prediction is camera motion removal — if the training videos are characterized by camera motion, the SRF is bound to learn the distinction between foreground and background motion (fig. 7, 8).

Acknowledgements. This research is supported by the Dutch national program COMMIT.

References

1. Breiman, L.: Random forests. In: Machine learning (2001)
2. Butler, D.J., Wulff, J., Stanley, G.B., Black, M.J.: A naturalistic open source movie for optical flow evaluation. In: Fitzgibbon, A., Lazebnik, S., Perona, P., Sato, Y., Schmid, C. (eds.) ECCV 2012, Part VI. LNCS, vol. 7577, pp. 611–625. Springer, Heidelberg (2012)
3. Cabral, B., Leedom, L.C.: Imaging vector fields using line integral convolution. In: Computer Graphics and Interactive Techniques (1993)
4. Cifuentes, C.G., Sturzel, M., Jurie, F., Brostow, G.J.: et al.: Motion models that only work sometimes. In: BMVC (2012)
5. Criminisi, A., Shotton, J., Konukoglu, E.: Decision forests: A unified framework for classification, regression, density estimation, manifold learning and semi-supervised learning. In: Foundations and Trends® in Computer Graphics and Vision (2012)
6. Dai, S., Wu, Y.: Motion from blur. In: CVPR (2008)
7. Dalal, N., Triggs, B., Schmid, C.: Human detection using oriented histograms of flow and appearance. In: Leonardis, A., Bischof, H., Pinz, A. (eds.) ECCV 2006. LNCS, vol. 3952, pp. 428–441. Springer, Heidelberg (2006)
8. Delaitre, V., Laptev, I., Sivic, J.: Recognizing human actions in still images: a study of bag-of-features and part-based representations. In: BMVC (2010)
9. Dollár, P., Zitnick, C.L.: Structured forests for fast edge detection. In: ICCV (2013)
10. Everts, I., van Gemert, J., Gevers, T.: Evaluation of color stips for human action recognition. In: CVPR (2013)
11. Fanello, S., Keskin, C., Kohli, P., Izadi, S., Shotton, J., Criminisi, A., Pattaccini, U., Paek, T.: Filter forests for learning data-dependent convolutional kernels
12. Freeman, W.T., Adelson, E.H., Heeger, D.J.: Motion without movement. In: Computer Graphics (1991)
13. van Gemert, J.: Exploiting photographic style for category-level image classification by generalizing the spatial pyramid. In: ICMR (2011)
14. Hastie, T., Tibshirani, R., Friedman, J.J.H.: The elements of statistical learning (2001)
15. Ikizler-Cinbis, N., Cinbis, R., Sclaroff, S.: Learning actions from the web. In: ICCV (2009)
16. Kitani, K.M., Ziebart, B.D., Bagnell, J.A., Hebert, M.: Activity forecasting. In: Fitzgibbon, A., Lazebnik, S., Perona, P., Sato, Y., Schmid, C. (eds.) ECCV 2012, Part IV. LNCS, vol. 7575, pp. 201–214. Springer, Heidelberg (2012)
17. Klaser, A., Marszałek, M., Schmid, C., et al.: A spatio-temporal descriptor based on 3d-gradients. In: BMVC (2008)
18. Kontschieder, P., Rota Bulò, S., Bischof, H., Pelillo, M.: Structured class-labels in random forests for semantic image labeling. In: ICCV (2011)
19. Lafferty, J., McCallum, A., Pereira, F.: Conditional random fields: probabilistic models for segmenting and labeling sequence data. In: ICML (2001)
20. Laptev, I., Marszalek, M., Schmid, C., Rozenfeld, B.: Learning realistic human actions from movies. In: CVPR (2008)
21. Lazebnik, S., Schmid, C., Ponce, J.: Beyond bags of features: Spatial pyramid matching for recognizing natural scene categories. In: CVPR (2006)
22. Liu, C., Yuen, J., Torralba, A., Sivic, J., Freeman, W.T.: SIFT flow: Dense correspondence across different scenes. In: Forsyth, D., Torr, P., Zisserman, A. (eds.) ECCV 2008, Part III. LNCS, vol. 5304, pp. 28–42. Springer, Heidelberg (2008)

23. Max, N., Crawfis, R., Grant, C.: Visualizing 3d velocity fields near contour surfaces. In: Conference on Visualization (1994)
24. Prest, A., Leistner, C., Civera, J., Schmid, C., Ferrari, V.: Learning object class detectors from weakly annotated video. In: CVPR (2012)
25. Schuldt, C., Laptev, I., Caputo, B.: Recognizing human actions: a local svm approach. In: ICPR (2004)
26. Shotton, J., Sharp, T., Kohli, P., Nowozin, S., Winn, J., Criminisi, A.: Decision jungles: Compact and rich models for classification. In: NIPS (2013)
27. Smeaton, A., Over, P., Kraaij, W.: Evaluation campaigns and trecvid. In: ACM-mir (2006)
28. Tsochantaridis, I., Joachims, T., Hofmann, T., Altun, Y., Singer, Y.: Large margin methods for structured and interdependent output variables. In: JMLR (2006)
29. Van De Sande, K.E., Gevers, T., Snoek, C.G.: Evaluating color descriptors for object and scene recognition. In: PAMI (2010)
30. Van Gemert, J.C., Veenman, C.J., Geusebroek, J.M.: Episode-constrained cross-validation in video concept retrieval. Transactions on Multimedia (2009)
31. Wang, H., Ulla, M.M., Klaser, A., Laptev, I., Schmid, C.: Evaluation of local spatio-temporal features for action recognition. In: BMVC (2009)

Transfer Learning Based Visual Tracking with Gaussian Processes Regression

Jin Gao[1,2], Haibin Ling[2], Weiming Hu[1], and Junliang Xing[1]

[1] National Laboratory of Pattern Recognition, Institute of Automation, CAS, Beijing, China
{jin.gao,wmhu,jlxing}@nlpr.ia.ac.cn
[2] Department of Computer and Information Sciences, Temple University, Philadelphia, USA
hbling@temple.edu

Abstract. Modeling the target appearance is critical in many modern visual tracking algorithms. Many tracking-by-detection algorithms formulate the probability of target appearance as exponentially related to the confidence of a classifier output. By contrast, in this paper we directly analyze this probability using Gaussian Processes Regression (GPR), and introduce a latent variable to assist the tracking decision. Our observation model for regression is learnt in a semi-supervised fashion by using both labeled samples from previous frames and the unlabeled samples that are tracking candidates extracted from the current frame. We further divide the labeled samples into two categories: *auxiliary samples* collected from the very early frames and *target samples* from most recent frames. The auxiliary samples are dynamically re-weighted by the regression, and the final tracking result is determined by fusing decisions from two individual trackers, one derived from the auxiliary samples and the other from the target samples. All these ingredients together enable our tracker, denoted as TGPR, to alleviate the drifting issue from various aspects. The effectiveness of TGPR is clearly demonstrated by its excellent performances on three recently proposed public benchmarks, involving 161 sequences in total, in comparison with state-of-the-arts.

1 Introduction

Visual tracking is a fundamental problem in computer vision with a wide range of applications such as augmented reality, event detection and human-computer interaction, to name a few. Due to the challenges in tracking arbitrary objects, especially the drastic object appearance changes caused by lighting conditions, object pose variations, and occlusion, a tracking system needs to adaptively update the observation model on-the-fly. A well-known danger of this updating over time, however, is the tendency to "drift".

There are several popular strategies in previous studies toward alleviating drift (§2). First, background information should be take into consideration to develop a discriminative tracker, as followed by many tracking-by-detection methods. Second, unlabeled samples from the current frame provide rich information in a semi-supervised manor, and can be used for enhancing the tracking inference. Third, re-weighting the training samples appropriately may help reduce the impact of the noisy and potential sample misalignment during model updating. Fourth, training samples should be adaptively to avoid the loss of sample diversity. Fifth, using the auxiliary data to assist the current online tracking task (e.g., using a transfer learning strategy) is preferable, because it can

D. Fleet et al. (Eds.): ECCV 2014, Part III, LNCS 8691, pp. 188–203, 2014.

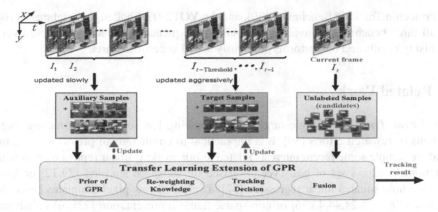

Fig. 1. Overview of the proposed TGPR tracking algorithm

reduce the drift resulting from the direct *Maximum a Posterior* (MAP) estimation over the noisy observation. Sixth, some part-based local representation methods are robust to the partial occlusion and small non-rigid deformation. Although these strategies have been exploited before, integrating all of them together remains challenging.

In this paper, we attack the challenge by proposing a new transfer learning based visual tracker using *Gaussian Processes Regression* (GPR). The new tracker, denoted as TGPR, naturally addresses the drifting issue from six aforementioned aspects.

First, we explicitly model the probability of target appearances in a GPR framework, and then a latent variable is naturally introduced to locate the best tracking candidates. In this process, the background information consists of the negative samples for regression. Also, the unlabeled samples (tracking candidates) are exploited when the prior of GPR is defined, so that the observation model is inferred in a semi-supervised fashion.

Second, we divide the training samples into two categories and treat them differently: the *auxiliary samples* (collected from the very early frames) are updated slowly and carefully; the *target samples* (from most recent frames) are updated quickly and aggressively. Such strategy allows us to re-weight the auxiliary samples, which is closely related to the current tracking status. The re-weighting helps to reduce the impact of the noisy and potential sample misalignment when the auxiliary samples are locate the best tracking candidates.

Third, the re-weighting of the auxiliary samples can be viewed as the knowledge that can be effectively exploited in a transfer learning framework. In particular, we adopt the task-transfer strategy [38], where the tracking decision using the re-weighted auxiliary samples assists the decision using target samples by fusing these two decisions. Their collaboration circumvents the direct *Maximum a Posterior* (MAP) estimation over the most likely noisy observation model, and allows the use of a new strategy similar to the *Minimum Uncertainty Gap* (MUG) estimation [19]. In addition, we define the prior of GPR by a local patch representation method to achieve robustness against occlusion.

Figure 1 overviews the proposed approach. For fairly evaluating the proposed tracker and reducing subjective bias as suggested by [28], we test TGPR on three recently proposed online tracking benchmarks: the CVPR2013 Visual Tracker Benchmark [35], the Princeton Tracking Benchmark [30], and the VOT2013 Challenge Benchmark [16]. On all three benchmarks, involving in total 161 sequences, TGPR has achieved very promising results and outperforms previously tested state-of-the-arts.

2   Related Work

Model-Free Tracking. Single target visual tracking has long been attracting large amounts of research efforts [39]. It is impractical to enumerate all previous work, instead we sample some recent interests related to our work: i) linear representation with a dictionary, e.g., a set of basis vectors based on subspace learning [29,12] or least soft-threshold squares linear regression [32], a series of raw pixel templates based on sparse coding [25,24,44,43,36] or non-sparse linear representation [22]; ii) collaboration of multiple tracking models, e.g., Interacting *Markov Chain Monto Carlo* (MCMC) based [17,18,19], local/global combination based [45]; iii) part-based models, e.g., fragments voting based [1,9,5], incorporating spatial constraints between the parts [42,37], alignment-pooling across the local patches [14]; iv) and the widely followed tracking-by-detection (or discriminative) methods [6,7,20,2,8,21,31,45], which treat the tracking problem as a classification task. All these trackers adaptively update tracking models to accommodate the appearance changes and new information during tracking.

Alleviate Drifts. Much progress has been made in alleviating drifts. Previous strategies mainly consist of following aspects. i) Some studies [14,36,23] observe that straight-forward and frequent update of new observations may cause gradual drifting due to accumulated errors and loss of sample diversity. So some strategies, e.g., slow update of old templates and quick update of new ones by assigning different update probability to them [14], multi-lifespan setting [36,23], are adopted. ii) Some studies [7,41,45,19] notice that appearance models are often updated with noisy and potentially misaligned samples, which often leads to drifting. So their solutions incorporate the data-independent knowledge, e.g., a fixed prior classifier trained by the labeled samples from the first frame [7], a measurement matrix for compressive sensing [41], a fixed dictionary for histogram generation [45], or utilize the MUG estimation instead of the MAP estimation [19]. iii) Some work [9,14], based on the part-based model, focuses on selectively updating the parts of the object to handle the tracking drift caused by heavy occlusion; other work [26,3,45] use occlusion detection strategy to determine whether the template should be updated with the new observation. iv) Many tracking-by-detection methods and some others [43,22] reduce the drifting effects by incorporating background samples.

Re-weight the Training Samples. Re-weighting tracking samples has been widely used in the sparse coding based tracking methods (e.g., [44,43]), however the importance of re-weighting the training samples is hardly observed in the tracking-by-detection methods with a few exceptions such as [22,8,31]. In [22] larger weights are assigned to the recently added samples while smaller weights to old ones using a time-weighted reservoir sampling strategy. Their re-weighting method is prone to drifting when the recently added samples are noisy or misaligned with the current tracking. In [8] the focus

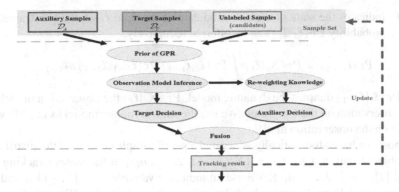

Fig. 2. The relationship among the components of the proposed TGPR tracker

is on re-weighting the support vectors by taking into account the current learner and a bounding box overlap based loss function. In [31] "good" frames are selected to learn a new model while revisiting past frames to correct mistakes made by previous models, which means that past frames are re-weighted to learn a new model. By contrast, our GPR-based solution re-weights all auxiliary samples by considering distances between all pairs of samples. Thus, distribution of unlabeled samples collected from the current frame strongly influences the modelling process.

Transfer Learning Based Tracking. Transfer learning has recently been applied to visual tracking (e.g., [20,34,33]). In [20], the "Covariate Shift" extension of the semi-supervised on-line boosting tracker [7] is proposed. Different than in our work, the auxiliary samples' re-weighting in [20] is based on the online boosting classifier. The methods in [34,33] transfer the prior knowledge from offline training on the real-world natural images to the current online target tracking task. By contrast, in our algorithm the prior knowledge is based on the online regression on the auxiliary samples.

3 The Proposed Tracking Approach

In this section, we first analyze the probability of the observation model in the Bayesian tracking framework and re-formulate it as a new objective. Then, we use GPR to solve this new formulation. Fig. 2 depicts the whole process.

3.1 New Objective of the Observation Model

Visual tracking can be cast as a sequential Bayesian inference problem [13]. Given a set of observed image patches $\mathcal{I}_t$ up to the t-th frame, we aim to estimate the value of the state variable ℓ_t, which describes the target location at time t. The true posterior state distribution $\Pr(\ell_t | \mathcal{I}_t)$ is commonly approximated by a set of n_U samples, called tracking candidates, $\{\ell_t^i, i = 1, 2, \ldots, n_U\}$, and ℓ_t is estimated by MAP:

$$\hat{\ell}_t = \arg\max_{\ell_t^i} \Pr\left(\ell_t^i | \mathcal{I}_t\right), \tag{1}$$

where ℓ_t^i indicates the state of the i-th candidate of the state ℓ_t on the t-th frame. The posterior probability $\Pr(\ell_t|\mathcal{I}_t)$ can be inferred recursively,

$$\Pr(\ell_t|\mathcal{I}_t) \propto \Pr(\mathbf{X}_t|\ell_t) \int \Pr(\ell_t|\ell_{t-1}) \Pr(\ell_{t-1}|\mathcal{I}_{t-1}) \, d\ell_{t-1}, \tag{2}$$

where $\Pr(\ell_t|\ell_{t-1})$ denotes the dynamic model, $\Pr(\mathbf{X}_t|\ell_t)$ the observation model, and $\mathbf{X}_t$ the observation on the t-th frame. We use the same dynamic model as in [29], while focusing on the observation model.

Suppose we have stochastically generated a set of samples to model the distribution of the object location, i.e., $\mathcal{X}_U = \{\mathbf{X}_t^i, i = 1, 2, \ldots, n_U\}$ at the states (tracking candidates) $\{\ell_t^i, i = 1, 2, \ldots, n_U\}$. We use an indicator variable $y_i \in \{1, -1\}$ to indicate "same" ($y_i = +1$) or "completely different" ($y_i = -1$) for $\mathbf{X}_t^i$. We call $\mathcal{X}_U$ as the unlabeled sample set. Then, we can re-formulate the observation model as

$$\Pr(\mathbf{X}_t^i|\ell_t^i) \propto \Pr(y_i = +1|\mathbf{X}_t^i) \tag{3}$$

where the right hand is the likelihood that an observed image patch $\mathbf{X}_t^i$ having the "same" observation of the tracking object.

From the tracking results $\{\hat{\ell}_f, f = 1, 2, \ldots, t - 1\}$ up to the $(t - 1)$-th frame, we extract n_L labeled training samples with the labels in $\{-1, +1\}$. Furthermore, we divide these samples into two categories and treat them differently: the *auxiliary samples* (from the very early frames) are updated slowly and carefully; the *target samples* (from most recent frames) are updated quickly and aggressively. Hereafter we denote $\mathcal{D}_T = \{(\mathbf{X}^j, y_j), j = 1, 2, \ldots, n_T\}$ as the target sample set, and $\mathcal{D}_A = \{(\mathbf{X}^j, y_j), j = n_T + 1, n_T + 2, \ldots, n_T + n_A\}$ the auxiliary sample set, where $n_L = n_T + n_A$ and y_j is the label in the sense of Eq. (3). Let $\mathbf{1} = [+1, +1, \ldots, +1]^\top$, the regression function for the indicators of the unlabeled samples $\mathbf{y}_U = [y_1, y_2, \ldots, y_{n_U}]^\top$ can be written as

$$\mathcal{R} = \Pr(\mathbf{y}_U = \mathbf{1}|\mathcal{X}_U, \mathcal{D}_A, \mathcal{D}_T) . \tag{4}$$

3.2 Analyses

To analyze the regression $\mathcal{R}$ directly, we introduce two *real valued* latent vectors $\mathbf{z}_A \in \mathbb{R}^{n_A}$ and $\mathbf{z}_U \in \mathbb{R}^{n_U}$, underpinning the labels in $\mathbf{y}_A$ and $\mathbf{y}_U$, respectively. This way, $\mathcal{R}$ can be derived as marginalize over $\mathbf{z}_A, \mathbf{z}_U$:

$$\Pr(\mathbf{y}_U = \mathbf{1}|\mathcal{X}_U, \mathcal{D}_A, \mathcal{D}_T) = \int\int \Pr(\mathbf{y}_U = \mathbf{1}|\mathbf{z}_A, \mathbf{z}_U, \mathcal{X}_U, \mathcal{D}_A, \mathcal{D}_T) \, d\mathbf{z}_A \, d\mathbf{z}_U$$

$$= \int\int \Pr(\mathbf{y}_U = \mathbf{1}|\mathbf{z}_U) \mathbf{f}(\mathbf{z}_A, \mathbf{z}_U|\mathcal{X}_U, \mathcal{D}_A, \mathcal{D}_T) \, d\mathbf{z}_A \, d\mathbf{z}_U , \tag{5}$$

where $\mathbf{f}(\mathbf{z}_A, \mathbf{z}_U|\mathcal{X}_U, \mathcal{D}_A, \mathcal{D}_T)$ is the joint probability density.

Analysis 1. Let $\mathbf{z}_U = [z_1, z_2, \ldots, z_{n_U}]^\top$, we model $\Pr(\mathbf{y}_U|\mathbf{z}_U)$ as a noisy label generation process $\mathcal{X}_U \rightarrow \mathbf{z}_U \rightarrow \mathbf{y}_U$ with the following sigmoid noise output model:

$$\Pr(y_i|z_i) = \frac{e^{\gamma z_i y_i}}{e^{\gamma z_i y_i} + e^{-\gamma z_i y_i}} = \frac{1}{1 + e^{-2\gamma z_i y_i}} , \quad \forall i = 1, 2, \ldots, n_U \tag{6}$$

where γ is a parameter controlling the steepness of the sigmoid.

The label generation process is similar for the auxiliary data, i.e., $\mathcal{X}_A \rightarrow \mathbf{z}_A \rightarrow \mathbf{y}_A$, where $\mathcal{X}_A = \{\mathbf{X}^j, j = n_T + 1, n_T + 2, \ldots, n_T + n_A\}$, $\mathbf{z}_A = [z_{n_T+1}, z_{n_T+2}, \ldots, z_{n_T+n_A}]^{\top}$, and $\mathbf{y}_A = [y_{n_T+1}, y_{n_T+2}, \ldots, y_{n_T+n_A}]^{\top}$. In this case, $\mathbf{z}_A$ can be viewed as the re-weighting knowledge extracted from the regression $\mathcal{R}$. Thus, $\mathbf{z}_A$ bridges the gap between the regression of the current tracking task and the indicators of the auxiliary samples. $\mathbf{z}_A$ can also be viewed as a soft substitution of $\mathbf{y}_A$, and is therefore less sensitive to noisy and potential sample misalignment.

Analysis 2. Applying the Bayes' theorem to $\mathbf{f}(\mathbf{z}_A, \mathbf{z}_U | \mathcal{X}_U, \mathcal{D}_A, \mathcal{D}_T)$, we have

$$
\begin{aligned}
\mathbf{f}(\mathbf{z}_A, \mathbf{z}_U | \mathcal{X}_U, \mathcal{D}_A, \mathcal{D}_T) &= \mathbf{f}(\mathbf{z}_A, \mathbf{z}_U | \mathcal{X}_U, \mathcal{X}_A, \mathbf{y}_A, \mathcal{D}_T) \\
&= \frac{\Pr(\mathbf{y}_A | \mathbf{z}_A, \mathbf{z}_U, \mathcal{X}_A, \mathcal{X}_U, \mathcal{D}_T) \bullet \mathbf{f}(\mathbf{z}_A, \mathbf{z}_U | \mathcal{X}_A, \mathcal{X}_U, \mathcal{D}_T)}{\Pr(\mathbf{y}_A | \mathcal{X}_A, \mathcal{X}_U, \mathcal{D}_T)} \\
&\propto \Pr(\mathbf{y}_A | \mathbf{z}_A) \bullet \mathbf{f}(\mathbf{z}_A, \mathbf{z}_U | \mathcal{X}_A, \mathcal{X}_U, \mathcal{D}_T) \ .
\end{aligned} \tag{7}
$$

We model $\mathbf{f}(\mathbf{z}_A, \mathbf{z}_U | \mathcal{X}_A, \mathcal{X}_U, \mathcal{D}_T)$ with a Gaussian process, which can be specified by the mode $\boldsymbol{\mu}$ and the covariance matrix $\mathbf{G} \in \mathbb{R}^{(n_A+n_U) \times (n_A+n_U)}$, i.e.,

$$
\Pr(\mathbf{z}_A, \mathbf{z}_U | \mathcal{X}_A, \mathcal{X}_U, \mathcal{D}_T) \sim \mathcal{N}(\boldsymbol{\mu}, \mathbf{G}) \ . \tag{8}
$$

The non-Gaussianity of $\Pr(\mathbf{y}_A | \mathbf{z}_A)$ (see Analysis 1) makes the $\mathbf{f}(\mathbf{z}_A, \mathbf{z}_U | \mathcal{X}_U, \mathcal{D}_A, \mathcal{D}_T)$ no longer Gaussian, consequently Eq. (5) becomes analytically intractable. According to [11], assuming $\mathbf{f}(\mathbf{z}_A, \mathbf{z}_U | \mathcal{X}_U, \mathcal{D}_A, \mathcal{D}_T)$ to be uni-modal, we can consider instead its *Laplace approximation*. In place of the correct density we use an $(n_A + n_U)$-dimensional Gaussian measure with mode $\boldsymbol{\mu}' \in \mathbb{R}^{n_A+n_U}$ and covariance $\boldsymbol{\Sigma} \in \mathbb{R}^{(n_A+n_U) \times (n_A+n_U)}$, where $\boldsymbol{\mu}' = \arg\max_{\mathbf{z}_A \in \mathbb{R}^{n_A}, \mathbf{z}_U \in \mathbb{R}^{n_U}} \mathbf{f}(\mathbf{z}_A, \mathbf{z}_U | \mathcal{X}_U, \mathcal{D}_A, \mathcal{D}_T)$. In the next we decompose this maximization over $\mathbf{z}_A$ and $\mathbf{z}_U$ separately.

Taking the logarithm of Eq. (7), we get the following objective function to maximize

$$
\mathcal{J}(\mathbf{z}_A, \mathbf{z}_U) = \underbrace{\ln(\Pr(\mathbf{y}_A | \mathbf{z}_A))}_{Q_1(\mathbf{z}_A)} + \underbrace{\ln(\mathbf{f}(\mathbf{z}_A, \mathbf{z}_U | \mathcal{X}_A, \mathcal{X}_U, \mathcal{D}_T))}_{Q_2(\mathbf{z}_A, \mathbf{z}_U)} \ . \tag{9}
$$

Denote $\mathbf{z}^{\top} = (\mathbf{z}_A^{\top} \ \mathbf{z}_U^{\top})$, $\mathbf{y}^{\top} = (\mathbf{y}_T^{\top} \ \mathbf{z}_A^{\top})$, where $\mathbf{y}_T = [y_1, y_2, \ldots, y_{n_T}]^{\top}$. According to Eq. (8), we define Q_2 as

$$
\begin{aligned}
Q_2(\mathbf{z}_A, \mathbf{z}_U) &= -\frac{1}{2}\left(\ln(2\pi)^{n_A+n_U} + \ln|\mathbf{G}| + (\mathbf{z}-\boldsymbol{\mu})^{\top}\mathbf{G}^{-1}(\mathbf{z}-\boldsymbol{\mu})\right) \\
&= -\frac{1}{2}\left(\ln|\mathbf{G}_{\mathrm{all}}| + (\mathbf{y}_T^{\top} \ \mathbf{z}^{\top})\mathbf{G}_{\mathrm{all}}^{-1}\begin{pmatrix}\mathbf{y}_T \\ \mathbf{z}\end{pmatrix}\right) + c_1 \tag{10} \\
&= -\frac{1}{2}\left(\ln|\mathbf{G}_{\mathrm{all}}| + (\mathbf{y}^{\top} \ \mathbf{z}_U^{\top})\mathbf{G}_{\mathrm{all}}^{-1}\begin{pmatrix}\mathbf{y} \\ \mathbf{z}_U\end{pmatrix}\right) + c_1 \ , \tag{11}
\end{aligned}
$$

where $\mathbf{G}_{\mathrm{all}} = \begin{pmatrix} \mathbf{G}_{LL} & \mathbf{G}_{LU} \\ \mathbf{G}_{UL} & \mathbf{G}_{UU} \end{pmatrix}$ and $\mathbf{G}_{\mathrm{all}}^{-1} = \begin{pmatrix} \mathbf{A} & \mathbf{B} \\ \mathbf{B}^{\top} & \mathbf{M} \end{pmatrix}$ are the $(n_L + n_U) \times (n_L + n_U)$ Gram matrix (symmetric, non-singular) and its inverse, and $c_1 \in \mathbb{R}$ summarizes all terms independent of $\mathbf{z}$. As the prior of GPR for our observation model, the matrix $\mathbf{G}_{\mathrm{all}}$ is defined over all samples. $\boldsymbol{\mu}$ and $\mathbf{G}$ in Eq. (8) can be derived from $\mathbf{G}_{\mathrm{all}}$ as follows.

Proposition 1. *By defining the prior Gram matrix $\mathbf{G}_{\text{all}}$ over all samples, we can determine μ and $\mathbf{G}$ in Eq. (8) by* $\mu = -\mathbf{M}^{-1}\mathbf{B}^{\top}\mathbf{y}_T$ *and* $\mathbf{G} = \mathbf{M}^{-1}$.

The derivation is based on Eq. (10) and can be found in the supplementary material[1].

Note $\mathbf{z}_U$ appears only in Q_2, and we can independently optimize $Q_2(\mathbf{z}_A, \bullet)$ w.r.t. $\mathbf{z}_U$ given $\hat{\mathbf{z}}_A$, where $(\hat{\mathbf{z}}_A, \hat{\mathbf{z}}_U) = \arg\max_{\mathbf{z}_A, \mathbf{z}_U} \mathcal{J}$. According to [11,47], by taking derivative of $Q_2(\mathbf{z}_A, \bullet)$ w.r.t. $\mathbf{z}_U$, the optimal value $\hat{\mathbf{z}}_U$ can be derived as:

$$\hat{\mathbf{z}}_U = \mathbf{G}_{UL}\mathbf{G}_{LL}^{-1}\begin{pmatrix} \mathbf{y}_T \\ \hat{\mathbf{z}}_A \end{pmatrix} . \tag{12}$$

Then, let $\mathbf{z}_U = \mathbf{G}_{UL}\mathbf{G}_{LL}^{-1}\begin{pmatrix} \mathbf{y}_T \\ \mathbf{z}_A \end{pmatrix}$ in Eq. (11), we can derive $\hat{\mathbf{z}}_A$ by Proposition 2.

Proposition 2. *The optimal value $\hat{\mathbf{z}}_A$ is given by*

$$\hat{\mathbf{z}}_A = \arg\max_{\mathbf{z}_A \in \mathbb{R}^{n_A}} \mathcal{J} = \arg\max_{\mathbf{z}_A \in \mathbb{R}^{n_A}} \sum_{j=n_T+1}^{n_L} \ln\left(\Pr\left(y_i|z_i\right)\right) - \frac{1}{2}\left(\mathbf{y}_T^{\top}\ \mathbf{z}_A^{\top}\right)\mathbf{G}_{LL}^{-1}\begin{pmatrix} \mathbf{y}_T \\ \mathbf{z}_A \end{pmatrix} + c_2 , \tag{13}$$

where $Q_1(\mathbf{z}_A) = \sum_{j=n_T+1}^{n_L} \ln\left(\Pr\left(y_i|z_i\right)\right)$ *and* $c_2 = c_1 - \frac{1}{2}\ln|\mathbf{G}_{\text{all}}|$.

The derivation is based on Eq. (11) and can be found in the supplementary material[1].

The above derivations in (12) and (13) help us to estimate the mode μ'. In fact, we can also estimate the covariance $\boldsymbol{\Sigma}$ and thus Eq. (5) is computationally feasible. That is because determining Eq. (5) reduces to computing $\Pr\left(\mathbf{y}_U = \mathbf{1}|\mathcal{X}_U, \mathcal{D}_A, \mathcal{D}_T\right) = \int \Pr\left(\mathbf{y}_U = \mathbf{1}|\mathbf{z}_U\right)\mathbf{f}\left(\mathbf{z}_U|\hat{\mathbf{z}}_A, \mathcal{X}_U, \mathcal{D}_A, \mathcal{D}_T\right)d\mathbf{z}_U$, and $\mathbf{f}\left(\mathbf{z}_U|\hat{\mathbf{z}}_A, \mathcal{X}_U, \mathcal{D}_A, \mathcal{D}_T\right)$ is approximated by a Gaussian parameterized by μ' and $\boldsymbol{\Sigma}$ (see [11] for more details).

Analysis 3. We use an iterative Newton-Raphson scheme to find the optimal value $\hat{\mathbf{z}}_A$ in Proposition 2. Let $\rho(z_j) = (1+e^{-2\gamma z_j})^{-1}$, where $j = n_T+1, n_T+2, \ldots, n_T+n_A$. Since $y_j \in \{-1, +1\}$, the auxiliary data generation model can be written as

$$\Pr\left(y_j|z_j\right) = \frac{e^{\gamma z_j y_j}}{e^{\gamma z_j y_j} + e^{-\gamma z_j y_j}} = \rho(z_j)^{\frac{y_j+1}{2}}(1-\rho(z_j))^{\frac{1-y_j}{2}} , \tag{14}$$

therefore

$$Q_1(\mathbf{z}_A) = \gamma\left(\mathbf{y}_A - 1\right)^{\top}\mathbf{z}_A - \sum_{j=n_T+1}^{n_L} \ln\left(1 + e^{-2\gamma z_j}\right) . \tag{15}$$

Let $\mathbf{G}_{LL}^{-1} = \begin{pmatrix} \mathbf{F}_{TT} & \mathbf{F}_{TA} \\ \mathbf{F}_{AT} & \mathbf{F}_{AA} \end{pmatrix}$, we can estimate $\hat{\mathbf{z}}_A$ by taking derivative of $\mathcal{J}$ w.r.t. $\mathbf{z}_A$,

$$\frac{\partial\mathcal{J}}{\partial\mathbf{z}_A} = \gamma(\mathbf{y}_A - 1) + 2\gamma\left(1 - \rho(\mathbf{z}_A)\right) - \mathbf{F}_{AA}\mathbf{z}_A - \frac{1}{2}\mathbf{F}_{TA}^{\top}\mathbf{y}_T - \frac{1}{2}\mathbf{F}_{AT}\mathbf{y}_T , \tag{16}$$

---

[1] http://www.dabi.temple.edu/~hbling/code/TGPR.htm

where $\rho(z_A) = [\rho(z_{n_T+1}), \rho(z_{n_T+2}), \ldots, \rho(z_{n_L})]^\top$. The term $\rho(z_A)$ makes it impossible to compute $\hat{z}_A$ in a closed form. Instead we use Newton-Raphson algorithm,

$$z_A^{m+1} \leftarrow z_A^m - \eta \mathbf{H}^{-1} \frac{\partial \mathcal{J}}{\partial z_A}\Big|_{z_A^m} \tag{17}$$

where $\eta \in \mathbb{R}^+$ is chosen so that $\mathcal{J}^{m+1} > \mathcal{J}^m$, and $\mathbf{H}$ is the Hessian matrix defined as

$$\mathbf{H} = \left[\frac{\partial^2 \mathcal{J}}{\partial z_i \partial z_j}\Big|_{z_A} \right] = -\mathbf{F}_{AA} - \mathbf{P} \tag{18}$$

where $\mathbf{P}$ is a diagonal matrix with elements $P_{ii} = 4\gamma^2 \rho(z_i)(1 - \rho(z_i))$.

Analysis 4. An important aspect of GPR in our model lies in constructing the prior Gram or kernel matrix $\mathbf{G}_{\text{all}}$ in (11). A popular way is to define the matrix entries in a "local" manner. For example, in a radial basis function (RBF) kernel $\mathbf{K}$, the matrix element $k_{ij} = \exp(-d_{ij}^2/\alpha^2)$ depends only on the distance d_{ij} between the i, j-th items. Such definition ignores the information encoded in unlabeled samples. Addressing this issue, we define the Gram matrix $\mathbf{G}_{\text{all}}$ based on a weighted graph to explore the manifold structure of all samples (both labelled and unlabeled), as suggested in [46,47] following the intuition that similar samples often share similar labels.

Consider a graph $\mathcal{G} = (V, E)$ with the node set $V = T \cup A \cup U$ corresponding to all $n = n_L + n_U$ samples, where $T = \{1, \ldots, n_T\}$ denotes labeled target samples, $A = \{n_T+1, \ldots, n_T+n_A\}$ the labeled auxiliary samples, and $U = \{n_L+1, \ldots, n_L+n_U\}$ the unlabeled samples. We define weight matrix $\mathbf{W} = [w_{ij}] \in \mathbb{R}^{n \times n}$ on the edges of the graph using the local patch representation in [12]. This benefits the robust tracking, especially under partial occlusion. For the i-th and j-th samples, the weight w_{ij} is defined by the spatially weighted log-Euclidean Riemannian Metric over block-based covariance descriptors. Specifically, for the i-th sample, we first divide its image patch into $N_r \times N_c$ blocks, and then describe its (p, q)-th block by a covariance matrix $\mathbf{C}_i^{pq}$. Specifically, w_{ij} is defined as

$$w_{ij} = \frac{1}{\sum_{p,q} \beta_{p,q}} \sum_{p,q} \beta_{p,q} \exp\left(-\frac{\|\log \mathbf{C}_i^{pq} - \log \mathbf{C}_j^{pq}\|^2}{\sigma_i^{pq} \sigma_j^{pq}} \right) \tag{19}$$

where σ_i^{pq} is a local scaling factor proposed by [40]; $\beta_{p,q} = \exp(-\frac{\|\text{pos}^{pq} - \text{pos}^o\|^2}{2\sigma_{\text{spatial}}^2})$ is the spatial weight, in which pos^{pq} indicates the position of the (p, q)-th block, pos^o the position of the block center, and σ_{spatial} the scaling factor.

Instead of connecting all pairs of nodes in V, we restrict the edges to be within the k-nearest-neighborhood, where k controls the density of the graph and the sparsity of $\mathbf{W}$. We can hence define the combinatorial Laplacian Δ of $\mathcal{G}$ in the matrix form as $\Delta = \mathbf{D} - \mathbf{W}$, where $\mathbf{D} = \text{diag}(D_{ii})$ is the diagonal matrix with $D_{ii} = \sum_j w_{ij}$.

Finally, we define the Gram matrix as $\mathbf{G}_{\text{all}} = (\Delta + \mathbf{I}/\lambda^2)^{-1}$, where the regularization term $\mathbf{I}/\lambda^2$ guards $\Delta + \mathbf{I}/\lambda^2$ from being singular. From the definition of $\mathbf{G}_{\text{all}}$ we can see that, the prior covariance in Eq. (11) between any two samples i, j in general depends

---

Algorithm 1. Transfer with GPR for Tracking

Input: Target sample set $\mathcal{D}_T$, auxiliary sample set $\mathcal{D}_A$, and unlabeled sample dataset $\mathcal{X}_U$
Output: The node set V_{res} (with size limit n_V) of the unlabeled samples that are most likely to belong to the tracking object.

1: **if** $n_A \leq$ Threshold **then**
2:     Calculate $\mathbf{W}_t$ over the target and unlabeled samples from Eq. (19);
3:     Construct $\mathbf{G}_{\text{all}}^t$ according to Analysis 4;
4:     **Target tracking:** $\mathbf{z}_U^{\hat{t}} = \mathbf{G}_{UT}\mathbf{G}_{TT}^{-1}\mathbf{y}_T$;
5:     $[\bullet, \text{Idx}_t] = \text{sort}(\mathbf{z}_U^{\hat{t}}, \text{'descend'})$;
6:     $V_{\text{res}} = \text{Idx}_t(1 : n_V)$;
7: **else**
8:     Calculate $\mathbf{W}$ over all the target, auxiliary and unlabeled samples from Eq. (19);
9:     Construct $\mathbf{G}_{\text{all}}$ according to Analysis 4;
10:     Calculate $\hat{\mathbf{z}}_A$ from Eq. (17) until convergence;
11:     Let $\mathbf{W}_a = \mathbf{W}(n_T + 1 : n, \ n_T + 1 : n)$ and construct $\mathbf{G}_{\text{all}}^a$ according to Analysis 4;
12:     **Auxiliary tracking:** $\mathbf{z}_U^{\hat{a}} = \mathbf{G}_{UA}\mathbf{G}_{AA}^{-1}\hat{\mathbf{z}}_A$;
13:     Construct $\mathbf{W}_t = \begin{pmatrix} \mathbf{W}(1 : n_T, \ 1 : n_T) & \mathbf{W}(1 : n_T, \ n_L + 1 : n) \\ \mathbf{W}(n_L + 1 : n, \ 1 : n_T) & \mathbf{W}(n_L + 1 : n, \ n_L + 1 : n) \end{pmatrix}$;
14:     Construct $\mathbf{G}_{\text{all}}^t$ according to Analysis 4;
15:     **Target tracking:** $\mathbf{z}_U^{\hat{t}} = \mathbf{G}_{UT}\mathbf{G}_{TT}^{-1}\mathbf{y}_T$;
16:     /* Fusing two trackers, 'pool' is the size of candidate pool */
17:     $[\bullet, \text{Idx}_a] = \text{sort}(\mathbf{z}_U^{\hat{a}}, \text{'descend'})$;
18:     $[\bullet, \text{Idx}_t] = \text{sort}(\mathbf{z}_U^{\hat{t}}, \text{'descend'})$;
19:     $V_A = \text{Idx}_a(1 : \text{pool}) \setminus \{i : \text{Idx}_a(i) \notin \text{Idx}_t(1 : \text{pool})\}$;
20:     $V_T = \text{Idx}_t(1 : \text{pool}) \setminus \{i : \text{Idx}_t(i) \notin \text{Idx}_a(1 : \text{pool})\}$;
21:     **if** $|V_A| >$ pool/2 **then**
22:         $V_{\text{res}} = V_A(1 : \min(n_V, \text{pool}/2))$;
23:     **else if** $|V_A| = 0$ **then**
24:         $V_{\text{res}} = \text{Idx}_a(1 : n_V)$;
25:     **else**
26:         $V_{\text{res}} = V_T(1 : \min(n_V, |V_A|))$;
27:     **end if**
28: **end if**

---

on all samples – all the target and unlabeled samples are used to define the prior. Thus, distribution of target and unlabeled samples may strongly influence the kernel, which is desired when we extract the re-weighting knowledge $\mathbf{z}_A$.

3.3 Fusion Based Transfer Learning Extension

The value of a latent variable in $\hat{\mathbf{z}}_U$ can be viewed as a soft version of tracking decision. Consequently, our tracker can be based on using $\hat{\mathbf{z}}_U$ to decide which samples most likely have the "same" observations to the object. The larger the value of $\hat{z}_i$ in $\hat{\mathbf{z}}_U$, the more likely the sample has the "same" observation. However, we do not directly use Eq. (12) to compute $\hat{\mathbf{z}}_U$ for tracking. This is because the unlabeled samples relate more to the target samples than to the auxiliary ones, and direct use of Eq. (12) may overfit the target samples and is vulnerable to the misaligned target samples or occlusion. Alternatively, we use the re-weighted auxiliary samples and the target samples to build two individual trackers. Then, the auxiliary decision (made by the re-weighted auxiliary samples) assists the target decision (made by the target samples) by fusing the two trackers. This can be thought as a task-transfer process, in which the re-weighting knowledge is transferred from the auxiliary decision to the target decision.

These two trackers can be derived based on §3.2. Given all the labeled (auxiliary and target) and unlabeled samples, i.e., $(\mathcal{X}_L, \mathbf{y}_L)$ and $\mathcal{X}_U$, Eq. (5) can be reduced to $\Pr(\mathbf{y}_U = 1 | \mathcal{X}_U, \mathcal{X}_L, \mathbf{y}_L) = \int \Pr(\mathbf{y}_U = 1 | \mathbf{z}_U) \, \mathbf{f}(\mathbf{z}_U | \mathcal{X}_U, \mathcal{X}_L, \mathbf{y}_L) \, d\mathbf{z}_U$. Meanwhile, the Gaussian distribution in Eq. (8) is reduced to $\Pr(\mathbf{z}_U | \mathcal{X}_U, \mathcal{X}_L, \mathbf{y}_L) \sim \mathcal{N}(\boldsymbol{\mu}_L, \mathbf{G}_L)$. According to Proposition 1, let $\mathbf{y}_T = \mathbf{y}_L$ and $\mathbf{z} = \mathbf{z}_U$ in Eq. (11), we can find the optimal estimation of $\mathbf{z}_U$ by $\hat{\mathbf{z}}_U = \boldsymbol{\mu}_L = -\mathbf{M}_L^{-1}\mathbf{B}_L^{\top}\mathbf{y}_L$, where $\mathbf{G}_{\mathrm{all}} = \begin{pmatrix} \mathbf{G}_{LL} & \mathbf{G}_{LU} \\ \mathbf{G}_{UL} & \mathbf{G}_{UU} \end{pmatrix}$ and $\mathbf{G}_{\mathrm{all}}^{-1} = \begin{pmatrix} \mathbf{A}_L & \mathbf{B}_L \\ \mathbf{B}_L^{\top} & \mathbf{M}_L \end{pmatrix}$ are the Gram matrix and its inverse over all samples. The blocks in $\mathbf{G}_{\mathrm{all}}^{-1}$ can be derived as $\mathbf{B}_L^{\top} = -\mathbf{M}_L \mathbf{G}_{UL} \mathbf{G}_{LL}^{-1}$. Consequently, we have $\hat{\mathbf{z}}_U = \mathbf{G}_{UL} \mathbf{G}_{LL}^{-1} \mathbf{y}_L$. This is consistent to the harmonic property proposed in [46,47], which shows that the value of soft label $\hat{z}_i$ at each unlabeled sample is the average of label values from its neighborhood.

With the above derivation, we can perform the two tracking algorithms respectively using the re-weighted auxiliary samples and the target samples:

- **Auxiliary Tracking Using $\mathbf{z}_U^{\hat{a}}$:** use the auxiliary samples $\mathcal{X}_A$ as labeled samples with labels $\hat{\mathbf{z}}_A$; construct the prior Gram matrix $\mathbf{G}_{\mathrm{all}}^a = \begin{pmatrix} \mathbf{G}_{AA} & \mathbf{G}_{AU} \\ \mathbf{G}_{UA} & \mathbf{G}_{UU} \end{pmatrix}$ according to Analysis 4; then the soft labels of unlabeled samples can be determined by the auxiliary samples as $\mathbf{z}_U^{\hat{a}} = \mathbf{G}_{UA} \mathbf{G}_{AA}^{-1} \hat{\mathbf{z}}_A$.

- **Target Tracking Using $\mathbf{z}_U^{\hat{t}}$:** use the target samples $\mathcal{X}_T$ as labeled samples with labels $\mathbf{y}_T$; construct the prior Gram matrix $\mathbf{G}_{\mathrm{all}}^t = \begin{pmatrix} \mathbf{G}_{TT} & \mathbf{G}_{TU} \\ \mathbf{G}_{UT} & \mathbf{G}_{UU} \end{pmatrix}$ according to Analysis 4; then the soft labels of unlabeled samples can be determined by the target samples as $\mathbf{z}_U^{\hat{t}} = \mathbf{G}_{UT} \mathbf{G}_{TT}^{-1} \mathbf{y}_T$.

Finally, we use a heuristic fusion method to regularize the target decision with the assistance of the auxiliary decision. Specifically, when obtaining two positive candidate sets according to these two decisions separately, we check the two sets' coincidence degree, e.g., $|V_A|$ in Algorithm 1. When the degree is high, it does not matter whether we rely on the auxiliary decision or the target decision; when the degree is small, we rely more on the target decision to ensure the consistency of the tracking results; when the degree is zero, we rely more on the auxiliary decision to recover from the severe appearance variation and heavy occlusion. We detail this procedure in Algorithm 1. When the node set V_{res} in Algorithm 1 is obtained, the object location can be determined by the average over locations of the samples indexed by these nodes.

4 Experiments

It is not easy to thoroughly evaluate a tracking algorithm without subjective bias [28], due to the influence from many factors such as sequence selection and parameter tuning. Several notable recent efforts [35,30,16] have been devoted to address this issue by proposing tracking benchmarks. Aligning with these efforts, we evaluate the proposed TGPR tracker over these benchmarks by following rigorously their evaluation protocols. In summary, TGPR is run on a total of 161 sequences and has achieved excellent performances in all the benchmarks.

4.1 Implementation Details

The proposed algorithm is implemented in C++ and evaluated on a desktop with a 3.40GHz CPU and 8GB RAM. The running time is about 3~4 frames per second. This C++ implementation of TGPR is publicly available[1].

Samples Collection. We use the dynamic model proposed by [29] for collecting unlabeled samples $\mathcal{X}_U$ from the current frame I_t, where we only consider the variations of 2D translation $(\vec{x}_t, \vec{y}_t)$ and scale (s_t) in the affine transformation, and set the number n_U of particles to 300. When the conditions of lines 22 and 24 in Algorithm 1 are met, the parameter settings of $(\vec{x}_t, \vec{y}_t)$ and n_U are increased by a factor of 1.5. As for $\mathcal{D}_T$, we use the tracking results of past 10 frames $I_{t-10}, \ldots, I_{t-1}$ (or less than 10 in the beginning of tracking) as the positive target samples; the negative target samples are sampled from the frame I_{t-1} around its tracking result $(\vec{x}_{t-1}^*, \vec{y}_{t-1}^*, s_{t-1}^*)$, using dense sampling method similar to [20] (overlap ratio is 0.11) in the sliding region, i.e., $\{\mathbf{X} : \ell(\mathbf{X}) \in (\mathrm{R}(\vec{x}_{t-1}^*, \vec{y}_{t-1}^*, 2s_{t-1}^*) - R(\vec{x}_{t-1}^*, \vec{y}_{t-1}^*, s_{t-1}^*))\}$, where $\ell(\mathbf{X})$ denotes the location of negative target sample $\mathbf{X}$, $\in$ means the center location of $\mathbf{X}$ lies in a certain image region, and $R(\vec{x}, \vec{y}, s)$ denotes the image region corresponding to the affine transformation $(\vec{x}, \vec{y}, s)$. Then, we randomly sample 64 negative target samples. For the purpose of updating the auxiliary set slowly, we collect the auxiliary samples $\mathcal{D}_A$ from the frames before $t - 10$ at intervals of 3 (or 6 for long-term tracking) frames, if these frames are available. The collection in such frames is the same to the collection of labeled samples in [20]. We set the size limit of positive auxiliary sample buffer to 50, and negative auxiliary sample buffer to 200.

Parameter Settings. Note that these settings are fixed for all experiments. In Analysis 4, the weight (Eq. (19)) of $\mathbf{W}$ is calculated by setting $N_r = N_c = 3$, $\sigma_{\mathrm{spatial}} = 3.9$ and σ_i^{pq} calculated from the $7th$ nearest neighbor. The hyperparameter k for controlling the sparsity of $\mathbf{W}$ is set to 50. The Gram matrix is defined by setting $\lambda = 1000$. In Analysis 3, γ in Eq. (6) is set to be 10, η in Eq. (17) is 0.4, and the number of iterations for calculating $\hat{\mathbf{z}_A}$ from Eq. (17) is 15. In Algorithm 1, the size limit n_V of the output V_{res} is set to be 5, Threshold is 30, and pool is 20.

4.2 Experiment 1: CVPR2013 Visual Tracker Benchmark

The CVPR2013 Visual Tracker Benchmark [35] contains 50 fully annotated sequences. These sequences include many popular sequences used in the online tracking literature

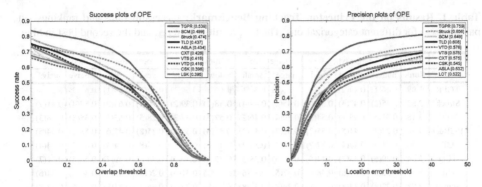

Fig. 3. Plots of OPE on the CVPR2013 Visual Tracker Benchmark. The performance score for each tracker is shown in the legend. For each figure, the top 10 trackers are presented for clarity (best viewed on high-resolution display.

over the past several years. For better evaluation and analysis of the strength and weakness of tracking approaches, these sequences are annotated with the 11 attributes including illumination variation, scale variation, occlusion, deformation, motion blur, fast motion, in-plane rotation, out-of-plane rotation, out-of-view, background clutters, and low resolution.

The providers have evaluated 29 tracking algorithms and released their results along with the sequences. To analyze the performances of different algorithms, the **precision plots** based on the location error metric and the **success plots** based on the overlap metric are adopted. In addition, the providers propose three kinds of robustness evaluation strategies: **OPE** (one-pass evaluation), **TRE** (temporal robustness evaluation), **SRE** (spatial robustness evaluation).

Results. Due to space limitations, we only show the overall performance of OPE for our tracker and compare it with some other state-of-the-arts (ranked within top 10) as shown in Fig. 3. These trackers include Struck [8], SCM [45], TLD [15], ASLA [14], VTD [17], VTS [18], CXT [4], LSK [24], CSK [10], MTT [44] and LOT [27]. Note that all the plots are automatically generated by the code library supported by the benchmark providers. From Fig. 3, we see that: (1) in the success plot, our proposed tracker TGPR outperforms the second best tracker SCM by 8.0%; and (2) in the precision plot, TGPR outperforms the second best tracker Struck by 15.7%.

Note that due to space limitation, we only include the above representative results and leaves more details in the supplementary material. It worth pointing out that, as shown in [35], the results (especially the top ones) in OPE are in general consistent with those in TRE and SRE.

4.3 Experiment 2: Princeton Tracking Benchmark

In the Princeton Tracking Benchmark [30], the providers captured a new benchmark by recording 100 video clips with both RGB and depth data using a standard Microsoft Kinect 1.0. In spite of some constraints due to acquisition (e.g., captured indoors, with

Table 1. Results on the Princeton Tracking Benchmark: successful rates and rankings (in parentheses) for different categorizations. The best results are in red and the second best in blue.

Alg.	Avg. Rank	target type			target size		movement		occlusion		motion type	
		human	animal	rigid	large	small	slow	fast	yes	no	passive	active
TGPR	1.09	0.46(1)	0.49(2)	0.67(1)	0.56(1)	0.53(1)	0.66(1)	0.50(1)	0.44(1)	0.69(1)	0.67(1)	0.50(1)
Struck	2.82	0.35(2)	0.47(3)	0.53(4)	0.45(2)	0.44(4)	0.58(2)	0.39(2)	0.30(4)	0.64(2)	0.54(4)	0.41(2)
VTD	3.18	0.31(5)	0.49(1)	0.54(3)	0.39(4)	0.46(2)	0.57(3)	0.37(3)	0.28(5)	0.63(3)	0.55(3)	0.38(3)
RGBdet	4.36	0.27(7)	0.41(5)	0.55(2)	0.32(7)	0.46(3)	0.51(5)	0.36(4)	0.35(2)	0.47(6)	0.56(2)	0.34(5)
CT	5.36	0.31(4)	0.47(4)	0.37(7)	0.39(3)	0.34(7)	0.49(6)	0.31(5)	0.23(8)	0.54(4)	0.42(7)	0.34(4)
TLD	5.64	0.29(6)	0.35(7)	0.44(5)	0.32(6)	0.38(5)	0.52(4)	0.30(7)	0.34(3)	0.39(7)	0.50(5)	0.31(7)
MIL	5.82	0.32(3)	0.37(6)	0.38(6)	0.37(5)	0.35(6)	0.46(7)	0.31(6)	0.26(6)	0.49(5)	0.40(8)	0.34(6)
SemiB	7.73	0.22(8)	0.33(8)	0.33(8)	0.24(8)	0.32(8)	0.38(8)	0.24(8)	0.25(7)	0.33(8)	0.42(6)	0.23(8)
OF	9.00	0.18(9)	0.11(9)	0.23(9)	0.20(9)	0.17(9)	0.18(9)	0.19(9)	0.16(9)	0.22(9)	0.23(9)	0.17(9)

object depth values ranging from 0.5 to 10 meters), the dataset is valuable for evaluating the state-of-the-art visual tracking algorithms (only use the RGB data). This benchmark dataset presents varieties in the following aspects: target type, scene type, presence of occlusion, bounding box location and size distribution, and bounding box variation over time.

Along with the dataset, the providers also provide the evaluation results of the success rates measured by overlap ratio for eight state-of-the-art trackers (with RGB input) and eight RGBD competitors (with RGBD input). For fair comparison, we only compare the proposed TGPR tracker with the eight RGB competitors, including Struck [8], VTD [17], CT [41], TLD [15], MIL [2], SemiB [7] and the other 2 RGB baseline algorithms provided by the benchmark providers, RGBdet [30] and OF [30].

Results. The groundtruth of 95 out of the 100 sequences is reserved by the providers to reduce the chance for data-specific tuning. Following the instruction in http://tracking.cs.princeton.edu/submit.php, we submitted our tracking results online and obtained the evaluation results compared with the other RGB trackers as shown in Table 1. The results show that TGPR again outperforms other state-of-the-arts in almost all categories.

4.4   Experiment 3: VOT2013 Challenge Benchmark

The visual object tracking VOT2013 Challenge Benchmark [16] provides an evaluation kit and the dataset with 16 fully annotated sequences for evaluating tracking algorithms in realistic scenes subject to various common conditions. Following the protocol, we integrate our tracker TGPR into the VOT2013 evaluation kit, which automatically performs a standardized experiment on the tracking algorithm.

The tracking performance in the VOT2013 Challenge Benchmark is primarily evaluated by the following measures with a different view from the common evaluation criteria. **Accuracy (acc.):** This measure is the average of the overlap ratios over the valid frames of each sequence. The possible values are in the range of $[0, 1]$. **Robustness (rob.):** The tracker's robustness is evaluated by the total number of failures over

Table 2. The results of our tracker TGPR on the VOT2013 Challenge Benchmark. All the values are averaged by running each test on each sequence 15 times.

		bicycle	bolt	car	cup	david	diving	face	gym.	hand	iceskater	juice	jump	singer	sunshade	torus	woman
A	acc.	0.60	0.57	0.45	0.83	0.58	0.33	0.85	0.57	0.56	0.60	0.76	0.59	0.65	0.73	0.78	0.74
	rob.	0	1.27	0.40	0	0.27	2.87	0	2.87	1.67	0	0	0	0.60	0.20	0.13	1.00
B	acc.	0.57	0.57	0.41	0.75	0.58	0.32	0.77	0.53	0.53	0.57	0.73	0.57	0.45	0.64	0.65	0.67
	rob.	0	1.27	0.20	0	0.27	2.87	0.07	3.00	2.07	0	0	0	0.33	0.07	0.60	1.00

15 runs. In particular, a failure is detected once the overlap ratio measure drops to zero. When a failure happens, an operator re-initializes the tracker so it can continue. An equivalent of the number of required manual interventions per sequence is recorded and used as a comparative score.

We run TGPR in two types of test following the benchmark protocol. **Test A:** TGPR was run on each sequence in the dataset 15 times by initializing it on the ground truth bounding box, obtaining average statistic scores of the measures. **Test B:** TGPR was run, initialized with 15 noisy bounding boxes in each sequence, i.e., bounding boxes randomly perturbed in order of ten percent of the ground truth bounding box size. Then, average statistic scores of the measures are obtained.

Results. Because the VOT does not provide their ranking-based evaluation systems to public, we can report the results of our tracker in Table 2. That said, the table shows the great effectiveness of TGPR, with the failure rate often equal to 0, and most overlapping ratios above 0.5. Meanwhile, Table 2 shows that our tracker is not that sensitive to different initializations.

5 Conclusion

We proposed a new transfer learning based tracking algorithm with Gaussian Processes Regression (GPR). Specifically, GPR is innovatively exploited to make a new objective of the observation model, and then a simple but effective task-transfer tracking framework is extended so that drift problems can be alleviated from various aspects. We have also used a local patch representation method based graph Laplacian to define the prior Gram matrix in GPR, so that the distribution of target and unlabeled samples may strongly influence the transferred re-weighting knowledge. We have performed thorough evaluations on three public benchmarks and TGPR has generated very promising results by outperforming many state-of-the-arts.

Acknowledgement. Ling is supported in part by the US NSF Grant IIS-1218156 and the US NSF CAREER Award IIS-1350521. The others are partially supported by NSFC (Grant No. 60935002, Grant No. 61303178), the National 863 High-Tech R&D Program of China (Grant No. 2012AA012504), the Natural Science Foundation of Beijing (Grant No. 4121003), and The Project Supported by Guangdong Natural Science Foundation (Grant No. S2012020011081).

References

1. Adam, A., Rivlin, E., Shimshoni, I.: Robust fragments-based tracking using the integral histogram. In: CVPR (2006)
2. Babenko, B., Yang, M.-H., Belongie, S.: Visual tracking with online multiple instance learning. In: CVPR (2009)
3. Bao, C., Wu, Y., Ling, H., Ji, H.: Real time robust ℓ_1 tracker using accelerated proximal gradient approach. In: CVPR (2012)
4. Dinh, T.B., Vo, N., Medioni, G.: Context tracker: Exploring supporters and distracters in unconstrained environments. In: CVPR (2011)
5. Erdem, E., Dubuisson, S., Bloch, I.: Fragments based tracking with adaptive cue integration. Computer Vision and Image Understanding 116(7), 827–841 (2012)
6. Grabner, H., Grabner, M., Bischof, H.: Real-time tracking via on-line boosting. In: BMVC (2006)
7. Grabner, H., Leistner, C., Bischof, H.: Semi-supervised on-line boosting for robust tracking. In: Forsyth, D., Torr, P., Zisserman, A. (eds.) ECCV 2008, Part I. LNCS, vol. 5302, pp. 234–247. Springer, Heidelberg (2008)
8. Hare, S., Saffari, A., Torr, P.H.S.: Struck: Structured output tracking with kernels. In: ICCV (2011)
9. He, S., Yang, Q., Lau, R., Wang, J., Yang, M.-H.: Visual tracking via locality sensitive histograms. In: CVPR (2013)
10. Henriques, J.F., Caseiro, R., Martins, P., Batista, J.: Exploiting the circulant structure of tracking-by-detection with kernels. In: Fitzgibbon, A., Lazebnik, S., Perona, P., Sato, Y., Schmid, C. (eds.) ECCV 2012, Part IV. LNCS, vol. 7575, pp. 702–715. Springer, Heidelberg (2012)
11. Herbrich, R.: Kernel classifiers from a bayesian perspective. Learning Kernel Classifiers: Theory and Algorithms. MIT Press (2002)
12. Hu, W., Li, X., Luo, W., Zhang, X., Maybank, S., Zhang, Z.: Single and multiple object tracking using log-euclidean riemannian subspace and block-division appearance model. Trans. on PAMI 34(12), 2420–2440 (2012)
13. Isard, M., Blake, A.: Condensation - conditional density propagation for visual tracking. International Journal of Computer Vision 29(1), 5–28 (1998)
14. Jia, X., Lu, H., Yang, M.-H.: Visual tracking via adaptive structural local sparse appearance model. In: CVPR (2012)
15. Kalal, Z., Mikolajczyk, K., Matas, J.: Tracking-learning-detection. Trans. on PAMI 34(7), 1409–1422 (2012)
16. Kristan, M., Pflugfelder, R., et al.: The visual object tracking vot2013 challenge results. In: Vis. Obj. Track. Challenge VOT 2013, In conjunction with ICCV (2013)
17. Kwon, J., Lee, K.M.: Visual tracking decomposition. In: CVPR (2010)
18. Kwon, J., Lee, K.M.: Tracking by sampling trackers. In: ICCV (2011)
19. Kwon, J., Lee, K.M.: Minimum uncertainty gap for robust visual tracking. In: CVPR (2013)
20. Li, G., Qin, L., Huang, Q., Pang, J., Jiang, S.: Treat samples differently: object tracking with semi-supervised online covboost. In: ICCV (2011)
21. Li, X., Shen, C., Dick, A., van den Hengel, A.: Learning compact binary codes for visual tracking. In: CVPR (2013)
22. Li, X., Shen, C., Shi, Q., Dick, A., van den Hengel, A.: Non-sparse linear representations for visual tracking with online reservoir metric learning. In: CVPR (2012)
23. Li, Y., Ai, H., Yamashita, T., Lao, S., Kawade, M.: Tracking in low frame rate video: A cascade particle filter with discriminative observers of different lifespans. In: CVPR (2007)

24. Liu, B., Huang, J., Yang, L., Kulikowsk, C.: Robust tracking using local sparse appearance model and k-selection. In: CVPR (2011)
25. Mei, X., Ling, H.: Robust visual tracking and vehicle classification via sparse representation. Trans. on PAMI 33(11), 2259–2272 (2011)
26. Mei, X., Ling, H., Wu, Y., Blasch, E., Bai, L.: Minimum error bounded efficient ℓ_1 tracker with occlusion detection. In: CVPR (2011)
27. Oron, S., Bar-Hillel, A., Levi, D., Avidan, S.: Locally orderless tracking. In: CVPR (2012)
28. Pang, Y., Ling, H.: Finding the best from the second bests - inhibiting subjective bias in evaluation of visual tracking algorithms. In: ICCV (2013)
29. Ross, D.A., Lim, J., Lin, R., Yang, M.-H.: Incremental learning for robust visual tracking. Int. J. Comp. Vis. 77(1), 125–141 (2008)
30. Song, S., Xiao, J.: Tracking revisited using rgbd camera: Unified benchmark and baselines. In: ICCV (2013)
31. Supančič, J.S., Ramanan, D.: Self-paced learning for long-term tracking. In: CVPR (2013)
32. Wang, D., Lu, H., Yang, M.-H.: Least soft-thresold squares tracking. In: CVPR (2013)
33. Wang, N., Yeung, D.Y.: Learning a deep compact image representation for visual tracking. In: NIPS (2013)
34. Wang, Q., Chen, F., Yang, J., Xu, W., Yang, M.-H.: Transferring visual prior for online object tracking. Trans. on IP 21(7), 3296–3305 (2012)
35. Wu, Y., Lim, J., Yang, M.-H.: Online object tracking: A benchmark. In: CVPR (2013)
36. Xing, J., Gao, J., Li, B., Hu, W., Yan, S.: Robust object tracking with online multi-lifespan dictionary learning. In: ICCV (2013)
37. Yao, R., Shi, Q., Shen, C., Zhang, Y., van den Hengel, A.: Part-based visual tracking with online latent structural learning. In: CVPR (2013)
38. Yao, Y., Doretto, G.: Boosting for transfer learning with multiple sources. In: CVPR (2010)
39. Yilmaz, A., Javed, O., Shah, M.: Object tracking: A survey. ACM Comput. Surv. 38(4) (2006)
40. Zelnik-Manor, L., Perona, P.: Self-tuning spectral clustering. In: NIPS (2005)
41. Zhang, K., Zhang, L., Yang, M.-H.: Real-time compressive tracking. In: Fitzgibbon, A., Lazebnik, S., Perona, P., Sato, Y., Schmid, C. (eds.) ECCV 2012, Part III. LNCS, vol. 7574, pp. 864–877. Springer, Heidelberg (2012)
42. Zhang, L., van der Maaten, L.: Structure preserving object tracking. In: CVPR (2013)
43. Zhang, T., Ghanem, B., Liu, S., Ahuja, N.: Low-rank sparse learning for robust visual tracking. In: Fitzgibbon, A., Lazebnik, S., Perona, P., Sato, Y., Schmid, C. (eds.) ECCV 2012, Part VI. LNCS, vol. 7577, pp. 470–484. Springer, Heidelberg (2012)
44. Zhang, T., Ghanem, B., Liu, S., Ahuja, N.: Robust visual tracking via multi-task sparse learning. In: CVPR (2012)
45. Zhong, W., Lu, H., Yang, M.-H.: Robust object tracking via sparsity-based collaborative model. In: CVPR (2012)
46. Zhu, X., Ghahramani, Z., Lafferty, J.: Semi-supervised learning using gaussian fields and harmonic functions. In: ICML (2003)
47. Zhu, X., Lafferty, J., Ghahramani, Z.: Semi-supervised learning: From gaussian fields to gaussian processes. Tech. Rep. CMU-CS-03-175, School of Computer Science, Carnegie Mellon University, Pittsburgh, Pennsylvania (August 2003)

Separable Spatiotemporal Priors
for Convex Reconstruction of
Time-Varying 3D Point Clouds

Tomas Simon[1], Jack Valmadre[2,3], Iain Matthews[4,1], and Yaser Sheikh[1]

[1] Carnegie Mellon University, USA
[2] Queensland University of Technology, Australia
[3] Commonwealth Scientific and Industrial Research Organisation, Australia
[4] Disney Research Pittsburgh, USA
{tsimon,yaser,iainm}@cs.cmu.edu, j.valmadre@qut.edu.au

Abstract. Reconstructing 3D motion data is highly under-constrained due to several common sources of data loss during measurement, such as projection, occlusion, or miscorrespondence. We present a statistical model of 3D motion data, based on the Kronecker structure of the spatiotemporal covariance of natural motion, as a prior on 3D motion. This prior is expressed as a matrix normal distribution, composed of separable and compact row and column covariances. We relate the marginals of the distribution to the shape, trajectory, and shape-trajectory models of prior art. When the marginal shape distribution is not available from training data, we show how placing a hierarchical prior over shapes results in a convex MAP solution in terms of the trace-norm. The matrix normal distribution, fit to a single sequence, outperforms state-of-the-art methods at reconstructing 3D motion data in the presence of significant data loss, while providing covariance estimates of the imputed points.

Keywords: Matrix normal, trace-norm, spatiotemporal, missing data.

1 Introduction

Dynamic 3D reconstruction is the problem of recovering the time-varying 3D configuration of points from incomplete observations. The theoretical and practical challenges in this problem center on the issue of missing data. In theory, dynamic 3D reconstruction is often an ill-posed problem because of *projection loss* due to the imaging of 3D information to 2D. In practice, a number of additional sources of missing data arise. First, occlusions, self-occlusions, and imaging artifacts (such as motion blur) can cause *detection loss* where points of interest are simply not detected in particular frames. Second, if points are not re-associated to their earlier detection, the system may break one trajectory into two separate trajectories, causing *correspondence loss*. While missing data issues are present in static 3D reconstruction, they are of greater significance in dynamic 3D reconstruction, as the observation system has only one opportunity to directly measure information about the structure at a particular time instant.

D. Fleet et al. (Eds.): ECCV 2014, Part III, LNCS 8691, pp. 204–219, 2014.

Thus, the question at the core of dynamic 3D reconstruction is what internal model a system should refer to when there is insufficient information.

Ideally, a good model should capture all available correlations in the data—spatial, temporal, and spatiotemporal—as these correlations allow us to reason about the information that is missing. Because dynamic structure is high dimensional (e.g., 100 points over 120 frames is 36,000 degrees of freedom), the number of possible correlations is very large (i.e., ~648 million parameters), and learning these correlations therefore requires a large quantity of samples, where each sample is a full spatiotemporal sequence. For most applications, such large numbers of sequences are not accessible. In this paper, we present a probabilistic model of 3D data that captures most salient correlations and can still be estimated from a few or even one sequence.

The correlations present in spatiotemporal sequences are primarily a result of separable correlations across time and correlations across structure or shape [15,1]. Our model represents these correlations as a matrix normal distribution (MND) over dynamic structure, which translate into a Kronecker pattern in the spatiotemporal covariance matrix. We show that this pattern is observed empirically. Additionally, we show that analytical models of the trajectory covariance capture most of the covariance of natural motions. Because such an analytical distribution over shape or structure is generally not available, we instead place a prior over the shape covariance, and derive a convex MAP solution to this problem in terms of the trace-norm. The model presented here applies to any dynamic 3D reconstruction problem, including nonrigid structure from motion, stereo, and multi-view dynamic 3D reconstruction.

Summary. In Sect. 4, we identify the Kronecker pattern in time-varying 3D point cloud covariance matrices, and present a generative probabilistic model based on the MND that explains this pattern. In Sect. 5, we establish a connection between MND and the trace-norm that leads to a convex MAP objective for 3D reconstruction. In Sect. 7, we show how this model unifies a number of shape and trajectory models, both probabilistic and algebraic, used in prior art.

2   Prior Art

The literature on reconstructing dynamic 3D structure is large and we focus our review on methods that directly deal with issues of information loss (either in the monocular or multi-camera case). There are largely two approaches: physically-based approaches, where ill-posed systems are conditioned according to a physically-grounded model, and statistically-based methods, where expected statistical properties of the data are used to regularize the ill-posed system without explicitly appealing to any physical grounding.

The earliest physically-based representation, in this context, was by Terzopoulos et al. [31]; subsequent work [19] presented a physically-based approach using nonlinear filtering over a superquadratic representation. Concurrently, Pentland and Horowitz [23] presented an approach where a finite element model described deformations in terms of a small number of free vibration modes, equivalent to a Kalman filter accounting for dynamics. Taylor et al. [30] revisited the idea of using rigidity but at a local scale using a minimal configuration orthographic reconstruction. Salzmann and Urtasun [26] described a number of physically-based constraints on trajectories of points that could be applied via convex priors. Investigation into statistically-based methods began with Tomasi and Kanade's rank 3 theorem [32], which established that image measurements of a rigidly rotating 3D object lay in a three dimensional subspace. The associated factorization algorithm was extended by Bregler et al. for nonrigid objects [8], positing that a shape space spanned the set of possible shapes. Unlike the rigid case, where the bilinear form could be solved using singular value decomposition (SVD), this formulation had a trilinear form. Bregler et al. proposed a nested SVD routine, which proved to be sensitive to initialization and missing data. A series of subsequent papers investigated various constraints to better constrain the solution or relax the optimization (a sample of major work includes [7,38,35,13,25]). Recently, Dai et al. [10] presented a method that uses a trace-norm minimization to enforce a low rank shape space, and Garg et al. [14] showed that the method can be applied to recover dense, non-rigid structure. Lee et al. [17] formulated a normal distribution over shapes in a Procrustes aligned space.

In conjunction, trajectory space representations were proposed by Sidenbladh et al. [27], which they referred to as *eigenmotions*. Akhter et al. [2] noted that, in trajectory space, a predefined basis could be used, which reduced the trilinear form to a bilinear form and allowed the use of SVD once again to recover the nonrigid structure. Unfortunately, the solution was shown to be sensitive to missing data and cases where the camera motion is smooth [21]. Park et al. [21] used static background structure to estimate camera motion, reducing the optimization into a linear system, and were able to handle missing data. Valmadre and Lucey [34] presented various priors on trajectories in terms of 3D point differentials, showing better noise performance.

A number of approaches have combined spatial and temporal constraints [23,19,20,33,15]. Torresani et al. [33] presented a probabilistic representation, using probabilistic PCA within a linear dynamical system. The shape space and trajectory space approach were combined by Gotardo and Martinez [15], and Lee et al. [18] embedded the Procrustean distribution within a Markov process.

In contrast to prior work, our model describes an explicit parametric distribution over spatiotemporal data that allows us to define a spatiotemporal covariance matrix relating any point in time to any other point in time. The distribution can be estimated from a single sequence and used to calculate covariance estimates for missing data. As summarized in Table 1, we take a step towards reconciling a number of recent statistically-based linear representations in nonrigid structure from motion [8,33,20,2,15,34,10,4].

3   Observation Model for Time-Varying 3D Point Clouds

The time-varying structure of a configuration of P 3D points across F frames can be represented by a matrix $\mathbf{X} \in \mathbb{R}^{F \times 3P}$. The row f corresponds to the

3D shape in frame f, and is formed by the horizontal concatenation of points $X_p^f \in \mathbb{R}^{1 \times 3}$, denoting the p-th 3D point. We will denote by $\text{vec}(\mathbf{X})$ the column-major vectorization of the matrix $\mathbf{X}$, and we will interchangeably use lowercase bold letters to denote the vectorized matrices, i.e., $\mathbf{x} = \text{vec}(\mathbf{X})$.

In practice, due to missing data and camera projection, only a reduced set of measurements of $\mathbf{X}$ are observed. We model observations linearly as

$$\mathbf{y} = \mathbf{O}\,\text{vec}(\mathbf{X}) + \epsilon, \tag{1}$$

where $\mathbf{y}$ is a vector of observations of size n_{obs} (the number of observations), $\mathbf{O} \in \mathbb{R}^{n_{\text{obs}} \times 3FP}$ is the observation matrix, and ϵ is noise sampled from a normal distribution. In the simplest case of fully observed data, $\mathbf{O}$ is an identity matrix of size $3FP \times 3FP$. For entries x, y, or z that are missing, we would remove the corresponding rows of the identity matrix, yielding a matrix $\mathbf{O}_{\text{miss}}$ containing a subset of the rows.

The action of camera projection can also be modeled by $\mathbf{O}$. For ease of notation, let us briefly consider the row-major vectorization $\text{vec}_r(\mathbf{X})$. For this arrangement, the effect of orthographic projection from a single camera can be expressed as a matrix $\mathbf{O}_{\text{ortho}}$ such that

$$\mathbf{y} = \begin{pmatrix} \mathbf{R}_1 \otimes \mathbf{I}_P & & \\ & \ddots & \\ & & \mathbf{R}_F \otimes \mathbf{I}_P \end{pmatrix} \text{vec}_r(\mathbf{X}) + \epsilon, \tag{2}$$

i.e., each of the P points is transformed by a camera matrix for frame f, equal to $\mathbf{R}_f \in \mathbb{R}^{2 \times 3}$. A rearrangement of this matrix can be used with the column-major vectorization $\text{vec}(\mathbf{X})$. The case of a single camera observing the scene with unknown rotations $\mathbf{R}_f$ is the problem of NRSfM. For multiview reconstruction, several $\mathbf{O}_{\text{ortho}}$ matrices can be stacked, one for each camera observing the scene. If some of the projected points are missing, we can concatenate the effect of the matrices: $\mathbf{O} = \mathbf{O}_{\text{miss}}\mathbf{O}_{\text{ortho}}$. In this paper, we assume that the observation matrix $\mathbf{O}$ is known (e.g., via rigid SfM [11] or IMUs); simultaneous recovery of the camera matrices (as in NRSfM) is not the focus of this paper.

Our objective is to estimate the most likely spatiotemporal structure $\hat{\mathbf{X}}$ given the observations $\mathbf{y}$. Note, however, that $n_{\text{obs}} \ll 3FP$, and the problem $\min_{\mathbf{X}} \sigma^{-2} \|\mathbf{y} - \mathbf{O}\,\text{vec}(\mathbf{X})\|_2^2$ is therefore severely under constrained. We therefore take a Bayesian approach to the estimation problem,

$$\hat{\mathbf{X}} = \underset{\mathbf{X}}{\text{argmax}}\, p(\mathbf{X}|\mathbf{y}) \propto p(\mathbf{y}|\mathbf{X})p(\mathbf{X}), \tag{3}$$

where $p(\mathbf{y}|\mathbf{X}) = \mathcal{N}\left(\mathbf{O}\,\text{vec}(\mathbf{X}), \sigma^2 \mathbf{I}\right)$ from Eq. (1). The goal is then to design a prior $p(\mathbf{X})$ that models the data well while remaining amenable to global optimization.

4 Spatiotemporal Prior for Time-Varying 3D Point Clouds

We model the time-varying structure $\mathbf{X} \in \mathbb{R}^{F \times 3P}$ as the sum of a mean component $\mathbf{M}$ and a residual non-rigid component $\mathbf{Z}$,

$$\mathbf{X} = \mathbf{M} + \mathbf{Z}. \tag{4}$$

While this does not reduce the number of variables to estimate, this decomposition will allow us to set sensible priors over the individual components.

Mean Component M. The purpose of the mean component is to capture the rigid shape of the object and its translational motion. We model this component as $\mathbf{M} = \mathbf{1}_F \mathbf{m}_{\text{shape}} + \mathbf{M}_{\text{trans}} \mathbf{P}_{\text{trans}}$, where the mean 3D shape is $\mathbf{m}_{\text{shape}} \in \mathbb{R}^{1 \times 3P}$, and the mean 3D trajectory is $\mathbf{M}_{\text{trans}} \in \mathbb{R}^{F \times 3}$ (containing the per-frame translation of the object), where[1] $\mathbf{P}_{\text{trans}} = \text{blkdiag}(\mathbf{1}_P^T; \mathbf{1}_P^T; \mathbf{1}_P^T) \in \mathbb{R}^{3 \times 3P}$.

We set a uniform prior over the mean shape: a priori, we do not have a preferred shape for objects. Because translational motion of objects that have mass is necessarily smooth, we will choose a prior for the translational component that encourages smooth motion of the object. We specify this prior using a complete trajectory basis $\mathbf{\Theta} \in \mathbb{R}^{F \times F}$, where $\mathbf{\Theta} = \tilde{\mathbf{\Theta}} \mathbf{W}_t$ with $\tilde{\mathbf{\Theta}}$ an orthonormal basis and $\mathbf{W}_t$ a diagonal weighting matrix. The basis vectors and corresponding weights in $\mathbf{W}_t$ are chosen such that smooth trajectories are more likely, resulting in a covariance over trajectories $\mathbf{\Sigma} = \mathbf{\Theta}\mathbf{\Theta}^T$ that characterizes the prior distribution over trajectories:

$$\mathbf{M}_{\text{trans}} \sim \mathcal{MN}(\mathbf{0}, \mathbf{\Sigma}, \mathbf{I}_3), \tag{5}$$

where $\mathcal{MN}$ denotes the Matrix Normal Distribution (MND) [12], with mean $\mathbf{0}$, column covariance $\mathbf{\Sigma}$ (describing correlations across time), and row covariance $\mathbf{I}_3$ (describing that there are no a priori correlations between the x, y, and z components).

Residual Component Z. We model the residual non-rigid deformations of the object as

$$\mathbf{Z} = \mathbf{\Theta}\mathbf{C}\mathbf{B}^T, \tag{6}$$

where $\mathbf{C} \in \mathbb{R}^{F \times 3P}$ is a matrix of mixing coefficients, $\mathbf{B} \in \mathbb{R}^{3P \times 3P}$ is a complete shape basis such that $\mathbf{B} = \tilde{\mathbf{B}} \mathbf{W}_b$ where $\tilde{\mathbf{B}}$ is orthonormal and $\mathbf{W}_b$ a diagonal weighting matrix. Additionally, we model the distribution over coefficients $\mathbf{C}$ as $\mathbf{c} \sim \mathcal{N}(\mathbf{0}, \mathbf{I})$. This corresponds to a probabilistic formulation of the bilinear model of Akhter et al. [1], and results in a matrix normal distribution

$$\mathbf{Z} \sim \mathcal{MN}(\mathbf{0}, \mathbf{\Sigma}, \mathbf{\Delta}), \tag{7}$$

where $\mathbf{\Delta} = \mathbf{B}\mathbf{B}^T$ is the row covariance (describing shape correlations) and $\mathbf{\Sigma} = \mathbf{\Theta}\mathbf{\Theta}^T$ is the column covariance (describing trajectory correlations). Equivalently,

---

[1] $\mathbf{1}_P$ denotes a column vector of ones of size P, and blkdiag produces a block diagonal matrix.

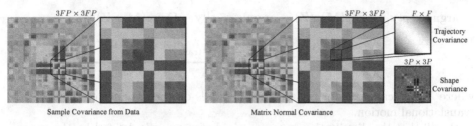

Sample Covariance from Data   Matrix Normal Covariance

Fig. 1. Human spatiotemporal point cloud data exhibits a Kronecker structured co-variance matrix, allowing us to model the distribution over sequences as matrix normal. (Left) The spatiotemporal covariance computed from 5402 vectorized sequences shows a distinct block structure, highlighted in the inset. (Right) The corresponding covari-ance of the matrix normal model, where the full $(3FP) \times (3FP)$ matrix is separable into two smaller covariance matrices, the $F \times F$ trajectory (row) and $3P \times 3P$ shape (column) covariances respectively. Here, $F = 30$ frames and $P = 16$ points.

the distribution over dynamic 3D structure is multivariate normal with a Kro-necker structured covariance matrix [3], with $\mathbf{z} = (\mathbf{B} \otimes \mathbf{\Theta})\mathbf{c}$ and,

$$\mathbf{z} \sim \mathcal{N}(\mathbf{0}, \mathbf{\Delta} \otimes \mathbf{\Sigma}). \tag{8}$$

Fig. 1 illustrates the intuition for choosing this prior over dynamic 3D struc-ture: the spatiotemporal covariance matrix of natural motions is dominated by a Kronecker product block pattern. This Kronecker pattern of the covariance is precisely the one induced by the MND distribution.

This is a significant finding for the purposes of estimation because the MND model allows us to parameterize the spatiotemporal covariance of a dynamic 3D structure with far fewer free variables than are needed for a general, unstructured covariance matrix. The number of covariance parameters in an MND distribu-tion is approximately $(3P)^2/2 + (F)^2/2$, versus $\sim(3FP)^2/2$ for a full covariance matrix. Even for small values of $F=30$ frames and $P=31$ points, this results in ~5000 variables for the MND versus ~3.9 million for a full spatiotemporal covariance.

5 Convex MAP Reconstruction

Reconstructing the 3D shape of the object can now be formulated as finding the most likely spatiotemporal configuration of points $\mathbf{X}$ given the image measure-ments $\mathbf{y}$ under our new probabilistic parameterization for dynamic structures,

$$p(\mathbf{y}|\mathbf{X})p(\mathbf{X}) = p(\mathbf{y}|\mathbf{M}, \mathbf{Z})p(\mathbf{M}, \mathbf{Z}). \tag{9}$$

We assume independence between the mean and non-rigid components, $p(\mathbf{M}, \mathbf{Z}) = p(\mathbf{M})p(\mathbf{Z})$, with each of the priors described by an MND as defined above. The negative log-likelihood of the MND is quadratic, and inference under an MND prior can be posed as a least-squares problem:

$$\operatorname*{argmax}_{\mathbf{M},\mathbf{Z}} p(\mathbf{y}|\mathbf{M},\mathbf{Z})p(\mathbf{M})p(\mathbf{Z}) = \operatorname*{argmin}_{\mathbf{M},\mathbf{Z}} \sigma^{-2}\|\mathbf{y} - \mathbf{O}\operatorname{vec}(\mathbf{M}+\mathbf{Z})\|_F^2$$

$$+ \lambda \underbrace{\operatorname{tr}\left[\mathbf{M_{trans}}^T\mathbf{\Sigma}^{-1}\mathbf{M_{trans}}\right]}_{-\log(p(\mathbf{M}))+c_2} + \underbrace{\operatorname{tr}\left[\mathbf{\Delta}^{-1}\mathbf{Z}^T\mathbf{\Sigma}^{-1}\mathbf{Z}\right]}_{-\log(p(\mathbf{Z}))+c_1}, \quad (10)$$

where λ is a scaling factor related that depends on the variance of the object's translational motion.

Recall that the distribution over non-rigid structures is defined by the generative model $\mathbf{Z} = \mathbf{\Theta}\mathbf{C}\mathbf{B}^T$, where $\mathbf{\Theta}$ and $\mathbf{B}$ parameterize the shape and trajectory covariances. These covariances may depend on the object and are unknown a priori, and therefore need to be estimated:

$$p(\mathbf{\Theta},\mathbf{C},\mathbf{B},\mathbf{M}|\mathbf{y}) \propto p(\mathbf{y}|\mathbf{\Theta},\mathbf{C},\mathbf{B},\mathbf{M})p(\mathbf{\Theta}|\mathbf{C},\mathbf{B})p(\mathbf{B}|\mathbf{C})p(\mathbf{C})p(\mathbf{M}). \quad (11)$$

At this point, we have added optimization variables without reducing the number of unknowns. The benefit of this seemingly more complex parameterization is that we can set priors over the individual terms. The two priors that remain to be specified are:

(1) $p(\mathbf{\Theta}|\mathbf{C},\mathbf{B})$. Because the MND covariance is separable into shape and trajectory covariances, we can make use of a generic analytical model for the trajectory covariance $\mathbf{\Sigma} = \mathbf{\Theta}\mathbf{\Theta}^T$. Consider the trajectory $\mathbf{X}_p \in \mathbb{R}^{F\times 3}$ of a point p. Minimizing the kinetic energy is equivalent to minimizing $\operatorname{tr}\left[\mathbf{X}_p^T\mathbf{D}^T\mathbf{D}\mathbf{X}_p\right]$, where $\mathbf{D}$ is a first order difference matrix, which is proportional to the negative log-likelihood of a Gaussian distribution over trajectories. Define $\mathbf{G} = \mathbf{D}^T\mathbf{D}$, the second order difference matrix. It is known that $\mathbf{G} = \tilde{\mathbf{\Theta}}\mathbf{\Lambda}\tilde{\mathbf{\Theta}}^T$, where $\tilde{\mathbf{\Theta}}$ is the orthogonal DCT transform and $\mathbf{\Lambda}$ is a diagonal matrix (subject to boundary conditions), and therefore $\mathbf{\Theta} = \tilde{\mathbf{\Theta}}\mathbf{\Lambda}^{-1/2}$ [29]. The term $\mathbf{\Theta}$ is therefore known and drops from the expression

$$\operatorname*{argmax}_{\mathbf{M},\mathbf{C},\mathbf{B}} p(\mathbf{y}|\mathbf{\Theta},\mathbf{C},\mathbf{B},\mathbf{M})p(\mathbf{B}|\mathbf{C})p(\mathbf{C})p(\mathbf{M}). \quad (12)$$

(2) $p(\mathbf{B}|\mathbf{C})$. To obtain a convex solution, we assume that $p(\mathbf{B}|\mathbf{C}) = p(\mathbf{B})$, i.e., the distribution over shape covariance is independent of the particular shape configurations observed in a given sequence. We choose a normal prior over the entries of $\mathbf{B}$ (equivalently, a Wishart prior over $\mathbf{\Delta}$). This is computationally convenient, but more importantly, the effect is similar to the traditional low-rank shape assumption. Intuitively, the prior minimizes non-rigid deformations by encouraging that the singular values of the shape covariance matrix should decrease rapidly (see Sect. 6.1).

Using the specified priors and writing this optimization in terms of the component negative log-likelihoods,

$$\operatorname*{argmin}_{\mathbf{M},\mathbf{C},\mathbf{B}} \sigma^2\|\mathbf{y} - \mathbf{O}\operatorname{vec}(\mathbf{M}+\mathbf{\Theta}\mathbf{C}\mathbf{B}^T)\|_F^2 + \|\mathbf{C}\|_F^2 + \|\mathbf{B}\|_F^2 + \lambda\|\mathbf{\Theta}^+\mathbf{M_{trans}}\|_F^2.$$

$$(13)$$

This expression is bilinear in $\mathbf{C}$ and $\mathbf{B}$. A change of variables suffices to transform this bilinear equation into a convex problem using the matrix trace-norm

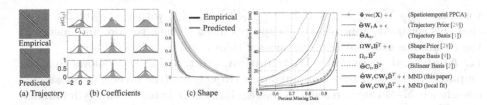

Fig. 2. (Left) Empirical and predicted parameter distributions. (a) Top: the empirical trajectory precision matrix. Below, the second order differences matrix predicted by energy minimization. (b) Each plot corresponds to a coefficient $C_{i,j}$ in the matrix $\mathbf{C}$. The red curve shows the predicted standard normal pdf, the histogram shows the empirical distribution. (c) Distribution of singular values for empirical shape covariances (black), compared to the predicted fall-off induced by $p(\mathbf{B})$ (red). (Right) Inference of missing data with known distribution parameters. Subscript tr indicates truncation.

$\|\cdot\|_*$. Using a result from [28], the trace-norm can also be written as $\|\mathbf{R}\|_* = \min_{\mathbf{U},\mathbf{V}}\{\frac{1}{2}\|\mathbf{U}\|_F^2 + \frac{1}{2}\|\mathbf{V}\|_F^2\}$ subject to $\mathbf{R} = \mathbf{U}\mathbf{V}^T$. With a change of variables $\mathbf{\Theta}^+\mathbf{X}\mathbf{P}_\perp^T = \mathbf{C}\mathbf{B}^T$ we have

$$\operatorname*{argmax}_{\mathbf{X}} p(\mathbf{X}|\mathbf{y}) = \operatorname*{argmin}_{\mathbf{X}} \sigma^{-2}\|\mathbf{y} - \mathbf{O}\operatorname{vec}(\mathbf{X})\|_2^2 + \|\mathbf{\Theta}^+\mathbf{X}\mathbf{P}_\perp\|_* + \frac{\lambda}{\sqrt{P}}\|\mathbf{\Theta}^+\mathbf{X}\mathbf{P}_{\text{trans}}^T\|_F^2,$$

(14)

where $\mathbf{P}_\perp$ is a projection matrix that removes the per-frame translation component (i.e., $\mathbf{P}_\perp = \mathbf{I} - \mathbf{P}_{\text{trans}}^T(\mathbf{P}_{\text{trans}}\mathbf{P}_{\text{trans}}^T)^{-1}\mathbf{P}_{\text{trans}}$). Note that this is the inverse operation of $\mathbf{P}_{\text{trans}}^T$, which isolates the per-frame translation such that $\mathbf{X}\mathbf{P}_{\text{trans}}^T = P\mathbf{M}_{\text{trans}}$. This objective lends itself to optimization by the Alternating Direction Method of Multipliers (ADMM) [6], being decomposable into readily solvable sub-problems (see supplementary materials for details), or as a generalized trace-norm problem [5].

6   Results

6.1   Validation on Natural Motions

We validate the proposed distribution and the four components of our model by computing statistics on a large set of natural motions. We use the CMU Motion Capture database, where we subsample the data to retain point tracks for 15 joint locations on the body, yielding $N = 5402$ 30-frame sub-sequences $\mathbf{X}_n$ which we also align using Procrustes analysis and center around their mean shape.

I. Kronecker Covariance Structure. (Sect. 4) Fig. 1(left) shows the empirical sample covariance matrix $\frac{1}{N}\sum_n \operatorname{vec}(\mathbf{X}_n)\operatorname{vec}(\mathbf{X}_n)^T$ computed on the full set of sequences. On the right, we show the covariance associated with the matrix normal distribution, i.e., $\mathbf{\Delta} \otimes \mathbf{\Sigma}$, where $\mathbf{\Delta}$ is computed[2] as the covariance of the

---

[2] ML estimates of the parameters for noiseless data can be obtained using a "flip-flop" algorithm [12], but in practice we obtained better results with this procedure.

rows $\Delta = \frac{1}{NF} \sum_n \mathbf{X}_n^T \mathbf{X}_n$, and $\Sigma = \frac{1}{vN3P} \sum_n \mathbf{X}_n \mathbf{X}_n^T$, with $v = \frac{1}{3P} \text{tr}(\Delta)$. Note that this separable approximation captures most of the structure and energy in the covariance using far fewer parameter than a full covariance matrix.

II. Analytical Trajectory Distribution. (Sect. 5) Fig. 2(a) shows that the empirical precision matrix computed over trajectories (the inverse of the sample covariance, Σ^{-1}) closely resembles the regularizer predicted by energy minimization. Most correlations in the data are captured by the analytical model.

III. Distribution of Coefficients. (Sect. 4) The matrix normal model assumes a standard normal distribution over the latent coefficients, i.e., $C_{i,j} \sim \mathcal{N}(0, 1)$. Given a large set of natural motion sequences, we can verify the accuracy of this assumption by fitting the model coefficients $\mathbf{C}_n \in \mathbb{R}^{F \times 3P}$ to each sequence $\mathbf{X}_n$, and plotting the resulting histogram of coefficient values. Fig. 2(b) shows that the empirical distribution can be more spiked, closer to Laplacian or Cauchy.

IV. Hierarchical Prior on Shape Covariance. (Sect. 5) We sample shape covariance matrices from the prior $\mathbf{B} \sim \mathcal{MN}(0, \mathbf{I}_{3P}, \mathbf{I}_{3P})$ and compute their singular values (SVs). Fig. 2(c) compares the energy fall-off in SVs from sampled matrices to that of empirically computed covariance matrices. The plot shows the mean SVs and ± 3 standard deviations. The fall-off in the energy of the singular values by the induced prior on $\mathbf{B}$ is not as quick as that observed from data, but this particular choice allows for a convex optimization. Finding priors with faster fall-off but that still remain amenable to global minimization is an interesting direction for future research.

6.2   Missing Data in Motion Capture

The objective of these experiments is to characterize the resilience of the model to typical patterns of missing data encountered in dynamic reconstruction. We decouple the problem of missing data from projection loss and reconstructibility [34] by studying inference on 3D observations (e.g., the output from a motion capture system). The task is to infer the complete sequences from a reduced set of 3D observations. We use the observation model $\mathbf{O}_{\text{miss}}$ as per Sect. 3.

Known Distribution Parameters. When 3D training data is available, we can learn the parameters for MND distribution and perform inference with Eq. (10). We compare with the models corresponding to *probabilistic* and *truncated* versions of shape, trajectory, and shape-trajectory distributions (summarized in Table 1). Additionally, we evaluate against a probabilistic Principal Component Analysis (PCA) model trained on the vectorized spatiotemporal sequences, i.e., $\mathbf{y} = \Phi \text{vec}(\mathbf{X}) + \epsilon$. We report mean 3D error in Figure 2. As a reference, the error incurred when using the mean shape at every frame as an estimation is $\sim$175cm.

For this experiment, we use data from the CMU Motion Capture database. We take 50 random sequences of $20s$ in duration, sample them at 30Hz and Procrustes align and mean center them. There are 31 markers on the body, and we subdivide each sequence into $1s$ windows resulting in F=30 and P=31. We train all models on 49 of the sequences, and test on a random $1s$ segment of the left out sequence. We simulate random occlusion on a percentage of the points and report the average over 50 trials. For the probabilistic models, we set the

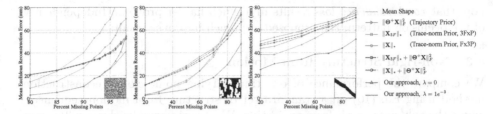

Fig. 3. Inferring missing data under three different occlusion patterns when the shape distribution is unknown. The graphs show mean Euclidean error in the reconstruction under the occlusion models discussed in Section 6.2. The bottom two results correspond to the method of Sect. 5. We investigate two different arrangements for the data matrix, $3F \times P$ and $F \times 3P$, which capture different correlations of the data. For this experiment, $3F \times P$ usually offered better performance, which we report on our method. The data is from dense human motion capture originally intended to measure non-rigid skin deformation while running in place.

noise variance to 0. For models relying on truncation of the basis, we sweep over all possible levels of truncation and pick the best number *a posteriori*. Note that the MND model with factored covariance performs equally well or better than PCA on the vectorized sequences, while requiring less training data (50 times less in this experiment). This allows us to train a *local* model only on the subsequences neighboring the test subsequence; the model is more specific and results in lower error.

Unknown Distribution Parameters. When no training data is available, we rely on the convex inference procedure described in Sect. 5. We compare our approach with three different priors: (1) a trajectory-only prior, (2) a trace-norm prior, and (3) a naive combination of the trace-norm and trajectory priors. We assume $\sigma = 1$mm for all methods. We use dense motion capture data from Park and Hodgins [22]. The sequences are captured at 120Hz with a dense spatial sampling across the body. We downsample by four spatially and temporally, yielding a point cloud of 118 points at 30Hz across 162 frames. We measure reconstruction error as mean Euclidean distance over all points, under three different patterns of missing data: **(a) Random:** We occlude points (x, y, z) at random until we achieve a percentage of missing data. This pattern of occlusion is not common in practical situations. Nonetheless, it is of interest here because under this pattern, the trace-norm is known to provide minimum rank solutions with high probability [24]. **(b) Detection loss:** We model detection loss by occluding spatially proximal points during 1 second durations (30 frames), simulating an occlusion. We superimpose these simulated occlusions to increase the amount of missing data. **(c) Correspondence loss:** We duplicate every point trajectory. Each of the resulting trajectories is observable during a non-overlapping duration, resulting in a pattern similar to that observed when tracking from visual features. The track length is modified to achieve a particular level of missing data (with respect to the original sequence).

The resulting occlusion patterns are shown as insets on the graphs in Fig. 3, laid out as a matrix of frames by points, where black denotes observed entries. We note that *correspondence loss* results in a much harder problem. Independently of the occlusion pattern, the proposed approach improves results.

6.3 Non-rigid Structure from Motion

We compare the performance of our time-varying point cloud reconstruction method using Eq. (10) on a standard set of structure from motion sequences, where the only data loss is from projection. We report normalized mean 3D error as computed in [15] for four methods, (1) KSTA [15], a non-linear kernelized shape-trajectory method, (2) Dai et al. [10], (3) a trajectory-only prior, and (3) our approach. For our method, we compute the camera matrices as in Dai et al. [10] [3], and set $\sigma=1$ and $\lambda=0$. For Dai et al. and KSTA, the optimal parameter k was chosen for each test.

Dataset	KSTA	Dai	Traj.	Ours
Drink	0.0156	0.0266	0.0102	**0.0099**
Pick-up	0.2322	0.1731	**0.1707**	**0.1707**
Yoga	0.1476	0.1150	0.1125	**0.1114**
Stretch	**0.0674**	0.1034	0.0972	0.0940
Dance	0.2504	0.1842	0.1385	**0.1347**
Face2	0.0339	0.0303	0.0408	**0.0299**
Walking2	**0.1029**	0.1298	0.3111	0.1615
Shark2	**0.0160**	0.2358	0.1380	0.1297
Capoeira	**0.2376**	0.3931	0.4394	0.3786

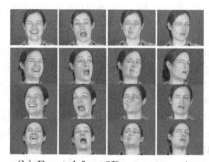

(a) Performance on NR-SfM data sets   (b) Frontal face 3D reconstruction

Fig. 4. (a) Comparison on standard NRSfM sequences using normalized mean 3D error as reported by [10] and [15]. For our method, we compute the camera matrices as Dai et al. Our method shows improved performance on 5 of 8 sequences, while the non-linear KSTA method can achieve better performance on some sequences. (b) Reconstructing a dynamic face from a frontal view. The top row shows frames from a video with superimposed detected 2D landmarks (green circles) provided by IntraFace [37]. We reconstruct the face in full 3D using Eq. (14) and show the reprojection onto three other (held out) views for comparison (yellow dots).

6.4 Monocular Reconstruction

In Fig. 4(b) we show a 3D point cloud reconstruction example from a frontal view of a face using 2D landmark detections provided by IntraFace [37]. The original video is around 1500 frames long and is reconstructed simultaneously. Only a subset of frames is shown here. We directly use the model of Eq. (14) and build an observation matrix $\mathbf{O}_{ortho}$ using the head pose estimation matrices provided by IntraFace. Our method recovers a time-varying 3D point cloud of the face, which we can project onto three other views (not used during reconstruction) to evaluate the accuracy.

---

[3] For KSTA [15], the camera matrices are computed as per Akhter et al. [2]. The implementation of Dai et al. and KSTA was provided by the respective authors.

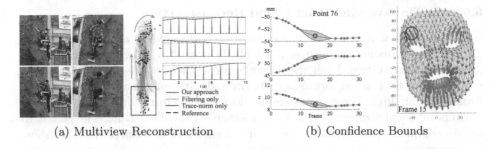

(a) Multiview Reconstruction   (b) Confidence Bounds

Fig. 5. (a) Multiview reconstruction on the "Rock Climbing" sequence from [21]. Annotated labels are shown in white. (Left) Qualitative comparison. The top row shows a result on the full data (104 camera snapshots of 45 points). All methods perform similarly for fully observed frames. The bottom row shows a result on a simulated occlusion (see text). (Center) Reconstructed 3D trajectories of the points, side view of the climbing wall. The arrows denote the direction of motion of the climber. (Right) x,y,z-plot of the mean trajectories of the imputed points. (b) The matrix normal prior allows us to compute the expected value and spatiotemporal covariance of missing data. For this 30 frame sequence, points have been removed completely from frames 10–20. Observed points are marked by red dots. We infer missing values and visualize the mean and 95% confidence bound.

6.5   Multiview Dynamic Reconstruction

We perform a qualitative evaluation of the method of Sect. 5 on a dynamic reconstruction sequence from Park et al. [21]. This sequence is observed very sparsely by multiple cameras taking snapshots of the scene at a rate of around 1 per second. We aim to reconstruct the original motion at 30Hz. Because the observations are now 2D image measurements under 3D-to-2D perspective projection, we use an observation model $\mathbf{O}_{\mathrm{proj}}$ corresponding to a matrix re-arrangement of the observation model described in [21]. Fig. 5(a) shows reconstructions on two sequences, where we have simulated two types of occlusion. Because ground truth is not available, we first run all methods on the full data to obtain a reference reconstruction and we average the resulting structure. This result is shown in black. Fig. 5(a)(left) shows a simulated occlusion of the points on the left foot during the first 6 seconds of the sequence. The trajectory-only prior $\|\mathbf{\Theta}^+\mathbf{X}\|_F^2$ gives a smooth solution, but the foot is not at a coherent location with respect to the body. Conversely, all trace-norm based methods are able to infer the position of the left foot (bottom row of images) fairly plausibly. However, when we look at the temporal domain Fig. 5(a)(right), we observe that the trace-norm penalization $\|\mathbf{X}\|_*$ results in temporal artifacts—rows in the matrix with no observations are set to zero. This model is not adequate for data interpolation: as observed in the matrix completion literature, the non-uniformity of the missing entries (as happens when interpolating a sparsely observed signal at 30Hz) negatively affect the performance of trace-norm based methods. Our method is able to achieve a smoother interpolation while maintaining a low-rank structure.

6.6   3D Time-varying Point Cloud Reconstruction

In Fig. 6 we show a reconstruction of the baseball sequence acquired by Joo et al. [16]. The sequence is given as a set of 3D point trajectories obtained from a multi-camera system. Each trajectory is only partially observed (i.e., once a point cannot be tracked forwards or backwards, its coordinates in subsequent frames are missing). These sequences are 30-frames in duration and have around ~800 points, which where occluded on average ~15% of the time. The goal is to obtain complete trajectories for the entire duration of the video. Here, we show two reconstructions for two overlapping 30-frame subsets of these sequences. The graphs show the trajectories for subsets of points. Note how the recovered trajectories are smooth, and motion occurs in groups because of the low-rank effect of the shape prior.

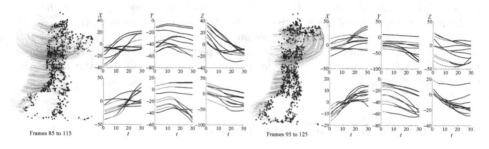

Fig. 6. Reconstructing a baseball motion sequence. Black lines indicate observed points, red lines are inferred trajectories. Two motion trail diagrams of 30-frame overlapping parts of a baseball swing are shown. The graphs show a close up reconstruction for different subsets of the points.

7   Discussion

The model over dynamic 3D structure we describe can be related to shape, trajectory, and shape-trajectory representations used in prior art [15,8,9,27,36,33,2,34] (see Table 1). The convex MAP minimization of Eq. (14). when using a normal prior over $\mathbf{B}$ can be related to the use of the trace-norm in rigid and non-rigid structure from motion [5,10]. In the following, consider the MND prior over point cloud data $\mathbf{X} \sim \mathcal{MN}(\mathbf{M}, \mathbf{\Delta}, \mathbf{\Sigma})$ with known distribution parameters $\mathbf{M}$, $\mathbf{\Delta}$, and $\mathbf{\Sigma}$.

Trajectory Methods. The MND describes a joint shape-trajectory distribution, but it is illustrative to consider the marginal distribution it induces for a particular trajectory $\mathbf{x}^j$ (a column j of $\mathbf{X}$) independent of all other points. This corresponds to an equivalent basis representation over trajectories, as described by Sidenbladh et al. [27]. The marginal distribution is then $\mathbf{x}_j \sim \mathcal{N}(\mathbf{M}^j, \mathbf{\Delta}_{j,j}\mathbf{\Sigma})$, where $\mathbf{\Sigma} = \mathbf{\Theta}\mathbf{\Theta}^T$ is the trajectory covariance matrix, and $\mathbf{\Delta}_{j,j}$ loosely corresponds to the mass of each point. This expression is equivalent to the *filtering* solution

Table 1. Comparison of linear methods for structure reconstruction. See Sect. 4.

	Truncation	Probabilistic	Convex Approx.
Shape	Bregler et al. [8] $X = \Omega \tilde{B}^T$	Torresani et al. [33] $X = \Omega W_b \tilde{B}^T + \epsilon$	Dai et al.[10] $\|X\|_*$
Trajectory	Akhter et al. [2] $X = \tilde{\Theta} A$	Valmadre et al. [34] $X = \tilde{\Theta} W_b A + \epsilon$	
Shape-Trajectory	Gotardo and Martinez [15] $X = \tilde{\Theta} C \tilde{B}^T$	(This Paper) $X = \tilde{\Theta} W_t C W_b \tilde{B}^T + \epsilon$ $\|\Theta^+ X P_\perp\|_*$	

proposed by Valmadre and Lucey [34], who observe that a combination of first and second-order differences fit natural motions well. See also [26].

Shape Methods. The marginal distribution of a particular shape x^i (a row i of X arranged as a column) independent of all other time instants corresponds exactly to shape-only distributions used in prior art, such as the Point Distribution Model (PDM) of Cootes et al. [9], and the shape basis model of Torresani et al. [33]. It follows from the matrix normal model that $x^i \sim \mathcal{N}(M^i, \Sigma_{i,i}\Delta)$,, where $\Sigma_{i,i}$ is the entry (i, i) in Σ and $\Delta = BB^T$ is the shape covariance matrix. An equivalent shape basis B is usually computed with PCA [8,36,2,33].

Bilinear Spatiotemporal Methods. The model we present is a probabilistic formulation of the shape-trajectory basis models described in [15,1]. These models describe spatiotemporal sequences as a linear combination of the outer product of a reduced set of trajectory basis vectors and a set of shape basis vectors. They rely on truncation of the basis to achieve compaction, while the probabilistic MND model describes the relative variance of each spatiotemporal mode with the weighting matrices W_t and W_b. Additionally, the MND allows us to compute a confidence bound on the imputed missing data. We visualize this distribution in Fig. 5(b) on a facial motion capture sequence from [1].

Trace-norm Methods. The trace-norm term in Eq. (14) can be written in terms of the "generalized trace-norm" developed by Angst et al. for rigid SfM [5]. Compared to the rigid model of Angst et al., our work draws an explicit connection between the row and column spaces of an MND distribution of a time-varying 3D structure. Compared to the trace-norm regularizer of Dai et al. [10], we obtain an equivalent minimization if we assume that the temporal covariance is an identity matrix (and set $\lambda=0$). The effect of this is most easily understood for the case of interpolation: frames (rows) for which all points are missing will be set to zero by the $\|X\|_*$ penalizer. This effect can result in abrupt changes in the reconstruction, and can be seen in the spiked blue curves in Fig. 5(a) (right).

References

1. Akhter, I., Simon, T., Matthews, I., Khan, S., Sheikh, Y.: Bilinear spatiotemporal basis models. In: TOG (2012)
2. Akhter, I., Sheikh, Y., Khan, S., Kanade, T.: Nonrigid structure from motion in trajectory space. In: NIPS (2008)

3. Allen, G., Tibshirani, R.: Transposable regularized covariance models with an application to missing data imputation. Annals of Applied Statistics (2010)
4. Angst, R., Pollefeys, M.: A unified view on deformable shape factorizations. In: Fitzgibbon, A., Lazebnik, S., Perona, P., Sato, Y., Schmid, C. (eds.) ECCV 2012, Part VI. LNCS, vol. 7577, pp. 682–695. Springer, Heidelberg (2012)
5. Angst, R., Zach, C., Pollefeys, M.: The generalized trace-norm and its application to structure-from-motion problems. In: ICCV (2011)
6. Boyd, S., Parikh, N., Chu, E., Peleato, B., Eckstein, J.: Distributed optimization and statistical learning via the alternating direction method of multipliers. Foundations and Trends in Machine Learning (2011)
7. Brand, M.: A direct method for 3d factorization of nonrigid motion observed in 2d. In: ICCV (2005)
8. Bregler, C., Hertzmann, A., Biermann, H.: Recovering non-rigid 3d shape from image streams. In: CVPR (2000)
9. Cootes, T.F., Taylor, C.J., Cooper, D.H., Graham, J.: Active shape models, their training and application. In: CVIU (1995)
10. Dai, Y., Li, H., He, M.: A simple prior-free method for non-rigid structure-from-motion factorization. In: CVPR (2002)
11. Del Bue, A., Lladó, X., Agapito, L.: Non-rigid face modelling using shape priors. In: Analysis & Modelling of Faces & Gestures (2005)
12. Dutilleul, P.: The mle algorithm for the matrix normal distribution. Statistical Computation and Simulation (1999)
13. Fayad, J., Del Bue, A., Agapito, L., Aguiar, P.: Non-rigid structure from motion using quadratic deformation models. In: BMVC (2009)
14. Garg, R., Roussos, A., Agapito, L.: Dense variational reconstruction of non-rigid surfaces from monocular video. In: CVPR (2013)
15. Gotardo, P., Martinez, A.: Computing smooth time trajectories for camera and deformable shape in structure from motion with occlusion. PAMI (2011)
16. Joo, H., Park, H., Sheikh, Y.: Optimal visibility estimation for large-scale dynamic 3d reconstruction. In: CVPR (2014)
17. Lee, M., Cho, J., Choi, C., Oh, S.: Procrustean normal distribution for non-rigid structure from motion. In: CVPR (2013)
18. Lee, M., Choi, C., Oh, S.: A procrustean markov process for non-rigid structure recovery. In: CVPR (2014)
19. Metaxas, D., Terzopoulos, D.: Shape and nonrigid motion estimation through physics-based synthesis. PAMI (1993)
20. Olsen, S., Bartoli, A.A.: Implicit non-rigid structure-from-motion with priors. Journal of Mathematical Imaging and Vision (2008)
21. Park, H.S., Shiratori, T., Matthews, I., Sheikh, Y.: 3D reconstruction of a moving point from a series of 2D projections. In: Daniilidis, K., Maragos, P., Paragios, N. (eds.) ECCV 2010, Part III. LNCS, vol. 6313, pp. 158–171. Springer, Heidelberg (2010)
22. Park, S.I., Hodgins, J.K.: Data-driven modeling of skin and muscle deformation. In: TOG (2008)
23. Pentland, A., Horowitz, B.: Recovery of nonrigid motion & structure. PAMI (1993)
24. Recht, B., Fazel, M., Parrillo, P.: Guaranteed minimum-rank solutions of linear matrix equations via nuclear norm minimization. In: SIAM (2010)
25. Russell, C., Fayad, J., Agapito, L.: Energy based multiple model fitting for non-rigid structure from motion. In: CVPR (2011)
26. Salzmann, M., Urtasun, R.: Physically-based motion models for 3d tracking: A convex. formulation. In: ICCV (2011)

27. Sidenbladh, H., Black, M.J., Fleet, D.J.: Stochastic tracking of 3D human figures using 2D image motion. In: Vernon, D. (ed.) ECCV 2000. LNCS, vol. 1843, pp. 702–718. Springer, Heidelberg (2000)

28. Srebro, N., Rennie, J., Jaakkola, T.: Maximum margin matrix factorizations. In: NIPS (2005)

29. Strang, G.: The discrete cosine transform. SIAM Review (1999)

30. Taylor, J., Jepson, A., Kutulakos, K.: Non-rigid structure from locally-rigid motion. In: CVPR (2010)

31. Terzopoulos, D., Witkin, A., Kass, M.: Constraints on deformable models: Recovering 3d shape and nonrigid motion. Artificial Intelligence (1988)

32. Tomasi, C., Kanade, T.: Shape and motion from image streams under orthography: a factorization method. IJCV (1992)

33. Torresani, L., Hertzmann, A., Bregler, C.: Non-rigid structure-from-motion: Estimating shape and motion with hierarchical priors. PAMI (2008)

34. Valmadre, J., Lucey, S.: A general trajectory prior for non-rigid reconstruction. In: CVPR (2012)

35. Vidal, R., Abretske, D.: Nonrigid shape and motion from multiple perspective views. In: Leonardis, A., Bischof, H., Pinz, A. (eds.) ECCV 2006. LNCS, vol. 3952, pp. 205–218. Springer, Heidelberg (2006)

36. Xiao, J., Chai, J.-X., Kanade, T.: A closed-form solution to non-rigid shape and motion recovery. In: Pajdla, T., Matas, J(G.) (eds.) ECCV 2004. LNCS, vol. 3024, pp. 573–587. Springer, Heidelberg (2004)

37. Xiong, X., De La Torre, F.: Supervised descent method and its applications to face alignment. In: CVPR (2013)

38. Yan, J., Pollefeys, M.: A factorization-based approach to articulated motion recovery. In: CVPR (2005)

Highly Overparameterized Optical Flow Using PatchMatch Belief Propagation

Michael Hornáček[1,*], Frederic Besse[2,*], Jan Kautz[2], Andrew Fitzgibbon[3], and Carsten Rother[4]

[1] TU Vienna, Austria
michael.hornacek@tuwien.ac.at
[2] University College London, UK
{f.besse,j.kautz}@cs.ucl.ac.uk
[3] Microsoft Research Cambridge, UK
awf@microsoft.com
[4] TU Dresden, Germany
carsten.rother@tu-dresden.de

Abstract. Motion in the image plane is ultimately a function of 3D motion in space. We propose to compute optical flow using what is ostensibly an extreme overparameterization: depth, surface normal, and frame-to-frame 3D rigid body motion at every pixel, giving a total of 9 DoF. The advantages of such an overparameterization are twofold: first, geometrically meaningful reasoning can be called upon in the optimization, reflecting possible 3D motion in the underlying scene; second, the 'fronto-parallel' assumption implicit in the use of traditional matching pixel windows is ameliorated because the parameterization determines a plane-induced homography at every pixel. We show that optimization over this high-dimensional, continuous state space can be carried out using an adaptation of the recently introduced PatchMatch Belief Propagation (PMBP) energy minimization algorithm, and that the resulting flow fields compare favorably to the state of the art on a number of small- and large-displacement datasets.

Keywords: Optical flow, large displacement, 9 DoF, PatchMatch, PMBP.

1 Introduction

One statement of the goal of optical flow computation is the recovery of a dense correspondence field between a pair of images, assigning to each *pixel* in one image a 2D translation vector that points to the pixel's correspondence in the other. Sun et al. [22] argue that classical models, such as the Horn and Schunck [11] can achieve good performance when coupled to modern optimizers. They point out the key elements that contribute to quality of the solution, including image pre-processing, a coarse-to-fine scheme, bicubic interpolation, robust

---

* Michael Hornáček and Frederic Besse were funded by Microsoft Research through its European Ph.D. scholarship programme.

D. Fleet et al. (Eds.): ECCV 2014, Part III, LNCS 8691, pp. 220–234, 2014.

penalty functions, and median filtering, which they integrate into a new energy formulation. Xu et al. [28] observe that while a large number of optical flow techniques use a multiscale approach, pyramidal schemes can lead to problems in accurately detecting the large motion of fine structures. They propose to combine sparse feature detection with a classic pyramidal scheme to overcome this difficulty. Additionally, they selectively combine color and gradient in the similarity measure on a per pixel basis to improve robustness, and use a Total Variation/L1 (TVL1) optimizer [31]. Similarly, Brox et al. [6] integrate SIFT feature matching [14] into a variational framework to guide the solution towards large displacements.

Another way to define a correspondence is in terms of the similarity of *pixel windows* centered on each image pixel. Immediately, the size of the window becomes an important algorithm parameter: a small window offers little robustness to intensity variations such as those caused by lighting change, differences in camera response, or image noise; a large window can overcome these difficulties but most published work suffers from what we loosely term the 'fronto-parallel' (FP) assumption, according to which each point in the window is assumed to undergo the same 2D translation. The robustness of small-window models can be improved by means of priors over motion at neighboring pixels, but first-order priors themselves typically imply the fronto-parallel limitation, second-order priors are expensive to optimize for general energies [27] although efficient schemes exist for some cases [23]. Beyond second order, higher-order priors impose quite severe limitations on the state spaces they can model. In the case of optical flow, the state space is essentially continuous, and certainly any discretization must be very dense.

An alternative strategy to relax the FP assumption is to *overparameterize* the motion field. Previous work in optical flow has considered 3 DoF similarity transformations [3], 6 DoF affine transformations [18], or 6 DoF linearized 3D motion models [18]. In the case of stereo correspondence, the 1 DoF disparity field has been overparameterized in terms of a 3 DoF surface normal and depth field [4,5,13]. With such models, even first order priors can be expressive (e.g., piecewise constant surface normal is equivalent to piecewise constant depth derivatives rather than piecewise constant depth). However, effective optimization of such models has required linearization of brightness constancy [18] or has suffered from local optimality [13]. Recently, however, algorithms based on PatchMatch [2,3] have been applied to 3 DoF (depth+normal) stereo matching [4,5,10] and 6 DoF (3D rigid body motion) RGB-D scene flow [12], and it is to this class of algorithms that ours belongs.

In this paper, we employ an overparameterization not previously applied to the computation of optical flow, assigning a 9 DoF plane-induced homography to each pixel. In addition to relaxing the FP assumption, such a model allows for geometrically meaningful reasoning to be integrated in the optimization, reflecting possible 3D motion in the underlying scene. Vogel et al. [25] recover scene flow over consecutive calibrated stereo pairs by jointly computing a segmentation of a keyframe and assigning to each segment a 9 DoF plane-induced homography, optimized using QPBO [21] over a set of proposal homographies. For optical flow from a pair of images without strictly enforcing epipolar geometry, we show that PatchMatch Belief Propagation (PMBP) of Besse et al. [4] can be adapted to optimize the high-dimensional, non-convex optimization problem of assigning a 9 DoF plane-induced homography to each pixel and that the resulting flow fields compare favorably to the state of the art on a number of datasets. The model parameterizes, at each pixel, a 3D plane undergoing rigid body motion, and can be specialized for piecewise rigid motion, or indeed for a single global rigid motion [24,26].

2   Algorithm

Let (I_1, I_2) be an ordered pair of images depicting a static or moving scene at different points in time and/or from different points of view, and let (G_1, G_2) be the analogous gradient images, each consisting of a total of p pixels. For one of the two views $i \in \{1, 2\}$, let $\mathbf{x}_s = (x_s, y_s)^\top$ denote such a pixel, indexed by $s \in \{1, \ldots, p\}$. Let $N(s)$ denote the set of indices of the 4-connected neighbors of $\mathbf{x}_s$ and $W(s)$ the set of indices of pixels in the patch centered on $\mathbf{x}_s$. At every pixel $\mathbf{x}_s$, rather than seek a 2D flow vector, we shall aim to obtain a state vector $\boldsymbol{\theta}_s$ that determines a plane-induced homography $H(\boldsymbol{\theta}_s)$ to explain the motion of the pixels $\mathbf{x}_t, t \in W(s)$. We solve for the flow field by minimizing an energy defined over such state vectors, comprising *data terms* ψ_s and *smoothness terms* ψ_{st}:

$$E(\boldsymbol{\theta}_1, \ldots, \boldsymbol{\theta}_p) = \sum_{s=1}^{p} \psi_s(\boldsymbol{\theta}_s) + \sum_{s=1}^{p} \sum_{t \in N(s)} \psi_{st}(\boldsymbol{\theta}_s, \boldsymbol{\theta}_t). \tag{1}$$

In the remainder of this section, we proceed first to introduce the parameterization and the data term, and follow by detailing the smoothness term.

2.1   Model and Data Term

Ignoring for the moment the details of the parameterization, let $I_i(\mathbf{x}_s)$ and $G_i(\mathbf{x}_s)$ denote the color and gradient, respectively, at pixel $\mathbf{x}_s$ in view i, $i \in \{1, 2\}$. Given a pixel $\mathbf{x}$ in floating point coordinates, we obtain $I_i(\mathbf{x}), G_i(\mathbf{x})$ by interpolation. Let $\tilde{\mathbf{x}} = (x_1, x_2, x_3)^\top \in \mathbb{P}^2$ denote a pixel in projective 2-space, and $\epsilon(\tilde{\mathbf{x}}) = (x_1/x_3, x_2/x_3)^\top \in \mathbb{R}^2$ its analogue in Euclidean 2-space. Let H_s be shorthand for $H(\boldsymbol{\theta}_s)$ and H_s denote the 3×3 matrix form of H_s, and let $H_s * \mathbf{x} = \epsilon(\mathsf{H}_s(\mathbf{x}^\top, 1)^\top) \in \mathbb{R}^2$ be the pixel obtained by applying the homography H_s to the pixel $\mathbf{x}$. This lends itself to a data term that, at pixel $\mathbf{x}_s$ in view i—which we shall call the *source* view—sums over the pixels of the patch $W(s)$:

$$\psi_s(\boldsymbol{\theta}_s) = \frac{1}{|W(s)|} \tag{2}$$

$$\sum_{t \in W(s)} w_{st} \cdot \Big((1-\alpha)\|I_i(\mathbf{x}_t) - I_j(H_s * \mathbf{x}_t)\| + \alpha \|G_i(\mathbf{x}_t) - G_j(H_s * \mathbf{x}_t)\| \Big),$$

where $j \in \{1, 2\}, i \neq j$, indexes the *destination* view, $w_{st} = \exp(-\|I_i(\mathbf{x}_s) - I_i(\mathbf{x}_t)\|/\gamma)$ implements a form of adaptive support weighting [30], and $\alpha \in [0, 1]$ controls the relative influence of the color and gradient components of the data term. The data term is scaled by $1/|W(s)|$ in the aim of rendering the strength of the smoothness term in (1) invariant to the patch size.

Casting the standard FP model in these terms, one could define $\boldsymbol{\theta}^{\mathrm{FP}} = (\delta_x, \delta_y)^\top$ to be the 2D flow vector at pixel $\mathbf{x}_s$, and express the homography $H(\boldsymbol{\theta}^{\mathrm{FP}})$ in matrix form as

$$\mathrm{H}(\boldsymbol{\theta}^{\mathrm{FP}}) = \begin{bmatrix} 1 & 0 & \delta_x \\ 0 & 1 & \delta_y \\ 0 & 0 & 1 \end{bmatrix}. \tag{3}$$

Nir et al. [18] propose a number of further variants of $H(\boldsymbol{\theta})$ including a 6 DoF affine transformation and a 6 DoF linearized 3D motion model. In [20], the fundamental matrix $\mathbf{F}$ is assumed to be known, and homographies consistent with $\mathbf{F}$ are parameterized by three parameters per pixel, yielding essentially an unrectified dense stereo algorithm. The three parameters are related to the 3 DoF parameterization of a scene plane at pixel $\mathbf{x}_s$, as used in [4,5]. We take the parameterization a step further, parameterizing not only a 3D plane at each pixel, but also a 3D rigid body motion transforming the points in the plane.

Let $\mathbf{n}_s$ denote the unit surface normal of a plane in 3D and Z_s the depth of the point of intersection of that plane with the back-projection $\mathbf{p}_s = \mathrm{K}^{-1}(\mathbf{x}_s^\top, 1)^\top$ of the pixel $\mathbf{x}_s$, where K is the 3×3 camera calibration matrix. The point of intersection is then given by $Z_s \mathbf{p}_s \in \mathbb{R}^3$. Let $\mathrm{R}_s, \mathbf{t}_s$ denote a rigid body motion in 3D. We write our overparameterized motion model $H(\boldsymbol{\theta}_s)$ in matrix form as

$$\mathrm{H}(\boldsymbol{\theta}_s) = \mathrm{K}\left(\mathrm{R}_s + \frac{1}{Z_s \mathbf{n}_s^\top \mathbf{p}_s} \mathbf{t}_s \mathbf{n}_s^\top \right) \mathrm{K}^{-1}, \tag{4}$$

where $\boldsymbol{\theta}_s = (Z_s, \mathbf{n}_s, \mathrm{R}_s, \mathbf{t}_s)^\top$, for a total of 9 DoF. Setting $Z_s \mathbf{n}_s^\top \mathbf{p}_s = -d_s$, we obtain the familiar *homography induced by the plane* [9], with plane $\boldsymbol{\pi}_s = (\mathbf{n}_s^\top, d_s)^\top \in \mathbb{P}^3$. For static scenes undergoing only camera motion, $\mathrm{R}_s, \mathbf{t}_s$ determine the pose of the camera of the destination view, expressed in the camera coordinate frame of the source view. More generally, such a homography lends itself to interpretation as $\mathrm{R}_s, \mathbf{t}_s$ applied to the point obtained by intersecting $\boldsymbol{\pi}_s$ with a pixel back-projection in the source view, and projecting the resulting point into the destination view (cf. Fig. 1), with the pose of both cameras kept identical. On this interpretation, we may reason about scenes undergoing pure camera motion, pure object motion, or joint camera and object motion in the same conceptual framework.

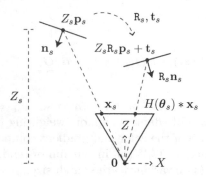

Fig. 1. Depiction of the geometric interpretation of a homography $H(\boldsymbol{\theta}_s)$, $\boldsymbol{\theta}_s = (Z_s, \mathbf{n}_s, \mathbf{R}_s, \mathbf{t}_s)^\top$, assigned to a pixel $\mathbf{x}_s$ as a 3D plane with unit normal $\mathbf{n}_s$ intersecting the back-projection of the pixel $\mathbf{x}_s$ at depth Z_s and undergoing the rigid body motion $\mathbf{R}_s, \mathbf{t}_s$. Applying $H(\boldsymbol{\theta}_s)$ to an arbitrary pixel $\mathbf{x}_t$ has the effect of intersecting the back-projection of $\mathbf{x}_t$ with this plane to obtain a point $\mathbf{P}_t \in \mathbb{R}^3$, transforming $\mathbf{P}_t$ by the motion $\mathbf{R}_s, \mathbf{t}_s$ to obtain $\mathbf{P}'_t = \mathbf{R}_s \mathbf{P}_t + \mathbf{t}_s$, and finally projecting $\mathbf{P}'_t$ back to image space.

Recognizing that a plane whose normal does not point toward the camera is meaningless, and one that is close to orthogonal to the look direction is of no practical use in obtaining matches, we additionally wish to flatly reject such *invalid* states without taking the time to compute the data term in (2). Accordingly, a homography $H(\boldsymbol{\theta}_s)$ is deemed invalid if the source and destination normals $\mathbf{n}_s, \mathbf{R}_s \mathbf{n}_s$ do not both face toward the camera and are not both within $85°$ of the source and destination look direction vectors, respectively. We additionally deem invalid states that encode negative source or destination depth or states for which $H(\boldsymbol{\theta}_s) * \mathbf{x}_s$ lies outside the destination image.

2.2   Smoothness Term

The role of the smoothness term ψ_{st} is to encourage the action of the homographies parametrized by states $\boldsymbol{\theta}_s, \boldsymbol{\theta}_t$ assigned to neighboring pixels to be similar. One approach to defining a such a smoothness term could be to define distances between the geometric quantities encoded in the state vectors, specifically depth, normal, and rigid body motion. Reasoning directly in terms of the similarity of the parameters of the model would introduce a number of algorithm tuning parameters, as the natural scales of variation of each parameter type are not commensurate. While these could be determined using a training set, a large training set may be required. We instead focus our attention directly on the smoothness of the resulting 2D flow—since it is a smooth 2D flow field that we aim to obtain as output of our algorithm—and introduce a considerably more intuitive smoothness term:

$$\psi_{st}(\boldsymbol{\theta}_s, \boldsymbol{\theta}_t) = \lambda \cdot \min\left(\kappa, \left\| H_s * \mathbf{x}_s - H_t * \mathbf{x}_s \right\| + \left\| H_t * \mathbf{x}_t - H_s * \mathbf{x}_t \right\| \right), \quad (5)$$

where $\lambda \geq 0$ is a smoothness weight and $\kappa > 0$ is a truncation constant intended to add robustness to large state discontinuities, particularly with object boundaries in mind. This smoothness term has only two parameters (λ and κ) and is in units of pixels.

2.3   Energy Minimization

While it may be easy to formulate a realistic energy function, such a function is of little practical use if it cannot be minimized in reasonable time. Minimizing the energy in (1) is a non-convex optimization problem over a high-dimensional, continuous state space. The recently introduced PatchMatch Belief Propagation (PMBP) algorithm of Besse et al. [4] provides an avenue to optimizing over such a state space by leveraging PatchMatch [2,3] for exploiting the underlying spatial coherence of the parameter space by sampling from pixel neighbors (spatial propagation), and belief propagation [29] for the explicit promotion of smoothness.

We adapt PMBP in the aim of assigning to each pixel $\mathbf{x}_s$ an optimal state $\boldsymbol{\theta}_s$, mapping the projectively warped patch centered on $\mathbf{x}_s$ in the source view to its analogue in the destination view. Since our parameterization has a geometric interpretation in terms of rigidly moving planes in 3D, we are able to tailor PMBP to make moves that are sensible in 3D. We begin by (i) initializing the state space in a semi-random manner, making use of knowledge about the scene that we are able to recover from the input image pair (*initialization*). Next, for i iterations, we traverse each pixel $\mathbf{x}_s$ in scanline order, first (ii) attempting to propagate the states assigned to neighbors of $\mathbf{x}_s$ (*spatial propagation*) and then (iii) trying to refine the state vector (*random search*), in each case adopting a candidate state if doing so yields lower disbelief than the current assignment. We do this in both directions (view 1 to view 2, view 2 to view 1) *in parallel* and in opposite traversal orders, and as a last step when visiting $\mathbf{x}_s$ we additionally (iv) attempt to propagate the state at $\mathbf{x}_s$ from the source view to $H(\boldsymbol{\theta}_s) * \mathbf{x}_s$ in the destination, rounded to the nearest integer pixel (*view propagation*); accordingly, by the time a pixel is reached in one view, the most recent match available from the other has already been considered.

Initialization. In order to promote convergence to correct local minima, we constrain our choice of initializing state vectors using knowledge we are able to recover from the input image pair. We estimate the dominant rigid body motion of the scene by feeding pairs of keypoint matches obtained using ASIFT[-3] [17] to the 5 point algorithm [19] with RANSAC [8], giving an essential matrix $\mathbf{E} = [\mathbf{t_E}]_\times \mathbf{R_E}$ that we subsequently decompose into a rigid body motion $\mathbf{R_E}, \mathbf{t_E}$ [9]. One might consider iteratively recovering additional dominant rigid body motions by culling inlier matches and re-running the 5 point algorithm with RANSAC on the

---

[-3] The publicly available ASIFT code carries out a form of epipolar filtering using the Moisan-Stival Optimized Random Sampling Algorithm (ORSA) [16]. We remove this feature in order to obtain all matches recovered by the ASIFT matcher.

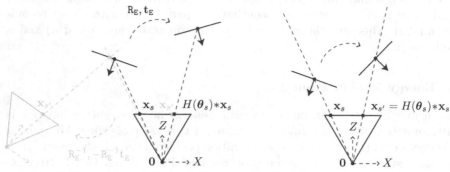

(a) Initialization from inlier matches.   (b) Initialization from general matches.

Fig. 2. (a) Initialization from ASIFT match pairs $(\mathbf{x}_s, \mathbf{x}_{s'})$ that are inliers of a recovered dominant rigid body motion $\mathsf{R}_E, \mathbf{t}_E$, with depth Z_s determined by triangulation and $\mathbf{n}_s$ as the only free parameter. (b) Initialization from general ASIFT match pairs $(\mathbf{x}_s, \mathbf{x}_{s'})$, constrained in that $\mathbf{x}_{s'} = H(\boldsymbol{\theta}_s) * \mathbf{x}_s$; an alternative expression of this constraint is the requirement that $Z_s \mathsf{R}_s \mathbf{p}_s + \mathbf{t}_s$ project exactly to the pixel $\mathbf{x}_{s'}$.

matches that remain, or consider alternative rigid motion segmentation techniques [7]. We triangulate the ASIFT matches that are inliers of the recovered dominant motion, giving seed points for which only the plane normal $\mathbf{n}_s$ remains a free parameter (cf. Fig. 2a). Since we wish to allow deviation from recovered dominant motions yet would like to leverage all of the available ASIFT matches, we additionally use the full set of ASIFT match pairs $(\mathbf{x}_s, \mathbf{x}_{s'})$ for seeding by estimating, for each pair, a tailored rigid body motion constrained by the requirement that $\mathbf{x}_{s'} = H(\boldsymbol{\theta}_s) * \mathbf{x}_s$ (cf. Fig. 2b), with depth Z_s in addition to normal $\mathbf{n}_s$ as free parameters. At pixels where more than one such seed is available, we choose one at random. For unseeded pixels, we set $\mathsf{R}_s, \mathbf{t}_s$ to one of the recovered dominant motions, with depth Z_s and normal $\mathbf{n}_s$ again free.

Spatial Propagation. In the usual manner of PatchMatch [2,3,4], we traverse the pixels of the source image in scanline order and consider, at the current pixel $\mathbf{x}_s$, the subset of states $\{\boldsymbol{\theta}_t \mid t \in N(s)\}$ assigned to the 4-connected neighbors of $\mathbf{x}_s$ that have already been visited in the iteration, and adopt such a state $\boldsymbol{\theta}_t$ if doing so gives lower disbelief than the current assignment. Note that owing to our parameterization, adopting the state $\boldsymbol{\theta}_t = (Z_t, \mathbf{n}_t, \mathsf{R}_t, \mathbf{t}_t)^\top$ at pixel $\mathbf{x}_s$ calls for recomputing the depth by intersecting the plane π_t with the back-projection of $\mathbf{x}_s$; the remaining components of the state vector $\boldsymbol{\theta}_t$ are simply copied.

Random Search. We perturb, at random, either depth Z_s and normal $\mathbf{n}_s$ or the rigid body motion $\mathsf{R}_s, \mathbf{t}_s$ of the state vector $\boldsymbol{\theta}_s$ currently assigned to the pixel $\mathbf{x}_s$. When $\mathsf{R}_s, \mathbf{t}_s$ are locked, we are effectively carrying out stereo matching. When $Z_s, \mathbf{n}_s$ are locked, we perturb the translational component of the motion with the effect of sampling within a 3D radius around $Z_s \mathsf{R}_s \mathbf{p}_s + \mathbf{t}_s$; perturbation of

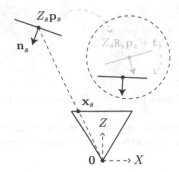

Fig. 3. Refinement of the rigid motion R_s, t_s for plane parameters Z_s, n_s fixed. Perturbation of the translational component t_s is carried out with the effect of applying a translation to the current $P'_s = Z_s R_s p_s + t_s$ within a radius of P'_s in 3D (depicted by the dashed circle). Perturbation of the rotational component R_s serves effectively to rotate the transformed plane around the current P'_s.

the rotational component serves effectively to change the normal of the transformed plane (cf. Fig. 3). We carry out several such perturbations of the four components of the assigned state vector, reducing the search range with every try. We adopt a proposed perturbation if doing so gives lesser disbelief than the current assignment.

If R_s, t_s are reasonable and if at least parts of the reconstructed depth map are already plausible, a geometrically sensible move to promote convergence to correct local minima is to attempt to refine n_s, Z_s by fitting a plane to the already computed minimum disbelief recovered 3D points $\{Z_t p_t \mid t \in W(s), \theta_t = (Z_t, n_t, R_t, t_t)^\top\}$, using RANSAC. The candidate normal is simply the normal vector—constrained to point toward the camera—of this plane, and the candidate depth is obtained by intersecting the plane with the back-projection of x_s. We carry out such a plane fit as the first step in random search, and follow with the perturbations described above.

View Propagation. Most similarly to [12], which in turn builds upon [4,5], as a last step when visiting a pixel x_s and given its assigned state vector $\theta_s = (Z_s, n_s, R_s, t_s)^\top$, we propose the inverted state $\theta'_s = (Z'_s, n'_s, R'_s, t'_s)^\top$ in the destination view. We compute θ'_s by $n'_s = R_s n_s$, $R'_s = R_s^{-1}$, $t'_s = -R_s^{-1} t$; the depth Z'_s is obtained by intersecting the transformed plane with the back-projection of $Z_s R_s p_s + t_s$ projected to the nearest integer pixel, which is where in the destination view we then evaluate θ'_s. Geometrically, this amounts to considering the inverse rigid body motion applied to the transformed plane. Since we carry out our algorithm on both views in parallel and in opposite traversal orders, the most recent corresponding match available from the destination view has thus already been considered by the time x_s is reached.

2.4   Post-processing

In areas of the scene that are occluded in one of the two views, subject to the aperture problem, or poorly textured, our algorithm is likely to assign states

| Raw | Inconsistent pixels | Post-processed | Ground truth |

Fig. 4. Effect of our post processing on the Crates1Htxtr2 data set. Only the pixels that fail the consistency check (indicated in gray) undergo post-processing.

that do not correspond to the correct flow (cf. Fig. 4). If flow is computed in both directions, we can identify inconsistent state assignments by running a consistency check over 'forward' and 'backward' flow, labelling as inconsistent each pixel $\mathbf{x}_s$ that fails the following condition:

$$\left\| \mathbf{x}_s - H(\boldsymbol{\theta}_s^{\mathrm{B}}) * \left(H(\boldsymbol{\theta}_s^{\mathrm{F}}) * \mathbf{x}_s \right) \right\| \leq 1, \tag{6}$$

where $\boldsymbol{\theta}_s^{\mathrm{F}}$ determines the forward flow assigned in the source view to pixel $\mathbf{x}_s$, and $\boldsymbol{\theta}_s^{\mathrm{B}}$ the backward flow assigned in the destination view to the pixel $\boldsymbol{\theta}_s^{\mathrm{F}} * \mathbf{x}_s$ rounded to the nearest integer coordinates. This generates a pixel mask that identifies pixels that subsequently undergo post-processing. For each $\mathbf{x}_s$ that failed the check, we first consider the pixels in a window around $\mathbf{x}_s$ that passed, adopting the homography of the pixel that is closest in appearance. Next, for pixels $\mathbf{x}_s$ that still fail the check, we seek the nearest pixels above and below $\mathbf{x}_s$ that passed, and adopt the homography of the pixel closest in appearance. Finally, we proceed similarly for left and right.

3   Evaluation

We tested our method on the UCL optical flow data set [15] and on a subset of the Middlebury optical flow benchmark [1] for which ground truth flow was available. Accordingly, we considered data sets exhibiting flow at small and large displacements (we set the threshold between the two at 25 pixels) and undergoing rigid, piecewise rigid, and non-rigid motions. A comparison over end point error (EPE) is provided in Table 1 with respect to four competing methods. We ran our algorithm on all data sets in the table with a patch size of 21 × 21 for three iterations on a single particle. As in [4,5], we set the weight α that balances the influence of gradient over color in (2) to 0.9, and γ in the adaptive support weighting to 10. The truncation constant κ of the smoothness term in (5) was set to 1 in all our experiments. Only a single dominant rigid body motion was recovered per data set, in the manner described in Sec. 2.3. Minimum depth was fixed to 0; maximum depth per view was set to the maximum depth of triangulated matches that were inliers of the dominant motion. In the random search stage, maximum allowable deviation from the current rigid body motion was set to 0.01 for both the rotational (expressed in terms of quaternions) and translational components of the motion. Analogously to [4,5], we set maximum flow per dataset. Camera calibration matrix K was fixed such that the focal length was 700 pixels and the principal point was in the image center.

UCL Lg. Displ.

	TV	LD	CN	MDP	Ours$_{\lambda=0.005}$	Ours$_{\lambda=0}$	Ours$_{\lambda=0.01}$
Crates1	3.45	3.10	3.15	1.65	2.37	2.62	2.9
Crates2	4.02	2.51	10.4	1.35	1.71	1.84	1.73
Mayan1	2.33	7.96	1.71	0.48	0.16	0.17	0.18
Robot	2.34	1.21	1.53	0.7	1.85	2.14	1.96
Crates1Htxtr2	1.11	0.54	1.64	0.28	0.29	0.39	0.3
Crates2Htxtr1	3.13	0.81	6.88	0.37	0.47	0.45	0.64
Brickbox1t1	1.09	2.6	0.22	0.2	0.15	0.16	0.15
Brickbox2t2	7.48	3.51	2.19	0.56	0.22	0.2	0.22
GrassSky0	2.1	1.04	1.3	0.47	0.27	0.3	0.27
GrassSky9	6.72	0.51	0.27	0.29	0.25	0.34	0.26
blow19Txtr2†	0.53	0.32	0.19	0.26	0.22	0.23	0.27
drop9Txtr2†	3.2	4.37	2.71	1.15	0.65	0.75	0.86
street1Txtr1†	3.65	2.66	4.89	3.19	0.92	1.72	1.45

UCL Sm. Displ.

	TV	LD	CN	MDP	Ours$_{\lambda=0.005}$	Ours$_{\lambda=0}$	Ours$_{\lambda=0.01}$
Mayan2	0.44	0.35	0.21	0.23	0.17	0.19	0.18
YosemiteSun†	0.31	0.18	0.23	3.79	0.33	0.35	0.38
GroveSun	0.58	0.48	0.23	0.43	0.24	0.24	0.23
Sponza1	1.01	0.91	1.1	1.08	2.75	2.84	2.8
Sponza2	0.53	0.48	1.6	1.77	2.61	2.58	2.61
TxtRMovement	3.17	0.36	0.13	0.19	1.71	1.7	1.72
TxtLMovement	1.52	0.6	0.12	0.23	1.73	1.76	1.76
blow1Txtr1†	0.09	0.08	0.03	0.05	0.04	0.04	0.04
drop1Txtr1†	0.12	0.08	0.05	0.06	0.04	0.04	0.04
roll1Txtr1†	0.004	0.002	0.002	0.002	0.002	0.002	0.002
roll9Txtr2†	0.04	0.02	0.01	0.02	0.01	0.01	0.01
Middlebury							
Dimetrodon†	0.211	0.117	0.115	0.153	0.169	0.174	0.17
Grove2	0.220	0.149	0.091	0.15	0.184	0.187	0.3
Grove3	0.715	0.657	0.438	0.53	0.517	0.455	0.97
Hydrangea†	0.196	0.178	0.154	0.164	0.222	0.207	0.234
RubberWhale†	0.135	0.120	0.077	0.09	0.114	0.12	0.125
Urban2	0.506	0.334	0.207	0.32	0.3	0.312	0.29
Urban3	1.132	0.600	0.377	0.42	0.905	1.27	1.03
Venus	0.408	0.433	0.229	0.28	0.342	0.342	0.434

Table 1. End point error (EPE) comparison. TV = A Duality Based Approach for Realtime TV-L1 Optical Flow [31]. LD = Large Displacement Optical Flow [6]. CN = Secrets of Optical Flow [22]. MDP = Motion Detail Preserving Optical Flow [28]. Cell colors indicate ranking among the five methods, from best to worst: green, light green, yellow, orange, red. Gray cells are shown for comparison but are not included in the ranking. † indicates that the scene is non-static.

Our method performs particularly well on the large displacement cases of the UCL dataset, and produces reasonable results for smaller displacements. Quantitative results show that our technique outperforms all four other methods in ca. 1/3 of the data sets (ca. 1/2 of the cases for large motion), while the end point error is lower than that of TV and LD in most of the cases. The color scheme used in Table 1 indicates that our approach is the one that is most frequently ranked in the first two positions (ca. 2/3 of the cases), when compared to the other four techniques. A visual comparison for four data sets is given in Fig. 5. The effect of the smoothness term can be seen in Fig. 6, where we compare the resulting 2D flow for our algorithm with $\lambda = 0$ (no smoothness) and $\lambda = 0.005$ on the Middlebury Dimetrodon data set. Additionally, we give the EPE results for $\lambda = 0$ and $\lambda = 0.01$ for all data sets in Table 1.

(Piecewise) Unrectified Stereo. For scenes undergoing only a single dominant rigid body motion, one could run our algorithm with no deviation allowed from the recovered dominant rigid body motion R_E, t_E. We show precisely such a reconstruction for the Brickbox2t2 data set in Fig. 7, providing a coloring of the recovered normals, the depth map, and a colored point cloud rendered at a novel view. Locking the motion reduces our algorithm to an unrectified stereo matcher with slanted support windows, most closely akin to [4].

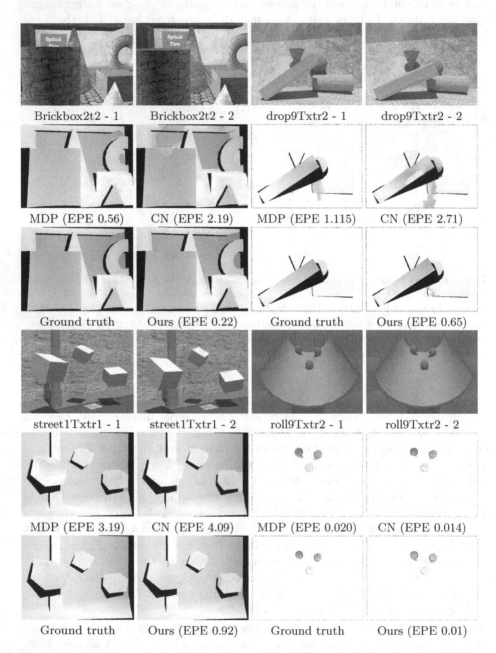

Fig. 5. Optical flow colorings for a subset of the UCL optical flow data set. EPE = End Point Error. CN = Secrets of Optical Flow [22]. MDP = Motion Detail Preserving Optical Flow [28]. Results correspond to Table 1.

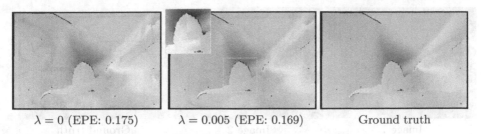

$\lambda = 0$ (EPE: 0.175) $\lambda = 0.005$ (EPE: 0.169)   Ground truth

Fig. 6. The effect of the smoothness term on the Dimetrodon data set for $\lambda = 0$ (no smoothness) and $\lambda = 0.005$. Inlay shown with contrast stretch; results best viewed zoomed in. Flow coloring and EPE without post-processing.

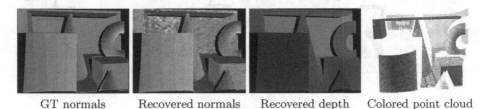

GT normals   Recovered normals   Recovered depth   Colored point cloud

Fig. 7. Restriction to the recovered dominant rigid body motion R_E, t_E for the Brickbox2t2 data set. Estimation of the plane normals and depth on a static scene, and rendering as a colored point cloud.

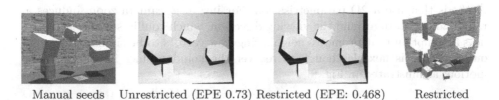

Manual seeds   Unrestricted (EPE 0.73)   Restricted (EPE: 0.468)   Restricted

Fig. 8. Result obtained on the street1Txtr1 data set by seeding with the dominant motion obtained by the 5 point algorithm with RANSAC on all ASIFT matches and on the three additional sets of manually provided matches (indicated in red, yellow, and green), giving four motions in total. Results shown for deviation allowed from those four motions, and for no deviation allowed. Otherwise, we used the same parameter settings to compute our results as in Table 1.

In order to give an impression of the limits of the approach, we recover the dominant rigid body motion on the street1Txtr1 data set in the manner described in Sec. 2.3 and obtain motions on the three independently moving cubes by manually supplying correspondences to the 5 point algorithm using RANSAC (cf. Fig. 8). We show the result for allowing deviations from those four motions, and for allowing no deviation. We additionally show the resulting point cloud where no deviation is allowed. Note that the three cubes are not reconstructed with commensurate size; this is a consequence of each piecewise reconstruction being individually up to a scale ambiguity.

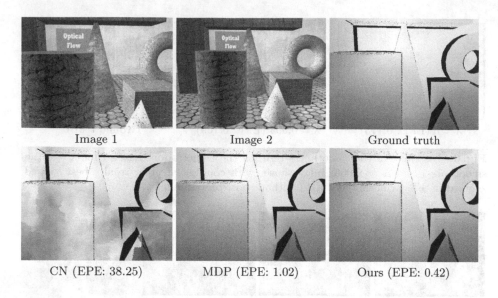

| Image 1 | Image 2 | Ground truth |
| CN (EPE: 38.25) | MDP (EPE: 1.02) | Ours (EPE: 0.42) |

Fig. 9. Result on a challenging case with large displacement camera zoom, causing a radial flow pattern. Note that this sequence is not part of the published UCL optical flow data set. We used the same parameter settings to compute our results as in Table 1.

Radial Flow. Certain types of camera motions can be difficult to handle for flow methods that use a 2D parametrisation. For instance, camera zoom induces a radial flow pattern around the viewing direction, which conflicts with a smoothness assumption that promotes neighboring flow vectors to be similar. However, our approach is flexible enough to recover the homographies induced by this motion, as illustrated in Fig. 9.

Limitations. We kept the patch size identical across all our experiments, regardless of image size or scale. As in patch-based stereo techniques, our approach is sensitive to the aperture problem, and more generally to poorly textured surfaces. It is this problem of inadequate match discriminability that accounts for the comparatively poor performance of our algorithm for the Robot, Sponza1, Sponza2, TxtRMovement, and TxtLMovement data sets. An obvious way to alleviate this problem where applicable is to set the patch size appropriately. A direction for future work could be to develop a smoothness term that promotes not only smoothness of the 2D flow, but explicitly exploits the geometric interpretation of the paramterization to promote similarity of the 9 DoF states themselves.

4   Conclusion

We have presented a new optical flow technique that uses a simple and geometrically motivated model and exploits that model to carry out the optimization in a manner that makes geometrically reasonable moves. While the model lives in a high-dimensional space that would prove challenging to optimize using conventional methods, we show PMBP to be well suited for the task. We obtain a 2D flow that compares favorably to other state-of-the-art techniques and manage to handle both small and large displacements. Our smoothness term helps promote smoothness of the obtained 2D flow fields. A side effect of our approach is that—provided rigid body motions are reasonable—depth can be directly extracted from the parameterization, which can be used to construct a point cloud and flowed to intermediate time steps.

References

1. Baker, S., Scharstein, D., Lewis, J., Roth, S., Black, M., Szeliski, R.: A database and evaluation methodology for optical flow. Intl. J. of Comp. Vis. (2011)
2. Barnes, C., Shechtman, E., Finkelstein, A., Goldman, D.: PatchMatch: a randomized correspondence algorithm for structural image editing. ACM Transactions on Graphics (2009)
3. Barnes, C., Shechtman, E., Goldman, D.B., Finkelstein, A.: The generalized patchMatch correspondence algorithm. In: Daniilidis, K., Maragos, P., Paragios, N. (eds.) ECCV 2010, Part III. LNCS, vol. 6313, pp. 29–43. Springer, Heidelberg (2010)
4. Besse, F., Rother, C., Fitzgibbon, A., Kautz, J.: PMBP: PatchMatch belief propagation for correspondence field estimation. In: Proc. BMVC (2012)
5. Bleyer, M., Rhemann, C., Rother, C.: PatchMatch stereo-Stereo matching with slanted support windows. In: Proc. BMVC (2011)
6. Brox, T., Bregler, C., Malik, J.: Large displacement optical flow. In: Proc. CVPR (2009)
7. Delong, A., Osokin, A., Isack, H.N., Boykov, Y.: Fast approximate energy minimization with label costs. Intl. J. of Comp. Vis. (2012)
8. Fischler, M.A., Bolles, R.C.: Random sample consensus: A paradigm for model fitting with applications to image analysis and automated cartography. Commun. ACM (1981)
9. Hartley, R., Zisserman, A.: Multiple view geometry in computer vision, vol. 2. Cambridge University Press (2000)
10. Heise, P., Klose, S., Jensen, B., Knoll, A.: PM-Huber: PatchMatch with Huber regularization for stereo matching. In: Proc. CVPR (2013)
11. Horn, B., Schunck, B.: Determining optical flow. Artificial Intelligence (1981)
12. Hornáček, M., Fitzgibbon, A., Rother, C.: SphereFlow: 6 DoF scene flow from RGB-D pairs. In: Proc. CVPR (June 2014)
13. Li, G., Zucker, S.W.: Surface geometric constraints for stereo in belief propagation. In: Proc. CVPR (2006)
14. Lowe, D.: Object recognition from local scale-invariant features. In: Proc. ICCV (1999)
15. Mac Aodha, O., Humayun, A., Pollefeys, M., Brostow, G.: Learning a confidence measure for optical flow. IEEE T-PAMI (2012)
16. Moisan, L., Stival, B.: A probabilistic criterion to detect rigid point matches between two images and estimate the fundamental matrix. Intl. J. of Comp. Vis. (2004)
17. Morel, J.M., Yu, G.: Asift: A new framework for fully affine invariant image comparison. SIAM Journal on Imaging Sciences (2009)

18. Nir, T., Bruckstein, A., Kimmel, R.: Over-parameterized variational optical flow. Intl. J. of Comp. Vis. (2008)
19. Nistér, D.: An efficient solution to the five-point relative pose problem. IEEE T-PAMI (2004)
20. Rosman, G., Shem-Tov, S., Bitton, D., Nir, T., Adiv, G., Kimmel, R., Feuer, A., Bruckstein, A.: Over-parameterized optical flow using a stereoscopic constraint. Scale Space and Variational Methods in Computer Vision (2012)
21. Rother, C., Kolmogorov, V., Lempitsky, V., Szummer, M.: Optimizing binary MRFs via extended roof duality. In: Proc. CVPR (2007)
22. Sun, D., Roth, S., Black, M.: Secrets of optical flow estimation and their principles. In: Proc. CVPR (2010)
23. Trobin, W., Pock, T., Cremers, D., Bischof, H.: An unbiased second-order prior for high-accuracy motion estimation. Pattern Recognition (2008)
24. Valgaerts, L., Bruhn, A., Weickert, J.: A variational model for the joint recovery of the fundamental matrix and the optical flow. Pattern Recognition (2008)
25. Vogel, C., Schindler, K., Roth, S.: Piecewise rigid scene flow. In: Proc. ICCV (2013)
26. Wedel, A., Pock, T., Braun, J., Franke, U., Cremers, D.: Duality TV-L1 flow with fundamental matrix prior. Image and Vision Computing (2008)
27. Woodford, O., Torr, P., Reid, I., Fitzgibbon, A.: Global stereo reconstruction under second-order smoothness priors. IEEE T-PAMI (2009)
28. Xu, L., Jia, J., Matsushita, Y.: Motion detail preserving optical flow estimation. IEEE T-PAMI (2012)
29. Yedidia, J.S., Freeman, W.T., Weiss, Y.: Generalized belief propagation. In: NIPS (2000)
30. Yoon, K., Kweon, I.: Adaptive support-weight approach for correspondence search. IEEE T-PAMI (2006)
31. Zach, C., Pock, T., Bischof, H.: A duality based approach for realtime TV-L1 optical flow. Pattern Recognition (2007)

Local Estimation of High Velocity Optical Flow with Correlation Image Sensor

Hidekata Hontani, Go Oishi, and Tomohiro Kitagawa

Department of Computer Science
Nagoya Institute of Technology, Japan

Abstract. In this article, the authors address a problem of the estimation of high velocity optical flow. When images are captured by conventional image sensors, the problem of the optical flow estimation is ill-posed if only the temporal constancy of the image brightness is the valid assumption. When given images are captured by the correlation image sensors, though, you can make the problem of the optical flow estimation well-posed under some condition and can locally estimate the unique optical flow at each pixel in each single frame. The condition though would not be satisfied when the flow velocity is high. In this article, we propose a method that can estimate the normal component of high velocity optical flow using only the local image values in each single frame. The equation used for estimating the normal velocity is theoretically derived and the condition the equation holds is also revealed.

Keywords: optical flow, high velocity flow, real time estimation, time correlation image sensor.

1 Introduction

Ill-posedness is a fundamental problem for estimating optical flow. Most techniques of the optical flow estimation use one basic model that represents the temporal constancy of image brightness, $I(x, y)$: the image brightness of a particular point in the moving pattern is assumed temporally constant. Horn and Schunk derived one linear equation from this assumption[1]:

$$(u\partial_x + v\partial_y + \partial_t)I(x, y, t) = 0, \tag{1}$$

where ∂_* denotes the partial derivative with respect to the subscript variable, and a two-vector, $v = [u, v]^T$, denotes the flow vector at (x, y). The problem of the flow estimation is ill-posed[2] because one single constraint (1) cannot determine the values of the two unknowns u and v, uniquely. Even if the corresponding edge is curved, as long as you use only the model (1), you cannot make the problem well-posed: Multiple pixels bring more unknowns than constraints. You can estimate only the component of the flow parallel to the spatial gradient of $I(x, y)$ if only the linear constraint equation (1) is available[2].

For determining the 2D flow uniquely, you need another model that constrains the flow based on a different aspect of the optical flow. Many models have

D. Fleet et al. (Eds.): ECCV 2014, Part III, LNCS 8691, pp. 235–249, 2014.

been proposed for that purpose[3] and they can be classified into two categories – local models and global ones. The former represents local coherence of the flow[4][5]: e.g., the unknown optical flow vector is assumed constant within some neighborhood[5]. The latter represents some global characteristics of the flow distribution, e.g. partly smooth distribution, and is employed by the variational methods[6][7][8] and by the discrete optimization ones[9][10]. You can find large varieties of the models for representing the characteristics of optical flow field and of the optimization algorithms, and the temporal constancy of the image brightness is still a basic assumption for all of these methods[3]. Those local/global models represent the prior knowledge of flow fields and are distinct from the temporal constancy model, which represents an aspect of measurement. In this article, the temporal constancy model is focused on.

Recently, a correlation image sensor has been developed by Wei et al. [11]. It has been demonstrated that, under certain conditions, you can estimate optical flows based only on the temporal constancy model when the input images are captured by the correlation image sensor[11]. Conventional image sensors capture images by integrating light intensity over the period the shutter is open, and this time integration eliminates the information of the temporal change of the light intensity. On the other hand, a correlation image sensor has three channels and measures not only the brightness but also the cross-correlation between the temporal change of the incident light intensity and reference signals supplied by you. The value of the cross-correlation measured at each pixel contains some information of the temporal change of the light intensity during the shutter is open, and is independent of the brightness. You can hence make the problem of the optical flow estimation well-posed and can uniquely estimate the optical flow by using the measurements obtained in a local small aperture based only on the temporal constancy model, under some conditions. The details will be described later.

Unfortunately, you can not always make the problem of the optical flow estimation well-posed even if the images are captured by correlation image sensors. The estimation would be ill-posed when the flow velocity is high and when the brightness pattern is heavily blurred by the high velocity motion. When the velocity is high, the linear constraint equation (1) does not hold well and the heavy motion blur smooths out the local structures of the pattern that are required for the optical flow estimation. This is why the proposed method is required for estimating high velocity flows. Figure 1 shows the outlines of the methods of optical flow estimation. The conventional methods estimate flows by using two images consecutively captured by a conventional image sensor (Fig.1(A)). The Wei's method[11] estimates flows by using three images simultaneously captured by a time correlation image sensor (Fig.1(B)), and the proposed method computes the normal components of the flows from the spatial gradient of the phase computed from two of the three images (Fig.1(C)).

In this article, we propose a method that estimates the normal components of high velocity flows based only on the measurements obtained in a small spatial window, e.g., a 3×3 pixels, in each *single* frame, even when the image brightness

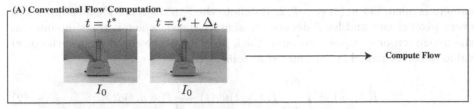

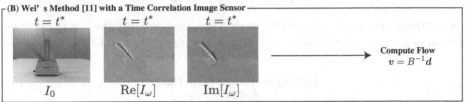

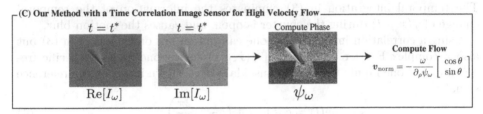

Fig. 1. Comparison between conventional methods(A), Wei's method(B)[11], and our proposed method(C). Conventional methods use two consecutive images captured at different times. The Wei's method[11] computes optical flows by using three images simultaneously captured by a time correlation image sensor. Our method computes normal components of high velocity flows by using two of the images captured by the time correlation image sensor.

pattern is heavily blurred by the motion. Analogous to the Wei's method, our proposed method uses the time correlation image sensor for measuring both the brightness and the complex Fourier coefficient corresponding to a specific frequency determined by the reference signals at each pixel. Then, the proposed method computes the spatial gradients of the phases of the complex Fourier coefficient, and estimates the normal component of the high velocity flow at each pixel by using the computed spatial gradient of the phase. The details of the correlation image sensors and of the algorithm of the Wei's method[11] are explained in the remainder of this section. Our proposed method is then described in the next section.

1.1   Correlation Image Sensor

A correlation image sensor has an array of pixel circuits, each of which measures the temporal cross-correlations between the light intensity and three reference signals. Let $f(x, y, t)$ denote the light intensity, where (x, y) denotes the location of the pixel circuit on the sensor and t denotes the time during the shutter of the camera is open. Let $w_i(t)$ $(i = 1, 2, 3)$ denote the i-th reference signal supplied to every pixel circuit and let T denote the shutter speed, which is the time interval the image sensor is exposed to light. Each pixel has three channels and the pixel value of each channel is determined as follows[11]:

$$R_i(x, y) = \int_{-T/2}^{T/2} f(x, y, t) w_i(t) + \frac{1}{3} f(x, y, t) dt. \tag{2}$$

Conventional image sensors, on the other hand, measure just the temporal integration of $f(x, y, t)$ at each pixel and obtains the pixel values, $I_0(x, y)$, as follows:

$$I_0(x, y) = \int_{-T/2}^{T/2} f(x, y, t) dt. \tag{3}$$

The temporal integration in (3) eliminates the information of the temporal change of $f(x, y, t)$ during the shutter is open, and causes the motion blur.

Using a correlation image sensor, one can obtain not only $I_0(x, y)$ in (3) but also a complex Fourier coefficient of $f(x, y, t)$ corresponding to a specific frequency, ω, if one inputs the three sinusoidal waves shown in (4) as the reference signals:

$$w_i(t) = \cos\left(\omega t + (i - 1)\frac{2\pi}{3}\right). \tag{4}$$

In this paper, we assume that the Fourier coefficients of the temporal signal, $f(x, y, t)$, are well defined. Let f_ω denote the temporal Fourier coefficient: $f_\omega = A_\omega e^{j\phi_\omega}$, where A_ω denotes the amplitude and ϕ_ω denotes the phase. One can estimate A_ω and ϕ_ω as shown in (5) and (6) when $w_i(t)$ in (4) are the reference signals[11]:

$$\phi_\omega = \tan^{-1}\left(\frac{\sqrt{3}(R_2 - R_3)}{2R_1 - R_2 - R_3}\right), \tag{5}$$

$$A_\omega = \frac{2\sqrt{2}}{3}\sqrt{(R_1 - R_2)^2 + (R_2 - R_3)^2 + (R_3 - R_1)^2}. \tag{6}$$

In addition to the values of ϕ_ω and A_ω, one can estimate the value of I_0 shown in (3) as follows:

$$I_0(x, y) = R_1 + R_2 + R_3. \tag{7}$$

R_1, R_2, and R_3 are measured by a correlation sensor, and the values of I_0, A_ω, and ϕ_ω are calculated by a computer for each pixel in every frame. Using these values, you can represent the temporal signal $f(x, y, t)$ as follows:

$$f(x, y, t) = \frac{I_0}{T} + A_\omega \cos(\omega t + \phi_\omega) + \xi(t), \quad (-T/2 < t < T/2) \tag{8}$$

where $\xi(t)$ denotes any time-varying components except for the frequency, ω. A_ω and ϕ_ω carry some information of the temporal change of $f(x, y, t)$. Here, it should be reminded that a target signal is (implicitly) assumed to be periodic when you compute its Fourier coefficients: A signal, $f_{\text{recon}}(x, y, t)$, reconstructed from the Fourier coefficients is periodic and satisfies $f_{\text{recon}}(x, y, t + mT) = f(x, y, t)$ $(-T/2 < t < T/2)$ where m is an integer.

1.2 Making Optical Flow Problem Well-Posed

The optical flow estimation is an ill-posed problem if a conventional image sensor is used and if only the temporal constancy is the valid assumption. Under the constancy assumption, the following equation is satisfied for any $t \in [-T/2, T/2]$:

$$\frac{df}{dt}(x(t), y(t), t) = 0. \tag{9}$$

For small displacement, a first order Taylor expansion yields the optical flow constraint of the incident light intensity:

$$(u\partial_x + v\partial_y + \partial_t)f(x, y, t) = 0. \tag{10}$$

You cannot use directly the equation (10) for the flow estimation because no image sensor can measure the instantaneous light intensity, $f(x, y, t)$. The flow, (u, v), should be constrained by the pixel values, $I_0(x, y)$, if images are captured by conventional image sensors. Integrating the equation (10) over the period the shutter is open, one obtains the optical flow constraint equation proposed by Horn and Schunk[1] that represents the relationship between the flow, (u, v), and the partial differential coefficients of $I_0(x, y)$:

$$\int_{-T/2}^{T/2} (u\partial_x + v\partial_y + \partial_t)f(x, y, t)dt = (u\partial_x + v\partial_y + \partial_t)I_0(x, y) = 0. \tag{11}$$

This single linear equation is well satisfied in many cases[3], but is evidently insufficient for estimating unique values of the two variables, u and v, for each pixel: The estimation of (u, v) is ill-posed here, and you need other information of (u, v) for restricting the solutions. For example, some local methods assume that the flow is spatially constant in each local area[5] and some global methods assume optical flow fields are partly smooth[6]. In our proposed method, the information comes from the Fourier coefficient measured by a correlation image sensor.

The optical flow estimation can be a well-posed problem under some conditions even when only the temporal constancy is the valid assumption, if the images are captured by correlation image sensors[11]. You can derive a system of independent linear equations of (u, v) from the constancy assumption (10). Integrating the equation (10) with a modulating function, $w(t) = e^{-j\omega t}$, over the exposure time interval, one obtains the following equation, which describes the relationship between the Fourier coefficient and the flow:

$$\int_{-T/2}^{T/2} \{(u\partial_x + v\partial_y + \partial_t)f(x,y,t)\} e^{-j\omega t} dt =$$

$$(u\partial_x + v\partial_y + j\omega)I_\omega(x,y) + [f(x,y,t)e^{-j\omega t}]_{-T/2}^{T/2} = 0,$$

$$(12)$$

where $I_\omega(x,y,t)$ is the complex Fourier coefficient, which can be obtained by a correlation sensor as

$$I_\omega(x,y) = \int_{-T/2}^{T/2} f(x,y,t)e^{-j\omega t} dt = A_\omega(\cos\phi_\omega - j\sin\phi_\omega). \quad (13)$$

It should be noted that the temporal partial differentiation is eliminated in (12) by using the integration by parts. As described in [11], setting the angular frequency of the reference signals as

$$\omega = \frac{2n\pi}{T}, \quad (14)$$

you can derive from (12) a system of two linear equations such that

$$Bv = d, \quad (15)$$

where $v = [u,v]^T$, $d = [\omega \mathrm{Im}[I_\omega], -\omega \mathrm{Re}[I_\omega]]^T$, and

$$B = \begin{bmatrix} \partial_x\{\mathrm{Re}[I_\omega] - (-1)^n I_0\} & \partial_y\{\mathrm{Re}[I_\omega] - (-1)^n I_0\} \\ \partial_x \mathrm{Im}[I_\omega] & \partial_y \mathrm{Im}[I_\omega] \end{bmatrix}. \quad (16)$$

You can estimate the flow, v, by solving (16) as $v = B^{-1}d$. The equation shown in (15) is employed for the estimation in the remainder of this article.

The information used for the estimation of the flow is very local. When you use a $\Delta \times \Delta$ difference operator (e.g. $\Delta = 3$ pixels) for computing each of the spatial differentiations in (16), you can estimate the flow vector for each pixel based only on the measurements, I_0 and I_ω, obtained at the neighboring $\Delta \times \Delta$ pixels in each single frame. Temporal difference operations are not required for the flow estimation because the temporal differentiation is eliminated in (12). The estimation of the optical flow is now well-posed if $\det B \neq 0$. This condition is well satisfied, e.g., around the boundaries of moving objects and in moving textured regions.

2   Local Estimation of Optical Flow

In this section, our proposed method for locally estimating high velocity optical flow is described. Before describing the method, we discuss the spatio-temporal characteristics of $f(x,y,t)$ and the aperture problem.

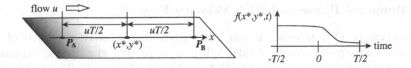

Fig. 2. A spatial trajectory of a point moving at the velocity, $\bar{u}$. The right graph shows the temporal change of $f(x^*, y^*, t)$.

2.1 Spatio-Temporal Structures of Light Intensity

A spatial trajectory of a point during the time the shutter is open is firstly considered. As shown in (3) and in (13), the pixel values, $I_0(x^*, y^*)$ and $I_\omega(x^*, y^*)$ measured at a point (x^*, y^*) are determined by the temporal change of the instantaneous light intensity, $f(x^*, y^*, t)$ $(t \in (-T/2, T/2))$. In this subsection, we assume that $v(x^*, y^*) = [\bar{u}, 0]^T$ $(\bar{u} \neq 0)$ without loss of generality and that the velocity is spatially and temporally coherent in a local aperture around $(x^*, y^*, 0)$. The unit of the velocity is pixel per second and the time needed for moving to a neighbor pixel is $1/\bar{u}$ seconds. Then, the location of a point that passes through (x^*, y^*) at $t = 0$ is described as follows:

$$[x(t), y(t)]^T = [\bar{u}t + x^*, y^*]^T. \tag{17}$$

The spatial trajectory of the point between $[-T/2, T/2]$ is a line segment between two points, $P_A = (x^* - \bar{u}T/2, y^*)$ and $P_B = (x^* + \bar{u}T/2, y^*)$ as shown in Fig.2. Using $x^* = x(t) - \bar{u}t$, you can transform the temporal integrations shown in (3) and in (13) into spatial ones:

$$I_0(x^*, y^*) = \frac{1}{\bar{u}} \int_{-\bar{u}T/2}^{\bar{u}T/2} f(x^* - s, y^*, 0) ds, \tag{18}$$

$$I_\omega(x^*, y^*) = \frac{1}{\bar{u}} \int_{-\bar{u}T/2}^{\bar{u}T/2} f(x^* - s, y^*, 0) e^{-j\omega s/\bar{u}} ds, \tag{19}$$

where $s = \bar{u}t$. $I_0(x, y)$ is a spatial convolution between $f(x, y, 0)$ and a box filter, $b_u(x)$, where

$$b_u(x) = \begin{cases} 1/\bar{u}, & -\bar{u}T/2 < x < \bar{u}T/2, \\ 0, & \text{otherwise.} \end{cases} \tag{20}$$

This convolution represents the motion blur, of which scale is proportional to $\bar{u}$ and T[1]. $I_\omega(x, y)$ is a spatial convolution between $f(x, y, 0)$ and a complex partial sinusoidal wave, $g_u(x)$, where

$$g_u(x) = \begin{cases} \bar{u}^{-1} e^{-j\omega x/\bar{u}}, & -\bar{u}T/2 \leq x \leq \bar{u}T/2, \\ 0, & \text{otherwise.} \end{cases} \tag{21}$$

This convolution extracts the component of a specific spatial frequency, $\omega/\bar{u}$, from the profile of $f(x, y, 0)$ along the line segment $\overline{P_A P_B}$.

---

[1] $\int b_u(x) dx = T$ means the images become brighter when the exposure time is longer.

2.2 Temporal Phase and High Velocity Flow

The solution of (15) is exact if the first order Taylor expansion (10) of the constancy assumption exactly holds. When $v = [\bar{u}, 0]^T$, the Taylor expansion of the constancy assumption yields $(\bar{u}\partial_x + \partial_t)f(x, y^*, t) = 0$. The term of ∂_y disappears from the constraint equation (10) because $dy(t)/dt = 0$. Let us assume that $f(x, y^*, 0)$ is linear with respect to x and that the first order Taylor expansion exactly holds: i.e., $f(x, y^*, 0) = ax + b$ $(a \neq 0)$. Then, setting $n = 1$ in (14) for simplicity, you obtain $I_0(x, y^*) = (ax + b) \otimes b_u(x) = (ax + b)T/\bar{u}$ and $I_\omega(x, y^*) = (ax + b) \otimes g_u(x) = -aT/j\omega$, and have the system of the equations in (15) as follows:

$$Bv = \begin{bmatrix} aT/\bar{u} & \epsilon \\ 0 & \delta \end{bmatrix} \begin{bmatrix} u \\ v \end{bmatrix} = \begin{bmatrix} aT \\ 0 \end{bmatrix}. \tag{22}$$

where ϵ and δ are not determined by the constraint equation. You can obtain a unique and exact solution, $\hat{u} = [\bar{u}, 0]^T$, if $\epsilon \neq 0$ or $\delta \neq 0$. In other words, you do not have the aperture problem when $\partial_y \mathrm{Re}[I_\omega] \neq (-1)^n \partial_y I_0$ or $\partial_y \mathrm{Im}[I_\omega] \neq 0$. These conditions would be satisfied when I_0 or I_ω spatially changes along the direction perpendicular to the flow vector.

When the flow velocity is high, though, the solution of (15) might be inaccurate even if the light intensity of each moving point is temporally constant as assumed in (9). Higher velocity flow smooths out the spatial structures of $f(x, y, 0)$ heavily and generates more blurred images, $I_0(x, y)$. This results in that $\partial_x I_0(x, y) \simeq 0$ when $v = [\bar{u}, 0]^T$ and that the calculated values of $\partial_x I_0(x, y)$ in (16) are unreliable because of noises and of quantization. In other words, the constraint equation of I_0 shown in (11) constrains little about the optical flow. This is one of the main reasons why you need some information other than the optical flow constraint for obtaining large displacement flow(e.g. [12]). When the equation (11) constrains u and v little, the estimation of the optical flow is again ill-posed even if the images are captured by correlation sensors. Now, the aperture problem returns and only the complex image, $I_\omega(x, y)$, contains information useful for locally estimating the optical flow.

Let an isophase curve that passes through (x^*, y^*) be denoted by $\mathcal{C}$, where $\mathcal{C} = \{(x, y) | \phi_\omega(x, y) = \phi_\omega(x^*, y^*)\}$. Assuming some coherency on the spatial pattern of $f(x, y, 0)$ and on the spatial distribution of optical flow, you can assume $\mathcal{C}$ is continuous and smooth, and the temporal signals, $f(x, y, t)$, measured on $\mathcal{C}$ are similar. The normal component estimated by the proposed method is a component of the optical flow perpendicular to the isophase curve, $\mathcal{C}$. Let an orthogonal curve of the isophase curves that passes through (x^*, y^*) be denoted by $\mathcal{T}$ (see Fig.3). This curve, $\mathcal{T}$, is a pseudo trajectory of a moving point that passes through (x^*, y^*), and let assume, without loss of generality, $\mathcal{T}$ is a line parallel to the x-axis around (x^*, y^*). The coordinates of a point in $\mathcal{T}$ is represented by $(x^* + \rho, y^*)$ and the positive direction of ρ is identical with that of the flow. The temporal signal, $f(x^*, y^*, t)$ $(t \in (-T/2, T/2))$, is determined by the spatial profile of the light intensity along $\mathcal{T}$, $f_{\mathcal{T}}^*(\rho) = f(x^* + \rho, y^*, 0)$.

Fig. 3. The time delay observed at a neighboring pixel. The red curve in the right graph is measured at $(x^* + \rho, y^*)$ when the black one is measured at (x^*, y^*).

At the neighboring point, you measure a temporal signal identical to $f(x^*, y^*, t)$ with a time delay, $\rho/\bar{u}$:

$$f(x^* + \rho, y^*, t) = f(x^*, y^*, t - \rho/\bar{u}) = f(x^*, y^*, t) \otimes \delta(t - \rho/\bar{u}), \qquad (23)$$

where the convolution with the delta function is estimated with respect to the time t. Let again

$$I_\omega(x^*, y^*) = A_\omega e^{-j\phi_\omega} = \int_{-T/2}^{T/2} f(x^*, y^*, t) e^{-j\omega t} dt, \qquad (24)$$

where A_ω is the amplitude and ϕ_ω is the phase at (x^*, y^*). Substituting (24) for (23), you obtain the following equation, in which the phase of $I_\omega(x^* + \rho, y^*)$ is proportional to the spatial distance, ρ:

$$I_\omega(x^* + \rho, y^*) = A_\omega e^{-j\phi_\omega(\rho)} = A_\omega e^{-j(\phi_\omega - \rho\omega/\bar{u})}. \qquad (25)$$

In case the equation (25) holds, you can estimate the normal speed, $\bar{u} = \|v_{\text{norm}}\|$, by using the value of the spatial derivative of the phase,

$$\frac{\partial \phi_\omega(\rho)}{\partial \rho} = -\frac{\omega}{\bar{u}}. \qquad (26)$$

Unfortunately, though equation (23) always holds, equation (25) does not always hold because of the fixed and bounded integration interval. At least the condition, $f(x^*, y^*, -T/2) = f(x^*, y^*, T/2)$, should be satisfied in order for equation (25) to hold. This is because, if $f(x^*, y^*, -T/2) \neq f(x^*, y^*, T/2)$, the reconstructed signal, $f_{\text{recon}}(t)$, is discontinuous at $t = -T/2 + mT$ and these discontinuous points are fixed and independent from the time-delay. For example, when a flying bright particle passes in front of the sensor with a high speed, $\bar{u}$, then the temporal change of the light intensity can be well represented by a delta function: $f(x^* + \rho, y^*, t) = A\delta(t - \rho/\bar{u})$, and you obtain $I_\omega(x^* + \rho, y^*) = Ae^{-j\omega\rho/\bar{u}}$ from (24). In this example, equation (25) holds and you can estimate the speed as $\bar{u} = \omega/(\partial_\rho\phi_\omega)$. On the other hand, for example, when the temporal change of the light intensity is represented by a step function: $f(x^* + \rho, y^*, t) = B \times h(t - \rho/\bar{u})$, where

$$h(t) = \begin{cases} 1, & \text{if } t \geq 0, \\ 0, & \text{otherwise,} \end{cases} \qquad (27)$$

then you obtain $I_\omega(x^* + \rho, y^*) = I_\omega^{(h)}(\rho)$, where

$$I_\omega^{(h)}(\rho) = \int_{-T/2}^{T/2} h(t - \rho/\bar{u})e^{-j\omega t}dt = \begin{cases} -(e^{-j\omega\rho/\bar{u}} - j)/\omega, & \text{if } \rho > 0, \\ -(e^{-j\omega\rho/\bar{u}} + j)/\omega, & \text{otherwise.} \end{cases} \qquad (28)$$

In this case, $f(x^*, y^*, -T/2) \neq f(x^*, y^*, T/2)$ and the imaginary part of I_ω has a non-zero constant term. As a result, the equation (25) does not hold and you cannot estimate the velocity accurately by using the phase delay because $\bar{u} \neq \omega/(\partial_\rho\phi_\omega)$. From an application's point of view, a step function well represents the temporal changes of the light intensities measured near the boundaries of rapidly moving objects, and we need a method that can accurately estimate $\bar{u}$ even if the temporal change of the light intensity has a form like a step function.

Let the function of the temporal change of the light intensity be decomposed as follows:

$$f(x^*, y^*, t) = A \times b(t) + B \times h(t) + \eta(t), \qquad (29)$$

where $h(t)$ is a step function described above, and $b(t)$ is any bounded function that has non-zero values only in a limited region as follows:

$$b(t) = \begin{cases} b_{\text{in}}(t), & \text{if } -\epsilon < t < \epsilon \\ 0, & \text{otherwise.} \end{cases} \qquad (30)$$

Here, $0 < \epsilon < T/2$ and $b_{\text{in}}(t)$ can have non-zero values. $b(t)$ represents the temporal change of the light intensity that would be measured when a small or thin object rapidly passes in front of the sensor, and $h(t)$ would be measured at around the boundaries of rapidly moving large objects. The last term of the right hand side of (29), $\eta(t)$, denotes a component of $f(x^*, y^*, t)$ other than $b(t)$ and $h(t)$.

In the proposed method, we assume that the values, $I_\omega(x, y)$, measured by a correlation sensor are mainly determined by $b(t)$ and $h(t)$: The component of $\eta(t)$ corresponding to the frequency of ω has a power smaller than those of $b(t)$ and of $h(t)$, and is ignorable. This assumption does not hold in general but is satisfied by variety of signals including impulse signals, Gaussian pulses, and blurred step functions, which cover main signals measured when high speed objects are observed. Let $I_\omega^{(b)}(\rho)$ denote the Fourier coefficient of $b(t - \rho/\bar{u})$. Computing the coefficient, you obtain

$$I_\omega^{(b)}(\rho) = A_b e^{-j(\phi_\omega^{(b0)} + \rho/\bar{u})}, \qquad (31)$$

where

$$\int_{-T/2}^{T/2} b(t)e^{-j\omega t}dt = A_b e^{-j\phi_\omega^{(b0)}}, \qquad (32)$$

and A_b is a real coefficient. Under the condition that $\eta(t)$ is ignorable, you obtain

$$I_\omega(x^* + \rho, y^*) = \alpha e^{-j\omega\rho/\bar{u}} + \beta \qquad (33)$$

by inserting (28) and (31) to (29), where $\alpha = A \cdot A_b \cdot e^{-j\phi_\omega^{(b0)}} - B/\omega$ and $\beta = -jB/\omega$. Here, it should be noted that the phase of $I_\omega(x^* + \rho, y^*)$ is not proportional to ρ because of β. For eliminating β, we compute the spatial differentiation of $I_\omega(x^* + \rho, y^*)$:

$$\frac{\partial I_\omega(x^* + \rho, y^*)}{\partial \rho} = -\frac{j\omega}{\bar{u}} \alpha e^{-j\omega\rho/\bar{u}}. \tag{34}$$

Now, the phase of $\partial_\rho I_\omega$ is proportional to ρ as shown in (34). Let the phase of $\partial_\rho I_\omega$ be denoted by ψ_ω, where $\psi_\omega = \mathrm{Im}[\partial_\rho I_\omega]/\mathrm{Re}[\partial_\rho I_\omega]$. Then, you can compute the speed, $\bar{u}$ by using the following equation:

$$\partial_\rho \psi_\omega = -\omega/\bar{u}. \tag{35}$$

As described above, the normal speed, $\bar{u}$, can be obtained by computing the directional derivative of I_ω and of ψ_ω with respect to ρ, and the direction of ρ is parallel to the spatial gradient of the phase of $I_\omega(x, y)$. Let the phase of $I_\omega(x, y)$ be denoted by $\phi_\omega(x, y) = \tan^{-1}(\mathrm{Im}[I_\omega]/\mathrm{Re}[I_\omega])$ and the angle between the direction of the spatial gradient $\nabla\phi_\omega$ and the x-axis be denoted by θ. Then, the direction of ρ is parallel to $[\cos\theta, \sin\theta]^T$. The proposed method computes v_{norm} as followings:

1. Compute the direction of $\nabla\phi_\omega = [\partial_x\phi_\omega, \partial_y\phi_\omega]^T$ as follows:

$$\cos\theta = \frac{\partial_x\phi_\omega}{\sqrt{(\partial_x\phi_\omega)^2 + (\partial_y\phi_\omega)^2}}, \text{ and } \sin\theta = \frac{\partial_y\phi_\omega}{\sqrt{(\partial_x\phi_\omega)^2 + (\partial_y\phi_\omega)^2}} \tag{36}$$

2. Compute the directional derivative of $I_\omega(x, y)$ with respect to ρ as

$$\partial_\rho I_\omega = (\partial_x I_\omega)\cos\theta + (\partial_y I_\omega)\sin\theta, \tag{37}$$

   where $\cos\theta$ and $\sin\theta$ are given in (36). Let $\psi_\omega = \tan^{-1}\mathrm{Im}[\partial_\rho I_\omega]/\mathrm{Re}[\partial_\rho I_\omega]$.
3. Compute

$$\partial_\rho \psi_\omega = (\partial_x\psi_\omega)\cos\theta + (\partial_y\psi_\omega)\sin\theta. \tag{38}$$

   The resultant two-vector, v_{norm} is obtained as follows:

$$v_{\mathrm{norm}} = -\frac{\omega}{\partial_\rho\psi_\omega}\begin{bmatrix}\cos\theta \\ \sin\theta\end{bmatrix}. \tag{39}$$

3   Experiments

The performance of the proposed method was evaluated by using artificial images and by using real ones captured by a correlation sensor.

3.1   Simulation Experiments

The accuracy of the proposed estimation method was experimentally evaluated using artificial images. Setting the shutter speed $T = 1/30$ seconds and $n = 1$ in (14), we simulated image capturing of the correlation sensor. this paper, we

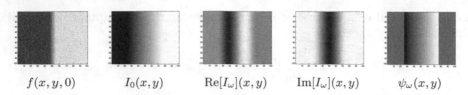

$f(x,y,0)$ $\qquad I_0(x,y)$ $\qquad \mathrm{Re}[I_\omega](x,y)$ $\qquad \mathrm{Im}[I_\omega](x,y)$ $\qquad \psi_\omega(x,y)$

Fig. 4. Artificial images generated in the simulation experiments

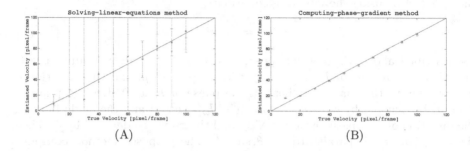

(A) $\qquad\qquad\qquad\qquad\qquad\qquad$ (B)

Fig. 5. Distributions of the estimates obtained by the Wei's method(A) and by the proposed method(B). In each graph, the horizontal axis shows the true normal velocity and the vertical one shows the estimated values. Mean values and one-sigma error bars are indicated in the graphs. The Wei's method cannot accurately estimate the flow when $\bar{u}T$ is larger than $\sigma = 10$.

report the results obtained when we set the light intensity, $f(x,y,0)$, as a blurred step function contaminated by a Gaussian noise as follows:

$$f(x,y,0) = (B \cdot h(t)) * G(\sigma^2) + \xi, \qquad (40)$$

where $G(\sigma^2)$ is a Gaussian blurring filter of which scale is σ^2 and ξ is a Gaussian noise of which variance is s_f^2. Examples of the simulated images, $f(x,y,0)$, $I_0(x,y)$, $\mathrm{Re}[I_\omega](x,y)$, $\mathrm{Im}[I_\omega](x,y)$, and $\phi_\omega(x,y)$, which were obtained when $\boldsymbol{v}_{\mathrm{norm}} = [\bar{u},0]^T = [50,0]^T$ pixel/sec and when $\sigma = 10$ pixel, are shown in Fig.4.

For a comparison purpose, two flow estimation methods were applied to the identical set of simulated images: One was the proposed method and the other was the Wei's method[11] that solves the system of the linear-equations (15). The graphs shown in Fig.5(A) and (B) show the distributions of the estimated velocities. In the graphs, the horizontal-axis indicates the true velocity, $\bar{u}$, the vertical-axis indicates the estimated values, and the blue line shows the ideal estimates. The red colored results were obtained when the noise level, s_f, was 5% of the step size of B in (40) and the green ones were obtained when the noise level was 10% of B. In case the $f(x,y,0)$ is given as shown in (40), the Wei's method works well only when the moving distance of $f(x,y,0)$, $\bar{u}T$, and the spatial blurring scale, σ, is comparable: If $\bar{u}$ is so large that $\bar{u}T \gg \sigma$, then the spatial gradients of I_0 supply little information about the target motion and the solution of the system of the linear equations (15) is unreliable. As shown in

Fig. 6. A camera with the correlation image sensor (left) and the experimental setting (right)

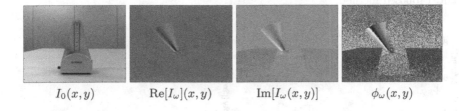

$I_0(x,y)$ $\mathrm{Re}[I_\omega](x,y)$ $\mathrm{Im}[I_\omega(x,y)]$ $\phi_\omega(x,y)$

Fig. 7. Examples of images captured by the correlation image sensor

the graph (A), the Wei's method[11] estimates the flows accurately only when the true velocity is equal or less than $\sigma = 10$. On the other hand, the proposed method estimates the flows accurately when $\bar{u}$ is enough large, as shown in the graph (B).

3.2 Experiments Using a Real Correlation Image Sensor

Capturing real image sequences of a metronome by the correlation image sensor (Fig.6), we evaluated the performance of our proposed method. Figure 7 shows examples of the images captured by the sensor. Using these images, the flows were computed by our proposed method and by the Wei's method[11], and the results were compared with gold standards manually made from $I_0(x,y)$. An example of the flow estimated by each of the methods is shown in Fig.8. The color shows the direction of the flow. The flow obtained by the Wei's method is contaminated by the textures behind the swinging pendulum. On the other hand, the proposed method accurately estimated the flow. It should be noted that these flows are computed in real time for each single frame. The results of the quantitative evaluation are shown in Fig.9. As shown in the graph (A), the Wei's method underestimated the flows of the pendulum when it moved fast, but the proposed one accurately estimated the high-speed flows, as shown in the graph (B).

Fig. 8. Examples of estimated optical flow. Left: $I_0(x, y)$. Middle: Wei's method[11]. Right: Proposed method.

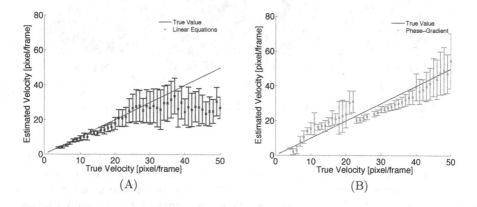

Fig. 9. Distributions of the velocities estimated by the Wei's method (A) and by the proposed method (B)

4   Conclusion

In this article, we proposed a method that can estimate the normal component of high velocity optical flow using the local measurements obtained by the correlation image sensor. When given images are captured by the correlation image sensor, you can make the optical flow estimation well-posed if the corresponding system of the linear equations is not degenerated. In our proposed method, the normal component of the flow is estimated by using the spatial gradient of the phase, $\psi_\omega(x, y)$ when the system of the equations is degenerated. The equation used for estimating the normal velocity was theoretically derived in this paper. Our future works include to develop a vision system that can compute a wide rage of optical flows in real time by combining the Wei's method and our proposed one.

References

1. Horn, B.K., Schunck, B.G.: Determining optical flow. Artificial Intelligence 17(1), 185–203 (1981)
2. Bertero, M., Poggio, T.A., Torre, V.: Ill-posed problems in early vision. Proceedings of the IEEE 76(8), 869–889 (1988)
3. Sun, D., Roth, S., Black, M.J.: Secrets of optical flow estimation and their principles. In: 2010 IEEE Conference on Computer Vision and Pattern Recognition (CVPR), pp. 2432–2439. IEEE (2010)
4. Bigun, J., Granlund, G.H.: Optical flow based on the inertia matrix of the frequency domain. In: Proceedings from SSAB Symposium on Picture Processing, pp. 132–135. Lund University, Sweden (1988)
5. Lucas, B.D., Kanade, T., et al.: An iterative image registration technique with an application to stereo vision. In: IJCAI, vol. 81, pp. 674–679 (1981)
6. Ayvaci, A., Raptis, M., Soatto, S.: Sparse occlusion detection with optical flow. International Journal of Computer Vision 97(3), 322–338 (2012)
7. Garg, R., Roussos, A., Agapito, L.: Robust trajectory-space tv-l1 optical flow for non-rigid sequences. In: Boykov, Y., Kahl, F., Lempitsky, V., Schmidt, F.R. (eds.) EMMCVPR 2011. LNCS, vol. 6819, pp. 300–314. Springer, Heidelberg (2011)
8. Steinbrucker, F., Pock, T., Cremers, D.: Large displacement optical flow computation withoutwarping. In: 2009 IEEE 12th International Conference on Computer Vision, pp. 1609–1614. IEEE (2009)
9. Cosker, D., Li, W., Brown, M., Tang, R.: Optical flow estimation using laplacian mesh energy. In: IEEE International Conference on Computer Vision and Pattern Recognition (CVPR). University of Bath (2013)
10. Trobin, W., Pock, T., Cremers, D., Bischof, H.: Continuous energy minimization via repeated binary fusion. In: Forsyth, D., Torr, P., Zisserman, A. (eds.) ECCV 2008, Part IV. LNCS, vol. 5305, pp. 677–690. Springer, Heidelberg (2008)
11. Wei, D., Masurel, P., Kurihara, T., Ando, S.: Optical flow determination with complex-sinusoidally modulated imaging. In: 2006 8th International Conference on Signal Processing, vol. 2. IEEE (2009)
12. Brox, T., Malik, J.: Large displacement optical flow: descriptor matching in variational motion estimation. IEEE Transactions on Pattern Analysis and Machine Intelligence (99), 1 (2011)

Rank Minimization
with Structured Data Patterns

Viktor Larsson[1], Carl Olsson[1], Erik Bylow[1], and Fredrik Kahl[1,2]

[1] Centre for Mathematical Sciences
Lund University, Sweden
[2] Department of Signals and Systems
Chalmers University of Technology, Sweden

Abstract. The problem of finding a low rank approximation of a given measurement matrix is of key interest in computer vision. If all the elements of the measurement matrix are available, the problem can be solved using factorization. However, in the case of missing data no satisfactory solution exists. Recent approaches replace the rank term with the weaker (but convex) nuclear norm. In this paper we show that this heuristic works poorly on problems where the locations of the missing entries are highly correlated and structured which is a common situation in many applications.

Our main contribution is the derivation of a much stronger convex relaxation that takes into account not only the rank function but also the data. We propose an algorithm which uses this relaxation to solve the rank approximation problem on matrices where the given measurements can be organized into overlapping blocks without missing data. The algorithm is computationally efficient and we have applied it to several classical problems including structure from motion and linear shape basis estimation. We demonstrate on both real and synthetic data that it outperforms state-of-the-art alternatives. [1]

1 Factorization Methods and Convex Relaxations

The ability to find the best fixed rank approximation of a matrix has been proven useful in applications such as structure from motion, photometric stereo and optical flow [5,23,9,3,10]. The rank of the approximating matrix typically describes the complexity of the solution. For example, in non-rigid structure from motion the rank measures the number of basis elements needed to describe the point motions [5]. Therefore a good optimization criterion consists of a trade-off between rank and residual errors, leading to formulations of the type

$$\min_X \mu \operatorname{rank}(X) + \|X - M\|_F^2, \tag{1}$$

where M is a matrix of measurements. The above problem can be solved using the singular value decomposition (SVD) followed by truncation of the singular

---

[1] This work has been funded by the Swedish Research Council (grants no. 2012-4213 and 2012-4215) and the Crafoord Foundation.

D. Fleet et al. (Eds.): ECCV 2014, Part III, LNCS 8691, pp. 250–265, 2014.

values, but the strategy is limited to problems without missing data and outliers. The issue of outliers has received a lot of attention lately. In [8,21,24] the
more robust ℓ_1 norm is used. While experimental results indicate robustness to
suboptimal solutions, these methods are still local in that updates are computed
using a local approximation of the objective function. To handle missing data
[2] replaces the Frobenious norm with the spectral norm. It is shown that if the
missing data forms a Young pattern the globally optimal solution can be computed. For general problems [2] proposes an alternation over Young patterns.

A recent heuristic that has been shown to work well is to replace the rank
function with the nuclear norm [19,7,9,18,1]. This leads to formulations of the
type

$$\min_X \mu\|X\|_* + \|W \odot (X - M)\|_F^2, \tag{2}$$

where W is a matrix with entry $W_{ij} = 1$ if M_{ij} has been observed, $W_{ij} = 0$ otherwise and $\odot$ denotes elementwise multiplication. It can be shown [19,7] that if the
location of the missing entries are random then problem (2) provides the correct
low rank solution. However, in many applications such as structure from motion,
missing entries are highly correlated. When a scene point cannot be tracked any
longer (either due to occlusion or appearance change) it rarely appears again.
This gives rise to certain sparsity patterns (often diagonally dominant) in W
which are not random.

Figure 1 shows the results of a synthetic experiment. Here we generated a
100×100 matrix $A = UV^T$ of rank 3 by randomly selecting 100×3 matrices
U and V with elements selected from a Gaussian distribution (with mean 0 and
standard deviation 1). To generate the measurement matrix M we then added
Gaussian noise with standard deviation 0.05 to each entry in A.

Fig. 1. *Left*: The pattern of missing data (red lines show the blocks used by our algorithm). Available measurements are located close to the diagonal. *Middle*: Absolute
errors of the (rank 3) solution obtained using $(2)^2$. *Right*: Absolute errors of the (rank
3) solution obtained using the proposed approach.

---

[2] μ was chosen so that the first three singular values accounted for 99% of the solution.

In an effort to strengthen the nuclear norm formulation, [1] adds prior information using the generalized trace norm. The formulation is related to (2) by a reweighing of the data term and can incorporate knowledge such as smoothness priors. The availability of such information can improve the estimation, however the formulation still uses the nuclear norm for regularization. On a high level our approach is similar to [1] in that it also attempts to find a stronger convex relaxation by considering not just the rank function but also the data. However, in contrast to [1] we do not add priors to the problem but simply use the information in the available measurements.

The motivation for replacing the rank function with the nuclear norm in (2) is that it is the convex envelope of the rank function on the set $\{X; \sigma_{max}(X) \leq 1\}$. That is, it is the tightest possible convex relaxation on this set. The constraint $\sigma_{max}(X) \leq 1$ is however not present in (2). In fact, the convex envelope of an unconstrained rank function is the zero function. In this paper we show that a significantly more accurate convex envelope can be computed if a solution estimate X_0 is available. Specifically, we compute the convex envelope of

$$f(X) = \mu \operatorname{rank}(X) + \|X - X_0\|_F^2. \tag{3}$$

We will refer to this function as the **localized rank function**. Compared to the nuclear norm constraint $\sigma_{max}(X) \leq 1$, the term $\|X - X_0\|_F^2$ effectively translates the feasible region to a neighborhood around X_0 instead of the trivial solution 0. Therefore our convex envelope can penalize smaller singular values harder than larger ones, while the nuclear norm tries to force all singular values to be zero.

The work most similar to ours is perhaps [13] where the convex envelope of a vector version of our problem (the cardinality function and the ℓ_2-norm) is computed. In contrast, here we are interested in the matrix setting. Furthermore, in [13] the ℓ_2-norm is centered around the origin. In our work the translation is an essential component required to avoid penalizing large singular values.

Minimizing the convex envelope of (3) gives the same result as $\min f(X)$. The significant advantage of using the envelope instead is that it is convex and therefore can be combined with other convex constraints and functions. We propose to utilize it for problems with missing data patterns as exemplified in Figure 1. More specifically, our convex relaxation is applied to sub-blocks of the matrix with no missing entries rather than the nuclear norm of the entire matrix X. In effect, this can be seen as minimizing the rank of each sub-block separately and due to the convexity of our approximation, it is possible to enforce that the sub-blocks agree on their overlap. Furthermore, we show that under mild assumptions it possible to extract a solution to the full matrix X that has rank equal to the largest rank of the sub-blocks. We present an ADMM [4] based approach for obtaining a solution which only requires to compute SVDs of the sub-blocks rather than the whole matrix resulting in an efficient implementation. In summary, we derive tight convex relaxations for a class of problems with a large amount of missing entries that outperform state-of-the-art methods.

Notation. Throughout the paper we use $\sigma_i(X)$ to denote the ith singular value of a matrix X. The vector of all singular values is denoted $\boldsymbol{\sigma}(X)$. With some abuse of notation we write the SVD of X as $U \operatorname{diag}(\boldsymbol{\sigma}(X))V^T$. For ease of notation we do not explicitly indicate the dependence of U and V on X. The scalar product is defined as $\langle X, Y \rangle = \operatorname{tr}(X^T Y)$, where tr is the trace function, and the Frobenius norm $\|X\|_F = \sqrt{\langle X, X \rangle} = \sqrt{\sum \sigma_i^2(X)}$. Truncation at zero is denoted $[a]_+$, that is, $[a]_+ = 0$ if $a < 0$ and a otherwise.

2 The Convex Envelope

In this section we show that it is possible to compute a closed form expression for the convex envelope of the localized rank function (3).

Finding the envelope of f is equivalent to computing $f^{**} = (f^*)^*$, where

$$f^*(Y) = \max_X \ \langle Y, X \rangle - f(X), \tag{4}$$

is the Fenchel conjugate of f [20]. By completing squares, $f^*(Y)$ can be written

$$f^*(Y) = \max_k \ \max_{\operatorname{rank}(X)=k} \left\| \frac{1}{2}Y + X_0 \right\|_F^2 - \|X_0\|_F^2 - \left\| X - (\frac{1}{2}Y + X_0) \right\|_F^2 - \mu k. \tag{5}$$

Note that the first two terms are independent of X and can be considered as constants in the maximization over X and k. In addition k is fixed in the inner maximization. For a fixed k, the maximizing X is given by the best rank k approximation of $\frac{1}{2}Y + X_0$ which can be obtained via an SVD of $\frac{1}{2}Y + X_0$ by setting all singular values but the k largest to zero. Inserting into (5) we get

$$f^*(Y) = \max_k \left\| \frac{1}{2}Y + X_0 \right\|_F^2 - \|X_0\|_F^2 - \sum_{i=k+1}^n \sigma_i^2(\frac{1}{2}Y + X_0) - \mu k \tag{6}$$

$$= \max_k \left\| \frac{1}{2}Y + X_0 \right\|_F^2 - \|X_0\|_F^2 - \sum_{i=k+1}^n \sigma_i^2(\frac{1}{2}Y + X_0) - \sum_{i=1}^k \mu. \tag{7}$$

To select the best k we note that the largest value is achieved when k fulfills

$$\sigma_k^2(\frac{1}{2}Y + X_0) \geq \mu \geq \sigma_{k+1}^2(\frac{1}{2}Y + X_0). \tag{8}$$

For the maximizing k the last two sums can be written

$$\sum_{i=k+1}^n \sigma_i^2(\frac{1}{2}Y + X_0) + \sum_{i=1}^k \mu = \sum_{i=1}^n \min\left(\mu, \ \sigma_i^2(\frac{1}{2}Y + X_0) \right). \tag{9}$$

Therefore we get the conjugate function

$$f^*(Y) = \left\| \frac{1}{2}Y + X_0 \right\|_F^2 - \|X_0\|_F^2 - \sum_{i=1}^n \min\left(\mu, \ \sigma_i^2(\frac{1}{2}Y + X_0) \right). \tag{10}$$

We next proceed to compute the bi-conjugate $f^{**}(X) = \max_Y \langle X, Y \rangle - f^*(Y)$. To simplify computations we change variables to $Z = \frac{1}{2}Y + X_0$ and maximize over Z instead. We get

$$f^{**}(X) = \max_Z 2\langle X, Z - X_0 \rangle - \|Z\|_F^2 + \|X_0\|_F^2 + \sum_{i=1}^{n} \min(\mu, \sigma_i^2(Z)). \quad (11)$$

The first three terms can, by completing squares, be simplified into $\|X - X_0\|_F^2 - \|Z - X\|_F^2$. Furthermore, since $\|X - X_0\|_F^2$ does not depend on Z we get

$$f^{**}(X) = \|X - X_0\|_F^2 + \max_Z \left(\sum_{i=1}^{n} \min\left(\mu, \sigma_i^2(Z)\right) - \|Z - X\|_F^2 \right). \quad (12)$$

The sum in (12) only depends on the singular values of Z and is therefore unitarily invariant. We also note that $-\|Z - X\|_F^2 = -\|Z\|_F^2 + 2\langle Z, X \rangle - \|X\|_F^2$. The term $\|Z\|_F^2$ is unitarily invariant and by von Neumann's trace inequality, we know that $\langle Z, X \rangle \leq \sum_{i=1}^{n} \sigma_i(Z)\sigma_i(X)$. Equality is achieved if X and Z have SVDs with the same U and V. Hence, for Z to maximize the sum in (12), its SVD should be of the form $Z = U \operatorname{diag}(\boldsymbol{\sigma}(Z))V^T$ if $X = U \operatorname{diag}(\boldsymbol{\sigma}(X))V^T$.

What is left now is to determine the singular values of Z and because both terms containing $\sigma_i(Z)$ are separable, we can consider one at a time. Hence we need to solve $\max_{\sigma_i(Z)} \min(\mu, \sigma_i^2(Z)) - (\sigma_i(Z) - \sigma_i(X))^2$. There are two cases:

(i) If $\sigma_i(Z) \leq \sqrt{\mu}$ then the problem simplifies to $\max_{\sigma_i(Z)} \sigma_i^2(Z) - (\sigma_i(Z) - \sigma_i(X))^2$. Expanding the square, this objective function is $2\sigma_i(X)\sigma_i(Z) - \sigma_i^2(X)$. The singular value $\sigma_i(X)$ is positive and the optimal choice is therefore $\sigma_i(Z) = \sqrt{\mu}$.

(ii) If $\sigma_i(Z) \geq \sqrt{\mu}$ we need to solve $\max_{\sigma_i(Z)} \mu - (\sigma_i(Z) - \sigma_i(X))^2$. The maximum is clearly achieved in $\sigma_i(Z) = \sigma_i(X)$.

Summarizing the two cases, the optimal Z has $\sigma_i(Z) = \max(\sqrt{\mu}, \sigma_i(X))$.

We now insert Z into (12) to find the expression for the bi-conjugate. Note that $\min\left(\mu, \sigma_i^2(Z)\right) = \min\left(\mu, \max(\mu, \sigma_i^2(X))\right) = \mu$, and that $\|Z - X\|_F^2 = \sum_{i=1}^{n} \left[\sqrt{\mu} - \sigma_i(X)\right]_+^2$. Hence, the convex envelope is given by

$$f^{**}(X) = \mathcal{R}_\mu(X) + \|X - X_0\|_F^2, \quad (13)$$

where

$$\mathcal{R}_\mu(X) = \sum_{i=1}^{n} \left(\mu - [\sqrt{\mu} - \sigma_i(X)]_+^2 \right). \quad (14)$$

In [22] the authors propose a rank regularizer which for some parameter choices is equivalent to $\mathcal{R}_\mu$. However, they make no connection to the convex envelope of f and simply minimize it in a non-convex framework.

Figure 2 shows a one dimensional version of (13). To the left is the term $\mu - \left[\sqrt{\mu} - \sigma\right]_+^2$ which is in itself not convex. For singular values larger than $\sqrt{\mu}$

it gives a constant penalty. When the quadratic term σ^2 is added the result is a convex penalty, see the middle graph in Figure 2. For $\sigma < \sqrt{\mu}$ the function has a linear shape (red dashed curve) similar to the nuclear norm, while for $\sigma \geq \sqrt{\mu}$ it behaves like the quadratic function $\mu + \sigma^2$. Note that the one dimensional version of f is identical to $\mu + \sigma^2$ everywhere except for $\sigma = 0$. In the right image we plotted the graphs of $\mu - \left[\sqrt{\mu} - \sigma\right]_+^2 + (\sigma - \sigma_0)^2$ for $\sigma_0 = 0, 1, 2$. If σ_0 is large enough the function will not try to force σ to be zero.

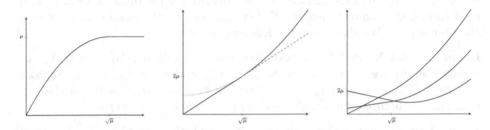

Fig. 2. One dimensional visualizations of (13) for $\mu = 2$. Left: The graph of $\mu - \left[\sqrt{\mu} - \sigma\right]_+^2$. Middle: The graph of $\mu - \left[\sqrt{\mu} - \sigma\right]_+^2 + \sigma^2$. If μ is large its shape resembles the nuclear norm. Right: The graphs of $\mu - \left[\sqrt{\mu} - \sigma\right]_+^2 + (\sigma - \sigma_0)^2$ for $\sigma_0 = 0, 1, 2$.

3   A Block Decomposition Approach

Next we present our approach for solving the missing data problem. The idea is to try to enforce low rank of sub-blocks of the matrix where no measurements are missing using our convex relaxation.

Let R_i and C_i, $i = 1, .., K$ be a subset of row and column indices for each block. By $\mathcal{P}_i : \mathbb{R}^{m \times n} \mapsto \mathbb{R}^{|R_i| \times |C_i|}$ we will mean the (linear) operator that extracts the elements with indices in $R_i \times C_i$ and forms a sub-matrix of size $|R_i| \times |C_i|$. If M is our (partially filled) measurement matrix, then the submatrix $\mathcal{P}_i(M)$ has no missing values. We seek to minimize the non-convex function

$$f(X) = \sum_{i=1}^{K} \mu_i \operatorname{rank}(\mathcal{P}_i(X)) + \|\mathcal{P}_i(X) - \mathcal{P}_i(M)\|_F^2, \qquad (15)$$

by replacing it with the convex envelopes of the localized rank function (13),

$$f_{\mathcal{R}}(X) = \sum_{i=1}^{K} \mathcal{R}_{\mu_i}(\mathcal{P}_i(X)) + \|\mathcal{P}_i(X) - \mathcal{P}_i(M)\|_F^2. \qquad (16)$$

Note that we do not explicitly enforce that the rank of X is penalized, but instead this is accomplished via the rank penalization of the sub-matrices. In the next subsection, we shall see that the rank of the full matrix X and the rank of its sub-matrices $\mathcal{P}_i(X)$ are strongly related. Also note that since the blocks have overlaps this formulation counts some residuals more than others. It is possible to add a term $\|W^r \odot (X - M)\|_F^2$ to ensure that each residual error is counted equally many times, but we have experimentally found that this makes little difference and we therefore ignore this term for ease of presentation.

3.1   Constructing the Full Matrix X

Let us now assume that we have solved the convex relaxation of problem (16). However, as only the sub-matrices of X are involved in the optimization, we still need to find the complete matrix X. Let $r_{\max}$ denote the maximum rank over all sub-matrices. We shall show the following result:

Lemma 1. *Let X_1 and X_2 be two given matrices with overlap matrix X_{22} as depicted in Figure 3, and let $r_1 = \text{rank}(X_1)$ and $r_2 = \text{rank}(X_2)$. Suppose that $\text{rank}(X_{22}) = \min(r_1, r_2)$, then there exists a matrix X with $\text{rank}(X) = \max(r_1, r_2)$. Additionally if $\text{rank}(X_{22}) = r_1 = r_2$ then X is unique.*

Proof. We will assume (w.l.o.g) that $r_2 \leq r_1$, and look at the block X_2. The overlap X_{22} is of rank r_2 so there are r_2 linearly independent columns in $[X_{22}^T \ X_{32}^T]^T$ and rows in $[X_{22} \ X_{23}]$. Now the rank of X_2 is r_2 and we can find coefficient matrices C_1 and C_2 such that

$$\begin{bmatrix} X_{23} \\ X_{33} \end{bmatrix} = \begin{bmatrix} X_{22} \\ X_{32} \end{bmatrix} C_1 \quad \text{and} \quad \begin{bmatrix} X_{32} \ X_{33} \end{bmatrix} = C_2 \begin{bmatrix} X_{22} \ X_{23} \end{bmatrix}. \tag{17}$$

We therefore set $X_{13} := X_{12}C_1$ and $X_{31} := C_2X_{21}$. To determine the rank of the resulting X we first look at the number of linearly independent columns. By construction, the columns $[X_{13}^T \ X_{23}^T \ X_{33}^T]^T$ are linear combinations of the other columns, and similarly, the rows $[X_{31} \ X_{32} \ X_{33}]$ are linear combinations of the other rows. Hence, the number of linear independent columns (or rows) has not increased. Therefore X has the same rank as X_1. The uniqueness in the case of $r_1 = r_2$ can easily be proven by contradiction.   □

We now present a simple way to extend the solution beyond the blocks. The completion of two blocks is in practice performed by finding rank $r_{\max}$ factorizations of X_1 and X_2 using SVD (see Figure 3),

$$X_1 = U_1 V_1^T \quad \text{and} \quad X_2 = U_2 V_2^T \quad \text{where} \quad U_k \in \mathbb{R}^{m_k \times r}, V_k \in \mathbb{R}^{n_k \times r}. \tag{18}$$

The low rank factorizations are however not unique because for any invertible H, $U_1 V_1^T = (U_1 H)(H^{-1} V_1^T)$. To find the unknown H we consider the block $X_{22} = \hat{U}_1 \hat{V}_1^T = \hat{U}_2 \hat{V}_2^T$, where $\hat{U}_i \hat{V}_i^T$ is the restriction of the $U_i V_i^T$ to X_{22}. Then

$$\hat{U}_1 = \hat{U}_2 H \quad \text{and} \quad \hat{V}_1^T = H^{-1} \hat{V}_2^T \implies H \hat{V}_1^T = \hat{V}_2^T, \tag{19}$$

which we solve in a least squares sense. In this way we iteratively combine the sub-blocks. Other approaches, such as nullspace matching methods used in [17] and [12], are also possible. Note however, that in each iteration we only compute the SVD of the new (smaller) block allowing efficient implementation.

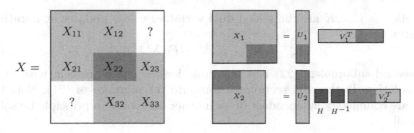

Fig. 3. *Left:* The matrix X contains two overlapping blocks X_1 and X_2. The goal is to fill in the missing entries X_{13} and X_{31} such that rank(X) is kept to a minimum. *Right:* The low-rank factorizations of the two blocks X_1 and X_2. The overlap is marked in both the blocks and the factorizations.

3.2 Selecting μ

The regularizer $\mathcal{R}_\mu$ in (14) only penalizes singular values less than $\sqrt{\mu}$. This gives a clear way to set how much variation in the data we allow to be explained by measurement noise.

If a fixed rank r solution is desired, then the parameters μ_i in (15) can be found iteratively by solving the problem and then updating each μ_i to be slightly smaller than $\sigma_r^2(\mathcal{P}_i(X))$. This ensures that only singular values less than $\sigma_r(\mathcal{P}_i(X))$ are penalized in each block.

4   An ADMM Implementation

In this section we present a simple approach for computing a solution to our formulation. Working with the sub-blocks of a matrix, the ADMM scheme is a natural choice for implementation. Furthermore, our objective function is convex, so convergence to the optimal value is guaranteed [4].

For each block $\mathcal{P}_i(X)$ we introduce a separate set of variables X_i and enforce consistency via the linear constraints $X_i - \mathcal{P}_i(X) = 0$. We formulate an augmented Lagrangian of (15) as

$$\sum_{i=1}^{K} \left(\mathcal{R}_{\mu_i}(X_i) + \|X_i - \mathcal{P}_i(M)\|_F^2 + \rho\|X_i - \mathcal{P}_i(X) + \Lambda_i\|_F^2 - \rho\|\Lambda_i\|_F^2 \right). \quad (20)$$

At each iteration t of ADMM we solve the subproblems

$$X_i^{t+1} = \arg\min_{X_i} \mathcal{R}_{\mu_i}(X_i) + \|X_i - \mathcal{P}_i(M)\|_F^2 + \rho\|X_i - \mathcal{P}_i(X^t) + \Lambda_i^t\|_F^2, \quad (21)$$

for $i = 1, ..., K$ and

$$X^{t+1} = \arg\min_X \sum_{i=1}^{K} \rho\|X_i^{t+1} - \mathcal{P}_i(X) + \Lambda_i^t\|_F^2. \quad (22)$$

Here Λ_i^t, $i = 1, ..., K$ are the scaled dual variables whose updates at iteration t are given by

$$\Lambda_i^{t+1} = \Lambda_i^t + X_i^{t+1} - P_i(X^{t+1}). \tag{23}$$

The second subproblem (22) is a separable least squares problem with closed form solution. In the next section we compute the solutions of (21). Note that these are completely independent of each other and could in principle be solved in parallel.

4.1   The Proximal Operator

Ignoring constants, the objective function in (21) can be written

$$F(X_i) = G(X_i) - 2\langle Y, X_i \rangle, \tag{24}$$

where

$$G(X_i) = \sum_{j=1}^{n} \left(-[\sqrt{\mu} - \sigma_j(X_i)]_+^2 \right) + (1 + \rho)\|X_i\|_F^2, \tag{25}$$

and $Y = P_i(M) + \rho(P_i(X^t) - \Lambda_i^t)$. Due to convexity it is sufficient to find X_i such that $0 \in \partial F(X_i)$ to optimize F. Define the function $g : \mathbb{R}^n \mapsto \mathbb{R}$ by

$$g(\boldsymbol{\sigma}) = \sum_{i=1}^{n} g_i(\sigma_i), \tag{26}$$

where $g_i(\sigma) = -\left[\sqrt{\mu} - |\sigma|\right]_+^2 + (1 + \rho)\sigma^2$. Then g is an absolutely symmetric convex function and G can be written $G(X) = g \circ \boldsymbol{\sigma}(X)$. If $X = U \operatorname{diag}(\boldsymbol{\sigma}(X))V^T$ then according to [15], the sub-differentials of G and g are related by

$$\partial G(X) = U \operatorname{diag}(\partial g \circ \boldsymbol{\sigma}(X))V^T. \tag{27}$$

The function $g(\boldsymbol{\sigma})$ is a sum of one dimensional functions and therefore its sub-differential can easily be computed by considering the components of the sum separately. The functions $g_i(\sigma)$ are differentiable everywhere except in $\sigma = 0$ where $\partial g_i(0) = [-2\sqrt{\mu}, 2\sqrt{\mu}]$. For any other σ we have

$$\frac{\partial g_i}{\partial \sigma} = -2\operatorname{sgn}(\sigma)\left[\sqrt{\mu} - |\sigma|\right]_+ + 2(1 + \rho)\sigma. \tag{28}$$

To solve $0 \in \partial F(X_i)$ we now construct a solution to $2Y \in \partial G(X_i)$. If $Y = U \operatorname{diag}(\boldsymbol{\sigma}(Y))V^T$ then it can be verified that $X_i = U \operatorname{diag}(\boldsymbol{\sigma}(X_i))V^T$ where

$$\sigma_i(X) = \begin{cases} \frac{\sigma_i(Y)}{1+\rho} & \text{if } \sigma_i(Y) \geq (1+\rho)\sqrt{\mu} \\ \frac{\sigma_i(Y) - \sqrt{\mu}}{\rho} & \text{if } \sqrt{\mu} \leq \sigma_i(Y) \leq (1+\rho)\sqrt{\mu} \\ 0 & \text{if } \sigma_i(Y) \leq \sqrt{\mu} \end{cases} \tag{29}$$

fulfills all the required constraints.

5   Experiments

In this section we evaluate the quality of our relaxation on both synthetic and real data. All experiments were run on a computer running Ubuntu 13.04 with an Intel I7-3930K CPU and 64 GB of RAM. The algorithms were implemented in Matlab and the block update in ADMM was not parallelized.

5.1   Evaluation of the Convex Relaxation

We emprically evaluate the performance of the convex relaxation $f_{\mathcal{R}}(X)$ in (16) for the non-convex objective function $f(X)$ in (15). Note that in the case of a single block $K = 1$, $f_{\mathcal{R}}(X)$ is a tight convex relaxation of $f(X)$. Therefore we test the performance when we have more blocks ($K = 7$).

We generated random 100×100 rank 3 matrices. This was done by sampling $U, V \in \mathbb{R}^{100 \times 3}$ from a Gaussian distribution with zero mean and unit variance and then forming the measurement matrix $M = UV^T$. The observation matrix W was chosen to be a band-diagonal matrix with bandwidth 40 similar to the matrix in Figure 1. The blocks were laid out along the diagonal such that their overlap was 6×6 and contained no missing data. We then solved $X_{\mathcal{R}}^* = \arg\min_X f_{\mathcal{R}}(X)$ with $\mu_i = 1$ and varying degrees of Gaussian noise added to M. For each noise level, the test was repeated 1000 times and the results averaged. In the left of Figure 4 we plot the averages of $f(X_{\mathcal{R}}^*)$ and $f_{\mathcal{R}}(X_{\mathcal{R}}^*)$. Note that if $f(X_{\mathcal{R}}^*) = f_{\mathcal{R}}(X_{\mathcal{R}}^*)$ then $X_{\mathcal{R}}^*$ is a global minimizer of f.

For comparison we substituted the rank function for the nuclear norm. The nuclear norm is also convex, hence it can be used in our block decomposition framework. Therefore we did the same experiment with

$$f_N(X) = \sum_{i=1}^{K} \mu_i \|\mathcal{P}_i(X)\|_* + \|\mathcal{P}_i(X) - \mathcal{P}_i(M)\|_F^2. \qquad (30)$$

The comparative results can be seen in the left graph of Figure 4. Note that the constraint $\sigma_{\max}(\mathcal{P}_i(X)) \leq 1$ can be violated, so f_N is not necessarily a lower bound on f.

5.2   Comparison to Non-Convex Approaches

Next we compare our methods performance to two state-of-the-art non-convex methods: OptSpace [14] and Truncated Nuclear Norm Regularization (TNNR) [11]. OptSpace is based on local optimization on Grassmann manifolds and in TNNR an energy which penalizes the last $(n-r)$ singular values is minimized. In [11] the authors propose three algorithms. In our experiments TNNR-ADMMAP performed the best and therefore we only include this in our comparison.

The experiment was generated in the same way as in Section 5.1. Both OptSpace and TNNR-ADMMAP try to find the best fixed rank approximation. In contrast our method penalizes a trade-off between the rank and residual

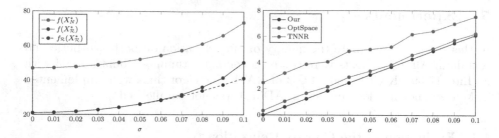

Fig. 4. Evaluation of the proposed formulation on synthetic data with varying noise levels. *Left*: Comparison of our convex relaxation solution $X_\mathcal{R}^*$ with the nuclear norm X_N^*. *Right*: The error $\|W \odot (X - M)\|_F$ for varying noise levels.

errors. We therefore iterate our method over μ_i to achieve the correct rank. Typically only one or two iterations are required. To the right in Figure 4, we plot the average values of $\|W \odot (X - M)\|_F$ for the different approaches.

It should be noted that on most problem instances OptSpace and TNNR performed similarly or even slightly better than our approach. The reason for this is that these non-convex approaches try to directly optimize the correct criterion while we use a convex relaxation (and, in addition, our blocks do not cover all the data). Hence, if they converge to the correct solution it will be at least as good as ours. However, as can be seen in Figure 4, local minima raise their average errors.

For the experiment the average run times were 0.88s (our), 20.94s (OptSpace) and 21.44s (TNNR). It is hard to make a fair comparison of different algorithms since it depends on implementations and various tuning parameters. Though we think these running times reflect the fact that we only need to optimize over the blocks and need not keep track of the full matrix while solving our convex problem.

5.3   Real Data

Structure from Motion. We now consider the well-known Oxford dinosaur sequence[3]. The measurement matrix M contains the 2D coordinates of the tracked 3D points. The measurement matrix M will have rank 4 since we do not account for the translation in the affine camera model. In this experiment we consider an outlier free subset consisting of 321 3D points where each point is seen in at least six images. The observation matrix W contains 77% missing data and exhibits the band diagonal structure which is typical for structure from motion problems. The matrix W and the selected blocks for this experiment can be seen in the left graph of Figure 5.

In Figure 6 we show the resulting image point trajectories of our method versus the nuclear norm approach with missing data, cf. (2). We optimize (2)

---

[3] http://www.robots.ox.ac.uk/$\sim$vgg/data/data-mview.html

Fig. 5. Structured data patterns of observations (matrix W) and sub-blocks for the *dino*, *book*, *hand* and *banner* sequences.

using ADMM with the shrinkage operator from [6]. For comparison we also show the matrix found by performing a full perspective reconstruction (using bundle adjustment) followed by truncating the reprojections to rank 4. The errors $||W \odot (X - M)||_F$ for the three solutions were 73.2 (our), 1902.5 (nuclear) and 116.2 (perspective). The nuclear norm favors solutions where elements away from the observed data have small values. Therefore its trajectories are stretched towards the origin. Out of the three, the perspective reconstruction captures the turntable motion best. However, its error is higher than our solution and therefore, seen as a low-rank approximation problem, our solution is better. The run times were 14.58s (our) and 18.11s (nuclear).

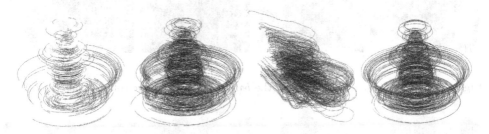

Fig. 6. *From Left to Right*: Observed image point trajectories, results obtained with the proposed algorithm, with the nuclear norm formulation (2) and with perspective reconstruction followed by projecting onto rank 4 using SVD.

Linear Shape Basis Models. Next we consider the linear shape basis model common in non-rigid structure from motion. Let X_f be the 2D- or 3D- coordinates of N tracked points in frame f. The model assumes that in each frame the coordinates are a linear combination of some unknown shape basis vectors, i.e.

$$X_f = \sum_{k=1}^{K} C_{fk} S_k, \quad f = 1, ..., F, \tag{31}$$

where S_k is the shape basis and C is the coefficient matrix. The measurement matrix M consists of the observations of X_f stacked on top of each other. The elements of the observation matrix W indicate if the point was successfully tracked in the particular frame. We search for a solution with as few basis elements as possible by finding a low rank approximation of M.

Fig. 7. Frames 1, 121, 380 and 668 of the *book* sequence. The solution has rank 3.

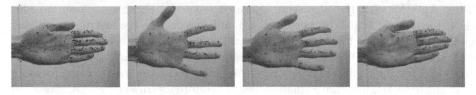

Fig. 8. Frames 1, 210, 340 and 371 of the *hand* sequence. The solution has rank 5.

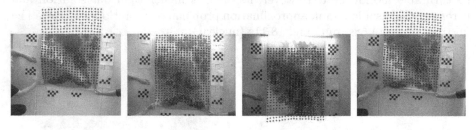

Fig. 9. Frames 70, 155, 357 and 650 of the *banner* sequence. The solution has rank 9.

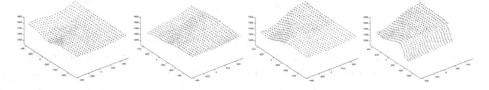

Fig. 10. *From left to right:* Our solution (frame 329), nuclear norm solution (frame 329), our solution (frame 650), nuclear norm solution (frame 650)

We consider three problem instances of varying rank. In the first two (see Figures 7 and 8) we track image points through a video sequence using the standard KLT tracker [16]. Due to occlusion and appearance changes only a subset of the points were successfully tracked throughout the entire sequence. Using (16) we found a low-rank approximation of the measurement matrix. The results can be seen in Figures 7 and 8. Blue dots correspond to the reconstructions of the successfully tracked points. The available measurements for these points are indicated by green crosses. Red dots are the reconstructed point positions for points with no measurements available. The run times for the *book* and *hand* sequences were 34.3s and 35.1s.

In the third problem we used an RGB-D camera to track the 3D-position of a point grid on a moving piece of fabric (see Figure 9). Here missing data is due to limited field of view of the camera and missing depth values. To obtain 3D grid coordinates in a common coordinate system from each video frame we registered the cameras using the patterns visible on the wall. Figures 9 and 10 show the results in 2D and 3D. In Figure 10 we also plot the nuclear norm solution of (2) for comparison. The same tendency to move undetected points towards the origin is visible. The run times for the *banner* sequence were 17.7 min (our) and 2.7 min (nuclear). In this instance we used a large number of blocks. With these blocks and this size of matrix, it is still faster to factorize the entire matrix compared to factorizing all the blocks without parallelization. On average our method spends 0.6s while the nuclear norm approach spends 0.2s per iteration computing SVDs.

The right of Figure 5 shows the data patterns and the selected blocks for the three problems. Note that in the *book* sequence, the blocks leave a relatively large portion of the available measurements unused.

6   Conclusions and Future Work

In this paper we have proposed a method for low-rank approximation of matrices with missing elements. The approach is based on a new convex relaxation - the strongest one possible - of the localized rank function. Unlike the nuclear norm, it is able to avoid penalizing large singular values. Our experiments clearly show the benefits of being able to do so in a convex framework. It should be noted that the presented results are the outputs of our approach without refinement. In cases where the relaxation is not tight, the solution can be used as a starting point for local optimization to obtain even better results.

The proposed method only has to compute the SVD of small sub-matrices, therefore it has potential to tackle large-scale problems. Furthermore, the ADMM approach allows to perform computations in a parallel and distributed manner.

A limitation of the formulation is that in its current form it is sensitive to outliers. The issue has received a lot of attention lately, for example, using the arguably more robust ℓ_1-norm [8,21,24] and it is something that we intend to address in the near future.

In our experiments we have exclusively used rectangular (manually selected) sub-blocks of the measurement matrix. This is however not a limitation. Blocks can be formed from any rows and columns in the matrix. How to select these blocks so as to cover as many measurements as possible and achieve sufficiently large overlaps is still an open problem.

References

1. Angst, R., Zach, C., Pollefeys, M.: The generalized trace-norm and its application to structure-from-motion problems. In: International Conference on Computer Vision (2011)

2. Aquiar, P.M.Q., Stosic, M., Xavier, J.M.F.: Spectrally optimal factorization of incomplete matrices. In: IEEE Conference on Computer Vision and Pattern Recognition (2008)
3. Basri, R., Jacobs, D., Kemelmacher, I.: Photometric stereo with general, unknown lighting. Int. J. Comput. Vision 72(3), 239–257 (2007)
4. Boyd, S., Parikh, N., Chu, E., Peleato, B., Eckstein, J.: Distributed optimization and statistical learning via the alternating direction method of multipliers. Found. Trends Mach. Learn. 3(1), 1–122 (2011)
5. Bregler, C., Hertzmann, A., Biermann, H.: Recovering non-rigid 3d shape from image streams. In: IEEE Conference on Computer Vision and Pattern Recognition (2000)
6. Cai, J.F., Candès, E.J., Shen, Z.: A singular value thresholding algorithm for matrix completion. SIAM J. on Optimization 20(4), 1956–1982 (2010)
7. Candès, E.J., Li, X., Ma, Y., Wright, J.: Robust principal component analysis? J. ACM 58(3), 11:1–11:37 (2011)
8. Eriksson, A., Hengel, A.: Efficient computation of robust weighted low-rank matrix approximations using the L_1 norm. IEEE Trans. Pattern Anal. Mach. Intell. 34(9), 1681–1690 (2012)
9. Garg, R., Roussos, A., de Agapito, L.: Dense variational reconstruction of non-rigid surfaces from monocular video. In: IEEE Conference on Computer Vision and Pattern Recognition (2013)
10. Garg, R., Roussos, A., Agapito, L.: A variational approach to video registration with subspace constraints. Int. J. Comput. Vision 104(3), 286–314 (2013)
11. Hu, Y., Zhang, D., Ye, J., Li, X., He, X.: Fast and accurate matrix completion via truncated nuclear norm regularization. IEEE Trans. Pattern Anal. Mach. Intell. 35(9), 2117–2130 (2013)
12. Jacobs, D.: Linear fitting with missing data: applications to structure-from-motion and to characterizing intensity images. In: IEEE Conference on Computer Vision and Pattern Recognition (1997)
13. Jojic, V., Saria, S., Koller, D.: Convex envelopes of complexity controlling penalties: the case against premature envelopment. In: International Conference on Artificial Intelligence and Statistics (2011)
14. Keshavan, R.H., Montanari, A., Oh, S.: Matrix completion from a few entries. IEEE Trans. Inf. Theory 56(6), 2980–2998 (2010)
15. Lewis, A.S.: The convex analysis of unitarily invariant matrix functions (1995)
16. Lucas, B.D., Kanade, T.: An iterative image registration technique with an application to stereo vision. In: International Joint Conference on Artificial Intelligence (1981)
17. Olsen, S., Bartoli, A.: Implicit non-rigid structure-from-motion with priors. Journal of Mathematical Imaging and Vision 31(2-3), 233–244 (2008)
18. Olsson, C., Oskarsson, M.: A convex approach to low rank matrix approximation with missing data. In: Scandinavian Conference on Image Analysis (2009)
19. Recht, B., Fazel, M., Parrilo, P.A.: Guaranteed minimum-rank solutions of linear matrix equations via nuclear norm minimization. SIAM Rev. 52(3), 471–501 (2010)
20. Rockafellar, R.: Convex Analysis. Princeton University Press (1997)
21. Strelow, D.: General and nested Wiberg minimization. In: IEEE Conference on Computer Vision and Pattern Recognition (2012)
22. Wang, S., Liu, D., Zhang, Z.: Nonconvex relaxation approaches to robust matrix recovery. In: International Joint Conference on Artificial Intelligence (2013)

23. Yan, J., Pollefeys, M.: A factorization-based approach for articulated nonrigid shape, motion and kinematic chain recovery from video. IEEE Trans. Pattern Anal. Mach. Intell. 30(5), 865–877 (2008)
24. Zheng, Y., Liu, G., Sugimoto, S., Yan, S., Okutomi, M.: Practical low-rank matrix approximation under robust L_1-norm. In: IEEE Conference on Computer Vision and Pattern Recognition (2012)

Duality and the Continuous Graphical Model

Alexander Fix[1] and Sameer Agarwal[2]

[1] Cornell University, USA
[2] Google Inc., USA

Abstract. Inspired by the Linear Programming based algorithms for discrete MRFs, we show how a corresponding infinite-dimensional dual for continuous-state MRFs can be approximated by a hierarchy of tractable relaxations. This hierarchy of dual programs includes as a special case the methods of Peng et al. [17] and Zach & Kohli [33]. We give approximation bounds for the tightness of our construction, study their relationship to discrete MRFs and give a generic optimization algorithm based on Nesterov's dual-smoothing method [16].

1 Introduction

Consider an optimization problem of the form

$$\min_{\mathbf{x}} \sum_{\alpha} f_\alpha(\mathbf{x}_\alpha). \tag{1}$$

Here, $\mathbf{x}$ is n-dimensional parameter vector. The index α varies over subsets of the variables of $\mathbf{x} = \{x_1, \ldots, x_n\}$, $\mathbf{x}_\alpha$ denotes the the corresponding sub-vector of $\mathbf{x}$, and $f_\alpha(\mathbf{x}_\alpha)$ is a function that only depends on $\mathbf{x}_\alpha$. For problems of interest to us $|\alpha| \ll n$, i.e., the number of parameters that f_α depends on is much smaller than the total number of parameters.

Problems of this form abound in computer vision and machine learning, including image denoising [3], bundle adjustment [26], and stereo matching [25], among many others. One particularly important case is the inference problem in Markov Random Fields(MRFs) [8]. MRFs are probability distributions that can be written in the form

$$p(\mathbf{x}) \propto \prod_{\alpha} e^{-f_\alpha(\mathbf{x}_\alpha)}. \tag{2}$$

Where, α are cliques in the underlying graph and f_α are the associated clique potentials. It is straightforward to see that the MAP inference problem for $p(\mathbf{x})$ is equivalent to solving (1).

In the case where the domain of the f_α (commonly known as the state-space of $\mathbf{x}$) is a finite discrete set, (2) is known as a discrete MRF and finding the optimal solution to (1) is NP-Hard [22]. Despite this, a variety of algorithms have been developed to efficiently compute an approximately optimal solution. These include graph cuts [4], belief propagation [30], and (most relevant to this

D. Fleet et al. (Eds.): ECCV 2014, Part III, LNCS 8691, pp. 266–281, 2014.

work) dual and primal-dual methods [12,31,21]. Most of these methods have been developed for the case of *pairwise discrete* MRFs, i.e., $|\alpha| \leq 2$.

There is however considerable interest in problems where the states are continuous and/or the cliques have size greater than 2, including pose tracking [23,24], structure from motion [27,6], stereo estimation [9,32], and protein folding [17]. Given the success of the methods used for solving discrete pairwise MRFs, it is natural that a number of attempts have been made to extend them to continuous domains and larger clique sizes [10,17,33]. But it is fair to say that their success is limited and the development of these methods is still in its infancy. Current methods for optimizing continuous MRFs include [17], [33] (which we will discuss at greater length below) as well as [1], which can only handle convex hinge-loss functions, but does allow constraints between the variables.

One of the most powerful tools for developing and analyzing discrete optimization algorithms (exact and approximate) is linear programming [14,28]. So it is no surprise that linear programming is at the heart of some of the most successful methods for solving MRFs including [12,31,21] (see [29] for a review). It is straightforward to construct a linear program relaxation of (1), as well as its dual, but both of these end up being abstract infinite dimensional problems that are not amenable to computation.

In this paper we offer a systematic procedure for approximating the infinite dimensional dual using a hierarchy of piecewise polynomial functions. Doing so allows us to handle both the issue of continuous domain as well as larger clique size in a principled manner. It also allows us to unify and generalize the works of Peng et al. [17] and Zach & Kohli [33]. As one would expect, the degree of the polynomial and the granularity of the piecewise construction affect the fidelity of the approximation. We analyze this and provide explicit approximation bounds. We also study the cases where the elements of the hierarchy coincide with a suitably constructed discrete optimization problem thereby enabling the use of existing optimization algorithms. Last but not the least, we propose a dual optimization algorithm applicable to a slice of our hierarchy based on Nesterov's dual-smoothing methods [16], which has recently been used successfully to solve discrete MRFs [11,21].

The rest of the paper is organized as follows. In section 2 we construct the linear programming relaxation to (1), its dual, and make some elementary observations about their structure. In section 3 we present a hierarchy of polynomial approximations to the dual, and in section 4 we generalize to piecewise polynomial approximations to the dual. Section 5 considers the special case of piecewise constant and linear f_α. Section 6 presents optimization methods for solving the dual hierarchy. We conclude with a discussion in Section 7.

1.1 Preliminaries

Without loss, we assume that unary terms exist for each $i \in \{1, \dots n\}$ [1]. Furthermore the vector $\mathbf{x}$ lives in some $\Omega = \Omega_1 \times \cdots \times \Omega_n$. We will assume that the

---

[1] This is a notational convenience. If an f_i is not part of the input, set $f_i = 0$, which does not change the optimization problem.

domains Ω_i are 1-dimensional, i.e., $\Omega_i \subseteq \mathbb{R}$ and compact. Compactness ensures that the minimum value is attained. This allows us to re-write (1) as

$$\min_{\mathbf{x} \in \Omega} \sum_i f_i(x_i) + \sum_\alpha f_\alpha(\mathbf{x}_\alpha). \tag{F}$$

Where, $|\alpha| \geq 2$. Let $M = \sum_\alpha |\alpha|$ which is one convenient measure for the size of the input.

We will distinguish between two cases for the domain. If Ω is finite, we will refer to (F) as a discrete problem. If each Ω_i is an interval $[a, b]$ we will refer to (F) as a continuous problem. f_i and f_α will be assumed to be lower semi-continuous (l.s.c.) as functions $\Omega \to \mathbb{R}$. Note that if Ω is discrete then all functions $\Omega \to \mathbb{R}$ are continuous.

For any Ω, $\mathcal{P}[\Omega]$ is the space of all regular[2] probability distributions on Ω. $\langle f, \mu \rangle$ is the expectation of f with respect to the probability distribution μ. $C[\Omega]$ denotes the space of continuous functions $\Omega \to \mathbb{R}$, and $\mathrm{Lip}_L[\Omega] \subseteq C[\Omega]$ are the L-Lipschitz continuous functions, i.e., functions f with $|f(x) - f(y)| \leq L\|x - y\|_1$ for all $x, y \in \Omega$.

The Fenchel Conjugate of a function g is $g^*(\mathbf{y}) = \sup_{\mathbf{x}} \mathbf{y}^\top \mathbf{x} - g(\mathbf{x})$; it is always convex. The double Fenchel Conjugate g^{**} is the convex envelope of g.

For an optimization problem A, $\mathrm{OPT}(A)$ will denote the optimal objective function value.

2   The Linear Programming Relaxation

If $\mu \in \mathcal{P}[\Omega]$, then for every subset α, let $\mu|_\alpha \in \mathcal{P}[\Omega_\alpha]$ be the marginal distribution of μ over the variables in α. Consider the optimization problem

$$\min_{\substack{\mu \in \mathcal{P}[\Omega] \\ \mu_\alpha \in \mathcal{P}[\Omega_\alpha]}} \sum_\alpha \langle f_\alpha, \mu_\alpha \rangle, \text{ s.t. } \mu_\alpha = \mu|_\alpha. \tag{3}$$

This is the *Full Marginal Polytope LP*. It has the same optimum as (1). It is however intractable. Even in the discrete case it involves exponentially many variables (it requires specifying a probability for each value of $\mathbf{x} \in \Omega$). To get around this, a standard relaxation is [3]:

$$\min_{\substack{\mu_i \in \mathcal{P}[\Omega_i] \\ \mu_\alpha \in \mathcal{P}[\Omega_\alpha]}} \sum_i \langle f_i, \mu_i \rangle + \sum_\alpha \langle f_\alpha, \mu_\alpha \rangle, \text{ s.t. } \mu_\alpha|_i = \mu_i. \tag{P-F}$$

---

[2] A measure μ is regular if for each $A \subseteq \Omega$ we have $\mu(A) = \inf\{\mu(O) \mid O \supseteq A, O \text{ open}\} = \sup\{\mu(K) \mid K \subseteq A, K \text{ compact}\}$. Many nice distributions, in particular, delta distributions, are regular.

[3] Sometimes, if more is known about the structure of f_α, then more specialized relaxations can be constructed. e.g. if f_α is a polynomial, then problem (3) is the same starting point as that of the Lasserre Heirarchy [13]. The Lasserre hierarchy exploits the fact that expectations of polynomials are linear in the moment variables of a distribution $y_d = \langle x^d, \mu \rangle$. Then, the inverse Moment Problem allows relaxing the original problem to a hierarchy of Semi-Definite Programs.

This is the *Local Marginal Polytope LP*. The constraints $\mu_\alpha|_i = \mu_i$ (indexed by α, i for all α and $i \in \alpha$.) are equivalent to saying that the signed measures[4] $\mu_\alpha|_i - \mu_i$ are identically 0. By dualizing these constraints, we get the following unconstrained optimization problem [17]:

$$\max_{\boldsymbol{\lambda}} \sum_i \min_{x_i \in \Omega_i} \left[f_i(x_i) - \sum_{\alpha \ni i} \lambda_{\alpha,i}(x_i) \right] + \sum_\alpha \min_{\mathbf{x}_\alpha \in \Omega_\alpha} \left[f_\alpha(\mathbf{x}_\alpha) + \sum_{i \in \alpha} \lambda_{\alpha,i}(x_i) \right] \quad \text{(D-F)}$$

From [19], we know that the dual variables $\lambda_{\alpha,i}$ are arbitrary continuous univariate functions defined on Ω_i, i.e., $\lambda_{\alpha,i} \in C[\Omega_i]$. Furthermore, we have strong-duality: OPT(P-F) = OPT(D-F). Here, we have not assumed anything about f_α. In fact, if the f_α satisfy certain smoothness properties, then the optimal dual variables do as well. The proof of the following lemma can be found in Appendix A.

Lemma 1. *If all $f_\alpha \in Lip_L[\Omega_\alpha]$, then there is a dual-optimal $\boldsymbol{\lambda}$ where each $\lambda_{\alpha,i} \in Lip_L[\Omega_i]$.*

Before we go further, let us define some notation. We will use $q(\boldsymbol{\lambda})$ to denote the value of the objective in (D-F) and $q_i(\boldsymbol{\lambda})$ and $q_\alpha(\boldsymbol{\lambda})$ to denote the individual terms of the summation. For convenience, we define $\lambda_i(x_i) = \sum_{\alpha \ni i} \lambda_{\alpha,i}(x_i)$ and $\lambda_\alpha(\mathbf{x}_\alpha) = \sum_{i \in \alpha} \lambda_{\alpha,i}(x_i)$. Given this notation we can write

$$q_i(\boldsymbol{\lambda}) = \min_{x_i} f_i(x_i) - \lambda_i(x_i) \tag{4}$$

$$q_\alpha(\boldsymbol{\lambda}) = \min_{\mathbf{x}_\alpha} f_\alpha(\mathbf{x}_\alpha) + \lambda_\alpha(\mathbf{x}_\alpha) \tag{5}$$

$$q(\boldsymbol{\lambda}) = \sum_i q_i(\boldsymbol{\lambda}) + \sum_\alpha q_\alpha(\boldsymbol{\lambda}). \tag{6}$$

Since the dual variables $\boldsymbol{\lambda}$ are allowed to be arbitrary continuous functions, the dual problem (D-F) is infinite dimensional and hence not computationally tractable. We will instead consider subspaces $\Lambda \subset C[\Omega]$ that lead to computationally tractable duals:

$$\max_{\boldsymbol{\lambda} \in \Lambda} \sum_i q_i(\boldsymbol{\lambda}) + \sum_\alpha q_\alpha(\boldsymbol{\lambda}). \tag{D-Λ}$$

Lemma 2. *Let $\Lambda \subset \Lambda' \subseteq C[\Omega]$, and let $\boldsymbol{\lambda}^*$ and $\boldsymbol{\lambda}'^*$ be the solution of the corresponding optimization problems (D-Λ) and (D-Λ'). Then*

$$q(\boldsymbol{\lambda}^*) \leq q(\boldsymbol{\lambda}'^*) \leq q(\boldsymbol{\lambda}^*) + 2M\epsilon \tag{7}$$

where, $M = \sum_\alpha |\alpha|$ and $\epsilon = \max_{\alpha,i} \sup_{x_i} |\lambda_{\alpha,i}^*(x_i) - \lambda_{\alpha,i}'^*(x_i)|$.

---

[4] $\mu_\alpha|_i - \mu_i$ are signed measures on Ω_i, since we may have $\mu_\alpha|_i > \mu_i$ for some events, and $\mu_\alpha|_i < \mu_i$ elsewhere.

Proof. The left inequality holds because (D-Λ') optimizes over a larger set than (D-Λ). For the right inequality, let $\Delta_i = |\{\alpha \ni i\}|$ and $\Delta_\alpha = |\{i \in \alpha\}|$. Then

$$\min_{x_i} f_i(x_i) - \sum_\alpha \lambda^*_{\alpha,i}(x_i) \geq \min_{x_i} f_i(x_i) - \sum_\alpha \lambda'^*_{\alpha,i}(x_i) - \Delta_i \epsilon \tag{8}$$

$$\min_{\mathbf{x}_\alpha} f_\alpha(\mathbf{x}_\alpha) + \sum_i \lambda^*_{\alpha,i}(x_i) \geq \min_{\mathbf{x}_\alpha} f_\alpha(\mathbf{x}_\alpha) + \sum_i \lambda'^*_{\alpha,i}(x_i) - \Delta_\alpha \epsilon \tag{9}$$

hence $q(\boldsymbol{\lambda}^*) \geq \sum_i q_i(\boldsymbol{\lambda}'^*) + \sum_\alpha q_\alpha(\boldsymbol{\lambda}'^*) - (\sum_i \Delta_i + \sum_\alpha \Delta_\alpha)\epsilon = q(\boldsymbol{\lambda}'^*) - 2M\epsilon$.

3 Polynomial Dual Variables

We begin by considering polynomial dual variables. The subspace $\Lambda^{(d)} \subset C[\Omega]$ will denote dual variables that are polynomials of degree d i.e.,

$$\lambda_{\alpha,i}(x_i) = \lambda^{(0)}_{\alpha,i} + \lambda^{(1)}_{\alpha,i} x_i + \cdots + \lambda^{(d)}_{\alpha,i} x_i^d. \tag{10}$$

Since $\Lambda^{(d-1)} \subset \Lambda^{(d)}$, this forms a hierarchy. Let us look at some special cases.

3.1 Constant Dual Variables

The simplest subspace of dual variables is $\Lambda^{(0)}$, the space of constant functions, i.e., $\lambda_{\alpha,i}(x_i) = \lambda^{(0)}_{\alpha,i}$. Then we have

Lemma 3. *Let* $\boldsymbol{\lambda}^{(0)} \in \Lambda^{(0)}$, *then for all* $\boldsymbol{\lambda} \in C[\Omega]$, $q(\boldsymbol{\lambda} + \boldsymbol{\lambda}^{(0)}) = q(\boldsymbol{\lambda})$.

Proof. Observe that $q_i(\boldsymbol{\lambda} + \boldsymbol{\lambda}^{(0)}) = q_i(\boldsymbol{\lambda}) - \lambda^{(0)}_i$ and $q_\alpha(\boldsymbol{\lambda} + \boldsymbol{\lambda}^{(0)}) = q_\alpha(\boldsymbol{\lambda}) + \lambda^{(0)}_\alpha$ and $\sum_i \lambda^{(0)}_i = \sum_{\alpha,i} \lambda^{(0)}_{\alpha,i} = \sum_\alpha \lambda^{(0)}_\alpha$. Therefore,

$$q(\boldsymbol{\lambda} + \boldsymbol{\lambda}^{(0)}) = \sum_i q_i(\boldsymbol{\lambda}) + \sum_\alpha q_\alpha(\boldsymbol{\lambda}) - \sum_i \lambda^{(0)}_i + \sum_\alpha \lambda^{(0)}_\alpha = q(\boldsymbol{\lambda}) \tag{11}$$

In other words, we can ignore constants added to $\lambda_{\alpha,i}$. In addition, this allows us to simplify the optimization problem (D-$\Lambda^{(0)}$).

Corollary 1. OPT(D-$\Lambda^{(0)}$) = $q(\mathbf{0})$ = $\sum_i \min_{x_i} f_i(x_i) + \sum_\alpha \min_{\mathbf{x}_\alpha} f_\alpha(\mathbf{x}_\alpha)$

Proof. OPT(D-$\Lambda^{(0)}$) = $q(\mathbf{0})$ is a straightforward consequence of Lemma 3. Then

$$q(\mathbf{0}) = \sum_i q_i(\mathbf{0}) + \sum_\alpha q_\alpha(\mathbf{0}) \tag{12}$$

$$= \sum_i \min_{x_i} f_i(x_i) + \sum_\alpha \min_{\mathbf{x}_\alpha} f_\alpha(\mathbf{x}_\alpha) \tag{13}$$

Thus OPT(D-$\Lambda^{(0)}$) is the obvious lower bound of f obtained by simply minimizing each term separately.

3.2   Affine Dual Variables

Next, we consider the space $\Lambda^{(1)}$ of affine dual variables $\lambda_{\alpha,i}(x_i) = \lambda_{\alpha,i}^{(0)} + \lambda_{\alpha,i}^{(1)} x_i$. From Lemma 3 we know that constant offsets cancel out, so we can assume that $\lambda_{\alpha,i}^{(0)} = 0$, i.e., optimizing over affine dual variables is the same as optimizing over linear dual variables. With $\boldsymbol{\lambda} \in \Lambda^{(1)}$ we have:

$$q_i(\boldsymbol{\lambda}) = \min_{x_i} f_i(x_i) - \lambda_i^{(1)} x_i = -f_i^*(\lambda_i^{(1)}) \tag{14}$$

$$q_\alpha(\boldsymbol{\lambda}) = \min_{\mathbf{x}_\alpha} f_\alpha(\mathbf{x}_\alpha) + \boldsymbol{\lambda}_\alpha^{(1)T} \mathbf{x}_\alpha = -f_\alpha^*(-\boldsymbol{\lambda}_\alpha^{(1)}) \tag{15}$$

Here $\boldsymbol{\lambda}_\alpha^{(j)}$ is the vector $(\lambda_{\alpha,i}^{(j)})_{i \in \alpha}$ and $\lambda_i^{(j)}$ is the sum $\sum_\alpha \lambda_{\alpha,i}^{(j)}$. Recall that f^* is the Fenchel conjugate of f. Combining these, D-$\Lambda^{(1)}$ can be simplified to

$$\max_{\boldsymbol{\lambda}} \sum_i -f_i^*(\lambda_i^{(1)}) + \sum_\alpha -f_\alpha^*(-\boldsymbol{\lambda}_\alpha^{(1)}) \tag{D-$\Lambda^{(1)}$}$$

The Fenchel Conjugate can be explicitly computed for certain analytically defined functions (such as truncated quadratics). In cases where an analytical solution is not possible, there are numerical algorithms that can compute the Fenchel conjugate of a sampled function in linear time (e.g., [15]).

More interestingly, we have

Theorem 1. *Let*

$$\min_{\mathbf{x}} \sum_i f_i^{**}(x_i) + \sum_\alpha f_\alpha^{**}(\mathbf{x}_\alpha) \tag{P-SC}$$

be the convex optimization problem obtained by separately convexifying each term of (F), *then* $\mathrm{OPT(P\text{-}SC)} = \mathrm{OPT(D\text{-}\Lambda^{(1)})}$.

Proof. Introduce copies of the variables $\mathbf{y}_\alpha$ for each clique α in (P-SC) to get the equivalent optimization problem

$$\min_{\mathbf{x}, \{\mathbf{y}_\alpha\}} \sum_i f_i^{**}(x_i) + \sum_\alpha f_\alpha^{**}(\mathbf{y}_\alpha), \text{ s. t. } \mathbf{y}_{\alpha,i} = x_i \tag{16}$$

Dualizing the equality constraints with dual-multipliers $\lambda_{\alpha,i}^{(1)}$ we get (D-SC)

$$\max_{\boldsymbol{\lambda}^{(1)}} \min_{\mathbf{x}, \{\mathbf{y}_\alpha\}} \sum_i \left[f_i^{**}(x_i) - \lambda_i^{(1)} x_i \right] + \sum_\alpha \left[f_\alpha^{**}(\mathbf{y}_\alpha) + \boldsymbol{\lambda}_\alpha^{(1)T} \mathbf{y}_\alpha \right] \tag{D-SC}$$

$$= \max_{\boldsymbol{\lambda}^{(1)}} \sum_i \min_{x_i} \left[f_i^{**}(x_i) - \lambda_i^{(1)} x_i \right] + \sum_\alpha \min_{\mathbf{y}_\alpha} \left[f_\alpha^{**}(\mathbf{y}_\alpha) + \boldsymbol{\lambda}_\alpha^{(1)T} \mathbf{y}_\alpha \right] \tag{17}$$

$$= \max_{\boldsymbol{\lambda}^{(1)}} \sum_i -f_i^{***}(\lambda_i^{(1)}) + \sum_\alpha -f_\alpha^{***}(-\boldsymbol{\lambda}_\alpha^{(1)}) \tag{18}$$

For any f it is the case that $f^{***} = f^*$, i.e., the convex envelope of a convex function is the function itself. Therefore (18) is the same optimization problem as $\mathrm{OPT(D\text{-}\Lambda^{(1)})}$, and then by strong duality, $\mathrm{OPT(P\text{-}SC)} = \mathrm{OPT(D\text{-}\Lambda^{(1)})}$.

3.3   Degree d Polynomial Dual Variables

Let us now consider the subspaces $\Lambda^{(d)}$ when $d > 1$. Recall that $\lambda_{\alpha,i}(x_i) = \lambda_{\alpha,i}^{(1)} x_i + \cdots + \lambda_{\alpha,i}^{(d)} x_i^d$. This gives subproblems of the form

$$q_i(\boldsymbol{\lambda}) = \min_{x_i} f_i(x_i) - \lambda_i^{(1)} x_i - \cdots - \lambda_i^{(d)} x_i^d \tag{19}$$

$$q_\alpha(\boldsymbol{\lambda}) = \min_{\mathbf{x}_\alpha} f_\alpha(\mathbf{x}_\alpha) + \sum_{i \in \alpha} (\lambda_{\alpha,i}^{(1)} x_i + \cdots + \lambda_{\alpha,i}^{(d)} x_i^d) \tag{20}$$

These subproblems look almost like a Fenchel conjugate, with the linear form $\lambda_{\alpha,i}^{(1)} x_i$ replaced with a polynomial. In fact, optimization problems of this form have been studied, under the name of Φ-conjugates [7].

For a function $\Phi : \mathbb{R}^n \times \mathbb{R}^m \to \mathbb{R}$, the Φ-conjugate transforms functions $f : \mathbb{R}^n \to \mathbb{R}$ to their conjugate $f^\Phi : \mathbb{R}^m \to \mathbb{R}$, defined by

$$f^\Phi(\mathbf{y}) = \sup_{\mathbf{x}} \Phi(\mathbf{x}, \mathbf{y}) - f(\mathbf{x}) \tag{21}$$

If $\Phi(\mathbf{x}, \mathbf{y}) = \mathbf{x}^T \mathbf{y}$, then the Φ-conjugate is just the Fenchel Conjugate. In the case of polynomial dual variables, we can define Φ to be the polynomial evaulation map: $\Phi_{i,d}(x_i, y^{(1)}, \ldots, y^{(d)}) = y^{(1)} x_i + \cdots + y^{(d)} x_i^d$ and $\Phi_{\alpha,d}(\mathbf{x}_\alpha, \mathbf{y}_\alpha^{(1)}, \ldots, \mathbf{y}_\alpha^{(d)}) = \sum_{i \in \alpha} \Phi_{i,d}(x_i, y_i^{(1)}, \ldots, y_i^{(d)})$. Then, the dual for degree d polynomials becomes

$$\max_{\boldsymbol{\lambda}} \sum_i \left[-f_i^{\Phi_{i,d}} \left(\lambda_i^{(1)}, \ldots, \lambda_i^{(d)} \right) \right] + \sum_\alpha \left[-f_\alpha^{\Phi_{\alpha,d}} \left(-\boldsymbol{\lambda}_\alpha^{(1)}, \ldots, -\boldsymbol{\lambda}_\alpha^{(d)} \right) \right] \tag{22}$$

In this case, the Φ-conjugate can be computed in terms of the Fenchel conjugate (this is a straightforward generalization of the full quadratic transform, Example 11.65 of [18]).

4   Piecewise Defined Dual Variables

A separate hierarchy, orthogonal to the polynomial hierarchy above, is obtained by considering dual-variables defined piecewise on their domain. That is, each dual variable has some fixed number of pieces and each piece belongs to $\Lambda^{(d)}$ for some fixed degree d, e.g., piecewise constant or piecewise linear functions.

To simplify notation, we assume the domain of x_i is $\Omega_i = [0, K]$ for some integer K and consider dual variables $\lambda_{\alpha,i}$ which are piecewise defined on the subintervals $I_k = [k-1, k)$ for $k = 1, \ldots, K$. We will use superscript notation to denote the pieces of $\boldsymbol{\lambda}$, so that $\lambda_{\alpha,i}(x_i) = \lambda_{\alpha,i}^k(x_i)$ for $x_i \in I_k$. We'll define $\lambda_{\alpha,i}^k = 0$ outside I_k so that $\lambda_{\alpha,i} = \sum_k \lambda_{\alpha,i}^k$.

It will be convenient to correspondingly subdivide the domains of f_i, f_α, so let $f_i^k(x_i) = f_i(x_i)$ for $x_i \in I_k$ and 0 otherwise. For the higher-order functions, we subdivide the cube $[0, K]^{|\alpha|}$ into grid-cells, indexed by $\mathbf{k}_\alpha = (k_i)_{i \in \alpha}$. Then, the grid cells are $I_{\mathbf{k}_\alpha} = \prod_{i \in \alpha} I_{k_i}$, and the pieces of f_α are $f_\alpha^{\mathbf{k}_\alpha}$, where $f_\alpha^{\mathbf{k}_\alpha}(\mathbf{x}_\alpha) =$

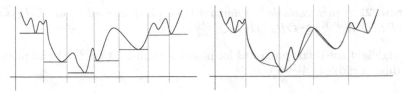

Fig. 1. (left) Piecewise constant dual variables find the minimum value in each "piece". (right) Piecewise linear dual variables convexify each piece separately. Note that the overall function is non-convex.

$f_\alpha(\mathbf{x}_\alpha)$ for $\mathbf{x}_\alpha \in I_{\mathbf{k}_\alpha}$ and 0 otherwise. Finally let us define subproblems for each piece:

$$q_i^k(\boldsymbol{\lambda}) = \min_{x_i \in I_k} f_i^k(x_i) - \lambda_i^k(x_i) \tag{23}$$

$$q_\alpha^{\mathbf{k}_\alpha}(\boldsymbol{\lambda}) = \min_{\mathbf{x}_\alpha \in I_{\mathbf{k}_\alpha}} f_\alpha^{\mathbf{k}_\alpha}(\mathbf{x}_\alpha) + \lambda_\alpha^{\mathbf{k}_\alpha}(x_i) \tag{24}$$

where we have extended our summation-shorthand with $\lambda_i^k = \sum_{\alpha \ni i} \lambda_{\alpha,i}^k$ and $\lambda_\alpha^{\mathbf{k}_\alpha} = \sum_{i \in \alpha} \lambda_{\alpha,i}^{k_i}$.

Lemma 4. *For piecewise defined dual-variables, the dual problem is given by*

$$q(\boldsymbol{\lambda}) = \sum_i \min_k q_i^k(\boldsymbol{\lambda}) + \sum_\alpha \min_{\mathbf{k}_\alpha} q_\alpha^{\mathbf{k}_\alpha}(\boldsymbol{\lambda}). \tag{25}$$

Proof. For piecewise dual variables, we know that $\lambda_{\alpha,i} = \sum_k \lambda_{\alpha,i}^k$, and that $\lambda_{\alpha,i}^k$ and f_i^k (resp. $f_\alpha^{\mathbf{k}_\alpha}$) are 0 for $x_i \notin I_k$ (resp. for $\mathbf{x}_\alpha \notin I_{\mathbf{k}_\alpha}$). Therefore, we have

$$q_i(\boldsymbol{\lambda}) = \min_{x_i} \sum_k [f_i^k(x_i) - \lambda_i^k(x_i)] \tag{26}$$

$$= \min_k \min_{x_i \in I_k} [f_i^k(x_i) - \lambda_i^k(x_i)] = \min_k q_i^k(\boldsymbol{\lambda}) \tag{27}$$

$$q_\alpha(\boldsymbol{\lambda}) = \min_{\mathbf{x}_\alpha} \sum_{\mathbf{k}_\alpha} [f_\alpha^{\mathbf{k}_\alpha}(\mathbf{x}_\alpha) + \lambda_\alpha^{k_\alpha}(\mathbf{x}_\alpha)] \tag{28}$$

$$= \min_{\mathbf{k}_\alpha} \min_{\mathbf{x}_\alpha \in I_{\mathbf{k}_\alpha}} [f_\alpha^{\mathbf{k}_\alpha}(\mathbf{x}_\alpha) + \lambda_\alpha^{k_\alpha}(\mathbf{x}_\alpha)] = \min_{\mathbf{k}_\alpha} q_\alpha^{\mathbf{k}_\alpha}(\boldsymbol{\lambda}) \tag{29}$$

So, if we know the dual subproblems q_i and q_α for a given class of functions, then adding piecewise defined functions just requires a finite minimum over the $K^{|\alpha|}$ subproblems for each piece.

We can combine this approach with the polynomial hierarchy of Sections 3.2 and 3.3 by letting (D-$\Lambda^{(d),K}$) be the dual program with piecewise polynomial dual variables — each piece is a degree d polynomial, and the pieces are K equally-sized intervals of the domain Ω_i. We can bound how close each approximation is to the true dual solution: as we increase the number of pieces of the domain, or the degree of polynomials allowed as dual variables, these bounds converge to 0, as characterized by the following theorem (proof in the Appendix).

Theorem 2. *If each variable has domain* $\Omega_i = [0,1]$, *and all* f_α *are L-Lipschitz, then* $OPT(\text{D-}\Lambda^{(d),K}) \geq OPT(D) - O(\frac{ML}{dK})$.

We highlight the duals programs for piecewise constant ($\Lambda^{(0),K}$) and piecewise linear dual variables ($\Lambda^{(1),K}$).

4.1   Piecewise Constant Dual Variables

Substituting the appropriate subproblems $q_i^k, q_\alpha^{\mathbf{k}_\alpha}$ into Lemma 4, we get

$$\max_{\boldsymbol{\lambda}} \left[\sum_i \min_k \left[\min_{x_i}(f_i^k(x_i)) + \lambda_i^{(0),k} \right] + \right. \qquad\qquad (\text{D-}\Lambda^{(0),K})$$

$$\left. \sum_\alpha \min_{\mathbf{k}_\alpha} \left[\min_{\mathbf{x}_\alpha}(f_\alpha^{\mathbf{k}_\alpha}(\mathbf{x}_\alpha)) + \lambda_\alpha^{(0),\mathbf{k}_\alpha} \right] \right]$$

Recall that the pieces of Ω_i and Ω_α are indexed by $k_i, \mathbf{k}_\alpha$. Define the following discrete functions

$$\overline{f}_i(k_i) = \min_{x_i \in I_k} f_i(x_i) \qquad\qquad (30)$$

$$\overline{f}_\alpha(\mathbf{k}_\alpha) = \min_{\mathbf{x}_\alpha \in I_{\mathbf{k}_\alpha}} f_\alpha(\mathbf{x}_\alpha) \qquad\qquad (31)$$

and the discrete optimization problem

$$\min_{\mathbf{k}} \sum_i \overline{f}_i(k_i) + \sum_\alpha \overline{f}(\mathbf{k}_\alpha). \qquad\qquad (\text{F})$$

Note that $\overline{f} = \sum_i \overline{f}_i + \sum_\alpha \overline{f}_\alpha$ is obtained by taking the minimum value in each piece of the domain (see Figure 1 (left) for illustration). The primal LP relaxation of this problem using the Local Marginal Polytope is

$$\min_{\substack{\mu_i \in \mathcal{P}(K) \\ \mu_\alpha \in \mathcal{P}^\alpha(K)}} \sum_i \langle \overline{f}_i, \mu_i \rangle + \sum_\alpha \langle \overline{f}_\alpha, \mu_\alpha \rangle, \text{ s.t. } \mu_\alpha|_i = \mu_i. \qquad (\text{P-}\overline{\text{F}})$$

Where, $\mathcal{P}(K)$ is the space of discrete probability distributions on the integers $\{1, \ldots, K\}$ and $\mathcal{P}^\alpha(K)$ is the space of discrete probability distributions on corresponding $|\alpha|$-dimensional integer grid. Then we have,

Theorem 3. $OPT(\text{D-}\Lambda^{(0),K}) = OPT(\text{P-}\overline{\text{F}})$.

Proof. Substituting (30) and (31) into (D-$\Lambda^{(0),K}$), we get

$$\max_{\boldsymbol{\lambda}} \sum_i \min_{k_i} \left[\overline{f}_i(k_i) - \lambda_i^{(0),k} \right] + \sum_\alpha \min_{\mathbf{k}_\alpha} \left[\overline{f}_\alpha(\mathbf{k}_\alpha) + \lambda_\alpha^{(0),\mathbf{k}_\alpha} \right] \qquad (32)$$

This is exactly the dual of (P-$\overline{\text{F}}$), and by strong duality our claim holds.

Note that this means we can solve D-$\Lambda^{(0),K}$ by using $\overline{f}$ as input to any Discrete MRF solver which optimizes the dual, such as [31,21].

4.2   Piecewise Linear Dual Variables

Again, substituting the appropriate subproblems $q_i^k, q_\alpha^{\mathbf{k}_\alpha}$ into Lemma 4, we get

$$\max_{\boldsymbol{\lambda}} \left[\sum_i \min_k \left[-(f_i^k)^*(\lambda_i^{(1),k}) + \lambda_i^{(0),k} \right] + \right.$$
$$\left. \sum_\alpha \min_{\mathbf{k}_\alpha} \left[-(f_\alpha^{\mathbf{k}_\alpha})^*(-\boldsymbol{\lambda}_\alpha^{(1),\mathbf{k}_\alpha}) + \lambda_\alpha^{(0),\mathbf{k}_\alpha} \right] \right] \qquad (\text{D-}\Lambda^{(1),K})$$

This problem turns out to be closely related to the method proposed by Zach and Kohli [33]. Their method first subdivides the functions f_i, f_α on a grid, and separately convexifies each piece (see Figure 1 (right) for illustration). The resulting problem is solved using a convex program with marginalization constraints. More specifically, their method solves the following convex program[5]:

$$\min_{\mathbf{x},\mathbf{y}} \sum_{i,k} y_i^k (f_i^k)^{**} \left(\frac{x_i^k}{y_i^k} \right) + \sum_{\alpha,\mathbf{k}_\alpha} y_\alpha^{\mathbf{k}_\alpha} (f_\alpha^{\mathbf{k}_\alpha})^{**} \left(\frac{\mathbf{x}_\alpha^{\mathbf{k}_\alpha}}{y_\alpha^{\mathbf{k}_\alpha}} \right) \qquad (\text{P-ZK})$$

$$\sum_{\mathbf{k}_\alpha : k_i = k} y_\alpha^{\mathbf{k}_\alpha} = y_i^k \qquad (33)$$

$$\sum_{\mathbf{k}_\alpha : k_i = k} x_{\alpha,i}^{\mathbf{k}_\alpha} = x_{i,k} \qquad (34)$$

$$\langle y_i, 1 \rangle = \langle y_\alpha, 1 \rangle = 1 \qquad (35)$$

$$0 \le x_i^k \le y_i^k \qquad 0 \le x_{\alpha,i}^{\mathbf{k}_\alpha} \le y_\alpha^{\mathbf{k}_\alpha} \qquad (36)$$

Theorem 4. $\text{OPT}(\text{D-}\Lambda^{(1),K}) = \text{OPT}(\text{P-ZK})$.

Proof. We can dualize the constraints (33) and (34) with dual variables $\lambda_{\alpha,i}^{(1),k}$ and $\lambda_{\alpha,i}^{(0),k}$ respectively. This gives the program:

$$\max_{\boldsymbol{\lambda}} \min_{\mathbf{x},\mathbf{y}} \sum_{i,k} y_i^k \left[(f_i^k)^{**} \left(\frac{x_i^k}{y_i^k} \right) - \lambda_i^{(1),k} \frac{x_i^k}{y_i^k} - \lambda_i^{(0),k} \right] \qquad (37a)$$

$$+ \sum_{\alpha,\mathbf{k}_\alpha} y_\alpha^{\mathbf{k}_\alpha} \left[(f_\alpha^{\mathbf{k}_\alpha})^{**} \left(\frac{\mathbf{x}_\alpha^{\mathbf{k}_\alpha}}{y_\alpha^{\mathbf{k}_\alpha}} \right) + (\boldsymbol{\lambda}_\alpha^{(1),\mathbf{k}_\alpha})^T \frac{\mathbf{x}_\alpha^{\mathbf{k}_\alpha}}{y_\alpha^{\mathbf{k}_\alpha}} + \lambda_\alpha^{(0),\mathbf{k}_\alpha} \right] \qquad (37b)$$

$$\langle y_i, 1 \rangle = \langle y_\alpha, 1 \rangle = 1 \qquad (37c)$$

$$0 \le x_i^k \le y_i^k \qquad 0 \le x_{\alpha,i}^{\mathbf{k}_\alpha} \le y_\alpha^{\mathbf{k}_\alpha} \qquad (37d)$$

Then, minimizing over $\mathbf{x}$ and then $\mathbf{y}$ (and using the fact that $f^{***} = f^*$), this simplifies to $(\text{D-}\Lambda^{(1),K})$. Therefore, $(\text{D-}\Lambda^{(1),K})$ is dual to (P-ZK).

---

[5] (P-ZK) generalizes equation (8) from [33] to higher-order cliques (they consider only pairwise terms), with slight changes in notation to match our own. Additionally, throughout this section we'll define $0/0 = 0$, to make the divisions above always be well-defined.

5 Piecewise Defined f_i and f_α

In the last two sections we studied versions of (D-F) where the dual variables are restricted to subspaces of $C[\Omega_i]$ without any restrictions on f_i and f_α. Let us now consider the case where the functions f_i and f_α are also defined piecewise.

Theorem 5. *If f_i, f_α are piecewise constant on $I_k, I_{\mathbf{k}_\alpha}$ respectively, and if $\overline{F}$ is the optimization problem obtained by discretizing F (via (30) and (31)), then*

$$\mathrm{OPT}(\text{P-F}) = \mathrm{OPT}(\text{P-}\overline{\text{F}}) = \mathrm{OPT}(\text{D-}\Lambda^{(0),K})$$

Proof. Since f_i, f_α are all piecewise constant on the grid cells $I_k, I_{\mathbf{k}_\alpha}$, then the construction (30) and (31) reduces to

$$\overline{f}_i(k_i) = \min_{x_i \in I_k} f_i(x_i) = f_i(I_k) \tag{38}$$

$$\overline{f}_\alpha(\mathbf{k}_\alpha) = \min_{\mathbf{x}_\alpha \in I_{\mathbf{k}_\alpha}} f_\alpha(\mathbf{x}_\alpha) = f(I_{\mathbf{k}_\alpha}) \tag{39}$$

Observe that the optimal dual variables $\boldsymbol{\lambda}^*$ for (D) will also be piecewise constant, here is why. Since f_i, f_α are constant on $I_k, I_{\mathbf{k}_\alpha}$, setting $\lambda_{\alpha,i}(x_i)$ to its average value on the interval, $\lambda_{\alpha,i}(x_i) = \frac{1}{|I_k|} \int_{I_k} \lambda_{\alpha,i}(x_i)dx$ for $x_i \in I_k$, does not decrease the objective q. Therefore, we have $\mathrm{OPT}(D) = \mathrm{OPT}(\text{D-}\Lambda^{(0),K})$, which combined with $\mathrm{OPT}(D) = \mathrm{OPT}(\text{P-F})$ and Lemma 3 gives our result.

For piecewise-linear functions, we have a similar result (proof in Appendix).

Theorem 6. *Let the functions f_i, f_α be continuous piecewise-linear on a regular grid[6] and let $\widetilde{f}_i$ be f_i restricted to $\{0, \dots, K\}$, and $\widetilde{f}_\alpha$ be f_α restricted to $\{0, \dots, K\}^\alpha$. Then consider the discrete optimization problem:*

$$\min_{\substack{\mu_i \in \mathcal{P}(K) \\ \mu_\alpha \in \mathcal{P}^\alpha(K)}} \sum_i \left\langle \widetilde{f}_i, \mu_i \right\rangle + \sum_\alpha \left\langle \widetilde{f}_\alpha, \mu_\alpha \right\rangle, \ \ s.t. \ \mu_\alpha|_i = \mu_i \tag{P-$\widetilde{\text{F}}$}$$

$\mathrm{OPT}(\text{P-F}) = \mathrm{OPT}(\text{P-}\widetilde{\text{F}})$.

According to these theorems, for piecewise-constant and piecewise-linear objective functions, the infinite dimensional primal and dual problems have the same value as the finite dimensional problems for the discrete MRF $\widetilde{f}$. This means that the classic discrete MRF optimization methods can be used to solve this class of problems effectively.

6 Solving D-$\Lambda^{(d),K}$

The problem D-$\Lambda^{(d),K}$ is a finite dimensional, unconstrained convex non-smooth optimization problem. For non-smooth problems, the best general-purpose optimization algorithms are subgradient methods [2]. However, because subgradient

---

[6] f_i is linear on each interval I_k, and that there's a triangulation T of the grid Ω_α such that f_α is linear on each triangle (or simplex) $\tau \in T$.

algorithms have slow convergence, requiring $O(\frac{1}{\epsilon^2})$ function evaluations to obtain an ϵ-optimal solution [2]) it is worth considering more specialized methods.

As we noted earlier, as consequence of Theorem 3, (D-$\Lambda^{(0),K}$) can be solved efficiently using discrete MRF solvers that operate on the dual.

Sometimes it is preferable to slightly modify the problem and instead optimize a smooth approximation to the dual and this can lead to a convergence rate of $O(1/\epsilon)$ [16]. For discrete problems, this approach has been used in the Adaptive Diminishing Smoothing method of [21] to obtain state of the art optimization results for discrete MRFs. This can also be applied to (D-$\Lambda^{(1),K}$). There are two sources of discontinuity in dual: the finite minimization from the piecewise part, where $q_i(\boldsymbol{\lambda}) = \min_k q_i^k(\boldsymbol{\lambda})$; and the Fenchel conjugate $q_i^k(\boldsymbol{\lambda}) = -(f_i^k)^*(\lambda_i^{(1),k})$, which may also be non-differentiable. To get a smooth approximation for the finite minimization, we replace min with soft-min[7] as in the work of [21]. For the Fenchel conjugate, we have

Lemma 5. *For $f : [0,1]^n \to \mathbb{R}$ and $t > 0$, let $f_t(\mathbf{x}) = f^{**} + t\|x\|^2$. Then f_t^* is differentiable, and $f^*(\mathbf{y}) \geq f_t^*(\mathbf{y}) \geq f^*(\mathbf{y}) - tn$.*

Proof. We note that (by Lemma 26.3 of [20]) f^* is differentiable if and only if f is strictly-convex, and f^{**} is convex and $t > 0$ so f_t is strictly convex. Then, $f_t \geq f$ for all $\mathbf{x}$, so $f_t^* \leq f^*$ (the Fenchel conjugate is order reversing). Finally,

$$f_t^*(\mathbf{y}) = \sup_{\mathbf{x}} \mathbf{y}^T \mathbf{x} - f^{**}(\mathbf{x}) - t\|x\|^2 \tag{40}$$

$$\geq \sup_{\mathbf{x}} \mathbf{y}^T \mathbf{x} - f^{**}(\mathbf{x}) - tn = f^*(\mathbf{y}) - tn. \tag{41}$$

Combining these two smoothing techniques gives us a differentiable approximation to (D-$\Lambda^{(1),K}$) which can then be efficiently optimized, either using conventional quasi-Newton methods such as L-BFGS, or the special-purpose optimal method of Nesterov [16].

For $d > 1$, the story is less nice. Recall that if there are multiple minimizers for $f(\mathbf{x}) = \min_{i \in I} g_i(\mathbf{x})$, then f is non-differentiable. In particular, for quadratic dual variables, the Φ-conjugate $f^\Phi(a_1, a_2) = \sup_x a_1 x + a_2 x^2 - f(x)$ may have multiple minimizers. Ensuring strict convexity does not help this situation: if $f(x) = x^2$, then $f^\Phi(0,1) = \sup_x 0 \cdot x + 1 \cdot x^2 - x^2 = \sup_x 0$, which is minimized by every x. So for $d > 1$, the smoothing method of Lemma 5 doesn't work. We do not know a practical way to smooth these subproblems, so we can only propose to use subgradient methods for optimization in this case.

7   Discussion

We have given a sequence of dual programs (D-$\Lambda^{(d),K}$), which get increasingly close to the infinite-dimensional dual (D) as d, K increase. To see the tradeoffs in

---

[7] Defined by soft-min$_{i \in I} g_i(\mathbf{x}) = -t \log \sum_i e^{-g_i(\mathbf{x})/t}$.

choosing d, K, the bounds from Theorem 2 are $O(\frac{1}{dK})$. If we consider either doubling the number of pieces K, or the degree d, then we get the same improvement in error bound, but both choices use twice as many coefficients $\lambda_{\alpha,i}^{(j),k}$.

However, the computation of the soft-min for the gradient of f_α scales as $K^{|\alpha|}$, whereas if our f_α are analytically defined, our Fenchel conjugate computation may be much cheaper to compute (potentially in constant time). Therefore, depending on the specifics of the problem, increasing the degree d is likely to be a better tradeoff in terms of computational efficiency. Unfortunately, (D-$\Lambda^{(d),K}$) cannot use smooth optimization methods for $d > 1$, which suggests that (D-$\Lambda^{(1),K}$) is the best choice.

A further attractive feature of the dual construction is that it unifies both higher order cliques α, and continuous domains in a single framework. The main complexity of the dual (D) is due to the continuous variables, causing it to be infinite dimensional. The higher-order cliques do cause the number of pieces I_{k_α} in the piecewise dual variable case to grow exponentially with the clique size, but the same is true for discrete MRFs as well.

Going forward we plan on exploring the practical performance and specialized algorithms for computing the dual for specific f_α of interest in applications. In particular, we will consider the truncated L_1 and L_2 priors, because their Fenchel conjugates can be analytically derived and computed in constant time. We will also investigate the Fast Fenchel Conjugate [15] for handling more general f_α. Using these duals as building blocks, we then plan on building a practical implementation of smoothing based optimization algorithm for (D-$\Lambda^{(1),K}$).

A   Proofs

Lemma 1. *If all $f_\alpha \in Lip_L[\Omega_\alpha]$, then there is a dual-optimal λ where each $\lambda_{\alpha,i} \in Lip_L[\Omega_i]$.*

Proof. Let λ be dual-optimal. We will iterate through α, i updating each $\lambda_{\alpha,i}$ to become L-Lipschitz, without reducing the objective $q(\lambda)$. So, let $\lambda'_{\alpha,i}(x_i) = \min_{x'_i} \lambda_{\alpha,i}(x'_i) + L|x_i - x'_i|$. First, note that $\lambda'_{\alpha,i} \leq \lambda_{\alpha,i}$. We also have that $\lambda'_{\alpha,i}$ is L-Lipschitz: for any x there is some z with $\lambda'_{\alpha,i}(x) = \lambda_{\alpha,i}(z) + L|x - z|$ and for all y, $\lambda'_{\alpha,i}(y) \leq \lambda'_{\alpha,i}(z) + L|y - z|$ hence $\lambda'_{\alpha,i}(y) - \lambda'_{\alpha,i}(x) \leq L|y - z| - L|x - z| \leq L|y - x|$. By symmetry, $|\lambda'_{\alpha,i}(y) - \lambda'_{\alpha,i}(x)| \leq L|y - x|$.

Let λ' be λ where we've updated one $\lambda_{\alpha,i}$ to $\lambda'_{\alpha,i}$. Since $\lambda'_{\alpha,i} \leq \lambda_{\alpha,i}$ we know $q_i(\lambda') \geq q_i(\lambda)$. To show $q_\alpha(\lambda') \geq q_\alpha(\lambda)$, pick any $\mathbf{x}_\alpha$. There is some x'_i such that $\lambda'_{\alpha,i}(x_i) = \lambda_{\alpha,i}(x'_i) + L|x'_i - x_i|$. Let $\mathbf{x}'_\alpha$ be $\mathbf{x}_\alpha$ with x'_i replacing x_i. Then:

$$f_\alpha(\mathbf{x}_\alpha) + \sum_i \lambda'_{\alpha,i}(x_i) = f_\alpha(\mathbf{x}_\alpha) + \sum_j \lambda_{\alpha,j}(x'_j) + L|x_i - x'_i| \tag{42}$$

$$\geq f_\alpha(\mathbf{x}'_\alpha) + \sum_i \lambda_{\alpha,i}(x'_i) \geq q_\alpha(\lambda) \tag{43}$$

Therefore, $q_\alpha(\lambda') = \min_{\mathbf{x}_\alpha} f_\alpha(\mathbf{x}_\alpha) + \lambda'_\alpha(\mathbf{x}_\alpha) \geq q_\alpha(\lambda)$, so $q(\lambda') \geq q(\lambda)$.

Theorem 2. *If each variable has domain $\Omega_i = [0,1]$, and all f_α are L-Lipschitz, then $OPT(\text{D-}\Lambda^{(d),K}) \geq OPT(D) - O\left(\frac{ML}{dK}\right)$.*

Proof. We use Jackson's theorem (Corollary 7.5 of [5]): there is a constant C such that if $f \in \text{Lip}_L[0,1]$ then there is a polynomial p_n of degree n with $\|f - p_n\|_\infty \leq O\left(\frac{L}{n}\right)$. This bound may not be tight for small n; however for constant and linear functions, we have $p_0(x) = f(\frac{1}{2})$ and $p_1(x) = f(\frac{1}{4}) + (f(\frac{3}{4}) - f(\frac{1}{4}))x$ with $\|f - p_0\| \leq \frac{L}{2}$ and $\|f - p_1\| \leq \frac{L}{4}$ (the functions $f_0(x) = Lx$ and $f_1(x) = L|x - \frac{1}{2}|$ show that these bounds are tight).

Since the f_α are L-Lipschitz, by lemma 1 there is a dual-optimal $\boldsymbol{\lambda}$ where each $\lambda_{\alpha,i}$ is L-Lipschitz. Then, apply the Jackson-inequality to each piece $[\frac{i}{K}, \frac{i+1}{K}]$ of the domain $[0,1]$ to get a K-piecewise d-degree $\overline{\boldsymbol{\lambda}}$ with $\|\overline{\lambda}_{\alpha,i} - \lambda^*_{\alpha,i}\|_\infty \leq O\left(\frac{L}{dK}\right)$. Consequently, by lemma 2, $OPT(\text{D-}\Lambda^{(d),K}) \geq q(\overline{\boldsymbol{\lambda}}) \geq OPT^* - O\left(\frac{ML}{dK}\right)$.

Theorem 6. *If f_i, f_α are continuous piecewise-linear functions on a regular grid, then $OPT(\text{P-F}) = OPT(\text{P-}\widetilde{F})$.*

Proof. Since $\widetilde{f}$ is just a sampled version of f, the discrete LP (P-$\widetilde{F}$) is identical to (P-F) with the restriction that $\widetilde{\mu}_\alpha \in \mathcal{P}^\alpha(K)$. Since $\mathcal{P}^\alpha(K) \subseteq \mathcal{P}[\Omega_\alpha]$ it's clear that the continuous LP is a lower bound on the discrete LP.

For the other direction, take a feasible primal $\mu_\alpha \in \mathcal{P}[\Omega_\alpha]$: we'll construct a feasible $\widetilde{\mu}_\alpha \in \mathcal{P}^\alpha(K)$ with the same objective.

Let T_α be the standard triangulation of the grid $\{0, \dots, K\}^\alpha$. Each simplex $\tau \in T_\alpha$ has vertices in $\{0, \dots, K\}^\alpha$ and the projection of τ onto the i-th component is an interval $[j, j+1]$. For each $\widetilde{\mathbf{x}} \in \{0, \dots, K\}^\alpha$, there is a set of simplices with $\widetilde{\mathbf{x}}$ as a vertex, we will denote this set as $\tau \sim \widetilde{\mathbf{x}}$. Each simplex comes with barycentric coordinates: every point $\mathbf{x} \in \tau$ is a convex combination of the vertices. We'll write these as $\xi_{\tau,\widetilde{\mathbf{x}}}(\mathbf{x})$ which satisfy $\sum_{\widetilde{\mathbf{x}} \sim \tau} \xi_{\tau,\widetilde{\mathbf{x}}}(\mathbf{x})\widetilde{\mathbf{x}} = \mathbf{x}$.

We construct $\widetilde{\mu}_\alpha$ by taking all the mass from μ_α on a simplex τ, and gathering it to each vertex $\widetilde{\mathbf{x}}$, weighted by the barycentric coordinates $\xi_{\tau,\widetilde{\mathbf{x}}}$. More specifically, define $\widetilde{\mu}_\alpha(\widetilde{\mathbf{x}}) := \sum_{\tau \sim \widetilde{\mathbf{x}}} \int_\tau \xi_{\tau,\widetilde{\mathbf{x}}}(\mathbf{x}) d\mu_\alpha$.

The fact that the barycentric coordinates sum to 1 ensures that $\widetilde{\mu}_\alpha$ is a probability distribution on $\widetilde{\Omega}_\alpha$, and since the projections of τ onto the i-th component are intervals $[j, j+1]$ we get that $\{\widetilde{\mu}_\alpha\}$ satisfy the marginalization constraints. Finally, since our objective is linear on each τ, we have $f_\alpha(\mathbf{x}_\alpha) = \sum_{\widetilde{\mathbf{x}} \sim \tau} \xi_{\tau,\widetilde{\mathbf{x}}}(\mathbf{x}_\alpha) f(\widetilde{\mathbf{x}})$. Therefore, we have

$$\langle f_\alpha, \widetilde{\mu}_\alpha \rangle = \sum_{\widetilde{\mathbf{x}}} f_\alpha(\widetilde{\mathbf{x}})\left(\sum_{\tau \sim \widetilde{\mathbf{x}}} \int_\tau \xi_{\tau,\widetilde{\mathbf{x}}}(\mathbf{x}_\alpha) d\mu_\alpha\right) = \sum_\tau \int_\tau \sum_{\widetilde{\mathbf{x}} \sim \tau} f(\widetilde{\mathbf{x}})\xi_{\tau,\widetilde{\mathbf{x}}}(\mathbf{x}_\alpha) d\mu_\alpha \quad (44)$$

$$= \sum_\tau \int_\tau f(\mathbf{x}_\alpha) d\mu_\alpha = \langle f_\alpha, \mu_\alpha \rangle. \quad (45)$$

References

1. Bach, S.H., Broecheler, M., Getoor, L., O'Leary, D.P.: Scaling MPE inference for constrained continuous markov random fields with consensus optimization. In: Advances in Neural Information Processing Systems, pp. 2663–2671 (2012)

2. Bertsekas, D.: Nonlinear Programming. Athena Scientific (1995)
3. Besag, J., Besag, J.: On the statistical analysis of dirty pictures. Journal of the Royal Statistical Society B, 48–259 (1986)
4. Boykov, Y., Veksler, O., Zabih, R.: Fast approximate energy minimization via graph cuts. IEEE Transactions on Pattern Analysis and Machine Intelligence 23(11), 1222–1239 (2001)
5. Carothers, N.L.: A short course on approximation theory (2009)
6. Crandall, D.J., Owens, A., Snavely, N., Huttenlocher, D.P.: SfM with MRFs: Discrete-continuous optimization for large-scale structure from motion. IEEE Transactions on Pattern Analysis and Machine Intelligence 35(12), 2841–2853 (2013)
7. Dolecki, S., Kurcyusz, S.: On ϕ-convexity in extremal problems. SIAM Journal on Control and Optimization 16(2), 277–300 (1978)
8. Geman, S., Geman, D.: Stochastic relaxation, Gibbs distributions, and the Bayesian restoration of images. IEEE Transactions on Pattern Analysis and Machine Intelligence 6(6), 721–741 (1984)
9. Ihler, A., McAllester, D.: Particle belief propagation. In: Artificial Intelligence and Statistics, pp. 256–263 (2009)
10. Ishikawa, H.: Higher-order gradient descent by fusion-move graph cut. In: IEEE International Conference on Computer Vision, pp. 568–574 (2009)
11. Jojic, V., Gould, S., Koller, D.: Fast and smooth: Accelerated dual decomposition for MAP inference. In: International Conference on Machine Learning (2010)
12. Komodakis, N., Tziritas, G.: Approximate labeling via graph cuts based on linear programming. IEEE Transactions on Pattern Analysis and Machine Intelligence 29(8), 1436–1453 (2007)
13. Lasserre, J.B.: Global optimization with polynomials and the problem of moments. SIAM Journal on Optimization 11, 796–817 (2001)
14. Lee, J.: A first course in combinatorial optimization, vol. 36. Cambridge University Press (2004)
15. Lucet, Y.: Faster than the fast Legendre transform, the linear-time Legendre transform. Numerical Algorithms 16(2), 171–185 (1997)
16. Nesterov, Y.: Smooth minimization of non-smooth functions. Mathematical Programming 103(1), 127–152 (2005)
17. Peng, J., Hazan, T., Mcallester, D., Urtasun, R.: Convex max-product algorithms for continuous MRFs with applications to protein folding. In: International Conference on Machine Learning (2011)
18. Rockafellar, R.T., Wets, R.J.B., Wets, M.: Variational analysis, vol. 317. Springer (1998)
19. Rockafellar, R.: Conjugate Duality and Optimization. Society for Industrial and Applied Mathematics (1974)
20. Rockafellar, R.: Convex Analysis. Princeton University Press (1997)
21. Savchynskyy, B., Schmidt, S., Schnrr, C.: Efficient MRF energy minimization via adaptive diminishing smoothing. In: Uncertainty in Artificial Intelligence (2012)
22. Shimony, S.E.: Finding MAPs for belief networks is NP-hard. Artificial Intelligence 68(2), 399–410 (1994)
23. Sigal, L., Bhatia, S., Roth, S., Black, M., Isard, M.: Tracking loose-limbed people. In: IEEE Conference on Computer Vision and Pattern Recognition (2004)
24. Sudderth, E.B., Michael, I.M., Freeman, W.T., Willsky, A.S.: Distributed occlusion reasoning for tracking with nonparametric belief propagation. In: Advances in Neural Information Processing Systems, pp. 1369–1376 (2004)

25. Sun, J., Zheng, N.N., Shum, H.Y.: Stereo matching using belief propagation. IEEE Transactions on Pattern Analysis and Machine Intelligence 25(7), 787–800 (2003)
26. Triggs, B., McLauchlan, P.F., Hartley, R.I., Fitzgibbon, A.W.: Bundle adjustment a modern synthesis. In: Triggs, B., Zisserman, A., Szeliski, R. (eds.) Vision Algorithms 1999. LNCS, vol. 1883, pp. 298–372. Springer, Heidelberg (2000)
27. Trinh, H., McAllester, D.: Particle-based belief propagation for structure from motion and dense stereo vision with unknown camera constraints. In: Sommer, G., Klette, R. (eds.) RobVis 2008. LNCS, vol. 4931, pp. 16–28. Springer, Heidelberg (2008)
28. Vazirani, V.V.: Approximation algorithms. Springer (2001)
29. Wainwright, M.J., Jordan, M.I.: Graphical models, exponential families, and variational inference. Found. Trends Mach. Learn. 1(1-2), 1–305 (2008)
30. Weiss, Y., Freeman, W.T.: On the optimality of solutions of the max-product belief-propagation algorithm in arbitrary graphs. IEEE Trans. Inf. Theor. 47(2), 736–744 (2006)
31. Werner, T.: A linear programming approach to max-sum problem: A review. IEEE Transactions on Pattern Analysis and Machine Intelligence 29(7), 1165–1179 (2007)
32. Yamaguchi, K., Hazan, T., McAllester, D., Urtasun, R.: Continuous Markov random fields for robust stereo estimation. In: Fitzgibbon, A., Lazebnik, S., Perona, P., Sato, Y., Schmid, C. (eds.) ECCV 2012, Part V. LNCS, vol. 7576, pp. 45–58. Springer, Heidelberg (2012)
33. Zach, C., Kohli, P.: A convex discrete-continuous approach for Markov random fields. In: Fitzgibbon, A., Lazebnik, S., Perona, P., Sato, Y., Schmid, C. (eds.) ECCV 2012, Part VI. LNCS, vol. 7577, pp. 386–399. Springer, Heidelberg (2012)

Spectral Clustering with a Convex Regularizer on Millions of Images

Maxwell D. Collins[1], Ji Liu[2], Jia Xu[1],
Lopamudra Mukherjee[3], and Vikas Singh[1]

[1] University of Wisconsin–Madison, USA
[2] University of Rochester, USA
[3] University of Wisconsin–Whitewater, USA
mcollins@cs.wisc.edu, jliu@cs.rochester.edu, jiaxu@cs.wisc.edu,
mukherj1@uww.edu, vsingh@biostat.wisc.edu

Abstract. This paper focuses on efficient algorithms for single and multi-view spectral clustering with a convex regularization term for very large scale image datasets. In computer vision applications, multiple views denote distinct image-derived feature representations that inform the clustering. Separately, the regularization encodes high level advice such as tags or user interaction in identifying similar objects across examples. Depending on the specific task, schemes to exploit such information may lead to a smooth or non-smooth regularization function. We present stochastic gradient descent methods for optimizing spectral clustering objectives with such convex regularizers for datasets with up to a hundred million examples. We prove that under mild conditions the local convergence rate is $O(1/\sqrt{T})$ where T is the number of iterations; further, our analysis shows that the convergence improves linearly by increasing the number of threads. We give extensive experimental results on a range of vision datasets demonstrating the algorithm's empirical behavior.

1 Introduction

The need to *process* and make sense of the large number of images on the internet — for search, categorization, and ranking, motivates problems that are fundamental to vision and machine learning research today. To facilitate such inference tasks, the image is first expressed in terms of its response to a large set of specialized filters pertaining to texture, distinct object categories and appearance, among others. This information may be further complemented by textual cues that co-occur with the images, image tags, or hyperlinks to the image. With these representations in hand, the goal is to leverage all views simultaneously and derive a solution that best explains the given set of examples in the context of the inference objective of interest.

Clustering serves as an important exploratory tool for categorizing sets of images into semantically meaningful concepts. Mixture modeling and k-means remain traditional workhorses for this task and provide estimates of the parameters of an explicit model for the data. Spectral objectives, which are a focus

D. Fleet et al. (Eds.): ECCV 2014, Part III, LNCS 8691, pp. 282–298, 2014.
© Springer International Publishing Switzerland 2014

of this paper, instead analyze the eigen structure (or spectrum) of a matrix derived from the pairwise similarities of nodes, and are especially useful when the cluster distributions correspond to more complex shapes [35]. Despite these advantages, spectral clustering is expensive for larger datasets. The most common optimization is to sparsify [7] or subsample [13,24] the matrix of similarities between examples. Even with these optimizations, solving the spectral clustering problem for very large datasets is expensive — partly due to the need for an eigen-decomposition of big matrices. These issues clearly intensify when operating with multiple views of the data, and if we seek to incorporate side advice such as tags. To address these limitations, there is significant recent interest in making spectral clustering efficient in the large dataset setting — with user interaction [8], 'activization' schemes [17], random projections [28], Spielman-Teng's near linear Laplacian solver [16], and parallelized versions of the Lanczos solver [7]. These solutions are highly effective for the standard spectral clustering objective and several also come with nice guarantees.

These advantages notwithstanding, the algorithms above can rarely be used in an off the shelf manner to address and exploit the specific needs and characteristics of the vision application above. First, few of these formulations support multiple views natively. Second, it is not straightforward to adapt the key optimization schemes to run in a distributed manner over tens of cores — this is essential if the system is expected to work efficiently on massive datasets and on distributed platforms such as CloudCV [2]. Finally, incorporating weak (or distant) supervision, user interaction and/or auxiliary domain specific priors beyond must-link/cannot-link constraints is challenging. Such side information is ubiquitous in most real world datasets and seems like a desirable feature for a system deployed in practice.

Motivated by these core issues, our primary **goal** is to develop stochastic methods, with a focus on spectral clustering for both single and multi-view data, that satisfy three criteria: **a)** Allow scaling to very large datasets ($\sim$ 100M) in a distributed manner; **b)** Show provably good convergence behavior; **c)** Offer the ability to incorporate high level priors (e.g., images share 'tags', user interaction) as a regularization term. The **contribution** of this paper is to provide an optimization scheme that meets these theoretical and practical considerations.

Related Work. The preceding section covered several relevant results on scaling spectral clustering to large datasets. Therefore, here we review related work on multi-view models. To our knowledge, among the earliest methods for multi-view clustering is a paper by Bickel & Scheffer [4] where the authors emulate co-training for clustering with two views (e.g., the webpage and in-coming hyperlinks). More recently, [5] studied multi-view clustering for images. Using a kernel CCA over *two* views, they showed that the clustering of images is facilitated by the textual description that comes with the image data. Subsequently, [6] described a nice theoretical analysis of the scenario where we infer an underlying mixture model (i.e., mixing weights), given independently drawn samples from the mixture. The authors showed that the low-dimensional subspace spanned by the means of the component distributions can be identified when the views are conditionally uncorrelated. Strategies based on Non-negative Matrix Factorization [25], Co-training [19], Linked Matrix Factorization [30] and Random Walks [36] have also been proposed. The multi-view problem was investigated for a spectral clustering objective by [20]. This paper, which is the most closely related to ours, uses alternating maximization to co-regularize the clustering across views by requiring that the hypotheses learned from different views of the set of examples agree with each other. Like [20], our proposed approach will also operate with multiple views of the data. However, for scalability reasons, we will not impose inter-view consistency or differentially weight the given views, though our model easily permits this extension. We will instead adopt a simpler objective that considers all views to be equally informative, but still remains competitive with the more sophisticated strategies above in experiments.

2   Multi-View Spectral Clustering Model

Assume we are given l views of a dataset, $X = \{\mathbf{x}_1, \cdots, \mathbf{x}_n\}$, consisting of examples to be grouped into p clusters. Classically, for a single view, spectral clustering achieves this task by finding the p minimum eigenvectors of a Laplacian matrix $L \in \mathbb{R}^{n \times n}$, which encodes an appropriate graph over the examples. Typically, the eigenvectors are found via iterative methods such as Lanczos and its variations [22] that allow for implementations that can exploit the underlying sparsity of L. Spectral clustering may be viewed as a minimization of the trace of $V^T L V$ over the set $S_{n,p} \subseteq \mathbb{R}^{n \times p}$ of orthonormal $n \times p$ matrices V. $S_{n,p}$ is known as the *Stiefel manifold*. At the optimum, the columns of V must span the same subspace as the eigenvectors of the p least eigenvalues of L. To extend this to the multiview case, where we have a Laplacian denoted as $L^{(u)}$ for the uth view of the data, one possibility is to penalize the Frobenius norm of variations between the V-representations of each view-pair [20]. Here, the number of additional terms grows quadratically with the number of views. Instead, the 'centroid' based formalization in [20] enforces the view-specific eigenvectors to be similar by requiring that they lie close to a common centroid. Similar to this intuition, we look for a common V that balances the solution over all the views. This translates into the following model,

$$\min_{V \in \mathbb{R}^{n \times p}} h(V) := \sum_u \text{tr}(V^T L^{(u)} V) \quad \text{s.t.} \quad V^T V = I \qquad (1)$$

The simple formulation above offers important scalability benefits. However, it has the limitation of uniformly weighting the views — which is mathematically equivalent to summing up the view-wise Laplacians. This raises two issues: (a) Experimentally, is the unweighted sum of features much worse than multi-view methods that impose consistency across V's for each pair of views? (b) If not, is it attractive to pre-compute the combined Laplacian and then run a single view spectral clustering on it? We will present results in Section 5 to show that the objective in (1) is empirically competitive with multi-view approaches in [20] (note that analogously, feature concatenation remains a powerful baseline for MKL methods [14]). Regarding the second issue, rather than sum up the Laplacians beforehand, we will work with the views separately. Besides being a natural point at which to decompose the objective for stochastic gradient descent (as described later), dividing the Laplacians between separate computational nodes has useful performance advantages. For instance, in a distributed optimization setting, one does not need to copy these matrices (that exceed 50GB for large datasets) across each participating core. The entries of these matrices can also be lazily computed, with nearest neighbor lookups performed lazily to save unneeded work.

Incorporating Group Priors. Separate from Laplacians, there is typically a great deal of side information available suggesting (with varying degrees of confidence) that certain subsets of examples are likely to belong to the same class. Must-link constraints are tedious to deploy via user supervision for a large set of examples — instead, one may impose this prior indirectly. For example, if a set of images share five or more tags and the data source is somewhat reputable, it yields valuable group level advice to regularize (1) and complements the information extracted from the image.

Assume that we have a group prior information about examples where a group is defined as $C = \{v_1, v_2, \cdots, v_{|C|}\}$ where each v_j is a row of V corresponding to an example. To encode similarity in how their respective representations in V behave, we have a group concentration term, which measures the distance of each example (in the group) to the group's center $\bar{v}$:

$$g_C(V) = \sqrt{\frac{1}{|C|} \sum_{t=1}^{|C|} d(v_t, \bar{v})^2}, \qquad (2)$$

where $\bar{v} = \frac{1}{|C|} \sum_{t=1}^{|C|} v_t$ and $d(\cdot, \cdot)$ is a suitable distance function. This regularization essentially measures intra-group distances, and we obtain a multi-view spectral clustering problem with a group prior:

$$\min_{V \in \mathbb{R}^{n \times p}} \quad f(V) := h(V) + g(V) \quad \text{s.t.} \quad V^T V = I, \qquad (3)$$

where $g(V) = \lambda \sum_{\forall C} g_C(V)$ is a convex real-valued function that is the sum of the concentration terms for all groups (e.g. tags) in the dataset, with hyperparameter weight λ. We should point out that (2) is merely a simple example to make the following presentation concrete. Our subsequent analysis of this problem allows for non-smooth g, and group norms such as $\ell_{2,1}$ and others may be used based on specific needs. Some priors can be subsumed into the Laplacians whereas others can not, we make no assumptions on this. We denote the overall objective by $f(V)$.

3   Stochastic Gradient Descent Procedure

Our optimization scheme seeks to distribute the problem in such a way that at any given step, one only needs to consider a subset of the examples. This is done using the method of *stochastic gradient descent* [9]. It is easy to see that the objective for $h(V)$ can be expressed as

$$\sum_u \sum_{ij} L_{ij}^{(u)} \langle V_{i\cdot}, V_{j\cdot} \rangle = \sum_u \sum_{i \sim j} w_{ij}^{(u)} \|V_{i\cdot} - V_{j\cdot}\|_2^2$$

where the inner sum is over non-zero entries of the Laplacian matrix for the uth view in the first instance and edges of the corresponding graph with weights $w_{ij}^{(u)}$ in the second expression. Each term of the sum can be considered a subfunction of the objective, and so we can descend along the gradient of a randomly selected subset of the terms. Depending on the sampling strategy (discussed shortly), we want the resulting descent direction, *in expectation*, to be equivalent to an ordinary gradient descent on the full objective. Later, this will provide convergence guarantees.

At iteration t, one only obtains $\hat{L}_t$ that is a sample of L satisfying $\mathbb{E}(\hat{L}_t) = L$. To keep the notations and the presentation simple, we write our results and sampling strategy in the context of a single Laplacian L. For the following, we assume a simple procedure that uniformly selects edges from the graph, though our analysis also applies to additional sampling strategies discussed in Section 3.2, including the multi-view case. The stochastic gradient descent algorithm can then be applied to the entire objective of (3), resulting in the following update:

$$V_{t+1} = \mathcal{P}_\Omega(V_t - \gamma_t(2\hat{L}_t V_t + \partial g(V_t))), \tag{4}$$

where $\Omega := S_{n,p}$, γ_t the stepsize, and $\mathcal{P}_\Omega$ is a projection onto the feasible set.

Note that stochastic optimization on the Grassmannian and Stiefel manifolds has been considered in the context of GROUSE [1] and related work [34], and is not novel to this work specifically. In particular, [1] considers rank-one updates of the orthogonal solution matrix V on incomplete portions of the data.

3.1   Convergence of Stochastic Gradient

Generally, it is difficult to assess the convergence rate for non-convex optimization, but in our case the convergence can be obtained easily by properly choosing the stochastic gradient such that the objective decreases monotonically, for example, full gradient and (block) coordinate gradient. Therefore, based on the convergence "assumption," the following result shows that under some mild conditions, the *local* convergence rate is $O(1/\sqrt{T})$, where T is the number of iterations. We provide a brief outline of the proof in this section. Note that the convergence rate analysis is not only useful as a performance measure but helps provide the optimal sampling strategy for our optimization method and also shows how the framework will behave with parallelization across additional cores. To our knowledge, this is the first result of this kind for spectral clustering with regularization. Let $\Delta_t = \hat{L}_t - L$ where $\hat{L}_t$ is the sampled Laplacian at the tth iteration and $L := \sum_u L^{(u)}$. We first define:

$$\sigma^2 := \max_{V^T V = I, t} \mathbb{E}(\|\Delta_t V\|_F^2); \quad M := \max_{V^T V = I} \|LV\|_F; \quad N := \max_{V^T V = I} \|\partial g(V)\|_F.$$

Notice that M and N are constants decided by L and g respectively, while σ^2 directly depends on the sampling strategy. For convenience, we define a function Υ as $\Upsilon(M, N, \sigma^2, T) := \sqrt{((M+N)^2 + \sigma^2)/T}$. Our convergence result states:

Theorem 1. *Let V^* be a convergent point of the sequence $\{V_t\}$ generated from (4). Suppose $\{V_t\}$ is contained in a small ball with radius $\delta > 0$. Denote $f(V^*)$ as f^*, and let ϕ be a positive value. If $\mathcal{P}_\Omega \left(V_t - \gamma_t(\hat{L}_t V_t + \partial g(V_t)) \right)$ is a nonexpansive projection on this ball, we have:*
i) If the stepsize is chosen as $\gamma_t = \dfrac{\phi \delta}{\sqrt{((M+N)^2 + \sigma^2)T}}$ and
$\bar{V}_T = (\sum_{t=1}^{T} \gamma_t)^{-1} \sum_{t=1}^{T} \gamma_t V_t$*, then $\mathbb{E}\left(f(\bar{V}_T) \right) - f^* \le (\phi + \phi^{-1}) \frac{\delta}{2} \Upsilon$.*
ii) If the step size is chosen as $\gamma_t = \theta_t \dfrac{f(V_t) - f^*}{(M+N)^2 + \sigma^2}$, then $\mathbb{E}(f(\tilde{V}_T)) - f^* \le \dfrac{\delta}{\sqrt{\theta_{\min}}} \Upsilon$
where $\tilde{V}_T = \frac{1}{T} \sum_{t=1}^{T} V_t$, $\theta_t \in (0, 2)$ and $\theta_{\min} = \min_t 1 - (\theta_t - 1)^2$.

From Theorem 1, it is clear that independent of how the stepsize is chosen, the local convergence rate is essentially bounded by $\Upsilon \in O(1/\sqrt{T})$. Theorem 1 is proved in the extended version of this paper. Next, we further investigate the behavior of σ^2, and introduce sampling strategies based on nodes and edges.

Similar convergence can also be achieved by the partial stochastic gradient projection method, that is,

$$V_{t+1} = \mathcal{P}_\Omega(V_t - \gamma_t \partial_{[t]} f(V_t)) \tag{5}$$

where $\partial f(V_t) := LV_t + \partial g(V_t)$ is the subgradient of $f(V)$ at V_t and $\partial_{[t]} f(V)$ is a vector with the same size as $\partial f(V)$ taking the same values on the set $[t]$ and setting the rest as 0. More details are provided in the supplemental material.

3.2   Sampling

To meet the requirement of stochastic gradient, the randomly generated $\hat{L}_t$ should satisfy $\mathbb{E}(\hat{L}_t) = L$. The following discusses a sampling strategy that only uniformly samples the nonzero elements in L. Note that nonzero elements in L correspond to edges in the graph. Define $\bar{L}_{ij} \in \mathbb{R}^{n \times n}$ to be an extended matrix with L_{ij} at the ij^{th} element and zeros at the rest. We generate the stochastic gradient at the current iteration as $\hat{L}_t = \frac{\|L\|_0}{|\mathcal{E}|} \sum_{ij \in \mathcal{E}} \bar{L}_{ij}$ where $\mathcal{E}$ is the set of randomly selected edges.

In order to simplify the following discussion, we assume that the sampling strategy chooses a fixed number of edges at each iteration. These assumptions imply that every nonzero element (edge) in L has equal probability to be chosen. Let $\lambda_i(\Delta_t^T \Delta_t)$ denote the ith largest eigenvalue of $\Delta_t^T \Delta_t$. From the definition of σ^2, we have

$$\sigma^2 = \mathbb{E}\left(\max_{V^T V = I} \|\Delta_t V\|_F^2 \right) = \mathbb{E}\left(\sum_{i=1}^{p} \lambda_i(\Delta_t^T \Delta_t) \right) \le \mathbb{E}(\|\Delta_t\|_F^2) = \sum_{ij \in \mathcal{E}} \mathbb{E}((\Delta_t)_{ij}^2) \tag{6}$$

To estimate the upper bound of $\mathbb{E}((\Delta_t)_{ij}^2)$, we consider the sampling strategy without replacement (the replacement case can be handled similarly).

$$(\Delta_t)_{ij} = \begin{cases} \left(\frac{\|L\|_0}{|\mathcal{E}|} - 1\right) L_{ij} & \text{w. p. } \frac{|\mathcal{E}|}{\|L\|_0} \\ -L_{ij} & \text{w. p. } 1 - \frac{|\mathcal{E}|}{\|L\|_0} \end{cases} \tag{7}$$

One can easily verify that $\mathbb{E}((\Delta_t)_{ij}^2) = \left(\frac{\|L\|_0}{|\mathcal{E}|} - 1\right) L_{ij}^2$. Thus, from (6) we have $\sigma^2 \leq \left(\frac{\|L\|_0}{|\mathcal{E}|} - 1\right) \|L\|_F^2$. When the cardinality of L is large, $\|L\|_0 \gg |\mathcal{E}|$. In other words, σ^2 dominates the convergence rate. Further, M^2 is bounded by $\|L\|_F^2$, which indicates that the convergence rate is bounded by

$$O\left(T^{-1/2}\sqrt{(\|L\|_0/|\mathcal{E}| - 1)\|L\|_F^2 + (M + N)^2}\right)$$
$$\leq O\left(T^{-1/2}\left(\sqrt{\|L\|_0/|\mathcal{E}|}\|L\|_F + N + \sqrt{N\|L\|_F}\right)\right).$$

When $\sqrt{\frac{\|L\|_0}{|\mathcal{E}|}}$ is large, the bound is dominated by

$$O\left(\sqrt{\|L\|_0/(T|\mathcal{E}|)}\|L\|_F\right) = O((T|\mathcal{E}|)^{-1/2})$$

Note that the size of $\mathcal{E}$ is proportional to the number of threads. It means that the convergence can be speeded up linearly by increasing the number of threads (on different cores or slave computers) — exactly the behavior one hopes to achieve in the ideal situation. In addition, this linear speedup property is also achieved by the *partial* stochastic gradient projection method.

This edge sampling strategy can be easily extended to the setting where multiple separable views live in a distributed environment. The basic change here is that one needs to sample edges across all views, satisfying the condition $\mathbb{E}(\hat{L}_t) = \sum_u L^{(u)}$. This condition is true for a sampling strategy that first chooses a single u with probability proportional to the number of edges in $L^{(u)}$ from which edges are sampled identically to the single-view case. Similar linear speedup properties can be obtained; the result above carries through with essentially mechanical changes. Besides sampling edges, one may sample nodes (nodes correspond to the coordinates of V) to generate the stochastic gradient. However, when sampling nodes, the probability of sampling a given node must be weighted by its degree in order to achieve the same consistency conditions.

Projection vs Manifold Optimization. In order to realize the full benefits of parallelizing the optimization across multiple threads, we propose the manifold optimization method of Section 4. This does not satisfy the conditions of a non-expansive projection P_Ω in Theorem 1. Rather, it has the properties of a block coordinate descent method and does not leave the feasible region. While the manifold optimization has weaker convergence guarantees, it avoids the *projection* step, which requires synchronization between the parallel threads. See Fig. 1 side-by-side pseudocode showing the distinction.

Require: $f : \mathbb{R}^{n \times p} \to \mathbb{R},\ V_0 \in S_{n,p}$
   for $t = 1,\ \dots,\ T$ **do**
      Pick some u
      Sample $\hat{L}_t$ from $L^{(u)}$'s (see Section 3.2)

      Get subgradient $d \in 2\hat{L}_t V_t + \partial g(V_t)$
      Pick step size γ_t
      Take step in $\mathbb{R}^{n \times p}$: $V_{t+1}' \leftarrow V_t - \gamma_t d$
      Project onto feasible set:
         $V_{t+1} \leftarrow \mathcal{P}_{S_{n,p}}(V_{t+1}')$
end for

Require: $f : S_{n,p} \to \mathbb{R},\ V_0 \in S_{n,p}$
   for $t = 1,\ \dots,\ T$ **do**
      Select $\mathcal{K} \subseteq \{1,\ \dots,\ n\}$
      Take *descent curve* $Y(\tau)$ in $S_{n,p}$ s.t.
         $Y(0) = V_t$
         $\left.\dfrac{d(f \circ Y)}{d\tau}\right|_{\tau=0} \leq 0$
         $(Y(\tau))_{ij} = (V_t)_{ij} \quad \forall \tau, i \notin \mathcal{K}$
      Pick step size τ_t
      $V_{t+1} \leftarrow Y(\tau_t)$
end for

Fig. 1. Comparison on projection (discussed in Section 3) and projection-free manifold (see Section 4) algorithms for solving optimization problems over the Stiefel manifold $S_{n,p}$. When done in parallel, multiple processors may perform independent iterations on different choices of $\hat{L}_t$ and $\mathcal{K}$.

4 Projection-Free Manifold Optimization Procedure

Ideally, we want to be able to split up the problem into subsets of examples, while *also* producing iterates that satisfy the constraints $V^T V = I$. Say we have a subset $\mathcal{K}$ of k row indices, corresponding to rows of V (the submatrix corresponding to these rows is denoted by $V_{\mathcal{K}.} \in \mathbb{R}^{k \times p}$). We are given a feasible iterate V, and seek to compute the next iterate W such that it *also* lies in the Stiefel manifold $S_{n,p}$ and is thus feasible for the problem in (3), *and* W only differs from V in the rows selected by $\mathcal{K}$. This means that any number of parallel computational units, asynchronously modifying mutually disjoint subsets of the rows of V, will still produce feasible iterates.

Taking an optimization problem over only the rows in $\mathcal{K}$, we will show this produces a subproblem that seeks a rotation of the linearly independent columns of $V_{\mathcal{K}.}$. W.l.o.g., assume $V_{\mathcal{K}.} = [V_{\mathcal{K}\mathcal{I}}, V_{\mathcal{K}\mathcal{I}}R]$, where $V_{\mathcal{K}\mathcal{I}} \in \mathbb{R}^{k \times |\mathcal{I}|}$ is a maximal subset of linearly independent columns of $V_{\mathcal{K}.}$ and $R \in \mathbb{R}^{|\mathcal{I}| \times (p-|\mathcal{I}|)}$ is the linear mapping from $V_{\mathcal{K}\mathcal{I}}$ to the dependent columns. Let $P = V_{\mathcal{K}\mathcal{I}}{}^T V_{\mathcal{K}\mathcal{I}} \in \mathbb{R}^{|\mathcal{I}| \times |\mathcal{I}|}$ be the matrix of inner products of these columns. We know by construction that $P \succ 0$. Taking any orthonormal $U \in S_{k,|\mathcal{I}|}$,

$$W(U) = \begin{bmatrix} UP^{1/2} & UP^{1/2}R \\ V_{\bar{\mathcal{K}},\mathcal{I}} & V_{\bar{\mathcal{K}},\bar{\mathcal{I}}} \end{bmatrix} \in \mathbb{R}^{n \times p} \tag{8}$$

assuming w.l.o.g. above that $\mathcal{K}$ selects the first $|\mathcal{K}|$ rows of the matrix. This is constructed such that those rows of V in the *complement* of $\mathcal{K}$ (denoted by $\bar{\mathcal{K}}$) are unchanged in W and the constraints are preserved:

$$W_{\mathcal{K}.}{}^T W_{\mathcal{K}.} = \begin{bmatrix} P^{1/2}U^T U P^{1/2} & P^{1/2}U^T U P^{1/2}R \\ R^T P^{1/2}U^T U P^{1/2} & R^T P^{1/2}U^T U P^{1/2}R \end{bmatrix}$$

$$= \begin{bmatrix} P & PR \\ R^T P & R^T PR \end{bmatrix} = V_{\mathcal{K}.}^T V_{\mathcal{K}.}.$$

so that

$$W^T W = W_{\mathcal{K}}^T W_{\mathcal{K}} + W_{\bar{\mathcal{K}}}^T W_{\bar{\mathcal{K}}} = V_{\mathcal{K}}^T V_{\mathcal{K}} + V_{\bar{\mathcal{K}}}^T V_{\bar{\mathcal{K}}} = V^T V.$$

Therefore, if V lies on the Stiefel manifold $S_{n,p}$, so must W.

The above construction successfully reduces the problem of finding a feasible iterate W to modifying a subset of the rows given an appropriately constructed matrix $U \in S_{k,|\mathcal{I}|}$. The specific choice of U is determined by moving along a curve in the smaller Stiefel manifold. The starting point is given as $U_0 = V_{\mathcal{KI}} P^{-1/2}$, for which $W(U_0) = V$. To generate a *geodesic* [12] that serves as a descent curve, we can project a subgradient of $f \circ W$ onto the tangent space of the manifold $S_{k,|\mathcal{I}|}$ at U_0, and take the manifold exponential map. An analogous procedure generates curves from the Cayley transformation [33], which can be calculated more cheaply. This curve on $S_{k,|\mathcal{I}|}$ can be mapped by W to a curve on Stiefel manifold $S_{n,p}$ in the original problem. This construction produces a descent curve meeting the conditions in Fig. 1.

If we perform a line search over this descent curve such that the objective function is monotonically nonincreasing, the convergence of this algorithm is apparent. However, there is no guarantee to converge to the global solution because of the non-convexity of problem (1).

5   Experiments

We have performed a number of experiments to evaluate our methods on several aspects: (a) performance w.r.t. to a variety of datasets with special emphasis on scalability as a function of size (b) comparison with state of the art method [20] when appropriate (c) performance when incorporating high level priors into the model. Though our focus is to show that the method is applicable for multi-view spectral clustering (with convex regularization) for larger computer vision datasets, for which few alternatives are available, we also performed some experiments on machine learning datasets as a sanity check, where we match reported results. Our vision datasets cover Caltech 101, Caltech 256, LabelMe and TinyImages. For experiments with very large datasets, we also used simulated datasets with on the order of hundreds of millions of examples. As a performance comparison measure we report on Normalized Mutual Information (NMI).

5.1   Multi-view ML Datasets

UCI Digits: The first dataset we use is the handwritten digits (0-9) data from the UCI repository. The dataset consists of 2000 examples, with six sets of features for each image from which we construct six views. These results are summarized in Figure 2b. Since our method depends on initialization, we repeat the experiments 10 times (different initializations) and report on the best NMI value obtained and standard deviations. The authors of [20] provide an initialization in their code using eigenvectors of individual views.

Reuters Multilingual: In addition, we consider multiview spectral clustering on a natural language dataset. We subsample the dataset in a manner consistent with [20]. Since the features for this dataset are sparse and high-dimensional, we first use Latent Semantic Analysis (LSA) [15] to reduce the dimensionality.

5.2   Multi-view Vision Datasets

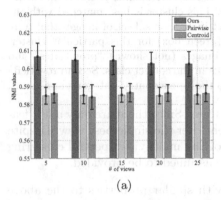

	Digits	Reuters
Ours	0.798(0.03)	0.312(0.01)
[20] Pairwise	0.659	0.305
[20] Centroid	0.669	0.308
Best 1-view	0.641	0.288

(a)   (b)

Fig. 2. (a) Caltech101, showing the NMI values for different choices of views for ours and [20]. (b) Comparison on UCI Digits and Reuters, with mean (and s.d.) NMI.

Caltech101: We evaluated the method on Caltech101, a popular benchmark for object categorization with 102 categories of images (101 distinct objects and background), and 30 images per category. To generate the views, we use the UCSD-MKL dataset — a collection of kernels derived from various visual features (up to 25) for Caltech101 data. We used only the training class kernels in an unsupervised setting. Kernels for 5 random splits, with each split containing information regarding 1515 images (15 images for each of the 101 categories) is provided. We report also results randomly selecting subsets of the views. In each case, we report our summaries as well as [20] by averaging across all 5 splits. The results in Figure 2a suggest that the method compares well to [20].

Caltech256: A similar but bigger dataset is Caltech256, which contains 256 object classes and more than 30000 images across all classes, We restrict our evaluations to three main features for each image: V1-like [29], SURF [3] and Region Covariance (RegCov) [32], for generating views for this data. The Spectral Hashing method in [18] was then adapted to construct the graph for the Laplacians. Note that here we cannot perform comparisons with [20] since their method requires a dense kernel construction. Because of the nature of this dataset, the V1-like view alone yields a NMI of 0.267, SURF gives 0.207, whereas RegCov performs poorly at 0.088. Contrary to the results from other datasets above, here, the multi-view performance at 0.181 is close to but worse than the best view (with two views, SURF and V1-like, multi-view NMI is 0.22). There are two primary reasons. First, the views do not seem to be uncorrelated and the

Fig. 3. Example results from LabelMe. The first row corresponds to a certain cluster from our multi-view method *without* tag prior. This cluster is best matched with the 'opencountry' category in the ground truth, but includes a subset of images that were false positives (red box) and false negatives (green box) for this particular cluster. Introducing group prior on a *separate* set of images (not shown) "propagates" and helps correctly put both the red and green blocks in the correct class. Second row (left) shows the new images that were introduced into the 'opencountry' category, as a result.

best view, V1-like, seems to dominate the others. Since there are only a few feature types, we cannot expect an improvement over the single best view. Despite these issues, the evaluations suggest that solving multi-view spectral clustering for these sizes *is* feasible, if the features are assumed to be provided.

ImageNet: We can construct a dataset with similar properties to the above following a similar procedure in [24]. We use ILSVRC 2013 [10], an updated version of the challenge set that is the basis of the dataset in [24]. ImageNet categories consist of Wordnet noun synsets, which precisely defines the object in the image. From ILSVRC 2013 [10] we select 100 categories at random, with a total of 127885 images selected. We use four views derived from Decaf [11], GIST [27], TinyImage [31], and SIFT [26] features. Each view considered separately produces NMIs of 0.198, 0.181, 0.181, and 0.184 respectively. The multiview objective combining all four produces a labeling with an NMI of 0.203.

5.3 Incorporating Group Structure

LabelMe: To evaluate the group prior effect, we used the LabelMe data [27], which includes eight outdoor scene categories: coast, forest, highways, inside city, mountain, open country, street and tall buildings. There are 2688 color images and each category contains at least 260 images. We employ three views of visual features: Gist [27], Spatial Pyramid Matching (SPM) [21], and Object Bank (OB) [23]. The group prior information comes from the text tags available in LabelMe annotations. We ask users to study the text tags and pick 19 'major' tags out of 781. With each tag, we build 19 groups, each of which is a set of images that share a single tag (like beach, tree trunks, car). We note these groups are only about 70–90% correct with respect to the ground truth. For example, 'insidecity' images and 'street' images both include the "building" tag. Our prior regularization term $g(V)$ is the sum of Frobenius norm of 19 groups. These groups covered only about 1500 of $\sim$ 2700 images.

To evaluate how such a prior incrementally improves performance, we add sub-sampling schemes at levels $\{0\%, 10\%, 60\%, 100\%\}$, where 100% means we use all 1500 images that have tags and 0% is standard multi-view spectral clustering. For all of our experiments with the prior, we set $\lambda = \frac{10^2\|L\|_1}{\|L\|_0}$. Representative examples are shown in Figure 3 and demonstrate how priors on some images may in fact help correctly classify a subset of images that do *not* have this auxiliary data available. The NMI values for GIST [27], SPM [21] and OB [23] in a single view setting were 0.448, 0.419, and 0.511 respectively. The no-prior model improves the NMI to 0.561. Tag priors at the 10%, 60%, and 100% (i.e., 1500 images) incrementally improve NMI from 0.561 to 0.613, 0.633 and finally 0.679, suggesting their utility in this setting.

5.4 Jumbo-Sized Datasets

We summarize our main experiments on very large datasets here. Note that there are significant implementation issues (e.g., memory management, data structures, queries) in successfully running a system on tens of millions of examples.

TinyImages: TinyImages [31] is a set of nearly eighty million 32×32 color images collected from internet searches. The dataset is distributed along with GIST features computed on each image, which were used as the basis of our clustering. Nearest neighbors were computed using [18], from which a weighted graph with 320 million edges was constructed. The dataset includes a keyword associated with each image, for 24690 images the dataset authors evaluated the accuracy of this keyword out of which 5660 images depicted the associated keyword. This keyword is the only form of label provided with the TinyImage dataset, no ground truth is available.

We split the entire TinyImages dataset into two clusters using spectral clustering with the manifold optimization method. With 34 CPU cores, the optimization averaged one iteration every 0.015 seconds. To qualitatively evaluate the clustering at a local scale, we look at how individual keywords are split between the clusters. While most keywords are split by this clustering, some keywords corresponding to more homogeneous sets of images are well separated into one cluster or the other. In Figure 4, we show a subset of the keywords sampled from both well-clustered and poorly clustered images.

ImageNet: We can also test a clustering task on the full ILSVRC2013 dataset. This full dataset has 1000 categories and 1281165 images. Since our optimization procedure considers a high-n low-p regime, we find a two-way split as in the TinyImages. The (non-normalized) MI of the two-way labelling versus the ground truth is 0.229.

Mixture Model: To assess the scalability of our optimization scheme, independent of issues related to generating a diverse set of feature descriptors and side information on a large vision dataset, we performed experiments to evaluate if we can reliably process a Gaussian Mixture Model. We ran the model on mixtures comprising of 10^6 and 10^8 examples distributed concurrently across (up to 36) heterogeneous CPU cores. For $|\mathcal{K}| = 1024$, this setup computed iterations at a rate of one iteration every 0.016 seconds and 0.034 seconds respectively. Within 50000 iterations, the 10^6 case reaches an objective value of 0.054 with an NMI of 0.769 against the true label of which Gaussian distribution from which each point is sampled. On the 10^8 case an NMI of 0.683 was seen with the objective reduced to 2.685.

5.5 Model Characteristics

Varying $|\mathcal{K}|$ and Number of Iterations: The size of $\mathcal{K}$, the number of examples chosen in sampling in each iteration, is a key parameter in our approach. To show how this choice impacts the performance of the model, we use 5 kernels chosen from the Caltech101 experiments as our views. The kernels and the initialization are kept fixed in different runs, whereas $|\mathcal{K}|$ and the number of iterations are varied from 100 to 1000, and the objective is shown in Figure 5. The objective is progressively lower for increasing values of $|\mathcal{K}|$ and the iterations converge sooner with increasing values, as it approaches the full gradient. The

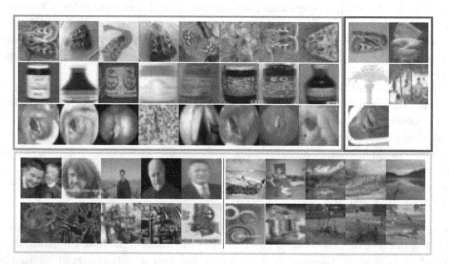

Fig. 4. Results of our method applied to the TinyImages dataset, looking at how five selected keywords (top to bottom: `antler_moth`, `cassareep`, `true_vocal_cord`, `john`, and `machinery`) are split by the clustering. To the left of the divide is a sampling of images for which spectral clustering produces a "dominant" label for this keyword, and the rightmost columns are given the "wrong" label. Green and red boxes mark these groups for the three keywords shown for which we achieved a good separation of the clusters. The keywords in the yellow box do not have an informative cluster.

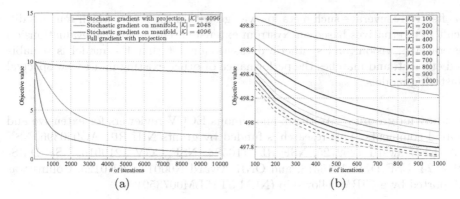

(a)   (b)

Fig. 5. (a) Plot showing the convergence rate of ordinary gradient descent with projection onto the Stiefel manifold, stochastic gradient descent with projection, and stochastic gradient descent using manifold optimization. (b) Plot showing the variation in objective with increasing iterations and different values of $|\mathcal{K}|$ from 100 to 1000. The objective value is drawn against iterations, demonstrating that quicker convergence is achieved with larger samples at the expense of increasing per-iteration cost.

rate of change in the objective as a function of iterations is similar for $|\mathcal{K}| \geq 300$, which suggests that a relatively small value should suffice.

Comparison of Projection and Manifold Optimization Techniques: We compare the manifold optimization of Section 4 and the method using projection on synthetic data. These use a single normalized Laplacian of a random graph over $n = 10^5$ points in 4 clusters. All three methods are applied to solve (1). As we can see from Figure 5, ordinary gradient descent converges in the fewest iterations due to using the entire matrix and $O(n^2)$ computations in *each* iteration. The manifold optimization method converges faster than projection in part because of heuristics used in selecting the step size. Further, the convergence rate increases when the sample size is increased. The Lanczos method (i.e., MATLAB's `eigs`) fails due to excessive memory requirements ($> 32\text{GB}$).

6   Conclusion

We describe a scalable stochastic optimization approach for Multi-view spectral clustering with a convex regularizer. A useful feature of this approach is that at any given step, the gradient is computed only for a subset of the examples — the direct consequence is that with an increase in the number of examples, the optimization can still make progress without having to compute the full gradient at each step. We provide a detailed analysis of its convergence properties, which sheds light on how adding a large number of processors in a distributed environment will affect its performance. Finally, we discuss how high-level priors can be easily leveraged within this framework. The highly scalable implementation accompanying this paper is particularly useful in applications where would want to effectively leverage such meta knowledge within inference, which remains difficult in alternatives based on Nyström extension. Our empirical evaluations on several ML, vision, and synthetic datasets suggest that the model is scalable and efficient, and matches the performance of other existing multi-view spectral clustering models.

Acknowledgments. We thank anonymous ECCV reviewers for extensive and helpful comments. This research is funded by grants NIH R01 AG040396, NSF CAREER award 1252725, NSF RI 1116584, NSF CGV 1219016, NSF DMS-0914524, NSF DMS-1216318, and ONR Award N00014-13-1-0129. Collins was supported by a CIBM fellowship (NLM 5T15LM007359).

References

1. Balzano, L., Nowak, R., Recht, B.: Online identification and tracking of subspaces from highly incomplete information. In: Proceedings of the Allerton Conference on Communication, Control and Computing (2010)
2. Batra, D., Agrawal, H., Banik, P., Chavali, N., Alfadda, A.: CloudCV: Large-scale distributed computer vision as a cloud service (2013), http://www.cloudcv.org
3. Bay, H., Tuytelaars, T., Van Gool, L.: Surf: Speeded up robust features. In: Leonardis, A., Bischof, H., Pinz, A. (eds.) ECCV 2006, Part I. LNCS, vol. 3951, pp. 404–417. Springer, Heidelberg (2006)
4. Bickel, S., Scheffer, T.: Multi-view clustering. In: Proceedings of the IEEE International Conference on Data Mining (2004)
5. Blaschko, M.B., Lampert, C.H.: Correlational spectral clustering. In: Proceedings of the IEEE Conference on Computer Vision and Pattern Recognition (2008)
6. Chaudhuri, K., Kakade, S.M., Livescu, K., Sridharan, K.: Multi-view clustering via canonical correlation analysis. In: Proceedings of the International Conference on Machine Learning (2009)
7. Chen, W., Song, Y., Bai, H., Lin, C., Chang, E.Y.: Parallel spectral clustering in distributed systems. IEEE Transactions on Pattern Analysis and Machine Intelligence 33(3), 568–586 (2011)
8. Chen, X., Cai, D.: Large scale spectral clustering with landmark-based representation. In: Proceedings of the AAAI Conference on Artificial Intelligence (2011)
9. Darken, C., Moody, J.: Towards faster stochastic gradient search. In: Advances in Neural Information Processing Systems (1993)
10. Deng, J., Dong, W., Socher, R., Li, L.J., Li, K., Fei-Fei, L.: ImageNet: A Large-Scale Hierarchical Image Database. In: Proceedings of the IEEE Conference on Computer Vision and Pattern Recognition (2009)
11. Donahue, J., Jia, Y., Vinyals, O., Hoffman, J., Zhang, N., Tzeng, E., Darrell, T.: Decaf: A deep convolutional activation feature for generic visual recognition. ArXiv preprint ArXiv:1310.1531 (2013)
12. Edelman, A., Arias, T.A., Smith, S.T.: The geometry of algorithms with orthogonality constraints. SIAM Journal on Matrix Analysis and Applications 20(2), 303–353 (1998)
13. Fowlkes, C., Belongie, S., Chung, F., Malik, J.: Spectral grouping using the Nyström method. IEEE Transactions on Pattern Analysis and Machine Intelligence 26(2), 214–225 (2004)

14. Gehler, P., Nowozin, S.: On feature combination for multiclass object classification. In: Proceedings of the IEEE International Conference on Computer Vision (2009)
15. Hofmann, T.: Probabilistic latent semantic analysis. In: Proceedings of the Conference on Uncertainty in Artificial Intelligence (1999)
16. Khoa, N.L.D., Chawla, S.: Large scale spectral clustering using resistance distance and Spielman-Teng solvers. In: Ganascia, J.-G., Lenca, P., Petit, J.-M. (eds.) DS 2012. LNCS, vol. 7569, pp. 7–21. Springer, Heidelberg (2012)
17. Krishnamurthy, A., Balakrishnan, S., Xu, M., Singh, A.: Efficient active algorithms for hierarchical clustering. In: Proceedings of the International Conference on Machine Learning (2012)
18. Kulis, B., Grauman, K.: Kernelized locality-sensitive hashing for scalable image search. In: Proceedings of the IEEE International Conference on Computer Vision (2009)
19. Kumar, A., Daumé III, H.: A co-training approach for multi-view spectral clustering. In: Proceedings of the International Conference on Machine Learning (2011)
20. Kumar, A., Rai, P., Daumé III, H.: Co-regularized multi-view spectral clustering. In: Advances in Neural Information Processing Systems (2011)
21. Lazebnik, S., Schmid, C., Ponce, J.: Beyond bags of features: Spatial pyramid matching for recognizing natural scene categories. In: Proceedings of the IEEE Conference on Computer Vision and Pattern Recognition (2006)
22. Lehoucq, R.B., Sorensen, D.C., Yang, C.: ARPACK users' guide: Solution of large-scale eigenvalue problems with implicitly restarted Arnoldi methods, vol. 6 (1998)
23. Li, L., Su, H., Xing, E.P., Fei-Fei, L.: Object bank: A high-level image representation for scene classification & semantic feature sparsification. In: Advances in Neural Information Processing Systems (2010)
24. Li, M., Lian, X.C., Kwok, J., Lu, B.L.: Time and space efficient spectral clustering via column sampling. In: Proceedings of the IEEE Conference on Computer Vision and Pattern Recognition (2011)
25. Liu, J., Wang, C., Gao, J., Han, J.: Multi-view clustering via joint nonnegative matrix factorization. In: SIAM International Conference on Data Mining (2013)
26. Lowe, D.G.: Distinctive image features from scale-invariant keypoints. International Journal of Computer Vision 60(2), 91–110 (2004)
27. Oliva, A., Torralba, A.: Modeling the shape of the scene: A holistic representation of the spatial envelope. International Journal of Computer Vision 42(3), 145–175 (2001)
28. Sakai, T., Imiya, A.: Fast spectral clustering with random projection and sampling. In: Machine Learning and Data Mining in Pattern Recognition (2009)
29. Serre, T., Wolf, L., Poggio, T.: Object recognition with features inspired by visual cortex. In: Proceedings of the IEEE Conference on Computer Vision and Pattern Recognition (2005)
30. Tang, W., Lu, Z., Dhillon, I.S.: Clustering with multiple graphs. In: Proceedings of the IEEE International Conference on Data Mining (2009)
31. Torralba, A., Fergus, R., Freeman, W.T.: 80 million tiny images: a large dataset for non-parametric object and scene recognition. IEEE Transactions on Pattern Analysis and Machine Intelligence 30(11), 1958–1970 (2008)
32. Tuzel, O., Porikli, F., Meer, P.: Region covariance: A fast descriptor for detection and classification. In: Leonardis, A., Bischof, H., Pinz, A. (eds.) ECCV 2006. LNCS, vol. 3952, pp. 589–600. Springer, Heidelberg (2006)
33. Wen, Z., Yin, W.: A feasible method for optimization with orthogonality constraints. Mathematical Programming, 1–38 (2012)

34. Xu, J., Ithapu, V.K., Mukherjee, L., Rehg, J.M., Singh, V.: GOSUS: Grassmannian Online Subspace Updates with Structured-sparsity. In: Proceedings of the IEEE International Conference on Computer Vision (2013)
35. Zelnik-Manor, L., Perona, P.: Self-tuning spectral clustering. In: Advances in Neural Information Processing Systems (2004)
36. Zhou, D., Burges, C.J.C.: Spectral clustering and transductive learning with multiple views. In: Proceedings of the International Conference on Machine Learning (2007)

Riemannian Sparse Coding
for Positive Definite Matrices

Anoop Cherian[1] and Suvrit Sra[2]

[1] LEAR team, Inria Grenoble Rhône-Alpes, France
[2] Max Planck Institute for Intelligent Systems, Tübingen, Germany

Abstract. Inspired by the great success of sparse coding for vector valued data, our goal is to represent symmetric positive definite (SPD) data matrices as sparse linear combinations of atoms from a dictionary, where each atom itself is an SPD matrix. Since SPD matrices follow a non-Euclidean (in fact a Riemannian) geometry, existing sparse coding techniques for Euclidean data cannot be directly extended. Prior works have approached this problem by defining a sparse coding loss function using either extrinsic similarity measures (such as the log-Euclidean distance) or kernelized variants of statistical measures (such as the Stein divergence, Jeffrey's divergence, etc.). In contrast, we propose to use the intrinsic Riemannian distance on the manifold of SPD matrices. Our main contribution is a novel mathematical model for sparse coding of SPD matrices; we also present a computationally simple algorithm for optimizing our model. Experiments on several computer vision datasets showcase superior classification and retrieval performance compared with state-of-the-art approaches.

Keywords: Sparse coding, Riemannian distance, Region covariances.

1 Introduction

Symmetric positive definite matrices—in the form of region covariances [1]—play an important role as data descriptors in several computer vision applications. Notable examples where they are used include object recognition [2], face recognition [3], human detection and tracking [4,5], visual surveillance [6], 3D object recognition [7], among others. Compared with popular vectorial descriptors, such as bag-of-words, Fischer vectors, etc., the second-order structure that covariance matrices offer makes them particularly appealing. For instance, covariance descriptors offer a convenient platform for fusing multiple features into a compact form independent of the number of data points. By choosing appropriate features, this fusion can be made invariant to image affine distortions [8], or robust to static image noise and illumination variations, while generating these matrices remains efficient using integral image transforms [4].

In this paper, we study SPD matrices in the context of sparse coding. The latter is now an important, established tool in signal processing and computer vision: it helps understand the inherent structure of the data [9,10], leading to

D. Fleet et al. (Eds.): ECCV 2014, Part III, LNCS 8691, pp. 299–314, 2014.

state-of-the-art results for a variety of vision applications [11,12,13]. Given an input data point and an overcomplete dictionary of basis atoms, Euclidean sparse coding seeks a representation of this point as sparse linear combination of atoms so that a squared Euclidean loss is minimized. Formally, if $\mathcal{B}$ is the dictionary and z the input data point, generic sparse coding may be formulated as

$$\min_\theta \quad \mathcal{L}(z, \mathcal{B}, \theta) + \lambda \operatorname{Sp}(\theta), \tag{1}$$

where the loss function $\mathcal{L}$ measures reconstruction accuracy obtained by using the "code" θ, while λ regulates the impact of the sparsity penalty $\operatorname{Sp}(\theta)$.

Sparse coding has found great success for vector valued data, so it is natural to hope for similar benefits when applying it to the more complex setting of data represented via SPD matrices. However, applying sparse coding to SPD matrices is not straightforward, a difficulty that arises primarily because SPD matrices form a curved Riemannian manifold of negative sectional curvature (so that distances along the manifold are lower than corresponding Euclidean distances). As a result, this manifold cannot be isometrically embedded into Euclidean space through operations such as mere vectorization, without introducing embedding errors. Such errors can affect the application performance [14,4]. On the other hand, computing distances and solving optimization problems on the SPD manifold is computationally demanding (see Section 3). Thus care must be taken to select an appropriate loss function.

The main goal of this paper is to study sparse coding of SPD matrices in their native Riemannian geometric context by using a dictionary comprised of SPD matrices as atoms. Towards this end, we make the following contributions.

- *Formulation:* We propose a novel model that finds nonnegative sparse linear combinations of SPD atoms from a given dictionary to well-approximate an input SPD matrix. The approximation quality is measured by the squared intrinsic Riemannian distance. As a theoretical refinement to our model, we describe a surprising but intuitive geometric constraint under which the nonconvex Riemannian sparse coding task actually becomes convex.
- *Optimization:* The main challenge in using our formulation is its higher computational cost relative to Euclidean sparse coding. However, we describe a simple and effective approach for optimizing our objective function.
- *Experiments:* We present results on a few computer vision tasks on several state-of-the-art datasets to demonstrate superior performance obtained by using our new sparse coding model.

To set the stage for presenting our contributions, we first survey some recent methods suggested for sparse coding. After that we review key tools from Riemannian geometry that we will use to develop our ideas. Throughout we work with real matrices. The space of $d \times d$ SPD matrices is denoted as $\mathcal{S}_+^d$, symmetric matrices by $\mathcal{S}^d$, and the space of (real) invertible matrices by $\operatorname{GL}(d)$. By $\operatorname{Log}(X)$, for $X \in \mathcal{S}_+$, we mean the principal matrix logarithm.

2   Related Work

Sparse coding of SPD matrices has recently received a significant attention in the vision community due to the performance gains that it brings to the respective applications. As alluded to earlier, the manifold geometry hinders a straight-forward extension of classical sparse coding techniques to these objects. Prior methods typically use one of the following proxies: (i) rather than Riemannian geometry, use an information geometric perspective using an appropriate statistical measure; (ii) map the matrices into a flat Riemannian symmetric space; or (iii) use a kernelizable similarity measure to embed the matrices into an RKHS. We briefly review each of these schemes below.

Statistical measures. In [15], a sparse coding framework is proposed based on the log-determinant divergence (Burg loss) to model the loss function. Their formulation requires sophisticated interior point methods for the optimization, and as a result it is often slow even for moderately large covariances (more than 5×5). In [16], a data matrix is approximated by a sparse linear combination of rank-one matrices under a Frobenius norm based loss. Although this scheme is computationally efficient, it discards the manifold geometry.

Differential geometric schemes. Among the several computationally efficient variants of Riemannian distances, one of the most popular is the log-Euclidean distance d_{le} [17] defined for $X, Y \in \mathcal{S}_+^d$ as $d_{le}(X, Y) := \|\text{Log}(X) - \text{Log}(Y)\|_F$. The Log operator maps an SPD matrix isomorphically and diffeomorphically into the flat space of symmetric matrices; the distances in this space are Euclidean. Sparse coding with the squared log-Euclidean distance has been proposed in the past [18] with promising results. A similar framework was suggested recently [19] in which a local coordinate system is defined on the tangent space at the given data matrix. While, their formulation uses additional constraints that make their framework coordinate independent, their scheme restricts sparse coding to specific problem settings.

Kernelized Schemes. In [20], a kernelized sparse coding scheme is presented for SPD matrices using the Stein divergence [21] for generating the underlying kernel function. But this divergence does not induce a kernel for all bandwidths. To circumvent this issue [22,23] propose kernels based on the log-Euclidean distance. It is well-known (and also shown in our experiments) that a kernelized sparse coding scheme suffers significantly when the number of dictionary atoms is high.

In contrast to all these methods, our scheme directly uses the intrinsic Riemannian distance to design our sparse reconstruction loss, which is the natural distance for covariances. To circumvent the computational difficulty we propose an efficient algorithm based on spectral projected gradient. Our experiments demonstrate that our scheme is efficient and provides state of the art results on several computer vision problems that use covariance matrices.

3 Preliminaries

We provide below a brief overview of the Riemannian geometry of SPD matrices. An SPD matrix has the property that all its eigenvalues are positive. For an $n \times n$ SPD matrix, such a property restricts it to span only the convex half-cone of the n^2 dimensional Euclidean space of symmetric matrices. A manifold is a Hausdorff space that is locally Euclidean and second-countable. The former property means that there is a distinct neighborhood for every point belonging to this manifold. Second countability suggests that there exists a countable collection of open sets such that every open set is the union of these sets. These properties are often useful for analyzing stationary points for optimization problems on the manifold.

For a point X on the manifold, its tangent space is a vector space consisting of all the tangent vectors at that point. SPD matrices form a differentiable Riemannian manifold, which implies that every point on it has a well-defined continuous collection of scalar products defined on its tangent space and is endowed with an associated Riemannian metric [24, Ch. 6]. This metric provides a measure on the manifold for computing distances between points. As the manifold is curved, this distance specifies the length of the shortest curve that connects the points, i.e., *geodesics*. A manifold is Riemannian if it is locally Euclidean, that is its geodesics are parallel to the tangent vectors.

There are predominantly two operations that one needs for computations on the Riemannian manifold, namely (i) the exponential map $\exp_P : \mathcal{S}^d \to \mathcal{S}^d_+$ and (ii) the logarithmic map $\log_P = \exp_P^{-1} : \mathcal{S}^d_+ \to \mathcal{S}^d$, where $P \in \mathcal{S}^d_+$. While the former projects a symmetric point on the tangent space onto the manifold, the latter does the reverse. Note that these maps depend on the manifold point P at which the tangent spaces are computed. In our analysis, we will be measuring distances assuming P to be the identity matrix[1], I. A popular intrinsic (i.e., distances are computed along the curvature of the manifold) metric on the SPD manifold is the affine invariant *Riemannian distance* [14]:

$$d_{\mathcal{R}}(X, Y) = \left\| \operatorname{Log} X^{-1/2} Y X^{-1/2} \right\|_{\mathrm{F}}. \tag{2}$$

4 Problem Formulation

We are now ready to introduce our new model for sparse coding of SPD matrices. Figure 1 provides a schematic of our sparse coding model on the manifold.

Model. Let $\mathcal{B}$ be a dictionary with n atoms $B_1, B_2, \cdots, B_n$, where each $B_i \in \mathcal{S}^d_+$. Let $X \in \mathcal{S}^d_+$ be an input matrix that must be sparse coded. Our basic sparse coding objective is to solve

---

[1] As the metric that we use in this paper is affine invariant, such a choice will not distort the geometry of the manifold and is achieved by scaling the SPD matrices by $X^{-1/2}$ on the left and the right.

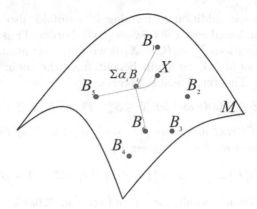

Fig. 1. A schematic illustration of our sparse coding objective formulation. For the SPD manifold M and given SPD basis matrices B_i on the manifold, our objective seeks a non-negative sparse linear combination $\sum_i \alpha_i B_i$ of the B_i's that is closest (in a geodesic sense) to the given input SPD matrix X.

$$
\begin{aligned}
\min_{\alpha \geq 0} \quad \phi(\alpha) &:= \frac{1}{2} d_{\mathcal{R}}^2 \left(\sum\nolimits_{i=1}^{n} \alpha_i B_i, X \right) + \mathrm{Sp}(\alpha) \\
&= \frac{1}{2} \left\| \mathrm{Log} \sum\nolimits_{i=1}^{n} \alpha_i X^{-\frac{1}{2}} B_i X^{-\frac{1}{2}} \right\|_{\mathrm{F}}^2 + \mathrm{Sp}(\alpha),
\end{aligned}
\tag{3}
$$

where α_i is the i-th component of α, and Sp is a sparsity inducing function.

Problem (3) measures reconstruction quality offered by a sparse non-negative linear combination of the atoms to a given input point X. It will turn out (see experiments in Section 6) that the reconstructions obtained via this model actually lead to significant improvements in performance over sparse coding models that ignore the rich geometry of SPD matrices. However, this gain comes at a price: model (3) is a difficult nonconvex problem, which remains nonconvex even if we take into account the geodesic convexity of $d_{\mathcal{R}}$.

While in practice this nonconvexity does not seem to impede the use of our model, we show below a surprising but highly intuitive constraint under which Problem 3 actually becomes convex!

Theorem 1. *The function* $\phi(\alpha) := d_{\mathcal{R}}^2(\sum_i \alpha_i B_i, X)$ *is convex on the set*

$$
\mathcal{A} := \{\alpha \mid \sum_i \alpha_i B_i \preceq X, \text{ and } \alpha \geq 0\}.
\tag{4}
$$

Before we prove this theorem, let us intuitively describe what it is saying. While sparsely encoding data we are trying to find sparse coefficients $\alpha_1, \ldots, \alpha_n$, such that in the ideal case we have $\sum_i \alpha_i B_i = X$. But in general this equality cannot be satisfied, and one only has $\sum_i \alpha_i B_i \approx X$, and the quality of this approximation is measured using $\phi(\alpha)$ or some other desirable loss-function. The loss $\phi(\alpha)$ from (3) is nonconvex while convexity is a "unilateral" property—it lives in the world of inequalities rather than equalities [25]. And it is known that SPD matrices in addition to forming a manifold also enjoy a rich conic geometry that is endowed with the Löwner partial order. Thus, instead of seeking arbitrary approximations $\sum_i \alpha_i B_i \approx X$, if we limit our attention to those that underestimate X as in (4), we might benefit from the conic partial order. It is this intuition that Theorem 1 makes precise.

Lemma 1. *Let $Z \in \mathrm{GL}(d)$ and let $X \in \mathcal{S}_+^d$. Then, $Z^T X Z \in \mathcal{S}_+^d$.*

Lemma 2. *The Fréchet derivative [26, see e.g., Ch. 1] of the map $X \mapsto \log X$ at a point Z in the direction E is given by*

$$D\log(Z)(E) = \int_0^1 (\beta Z + (1-\beta)I)^{-1} E (\beta Z + (1-\beta)I)^{-1} d\beta. \tag{5}$$

Proof. This is a classical result, for a proof see e.g., [26, Ch. 11].

Corollary 1. *Consider the map $\ell(\alpha) := \alpha \in \mathbf{R}_+^n \mapsto \mathrm{Tr}(\log(SM(\alpha)S)H)$, where M is a map from $\mathbf{R}_+^n \to \mathcal{S}_+^d$ and $H \in \mathcal{S}^d$, $S \in \mathcal{S}_+^d$. Then, for $1 \le p \le n$, we have*

$$\frac{\partial \ell(\alpha)}{\partial \alpha_p} = \int_0^1 \mathrm{Tr}[K_\beta S \frac{\partial M(\alpha)}{\partial \alpha_p} S K_\beta H] d\beta,$$

where $K_\beta := (\beta S M(\alpha) S + (1-\beta)I)^{-1}$.

Proof. Simply apply the chain-rule of calculus and use linearity of $\mathrm{Tr}(\cdot)$.

Lemma 3. *The Fréchet derivative of the map $X \mapsto X^{-1}$ at a point Z in direction E is given by*

$$D(Z^{-1})(E) = -Z^{-1} E Z^{-1}. \tag{6}$$

We are now ready to prove Theorem 1.

Proof (Thm. 1). We show that the Hessian $\nabla^2 \phi(\alpha) \succeq 0$ on $\mathcal{A}$. To ease presentation, we write $S = X^{-1/2}$, $M \equiv M(\alpha) = \sum_i \alpha_i B_i$, and let D_q denote the differential operator D_{α_q}. Applying this operator to the first-derivative given by Lemma 4 (in Section 5), we obtain (using the product rule) the sum

$$\mathrm{Tr}\big([D_q \log(SMS)](SMS)^{-1} S B_p S\big) + \mathrm{Tr}\big(\log(SMS) D_q[(SMS)^{-1} S B_p S]\big).$$

We now treat these two terms individually. To the first we apply Corr. 1. So

$$
\begin{aligned}
\mathrm{Tr}\big([D_q \log(SMS)](SMS)^{-1} S B_p S\big) &= \int_0^1 \mathrm{Tr}(K_\beta S B_q S K_\beta (SMS)^{-1} S B_p S) d\beta \\
&= \int_0^1 \mathrm{Tr}(S B_q S K_\beta (SMS)^{-1} S B_p S K_\beta \cdot) d\beta \\
&= \int_0^1 \langle \Psi_\beta(p), \Psi_\beta(q) \rangle_M \, d\beta,
\end{aligned}
$$

where the inner-product $\langle \cdot, \cdot \rangle_M$ is weighted by $(SMS)^{-1}$ and the map $\Psi_\beta(p) := S B_p S K_\beta$. We find a similar inner-product representation for the second term too. Starting with Lemma 3 and simplifying, we obtain

$$
\begin{aligned}
\mathrm{Tr}\big(\log(SMS) D_q[(SMS)^{-1} S B_p S]\big) &= -\mathrm{Tr}\big(\log(SMS)(SMS)^{-1} S B_q M^{-1} B_p S\big) \\
&= \mathrm{Tr}\big(-S \log(SMS) S^{-1} M^{-1} B_q M^{-1} B_p\big) \\
&= \mathrm{Tr}\big(M^{-1} B_p [-S \log(SMS) S^{-1}] M^{-1} B_q\big).
\end{aligned}
$$

By assumption $\sum_i \alpha_i B_i = M \preceq X$, which implies $SMS \preceq I$. Since $\log(\cdot)$ is operator monotone [24], it follows that $\log(SMS) \preceq 0$; an application of Lemma 1 then yields $S\log(SMS)S^{-1} \preceq 0$. Thus, we obtain the weighted inner-product

$$\text{Tr}\big(M^{-1}B_p[-S\log(SMS)S^{-1}]M^{-1}B_q\big) = \langle M^{-1}B_p, M^{-1}B_q \rangle_L,$$

where $L = [-S\log(SMS)S^{-1}] \succeq 0$, whereby $\langle \cdot, \cdot \rangle_L$ is a valid inner-product.

Thus, the second partial derivatives of ϕ may be ultimately written as

$$\frac{\partial^2 \phi(\alpha)}{\partial \alpha_p \partial \alpha_q} = \langle \Gamma(B_q), \Gamma(B_p) \rangle,$$

for some map Γ and some corresponding inner-product (the map and the inner-product are defined by our analysis above). Thus, we have established that the Hessian is a Gram matrix, which shows it is semidefinite. Moreover, if the B_i are different $(1 \leq i \leq n)$, then the Hessian is strictly positive definite.   □

5   Optimization

We briefly describe below our optimization approach for solving our main problem (3). In particular, we propose to use a first-order method, i.e., a method based on the gradient $\nabla \phi(\alpha)$. The following lemma proves convenient towards this gradient computation.

Lemma 4. *Let B, C, and X be fixed SPD matrices. Consider the function $f(x) = d_\mathcal{R}^2(xB + C, X)$. The derivative $f'(x)$ is given by*

$$f'(x) = 2\,\text{Tr}(\log(X^{-1/2}(xB+C)X^{-1/2})X^{1/2}(xB+C)^{-1}BX^{-1/2}). \quad (7)$$

Proof. Introduce the shorthand $S \equiv X^{-1/2}$ and $M(x) \equiv xB + C$. From definition (2) and using $\|Z\|_F^2 = \text{Tr}(Z^T Z)$ we have

$$f(x) = \text{Tr}(\log(SM(x)S)^T \log(SM(x)S)).$$

Differentiating this the chain-rule of calculus immediately yields

$$f'(x) = 2\,\text{Tr}(\log(SM(x)S)(SM(x)S)^{-1}SM'(x)S),$$

which is nothing but (7).   □

Writing $M(\alpha_p) = \alpha_p B_p + \sum_{i \neq p} \alpha_i B_i$ and using Lemma 4 we obtain

$$\frac{\partial \phi(\alpha)}{\partial \alpha_p} = \text{Tr}\left(\log(SM(\alpha_p)S)\big(SM(\alpha_p)S\big)^{-1}SB_p S\right) + \frac{\partial \text{Sp}(\alpha)}{\partial \alpha}. \quad (8)$$

Computing (8) for all α is the dominant cost in a gradient-based method for solving (3). We present pseudocode (Alg. 1) that efficiently implements the gradient for the first part of (8). The total cost of Alg. 1 is $O(nd^2) + O(d^3)$—a naïve implementation of (8) costs $O(nd^3)$, which is substantially more expensive.

Input: $B_1, \ldots, B_n, X \in \mathcal{S}_+^d, \alpha \geq 0$
$S \leftarrow X^{-1/2}$; $M \leftarrow \sum_{i=1}^n \alpha_i B_i$;
$T \leftarrow \log(SMS)(MS)^{-1}$;
for $i = 1$ **to** n **do**
| $\quad g_i \leftarrow \mathrm{Tr}(TB_p)$;
end
return g

Algorithm 1. Subroutine for efficiently computing gradients

For simplicity, in (8) that defines $\phi(\alpha)$ we use the sparsity penalty $\mathrm{Sp}(\alpha) = \lambda\|\alpha\|_1$, where $\lambda > 0$ is a regularization parameter. Since we are working with $\alpha \geq 0$, we replace this penalty by $\lambda \sum_i \alpha_i$, which is differentiable. This allows us to use Alg. 1 in conjunction with a gradient-projection scheme that essentially runs the iteration

$$\alpha^{k+1} \leftarrow \mathscr{P}[\alpha^k - \eta_k \nabla\phi(\alpha^k)], \qquad k = 0, 1, \ldots, \tag{9}$$

where $\mathscr{P}[\cdot]$ denotes the projection operator defined as

$$\mathscr{P}[\alpha] \equiv \alpha \mapsto \mathrm{argmin}_{\alpha'} \tfrac{1}{2}\|\alpha' - \alpha\|_2^2, \quad \text{s.t. } \alpha' \geq 0, \ \alpha' \in \mathcal{A}. \tag{10}$$

Iteration (9) has three major computational costs: (i) computing the stepsize η_k; (ii) obtaining the gradient $\nabla\phi(\alpha^k)$; and (iii) computing the projection (10). Alg. 1 shows how to efficiently obtain the gradient. The projection task (10) is a special least-squares (dual) semidefinite program (SDP), which can be solved using any SDP solver or by designing a specialized routine. However, for the sake of speed, we could drop the constraint $\alpha' \in \mathcal{A}$ in practice, in which case $\mathscr{P}[\alpha]$ reduces to the truncation $\max(0, \alpha)$, which is trivial. We stress at this point that developing efficient subroutines for the full projection (10) is rather nontrivial, and a task worthy of a separate research project, so we defer it to the future. It only remains to specify how to obtain the stepsize η_k.

There are several choices available in the nonlinear programming literature [27] for choosing η_k, but most of them can be quite expensive. In our quest for an efficient sparse coding algorithm, we choose to avoid expensive line-search algorithms for selecting η_k and prefer to use the Barzilai-Borwein stepsizes [28], which can be computed in closed form and lead to remarkable gains in performance [28,29]. In particular, we use the Spectral Projected Gradient (SPG) method [30] by adapting a simplified implementation of [29].

SPG runs iteration (9) using Barzilai-Borwein stepsizes with an occasional call to a nonmontone line-search strategy to ensure convergence of $\{\alpha^k\}$. Without the constraint $\alpha' \in \mathcal{A}$, we cannot guarantee anything more than a stationary point of (3), while if we were to use the additional constraint then we can even obtain global optimality for iterates generated by (9).

6   Experiments and Results

In this section, we provide experimental results on simulated and real-world data demonstrating the effectiveness of our algorithm compared to the state-of-the-art methods on covariance valued data. For all the datasets, we will be using the classification accuracy as the performance metric. Our implementations are in MATLAB and the timing comparisons used a single core Intel 3.6GHz CPU.

6.1   Comparison Methods

We denote our Riemannian Sparse coding setup as Riem-SC. We will compare against six other methods, namely (i) log-Euclidean sparse coding (LE-SC) [18] that projects the data into the Log-Euclidean symmetric space, followed by sparse coding the matrices as Euclidean objects, (ii) Frob-SC, in which the manifold structure is discarded, (iii) Stein-Kernel-SC [20] using a kernel defined by the symmetric Stein divergence [21], (iv) Log-Euclidean Kernel-SC which is similar to (iii) but uses the log-Euclidean kernel [23], (v) tensor sparse coding (TSC) [15] which uses the log-determinant divergence, and generalized dictionary learning (GDL) [16].

6.2   Simulated Experiments

Simulation Setup: In this subsection, we evaluate in a controlled setting, some of the properties of our scheme. For all our simulations, we used covariances generated from data vectors sampled from a zero-mean unit covariance normal distribution. For each covariance sample, the number of data vectors is chosen to be ten times its dimensionality. For fairness of the comparisons, we adjusted the regularization parameters of the sparse coding algorithms so that the codes generated are approximately 10% sparse. The plots to follow show the performance averaged over 50 trials. Further, all the algorithms in this experiment used the SPG method to solve their respective formulations so that their performances are comparable. The intention of these timing comparisons is to empirically point out the relative computational complexity of our Riemannian scheme against the baselines rather than to show exact computational times. For example, for the comparisons against the method Frob-SC, one can vectorize the matrices and then use a vectorial sparse coding scheme. In that case, Frob-SC will be substantially faster, and incomparable to our scheme as it solves a different problem.

Increasing Dictionary Size: In this experiment, we fixed the matrix dimensionality to 10, while increased the number of dictionary atoms from 20 to 1000. Figure 2(a) shows the result. As is expected, the sparse coding performance of all the kernelized schemes drops significantly for larger dictionary sizes, while our scheme performs fairly.

Increasing Matrix Dimensionality: In this experiment, we fixed the number of dictionary atoms to be 200, while increased the matrix dimensionality from 3 to 100. Figure 2(b) shows the result of this experiment. The plot shows that the extra computations required by Riem-SC is not substantial compared to Frob-SC.

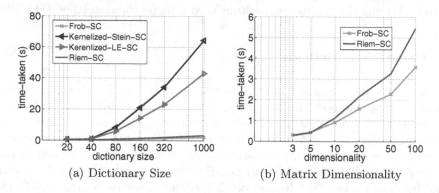

(a) Dictionary Size   (b) Matrix Dimensionality

Fig. 2. Sparse coding time against (a) increasing number of dictionary atoms and (b) increasing matrix dimensionality. We used a maximum of 100 iterations for all the algorithms.

6.3   Experiments with Public Datasets

Now let us evaluate the performance of our framework on real-world computer vision datasets. We experimented on four datasets, namely (i) texture recognition, (ii) person re-identification, (iii) view-invariant object recognition, and (iv) 3D object recognition. We describe these datasets below.

Brodatz Texture: Covariances have shown promising results for texture recognition [1,31] problems. Following the work of [15], we use the Brodatz texture dataset[2] for this experiment, which consists of 110 gray scale texture images. Each image is of dimension 512×512. We sampled approximately 300 patches, each of dimension 25×25, from random locations of each image, from which we removed patches without any useful textures (low entropy). This resulted in approximately 10K patches. We used a five dimensional feature descriptor to compute the covariances, with features given by: $F_{textures} = [x, y, I, |I_x|, |I_y|]^T$. The first two dimensions are the coordinates of a pixel from the top-left corner of a patch, the last three dimensions capture the image intensity, and gradients in the x and y directions respectively. Covariances of size 5×5 are generated from all features in a patch.

---

[2] http://www.ux.uis.no/~tranden/brodatz.html

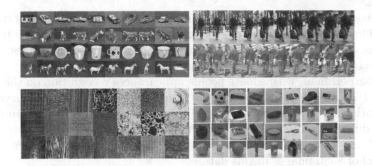

Fig. 3. Montage of sample images from the four datasets used in our experiments. Top-left are samples from the ETH80 object dataset, bottom-left are the Brodatz textures, top-right are the samples from ETHZ people dataset, and images from the RGB-D object recognition dataset are shown on bottom right.

ETH80 Object Recognition: Region covariances are studied for object recognition applications in [2] demonstrating significant performance gains. In this experiment, we loosely follow their experimental setup and evaluate our scheme on the object recognition problem using the ETH80 dataset. This dataset consists of eight ground truth object categories, each consisting of ten different instances (see Figure 3) from 41 different views, for a total of 3280 images. These objects undergo severe view point change, posing significant challenges to recognition due to the high intra-class diversity.

To generate covariances, we use a combination of texture and color features. First, we segment out the objects from the images using the given ground truth masks. Next, we generate texture features from these segmented objects using a bank of Laws texture filters [32] defined as: let $H_1 = [1\ 2\ 1]^T$, $H_2 = [-1\ 0\ 1]^T$, and $H_3 = [-1\ 2\ -1]^T$ denote the filter templates, then the filter bank is:

$$L_{bank} = \begin{bmatrix} H_1 H_1^T & H_1 H_2^T & H_1 H_3^T & H_2 H_1^T & H_2 H_2^T & H_2 H_3^T & H_3 H_1^T & H_3 H_2^T & H_3 H_3^T \end{bmatrix}^T.$$
(11)

Let F_{Laws} be a 9D feature vector obtained from every pixel after applying L_{bank}. Appending other texture and color features as provided by the pixel color, and gradients, our complete feature vector for every pixel on the object is:

$$F_{ETH80} = \begin{bmatrix} F_{Laws} & x & y & I_r & I_g & I_b & |I_x| & |I_y| & |I_{LoG}| & \sqrt{I_x^2 + I_y^2} \end{bmatrix}^T,$$
(12)

where I_{LoG} stands for the Laplacian of Gaussian filter, useful for edge detection. With this feature set, we generate covariances of size 19×19 for each image.

ETHZ Person Re-identification Dataset: Recognition and tracking of people are essential components of a visual surveillance system. Typically, the visual data from such systems are more challenging compared to other sub-areas of computer vision. These challenges arise mainly because the images used are generally shot in low-resolution or low-lighting conditions and the appearances of the same person differ significantly from one camera to the next due to changes in poses, occlusions, etc. Covariances have shown to be robust to these challenges, making it an attractive option for person re-identification tasks [20,5].

In this experiment, we evaluate people appearances recognition on the benchmark ETHZ dataset [33]. This dataset consists of low-resolution surveillance images with sizes varying between 78×30 to 400×200 pixels. The images are from 146 different individuals and the number of images for a single person varies between 5 and 356. Sample images from this dataset are shown in Figure 3. There are a total of 8580 images in this dataset.

In literature, there exist several proposals for features on this task; examples include Gabor wavelet [5], color gradients [20], etc. Rather than demonstrating the performances of various feature combinations, we detail below the combination that worked best in our experiments (on a small validation set). Our feature vector for this task is obtained by combining nine features:

$$F_{ETHZ} = [x \ I_r \ I_g \ I_b \ Y_i \ |I_x| \ |I_y| \ |\sin(\theta) + \cos(\theta)| \ |H_y|]^T , \qquad (13)$$

where x is the x-coordinate of a pixel location, I_r, I_g, I_b are the RGB color of a pixel, Y_i is the pixel intensity in the YCbCr color space, I_x, I_y are the gray scale pixel gradients, and H_y is the y-gradient of pixel hue. Further, we also use the gradient angle $\theta = \tan^{-1}(I_y/I_x)$. We resized each image to a fixed size of 300×100, dividing it into upper and lower parts. We compute a different covariance matrix for each part, which are then merged as two block diagonal matrices to form a single 18×18 covariance for each image.

3D Object Recognition Dataset: The goal of this experiment is to recognize objects in 3D point clouds. To this end, we used the public RGB-D Object dataset [34], which consists of about 300 objects belonging to 51 categories and spread in about 250K frames. We used approximately 15K frames for our evaluation with approximately 250-350 frames devoted to every object seen from three different view points (30, 45, and 60 degrees above the horizon). Following the procedure suggested in [35][Chap. 5], for every frame, the object was segmented out and 18 dimensional feature vectors generated for every 3D point in the cloud (and thus 18×18 covariance descriptors); the features we used are as follows:

$$F_{RGBD} = [x, y, z, I_r, I_g, I_b, I_x, I_y, I_{xx}, I_{yy}, I_{xy}, I_m, \delta_x, \delta_y, \delta_m, \nu_x, \nu_y, \nu_z], \qquad (14)$$

where the first three dimensions are the spatial coordinates, I_m is the magnitude of the intensity gradient, δ's represent gradients over the depth-maps, and ν represents the surface normal at the given 3D point. Sample images from this dataset are given in Figure 3.

Experimental Setup: We used 80% of the Brodatz texture and the ETH80 objects datasets to form the training set and the remaining as the test set. Further, 20% of the training set was used as a validation set. For both these datasets, we used a linear SVM for training and classification. For the ETHZ dataset and the RGB-D objects dataset, since there might not be enough images from a single class to train a classifier, we resort to a nearest neighbor classification scheme using our sparse coding framework. For this setup, we used 20% for learning the dictionary, while the remaining data points were used as the query database. The splitting was such that there is at least one data matrix from each class in the training and the test set respectively. We used a dictionary of fixed size, which is 10 times the matrix dimensionality, for all the experiments. This dictionary was learned from the training set using Log-Euclidean K-Means followed by projecting the cluster centroids onto the SPD manifold (exponential map). The regularizations in the sparse coding objective was adjusted for all the datasets (and all the experiments) to generate 10% sparse vectors. The slack parameter for the SVM was selected via cross-validation.

Results: In Tables 1, 2, 3, 4, we report results of our Riem-SC scheme against several state-of-the-art methods. For the texture and the object classification problems, we report the average SVM classification accuracy after 5-fold cross-validation. For the ETHZ people re-identification and RGB-D object recognition, our experiments were as follows: every data point in the test set was selected as a query point, and its nearest neighbor, in the Euclidean sense, is found (recall that the database points and this query point are sparse coded), and is deemed correct if their ground truth labels matched. The table shows that Riem-SC shows consistent and state-of-the-art performance against other schemes. Other methods, especially TSC and GDL are seen to perform poorly, while the kernelized schemes perform favorably. Along with the accuracies, we also report the respective standard deviations over the trials.

Discussion: Overall, our real-world and simulated experiments reveal that our sparse coding scheme demonstrates excellent application performance, while remaining computationally tractable. The kernelized schemes show a close match in accuracy to our scheme which is not unsurprising as they project the data points onto a linear feature space. However, these methods suffer when working with larger dictionary sizes, as our results in Figure 2 show. Other sparse coding schemes such as TSC are difficult to optimize while their performances are poor. In summary, our algorithm offers a practical trade off between accuracy and performance.

7 Conclusion and Future Work

In this paper, we proposed a novel scheme for representing symmetric positive definite matrices as sparse linear combinations of atoms from a given dictionary; these atoms themselves being SPD matrices. In contrast to other approaches that use proxy distances on the manifold to define the sparse reconstruction loss, we propose to use the most natural Riemannian metric on the manifold, namely the

Table 1. Brodatz texture dataset

Method	Accuracy (%)
LE-SC	47.4 (11.1)
Frob-SC	32.3 (4.4)
K-Stein-SC	39.2 (0.79)
K-LE-SC	47.9 (0.46)
TSC	35.6 (7.1)
GDL	43.7 (6.3)
Riem-SC(ours)	**53.9** (3.4)

Table 2. ETH80 object recognition

Method	Accuracy (%)
LE-SC	68.9 (3.3)
Frob-SC	67.3 (1.4)
K-Stein-SC	**81.6** (2.1)
K-LE-SC	76.6 (0.4)
TSC	37.1 (3.9)
GDL	65.8 (3.1)
Riem-SC(ours)	77.9 (1.9)

Table 3. ETHZ Person Re-identification

Method	Accuracy (%)
LE-SC	78.5 (2.5)
Frob-SC	83.7 (0.2)
K-Stein-SC	88.3 (0.4)
K-LE-SC	87.8 (0.8)
TSC	67.7 (1.2)
GDL	30.5 (1.7)
Riem-SC(ours)	**90.1** (0.9)

Table 4. RGB-D Object Recognition

Method	Accuracy (%)
LE-SC	**86.1** (1.0)
Frob-SC	80.3 (1.1)
K-Stein-SC	75.6 (1.1)
K-LE-SC	83.5 (0.2)
TSC	72.8 (2.1)
GDL	61.9 (0.4)
Riem-SC(ours)	84.0 (0.6)

Affine Invariant Riemannian distance. Further, we proposed a simple scheme to optimize the resultant sparse coding objective. Our experiments demonstrate that our scheme is computationally efficient and produces superior results compared to other schemes on several computer vision datasets. Going forward, an important future direction is the problem of efficient dictionary learning under these formulations.

Acknowledgements. AC would like to thank Dr. Duc Fehr for sharing the RGB-D objects covariance data.

References

1. Tuzel, O., Porikli, F., Meer, P.: Region Covariance: A Fast Descriptor for Detection and Classification. In: Leonardis, A., Bischof, H., Pinz, A. (eds.) ECCV 2006. LNCS, vol. 3952, pp. 589–600. Springer, Heidelberg (2006)
2. Sandeep, J., Richard, H., Mathieu, S., Li, H., Harandi, M.: Kernel methods on the Riemannian manifold of symmetric positive definite matrices. In: CVPR (2013)
3. Pang, Y., Yuan, Y., Li, X.: Gabor-based region covariance matrices for face recognition. IEEE Transactions on Circuits and Systems for Video Technology 18(7), 989–993 (2008)
4. Porikli, F., Tuzel, O.: Covariance tracker. In: CVPR (June 2006)
5. Ma, B., Su, Y., Jurie, F., et al.: Bicov: A novel image representation for person re-identification and face verification. In: BMVC (2012)

6. Cherian, A., Morellas, V., Papanikolopoulos, N., Bedros, S.J.: Dirichlet process mixture models on symmetric positive definite matrices for appearance clustering in video surveillance applications. In: IEEE CVPR, pp. 3417–3424 (2011)
7. Fehr, D., Cherian, A., Sivalingam, R., Nickolay, S., Morellas, V., Papanikolopoulos, N.: Compact covariance descriptors in 3d point clouds for object recognition. In: IEEE ICRA (2012)
8. Ma, B., Wu, Y., Sun, F.: Affine object tracking using kernel-based region covariance descriptors. In: Wang, Y., Li, T. (eds.) ISKE 2011. AISC, vol. 122, pp. 613–623. Springer, Heidelberg (2011)
9. Elad, M., Aharon, M.: Image denoising via learned dictionaries and sparse representation. In: CVPR (2006)
10. Olshausen, B., Field, D.: Sparse coding with an overcomplete basis set: A strategy employed by V1. Vision Research 37(23), 3311–3325 (1997)
11. Guha, T., Ward, R.K.: Learning sparse representations for human action recognition. PAMI 34(8), 1576–1588 (2012)
12. Wright, J., Yang, A.Y., Ganesh, A., Sastry, S.S., Ma, Y.: Robust face recognition via sparse representation. PAMI 31(2), 210–227 (2009)
13. Yang, J., Yu, K., Gong, Y., Huang, T.: Linear spatial pyramid matching using sparse coding for image classification. In: IEEE CVPR (2009)
14. Pennec, X., Fillard, P., Ayache, N.: A Riemannian framework for tensor computing. IJCV 66(1), 41–66 (2006)
15. Sivalingam, R., Boley, D., Morellas, V., Papanikolopoulos, N.: Tensor sparse coding for region covariances. In: Daniilidis, K., Maragos, P., Paragios, N. (eds.) ECCV 2010, Part IV. LNCS, vol. 6314, pp. 722–735. Springer, Heidelberg (2010)
16. Sra, S., Cherian, A.: Generalized dictionary learning for symmetric positive definite matrices with application to nearest neighbor retrieval. In: Gunopulos, D., Hofmann, T., Malerba, D., Vazirgiannis, M. (eds.) ECML PKDD 2011, Part III. LNCS (LNAI), vol. 6913, pp. 318–332. Springer, Heidelberg (2011)
17. Arsigny, V., Fillard, P., Pennec, X., Ayache, N.: Log-Euclidean metrics for fast and simple calculus on diffusion tensors. Magnetic Resonance in Medicine 56(2), 411–421 (2006)
18. Guo, K., Ishwar, P., Konrad, J.: Action recognition using sparse representation on covariance manifolds of optical flow. In: IEEE AVSS (2010)
19. Ho, J., Xie, Y., Vemuri, B.: On a nonlinear generalization of sparse coding and dictionary learning. In: ICML (2013)
20. Harandi, M.T., Sanderson, C., Hartley, R., Lovell, B.C.: Sparse coding and dictionary learning for symmetric positive definite matrices: A kernel approach. In: Fitzgibbon, A., Lazebnik, S., Perona, P., Sato, Y., Schmid, C. (eds.) ECCV 2012, Part II. LNCS, vol. 7573, pp. 216–229. Springer, Heidelberg (2012)
21. Sra, S.: Positive definite matrices and the S-divergence. ArXiv preprint ArXiv:1110.1773 (2011)
22. Jayasumana, S., Hartley, R., Salzmann, M., Li, H., Harandi, M.: Kernel methods on the riemannian manifold of symmetric positive definite matrices. In: CVPR (2013)
23. Li, P., Wang, Q., Zuo, W., Zhang, L.: Log-euclidean kernels for sparse representation and dictionary learning. In: IEEE ICCV (2013)
24. Bhatia, R.: Positive Definite Matrices. Princeton University Press (2007)
25. Hiriart-Urruty, J.B., Lemaréchal, C.: Fundamentals of convex analysis. Springer (2001)
26. Higham, N.: Functions of Matrices: Theory and Computation. SIAM (2008)

27. Bertsekas, D.P.: Nonlinear Programming, 2nd edn. Athena Scientific (1999)
28. Barzilai, J., Borwein, J.M.: Two-Point Step Size Gradient Methods. IMA J. Num. Analy. 8(1) (1988)
29. Schmidt, M., van den Berg, E., Friedlander, M., Murphy, K.: Optimizing Costly Functions with Simple Constraints: A Limited-Memory Projected Quasi-Newton Algorithm. In: AISTATS (2009)
30. Birgin, E.G., Martínez, J.M., Raydan, M.: Algorithm 813: SPG - Software for Convex-constrained Optimization. ACM Transactions on Mathematical Software 27, 340–349 (2001)
31. Luis-García, R., Deriche, R., Alberola-López, C.: Texture and color segmentation based on the combined use of the structure tensor and the image components. Signal Processing 88(4), 776–795 (2008)
32. Laws, K.I.: Rapid texture identification. In: 24th Annual Technical Symposium, International Society for Optics and Photonics, pp. 376–381 (1980)
33. Schwartz, W., Davis, L.: Learning Discriminative Appearance-Based Models Using Partial Least Squares. In: Proceedings of the XXII Brazilian Symposium on Computer Graphics and Image Processing (2009)
34. Lai, K., Bo, L., Ren, X., Fox, D.: A large-scale hierarchical multi-view rgb-d object dataset. In: ICRA (2011)
35. Fehr, D.A.: Covariance based point cloud descriptors for object detection and classification. University of Minnesota (2013)

Robust Sparse Coding and Compressed Sensing with the Difference Map

Will Landecker[1,2,*], Rick Chartrand[3], and Simon DeDeo[2,4]

[1] Portland State University, USA
[2] Santa Fe Institute, USA
[3] Los Alamos National Laboratory, USA
[4] Indiana University, USA

Abstract. In compressed sensing, we wish to reconstruct a sparse signal x from observed data y. In sparse coding, on the other hand, we wish to find a representation of an observed signal y as a sparse linear combination, with coefficients x, of elements from an overcomplete dictionary. While many algorithms are competitive at both problems when x is very sparse, it can be challenging to recover x when it is *less* sparse. We present the *Difference Map*, which excels at sparse recovery when sparseness is lower. The Difference Map out-performs the state of the art with reconstruction from random measurements and natural image reconstruction via sparse coding.

Keywords: Sparse coding, compressed sensing.

1 Introduction

In compressed sensing (CS), we are given a measurement matrix $\Phi \in \mathbb{R}^{m \times n}$ (where $m < n$), observed data $y \in \mathbb{R}^m$, and we wish to recover a *sparse* $x \in \mathbb{R}^n$ such that

$$y = \Phi x.$$

The compressed sensing problem can then be written as

$$\arg \min_x \|x\|_0 \text{ subject to } y = \Phi x, \tag{1}$$

where $\| \cdot \|_0$ is the ℓ^0 penalty function, giving the number of nonzero elements. In the noisy case, where

$$\tilde{y} = \Phi x + \epsilon \cdot \mathcal{N}(0, 1)$$

is assumed to be a noisy observation, we often replace the linear constraints with quadratic ones:

$$\arg \min_x \|x\|_0 \text{ subject to } \|\tilde{y} - \Phi x\|_2^2 \leq \delta \tag{2}$$

for some $\delta > 0$. The problem (2) can also be used for sparse coding (SC); in this setting, Φ is an overcomplete dictionary, y is a signal (such as an image patch), and we seek a sparse coefficient vector x.

---

* Corresponding author: landeckw@cecs.pdx.edu

D. Fleet et al. (Eds.): ECCV 2014, Part III, LNCS 8691, pp. 315–329, 2014.

Recently, a variety of algorithms have achieved good results for a variety of CS and SC problems, including Least Angle Regression (LARS) [1], Iterative Soft Thresholding and its variants [2,3], Subspace Pursuit [4], Matching Pursuit and its variants [5,6], Iterative Hard Thresholding (IHT) and its variants [7,8,9], Iteratively Reweighted Least Squares (IRLS) [10], and the Alternating Direction Method of Multipliers (ADMM) [11,12].

Because solving problems (1) and (2) directly is known to be NP-hard [13], some approaches relax the ℓ^0 penalty to the convex ℓ^1 norm [14,1], while some attempt to address the ℓ^0 case directly [4,6,7], and still others consider any number of ℓ^p (quasi-)norms for $0 < p \leq 1$ [10,11,12]. In general, the challenge for CS and SC algorithms is to balance two competing constraints on the solution x^*: to accurately reconstruct the observed data y, and to be sparse.

This paper presents a method for solving CS and SC problems without relaxing the ℓ^0 constraint, using a general method known as the Difference Map [15]. The Difference Map (DM) has been used to solve a wide variety of constraint-intersection problems. Given sets A and B and distance-minimizing projections P_A and P_B[1], respectively, DM searches for a point $x^* \in A \cap B$. One iteration of DM is defined by $x \leftarrow D(x)$, where

$$D(x) = x + \beta \left[P_A \circ f_B(x) - P_B \circ f_A(x) \right], \qquad (3)$$

in which

$$f_A(x) = P_A(x) - (P_A(x) - x) / \beta,$$
$$f_B(x) = P_B(x) + (P_B(x) - x) / \beta,$$

and $\beta \neq 0$. One can test for convergence by monitoring the value $\| P_A \circ f_B(x) - P_B \circ f_A(x) \|_2$, which vanishes when a solution is found. Recently, DM has achieved state-of-the-art performance on a variety of NP-hard nonconvex optimization problems including protein folding, k-SAT, and packing problems [15].

The rest of this paper is organized as follows. In Section 2, we introduce an adaptation of the Difference Map for compressed sensing and sparse coding, which we compare at a high level to other well-known algorithms. In Section 3, we compare the algorithms on CS problems using random measurements, and we reconstruct natural images via SC in Section 4.

2   Compressed Sensing and Sparse Coding with the Difference Map

Given a matrix $\Phi \in \mathbb{R}^{m \times n}$ (where $m < n$) and data $y \in \mathbb{R}^m$, we wish to find a sparse vector $x^* \in \mathbb{R}^n$ that is a solution to problem (2). We apply the Difference Map to this problem by defining the constraint sets

$$A = \{ x \in \mathbb{R}^n : \|x\|_0 \leq s \},$$
$$B = \{ x \in \mathbb{R}^n : \|\Phi x - y\|_2^2 \leq \delta \},$$

---

[1] By distance-minimizing projection, we mean that $P_A(x_0) = \arg\min_x \|x_0 - x\|_2$ subject to $x \in A$, and likewise for P_B.

for a pre-defined positive integer s and scalar $\delta > 0$.

The minimum-distance projection onto A is known as *hard thresholding*, and is defined by

$$P_A(x) = [x]_s, \tag{4}$$

where $[x]_s$ is obtained by setting to zero the $n - s$ components of x having the smallest absolute values.

A minimum-distance projection onto the set B involves solving a quadratically-constrained quadratic programming problem (QCQP), which can be very costly. We approximate this projection with:

$$P_B(x) = x - \Phi^+(\Phi x - y), \tag{5}$$

where $\Phi^+ = \Phi^T(\Phi\Phi^T)^{-1}$ is the Moore-Penrose pseudo-inverse of Φ.

The motivation for (5) comes from a simplification of our definition for B. Consider the set with linear constraints (as in (1)):

$$\{x \in \mathbb{R}^n : \Phi x = y\}.$$

The minimum distance projection onto this set is given by the linearly constrained quadratic programming (LCQP) problem

$$P(x_0) = \arg\min_{x\in\mathbb{R}^n} \tfrac{1}{2}\|x - x_0\|_2^2 \text{ such that } \Phi x = y. \tag{6}$$

The Lagrangian of this LCQP is

$$\mathcal{L}(x, \lambda) = \tfrac{1}{2}\|x - x_0\|_2^2 + \lambda(\Phi x - y).$$

The x that solves the LCQP (6) is a minimizer of $\mathcal{L}$, and is found by setting $\nabla_x(\mathcal{L}) = 0$, which yields

$$x = x_0 + \Phi^T\lambda. \tag{7}$$

Plugging (7) into $y = \Phi x$ and solving for λ gives

$$\lambda = (\Phi\Phi^T)^{-1}(\Phi x_0 - y).$$

Finally, we plug this into (7) to get

$$x = x_0 - \Phi^T(\Phi\Phi^T)^{-1}(\Phi x_0 - y),$$

as in (5).

Although the motivation for (5) comes from the assumption of non-noisy observations $y = \Phi x$, it in fact performs very well in the noisy case. In Figure 1, we see that the linearly-constrained P_B (LCQP) allows DM to converge much more quickly than the quadratically-constrained P_B (QCQP), even when given noisy observations. In this experiment, we chose a random $\Phi \in \mathbb{R}^{400\times1000}$ and $\|x\|_0 = 150$ (see Section 3 for details on constructing Φ and x). We calculated the noiseless $y = \Phi x$ and the noisy $\tilde{y} = y + \epsilon \cdot \mathcal{N}(0,1)$ such that $\text{SNR}(y, \tilde{y}) = 20$ dB. The Difference Map was then given Φ and $\tilde{y}$, and asked to recover x using

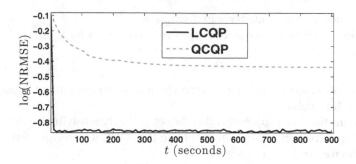

Fig. 1. The linearly constrained approximation (LCQP) of P_B allows the Difference Map to recover the signal x much more quickly than the quadratically constrained (QCQP) version of P_B, even when given the noisy observation $\tilde{y} = \Phi x + \epsilon \cdot \mathcal{N}(0, 1)$. We measure the log(NRMSE) of the estimate $\hat{x}$, computed by $\log(\|x - \hat{x}\|_2 / \|x\|_2)$. See text for additional details.

either the quadratically constrained P_B (QCQP) or the linearly constrained P_B (LCQP). The computationally expensive QCQP at each iteration causes DM to perform much more slowly. Thus we only consider the LCQP version of DM for the remainder of this work.

As stated above, the LCQP assumes that $\delta = 0$. Note that this assumption may reduce or even eliminate the intersection between the sets A and B. Nonetheless, Figure 1 shows that the speed improvement gained by this assumption far outweighs the disadvantages of the approximation, while still giving superior reconstruction for moderate noise (meaning $\delta > 0$).

It is worth noting that the pseudo-inverse is expensive to compute, though it only needs to be computed once. Thus in the case of sparse image reconstruction where each image patch is reconstructed independently, amortizing the cost of computing Φ^+ over all image patches significantly reduces the pre-computation overhead.

2.1 Comparison to other Algorithms

In what follows, we compare the Difference Map to a representative sample of commonly-used algorithms for solving CS and SC problems: Least Angle Regression (LARS) [1], Fast Iterative Soft Thresholding Algorithm (FISTA) [3], Stagewise Orthogonal Matching Pursuit (StOMP) [5], Accelerated Iterative Hard Thresholding (AIHT) [9], Subspace Pursuit (SP) [4], Iteratively-Reweighted Least Squares (IRLS) [10] and Alternating Direction Method of Multipliers (ADMM) [11,12]. As a final point of comparison, we test the Alternating Map (AM) defined by $x \leftarrow P_A(P_B(x))$, with P_A and P_B defined as in (4) and (5), respectively, which resembles the ECME algorithm for known sparsity levels [16].

The projection P_A (4), known as hard thresholding, is an important part of many CS algorithms [9,8,7,4,16,17]. The projection P_B (5) also appears in the ECME algorithm [16,17]. Normalized Iterative Hard Thresholding (NIHT) [8] uses a calculation similar to P_B, replacing the pseudo-inverse with $\mu_t \Phi^T$ for an appropriately chosen scalar μ_t.

Given that many algorithms consider the same types of projections as DM, any advantage achieved by DM must not come from the individual projections P_A and P_B, but rather the way in which DM combines the two projections into a single iterative procedure. This is particularly true when comparing DM to the simple alternating map. Alternating between projections is guaranteed to find a point at the intersection of the two constraints if both are convex; however, if either of the constraints is not convex, it is easy for this scheme to get stuck in a local minimum that does not belong to the intersection.

While many of the theoretical questions about the Difference Map remain open, it does come with a crucial guarantee here: even on nonconvex problems, a fixed point (meaning $D(x) = x$) implies that we have found a solution (meaning a point in $A \cap B$). To see this, note that $D(x) = x$ implies

$$P_A \circ f_B(x) = P_B \circ f_A(x). \tag{8}$$

Thus we have found a point that exists in both A and B. This leads us to believe that DM will find better sparse solutions when other algorithms are stuck in local minima.

Note that we are not the first to consider applying DM to compressed sensing. Qiu and Dogandžić [17] apply DM to the ECME algorithm (a variant of expectation maximization) in order to improve upon one of the two projections inside that algorithm. Although one of ECME's two projections uses DM *internally*, ECME continues to combine the two projections in a simple alternating fashion. This is in stark contrast to our proposed algorithm, which uses DM *externally* to the individual projections as a more intricate way of combining them. The resulting algorithm, called DM-ECME, is intended only for compressed sensing with non-negative signals. Because we consider different types of problems in this paper, we do not include DM-ECME in the comparisons below.

2.2 Implementation Details

We implemented the Difference Map in Matlab [18]. All experiments were performed on a computer with a 2.7 GHz quad-core Intel i7 processor, running Matlab R2013a. We obtained Matlab implementations of LARS and StOMP from SparseLab v2.1 [19]. Implementations of AIHT [9] and Subspace Pursuit [4] were found on the websites of the papers' authors. We also obtained Matlab implementations of ADMM [12] and IRLS [10] directly from the authors of the cited papers.

The implementations of LARS, Subspace Pursuit, AIHT, and StOMP are parameter-free. It was necessary to tune a single parameter for DM, and two parameters each for ADMM and IRLS. We tuned the parameters in two iterations of grid search. ADMM and IRLS required different parameters for the two different experiments presented in this paper (reconstruction from random measurements, and natural image reconstruction). Interestingly, DM performed well with the same parameter for both types of experiments.

We use "training" matrices of the same dimension, sparsity, and noise level as the ones presented in the figures of this paper in order to tune parameters. We chose parameters to minimize the MSE of the recovering x, averaged over all training problems. When tuning parameters for natural image reconstruction, we used a training set of 1000 image patches taken from the *person* and *hill* categories of ImageNet [20], providing a good variety of natural scenery.

When tuning β for DM, note that the values $\beta = 1$ and $\beta = -1$ greatly simplify the definitions of f_A and f_B and reduce the amount of computation per iteration by approximately one half. Thus these values are preferable when they lead to good performance. If they do not, one must resort to heuristics like grid search, as we do here. We first perform grid search with an interval of 0.1, between -1.2 and 1.2^2. Next, in a radius of 0.05 around the best β, we performed another grid search with an interval of 0.01. Surprisingly, all β in the interval $[-0.9, -0.1]$ appeared to be equally good for all problems reported in this paper. We chose $\beta = -0.14$ because it performed slightly better during our experiments, but the advantage over other $\beta \in [-0.9, -0.1]$ was not significant.

We use logarithmic grid search to tune the two parameters for ADMM and IRLS. First, we search parameter values by powers of ten, meaning 10^α, for $\alpha = -5, -4, \ldots, 5$. We then search in the neighborhood of best exponent c by $\frac{1}{10}$ powers of ten, meaning $10^{c+\alpha}$ for $\alpha = -0.5, -0.4, \ldots, 0.5$.

For random measurements (the experiments in Section 3), this results in parameter values $\mu = 1.26 \times 10^2, \lambda = 3.98 \times 10^{-1}$ for ADMM, and $\alpha = 3.16 \times 10^{-3}; \beta = 2.51 \times 10^{-1}$. For natural image reconstruction (Section 4), we found $\mu = 1.58 \times 10^2, \lambda = 1.0 \times 10^{-1}$ for ADMM and $\alpha = 2.5 \times 10^{-4}, \beta = 5 \times 10^{-3}$ for IRLS. Note that the β parameter for IRLS has nothing to do with the β parameter for DM. We refer to both as β only to remain consistent with the respective bodies of literature about each algorithm, but in what follows we will only refer to the parameter for DM. IRLS is capable of addressing the ℓ^p quasi-norm for a variety of values $0 < p \le 1$, while ADMM uses modifications of the ℓ^p quasi-norm designed to have a simple proximal mapping [21]. In both cases we tried $p = \frac{1}{2}$ and $p = 1$, and found $p = \frac{1}{2}$ to perform better.

3   Random Measurements

In this Section, we compare the performance of DM to other algorithms when reconstructing signals from random measurements, testing a wide variety of matrix sizes, sparsity, and noise levels. Given positive integers m, n, and s, we generate the random matrix $\Phi \in \mathbb{R}^{m \times n}$ with entries drawn from $\mathcal{N}(0, 1)$. We then ensure that columns have zero mean and unit norm. We generate the s-sparse vector $x \in \mathbb{R}^n$ whose nonzero elements are drawn from $\mathcal{N}(0, 1)$. We then calculate $y = \Phi x$, and the noisy "observation" $\tilde{y} = y + \epsilon \cdot \mathcal{N}(0, 1)$. Finally, we ask each algorithm to reconstruct x given only Φ and $\tilde{y}$.

---

[2] The natural range for the parameter β is [-1,1] (excluding 0), but Elser *et al.* [15] report that occasionally values outside of this interval work well.

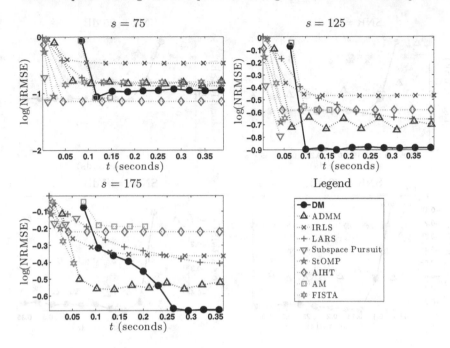

Fig. 2. Reconstructing signals with various levels of sparsity s. Given y and Φ, we try to recover x such that $y = \Phi x$ and $\|x\|_0 \leq s$. We measure the normalized root mean squared error (NRMSE) at time t by estimating x_t and calculating $\|x - x_t\|/\|x\|$. With sparser signals (upper left), most algorithms get equally close to recovering the true signal. With less sparse signals (upper right, lower left), the Difference Map gets closer than other algorithms to recovering the signal. Each plot is averaged over ten runs, with ϵ chosen to give an SNR of approximately 20 dB, and $\Phi \in \mathbb{R}^{400 \times 1000}$.

We measure runtime instead of iterations, as the time required per iteration varies widely for the algorithms considered. Additionally, the pre-computation for DM is the longest of any algorithm, requiring the pseudo-inverse of the dictionary. This pre-computation overhead is included in the timekeeping.

In the first experiment, each algorithm attempts to reconstruct x as we vary the sparsity level s. We choose ϵ so that the signal-to-noise ratio (SNR) is close to 20 dB. The results in Figure 2 demonstrate that for small values of s (upper left), meaning sparser signals, most algorithms are able to recover x about equally well. As we increase the value of s (upper right, lower left), meaning denser signals, other algorithms converge to undesirable minima. The Difference Map, however, continues to get very close to recovering x.

In the next experiment, each algorithm attempts to reconstruct x as we vary the noise by changing ϵ. We fix s at 150. The results in Figure 3 show that with very little noise (upper left) and very high noise (lower right), the Difference Map performs as well as several algorithms at recovering the true signal x, though it requires more time. For moderate amounts of noise (upper right, lower left), the Difference Map is able to get closer to recovering the signal than any other algorithm.

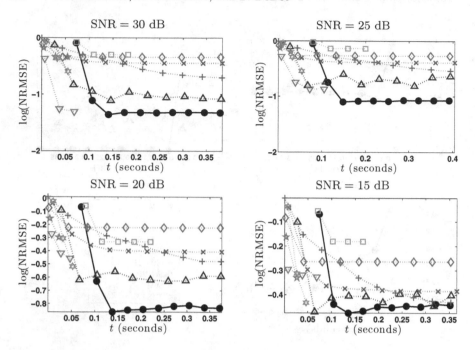

Fig. 3. Reconstructing signals with various levels of noise ϵ. Legend is the same as Figure 2. With very little noise (upper left) and large amounts of noise (bottom right), the Difference Map recovers the signal as well as the best algorithms, though requiring more time. With moderate amounts noise (upper right, lower left), the Difference Map gets closer than other algorithms to recovering the signal. Each plot is averaged over ten runs, with $s = 150$ and $\Phi \in \mathbb{R}^{400 \times 1000}$.

Note that DM and AM start "late" in all plots from Figures 2 and 3 because their pre-computation time is the longest (calculating Φ^+). Despite using the same projections, we notice a large disparity in performance between DM and AM when $s > 75$. Because the two algorithms both use the same two projections P_A and P_B, this performance gap shows the power of combining two simple projections in a more elaborate way than simply alternating between them.

From the results in Figures 2 and 3, we hypothesize that DM has a significant advantage with less sparse signals containing a moderate amount of noise, where other state-of-the-art compressed sensing algorithms get stuck in local minima or require a large amount of time to reach a good solution. We test this hypothesis with a variety of different matrix sizes and sparsity ratios in Figure 4, each time with an SNR of approximately 20 dB. The results show that DM does indeed outperform other algorithms in this setting, for all cases tested.

For all experiments reported above, the Difference Map's ℓ^0 constraint in (4) was the same as the true s used to generate the data. In many settings, however, the true s is unknown. We measure the robustness of DM in this setting by fixing the true value s (used to generate x) while varying the ℓ^0 constraint in (4). We then measure the log-NRMSE of the reconstructed signal $\hat{x}$. The results in Figure

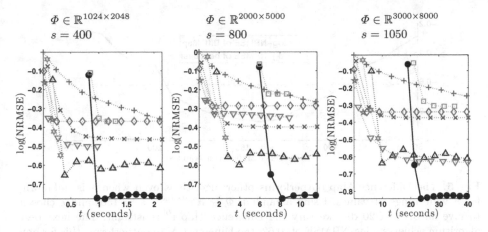

Fig. 4. In the low sparsity regime, the difference map outperforms other algorithms at recovering x from a noisy observed signal with a wide variety of matrix sizes $\mathbb{R}^{m \times n}$. Legend is the same as Figure 2. The noisy observation $\tilde{y} = \Phi x + \epsilon \cdot \mathcal{N}(0, 1)$ has an SNR of approximately 20 dB. Each plot is averaged over ten runs.

5 show that when s is fixed at 150, DM continues to recover x better than any other algorithm for an ℓ^0 constraint down to 90 and up to 190. Thus DM appears quite robust to the specific ℓ^0 constraint value used when implementing the algorithm; we explore this property further when reconstructing natural images in Section 4, for which the "true s" is unknown.

4   Sparse Coding Image Reconstruction

The results from Section 3 indicate that DM offers an advantage over other algorithms when the underlying signal is *less* sparse and the observation is noisy. The less-sparse, noisy setting corresponds well to images which contain a large variety of textures, such as natural images. In this Section, we measure the sparse coding performance of the same algorithms as in the previous section (with the exception of AM, whose sparse coding performance was not competitive), by comparing reconstruction quality for a variety of images.

When reconstructing a large image, we treat each $w \times w$ patch as an independent signal to reconstruct. Because our dictionary is constant, we only need to compute the pseudo-inverse in (5) once. By amortizing the cost of the pseudo-inversion over all patches, this effectively allows DM to converge in less time per patch. We amortize the cost of pre-computation for other algorithms as well (most notably ADMM and IRLS).

In order to test the performance of the algorithms when reconstructing natural images, we require a dictionary learned for sparse image reconstruction. Dictionary learning is not the focus of this paper, but we present our method for completeness. The dictionary is trained with 10 million 20×20 image patches, and we choose to learn 1000 atoms, resulting in a dictionary of size 400×1000.

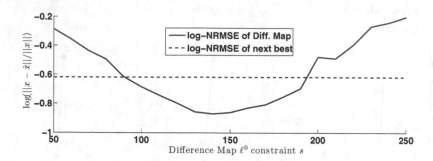

Fig. 5. The Difference Map outperforms other algorithms even when s is unknown, for a wide range of values. Using a random $\Phi \in \mathbb{R}^{400 \times 1000}$, $s = 150$, and ϵ chosen to give an SNR of 20 dB, we vary the Difference Map ℓ^0 constraint. The next best algorithm achieves a log-NRMSE of -0.62; the Difference Map outperforms this for any ℓ^0 constraint between 90 and 190.

We train the dictionary with patches from the *person* and *hills* category of ImageNet [20], which provide a variety of natural scenery. We alternate sparse coding using 20 iterations of ADMM using p-shrinkage with $p = 1/2$ (see [21] for details), with a dictionary update using the method of optimal directions [22]. We used ADMM as the sparse-coding algorithm simply because we had access to MPI-parallelized C code for this purpose. We do not believe that this gave an unfair advantage to ADMM, because the reconstructed images presented in this paper are separate from the dataset used to train the dictionary.

Using 1,000 processors, the dictionary converged in about 2.5 hours. The training patches were reconstructed by the dictionary with an average of 29 nonzero components (out of 1000), and the reconstruction of the training images had a relative error of 5.7%. The dictionary contains the typical combination of high- and low-frequency edges, at various orientations and scales. Some examples are shown in Figure 6.

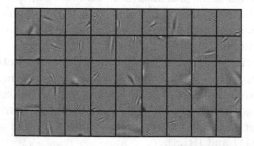

Fig. 6. Example atoms from the dictionary $\Phi \in \mathbb{R}^{400 \times 1000}$ used for reconstruction. The dictionary contains elements of size 20×20, learned from 10 million image patches from the *person* and *hill* categories of ImageNet [20].

Table 1. Signal to noise ratio (SNR, in decibels) of the reconstructed image from Figure 7. We test various sparsity levels s and various runtimes t (seconds per entire image). The difference map consistently achieves high SNR.

	$s = 100$			$s = 200$		
	$t = 10$	$t = 20$	$t = 30$	$t = 10$	$t = 20$	$t = 30$
Diff. Map	15.91	**17.55**	**17.45**	**20.28**	**22.38**	**23.34**
FISTA	4.80	12.04	17.21	4.82	12.13	21.71
ADMM	15.51	16.71	17.31	19.80	21.96	23.00
IRLS	9.62	13.52	14.92	13.47	18.38	20.62
Sub. Pursuit	**16.47**	16.78	16.84	16.94	16.88	16.87
LARS	10.62	12.66	14.16	10.63	12.68	14.24
AIHT	14.71	15.62	16.18	18.72	19.91	20.69
StOMP	15.55	15.50	15.50	17.65	17.92	17.93

Original	LARS	StOMP	IRLS	ADMM	SP	AIHT	FISTA	Diff. Map
	14.24 dB	17.93 dB	20.62 dB	23.00 dB	16.87 dB	20.69 dB	21.71 dB	**23.34 dB**

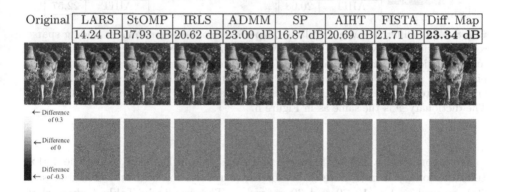

← Difference of 0.3

← Difference of 0

Difference of -0.3 ←

Fig. 7. Reconstructing a natural image. The Difference Map outperforms the other algorithms (SNR shown in decibels, top row) when reconstructing a 320×240 image of a dog (reconstructions shown in middle row). Difference images (bottom row) show the difference between the reconstruction and the original image, which ranges from -0.3 (black) to 0.3 (white) – original grayscale values are between 0 (black) and 1 (white). Results for $s = 200$ and $t = 30$.

We reconstruct several natural images and measure the quality of the sparse reconstruction as a function of time. At time t, we measure the reconstruction quality of patch y as follows. First, we perform hard-thresholding on the algorithm's current guess x_t, setting the $n - s$ smallest absolute values to zero, yielding the s-sparse vector $[x_t]_s$. We then calculate the reconstruction

$$y_t = \Phi[x_t]_s$$

and measure the SNR of y (the true image patch) to y_t. Thus we are measuring how well, at time t, the algorithm can create a *sparse* reconstruction of y. Note that algorithms returning a solution that is *sparser* than required will not be affected by the hard-thresholding step.

Diff. Map	23.19
FISTA	19.49
ADMM	22.16
IRLS	20.58
LARS	14.51
SP	17.85
StOMP	19.32
AIHT	20.37

Diff. Map	24.84
FISTA	18.96
ADMM	23.78
IRLS	23.31
LARS	18.02
SP	20.81
StOMP	23.23
AIHT	22.65

Diff. Map	22.79
FISTA	19.00
ADMM	21.92
IRLS	20.51
LARS	14.81
SP	17.89
StOMP	18.81
AIHT	20.08

Diff. Map	24.80
FISTA	19.31
ADMM	24.06
IRLS	23.28
LARS	18.00
SP	20.38
StOMP	21.13
AIHT	22.57

Fig. 8. The Difference Map regularly outperforms other algorithms in finding sparse reconstructions of a variety of images. We measure the SNR in decibels between the reconstruction and the original image (left column). Images are scaled to 240×320 pixels (320×240 for horizontal images). Reconstructions have sparsity $s = 200$, and are completed in 30 seconds per image (approximately 0.15 seconds per 20×20 patch). The dictionary Φ is the same as in Figure 6.

We reconstruct a 320×240 image of a dog, seen in Figure 7, using the 400×1000 dictionary from Figure 6. We measure results for both $s = 100$ and $s = 200$, as well as $t = 10, 20$ and 30 seconds[3]. The results in Table 1 show that DM consistently achieves a very good SNR of the reconstruction. As would be expected, increasing s and t tend to improve each algorithm's reconstruction performance.

The highest quality reconstructions, achieved with $s = 200$ and $t = 30$, are shown in Figure 7. While some algorithms fail to reconstruct details in the animal's fur and the grass, many algorithms reconstruct the image well enough to make it difficult to find errors by mere visual inspection. We show the difference between the reconstructions and the original image (Figure 7, bottom row), where a neutral gray color in the difference image corresponds to a perfect reconstruction of that pixel; white and black are scaled to a difference of 0.3 and -0.3, respectively (the original image was scaled to the interval [0,1]).

---

[3] We measure time in seconds per full-image reconstruction, which is actually performed independently for each 20×20 patch. Thus $t = 10, 20$ and 30 correspond to approximately $0.05, 0.1$, and 0.15 seconds per patch, respectively. The astute reader will notice that when Φ has dimension 400×1000, it takes longer than 0.05 seconds to compute Φ^+. This can be seen in Figure 3, where it takes almost 0.1 seconds for DM to finish calculating Φ^+ and begin searching for x. However, because we only need to calculate the pseudo-inverse once for the entire image, this start-up cost is amortized over all patches and becomes negligible.

The advantage of DM over other algorithms, when sparsely reconstructing images, can be seen with a large variety of images. In Figure 8, we see that DM consistently achieves the best reconstruction. All original images are included in the Supplementary Material.

5   Conclusions

We have presented the Difference Map, a method of finding a point at the intersection of two constraint sets, and we have introduced an implementation of DM for sparse coding and compressed sensing. The constraint-set formulation is a natural fit for sparse recovery problems, in which we have two competing constraints for x: to be consistent with the data y, and to be sparse.

When the solution x is very sparse and the observation $\tilde{y}$ is not too noisy, DM takes more time in finding the same solution as competing algorithms. However, when the solution x is *less* sparse and when the observation $\tilde{y}$ is noisy, DM outperforms state of the art sparse recovery algorithms. The noisy, less sparse setting corresponds well to reconstructing natural images, which can often require a large number of components in order to accurately reconstruct. Experiments show that DM performs favorably in reconstructing a variety of images, with a variety of parameter settings.

Parameter tuning can present a laborious hurdle to the researcher. DM requires tuning only a single parameter β. For all experiments in this paper (natural image reconstruction for various images; reconstruction with random matrix dictionaries of various sizes, with varying amounts of sparsity and noise), we found DM to work almost equally as well for all $-0.9 \leq \beta \leq -0.1$. The robustness of DM under such a wide variety of parameter values and problems makes DM a very competitive choice for compressed sensing.

In the case where s is unknown, it effectively becomes a separate parameter for many algorithms, including DM. However, we have shown in Figure 5 and in all experiments in Section 4 that DM maintains superior performance over competing algorithms even when s is unknown.

The robustness of DM comes from how it combines two simple projections into a single iterative procedure. The Alternating Map (AM) combines the same projections in a simple alternating fashion, and struggles in almost all experiments. The gap in performance between these two methods demonstrates the power of combining multiple constraints in a more perspicacious way.

Finally, we recall that performance in all experiments was measured as a function of time, which would seem to put DM at a natural disadvantage to other algorithms: DM requires the pseudo-inverse of the dictionary, computing which requires more time than any other algorithm's pre-computation. Despite this, DM consistently outperforms other algorithms.

Acknowledgements. SD and WL were supported by National Science Foundation Grant EF- 1137929, "The Small Number Limit of Biological Information Processing," and the Emergent Institutions Project.

RC was supported by the U.S. Department of Energy through the LANL/LDRD Program, and by the University of California Laboratory Fees Research Program.

References

1. Efron, B., Hastie, T., Johnstone, I., Tibshirani, R.: Least angle regression. Annals of Statistics 32, 407–499 (2004)
2. Daubechies, I., Defrise, M., De Mol, C.: An iterative thresholding algorithm for linear inverse problems with a sparsity constraint. Communications in Pure and Applied Mathematics 57(11), 1413–1457 (2004)
3. Beck, A., Teboulle, M.: A fast iterative shrinkage-thresholding algorithm for linear inverse problems. SIAM Journal on Imaging Sciences 2(1), 183–202 (2009)
4. Dai, W., Milenkovic, O.: Subspace pursuit for compressive sensing signal reconstruction. IEEE Transactions on Information Theory 55(5), 2230–2249 (2009)
5. Donoho, D.L., Tsaig, Y., Drori, I., Starck, J.L.: Sparse solution of underdetermined systems of linear equations by stagewise orthogonal matching pursuit. IEEE Transactions on Information Theory 58(2), 1094–1121 (2012)
6. Tropp, J.A., Gilbert, A.C.: Signal recovery from random measurements via orthogonal matching pursuit. IEEE Transactions on Information Theory 53(12), 4655–4666 (2007)
7. Blumensath, T., Davies, M.E.: Normalized iterative hard thresholding: Guaranteed stability and performance. IEEE Journal of Selected Topics in Signal Processing, 298–309 (2010)
8. Blumensath, T., Davies, M.E.: Iterative hard thresholding for compressed sensing. Applied and Computational Harmonic Analysis 27(3), 265–274 (2009)
9. Blumensath, T.: Accelerated iterative hard thresholding. Signal Processing 92(3), 752–756 (2012)
10. Chartrand, R., Yin, W.: Iteratively reweighted algorithms for compressive sensing. In: IEEE International Conference on Acoustics, Speech and Signal Processing, pp. 3869–3872 (2008)
11. Boyd, S., Parikh, N., Chu, E., Peleato, B., Eckstein, J.: Distributed optimization and statistical learning via the alternating direction method of multipliers. Foundations and Trends in Machine Learning 3(1), 1–122 (2011)
12. Chartrand, R., Wohlberg, B.: A nonconvex ADMM algorithm for group sparsity with sparse groups. In: IEEE International Conference on Acoustics, Speech, and Signal Processing (2013)
13. Natarajan, B.K.: Sparse approximate solutions to linear systems. SIAM Journal on Computing 24(2), 227–234 (1995)
14. Tibshirani, R.: Regression shrinkage and selection via the lasso. Journal of the Royal Statistical Society. Series B (Methodological), 267–288 (1996)
15. Elser, V., Rankenburg, I., Thibault, P.: Searching with iterated maps. Proceedings of the National Academy of Sciences 104(2), 418–423 (2007)
16. Qiu, K., Dogandžić, A.: Double overrelaxation thresholding methods for sparse signal reconstruction. In: IEEE Information Sciences and Systems, pp. 1–6 (2010)
17. Qiu, K., Dogandžić, A.: Nonnegative signal reconstruction from compressive samples via a difference map ECME algorithm. In: IEEE Workshop on Statistical Signal Processing, pp. 561–564 (2011)
18. Landecker, W., Chartrand, R., DeDeo, S.: Matlab code for sparse coding and compressed sensing with the Difference Map,
http://santafe.edu/~simon/dm-cs0.zip

19. Stodden, V., Carlin, L., Donoho, D., Drori, I., Dunson, D., Elad, M., Ji, S., Starck, J., Tanner, J., Temlyakov, V., Tsaig, Y., Xue, Y.: SparseLab. Matlab software package,
    http://sparselab.stanford.edu/
20. Deng, J., Dong, W., Socher, R., Li, L.J., Li, K., Fei-Fei, L.: ImageNet: A Large-Scale Hierarchical Image Database. In: IEEE Conference on Computer Vision and Pattern Recognition (2009)
21. Chartrand, R.: Nonconvex splitting for regularized low-rank + sparse decomposition. IEEE Transactions on Signal Processing 60, 5810–5819 (2012)
22. Engan, K., Aase, S., Hakon Husoy, J.: Method of optimal directions for frame design. In: IEEE International Conference on Acoustics, Speech, and Signal Processing, pp. 2443–2446 (1999)

Object Co-detection via Efficient Inference in a Fully-Connected CRF*

Zeeshan Hayder, Mathieu Salzmann, and Xuming He

Australian National University (ANU)
NICTA, Canberra, Australia

Abstract. Object detection has seen a surge of interest in recent years, which has lead to increasingly effective techniques. These techniques, however, still mostly perform detection based on local evidence in the input image. While some progress has been made towards exploiting scene context, the resulting methods typically only consider a single image at a time. Intuitively, however, the information contained jointly in multiple images should help overcoming phenomena such as occlusion and poor resolution. In this paper, we address the co-detection problem that aims to leverage this collective power to achieve object detection simultaneously in all the images of a set. To this end, we formulate object co-detection as inference in a fully-connected CRF whose edges model the similarity between object candidates. We then learn a similarity function that allows us to efficiently perform inference in this fully-connected graph, even in the presence of many object candidates. This is in contrast with existing co-detection techniques that rely on exhaustive or greedy search, and thus do not scale well. Our experiments demonstrate the benefits of our approach on several co-detection datasets.

Keywords: Object co-detection, fully-connected CRFs.

1 Introduction

Object detection has been a central problem in modern computer vision, and much progress has been made in recent years, as demonstrated by the PASCAL challenge [12] and the ImageNet challenge [7]. Whether working at instance [22] or category [14] level, most of the research has focused on detecting objects in a single image and in a sliding window manner. It is widely acknowledged, however, that such a myopic view is too restrictive as it ignores all contextual information [15]. On their own, the appearance cues of an object instance are often ambiguous due to poor resolution, occlusions, or challenging lighting conditions.

Previous work on object detection with context mainly exploits the 2D or 3D scene context observed in the same image as the detected objects [19,8]. Recently, simultaneously exploiting multiple images has been proposed as a means

---

* NICTA is funded by the Australian Government as represented by the Department of Broadband, Communications and the Digital Economy, as well as by the Australian Research Council through the ICT Centre of Excellence program.

D. Fleet et al. (Eds.): ECCV 2014, Part III, LNCS 8691, pp. 330–345, 2014.

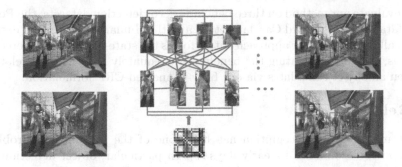

Fig. 1. Overview of our method. Left: Original input images and candidates generated with a DPM; Middle: Fully-connected CRF on the candidates and corresponding learned pairwise similarities; Right: Jointly detected objects by efficient inference in the fully-connected CRF (actual result).

to gather broader contextual information for detection. The resulting *object co-detection* techniques [3,18,24] aim to jointly detect multiple instances of an object class from a pool of images. Intuitively, object co-detection leverages the weak appearance cues of object instances seen in multiple images to improve the robustness of object detection.

A critical challenge in object co-detection is to incorporate many object hypotheses from multiple images while keeping the joint classification of those object hypotheses tractable. Typically, the problem is formulated as that of inferring the (binary) activation labels of object candidates, which is a combinatorial search problem. The existing methods rely on either exhaustive search [3], or ad hoc greedy search [24]. While these strategies are effective for a small number of images, they are in general suboptimal, and become impractical when considering large image pools or number of classes.

In this paper, we introduce a principled and efficient inference method for object co-detection. Given a pool of object candidates obtained by applying a pre-trained detector with a high recall rate (e.g., the Deformable Part-based Model (DPM) [14]), we construct a fully-connected Conditional Random Field (CRF) where the nodes represent the candidate labels, and the edges encode the appearance similarity between two candidates. Inference in this CRF lets us predict the labels of all the object candidates simultaneously.

For our formulation to remain tractable, we need to be able to leverage efficient inference techniques in fully-connected CRFs. To this end, we model the similarity between two candidates as a linear combination of Gaussian kernels defined on multiple image features. The weights of this combination can be efficiently learned from training data. We make use of this similarity in the edge potentials of our CRF, which encode a data-dependent Potts model. The form of these potentials lets us utilize the efficient mean field inference algorithm of [21], which not only yields the candidate labels, but also confidence in our predictions. Fig. 1 depicts an overview of our framework.

We evaluate our method on three benchmark co-detection datasets: the Pedestrian dataset [11], the Ford Car dataset [3] and the Human Co-Detection dataset [24]. In all three cases, our approach outperforms the state-of-the-art co-detection methods, thus demonstrating the benefits of adequately modeling the relations between all object candidates via our fully-connected CRF formulation.

2   Related Work

Object modeling and recognition has been one of the fundamental problems in computer vision since its early days [9]. In particular, object detection has evolved into a core challenge in vision research [12,7], and much progress has been made recently due to advances in deformable part-based object models, e.g., DPM [14], as well as in deep network models [16].

Traditionally, object detection methods take a scanning window approach and exhaustively search for object candidates at every location and scale in an image [28,6,14]. More recently, objectness criteria have been used to propose potential candidates, which drastically reduces the search space [10,1,25]. Objectness, however, is very challenging to adequately represent, since it has to account for the huge intra-class variations of the general *object* category, while still being able to differentiate it from the *background* class. As a matter of fact, these challenges remain unsolved even when detecting specific objects.

A natural perspective to improve the robustness of detectors to phenomena such as poor resolution, occlusions, and challenging lighting conditions, consists in putting objects into context. To this end, the scene properties of the target image are exploited to boost the object detection performance. For instance, Desai et al. [8] propose to jointly detect multiple object classes by defining a CRF on top of DPMs. In [4], multiple instances of the same object class are jointly detected to address the occlusion problem. Hoiem et al. [19] consider the geometric context of the scene to improve detection by reducing the number of false positives. While these approaches have proven more effective than context-free detectors, they focus on exploiting the context from a single image. Intuitively, however, the information available in multiple images should be helpful to disambiguate detection.

Object co-detection methods [3,18,24] were recently introduced to exploit the collective power of a set of images. In particular, the term *co-detection* was coined by Bao et al. [3], who tackle the problem by exhaustively searching for matching object instances in a set of object candidates. Generally speaking, co-detection has been considered for both 2D and 3D object models, as well as at category- and instance-levels. Category-level co-detection involves matching objects belonging to the same class (e.g., a person with another person) and appearing either in the same image, or in multiple images. In contrast, instance-level co-detection compares specific object instances (e.g., a specific person) that appear simultaneously in a pool of input images (e.g., [24]). While the original work of Bao et al. [3] could only handle pairs of images, Guo et al. [18] introduced a robust approach to multi-image co-detection that builds a shared low-rank representation of the object instances in multiple feature spaces. Unlike these works, our method is based on a principled CRF formulation. Therefore, it enables us to perform joint inference efficiently for many object instances extracted from multiple images.

Our work is inspired by the fully-connected CRF model for semantic labeling of [21,27,30]. By restricting the functional form of the pairwise potentials to a weighted mixture of Gaussian kernels defined on the input feature space, inference in this fully-connected CRF can be performed efficiently as a filtering operation. Here, instead of labeling the pixels in an image, we aim to label object candidates from multiple images in a principled and yet efficient manner. To the best of our knowledge, our work is the first attempt to extend the fully-connected CRF model of [21] to another vision problem domain.

In this context, we propose to learn the pairwise potentials in our CRF by fitting a linear combination of kernels to a target similarity measure. This bears some connections with the multiple kernel learning literature [17,26]. However, our objective is not to build a kernel-based similarity classifier as in [24], since this would not yield a mixture of Gaussian kernels adapted to our fully-connected CRF framework. Instead, our similarity learning approach is closer to metric learning [29]. In contrast, however, we jointly consider multiple kernels defined on separate feature spaces, thus yielding more flexibility than the single linear transformation typically used in metric learning methods.

3 A Fully-Connected CRF for Co-detection

In this paper, we tackle the object co-detection problem, in which we aim to detect simultaneously all the instances of an object class in a group of S input images $\mathcal{I} = \{I^1, \cdots, I^S\}$. As in [3,18,24], when dealing with $C > 1$ object classes, we handle each class separately. Note that, while we discuss the case of category-level detection, our framework also applies to detecting the instances of specific objects (instance-level). Furthermore, we do not assume that each image contains only a single instance of an object class.

For each object class, our approach consists of two stages: first we generate a pool of object candidates in the form of bounding boxes obtained with a pre-trained object detector; then we formulate co-detection as a two-class labeling problem, where each candidate must be assigned either to the current object class of interest, or to a background class. These two steps are described in more detail in the remainder of this setion.

3.1 Object Candidate Generation

Following [3], given a target object class c, we first apply a pre-trained DPM [14] to each input image and extract a set of object candidates, denoted by $\mathcal{X}^c = \{\mathbf{X}_1^c, \cdots, \mathbf{X}_{N_c}^c\}$. To prevent entirely missing some objects in this first stage, we adjust the threshold of each detector and the non-maximum suppression parameters so as to achieve a high recall rate for all target classes. Note that, while we employ DPMs, any object detector that outputs a bounding box can

Fig. 2. Sample object candidates in three datasets. Left: Pedestrian dataset [11]; Middle: Ford Car dataset [3]; Right: Human Co-detection dataset [24].

be employed in our candidate generation stage. Fig. 2 shows some examples of object candidates generated for three different object classes.

Given the set of candidates $\mathcal{X}^c$ for class c, we then adopt a part-based representation as in the DPM. An object candidate $\mathbf{X}_i^c$ is represented by its root $\mathbf{r}_i^c$ and a set of k parts $\mathcal{P}_i^c = \{\mathbf{p}_{i,1}^c, \cdots, \mathbf{p}_{i,k}^c\}$, together with the image window $\mathbf{W}_i^c$ corresponding to the object bounding box. For each candidate $\mathbf{X}_i^c$, we also compute a set of appearance features from its image window $\mathbf{W}_i^c$. These features, denoted by $\mathbf{f}_{i,s}^c$ for a specific feature type s, capture the color and texture properties of the candidate.

3.2   CRF Formulation

Given the candidate pool $\mathcal{X}^c$, we formulate object co-detection as the problem of jointly labeling the candidates with the corresponding object or background class. More specifically, we introduce a label variable y_i^c for each object candidate $\mathbf{X}_i^c$, which takes either the object class label l^c, or the background label l^0.

To appropriately capture the dependencies of our object candidates, we build a fully-connected Conditional Random Field (CRF) on the label variables $\mathcal{Y}^c = \{y_1^c, \cdots, y_{N_c}^c\}$. Each node in the CRF corresponds to the label of one object candidate, and any pair of two candidates are connected by an edge that encodes their relationship. Formally, we define the joint distribution over the label variables $\mathcal{Y}^c$ given the observed candidates $\mathcal{X}^c$ as

$$P(\mathcal{Y}^c|\mathcal{X}^c) = \frac{1}{Z(\mathcal{X}^c)} \exp\left(-\sum_{i=1}^{N_c} \phi_u(y_i^c|\mathbf{X}_i^c) - \alpha \sum_{i=1}^{N_c} \sum_{j>i} \psi_p(y_i^c, y_j^c|\mathbf{X}_i^c, \mathbf{X}_j^c)\right), \quad (1)$$

where $Z(\cdot)$ is the partition function, α is a weight learned by cross-validation, and ϕ_u and ψ_p are the unary and pairwise potential functions, respectively. The unary potential ϕ_u encodes how likely a candidate is to be associated with each class, while the pairwise potential ψ_p measures the affinity between the different possible class assignments of two candidates.

Object co-detection then boils down to inferring the optimal label configuration of this CRF model, which jointly labels all the object candidates. In our work, we do not put any restriction on the number of input images. Consequently, we may have a large number of object candidates (nodes) in our CRF. Inference in such a large, fully-connected CRF is in general intractable and difficult to approximate. The key challenge therefore lies in finding an efficient inference procedure in our fully-connected CRF.

To address joint inference in a principled way, we rely on the formulation of [21] to design our CRF model. The main requirement of this formulation is that the pairwise potentials must have the form of a mixture of Gaussian kernels. In the following, we discuss the potential functions employed in our model, and, in particular, introduce pairwise potentials that meet this mixture-of-Gaussian-kernels requirement and, as we will show, are effective for co-detection.

Unary Potentials. The unary potentials measure the likelihood that a candidate $\mathbf{X}_i^c$ belongs to the object class and to the background class. Following [3], we use a rescaled DPM score as unary potential. This lets us write our unary term as

$$\phi_u(y_i^c|\mathbf{X}_i^c) = \begin{cases} E_r(\mathbf{r}_i^c, \mathbf{W}_i^c) + \sum_{j=1}^{k} \left(E_p(\mathbf{p}_{i,j}^c, \mathbf{W}_i^c) + E_d(\mathbf{r}_i^c, \mathbf{p}_{i,j}^c) \right) & \text{if } y_i^c = l^c \\ 0 & \text{if } y_i^c = l^0, \end{cases} \tag{2}$$

where E_r and E_p are the unary potentials for the root and part filters respectively. E_d encodes the deformation cost between the root $\mathbf{r}_i^c$ and each part $\mathbf{p}_{i,j}^c$. E_r, E_p and E_d are directly defined as in the original DPM [14]. Note that, in principle, if the candidate was generated by another detector, we could still extract the DPM model parameters from $\mathbf{W}_i^c$ and make use of this unary potential.

Pairwise Potentials. The pairwise potential ψ_p is a data-dependent smoothing term that encourages similar hypotheses to share the same object label. As in [21], we restrict our pairwise potential to take the form of a weighted mixture of Gaussian kernels, which can be expressed as

$$\psi_p(y_i^c, y_j^c|\mathbf{X}_i^c, \mathbf{X}_j^c) = \mu(y_i^c, y_j^c) \sum_{m=1}^{M} w^m k^{(m)}(\mathbf{f}_i^c, \mathbf{f}_j^c), \tag{3}$$

where $\{w^m\}$ are the weights of the Gaussian kernels $\{k^{(m)}\}$, and μ is a label compatibility function. In particular, we make use of this function to encode a data-dependent Potts model, i.e., $\mu(y_i, y_j) = \mathbf{1}_{y_i \neq y_j}$.

The mixture of Gaussian kernels measures the appearance similarity between two object candidates. To this end, we use multiple feature types, as well as multiple kernel parameters. For each feature type $\mathbf{f}_s$, we construct a series of kernel functions of the form

$$k(\mathbf{f}_{i,s}^c, \mathbf{f}_{j,s}^c; t, \sigma_s) = \exp\left(-\frac{\|\mathbf{f}_{i,s}^c - \mathbf{f}_{j,s}^c\|^2}{2^t \sigma_s^2} \right), \tag{4}$$

where σ_s is the minimum kernel width and t is an integer. We enumerate the value of t from 1 to T to define our series of kernels. Using kernels with different widths provides us with more flexibility in the representation of the similarity. The mixture of Gaussian kernels in Eq. 3 is then obtained by summing over all feature types and all values of t in each type. As will be discussed in Section 3.3, to avoid having to manually tune the weights $\{w^m\}$ of this mixture, we propose an efficient supervised learning procedure to estimate these weights.

Efficient co-detection. Given our fully-connected CRF model, we jointly detect the object instances in the input images by performing maximum posterior marginal inference. Following [21], we adopt a fast mean field approximation algorithm to compute the marginals. Given the current mean field estimates $\{Q_i\}$ of the marginals, the update equation can be written as

$$Q_i(y_i^c = l) \propto \exp\left(-\phi_u(y_i^c) - \sum_{l' \neq l}\sum_{j \neq i} Q_j(y_j^c = l')\psi_p(y_i^c, y_j^c)\right) . \tag{5}$$

Due to the mixture of Gaussian kernels form of the pairwise term, the updates can be computed in parallel by convolution with Gaussian kernels. This can be achieved efficiently by exploiting fast Gaussian filtering techniques, such as the permutohedral lattice-based method of [2].

After convergence, we obtain an (approximate) posterior distribution of object labels for each node (i.e., object candidate). To obtain the final co-detection results, we can then compute the most likely label for each object candidate, $\hat{y}_i^c = \arg\max_{y_i^c} Q_i(y_i^c)$. Furthermore, we can also exploit the mean field approximate marginal probability $Q_i(\hat{y}_i^c)$ as a detection score.

Note that, with our pairwise potential and since we treat each class separately, our CRF models a binary problem with a submodular energy function. As such, it could in principle be solved exactly by the graph-cut algorithm [5,20]. However, to achieve efficiency, the conventional graph-cut algorithm [5] relies on the sparse connectivity of the graph. As will be shown in Section 4, a graph-cut solution to our inference problem becomes significantly slower than our efficient filtering-based mean field solution when dealing with large densely connected random fields. Furthermore, note also that the MAP estimate from graph-cut does not provide a confidence score for the detection. Finally, despite that in this work we focus on a binary labeling problem, our formulation easily extends to the multi-class scenario.

3.3   Learning Object Similarity

Recall that our pairwise potentials encode the appearance similarity between two object candidates as a mixture of Gaussian kernels. To suitably adjust the weights of the mixture to the problem at hand, we can exploit training data and learn the weights that minimize the deviation from an ideal similarity measure. Here we formulate kernel weights estimation as a least-squares regression problem, where the ground-truth (binary) similarity is directly defined by the compatibility of the labels of two object instances.

More specifically, we build a training set of object pairs, $\mathcal{D} = \{(\mathbf{X}_{i,1}, \mathbf{X}_{i,2}, s_i)\}$, where s_i is the ground-truth similarity, taking value 1 if $\mathbf{X}_{i,1}$ and $\mathbf{X}_{i,2}$ belong to the same class (excluding background) and 0 otherwise. The weights of the kernels can then be estimated by solving the optimization problem

$$\hat{\mathbf{w}} = \operatorname*{argmin}_{\mathbf{w}} \frac{1}{|\mathcal{D}|} \sum_{i=1}^{|\mathcal{D}|} \left(s_i - \sum_{m=1}^{M} w^m k^{(m)}(\mathbf{f}_{i,1}, \mathbf{f}_{i,2}) \right)^2 , \qquad (6)$$

where $\mathbf{w} = \{w^1, \cdots, w^M\}$ contains the weights of all kernels for all feature types. Note that this is a least-squares problem, and that its solution can therefore be obtained in closed-form.

To compute ground-truth similarities for category-level co-detection, we employ the following procedure. For each object class c, we first apply the same pre-trained object detector with high recall on the training images, and compute the intersection-over-union (IOU) of each detected bounding box with respect to the ground-truth bounding boxes. A detected bounding box is said to belong to class c if its maximum IOU w.r.t. ground-truth bounding boxes is larger than 50%. Otherwise, it is labeled as background. The training set $\mathcal{D}$ can then be constructed by collecting all possible pairs of detected bounding boxes and setting their similarity to 1 if they were both found to belong to class c, and 0 otherwise. In practice, the number of such pairs grows quickly, and we therefore randomly subsample the dissimilar pairs to build a balanced training set. Note that, as will be shown in our experiments, this procedure can also make use of instance-level labels when available, even if the final task remains category-level co-detection. In this scenario, two bounding boxes are considered similar only if they depict the same instance from the general category c.

4   Experiments

In this section, we study the effectiveness of our approach and compare it against state-of-the-art co-detection baselines.

4.1   Datasets and Setup

We evaluate our framework on several standard object co-detection datasets. These datasets include the Ford Car dataset of [3] and the Pedestrian dataset of [11], which provide category-level labels for the bounding boxes. Furthermore, we also employ the Human Co-detection (HCD) dataset of [24], which provides instance-level annotations of the bounding boxes. Note, however, that the task for HCD remains that of category-level co-detection, but, as suggested in [24], the instance-level annotations can be employed to better model object similarities.

In our experiments, we used the version 4 of DPMs [13], since it was also employed in [18,24]. This version provides one root and eight parts for each object. For each object candidate, we computed a 59 dimensional Local Binary Patterns (LBP) feature and a 32 dimensional color histogram feature on the H channel of the HSV color-space. Note that the dimensionality of these features can be reduced using PCA to speed up inference. Our method has three hyper-parameters: the number of kernels, the widths σ_s and the pairwise weight α. These parameters were obtained by two-fold cross validation.

In our results, each bounding box is labeled based on the mean field approximate marginal probability of the object class. This lets us compute precision-recall curves, as opposed to a single point on these curves if we used the MAP estimate. We report average precision (AP) at category level following the evaluation metric in the PASCAL VOC challenge. For a bounding box to be considered correct, it must have at least 50% overlap with one of the ground truth bounding boxes in that image. This also has the advantage of making our results directly comparable to previously-reported ones. Therefore, for the baselines, we directly quote results reported in [3,18,24]. Our results for all experiments were averaged over 10 random training/test partitions.

We compare our method with the DPM baseline [14] and the following state-of-the-art co-detection approaches: 1) Object Co-detection [3]; 2) Multi-feature Joint Low-Rank Reconstruction [18]; 3) Human Co-detection and Labeling [24]. To study the effect of using different image features in our similarity kernels, we also consider two simpler versions of our approach, each of which uses only one feature type (either LBP [23] or color histograms). We refer to these two systems as LBP-CRF and Color-CRF, respectively, and to our full system as Joint-CRF.

4.2   Results and Discussion

Pedestrian Dataset. The Pedestrian dataset consists of 476 training images and 374 test images from two video sequences of street scenes acquired with a stereo setup. Each image has a resolution of 640×480 and contains multiple people. To evaluate our co-detection framework, we follow the same scenario as other co-detection work, which address the problem of jointly detecting people in a pair of images. Note that this dataset provides ground truth labels only for the left images in the stereo pairs. To mimic the stereo scenario, we therefore follow the same strategy as [18] and generate pseudo-stereo pairs by randomly drawing pairs of images that are no more than 3 frames apart in the left sequences. We generate 476 training pairs from the left training sequence and 300 test pairs from the left test sequence in this manner.

In Table 1, we report the results of our approach and the baselines on this dataset. Note that our approach significantly improves the results of the DPMs. More importantly, we also outperform all the baselines, even [24] that is specifically dedicated to the human co-detection case. This is also true for the single-feature versions of our model (LBP-CRF and Color-CRF). Combining these two features in our Joint-CRF model nonetheless lets us further improve performance. Sample co-detection results are given in Fig. 3. We also evaluate our method with random pairs as in [3] and achieve a similar performance, as shown in Table 1.

Table 1. Pedestrian co-detection: Comparison of our approach with state-of-the-art co-detection methods on the Pedestrian dataset

	Stereo Pairs		Random Pairs	
Methods	Ped(all)	Ped(h>120)	Ped(all)	Ped(h>120)
DPM [13]	59.7	55.4	59.7	55.4
Obj. Co-detection [3]	62.7	63.4	58.1	58.1
Robust Obj. Co-detection [18]	67.8	70.1	67.7	70.3
Human CoDeL [24]	74.4	73.8	-	-
LBP-CRF	77.04	79.43	-	-
Color-CRF	77.99	79.70	-	-
Joint-CRF	**78.73**	**81.25**	**77.7**	**80.43**

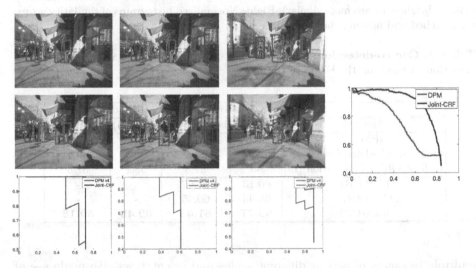

Fig. 3. Sample Results: Examples of our co-detection results on test pairs of the Pedestrian dataset. Top two rows: Input image pairs (Green dash: our results, Red solid: DPM results); Bottom row: Precision-recall curves of our method and DPM for the three image pairs. The precision-recall curves over all pairs are shown on the right.

We then study the quality of the similarity function learned from the training pairs using the method described in Section 3.3. To this end, in Fig. 4, we compare the similarity matrix obtained by applying the learned function to the candidates in one test pair with the corresponding ground-truth similarity computed from the correct labels (pedestrian vs background). Note that the predicted similarity depicts a similar pattern to the ground-truth one. This is further evidenced by the histogram that shows that pedestrian candidates have a high similarity score.

Ford Car Dataset. The Ford Car dataset consists of five scenes, each of which contains 86 stereo images. Each image has a resolution of 781×601 and depicts

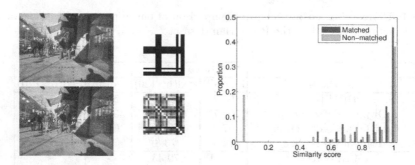

Fig. 4. Predicting similarity: Sample similarity matrix obtained by applying our learned similarity function to one test pair of the Pedestrian dataset. Left: Input image pair; Middle: (Top) target (ground truth) similarity matrix, (Bottom) learned similarity matrix (brighter means more similar); Right: Normalized histograms of similarity scores for matched and non-matched candidate pairs.

Table 2. Car co-detection: Comparison of our approach with state-of-the-art co-detection methods on the Ford Car dataset

Method	Stereo Pairs		Random Pairs	
	Ford(all)	Ford(h>80)	Ford(all)	Ford(h>80)
DPM [13]	49.8	47.1	49.8	47.1
Obj. Co-detection [3]	53.5	55.5	50.0	49.1
Robust Obj. Co-detection [18]	55	57.5	55.1	57.5
LBP-CRF	60.13	61.67	-	-
Color-CRF	59.44	60.45	-	-
Joint-CRF	**60.77**	**61.45**	**62.49**	**59.13**

multiple instances of cars at different scales and orientations. We made use of the 300 pseudo-stereo pairs provided by [3], which were generated in the same manner as described above for the Pedestrian dataset. Since no training pairs are provided, we extracted them in the same fashion, while ensuring no overlap with the test pairs. This resulted in a total of 410 training pairs.

The results of our approach and the baselines on this dataset are reported in Table 2. Note that, since it is dedicated to human co-detection, the method of [24] does not apply to this dataset. As in the Pedestrian case, our approach yields a significant performance improvement over the baselines. This is the case both with the single-feature models and with our Joint-CRF model. Sample co-detections are provided in Fig. 5. In addition, we also use random pairs, as in [3], for evaluation and obtain similar results. This shows that our method does not rely on the temporal information in the dataset.

Similarly to the Pedestrian case, in Fig. 6, we illustrate the quality of the learned similarity function by depicting the similarity matrix obtained when applying this function to one test pair. We can again see that the predicted similarity correctly reflects the ground-truth one.

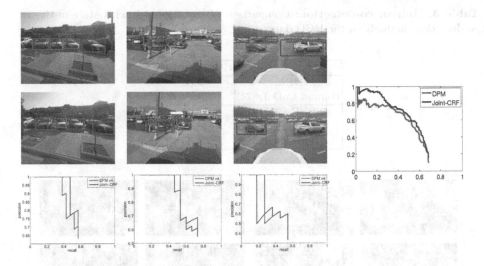

Fig. 5. Sample Results: Examples of our co-detection results on test pairs of the Ford Car dataset. Top two rows: Input image pairs (Green dash: our results, Red solid: DPM results); Bottom row: Precision-recall curves of our method and DPM for the three image pairs. The precision-recall curves over all pairs are shown on the right.

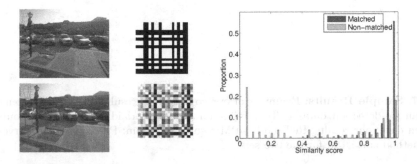

Fig. 6. Predicting similarity: Sample similarity matrix obtained by applying our learned similarity function to one test pair of the Ford Car dataset. Left: Input image pair; Middle: (Top) target (ground truth) similarity matrix, (Bottom) learned similarity matrix (brighter means more similar); Right: Normalized histograms of similarity scores for matched and non-matched candidate pairs.

Human Co-Detection Dataset. The HCD [24] comprises 387 images separated into 26 sets. Each image may contain multiple people, and the appearance of these people is consistent within one set. As opposed to the Ford Car and Pedestrian datasets where only two images with relatively small viewpoint difference are employed for co-detection, all the images in one set of HCD are considered simultaneously and typically depict large viewpoint changes. For our experiments, we followed a leave-five-sets-out strategy, which amounts to using roughly 80% of the images as training data and the remaining 20% (coming from

Table 3. Human co-detection: Comparison of our approach with state-of-the-art co-detection methods on the HCD dataset

	HCD Dataset
DPM	69.64
Human CoDeL [24]	74.94
LBP-CRF	78.81
Color-CRF	79.19
Joint-CRF	**79.41**

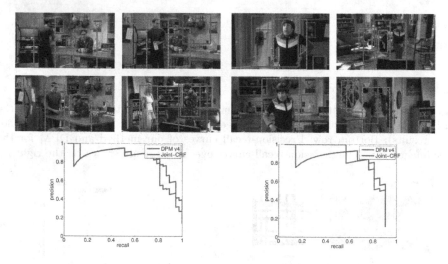

Fig. 7. Sample Results: Examples of our co-detection results on two sets from the Human Co-detection dataset. Top: Input image set overlaid with detection output (Green dash: our results, Red solid: DPM results); Bottom: Precision-recall curves of our method and DPM for the two sets.

five independent sets) as test images. For this dataset, we employed the provided instance-level labels to learn our similarity function. Note however that the main task remains category-level (human) co-detection.

We report our results on this dataset in Table 3. Note that the only reported results on HCD are those of [24]. As for the other datasets, we outperform the baselines, whether using a single feature type or multiple ones. Fig. 7 depicts some of our co-detection results on HCD. For this dataset, we also compare our results with those of a sparse CRF constructed by connecting only the first k nearest neighbors (based on our similarity) of each node, with k ranging from 1 to 50. The best F1 score of this sparse CRF (over all values of k) is 80.45%. This is clearly outperformed by our F1 score of 85.3%.

In Fig. 8, we also show the predicted similarity function for one of the sets in the dataset. Note that, because of the instance-level annotations, the similarity matrix is more complex than before. Nonetheless, our predicted similarity matrix still yields a good approximation of the ground-truth one.

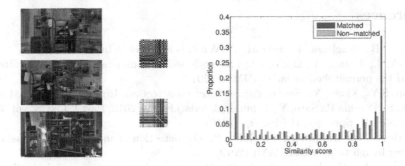

Fig. 8. Predicting similarity: Sample similarity matrix obtained by applying our learned similarity function to one test set in the Human Co-Detection dataset. Left: Input images (three examples); Middle: (Top) target (ground truth) similarity matrix, (Bottom) learned similarity matrix (brighter means more similar); Right: Normalized histograms of similarity scores for matched and non-matched candidate pairs.

Scaling up. As mentioned earlier, inference in our model could in principle also be performed using the Graph-cut algorithm [5]. Here, we study the scalability of both inference strategies with respect to the number of images considered jointly at test time. To this end, we build two fully-connected CRF models with different numbers of test images from the HCD dataset. The first CRF has 330 nodes. In this case, our mean field filtering inference takes 6.5 seconds and the Graph-cut only takes 0.6 second (this includes the time to compute the potential functions). However, when the size of the CRF increases by a factor 10, our method takes 8.5 seconds, which is only mildly slower compared to the previous setting. In contrast, the Graph-cut spends 30 seconds in potential calculation and 60 seconds in inference. This shows that the Graph-cut algorithm does not scale up to larger test sets for fully connected graphs, and thus confirms our choice of inference strategy.

5 Conclusion

In this paper, we have introduced a formulation of object co-detection from a pool of images that expresses the problem as inference in a fully-connected CRF whose nodes represent object candidates. We have then shown that modeling the similarity between pairs of candidates as a weighted mixture of Gaussian kernels allowed us to efficiently perform inference in our graph, while yielding an effective representation for co-detection. Our experimental evaluation has demonstrated that our approach could effectively leverage the information in multiple images to improve detection accuracy, thus outperforming existing co-detection techniques on benchmark datasets. In the future, we intend to study how our framework can be applied to jointly co-detecting different object categories, thus leveraging the collective power not only of multiple images, but also of multiple classes.

References

1. Alexe, B., Deselaers, T., Ferrari, V.: What is an object? In: CVPR (2010)
2. Baek, J., Adams, A., Dolson, J.: Lattice-based high-dimensional gaussian filtering and the permutohedral lattice. JMIV (2013)
3. Bao, S.Y., Xiang, Y., Savarese, S.: Object co-detection. In: Fitzgibbon, A., Lazebnik, S., Perona, P., Sato, Y., Schmid, C. (eds.) ECCV 2012, Part I. LNCS, vol. 7572, pp. 86–101. Springer, Heidelberg (2012)
4. Barinova, O., Lempitsky, V., Kohli, P.: On detection of multiple object instances using hough transforms. PAMI (2012)
5. Boykov, Y., Veksler, O., Zabih, R.: Fast approximate energy minimization via graph cuts. IEEE Trans. PAMI 23(11) (2001)
6. Dalal, N., Triggs, B.: Histograms of oriented gradients for human detection. In: CVPR (2005)
7. Deng, J., Dong, W., Socher, R., Li, L.J., Li, K., Fei-Fei, L.: Imagenet: A large-scale hierarchical image database. In: CVPR (2009)
8. Desai, C., Ramanan, D., Fowlkes, C.: Discriminative models for multi-class object layout. In: ICCV (2009)
9. Dickinson, S.J., Leonardis, A., Schiele, B., Tarr, M.J.: Object Categorization: Computer and Human Vision Perspectives. Cambridge University Press (2009)
10. Endres, I., Hoiem, D.: Category independent object proposals. In: Daniilidis, K., Maragos, P., Paragios, N. (eds.) ECCV 2010, Part V. LNCS, vol. 6315, pp. 575–588. Springer, Heidelberg (2010)
11. Ess, A., Leibe, B., Gool, L.V.: Depth and appearance for mobile scene analysis. In: International Conference on Computer Vision, ICCV 2007 (October 2007)
12. Everingham, M., Van Gool, L., Williams, C.K.I., Winn, J., Zisserman, A.: The pascal visual object classes (voc) challenge. IJCV (2010)
13. Felzenszwalb, P.F., Girshick, R.B., McAllester, D.: Discriminatively trained deformable part models, release 4,
   http://people.cs.uchicago.edu/~pff/latent-release4/
14. Felzenszwalb, P.F., Girshick, R.B., McAllester, D., Ramanan, D.: Object detection with discriminatively trained part based models. IEEE PAMI (2010)
15. Galleguillos, C., Belongie, S.: Context based object categorization: A critical survey. CVIU 114, 712–722 (2010)
16. Girshick, R.B., Donahue, J., Darrell, T., Malik, J.: Rich feature hierarchies for accurate object detection and semantic segmentation. ArXiv 1311.2524 (2013)
17. Gönen, M., Alpaydın, E.: Multiple kernel learning algorithms. JMLR 12 (2011)
18. Guo, X., Liu, D., Jou, B., Zhu, M., Cai, A., Chang, S.F.: Robust Object Co-detection. In: CVPR (2013)
19. Hoiem, D., Efros, A.A., Hebert, M.: Putting Objects in Perspective. IJCV 80, 3–15 (2008)
20. Kolmogorov, V., Zabin, R.: What energy functions can be minimized via graph cuts? IEEE Trans PAMI 26(2) (2004)
21. Krähenbühl, P., Koltun, V.: Efficient inference in fully connected crfs with gaussian edge potentials. In: NIPS (2011)
22. Lowe, D.G.: Object recognition from local scale-invariant features. In: ICCV (1999)
23. Ojala, T., Pietikainen, M., Maenpaa, T.: Multiresolution gray-scale and rotation invariant texture classification with local binary patterns. IEEE Trans. PAMI 24(7) (2002)

24. Shi, J., Liao, R., Jia, J.: CoDeL: An efficient human co-detection and labeling framework. In: ICCV (2013)
25. Uijlings, J., van de Sande, K., Gevers, T., Smeulders, A.: Selective search for object recognition. IJCV (2013)
26. Vedaldi, A., Gulshan, V., Varma, M., Zisserman, A.: Multiple kernels for object detection. In: ICCV (2009)
27. Vineet, V., Warrell, J., Torr, P.H.S.: Filter-based mean-field inference for random fields with higher-order terms and product label-spaces. In: Fitzgibbon, A., Lazebnik, S., Perona, P., Sato, Y., Schmid, C. (eds.) ECCV 2012, Part V. LNCS, vol. 7576, pp. 31–44. Springer, Heidelberg (2012)
28. Viola, P., Jones, M.J.: Robust real-time face detection. Int. J. Comput. Vision 57(2) (2004)
29. Weinberger, K., Blitzer, J., Saul, L.: Distance metric learning for large margin nearest neighbor classification. In: NIPS (2006)
30. Zhang, Y., Chen, T.: Efficient inference for fully-connected crfs with stationarity. In: CVPR (2012)

Spatial Pyramid Pooling in Deep Convolutional Networks for Visual Recognition

Kaiming He[1], Xiangyu Zhang[2,*], Shaoqing Ren[3,*], and Jian Sun[1]

[1] Microsoft Research, China
[2] Xi'an Jiaotong University, China
[3] University of Science and Technology of China

Abstract. Existing deep convolutional neural networks (CNNs) require a fixed-size (*e.g.* 224×224) input image. This requirement is "artificial" and may hurt the recognition accuracy for the images or sub-images of an arbitrary size/scale. In this work, we equip the networks with a more principled pooling strategy, "spatial pyramid pooling", to eliminate the above requirement. The new network structure, called SPP-net, can generate a fixed-length representation regardless of image size/scale. By removing the fixed-size limitation, we can improve all CNN-based image classification methods in general. Our SPP-net achieves state-of-the-art accuracy on the datasets of ImageNet 2012, Pascal VOC 2007, and Caltech101.

The power of SPP-net is more significant in object detection. Using SPP-net, we compute the feature maps from the entire image only once, and then pool features in arbitrary regions (sub-images) to generate fixed-length representations for training the detectors. This method avoids repeatedly computing the convolutional features. In processing test images, our method computes convolutional features 30-170× faster than the recent leading method R-CNN (and 24-64× faster overall), while achieving better or comparable accuracy on Pascal VOC 2007.[1]

1 Introduction

We are witnessing a rapid, revolutionary change in our vision community, mainly caused by deep convolutional neural networks (CNNs) [18] and the availability of large scale training data [6]. Deep-networks-based approaches have recently been substantially improving upon the state of the art in image classification [16,31,24], object detection [12,33,24], many other recognition tasks [22,27,32,13], and even non-recognition tasks.

However, there is a technical issue in the training and testing of the CNNs: the prevalent CNNs require a *fixed* input image size (*e.g.*, 224×224), which limits both the aspect ratio and the scale of the input image. When applied to images of arbitrary sizes, current methods mostly fit the input image to the fixed

---

* This work was done when X. Zhang and S. Ren were interns at Microsoft Research.
[1] A longer technical report of our paper is in http://arxiv.org/abs/1406.4729v1.pdf

D. Fleet et al. (Eds.): ECCV 2014, Part III, LNCS 8691, pp. 346–361, 2014.

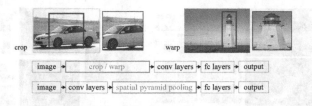

Fig. 1. Top: cropping or warping to fit a fixed size. Middle: a conventional deep convolutional network structure. Bottom: our spatial pyramid pooling network structure.

size, either via cropping [16,31] or via warping [7,12], as shown in Fig. 1 (top). But the cropped region may not contain the entire object, while the warped content may result in unwanted geometric distortion. Recognition accuracy can be compromised due to the content loss or distortion. Besides, a pre-defined scale (*e.g.*, 224) may not be suitable when object scales vary. Fixing the input size overlooks the issues involving scales.

So why do CNNs require a fixed input size? A CNN mainly consists of two parts: convolutional layers, and fully-connected layers that follow. The convolutional layers operate in a sliding-window manner and output feature maps which represent the spatial arrangement of the activations (Fig. 2). In fact, convolutional layers do not require a fixed image size and can generate feature maps of any sizes. On the other hand, the fully-connected layers need to have fixed-size/length input by their definition. Hence, the fixed-size constraint comes only from the fully-connected layers, which exist at a deeper stage of the network.

In this paper, we introduce a *spatial pyramid pooling* (SPP) [14,17] layer to remove the fixed-size constraint of the network. Specifically, we add an SPP layer on top of the last convolutional layer. The SPP layer pools the features and generates fixed-length outputs, which are then fed into the fully-connected layers (or other classifiers). In other words, we perform some information "aggregation" at a deeper stage of the network hierarchy (between convolutional layers and fully-connected layers) to avoid the need for cropping or warping at the beginning. Fig. 1 (bottom) shows the change of the network architecture by introducing the SPP layer. We call the new network structure *SPP-net*.

We believe that aggregation at a deeper stage is more physiologically sound and more compatible with the hierarchical information processing in our brains. When an object comes into our field of view, it is more reasonable that our brains consider it as a whole instead of cropping it into several "views" at the beginning. Similarly, it is unlikely that our brains distort all object candidates into fixed-size regions for detecting/locating them. It is more likely that our brains handle arbitrarily-shaped objects at some deeper layers, by aggregating the already deeply processed information from the previous layers.

Spatial pyramid pooling [14,17] (popularly known as spatial pyramid matching or SPM [17]), as an extension of the Bag-of-Words (BoW) model [25], is one of the most successful methods in computer vision. It partitions the image into divisions from finer to coarser levels, and aggregates local features in them. SPP has long been a key component in the leading and competition-winning systems

Fig. 2. Visualization of the feature maps. (a) Two images in Pascal VOC 2007. (b) The feature maps of some conv5 (the fifth convolutional layer) filters. The arrows indicate the strongest responses and their corresponding positions in the images. (c) The ImageNet images that have the strongest responses of the corresponding filters. The green rectangles mark the receptive fields of the strongest responses.

for classification (*e.g.*, [30,28,21]) and detection (*e.g.*, [23]) before the recent prevalence of CNNs. Nevertheless, SPP has not been considered in the context of CNNs. We note that SPP has several remarkable properties for deep CNNs: 1) SPP is able to generate a fixed-length output regardless of the input size, while the sliding window pooling used in the previous deep networks [16] cannot; 2) SPP uses multi-level spatial bins, while the sliding window pooling uses only a single window size. Multi-level pooling has been shown to be robust to object deformations [17]; 3) SPP can pool features extracted at variable scales thanks to the flexibility of input scales. Through experiments we show that all these factors elevate the recognition accuracy of deep networks.

The flexibility of SPP-net makes it possible to generate a full-image representation for testing. Moreover, it also allows us to feed images with varying sizes or scales during training, which increases scale-invariance and reduces the risk of over-fitting. We develop a simple multi-size training method to exploit the properties of SPP-net. Through a series of controlled experiments, we demonstrate the gains of using multi-level pooling, full-image representations, and variable scales. On the ImageNet 2012 dataset, our network reduces the top-1 error by 1.8% compared to its counterpart without SPP. The fixed-length representations given by this pre-trained network are also used to train SVM classifiers on other datasets. Our method achieves 91.4% accuracy on Caltech101 [9] and 80.1% mean Average Precision (mAP) on Pascal VOC 2007 [8] using only a *single* full-image representation (single-view testing).

SPP-net shows even greater strength in object detection. In the leading object detection method R-CNN [12], the features from candidate windows are extracted via deep convolutional networks. This method shows remarkable detection accuracy on both the VOC and ImageNet datasets. But the feature computation in R-CNN is time-consuming, because it repeatedly applies the deep convolutional networks to the raw pixels of thousands of warped regions per image. In this paper, we show that we can run the convolutional layers only *once* on the entire image (regardless of the number of windows), and then extract features by SPP-net on the feature maps. This method yields a speedup of over one hundred times over R-CNN. Note that training/running a detector on the feature maps (rather than image regions) is actually a more popular idea [10,5,23,24]. But SPP-net inherits the power of the deep CNN feature maps and also the flexibility of SPP on arbitrary window sizes, which leads to outstanding accuracy and efficiency. In our experiment, the SPP-net-based system (built upon the R-CNN pipeline) computes convolutional features 30-170× faster than R-CNN, and is overall 24-64× faster, while has better or comparable accuracy. We further propose a simple model combination method to achieve a new state-of-the-art result (mAP 60.9%) on the Pascal VOC 2007 detection task.

2   Deep Networks with Spatial Pyramid Pooling

2.1   Convolutional Layers and Feature Maps

Consider the popular seven-layer architectures [16,31]. The first five layers are convolutional, some of which are followed by pooling layers. These pooling layers can also be considered as "convolutional", in the sense that they are using sliding windows. The last two layers are fully connected, with an N-way softmax as the output, where N is the number of categories.

The deep network described above needs a fixed image size. However, we notice the requirement of fixed sizes is only due to the fully-connected layers that demand fixed-length vectors as inputs. On the other hand, the convolutional layers accept inputs of arbitrary sizes. The convolutional layers use sliding filters, and their outputs have roughly the same aspect ratio as the inputs. These outputs are known as *feature maps* [18] - they involve not only the strength of the responses, but also their spatial positions. In Fig. 2, we visualize some feature maps. They are generated by some filters of the conv$_5$ layer.

It is worth noticing that we generate the feature maps in Fig. 2 without fixing the input size. These feature maps generated by deep convolutional layers are analogous to the feature maps in traditional methods [2,4]. In those methods, SIFT vectors [2] or image patches [4] are densely extracted and then encoded, *e.g.*, by vector quantization [25,17,11], sparse coding [30,28], or Fisher kernels [21]. These encoded features consist of the feature maps, and are then pooled by Bag-of-Words (BoW) [25] or spatial pyramids [14,17]. Analogously, the deep convolutional features can be pooled in a similar way.

2.2   The Spatial Pyramid Pooling Layer

The convolutional layers accept arbitrary input sizes, but they produce outputs of variable sizes. The classifiers (SVM/softmax) or fully-connected layers require fixed-length vectors. Such vectors can be generated by the Bag-of-Words (BoW) approach [25] that pools the features together. Spatial pyramid pooling [14,17] improves BoW in that it can maintain spatial information by pooling in local spatial bins. These spatial bins have sizes proportional to the image size, so the number of bins is fixed regardless of the image size. This is in contrast to the

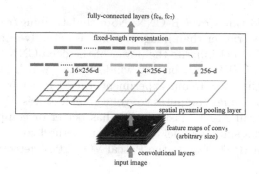

Fig. 3. The network structure with a **spatial pyramid pooling layer**

sliding window pooling of the previous deep networks [16], where the number of sliding windows depends on the input size.

To adopt the deep network for images of arbitrary sizes, we replace the pool_5 layer (the pooling layer after conv_5) with a *spatial pyramid pooling layer*. Fig. 3 illustrates our method. In each spatial bin, we pool the responses of each filter (throughout this paper we use max pooling). The outputs of SPP are $256M$-d vectors with the number of bins denoted as M (256 is the number of conv_5 filters). The fixed-dimensional vectors are the input to the fc layer (fc_6).

With SPP, the input image can be of any sizes; this not only allows arbitrary aspect ratios, but also allows arbitrary scales. We can resize the input image to any scale (*e.g.*, $\min(w, h)$=180, 224, ...) and apply the same deep network. When the input image is at different scales, the network (with the same filter sizes) will extract features at different scales. The scales play important roles in traditional methods, *e.g.*, the SIFT vectors are often extracted at multiple scales [19,2] (determined by the sizes of the patches and Gaussian filters). We will show that the scales are also important for the accuracy of deep networks.

2.3 Training the Network with the Spatial Pyramid Pooling Layer

Theoretically, the above network structure can be trained with standard back-propagation [18], regardless of the input image size. But in practice the GPU implementations (such as *convnet* [16] and *Caffe* [7]) are preferably run on fixed input images. Next we describe our training solution that takes advantage of these GPU implementations while still preserving the SPP behaviors.

Single-Size Training. As in previous works, we first consider a network taking a fixed-size input (224×224) cropped from images. The cropping is for the purpose of data augmentation. For an image with a given size, we can pre-compute the bin sizes needed for spatial pyramid pooling. Consider the feature maps

```
[pool3x3]        [pool2x2]        [pool1x1]        [fc6]
type=pool        type=pool        type=pool        type=fc
pool=max         pool=max         pool=max         outputs=4096
inputs=conv5     inputs=conv5     inputs=conv5     inputs=pool3x3,pool2x2,pool1x1
sizeX=5          sizeX=7          sizeX=13
stride=4         stride=6         stride=13
```

Fig. 4. An example 3-level pyramid pooling in the convnet style [16]. Here sizeX is the size of the pooling window. This is for a network whose feature map size of conv$_5$ is 13×13, so pool$_{3\times3}$, pool$_{2\times2}$, and pool$_{1\times1}$ will have 3×3, 2×2, and 1×1 bins respectively.

after conv$_5$ that have a size of $a\times a$ (e.g., 13×13). With a pyramid level of $n\times n$ bins, we implement this pooling level as a sliding window pooling, where the window size $win = \lceil a/n \rceil$ and stride $str = \lfloor a/n \rfloor$ with $\lceil \cdot \rceil$ and $\lfloor \cdot \rfloor$ denoting ceiling and floor operations. With an l-level pyramid, we implement l such layers. The next fc layer (fc$_6$) will concatenate the l outputs. Fig. 4 shows an example configuration of 3-level pyramid pooling (3×3, 2×2, 1×1) in the *convnet* style [16].

The main purpose of our single-size training is to enable the multi-level pooling behavior. Experiments show that this is one reason for the gain of accuracy.

Multi-size Training. Our network with SPP is expected to be applied on images of any sizes. To address the issue of varying image sizes in training, we consider a set of pre-defined sizes. We use two sizes (180×180 in addition to 224×224) in this paper. Rather than crop a smaller 180×180 region, we resize the aforementioned 224×224 region to 180×180. So the regions at both scales differ only in resolution but not in content/layout. For the network to accept 180×180 inputs, we implement another fixed-size-input (180×180) network. The feature map size after conv$_5$ is $a\times a = 10\times10$ in this case. Then we still use $win = \lceil a/n \rceil$ and $str = \lfloor a/n \rfloor$ to implement each pyramid level. The output of the SPP layer of this 180-network has the same fixed length as the 224-network. As such, this 180-network has exactly the same parameters as the 224-network in each layer. In other words, during training we implement the varying-size-input SPP-net by two fixed-size-input networks that share parameters.

To reduce the overhead to switch from one network (e.g., 224) to the other (e.g., 180), we train each full epoch on one network, and then switch to the other one (copying all weights) for the next full epoch. This is iterated. In experiments, we find the convergence rate of this multi-size training to be similar to the above single-size training. We train 70 epochs in total as is a common practice.

The main purpose of multi-size training is to simulate the varying input sizes while still leveraging the existing well-optimized fixed-size implementations. In theory, we could use more scales/aspect ratios, with one network for each scale/aspect ratio and all networks sharing weights, or we could develop a varying-size implementation to avoid switching. We will study this in the future.

Note that the above single/multi-size solutions are for training only. At the testing stage, it is straightforward to apply SPP-net on images of any sizes.

Table 1. Error rates in the validation set of ImageNet 2012. All the results are based on **a single network**. The number of views in Overfeat depends on the scales and strides, for which there are several hundreds at the finest scale.

	method	test scale	test views	top-1 val	top-5 val
(a)	Krizhevsky et al.[16]	1	10	40.7	18.2
(b1)	Overfeat (fast) [24]	1	-	39.01	16.97
(b2)	Overfeat (fast) [24]	6	-	38.12	16.27
(b3)	Overfeat (big) [24]	4	-	35.74	14.18
(c1)	Howard (base) [15]	3	162	37.0	15.8
(c2)	Howard (high-res) [15]	3	162	36.8	16.2
(d1)	Zeiler & Fergus (ZF) (fast) [31]	1	10	38.4	16.5
(d2)	Zeiler & Fergus (ZF) (big) [31]	1	10	37.5	16.0
(e1)	our impl of ZF (fast)	1	10	35.99	14.76
(e2)	SPP-net$_4$, single-size trained	1	10	35.06	14.04
(e3)	SPP-net$_6$, single-size trained	1	10	34.98	14.14
(e4)	SPP-net$_6$, multi-size trained	1	10	34.60	13.64
(e5)	SPP-net$_6$, multi-size trained	1	8+2full	**34.16**	**13.57**

3   SPP-Net for Image Classification

3.1   Experiments on ImageNet 2012 Classification

We trained our network on the 1000-category training set of ImageNet 2012. Our training details follow the practices of previous work [16,31,15]. The images are resized so that the smaller dimension is 256, and a 224×224 crop is picked from the center or the four corners from the entire image[2]. The data are augmented by horizontal flipping and color altering [16]. Dropout [16] is used on the two fully-connected layers. The learning rate starts from 0.01, and is divided by 10 (twice) when the error plateaus. Our implementation is based on the publicly available code of *convnet* [16]. Our experiments are run on a GTX Titan GPU.

As our baseline model, we implement the 7-layer network of Zeiler and Fergus's (ZF) "fast" (smaller) model [31], which produces competitive results with a moderate training time (two weeks). The filter numbers (sizes) of the five convolutional layers are: $96(7 \times 7)$, $256(5 \times 5)$, $384(3 \times 3)$, $384(3 \times 3)$, and $256(3 \times 3)$. The first two layers have a stride of 2, and the rest have a stride of 1. The first two layers are followed by (sliding window) max pooling with a stride of 2, window size of 3, and contrast normalization operations. The outputs of the two fully-connected layers are 4096-d. At the testing stage, we follow the standard 10-view prediction in [16]: each view is a 224×224 crop and their scores are averaged. Our replication of this network gives 35.99% top-1 error (Tab. 1 (e1)), better than 38.4% (Tab. 1 (d1)) as reported in [31]. We believe this margin is because the corner crops are from the entire image (rather than from the corners of the central 256×256 square), as is reported in [15].

Tab. 1 (e2)(e3) show our results using single-size training. The training and testing sizes are both 224×224. In these networks, the convolutional layers have the same structures as the ZF fast model, whereas the pooling layer after conv$_5$ is replaced with the SPP layer. We use a 4-level pyramid. The pyramid is {4×4,

---

[2] In [16], the four corners are picked from the corners of the central 256×256 crop.

Table 2. Error rates in the validation set of ImageNet 2012 using a single view. The images are resized so $\min(w, h) = 256$. The crop view is the central 224×224

method	test view	top-1 val
SPP-net$_6$, single-size trained	1 crop	38.01
SPP-net$_6$, single-size trained	1 full	**37.55**
SPP-net$_6$, multi-size trained	1 crop	37.57
SPP-net$_6$, multi-size trained	1 full	**37.07**

3×3, 2×2, 1×1}, totally 30 bins and denoted as SPP-net$_4$ (e2), or {6×6, 3×3, 2×2, 1×1}, totally 50 bins and denoted as SPP-net$_6$ (e3). In these results, we use 10-view prediction with each view a 224×224 crop. The top-1 error of SPP-net$_4$ is 35.06%, and of SPP-net$_6$ is 34.98%. These results show considerable improvement over the no-SPP counterpart (e1). Since we are still using the same 10 cropped views as in (e1), this gain is solely because of multi-level pooling. Note that SPP-net$_4$ has even fewer parameters than the no-SPP model (fc$_6$ has 30×256-d inputs instead of 36×256-d). So the gain of the multi-level pooling is **not** simply due to more parameters. Rather, it is because the multi-level pooling is robust to the variance in object deformations and spatial layout [17].

Tab. 1 (e4) shows our result using multi-size training. The training sizes are 224 and 180, while the testing size is still 224. In (e4) we still use the 10 cropped views for prediction. The top-1 error drops to 34.60%. Note the networks in (e3) and (e4) have exactly the same structure and the same method for testing. So the gain is solely because of the multi-size training.

Next we investigate the accuracy of the full-image views. We resize the image so that $\min(w, h)$=256 while maintaining its aspect ratio. The SPP-net is applied on this full image to compute the scores of the full view. For fair comparison, we also evaluate the accuracy of the single view in the center 224×224 crop (which is used in the above evaluations). The comparisons of single-view testing accuracy are in Tab. 2. The top-1 error rates are reduced by about 0.5%. This shows the importance of maintaining the complete content. Even though our network is trained using square images only, it generalizes well to other aspect ratios.

In Tab. 1 (e5), we replace the two center cropped views with two full-views (with flipping) for testing. The top-1 error is further reduced to 34.16%. This again indicates that the full-image views are more representative than the cropped views[3]. The SPP-net in (e5) is better than the no-SPP counterpart (e1) by 1.8%.

There are previous CNN solutions [24,15] that deal with various scales/sizes, but they are based on model averaging. In Overfeat [24] and Howard's method [15], the single network is applied at multiple scales in the testing stage, and the scores are averaged. Howard further trains two different networks on low/high-resolution image regions and averages the scores. These methods generate much more views (*e.g.*, over hundreds), but the sizes of the views are still pre-defined beforehand. On the contrary, our method builds the SPP structure into the

---

[3] However, the combination of the 8 cropped views is still useful.

Table 3. Classification mAP in Pascal VOC 2007

model size	(a) plain net crop 224×224	(b) SPP-net crop 224×224	(c) SPP-net full 224×-	(d) SPP-net full 392×-
conv$_4$	59.96	57.28	-	-
conv$_5$	66.34	65.43	-	-
pool$_5$ (6×6)	69.14	68.76	70.82	71.67
fc$_6$	74.86	75.55	77.32	78.78
fc$_7$	75.90	76.45	78.39	**80.10**

Table 4. Classification accuracy in Caltech101

model size	(a) plain net 224×224 crop	(b) SPP-net 224×224 crop	(c) SPP-net 224×- full
conv$_4$	80.12	81.03	-
conv$_5$	84.40	83.76	-
pool$_5$ (6×6)	87.98	87.60	89.46
SPP pool$_5$	-	89.47	**91.44**
fc$_6$	87.86	88.54	89.50
fc$_7$	85.30	86.10	87.08

network, and uses multi-size images to train a single network. Our method also enables the use of full-view as a single image representation.

Our results can be potentially improved further. The usage of the SPP layer does not depend on the design of the convolutional layers. So our method may benefit from, *e.g.*, increased filter numbers or smaller strides [31,24]. Multiple-model averaging also may be applied. We will study these in the future.

3.2   Experiments on Pascal VOC 2007 Classification

With the networks pre-trained on ImageNet, we extract representations from the images in other datasets and re-train SVM classifiers [1] for the new datasets. In the SVM training, we intentionally do not use any data augmentation (flip/multi-view). We l_2-normalize the features and fix the SVM's soft margin parameter C to 1. We use our multi-size trained model in Tab. 1 (e5).

The classification task in Pascal VOC 2007 [8] involves 9,963 images in 20 categories. 5,011 images are for training, and the rest are for testing. The performance is evaluated by mAP. Tab. 3 summarizes our results for different settings.

We start from a baseline in Tab. 3 (a). The model is the one in Tab. 1 (e1) without SPP ("plain net"). To apply this model, we resize the image so that $\min(w, h) = 224$, and crop the center 224×224 region. The SVM is trained via the features of a layer. On this dataset, the deeper the layer is, the better the result is. In col.(b), we replace the plain net with our SPP-net. As a first-step comparison, we still apply the SPP-net on the center 224×224 crop. The results of the fc layers improve. This gain is mainly due to multi-level pooling.

Tab. 3 (c) shows our results on the full images which are resized so that $\min(w, h) = 224$. The results are considerably improved (78.39% *vs.* 76.45%). This is due to the full-image representation that maintains the complete content.

Because the usage of our network does not depend on scale, we resize the images so that $\min(w, h) = s$ and use the same network to extract features. We

Table 5. Classification results for Pascal VOC 2007 (mAP) and Caltech101 (accuracy). [†]numbers reported by [2]. [‡]our implementation as in Tab. 3 (a)

method	VOC 2007	Caltech101
VQ [17][†]	56.07	74.41±1.0
LLC [28][†]	57.66	76.95±0.4
FK [21][†]	61.69	77.78±0.6
DeCAF [7]	-	86.91±0.7
Zeiler & Fergus [31]	75.90[‡]	86.5±0.5
Oquab et al.[20]	77.7	-
ours	**80.10**	**91.44±0.7**

find that $s = 392$ gives the best results (Tab. 3 (d)) based on the validation set. This is mainly because the objects occupy smaller regions in VOC 2007 but larger regions in ImageNet, so the relative object scales are different between the two sets. These results indicate scale matters in the classification tasks, and SPP-net can partially address this "scale mismatch" issue.

Tab. 5 summarizes our results and the comparisons with previous state-of-the-art methods. Among these methods, VQ [17], LCC [28], and FK [21] are all based on spatial pyramids matching, and [7,31,20] are based on deep networks. Our method outperforms these methods. We note that Oquab et al.[20] achieves 77.7% with 500 views per image, whereas we achieve **80.10%** with a single full-image view. Our result may be further improved if data argumentation, multi-view testing, or network fine-tuning is used.

3.3 Experiments on Caltech101

Caltech101 [9] contains 9,144 images in 102 categories (one background). We randomly sample 30 images/category for training and up to 50 images/category for testing. We repeat 10 random splits and average the accuracy.

Tab. 4 summarizes our results. There are some common observations in the Pascal VOC 2007 and Caltech101 results: SPP-net is better than the plain net (Tab. 4 (b) vs. (a)), and the full-view representation is better than the crop ((c) vs. (b)). But the results in Caltech101 have some differences with Pascal VOC. The fully-connected layers are less accurate, and the $pool_5$ and SPP layers are better. This is possibly because the object categories in Caltech101 are less related to those in ImageNet, and the deeper layers are more category-specialized. Further, we find that the scale 224 has the best performance among the scales we tested on this dataset. This is mainly because the objects in Caltech101 also occupy large regions of the images, as is the case of ImageNet.

Tab. 5 summarizes our results compared with several previous state-of-the-art methods on Caltech101. Our result (**91.44%**) exceeds the previous state-of-the-art results (86.91%) by a substantial margin (4.5%).

4   SPP-Net for Object Detection

Deep networks have been used for object detection. We briefly review the recent state-of-the-art R-CNN method [12]. R-CNN first extracts about 2,000 candidate windows from each image via selective search [23]. Then the image region in each window is warped to a fixed size (227×227). A pre-trained deep network is used to extract the feature of each window. A binary SVM classifier is then trained on these features for detection. R-CNN generates results of compelling quality and substantially outperforms previous methods (30% relative improvement!). However, because R-CNN repeatedly applies the deep convolutional network to about 2,000 windows per image, it is time-consuming.

Our SPP-net can also be used for object detection. We extract the feature maps from the entire image only once. Then we apply the spatial pyramid pooling on each candidate window of the feature maps to pool a fixed-length representation of this window (see Fig. 5). Because the time-consuming convolutional network is only applied once, our method can run *orders of magnitude* faster.

Our method extracts window-wise features from regions of the feature maps, while R-CNN extracts directly from image regions. In previous works, the Deformable Part Model (DPM) [10] extracts from windows in HOG [5] feature maps, and Selective Search [23] extracts from windows in encoded SIFT feature maps. The Overfeat detection method [24] also extracts from windows in CNN feature maps, but needs to pre-define the window size. On the contrary, our method enables feature extraction in any windows from CNN feature maps.

4.1 Detection Algorithm

We use the "fast" mode of selective search [23] to generate about 2,000 candidate windows per image. Then we resize the image such that $\min(w, h) = s$, and extract the feature maps of conv$_5$ from the entire image. We use our pre-trained model of Tab. 1 (e3) for the time being. In each candidate window, we use a 4-level spatial pyramid (1×1, 2×2, 3×3, 6×6, totally 50 bins) to pool the features. This generates a 12,800-d (256×50) representation for each window. These representations are provided to the fully-connected layers of the network. Then we train a binary linear SVM classifier for each category on these features.

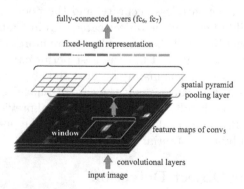

Fig. 5. SPP-net for object detection. The feature maps are computed from the entire image. The pooling is performed in candidate windows.

Our implementation of the SVM training follows [23,12]. We use the ground-truth windows to generate the positive samples. The negative samples are those overlapping a positive window by at most 30% . Any negative sample is removed if it overlaps another negative sample by more than 70%. We apply the standard hard negative mining [10] to train the SVM. This step is iterated once. It takes less than 1 hour to train SVMs for all 20 categories. In testing, the classifier is used to score the candidate windows. Then we use non-maximum suppression [10] (threshold of 30%) on the scored windows.

Our method can be improved by multi-scale feature extraction. We resize the image such that $\min(w, h) = s \in \mathcal{S} = \{480, 576, 688, 864, 1200\}$, and compute the feature maps of conv_5 for each scale. One strategy of combining the features from these scales is to pool them channel-by-channel. But we empirically find that another strategy provides better results. For each candidate window, we choose a single scale $s \in \mathcal{S}$ such that the scaled candidate window has a number of pixels closest to 224×224. Then we only use the feature maps extracted from this scale to compute the feature of this window. If the pre-defined scales are dense enough and the window is approximately square, our method is roughly equivalent to resizing the window to 224×224 and then extracting features from it. Nevertheless, our method only requires computing the feature maps once (at each scale) from the entire image, regardless of the number of candidate windows.

We also fine-tune our pre-trained network, following [12]. Since our features are pooled from the conv_5 feature maps from windows of any sizes, for simplicity we only fine-tune the fully-connected layers. In this case, the data layer accepts the fixed-length pooled features after conv_5, and the $\mathrm{fc}_{6,7}$ layers and a new 21-way (one extra negative category) fc_8 layer follow. The fc_8 weights are initialized with a Gaussian distribution of $\sigma{=}0.01$. We fix all the learning rates to 1e-4 and then adjust to 1e-5 for all three layers. During fine-tuning, the positive samples are those overlapping with a ground-truth window by $[0.5, 1]$, and the negative samples by $[0.1, 0.5)$. In each mini-batch, 25% of the samples are positive. We train 250k mini-batches using the learning rate 1e-4, and then 50k mini-batches using 1e-5. Because we only fine-tune the fc layers, the training is very fast and takes about 2 hours on the GPU. Also following [12], we use bounding box regression to post-process the prediction windows. The features used for regression are the pooled features from conv_5 (as a counterpart of the pool_5 features used in [12]). The windows used for the regression training are those overlapping with a ground-truth window by at least 50%.

We will release the code to facilitate reproduction of the results[4].

4.2   Detection Results

We evaluate our method on the detection task of the Pascal VOC 2007 dataset. Tab. 6 shows our results on various layers, by using 1-scale ($s{=}688$) or 5-scale. Using the pool_5 layers (in our case the pooled features), our result (44.9%) is comparable with R-CNN's result (44.2%). But using the non-fine-tuned fc_6

---

[4] research.microsoft.com/en-us/um/people/kahe/

Table 6. Detection results (mAP) on Pascal VOC 2007. "ft" and "bb" denote fine-tuning and bounding box regression. More details are in our technical report

	SPP (1-sc)	SPP (5-sc)	R-CNN
pool$_5$	43.0	44.9	44.2
fc$_6$	42.5	44.8	46.2
ftfc$_6$	52.3	53.7	53.1
ftfc$_7$	54.5	55.2	54.2
ftfc$_7$ bb	58.0	59.2	58.5
conv time (GPU)	0.053s	0.293s	8.96s
fc time (GPU)	0.089s	0.089s	0.07s
total time (GPU)	0.142s	0.382s	9.03s
speedup (vs. RCNN)	64×	24×	-

Table 7. Comparisons of detection results on Pascal VOC 2007

method	mAP	areo	bike	bird	boat	bottle	bus	car	cat	chair	cow	table	dog	horse	mbike	person	plant	sheep	sofa	train	tv
DPM [10]	33.7	33.2	60.3	10.2	16.1	27.3	54.3	58.2	23.0	20.0	24.1	26.7	12.7	58.1	48.2	43.2	12.0	21.1	36.1	46.0	43.5
SS [23]	33.8	43.5	46.5	10.4	12.0	9.3	49.4	53.7	39.4	12.5	36.9	42.2	26.4	47.0	52.4	23.5	12.1	29.9	36.3	42.2	48.8
Regionlet [29]	41.7	54.2	52.0	20.3	24.0	20.1	55.5	68.7	42.6	19.2	44.2	49.1	26.6	57.0	54.5	43.4	16.4	36.6	37.7	59.4	52.3
DetNet [26]	30.5	29.2	35.2	19.4	16.7	3.7	53.2	50.2	27.2	10.2	34.8	30.2	28.2	46.6	41.7	26.2	10.3	32.8	26.8	39.8	47.0
RCNN ftfc$_7$	54.2	64.2	69.7	50.0	41.9	32.0	62.6	71.0	60.7	32.7	58.5	46.5	56.1	60.6	66.8	54.2	31.5	52.8	48.9	57.9	64.7
SPP ftfc$_7$	55.2	65.5	65.9	51.7	38.4	32.7	62.6	68.6	69.7	33.1	66.6	53.1	58.2	63.6	68.8	50.4	27.4	53.7	48.2	61.7	64.7
RCNN ftfc$_7$ bb	58.5	68.1	72.8	56.8	43.0	36.8	66.3	74.2	67.6	34.4	63.5	54.5	61.2	69.1	68.6	58.7	33.4	62.9	51.1	62.5	64.8
SPP ftfc$_7$ bb	59.2	68.6	69.7	57.1	41.2	40.5	66.3	71.3	72.5	34.4	67.3	61.7	63.1	71.0	69.8	57.6	29.7	59.0	50.2	65.2	68.0

layers, our results are inferior. An explanation is that our fc layers are pre-trained using image regions, while in the detection case they are used on the feature map regions. The feature map regions can have strong activations near the window boundaries, while the image regions may not. This difference of usages can be addressed by fine-tuning. Using the fine-tuned fc layers (ftfc$_{6,7}$), our results are comparable with or slightly better than the fine-tuned results of R-CNN. After bounding box regression, our 5-scale result (**59.2%**) is 0.7% better than R-CNN (58.5%), and our 1-scale result (58.0%) is 0.5% worse. In Tab. 7, we show the results for each category. Our method outperforms R-CNN in 11 categories, and has comparable numbers in two more categories.

In Tab. 7, Selective Search (SS) [23] applies spatial pyramid matching on SIFT feature maps. DPM [10] and Regionlet [29] are based on HOG features [5]. Regionlet improves to 46.1% [33] by combining various features including conv$_5$. DetectorNet [26] trains a deep network that outputs pixel-wise object masks. This method only needs to apply the deep network once to the entire image, as is the case for our method. But this method has lower mAP (30.5%).

4.3   Complexity and Running Time

Despite having comparable accuracy, our method is much faster than R-CNN. The complexity of the convolutional feature computation in R-CNN is $O(n \cdot 227^2)$ with the window number n (~2000). This complexity of our method is $O(r \cdot s^2)$ at a scale s, where r is the aspect ratio. Assume r is about 4/3. In the single-scale version when $s = 688$, this complexity is about 1/160 of R-CNN's; in the 5-scale version, this complexity is about 1/24 of R-CNN's.

Table 8. Detection results on Pascal VOC 2007 using model combination

method	mAP	areo	bike	bird	boat	bottle	bus	car	cat	chair	cow	table	dog	horse	mbike	person	plant	sheep	sofa	train	tv
SPP-net (1)	59.2	**68.6**	69.7	57.1	41.2	40.5	66.3	71.3	72.5	34.4	**67.3**	61.7	63.1	71.0	69.8		57.6	29.7	59.0	50.2	65.2	68.0
SPP-net (2)	59.1	65.7	71.4	57.4	**42.4**	39.9	67.0	71.4	70.6	32.4	66.7	61.7	64.8	71.7	70.4		56.5	30.8	59.9	53.2	63.9	64.6
combination	**60.9**	68.5	**71.7**	**58.7**	41.9	**42.5**	**67.7**	**72.1**	**73.8**	34.7	67.0	**63.4**	**66.0**	**72.5**	**71.3**		**58.9**	**32.8**	**60.9**	**56.1**	**67.9**	**68.8**

In Tab. 6, we compare the experimental running time of the convolutional feature computation. The implementation of R-CNN is from the code published by the authors implemented in *Caffe* [7]. For fair comparison, we also implement our feature computation in *Caffe*. In Tab. 6 we evaluate the average time of 100 random VOC images using GPU. R-CNN takes 8.96s per image, while our 1-scale version takes only 0.053s per image. So ours is 170× faster than R-CNN. Our 5-scale version takes 0.293s per image, so is 30× faster than R-CNN.

Our convolutional feature computation is so fast that the computational time of fc layers takes a considerable portion. Tab. 6 shows that the GPU time of computing the 4,096-d fc_7 features (from the $conv_5$ feature maps) is 0.089s per image. Considering both convolutional and fully-connected features, our 1-scale version is 64× faster than R-CNN and is just 0.5% inferior in mAP; our 5-scale version is 24× faster and has better results. The overhead of the fc computation can be significantly reduced if smaller fc layers are used, *e.g.*, 1,024-d.

We do not consider the window proposal time in the above comparison. The selective search window proposal [23] takes about 1-2 seconds per image on the CPU. There are recent works (*e.g.*, [3]) on reducing window proposal time to milliseconds. We will evaluate this and expect a fast entire system.

4.4 Model Combination for Detection

Model combination is an important strategy for boosting CNN-based classification accuracy [16]. Next we propose a simple model combination method for detection. We pre-train another network in ImageNet, using the same structure but different random initializations. Then we repeat the above detection algorithm. Tab. 8 (SPP-net (2)) shows the results of this network. Its mAP is comparable with the first network (59.1% *vs.* 59.2%), and outperforms the first network in 11 categories. Given the two models, we first use either model to score all candidate windows on the test image. Then we perform non-maximum suppression on the union of the two sets of candidate windows (with their scores). A more confident window given by one method can suppress those less confident given by the other method. After combination, the mAP is boosted to **60.9%** (Tab. 8). In 17 out of all 20 categories the combination performs better than either individual model. This indicates that the two models are complementary.

5   Conclusion

Image scales and sizes are important in visual recognition, but received little consideration in the context of deep networks. We have suggested a solution to train a deep network with an SPP layer. The resulting SPP-net shows outstanding accuracy in classification/detection tasks and greatly accelerates DNN-based detection. Our studies also show that many time-proven techniques/insights in computer vision can still play important roles in deep-networks-based recognition.

References

1. Chang, C.C., Lin, C.J.: Libsvm: A library for support vector machines. ACM Transactions on Intelligent Systems and Technology, TIST (2011)
2. Chatfield, K., Lempitsky, V., Vedaldi, A., Zisserman, A.: The devil is in the details: An evaluation of recent feature encoding methods. In: BMVC (2011)
3. Cheng, M.M., Zhang, Z., Lin, W.Y., Torr, P.: BING: Binarized normed gradients for objectness estimation at 300fps. In: CVPR (2014)
4. Coates, A., Ng, A.: The importance of encoding versus training with sparse coding and vector quantization. In: ICML (2011)
5. Dalal, N., Triggs, B.: Histograms of oriented gradients for human detection. In: CVPR (2005)
6. Deng, J., Dong, W., Socher, R., Li, L.J., Li, K., Fei-Fei, L.: Imagenet: A large-scale hierarchical image database. In: CVPR (2009)
7. Donahue, J., Jia, Y., Vinyals, O., Hoffman, J., Zhang, N., Tzeng, E., Darrell, T.: Decaf: A deep convolutional activation feature for generic visual recognition. ArXiv:1310.1531 (2013)
8. Everingham, M., Van Gool, L., Williams, C.K.I., Winn, J., Zisserman, A.: The PASCAL Visual Object Classes Challenge, VOC 2007 Results (2007)
9. Fei-Fei, L., Fergus, R., Perona, P.: Learning generative visual models from few training examples: An incremental bayesian approach tested on 101 object categories. CVIU (2007)
10. Felzenszwalb, P.F., Girshick, R.B., McAllester, D., Ramanan, D.: Object detection with discriminatively trained part-based models. PAMI (2010)
11. van Gemert, J.C., Geusebroek, J.-M., Veenman, C.J., Smeulders, A.W.M.: Kernel codebooks for scene categorization. In: Forsyth, D., Torr, P., Zisserman, A. (eds.) ECCV 2008, Part III. LNCS, vol. 5304, pp. 696–709. Springer, Heidelberg (2008)
12. Girshick, R., Donahue, J., Darrell, T., Malik, J.: Rich feature hierarchies for accurate object detection and semantic segmentation. In: CVPR (2014)
13. Gong, Y., Wang, L., Guo, R., Lazebnik, S.: Multi-scale orderless pooling of deep convolutional activation features. ArXiv:1403.1840 (2014)
14. Grauman, K., Darrell, T.: The pyramid match kernel: Discriminative classification with sets of image features. In: ICCV (2005)
15. Howard, A.G.: Some improvements on deep convolutional neural network based image classification. ArXiv:1312.5402 (2013)
16. Krizhevsky, A., Sutskever, I., Hinton, G.: Imagenet classification with deep convolutional neural networks. In: NIPS (2012)
17. Lazebnik, S., Schmid, C., Ponce, J.: Beyond bags of features: Spatial pyramid matching for recognizing natural scene categories. In: CVPR (2006)
18. LeCun, Y., Boser, B., Denker, J.S., Henderson, D., Howard, R.E., Hubbard, W., Jackel, L.D.: Backpropagation applied to handwritten zip code recognition. Neural Computation (1989)
19. Lowe, D.G.: Distinctive image features from scale-invariant keypoints. IJCV (2004)

20. Oquab, M., Bottou, L., Laptev, I., Sivic, J., et al.: Learning and transferring mid-level image representations using convolutional neural networks. In: CVPR (2014)
21. Perronnin, F., Sánchez, J., Mensink, T.: Improving the fisher kernel for large-scale image classification. In: Daniilidis, K., Maragos, P., Paragios, N. (eds.) ECCV 2010, Part IV. LNCS, vol. 6314, pp. 143–156. Springer, Heidelberg (2010)
22. Razavian, A.S., Azizpour, H., Sullivan, J., Carlsson, S.: Cnn features off-the-shelf: An astounding baseline for recogniton. In: CVPR 2014, DeepVision Workshop (2014)
23. van de Sande, K.E., Uijlings, J.R., Gevers, T., Smeulders, A.W.: Segmentation as selective search for object recognition. In: ICCV (2011)
24. Sermanet, P., Eigen, D., Zhang, X., Mathieu, M., Fergus, R., LeCun, Y.: Overfeat: Integrated recognition, localization and detection using convolutional networks. ArXiv:1312.6229 (2013)
25. Sivic, J., Zisserman, A.: Video google: A text retrieval approach to object matching in videos. In: ICCV (2003)
26. Szegedy, C., Toshev, A., Erhan, D.: Deep neural networks for object detection. In: NIPS (2013)
27. Taigman, Y., Yang, M., Ranzato, M., Wolf, L.: Deepface: Closing the gap to human-level performance in face verification. In: CVPR (2014)
28. Wang, J., Yang, J., Yu, K., Lv, F., Huang, T., Gong, Y.: Locality-constrained linear coding for image classification. In: CVPR (2010)
29. Wang, X., Yang, M., Zhu, S., Lin, Y.: Regionlets for generic object detection. In: ICCV (2013)
30. Yang, J., Yu, K., Gong, Y., Huang, T.: Linear spatial pyramid matching using sparse coding for image classification. In: CVPR (2009)
31. Zeiler, M.D., Fergus, R.: Visualizing and understanding convolutional neural networks. ArXiv:1311.2901 (2013)
32. Zhang, N., Paluri, M., Ranzato, M., Darrell, T., Bourdevr, L.: Panda: Pose aligned networks for deep attribute modeling. In: CVPR (2014)
33. Zou, W.Y., Wang, X., Sun, M., Lin, Y.: Generic object detection with dense neural patterns and regionlets. ArXiv:1404.4316 (2014)

Context as Supervisory Signal:
Discovering Objects with Predictable Context

Carl Doersch, Abhinav Gupta, and Alexei A. Efros

[1] Carnegie Mellon University, USA
[2] UC Berkeley, USA

Abstract. This paper addresses the well-established problem of unsupervised object discovery with a novel method inspired by weakly-supervised approaches. In particular, the ability of an object patch to predict the rest of the object (its context) is used as supervisory signal to help discover visually consistent object clusters. The main contributions of this work are: 1) framing unsupervised clustering as a leave-one-out context prediction task; 2) evaluating the quality of context prediction by statistical hypothesis testing between *thing* and *stuff* appearance models; and 3) an iterative region prediction and context alignment approach that gradually discovers a visual object cluster together with a segmentation mask and fine-grained correspondences. The proposed method outperforms previous unsupervised as well as weakly-supervised object discovery approaches, and is shown to provide correspondences detailed enough to transfer keypoint annotations.

Keywords: Context, prediction, unsupervised object discovery, mining.

1 Introduction

Proponents of unsupervised representation learning [1,2,3,4] and unsupervised object discovery [5,6,7,8,9,10,11,12] have long argued that these approaches have the potential to solve two fundamental problems with supervised methods. The first is obvious: training labels are expensive to collect. More subtly, human annotations can introduce unwanted biases into representations [13]. Unsupervised object discovery has, however, proven extremely difficult; one state-of-the-art result [3] uses a million CPU-hours, yet reports only three discovered objects (cats, faces, and bodies), and the "neurons" sensitive to these objects could only be identified through the use of labeled data.

At its core, object discovery is a clustering problem; the goal is to group together image regions (patches or segments) that depict the same object. Standard clustering algorithms like K-means rely on a good distance metric, but unfortunately, distances in different regions of the feature space often aren't comparable [14]. This means that the "tightness" of each cluster will be a poor measure of whether it actually depicts an object. A number of recent works have argued that weak supervision can be an effective way to get more visually meaningful clusters [14,15,16,17,18,19,20,21,22,23]. The supervision (e.g., scene labels,

D. Fleet et al. (Eds.): ECCV 2014, Part III, LNCS 8691, pp. 362–377, 2014.

Fig. 1. Suppose we want to create a visually meaningful cluster containing the cat eye patch in (a). (b) shows a cluster produced by simple nearest neighbors, but there is too little information in just a cat eye, so it is confused with a motorbike. Nearest neighbors on a larger patch (c) introduces new errors because the patch now captures too much variation. Our proposed method (d) starts with the cluster in (b) and uses the context as a "supervisory signal" to discard the incorrect match.

GPS coordinates, etc.) gives information about which image regions should be close together (e.g., belong to the same cluster) and which should be far apart. But can a similar effect be achieved without any supervision?

The main contribution of this paper is the use of *context* [24] as a supervisory signal. At a high level, context provides similar information as a weak label: e.g., given a set of matched cat eye patches on Figure 1a, we expect the context surrounding those patches to depict cat faces. Errors in the matching (e.g. the motorcycle wheel) can then be detected and discarded because the context will not match. (One might object that we could simply include context as part of the feature used for matching, but Figure 1b shows that this performs poorly, as it is unable to handle the large variations between the cat faces).

Using context as a supervisory signal means we need a way to determine whether two contexts are sufficiently similar. However, standard distance metrics will be just as unreliable at measuring the visual similarity of the context as the visual similarity of the patches themselves. An 'easy' context (e.g., a uniform region) will have too many matches, whereas a 'difficult' context (e.g., a complex shape) will potentially match nothing. Our key insight is to normalize for this, by modeling the 'difficulty' of the context. Mathematically, our formulation is reminiscent of statistical hypothesis testing for object recognition [25]. For a given image, we have two competing hypotheses: 1) that the context in that image is best described as a 'thing,' i.e. an object with a well-defined shape, versus 2) that the image is best described as 'stuff' [26], i.e. that it is best modeled using low-level image statistics. Both models "predict" what the context will contain, i.e. they produce a probability distribution in image feature space, such that we can compute a single probability value for the image context. If the *thing* model predicts better, then the cluster is likely a good one, and the patch is likely a member of it. We perform a simple likelihood ratio test to determine if this is the case.

At what granularity should our models be allowed to predict? If we force the *thing* model to predict a cat face all at once, even a correct prediction might align poorly with the ground truth. Evaluating whether such a prediction is correct

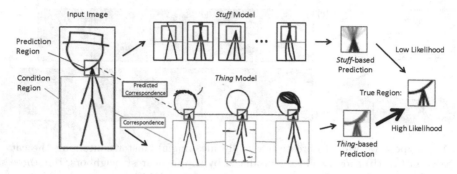

Fig. 2. Algorithm overview. Given a "condition" region (in green), our algorithm predicts the "prediction" region (in red) twice: once using a model that assumes correspondence with some complex shape (the *thing* model, bottom), and once assuming that the region is best modeled as texture (the *stuff* model, top). Both models' predictions are compared to the true region. If *thing* outperforms *stuff*, the prediction region is considered to be part of the discovered object. This process then repeats with the a new prediction region (anatomically accurate stick-figures from xkcd [28])

then becomes difficult. Making small predictions near the initial patch will be easier because errors due to misalignment will be small, but they will contain little information. Our approach finds middle ground by iteratively predicting small regions over a larger area. Between each prediction, we align the model to the true data. That is, we "grow" the predicted region one small step at a time, reminiscent of texture synthesis [27]. The model's alignment errors are thus corrected before they drift too far.

2   Overview

At a high level, our pipeline is similar to algorithms for mid-level patch discovery [16,15], especially in the early stages. Like [16], we first sample a large number of random patches (10,000 for our PASCAL VOC experiments), and then find the top few nearest neighbors in HOG feature space for each of them, across the entire dataset. ([16] uses normalized correlation as a distance metric, but we found Exemplar LDA [29], with a Gaussian learned from the entire unlabeled dataset, to give slightly better matches). These cluster proposals form the input to our object discovery algorithm. At the high level, the algorithm: 1) discards patches within each cluster whose context is inconsistent with the other patches, 2) ranks the clusters, and 3) discards clusters that do not contain visually consistent objects. The ranking (i.e. 'score' of a cluster) is simply the sum of the scores of patches that weren't discarded. Thus, the meat of our algorithm boils down to the process of scoring the context around a single patch. A given patch is scored using all the other patches in the cluster using *leave-one-out prediction*. That is, given n patches in a cluster, we use the context associated with patch 1 through patch $n-1$ to predict the context around the n'th patch.

But as was discussed earlier, a major difficulty is that some contexts are easier to predict than others. For instance, given a patch of blank wall, it's easy to predict that the context will be similarly blank. If we don't account for this, then any cluster that's full of blank patches (or any other simple texture) might be declared an object. Note, however, that this prediction doesn't really require the algorithm to understand that the patch is a wall; a highly accurate prediction could be made just based on low-level statistics. Hence, we don't measure how well the context of a patch can be predicted, but instead, how much the clustering *helps* us predict the context. Specifically, our algorithm uses two models that produce two predictions. The first—the *stuff* model—produces predictions based solely on knowledge of low-level image/texture statistics, which it extrapolates from the single patch whose context it is predicting. This model could easily predict that a blank wall will continue indefinitely. The other—the *thing* model—uses the specific correspondence defined by the cluster to make its predictions. Figure 2 illustrates why this is effective. The initial patch cluster (which generates the correspondence outlined in green) contains the bodies of the stick figures. The *thing* model can align these bodies and predict the presence of the neck. The *stuff* model, however, uses only low-level image statistics and predicts (incorrectly) that the contours will most likely continue straight. We then compare the likelihoods; the patch is considered a member of the cluster if the *thing* likelihood is significantly higher than the *stuff* likelihood.

To make this algorithm work as stated, however, we must compute the likelihood $P(c|p)$ of the context c given the patch p, under two separate models, and do so with reasonable accuracy. The problem of generative image modeling has a long history in computer vision [1,4,25,30,31,32], but historically these algorithms have performed poorly for object recognition problems, especially compared to the discriminative methods that have, of late, largely displaced them in the field. A core difficulty shared by generative methods is that they assume the image features are independent, conditioned on some set of latent variables. Obtaining a likelihood $P(c|p)$ requires integrating out those latent variables, which is generally intractable. Approximations (e.g. MCMC or variational methods) either do not scale well, or produce probability estimates that cannot be compared between different models. To get around this problem, our algorithm partitions the context c into small regions c_k (for example, if c is the HOG representation of the context, each c_k may be a single cell.) Next, we factorize the conditional likelihood as follows:

$$P(c|p) = \prod_{k=1}^{m} P(c_k|c_1, ..., c_{k-1}, p) \tag{1}$$

Here, the ordering of the c_k's can be whatever makes the computation easiest (in the case of HOG, c_i may be adjacent to the region covered by $\{c_k, ..., c_{k-1}, p\}$.) This deceptively simple algebraic manipulation—really just an application of the probability chain rule—is remarkably powerful. First, note that it is not an approximation, even though it makes no independence assumptions. It remains tractable because the c_k's are actually observed values; unlike in latent-variable models, the c_k's do not need to be integrated out in order to compute a valid likelihood. Furthermore, each c_k may be chosen so that its conditional distribution is well approximated with a simple parametric distribution (we find that a single HOG cell is well approximated by a Gaussian), even though we do not assume anywhere that the joint distribution has a parametric representation. Despite these good properties, we have found no previous work which attempts to compute image likelihoods using such a factorization (note that [31] comes close; however, their model still contains higher-order potentials, meaning that the terms in the product cannot be computed independently, and that inference still requires MCMC). We show that these incremental predictions can be made efficiently and with surprising accuracy, enough that the resulting likelihoods can be compared between our *thing* and *stuff* models.

3 Algorithm

We first formalize our notation. Assume we have a cluster proposal containing n patches. We select one 'held out' patch, and number it 0 (the others are numbered 1 through $n-1$). Let H^0 denote the feature representation for the image containing patch number 0, which we will call the *query* image. Let H_k^0 be the k'th feature in H^0, in our case, a single HOG cell. Let $\mathcal{P}$ index the subset of features in H^0 that were inside patch 0 (in Figure 2, $\mathcal{P}$ would be a strict subset of the region outlined in green for all but the first term in the product in Equation 1). Finally, let $\mathcal{C}$ be an *ordered* set of indices for the features in the context, i.e. the complement of $\mathcal{P}$ (in Figure 2, $\mathcal{C}$ indexes the remainder of the green, the red, and also the rest of the image). This means we predict $\mathcal{C}[1]$ using $\mathcal{P}$ alone, $\mathcal{C}[2]$ using $\mathcal{P} \cup \mathcal{C}[1]$, and so on. $\mathcal{C}[1:t]$ indexes the first t HOG cells in the context that get predicted. Our original factorization (Eq. 1) for the *thing* model can now be written more formally as:

$$P_T(H_\mathcal{C}^0|H_\mathcal{P}^0) = \prod_{t=1}^{|\mathcal{C}|} P_T(H_{\mathcal{C}[t]}^0|H_{\mathcal{C}[1:t-1]}^0, H_\mathcal{P}^0) \tag{2}$$

We will have a similar factorization for P_S of the *stuff* model. In Figure 2, the region outlined in red corresponds to $H_{\mathcal{C}[t]}^0$, and those outlined in green correspond to $\{H_{\mathcal{C}[1:t-1]}^0, H_\mathcal{P}^0\}$. We repeat this computation of $P.(H_{\mathcal{C}[t]}^0|H_{\mathcal{C}[1:t-1]}^0, H_\mathcal{P}^0)$ for all t; i.e. at the next iteration, the red region will get added to the green region and we'll choose a new red region.

For simplicity, we assume that the conditional distributions are Gaussian for both *thing* and *stuff* models; we find empirically that forcing both *thing* and *stuff* predictions into the same, simple family makes the likelihoods more comparable. To ease exposition, we'll call the HOG cells $\{H_{\mathcal{C}[1:t-1]}^0, H_\mathcal{P}^0\}$ the "condition" region, and $H_{\mathcal{C}[t]}^0$ the "prediction" region. We choose the order of $\mathcal{C}$ by increasing distance from the center of the patch; this means that, for each HOG cell we predict, at least one of its neighbors will be in the condition region.

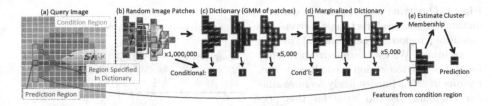

Fig. 3. Summary of our *stuff* model. (a) Given a condition region (green), we extract cells (blue) that are near to the prediction region (red). We assume we have a dictionary reminiscent of visual words (in our case, a GMM) learned from many sampled patches (b-c). For each dictionary element, we estimate the conditional distribution over the prediction region (red). We remove cells that aren't in the condition region (d) before assigning the extracted cells to the dictionary. Finally, we use the associated conditional distribution as our prediction.

3.1 *Stuff* Model

To construct the *stuff* prediction $P_S(H^0_{C[t]}|H^0_{C[1:t-1]}, H^0_P)$ (which we will abbreviate as $p^S_{C[t]}$), the simplest approach is to 1) extract a subset of the condition region that is spatially close to $C[t]$, 2) find nearest neighbors for that subset from a large database of images, and 3) use the context around those retrieved neighbors to form our prediction. Of course, this would be extremely computationally expensive, so we instead summarize our dataset using clustering, in a manner reminiscent of visual words.

Our more efficient approach is shown in Figure 3. We begin with a query image (Figure 3a), with a condition region (in green) and a prediction region (in red). We assume that we have available a 'dictionary' (Figure 3c) constructed from a large sample of image patches (Figure 3b), each of which was in a shape that's similar (but not necessarily identical) to the shape of the selected subset of the condition region (which is outlined in blue in Figure 3a). We learn 12 separate dictionaries to ensure that we always have a reasonably good match to a given local condition region. To construct these dictionaries, we first sample about a million such patches (Figure 3b), and learn a Gaussian Mixture Model (GMM) from the HOG features of these image patches. We temporarily ignore the region of these patches that corresponds to the prediction region (outlined in red in Figure 3b) and learn the GMM only on the rest. We restrict each GMM component to have a diagonal covariance matrix for computational efficiency. We use 5000 GMM components, and show some centroids in Figure 3c. We also estimate, for each component of the GMM, the prediction that will be made by this component for the red region. For this, we first soft-assign each of our sampled patches to the components of the GMM, and compute the empirical mean and covariance of the associated red cells for each component. This mean and covariance are interpreted as the parameters a Gaussian conditional distribution; we show the means of these conditional distributions outlined in red in Figure 3c.

Fig. 4. Our *thing* model predicts the prediction region (red rectangle) given the condition region (green border) in the query image. We estimate correspondence for the prediction region (red ellipse)—i.e. regions in other images likely to have similar contents—as the basis for this prediction. The red correspondence must be obtained without observing the prediction region, so we first estimate correspondence for the condition region (green ellipses) and extrapolate to the prediction region.

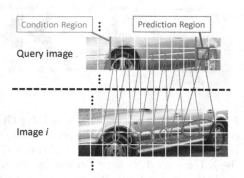

To actually make a prediction, we first determine which components of the GMM should be responsible for the prediction. We soft-assign the condition region of our query image (specifically, the subset outlined in blue) to the components of our GMM. Unfortunately, there may be dimensions of our GMM components that correspond to HOG cells outside the condition region; for instance, the leftmost cells highlighted in blue in Figure 3a). To deal with this, we marginalize out any such cells from the GMM as shown in Figure 3d (Hence why we use GMM's instead of K-means, as the marginalization of a GMM is well-defined). We next soft-assign the image data to the components of the GMM, which gives us a weighted set of conditional distributions over the prediction region. We average these predictions into a single Gaussian (specifically, we treat the set of predictions as a GMM over a single HOG cell, and compute a single Gaussian that matches the mean and variance of this GMM).

3.2   *Thing* Model

The *thing* model attempts to capture the details of a complex shape using the set of images that were retrieved when we built our initial patch cluster. Making a prediction for a particular prediction region $P_T(H^0_{\mathcal{C}[t]}|H^0_{\mathcal{C}[1:t-1]}, H^0_{\mathcal{P}})$ (which we will abbreviate as $p^T_{\mathcal{C}[t]}$) boils down to the problem of correspondence: if we can estimate which regions in the other images are likely to correspond to our current prediction region, then we can predict that the features will be the same. To avoid biasing the likelihood value, we must not to access the features $H^0_{\mathcal{C}[t]}$ while making the prediction, but there are cells in the condition region near the prediction region that we could use. Hence, we find the correspondence for each cell in the condition region (a standard image warping problem). Once we have this correspondence, we extrapolate it to the prediction region. Note, though, that we cannot assume this correspondence will exist for every image. Besides the standard problem of occlusion, we also have to deal with the many errors in the Exemplar-LDA matching. We have found that the top 20 matches are usually reasonably pure, but for some interesting objects the lower-ranked matches may be wrong. Hence, we only use the top 20 images per prediction, meaning we must use the data extremely efficiently.

Formally, recall that $\mathcal{C}$ and $\mathcal{P}$ index the HOG cells in our query image, and so each index in these sets can be written as 2-dimensional points (x, y) on the grid of HOG cells. We represent the correspondence as a mapping $f^i(x, y)$ from the cell (x, y) in the query image to cells in the HOG grid for image i, where i ranges from 1 to $n - 1$ (we'll call these the 'predictor' images). We optimize our mapping such that $H^i_{f^i(x,y)}$ is as similar as possible to $H^0_{(x,y)}$ for all (x, y) *in the condition region* (we defer the computation of f to Appendix A). Note that we are interested in correspondence for $\mathcal{C}[t] = (x_t, y_t)$, the *prediction* region, but we aren't allowed to access the HOG feature at $H^0_{\mathcal{C}[t]}$; therefore (x_t, y_t) isn't, strictly speaking, in the domain of f^i. To find correspondence for the prediction region, we find the nearest point (x_t^*, y_t^*) in the condition region and compute a simple linear extrapolation:

$$f^i(x_t, y_t) = f^i(x^*, y^*) + (x_t, y_t) - (x_t^*, y_t^*) \tag{3}$$

Thus far, we've treated $f^i(x_t, y_t)$ as if it indexed a single HOG cell, but is that enough? Recall that we have about 20 images; actually less than the dimensionality of HOG! Worse, correspondence is often ambiguous. Consider the example in Figure 4. The condition region contains the front wheel of a car and some of the car's side panel, and we are interested in a prediction region further to the right. Ideally, the algorithm should give some probability mass to the event that the panel will continue, and some mass to the event that it will end and a wheel will start. However, if $f^i(x_t, y_t)$ returns a single point as the correspondence for the prediction region, then the algorithm will be arbitrarily confident that *either* the prediction region should contain a continuation of the panel *or* that it will end. To address this, we alter our definition of f such that its range is the space of tuples of mean vectors and covariance matrices parameterizing 2-d Gaussian distributions.

$$f^i(x, y) := [\mu^i_{x,y}, \Sigma^i_{x,y}] \tag{4}$$

Thus, $f^i(x, y)$ defines Gaussian distribution over the HOG grid of image i. (In Equation 3, the addition is only performed on μ: i.e. $f^i(x, y) + (a, b) = [\mu^i_{x,y} + (a, b), \Sigma^i_{x,y}]$). Figure 4 visualizes these Gaussians as ellipses. In this illustration, note that the covariance of the Gaussians are small near the wheel (where there is less ambiguity), but they grow as the matching becomes more ambiguous. While this makes the optimization of f somewhat more complicated, ultimately it means the algorithm uses more data to make each prediction, and in the case of Figure 4 guesses that the prediction region could correspond to panel or to wheel.

This correspondence allows us to extract many HOG cells from each image that may correspond to the prediction region; to actually form a prediction, we aggregate these samples across all predictor images, with each sample weighted by the likelihood that it actually corresponds to the prediction region. Mathematically, we form our prediction by fitting a Gaussian in HOG feature space to the *weighted* set of HOG cells in $H^1...H^{n-1}$ that the prediction region potentially corresponds to:

Fig. 5. An example of our *thing* model running in "generative mode." As we run the alignment procedure, we generate each HOG cell in the prediction image as the average of the cells it corresponds to in the predictor images (we allow the algorithm to make a fresh prediction for each cell at each iteration, to allow better alignment). Starting only from the images on the left and the element-level correspondence shown by the red bounding boxes, we can synthesize a new, plausible car in HOG space, which we then render using inverse HOG [33].

$$p^T_{\mathcal{C}[t]} = \mathcal{N}(H^0_{\mathcal{C}[t]}; \mu^f_{\mathcal{C}[t]}, \Sigma^f_{\mathcal{C}[t]}) \tag{5}$$

where

$$\mu^f_{\mathcal{C}[t]} = \sum_{i,u,v} \eta^i_{\mathcal{C}[t],u,v} H^i_{u,v} \; ; \quad \Sigma^f_{\mathcal{C}[t]} = \sum_{i,u,v} \eta^i_{\mathcal{C}[t],u,v} (H^i_{u,v} - \mu^f_t)(H^i_{u,v} - \mu^f_t)^\top \tag{6}$$

There are two components of the weighting: $\eta^i_{\mathcal{C}[t],u,v} = w^i_{\mathcal{C}[t],u,v} \omega^i_{\mathcal{C}[t]}$. The first is based on the spatial correspondence f, and is defined as $w^i_{\mathcal{C}[t],u,v} = \mathcal{N}([u,v];$ $\mu^i_{x_t,y_t}, \Sigma^i_{x_t,y_t})$ for prediction region (x_t, y_t). This weight, however, is not sufficient by itself, because the correspondence from the prediction region to image i might be completely wrong (e.g. if there is nothing in image i that corresponds to the prediction region). Hence, we use $\omega^i_{\mathcal{C}[t]}$ to downweight the images where we expect the correspondence to be incorrect. Intuitively, we simply observe how useful image i was for the earlier predictions of other regions near to $\mathcal{C}[t]$. The mathematical details are somewhat involved and not required for understanding the rest of the algorithm, so we defer them to Appendix B.

3.3 Determining What to Predict

A remaining problem is that our *thing* model generally won't do a good job predicting every cell in the query image, since the object of interest may not fill the image, or it may be occluded. One possible resolution is to throw away any region where the *thing* model predicted poorly, but we find that this biases the entire algorithm toward overestimating the probability that the image is a *thing* (much like a gambler who judges his luck based only on the days when he won). A better solution is to have the *thing* model gracefully degrade to 'mimic' the *stuff* model when it believes it can't predict well. For simplicity, our algorithm makes a binary decision. Either it uses the correspondence-based algorithm (Equation 5) exclusively, or it 'mimics' the *stuff* model exactly (i.e. it sets its conditional distribution $P_T(h|H^0_{\mathcal{C}[1:t-1]}, H^0_{\mathcal{P}})$ equal to $P_S(h|H^0_{\mathcal{C}[1:t-1]}, H^0_{\mathcal{P}})$

for all h). Note that when the *thing* model mimics the *stuff* model, $p_{C[t]}^T$ will be equal to $p_{C[t]}^S$, and hence the value of H_C^0 will have no effect on the likelihood ratio score. To determine when the *thing* model should mimic the *stuff* model, we use two heuristics. First, we measure how well the *thing* model has predicted the query image in regions near the current prediction region. Second, to do a better job estimating the bounds of the object, we measure whether the *thing* model believes $C[t]$ corresponds to regions in other images that were predicted poorly. For implementation details, see Appendix C.

3.4   Details of Our Discovery Pipeline

The above sections outline a verification procedure that tells us whether the *thing* model predicted better than the *stuff* model for each individual element detection. However, one final difficulty is that a single cluster initialized by exemplar-LDA may actually contain two separate objects, and the verification procedure will happily verify both of them. To prevent this, we start by verifying a single patch, and attempt to grow the cluster in a way that selects for the object depicted in that first patch. After the first prediction, we can compute a "usage score" for every predictor image (see Appendix B), which captures how much that image helped predict the query image. We take the top image according to this score and compute its likelihood ratio, which produces more usage scores for the predictor images. We average the resulting usage scores for each image. We use 20 predictor images for each verification. To choose them, we first select at most 10 of the verified images with highest usage score, and for the rest we select the unverified images with the top exemplar-LDA score.

4   Results

Our goal is to demonstrate unsupervised object discovery on realistic databases with as little human intervention as possible. Our experiments focus on the PASCAL VOC, a challenging database for modern, supervised object detection algorithms. We evaluate discovery on PASCAL object categories, and also show results for keypoint transfer on the "car" category.

4.1   Quantitative Results: Purity-Coverage on PASCAL VOC 2007

Following the experimental setup of [15], we perform unsupervised object discovery on all PASCAL VOC 2007 images containing a dining table, horse, motorbike, bus, train, or sofa. We evaluate the quality of the discovered objects using the purity-coverage curve [14], which we compute in three steps: 1) for each of our discovered patch clusters, we select the top 10 patches (as scored by the likelihood ratio value); 2) we compute the purity of each cluster using these 10 patches, according to the majority VOC label in the cluster; 3) we sort the clusters by purity. To obtain the k'th point on the purity-coverage curve, we plot the average purity for the first through k'th clusters in this ranking versus

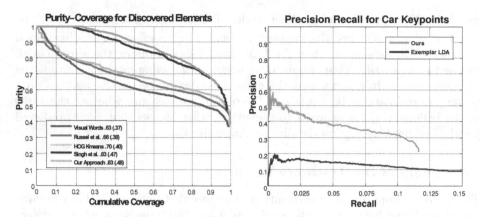

Fig. 6. Left: purity vs coverage for objects discovered on a subset of Pascal VOC 2007. The numbers in the legend indicate area under the curve (AUC). In parentheses is the AUC up to a coverage of .5 (lower ranked clusters generally aren't objects). Right: precision-recall for car keypoints transferred via unsupervised correspondence.

the total number of images that contribute at least one patch to the clusters 1 through k. (Note that, unlike [15], we follow [14] and plot purity and coverage on the same graph, since we find it makes the methods more comparable.) The result is shown in Figure 6 left. We slightly outperform [15], especially for the high purity regime (we get nearly 10% extra coverage before we make our first mistake). However, note that [15] is not completely unsupervised as it requires a "natural world" dataset, which typically contains a somewhat different distribution of visual data than the "discovery" dataset, providing an implicit, albeit very weak, supervision. Our method significantly outperforms other, truly unsupervised methods.

Implementation Details : We start with over 10,000 randomly-sampled image patches at multiple resolutions to initialize the clusters. Cluster verification is relatively computationally expensive, so in practice we terminate the verification of each cluster as soon as it appears to be producing low scores. We start by verifying a single patch for each cluster, and we kill the half of the clusters with low *thing* likelihood. We repeat this procedure iteratively, doubling the number of verifications before killing the worst half in terms of *thing* likelihood (keeping at least 1,000 at the end). We end when we have run 31 verifications per surviving element. To choose the elements to kill, one approach is to kill those with the lowest score. However, this can lead to many duplicates and poor coverage. Instead, we use a greedy selection procedure reminiscent of [34] Specifically, given a selection χ of clusters, let $s_{i,j}^{\chi}$ be the log likelihood ratio for the j'th highest-scoring patch in image i out of all clusters contained in χ. We greedily select clusters to include in χ to maximize $\sum_{i,j} 2^{-j} s_{i,j}^{\chi}$, i.e. exponentially discounting the scores of patches from the same image.

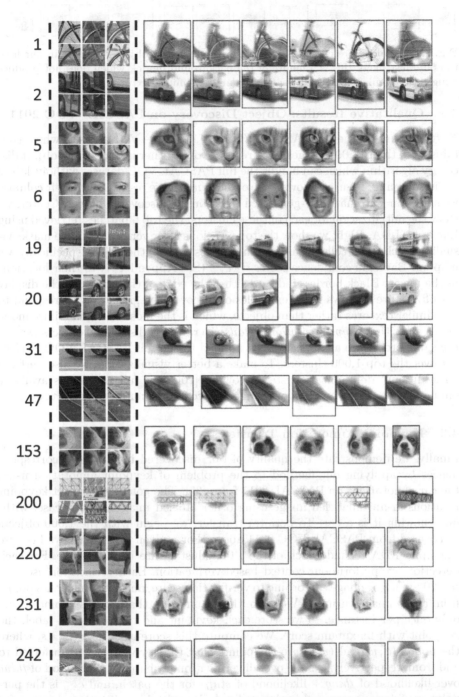

Fig. 7. Examples of regions discovered in PASCAL VOC 2011. Left: object rank. Center: initial top 6 patches from Exemplar LDA. Right: top 6 verifications. See text for details.

Fig. 8. Typical failure cases from our algorithm. These "objects" appear in our final top 50. Most likely this is a failure of the background model, which does not produce a high enough likelihood for these particular self-similar textures.

4.2   Qualitative Results: Object Discovery on PASCAL VOC 2011

Next, we turn to the full PASCAL VOC 2011 (Train+Val) dataset, which contains more than 11,000 images. We are aware of no other unsupervised object discovery algorithm which can handle the full PASCAL VOC dataset without labels or subsampling. Figure 7 shows some of our qualitative results. In the left column, we show our automatically-generated rank for the discovered object. Center, we show the initialization for each of these clusters: the top 6 patches retrieved using Exemplar LDA. Right we show the top 6 regions after verification. The masks visualize which HOG cells the algorithm believes contain the object: specifically, we map our Bayesian confidence scores $\beta * c_{x,y}$ (See Appendix A) to their locations in the image. Black borders indicate either the edge of the image, or the display cut off. Figure 8 shows a few examples of discovered regions that correspond to self-similar textures rather than objects, which is the most common failure mode of our algorithm. *Implementation Details:* To rank the discovered objects, we use the same procedure as in Section 4.1 applied to the full PASCAL VOC 2011 to discover the top 1,000 clusters. To make a better visualization, we also perform an additional de-duplication step following [16]. Our full ranking is available online at: http://graphics.cs.cmu.edu/projects/contextPrediction/.

4.3   Keypoint Annotation Transfer

Finally, we demonstrate the quality of our discovered intra-cluster correspondences by applying our method to the problem of keypoint annotation using the car annotations on PASCAL 2011 from [35]. The goal is to predict keypoint locations in an unlabeled image using other labeled images, in our case, without knowing it is a car. To perform transfer, we begin with the 1,000 objects discovered from PASCAL VOC 2011 above. For a given test image, we first use Exemplar-LDA to find which of the 1,000 clusters fire in this image. For each detection, we perform our context-based verification. Each verification uses the top 20 predictor images according to verification score, and we transfer keypoints from all 20 images using f. We make the assumption that each keypoint occurs only once per instance, so we score each keypoint and take, for each label, the keypoint with maximum score. We compute this score as $c_{x,y} * w_{u,v}^i * s$, where the points (x, y) and (u, v) are the points that the keypoint was transferred to and from, respectively, s is the overall verification probability (likelihood of *thing* over likelihood of *thing* + likelihood of *stuff*) for the patch, and $c_{x,y}$ is the per-point confidence computed in Appendix A. If multiple verifications happen for the same image (i.e. multiple patches are detected) and the regions considered to be *thing* overlap (intersection over union greater than .2), then the keypoints

Fig. 9. An example of keypoint transfer. For each predicted keypoint, we show a patch from the image where that keypoint was transferred from. These correspondences are discovered without any supervision. Note that multiple different labels are predicted for the wheel centers. This happens because our algorithm finds all wheels somewhat visually similar, and proposes as many correspondences as possible.

predicted for those verifications are merged and de-duplicated so that there is only one prediction per label.

Unfortunately, the evaluation of [35] isn't suitable in our situation, since they only measure keypoint accuracy conditioned on correctly-predicted bounding boxes. Since our algorithm may discover partial correspondences (e.g. only the wheel), we wish to evaluate on keypoints directly. We consider a keypoint prediction "correct" if there is a ground-truth keypoint of the same label within a distance less than 10% of the max dimension of the associated bounding box. We penalize repeated keypoint detections. Each predicted keypoint has a confidence score, so we can compute a precision-recall curve. For reasons of computation time, we only evaluate on images containing at least one car that's larger than 150 pixels on its minimum dimension (476 images total), and predict keypoints in a leave-one-out paradigm. Note that while we measure performance only on these images, we allow our algorithm to find correspondence in all images, even those containing no cars. Labels were never used to find or score correspondences (though we assume at most one instance of each keypoint label per object, which helps us de-duplicate). Figure 6 shows our precision-recall curve. Admittedly our recall is low, but note that out of 1,000 clusters, few correspond to cars (on the order of 50). For comparison, we include a baseline that uses Exemplar-LDA directly, explained in Appendix D. Chance performance is well below 1% precision. Figure 9 shows the raw output for one image, after thresholding the confidence of keypoint transfers.

5   Conclusion

In this work, we have presented a method for validating whether a cluster of patches depicts a coherent visual concept, by measuring whether the correspondence provided by that cluster helps to predict the context around each patch. However, many questions remain about the best ways to implement and use the prediction models presented here. For instance, can we predict color in a prediction region conditioned on the color of the condition region? If so, color may become an important cue in detecting these regions. Texture and even brightness information may be similarly useful. Another extension may be to treat $P(H^0_{C[t]}|H^0_{C[1:t-1]}, H^0_{\mathcal{P}})$ as a more classical machine learning problem: estimating conditional distributions is, after all, a classical *discriminative* learning setup. Our algorithm did not use standard discriminative learning algorithms due to a lack of reliable training data, but in a supervised setting our *thing* model might be replaced with a far simpler regression model trained discriminatively.

Acknowledgements: We thank Shiry Ginosar, Yong Jae Lee, Dinesh Jayaraman, and anonymous reviewers for suggesting improvements to the writing. This work was partially supported by an Amazon Web Services grant, a Google Research grant, and ONR MURI N000141010934. This research was conducted with Government support under and awarded by DoD, Air Force Office of Scientific Research, National Defense Science and Engineering Graduate (NDSEG) Fellowship, 32 CFR 168a.

References

1. Hinton, G.E., Dayan, P., Frey, B.J., Neal, R.M.: The "wake-sleep" algorithm for unsupervised neural networks. IEEE Proceedings (1995)
2. Olshausen, B.A., et al.: Emergence of simple-cell receptive field properties by learning a sparse code for natural images. Nature (1996)
3. Le, Q.V.: Building high-level features using large scale unsupervised learning. In: ICASSP (2013)
4. Fergus, R., Perona, P., Zisserman, A.: Object class recognition by unsupervised scale-invariant learning. In: CVPR (2003)
5. Sivic, J., Russell, B.C., Efros, A.A., Zisserman, A., Freeman, W.T.: Discovering objects and their location in images. In: ICCV (2005)
6. Russell, B.C., Freeman, W.T., Efros, A.A., Sivic, J., Zisserman, A.: Using multiple segmentations to discover objects and their extent in image collections. In: CVPR (2006)
7. Lee, Y.J., Grauman, K.: Foreground focus: Unsupervised learning from partially matching images. IJCV (2009)
8. Payet, N., Todorovic, S.: From a set of shapes to object discovery. In: Daniilidis, K., Maragos, P., Paragios, N. (eds.) ECCV 2010, Part V. LNCS, vol. 6315, pp. 57–70. Springer, Heidelberg (2010)
9. Kim, G., Faloutsos, C., Hebert, M.: Unsupervised modeling of object categories using link analysis techniques. In: CVPR (2008)
10. Grauman, K., Darrell, T.: Unsupervised learning of categories from sets of partially matching image features. In: CVPR (2006)
11. Faktor, A., Irani, M.: "Clustering by composition" – unsupervised discovery of image categories. In: Fitzgibbon, A., Lazebnik, S., Perona, P., Sato, Y., Schmid, C. (eds.) ECCV 2012, Part VII. LNCS, vol. 7578, pp. 474–487. Springer, Heidelberg (2012)
12. Rubinstein, M., Joulin, A., Kopf, J., Liu, C.: Unsupervised joint object discovery and segmentation in internet images. In: CVPR (2013)
13. Torralba, A., Efros, A.A.: Unbiased look at dataset bias. In: CVPR (2011)
14. Doersch, C., Gupta, A., Efros, A.A.: Mid-level visual element discovery as discriminative mode seeking. In: NIPS (2013)

15. Singh, S., Gupta, A., Efros, A.A.: Unsupervised discovery of mid-level discriminative patches. In: Fitzgibbon, A., Lazebnik, S., Perona, P., Sato, Y., Schmid, C. (eds.) ECCV 2012, Part II. LNCS, vol. 7573, pp. 73–86. Springer, Heidelberg (2012)

16. Doersch, C., Singh, S., Gupta, A., Sivic, J., Efros, A.A.: What makes Paris look like Paris? In: SIGGRAPH (2012)

17. Endres, I., Shih, K., Jiaa, J., Hoiem, D.: Learning collections of part models for object recognition. In: CVPR (2013)

18. Jain, A., Gupta, A., Rodriguez, M., Davis, L.: Representing videos using mid-level discriminative patches. In: CVPR (2013)

19. Juneja, M., Vedaldi, A., Jawahar, C.V., Zisserman, A.: Blocks that shout: Distinctive parts for scene classification. In: CVPR (2013)

20. Li, Q., Wu, J., Tu, Z.: Harvesting mid-level visual concepts from large-scale internet images. In: CVPR (2013)

21. Sun, J., Ponce, J.: Learning discriminative part detectors for image classification and cosegmentation. In: ICCV (2013)

22. Wang, X., Wang, B., Bai, X., Liu, W., Tu, Z.: Max-margin multiple-instance dictionary learning. In: ICML (2013)

23. Zeiler, M.D., Fergus, R.: Visualizing and understanding convolutional neural networks. ArXiv preprint ArXiv:1311.2901 (2013)

24. Oliva, A., Torralba, A.: The role of context in object recognition. Trends in Cognitive Sciences (2007)

25. Weber, M., Welling, M., Perona, P.: Unsupervised learning of models for recognition. In: CVPR (2000)

26. Adelson, E.H.: On seeing stuff: The perception of materials by humans and machines. In: Photonics West 2001-Electronic Imaging, International Society for Optics and Photonics (2001)

27. Efros, A.A., Leung, T.K.: Texture synthesis by non-parametric sampling. In: ICCV (1999)

28. Munroe, R.: xkcd, a webcomic of romance, sarcasm, math and language. Creative Commons Attribution-Noncommercial (2014)

29. Hariharan, B., Malik, J., Ramanan, D.: Discriminative decorrelation for clustering and classification. In: Fitzgibbon, A., Lazebnik, S., Perona, P., Sato, Y., Schmid, C. (eds.) ECCV 2012, Part IV. ECCV, vol. 7575, pp. 459–472. Springer, Heidelberg (2012)

30. Fei-Fei, L., Fergus, R., Perona, P.: Learning generative visual models from few training examples: An incremental bayesian approach tested on 101 object categories. CVIU (2007)

31. Wang, G., Zhang, Y., Fei-Fei, L.: Using dependent regions for object categorization in a generative framework. In: CVPR (2006)

32. Sudderth, E.B., Torralba, A., Freeman, W.T., Willsky, A.S.: Learning hierarchical models of scenes, objects, and parts. In: ICCV (2005)

33. Vondrick, C., Khosla, A., Malisiewicz, T., Torralba, A.: HOG-gles: Visualizing object detection features. In: ICCV (2013)

34. Song, H.O., Girshick, R., Jegelka, S., Mairal, J., Harchaoui, Z., Darrell, T.: On learning to localize objects with minimal supervision. In: ICML (2014)

35. Hejrati, M., Ramanan, D.: Analyzing 3d objects in cluttered images. In: NIPS (2012)

Learning to Hash with Partial Tags: Exploring Correlation between Tags and Hashing Bits for Large Scale Image Retrieval

Qifan Wang[1], Luo Si[1], and Dan Zhang[2]

[1] Department of Computer Science, Purdue University
West Lafayette, IN, USA, 47907-2107
{wang868,lsi}@purdue.edu
[2] Facebook Incorporation, Menlo Park, CA 94025, USA
danzhang@fb.com

Abstract. Similarity search is an important technique in many large scale vision applications. Hashing approach becomes popular for similarity search due to its computational and memory efficiency. Recently, it has been shown that the hashing quality could be improved by combining supervised information, e.g. semantic tags/labels, into hashing function learning. However, tag information is not fully exploited in existing unsupervised and supervised hashing methods especially when only partial tags are available. This paper proposes a novel semi-supervised tag hashing (SSTH) approach that fully incorporates tag information into learning effective hashing function by exploring the correlation between tags and hashing bits. The hashing function is learned in a unified learning framework by simultaneously ensuring the tag consistency and preserving the similarities between image examples. An iterative coordinate descent algorithm is designed as the optimization procedure. Furthermore, we improve the effectiveness of hashing function through orthogonal transformation by minimizing the quantization error. Extensive experiments on two large scale image datasets demonstrate the superior performance of the proposed approach over several state-of-the-art hashing methods.

Keywords: Hashing, Tags, Similarity Search, Image Retrieval.

1 Introduction

Due to the explosive growth of the Internet, a huge amount of image data has been generated, which indicates that efficient similarity search becomes more important. Traditional similarity search methods are difficult to be directly used for large scale datasets since the computational cost of similarity calculation using the original visual features is impractical for large scale applications. Recently, hashing has become a popular approach in large scale vision problems including image retrieval [5], object recognition [20], image matching [19], etc. Hashing methods design compact binary codes for a large number of images so that visually similar images are mapped into similar codes. In the retrieving process, these hashing methods first transform query images into the corresponding

D. Fleet et al. (Eds.): ECCV 2014, Part III, LNCS 8691, pp. 378–392, 2014.
© Springer International Publishing Switzerland 2014

hashing codes and then similarity search can be simply conducted by calculating the Hamming distances between the codes of available images and the query, and selecting images within small Hamming distances.

Recently hashing methods have shown that the hashing performance could be boosted by leveraging supervised information into hashing function learning such as semantic tags/labels. Although existing hashing methods generate promising results in large scale similarity search, tag information is not fully exploited especially when tags are incomplete and noisy. Most of the existing hashing methods only utilize a small portion of the information contained in tags, e.g., pairwise similarity or listwise ranking information, which might not be accurate or reliable under the situation where only partial tags are available. There are three main challenges to incorporate tags into hashing function learning: (1) we have no knowledge about how tags are related to the hashing bits; (2) we need to deal with noisy and incomplete tags when only partial tags are available; (3) we need to deal with the ambiguity of semantically similar tags.

This paper proposes a novel semi-supervised tag hashing (SSTH) approach to fully exploits tag information in learning effective hashing function by modeling the correlation between tags and hashing bits. The hashing function is learned in a unified framework by simultaneously ensuring the tag consistency and preserving the similarities between image examples. In particular, the objective function of the proposed SSTH approach is composed of two parts: (1) Tag consistency term (supervised), which ensures the hashing codes to be consistent with the observed tags via modeling the correlation between tags and hashing bits. (2) Similarity preservation term (unsupervised), which aims at preserving the visual similarity between images in the learned hashing codes. An iterative algorithm is then derived based on the relaxed objective function using a coordinate descent optimization procedure. We further improve the quality of hashing function by minimizing the quantization error.

We summarize the contributions in this paper as follows: (1) propose a unified framework to incorporate the supervised tag information for jointly learning effective hashing function and correlation between tags and hashing codes; (2) propose a coordinate descent method for the relaxed joint optimization problem; (3) prove the orthogonal invariant property of the optimal relaxed solution and learn an orthogonal matrix by minimizing the quantization error to further improve the code effectiveness.

2   Related Work

Hashing methods [1,15,16,17,24,25,27,30,32] are proposed to generate reasonably accurate search results in a fast process with compact binary vector representation. Hashing based fast similarity search methods transform the original visual features into a low dimensional binary space, while at the same time preserve the visual similarity between images as much as possible. Existing hashing methods can be divided into two groups: unsupervised and supervised/semi-supervised hashing methods.

Among the unsupervised hashing approaches, Locality-Sensitive Hashing (LSH) [3] is one of the most popular methods, which uses random linear projections to map images from a high dimensional Euclidean space to a binary space. This method has been extended to Kernelized LSH [7] by exploiting kernel similarity. Traditional dimensionality reduction methods try to solve the hashing problem based on the original feature information via simple thresholding. For example, the Principle Component Analysis (PCA) Hashing [8] method represents each example by coefficients from the top k principal components of the training set, and the coefficients are further binarized to 1 or -1 based on the median value. Restricted Boltzman Machine (RBM) is used in [17] to generate compact binary hashing codes. Recently, Spectral Hashing (SH) [28] is proposed to design compact binary codes with balanced and uncorrelated constraints in the learned codes that preserve the similarity between data examples in the original space. The work in [11] proposes a graph-based hashing method to automatically discover the neighborhood structure inherent in the data to learn appropriate compact codes. More recently, a bit selection method [12] has been proposed to select the most informative hashing bits from a pool of candidate bits generated from different hashing methods.

For the supervised/semi-supervised hashing methods, a Canonical Correlation Analysis with Iterative Quantization (CCA-ITQ) method has been proposed in [4,5] which treats the image features and tags as two different views. The hashing function is then learned by extracting a common space from these two views. The work in [26] combines tag information with topic modeling by extracting topics from texts for document retrieval. Recently, several pairwise hashing methods have been proposed. The semi-supervised hashing (SSH) method in [22] utilizes pairwise knowledge between image examples besides their visual features for learning more effective hashing function. A kernelized supervised hashing (KSH) framework proposed in [10] imposes the pairwise relationship between image examples to obtain good hashing codes. Complementary Hashing (CH) [29] uses pairwise information to learn multiple complementary hash tables in a boosting manner. Most recently, a ranking-based supervised hashing (RSH) [23] method is proposed to leverage the listwise ranking information to improve the search accuracy. However, these pairwise/listwise information is usually extracted from the image tags, and thus only represents a small portion of tag information rather than the complete supervised information contained in tags. Moreover, tags may have different representations for a similar semantic meaning (e.g.,'car' versus 'automobile') and could be missing or incomplete, which makes the pairwise/listwise information not reliable.

3   Semi-Supervised Tag Hashing

3.1   Problem Setting

Assume there are total n training image examples. Let us denote their features as: $X = \{x_1, x_2, \ldots, x_n\} \in R^{d \times n}$, where d is the dimensionality of the visual feature. Denote the observed/partial tags as: $T = \{t_1, t_2, \ldots, t_l\} \in \{0,1\}^{n \times l}$, where l is the total number of possible tags for each image. A label 1 in T means an image is associated with a certain tag, while a label 0 means a missing tag or the tag is not associated with that image. The goal is to obtain a linear hashing function $f : \mathbb{R}^d \rightarrow \{-1, 1\}^k$, which maps image examples X to their binary hashing codes $Y = \{y_1, y_2, \ldots, y_n\} \in \{-1, 1\}^{k \times n}$ (k is the length of hashing code). The linear hashing function is defined as:

$$y_i = f(x_i) = sgn(W^T x_i) \tag{1}$$

where $W \in \mathbb{R}^{d \times k}$ is the coefficient matrix representing the hashing function and sgn is the sign function. $y_i \in \{-1, 1\}^k$ is the binary hashing code of x_i.

The objective function of SSTH is composed of two components: (1) Tag consistency term, the supervised part which ensures that the hashing codes are consistent with the observed tags. (2) Similarity preservation term, the unsupervised part which aims at preserving the visual similarity in the learned hashing codes. In the rest of this section, we will present the formulation of these two components respectively. Then in the next section, we will describe the optimization algorithm together with a scheme that can further improve the quality of the hashing function by minimizing the quantization error.

3.2   Tag Consistency

Image data is often associated with various tags in many vision applications. These tag information provides useful supervised knowledge in learning effective hashing function. Therefore, it is necessary to design a scheme for leveraging tag information. There are three main challenges to incorporate tags. (1) We have no knowledge about how tags are related to the hashing bits. Therefore, we need to explore the correlation between them in order to bridge tags with hashing codes. (2) Tags could be partial and missing, and we need to deal with the situation of incomplete tags. (3) We need to deal with the ambiguity of semantically similar tags (e.g., 'human' versus 'people', 'car' versus 'automobile').

In this work, we propose to model the consistency between tags and hashing codes via matrix factorization using the latent factor model [21]. Semantically similar tags are represented by different tags (e.g., 'human' and 'people' are two distinct tags) in our model and we will discuss how this issue can be addressed later. In the latent factor model, a set of latent variables c_j for each tag t_j is first introduced to model the correlation between tags and hashing bits, where $j \in \{1, 2, \ldots, l\}$ and c_j is a $k \times 1$ vector indicating the correlation between the j-th tag and k hashing bits. Then a tag consistency component can be naturally formulated as:

$$\sum_{i=1}^{n} \sum_{j=1}^{l} \|T_{ij} - y_i^T c_j\|^2 + \alpha \sum_{j=1}^{l} \|c_j\|^2 \tag{2}$$

here T_{ij} is the label of j-th tag on the i-th image. Intuitively, $y_i^T c_j$ can be essentially viewed as a weighted sum that indicates how the j-th tag is related to the i-th image, and this weighted sum should be consistent with the observed label T_{ij} as much as possible. $\sum_{j=1}^{l} \|c_j\|^2$ is a regularizer to avoid overfitting and α is the trade-off parameter. In this way, the latent correlation between tags and hashing bits can be learned by ensuring this consistency term.

The ambiguity issue for semantically similar tags is addressed by the latent factor model since these tags often appear in common images, and thus the learned corresponding latent variables will be similar by ensuring the tag consistency term. This can also be explained by the formulation above, which ensures the consistency between tag t and $\boldsymbol{Y}c$ (i.e., $t \approx \boldsymbol{Y}c$). Therefore, if two tags t_i and t_j are associated with similar images, their corresponding c_i and c_j will be close as well. In the extreme case, if two tags appear in exactly the same set of images, their latent variables will be identical.

An importance matrix $\boldsymbol{I} \in R^{n \times l}$ is introduced to deal with the missing tag problem. As mentioned above, $\boldsymbol{T}_{ij} = 0$ can be interpreted into two ways: j-th tag on the i-th image is either missing or not related. Therefore, we set $\boldsymbol{I}_{ij} = a$ with a higher value when $\boldsymbol{T}_{ij} = 1$ than $\boldsymbol{I}_{ij} = b$ when $\boldsymbol{T}_{ij} = 0$, where a and b are parameters satisfying $a > b > 0$[1]. Then the whole tag consistency term becomes:

$$\sum_{i=1}^{n} \sum_{j=1}^{l} \boldsymbol{I}_{ij} \|\boldsymbol{T}_{ij} - y_i^T c_j\|^2 + \alpha \sum_{j=1}^{l} \|c_j\|^2 \tag{3}$$

By substituting Eqn.1, the above equation can be rewritten as a compact matrix form:

$$\|\boldsymbol{I}^{\frac{1}{2}} \cdot (\boldsymbol{T} - sgn(\boldsymbol{X}^T \boldsymbol{W})\boldsymbol{C})\|_F^2 + \alpha \|\boldsymbol{C}\|_F^2 \tag{4}$$

where $\boldsymbol{I}^{\frac{1}{2}}$ is the element-wise square root matrix of $\boldsymbol{I}$, and $\cdot$ is the element-wise matrix multiplication. $\|\|_F$ is the matrix *Frobenius* norm and $\boldsymbol{C}$ is a $k \times l$ correlation matrix bridging the hashing codes with tags. By minimizing this term, the consistency between tags and the learned hashing codes is ensured.

3.3 Similarity Preservation

One of the key problems in hashing algorithms is similarity preserving, which indicates that visually similar images should be mapped to similar hashing codes within a short Hamming distance. The Hamming distance between two binary codes y_i and y_j can be calculated as $\frac{1}{4}\|y_i - y_j\|^2$. To measure the similarity between image examples represented by the binary hashing codes, one natural way is to minimize the weighted average Hamming distance as follows:

$$\sum_{i,j} \boldsymbol{S}_{ij} \|y_i - y_j\|^2 \tag{5}$$

Here, $\boldsymbol{S}$ is the similarity matrix, which can be calculated from image features $\boldsymbol{X}$. In this paper, we adopt the local similarity [31], due to its nice property in many machine learning applications. To meet the similarity preservation criterion, we seek to minimize this quantity since it incurs a heavy penalty if two similar images are mapped far away.

---

[1] In our experiments, we set the importance parameters a=1 and b=0.01.

By introducing a diagonal $n \times n$ matrix D, whose entries are given by $D_{ii} = \sum_{j=1}^{n} S_{ij}$. Eqn.5 can be rewritten as:

$$tr\left(Y(D - S)Y^T\right) = tr\left(YLY^T\right) = tr\left(sgn(W^TX)Lsgn(X^TW)\right) \qquad (6)$$

where L is called graph *Laplacian* [28] and $tr()$ is the matrix trace function. The similarity preservation term plays an important role in hashing function learning especially when the supervised information is limit due to noisy and incomplete tags. By minimizing this term, the similarity between different image examples can be preserved in the learned hashing codes.

3.4 Overall Objective

The entire objective function consists of two components: the tag consistency term in Eqn.4 and the visual similarity preservation term given in Eqn.6 as follows:

$$\min_{W,C} \|I^{\frac{1}{2}} \cdot (T - sgn(X^TW)C)\|_F^2 + \gamma\, tr\left(sgn(W^TX)Lsgn(X^TW)\right) + \alpha\|C\|_F^2$$

$$s.t. \quad W^TW = I_k$$

$$(7)$$

where α and γ are trade-off parameters to balance the weights among the terms. The hard orthogonality constraints enforce the hashing bits to be uncorrelated with each other and therefore the learned hashing codes can hold least redundant information.

4   Optimization Algorithm

4.1 Relaxation

Directly minimizing the objective function in Eqn.7 is intractable since it is a constrained integer programming, which is proven to be NP-hard to solve. Therefore, we first convert the hard constraints into a soft penalty term by adding a regularizer to the objective and use the signed magnitude instead of the sign function as suggested in [10,23]. Then the relaxed objective function becomes:

$$\min_{\tilde{W},C} \|I^{\frac{1}{2}} \cdot (T - X^T\tilde{W}C)\|_F^2 + \gamma\, tr\left(\tilde{W}^T\tilde{L}\tilde{W}\right) + \alpha\|C\|_F^2 + \beta\|\tilde{W}^T\tilde{W} - I_k\|_F^2 \quad (8)$$

where $\tilde{L} \equiv XLX^T$ and can be pre-computed. However, even after the relaxation, the objective function is still difficult to optimize since $\tilde{W}$ and C are coupled together and it is non-convex with respect to $\tilde{W}$ and C jointly. We propose to split the optimization problem into two simpler sub-problems. The idea is that given $\tilde{W}$, C has a closed form solution with respect to $\tilde{W}$ (see details in $SP2$ below). Thus we split the relaxed objective with respect to $\tilde{W}$ and C and solve the two sub-problems iteratively using coordinate descent method. The two sub-problems are given as:

$$SP1 : \min_{\tilde{W}} \|I^{\frac{1}{2}} \cdot (T - X^T \tilde{W} C)\|_F^2 + \gamma\, tr\left(\tilde{W}^T \tilde{L} \tilde{W}\right) + \beta \|\tilde{W}^T \tilde{W} - I_k\|_F^2 \quad (9)$$

$$SP2 : \min_{C} \|I^{\frac{1}{2}} \cdot (T - X^T \tilde{W} C)\|_F^2 + \alpha \|C\|_F^2 \quad (10)$$

$SP1$ is still non-convex, but it is smooth and differentiable which enables gradient descent methods for efficient optimization. The gradient of $SP1$ is calculated as follows:

$$\partial \frac{SP1}{\tilde{W}} = 2X(I \cdot (X^T \tilde{W} C - T))C^T + 2\gamma \tilde{L} \tilde{W} + 4\beta \tilde{W}(\tilde{W}^T \tilde{W} - I_k) \quad (11)$$

With this obtained gradient, L-BFGS quasi-Newton method [9] is applied to solve $SP1$.

By taking the derivative of $SP2$ w.r.t. C and setting it to 0, we can obtain the closed form solution of $SP2$ below:

$$\partial \frac{SP2}{C} = 2\tilde{W}^T X(I \cdot (X^T \tilde{W} C - T)) + 2\alpha C = 0$$
$$\Rightarrow c_j = (\tilde{W}^T X I_j X^T \tilde{W} + \alpha I_k)^{-1} \tilde{W}^T X I_j T_j \quad (12)$$

where I_j is a $n \times n$ diagonal matrix with $I_{ij}, i = 1, 2, \ldots, n$ as its diagonal elements and $T_j = (T_{ij}), i = 1, 2, \ldots, n$ is a $n \times 1$ label vector of j-th tag.

We alternate the process of updating $\tilde{W}$ and C for several iterations to find a locally optimal solution. In practice, we have found that a reasonable small number of iterations (i.e., 30 in our experiments) can achieve good performance.

4.2   Orthogonal Transformation

After obtaining the optimal hashing function $\tilde{W}$ for the relaxation, the hashing codes Y can be generated using Eqn.1. It is obvious that the quantization error can be measured as $\|Y - \tilde{W}^T X\|_F^2$. Inspired by [5], we propose to further improve the hashing function by minimizing this quantization error using an orthogonal transformation. We first prove the following orthogonal invariant theorem.

Theorem 1. *Assume Q is a $k \times k$ orthogonal matrix, i.e., $Q^T Q = I_k$. If $\tilde{W}$ and C are an optimal solution to the relaxed problem in Eqn.8, then $\tilde{W} Q$ and $Q^T C$ are also an optimal solution.*

Proof. By substituting $\tilde{W} Q$ and $Q^T C$ into Eqn.8, we have:
$\|I^{\frac{1}{2}} \cdot (T - X^T \tilde{W} Q Q^T C)\|_F^2 = \|I^{\frac{1}{2}} \cdot (T - X^T \tilde{W} C)\|_F^2$,
$tr\left((\tilde{W} Q)^T \tilde{L} \tilde{W} Q\right) = tr\left(Q^T \tilde{W}^T \tilde{L} \tilde{W} Q\right) = tr\left(\tilde{W}^T \tilde{L} \tilde{W}\right)$, $\|Q^T C\|_F^2 = \|C\|_F^2$
and $\|(\tilde{W} Q)^T \tilde{W} Q - I_k\|_F^2 = \|Q^T(\tilde{W}^T \tilde{W} - I_k)Q\|_F^2 = \|\tilde{W}^T \tilde{W} - I_k\|_F^2$.
Thus, the value of the objective function in Eqn.8 does not change by the orthogonal transformation.

According to the above theorem, we propose to find a better hashing function $W = \tilde{W}Q$ by minimizing the quantization error between the binary hashing codes and the orthogonal transformation of the relaxed solution as follows:

$$\min_{Y,Q} \|Y - (\tilde{W}Q)^T X\|_F^2$$

$$s.t. \quad Y \in \{-1, 1\}^{k \times n}, \quad Q^T Q = I_k \tag{13}$$

Intuitively, we seek binary codes that are close to some orthogonal transformation of the relaxed solution. The orthogonal transformation not only preserves the optimality of the relaxed solution but also provides us more flexibility to achieve better hashing codes with low quantization error. The idea of orthogonal transformation is also utilized in ITQ [5]. However, ITQ method is not designed for incorporating partial tag information into learning effective hashing function and it does not preserve the local similarities among data examples. The above optimization problem can be solved by minimizing Eqn.13 with respect to Y and Q alternatively as follows:

Fix Q and update Y. The closed form solution can be expressed as:

$$Y = sgn\left((\tilde{W}Q)^T X\right) = sgn(W^T X) \tag{14}$$

which is identical with our linear hashing function in Eqn.1.

Fix Y and update Q. The objective function becomes:

$$\min_{Q^T Q = I_k} \|Y - Q^T \tilde{W}^T X\|_F^2 \tag{15}$$

In this case, the objective function is essentially the classic Orthogonal Procrustes problem [18], which can be solved efficiently by singular value decomposition using the following theorem (we refer to [18] for the detailed proof).

Theorem 2. *Let $S\Lambda V^T$ be the singular value decomposition of $YX^T\tilde{W}$. Then $Q = VS^T$ minimizes the objective function in Eqn.15.*

We then perform the above two steps alternatively to obtain the optimal hashing codes and the orthogonal transform matrix. In our experiments, we find that the algorithm usually converges in about 40~60 iterations. The full learning algorithm is described in Algorithm 1.

4.3 Complexity Analysis

This section provides some analysis on the training cost of the optimization algorithm. The optimization algorithm of SSTH consists of two main loops. In the first loop, we iteratively solve $SP1$ and $SP2$ to obtain the optimal solution, where the time complexities for solving $SP1$ and $SP2$ are bounded by $O(nlk + nkd + nk^2)$ and $O(nk^2 + nkl)$ respectively. The second loop iteratively optimizes the binary hashing codes and the orthogonal transformation matrix, where the

---

Algorithm 1. Semi-Supervised Tag Hashing (SSTH)

Input: Images X, Observed Tags T and trade-off parameters
Output: Hashing function W, Hashing codes Y and Correlation C
   Initialize $C = 0$ and $Q = I_k$, Calculate $\tilde{L}$.
   repeat
      Optimize $SP1$ using Eqn.11 and update $\tilde{W}$
      Optimize $SP2$ using Eqn.12 and update C
   until the solution converges
   repeat
      Update Y using Eqn.14
      Update $Q = VS^T$ according to Theorem 2.
   until the solution converges
   Compute hashing function $W = \tilde{W}Q$.

---

time complexities for updating Y and Q are bounded by $O(nk^2 + nkd + k^3)$. Moreover, both two loops take less than 60 iterations to converge as mentioned before. Thus, the total time complexity of the learning algorithm is bounded by $O(nlk + nkd + nk^2 + k^3)$, which scales linearly with n given $n \gg l > d > k$. For each query, the hashing time is constant $O(dk)$.

5   Experimental Results

5.1   Datasets

We evaluate our method for large scale image retrieval on two image benchmarks: *NUS-WIDE* and *FLICKR-1M*. *NUS-WIDE* [2] is created by NUS lab for evaluating image annotation and retrieval techniques. It contains $270k$ images associated with $5k$ unique tags. 500-dimensional visual features are extracted using a bag-of-visual-word model with local SIFT descriptor [13]. We randomly partition this dataset into two parts, $1k$ for testing and around $269k$ for training. *FLICKR-1M* [6] is collected from Flicker images for image retrieval tasks. This benchmark contains 1 million image examples associated with more than $7k$ unique tags. 512-dimensional GIST descriptors [14] are extracted from these images and are used as image features for hashing function learning. We randomly choose $990k$ image examples as the training set and $10k$ for testing.

    We implement our algorithm using Matlab on a PC with Intel Duo Core i5-2400 CPU 3.1GHz and 8GB RAM. The parameters α, β and γ in SSTH are tuned by 5-fold cross validation on the training set.

5.2   Evaluation Method

To conduct fair evaluation, we follow two criteria which are commonly used in the literature [5,10,23]: *Hamming Ranking* and *Hash Lookup*. *Hamming Ranking* ranks all the points in the database according to their Hamming distance from the query and the top k points are returned as the desired neighbors.

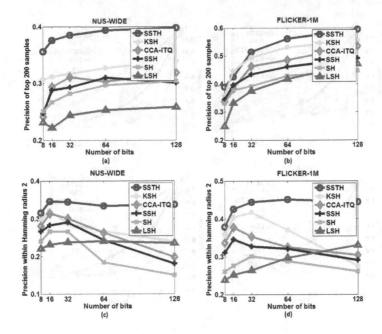

Fig. 1. Precision results on two datasets. (a)-(b): Precision of the top 200 returned examples using *Hamming Ranking*. (c)-(d): Precision within Hamming radius 2 using *Hash Lookup*.

Hash Lookup returns all the points within a small Hamming radius r of the query. The search results are evaluated based on whether the retrieved image and the query image share any ground-truth tags (i.e., if a returned image and the query image share any common semantic tags, then we treat this returned image as a true neighbor of the query image). We use several metrics to measure the performance of different methods. For *Hamming Ranking* based evaluation, we calculate the precision at top K which is the percentage of true neighbors among the top K returned examples, where we set K to be 200 in the experiments. We also compute the precision-recall value which is a widely used metric in information retrieval applications. A hamming radius of $R = 2$ is used to retrieve the neighbors in the case of *Hash Lookup*. The precision of the returned examples falling within Hamming radius 2 is reported.

5.3   Results and Discussion

The proposed SSTH approach is compared with five different algorithms, i.e., Spectral Hashing (SH) [28], Latent Semantic Hashing (LSH) [3], Canonical Correlation Analysis with Iterative Quantization (CCA-ITQ) [5,4], Semi-Supervised Hashing (SSH) [22] and Kernel Supervised Hashing (KSH) [10]. For LSH, we randomly select projections from a Gaussian distribution with zero-mean and identity covariance to construct the hash tables. For SSH and KSH, we sample $2k$

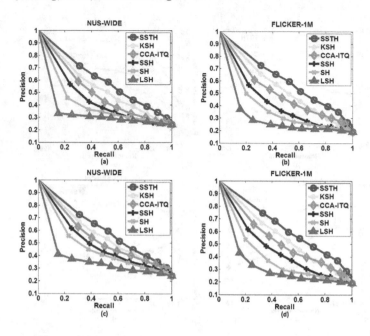

Fig. 2. Results of Precision-Recall behavior on two datasets. (a)-(b): Precision-Recall curve with 16 hashing bits. (c)-(d): Precision-Recall curve with 32 hashing bits.

random points from the training set to construct the pairwise constraint matrix. The reason we choose $2k$ points is that tags tend to be noisy and incomplete, and the constructed pairwise matrix based on these tags may be unreliable and inconsistent especially when tags are very sparse, resulting in even lower performance with more samples. Therefore, following the parameter settings in their papers, we also sample $2k$ points in our experiments.

In the first set of experiments, we report the precisions for the top 200 retrieved images and the precisions for retrieved images within Hamming ball with radius 2 by varying the number of hashing bits in the range of $\{8, 16, 32, 64, 128\}$ in Fig.1. The precision-recall curves with 16 and 32 hashing bits on both datasets are reported in Fig.2. From these comparison results, we can see that SSTH provides the best results among all six hashing methods on both benchmarks. LSH does not perform well in most cases since LSH method is data-independent, which may generate inefficient codes compared to those data-depend methods. The unsupervised SH method only tries to preserve image similarity in learned hashing codes, but does not utilize the supervised information contained in tags. SSH and KSH achieves better performance than SH and LSH due to the modeling of pairwise information. However, as pointed out in section 2, the coarse pairwise constraints generated from tags do not fully utilize tag information. The supervised method CCA-ITQ have similar performance to KSH since it also incorporates tags into learning better data representations. But in CCA-ITQ, it treats tags as another independent source where it may not be even reliable as tags can be incomplete, noisy and partially available. Moreover, the visual similarity is not well preserved in its hashing function learning. On the other hand, our SSTH not only exploits tag information via modeling the correlation between tags and hashing bits, but also preserves image similarity at the same time in the learned hashing function, which enables SSTH to generate higher quality hashing codes than the other supervised hashing methods. In Fig.1(c)-(d), we observe the precision of *Hash Lookup* for most of the compared methods decreases significantly with the increasing number of hashing bits. The reason is that the Hamming space becomes increasingly sparse with longer hashing bits and very few data points fall within the Hamming ball with radius 2, which makes many queries have 0 precision results. However, the precision of SSTH is still consistently higher than the other methods for *Hash Lookup*.

Table 1. Precision of the top 200 retrieved images under different training tag ratios on two datasets with 32 hashing bits

	NUS-WIDE					FLICKR-1M				
tag ratio	0.2	0.4	0.6	0.8	1.0	0.2	0.4	0.6	0.8	1.0
SSTH	**0.337**	**0.341**	**0.354**	**0.363**	**0.374**	**0.453**	**0.461**	**0.476**	0.480	**0.518**
SSTH^0	0.328	0.332	0.347	0.351	0.356	0.443	0.449	0.464	0.476	0.505
KSH [10]	0.288	0.296	0.301	0.308	0.316	0.422	0.448	0.459	**0.481**	0.484
CCA-ITQ [5,4]	0.287	0.290	0.305	0.330	0.348	0.410	0.427	0.445	0.467	0.494
SSH [22]	0.283	0.285	0.291	0.297	0.299	0.398	0.416	0.422	0.435	0.439

In the second set of experiments, we evaluate the effectiveness of the proposed SSTH if only partial tags are available. We progressively increase the number of training tags by varying the training tag ratio from $\{0.2, 0.4, 0.6, 0.8, 1\}^2$ and compare our SSTH with the other supervised hashing methods[3], CCA-ITQ, SSH and KSH on both datasets by fixing the hashing bits to 32. The precision results of top 200 retrieved images are reported in Table 1. We also evaluate our method without orthogonal transformation (by setting $Q = I_k$) and call this SSTH^0 in Table 1. It can be seen from the results that our SSTH gives the best performance among all supervised hashing methods in most cases. We also observe that the precision result of CCA-ITQ drops much faster than SSTH when the number of training tags decreases. Our hypothesis is that when training tags are very sparse, the common space learned from partial tags and visual features by CCA-ITQ is not accurate and reliable, resulting in low quality hashing codes. The comparison results of SSTH and SSTH^0 in Table 1 demonstrate that the orthogonal transformation can further improve the effectiveness of the hashing function, which is consistent with our expectation.

The third set of experiments demonstrate how the learned correlations, C, can bridge tags and hashing codes. We conduct the experiments on *FLICKR-1M*

---

[2] Tags are randomly sampled from the training data based on the ratio.

[3] SH and LSH do not utilize tags and thus are not necessary to be compared here.

Fig. 3. Results of top 3 predicted tags on *FLICKR-1M*

to predict tags for query images based on their hashing codes. In particular, we first generate hashing code for each query image by $y_q = W^T x_q$, and predict its tag vector using $t_q = C^T y_q$. Then we select the top 3 tags with largest values in tag vector t_q as the predicted tags for the query image. The comparison results of the top 3 predicted tags with ground truth tags on several images are shown in Fig.3. From this figure we can see that our SSTH can generate reasonable accurate tags for query images. The reason is that our method not only incorporates tags in learning effective hashing function, but also extracts the correlation between tags and hashing bits. Therefore, the tag information is fully explored in our SSTH.

In the fourth set of experiments, the training time for learning hashing function and testing time for encoding each query image on both datasets (with 32 bits) are reported in Table 2. Note that we do not include the cross-validation time and any offline calculation cost in all methods for fair comparison. We can see from this table that the training time of SSTH is comparable with most of the other hashing methods and it is efficient enough in practice. The test time is

Table 2. Training and testing time (in second) on two datasets with 32 hashing bits

| | NUS-WIDE | | FLICKR-1M | |
methods	training	testing	training	testing
SSTH	83.57	$0.4\text{x}10^{-4}$	219.03	$0.6\text{x}10^{-4}$
KSH [10]	248.85	$2.4\text{x}10^{-4}$	592.16	$2.5\text{x}10^{-4}$
CCA-ITQ [5,4]	46.13	$0.5\text{x}10^{-4}$	135.37	$0.5\text{x}10^{-4}$
SSH [22]	23.56	$0.4\text{x}10^{-4}$	40.83	$0.5\text{x}10^{-4}$
SH [28]	51.63	$3.6\text{x}10^{-4}$	173.68	$4.1\text{x}10^{-4}$
LSH [3]	2.75	$0.4\text{x}10^{-4}$	7.84	$0.4\text{x}10^{-4}$

sufficiently fast especially when compared to the nonlinear hashing method SH and kernel hashing method KSH.

6   Conclusions

This paper proposes a novel Semi-Supervised Tag Hashing (SSTH) framework that incorporates partial tag information by exploring the correlation between tags and hashing bits to fully exploit tag information. The framework simultaneously ensures the consistency between hashing codes and tags and preserves the similarities between images. Orthogonal transform is proposed for further improving the effectiveness of hashing bits. Experiments on two large scale datasets demonstrate the advantage of the proposed method over several state-of-the-art hashing methods. In future, we plan to investigate generalization error bound for the proposed learning method. We also plan to apply some sequential learning approach to accelerate the training speed of our method.

Acknowledgments. This work is partially supported by NSF research grants IIS-0746830, DRL-0822296, CNS-1012208, IIS-1017837, CNS-1314688 and a research grant from Office of Naval Research (ONR-11627465). This work is also partially supported by the Center for Science of Information (CSoI), an NSF Science and Technology Center, under grant agreement CCF-0939370.

References

1. Bergamo, A., Torresani, L., Fitzgibbon, A.W.: Picodes: Learning a compact code for novel-category recognition. In: NIPS, pp. 2088–2096 (2011)
2. Chua, T.S., Tang, J., Hong, R., Li, H., Luo, Z., Zheng, Y.: Nus-wide: A real-world web image database from national university of singapore. In: CIVR (2009)
3. Datar, M., Immorlica, N., Indyk, P., Mirrokni, V.S.: Locality-sensitive hashing scheme based on p-stable distributions. In: Symposium on Computational Geometry, pp. 253–262 (2004)
4. Gong, Y., Ke, Q., Isard, M., Lazebnik, S.: A multi-view embedding space for modeling internet images, tags, and their semantics. International Journal of Computer Vision 106(2), 210–233 (2014)
5. Gong, Y., Lazebnik, S., Gordo, A., Perronnin, F.: Iterative quantization: A procrustean approach to learning binary codes for large-scale image retrieval. IEEE TPAMI (2012)
6. Huiskes, M.J., Thomee, B., Lew, M.S.: New trends and ideas in visual concept detection: the mir flickr retrieval evaluation initiative. In: Multimedia Information Retrieval, pp. 527–536 (2010)
7. Kulis, B., Grauman, K.: Kernelized locality-sensitive hashing for scalable image search. In: ICCV, pp. 2130–2137 (2009)
8. Lin, R.S., Ross, D.A., Yagnik, J.: Spec hashing: Similarity preserving algorithm for entropy-based coding. In: CVPR, pp. 848–854 (2010)
9. Liu, D.C., Nocedal, J.: On the limited memory bfgs method for large scale optimization. Mathematical Programming 45, 503–528 (1989)

10. Liu, W., Wang, J., Ji, R., Jiang, Y.G., Chang, S.F.: Supervised hashing with kernels. In: CVPR, pp. 2074–2081 (2012)
11. Liu, W., Wang, J., Kumar, S., Chang, S.F.: Hashing with graphs. In: ICML, pp. 1–8 (2011)
12. Liu, X., He, J., Lang, B., Chang, S.F.: Hash bit selection: A unified solution for selection problems in hashing. In: CVPR, pp. 1570–1577 (2013)
13. Lowe, D.G.: Distinctive image features from scale-invariant keypoints. IJCV 60(2), 91–110 (2004)
14. Oliva, A., Torralba, A.: Modeling the shape of the scene: A holistic representation of the spatial envelope. IJCV 42(3), 145–175 (2001)
15. Raginsky, M., Lazebnik, S.: Locality-sensitive binary codes from shift-invariant kernels. In: NIPS, pp. 1509–1517 (2009)
16. Rastegari, M., Farhadi, A., Forsyth, D.: Attribute discovery via predictable discriminative binary codes. In: Fitzgibbon, A., Lazebnik, S., Perona, P., Sato, Y., Schmid, C. (eds.) ECCV 2012, Part VI. LNCS, vol. 7577, pp. 876–889. Springer, Heidelberg (2012)
17. Salakhutdinov, R., Hinton, G.E.: Semantic hashing. Int. J. Approx. Reasoning 50(7), 969–978 (2009)
18. Schonemann, P.: A generalized solution of the orthogonal procrustes problem. Psychometrika 31(1), 1–10 (1966)
19. Strecha, C., Bronstein, A.A., Bronstein, M.M., Fua, P.: Ldahash: Improved matching with smaller descriptors. IEEE TPAMI 34(1), 66–78 (2012)
20. Torralba, A., Fergus, R., Freeman, W.T.: 80 million tiny images: A large data set for nonparametric object and scene recognition. IEEE TPAMI 30(11), 1958–1970 (2008)
21. Wang, C., Blei, D.M.: Collaborative topic modeling for recommending scientific articles. In: KDD, pp. 448–456 (2011)
22. Wang, J., Kumar, S., Chang, S.F.: Semi-supervised hashing for large-scale search. IEEE TPAMI 34(12), 2393–2406 (2012)
23. Wang, J., Liu, W., Sun, A., Jiang, Y.G.: Learning hash codes with listwise supervision. In: ICCV (2013)
24. Wang, Q., Shen, B., Wang, S., Li, L., Si, L.: Binary codes emmbedding for fast image tagging with incomplete labels. In: ECCV (2014)
25. Wang, Q., Si, L., Zhang, Z., Zhang, N.: Active hashing with joint data example and tag selection. In: SIGIR (2014)
26. Wang, Q., Zhang, D., Si, L.: Semantic hashing using tags and topic modeling. In: SIGIR, pp. 213–222 (2013)
27. Wang, Q., Zhang, D., Si, L.: Weighted hashing for fast large scale similarity search. In: CIKM, pp. 1185–1188 (2013)
28. Weiss, Y., Torralba, A., Fergus, R.: Spectral hashing. In: NIPS, pp. 1753–1760 (2008)
29. Xu, H., Wang, J., Li, Z., Zeng, G., Li, S., Yu, N.: Complementary hashing for approximate nearest neighbor search. In: ICCV, pp. 1631–1638 (2011)
30. Ye, G., Liu, D., Wang, J., Chang, S.F.: Large scale video hashing via structure learning. In: ICCV (2013)
31. Zhang, D., Wang, J., Cai, D., Lu, J.: Self-taught hashing for fast similarity search. In: SIGIR, pp. 18–25 (2010)
32. Zhang, L., Zhang, Y., Tang, J., Lu, K., Tian, Q.: Binary code ranking with weighted hamming distance. In: CVPR, pp. 1586–1593 (2013)

Multi-class Open Set Recognition Using Probability of Inclusion

Lalit P. Jain[1], Walter J. Scheirer[1,2], and Terrance E. Boult[1,3,*]

[1] University of Coloradom, Colorado Springs, USA
[2] Harvard University, USA
[3] Securics, Inc., USA

Abstract. The perceived success of recent visual recognition approaches has largely been derived from their performance on classification tasks, where all possible classes are known at training time. But what about open set problems, where unknown classes appear at test time? Intuitively, if we could accurately model just the positive data for any known class without overfitting, we could reject the large set of unknown classes even under an assumption of incomplete class knowledge. In this paper, we formulate the problem as one of modeling positive training data at the decision boundary, where we can invoke the statistical extreme value theory. A new algorithm called the P_I-SVM is introduced for estimating the unnormalized posterior probability of class inclusion.

1 Introduction

Recent classification results reported for the ImageNet Large-Scale Visual Recognition Challenge [31,32] have captured the computer vision community's interest. With such low error rates (the top performing algorithm on the 2013 ImageNet challenge, a convolutional neural network, achieves an error rate of 11.1%), one might believe that we are closer to solving real-world visual object recognition than ever before. However, it is fair to ask if a scenario in which all classes are known during training time leads to an accurate assessment of the overall state of object recognition. Importantly, the *detection* results from the 2013 ImageNet challenge tell a different story. When unknown objects must be rejected in the process of detecting the location and label of a known object, no approach produces a result as impressive as what we see for classification: the best result is a mean average precision of just 22.6%. Detection falls under the general class of machine learning problems known as *open set recognition* [45], *i.e.* when the possibility of encountering novel classes not present in training exists during testing.

Emerging research that moves beyond typical binary models of positive/negative class association for open set recognition has examined the issues of detecting novel classes [16,5,4], rejecting outlier or unknown classes [24,57,2], and/or simultaneously detecting and recognizing known classes in the midst of unknown classes [45,11,14]. These approaches have been a good start, but they do not directly address the overarching problem: *multi-class open set recognition*, wherein models should account for multiple known classes as well as provide an option to detect novel classes or reject

* This work was supported in part by ONR MURI N00014-08-1-0638 and NSF IIS-1320956.

D. Fleet et al. (Eds.): ECCV 2014, Part III, LNCS 8691, pp. 393–409, 2014.
© Springer International Publishing Switzerland 2014

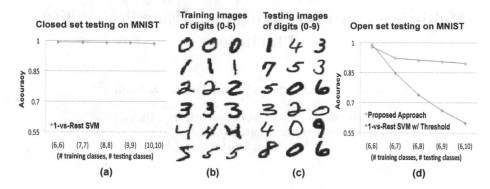

Fig. 1. What happens when the MNIST database of handwritten digits [33] is converted from a closed set classification task to an open set recognition task? (a) Standard supervised learning algorithms approach ceiling on the original MNIST classification problem. Here we show results for a 1-vs-Rest SVM with Platt [37] probability estimates using the same number of training and testing classes, where all classes are seen during training. (b) Training data consisting of six classes from MNIST. (c) Testing data consisting of all ten classes from MNIST, including four classes unseen during training. (d) By changing the testing regime to *cross-class-validation*, where some number of classes are held out during training (*e.g.* subfigure b) but included in testing (*e.g.* subfigure c), MNIST once again becomes a challenge. As soon as classes are with-held during training, the accuracy of the 1-vs-Rest SVM (with a rejection option provided by thresholding the Platt probability estimates) drops significantly. In this paper, we propose a new algorithm called the P_I-SVM, which retains higher levels of accuracy as the problem grows to be more open.

unknown classes. In this paper, we introduce a new and effective algorithm for this task. Moreover, in contrast to popular detection challenges such as PASCAL VOC [19] where background classes have the same distribution in the training and test sets, the problem considered here assumes that completely new background classes can appear at test time.

Careful experimental design is necessary to evaluate multi-class open set recognition. Ideally, we would like to use well-known data sets. However, open set recognition requires an experimental regime that provides classes unseen during training – using all testing classes during training inflates performance on recognition problems. To address this, we can extend the familiar idea of cross-validation to *cross-class-validation*, wherein we simulate the unknown classes of an open set scenario by defining the number of training classes, target classes to recognize, classifiers, and validation classes, leaving some classes out during training while including them in testing. After moving to the open set multi-class recognition scenario, even what appear to be very simple "solved" pattern recognition tasks become quite difficult. To illustrate this point, Fig. 1 demonstrates how cross-class-validation transforms a classic closed set classification problem such as the MNIST database of handwritten digits [33] into a challenging multi-class open set recognition problem. In closed set classification (Fig. 1(a)), standard approaches such as multi-class 1-vs-Rest SVM achieve an average accuracy rate of approximately 98%. However, their accuracy drops significantly when using open set cross-class-validation testing (Fig. 1(d)).

An obvious way [30,23,57] to approach the multi-class open set recognition problem is to incorporate a posterior probability estimator $P(y|x)$, where $y \in \mathbb{N}$ is a class label and $x \in \mathbb{R}^d$ is multi-dimensional feature data, and a decision threshold into an existing multi-class algorithm. Letting $\mathcal{C}$ be the set of known classes, testing is a two step process: 1) compute the maximum probability over known classes, and 2) label the data as "unknown" if that probability is below the threshold δ:

$$y^* = \begin{cases} \operatorname{argmax}_{y_i \in \mathcal{C}} P(y_i|x) & \text{if } P(y^*|x) \geq \delta. \\ \text{"unknown"} & \text{Otherwise} \end{cases} \tag{1}$$

Such a thresholded probability model can support a multi-class classifier with a rejection option, *e.g.* the 1-vs-Rest SVM with a threshold applied over Platt calibrated [37] decision scores as shown in Fig. 1(d). A key question when applying any probability estimator is: how do we build a consistent probability model without over-fitting or over-generalizing? While better than a strict multi-class SVM, which always assigns a known class label, SVM with a rejection option is still not very good for open set recognition. It is weak because it implicitly makes closed set assumptions during the decision score calibration process. In open set recognition, a sample that is *not* from a known negative class does not imply that it is from the positive class. Furthermore, because we must consider the possibility of unknown classes, Bayes' theorem does not directly apply. The best we can do is produce an unnormalized posterior estimate. In essence, we need a good way, in an open class setting, to consistently estimate the unnormalized posterior *probability of inclusion* for each class.

In this paper, we introduce the novel idea of fitting *a robust single-class probability model over the positive class scores from a discriminative binary classifier*. The use of an underlying binary classification model helps to discriminate the positive class from the known negative classes, while the single-class probability model adjusts the decision boundary so unknown classes are not frequently misclassified as belonging to the positive class. For consistency with open set assumptions, this model does not directly use negative data in its probabilistic modeling. Our algorithm, the P_I-SVM, follows this approach by modeling the unnormalized posterior probability of inclusion for multiple classes using a multi-class SVM as a basis, and fitting probability distributions consistent with the Statistical Extreme Value Theory (EVT) [12] to decision scores from positive training samples. This paper extends the recent statistical learning work of Scheirer et al. [43,42], which is limited to closed set problems. Our extension directly models the probability of inclusion for open set problems.

2   Related Work

The related work spans one-class classifiers, open set recognition, decision score calibration and probability-based rejection techniques for multi-class recognition. Of these topics, one-class classifiers, which require only positive training data, are a natural starting place for a solution to open set recognition. Density Estimation, Support Vector

Data Description (SVDD), and the One-class SVM are all prevalent techniques used for one-class classification. A simple way to obtain a one-class model is to fit a Gaussian distribution to the positive training data for a class and set a threshold on the resulting density [50]. A more sophisticated approach to accomplish the same goal is SVDD [49], where a hypersphere with the minimum radius is estimated around the positive class data that encompasses almost all training points. Using a different strategy, the training procedure for a one-class SVM [46] treats the origin in feature space as the only member of the second class, and maximizes the margin with respect to it. One-class models are typically less effective than binary classifiers [5,45,54].

More powerful binary classification models have been proposed specifically for open set visual recognition tasks. Scheirer et al. [45,41] offer a formalization of the risk of the unknown in open set recognition that is used to develop the 1-vs-Set Machine (a dual-plane linear classifier) [45] and W-SVM (a calibrated non-linear classifier) [41] algorithms. An approach similar to the 1-vs-Set Machine was described by Cevikalp and Triggs [8] for object detection. Unlike the approach we introduce here, none of these algorithms leverages a robust probability estimator for a single class that is derived from a binary classifier. Also related to the idea of unknown data is the "universum" [55], which constructs a data-dependent structure on the set of admissible functions by using a set of unlabeled training examples. However, the resulting model is still a traditional closed set binary classifier.

To estimate probabilities, various researchers [26,53,37,56,17,28,6] have proposed different techniques for converting a raw decision score to calibrated output. In all of these techniques a parametric model is assumed for the underlying distribution; parameters are estimated from calibration data and the raw scores mapped based on the resulting model. In practice, Gaussian modeling is common. The most widely used technique for score calibration is Platt's approach [37], which was originally proposed for SVM calibration, but has since been extended and evaluated on many types of learning systems [36]. In a cross-validation style training regime, a sigmoid function is fit to the decision scores from each fold, which is then used as a probability estimator for the overall classification model. Zadrozny and Elkan [56] note that "Platt scaling is most effective when the size of training/calibration data is small," which is potentially useful for open set recognition, where known negative class data in training is always smaller than the full domain of negative class data encountered during testing. Hybrid classifiers such as Naive Bayes Nearest Neighbor (NBNN) [3,34] can also provide probability estimation, but do so under a closed set assumption. It may be possible to adapt their estimates for an open setting, but we have not found an efficient means to do so.

In this paper, we propose using the Extreme Value Theory [12] for calibrating SVM decision scores to unnormalized posterior probabilities reflecting class inclusion. For recognition problems in computer vision, EVT has been demonstrated to be a powerful explanatory theory [43] and an effective tool for statistical modeling [7,22,21], including fitting probability estimators [44,42,41]. The most relevant work in EVT modeling is the multi-attribute spaces approach of Scheirer et al. [42], which applies EVT calibration over binary classifiers for visual attribute assignment. In essence, the algorithm estimates the probability of exclusion from the negative class. For example, in a gender classifier, the probability of being female is $1 - P(\text{male})$. This may be viable in a binary closed set problem, but is not an option for open set recognition. Moreover, Scheirer et al. do not describe how to estimate the critical "tail size" parameter.

Finally, using probabilities it is possible to reject "unlikely" samples (see Eq. 1), which can often improve our ability to reject unknown inputs. For multi-class recognition problems in computer vision, posterior probabilities are widely used to make decisions in applications such as pedestrian classification and orientation estimation [18], image retrieval [15], attribute fusion [42], part-based human tracking [47], large-scale multi-class object categorization [4], and activity recognition [39], among others. To operate in open set scenarios, a threshold for these algorithms can be set at a certain confidence interval to reject unknown classes. Chow [10] showed that the optimal decision rule is always a threshold over the posterior probability. Thus various score thresholds have been studied as rejection techniques, *e.g.* [30,23,57]. Recent prior work on thresholding [2,24] extends the notion of rejection via a threshold to the loss function of SVM to increase the cost of confusing samples. However, we note that in open set recognition the derivation of optimality in [10] does not hold, bringing the closed set modeling of all of these approaches into question for the general problem.

3   Single-Class Probability Estimation from a Binary Model

Intuitively, a one-class classifier such as the one-class SVM [46] seems like it should help us solve the open set recognition problem by providing a per-class model using just the positive data for each class. One-class classifiers do not assume a closed world, nor do they make any assumptions about negative or unknown classes. Unfortunately, it is precisely because they do not use any negative data that one-class classifiers have trouble enforcing separation between known positive and negative classes. The example in Fig. 2 highlights this issue.

To improve discrimination, binary classifiers such as RBF SVM use data from both positive and negative classes. But these models

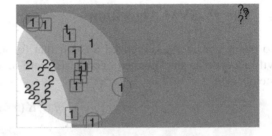

Fig. 2. Problems with existing models for two known classes ("1" and "2") when unknown classes ("?") are possible. If modeled by a one-class RBF SVM, the points with the red circles become support vectors defining the light red region as class 1. The model misclassifies most of class 2, but rejects unknowns. A binary RBF SVM separating 1 & 2 yields the blue region for class 1 with blue squares indicating positive support vectors. It can correctly classify class 1 and reject class 2, but it incorrectly classifies the unknowns with a cutting plane that over-extends rightward. SVM parameters in this example were optimized with 5-fold cross-validation grid-search.

do not have an effective mechanism for rejecting classes; unknown classes must be classified as either positive or negative. In Fig. 2, a binary RBF SVM will misclassify all of the "?" points because there is no distinction between class 1 and the unknown classes in the region where they appear. Converting decision scores to probabilities using the estimation technique of Platt [37] could provide an indication of class membership for a test sample. For the example in Fig. 2, this means that an unknown test sample should receive a low probability score for association with either class 1 or class 2. However, this technique (like other estimators [26,53,56,17,28,6]) assumes that all scores must be from a known positive or known negative class. Because of this, it is not very effective for open set recognition when combined with a threshold (see Sec. 6).

Thus we seek an approach for probability estimation that combines the ability to discriminate between known classes like a binary classifier, but with one-class-like rejection ability. To model this, the *probability of inclusion*, we only consider scores from the binary classifier that are associated with training data samples from a single class of interest in modeling. But what probabilty model should we use?

As shown by [1], for any $\zeta \in (1/2, 1)$ one can accurately estimate conditional probabilities in the interval $(1 - \zeta, \zeta)$ only if support vectors are not sparse over that interval. For efficient classifiers we need some degree of sparsity, thus ζ should be close to $1/2$ and probability calibration is only well defined close to the decision boundary. And since that boundary is defined by the training samples that are effectively extremes, we conclude that proper models for efficient SVM calibration should be based on extreme value theory [25]. Different from previous calibration work for visual recognition [44,42,41] that has applied EVT via rejection of a hypothesis, we use EVT to directly model probability of inclusion P_I for a class of interest.

4   The P_I-SVM Algorithm

To begin, consider a kernelized SVM h that for any d-dimensional feature vector x will generate an uncalibrated hypothesis score s, which can be used to assign class membership:

$$h(x) = \sum_{i=1}^{n} y_i \alpha_i K(x_i, x) + b \tag{2}$$

where α_i are support vectors, $K(x_i, x)$ is a radial basis function kernel, and b a bias term. A collection of such binary classifiers for each class $y \in C$ forms a multi-class SVM. For an uncalibrated SVM hypothesis score $s = h_y(x), s > 0$ we assume larger scores imply more likely inclusion in class y. We also assume such inclusion scores are bounded from below, though it is straightforward to adapt the model to unbounded scores, depending on the desired EVT distribution for probability estimation.

We consider a multi-class problem for the known training classes C where we do not assume that the list of classes is exhaustive, *i.e.* at test time other classes may occur. The objective of the P_I-SVM is to compute a per class unnormalized posterior probability estimate for any input sample x. For P_I-SVM training, let $\{(x_1, y), (x_2, y), \ldots, (x_n, y)\}$ be a collection of training samples that will be used to fit a probability estimator for a single class. Let our overall match set be represented by $\mathcal{M}_y$, with $s_j \in \mathcal{M}_y$ if $h_y(x_j) > 0$. Let ℓ_y be the lower extremes of $\mathcal{M}_y$ (for SVM, the scores closest to 0).

After fitting, we can use the probability model of inclusion defined by a set of parameters θ_y as a robust probability estimator for a classifier. If we let $\rho(y)$ be the prior

---

Algorithm 1. Multi-class EVT-based Probability Modeling for P_I-SVM Training

---

Require: A set of class labels C; a set of labeled training data points for each class $X_y, y \in C$; a pre-trained 1-vs-Rest RBF SVM h_y for each class $y \in C$, with positive support vectors α_y^+;

  for $y = 1 \to |C|$ **do**
    for $j = 1 \to |X_y|$ **do**   ▷ Generate decision scores for fitting
        $s_{y,j} = h_y(x_{y,j})$
        if $s_{y,j} > 0$ **then**
            $\mathcal{M}_y = \mathcal{M}_y \cup \{s_{y,j}\}$
        end if
    end for
    $p_y = 1.5 * |\alpha_y^+|$ ▷ See Sec. 5 for an explanation of this step
    Sort $\mathcal{M}_y$ retaining p_y smallest items as vector ℓ_y
    $[\tau_y, \kappa_y, \lambda_y] = \text{wblfit}(\ell_y)$ ▷ Fit a Weibull distribution
    $\theta_y = [\tau_y, \kappa_y, \lambda_y]$
  end for
  return $\mathcal{W} = [\theta_1 \ldots \theta_{|C|}]$ ▷ The result is a multi-class parameter set

---

probability of class y, then we can estimate the posterior probability of inclusion P_I for the input x and class label y conditioned on the parameters θ_y as:

$$P_I(y|x, \theta_y) = \xi \rho(y) P_I(x|y, \theta_y) = \xi \rho(y)(1 - e^{-(\frac{x - \tau_y}{\lambda_y})^{\kappa_y}}) \tag{3}$$

for some constant ξ. If all classes and priors are known, then Bayes' Theorem yields

$$\xi = \frac{1}{\sum_{y \in C} \rho(y) P_I(x|y, \theta_y)} \tag{4}$$

But we do not assume that all classes are known, so we let $\xi = 1$ and treat the posterior estimate as *unnormalized*. The use of unnormalized posterior estimation is well-known in computer vision [29,27,52,38,51], in part because as long as the missing normalization constant is consistent across all classes it still allows the use of maximum a posteriori estimation. Note that unnormalized posterior probabilities are always an approximation; the unknown constant ξ could be very large or very small which changes the true probability.

With a set of scores bounded from below, the correct EVT distribution to model ℓ_y is the Weibull [12]. The Weibull distribution has three parameters: location τ, shape κ, and scale λ (for details of the Weibull distribution, see Eq. 4 of [43]). For this work, we used the libMR library provided by the authors of [43], which uses Maximum Likelihood Estimation (MLE) to find the $\tau_y, \kappa_y, \lambda_y$ that best fit ℓ_y. In a multi-class setting, these three parameters are defined for each known class y, and we let θ_y represent the vector of those parameters. Alg. 1 provides a precise description of the Weibull probability modeling of class inclusion for each of the classes present during P_I-SVM training.

For multi-class open set recognition using a set of Weibull models we set a minimum threshold δ on class probability and select

$$y^* = \underset{y \in C}{\arg\max} \, P_I(y|x, \theta_y) \quad \text{subject to} \quad P_I(y^*|x, \theta_{y^*}) \geq \delta. \tag{5}$$

Algorithm 2. Multi-class Probability Estimation for P_I-SVM Testing

---

Require: A set of class labels $\mathcal{C}$; a pre-trained 1-vs-Rest RBF SVM h_y for each class y; parameter set $\mathcal{W}$ from Alg. 1; probability threshold δ for rejection; class prior probability $\rho(y)$ for each class y; a test sample x

> $y^* = $ "unknown"
> $\omega = 0$ ▷ Maximum probability score
> **for** $y = 1 \rightarrow |\mathcal{C}|$ **do**
> $P_I(x|y, \theta_y) = \text{wblcdf}(x, \theta_y)$ ▷ The Weibull CDF provides the probability of inclusion
> $P_I(y|x, \theta_y) = \rho(y)P_I(x|y, \theta_y)$ ▷ Unnormalized posterior probability
>   **if** $P_I(y|x, \theta_y) > \delta$ **then**
>   **if** $P_I(y|x, \theta_y) > \omega$ **then**
> $y^* = y$
> $\omega = P_I(y|x, \theta_y)$
>   **end if**
>   **end if**
> **end for**
> **return** $[y^*, \omega]$ ▷ The result is the label and unnormalized posterior probability

---

The formulation in Eq. 5 yields the most likely class, which is appropriate if the classes are exclusive (as in our testing). Alternatively, if the classes are overlapping, one might return all classes above a given probability threshold. Note that we are dealing with unnormalized posterior estimations so the priors $\rho(y)$ only need to be relatively scaled, *e.g.* they could sum to one even if there are unknown classes. It has been shown [10] that the optimal value for the threshold is a function of the risk associated with making a correct decision, making an error, or making a rejection respectively, as well as the prior probabilities of the known or unknown classes. In practice, these would come from the domain knowledge. In our experiments, we assume equal priors per class; accordingly, we set δ to be the prior probability of an unknown instance. Alg. 2 describes the P_I-SVM probability estimation process for a new test sample. The estimate for probability of inclusion $P_I(x|y, \theta_y)$ comes from the CDF of the Weibull model defined by the parameters θ_y (see the right-hand side of Eq. 3).

Algs. 1 & 2 can also be adapted to estimate the unnormalized posterior probability of class inclusion for a one-class SVM. We use this method as a performance baseline in Sec. 6. In the one-class variant P_I-OSVM, we fit a Weibull distribution to the lower extrema of the positive decision scores estimated from an RBF kernel machine trained over just the positive data for a single class. The multi-class EVT-based probability modeling and multi-class probability estimation for P_I-OSVM use the same steps of Algs. 1 and 2 – the only necessary change is the replacement of the 1-vs-Rest binary SVM with a one-class SVM for each class. To our knowledge, this is the first purely one-class kernel machine probability estimator.

5   A Principled Approach to Estimating Tail Size for EVT Fitting

While EVT helps us model extrema, the theory tells us nothing about how many samples to use in fitting the EVT distribution. Prior work in EVT models for visual recognition [44,43,42,22,21] simply recommends choosing a tail size as an arbitrary percentage (not exceeding 50%) of the available data. How much data can be considered a proper tail: 1%, 5%, 10%, 20%? We have found that the difference between a tail size of 5% and 20% of the data can produce a difference in recognition accuracy between 15-20%, with some models needing 5% and others needing 20% to achieve their best performance. Automatic estimation is a better strategy. One basic approach for estimating the tail size is to use cross-validation. However, our own experiments and those from others working in the area of financial modeling [40] have shown this approach to be unstable in practice. Why is this the case?

We believe the reason for this difficulty is that for visual learning, we apply EVT after mapping high-dimensional problems into one-dimensional scores. Inherent in our high-dimensional problems is a complex boundary where points can be near any part of it – there are many dimensions and directions in which points can appear as extrema. Reconsidering Fig. 2, what would the appropriate tail size be for modeling the score data from class 1? It depends not just on the training points but on the chosen classification model as well. When class 1 is modeled with a one-class SVM, the n-dimensional boundary is simpler (*i.e.* has fewer support vectors) than when it is modeled with a binary SVM. As the dimensionality of the data grows, the boundary can be far more complicated or it can be simple. With a complex dependency on dimensionality, sampling, and the problem, it should not be surprising that a tail defined by a fixed size or fixed percentage cannot easily predict how many points are on or near the boundary, or are extrema in general. We require a model that accounts for boundary complexity.

A useful insight is that, by construction, support vectors are a type of extreme sampling that effectively describes the class boundary. It is natural to ask if there is a known parametric relationship between training data size, dimensionality, and the number of support vectors. Unfortunately, there is not. Vapnik has shown [53] that the number of support vectors can be relatively independent of the number of training samples and dimensions. Subsequently, Steinward [48] has developed asymptotic sharp upper and lower bounds on the number of support vectors. For an RBF SVM with L_1 regularization, the fraction of data that are support vectors tends to be twice the Bayes risk. For an RBF SVM with L_2 regularization, the fraction of support vectors tends to be the probability of noise. In both cases, the fraction of data that are support vectors depends on a problem specific property that is not known *a priori* and which is difficult to estimate. These results reinforce the difficulty of estimating tail size based on the percentage of training data and/or dimensionality.

We are not, however, at a dead end. The above insights suggest a different approach: consider extrema to be those points close to the boundary in the original feature space and count them. Using this strategy a new optimization problem, similar to soft-margin SVM optimization, could be defined to locate and minimize the number of extreme training samples on either side of the boundary while minimizing a loss function related to our goal of probability estimation. However, we have found that the exact size of the tail can vary moderately and have only minimal impact on final multi-class recognition system performance. Thus defining and solving a new optimization just to estimate the tail size parameter is not warranted. Since we are applying the EVT model to calibrate an SVM classifier, and that classifier already has a well defined boundary, a much

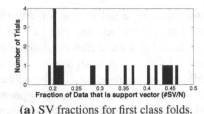   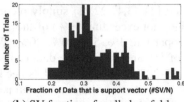

(a) SV fractions for first class folds.   (b) SV fractions for all class folds.

Fig. 3. What is the trouble with assuming a fixed tail size? Consider 20 random trials for the different classifiers in our LETTER [35] experiments (Sec. 6). The above plots show how many trials have a given ratio of support vectors in the training data. (a) shows the variation for just a single class, and (b) shows the variation over 15 classes. The overall distribution is broad and asymmetric – it is not consistent with a constant model implicit in assuming tail size is a fixed fraction; our approach in Eqs. 6 & 7 is different from assumptions made in prior EVT modeling.

simpler alternative is to consider points within some distance ϵ of the SVM decision boundary as the potential extrema. For problems not modeled by a binary SVM, *e.g.* those with only one class of data, a one-class SVM can still provide such an estimate. Given an SVM decision function, we define an indicator function B^+ and the positive tail size T_ϵ^+ via:

$$B^+(x; \epsilon) = \begin{cases} 1 & \text{if } h(x) \leq \epsilon \\ 0 & \text{otherwise} \end{cases} \quad \text{and} \quad T_\epsilon^+ = \sum_{x \in \mathcal{M}_y} B^+(x; \epsilon) \quad (6)$$

For a soft margin RBF SVM, which we use in this paper, support vectors include all points on or outside the positive-class region boundary as defined by the SVM decision function in Eq. 2. Thus T_0^+ is just the number of support vectors that belong to the positive class. For $\epsilon > 0$, some points inside the positive boundary would be included. An approximation that we have found to be both stable and effective is to use a small multiple of the number of support vectors from the positive class, thereby allowing a few points inside but near the class boundary. Letting $|\alpha^+|$ represent the number of support vectors from the positive class, we approximate the tail size via:

$$\hat{T}_\epsilon^+ = \max(3, \psi \times |\alpha^+|) \quad (7)$$

where we need ≥ 3 distinct points to ensure a well-defined EVT fitting. One free parameter ψ must be estimated. Empirically, we have found that any $\psi \in [1.25 - 2.5]$ works well. This range has provided relatively stable multi-class recognition across multiple problems. For the experiments presented in the next section, we fix $\psi = 1.5$.

To help illustrate the significant difference between a fixed fraction and our approach, Fig. 3 shows the variation in fraction of data that are support vectors for the different classifiers in the LETTER data set [35] considered in Sec. 6 below. The data consists of 15 classes over 20 random trials with a mean of 0.33, standard deviation of 0.08, minimum of 0.19, and maximum of 0.59. The distribution is broad and choosing a fixed tail size across all classes results in a large measure of inconsistency. The number of support vectors is always a fraction of the data. Thus a post-hoc approach could choose any arbitrary fraction, but as a fixed size, would still be a poor approximation compared to Eqs. 6 & 7. The experiments in the next section show that in conjunction with the P_I-SVM, this principled approach to tail size estimation for SVM is quite effective.

6   Experimental Evaluation

Experiments are performed for two different open set scenarios: (1) the decision component of object detection, where individual classifiers are evaluated separately; and (2) multi-class open set recognition, where ensembles of classifiers are evaluated together. While our focus is on multi-class open set recognition, we chose to also evaluate a detection problem in order to compare the P_I-SVM[1] with recent published work in open set recognition, and to first establish viability in a more restrictive open set context.

Preliminaries. In all experiments we make use of the cross-class-validation evaluation methodology described in Sec. 1. Extending typical cross-validation for machine learning evaluation, cross-class-validation leaves out not only some training data on each fold to be used for validation purposes, but also some number of classes. Four parameters control how open the validation problem is: the number of training classes t, the target number of known classes $\eta \leq t$ that we would like to identify using m classifiers for the problem, and the number of validation classes $e \geq t$. The steps for the process are shown in Alg. 3 (for simplicity, we show 1-fold), with the final result being a set of validation statistics (*e.g.* accuracies or F-measures) that provides a realistic reflection of how well a particular classifier is performing in the midst of $e - t$ unknown classes during testing.

Cross-class-validation can be used for either detection-oriented problems or multi-class open set recognition problems. To evaluate a detection problem, the number of target classes η is set to 1 and the number of validation classes e is set to a value greater than t. To evaluate a multi-class open set recognition problem, η is set to a number greater than 1, and e is set to a value greater than η and t. A fully closed problem would set $e = t$, meaning the set of unknown classes $\mathcal{C}_u$ is empty. The parameters m, t, η, and e also allow us to quantify "openness" as a single number (where a larger value means a more open problem), providing a consistent frame of reference for plotting results. Like the prior work of Scheirer et al. [45], we plot "openness" vs. F-measure for the experiments in this section[2]. Adapting Eq. 1 from [45], openness is defined as:

$$\text{openness} = 1 - \sqrt{(2 \times t)/(m \times \eta + e)} \qquad (8)$$

The primary question we seek to answer is how much improvement is achieved by the P_I-SVM over viable alternative approaches. To this end, we compare against a lengthy list of supervised learning algorithms including common classifiers and state-of-the-art algorithms for open set recognition. With respect to approaches that are suitable for detection[3], we consider standard SVM variants including the 1-vs-Rest binary

---

[1] Source code is available at https://github.com/ljain2/libsvm-openset.

[2] For comparison, accuracy plots are provided in the supplemental material.

[3] We also tried reference code for the optimal Naive Bayes Nearest Neighbor algorithm [3], but at 72 hours per test, and with 2,640 tests (88 classes × 6 levels of openness × 5 folds) needed to add it to Fig. 4, including it was beyond the scope of this paper. See the longer note in the supplemental material.

Algorithm 3. Cross-Class-Validation (1-Fold)

Require: A set of class labels $\mathcal{C}$; a set of labeled data points for each class $X_y, y \in \mathcal{C}$; number of top-level classifiers to train m; number of training classes t; number of target classes $\eta \leq t$, number of validation classes $e \geq t$; a training objective ϕ, a fusion function F combining η bottom-level classifiers, and a ground-truth operator $\mathcal{Y}(x)$ returning label for x

for $i = 1 \to m$ **do**
    Randomly choose t classes for training label set $\mathcal{C}_t \subseteq \mathcal{C}$ ▷ Different on each iteration
    Randomly choose η classes for target label set $[y_1 \ldots y_\eta] \in \mathcal{C}_t$
    for $y = y_1 \to y_\eta$ **do**
        Randomly choose positive training set T_y^+ from X_y
        Randomly choose negative training set T_y^- sampling each $X_j; j \in \mathcal{C}_t, j \neq y$
        $f_y = \phi(T_y^+ \cup T_y^-)$ ▷ Train a decision model; one-class objectives ignore T_y^-
    end for
    Randomly choose $e - t$ additional class labels $\mathcal{C}_u \subset \mathcal{C}, \mathcal{C}_u \cap \mathcal{C}_t = \varnothing$
    Randomly choose known class validation set E^t sampling each $X_j, j \in \mathcal{C}_t; E_j^t \cap T_j^+ = \varnothing$
    Randomly choose unknown class validation set E^u sampling each $X_j, j \in \mathcal{C}_u$
    $v_i = \cup_{x \in (E^t \cup E^u)} \{\mathcal{Y}(x), F(f_{y_1}(x), \ldots, f_{y_\eta}(x))\}$ ▷ Fuse classifiers; combine with label
    $\mathcal{V} = \mathcal{V} \cup \text{stats}(v_i)$ ▷ Accumulate overall evaluation statistics
end for
return $\mathcal{V}$ ▷ Return complete validation statistics for each classifier

---

RBF SVM, 1-vs-Rest binary linear SVM, and 1-vs-Rest binary RBF SVM with Platt Probability Estimation [37] and a threshold (all using LIBSVM implementations [9]). We also compare against the state-of-the-art EVT-based probability estimator Multi-Attribute Spaces (MAS) [42] with a threshold, and the 1-vs-Set Machine [45], a state-of-the-art algorithm for open set detection problems. For these latter two approaches, code was obtained from the public source repositories for the associated references.

With respect to approaches that are suitable for multi-class open set recognition, we consider standard multi-class SVM variants including the 1-vs-Rest Multi-class RBF SVM (LIBSVM ErrorCode implementation [28]), Pairwise Multi-class RBF SVM (LIBSVM implementation [9]), 1-vs-Rest Multi-class RBF SVM with Platt Probability Estimation and a threshold (LIBSVM ErrorCode implementation [28]), and Pairwise Multi-class RBF SVM with Platt Probability Estimation and a threshold (LIBSVM implementation [9]). As alternatives to standard SVM, we look at Logistic Regression analysis for multi-class probabilistic linear classification (LIBLINEAR implementation [20]), and MAS in a multi-class setting. Finally, the purely single-class P_I-OSVM is also used as a baseline in all experiments.

The first experiment uses a subset of Caltech 256 for training and images from Caltech 256 and ImageNet for separately testing open set "detection" for different classes. The setup is a replication of the experiment described in Sec. 5 of [45] (Fig. 7 of that article). 532,400 images are considered in total. Features are a 3,780-dimension vector of Histogram of Oriented Gradients (HOG) [13]. Using cross-class-validation (Alg. 3), we set $m = 88$, $\eta = 1$, and $e = 88$. The number of training classes t always includes one positive class and a varying number of negative classes to control the openness of

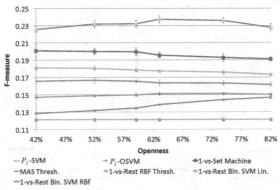

Fig. 4. Performance for the binary decision component of an *open set object detection task* for an open universe of 88 classes [45]. Results are calculated over a five-fold cross-data-set test with images from Caltech 256 used for training and images from Caltech 256 and ImageNet for testing; error bars reflect standard deviation. Approaches marked with "Thresh." have been augmented to support rejection. The P_I-SVM significantly outperforms the prior state-of-the-art (1-vs-Set Machine) with a 12%–22% improvement in F-measure, as well as the pure single-class P_I-OSVM model. We note that the P_I-OSVM is still measurably better than a standard one-class SVM (not plotted because its F-measures fall below the y-axis scale used in this figure), and is superior to other binary classifiers making use of probability estimation.

the problem. Alg. 3 is invoked five times, always choosing a new set of 88 classes from the 256 we have available in $\mathcal{C}$. We report the average result over all trials.

The second experiment uses data from two classic visual learning benchmarks, LETTER [35] and MNIST [33], both of which are considered to be solved in their original closed set forms. To evaluate LETTER in a multi-class open set recognition mode using Alg. 3, we set $m = 1$, $t = 15$, and $\eta = 15$. In this case, we vary the number of validation classes e by adding some number of additional class labels (not exceeding 11, the number of remaining letters outside of training) to the number of training classes t. To evaluate MNIST, we set $m = 1$, $t = 6$, and $\eta = 6$. We vary the number of validation classes e by adding some number of additional class labels (not exceeding 4, the number of remaining digits outside of training) labels to t. In both cases, we invoke Alg. 3 20 times and report the average, with standard deviation for error bars.

For multi-class open set recognition, the class with the maximum (depending on the operation of the algorithm) probability, decision score, or votes is the predicted class. Each approach producing a probability score has a rejection option via the threshold $\delta = 0.5 \times$ openness. Each approach producing an uncalibrated decision score assigns a sample with a score less than zero as either a true negative if an unknown class, or a false negative if a known class. For multi-class algorithms with a rejection option we consider a rejected sample as either a true negative if an unknown class, or a false negative if a known class. Multi-class SVMs without a rejection option produce no negative decisions. RBF kernel parameters are tuned via 5-fold cross-validation on the training data, giving us $(C = 2, \gamma = 2)$ for LETTER and $(C = 2, \gamma = 0.03125)$ for MNIST.

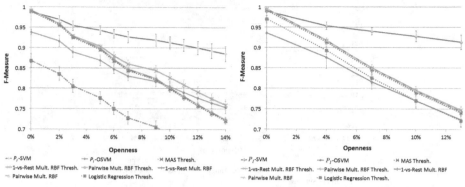

(a) Multi-Class Open Set Recog. for LETTER   **(b)** Multi-Class Open Set Recog. for MNIST

Fig. 5. Two classic data sets evaluated in a *multi-class open set recognition scenario*. All existing algorithms we tested have significant trouble achieving good performance as the problem grows to be more open. The P_I-SVM is more stable than existing algorithms, and achieves high F-measure scores across all levels of openness. Note the large gap between the P_I-SVM and MAS [42] algorithms, indicating the EVT fitting strategy of the P_I-SVM is significantly better.

Results. The results for the experiment evaluating the binary decision component of object detection are summarized in Fig. 4. The P_I-SVM significantly outperforms the prior state-of-the-art (1-vs-Set Machine) with a 12%–22% improvement in F-measure. An important effect in this experiment is the noticeable difference in F-measure between the P_I-SVM, which combines single-class probability estimation with a binary classification model, and the P_I-OSVM, which is purely single-class for probability estimation and classification. The extra discriminative power provided by the binary classifier addresses the limitations inherent in the one-class model. The P_I-OSVM, however, is still measurably better than a standard one-class SVM (off the plot; see supplemental material), and shows improvement over other binary probability estimators.

The results for the multi-class open set recognition experiments are shown in Fig. 5. We expected low F-measure scores for all approaches in the first experiment, which examined a large number of classes for object detection. In contrast, the low scores present for basic OCR tasks with far fewer classes indicate that existing approaches are fundamentally constrained to the closed set classification tasks for which they were designed. The P_I-SVM, which does not possess this same limitation, achieves more stability and considerably better performance over all comparison approaches. We also tested thresholding 1-vs-Rest Multi-class linear SVM and RBF one-class SVM, both of which performed worse than the methods in Fig. 5.

7   Conclusion

A surprising finding of this work has been the impact of recasting basic visual benchmarks like LETTER and MNIST as multi-class open set recognition problems. This suggests that we are much farther away from solving very basic recognition tasks than the classification performance numbers initially led us to believe. As a solution, one-class models are appealing in that they do not suffer from any of the problems associated with negative class modeling for open set recognition, but they almost always overfit their training data. Hybrid models such as the P_I-SVM we introduced in this paper may be the key to achieving good generalization through some measure of discrimination with known negative classes and an estimate of probability of positive class inclusion. Future work includes incorporating objectness or object saliency as a pre-processing step, as well as extending novelty detection [5] to multi-class recognition.

References

1. Bartlett, P.L., Tewari, A.: Sparseness vs estimating conditional probabilities: Some asymptotic results. Journal of Machine Learning Research 8, 775–790 (2007)
2. Bartlett, P.L., Wegkamp, M.H.: Classification with a reject option using a hinge loss. Journal of Machine Learning Research 9, 1823–1840 (2008)
3. Behmo, R., Marcombes, P., Dalalyan, A., Prinet, V.: Towards optimal naive bayes nearest neighbor. In: Daniilidis, K., Maragos, P., Paragios, N. (eds.) ECCV 2010, Part IV. LNCS, vol. 6314, pp. 171–184. Springer, Heidelberg (2010)
4. Bergamo, A., Torresani, L.: Meta-class features for large-scale object categorization on a budget. In: IEEE CVPR, pp. 3085–3092 (2012)
5. Bodesheim, P., Freytag, A., Rodner, E., Kemmler, M., Denzler, J.: Kernel null space methods for novelty detection. In: IEEE CVPR, pp. 3374–3381 (2013)
6. Bravo, C., Lobato, J.L., Weber, R., L'Huillier, G.: A hybrid system for probability estimation in multiclass problems combining svms and neural networks. In: Hybrid Intelligent Systems, pp. 649–654 (2008)
7. Broadwater, J., Chellappa, R.: Adaptive Threshold Estimation Via Extreme Value Theory. IEEE Transactions on Signal Processing 58(2), 490–500 (2010)
8. Cevikalp, H., Triggs, B.: Efficient object detection using cascades of nearest convex model classifiers. In: IEEE CVPR, pp. 886–893 (2012)
9. Chang, C.C., Lin, C.J.: LIBSVM: A library for support vector machines. ACM Transactions on Intelligent Systems and Technology 2, 27:1–27:27 (2011)
10. Chow, C.: On optimum recognition error and reject tradeoff. IEEE Transactions on Information Theory 16(1), 41–46 (1970)
11. Coates, A., Carpenter, B., Case, C., Satheesh, S., Suresh, B., Wang, T., Wu, D.J., Ng, A.Y.: Text detection and character recognition in scene images with unsupervised feature learning. In: Proceedings of the 2011 International Conference on Document Analysis and Recognition, pp. 440–445 (2011)
12. Coles, S.: An introduction to statistical modeling of extreme values. Springer Series in Statistics. Springer (2001)
13. Dalal, N., Triggs, B.: Histograms of oriented gradients for human detection. In: IEEE CVPR, pp. 886–893 (2005)
14. Dardas, N.H., Georganas, N.D.: Real-time hand gesture detection and recognition using bag-of-features and support vector machine techniques. IEEE Transactions on Instrumentation and Measurement 60, 3592–3607 (2011)
15. Deng, J., Berg, A.C., Li, F.F.: Hierarchical semantic indexing for large scale image retrieval. In: IEEE CVPR, pp. 785–792 (2011)
16. Ding, X., Li, Y., Belatreche, A., Maguire, L.P.: An experimental evaluation of novelty detection methods. Neurocomputing 135 (2014)
17. Duan, K.-B., Keerthi, S.S.: Which is the best multiclass SVM method? An empirical study. In: Oza, N.C., Polikar, R., Kittler, J., Roli, F. (eds.) MCS 2005. LNCS, vol. 3541, pp. 278–285. Springer, Heidelberg (2005)

18. Enzweiler, M., Gavrila, D.M.: Integrated pedestrian classification and orientation estimation. In: IEEE CVPR, pp. 982–989 (2010)
19. Everingham, M., Van Gool, L., Williams, C.K.I., Winn, J., Zisserman, A.: The PASCAL Visual Object Classes Challenge 2007 (VOC 2007) Results (2007), http://www.pascal-network.org/challenges/VOC/voc2007/workshop/index.html
20. Fan, R.E., Chang, K.W., Hsieh, C.J., Wang, X.R., Lin, C.J.: LIBLINEAR: A library for large linear classification. Journal of Machine Learning Research 9, 1871–1874 (2008)
21. Fragoso, V., Sen, P., Rodriguez, S., Turk, M.: EVSAC: accelerating hypotheses generation by modeling matching scores with extreme value theory. In: IEEE ICCV, pp. 2472–2479 (2013)
22. Fragoso, V., Turk, M.: SWIGS: a swift guided sampling method. In: IEEE CVPR, pp. 2770–2777 (2013)
23. Fumera, G., Roli, F.: Support vector machines with embedded reject option. In: Lee, S.-W., Verri, A. (eds.) SVM 2002. LNCS, vol. 2388, pp. 68–82. Springer, Heidelberg (2002)
24. Grandvalet, Y., Rakotomamonjy, A., Keshet, J., Canu, S.: Support vector machines with a reject option. In: NIPS, pp. 537–544 (2008)
25. Gumbel, E.: Statistical Theory of Extreme Values and Some Practical Applications. US Govt. Printing Office (1954)
26. Hastie, T., Tibshirani, R.: Classification by pairwise coupling. In: Annals of Statistics, pp. 507–513. MIT Press (1996)
27. Hinton, G.E., Ghahramani, Z., Teh, Y.W.: Learning to parse images. In: NIPS, pp. 463–469 (1999)
28. Huang, T.K., Weng, R.C., Lin, C.J.: Generalized bradley-terry models and multi-class probability estimates. Journal of Machine Learning Research 7, 85–115 (2006)
29. Jepson, A., Mann, R.: Qualitative probabilities for image interpretation. In: IEEE ICCV, pp. 1123–1130 (1999)
30. Kwok, J.T.Y.: Moderating the outputs of support vector machine classifiers. IEEE Transactions on Neural Networks 10(5), 1018–1031 (1999)
31. ImagetNet Large Scale Visual Recognition Challenge 2012 (ILSVRC2012), http://image-net.org/challenges/lsvrc/2012/index (Accessed: February 18, 2014)
32. ImagetNet Large Scale Visual Recognition Challenge 2013 (ILSVRC2013), http://image-net.org/challenges/lsvrc/2013/index (Accessed: February 18, 2014)
33. LeCun, Y., Bottou, L., Bengio, Y., Haffner, P.: Gradient-based learning applied to document recognition. Proceedings of the IEEE 86(11), 2278–2324 (1998)
34. McCann, S., Lowe, D.: Local naive Bayes nearest neighbor for image classification. In: CVPR (2012)
35. Michie, D., Spiegelhalter, D.J., Taylor, C.C., Campbell, J. (eds.): Machine Learning, Neural and Statistical Classification. Ellis Horwood (1994)
36. Niculescu-Mizil, A., Caruana, R.: Predicting good probabilities with supervised learning. In: ICML, pp. 625–632 (2005)
37. Platt, J.: Probabilistic outputs for support vector machines and comparison to regularized likelihood methods. In: Smola, A., Bartlett, P., Schölkopf, B. (eds.) Advances in Large Margin Classifiers. MIT Press (2000)
38. Ramanan, D., Sminchisescu, C.: Training deformable models for localization. In: IEEE CVPR, pp. 206–213 (2006)
39. Ryoo, M., Matthies, L.: First-person activity recognition: What are they doing to me? In: IEEE CVPR, pp. 2730–2737 (2013)
40. Samanta, R., LeBaron, B.: Extreme Value Theory and Fat Tails in Equity Markets. Computing in Economics and Finance 140, Society for Computational Economics (2005)

41. Scheirer, W., Jain, L., Boult, T.: Probability models for open set recognition. To appear in IEEE Transactions on Pattern Analysis and Machine Intelligence (2014)
42. Scheirer, W., Kumar, N., Belhumeur, P.N., Boult, T.E.: Multi-attribute spaces: Calibration for attribute fusion and similarity search. In: IEEE CVPR, pp. 2933–2940 (2012)
43. Scheirer, W., Rocha, A., Michaels, R., Boult, T.E.: Meta-recognition: The theory and practice of recognition score analysis. IEEE Transactions on Pattern Analysis and Machine Intelligence 33(8), 1689–1695 (2011)
44. Scheirer, W., Rocha, A., Micheals, R., Boult, T.: Robust fusion: Extreme value theory for recognition score normalization. In: Daniilidis, K., Maragos, P., Paragios, N. (eds.) ECCV 2010, Part III. LNCS, vol. 6313, pp. 481–495. Springer, Heidelberg (2010)
45. Scheirer, W., Rocha, A., Sapkota, A., Boult, T.: Toward open set recognition. IEEE Transactions on Pattern Analysis and Machine Intelligence 35(7), 1757–1772 (2013)
46. Schölkopf, B., Platt, J.C., Shawe-Taylor, J.C., Smola, A.J., Williamson, R.C.: Estimating the support of a high-dimensional distribution. Neural Computation 13, 1443–1471 (2001)
47. Shu, G., Dehghan, A., Oreifej, O., Hand, E., Shah, M.: Part-based multiple-person tracking with partial occlusion handling. In: IEEE CVPR, pp. 1815–1821 (2012)
48. Steinwart, I.: Sparseness of support vector machines–some asymptotically sharp bounds. In: NIPS, pp. 1069–1076 (2003)
49. Tax, D.M.J., Duin, R.P.W.: Support vector data description. Machine Learning 54, 45–66 (2004)
50. Tax, D.M.J.: One-class classification: Concept learning in the absence of counter-examples. Ph.D. thesis, Technische Universiteit Delft (2001)
51. Toronto, N., Morse, B.S., Ventura, D., Seppi, K.: The hough transform's implicit Bayesian foundation. In: IEEE ICIP, pp. 377–380 (2007)
52. Torr, P.H., Szeliski, R., Anandan, P.: An integrated Bayesian approach to layer extraction from image sequences. IEEE Transactions on Pattern Analysis and Machine Intelligence 23(3), 297–303 (2001)
53. Vapnik, V.N.: Statistical Learning Theory. Wiley Interscience (1998)
54. Wah, C., Belongie, S.: Attribute-based detection of unfamiliar classes with humans in the loop. In: IEEE CVPR, pp. 779–786 (2013)
55. Weston, J., Collobert, R., Sinz, F., Bottou, L., Vapnik, V.: Inference with universum. In: ICML, pp. 1009–1016 (2006)
56. Zadrozny, B., Elkan, C.: Transforming classifier scores into accurate multiclass probability estimates. In: Proceedings of the Eighth ACM SIGKDD International Conference on Knowledge Discovery and Data Mining, pp. 694–699 (2002)
57. Zhang, R., Metaxas, D.: RO-SVM: Support vector machine with reject option for image categorization. In: BMVC, pp. 1209–1218 (2006)

Sequential Max-Margin Event Detectors

Dong Huang, Shitong Yao*, Yi Wang*, and Fernando De La Torre

Robotics Institute, Carnegie Mellon University, Pittsburgh, PA, 15213. USA

Abstract. Many applications in computer vision (e.g., games, human computer interaction) require a reliable and early detector of visual events. Existing event detection methods rely on one-versus-all or multi-class classifiers that do not scale well to online detection of large number of events. This paper proposes Sequential Max-Margin Event Detectors (SMMED) to efficiently detect an event in the presence of a large number of event classes. SMMED sequentially discards classes until only one class is identified as the detected class. This approach has two main benefits w.r.t. standard approaches: (1) It provides an efficient solution for early detection of events in the presence of large number of classes, and (2) it is computationally efficient because only a subset of likely classes are evaluated. The benefits of SMMED in comparison with existing approaches is illustrated in three databases using different modalities: MSRDaliy Activity (3D depth videos), UCF101 (RGB videos) and the CMU-Multi-Modal Action Detection (MAD) database (depth, RGB and skeleton). The CMU-MAD was recorded to target the problem of event detection (not classification), and the data and labels are available at http://humansensing.cs.cmu.edu/mad/.

Keywords: Event Detection, Activity Recognition, Time Series Analysis, Multi-Modal Action Detection.

1 Introduction

Event detection in time series is a topic of growing interest in computer vision and machine learning. Many problems in surveillance [14], activity analysis [1], clinical monitoring [20] and human computer interaction [12] can be posed as detecting events in time series. While the type of data may vary (e.g., video, accelerometers, EEG, depth), the same techniques for event detection can be applied by changing the feature representation for each data type. At this point, it is important to notice that the vast majority of work on activity recognition in video does not address the detection problem, but rather focuses on classification (i.e., the start and the end of the action are given). This is surprising, since detection is of more practical use. While the methods developed for classification could be applied to detection by searching over different temporal scales and adding a null class (none of the existing classes), it is unclear how these methods will perform in practice. This paper focuses on developing a fast and efficient method to detect events from a large number of event classes, and shows its benefits on detecting human actions from a variety of sensing modalities (video, depth, skeleton).

---

* Both authors contributed equally to this paper.

D. Fleet et al. (Eds.): ECCV 2014, Part III, LNCS 8691, pp. 410–424, 2014.

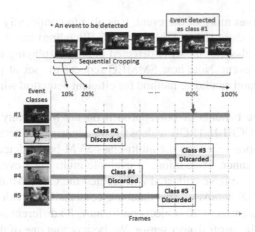

Fig. 1. Given a test event (sequence of a subject playing the violin in the top of the figure), SMMED sequentially evaluates partial events at $\{10\%, 20\%, \cdots, 100\%\}$. When SMMED is confident that the event is not from a given class, it automatically discards this class from further consideration. The blue bars illustrate that class #2(IceDancing), #4(BlowDryHair), #5(Blending), #3(Shaving) are sequentially discarded. Finally, the test event is identified as class #1(playing the violin): the remaining class (the longest blue bar), after 80% of the event has been evaluated.

Standard methods for event detection rely on one-vs-all classifiers [8, 11, 16]. Typically, for each event class, a one-vs-all detector is trained using temporal segments selected from training events. Applying one-vs-all detectors in the presence of a large number of event classes has three major drawbacks: (1) detection scores are not directly comparable, because they are not normalized, (2) detection is often slow because many detectors have to be run simultaneously, and (3) multiple detectors may fire at a given time because classes are not mutually exclusive. Using a multi-class event detector [3] would guarantee that the class label for a particular segment is unique. However, it still remains challenging to produce a consistent class label for non-overlapping but consecutive segments; typically the classifier with a higher score is selected. As a result, different consecutive segments of a given event might have different labels. This problem could be solved using off-line strategies (e.g., k-segmentation [16]), but it is unclear how to solve it online.

To address the above challenges, we propose Sequential Max-Margin Event Detectors (SMMED), which can efficiently scale to a large number of classes. Similar to [8, 21], SMMED is a maximum margin classifier learned using partial segments of training events. Unlike existing approaches, SMMED can sequentially select the most likely subset of classes while automatically enforcing a larger margin for the unlikely classes. As a result, SMMED can reliably discard many classes using only partially observed events.

Fig. 1 illustrates the basic idea of SMMED for multi-class event detection. In this case, we have five event classes (class #1-#5). The top part of Fig. 1 is the event to be detected. As it is common in online event detection, the frames of the event are provided sequentially. A five-class SMMED is sequentially run on partial segments of the event.

As SMMED observes more of the event, it is able to confidently discard classes such as #2 (Ice Dancing), #4 (Blow Dry Hair), #5 (Blending) and #3 (Shaving). Having ruled out all other classes, SMMED detected class #1 (playing the violin) after only seeing 80% of the event. Note how SMMED reduces the set of possible classes over time, making it a good candidate method for efficient detection when a large number of event classes exist.

We illustrate the benefits of our approach on the MSRDaily Activity (3D depth videos) [22] and UCF101 (RGB videos) [18] databases, where SMMED achieves slightly better performance than the multi-class SVM-based detectors, and does so in a more efficient manner. In addition, to evaluate multi-class event detection on continuous sequences, we have collected and labeled the CMU-Multi-modal Action Detection (CMU-MAD) database. This database contains RGB videos, 3D depth videos and body-joint sequences of 20 subjects performing 35 different actions. All data were recorded using a Microsoft Kinect sensor. We believe that one of the reasons for classification being more popular than detection is the limited number of databases with adequate labels. To encourage researchers to work on activity detection, we have released the CMU-MAD database (RGB, 3D depth and body-joint sequences) with frame-wise event labels and example codes to access the database.

2   Related Work

Activity recognition from video has been a long-standing problem in computer vision, and the vast majority of the literature deals with the problem of activity classification in video. Niebles et al. [13] used probabilistic Latent Semantic Analysis for unsupervised learning of human actions. Brand and Kettnaker [3] trained an HMM with entropy minimization and interpreted the hidden states for detection and segmentation of activities in video. [9, 19] modeled the temporal dynamics of activities for classification. Bengio et al. [2] applied tree-traversing to reduce the computational cost of multi-class activity classification in video.

The problem of detection, however, has been relatively unexplored. Early work of Sminchisescu et al. [17] used conditional models for human action detection. Ke et al. [10] detected human actions in videos of crowds. Oh et al. [15] proposed a parametric segmental switching linear dynamical system to model honey-bee behavior. This approach segments the video sequence off-line in a supervised manner. Recently, Gall et al. [6] used Hough Forests to segment the spatial-temporal cuboids of person from videos. Most related to our work is the work of Hoai et al. [7, 8]. [7] temporally segmented and detected events in video combining segment-based SVMs with Dynamic Programming (DP). [8] extended [7] to address the problem of early detection of events using a binary classifier trained to detect events as soon as possible. Unlike the aforementioned approaches, SMMED is a multi-class early event detection approach. SMMED sequentially discards the unlikely classes on consecutive segments, until a reliable class label can be identified from the remaining classes individually. Therefore, the number of detector scores that needs to be computed is reduced over time, making SMMED an efficient solution for a large number of event classes.

3 Structure Output SVM Event Detectors

Structured Output SVM (SO-SVM) [7, 8, 21] provides a natural formalism for event detection in time series, because the output of SO-SVM is the start and the end of the detected segment as well as the class label. More importantly, SVM is a discriminative model that is able to more efficiently model the null class [7] than generative models (e.g., HMMs), which is crucial in detection problems. This section reviews existing SO-SVM algorithms and reformulates SO-SVM as an unconstrained optimization problem.

Let c be the number of event classes, $\mathbf{x}_i^{y_i} \in \Re^d$ be a vector descriptor for the features of the ith segment that starts at the frame s_i and ends at the frame e_i, i.e., the temporal interval is $y_i = [s_i, e_i]$. The goal of event detection is to determine the temporal interval y_i and the class label of an event in a testing video. Let us denote $\delta_{\tilde{y}_i} \in [0, 1]$ to be a scalar that measures the overlap between a temporal segment $\tilde{y}_i = [\tilde{s}_i, \tilde{e}_i]$ and the ground truth segment $y_i = [s_i, e_i]$ of an event. That is, $\delta_{\tilde{y}_i} = 0$ if there is no overlap with the ground-truth, and $\delta_{\tilde{y}_i} = 1$ if there is a perfect overlap (i.e. $\tilde{y}_i = y_i$). The cost function for training Multi-class SO-SVM (MSO-SVM) event detectors can be written as:

$$\min_{\mathbf{W}} \ \|\mathbf{W}\|_F^2 + \lambda \sum_{p=1}^{c} \sum_{i \in \mathcal{N}_p} \xi_i^2 \tag{1}$$

$$s.t. \quad \delta_{\tilde{y}_i} - (\mathbf{w}_p - \mathbf{w}_q)^T \mathbf{x}_i^{\tilde{y}_i} \leq \xi_i; \quad \xi_i > 0,$$

$$\forall \tilde{y}_i; \ i \in \mathcal{N}_p \ ; \forall p \neq q; \ p, q = 1, \cdots, c,$$

where the column vectors of $\mathbf{W} = [\mathbf{w}_1, \cdots, \mathbf{w}_c] \in \Re^{d \times c}$ are the classifier vectors for the c event classes, and $\mathcal{N}_p$ is the index set of event instances belonging to the pth class. The constrains in Eq. 1 state that, for a segment feature $\mathbf{x}_i^{\tilde{y}_i}$ from the pth class ($i \in \mathcal{N}_p$), the classification score with the pth class $\mathbf{w}_p^T \mathbf{x}_i^{\tilde{y}_i}$ should be larger than the scores with any other class $\mathbf{w}_q^T \mathbf{x}_i^{\tilde{y}_i}$ ($p \neq q; p, q = 1, \cdots, c$) by a margin $\delta_{\tilde{y}_i}$. ξ_i is the slack variable that compensates for misclassification errors, and ξ_i^2 denotes the quadratic loss.

Although MSO-SVM is traditionally trained in the dual, we argue that formulating and optimizing the problem in the primal facilitates understanding and generalization of the method. Following Chapelle et al. [4] and using Lagrange multipliers, we can re-write Eq. 1 as an unconstrained optimization problem

$$\min_{\mathbf{W}} \|\mathbf{W}\|_F^2 + \lambda \sum_{p=1}^{c} \sum_{\{i \in \mathcal{N}_p; \tilde{y}\}} \|\mathbf{r}^{\tilde{y}_i} - (\mathbf{w}_p \mathbf{1}^T - \mathbf{W})^T \mathbf{x}_i^{\tilde{y}_i}\|_h, \tag{2}$$

where the second term in Eq. 2 measures the mis-classification error with the quadratic loss: $\|\mathbf{x}\|_h = \|max(0, \mathbf{x})\|_2^2 = \sum_i max(0, x_i)^2$. $\mathbf{r}^{\tilde{y}_i} \in \Re^{c \times 1}$ is a vector of which all the elements are $\delta^{\tilde{y}_i}$ expect for the pth element, which is zero because this element corresponds to $(\mathbf{w}_p - \mathbf{w}_p)^T \mathbf{x}_i^{\tilde{y}_i}$). The vector $\mathbf{r}^{\tilde{y}_i} - (\mathbf{w}_p \mathbf{1}^T - \mathbf{W})^T \mathbf{x}_i^{\tilde{y}_i}$ contains the scores for each of the c classes. Suppose that $\mathbf{x}_i^{\tilde{y}_i}$ belongs to the pth class ($i \in \mathcal{N}_p$). If the qth element of the scores is larger than 0, then $\mathbf{x}_i^{\tilde{y}_i}$ is considered a mis-classified sample between the pth class and the qth class. In addition, $\delta^{\tilde{y}_i}$ is larger for the higher over-lapped segments, which enforces higher penalty to the mis-classification of segments with higher overlap.

During testing, two popular approaches can be used for inference using MSO-SVM (i.e., detecting the segments where the event occurs): (1) The off-line approach, e.g., k-segmentation [16], which automatically selects the k non-overlapping segments that maximize the response of the classifier. This approach was proven to be optimal and has no local minima. However, it can only be implemented off-line and the number of segments k must be given a priori. (2) The Dynamic Programming (DP) approach [7] which can be adapted for online detection. Given a sliding window (maximum length of the training events) along the test time series, online DP solves for the optimal segment configuration such that the sum of the MSO-SVM classification scores is maximal. It then updates the class labels of segments in the sliding window and moves the sliding window forward until the end of the time series. However, consecutive segments around the true event may have inconsistent labels, and it can be computationally intensive to evaluate all classifiers in $\mathbf{W}$. To address these issues next section proposes SMMED.

4   Sequential Max-Margin Event Detectors

This section describes SMMED to overcome the drawbacks of standard MSO-SVM for event detection.

4.1   Cost Function for SMMED

Given the ith training event of the pth class ($i \in \mathcal{N}_p$) with temporal segment $y = [s, e]$, we split the segment y into m sub-segments of equal length l, i.e., $l = (e - s)/m$. We use these sub-segments to construct a set of partially overlapped temporal segments $\{[s, s + l], [s, s + 2l], \dots ,[s, e]\}$. In the left column of Fig. 2, we illustrate the partial temporal segmentation in four event classes.

The feature vector $\mathbf{x}_i^{y_f}$ is computed from the ith event at segment y_f. Note that the temporal segment $y_{f_2} = [s, s + 2l]$ overlaps with the previous segment $y_{f_1} = [s, s + l]$. $\mathbf{x}_i^{y_{f_2}}$ thus contains more information than $\mathbf{x}_i^{y_{f_1}}$ for discriminating the true class (#1) from the other classes. Therefore, if a class can already be discriminated from the true class using segment y_f, it is not necessary to consider this class for the larger segment y_{f_1}. To learn this property, SMMED uses larger margins to penalize mis-classification with this class. For instance, in Fig. 2, at the segment $y_{f_1} = [s, s + l]$ the 4th class can already be discriminated from the 1st class. Thus at the next larger segment, $y_{f_2} = [s, s + 2l]$, of the event $\mathbf{x}_i^{y_{f_2}}$, the 4th element in the margin vector $\mathbf{r}_1^{y_{f_2}}$ is increased by a positive scalar $\delta_{14}^{[s,f_2]}$. Similarly, at $y_{f_3} = [s, s + 3l]$, the term for the 3rd class is increased by $\delta_{13}^{[s,f_3]}$. The classifier of the 1st class $\mathbf{w}_1$ is learned by minimizing the sum of the three error terms above.

Including all partial event segments from the c classes in Eq. (2), the cost function of SMMED is

$$L(\mathbf{W}, \mathbf{r}_{(p)}^{y_f}) = \|\mathbf{W}\|_F^2 + \lambda \sum_{p=1}^{c} \sum_{f=s+l}^{e} \left\| \mathbf{r}_{(p)}^{y_f} \mathbf{1}^T - (\mathbf{W S}_p)^T \mathbf{X}_{(p)}^{y_f} \right\|_h \tag{3}$$

where $\mathbf{X}_{(p)} = [\mathbf{x}_i]_{i \in \mathcal{N}_p}$ is the matrix containing the vector descriptors for all partial events belonging to the pth class. $\mathbf{S}_p \in \Re^{c \times c}$ is a selection matrix for constructing the

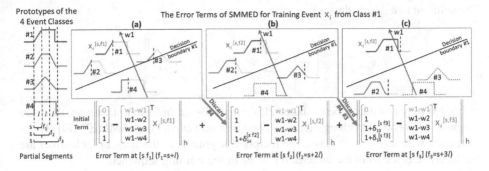

Fig. 2. A synthetic example that illustrates training SMMED. The sub-figures in the left column represent prototypes of four synthetic event classes. SMMED builds three partial segments for each class in the range $[s, f]$ ($f = s + l, s + 2l, s + 3l$). Let $\mathbf{x}_i$ be a training event instance from class #1. The sub-figures (a)-(c) illustrate training SMMED using the temporal segments of $\mathbf{x}_i$. The vectors $\mathbf{w}_1$, $\mathbf{w}_2$, $\mathbf{w}_3$ and $\mathbf{w}_4$ are the classifiers of the 4 classes. Note that in **(a)**, at segment $f_1 = s + l$, all the partial segments from classes #2 and #3 have a ramp, so they cannot be discriminated from class #1. The partial segment of #4 has a step, and thus can be discriminated from $\mathbf{x}_i^{[s,f_1]}$. SMMED therefore enforces that for all subsequent (larger) partial segments $f_2 = s + 2l$ (in **(b)**) and $f_3 = s + 3l$ (in **(c)**) class #4 remain discriminated from class #1. In order to enforce this property the error term associated with $\mathbf{w}_4$ is penalized by increasing its corresponding margin by $\delta_{14}^{[s,f_2]}$ and $\delta_{14}^{[s,f_3]}$ respectively. Similarly, in **(b)**, the training partial segment of class #3 has a peak and can be discriminated from #1. Therefore, in **(c)**, for partial segment $[s, s + 3l]$, the term for $\mathbf{w}_3$ is also penalized. Finally, the total error term for $\mathbf{x}_i$ is the sum of the three terms above.

difference between the $\mathbf{w}_p$ and all other classifiers, such that the product of $\mathbf{W} \in \Re^{d \times c}$ (the matrix of the c classifiers) and $\mathbf{S}_p$ is $\mathbf{WS}_p = [\mathbf{w}_p - \mathbf{w}_1, \mathbf{w}_p - \mathbf{w}_2, \cdots, \mathbf{w}_p - \mathbf{w}_c]$. The vector $\mathbf{r}_{(p)}^{y_f} \in \Re^{c \times 1}$ contains the margins for the partial events $y_f = [s, f]$ of the pth class. As illustrated in Fig. 2, the key to SMMED Eq. (3) is to update the elements of the vector $\mathbf{r}_{(p)}^{y_f}$ to penalize those classes that can already be discriminated from the true class. For instance, if at y_f, the qth class can be discriminated from p^{th} class, the qth element of vector $\mathbf{r}_{(p)}^{y_{f+l}}$ is updated to be $1 + \delta_{pq}^{y_{f+l}}$, where $\delta_{pq}^{y_{f+l}}$ is a scalar to be computed below.

SMMED uses a quadratic loss for $\| \cdot \|_h$. In this case, the optimal value of $\delta_{pq}^{y_{f+l}}$ can be estimated using a simple and efficient method. Note that the L_2-based norm of a matrix is minimal when the value of its elements are uniformly distributed. Assuming the classification error in the second term of Eq. 3 is class-wise uniform at y_{f+l}, the qth class is to be discarded from the pth class, Γ_p is the index set of remaining classes. It follows that

$$\left\| (1 + \delta_{pq}^{y_{f+l}}) \mathbf{1}^T - (\mathbf{w}_p - \mathbf{w}_q)^T \mathbf{X}_{(p)}^{y_{f+l}} \right\|_h = \frac{1}{|\Gamma_p|} \sum_{j \in \Gamma_p} \left\| \mathbf{1}^T - (\mathbf{w}_p - \mathbf{w}_j)^T \mathbf{X}_{(p)}^{y_{f+l}} \right\|_h.$$

The solution to $\delta_{pq}^{y_f+1}$ is thus

$$\delta_{pq}^{y_f+l} = \left\| \left(\frac{1}{|\Gamma_p|} \sum_{j \in \Gamma_p} \mathbf{w}_j - \mathbf{w}_q \right)^T \mathbf{X}_{(p)}^{y_f+l} \right\|_2. \tag{4}$$

Eq. (3) only considers the c labeled classes. However, in real applications, there are temporal segments not belonging to any class: the null event class. SMMED (Eq. 3) can be trained with a $(c+1)^{th}$ class. The temporal segments of the $(c+1)^{th}$ classifier are randomly selected from the unlabeled frames in the training sequences.

4.2 Solving SMMED

We solved SMMED (Eq. 3) in the primal following [4]. However, unlike [4] we used an efficient line search algorithm adapted to SMMED.

We initialized $\mathbf{W} = \mathbf{1}\mathbf{1}^T \in \Re^{d \times c}$ and $\mathbf{r}_{(p)}^{y_f} = \mathbf{1} \in \Re^{c \times 1}$ for all classes ($p = 1, \cdots, c$), and then iteratively updated the set of support vectors selected by $\| \cdot \|_h$, the classifiers $\mathbf{W}$, and the margin vectors ($\mathbf{r}_{(p)}^{y_f}$s) until convergence. The following steps were iterated:

(1) Identify the Mis-classified Sample-class Pairs. Let $\mathbf{H} = \mathbf{r}_{(p)}^{y_f} \mathbf{1}^T - (\mathbf{WS}_p)^T \mathbf{X}_{(p)}^{y_f} \in \Re^{c \times |\mathcal{N}_p|}$ be the matrix evaluated with the quadratic loss $\| \cdot \|_h$ for the pth class at the fth segment in Eq. 3. The quadratic loss $\| \cdot \|_h$ splits the elements in $\mathbf{H}$ into two sets: elements that fall into the zero part of the quadratic loss function (Ω_0) and those that fall into the quadratic part (Ω_2). Recall that the non-zero values in the SVM quadratic loss measure the classification error. The set Ω_2 is defined as the mis-classified class-sample pairs, i.e., $\{(q, \mathbf{x}_j)\}$, $(q = 1, 2, \cdots, c; j = 1, 2, \cdots, n)$. To simplify the derivation of the algorithm, in the following, we use the subindex "$\cdot_{\Omega_2}$" to denote both the classifier index p and the data index i that form a class-sample pair in the set Ω_2.

(2) Update the Classifiers W. Update $\mathbf{W}$ with gradient descent $\mathbf{W} = \mathbf{W} - \beta \frac{\partial L}{\partial \mathbf{W}}$, where

$$\frac{\partial L}{\partial \mathbf{W}} = 2\mathbf{W} + \lambda \sum_{p=1}^{c} \sum_{f=s+l}^{e} \left[-2[\mathbf{X}_{(p)}^{y_f}]_{\Omega_2} \mathbf{1}([\mathbf{r}_{(p)}^{y_f}]_{\Omega_2})^T [\mathbf{S}_p]_{\Omega_2}^T \right.$$
$$\left. +2[\mathbf{X}_{(p)}]_{\Omega_2}^{y_f}([\mathbf{X}_{(p)}^{y_f}]_{\Omega_2})^T \mathbf{W}[\mathbf{S}_p]_{\Omega_2}[\mathbf{S}_p^T]_{\Omega_2} \right]. \tag{5}$$

Substituting $\mathbf{W} = \mathbf{W} - \beta \frac{\partial L}{\partial \mathbf{W}}$ into L, and computing the partial derivative of L w.r.t. β, we have:

$$\frac{\partial L}{\partial \beta} = tr \left(-\mathbf{W}^T \frac{\partial L}{\partial \mathbf{W}} - \frac{\partial L}{\partial \mathbf{W}}^T \mathbf{W} + 2\beta \frac{\partial L}{\partial \mathbf{W}}^T \frac{\partial L}{\partial \mathbf{W}} \right)$$
$$+ \lambda \sum_{p=1}^{c} \sum_{f=s+l}^{e} tr[\mathbf{BA}^T + \mathbf{AB}^T + 2\beta \mathbf{AA}^T], \tag{6}$$

where the matrix $\mathbf{A} = [\mathbf{S}_p]_{\Omega_2}^T \frac{\partial L}{\partial \mathbf{W}} [\mathbf{X}_{(p)}^{y_f}]_{\Omega_2}$, and $\mathbf{B} = [\mathbf{r}_{(p)}]_{\Omega_2}^{y_f} \mathbf{1}^T - [\mathbf{S}_p]_{\Omega_2}^T \mathbf{W}^T [\mathbf{X}_{(p)}^{y_f}]_{\Omega_2}$. Then setting $\frac{\partial L}{\partial \beta^*} = 0$, the optimal step size is computed as

$$\beta^* = \frac{tr\left(\mathbf{W}^T \frac{\partial L}{\partial \mathbf{W}} + \frac{\partial L}{\partial \mathbf{W}}^T \mathbf{W} + \lambda \sum_{p=1}^c \sum_{f=s+l}^e \mathbf{B}\mathbf{A}^T + \mathbf{A}\mathbf{B}^T\right)}{tr\left(2\frac{\partial L}{\partial \mathbf{W}}^T \frac{\partial L}{\partial \mathbf{W}} - \lambda \sum_{p=1}^c \sum_{f=s+l}^e 2\mathbf{A}\mathbf{A}^T\right)}. \tag{7}$$

(3) Update the Margin Vector $\mathbf{r}_{(p)}^{y_{f+1}}$ **at Segment** y_{f+1} (See Fig. 2). Let $\mathbf{H} = \mathbf{r}_{(p)}^{y_{f-1}} \mathbf{1}^T - (\mathbf{W}\mathbf{S}_p)^T \mathbf{X}_{(p)}^{y_{f-1}} \in \Re^{c \times |\mathcal{N}_p|}$ be the matrix for the pth class at the segment $[s, f-l]$ in $\|\cdot\|_h$. Updating $\mathbf{r}_{(p)}^{y_f}$ consists of two sub-steps:

(a) Identify classes at $y_f = [s, f]$ that can already be discriminated from the true class. The qth class is discriminated from the pth class at y_f, if $\min(\mathbf{H}(q,:)) + \alpha(\max(\mathbf{H}(q,:)) - \min(\mathbf{H}(q,:))) < 0$, where α is a positive scalar, $\alpha \in [0,1]$. For instance, $\alpha = 0.9$ means 90% of samples in $\mathbf{X}_{(p)}^{y_f}$ are not classified as the pth class.

(b) Update the elements of $\mathbf{r}_{(p)}^{y_{f+1}}$ at segment $y_{f+1} = [s, f+1]$ to be $1 + \delta_{pq}^{y_{f+1}}$ where $\delta_{pq}^{y_{f+1}}$ is computed using Eq. 4.

Step **(1)**-**(3)** are repeated until the changes in $\mathbf{W}$ are small (i.e., $< 10^{-5}$).

4.3   Detecting Events in a Test Sequence

After the matrix $\mathbf{W}$ is learned, SMMED performs event detection as follows:

(1) Initialize Γ as the index set containing all $(c+1)$ classes, where the $(c+1)^{th}$ class is the null class. Recall that since this is a detection problem, many temporal segments will belong to the null class. Search the minimal temporal segment y_0 (e.g., 10% of the average length of training events, segment feature $\mathbf{x}^{y_0}$) and compute the classifier score of the null class $g_{c+1} = \mathbf{w}_{c+1}^T \mathbf{x}^{y_0}$. If g_{c+1} is smaller than the largest classifier score by 1, i.e., $g_{c+1} < \max_{p=1}^c g_p - 1$, remove the $(c+1)^{th}$ class from Γ; otherwise, label y_0 as a null class segment.

(2) If segment y_0 is not the null class, we sequentially construct a larger segment y by combining the segment y_0 with the incoming new frames. Remove the qth class from Γ if the $g_q < \max_{p \in \Gamma} g_p - 1$.

(3) If no additional class is removed for a certain number of incoming frames, e.g., 30% of the average training event length, output the current segment as a detected event with a class label $arg \max_{p \in \Gamma} g_p$.

(4) After an event is detected, go to step (1) until the end of the test sequence.

5   Experiments

We evaluated SMMED against Multi-class SVM-based detectors (Eq. 2) on three databases; the MSR3D-Daily [22] database (3D depth videos), the UCF101 [18] database (RGB videos), and our collected Multi-Modal Action Detection (MAD) database (video, depth and the 3D body joints). The event data in both the MSR3D-Daily and UCF101 databases are organized in isolated clips, which is ideal for a controlled evaluation of

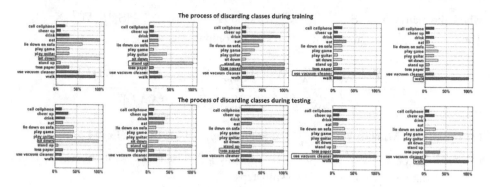

Fig. 3. Visualizing SMMED results on the MSRDaily database [22]. Each bar graph shows the portion of the event processed before the classes are discarded. The vertical axis depicts the class names (the red square highlights the true class), and the horizontal axis is the portion of the processed event. Each bar corresponds to one class. The end of the bar indicates when the class is discarded. For instance, for the class "sit down" (the top-left figure), the classes "call cellphone" and "cheer up" are discarded early because there is little overlap with the true action. **(Best viewed in color)**.

the detection performance. We used two metrics: (1) Percentage of Discarded Classes (PDC): the percentage of discarded classes when an event is detected; (2) Percentage of Early Labeling (PEL): the percentage of events that were reliably detected before the action ended (100% segment of an event). In addition, the MAD database has continuous events and the start and end of each action is provided, so the detection performance is easy to evaluate in a more realistic scenario.

5.1 MSRDaily Activity 3D Database

The MSRDaily Activity database [22] contains 3D depth clips of 10 subjects performing 16 daily activities. The resolution of the 3D depth frames is 640×480. Each subject performed each activity twice. There are a total of 320 activity instances organized in 10 groups (one group per person).

We used a fixed segmentation in each activity for a fair comparison. Each event was evenly split into 10 segments along time; The partial events were constructed as $[0\%, 10\%], [0\%, 20\%], \ldots, [0\%, 100\%]$ of each event for both training and testing, e.g., $[0\%, 100\%]$ includes all the frames of an event. For each partial event, we computed segment-based features using the DCSF (Depth Cuboid Similarity Feature) codes[1] provided by [23] and set the feature parameters according to [23]. As in [23], we used 12 of the 16 action classes. Note, our experiments are not directly comparable to [23](DCSF + SVM) because we are required to train and test on various temporal segments of the original event clips. In particular, [23] evaluated a classification problem: train and test only on the $[0\%, 100\%]$ segment of each event. Our experiments evaluated an event detection problem: the detectors must be trained over many temporal segments of each

---

[1] http://cvrc.ece.utexas.edu/lu/source_code.zip

event (the $[0\%, 20\%]$, $[0\%, 40\%]$,..., $[0\%, 100\%]$ segments), and test on many temporal segments in the test sequence.

We compared SMMED with the standard Multi-class SO-SVM (MSO-SVM), Eq. 1. MSO-SVM was trained using the Multi-Class SVM [5] of liblinear[2]. We used 5-fold-cross-validation on the 10 groups of sequences (2 groups per fold). For each cross-validation, 4 folds were used for training and the remaining 1 fold for testing. In the following experiments, we reported the best results for our SMMED (Eq.3) and the MSO-SVM detectors (Eq. 1) by tuning parameters over the 5-fold-cross-validation.

Fig.3 visualizes the training (the first row) and testing (the second row) process of discarding classes using SMMED. In each figure, the true classes are highlighted with a red square. Starting from the first column, the true classes are "sit down", "stand up", "toss papers", "use vacuum cleaner" and "walk". Each bar represents the percentage of time that an event class is considered as a candidate for the event. The end of the bar indicates the time when the action is discarded. Observe that in Fig. 3, many classes can be discriminated from the true class in the early stages (most bars stopped before 50% of the events). Moreover, the test bar graphs (the second row) and the training bar graphs (the first row) for the same true class show similar process of discarding classes. Recall that in SMMED, discarding a class means that the classification score for this class will not be computed in the later segments. This saves valuable time, especially when processing a large number of classes.

Table 1. Averaged recognition accuracy over 5-fold-cross-validation in MSRDaily database [22]. We compared the MSO-SVM detectors (different recognition results in different temporal segments) and our SMMED approach (the unique class labeling). Note, although we used the same DCSF codes provided by [23](DCSF+SVM), our experiment is not directly comparable to [23] because we address the detection problem not classification.

Segments	MSO-SVM	SMMED
$[0\%, 20\%]$	50.4%	
$[0\%, 40\%]$	63.8%	
$[0\%, 60\%]$	65.8%	**73.2%**
$[0\%, 80\%]$	68.8%	
$[0\%, 100\%]$	68.3%	

Table. 1 compares the average classification accuracy of SMMED against MSO-SVM. For all events, partial temporal segments were constructed using $[0\%, 20\%]$ to $[0\%, 100\%]$ frames of each event. Both MSO-SVM and SMMED were trained using all partial segments. Then MSO-SVM was tested on each partial segment of the test events respectively, and the recognition accuracy was computed at each segment by selecting the class with the highest score. SMMED, on the other hand, used all partial segments of the test events, and only discard classes until output a unique recognition accuracy at the last partial segment. Table. 1 shows that SMMED has higher recognition accuracy than the MSO-SVM for any segment. Moreover, we compared the detection

---

[2] http://www.csie.ntu.edu.tw/~cjlin/liblinear/

Fig. 4. Visualization of SMMED results of the true class "CricketBowling" in the UCF-101 dataset [18]. The horizontal axis lists the class names (the red square highlights the true class), and the vertical axis indicates the period or length that a particular class remains as a candidate action. Observe that most classes are discarded at very early stages (the short bars).

efficiency of SMMED against the MSO-SVM detectors in Table. 2. For a fair comparison against MSO-SVM, we used the same detection strategy described in Section 4.3 but the classifier matrix W trained by MSO-SVM. Table. 2 shows the average results over 5-fold-cross-validation for both SMMED and the MSO-SVM detector. Observe Table. 2, SMMED gets a higher Percentage of Discarded Classes (PDC) and Percentage of Early Labeling (PEL) than the MSO-SVM detector, being better suited for early activity detection. Specifically, 43.9% classes were discarded when test events were detected, and 39.2% of test events were identified without using all the frames.

Table 2. Averaged Percentage of Discarded Classes (PDC) and Percentage of Early Labeling (PEL) over 5-fold-cross-validation on MSRDaily [22]. We compared the MSO-SVM detectors and our SMMED approach.

	MSO-SVM	SMMED
PDC	29.1%	**43.9%**
PEL	13.8%	**39.2%**

5.2 UCF 101 Database

The UCF-101 database [18] contains 13320 video clips for 101 action classes. For each action class, the video clips were divided into 25 groups. Each group has 4-7 clips sharing common settings (e.g., similar background, same actors). All videos were recorded at 25fps and have a resolution of 320×240 pixels.

Similar to the MSRDaily experiment, we also constructed fixed partial segments for each event. The temporal segments used to evaluate the event detectors were $[0\%, 20\%]$, $[0\%, 40\%], \cdots , [0\%, 100\%]$, where the interval $[0\%, 100\%]$ covers all frames of an event. We built a Bag-of-Words (BoW) representation with 4000-cluster codebooks by clustering 162-dimensional space-time interest points (STIP) descriptors provided by [18]. The segment-based feature of each temporal segment was computed as a histogram on the codebooks, the standard BoW. 5-fold-cross-validation was computed over the 25 groups of sequences (5 groups per fold). For each cross-validation, 4 folds were used for training and the remaining 1 fold for testing.

Table 3. Averaged recognition accuracy over 5-fold-cross-validation on UCF101 [18] for SMMED and MSO-SVM

Segments	MSO-SVM	SMMED
[0%, 20%]	35.0%	
[0%, 40%]	37.1%	
[0%, 60%]	39.4%	40.6%
[0%, 80%]	40.3%	
[0%, 100%]	**40.9%**	

Table 4. Averaged Percentage of Discarded Classes (PDC) and Percentage of Early Labeling (PEL) over 5-fold-cross-validation in UCF-101 [18] for SMMED and MSO-SVM

	MSO-SVM	SMMED
PDC	20.4%	**97.6%**
PEL	0.5%	**95.9%**

Fig. 4 visualizes the training (the first row) and testing (the second row) used by SMMED to partially discard classes. In this case, we have more classes than in the MSRDaily database. The horizontal axis depicts the class types and the vertical axis is the portion of the event for which the classes are active. We can see in Fig. 4 that most classes were discarded very early-on for both training and testing (most classes were discarded within 40% of the event).

Table. 3 shows the average recognition accuracy of SMMED (which output a unique class label after using all temporal segments), against MSO-SVM detectors (which output different classes on different temporal segments). As in the previous experiment, we used the classifier matrix **W** trained by MSO-SVM in the detection strategy (described in Section 4.3). The MSO-SVM detector performs similar to SMMED when using partial events higher than 80%. On the other hand, Table. 4 shows that SMMED gets much a higher Percentage of Discarded Classes (PDC) and Percentage of Early Labeling (PEL) than the MSO-SVM detectors. SMMED is better suited for online detection: 97.6% classes were discarded when an event was identified, and 95.9% events were detected before all frames were observed.

5.3   Multi-modal Action Detection (MAD) Database

The event sequences in both the MSRDaily and UCF101 databases are only available as isolated clips. In real applications, event detection is performed on streaming data. Manually concatenating the isolated clips results in discontinuous time series, and is not a very realistic scenario. Unfortunately, there are very few publicly available databases with labels for practical human action detection. This section describes the Multi-Modal Action Detection (MAD) database[3] for multi-class event detection. MAD contains 40 sequences of 20 subjects (2 sequences per subject) performing 35 activities in each of the sequences. The length of each sequence is around 2-4 minutes (4000-7000 frames).

---

[3] The MAD database and labels can be downloaded from
humansensing.cs.cmu.edu/mad/.

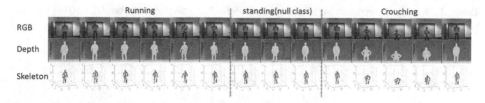

Fig. 5. Example frames of the Multi-Modal Action Detection (MAD) database

We recorded three modalities: RGB video (240 × 320), 3D depth (240 × 320), and a body-joint sequence (3D coordinates of 20 joints per frame). All data was recorded using the Microsoft Kinect sensor in an indoor environment. The 35 actions include full-body motion (e.g., Running, Crouching, jumping), upper-body motion(e.g., Throw, Basketball Dribble, Baseball swing), and lower-body motion (e.g., kicking). Each subject performs all the 35 activities continuously, and the segments between two actions are considered the null class (i.e., the subject is standing). Fig. 5 shows some example frames from the MAD database. The following experiments were performed using the 40 body-joint sequences.

We trained (35+ null class = 36)-class event detectors using both SMMED and MSO-SVM. The temporal segments used in training were the labeled event segments of the 35 event classes and the unlabeled segments (the null class, see the standing-by frames in Fig. 5). The feature for each temporal segment was computed in five steps: (1) Align all the body joints across frames using a 3D affine transformation; (2) Compute three descriptors using the aligned 3D-body-joints in each frame: the bone angles between joint pairs, differences of body-joint coordinates between the current and its previous frame, and average differences of body-joint coordinates between the current and its previous 10 frames; (3) Build a Bag-of-Word (BoW) with 100 codebooks for each of the three descriptors respectively; (4) Compute the frame features: For each frame, compute the three 100-dimensional BoW histograms, and concatenate them into a 100 × 3 = 300 dimensional frame feature vector; (5) Compute the segment features as the sum of frame features within each segment. After the SMMED and MSO-SVM classifiers were trained, SMMED-based action detection was done as described in Section 4.3. MSO-SVM was computed using [7] (i.e., MSO-SVM + Dynamic Programming(DP)), where DP searches the optimal temporal segmentation by enforcing the MSO-SVM objective. To allow MSO-SVM+DP [7] for on-line event detection, DP was solved in a sliding window (the maximum frame length of training events) moving through the test sequence.

For each method, we performed five-fold-cross-validation over the 20 subjects (4 subjects per fold). In each cross-validation, the labeled segments of four folds are used to train SMMED and MSO-SVM in [7]. The remaining sequence in the one fold is used for event detection. For instance, in the first cross-validation, the sequences of the 1st-4th subject are used for testing (4 × 2 = 8 sequences), and the sequences of the 5th-20th subject for training (16 × 2 = 32 sequences). Fig. 6 shows the frame-level detection results on 2 of the 8 test sequences. For each test sequence, the three bars are the ground truth frame-level labels, result of [7], and SMMED respectively. Different colors in the bars denote different class labels. Observe the bars, SMMED

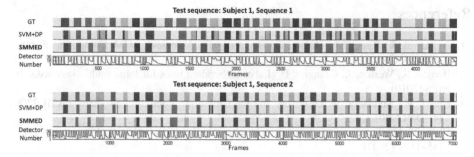

Fig. 6. Frame-level detection results on 2 test sequences in the MAD database. For each sequence, the three bars represent the ground truth frame-level labels (top), result of [7] (denoted as "SVM+DP" in the middle row), and SMMED respectively. In the curve figures below the detection bars shows the number of detectors used by SMMED detection. (**Best viewed in color**).

produces fewer fragmented class labels than [7] around each true event. Quantitatively, we compared two event-wise measures: (1) Precision(Prec): the percentage of correctly detected events over all the detected events, the detected event is correct if it overlaps with 50% segment of the ground truth event; (2) Recall (Rec): the percentage of correctly detected events over all the ground truth events. Averaging over the 5-fold cross-validation, SMMED reached higher Precision ($Prec = 59.2\%, Rec = 57.4\%$) than [7] ($Prec = 28.6\%, Rec = 51.4\%$)) with comparable recall. The figures in the top of Fig. 6 shows the number of detectors used by SMMED detection. Observe that for most frames, the detector numbers are much less than the total number of event classes, i.e., 36 classes (35 activity classes + 1 null class).

6 Conclusion

We have proposed SMMED, a maximum-margin multi-class early event detection method. Unlike standard multi-class approaches, SMMED sequentially discards classes that can be early discriminated from the true class, being more efficient when detecting large number of classes. In our experiments, SMMED typically discarded about half of the classes before detecting the event. Experiments on databases with three different modalities, i.e., depth videos, RGB videos and body-joint sequences have shown that SMMED is more efficient, temporally consistent and accurate for multi-class event detection than MSO-SVM. In addition, we have released the CMU-MAD database a multimodal activity detection database with 20 subjects performing 35 actions. SMMED is a supervised detection system, in future work, we will explore the use of SMMED in an unsupervised and semi-supervised setting.

Acknowledgments. This work was partially supported by Samsung Electronics and by the National Science Foundation (NSF) under the grant RI-1116583. Any opinions, findings, and conclusions or recommendations expressed in this material are those of the author(s) and do not necessarily reflect the views of the NSF.

References

1. Aggarwal, J., Ryoo, M.: Human activity analysis: A review. ACM Computing Surveys (CSUR) 43(3) (2011)
2. Bengio, S., Weston, J., Grangier, D.: Label embedding trees for large multi-class tasks. In: NIPS (2010)
3. Brand, M., Kettnaker, V.: Discovery and segmentation of activities in video. PAMI 22(8), 844–851 (2000)
4. Chapelle, O.: Training a support vector machine in the primal. Neural Computation 19(5), 1155–1178 (2007)
5. Crammer, K., Singer, Y.: On the algorithmic implementation of multi-class svms. JMLR, 265–292 (2001)
6. Gall, J., Yao, A., Razavi, N., Van Gool, L., Lempitsky, V.: Hough forests for object detection, tracking, and action recognition. PAMI 33(11), 2188–2202 (2011)
7. Hoai, M., Lan, Z., De la Torre, F.: Joint segmentation and classification of human actions in video. In: CVPR (2011)
8. Hoai, M., De la Torre, F.: Max-margin early event detectors. In: CVPR (2012)
9. Hongeng, S., Nevatia, R., Bremond, F.: Video-based event recognition: activity representation and probabilistic recognition methods. CVIU 96(2), 129–162 (2004)
10. Ke, Y., Sukthankar, R., Hebert, M.: Event detection in crowded videos. In: ICCV (2007)
11. Laptev, I., Marsza, M., Schmid, C., Rozenfeld, B.: Learning realistic human actions from movies. In: CVPR (2008)
12. Mitra, S., Acharya, T.: Gesture recognition: A survey. TSMC-C 37(3), 311–324 (2007)
13. Niebles, J., Wang, H., Fei-Fei, L.: Unsupervised learning of human action categories using spatial-temporal words. IJCV 79(3), 299–318 (2008)
14. Niu, W., Long, J., Han, D., Wang, Y.F.: Human activity detection and recognition for video surveillance. In: ICME (2004)
15. Oh, S., Rehg, J., Balch, T., Dellaert, F.: Learning and inferring motion patterns using parametric segmental switching linear dynamic systems. IJCV 77, 103–124 (2008)
16. Simon, T., Nguyen, M., De La Torre, F., Cohn, J.: Action unit detection with segment-based SVMs. In: CVPR (2010)
17. Sminchisescu, C., Kanaujia, A., Li, Z., Metaxas, D.: Conditional models for contextual human motion recognition. In: ICCV (2005)
18. Soomro, K., Zamir, A.R., Shah, M.: Ucf101: A dataset of 101 human action classes from videos in the wild. In: CRCV-TR-12-01 (2012)
19. Swears, E., Hoogs, A.: Learning and recognizing complex multi-agent activities with applications to american football plays. In: IEEE Workshop on the Applications of Computer Vision (2012)
20. Tapia, E., Intille, S., Haskell, W., Larson, K.: Real-time recognition of physical activities and their intensities using wireless accelerometers and a heart rate monitor. In: IEEE Int. Symp. Wearable Computers (2007)
21. Tsochantaridis, I., Joachims, T., Hofmann, T., Atun, Y.: Large margin methods for structured and interdependent output variables. JMLR 6, 1453–1484 (2005)
22. Wang, J., Liu, Z., Wu, Y., Yuan, J.: Mining actionlet ensemble for action recognition with depth cameras. In: CVPR (2012)
23. Xia, L., Aggarwal, J.: Spatio-temporal depth cuboid similarity feature for activity recognition using depth camera. In: CVPR (2013)

Which Looks Like Which:
Exploring Inter-class Relationships
in Fine-Grained Visual Categorization

Jian Pu[1], Yu-Gang Jiang[1], Jun Wang[2], and Xiangyang Xue[1]

[1] School of Computer Science, Shanghai Key Laboratory of Intelligent Information
Processing, Fudan University, Shanghai, China
[2] IBM T. J. Watson Research Center, Yorktown Heights, NY, USA
{jianpu,ygj,xyxue}@fudan.edu.cn, wangjun@us.ibm.com

Abstract. Fine-grained visual categorization aims at classifying visual
data at a subordinate level, e.g., identifying different species of birds. It
is a highly challenging topic receiving significant research attention recently. Most existing works focused on the design of more discriminative
feature representations to capture the subtle visual differences among
categories. Very limited efforts were spent on the design of robust model
learning algorithms. In this paper, we treat the training of each category
classifier as a single learning task, and formulate a *generic* multiple task
learning (MTL) framework to train multiple classifiers simultaneously.
Different from the existing MTL methods, the proposed generic MTL
algorithm enforces no structure assumptions and thus is more flexible in
handling complex inter-class relationships. In particular, it is able to automatically discover both clusters of similar categories and outliers. We
show that the objective of our generic MTL formulation can be solved
using an iterative reweighted ℓ_2 method. Through an extensive experimental validation, we demonstrate that our method outperforms several
state-of-the-art approaches.

Keywords: Fine-grained visual categorization, inter-class relationship,
multiple task learning.

1 Introduction

Object recognition has been extensively studied in computer vision. Significant
progress has been made in the recognition of basic categories like bird and
car. Recently, an increasing amount of attention is being paid to the study
of Fine-Grained Visual Categorization (FGVC), which aims at the identification and distinction of subcategories such as different species of birds or dogs
[5,11,18,19,34,37,40,41,42,43]. Algorithms and systems with such capabilities not
only enhance the performance of conventional object recognition, but also can
aid humans in specific domains, since even human experts may have difficulties
in recognizing some subcategories.

Generally, there are two critical challenges in the design of a robust FGVC
system. First, object categories under the same coarse semantic level often share

D. Fleet et al. (Eds.): ECCV 2014, Part III, LNCS 8691, pp. 425–440, 2014.

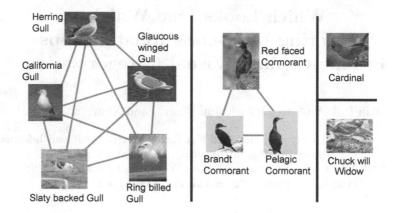

Fig. 1. Illustration of category relationships in fine-grained visual categorization problems, using birds as an example. There may exist multiple *clusters* containing highly similar categories (e.g., various species of Gull and Cormorant), as well as *outlier* categories that are distinct from others (e.g., Cardinal and Chuck will Widow). This paper proposes a generic multiple task learning algorithm, which is able to automatically discover and utilize the category grouping and outlier structure for improved fine-grained categorization performance.

similar appearances and the visual differences are very subtle. As shown in Figure 1, the subcategories within the same group (Gull or Cormorant) tend to share similar appearances. Therefore, very sophisticated features may be needed to distinguish such fine-grained categories. The second challenge is that fine-grained categorization tasks always lack in training data since the acquisition of clean positive samples for each subordinate category needs strong domain knowledge.

To address these challenges, we underline that FGVC systems should encode at least two characteristics of inter-class relationships: 1) sufficient discriminative capability to distinguish the subtle differences among the subcategories, and 2) strong learning power to explore similarities among categories to compensate for the lack of training samples. Most of the existing works only focused on solving the first issue by proposing new feature representations, as they emphasized that insufficient discriminative power resides in the way that features are encoded [19,41,18,43,34,40].

In this paper, we adopt and improve the *multiple task learning* (MTL) framework to design more discriminative classifiers. Instead of training classifiers independently, MTL trains multiple classifiers jointly and simultaneously to explore model commonalities in either structure or parameter space [3,12]. Since simultaneously learning multiple tasks will benefit from the learning of each other, the MTL paradigm often leads to better performance. However, standard MTL highly relies on the assumption of a clean model commonality, which is too idealistic to be practically used for FGVC. Although some recent works relaxed the strong assumption to *grouped structure* [25] or *outlier structure* [22] of tasks, the category relationships in the realistic FGVC problem could be more complicated and do not fit those existing structure assumptions.

Realizing the limitation of the existing MTL paradigms and the practical needs of FGVC, this paper presents a *generic* MTL framework without any specific structure assumptions. Our method exploits the relationships among the fine-grained categories by imposing a mixture norm penalty on the classifier coefficients to automatically learn the task structures, where a ridge term is used to reflect the categories' grouping structure and a lasso term represents outlier categories. Our objective is formulated as an unconstrained convex optimization problem, whose optimal solution can be obtained by iteratively solving a series of reweighted ℓ_2 problems. Extensive evaluations on two well-known FGVC benchmark datasets demonstrate the effectiveness our proposed method.

The remainder of this paper is organized as follows. Section 2 briefly reviews existing works in FGVC. Section 3 presents our proposed generic MTL framework. Section 4 provides experimental validations and comparative studies, and, finally, Section 5 concludes this paper.

2 Related Works

In this section we briefly review existing works on FGVC; the backgrounds of MTL will be discussed later in Section 3.1. Like any visual categorization applications, an FGVC system normally contains two major components: feature extraction and classifier learning. As mentioned earlier, most existing works focused on improving the discrimination power of the extracted feature representations (e.g., [19,26,43,41], among others), and a standard SVM classifier was often employed in the learning phase.

For feature representations used in FGVC, many researchers adopted local features as the basis to develop more powerful visual descriptors. For instance, locality-constrained linear coding [36], an effective bag-of-words quantization method, was adopted in [42] as a baseline. In [26], Khan et al. proposed a multi-cue method to build discriminative compound visual words from primitive cues. The kernel descriptors (KDES) [10] have also been adopted for FGVC and shown to be promising [40].

Another popular group of works used template-based feature representation and demonstrated good performance for FGVC applications. In [41], Yao et al. used randomly selected templates and generated visual features through concatenating the pooling results on template response maps. In [40], Yang et al. proposed an unsupervised template learning method to capture the common shape patterns across different categories. Several other factors such as the co-occurrence and diversity of templates were also taken into account.

In addition, Chai et al. [13] proposed a method called TriCoS to segment discriminative foregrounds. Segmentation based approaches were also explored in [1,14,39]. Several works further adopted localization approaches to identify discriminative parts or details of the target objects [44,21]. These methods, however, are computationally slow as both the segmentation and the part localization processes are expensive.

All the aforementioned approaches are less powerful in exploring the category relatedness and identifying the subtle differences across categories. Perhaps the most intuitive way to identify the subtle differences among categories is to use human-assisted techniques. Representative works include the human-in-the-loop approaches that asked humans to input object attributes [11,34], and the crowdsourcing-based method to identify more discriminative features [17]. Another approach that is loosely related to this category is the poselet-like methods [19,43], where human inputs were needed to label keypoint locations. The acquisition of manual annotations needed by these approaches is very expensive, and the inputs of the annotation tasks (e.g., the attribute questions) also need to be designed by experts with sufficient domain knowledge.

The lack of research on better model learning techniques in FGVC, especially those exploring the category relatedness, motivated us to propose the following generic MTL framework, which can automatically discover and utilize the complex inter-class relationships to achieve better performance. An intuitive way of using the category relationships is to explore domain knowledge. For example, adopting class taxonomies or hierarchies [6,23] may help train better prediction models by sharing appearance [20,30], visual parts [33], or classifiers [4]. However, the specific domain knowledge is not easy to be obtained, and the developed taxonomy for one FGVC application cannot be generalized to other different domains. The idea of using the class relationships was also exploited very recently in [8,9], where the authors proposed to use one-vs-*most* SVMs to find significant features that distinguish different species by omitting some similar classes, which is fundamentally different from our proposed solution.

3   Exploring Inter-class Relationships in FGVC

In this section, we present our proposed method to explore the inter-class relationships in FGVC. We start with introducing the notations and a brief background of MTL.

3.1   Notations and Background

Given a categorization problem, denote the training data containing n samples as $\{\mathbf{X}, \mathbf{z}\}$, where $\mathbf{X} = \{\mathbf{x}_i\}_{i=1}^{n}$ is the training set with $\mathbf{x}_i \in \mathbb{R}^D$ representing a D-dimensional feature of the i-th sample, and $\mathbf{z} = \{z_i\}_{i=1}^{n}, z_i \in \{1, \cdots, L\}$ is the label set for L categories. For a typical multi-class case, the one-vs-all strategy is widely used to train a classifier for each category. Hence, for the l-th category, we convert the multi-class label vector $\mathbf{z} = \{z_i\}_{i=1}^{n}$ to a binary label vector $\mathbf{y}_l = \{y_{li}\}_{i=1}^{n}, y_{li} \in \{-1, 1\}$ as $y_{li} = 1$ if $z_i = l$, otherwise $y_{li} = -1$. Assume that the classifier for the l-th category is defined in a linear form as $\hat{y}_l = \mathbf{w}_l^\top \mathbf{x} + b_l$, where $\hat{y}_l$ is the prediction; $\mathbf{w}_l \in \mathbb{R}^D$ and b_l are the coefficient vector and the bias[1], respectively. The cost function for training all the classifiers $\{\mathbf{w}_l\}_{l=1}^{L}$ is often written as

---

[1] In the following we omit the bias term b_l for simplicity.

$$\min_{\mathbf{W}} \sum_{l=1}^{L} \left(\sum_{i=1}^{n} \mathcal{V}(\mathbf{w}_l^\top \mathbf{x}_i, y_{li}) + \lambda \|\mathbf{w}_l\|_2 \right). \tag{1}$$

A major issue of the above formulation is that the relationships of different categories are ignored and the training for each category is performed independently. This normally leads to degraded performance particularly when the positive training samples are insufficient, which is often observed in FGVC applications. Simultaneously training multiple classifiers by MTL can effectively alleviate this problem. Formally, a basic MTL method is to replace the ℓ_2 penalty of each classifier with a structure penalty to constrain all the classifiers, with the following cost function:

$$\min_{\mathbf{W}} \sum_{l=1}^{L} \sum_{i=1}^{n} \mathcal{V}(\mathbf{w}_l^\top \mathbf{x}_i, y_{li}) + \lambda \|\mathbf{W}\|_{2,1}. \tag{2}$$

where the matrix $\mathbf{W}$ is formed through concatenating single classifiers as $\mathbf{W} = [\mathbf{w}_1, \mathbf{w}_2, \cdots, \mathbf{w}_l]$. The regularization term $\|\mathbf{W}\|_{2,1} = \sum_i \left(\sum_j w_{ij}^2 \right)^{1/2}$ induces row sparsity that encourages the elements of the same row to maintain similar zero/nonzero patterns. Minimizing the above cost to derive the optimal $\mathbf{W}$ can also be viewed as a feature selection process since the commonly shared discriminative features will be preserved as non-zero row vectors in the $\mathbf{W}$ matrix. The major limitation of this basic MTL formulation lies in the assumption that all the classifiers $\{\mathbf{w}_l\}_{l=1}^{L}$ share a common sparse structure.

To relax the common structure assumption, there are two major categories of advanced MTL methods. First, *cluster-based* MTL methods consider the existence of several task (category) clusters, where features are only shared within each cluster and irrelevant to tasks outside the cluster. Thus, several approaches introduced latent variables to indicate the cluster information or to select the features to be shared [25,28,45]. The optimization of the latent variables is usually merged into the main MTL procedure as a subroutine. Second, *robust* MTL methods assume that all the tasks consist of a major task group peppered with several outlier tasks. A popular way of tackling this robust MTL problem is to use a decomposition framework, which forms a learning objective with a structure term and an outlier penalty term [24,16,22]. Then, the target model is further decomposed into two components, i.e., a group component and an outlier component, which can be efficiently solved separately. Figure 2(a) illustrates the learned classifiers $\mathbf{W}$ by cluster-based MTL, where each column vector represents a single learning task and a total of two groups of tasks are identified. Similarly, Figure 2(b) demonstrates a structure of the learned classifiers from the robust MTL, where a major group of tasks and two outlier tasks can be observed.

3.2   Generic Multiple Task Learning (GMTL)

Since there always exist certain kinds of relationships between the categories in FGVC applications, performing MTL can help boost the classification performance

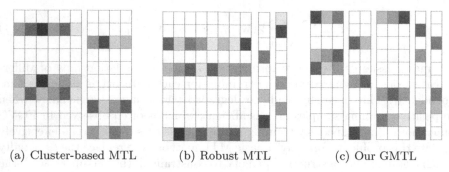

(a) Cluster-based MTL   (b) Robust MTL   (c) Our GMTL

Fig. 2. Illustration of the structures of the learned classifiers **W** using cluster-based MTL, robust MTL, and our GMTL. Each column represents a classifier $\mathbf{w}_l$ and each row represents the learned coefficients corresponding to a feature dimension. The white color indicates zero coefficient value, and the gray-scale colors reflect the magnitude of nonzero values. See text for more explanations.

through identifying the shared features across the categories. Especially, MTL is very suitable when the positive samples are inadequate for each classifier and the feature representation is in very high dimensions. However, due to the complex structures of the fine-grained categories, the aforementioned MTL models are infeasible for such applications since they all rely on strong assumptions of simple task structures. As illustrated by the bird examples in Figure 1, a usual FGVC problem may have the following structure characteristics: 1) some categories are strongly related and form a category group since they share similar visual signatures; 2) the similarity between different category groups may be very low (e.g., the Gull and Cormorant groups); 3) some categories are not similar to all the other categories, e.g., the Cardinal and Chuck will Widow (i.e., outlier categories).

Motivated by the above observations, we formulate a generic MTL (GMTL) framework without any specific structure assumption: the categories are related in a mixture manner with unknown clusters and outliers. As illustrated in Figure 2(c), the categories consist of multiple clusters and outliers. To capture such a complex task structure for FGVC applications, the proposed GMTL model explores a balanced mixture of the category clusters and outliers as

$$\min_{\mathbf{W}} \sum_{l=1}^{L} \sum_{i=1}^{n} \mathcal{V}(\mathbf{w}_l^\top \mathbf{x}_i, y_{li}) + \lambda \left(\alpha \|\mathbf{W}\|_{2,1} + (1-\alpha)\|\mathbf{W}\|_{1,1}\right). \tag{3}$$

The first term is the empirical loss of fitting the training data, and the regularization term consists of two parts: the feature sharing part for category grouping and the outlier detection part for category outliers. Accordingly, the $\|\mathbf{W}\|_{2,1}$ penalty reflects a grouping structure, and encourages feature sharing among tasks within each task group. The $\|\mathbf{W}\|_{1,1}$ penalty reflects an element-wise sparse structure, highlighting the outlier categories. The coefficient λ weighs the contribution of the total penalties, and the parameter α balances the two regularization terms.

In this paper, we particularly choose the squared hinge loss as our empirical loss for the FGVC problem:

$$\mathcal{V}(\mathbf{w}^\top \mathbf{x}, y) = \left[max(0, 1 - y\mathbf{w}^\top \mathbf{x})\right]^2. \tag{4}$$

Compared with the standard hinge loss, the above squared hinge loss penalizes less when the sign of prediction is correct but within the margin, and penalizes more when the sign of prediction is wrong. In addition, the squared hinge loss provides a better computational efficiency, which is extremely important when we need to solve the primal problem directly [15,29]. Note that a similar objective function with mixture norms and the hinge loss was investigated in a recent work [46] for other purposes using a different optimization strategy. However, the non-smoothness of the hinge loss may affect the convergence speed of their method. Another work used similar structural regularization forms with the mixture norms for regression problems [35], which is also different from the classification scenario of FGVC.

To further explore the role of these two penalties and better understand the above formulation, we rewrite Eq. 3 as:

$$\min_{\mathbf{W}} \sum_{l=1}^{L} \left(\sum_{i=1}^{n} \mathcal{V}(\mathbf{w}_l^\top \mathbf{x}_i, y_{li}) + \lambda(1-\alpha)\|\mathbf{w}_l\|_1 \right) + \lambda\alpha\|\mathbf{W}\|_{2,1}. \tag{5}$$

In contrast to the basic MTL formulation in Eq. 2, although we have the same MTL penalty $\mathbf{W}_{2,1}$ to encourage feature sharing among tasks, the term in the parentheses is different: we are solving an ℓ_1 regularized data fitting instead of the unregularized data fitting for each category. This ℓ_1 regularized term can shrink the small values of $\mathbf{w}_l$ to zero. Combining the effects of the two penalties, the optimization of Eq. 3 can satisfy all the three situations in fine-grained categorization: 1) the $\ell_{2,1}$ norm generally enforces categories to share features, including those categories from different groups; 2) since the categories in different groups are less relevant, the magnitude of feature sharing should be small; the $\ell_{1,1}$ penalty tends to shrink the corresponding weights to zero; 3) for the outliers, the mixture of the $\ell_{2,1}$ and $\ell_{1,1}$ penalties shrinks the unrelated features to be zero weighted. In summary, the above mixed structure regularization encourages category grouping, as well as identifies outlier categories.

3.3   Optimization Strategy

Solving the optimization problem in Eq. 3 is nontrivial due to the coupling of all the classifiers and the discontinuity of the regularization penalty. One way to optimize this problem is to employ the proximal gradient method [7]. However, for such a mixture norm penalty, it usually requires two shrinkage operations in the projection step [32], which are inefficient. Another way to optimize the mixture norm penalty is to iteratively solve a series of reweighted ℓ_2 problems [38]. With some derivations, the original problem in Eq. 3 can be rewritten as

$$\min_{\mathbf{W}} \sum_{l=1}^{L} \left(\sum_{i=1}^{n} \mathcal{V}(\mathbf{w}_l^{\top} \mathbf{x}_i, y_{li}) + \frac{\lambda}{2} \|\mathbf{C}_l \mathbf{w}_l\|_2 \right). \tag{6}$$

Here $\mathbf{C}_l = diag\,[(\mathbf{C}_l)_1, \cdots (\mathbf{C}_l)_d, \cdots, (\mathbf{C}_l)_D]$ is a diagonal weight matrix with the elements computed as:

$$(\mathbf{C}_l)_d = \alpha \|\mathbf{w}_{d\cdot}\|_2^{-1} + (1-\alpha)|w_{dl}|^{-1}, \tag{7}$$

where $\mathbf{w}_{d\cdot}$ represents the d-th row vector of $\mathbf{W}$. Note that $(\mathbf{C}_l)_d$ consists of two components: a group impact term $\|\mathbf{w}_{d\cdot}\|_2^{-1}$ imposing the global effect across all categories, and an individual term $|w_{dl}|^{-1}$ denoting the impact of the d-th feature on the l-th category.

Algorithm 1. Training Procedure of GMTL

Require: $\mathbf{X}$: feature representation of all the samples; $\{\mathbf{y}_l\}_{l=1}^{L}$: binary label vector for each category;
1. Initialize $\{\mathbf{C}_l\}_{l=1}^{L}$ with the identity matrix;
2. **while** not converged **do**
3.   **for** $l = 1$ to L **do**
4.   Reweight the training data:
           $\tilde{\mathbf{x}}_{li} = (\mathbf{C}_l)^{-1}\mathbf{x}_i$;
5.   Solve an ℓ_2 regularized minimization problem:
           $\tilde{\mathbf{w}}_l = \min_{\tilde{\mathbf{w}}_l} \left(\sum_{i=1}^{n} \mathcal{V}(\tilde{\mathbf{w}}_l^{\top} \tilde{\mathbf{x}}_{li}, y_{li}) + \frac{\lambda}{2}\|\tilde{\mathbf{w}}_l\|_2 \right)$;
6.   Compute the coefficient $\mathbf{w}_l$ for each classifier:
           $\mathbf{w}_l = (\mathbf{C}_l)^{-1}\tilde{\mathbf{w}}_l$;
7.   Update the weight matrix:
           $\mathbf{C}_l = diag\left(\alpha \|\mathbf{w}_{d\cdot}\|_2^{-1} + (1-\alpha)|w_{dl}|^{-1} \right)$;
8.   **end for**
9. **end while**

Compared with the formulation of basic MTL in Eq. 1, the key difference lies in the regularization term, where a diagonal matrix $\mathbf{C}_l$ is applied to weight the importance of the individual feature dimensions for each classification model $\mathbf{w}_l$. To further simplify such a weighted ℓ_2 form in Eq. 6, we can transform the problem to reweighted data instead of reweighted classifiers. Denoting $\tilde{\mathbf{w}}_l = \mathbf{C}_l \mathbf{w}_l$ and $\tilde{\mathbf{x}}_{li} = \mathbf{C}_l^{-1}\mathbf{x}_i$, we can derive a standard ℓ_2 regularized optimization problem with reweighted data as:

$$\min_{\tilde{\mathbf{W}}} \sum_{l=1}^{L} \left(\sum_{i=1}^{n} \mathcal{V}(\tilde{\mathbf{w}}_l^{\top} \tilde{\mathbf{x}}_{li}, y_{li}) + \frac{\lambda}{2} \|\tilde{\mathbf{w}}_l\|_2 \right). \tag{8}$$

Starting from any reasonable initialization, we can solve the above minimization problem iteratively, where during each iteration we need to update the weight matrices $\{\mathbf{C}_l\}_{l=1}^{L}$ using Eq. 7 and reweight the data. Algorithm 1 summarizes the training procedure of the proposed GMTL through the iterative reweighted ℓ_2 method. In each iteration, to learn a classifier, there are four

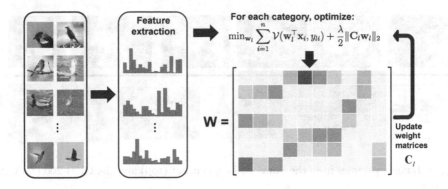

Fig. 3. Illustration of the iterative training process in GMTL

steps: *a*) reweight the data to obtain $\tilde{\mathbf{x}}_{li}$; *b*) solve an ℓ_2 regularized minimization problem; *c*) compute the coefficient vector of the classifier $\mathbf{w}_l$; *d*) update the weight matrix $\mathbf{C}_l$ (referring to step 4-7 in Algorithm 1). The first three steps are equivalent to solving an ℓ_2 reweighted classifier, and the last step updates the weight matrix $\mathbf{C}_l$. Therefore, the GMTL optimization is formed in nested loops, where the outer loop (while-loop) is for pursuing local convergence and the inner loop (for-loop) is for updating the classifier of each category. Detailed proof of the convergence of the GMTL is omitted due to space limitation. In our experiments, we have empirically observed that the convergence can be often achieved after just a few iterations. The conceptual pipeline of using the proposed GMTL for learning fine-grained categorization models is also demonstrated in Figure 3.

4 Experiments

In this section, we first introduce the used datasets and experimental settings. Then we discuss our results and present comparison studies with state-of-the-art methods. After that we visualize the automatically identified category groups.

4.1 Datasets and Settings

We evaluate our approach using mainly two public datasets: the Stanford Dog [27] and the Caltech-UCSD Bird-200-2010 [37], which are widely used in the FGVC literature. The Stanford Dog dataset contains $20,580$ images from 120 breeds of dogs. Following the standard setup of [27], 100 images from each category are used for training and the rest are used for testing. The Caltech-UCSD Bird-200-2010 (CUB-200-2010) contains $6,033$ images from 200 bird species in North America, with about 30 images per class and 15 of them for training [37]. Exemplar images from Dog and Bird datasets are shown in Figure 4. Following the standard procedure in existing FGVC works [27,37], all the images are cropped according to the provided dog/bird bounding boxes before feature extraction. The images are then

Fig. 4. Image examples from the Stanford Dog Dataset (top) and the CUB-200 Dataset (bottom)

resized to be no larger than 300 × 300 with the original aspect ratio preserved. At the end of the experiments, we also briefly discuss our results on the newer 2011 version of the bird dataset, which has more training and testing images per class.

We adopt the kernel descriptors (KDES) [10,40] to represent each image as a feature vector. Following [10,40], we use four types of the kernel descriptors: color-based, normalized color-based, gradient-based, and local-binary-pattern-based. The color and normalized color kernel descriptors are extracted from the original RGB images, and the other descriptors are extracted from converted gray scale images. All the kernel descriptors are computed on 16 × 16 image patches over dense regular grids with a step size of 8 pixels. Combining all the descriptors, we receive the final image representation as a 120, 000-dimension feature vector.

In addition to comparing our results with the state-of-the-art FGVC methods, we also compare with two representative MTL algorithms: Joint Feature Selection (JFS) [2] and Clustered MTL (CMTL) [45]. The formulation of JFS can be treated as a special case of our generic solution by setting $\alpha = 1$, and the CMTL method is based on the spectral-relaxed k-means clustering. We use the source codes provided by the authors of [45]. For all the MTL methods including ours, we use cross validation to estimate suitable parameters.

Table 1. Comparison of the classification accuracies on the Stanford Dog dataset

Approach		Accuracy (%)
State-of-the-art FGVC methods	SIFT [27]	22.0
	KDES [10]	36.0
	UTL [40]	38.0
	Symb+DPM [14]	45.6
MTL methods	JFS [2]	29.9
	CMTL [45]	30.4
	Our GMTL	39.3

4.2   Results and Discussions

Dog Categorization. We now discuss results on the Stanford Dog dataset. We compare with a SIFT-based method [27], KDES [10], an approach using unsupervised template learning (UTL) [40] and a recent work [14]. For all the approaches, the classification accuracies are reported using the same settings. In addition, the performance of JFS and CMTL are also reported, using the same KDES features. Table 1 gives the classification accuracies of various approaches. It is easy to see that the GMTL approach significantly outperforms the other two MTL methods. It is worth noting that both JFS and CMTL have worse performance than the KDES baseline. This is due to the existence of both subtle and drastic appearance variations among categories in FGVC datasets, which result in negative transfer or improper feature sharing in the JFS and CMTL methods. As discussed earlier in Section 3, our proposed GMTL is able to cope with the existence of both category clusters and outliers, which enables a more appropriate exploration of class relationships, and thus offers better performance. Our GMTL improves the KDES baseline by 3.3%, which is a significant gain considering the difficulty of the problem. Note that the recently developed approach [14] exploits symbiotic segmentation and part localization techniques to achieve strong performance on this dataset. However, this approach is computationally more expensive and the performance highly relies on the quality of segmentation and localization.

14 Bird Species Categorization. Next we experiment with the CUB-200-2010 dataset, which has more categories, less training data, and even more significant appearance variations across categories. Since this dataset is very challenging, in many existing works, a subset of 14 species was frequently used for evaluation. For the ease of comparison we also report results on this subset.

The subset contains two families of birds: Vireos and Woodpeckers [19]. Following [19,41], we produce a left-right mirrored image for each training and test image, which forms a total of 420 training images and 508 testing images. We compare with the following published approaches: multiple kernel learning (MKL) [11], Birdlet [19], a random template method [41], and the KDES [10]. A few very recent approaches are excluded from the comparison since they are designed under different settings and require additional human inputs like [17].

Following [41], we report the performance on this dataset using mean average precision (mAP) in Table 2. Again, we find that JFS and CMTL fail to improve the KDES baseline, and our GMTL significantly outperforms these two MTL methods. Compared with the state-of-the-art FGVC methods, our GMTL performs better than all of them. Table 3 further gives the per-class results for the three compared MTL approaches on this subset. For most of the bird subcategories, the proposed GMTL provides a visible performance gain over the compared JFS and CMTL methods.

All Bird Species Categorization. Finally, we test our method on the full bird dataset of 200 species. Results are summarized in Table 4. We compare with a multiple kernel learning (MKL) method [11], a bag-of-features approach using the LLC [36], a randomization based method [42], a multi-cue representation [26],

Table 2. Performance comparison on the bird subset of 14 species, measured by mean average precision (mAP)

Approach		mAP (%)
	MKL [11]	37.0
State-of-the-art	Birdlet [19]	40.3
FGVC methods	Random template [41]	44.7
	KDES [10]	42.5
	JFS [2]	38.9
MTL methods	CMTL [45]	40.6
	Our GMTL	45.7

Table 3. Per-class average precision (%) of the three MTL-based methods on the bird subset of 14 species. The best results of each row are shown in bold. We list abbreviated names of the bird species due to space limitation.

	JFS [2]	CMTL [45]	Our GMTL
BC Vireo	33.0	33.9	**39.5**
BH Vireo	**22.3**	20.9	**22.3**
P Vireo	33.1	35.6	**45.7**
RE Vireo	14.5	**14.8**	13.3
W Vireo	14.0	**18.1**	17.2
WE Vireo	49.1	48.4	**54.7**
YT Vireo	23.9	25.0	**28.3**
N Flicker	66.3	65.2	**76.0**
ATT Woodpecker	58.1	57.9	**63.6**
P Woodpecker	50.0	53.5	**67.6**
RB Woodpecker	41.1	41.2	**45.2**
RC Woodpecker	19.5	30.8	**33.9**
RH Woodpecker	89.7	92.7	**95.8**
D Woodpecker	29.4	30.6	**36.8**
mAP (%)	38.9	40.6	**45.7**

the TriCoS[13], the UTL [40], the KDES [10] and two recent approaches [1,14]. Results of most methods are from the corresponding references, except that the performances of LLC and KDES were reported in [42] and [40] respectively.

As shown in the table, GMTL outperforms most of the compared FGVC approaches, which again confirms the effectiveness of our method. Compared with UTL, the gain is marginal. However, UTL focuses on feature representation, while our method emphasizes on the use of the class relationships during the learning phase. Since the UTL and KDES results are based the same SVM classification pipeline, we expect that similar improvement can be attained using our GMTL over the UTL feature, which however is difficult to validate as the source codes of UTL are not available online. Several recent works [1,14,17] reported better performance on this dataset. However, the approaches of [1,14] include computationally expensive segmentation/detection, and [17] requires additional human inputs, which is therefore excluded from the table. In addition, similar to

Table 4. Performance comparison on the entire Caltech-UCSD Bird-200-2010 dataset

Approach		Accuracy (%)
State-of-the-art FGVC methods	MKL [11]	19.0
	LLC [42]	18.0
	Randomization [42]	19.2
	Multi-Cue [26]	22.4
	TriCoS [13]	25.5
	UTL [40]	28.2
	KDES [10]	26.4
	Detection+Segmentation [1]	30.2
	Symb+DPM [14]	47.3
MTL methods	JFS [2]	21.7
	CMTL [45]	22.0
	Our GMTL	28.4

the observations from the experiment on the subset, JFS and CMTL fail again for the same reason as discussed earlier.

We also evaluate our method on the newer 2011 version of the Bird dataset, which contains more samples per category. Comparing to the baseline KDES using SVM (43.0%), our GMTL method achieves an accuracy of 44.2%. The improvement on this dataset (1.2%) is less significant than that on the 2010 version

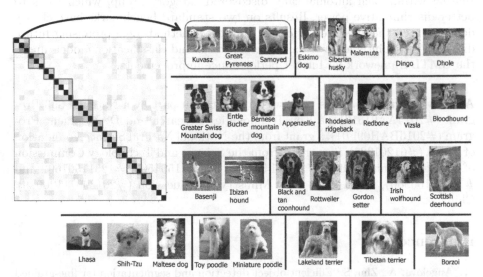

Fig. 5. Left: Similarity matrix of a subset of the learned tasks on the Stanford Dog dataset, where the red boxes indicate the automatically generated category groups. **Right:** Visual examples of the category groups (and the three outliers in the lower right corner) indicated on the similarity matrix, ordered from left to right and top to bottom. For instance, the first red box on the matrix corresponds to the upper left group of the example images.

(2.0%), indicating that our method is more effective when there is insufficient training data.

Visualization of Category Groups and Outliers. Finally, we analyze the power of our GMTL in identifying the inter-class relationships, including both the category groups and the outliers. The Stanford Dog dataset is adopted in this study for the ease of visualization as it contains less categories. We use $\mathbf{W}^\top\mathbf{W}$ to represent the similarity matrix of all the categories, and adopt the Normalized Cut [31] to group the categories, which are then reordered for visualization. A subset of the similarity matrix is displayed in Figure 5, which shows ten category groups and three outliers. Within each category group, the different species of dogs share similar color, shape and texture, while there exist significant differences across different groups.

5   Conclusion

We have presented a generic MTL method to explore inter-class relationships for improved fine-grained visual categorization. Different from the existing MTL algorithms that often rely on certain assumptions of the task structure, the proposed GMTL imposes no structural assumptions, making it more flexible to handle complex category relationships in the FGVC applications. We have shown that the training of our GMTL can be efficiently achieved using an iterative reweighted ℓ_2 method. The learned classification models enforce feature sharing within each automatically discovered category group, which leads to better discriminative power. Results on two standard benchmarks have clearly demonstrated the effectiveness of our proposed method. One promising future direction is to jointly learn visual representations and classification models under the GMTL framework for further performance improvements.

Acknowledgments. This work was supported in part by a National 863 Program (#2014AA015101), a Key Technologies Research and Development Program (#2013BAH09F01), a grant from the National Natural Science Foundation of China (#61201387), four grants from the Science and Technology Commission of Shanghai Municipality (#13PJ1400400, #13511504503, #12511501602 and #14511106900), and a grant from Ministry of Education (#20120071120026), China.

References

1. Angelova, A., Zhu, S.: Efficient object detection and segmentation for fine-grained recognition. In: CVPR (2013)
2. Argyriou, A., Evgeniou, T., Pontil, M.: Multi-task feature learning. In: NIPS (2007)
3. Argyriou, A., Evgeniou, T., Pontil, M.: Convex multi-task feature learning. Mach. Learn. 73(3), 243–272 (2008)
4. Babenko, B., Branson, S., Belongie, S.: Similarity metrics for categorization: From monolithic to category specific. In: ICCV (2009)

5. Bar-Hillel, A., Weinshall, D.: Subordinate class recognition using relational object models. In: NIPS (2006)
6. Bart, E., Porteous, I., Perona, P., Welling, M.: Unsupervised learning of visual taxonomies. In: CVPR (2008)
7. Beck, A., Teboulle, M.: A fast iterative shrinkage-thresholding algorithm for linear inverse problems. SIAM J. Img. Sci. 2(1), 183–202 (2009)
8. Berg, T., Belhumeur, P.N.: How do you tell a blackbird from a crow? In: ICCV (2013)
9. Berg, T., Liu, J., Lee, S.W., Alexander, M.L., Jacobs, D.W., Belhumeur, P.N.: Birdsnap: Large-scale fine-grained visual categorization of birds. In: CVPR (2014)
10. Bo, L., Ren, X., Fox, D.: Kernel Descriptors for Visual Recognition. In: NIPS (2010)
11. Branson, S., Wah, C., Schroff, F., Babenko, B., Welinder, P., Perona, P., Belongie, S.: Visual recognition with humans in the loop. In: Daniilidis, K., Maragos, P., Paragios, N. (eds.) ECCV 2010, Part IV. LNCS, vol. 6314, pp. 438–451. Springer, Heidelberg (2010)
12. Caruana, R.: Multitask learning. Mach. Learn. 28(1), 41–75 (1997)
13. Chai, Y., Rahtu, E., Lempitsky, V., Van Gool, L., Zisserman, A.: TriCoS: A tri-level class-discriminative co-segmentation method for image classification. In: Fitzgibbon, A., Lazebnik, S., Perona, P., Sato, Y., Schmid, C. (eds.) ECCV 2012, Part I. LNCS, vol. 7572, pp. 794–807. Springer, Heidelberg (2012)
14. Chai, Y., Lempitsky, V., Zisserman, A.: Symbiotic segmentation and part localization for fine-grained categorization. In: ICCV (2013)
15. Chapelle, O.: Training a support vector machine in the primal. Neural. Comput. 19(5), 1155–1178 (2007)
16. Chen, J., Zhou, J., Ye, J.: Integrating low-rank and group-sparse structures for robust multi-task learning. In: KDD (2011)
17. Deng, J., Krause, J., Fei-Fei, L.: Fine-grained crowdsourcing for fine-grained recognition. In: CVPR (2013)
18. Duan, K., Parikh, D., Crandall, D., Grauman, K.: Discovering localized attributes for fine-grained recognition. In: CVPR (2012)
19. Farrell, R., Oza, O., Zhang, N., Morariu, V.I., Darrell, T., Davis, L.S.: Birdlets: Subordinate categorization using volumetric primitives and pose-normalized appearance. In: ICCV (2011)
20. Fergus, R., Bernal, H., Weiss, Y., Torralba, A.: Semantic label sharing for learning with many categories. In: Daniilidis, K., Maragos, P., Paragios, N. (eds.) ECCV 2010, Part I. LNCS, vol. 6311, pp. 762–775. Springer, Heidelberg (2010)
21. Gavves, E., Fernando, B., Snoek, C.G.M., Smeulders, A.W.M., Tuytelaars, T.: Fine-grained categorization by alignments. In: ICCV (2013)
22. Gong, P., Ye, J., Zhang, C.: Robust multi-task feature learning. In: KDD (2012)
23. Griffin, G., Perona, P.: Learning and using taxonomies for fast visual categorization. In: CVPR (2008)
24. Jalali, A., Ravikumar, P.D., Sanghavi, S., Ruan, C.: A dirty model for multi-task learning. In: NIPS (2010)
25. Kang, Z., Grauman, K., Sha, F.: Learning with whom to share in multi-task feature learning. In: ICML (2011)
26. Khan, F.S., Van De Weijer, J., Bagdanov, A.D., Vanrell, M.: Portmanteau vocabularies for multi-cue image representation. In: NIPS (2011)
27. Khosla, A., Jayadevaprakash, N., Yao, B., Fei-Fei, L.: Novel dataset for fine-grained image categorization. In: First Workshop on FGVC, CVPR (2011)
28. Kumar, A., Daumé III, H.: Learning task grouping and overlap in multi-task learning. In: ICML (2012)

29. Melacci, S., Belkin, M.: Laplacian Support Vector Machines Trained in the Primal. JMLR 12, 1149–1184 (2011)
30. Salakhutdinov, R., Torralba, A., Tenenbaum, J.: Learning to share visual appearance for multiclass object detection. In: CVPR (2011)
31. Shi, J., Malik, J.: Normalized cuts and image segmentation. IEEE Trans. Pattern Anal. Mach. Intell. 22(8), 888–905 (2000)
32. Su, H., Yu, A.W., Fei-Fei, L.: Efficient euclidean projections onto the intersection of norm balls. In: ICML (2012)
33. Todorovic, S., Ahuja, N.: Learning subcategory relevances for category recognition. In: CVPR (2008)
34. Wah, C., Branson, S., Perona, P., Belongie, S.: Multiclass recognition and part localization with humans in the loop. In: ICCV (2011)
35. Wang, H., Nie, F., Huang, H., Risacher, S.L., Ding, C.H.Q., Saykin, A.J., Shen, L.: Adni: Sparse multi-task regression and feature selection to identify brain imaging predictors for memory performance. In: ICCV (2011)
36. Wang, J., Yang, J., Yu, K., Lv, F., Huang, T.S., Gong, Y.: Locality-constrained linear coding for image classification. In: CVPR (2010)
37. Welinder, P., Branson, S., Mita, T., Wah, C., Schroff, F., Belongie, S., Perona, P.: Caltech-UCSD Birds 200. Tech. Rep. CNS-TR-2010-001, California Institute of Technology (2010)
38. Wipf, D.P., Nagarajan, S.S.: Iterative reweighted ℓ_1 and ℓ_2 methods for finding sparse solutions. J. Sel. Topics Signal Processing 4(2), 317–329 (2010)
39. Xie, L., Tian, Q., Hong, R., Yan, S., Zhang, B.: Hierarchical Part Matching for Fine-Grained Visual Categorization. In: ICCV (2013)
40. Yang, S., Bo, L., Wang, J., Shapiro, L.: Unsupervised Template Learning for Fine-Grained Object Recognition. In: NIPS (2012)
41. Yao, B., Bradski, G., Fei-Fei, L.: A codebook-free and annotation-free approach for fine-grained image categorization. In: CVPR (2012)
42. Yao, B., Khosla, A., Fei-Fei, L.: Combining randomization and discrimination for fine-grained image categorization. In: CVPR (2011)
43. Zhang, N., Farrell, R., Darrell, T.: Pose pooling kernels for sub-category recognition. In: CVPR (2012)
44. Zhang, N., Farrell, R., Iandola, F., Darrell, T.: Deformable part descriptors for fine-grained recognition and attribute prediction. In: ICCV (2013)
45. Zhou, J., Chen, J., Ye, J.: Clustered multi-task learning via alternating structure optimization. In: NIPS (2011)
46. Zweig, A., Weinshall, D.: Hierarchical regularization cascade for joint learning. In: ICML (2013)

Object Detection and Viewpoint Estimation with Auto-masking Neural Network

Linjie Yang[1], Jianzhuang Liu[1,3], and Xiaoou Tang[1,2]

[1] Department of Information Engineering, The Chinese University of Hong Kong
[2] Shenzhen Key Lab of Computer Vision and Pattern Recognition
Shenzhen Institutes of Advanced Technology, Chinese Academy of Sciences, China
[3] Media Lab, Huawei Technologies Co. Ltd., China
{yl012,xtang}@ie.cuhk.edu.hk, liu.jianzhuang@huawei.com

Abstract. Simultaneously detecting an object and determining its pose has become a popular research topic in recent years. Due to the large variances of the object appearance in images, it is critical to capture the discriminative object parts that can provide key information about the object pose. Recent part-based models have obtained state-of-the-art results for this task. However, such models either require manually defined object parts with heavy supervision or a complicated algorithm to find discriminative object parts. In this study, we have designed a novel deep architecture, called Auto-masking Neural Network (ANN), for object detection and viewpoint estimation. ANN can automatically learn to select the most discriminative object parts across different viewpoints from training images. We also propose a method of accurate continuous viewpoint estimation based on the output of ANN. Experimental results on related datasets show that ANN outperforms previous methods.

1 Introduction and Related Work

Category-level object detection has attracted a great deal of attentions in computer vision research. Aside from locating the object in an image, determining the pose of the object is also essential for practical tasks such as autonomous driving and robotic operation. Due to the large variance of the appearance of the object category, pose estimation remains a challenging task and a popular research topic in recent years.

Part-based models have attracted a great deal of attention in object detection and viewpoint estimation. Recently proposed models include the star shape model [29], [24], [1], constellation model [7], [23], graphical model [25], and deformable part model (DPM) [6], [15], [19], [18]. The DPM in [6] initializes and learns object parts in a data-driven way without intensive human operations. Later, the DPM is extended to 3D DPM that can infer 3D positions of object parts [19], [18]. The integration of rendered images from CAD models provides viewpoint ground truth and more information about object appearance in training [14], [23].

To obtain viewpoint estimation, Pepik et al. [19] quantized the viewing circle into discrete bins and formulated the estimation as a multi-class classification

D. Fleet et al. (Eds.): ECCV 2014, Part III, LNCS 8691, pp. 441–455, 2014.

problem. Later, they used an interpolation scheme from the predefined viewpoint bins to approximate the continuous viewpoint [18]. Other works to have targeted continuous viewpoint estimation are [28] and [30]. Teney et al. [28] fit a Gaussian distribution to the main peaks of voted scores to obtain an estimation of the continuous viewpoint, while Torki et al. [30] designed a regression function based on local features and their spatial arrangement.

The part-based approaches have greatly improved the performance of object detection and viewpoint estimation. However, they require manually defined object parts with extensive human operation and intervention, or need to design a complicated algorithm to find object parts.

Deep models have been successfully used recently in computer vision tasks such as pedestrian detection [21], face verification [9], face parsing [16], and classification [13], [22]. The research works of deep models focus on designing network structures [10], [2], [26] and feature learning algorithms [11], [27].

The convolutional neural network (CNN) [10] is one of the most popular deep models currently used to deal with computer vision problems [13], [21], [9], [26]. However, it still faces difficulties when applied to fine-grained tasks such as viewpoint estimation. The main reason is that although CNN is good at extracting global features, it does not emphasize local discriminative features which are critical for fine-grained tasks. Besides, the capability of CNN for continuous output tasks such as viewpoint estimation has rarely been explored, despite the fact that it succeeds in multi-class classification [9], [13].

In this paper, based on CNN, we propose a novel network structure, called Auto-masking Neural Network (ANN) for object detection and viewpoint estimation. ANN contains multiple CNNs and a mask layer that can select the most discriminative features from the input and pass them to the next level. It can also deal with multiple tasks such as object detection and viewpoint estimation simultaneously. Besides, a new method is presented to estimate the continuous viewpoint, which makes the estimation more accurate. Our experimental results show ANN outperforms the state-of-the-art algorithms.

2   Auto-masking Neural Network (ANN)

We have designed a deep neural network for the combined task of object detection and viewpoint estimation. Specifically, we have focused on a long-lasting and challenging task: car detection and viewpoint estimation. Our method is based on sliding windows, similar to the related works. At evaluation, it makes a prediction for each image patch. The structure of ANN is shown in Fig. 1, which has the following three parts: (i) the *mask generator* takes an image (patch) as input, and generates a mask; (ii) the *mask operator* does a mask operation between the input image and the mask, resulting in a masked image; and (iii) the *target predictor* outputs a detection label and a viewpoint from the masked image.

ANN utilizes a mask layer and three CNNs to extract discriminative features from images. The three CNNs have different purposes. CNN_M finds the positions

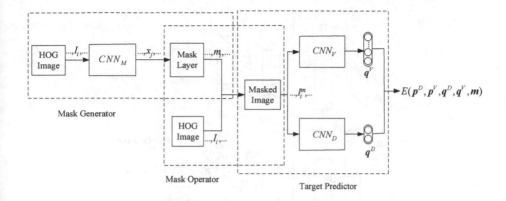

Fig. 1. Structure of ANN

of discriminative features from an input patch, while CNN_D detects the object and CNN_V estimates the viewpoint. The components of ANN are described in more detail in the following subsections.

2.1   Convolutional Neural Network (CNN)

CNNs have demonstrated their powerful capability in pedestrian detection [21], face verification [9], face alignment [26], and classification [13]. As an effective tool for learning global features, CNN's capability to select discriminative features for fine-grained tasks such as continuous viewpoint estimation has rarely been explored in the literature.

Fig. 2(a) shows the structure of CNN_M, which contains one convolution layer followed by max pooling [10], and one locally connected layer followed by another max pooling. The purpose of the convolution layer is to discover position-insensitive features in the image, while the purpose of the locally connected layer is to detect the position-sensitive patterns on top of the position-insensitive features. Fig. 2(b) shows the structure of CNN_D (or CNN_V). The first four layers of CNN_D (or CNN_V) have the same layer type as those of CNN_M, but one more fully connected layer is appended in CNN_D (or CNN_V). This fully connected layer is used to obtain the detection (or viewpoint estimation) result q^D (or q^V).

In our work, each image is rescaled to eight scales and image patches of size 200×200 are cropped using a sliding window. The input to ANN is a HOG image [3] with 23×23 blocks extracted from an image patch. The intensities of the HOG image are normalized to $[0, 1]$. The parameters (layer sizes) of the networks can be seen in Fig. 2.

2.2   Mask Layer

The mask layer is the key component of ANN. The whole network is trained automatically with the input HOG images and the target ground truth infor-

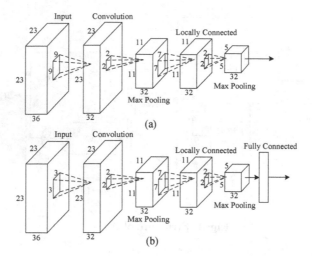

Fig. 2. (a) The structure of CNN_M, (b) The structure of CNN_D (or CNN_V). The sizes of the input, convolution, max pooling, and locally connected layers are illustrated by the cuboids with the numbers on their three dimensions. The local receptive fields of the neurons in the layers are illustrated by the small squares on the cuboids.

mation (detection labels and viewpoints) through back-propagation. For each HOG image, ANN generates a specific mask, automatically finding important parts from the input and allowing only these parts to pass to the target predictor. The mask layer is fully-connected to the output of CNN_M with bounded rectified linear neurons, the outputs of which are

$$m_i = \min\{1, \max\{0, \sum_j w_{ij}x_j\}\}, \ i = 1, 2, ..., N, \tag{1}$$

where $m_i \in [0, 1]$ is the response of a node in the mask layer, x_i is the response of a node in the output of CNN_M, w_{ij} is the weight between nodes i and j of the two layers, and N is the size of the mask, which is 529 (23×23) in our setting (see Figs. 1 and 2). The mask operation is an element-wise minimum operation between the HOG image and the mask, resulting in the masked image with its intensities being

$$I_i^m = \min\{m_i, I_i\}, \ i = 1, 2, ..., N, \tag{2}$$

where the mask and the HOG image are of the same size and $I_i \in [0, 1]$ is the ith intensity of the HOG image. It is easy to see the masking effect: when $m_i = 0$, the corresponding pixel i from the input is blocked by the mask; when $m_i \geq I_i$, it is passed completely ($I_i^m = I_i$).

Usually, only several key parts of an object in an image provide significant information for detection and viewpoint estimation. For example, the existence of a round wheel provides a strong indication that this image has a car that is viewed from the side. Therefore, we should enforce sparseness on the mask (i.e., m_i close to 1 are sparse and most m_i should be close to 0). Furthermore, considering that the features on the object should be more discriminative than those from the background, the positions with m_i close to 1 should concentrate on the object. When a region larger than the object is cropped as the input (see Section 3 for the detail), the positions with m_i close to 1 should form clusters on the object in the mask. Thus, considering m_i as mass points on a plane, we minimize the following moment of inertia of m_i in order to satisfy the sparseness and clustering requirements,

$$E_{sc} = \sum_i m_i r_i^2, \tag{3}$$

where r_i is the distance from pixel i to the center of the mass of m_i.

Figs. 5 and 6 in the section of experimental results provide some examples of the masks superimposed on the corresponding images. We can see that the masks are sparse and the positions (bright) with m_i close to 1 form clusters on the object.

2.3 Target Prediction

In the target predictor, two CNNs, CNN_D and CNN_V, are used for object detection and viewpoint estimation simultaneously. Since the two tasks are quite different and require different filters that aim at different features, we allow them to have separate CNNs but to share the same masked image as the input. Their outputs are both probability distributions, where CNN_D produces two outputs (object or non-object) and CNN_V has N_{vp} outputs. For discrete viewpoint estimation, the N_{vp} outputs of CNN_V represent N_{vp} probabilities of viewpoints within N_{vp} bins uniformly located on the viewing circle. The centers of the bins are $\theta_i = \frac{360}{N_{vp}} i$, $i = 0, 1, ..., N_{vp} - 1$.

In training, the cost for one input patch is the sum of the cross-entropy errors of the two CNNs and the sparseness and clustering cost,

$$E = -\sum_{i=0}^{1} p_i^D \log q_i^D - p_1^D \sum_{i=0}^{N_{vp}-1} p_i^V \log q_i^V + \lambda E_{sc}, \tag{4}$$

where $\boldsymbol{p}^D = (p_0^D, p_1^D)$ is the ground truth probability distribution for detection ($\boldsymbol{p}^D = (1, 0)$ for a negative sample and $\boldsymbol{p}^D = (0, 1)$ for a positive sample), $\boldsymbol{p}^V = (p_0^V, p_1^V, ..., p_{N_{vp}-1}^V)$ is the ground truth probability distribution for viewpoint (only one component of $\boldsymbol{p}^V$ is 1 and the others are 0), $\boldsymbol{q}^D$ and $\boldsymbol{q}^V$ are the corresponding estimates for detection and viewpoint, respectively, and λ is a weighting factor. Here, the cost for viewpoint estimation is meaningful only when the input is a positive sample, which is why the second term on the right-hand side of (4) is multiplied by p_1^D.

2.4 Discrete and Continuous Viewpoint Estimation

The most straightforward way of ANN training for viewpoint estimation is to set one of the $\boldsymbol{p}^V$'s components (say, p_j^V) to 1 and the other components to 0, where θ_j^V is the center of the jth bin within which the viewpoint of the training object is located. We refer to this training scheme as *discrete viewpoint training*. In testing, for a predicted positive sample, the estimated viewpoint is set to θ_i if the largest component of $\boldsymbol{q}^V$ is q_i^V.

However, from our experiments, we find that ANN trained this way does not generate sufficiently precise viewpoint estimation because a lot of the information is lost when each of the continuous viewpoints of the training objects is abruptly quantized to only one component of $\boldsymbol{p}^V$. Next, we present an interpolation method to handle this problem.

Let the ground truth viewpoint be θ, which is located between two neighboring viewpoint bin centers θ_j and θ_{j+1}. Then

$$p_j^V(\theta) = \frac{\theta_{j+1} - \theta}{L}, \quad p_{j+1}^V(\theta) = \frac{\theta - \theta_j}{L}, \quad p_k^V(\theta) = 0, \ k \notin \{j, j+1\}, \quad (5)$$

where $L = \frac{360}{N_{vp}}$ is the size of a bin, and p_j^V, p_{j+1}^V, and p_k^V are the components of $\boldsymbol{p}^V$. In this method, although there are only two non-zero components p_j^V and p_{j+1}^V in $\boldsymbol{p}^V$ when $\theta \in (\theta_j, \theta_{j+1})$, p_j^V and p_{j+1}^V implicitly encode all possible continuous viewpoint angles in $[\theta_j, \theta_{j+1}]$, because from (5) we can have $\theta = p_j^V \theta_j + p_{j+1}^V \theta_{j+1} \in [\theta_j, \theta_{j+1}]$. We call the training with $\boldsymbol{p}^V$ defined by (5) *continuous viewpoint training*. Since $\sum_{j=0}^{N_{vp}-1} p_j^V = 1$, $\boldsymbol{p}^V$ can still be considered as a probability distribution.

Objects of the same kind usually have similar appearances when they are in close viewpoints. The similarity between two objects in viewpoints θ_a and θ_b can be defined as

$$s(\theta_a, \theta_b) = \max\{0, 1 - \frac{|\theta_a - \theta_b|}{\theta_T}\}, \quad (6)$$

where θ_T is a threshold, which makes the similarity to be 0 when $|\theta_a - \theta_b| \geq \theta_T$. If θ_T is set to the size of a bin $\frac{360}{N_{vp}}$, then

$$p_j^V(\theta) = s(\theta, \theta_j), \ j = 0, 1, ..., N_{vp} - 1. \quad (7)$$

This relation indicates that $p_j^V(\theta)$ can also be regarded as the similarity between two objects in viewpoints θ and θ_j, respectively.

In testing, with the output $\boldsymbol{q}^V = (q_0^V, q_1^V, ..., q_{N_{vp}-1}^V)$ of ANN, on the manifold $\boldsymbol{p}^V(\theta)$ defined by (5), we find a point $\boldsymbol{p}^V(\theta^*)$ closest to $\boldsymbol{q}^V$ with the pseudo-distance Kullback-Leibler divergence [12], and use θ^* to be the estimated viewpoint; i.e.,

$$\theta^* = \underset{\theta}{\operatorname{argmin}} \{D_{KL}(\boldsymbol{p}^V(\theta) \| \boldsymbol{q}^V)\} = \underset{\theta}{\operatorname{argmin}} \{ \sum_{j=0}^{N_{vp}-1} p_j^V(\theta) \log \frac{p_j^V(\theta)}{q_j^V} \}. \quad (8)$$

To solve the problem (8), we can start by finding all the local optimal solutions $\theta_i^* \in [\theta_i, \theta_{i+1})$, $i = 0, 1, ..., N_{vp} - 1$, and then obtain the global optimal solution

$$\theta^* = \underset{\theta_i^*, 0 \leq i \leq N_{vp}-1}{\operatorname{argmin}} \{D_{KL}(\boldsymbol{p}^V(\theta_i^*) \| \boldsymbol{q}^V)\}. \quad (9)$$

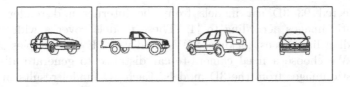

Fig. 3. Four examples of the non-photorealistic images of size 200×200 rendered from different 3D models in different views

Foreground Box

Background

Fig. 4. The foreground box and the background on an image patch of size 200×200. The center of the foreground box is also at the center of the image patch.

For $\theta \in [\theta_i, \theta_{i+1})$, the problem (8) becomes

$$\theta_i^* = \operatorname*{argmin}_{\theta \in [\theta_i, \theta_{i+1})} \{ \sum_{j=0}^{N_{vp}-1} p_j^V(\theta) \log \frac{p_j^V(\theta)}{q_j^V} \} \tag{10}$$

$$= \operatorname*{argmin}_{\theta} \{ p_i^V(\theta) \log \frac{p_i^V(\theta)}{q_i^V} + p_{i+1}^V(\theta) \log \frac{p_{i+1}^V(\theta)}{q_{i+1}^V} \}$$

$$= \operatorname*{argmin}_{\theta} \{ \frac{\theta_{i+1}-\theta}{L} \log \frac{\theta_{i+1}-\theta}{Lq_i^V} + \frac{\theta-\theta_i}{L} \log \frac{\theta-\theta_i}{Lq_{i+1}^V} \}.$$

By $\frac{d}{d\theta}(\frac{\theta_{i+1}-\theta}{L} \log \frac{\theta_{i+1}-\theta}{Lq_i^V} + \frac{\theta-\theta_i}{L} \log \frac{\theta-\theta_i}{Lq_{i+1}^V}) = 0$, we have

$$\theta_i^* = \theta_i + \frac{q_{i+1}^V L}{q_i^V + q_{i+1}^V}. \tag{11}$$

Since $q_i^V, q_{i+1}^V \in [0,1]$, it is easy to verify that $\theta_i^* \in [\theta_i, \theta_{i+1}]$.

3   ANN Training and Testing

Previous approaches [19], [18], [14], [23] have used not only real images but also non-photorealistic images rendered from 3D CAD models for training. These rendered objects are with known viewpoints (ground truth) and provide more information about object appearances. In our work, we also use the rendering of 3D CAD models for ANN training. Note that, like previous studies, we have only considered the estimation of viewpoint in horizontal directions without considering object tilt angles.

We collected 93 3D car models from the internet and render the non-photorealistic images according to [4]. These models cover a wide variety of cars, including limousines, pickups, SUVs, and vans. Four examples are shown in Fig. 3. We choose a fixed camera-to-car distance to generate all the non-photorealistic images from the 3D models. Each 3D model results in 180 projections (images) with a viewpoint difference of $2°$ between two neighboring projections. Each projected car is located approximately at the center of the image whose size is 200×200.

In order to cover more car appearances in training, each projected 2D car C is used to generate four more car images, as follows. (i) C is rotated by an angle that is a sample from the Gaussian distribution with zero mean and standard variance of $2°$. (ii) The rotated C is resized with these four scales 0.9, 0.95, 1.05, and 1.1. All these rendered (synthetic) images are used as positive samples for training.

The previous template-based object detection methods work with a set of sliding windows with different scales and aspect ratios [8]. The sliding windows of different aspect ratios are used to cover the large shape variations of the objects in images. For example, Gu et al. [8] used 4–16 aspect ratios in their experiments. To obtain training samples from real images, when moving a sliding window on an image, an image patch under the sliding window is regarded as a positive sample if a ratio T_1 is larger than a threshold (say, 60%). T_1 is defined by $\frac{A_1}{A_2}$, where A_1 is the area of the overlapping part between the sliding window and the bounding box of the object, and A_2 is the sum of the sliding window area and the bounding box area minus A_1.

We design a different sliding window method to obtain positive and negative training samples from real images, where the sliding window is square with size 200×200. An image patch covered by the sliding window is partitioned into two parts, the foreground and the background. The foreground is a rectangular region in the image patch called the *foreground box*, as shown in Fig. 4. The center of the foreground box is located at the center of the image patch. For an image patch containing an object, the size and shape of the foreground box are determined by the viewpoint of the object,

$$B(I) = f_B(\theta(I)), \tag{12}$$

where $B(I)$ denotes the foreground box in the image patch I, $\theta(I)$ is the viewpoint of the object in I, and $f_B(\theta)$ is a function producing the foreground box from the viewpoint θ. We derive $f_B(\theta)$ as follows. After normalizing the bounding boxes of all the objects to the same size (i.e., the same area = length $\times$ height), the bounding boxes of the objects in the same viewpoint have similar aspect ratios. Then, the average of the bounding boxes of the objects in the same viewpoint θ is defined as $f_B(\theta)$. For a training image patch containing an object in viewpoint θ, if a ratio T_2 is larger than a threshold, then the patch is regarded as a positive sample; otherwise a negative sample. T_2 is defined by $\frac{A_3}{A_4}$, where A_3 is the area of the overlapping part between the foreground box and the bounding box of the object, and A_4 is the sum of the foreground box area and the bounding box area minus A_3.

In testing, if $p_1^D \geq 0.5$ for an input image patch, then the patch is predicted as a positive sample. Suppose that the predicted viewpoint is θ for a positive sample; we then use the foreground box defined by $f_B(\theta)$ to be the bounding box for this positive sample. Although this foreground box may just be an approximation to the real bounding box of the object, it does show very good detection performance in our experiments.

Note that the mask generated by ANN cannot be directly used to infer the bounding box of the object in testing. The positions with m_i close to 1 may exist in the background of the patch, and there are only several clusters with m_i close to 1 on the object, which do not give enough information to cover the whole object and only the object.

HOG feature [3] is able to bridge the representation gap between real images and non-photorealistic images [19]. We extract HOG features (also called HOG images in this paper) from both the real image patches and the synthetic image patches. All these patches are of size 200×200, but the size of the HOG images is 23×23. In order to cover the size variations of the objects in real images, each real image is rescaled to eight scales in training and testing.

Compared with previous sliding window methods, ours does not need a set of sliding windows with different aspect ratios to accommodate different object shapes; instead, our sliding window has only one shape (square), as shown in Fig. 4, which greatly reduces the number of image patches sampled in training and testing. In addition, a positive image patch contains not only the object but also part of the background (see Fig. 4). Incorporating the background around the object can provides more cues for object detection, because objects and their backgrounds usually have certain patterns in the scenes. For example, cars mostly remain still or run on streets, and ships float on water.

4   Experimental Results

In this section, we evaluate our ANN model for car detection and viewpoint estimation, and compare it with several state-of-the-art methods in [19], [18], [28], and [30]. In [19], there are two models, DPM-VOC+VP and DPM-3D-Constraints. The former includes a distinct mixture component for each viewpoint bin, and the latter adds 3D constraints across viewpoints in the DPM model. In [18], the authors construct a 3D DPM model called $3D^2PM$. The methods in [28] and [30] give continuous viewpoint estimation via regression. Through cross-validation, the parameter λ in (4) is chosen to be 1E-6 for all the experiments. For the evaluation of the effectiveness of the mask layer, we design a baseline network called CNN-V&D as follows. From ANN, we remove the mask generator and mask operator, with the HOG images directly inputted into CNN_V and CNN_D, and obtain detection label and viewpoint estimation as output. In the following comparisons, all of the results, except those obtained by our models, come from [19], [18], [28], and [30].

We use the 3D Object Classes car dataset [20] and the EPFL car dataset [17] in our experiments because they provide ground truth for both detection and viewpoint estimation. We train the ANN model using not only the real images from these datasets, but also the synthetic images generated from the 3D models (note that [19] and [18] also use real and synthetic images to train their models). When ANN is trained and tested on one dataset, the training real images are only from this dataset. ANN takes less than 1 second to obtain the result of object detection and viewpoint estimation for one input image of size 300×400, on a PC with a NVIDIA GTX 670 GPU.

4.1   Detection and Discrete Viewpoint Estimation

Discrete viewpoint estimation can be regarded as a multi-class classification problem. 3D Object Classes annotates only eight different viewpoint bins, while EPFL provides degree-level annotations. We follow the previous protocols and report results of Mean Precision of Pose Estimation (MPPE) [19], [18], which is the average classification accuracy of multiple classes. The detection performance is evaluated by the widely used criterion Average Precision (AP) established in the Pascal VOC challenge [5].

Table 1 shows the results of AP (for object detection) and MPPE (for viewpoint estimation) obtained by five models on the 3D Object Classes car dataset. $3D^2PM$-D is a version of $3D^2PM$ for discrete viewpoint estimation. ANN-D and CNN-V&D-D are ANN and CNN-V&D trained with the discrete viewpoint training scheme (see Section 2.4), respectively. The studies in [28] and [30] only provide the results of continuous viewpoint estimation and are therefore not available for comparison here.

From Table 1, we can see that on this dataset, except CNN-V&D-D, all the models work very well in terms of AP, but ANN-D and DPM-VOC+VP perform the best in both AP and MPPE.

Unlike the 3D Object Classes car dataset that gives only eight coarse viewpoint bins, the EPFL car dataset allows much finer comparison in viewpoint estimation. Table 2 shows the comparison results between our work and [18] for 18 and 36 bins. Note that 36 bins are the finest viewpoint estimation in [18], and the work in [19] does not have experiment on this dataset. In Table 2, $3D^2PM$-C Lin and $3D^2PM$-C Exp are two versions of $3D^2PM$ targeting at continuous viewpoint estimation through linear and exponential combinations of the output scores in the discrete viewpoint bins, respectively. ANN-C and CNN-V&D-C are ANN and CNN-V&D trained with the continuous viewpoint training scheme (see Section 2.4) and evaluated in discrete viewpoints, respectively.

Table 2 shows that the performances of ANN-C and the previous sate-of-the-art method $3D^2PM$-D are similar for 18 bins, but ANN-C obtains the best results for 36 bins in both detection and viewpoint estimation. It has significant improvement over the models in [18] in fine viewpoint estimation. Our continuous viewpoint estimation model (ANN-C) performs better than the discrete viewpoint estimation model (ANN-D) both for 18 bins and 36 bins. ANN outperforms the baseline model CNN-V&D with a large margin both in discrete viewpoint training scheme and in continuous viewpoint training scheme, which shows the effectiveness of the mask layer.

Table 1. AP (for object detection) and MPPE (for viewpoint estimation) obtained by five models on the 3D Object Classes car dataset

	AP / MPPE		AP / MPPE
DPM-3D-Constraints [19]	99.7 / 96.3	DPM-VOC+VP [19]	**99.9 / 97.9**
3D²PM-D [18]	99.6 / 95.8	CNN-V&D-D	95.8 / 87.7
ANN-D	**99.9 / 97.9**		

Table 2. AP / MPPE obtained by seven models on the EPFL car dataset

	AP / MPPE			AP / MPPE	
	18 bins	36 bins		18 bins	36 bins
3D²PM-D [18]	99.2 / **71.8**	99.3 / 45.8	CNN-V&D-D	96.6 / 62.5	97.0 / 46.4
3D²PM-C Lin [18]	99.3 / 71.2	99.2 / 52.1	CNN-V&D-C	95.9 / 63.8	95.3 / 46.1
3D²PM-C Exp [18]	99.2 / 70.5	99.5 / 53.5	ANN-D	99.2 / 70.5	**99.9** / 53.1
ANN-C	**99.6** / 71.4	**99.9 / 58.1**			

4.2 Continuous Viewpoint Estimation

This section evaluates our model for continuous viewpoint estimation. Since the EPFL car dataset provides degree-level annotations, it is suitable for this experiment. Two measures are used for the evaluation: Median Angular Error (MAE) and Mean Angular Error (MnAE).

Table 3 shows the results obtained by six models that can be used for continuous viewpoint estimation. The authors of [18] do not provide MnAE results. The models in [28] and [30] estimate viewpoints without the need of the parameter of viewpoint bins, while 3D²PM-C Lin, 3D²PM-C Exp, CNN-V&D-C and ANN-C are related to this parameter. This table shows that ANN-C outperforms the other models greatly with the much smaller errors. ANN also outperforms CNN-V&D in this experiment.

Note that the two datasets are saturated for detection by the state-of-the-art methods, but they are not for viewpoint estimation, especially the EPFL car dataset. For example, under 36 bins, the best MPPE and MnAE are only 58.1 and 27.6, respectively, which show that there are still large gaps for improvement.

Table 3. MAE / MnAE obtained by different models on the EPFL car dataset

	MAE / MnAE			MAE / MnAE	
	18 bins	36 bins		18 bins	36 bins
[28]	5.8 / 39.0		3D²PM-C Lin [18]	5.6 / -	4.7 / -
[30]	11.3 / 34.0		3D²PM-C Exp [18]	6.9 / -	4.7 / -
CNN-V&D-C	4.8 / 30.8	4.9 / 32.5	ANN-C	**3.3 / 24.1**	**3.3 / 27.6**

4.3 Mask Layer

The mask layer plays a significant role for ANN to be the state of the art. It acts as a feature selector and finds the discriminative features for the object of

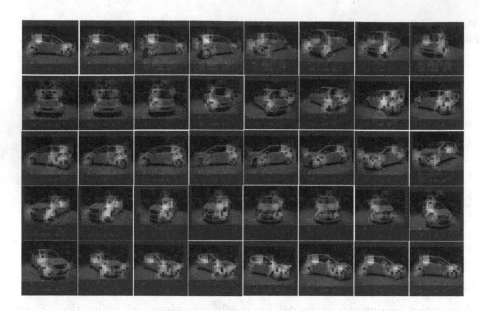

Fig. 5. Some positive sample images of the 11th car in the EPFL car dataset superimposed with their corresponding masks

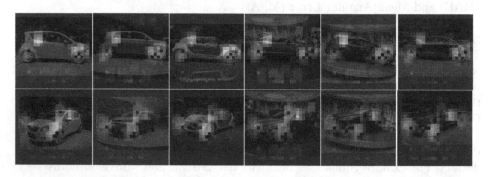

Fig. 6. Six different cars each in two views superimposed with their corresponding masks

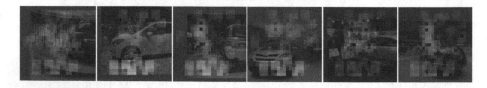

Fig. 7. Some negative samples from the EPFL car dataset superimposed with their corresponding masks

interest to pass to the next stage of ANN. In Fig. 5 and Fig. 6, we superimpose some masks obtained by ANN on their corresponding positive testing samples. The bright parts on the images indicate the large responses of the masks. From our experiments, we have made the following observations.

(i) Most large responses on the mask appear on or close to the car, meaning that the mask layer discriminates the car from the background in the image and prefers the features extracted from the car. Besides, the large responses in a mask are sparse and form clusters.

(ii) For cars in similar viewpoints, the mask layer generates similar masks, which indicates that ANN can find similar patterns across similar viewpoints. This is true even for the images of cars of different kinds. Fig. 6 shows six different cars each in two views. The masks in the first row (viewpoint 1) are similar, and the masks in the second row (viewpoint 2) are also similar.

(iii) Some car parts, such as the wheels, always have large responses on the mask. Wheels have similar shapes in different cars. Their appearances are also a strong indicator of the viewpoint of a car. For example, wheels are round in the side view and oval in the near-front and near-rear view of a car. ANN can capture the parts with discriminative features for the tasks of detection and viewpoint estimation.

In Fig. 7, we examine the mask's responses on negative samples. Note that a car or part of it can be in a negative sample if the overlapping between the bounding box of the car and the foreground box of the image patch is not large enough. The distributions of the large responses of these masks are clearly different from those in Figs. 5 and 6. These different distributions between positive and negative samples greatly benefit object detection and viewpoint estimation.

All the above experiments and observations indicate that ANN is effective in dealing with the combined task, object detection and viewpoint estimation. The mask layer in ANN bridges CNN_M with CNN_D and CNN_V, and plays an important role for feature extraction. We believe that the structure of ANN can also be successfully applied to the detection and/or viewpoint estimation of other object categories.

5   Conclusion

We have proposed a deep model, known as ANN, for object detection and viewpoint estimation. ANN automatically learns to select the most discriminative object parts from training images without human interaction. Despite the simple procedures of ANN training and testing, it achieves the best performance among the state-of-the-art models. The experiments and observations on the masks produced by ANN show its effectiveness to capture the discriminative features from the input for the combined task. We believe that our model can be applied to many other object categories, especially those with relatively rigid objects such as bicycles, chairs, motorcycles, and ships, because compared with cars, they have similar appearance variations in different viewpoints, which is our future work. We also plan to apply ANN to other vision tasks such as object segmentation, classification, and detection.

Acknowledgements. This work was supported by a grant from Guangdong Innovative Research Team Program (No. 201001D0104648280).

References

1. Arie-Nachimson, M., Basri, R.: Constructing implicit 3d shape models for pose estimation. In: ICCV (2009)
2. Ciresan, D., Meier, U., Schmidhuber, J.: Multi-column deep neural networks for image classification. In: CVPR (2012)
3. Dalal, N., Triggs, B.: Histograms of oriented gradients for human detection. In: CVPR (2005)
4. DeCarlo, D., Finkelstein, A., Rusinkiewicz, S., Santella, A.: Suggestive contours for conveying shape. In: SIGGRAPH (2003)
5. Everingham, M., Van Gool, L., Williams, C.K.I., Winn, J., Zisserman, A.: The PASCAL Visual Object Classes Challenge 2007 (VOC 2007) Results (2007), http://www.pascal-network.org/challenges/VOC/voc2007/workshop/index.html
6. Felzenszwalb, P.F., Girshick, R.B., McAllester, D., Ramanan, D.: Object detection with discriminatively trained part-based models. T-PAMI 32(9), 1627–1645 (2010)
7. Fergus, R., Perona, P., Zisserman, A.: Object class recognition by unsupervised scale-invariant learning. In: CVPR (2003)
8. Gu, C., Ren, X.: Discriminative mixture-of-templates for viewpoint classification. In: Daniilidis, K., Maragos, P., Paragios, N. (eds.) ECCV 2010, Part V. LNCS, vol. 6315, pp. 408–421. Springer, Heidelberg (2010)
9. Huang, G.B., Lee, H., Learned-Miller, E.: Learning hierarchical representations for face verification with convolutional deep belief networks. In: CVPR (2012)
10. Jarrett, K., Kavukcuoglu, K., Ranzato, M., LeCun, Y.: What is the best multi-stage architecture for object recognition? In: ICCV (2009)
11. Kavukcuoglu, K., Sermanet, P., Boureau, Y.L., Gregor, K., Mathieu, M., Cun, Y.L.: Learning convolutional feature hierarchies for visual recognition. In: NIPS (2010)
12. Kullback, S., Leibler, R.A.: On information and sufficiency. The Annals of Mathematical Statistics 22(1), 79–86 (1951)
13. Lee, H., Grosse, R., Ranganath, R., Ng, A.Y.: Convolutional deep belief networks for scalable unsupervised learning of hierarchical representations. In: ICML (2009)
14. Liebelt, J., Schmid, C., Schertler, K.: Viewpoint-independent object class detection using 3d feature maps. In: CVPR (2008)
15. Lopez-Sastre, R.J., Tuytelaars, T., Savarese, S.: Deformable part models revisited: A performance evaluation for object category pose estimation. In: ICCV Workshops (2011)
16. Luo, P., Wang, X., Tang, X.: Hierarchical face parsing via deep learning. In: CVPR (2012)
17. Ozuysal, M., Lepetit, V., Fua, P.: Pose estimation for category specific multiview object localization. In: CVPR (2009)
18. Pepik, B., Gehler, P., Stark, M., Schiele, B.: 3D^{2}PM – 3D deformable part models. In: Fitzgibbon, A., Lazebnik, S., Perona, P., Sato, Y., Schmid, C. (eds.) ECCV 2012, Part VI. LNCS, vol. 7577, pp. 356–370. Springer, Heidelberg (2012)
19. Pepik, B., Stark, M., Gehler, P., Schiele, B.: Teaching 3d geometry to deformable part models. In: CVPR (2012)

20. Savarese, S., Fei-Fei, L.: 3d generic object categorization, localization and pose estimation. In: ICCV (2007)
21. Sermanet, P., Kavukcuoglu, K., Chintala, S., LeCun, Y.: Pedestrian detection with unsupervised multi-stage feature learning. In: CVPR (2013)
22. Sohn, K., Zhou, G., Lee, C., Lee, H.: Learning and selecting features jointly with point-wise gated Boltzmann machines. In: ICML (2013)
23. Stark, M., Goesele, M., Schiele, B.: Back to the future: Learning shape models from 3d cad data. In: BMVC (2010)
24. Su, H., Sun, M., Fei-Fei, L., Savarese, S.: Learning a dense multi-view representation for detection, viewpoint classification and synthesis of object categories. In: ICCV (2009)
25. Sudderth, E.B., Torralba, A., Freeman, W.T., Willsky, A.S.: Learning hierarchical models of scenes, objects, and parts. In: ICCV (2005)
26. Sun, Y., Wang, X., Tang, X.: Deep convolutional network cascade for facial point detection. In: CVPR (2013)
27. Taylor, G.W., Fergus, R., LeCun, Y., Bregler, C.: Convolutional learning of spatio-temporal features. In: Daniilidis, K., Maragos, P., Paragios, N. (eds.) ECCV 2010, Part VI. LNCS, vol. 6316, pp. 140–153. Springer, Heidelberg (2010)
28. Teney, D., Piater, J.: Continuous pose estimation in 2d images at instance and category levels. In: Comp. and Rob. Vis. (2013)
29. Thomas, A., Ferrar, V., Leibe, B., Tuytelaars, T., Schiel, B., Van Gool, L.: Towards multi-view object class detection. In: CVPR (2006)
30. Torki, M., Elgammal, A.: Regression from local features for viewpoint and pose estimation. In: ICCV (2011)

Statistical and Spatial Consensus Collection for Detector Adaptation

Enver Sangineto

DISI, University of Trento, Italy
Enver.Sangineto@unitn.it

Abstract. The increasing interest in automatic adaptation of pedestrian detectors toward specific scenarios is motivated by the drop of performance of common detectors, especially in video-surveillance low resolution images. Different works have been recently proposed for unsupervised adaptation. However, most of these works do not completely solve the *drifting* problem: initial false positive target samples used for training can lead the model to drift. We propose to transform the outlier rejection problem in a weak classifier selection approach. A large set of weak classifiers are trained with random subsets of unsupervised *target* data and their performance is measured on a labeled *source* dataset. We can then select the most accurate classifiers in order to build an ensemble of weakly dependent detectors for the target domain. The experimental results we obtained on two benchmarks show that our system outperforms other pedestrian adaptation state-of-the-art methods.

Keywords: Pedestrian Detection, Unsupervised Domain Adaptation, RANSAC.

1 Introduction

There is an increasing interest of the Computer Vision research community in transfer learning and domain adaptation techniques in the recent years as witnessed by the large number of papers on these subjects. The motivation behind this interest is due to the bottleneck of the current classifiers' training procedures which usually need hundreds or thousands of manually labeled samples. Indeed, manual annotation is an expensive and time consuming activity, and, in some domains, data acquisition can be a difficult task. On the other hand, the performance of current detectors usually drastically drops when used (tested) in scenarios different from the training data [18,10,6]. This is sometimes called *the dataset bias* problem [18]: a classifier trained with a specific image resolution, viewpoint, illumination conditions, etc., will have a poor generalization ability in a testing situation not fitting the training dataset characteristics. In order to alleviate this problem different works have been recently proposed which directly or indirectly use labeled data from a known domain (the *source dataset*) together with unsupervised or semisupervised data, acquired from the specific *target domain* (i.e., the scenario of interest).

D. Fleet et al. (Eds.): ECCV 2014, Part III, LNCS 8691, pp. 456–471, 2014.

In this paper we focus on the pedestrian detection case, in which the human body is the class of interest. However, no specific assumption on the positive class is done, except the existence of a sufficiently reliable object detector which is used in the very first stage of our algorithm for extracting candidate target samples. Collecting target samples using a generic pedestrian detector is an approach adopted in different other works, such as, for instance [32,29,34,28]. However, the question is: since the generic detector is supposed to poorly perform on the target domain, and many false positives will presumably belong to the initial candidate set, can we train an *adapted* detector using these candidates and improve the accuracy of the generic detector?

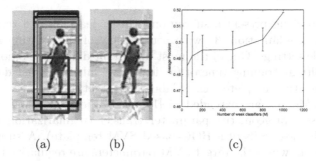

(a)   (b)   (c)

Fig. 1. (a)-(b) Spatial consensus collection. (a) Four out of five classifiers of our detector ensemble correctly hit the pedestrian in the figure. Bounding boxes of different colors correspond to positive answers of different classifiers. (b) The final answer of the ensemble. Note that the small blue rectangle on (a) has not been clustered together with all the other rectangles because of the scale difference and has not contributed to computing the average final rectangle on (b). (c) AP on the CUHK Square Test dataset as a function of M. Error bars show ± 1 standard deviation from the mean.

We propose to solve this issue transforming the target sample selection problem in a classifier selection problem. The target bounding boxes extracted using a baseline detector run on the target videos are randomly grouped in different overlapping subsets. In turn, each subset is used to train a different classifier. We train in this way a large vocabulary V of (weak) classifiers. Each element $C \in V$ will have an accuracy depending on the number of outliers (false positives of the baseline detector) included in its specific training set. If we could measure this accuracy, we could prune V. However, due to the lack of labeled target data (unsupervised training assumption), we cannot directly compute the accuracy of C. Nevertheless, we can use a different training set (the *source* dataset), for a rough estimate of this accuracy. There is an analogy between the approach we propose and RANSAC [13], where a statistical model is computed using a random subset of the available data and then it is verified using the rest of the data. In our case, the statistical model is C and the verification phase is performed using a different but similar dataset. V is pruned selecting the most promising classifiers which will be used at testing time as an ensemble of detectors.

The second novelty we propose concerns the way in which the ensemble detector reaches a decision on a test image. Rather than using a common voting approach [36], in which the final decision is taken *on each input subwindow*, our ensemble decisions are based on an agreement on *spatially related subwindows*. The underlying rationale is that different classifiers can disagree on a specific image window but they usually agree on windows which are close to a real instance of the class of interest (see Fig. 1(a)-1(b)).

The details of our approach are presented in Sec. 3-5, after a brief overview of the literature in Sec. 2. Experimental results using different protocols are illustrated in Sec. 6 and we finally conclude in Sec. 7.

2   Related Work

In [25] Pan and Yang present a survey on transfer learning and related areas, including domain adaptation [3], with a taxonomy of the existing approaches and the possible settings. One of the most important differences among settings is the availability at training time of (at least few) labeled target data. In this paper we assume the complete lack of labels for target data.

Adaptive-SVMs [35] are extended in [1] in an object detection scenario by introducing a sort of geometric parameter transfer (regularization is enforced among spatially close cells of a HOG-based SVM template). A similar idea is presented in [2], in which the target SVM parameters are regularized with parts borrowed from source templates. In [20] new object classes are learned borrowing *sample instances* from other similar classes, possibly after applying various geometric transformations. All these transfer learning approaches require at least a few target labeled data in order to refine the target classifier's parameters.

In [19] a shared intra-class representation, based on semantic attributes, is learned using only source samples, after that no training phase is necessary for the target class. In [27] an Information-theoretic Metric Learning is used to learn a linear transformation from the source to the target domain. A Transductive SVM together with virtual samples obtained using computer graphics techniques is used in [30] for adaptation in a pedestrian detection scenario.

In [26] a scene specific detection task is dealt with by a grid of classifiers, where each classifier needs only to learn the visual pattern of the corresponding cell on the image grid. In [22] a domain-specific classifier is selected from an initial set of pre-trained classifiers using model recommendation methods. In [23] background subtraction is used for collecting target samples. However, background subtraction can be unstable, especially in outdoor scenes.

In [32,34,29,28] a baseline pedestrian detector is run on the target videos in order to collect an initial set of positive samples. In [32] *source* samples (INRIA pedestrians) are weighted using the average distance (in HOG space) to the k nearest neighbours *target* samples and are used for training an adapted classifier. The new detector is run on the target video frames in order to acquire new target data and the process is iterated until convergence. However, if the initial target samples include a large number of false positives, the whole process can converge toward a wrong model (*drifting problem*).

In [34] a similarity score between the test image and the initial candidate pedestrian set is computed using a pre-built vocabulary tree and a threshold is used in order to reject non-pedestrian test images. However, the rejection threshold and different other parameters need to be manually set on each target scenario. In [29] the accuracy of a generic pedestrian detector is boosted using a second, adapted detector (a random fern classifier [24]) trained on target data only. Target data are acquired using the baseline detector and clustered in trajectories using position, size and appearance affinities. Different motion and spatial heuristics are used to partition the trajectories in positive and negative samples (similarly to [28]).

A problem common to all these methods is that the candidate set of pedestrians, acquired with the generic detector, is either pruned using a set of ad hoc heuristics and confidence thresholds (which need to be tuned on the target domain, an hard task if we suppose the lack of target labels) or used as it is, which likely leads to a drift of the train process. We show in Sec. 4 how a large amount of outliers can be tolerated in the initial training set using a RANSAC-like strategy and the source dataset for verifying the accuracy of the trained models.

3   Collecting Candidate Pedestrians

In the first phase of our algorithm we collect positive pedestrian samples running a generic pedestrian detector on the frames of the target videos. We use the Dalal and Triggs [7] pedestrian detector provided by the OpenCv implementation. Other more sophisticated baseline detectors can be used for this task, such as, for instance, [12], but, since the target videos used for our experiments have been acquired in far field traffic scenes (see Sec. 6), and the resulting resolution is very low, part based detectors have a very poor performance on this scenario [32]. Since false positives frequently happen in a same position along a video captured with a stationary camera, similarly to [32,33], we discard detections with a very large mutual overlapping on the same position. Other detections are discarded when they are close to the image borders because people entering and exiting from the scene are usually truncated (only partially visible).

Let $B = \{b_1, b_2, ...\}$ be the set of remaining bounding boxes obtained with the baseline detector. We estimate the mean μ and the standard deviation σ of the height values of the bounding boxes in B and we compute an upper (u) and a lower (l) bound on such values:

$$l = max(\mu - 3\sigma, min\{h(b)|b \in B\}), \tag{1}$$

where $h(b)$ is the height of the bounding box b and u is computed similarly. We prune B discarding those bounding boxes out of the range $[l, u]$, obtaining $B' = \{b|b \in B, l \leq h(b) \leq u\}$. Then we rank B' comparing its elements with our source dataset S (we use the INRIA dataset [7]). Specifically, let $S_P = \{p_1, p_2, ...\}$ be the set of the positive sample bounding boxes of S (recall that S is labeled). Moreover, let $f(b)$ be the feature vector of b. We use the common HOG features [7]. A dissimilarity score s for each $b \in B'$ can be computed by means of:

$$s(b) = \sum_{p \in S_P} ||f(b) - f(p)||_2^2. \tag{2}$$

Eq. (2) is conceptually similar to the function used in [17] for computing the similarity between source support vectors and target data. We use it to rank B' and we obtain $R = \{b_{i_1}, ..., b_{i_m}\}$ such that: $i_j < i_l \Rightarrow s(b_{i_j}) \leq s(b_{i_l})$ and $m = |B'|$. Before extracting HOG features, all the elements in B' and S_P are normalized to a standard bounding box whose height is l and the width is $l/2$. This operation is important because the elements in S_P (the INRIA pedestrian images) have a high resolution, while the elements in B', acquired from a low resolution video, have much less gradient information.

Instead of using the whole S_P in Eq. (2) we could restrict the sum to only the k nearest neighbours of $f(b)$ in S_P (e.g., similarly to the source sample weighting process in [32]). However, without using sophisticated data structures, this is computationally equivalent to our procedure and would require the estimation of the parameter k (sufficient number of neighbours). In our experiments, the results obtained with Eq. (2) and a k nearest neighbours approach with various values of k were basically equivalent, hence we decided in favour of the simplest solution.

We discard the second half of R based on the assumption that the baseline detector poorly performs on the target domain and, hence, most of the elements in B (R) are false positives. A finer solution is to discard a portion of R depending on a measure of the dissimilarity between the distributions generating B' and S_P, such as the Maximum Mean Discrepancy. However, in the current implementation we adopted this simple truncation because in our experiments we found it sufficient to achieve good results across different videos and fairly stable (e.g., ±10% in the truncation ratio gives basically the same overall system's accuracy). Let $T = \{b_1, ..., b_n\}$ correspond to the first half of R $(n = m/2)$. In the following we use T as our target positive sample set.

The values l and u are used also at testing time to limit the number of analysed subwindows (Sec. 5) and at training time (Sec. 4) to specialize the classifiers to a specific scale range. This is reasonable since our goal is the construction of a detector for a specific scenario and viewpoint, in which the pedestrian scales are supposed to be constant over time. In [32,33] Wang et al. used our same target videos and assumed a similar mono-modal Gaussian distribution over the pedestrian sizes but they used mean shift [5] as to estimate the main mode of the distribution and the range $[l, u]$. However, the bandwidth of the mean shift kernel needs to be manually set thus we preferred a simpler but completely automatic procedure.

4   Transforming the Sample Selection Problem into a Classifier Selection Problem

The ranking and pruning operations described in Sec. 3 help in eliminating a lot of false positives. However, they are not sufficient to guarantee the lack of outliers in T, whose number depends on the accuracy of the baseline detector and the difficulty of the target domain. Using visual inspection, in our experiments we empirically found an average of about $40 - 50\%$ of outliers in T (errors of the baseline detector). Since we want to use the elements in T for training our classifier, we would ideally need an oracle able to select a subset $T_G \subseteq T$ of "good" positive samples to use for training. This idea can be extended since we not only want that the elements in T_G are correct pedestrians images, but we also want that they are the most informative (or discriminative) for our learning task: for instance, we would like to avoid including images of the same pedestrian in the same pose. This problem can be formulated as follows:

$$T_G = \arg\min_{T_i \subseteq T} E(C_{T_i}, \mathcal{D}^t), \tag{3}$$

where C_{T_i} is a classifier trained using the set of positive samples T_i and a given random set of negatives N_i (see Sec. 4.1), $\mathcal{D}^t$ is the target domain and $E()$ is the generalization error. Since we do not have labeled samples extracted from $\mathcal{D}^t$, we use samples of the source domain $\mathcal{D}^s$, specifically, $S = S_P \cup S_N$, where S_N is the set of negatives in the INRIA dataset. Thus, Eq. (3) is approximated by:

$$T_G = \arg\min_{T_i \subseteq T} L(C_{T_i}, S), \tag{4}$$

where $L()$ is a suitable loss function for computing the empirical risk on S and

$$C_{T_i} = \arg\min_{C \in \mathcal{C}} \mathcal{R}(C) + \theta \lambda(T_i, N_i), \tag{5}$$

being $\mathcal{C}$ a model of classifiers (e.g., Support Vector Machines), $\lambda(T_i, N_i)$ a loss function computed over T_i and N_i (note that, generally speaking, $\lambda() \neq L()$), $\mathcal{R}()$ is a suitable regularization and finally θ is a weight.

The minimization involved in Eq. (4)-(5) is clearly non-convex. It can be easily shown that $L(C_{T_i}, S)$ is not submodular [14] and it is not adaptive-monotone [15] (see the Supplementary Material of this paper), thus Eq. (4)-(5) cannot be approximated using greedy submodular function optimization techniques [14,15,16]. Moreover, an exhaustive approach in which all the possible subsets of T are used for training a classifier is intractable. We propose to solve this problem using a RANSAC-like approach [13]. We fix the cardinality n_g ($n_g < n$) of T_i for all i and we build T_i randomly drawing n_g elements of T with replacement. T_i is then used to train a classifier C_{T_i}. We iterate this process a large number of times, obtaining a vocabulary V of weak classifiers. Then, we "verify" each statistical model (classifier) in V using S and $L()$ and we select a small subset of V forming an ensemble which is our final classifier. In the following we provide the details.

4.1   Training Details

The strategy above proposed is independent of the specific class of classifiers ($\mathcal{C}$) used for building C_{T_i}. In our implementation we used HOG features and holistic (non part-based) classifiers based on linear SVMs, as described in [7]. We also followed the suggestions contained in [7] for setting the training parameters, such as, for instance, the SVM parameter 'C', set to 0.01 (which corresponds to θ in Eq. (5)). Due to the limited number of candidate target pedestrians in T, we set n_g to be a small number: $n_g = 400$, but we actually draw only 200 elements from T and we obtain T_i by horizontally flipping all the selected bounding boxes. Jittering could also be used but we do not use it in the current implementation. The number of positives used for training a classifier is lower than the positive samples used in [7]. However, our weak classifiers are used at testing time as an ensemble of weakly-dependent classifiers (weak statistical dependence is due to the partial overlapping of training data), which mutually compensate their errors. Moreover, we will show in Sec. 5 how we can further boost the ensemble performance merging spatially coherent answers.

A set of negatives N_i for the i-th classifier is collected as follows. From the target videos we randomly extract a few frames. Then we randomly select a few tens of windows from each of these frames. The total number of elements of N_i is five times n_g, using the same proportion adopted in [7]. The size of the randomly selected windows in N_i is bounded by $[l, u]$ (Sec. 3). Occasionally, some of the windows in N_i can overlap with pedestrians, so some of them can actually be false negatives. However we follow [26], in which a similar technique is used for unsupervised selection of negatives, exploiting the assumption that false negatives (random overlap of the selected windows with instances of the class of interest) happen with a quite low probability. As a consequence, both the current positive sample set T_i and the current negative set N_i can be noisy. From T_i and N_i we extract HOG features and we train a linear SVM (for details we refer to [7]).

Finally, we bootstrap the obtained classifier collecting hard target negatives (again following the strategy proposed in [7]). Specifically, we randomly select a second set of frames from the target videos and we run the just trained classifier on all the subwindows of these frames whose size is bounded by $[l, u]$. Hard negatives are all the positive answers of the classifier on the input windows and they are merged with N_i for a second turn of training, finally obtaining our weak classifier C_i. During the bootstrap phase we discard those hard negatives which overlap with elements in T, using the intersection over union criterion adopted in the PASCAL challenge. Nevertheless, since T does not represent *all* the pedestrians in the target videos (because the recall rate of the baseline classifier is very low), some of the hard negatives are possibly true positives, hence hard negatives can be noisy. However, since each frame of the training videos is composed of a huge number of subwindows, this situation happens in a minor number of cases. In our experiments the noisy hard negatives and the bootstrap retraining of the classifier largely helps in boosting the performance of the final classifiers.

We iterate the whole procedure collecting a vocabulary $V = \{C_i\}_{i=1}^{M}$ of weak classifiers. We set $M = 1000$. Each element C_i in V is then scored using a loss function $L()$ (Eq. (4)). We tested different loss functions, based on the overall error, the recall or the precision of C_i on S. Surprisingly, the best results have been obtained with a precision-based criterion, which does not take into account false negatives on S. This is probably due to the way in which we compute the ensemble decision (Sec. 5), which exploits the precision of each single classifier (low number of false positive answers). More in details, our loss function is:

$$L(C_i, S) = 1 - \frac{TP}{TP + FP}, \tag{6}$$

where TP is the number of true positives on S (again using the PASCAL intersection over union criterion), while FP is the number of false positives, i.e., all the positively classified subwindows of all the images in S which do not sufficiently overlap with any true source positive sample. Size boundaries (l, u) here are not necessary and they are not used. We use Eq. (6) to associate each C_i with an error rate $e_i = L(C_i, S)$.

Training and computing the source dataset error of 1000 classifiers is a time consuming operation. With our non-optimized and non-parallelized C++ implementation, it takes about one day on a standard PC. However, it is a fully automatic process, in which there is no human intervention and can be faster and less expensive than manual annotation of hundreds or thousands of target samples. Moreover, since each classifier training and error computing procedure is completely independent from the other classifiers, the whole process can be easily parallelized.

Once the set of errors $\{e_i\}_{i=1}^M$ has been computed, we rank V in ascending order and we select the k top most elements. In our experiments we used $k = 5$. We show in Sec. 6 the influence of different values of k and M on the final performance of the ensemble detector. We indicate with $\mathcal{E} = \{C_i\}_{i=1}^k$ the final set of selected classifiers.

5   Spatial Consensus Collection

The common way to combine the outputs of a *classifier* ensemble is a (possibly weighted) voting procedure [36,11]. A test feature x is simultaneously input to all the classifiers of a given ensemble $\mathcal{E} = \{C_i\}_{i=1}^k$, obtaining k different outputs. Each output can be associated with a confidence weight which need to be *calibrated* [36]. Using a notation similar to [36], a simple, non-weighted *majority vote* rule can be expressed by means of:

$$\mathcal{E}(x) = \arg \max_{\omega \in \Omega} \sum_{1=1}^k v_{i,\omega}, \tag{7}$$

where Ω is the set of all the classes and, for each class $\omega \in \Omega$, $v_{i,\omega} = 1$ if classifier C_i chooses class ω, and 0 otherwise. This simple but effective rule is largely used in classifier ensembles and bagging approaches [36,11].

However, our final goal here is the construction of a *detector* ensemble. The difference is that, in a detection scenario, typically based on a sliding window scan of the input image, input features x are not each other independent, being those features extracted from nearby and possibly overlapping windows highly correlated. In [8] Ding and Xiao observe that "local windows with positive classifier responses often cluster densely around human figures but distribute sparsely in the background". They exploit this observation building a context feature which takes into account the detector's local responses.

We propose to take advantage of the same observation differently, by combining the outputs of our detector ensemble over different windows which are close in the scale and translation space. In our case we have only two classes: $\Omega = \{0, 1\}$, the positive (1) and the negative (0) class. As is well known, the negative class is much more frequent in a sliding window approach [31], thus the classifiers' responses corresponding to the two classes need to be managed asymmetrically. A spatially-dependent majority vote rule can be formulated as follows:

$$\mathcal{E}(G) = \mathbf{1}_{||\mathbf{v}_G||_0 > k/2}(G). \tag{8}$$

In Eq. (8) $\mathbf{1}()$ is the indicator function and k is the cardinality of the ensemble. $G = \{\mathbf{d}_1, \mathbf{d}_2, ...\}$ is a spatial cluster of *positive* detections. Each $\mathbf{d}_j = (b_j, i)$ in G is a pair composed of an image window b_j and the index i of the corresponding classifier C_i whose outcome on b_j was positive:

$$C_i(f(b_j)) = 1. \tag{9}$$

Note that a same image window b_j in G can be associated with more than one positive detection (e.g., $(b_j, i_1), (b_j, i_2) \in G$). $\mathbf{v}_G = (v_1, ..., v_k)^T$ is a k-dimensional *vote* vector, such that, for each i ($1 \leq i \leq k$):

$$v_i = min(1, |\{(b, i) \in G\}|), \tag{10}$$

and $|A|$ is the cardinality of set A. Note that $\mathbf{v}_G$ is a vote vector collecting votes *over classifiers* and not over classes. Finally, $||\mathbf{x}||_0$ is the 0-norm which counts the number of non-zero elements in vector $\mathbf{x}$.

The intuitive idea behind Eq. (8) is quite straightforward. Given a cluster of nearby positive detections G, we simply count the number of *different* classifiers which contributed to G. If this number is higher than half of the ensemble cardinality (simple, non-weighted majority), then the decision of the ensemble on G is 1, and 0 otherwise (see Fig. 1(a)-1(b)).

Also the implementation is quite straightforward. We independently run every C_i on the whole image, scanning all those windows whose size is included in the range $[l, u]$ (see Sec. 3). Then we collect all the positive detections of *all* the classifiers in a set $D = \{\mathbf{d}_1, \mathbf{d}_2, ...\}$. We do not use classifiers' confidences (and, thus, we do not need any calibration among classifiers). After that, we perform standard clustering of the rectangles in D. We adopted the common procedure described in [31] and briefly summarized in Sec. 5.1. The clustering outcome is a set of detection groups $G_1, G_2, ...$ Each G_h is composed of windows spatially close and with a similar scale. We can now apply Eq. (8) on each G_h. If $\mathcal{E}(G_h) = 1$, then we compute the average rectangle $\bar{b}_h$ using $\{b_j\}_{(b_j, i) \in G_h}$.

Fig. 2. Some detection results of our system (right) and the Dalal and Triggs method (left) on the MIT Traffic dataset (a) and the CUHK Square dataset (b). Black rectangles are false positives, white rectangles false negatives and blue rectangles true positives.

Finally, $\bar{b}_h$ is a positive window of our detector ensemble. Fig. 2 shows some examples of results. The *whole* testing phase on a large 1152×1440 image takes about 3 seconds on a standard PC (non-parallelized and non-optimized code).

The proposed spatially-dependent majority vote rule is similar to the context score used in [4,12] and in [21], which is based on a max-pool aggregation of the detection scores produced by different classifiers on overlapping image windows. However, in [4,12] the context score is then input to a context-score-based SVM which needs to be trained with supervised data that we do not have (since $\mathcal{D}^t$ is unlabeled). Similarly, in [21] the context score is linearly combined using the pre-computed pairwise co-occurrence frequencies of different classifiers, which need to be trained in a supervised manner.

5.1   Clustering Multiple Detections

Even if clustering of positive detection windows is a standard procedure for object detection approaches, for completeness we briefly summarize here the algorithm we adopted. We followed the well known approach described, for instance, in [31]. Given a set of bounding boxes $B = \{b_1, b_2, ...\}$, B is partitioned in disjoint subsets according to this simple relation: b_i and b_j are in the same subset if the ratio of the intersection area over their union area is greater than 0.6. The parameter 0.6 is commonly adopted by many authors (e.g., [4,9]). The algorithm's output is the resulting partition. When used for Non Maxima Suppression (NMS), for each cluster an average bounding box is also computed.

6   Experiments

We used the datasets and the experimental protocols adopted in [32] in order to compare our approach with the methods and the results reported in the same article. A detection window is considered a true positive when the intersection area with a ground truth bounding box over the union of the two rectangles is at least 50% (PASCAL rule). The x-axis of the ROC curves is the number of False Positive Per Image (FPPI).

Datasets. We used as target datasets the videos adopted in [32]: the MIT Traffic dataset and the CUHK Square dataset (see Fig. 2 for some examples). They are two videos of two different traffic scenes (respectively, 90 and 60 minutes long), captured with a stationary camera in far field. In both videos there are low resolution pedestrians, vehicles and frequent occlusions. In [32] 420 frames were uniformly sampled from the first 45 minutes of the MIT Traffic video and used for training, and other 100 frames were uniformly sampled from the last 45 minutes and used for testing. Similarly, 350 frames were uniformly sampled from the first 30 minutes of the CUHK Square video and used for training and other 100 frames were sampled from the last 30 minutes for testing. Note that the authors in [32] provide annotations also for the train frames, but these annotations *were not used for training* (neither by us nor by the other methods we compare with). Indeed they are used only for testing purposes in a *transductive* learning paradigm (testing is done on the same video used for training because labeled data are not used). We adopted the same protocol, using the same frames for training our system (i.e., collecting the candidate pedestrian set T, see Sec. 3: one T used for *both* CUHK Square Train and Test, and one T used for *both* MIT Traffic Train and Test) and then we tested our approach on both the train and the test frames (Fig. 3). Two different detector ensembles have been trained, one on the MIT Traffic and the second on the CUHK Square dataset. In both cases we used the INRIA dataset [7] as source dataset.

Parameter Setting. Few parameters need to be set in our approach because we followed the standard setting of the common HOG+SVM approach proposed in [7] for the training phase (Sec. 4.1) and we adopted the NMS setting of [4,9] for the spatial cluster of the positive windows (Sec. 5.1). The number of positive samples n_g for each weak classifier (Sec. 4.1) was set to 400 (200 not considering flipping) because of the low number of candidate pedestrians extracted by the baseline detector in the target videos (a few hundreds per video). We believe that our method can largely benefit of a possible higher number of initial candidates. We used the first half of the CUHK Square Train frames as a validation set in order to select the values of all the remaining parameters, such as k and M (Sec. 4.1) and *we kept constant these parameters in all the experiments and across all the target domains*. We show below the effects of different choices for k and M using the Test frames of the same target video.

Comparison with Other Methods. We compare our approach with other state-of-the-art systems tested on the same datasets: Wang CVPR12 [32], Wang CVPR11 [33], Nair CVPR 04, a modified version of [23] (see [32] for details) and Dalal CVPR 05, the baseline HOG+SVM detector trained on INRIA which we used for the initial candidate pedestrian extraction (Sec. 3). All the results, except ours (called Statistical and Spatial Consensus Collection, SSCC) and Dalal CVPR 05, have been taken from [32]. Note that in [32] the authors also use as a baseline a HOG+SVM detector but obtained different results. This is probably due to the fact that we used the OpenCv implementation of the Dalal and Triggs method. Moreover, for a fair comparison, we adopted for (Dalal CVPR 05) the same NMS algorithm used in our system and described in Sec. 5.1. In fact we observed that our self-implemented NMS procedure gives better results than the OpenCV NMS.

The results are shown in Fig. 3. The ROC curves are computed as follows. We use a unique threshold τ for all the k classifiers' confidence values discarding all those detections $\mathbf{d}_j$ (Sec. 5) whose SVM confidence is less than τ. Varying τ we obtain different points on the ROC. Note that the classifiers' confidences are not used in Eq. (8). In fact Eq. (8) is simple and effective because it collects spatially-close votes and it does not need supervised weight learning for combining the classifiers' confidences as it is necessary in [4,12,21]. ROC curves can also be computed thresholding $|G|$ without using confidences at all. However, since G is usually small, we obtained only few ROC points using this method.

As it is clear from Fig. 3, we outperform all the other methods and the improvement is particularly sharp in the CUHK Square dataset. Specifically, the (large) improvement with respect to our baseline detector (Dalal CVPR 05) shows that the completely unsupervised method we proposed here for detector adaptation in a specific scene can effectively obtain much better results than a generic detector without any need of manual sample annotation. In the Supplementary Material we show further experiments using these datasets.

Experiments on Different Parts of Our Method. In all the remaining experiments we used the CUHK Square Test dataset. Tab. 1 shows the Average Precision (AP) difference between the full approach with an ensemble of 5 classifiers (SSCC-5) and the case in which a different number k of final classifiers is selected (SSCC-k). Classifier selection is always performed using the loss function of Eq. (6). (SSCC-1) is a single classifier: all the others are ensembles in which an agreement is reached using Eq. (8). The results reported in Tab. 1 show that, with $k > 1$, the cardinality of the ensemble only marginally influences the accuracy of the system, which is a good news, because it means that this parameter does not need to be set using target data.

In the same table we report the results of a "standard", non-spatially dependent majority vote for the ensemble decision (see Sec. 5), which we call Standard Ensemble Decision Rule (SEDR-5). The results for (SEDR-5) were obtained as follows. We used exactly *the same* classifier ensemble $\mathcal{E}$ of (SSCC-5). The only difference is at testing time, because in (SEDR-5) we collect the ensemble consensus using the rule described in Eq. (7) instead of Eq. (8). More in details, *for each window b* of the sliding window process, we extract its HOG representation $f(b)$ and we input $f(b)$ to all the classifiers in $\mathcal{E}$. Then we use the majority vote (Eq. (7)) for computing the class of b. Positive windows are collected in a set B (note that we do not need classifier indexes here) and NMS is applied as described in Sec. 5.1. The improvement of (SSCC-5) over (SEDR-5) shows the advantage of a spatially-dependent consensus collection for a detector ensemble based on a sliding window image scan. Quite surprisingly, (SEDR-5) is even worse than

(SSCC-1) (no ensemble): 0.4845 AP versus 0.4959 AP, respectively. We believe that this is a consequence of the interaction with the NMS stage. In fact classifiers usually agree on neighbouring windows but rarely exactly on the same window (Fig. 1(a)-1(b)). Consequently, the set B (Sec. 5.1) is more fragmented, producing slightly more false positives. As an explanatory example, suppose the best classifier (SSCC-1) outputs a cluster of positive windows around a true pedestrian. If the other classifiers do not agree on the same windows, many of them are discarded using Eq. (7). The subsequent NMS can produce different clusters, some of which non-sufficiently overlapped with the true pedestrian.

Table 1. AP over the CUHK Test dataset with different ensembles and decision rules

SEDR5	SSCC1	SSCC3	SSCC5	SSCC7	SSCC9	SSCC11
0.4845	0.4959	0.5118	0.5184	0.5183	0.5172	0.5175

Table 2. AP over the CUHK Test dataset using different loss functions for classifier selection

Precision	Recall	Error	Random	Random-1
0.5184	0.4750	0.4789	0.4494 (0.0232)	0.4382 (0.0408)

In Fig. 1(c) we show how the AP of our method varies as a function of the cardinality M of the classifier vocabulary V (Sec. 4.1). In this experiment, the cardinality of the final ensemble is fixed ($k = 5$) and we always used the loss function of Eq. (6) and the decision rule of Eq. (8). For every discrete value of M we randomly pre-selected M classifiers from our vocabulary V (before computing their accuracy on S) and we averaged the results over 10 tests.

Finally, Tab. 2 shows the impact of using different loss functions when computing the classifier's error on S (Sec. 4.1). All the tested ensembles are composed of 5 classifiers. The only difference is the loss function adopted for scoring their accuracy. *Precision* indicates the approach presented in the other sections of this paper, based on Eq. (6). Conversely, *Recall* is defined by:

$$L(C_i, S) = 1 - \frac{TP}{TP + FN}, \tag{11}$$

where FN is the number of false negatives (missed detections of C_i on S) and TP is the same as in Sec. 4.1. *Error* is based on:

$$L(C_i, S) = FP + FN. \tag{12}$$

In *Random* we simply randomly chose 5 classifiers from the vocabulary V. In case of *Random*, we repeated the experiment 10 times and the results were averaged in order to decrease the variance of the outcome (in brackets the standard deviation). Tab. 2 motivates our choice in favour of Eq. (6). *Random-1* was computed as *Random* but using only one classifier (drawn at random from V). Comparing *Random-1* with SSCC1 it is clear that using the source dataset for selecting the best classifier(s) is of crucial importance.

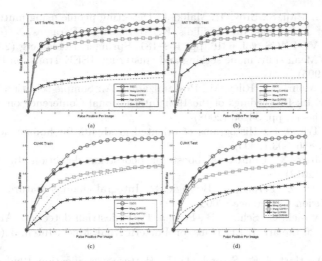

Fig. 3. ROC curves comparing our system (SSCC) with Wang CVPR12 [32], Wang CVPR11 [33], Nair CVPR 04 [23] and Dalal CVPR 05 [7]. The datasets used are: the MIT Traffic Train set (a), the MIT Traffic Test set (b), the CUHK Square Train set (c) and the CUHK Square Test set (d) (better seen at a high magnification).

7   Conclusions

In this paper we proposed two novelties: (1) Transforming the problem of rejecting outliers from an unsupervised target training dataset in a classifier selection problem using random subsets of the target data and a labeled source dataset for verification. (2) A spatially-dependent decision rule for detector ensembles. In contrast with most of the state-of-the-art people detector adaptation works, our method does not rely on sophisticated heuristics or target-dependent parameters for the rejection of outliers. Conversely, our proposed approach allows a simple yet effective and completely automatic construction of a small ensemble of detectors from a very noisy initial bunch of images.

We tested our approach on difficult, low resolution videos obtaining a large accuracy increment with respect to generic pedestrian detectors and state-of-the-art detector adaptation methods.

References

1. Aytar, Y., Zisserman, A.: Tabula rasa: Model transfer for object category detection. In: ICCV (2011)
2. Aytar, Y., Zisserman, A.: Enhancing exemplar svms using part level transfer regularization. In: British Machine Vision Conference (2012)
3. Ben-David, S., Blitzer, J., Crammer, K., Kulesza, A., Pereira, F., Vaughan, J.W.: A theory of learning from different domains. Mach. Learn. 79(1-2), 151–175 (2010)

4. Bourdev, L., Maji, S., Brox, T., Malik, J.: Detecting people using mutually consistent poselet activations. In: Daniilidis, K., Maragos, P., Paragios, N. (eds.) ECCV 2010, Part VI. LNCS, vol. 6316, pp. 168–181. Springer, Heidelberg (2010)
5. Cheng, Y.: Mean shift, mode seeking and clustering. IEEE Trans. on PAMI 17(8), 790–799 (1995)
6. Cortes, C., Mohri, M., Riley, M., Rostamizadeh, A.: Sample selection bias correction theory. In: Proceedings of the 19th International Conference on Algorithmic Learning Theory, pp. 38–53 (2008)
7. Dalal, N., Triggs, B.: Histograms of oriented gradients for human detection. In: CVPR. pp. 886–893 (2005)
8. Ding, Y., Jing, X.: Contextual boost for pedestrian detection. In: CVPR. pp. 2895–2902 (2012)
9. Dollár, P., Tu, Z., Perona, P., Belongie, S.: Integral channel features. In: British Machine Vision Conference (2009)
10. Dollár, P., Wojek, C., Schiele, B., Perona, P.: Pedestrian detection: An evaluation of the state of the art. IEEE Trans. on Pattern Anal. Mach. Intell. 34(4), 743–761 (2012)
11. Duda, R.O., Hart, P.E., Strorck, D.G.: Pattern classification (2nd ed.). Wiley Interscience (2000)
12. Felzenszwalb, P.F., Girshick, R.B., McAllester, D.A., Ramanan, D.: Object detection with discriminatively trained part-based models. IEEE Trans. on Pattern Anal. Mach. Intell. 32(9), 1627–1645 (2010)
13. Fischler, M., Bolles, R.: Random sample consensus: a paradigm for model fitting with applications to image analysis and automated cartography. Commun. ACM 24(6), 381–395 (1981)
14. Golovin, D., Krause, A.: Submodular Function Maximization. In: Tractability: Practical Approaches to Hard Problems (to appear)
15. Golovin, D., Krause, A.: Adaptive submodularity: Theory and applications in active learning and stochastic optimization. Journal of Artificial Intelligence Research (JAIR) 42, 427–486 (2011)
16. Guillory, A., Bilmes, J.: Simultaneous learning and covering with adversarial noise. In: ICML, pp. 369–376 (2011)
17. Jiang, W., Zavesky, E., Chang, S.F., Loui, A.C.: Cross-domain learning methods for high-level visual concept classification. In: ICIP, pp. 161–164 (2008)
18. Khosla, A., Zhou, T., Malisiewicz, T., Efros, A.A., Torralba, A.: Undoing the damage of dataset bias. In: Fitzgibbon, A., Lazebnik, S., Perona, P., Sato, Y., Schmid, C. (eds.) ECCV 2012, Part I. LNCS, vol. 7572, pp. 158–171. Springer, Heidelberg (2012)
19. Lampert, C.H., Nickisch, H., Harmeling, S.: Learning to detect unseen object classes by betweenclass attribute transfer. In: CVPR (2009)
20. Lim, J.J., Salakhutdinov, R., Torralba, A.: Transfer learning by borrowing examples for multiclass object detection. In: Neural Information Processing Systems, NIPS (2011)
21. Malisiewicz, T., Gupta, A., Efros, A.A.: Ensemble of exemplar-svms for object detection and beyond. In: ICCV (2011)
22. Matikainen, P., Sukthankar, R., Hebert, M.: Model recommendation for action recognition. In: CVPR, pp. 2256–2263 (2012)
23. Nair, V., Clark, J.J.: An unsupervised, online learning framework for moving object detection. In: CVPR, pp. 317–325 (2004)
24. Ozuysal, M., Calonder, M., Lepetit, V., Fua, P.: Fast keypoint recognition using random ferns. IEEE Trans. Pattern Anal. Mach. Intell. 32(3), 448–461 (2010)

25. Pan, S.J., Yang, Q.: A survey on transfer learning. IEEE Transaction on Knowledge and Data Engineering (2010)
26. Roth, P.M., Sternig, S., Grabner, H., Bischof, H.: Classifier grids for robust adaptive object detection. In: CVPR, pp. 2727–2734 (2009)
27. Saenko, K., Kulis, B., Fritz, M., Darrell, T.: Adapting visual category models to new domains. In: Daniilidis, K., Maragos, P., Paragios, N. (eds.) ECCV 2010, Part IV. LNCS, vol. 6314, pp. 213–226. Springer, Heidelberg (2010)
28. Sharma, P., Huang, C., Nevatia, R.: Unsupervised incremental learning for improved object detection in a video. In: CVPR, pp. 3298–3305 (2012)
29. Sharma, P., Nevatia, R.: Efficient detector adaptation for object detection in a video. In: CVPR, pp. 3254–3261 (2013)
30. Vázquez, D., López, A.M., Ponsa, D.: Unsupervised domain adaptation of virtual and real worlds for pedestrian detection. In: ICPR, pp. 3492–3495 (2012)
31. Viola, P., Jones, M.: Robust real-time face detection. Int. J. Computer Vision 57(2), 137–154 (2004)
32. Wang, M., Li, W., Wang, X.: Transferring a generic pedestrian detector towards specific scenes. In: CVPR, pp. 3274–3281 (2012)
33. Wang, M., Wang, X.: Automatic adaptation of a generic pedestrian detector to a specific traffic scene. In: CVPR, pp. 3401–3408 (2011)
34. Wang, X., Hua, G., Han, T.X.: Detection by detections: Non-parametric detector adaptation for a video. In: CVPR, pp. 350–357 (2012)
35. Yang, J., Yan, R., Hauptmann, A.G.: Adapting svm classifiers to data with shifted distributions, pp. 69–76. IEEE Computer Society (2007)
36. Zhang, C., Ma, Y.: Ensemble Machine Learning. Springer (2012)

Deep Learning of Scene-Specific Classifier for Pedestrian Detection

Xingyu Zeng[1], Wanli Ouyang[1], Meng Wang[1], and Xiaogang Wang[1,2]

[1] The Chinese University of Hong Kong, Shatin, Hong Kong
[2] Shenzhen Institutes of Advanced Technology, Chinese Academy of Sciences, China

Abstract. The performance of a detector depends much on its training dataset and drops significantly when the detector is applied to a new scene due to the large variations between the source training dataset and the target scene. In order to bridge this appearance gap, we propose a deep model to automatically learn scene-specific features and visual patterns in static video surveillance without any manual labels from the target scene. It jointly learns a scene-specific classifier and the distribution of the target samples. Both tasks share multi-scale feature representations with both discriminative and representative power. We also propose a cluster layer in the deep model that utilizes the scene-specific visual patterns for pedestrian detection. Our specifically designed objective function not only incorporates the confidence scores of target training samples but also automatically weights the importance of source training samples by fitting the marginal distributions of target samples. It significantly improves the detection rates at 1 FPPI by 10% compared with the state-of-the-art domain adaptation methods on MIT Traffic Dataset and CUHK Square Dataset.

1 Introduction

Pedestrian detection is a challenging task of great interest in computer vision. Significant progress has been achieved in recent years [8]. However, the performance of detectors depends much on the training dataset. For example, the performance of pedestrian detectors trained on the mostly used INRIA pedestrian dataset [5] drops significantly when they are tested on the MIT Traffic dataset [33]. Fig. 1 shows that the appearance differences between the samples from the two datasets are so large that it is difficult for a detector trained on one dataset to get a satisfactory performance when being applied to the other. Manually labeling examples in all specific scenes is impractical especially when considering the huge number of cameras used nowadays. On the other hand, for applications like video surveillance, the appearance variation of a scene captured by a camera is most likely to be small. Therefore, it is practical to train a scene-specific detector by transferring knowledge from a generic dataset in order to improve the detection performance on a specific scene. Much effort has been made to develop scene-specific detectors, whose training process is aided by generic detectors for automatically collecting training samples from target scenes without manually labeling them [33,34,23,32,1,30].

D. Fleet et al. (Eds.): ECCV 2014, Part III, LNCS 8691, pp. 472–487, 2014.

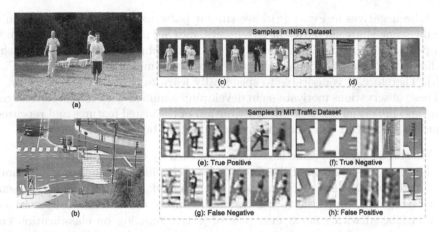

Fig. 1. (a): Image from INRIA dataset. (b): Image from MIT Traffic dataset. (c): Positive samples in INRIA. (d): Negatives in INRIA. (e)-(h): Detection results of a generic detector (HOG-SVM [5] trained on INRIA) on MIT Traffic. (e): True positives. (f): True negatives. (g): False negatives. (f): False positives. Best viewed in color.

Learning scene-specific detectors can be considered as a domain adaptation problem. It involves two distinct types of data: $\mathbf{x}_s$ from the source dataset and $\mathbf{x}_t$ from the target scene, with very different distributions $p_s(\mathbf{x}_s)$ and $p_t(\mathbf{x}_t)$. The source dataset contains a large amount of labeled data while the target scene contains no or a small amount of labeled training data. The objective is to adapt the classifier trained on the source dataset to the target scene, i.e. estimating the label y_t from $\mathbf{x}_t$ using a function $y_t = f(\mathbf{x}_t)$. As an important preprocessing, we can extract features from $\mathbf{x}_t$ and have $y_t = f(\phi(\mathbf{x}_t))$, where $\phi(\mathbf{x}_t)$ is the extracted features like HOG or SIFT. We also expect that the marginal distribution $p_s(\phi(\mathbf{x}_s))$ is very different from $p_t(\phi(\mathbf{x}_t))$. Our motivation of developing deep models for scene-specific detection is three-folds.

First, instead of only adaptively adjusting the weights of generic hand-crafted features as existing domain adaptation methods [33,34,23,32], it is desirable to automatically learn scene-specific features to best capture the discriminative information of a target scene. This can be well achieved with deep learning.

Second, it is important to learn $p_t(\phi(\mathbf{x}_t))$, which is challenging when the dimensionality of $\phi(\mathbf{x}_t)$ is high, while deep models can learn $p_t(\phi(\mathbf{x}_t))$ well in a hierarchical and unsupervised way [16]. 1) In the case that the number of labeled target training samples is small, it is beneficial to jointly learn the feature representations for both $p_t(\phi(\mathbf{x}_t))$ and $f(\phi(\mathbf{x}_t))$ to avoid overfitting of $f(\phi(\mathbf{x}_t))$ since regulation is added by $p_t(\phi(\mathbf{x}_t))$. 2) $p_t(\phi(\mathbf{x}_t))$ also helps to evaluate the importance of a source sample in learning the scene-specific classifier. Some source samples, e.g. the blue sky in Fig. 1(d), do not appear in the target scene and may mislead the training. Their influence should be reduced.

Third, a target scene has scene-specific visual patterns across true and false detections, which repeatedly appear. For example, the true positives in Fig. 1 (e) and false negatives in Fig. 1 (g) have similar patterns because pedestrians in a specific scene share similarity in viewpoints, moving modes, poses, backgrounds and pedestrian sizes when they walk on the same zebra crossing or wait for the traffic light at nearby locations. Similarly for the samples in Fig. 1 (f) and Fig. 1 (h). Therefore, it is desirable to specifically learn to capture these patterns.

These observations motivate us in developing a unified deep model that learns scene-specific visual features, the distribution of the visual features and repeated visual patterns. Our contributions are summarized below.

- Multi-scale scene-specific features are learned by the deep model.
- The deep model accomplishes both tasks of classification and reconstruction, which share feature representations with both discriminative and representative power. Since the target training samples are automatically selected and labeled with context cues, the objective function on classification encodes the confidence scores of target training samples, so that the learned deep model is robust to labeling mistakes on target training samples. In the meanwhile, an auto-encoder [16] reconstructs target training samples and models the distribution of samples in the target scene.
- With our specifically designed objective function, the influence of a training sample on learning the classifier is weighted by its probability of appearing in the target data.
- A new cluster layer is proposed in the deep model to capture the scene-specific patterns. The distribution of a sample over these patterns is used as additional features for detection.

Our innovation comes from the sights on vision problems and we well incorporate them into deep models. Compared with the state-of-the-art domain adaptation result [34], our deep learning approach has significantly improved the detection rates by 10% at 1 FPPI (False Positive Per Image) on two public datasets.

2   Related Work

Many generic human detection approaches learn features, clustered appearance mixtures, deformation and visibility using deep models [31,26,39,21,25] or part based models [9,38,24,27]. They assume that the distribution of source samples is similar to that of target samples. Our contributions aim at tackling the domain adaptation problem, where the distributions of data in the two domains vary significantly and the labeled target training samples are few or contain errors.

Many domain adaptation approaches learn features shared by source domain and target domain [14,12]. They project hand-crafted features into subspaces or manifolds, instead of learning features from raw data. Some deep models are investigated in the Unsupervised and Transfer Learning Challenge [15] and the Challenge on Learning Hierarchical Models [19]. And transfer learning using deep models has been proved to be effective in these challenges [22,13], in animal and vehicle recognition [13], and in sentiment analysis [11,3]. We are inspired by these works. However, they focus on unsupervised learning of features shared in different domains and use the same structures and objective functions as existing deep models for general learning. We have innovation in both aspects.

A group of works on scene-specific detection [23,29,35,33,34] construct auto-labelers for automatically obtaining confident samples from the target scene to retrain the generic detector. Wang et al. [34] explore a rich set of context cues to obtain reliable target-scene samples, predict their labels and confidence scores. Their training of classifiers incorporates confidence scores and is robust to labeling errors. Our approach is in this group. The confident samples obtained by these approaches can be used as the input of our approach in learning the deep model. Another group of works [36,20] are under the co-training framework [2], in which two different classifiers on two different sets of features are trained simultaneously for the same task. An experimental comparison in [34] shows that it is easy for co-training to drift when training pedestrian detectors and its performance is much lower than the adaptive detector proposed in [34].

Samples in the source and target datasets are re-weighted differently using SVM [35,33,34] and Boosting [4,28]. However, these approaches are heuristic but do not learn the distribution of target data. Our approach learns the distribution of target samples with a deep model and uses it for re-weighting samples.

3   The Proposed Deep Model at the Testing Stage

Our full model employed at the training stage is show in Fig. 3 and Fig. 4. It accomplishes both classification and reconstruction tasks, and takes input from source and target training samples. However, at the testing stage, we only keep the parts for classification and take target samples as input. An overview of the proposed deep model for pedestrian detection in the target scene is shown in Fig. 2. This deep model contains three convolutional neural network (CNN) layers [18], three fully connected layers, the proposed cluster layer and the classification label y on whether a window contains a pedestrian or not.

The three CNN layers contain three convolutional sub-layers and three average pooling sub-layers:
- The convolutional sub-layer convolves its input data with the learned filters and then the nonlinearity function $|\tanh(x)|$ is used for each filter response. The output is the filtered data map.
- Feature maps are obtained by average pooling of the filtered data maps.
- The next convolutional layer treats feature maps as the input data and this procedure repeats for three times.

Details for convolutional sub-layers and average pooling sub-layers are as follows:
- The first convolutional sub-layer has 64 $9\times9\times3$ filters, the second has 20 $2\times2\times64$ filters and the last has 12 $4\times4\times20$ filters.
- The average pooling sub-layer down-samples the filtered data map by sub-sampling step $K \times K$ using $K \times K$ boxcar filters. $K = 4$ in the first pooling sub-layer, $K = 2$ in the second and the third sub-layer.

The fully connected layers have 2888 hidden nodes at the first layer, 2400 nodes at the second layer, and 800 nodes at the third layer. The parameters of the

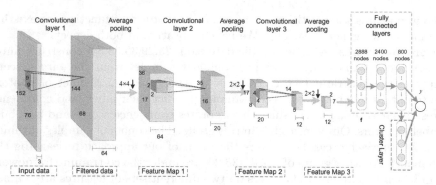

Fig. 2. Our deep model at the testing stage. There are three CNN layers, where each layer contains one convolutional sub-layer and one pooling sub-layer. The input data has three channels and is convolved with 64 9×9×3 filters, then averagely pooled within the 4 × 4 region to output the second layer. Similarly for the second layer and the third layer. The feature f is composed of the output from both the second layer and the third layer. Then the features are transferred to the fully connected layers and the cluster layer for estimating the class label y. Best viewed in color.

CNN structure are chosen by using the INRIA test set as the validation set. Details about the cluster layer is given in Section 4.5.

3.1   Input Data and Feature Preparation

We follow the approach in [26] for preparing the input data in Fig. 2. The only difference is the image size. The size of the input image is 152×76 in our implementation to have higher resolution images.

The output of all the CNN layers can be considered as features with different resolutions [31]. We concatenate the output of the second layer and the third layer in the CNN to form our features in order to use the information at different resolutions. The second layer has 20 maps of size 17×8, the third layer has 12 maps of size 7×2. Thus we obtain 2888-dimensional features, which is the f in Fig. 2. In this way, information at different resolutions are kept.

4   Training the Deep Model

4.1   Multi-stage Learning of the Deep Model

The overview of the stages in learning the deep model is shown in Fig. 3. It consists of the following steps:

– **(1) Obtaining Confident Target Training Samples.** Confident positive and negative training samples can be collected from the target scene using any existing approach. The method in [34] is used in our experiment. It starts with a generic detector trained on the source training set (INRIA dataset)

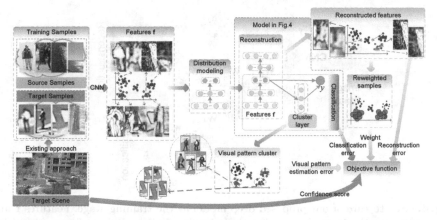

Fig. 3. Overview of our deep model. Confident samples are obtained from the target scene. Then features and their distributions in the target scene are learned. Scene-specific patterns are clustered and used for classification. Auto-encoder is used for reconstructing features and reweighting samples. The objective function is a combination of reconstruction error, visual pattern estimation error, and classification error weighted by reconstruction error and confidence score. Classification error, reconstruction error and visual pattern error are the first, second and third terms for the proposed objective function in (7) used for training the model in Fig. 4. Best viewed in color.

and automatically labels training samples from the target scene with additional context cues, such as motions, path models, and pedestrian sizes. Since automatic labeling contains errors, a score indicating the confidence on the predicated label is associated with each target training sample. Both target and source training samples are used to re-train the scene-specific detector.

- **(2) Feature Learning.** With target and source training samples, three CNN layers in Fig. 2 are used for learning discriminative features for the pedestrian detection task.
- **(3) Distribution Modeling.** The distribution of features in the target scene is learned with the deep belief net [16] using the target samples only.
- **(4) Scene-Specific Pattern Learning.** A cluster layer in our deep model is learned for capturing the scene-specific visual patterns.
- **(5) Joint Learning of Classification and Reconstruction.** Since target training samples are error prone, source samples are used to improve training. The target training samples have their classification estimation error weighted by their confidence scores in the objective function, in order to be robust to labeling mistakes. In addition to learning the discriminative information for the scene-specific classifier, an auto-encoder is included so that the deep model can learn the representative information in reconstructing the features. With a new objective function, the reconstruction error is used for reweighting the training samples. Samples better fitting the distribution of the target scene have smaller reconstruction errors and have larger influence on the objective function. At this stage, the parameters pre-trained in stage (2)-(4) are also jointly optimized with backpropagation.

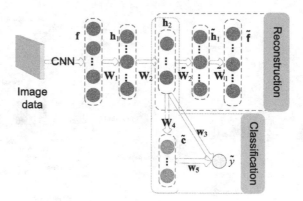

Fig. 4. Architecture of our proposed deep model at the training stage. Features **f** are extracted from the image data using three layers of CNN. In this figure, there are one input feature layer **f**, two hidden layers $\mathbf{h}_1$, $\mathbf{h}_2$, one cluster layer $\tilde{\mathbf{c}}$, one estimated classification label $\tilde{y}$, one reconstruction hidden layer $\tilde{\mathbf{h}}_1$, and one reconstructed feature layer $\tilde{\mathbf{f}}$. They are computed using Equations (1)-(6). Best viewed in color.

4.2 The Deep Model at the Training Stage

The architecture our deep model is shown in Fig. 4. The model for forward propagation is as follows:

$$\mathbf{h}_1 = \sigma(\mathbf{W}_1^{\mathrm{T}}\mathbf{f} + \mathbf{b}_1), \tag{1}$$

$$\mathbf{h}_2 = \sigma(\mathbf{W}_2^{\mathrm{T}}\mathbf{h}_1 + \mathbf{b}_2), \tag{2}$$

$$\tilde{\mathbf{c}} = softmax(\mathbf{W}_4^{\mathrm{T}}\mathbf{h}_2 + \mathbf{b}_4), \tag{3}$$

$$\tilde{y} = \sigma(\mathbf{w}_3^{\mathrm{T}}\mathbf{h}_2 + \mathbf{w}_5^{\mathrm{T}}\tilde{\mathbf{c}} + b_5), \tag{4}$$

$$\tilde{\mathbf{h}}_1 = \sigma(\tilde{\mathbf{W}}_2^{\mathrm{T}}\mathbf{h}_2 + \tilde{\mathbf{b}}_2), \tag{5}$$

$$\tilde{\mathbf{f}} = \sigma(\tilde{\mathbf{W}}_1^{\mathrm{T}}\mathbf{h}_i + \tilde{\mathbf{b}}_1), \tag{6}$$

where $\sigma(a) = 1/[1 + \exp(-a)]$ is the activation function.

- **f** is the feature obtained from CNN.
- $\mathbf{h}_i$ for $i = 1, \ldots, L$ denotes the vector containing hidden nodes in the ith hidden layer of the deep belief net used for capturing the shared representation of the target scene. As shown in Fig. 4, we use $L = 2$ hidden layers.
- $\tilde{\mathbf{c}}$ is the vector representing the cluster layer to be introduced in Section 4.5. Each node in this layer represents a scene-specific visual pattern.
- $\tilde{y}$ is the estimated classification label on whether a window contains a pedestrian or not.
- $\tilde{\mathbf{h}}_1$ is the hidden vector for reconstruction, with the same dimension as $\mathbf{h}_1$.
- $\tilde{\mathbf{f}}$ is the reconstructed feature vector for **f**.
- $\mathbf{W}_*$, $\mathbf{w}_*$, $\mathbf{b}_*$, $\tilde{\mathbf{W}}_*$, and $\tilde{\mathbf{b}}_*$ are the parameters to be learned.

The dimensionality of $\mathbf{h}_2$ is lower than that of $\mathbf{f}$. From $\mathbf{f}$ to $\mathbf{h}_1$ to $\mathbf{h}_2$, the features $\mathbf{f}$ are represented by low dimensional hidden nodes in $\mathbf{h}_2$. $\mathbf{h}_2$ is shared on the following two paths.

- The first path, from $\mathbf{h}_2$ to $\tilde{\mathbf{c}}$ to $\tilde{y}$, is used for estimating the classification label. This path is exactly the same as the model at the testing stage in Fig. 2. $\mathbf{h}_2$ is used for classification on this path.
- The second path, from the features $\mathbf{f}$, hidden nodes $\mathbf{h}_1$, $\mathbf{h}_2$, $\tilde{\mathbf{h}}_1$ to reconstructed features $\tilde{\mathbf{f}}$, is the auto-encoder used for reconstructing the features $\mathbf{f}$. This path is only used at the learning stage. $\mathbf{f}$ is reconstructed from the low dimensional nonlinear representation $\mathbf{h}_2$ on this path.

Denote the nth training sample with extracted feature $\mathbf{f}_n$ and label y_n as $\{\mathbf{f}_n, y_n, s_n, v_n\}$ for $n = 1, \ldots, N$, where $v_n = 1$ if $\mathbf{f}_n$ is from the target data and $v_n = 0$ if $\mathbf{f}_n$ is from the source data, s_n is the confidence score obtained by the existing approach [34] in our experiment. With the source samples and the target samples, the objective function for back-propagation (BP) learning of the deep model in Fig. 4 is as follows:

$$L = \sum_n e^{-\lambda_1 L^r(\mathbf{f}_n, \tilde{\mathbf{f}}_n)} L^c(y_n, \tilde{y}_n, s_n) + \lambda_2 v_n L^r(\mathbf{f}_n, \tilde{\mathbf{f}}_n) + v_n L_n^p, \quad (7)$$

where $L^r(\mathbf{f}_n, \tilde{\mathbf{f}}_n) = ||\mathbf{f}_n - \tilde{\mathbf{f}}_n||^2$, \hfill (8)

$$L^c(y_n, \tilde{y}_n, s_n) = s_n L^E(y_n, \tilde{y}_n), \quad (9)$$

$$L^E(y_n, \tilde{y}_n) = -y_n \log \tilde{y}_n - (1 - y_n) \log(1 - \tilde{y}_n). \quad (10)$$

- $L^r(\mathbf{f}_n, \tilde{\mathbf{f}}_n)$ is the error of the auto-encoder in reconstructing $\mathbf{f}_n$.
- $L^E(y_n, \tilde{y}_n)$ is the error in estimating the classification label y_n, which is implemented by the cross-entropy loss.
- $L^c(y_n, \tilde{y}_n, s_n)$ is the reweighted classification error. For the source sample, $s_n = 1$ and L^E is directly used. For the target sample, the confidence score $s_n \in [0\ 1]$ is used for reweighting the classification estimation error L^E so that the classifier is robust to the labeling mistake of the confident samples.
- L_n^p is the error in estimating the visual pattern membership of the target data, which is detailed in Section 4.5.
- $\lambda_1 = 0.00025$, $\lambda_2 = 0.1$ in all our experiments.

4.3   Motivation of the Objective Function

The Objective Function for Confident Target Samples. The objective function have three requirements for target samples:
- $\mathbf{h}_2$ should be representative so that the reconstruction error on target samples of the auto-encoder is small.
- $\mathbf{h}_2$ should be discriminative so that the class label estimation error is small.
- $\mathbf{h}_2$ should be able to recognize the scene-specific visual patterns.

Therefore, $\mathbf{h}_2$ should be a compact, nonlinear representation of the representative and discriminative information in the target scene.

The Objective Function for Source Samples. Denote the source sample by $\{\mathbf{f}_s, y_s, v_s\}$. Since $v_s = 0$ in (7), the source sample does not influence the learning of the auto-encoder and the cluster layer. Denote the probability of $\mathbf{f}_s$ appearing in the target scene by $p_t(\mathbf{f}_s)$.

- If $p_t(\mathbf{f}_s)$ is very low, this sample may not appear in the scene and may mislead the training procedure. Thus the influence of $\mathbf{f}_s$ on learning the scene-specific classifier should be reduced. The objective function in (7) fits this goal. In our model, the auto-encoder is used for learning the distribution of the target data. If the auto-encoder produces high reconstruction error for a source sample, this sample does not fit the representation of the target data and $p_t(\mathbf{f}_s)$ should be low. In the extreme case, $L^r(\mathbf{f}_s, \tilde{\mathbf{f}}_s) \to \infty$ and $e^{-aL^r(\mathbf{f}_s, \tilde{\mathbf{f}}_s)} \to 0$ in (7). Thus the weighted classification loss is 0 and this sample has no influence on learning the scene-specific classifier.

- If $p_t(\mathbf{f}_s)$ is high, it should be used. In this case, the sample can be well represented by the auto-encoder and has low reconstruction error. In our objective function, $e^{-aL^r(\mathbf{f}_s, \tilde{\mathbf{f}}_s)} \approx 1$ and the classification error L^c of this sample influences the scene-specific classifier.

In this way, the source samples are weighted by how they fit the low dimensional representation of the target domain. The other purpose of L^r in (7) is to require that the low-dimensional feature representation $\mathbf{h}_2$ used for classification can also well reconstruct most target samples. The regularization avoids overfitting when the number of training samples is not large and they have errors.

4.4 Learning Features and Distribution in the Target Scene

The CNN layers in Fig. 2 are used for extracting features from images. We train these layers by using source and target samples as input and putting their labels above the third CNN layer. The cross-entropy error function in (10) and BP are used for learning CNN. In this way, the features for the pedestrian detection task are pre-trained[1].

Then the distribution of features in the target scene is learned in an unsupervised way using targe samples only. This is done by treating $\mathbf{f}$, $\mathbf{h}_1$, $\mathbf{h}_2$ as a deep belief net (DBN) [16]. The weights $\mathbf{W}_1$ and $\mathbf{W}_2$ in Fig. 4 are pre-trained using the greedy layer-wise learning algorithm in [16] while all matrices connected to the cluster layer $\tilde{\mathbf{c}}$ are fixed to zero. Many studies have shown that DBN can well learn the distribution of high-dimensional data and its low-dimensional representation. Pre-trained with DBN, auto-encoder can well reconstruct high-dimensional data from this low-dimensional representation.

4.5 Unsupervised Learning of Scene-Specific Visual Patterns

This section introduces the cluster layer in Fig. 4 for capturing scene-specific visual patterns.

---

[1] They will be fine-tuned with other parts of the deep model in the final stage using BP.

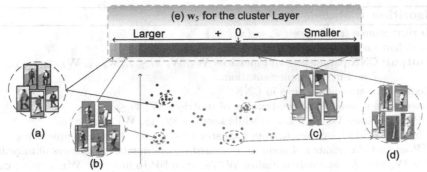

Fig. 5. Examples of scene-specific pattern clusters in the target scene and their learned weights $\mathbf{w}_5$. Pedestrians in cluster (a) are walking cross the road. Pedestrians in (b) are either waiting for green light or starting to cross the street. Samples in (c) are zebra crossings in different positions. Samples in cluster (d) contain lamp posts, trees and pedestrians. Each cluster share a similar appearance. Each cluster corresponds to a node in the cluster layer $\tilde{\mathbf{c}}$ and a weight in vector $\mathbf{w}_5$. The corresponding learned weights in $\mathbf{w}_5$ for estimating the class label $\tilde{y}$ are delineated for the patterns. $\tilde{y} = \sigma(\mathbf{w}_3^T\mathbf{h}_2 + \mathbf{w}_5^T\tilde{\mathbf{c}} + b_3)$. The clusters (a)(b), which mainly contain positive samples, have large positive weights in $\mathbf{w}_5$. The pattern (d), which contains mixed positive and negative samples, has its corresponding weight close to zero. Best viewed in color.

Scene-Specific Pattern Preparation. In order to capture scene-specific appearance patterns, e.g. pedestrians walking on the same road or zebra crossing, we cluster selected target samples into subsets with similar appearance. The features $\mathbf{f}$ learned from the CNN is used as the input for clustering.

We use the affinity propagation (AP) clustering method [10] to get initial clustering labels. AP fits our goal because it automatically determines the number of clusters and produces reasonable results. Fig. 5 shows some clustering results, where the visual patterns in the scene for positive and negative samples are well captured. The number of nodes in the cluster layer is set as the cluster number produced by AP. Each node in this layer corresponds to a cluster. The cluster labels of target samples are used for training the cluster layer. 51 clusters are found on the MIT Traffic dataset.

Training the Cluster Layer. The input of the nodes in the cluster layer take the combination of feature representation $\mathbf{h}_2$ with matrix $\mathbf{W}_4$. With CNN, $\mathbf{W}_1$, and $\mathbf{W}_2$ in Fig. 4 learned as introduced in Section 4.4, $\mathbf{W}_4$ in (3) is learned using the following cross-entropy error function for estimating the cluster label:

$$L_n^p = -\mathbf{c}_n^T \log \tilde{\mathbf{c}}_n, \tag{11}$$

where $\mathbf{c}_n$ is the cluster label obtained by AP, $\tilde{\mathbf{c}}_n$ is the predicted cluster label. Then $\mathbf{w}_3$ and $\mathbf{w}_5$ are fine-tuned using the objective function in (7). Finally, the parameters in the CNN, the cluster layer, and the fully connect layers are fine-tuned using (7). A summary of the overall training procedure is given in Al-

---

Algorithm 1. Stage-by-Stage Training

Input: Source training set: $\Psi_s = \{\mathbf{x}_s, y_s\}$
confident target scene set: $\Psi_t = \{\mathbf{x}_t, y_t\}$
Output: CNN parameters and matrices $\mathbf{W}_i, \tilde{\mathbf{W}}_i \ \forall i \leq L, \mathbf{w}_{L+1}, \mathbf{W}_{L+2}, \mathbf{w}_{L+3}$,
    $L = 2$ in our implementation.

1 Learn scene-specific features in CNN;
2 Layer-wise unsupervised pre-training of matrices $\mathbf{W}_i \ \forall i \leq L$;
3 BP to fine tune $\mathbf{W}_i \ \forall i \leq L+1$, while keeping $\mathbf{W}_{L+2}, \mathbf{W}_{L+3}$ as zero;
4 Cluster confident samples to obtain cluster label $\mathbf{c}_n$ for the nth sample using
    AP and set the number of nodes in $\mathbf{c}$ according the number of clusters obtained;
5 Fix $\mathbf{W}_i \ \forall i \leq L$, randomly initialize $\mathbf{W}_{L+2}$, then BP to fine tune $\mathbf{W}_{L+2}$ using $\mathbf{c}_n$
    as ground truth. L^p in (11) is used as the objective function ;
6 Randomly initialize $\mathbf{w}_{L+3}$. BP to fine tune $\mathbf{w}_{L+1}$ and $\mathbf{w}_{L+3}$ using the objective
    function in (7) ;
7 BP to fine tune all parameters using the objective function in (7) ;
8 Output parameters.

---

gorithm 1. L_n^p in (11) is used in (7) for constraining that the learned appearance pattern does not deviate far from the initial pattern found by AP clustering.

5 Experimental Results

5.1 Experimental Setting

All the experiments are conducted on the MIT Traffic dataset [33] and CUHK Square dataset [32]. The MIT Traffic dataset is a 90-minutes long video at 30 fps. 420 frames are uniformly sampled from the first 45 minutes video to train the scene-specific detector. 100 frames are uniformly sampled from the last 45 minutes video for test. The CUHK Square dataset is a 60-minutes long video. 350 frames are uniformly sampled from the first 30 minutes video for training. 100 frames uniformly sampled from the last 30 minutes video for testing. The INRIA training dataset [5] is used as the source dataset. The PASCAL criterion, i.e. the ratio of the overlap region compared to the union should be larger than 0.5, is adopted. The evaluation metric is recall rate versus false positive per image (FPPI). The same experimental setting has been used in [33,34,32].

We obtain 4262 confident positive samples, 3788 confident negative samples and their confident scores from the MIT Traffic training frames with the approach in [34]. For CUHK Square, we get 1506 positive samples and 37392 negative samples for training. They are used to train the scene-specific detector together with the source dataset. During test, for the sake of saving computation, we use a linear SVM trained on both source dataset and confident target samples to pre-scan all windows and prune candidate samples in the test images with conservative thresholds, and then apply our deep learning scene-specific detector to the remaining candidates. Compared with using SVM alone, about 50 % additional computation time is introduced. When we talk about detection rates, it is assumed that FPPI = 1.

Table 1. Comparison of detection rates with state-of-the-art generic detectors on the MIT Traffic dataset and the CUHK Square dataset. The training data for 'HOG+SVM', 'ChnFtrs', 'MultiSDP' and 'JointDeep' is the INRIA dataset.

	HOG+SVM [5]	ChnFtrs [7]	MultiSDP [39]	JointDeep [26]	ours
MIT Traffic	21%	23%	23%	17%	65%
CUHK Square	15%	32%	42%	22%	62%

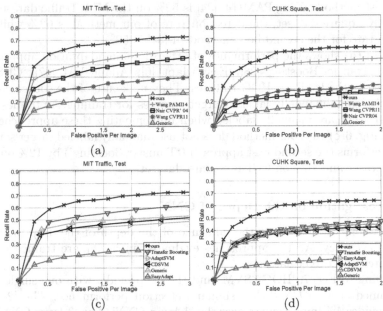

Fig. 6. Experimental results on the MIT Traffic dataset (left column) and the CUHK Square dataset (right column). (a) and (b): Comparison with methods requiring no manual labels from the target scene, i.e. Wang PAMI14 [34], Wang CVPR11 [33] and Nair CVPR04[23]. (c) and (d): Comparison with methods requiring manual labels on 50 frames from the target scene, i.e. Transfer Boosting [28], EasyAdapt [6], AdaptSVM [37] and CDSVM [17].

5.2   Overall Performance

We have compared our model with several state-of-the-art generic detectors [7,39,26]. The detection rates are shown in Table. 1. The training data for 'HOG+SVM', 'ChnFtrs', 'MultiSDP' and 'JointDeep' is the INRIA dataset. It is observed that the performance of the generic detectors on the MIT Traffic and CUHK Square datasets are quite poor due to the mismatch between the training data and the target scenes. They are far below the performance of our detector.

In Fig. 6(a)-(b), we compare our method with three other scene-specific approaches [23,33,34] on the two datasets. In addition to the source dataset, these approaches and ours do not require manually labeled samples from the target scene for training. 'Nair CVPR 04' in Fig. 6 represents the method in [23] which uses background subtraction to select target training samples. 'Wang CVPR11' [33] in Fig. 6 selects confident samples from the target scene by integrating multiple context cues, such as locations, sizes, appearance and motions, and train an HOG-SVM detector. 'Wang PAMI14' [34] in Fig. 6 selects target training samples in the same way as [33] and uses a proposed Confidence-Encode SVM, which better incorporates the confidence scores, to train the scene-specific detector. Our approach obtains the target training samples in the same way as [33] and [34]. As shown in Fig. 6(a)-(b), our approach performs better than the other three methods. The detection rate of our method reaches 65% while the second best method 'Wang PAMI14' [34] is 52% on the MIT Traffic dataset. On the CUHK Square dataset, the detection rate of our method is 62% while the detection rate for the second best method in [34] is 52%.

Fig. 6(c)-(d) shows the performance of other domain adaptation approaches, including 'Transfer Boosting' [28], 'EasyAdapt' [6], 'AdaptSVM' [37], 'CDSVM' [17]. These methods all use HOG features. They make use of the source dataset and require some manually labeled target samples for training. 50 frames from the target scene are manually labeled when implementing these approaches. As shown in Fig. 6(c)-(d), our method does not use manually labeled target samples but outperforms the second best approach ('Transfer Boosting') by 12% on MIT Traffic dataset and 16% on CUHK Square dataset.

5.3   Investigation on the Depth of CNN

In this section, we investigate the influence of the depth of the deep model on detection accuracy. All the approaches evaluated in Fig. 7 are trained on the same source and target datasets.

According to Fig. 7, 'HOG+SVM' and the deep model with one single CNN layer, named '1-layer-CNN', has similar detection performance. The '2-layer-CNN' provides 4% improvement over the '1-layer-CNN'. The '3-layer-CNN' provides 2% improvement over the '2-layer-CNN'. Therefore, the detection accuracy increases as the number of CNN layers increases from one to three. We did not observe obvious improvement by adding the fourth CNN layer. The performance increases by 2% and reaches 59% when the '3-layer-CNN' is added by two fully connected hidden layers, which is denoted by 'CNN-DBN' in Fig. 7 .

5.4   Investigation on Deep Model Design

In this section, we investiage the influence of our deep model design, i.e. the auto-encoder and the cluster layer, on the MIT Traffic dataset.

As shown in Fig. 7, the 'CNN-DBN' trained with our auto-encoder, denoted as 'CNN-DBN-AutoEncoder' in Fig. 7 , improves the detection rate by 3% compared with the 'CNN-DBN' without auto-encoder. Our final deep model with the cluster layer ('CNN-DBN-AutoEncocder-ClusterLayer') reaches detection rate 65%, which has 3% detection rate improvement compared with the deep model without the cluster layer ('CNN-DBN-AutoEncocder').

Different reweigting methods are also compared in Fig. 7. The 'CNN-DBN-Indegree' denotes the method in [34] which reweights source samples according to their indegrees from target samples. The 'CNN-DBN-AutoEncoder' denotes our

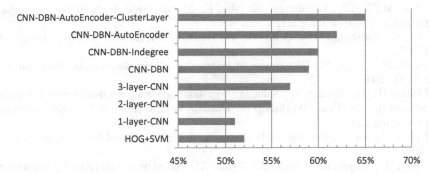

Fig. 7. Detection rates at FPPI =1 for the deep model with different number of layers and different deep model design on the MIT Traffic dataset. All the approaches, including 'HOG+SVM', are trained on the same INRIA data and the same confident target data. '1-layer-CNN' means network with only one CNN layer. '2-layer-CNN' means network with two CNN layers. '3-layer-CNN' means network with three CNN layers. 'CNN-DBN' means the model with three CNN layers and two fully connected layers. 'CNN-DBN-Indegree' means that the 'CNN-DBN' is retrained using the indegree-based reweighting method in [34]. 'CNN-DBN-AutoEncoder' is the 'CNN-DBN' retrained using our auto-encoder for reweighting samples. 'CNN-DBN-AutoEncoder-ClusterLayer' means the 'CNN-DBN-AutoEncoder' with the cluster layer. Best viewed in color.

reweighting method using the auto-encoder. Both methods are used for training the same network 'CNN-DBN'. Our reweighting method has 2% detection rate improvement compared with the indegree-based reweighting method in [34].

6 Conclusion

We propose a new deep model and a new objective function to learn scene-specific features, low dimensional representation of features and scene-specific visual patterns in static video surveillance without any manual labeling from the target scene. The new model and objective function guide learning both representative and discriminative feature representations from the target scene. Our approach is very flexible in incorporating with existing approaches that aim to obtain confident samples from the target scene.

Acknowledgement. This work is supported by the General Research Fund and Early Career Scheme sponsored by the Research Grants Council of Hong Kong (Project Nos. 417110, 417011, 419412), and Shenzhen Basic Research Program (JCYJ20130402113127496).

References

1. Benfold, B., Reid, I.: Stable multi-target tracking in real-time surveillance video. In: CVPR (2011)
2. Blum, A., Mitchell, T.: Combining labeled and unlabeled data with co-training. In: ACM COLT (1998)

3. Chen, M., Xu, Z., Weinberger, K., Sha, F.: Marginalized denoising autoencoders for domain adaptation (2012)
4. Dai, W., Yang, Q., Xue, G.R., Yu, Y.: Boosting for transfer learning. In: ICML (2007)
5. Dalal, N., Triggs, B.: Histograms of oriented gradients for human detection. In: CVPR (2005)
6. Daumé III, H., Kumar, A., Saha, A.: Frustratingly easy semi-supervised domain adaptation. In: Proc. Workshop on Domain Adaptation for Natural Language Processing (2010)
7. Dollár, P., Tu, Z., Perona, P., Belongie, S.: Integral channel features. In: BMVC (2009)
8. Dollár, P., Wojek, C., Schiele, B., Perona, P.: Pedestrian detection: An evaluation of the state of the art. PAMI 34(4), 743–761 (2012)
9. Felzenszwalb, P.F., Girshick, R.B., McAllester, D., Ramanan, D.: Object detection with discriminatively trained part-based models. PAMI 32(9), 1627–1645 (2010)
10. Frey, B.J., Dueck, D.: Clustering by passing messages between data points. Science 315(5814), 972–976 (2007)
11. Glorot, X., Bordes, A., Bengio, Y.: Domain adaptation for large-scale sentiment classification: A deep learning approach. In: ICML (2011)
12. Gong, B., Shi, Y., Sha, F., Grauman, K.: Geodesic flow kernel for unsupervised domain adaptation. In: CVPR (2012)
13. Goodfellow, I.J., Courville, A., Bengio, Y.: Spike-and-slab sparse coding for unsupervised feature discovery. NIPS Workshop Challenges in Learning Hierarchical Models (2012)
14. Gopalan, R., Li, R., Chellappa, R.: Domain adaptation for object recognition: An unsupervised approach. In: ICCV (2011)
15. Guyon, I., Dror, G., Lemaire, V., Taylor, G., Aha, D.W.: Unsupervised and transfer learning challenge. In: IJCNN (2011)
16. Hinton, G.E., Osindero, S., Teh, Y.W.: A fast learning algorithm for deep belief nets. Neural Computation 18(7), 1527–1554 (2006)
17. Jiang, W., Zavesky, E., Chang, S.F., Loui, A.: Cross-domain learning methods for high-level visual concept classification. In: ICIP (2008)
18. Krizhevsky, A., Sutskever, I., Hinton, G.E.: Imagenet classification with deep convolutional neural networks. In: NIPS, vol. 1, p. 4 (2012)
19. Le, Q.V., Ranzato, M., Salakhutdinov, R., Ng, A., Tenenbaum, J.: Challenges in learning hierarchical models: Transfer learning and optimization. In: NIPS Workshop (2011)
20. Levin, A., Viola, P., Freund, Y.: Unsupervised improvement of visual detectors using cotraining. In: ICCV (2003)
21. Luo, P., Tian, Y., Wang, X., Tang, X.: Switchable deep network for pedestrian detection. In: CVPR (2014)
22. Mesnil, G., Dauphin, Y., Glorot, X., Rifai, S., Bengio, Y., Goodfellow, I.J., Lavoie, E., Muller, X., Desjardins, G., Warde-Farley, D., et al.: Unsupervised and transfer learning challenge: a deep learning approach. JMLR-Proceedings Track 27, 97–110 (2012)
23. Nair, V., Clark, J.J.: An unsupervised, online learning framework for moving object detection. In: CVPR (2004)
24. Ouyang, W., Wang, X.: Single-pedestrian detection aided by multi-pedestrian detection. In: CVPR (2013)
25. Ouyang, W., Wang, X.: A discriminative deep model for pedestrian detection with occlusion handling. In: CVPR (2012)

26. Ouyang, W., Wang, X.: Joint deep learning for pedestrian detection. In: ICCV (2013)
27. Ouyang, W., Zeng, X., Wang, X.: Modeling mutual visibility relationship in pedestrian detection. In: CVPR (2013)
28. Pang, J., Huang, Q., Yan, S., Jiang, S., Qin, L.: Transferring boosted detectors towards viewpoint and scene adaptiveness. TIP 20(5), 1388–1400 (2011)
29. Rosenberg, C., Hebert, M., Schneiderman, H.: Semi-supervised self-training of object detection models. In: WACV (2005)
30. Roth, P.M., Sternig, S., Grabner, H., Bischof, H.: Classifier grids for robust adaptive object detection. In: CVPR (2009)
31. Sermanet, P., Kavukcuoglu, K., Chintala, S., LeCun, Y.: Pedestrian detection with unsupervised multi-stage feature learning. In: CVPR (2013)
32. Wang, M., Li, W., Wang, X.: Transferring a generic pedestrian detector towards specific scenes. In: CVPR (2012)
33. Wang, M., Wang, X.: Automatic adaptation of a generic pedestrian detector to a specific traffic scene. In: CVPR (2011)
34. Wang, X., Wang, M., Li, W.: Scene-specific pedestrian detection for static video surveillance. TPAMI 36, 361–374 (2014)
35. Wang, X., Hua, G., Han, T.X.: Detection by detections: Non-parametric detector adaptation for a video. In: CVPR (2012)
36. Wu, B., Nevatia, R.: Improving part based object detection by unsupervised, online boosting. In: CVPR (2007)
37. Yang, J., Yan, R., Hauptmann, A.G.: Cross-domain video concept detection using adaptive svms. ACM Multimedia (2007)
38. Yang, Y., Ramanan, D.: Articulated human detection with flexible mixtures of parts. PAMI 35(12), 2878–2890 (2013)
39. Zeng, X., Ouyang, W., Wang, X.: Multi-stage contextual deep learning for pedestrian detection. In: ICCV (2013)

A Contour Completion Model
for Augmenting Surface Reconstructions

Nathan Silberman[1], Lior Shapira[2], Ran Gal[2], and Pushmeet Kohli[3]

[1] Courant Institute, New York University, USA
[2] Microsoft Research, USA
[3] Microsoft Research, Cambridge, UK

Abstract. The availability of commodity depth sensors such as Kinect has enabled development of methods which can densely reconstruct arbitrary scenes. While the results of these methods are accurate and visually appealing, they are quite often incomplete. This is either due to the fact that only part of the space was visible during the data capture process or due to the surfaces being occluded by other objects in the scene. In this paper, we address the problem of completing and refining such reconstructions. We propose a method for scene completion that can infer the layout of the complete room and the full extent of partially occluded objects. We propose a new probabilistic model, Contour Completion Random Fields, that allows us to complete the boundaries of occluded surfaces. We evaluate our method on synthetic and real world reconstructions of 3D scenes and show that it quantitatively and qualitatively outperforms standard methods. We created a large dataset of partial and complete reconstructions which we will make available to the community as a benchmark for the scene completion task. Finally, we demonstrate the practical utility of our algorithm via an augmented-reality application where objects interact with the completed reconstructions inferred by our method.

Keywords: 3D Reconstruction, Scene Completion, Surface Reconstruction, Contour Completion.

1 Introduction

The task of generating dense 3D reconstruction of scenes has seen great progress in the last few years. While part of this progress is due to algorithmic improvements, large strides have been made with the adoption of inexpensive depth cameras and the fusion of color and depth signals. The combined use of depth and colour signals has been successfully demonstrated for the production of large-scale models of indoor scenes via both offline [1] and online [2] algorithms. Most RGB+D reconstruction methods require data that show the scene from a multitude of viewpoints and are not well suited for input sequences which contain a single-view or limited number of viewpoints. Moreover, these reconstruction methods are hindered by occlusion as they make no effort to infer the geometry of parts of the scene that are not visible in the input sequences. Consequently,

D. Fleet et al. (Eds.): ECCV 2014, Part III, LNCS 8691, pp. 488–503, 2014.

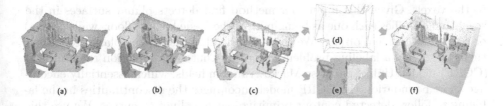

Fig. 1. Overview of the pipeline: Given a dense but incomplete reconstruction (a) we first detect planar regions (b) and classify them into ceiling (not shown), walls (tan), floor (green) and interior surfaces (pink) (c) Non-planar regions are shown in light blue. Next, we infer the scene boundaries(d) and shape of partially occluded interior objects, such as the dining table (e) to produce a complete reconstructed scene (f). Additional visualizations are found in the supplementary material.

the resulting 3D models often contain gaps or holes and do not capture certain basic elements of a scene, such as the true extent and shape of objects and scene surfaces.

Accurate and complete surface reconstruction is of special importance in Augmented Reality (AR) applications which are increasingly being used for both entertainment and commerce. For example, a recently introduced gaming platform [3] asks users to scan an interior scene from multiple angles. Using the densely reconstructed model, the platform overlays graphically generated characters and gaming elements. Furniture retailers (such as IKEA) enable customers to visualize how their furniture will look when installed without having to leave their homes. These applications often require a high fidelity dense reconstruction so that simulated physical phenomenon, such as lighting, shadow and object interactions (e.g. collisions) can be produced in a plausible fashion. Unfortunately, such reconstructions often require considerable effort on the part of the user. Applications either demand that users provide video capture of sufficient viewpoint diversity or operate using an incomplete model of the scene.

Our goal is to complement the surface reconstruction for an input sequence that is limited in viewpoint, and "fill in" parts of the scene that are occluded or not visible to the camera. This goal is driven by both a theoretical motivation and a practical application. Firstly, basic scene understanding requires high level knowledge of how objects interact and extend in 3D spaces. While most scene understanding research is concerned with semantics and pixel labeling, relatively little work has gone into inferring object or surface extent, despite the prevalence and elemental nature of this faculty in humans. Second, online surface reconstruction pipelines such as KinectFusion [2] are highly suitable for AR applications, and could benefit from a scene completion phase, integrated into the pipeline.

Our method assumes a partial dense reconstruction of the scene that is represented as a voxel grid where each voxel can be occupied, free or its state in unknown. We use the KinectFusion [2] method to compute this reconstruction which also assigns a surface normal and truncated signed distance function (TSDF) [4]

to the voxels. Given this input, our method first detects planar surfaces in the
scene and classifies each one as being part of the scene layout (floor, walls ceiling)
or part of an internal object. We then use the identities of the planes to extend
them by solving a labeling problem using our Contour-completion random field
(CCRF) model. Unlike pairwise Markov random fields, which essentially encourage short boundaries, the CCRF model encourages the discontinuities in the labeling to follow detected contour primitives such as lines or curves. We use this
model to complete both the floor map for the scene and estimate the extents of
planar objects in the room. This provides us with a watertight 3D model of the
room. Finally we augment the original input volume to account for our extended
and filled scene. The stages of our algorithm are demonstrated in figure 1.

Our Contributions: This paper makes the following technical contributions:
(1) We introduce the Contour Completion Random Field (CCRF), a novel algorithm for completing or extending contours in 2D scenes. (2) We describe an
algorithm for inferring the extent of a scene and its objects. (3) We demonstrate how to efficiently re-integrate the inferred scene elements into a 3D scene
representation to allow them to be used by a downstream application.

The rest of the paper is organized as follows. We discuss the relationship of
our work to the prior art in dense reconstruction in section 2. In section 3 we
describe how we detect and classify planar surfaces in the scene. In section 4
we discuss how we perform scene completion by inferring the extent of scene
boundaries and extending internal planes using our novel contour completion
MRF. The procedure for augmenting the original (TSDF) based reconstruction
with new values is discussed in section 5. In section 6 we perform qualitative
and quantitative evaluation of our methods and in section 7 discuss our results,
limitations and future work.

2   Related Work

KinectFusion [2] is a real-time dense surface mapping and tracking algorithm.
It maintains an active volume in GPU memory, updated regularly with new
depth observations from a Kinect camera. Each depth frame is tracked using the
iterative closest-point algorithm, and updates the reconstruction volume which
is represented as a truncated signed-distance function (TSDF) grid. At any point
the TSDF volume may be rendered (using ray casting) or transformed into an
explicit surface using marching cubes [5] (or similar algorithm). Our method
extends this pipeline by accessing the TSDF volume at certain key frames, and
augmenting it. As new depth observations reveal previously occluded voxels, our
augmentations are phased out. Our scene completion algorithm may be used to
augment other surface reconstruction methods such as [6,7] with little change.
However, most of these methods have different motivation, and are not real-time.
In SLAM++ [8], a database of 3D models is used during the reconstruction
process. This helps improve tracking, reduces representation size, and augments
the reconstructed scene. However, this method requires intensive preparation

time for each new scene in order to capture the various repeated objects found in each one.

In recent years there have been many papers on scene understanding from a single image. Barinova et al [9] geometrically parse a single image to identify edges, parallel lines and vanishing point, and a level horizon. Hoiem et al [10] estimate the layout of a room from a single image, by using a generalized box detector. This approach is not well suited to completing either highly occluded scenes or non-rectangular objects. Ruiqi and Hoiem [11] attempt to label occluded surfaces using a learning-based approach. This method is limited by the number of classes which can be learned, and does not infer the extent of the hidden objects. A more recent paper by the same authors [12] is more relevant to our approach. They detect a set of supporting horizontal surfaces in a single-image depth frame, and their extent is deduced using the features at each point and surrounding predictions. However, they do not attempt to infer the full scene layout and limit themselves to support-related objects.

Min Kim et al [13] augment and accelerate reconstruction of complex scenes by carefully scanning and modeling objects which repeat in the scene, in advance. These objects (e.g. office chairs, monitors) are then matched in the noisy and incomplete point cloud of the larger scene, and used to augment it. This approach is less suited to capturing a new environment, in which we cannot model the repeating objects independently (given that there are any). Kim et al[14] jointly estimate the 3D reconstruction of a scene, and the semantic labels associated with each voxel, on a coarse 3D volume. Their method works best with simple occlusions and does not extend the volume to estimate the overall shape of the room. Zheng et al [15] employ physical and geometrical reasoning to reconstruct a scene. Their method relies on successful object segmentation, and a Manhattan-world assumption. They fill occluded parts of objects by extrapolating along the major axes of the scene. However, none of these methods can handle previously unseen object and surfaces with non-linear boundaries.

3   Plane Detection and Classification

We now describe how our method detects the dominant planes from the partial voxel based reconstruction. We denote the space of all possible 3D planes by $\mathcal{H}$, and the set of planes present in the scene by H. Let the set of all 3D points visible in the scene be denoted by $\mathcal{P} = \{p_1, ... p_N\}$. We estimate the most probable labeling for H by minimizing the following energy function:

$$H* = \arg \min_{H \subset \mathcal{H}} \sum_{i=1}^{N} f_i(H) + \lambda |H|. \tag{1}$$

where λ is a penalty on the number of planes and f_i is a function that penalizes the number of points not explained by any plane: $f_i(H) = \min\{\min_{h \in H} [\delta(p_i, h), \lambda_b]\}$, where the function δ returns a value of 0 if point p_i falls on plane h and is infinity otherwise. Minimizing the first term alone has the trivial degenerate solution where we include a plane for every point p_i in the set H. However, this situation is avoided by the second terms of the energy which acts as a regularizer and adds a penalty that linearly increases with the cardinality of H.

Lemma 1. *The energy function defined in equation (1) is a supermodular set function.*

Proof in the supplemental material

Computing the Optimal H. Minimization of a super-modular function is an NP-hard problem even when the set of possible elements is finite (which is not true in our case). We employ a greedy strategy, starting from an empty set and repeatedly adding the element that leads to the greatest energy reduction. This method has been observed to achieve a good approximation [16]. We begin by using the Hough transform [17] to select a finite set of planes. In our method, each 3D point and its surface normal votes for a plane equation parameterized by its azimuth θ, elevation ψ and distance from the origin ρ. Each of these votes is accrued in an accumulator matrix of size $A \times E \times D$ where A is the number of azimuth bins, E is the number of elevation bins and D is the number of distance bins [1]. After each point has voted, we run non-maximal suppression to avoid accepting multiple planes that are too similar.

Once we have a set of candidate planes we sort them in descending order by the number of votes they have received and iteratively associate points to each plane. A point can be associated to a plane if it has not been previously associated to any other plane and if its planar disparity and local surface normal difference are small enough [2]. As an additional heuristic, each new plane and its associated points are broken into a set of connected components ensuring that planes are locally connected.

Semantic Labeling. Once we have a set of planes, we classify each one independently into one of four semantic classes: Floor, Wall, Ceiling and Internal. To do so, we train a Random Forest Classifier to predict each plane's class using the ground truth labels and 3D features from [18], which capture attributes of each plane including its height in the room, size and surface normal distribution. Planes classified as one of Floor, Wall and Ceiling will be used for inferring the floor plan and scene boundaries (section 4.6), whereas Internal planes will be extended and filled in a subsequent step (section 4.7).

4   Scene Completion

Given the set of detected and classified planes we infer the true extent of the scene, *ie.* obtain a water-tight room structure, and extend interior planes based on evidence from the scene itself.

---

[1] We use A=128, E=64 and D is found dynamically by spacing bin edges of size 5cm apart between the max and minimum points.
[2] Planar disparity threshold=.1, angular disparity threshold = .1.

4.1 Completion as a Labeling Problem

We now describe how to estimate the boundaries of planes as seen from a top-down view. We formulate boundary completion as a pixel labeling problem. Consider a set S of nodes that represent grid locations in the top-down view of the scene. We assume that a partial labeling of nodes $i \in S$ in the grid can be observed and is encoded by variables $y_i; i \in S$ where $y_i = 1$, $y_i = 0$ and $y_i = -1$ represent that i belongs to the plane, does not belong to the plane, and its membership is uncertain respectively. Given $\mathbf{y}$, we want to estimate the true extent of the plane which we denote by $\mathbf{x}$. Specifically, we will use the binary variable x_i to encode whether the plane covers the location of node i in the top-view. $x_i = 1$ represents that node i belongs to the plane while $x_1 = 0$ represents that it does not.

The traditional approach for pixel labeling problems is to use a pairwise Markov Random Field (MRF) model. The energy of any labeling $\mathbf{y}$ under the pairwise MRF model is defined as: $E(\mathbf{x}) = \sum_{i \in S} \phi_i(x_i) + \sum_{ij \in \mathcal{N}} \phi_{ij}(x_i, x_j)$, where ϕ_i encode the cost of assigning a label x_i and ϕ_{ij} are pairwise potentials that encourage neighboring ($\mathcal{N}$) nodes to take the same label. The unary potential functions force the estimated labels $\mathbf{x}$ to be consistent with the observations $\mathbf{y}$, ie. $\phi_i(x_i) = \inf$ if $y_i \neq -1$ and $x_i \neq y_i$, and $\phi_i(y_i) = 0$ for all other cases, while the pairwise potentials take the form an Ising model. The Maximum a Posteriori (MAP) labeling under the model can be computed in polynomial time using graph cuts. However, the results are underwhelming as the pairwise model does not encode any information about how boundaries should be completed. It simply encourages a labeling that has a small number of transitions.

4.2 Contour Completion Random Field

Unlike the standard MRF which penalizes the number of transitions in the labeling, our Contour Completion Random Field (CCRF) model adds a penalty based on the least number of curve primitives that can explain all the transitions. We implement this by introducing higher order potentials in the model. These potentials are defined over overlapping sets of edges where each set follows some simple (low-dimensional) primitive curve shape such as a line or a circle. Formally, the energy function for the CCRF model can be written as:

$$E(\mathbf{x}) = \sum_{i \in S} \phi_i(x_i) + \sum_{g \in \mathcal{G}} \Psi_g(\mathbf{x}) \tag{2}$$

where Ψ_g are our curve completion potentials, and $\mathcal{G}$ is a set where each curve g represents a set of nodes (edges) that follow a curve. The curve completion potentials have a diminishing returns property. More formally,

$$\Psi_g(\mathbf{x}) = F\left(\sum_{ij \in \mathcal{E}_g} \psi_{ij}(x_i, x_j) \right), \tag{3}$$

where $\mathcal{E}_g$ is the set of edges that defines the curve or edge group g. F is a non-decreasing concave function. In our experiments, we defined F as an upper-bounded linear function ie. $F(t) = \min\{\lambda * t, \theta\}$ where λ is the slope of the function and θ is the upper-bound. It can be seen that once a few edges are cut $t \geq \frac{\theta}{\lambda}$, the rest of the edges in the group can be cut without any penalty. This behavior of the model does not prevent the boundary in the labeling from including large number of edges as long as they belong to the same group (curve). The exact nature of these groups are described below.

4.3 Defining Edge Groups

We consider two types of edge groups: straight lines and parabolas. While previous work has demonstrated the ability of the hough transform [17] to detect other shapes, such as circles and ellipses, such high parameter shapes require substantially more memory and computation and we found lines and parabolas sufficiently flexible to capture most of the cases we encountered.

To detect lines, we used a modified Hough transform to not only detect lines in the image, but also the direction of the transition (the plane to free space or vice-versa). We use an accumulator with 3 parameters: ρ, the distance from the origin to the line, θ, the angle between the vector from the origin to the line and the X axis, and a quaternary variable d, which indicates the direction of the transition (both bottom-top and left-right directions) [3]. Following the accumulation of votes, we run non-maximal suppression and create an edge group for each resulting line.

The standard Hough transform for parabolas requires 4 parameters. To avoid the computational and memory demands of such a design, we introduce a novel and simple heuristic detailed in the supplemental material.

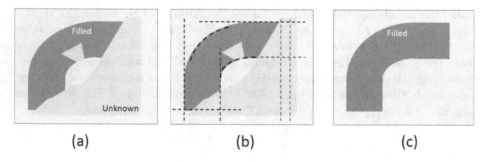

(a)   (b)   (c)

Fig. 2. Contour Completion Random Field: (a) A top-down view of a partially occluded plane (b) We detect lines and parabolas along the contour of the known pixels (stippled black lines), and hallucinate parallel lines (in red) (c) We apply CCRF inference to extend the plane

---

[3] We use 400 angular bins for θ and evenly spaced bins for ρ 1 unit apart. The minimum number of votes allowed was set to 10.

4.4   Hierarchical Edge Groups

While using detected lines or curves may encourage the correct surface boundaries to be inferred in many cases, in others, there is no evidence present in the image of how a shape should be completed. For example see the right side of the shape in figure 2 and the synthetic examples in figure 3(b). Motivated by the gestalt laws of perceptual grouping, we attempt to add edge groups whose use in completion would help provide for shapes that exhibited simple closure and symmetry. More specifically, for each observed line detected, we add addition parallel edge groups on the occluded side of the shape.

It is clear that defining edge groups that completely cover another edge group would lead to double counting. To prevent this, we modify the formulation to ensure that only one group from each hierarchy of edge groups is counted. To be precise, our CCRF model allows edge groups to be organized hierarchically so that a set of possible edges have a parent and only a single child per parent may be active. This formulation is formalised as:

$$E(\mathbf{x}) = \sum_{i \in \mathcal{S}} \phi_i(x_i) + \sum_{g \in \mathcal{G}} \min_{k \in c(g)} \Psi_k(\mathbf{x}) \tag{4}$$

where $c(g)$ denotes the set of child edge groups for each parent g.

To summarize, our edge groups are obtained by fitting lines and parabolas to the input image thus encouraging transitions that are consistent with these edges. As indicated in Equation 4, not all edge groups can be active simultaneously and in particular, any line used to hallucinate a series of edges is considered the parent to its child hallucinated lines. Consequently, we constrain only a single hallucinated line to be active (at most) at a time.

4.5   Inference with Hierarchical Edge Groups

Inference under higher order potentials defined over edges groups was recently shown to be NP-hard even for binary random variables by Jegelka et al. [19]. They proposed a special purpose iterative algorithm for performing approximate inference in this model. Later, Kohli et al. [20] proposed an approximate method that could deal with multi-label variables. Their method transformed edge group potentials into a sum of pairwise potentials with the addition of auxiliary variables that allowed the use of standard inference method like graph cuts. However, both these algorithms are unsuitable for CCRF because of the special hierarchical structure defined over our edge groups.

Inspired from [20], we transformed the higher-order curve completion potential (3) to the following pairwise form:

$$\Psi_g^p(\mathbf{x}) = T + \min_{h_g, \mathbf{z}} \Big\{ \sum_{ij \in \mathcal{E}_g} \theta_{ij}((x_i + x_j - 2z_{ij})h_g - 2(x_i + x_j)z_{ij} + 4z_{ij}) - Th_g \Big\}. \tag{5}$$

where h_g is the binary auxiliary corresponding to the group g, and $z_{ij}, \forall ij \in \mathcal{E}_g$ are binary auxiliary variables corresponding to the edges that constitute the edge group g. However, this transformation deviates from the energy of the hierarchical CCRF (equation 4) as it allows multiple edge groups in the hierarchy to be all active at once.

To enure that only one edge group is active in each edge group hierarchy, we introduce a series of constraints on the binary auxiliary variables corresponding to the edge groups. More formally, we minimize the following energy :

$$E(\mathbf{x}) = \sum_{i \in \mathcal{S}} \phi_i(x_i) + \sum_{g \in \mathcal{G}} \Psi_g^p(\mathbf{x}) \qquad \text{s.t.} \forall g, \qquad \sum_{k \in c(g)} h_k \leq 1 \qquad (6)$$

where $c(g)$ denotes the set of child edge groups for each parent edge group g. The minimum energy configuration of this formulation is equivalent to that of hierarchical CCRF (equation 4).

In order to find the MAP solution, we now need to minimize the constrained pairwise energy function (equation 6). We observe that on fixing the values of the group auxiliary variable (h's) the resulting energy becomes unconstrained and submodular, and thus, can be minimized using graph cuts. We use this observation to do inference by exhaustively searching over the space of edge group auxiliary variables and minimizes the rest of the energy using graph cuts. However, we can make the algorithm even more efficient by not allow the activity of a child edge group to be explored if its parent is not already active. In other words, we start by exhaustively searching over the auxiliary variables of the parent edge groups (at the top of the hierarchy), and if a group variable is found to be active, we check if its child variables can be made active instead of it.

4.6   Inferring Scene Boundaries

To extend and fill the scene boundaries, we begin by projecting the free space of the input TSDF and the Wall planes (predicted by our classifier) onto the floor plane. Given a 2D point cloud induced by these projections, we discretize the points to form a projection image illustrated by figure 2 where each pixel y_i takes on the value of free space, wall or unknown. To infer the full scene layout, we apply the CCRF (Equation 2) to infer the values of the unknown pixels. In this case, we consider free space to be the area to be expanded ($y_i = 1$) and the walls to be the surrounding area to avoid being filled ($y_i = 0$). We first detect the lines and curves of the walls to create a series of edge groups. Next, we set $\phi_i(x_i = 1) = \infty$ if $y_i = 0$ and $\phi_i(x_i = 0) = \infty$ if $y_i = 1$. Finally, we add a slight bias [6] to assigning free space $\phi_i(x_i = 0) = \epsilon$ [4].

4.7   Extending Planar Surfaces

Once the scene boundary has been completed, we infer the full extent of internal planar surfaces. For each internal plane, we project the TSDF onto the detected 2D plane as follows. First we find a coordinate basis for the plane using PCA

---

[4] ϵ=1e-6.

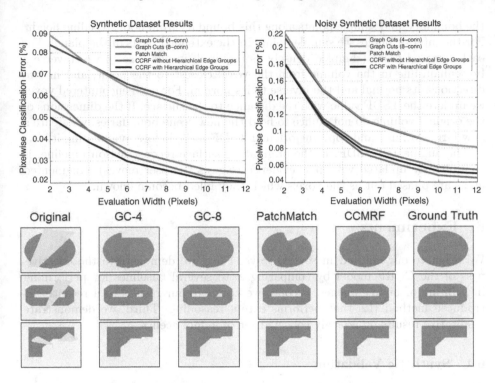

Fig. 3. (Top) Pixel-wise classification error on our synthetic dataset. The plot demonstrates performance as a function of the width of the evaluation region. (Bottom) Some examples from our dataset of synthetic images showing classification results for occluded pixels (yellow) using four methods.

and estimate the major and and minor axes of the plane, M and N, respectively. Next, we create an image of size $2N + 1 \times 2M + 1$ where the center pixel of the image corresponds to the centroid of the plane. We sample a grid along the plane basis of size $2N + 1 \times 2M + 1$ where the TSDF values sampled in each grid location are used to assign each of the image's pixels. If the sampled TSDF value is occupied, y_i is set to 1, if its free space y_i is set to 0 and if its unknown, y_i is set to -1. In practice, we also sample several voxels *away* from the plane (along the surface normal direction). This heuristic has the effect of reducing the effects of sensor noise and error from plane fitting.

Once Y has been created, we detect all lines and parabolas in the image and hallucinate the necessary lines to create our edge groups. Next, we assign the local potentials in the same manner as described in Section 4.6.

5 Augmenting the Original Volume

The result of our scene completion is a water-tight scene boundary, and extended interior planes. As the final step in our pipeline we augment the original TSDF we imported. For the scene boundary we simplify the resutling polyline representing the boundary, and sample points along this boundary from floor to ceiling height. For the interior planes we sample points in the extended parts of the planes. For each sampled point (sampled densely as required, in our case γ) we traverse a bresenham-line in the volume from the voxel closest to the point, and in two directions, its normal and the inverse to its normal. For each encountered voxel, we update the TSDF value with the distance to the surface. If the dimensions of the original volume do not suffice to hold the new scene boundaries, we create a new larger volume and copy the original TSDF to it, before augmenting it.

The augmented TSDF, in the originating surface reconstruction pipeline, is continuously updated with new evidence (e.g. as the user moves). Augmented areas are phased out as the voxels which they filled become known.

6 Experiments

We evaluate our method in several ways. First, we demonstrate the effectiveness of the CCRF model by comparing it to several baselines for performing in-painting of binary images. Second, we compare our results to a recently introduced method [12] that performs extent-reasoning. Third, we demonstrate qualitative results on a newly collected set of indoor scenes.

6.1 Synthetic Validation

We generated a dataset of synthetic images inspired by shapes of planar surfaces commonly found in indoor scenes. The dataset contained 16 prototypical shapes meant to resemble objects like desks, conference tables, beds, kitchen counters, etc. The set of 16 protypes were first divided into training and test sets so that we could identify the ideal parameters of each model using the training set. Each of the 8 training and testing prototypes were then randomly rotated and occluded 10 times resulting in 80 total training and 80 test images. Additionally, we created a noisy version of each image by randomly perturbing the observed labels near the boundaries of each shape.

Since we are primarily concerned with how these methods perform in predicting the boundaries of the input images, we use the evaluation metric of [21] in which we only evaluate the correctness of pixels immediately near the boundary areas. We computed evaluation scores for various widths of the evaluation region. Quantitative results can be found in Figure 3. We compare against several baseline methods that are commonly used for in-painting binary images. These include both 4 connected and 8 connected graph cuts and a non-parametric patch-matching algorithm for in-painting. The ideal parameters for each algorithm were fine tuned on the training set and then applied to the test set.

6.2 Single Frame Scene Completion

We compare our approach to the work of Guo and Hoiem [12] to demonstrate its applicability to single frame scene completion. While we produce a binary label indicating the voxels that are occupied, [12] output a heat map. Therefore, for each frame of the NYU V2 dataset [18] we computed the filled voxels using our regular pipeline. Since KinectFusion was not designed for single image inputs, a small number of images failed to be fused and were ignored during evaluation. For the rest we used the metric of [12] and report the accuracy using the same false positive rate as in our method.

[12] achieved 62.6% accuracy compared to our 60.6%. This demonstrates that while our method was not meant for single frame completion, and does not use RGB data, it achieves comparable results. For visual comparisons see figure 4.

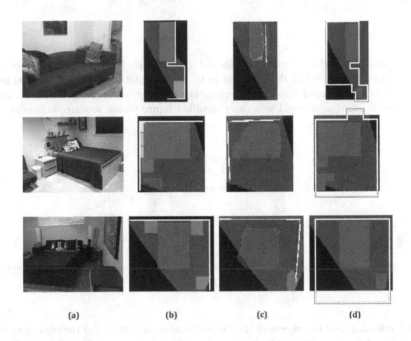

(a)   (b)   (c)   (d)

Fig. 4. Comparison with [12]: (a) Frames from the NYU2 dataset (b) Ground truth support extent. Support surfaces in red, observed free space in light blue, unobserved regions in black (c) Predicted extent from [12] (d) Our inferred object extents, with inferred room boundaries in white.

6.3 Qualitative Analysis

Using a Kinect Sensor attached to a notebook computer, we captured more than 100 scenes. Each scene is a collection of color and depth frames ranging from hundreds to thousands of frames. Each of these sequences was input into the KinectFusion pipeline, where for a large number of scenes we performed multiple reconstructions, sharing a starting frame, but varying in number of frames processed. This gave us a baseline for a qualitative and progressive evaluation of our results.

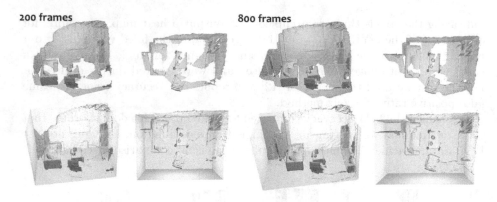

Fig. 5. Progressive surface reconstruction and scene completion. After 200 frames large parts of the room are occluded, and filled in by the completion model. After 800 previously occluded areas are observed and replace the completion, and overall the structure of the room is more accurate. For a more detailed figure please see supplementary material.

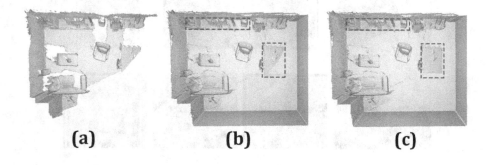

(a)   **(b)**   **(c)**

Fig. 6. Understanding the effects of the hierarchical edge groups. (a) the observed scene with predicted floors in line, walls in blue and internal planar surfaces in pink (b) the filled scene without hierarchical edge groups (c) the filled scene with hierarchical edge groups.

For each such scene we were able to evaluate the original augmented and original reconstruction at each step. As more evidence is revealed, extended planes are replaced with their physical counterparts, and the scene boundaries are updated to reflect reality. A sample progression can be seen in figure 5. Additional results can be seen in figure 8(top row) and the supplemental material.

We implemented a complete AR system in the Unity 3D framework, in which a user is able to navigate a captured scene, place virtual objects on horizontal supporting planes, and throw balls which bounce around the scene. As seen in figure 7, with scene completion, we are able to place figures on occluded planes, and bounce balls realistically off completed surfaces. Video captured results can be seen in the supplemental materials.

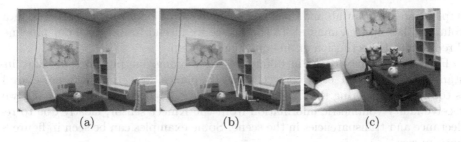

(a)   (b)   (c)

Fig. 7. We created an augmented reality application to demonstrate our results. (a) a ball bouncing on an occluded floor falls through (b) a ball bouncing on the floor in a completed scene bounces realistically (c) Virtual objects may be placed on any surface, including occluded planes in the completed scene. The scene shown is the same as in figure 5. *Video clips of this application can be seen in the supplemental material.*

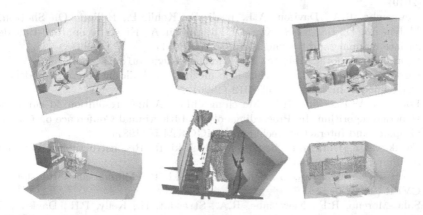

Fig. 8. Example scenes: darker colors represent completed areas, hues signify plane classification. The top row contains mostly successful completions. The bottom row contains failure cases, on the left the room is huge due to many reflective surfaces, the middle image is of a staircase, vertical in nature, which leads to incorrect plane classifications. And on the right a high ceiling and windows cause misclassification of the floor plane.

7   Discussion and Future Work

We have presented a complete and novel pipeline for surface reconstruction augmentation via scene completion. Our novel contour completion MRF algorithm is able to extend occluded surfaces in a believable manner, paving way for enhanced AR applications. In this work we have focused on extending planar surfaces and estimating scene boundaries, however we recognize the value in augmenting volumetric (non-planar) objects and intend to address it in future work. Moreover, in this work we do not rely on previously seen objects, nor on repetition in the scene, both of which we intend to employ in future work. Our current pipeline is implemented in Matlab and does not achieve online performance (processing a volume takes up to a minute). In the future we intend to integrate our pipeline directly into KinectFusion or an equivalent system.

Failure cases may occur in different stages along our pipeline. In some instances we fail to detect or correctly classify planes. Sometimes the noise level is too high, hampering the CCRF from fitting good contours. In some cases we receive faulty volumetric information from the Kinect sensor, mostly due to reflectance and transparencies in the scene. Some examples can be seen in figure 8 bottom row.

References

1. Henry, P., Krainin, M., Herbst, E., Ren, X., Fox, D.: Rgb-d mapping: Using depth cameras for dense 3d modeling of indoor environments. In: ISER, vol. 20, pp. 22–25 (2010)
2. Newcombe, R.A., Davison, A.J., Izadi, S., Kohli, P., Hilliges, O., Shotton, J., Molyneaux, D., Hodges, S., Kim, D., Fitzgibbon, A.: Kinectfusion: Real-time dense surface mapping and tracking. In: ISMAR (2011)
3. Qualcomm: Vuforia. Website (2011), https://www.vuforia.com/
4. Curless, B., Levoy, M.: A volumetric method for building complex models from range images. In: CGI, pp. 303–312 (1996)
5. Lorensen, W.E., Cline, H.E.: Marching cubes: A high resolution 3d surface construction algorithm. In: Proceedings of the 14th Annual Conference on Computer Graphics and Interactive Techniques, SIGGRAPH (1987)
6. Furukawa, Y., Curless, B., Seitz, S.M., Szeliski, R.: Reconstructing building interiors from images. In: ICCV (2009)
7. Furukawa, Y., Curless, B., Seitz, S., Szeliski, R.: Manhattan-world stereo. In: CVPR (2009)
8. Salas-Moreno, R.F., Newcombe, R.A., Strasdat, H., Kelly, P.H., Davison, A.J.: Slam++: Simultaneous localisation and mapping at the level of objects. In: CVPR (June 2013)
9. Barinova, O., Lempitsky, V., Tretiak, E., Kohli, P.: Geometric image parsing in man-made environments. In: Daniilidis, K., Maragos, P., Paragios, N. (eds.) ECCV 2010, Part II. LNCS, vol. 6312, pp. 57–70. Springer, Heidelberg (2010)
10. Hoiem, D., Hedau, V., Forsyth, D.: Recovering free space of indoor scenes from a single image (2012)
11. Guo, R., Hoiem, D.: Beyond the line of sight: Labeling the underlying surfaces. In: Fitzgibbon, A., Lazebnik, S., Perona, P., Sato, Y., Schmid, C. (eds.) ECCV 2012, Part V. LNCS, vol. 7576, pp. 761–774. Springer, Heidelberg (2012)
12. Guo, R., Hoiem, D.: Support surface prediction in indoor scenes. In: ICCV (2013)
13. Kim, Y.M., Mitra, N.J., Yan, D.M., Guibas, L.: Acquiring 3d indoor environments with variability and repetition. ACM Transactions on Graphics 31(6) (2012)
14. Soo Kim, B., Kohli, P., Savarese, S.: 3d scene understanding by voxel-crf. In: ICCV (2013)
15. Zheng, B., Zhao, Y., Yu, J.C., Ikeuchi, K., Zhu, S.C.: Beyond point clouds: Scene understanding by reasoning geometry and physics. In: CVPR (2013)
16. Nemhauser, G.L., Wolsey, L.A., Fisher, M.L.: An analysis of approximations for maximizing submodular set functions–I. Mathematical Programming 14(1), 265–294 (1978)

17. Duda, R.O., Hart, P.E.: Use of the hough transformation to detect lines and curves in pictures. Communications of the ACM 15(1), 11–15 (1972)
18. Silberman, N., Hoiem, D., Kohli, P., Fergus, R.: Indoor segmentation and support inference from RGBD images. In: Fitzgibbon, A., Lazebnik, S., Perona, P., Sato, Y., Schmid, C. (eds.) ECCV 2012, Part V. LNCS, vol. 7576, pp. 746–760. Springer, Heidelberg (2012)
19. Jegelka, S., Bilmes, J.: Submodularity beyond submodular energies: Coupling edges in graph cuts. In: CVPR (2011)
20. Kohli, P., Osokin, A., Jegelka, S.: A principled deep random field model for image segmentation. In: CVPR (2013)
21. Kohli, P., Torr, P.H., et al.: Robust higher order potentials for enforcing label consistency. IJCV 82(3) (2009)

Interactive Object Counting

Carlos Arteta[1], Victor Lempitsky[2], J. Alison Noble[1], and Andrew Zisserman[1]

[1] Department of Engineering Science, University of Oxford, UK
[2] Skolkovo Institute of Science and Technology (Skoltech), Russia

Abstract. Our objective is to count (and localize) object instances in an image *interactively*. We target the regime where individual object detectors do not work reliably due to crowding, or overlap, or size of the instances, and take the approach of estimating an object density.

Our main contribution is an interactive counting system, along with solutions for its main components. Thus, we develop a feature vocabulary that can be efficiently learnt on-the-fly as a user provides dot annotations – this enables densities to be generated in an interactive system. Furthermore, we show that object density can be estimated simply, accurately and efficiently using ridge regression – this matches the counting accuracy of the much more costly learning-to-count method. Finally, we propose two novel visualization methods for region counts that are efficient and effective – these enable integral count regions to be displayed to quickly determine annotation points for relevance feedback.

The interactive system is demonstrated on a variety of visual material, including photographs, microscopy and satellite images.

Keywords: Interactive vision systems, object counting, relevance feedback, visual recognition, biomedical image analysis.

1 Introduction

Counting instances of an object in crowded scenes is a tedious task frequently encountered in biology, remote sensing and surveillance data analysis. Towards this goal, several computer vision approaches that use machine learning in order to automate such tasks have been suggested [5, 8, 10, 12]. These methods are however limited to the scenarios where it is possible to collect and to manually annotate a representative set of training images. Systematic differences in the visual appearance or in the geometrical patterns between the training and the test images pose challenges for these methods and may result in systematic counting biases. This can be a serious limitation for practitioners, as e.g. any change of experimental protocol/conditions in a biological experiment might require reannotation and retraining.

Here, we present a system that addresses the counting task through *interactive* machine learning. In our case, the user annotates (i.e. with dots) the objects that belong to a representative but potentially small part of an image and the system propagates the annotations to the rest of the image. The results are then presented to the user, who then has the option to annotate another part of the image where the system has made significant errors. When the user is satisfied with the result, the system provides the count of the objects in the image. Our unoptimized MATLAB implementation takes at most a

D. Fleet et al. (Eds.): ECCV 2014, Part III, LNCS 8691, pp. 504–518, 2014.

few seconds for each iteration of the relevance feedback that includes recomputation of the features, discriminative (re)training, and visualization.

The approaches that cast the counting problem as one of object density estimation [5, 8, 10, 12] have so far been more accurate and also faster than approaches that detect individual instances. For this reason, we base our system around object density estimation. Counting through density estimation works by learning a mapping $\mathcal{F} : \mathcal{X} \mapsto \mathcal{Y}$ between local image features $\mathcal{X}$ and object density $\mathcal{Y}$, which then allows the derivation of an estimated object density map for unseen images (or non-annotated parts of an image in our case). If the learning is successful, integrating over regions in the estimated density map provides an object count within such regions. The accuracy of the density estimation depends crucially on the choice of local image features. Another important aspect of density-based counting is that density per se is not informative for a human user and cannot be used directly to verify the accuracy of the counting (and to provide feedback).

To address this aspect, and to achieve the processing speed demanded by the interactive scenario, we make the following three contributions. First, we propose a simplified approach for supervised density learning based on ridge regression (i.e. simple linear algebra operations). We show that even in the traditional batch mode (i.e. when learning from a set of annotated images and applying to a number of similar images) this approach achieves similar counting accuracy to the constraint-generation based learning in [12] (using the same features), while being dramatically faster to train, which is crucial for an interactive system. Furthermore, we propose two ways to visualize the estimated density, so that counting mistakes are easily identifiable by the user. This allows our system to incorporate user feedback in an interactive regime according to the user's own criterion of goodness. Finally, we propose an online codebook learning [20] that, in real-time, re-estimates low-level feature encoding as the user annotates progressively larger parts of an image. Such feature re-estimation (together with fast supervised density estimation) allows our system to avoid severe under- or over-fitting, whenever a small or a large part of an image is annotated.

In summary, this work presents a system for counting multiple instances of an object class in crowded scenes that *(i)* can be used interactively as it is fast to compute and can re-use the results from previous iterations, *(ii)* uses the simplicity and ease of computation of ridge regression, and *(iii)* presents the density estimation results in intuitive ways such that it is easy to know where further annotations may be required. We show the performance of the method in some of the typical applications for counting and detection methods such as counting cells in microscopy images, and various objects of interest in aerial images.

1.1 Related Work

Interactive Computer Vision: To the best of our knowledge, this is the first time an interactive counting system has been proposed. Nevertheless, interactive learning methods have been popular in computer vision as they provide the users with tools that can immediately and significantly alleviate tedious and time-consuming tasks, without the need to carefully prepare training datasets. The most common examples are the general purpose image segmentation methods [4, 16] which are still widely used today in real

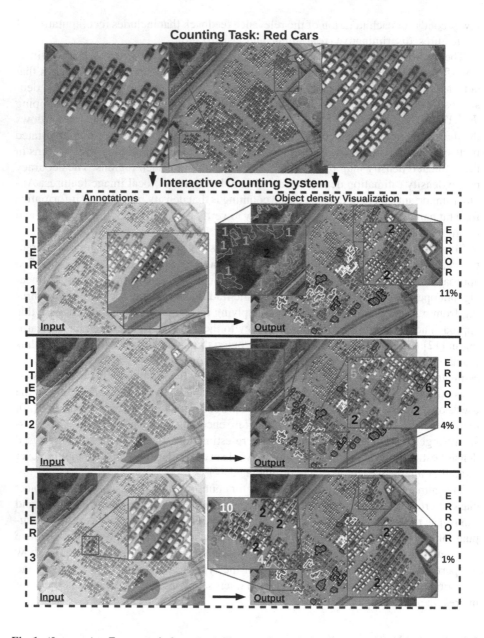

Fig. 1. *(Interactive Framework Overview)* Given an input image (or set of images) containing multiple instances of an object, our framework learns from regions with dot-annotations placed by the user in order to compute a map of *object density* for the non-annotated regions. The left column shows the annotated pixels provided by the user – all regions in the annotation images *outside* the green mask (i.e. with or without dot-annotations) are used as observations in the regression. The right column shown the intuitive visualization tool of the density estimation that allows the user to inspect the results and add further annotations where required in order to refine the output of the counting framework.

applications. Interactive image segmentation methods have also been widely adopted in medical imaging [9, 19, 20] where not only is it difficult to prepare datasets, but also users need to have the possibility of refining results in real-time. More recently, interactive methods have been applied to object detection [25] and learning of edge models for image partitioning [21], which is also highly relevant for biological image analysis. We expect this paper to bring the general benefits of interactive learning to counting problems.

Counting through Object Density Estimation: Counting objects in images without explicit object detection is a simplified alternative for cases where only the number of objects is required; it has proved to be especially useful in those tasks too challenging for object detectors such as crowded scenes. Initial efforts in this class of methods attempted to learn global counts through regressors from image-level [6, 11] or region-level [5, 13, 17] features to the total number of objects in it. However, these approaches ignored the local arrangements of the objects of interest. Towards this end, [12] proposed learning pixel-level object *density* through the minimization of the $MESA$ distance, a cost function specially tailored for the counting problem. Following [12], [8] proposed a simplified version of the object density estimator based on random forest, which represented an improvement in training time. Generating a pixel-level object density estimation not only has the advantage of estimating object counts in any region of the image, but can also be used to boost the confidence of object detectors as shown in [15]. Our approach follows the ideas in [8, 12] and further simplifies the learning to a few algebraic operations using a ridge regression, thus enabling an interactive application. Note that the learning approach proposed here should not be confused with the ridge regression used as baseline in [12], which belongs to the category of image-level regressors.

2 Interactive System Overview

Given an image $\mathcal{I}$, the counting proceeds within a feedback loop. At each iteration, the user marks a certain portion of an image using a freehand selection tool (we refer to pixels being included into such regions as *annotated pixels*). Then the user *dots* the objects, by clicking once on each object of interest within this annotation region. In the first iteration, the user also marks a diameter of a typical object of an image by placing a line segment over such a typical object.

At each iteration, given the set of dotted pixels $\mathcal{P}$ placed by the user on top of objects of interest in $\mathcal{I}$, our system aims to (1) build a codebook $\mathcal{X}$ of low-level features, (2) learn a mapping $\mathcal{F} : \mathcal{X} \mapsto \mathcal{Y}$ from the entries in the codebook $\mathcal{X}$ to an object density $\mathcal{Y}$, (3) use the learned mapping $\mathcal{F}$ to estimate the object density in the entire image $\mathcal{I}$, and (4) present the estimated object density map to the user through an intuitive visualization. The estimated object density map produced is such that integrating over a region of interest gives the estimated number of objects in it (e.g. integrating over the entire map gives an estimate of the total number of objects of interest in $\mathcal{I}$). By using the density visualization, the user can easily spot significant errors in the object density estimate, and can proceed to provide further annotations to refine the results in a next iteration of the process. An example with three iterations is shown in Figure 1. In practice, only a small portion or few small portions of a potentially large image have to be inspected in order to validate the correctness of the learned model or to identify parts with gross errors.

The first design requirement for an interactive counting system, such as the above, is that the codebook needs to be fast to compute, and adapt its size according to the amount of annotations in order to prevent under- or over-fitting. To address these problems, we propose in Section 3 a simple progressive codebook learning procedure, which builds a kd-tree that can grow from its current state as the user provides further annotations. The second requirement is a fast computation of the mapping $\mathcal{F}$. Our proposal is a pixel-level ridge regression presented in Section 4, which has a closed-form solution. Thus, the mapping $\mathcal{F}$ can be computed extremely fast through a few algebraic operations on sparse matrices. Finally, the system needs to present its current estimates to the user in such a way that identifying errors can be done through a quick visual inspection, which is not possible with the raw object density map and/or the global count. Therefore, we propose in Section 5 two methods to visualize object density maps by generating local "summaries" of it.

We show the performance of the interactive counting system through a series of examples in the experimental section, and videos of the interactive process are provided in [1].

3   Progressive Codebook Learning

Initially, we represent each pixel p of an image $\mathcal{I}$ with a d-dimensional real-valued vector $z_p \in \mathbf{R}^d$. The idea of building a codebook on top of these low-level features is to subdivide the feature space into k cells, so that the typical density for appearance patterns falling into each cell is roughly constant. Ideally, we want to strike a balance between two conflicting goals. Firstly, we want to partition the feature space finely enough to avoid underfitting. Secondly, we want each of the partitions to have at least several pixels that belong to the area annotated by the user in order to avoid overfitting. The latter requirement leads to the idea of interactive re-estimation of the feature space partition as more annotations become progressively available. This can be done very efficiently with the following algorithm.

We initialize the feature space partitioning by assigning all image pixels to the same partition. We then proceed recursively by splitting the partitions that contain more than N "annotated" pixels assigned to them ("annotated" here means belonging to the user-annotated area). Here, N is a meta-parameter selected by the user, which we set to 200 in our experiments. In more detail, the algorithms proceed as follows:

1. In the i-th iteration, find the partitions with more than N descriptors z_p assigned to it (only annotated pixels are taken into account).
2. For each of those partitions, find the feature dimension t of maximum variance (among the d dimensions), as well as the median of the values of all annotated pixels corresponding to this dimension.
3. Split such a partition into two according to whether a pixel value at the dimension t is greater or smaller then the median.
4. Repeat until every partition has less than N annotated pixels assigned to it.

The proposed algorithm thus constructs the kd-tree (w.r.t. the annotated pixels). Note, however, that we also maintain the partition assignments of the unannotated pixels (and the resulting partitions can be unbalanced w.r.t. the unannotated pixels). We finally note that there is no need to store the resulting kd-tree explicitly because the algorithm maintains the assignments of pixels to the leaves of the kd-tree (i.e. partitions). The partitioning algorithm is resumed whenever new annotations are added by the user. At this point, the codebook can grow from its current state by continuing the splitting (and is not re-learned from scratch).

Once the codebook has been learned, each pixel p in the image $\mathcal{I}$ is represented by a sparse k-dimensional vector x_p, where all entries are zero except the one corresponding to the partition to which the image descriptor z_p was assigned ("one-hot" encoding). The representation x_p is then used as the pixel features within the learning framework proposed in Section 4. Once again, we emphasize that the vector x_p changes (and becomes more high-dimensional) between the learning rounds as more user annotations become available.

4 Counting with Ridge Regression

We now introduce our simple alternative to [12] for learning an object density estimator. Our method here is similar to (and, arguably, simpler than) [8]. Most importantly, compared to [12], our approach reduces the training time from several dozens of seconds to a few seconds (for heavily annotated images), thus enabling the interaction.

Similarly to [8, 12], we define the ground truth density from the set of user dot-annotations $\mathcal{P}$ as the sum of delta functions centred on each of the annotation dots:

$$F^0(p) = \sum_{p' \in \mathcal{P}} \delta(p - p') , \qquad (1)$$

where p is the (x, y) position of a pixel.

We want to learn the mapping $\mathcal{F} : \mathcal{X} \mapsto \mathcal{Y}$ from local image features to a ground truth object density using ridge regression. Let us assume that each pixel p in a training image $\mathcal{I}$ is represented with a sparse vector $x_p \in R^k$ from a learned codebook. At the same time, each pixel is associated with a real-valued ground truth object density $y_p \in R$ according to $F^0(p)$. The ridge regression finds a k-dimensional vector of coefficients w that minimizes the following objective:

$$||Xw - Y||^2 + \lambda||w||^2 \to \min_w \qquad (2)$$

Here, X is the matrix of predictors (feature vectors) with each row containing x_p, Y is a vector of corresponding density values from the ground truth density F^0 and λ controls the balance between prediction error and regularization of w. Although computationally simple and efficient, the fitting procedure (2) tries to match the ground truth density values exactly in every pixel, which is unnecessary and leads to severe overfitting. Instead, as was argued in [12], the estimated densities Xw should match the ground truth densities Y when integrated over extended image regions (i.e. we do not care about very local deviations between Xw and Y as long as these deviations are unbiased and sum approximately to zero over extended regions).

Based on this motivation, [12] replaces the L2-distance between Xw and Y in (2) by the so called MESA-distance which looks at integrals over all possible box regions. While this change of distance dramatically improves the generalization, the learning with MESA-distance is costly as it employs constraint generation and has to solve a large number of quadratic programs. Here, we propose another, much simpler, alternative for the L2-distance in (2). Namely, we minimize a smoothed version of the objective by convolving the difference between the ground truth density and the estimated density with a Gaussian kernel:

$$||G * (Xw - Y)||^2 + \lambda||w||^2 \to \min_w \qquad (3)$$

Here, $G*$ denotes (with a slight abuse of notation) the Gaussian smoothing over the image plane (i.e. the column vector has to be reshaped back to the image dimensions and smoothed spatially). Typically, we use a sufficiently large isotropic covariance to ensure that the local unbiased deviations between Xw and Y are smoothed (so that "excesses" and "deficits" cancel each other). We found that the performance of the estimated w on the test set is not sensitive to large variation in the covariance (as long as the covariance parameter σ within G is greater than say half a typical object diameter). As we will show below, such smoothing is crucial for good performance of the counting.

Because of the linearity of the convolution, we can rewrite (3) as:

$$||(G * X)w - G * Y)||^2 + \lambda||w||^2 \to \min_w , \qquad (4)$$

where $(G * X)$ denotes Gaussian smoothing applied to each column of X.

Importantly, (4) can be regarded as ridge regression between the smoothed version of the feature maps $G * X$ and the smoothed ground truth density. The latter can be seen as the sum of Gaussian kernels centered on the user annotations:

$$F^0(p) = \sum_{p' \in \mathcal{P}} \mathcal{N}(p', \sigma) \qquad (5)$$

Similarly, the smoothed (but still sparse) matrix of predictors $G * X$ can be obtained by convolving independently each dimension of the feature vectors (i.e. each column of X), that is, spatially blurring each of the feature channels.

Using the vertically concatenated smoothed maps $X_s = [G * X]$ and $Y_s = [G * Y]$ respectively, w can be expressed using a standard ridge regression solution formula:

$$w = (X_s^T X_s + \lambda \Gamma^T \Gamma)^{-1} X_s^T Y_s , \qquad (6)$$

where Γ denotes the identity matrix and λ is a regularization parameter.

Finally, for a non-annotated region of image $\mathcal{I}$, the density value at pixel p can be obtained using the estimated w through a simple linear transform of the non-smoothed feature vectors x_p (i.e. in the same way as in [12]):

$$F(p) = w^T x_p \qquad (7)$$

It can be seen that learning the mapping vector w only involves simple matrix operations (mostly on sparse matrices) and Gaussian smoothing. Thus, w can be learned on-the-fly and with a low memory footprint.

We have found that the generalization performance is improved slightly if the non-negativity of the estimated w is enforced (which for non-negative x_p results in physically meaningful non-negative object densities at test time). Since it is computationally more expensive to include a non-negativity constraint within ridge regression in a principled manner (compared to the closed-form solution provided by unconstrained ridge regression), we use a simple trick of iteratively re-running ridge regression, while clipping the components of w having negative values to zero after each iteration.

4.1 Experimental Validation of Ridge Regression Counting

We now evaluate the counting method based on ridge regression and determine how it compares to previous work in the area that uses traditional batch processing (i.e. non-interactive). In particular, we compare to the most related approach [12] (using the same features, the same datasets, and the same experimental protocols as in [12]).

Table 1 shows the experimental results on the USCD pedestrian dataset [5], which consists of 2000 frames of dot-annotated pedestrians from a surveillance camera video. Table 2 shows the results on the synthetic cell dataset presented in [12]. The dataset

Table 1. Mean absolute errors for people counting in the UCSD surveillance camera video [5]. The columns correspond to four training/testing splits of the data ('maximal', 'downscale', 'upscale', 'minimal') proposed in [17]. The average number of people per image in each of the testing sets is shown in brackets on the top row. ⋆ indicates the methods tested with the same set of features. The proposed method (bottom line) matches on average the performance of the previous best method for the same features.

	'max' [28.25]	'down' [24.35]	'up' [29.68]	'min' [28.25]
Global count [11]	2.07	2.66	2.78	N/A
Segment+Count [17]	1.53	1.64	1.84	1.31
Density estimation (MESA) [12] ⋆	1.70	1.28	1.59	2.02
Density estimation (RF) [8]	1.70	2.16	1.61	2.20
Density estimation (proposed) ⋆	1.24	1.31	1.69	1.49

consists of 200 synthetic images of cells in fluorescence microscopy, with an average of 174 ± 64 cells per image. Between 1 and 32 images are used for training and validation,while testing is performed on a set of 100 images. The procedure is repeated for five different sets of N images, and the mean absolute counting errors and standard deviations are reported for different values of N. We additionally include the result of the method that does not blur the feature channels, and thus uses (2) rather than (3) as a learning criterion (in the special case of one-hot encoding and $\lambda = 0$, it simply corresponds to averaging the GT density value corresponding to each codeword in the dictionary). The inferior performance of this baseline highlights the importance of the smoothing in (3).

It can be seen from Table 1 and Table 2 that using simple ridge regression never results in a significant drop in performance compared to the more complex approach in [12], and thus, we use it as part of our interactive system (described next) without

Table 2. Mean absolute errors for cell counting in the synthetic cell dataset [12]. The columns correspond to the different sizes of the training and validation sets. ⋆ indicates the methods that use the same features. The proposed method (bottom line) matches the performance of the previous best method for the same features. The version that does not smooth the difference between the estimated and the GT density when evaluating the solution, performs considerably worse. The method [8] achieves lower counting error in this case, however it uses different and much stronger features learned in a supervised fashion.

	N = 1	N = 2	N = 4	N = 8	N = 16	N = 32
Img-level ridge reg. [12] ⋆	67.3 ± 25.2	37.7 ± 14.0	16.7 ± 3.1	8.8 ± 1.5	6.4 ± 0.7	5.9 ± 0.5
Dens. estim. (MESA) [12] ⋆	9.5 ± 6.1	6.3 ± 1.2	4.9 ± 0.6	4.9 ± 0.7	3.8 ± 0.2	3.5 ± 0.2
Dens. estim. (RF) [8]	N/A	4.8 ± 1.5	3.8 ± 0.7	3.4 ± 0.1	N/A	3.2 ± 0.1
Dens. estim. (no smooth) ⋆	13.8 ± 3.6	11.3 ± 3.1	10.6 ± 2.3	9.9 ± 0.7	10.6 ± 1.1	10.2 ± 0.4
Dens. estim. (proposed) ⋆	9.6 ± 5.9	6.4 ± 0.7	5.53 ± 0.8	4.5 ± 0.6	3.8 ± 0.3	3.5 ± 0.1

any compromise on the counting accuracy. Crucially for sustaining interactivity, our simplification yields a dramatic speedup of the learning procedure.

To avoid confusion, we note again that ridge regression was proposed as a baseline for counting in [12], as shown in Table 2, and tested with the same set of features we have used, but resulting in much poorer performance. This is because, the regression in that baseline was learned at the image level, i.e. it treated each of the training images as a single training example, which resulted in a severe overfitting due to a limited number of examples. This differs from learning w to match the pixel-wise object densities (it can be seen as an extreme case of infinitely wide Gaussian kernel G). Finally, we note a connection between the proposed approach and [8] that also performs smoothing of the output density function (at the testing stage) using structured-output random forests.

5 Object Density Visualizations

The visualization of the object density estimate plays a key role in our interactive counting system as it assists the user to identify the parts of the image where the system has estimated the counts with large errors, and thus, where to add further annotations. While the predicted densities are sufficient to estimate the counts in any region, the accuracy of these densities cannot be controlled by the user without further post-processing due to the mismatch between the continuous nature of the densities and the discrete nature of the objects. To address this problem, we propose two density visualization methods, which convert the estimated density into representations that are intuitive for the user. The first method is based on non-overlapping extremal regions and is algorithmically similar to [3], and aims to localize the objects from the density estimate. The second method is based on recursive image partitioning, and aims to split the image into a set of small regions where the number of objects can be easily eyeballed and compared to the density-based estimates.

For both visualization techniques, we start by generating a set of candidate regions with a nestedness property such that two regions R_i and R_j are either nested (i.e. $R_i \subset R_j$ or $R_j \subset R_i$) or they do not overlap (i.e. $R_i \cap R_j = \emptyset$). Therefore, the set of candidate regions in each case can be arranged into trees [2]. Both visualization approaches represent the densities by showing summations over a subset of those candidate regions and both approaches optimize the choice of this subset. In particular, each region R_i has a score V_i associated to it that indicates the *integrality* of the region, or how well the region encloses an entire object or a cluster of objects. The idea is that we want to show the user the regions that have near-integer integrals of the density over them. Given the integrality scores, both approaches compute the final representation by picking a non-overlapping subset of regions that maximize the sum of such integrality-driven scores.

In more detail, we begin by defining S_i to be the integral of the estimated density map over the region R_i, and I_i to be the approximation of S_i to its nearest integer. The score V_i for region R_i is then defined as:

$$V_i = (1 - (S_i - I_i))^2 \tag{8}$$

For N candidate regions, we introduce the indicator variables $\mathbf{y} = \{y_1, y_2, ..., y_N\}$, where $y_i = 1$ implies that R_i has been selected. Additionally, $\mathbf{y}$ must satisfy the constraint of only containing non-overlapping regions. That is, $\mathbf{y} \in \mathcal{Y}$, where $\mathcal{Y}$ is the set of all sub-sets of non-overlapping regions such that if $R_i \cap R_j \neq \emptyset$ then $y_i.y_j = 0$.

The global maximization objective is defined as follows:

$$F(y) = \max_{y \in \mathcal{Y}} \sum_{i=1}^{N} y_i (V_i + \lambda) \tag{9}$$

where λ is a constant that prevents from selecting the trivial solution (one biggest region containing the whole image) and biases the solution towards a set of small regions. The objective (9) is optimized efficiently by using dynamic programming due to the tree structure of the regions as in [3]. We now discuss the details of the two approaches and the difference between them.

Visualization Using Non-overlapping Extremal Regions. Extremal regions are the connected components on the binary images resulting from thresholding a gray image $\mathcal{I}$ with any arbitrary threshold τ. A key property of the extremal regions is the nestedness as described above. Therefore, the set of extremal regions of an image can be arranged into a tree (or a forest) according to the nestedness.

Following [3], we use extremal regions as candidates for object detection. In this case, extremal regions are extracted from the estimated object density map, and the ones selected by the optimization (9) should delineate entire objects or entire clusters of objects (Figure 2-c).

In practice, we collect these candidate regions using the method of Maximally Stable Extremal Regions (MSER) [14]. This method only keeps those extremal regions that are stable in the sense that they do not change abruptly between consecutive thresholds of the image (i.e. on regions with strong edges). During the inference, we exclude the regions which have an integral of density smaller than 0.5 from consideration as we have found that allowing any extremal region to be selected can result in very cluttered visualizations. Instead, this visualization aims to show only regions containing entire objects.

Visualization Using Hierarchical Image Partitioning. In this approach, we build a hierarchical image partition driven by the density. To obtain the partition, we iteratively apply spectral graph clustering, dividing image regions into two (akin to normalized cuts [18]). Unlike the extremal region visualization and unlike the traditional use of normalized cuts, we encourage the boundaries of this partition to go through regions of low density, thus creating a tile of regions that enclose entire objects (Figure 2-d). To achieve this, we build a 4-connected weighted graph $G = (V, E)$ with the adjacency matrix W defining the weights of the edges based on the estimated density map $F(p)$ as $w_{p,q}=0.5\,(F(p)+F(q))$ for $(p, q)\in E$.

The normalized cuts then tend to cut through the parts of the image where the density is near-zero, and also as usual have a bias towards equal-size partitions (which is desirable for our purpose).

Once the tree-structured graph is built, the inference selects the set of non-overlapping regions through the maximization of the sum of the integrality scores of the regions, as explained above. Additionally, we enforce at inference time that every pixel in the estimated density map must belong to one of the selected regions (i.e. that the selected subset of regions represent a cover). Therefore, the entire density distribution is "explained". Accordingly, all regions from the hierarchical partitioning of the image are considered, including those with near zero density integrals.

Compared to the visualization using the extremal regions, the visualization based on recursive partition does not tend to outline object boundaries, but represents the underlying ground truth density with greater fidelity due to the fact that the whole image ends up being covered by the selected regions (Figure 2).

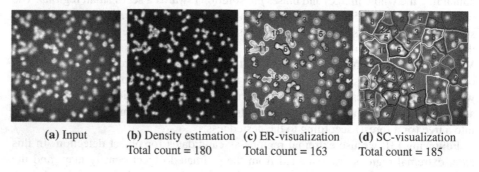

| (a) Input | (b) Density estimation
Total count = 180 | (c) ER-visualization
Total count = 163 | (d) SC-visualization
Total count = 185 |

Fig. 2. *(Density Visualization)* In order to assess the density estimation (b) of the original image (a), we propose two visualization methods. The first method (c) is based on non-overlapping extremal regions (ER) and aims to localize objects in the estimated density map (more intuitive but biased towards undercounting). The second method (d) is based on hierarchical image partitioning with spectral clustering (SC) and aims to explain the distribution of the density estimate across the entire image (higher fidelity but less intuitive visualization of the density). See text for details. In (c) and (d), the numbers indicate the objects contained within the region. Green regions contain a single object, but the number has been omitted for clarity. Non-outlined regions in (d) have zero counts.

Input	User Annotations	Estimated Density	Output

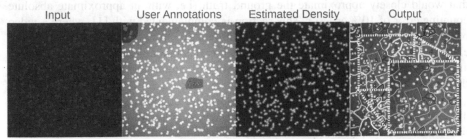

(a) **Synthetic cells. Number of dot-annotations = 16. Estimated count/GT = 476/484. Reference results from [24] = 482/500.**

(b) **Red cars. Number of dot-annotations = 19. Estimated count/GT = 220/230.**

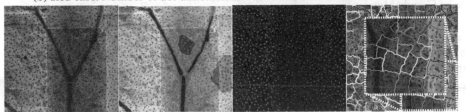

(c) **Stomata. Number of dot-annotations = 37. Estimated count/GT = 655/676. Reference results from [24] = 716/676.**

Fig. 3. *(Example results)* For the experiments shown, a large image (first column) is annotated interactively (second column) until qualitatively reasonable results are produced (fourth column). For all examples, the green masks on the annotation images (second column) indicate regions that have not been annotated by the user. All regions outside the green mask, with or without dot-annotations, are used as observations in the regression (Section 4). Annotated regions without dots can be seen as zero annotations. As expected, the number of annotations required increases with the difficulty of the problem. In cases where the background is complex, such as in aerial images (b), residual density tends to appear all over the image, which can be seen in the visualization. However, this can be easily fixed interactively using zero annotations, which are very fast and simple to add. Many more examples, as well as videos of the interactive process, are provided at [1].

6   Interactive Counting Experiments

We show the qualitative performance of the interactive counting system. The aim is to give a sense of the amount of annotations (and effort) required to obtain an object count that would closely approximate the ground truth (i.e. with an approximate absolute counting error of 10% or less). This section is complemented with [1], where a video of the system in use is shown, as well as additional example results including counting elongated objects using a scribble variant of the annotation. Note that, though results are shown here using the same images as input and output, it is possible to propagate the density estimation to other similar images in a batch.

Figure 3 shows example results of the interactive counting system, indicating the number of annotations added and the estimated object count for that amount of annotation. Part of the examples (Figures 3-a,c) have been taken from the benchmark dataset of [24], and we use their results *as reference* in Figure 3. We do not attempt to do a direct comparison of performance with [24] due to the fact that for the cases where a single image is given, our interactive method requires annotations on this image in order to produce results, and thus, disrupts the possibility of a fair comparison of performance. Moreover, due to the nature of the low-level features, our system crops the borders of the image by half the size of the texture patches (see implementation details), resulting in a possible difference of the ground truth count w.r.t. the original image. The additional examples (Figure 3-b and examples in [1]) correspond to aerial images extracted from Google Maps.

The same set of parameters have been used for all the examples shown, with the most relevant ones indicated in the implementation details. Due to space limitations, we use a single visualization method for each of the examples in Figure 3, but it can be seen that they are complementary. Nevertheless, depending on the image, one visualization can be more convenient than the other.

6.1   Implementation Details

Low-Level Features. We compute the initial (low-level) pixel descriptor z_p based on two types of local features on the Lab color-space. First, we use the contrast-normalized lightness values (L channel) of the pixels in a patch of size $n \times n$ centered at p [22]. The patches are rotated such that their dominant gradients are aligned in order to be invariant to the object's rotation in the image. Secondly, we collect the raw L, a and b values of the center pixel. The descriptor $z_p \in \mathbf{R}^d$ is the concatenation of the two local features. Therefore, the dimensionality d of the pixel descriptor for a color image is $n^2 + 3$. In the case of grayscale images, we do the feature computation on the given intensity channel, which results in $d = n^2 + 1$.

Collecting Extremal Regions. Extremal regions are extracted from the estimated density map using the MSER implementation from *VLFeat* [23]. In order to collect enough candidate regions for the inference to select from, we set a low stability threshold in the MSER algorithm.

Building a Binary Tree with Spectral Clustering. Computing the traditional spectral clustering as in [18] can be too slow for our interactive application, and the reason is the expensive computation of eigenvectors. Therefore, in practice we use the method from

Dhillon *et al.* [7] which solves the equivalent problem of weighted kernel k-means thus greatly reducing the computation time. We use the implementation from the authors of [7].

Setting Object-Size Dependent Parameters. Some of the parameters used in the implementation of the interactive counting system are better set with respect to the size of the object of interest. These are the size $n \times n$ of the patches for the low level features and the standard deviation σ for the Gaussian kernel used to smooth the dot-annotations and feature channels for the ridge regression. As discussed in Section 2, we chose to request an additional input from the user, where the approximate diameter of the object of interest is input by drawing a line segment over a single object in the image. The image is then rescaled with the scale factor of the object. For the experiments of the interactive system shown in the experimental section, we use an object size of 10 pixels, patches of 9×9 pixels and $\sigma = 3$ pixels.

Region Visualization. The boundaries of the regions that are chosen to visualize the density are superimposed on top of the original images. Alongside the boundaries, we show the density integrals over the highlighted regions rounded to the nearest integer (recall that regions are chosen so that such integrals tend to be near integer). We also color code the boundaries according to the counts (e.g. green for objects containing one object, blue for two objects, etc.).

7 Summary and Discussion

This paper is a first foray into enabling counting, previously treated as a traditional batch learning problem, to be handled interactively. To do this we have proposed a solution that speeds up the learning of object densities and overcomes the challenge of efficient density visualization. The result is an agile and flexible system which enables quite disparate visual material (spanning both microscopy images of cells and satellite imagery) to be annotated and counted in a matter of seconds.

There is certainly room for improvement: firstly, the features used can be extended to enable more local and contextual information to be captured. Secondly, our current system does not handle perspective geometry and cannot be directly applied to images with objects on a slanted ground plane. The latter, however, can easily be fixed by allowing a projective transformation to be imported or by the user providing additional object size annotations.

Acknowledgements. Financial support was provided by the RCUK Centre for Doctoral Training in Healthcare Innovation (EP/G036861/1) and ERC grant VisRec no. 228180.

References

1. http://www.robots.ox.ac.uk/~vgg/research/counting/
2. Arteta, C., Lempitsky, V., Noble, J.A., Zisserman, A.: Learning to detect cells using non-overlapping extremal regions. In: Ayache, N., Delingette, H., Golland, P., Mori, K. (eds.) MICCAI 2012, Part I. LNCS, vol. 7510, pp. 348–356. Springer, Heidelberg (2012)
3. Arteta, C., Lempitsky, V., Noble, J.A., Zisserman, A.: Learning to detect partially overlapping instances. In: CVPR (2013)

4. Boykov, Y., Jolly, M.P.: Interactive graph cuts for optimal boundary and region segmentation of objects in N-D images. In: Proc. ICCV, vol. 2, pp. 105–112 (2001)
5. Chan, A.B., Liang, Z.S.J., Vasconcelos, N.: Privacy preserving crowd monitoring: Counting people without people models or tracking. In: CVPR (2008)
6. Cho, S.Y., Chow, T.W.S., Leung, C.T.: A neural-based crowd estimation by hybrid global learning algorithm. Transactions on Systems, Man, and Cybernetics, Part B: Cybernetics 29(4), 535–541 (1999)
7. Dhillon, I.S., Guan, Y., Kulis, B.: Weighted graph cuts without eigenvectors a multilevel approach. IEEE Transactions on Pattern Analysis and Machine Intelligence 29(11), 1944–1957 (2007)
8. Fiaschi, L., Nair, R., Köethe, U., Hamprecht, F.: Learning to count with regression forest and structured labels. In: Proc. ICPR (2012)
9. Grady, L.: Random walks for image segmentation. TPAMI 28(11), 1768–1783 (2006)
10. Idrees, H., Saleemi, I., Seibert, C., Shah, M.: Multi-source multi-scale counting in extremely dense crowd images. In: CVPR (2013)
11. Kong, D., Gray, D., Tao, H.: A viewpoint invariant approach for crowd counting. In: Proc. ICPR (2006)
12. Lempitsky, V., Zisserman, A.: Learning to count objects in images. In: NIPS (2010)
13. Ma, W., Huang, L., Liu, C.: Crowd density analysis using co-occurrence texture features. In: 2010 5th International Conference on Computer Sciences and Convergence Information Technology (ICCIT), pp. 170–175 (November 2010)
14. Matas, J., Chum, O., Urban, M., Pajdla, T.: Robust wide-baseline stereo from maximally stable extremal regions. Image and Vision Computing (2004)
15. Mikel, R., Ivan, L., Josef, S., Jean-Yves, A.: Density-aware person detection and tracking in crowds. In: ICCV (2011)
16. Rother, C., Kolmogorov, V., Blake, A.: Grabcut: interactive foreground extraction using iterated graph cuts. Proc. ACM SIGGRAPH 23(3), 309–314 (2004)
17. Ryan, D., Denman, S., Fookes, C., Sridharan, S.: Crowd counting using multiple local features. In: Proc. DICTA (2009)
18. Shi, J., Malik, J.: Normalized cuts and image segmentation. TPAMI (2000)
19. Singaraju, D., Grady, L., Vidal, R.: Interactive image segmentation of quadratic energies on directed graphs. In: Proc. of CVPR 2008. IEEE Computer Society (June 2008)
20. Sommer, C., Straehle, C.N., Köthe, U., Hamprecht, F.A.: Ilastik: Interactive learning and segmentation toolkit. In: ISBI, pp. 230–233 (2011)
21. Straehle, C., Koethe, U., Hamprecht, F.A.: Weakly supervised learning of image partitioning using decision trees with structured split criteria. In: ICCV (2013)
22. Varma, M., Zisserman, A.: Texture classification: Are filter banks necessary? In: CVPR (2003)
23. Vedaldi, A., Fulkerson, B.: Vlfeat - an open and portable library of computer vision algorithms. In: ACM Multimedia (2010)
24. Verdié, Y., Lafarge, F.: Detecting parametric objects in large scenes by monte carlo sampling. International Journal of Computer Vision, 1–19 (2013)
25. Yao, A., Gall, J., Leistner, C., Gool, L.J.V.: Interactive object detection. In: CVPR, pp. 3242–3249 (2012)

Recognizing City Identity via Attribute Analysis of Geo-tagged Images

Bolei Zhou[1], Liu Liu[2], Aude Oliva[1], and Antonio Torralba[1]

[1] Computer Science and Artificial Intelligence Laboratory, Cambridge, MA, USA
[2] Department of Urban Studies and Planning
Massachusetts Institute of Technology, Cambridge, MA, USA
{bolei,lyons66,oliva,torralba}@mit.edu

Abstract. After hundreds of years of human settlement, each city has formed a distinct identity, distinguishing itself from other cities. In this work, we propose to characterize the identity of a city via an attribute analysis of 2 million geo-tagged images from 21 cities over 3 continents. First, we estimate the scene attributes of these images and use this representation to build a higher-level set of 7 city attributes, tailored to the form and function of cities. Then, we conduct the city identity recognition experiments on the geo-tagged images and identify images with salient city identity on each city attribute. Based on the misclassification rate of the city identity recognition, we analyze the visual similarity among different cities. Finally, we discuss the potential application of computer vision to urban planning.

Keywords: Geo-tagged image analysis, attribute, spatial analysis, city identity, urban planning.

1 Introduction

In Kevin Lynch's work *The Image of The City*, a city is described as a form of temporal art in vast scale. Over hundreds of years of human settlement, different cities have formed distinctive identities. City identity is defined as the sense of a city that distinguishes itself from other cities [22]. It appears in every aspects of urban life. For instance, Fig.1 shows photos taken by people in different cities, organized by different urban dimensions. Although there are no symbolic landmarks in those images, people who have lived in these cities or even just visited there can tell which image come from which cities. Such a capability suggests that some images from a city might have unique identity information that different urban observers may share knowledge of.

Akin to objects and scenes, cities are visual entities that differ in their shape and function [16,22]. As the growth of cities is highly dynamic, urban researchers and planners often describe cities through various attributes: they use the proportion of green space to evaluate living quality, take the land use to reflect transportation and social activity, or rely on different indicators to evaluate the urban development [26,16]. Here, we propose to characterize city identity

D. Fleet et al. (Eds.): ECCV 2014, Part III, LNCS 8691, pp. 519–534, 2014.

Fig. 1. City identity permeates every aspect of urban life. Can you guess from which cities these photos have been taken? Answer is below.[1]

via attribute analysis of geo-tagged images from photo-sharing websites. Photo-sharing websites like Instagram, Flickr, and Panoramio have amassed about 4 billion geo-tagged images, with over 2 million new images uploaded every day by users manually. These images contain a huge amount of information about the cities, which are not only used for landmark detection and reconstruction [12,3], but are also used to monitor ecological phenomena [29] and human activity [9] occurring in the city.

In this work a set of 7 high-level attributes is used to describe the spatial form of a city (amount of vertical buildings, type of architecture, water coverage, and green space coverage) and its social functionality (transportation network, athletic activity, and social activity). These attributes characterize the specific identity of various cities across Asia, Europe, and North America. We first collect more than 2 million geo-tagged images from 21 cities and build a large scale geo-tagged image database: the City Perception Database. Then based on the SUN attribute database [20] and deep learning features [5], we train the state-of-the-art scene attribute classifiers. The estimated scene attributes of images are further merged into 7 city attributes to describe each city within related urban dimensions. We conduct both city identity recognition experiment ("is it New York or Prague?") and city similarity estimation ("how similar are New York and Prague?"). Moreover, we discuss the potential application of our study to urban planning.

1.1 Related Work

The work on the geo-tagged images has received lots of attention in recent years. Landmarks of cities and countries are discovered, recognized, and reconstructed from large image collections [2,12,30,13,3]. Meanwhile, the IM2GPS approach [7] is used to predict image geolocation by matching visual appearance with geo-tagged images in dataset. Cross-view image matching is also used to correlate

---

[1] New York, London, Armsterdam, Tokyo; San Francisco, Armsterdam, Beijing, New Delhi; Barcelona, Paris, New York, London.

satellite images with ground-level information to localize images [14]. Additionally, geo-tagged images uploaded to social networking websites are also used to predict ecological phenomena [29] and people activity occurring in a city [9]. Besides, recent work [8] utilizes the visual cues of Google Street images to navigate the environment.

Our present work is inspired from discovering visual styles of architectures and objects in images [4,11], which use mid-level discriminative patches to characterize the identity of cities. Another relevant work [24] used Google street view images to estimate the inequality of urban perception with human's labeling. However, instead of detecting landmark images of cities and discovering local discriminative patches, our work aims at analyzing the city identity of the large geo-tagged image collection in the context of semantic attributes tailored to city form and function. *Attributes* are properties observable in images that have human-designated names (e.g. smooth, natural, vertical). Attribute-based representation has shown great potential for object recognition [1,19] and scene recognition [18,20]. Generally human-labeled attributes act as mid-level supervised information to describe and organize images. By leveraging attribute-based representations, we map images with a wide variety of image contents, from different cities, into the same semantic space with the common attribute dimension. Altogether, our approach presents an unified framework to measure the city identity and the similarity between cities. The proposed method not only automatically identifies landmarks and typical architectural styles of cities, but also detects unique albeit inconspicuous urban objects in cities. For instance, as shown in Fig.1 our results on the transportation attribute identify red double decker buses in London and yellow cabs in New York City as the objects with salient city identity value.

2   Describing City Perception by Attributes

In this section, we introduce a novel database of geo-tagged images[2] and its statistical properties. Then we propose a set of high-level city attributes from scene attributes to describe the city's spatial form (the amount of vertical buildings, type of architecture, water coverage, and green space coverage), as well as the city's social function (transportation network, athletic activity, and social activity). Attribute classifiers are trained using ground-truth from the SUN attribute database [20]. Furthermore, we analyze how the spatial distributions of city attributes vary across the urban regions and cities.

2.1   City Perception Database

Datasets of geo-tagged images can be either collected through cropping images from Google Street View as in [4] or downloading images from photo-sharing websites like Flickr and Panoramio as in [12,13,3]. These two data sources have

---

[2] Available at http://cityimage.csail.mit.edu.

different properties. Images from Google Street View are taken on roads where the Google vehicle can go, so the content of these images is limited, as a lot of content related to city perceptions, such as mountains and crowded indoor scenes are missing. Here we choose geo-tagged images from photo sharing websites. Interestingly, these images are power-law distributed on city maps (see Fig.3), given that people travel in a non-uniform way around a city, visiting more often the regions with historical, attractive tour sites as well as the regions with social events. Thus, these images represent *people's perception* of the city.

We build a new geo-tagged image dataset called City Perception Database. It consists of 2,034,980 geo-tagged images from 21 cities collected from Panoramio. To diversify the dataset, cities are selected from Europe, Asia, and North America. To get the geographical groundtruth for each city, we first outline the geographical area of the city, then segment the whole area into dense 500m×500m adjacent spatial cells. Geo-locations of these cells are further pushed to the API of Panoramio to query image URLs. Finally all the images lying within the city area are downloaded and the corrupted images are filtered out. The image numbers of the database along with their spatial statistics are listed in Fig.2. The negative Z-score of the Average Nearest Neighbor Index [23] indicates that the geo-locations of these images have the highly clustered pattern. Fig.3 shows the map plotting of all the images for two cities London and San Francisco.

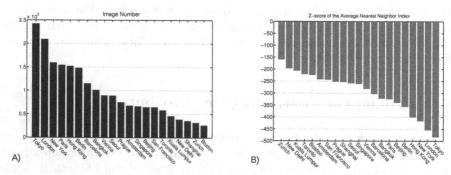

Fig. 2. A) The number of images obtained in each city. B) The Z-score of the Average Nearest Neighbor Index for each city. The more negative the value is, the more the geo-tagged images are spatially clustered. Thus images taken by people in a city are highly clustered.

2.2 From Scene Attributes to City Attributes

We propose to use attributes as a mid-level representation of images in our city perception database. Our approach is to train scene attribute classifiers, then to combine and calibrate various scene attribute classifiers into higher level city attribute classifiers.

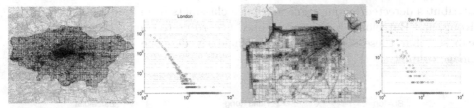

Fig. 3. The spatial plot of all the images, along with the spatial cells, on the city map of London and San Francisco. Each image is a black point on the map, while the color of the cell varies with the number of images it contains. Though these two cities have different areas and cell numbers, the distributions of image number per cell both follow a power law.

To train the scene attribute classifiers, we use the SUN attribute database [20], which consists of 102 scene attributes labeled on 14,340 images from 717 categories from the SUN database [28]. These scene attributes, such as 'natural', 'eating', and 'open area', are well tailored to represent the content of visual scenes. We use the deep convolutional network pre-trained on ImageNet [5] to extract features of images in the SUN attribute database, since deep learning features are shown to outperform other features in many large-scale visual recognition tasks [10,5]. Every image is then represented by a 4096 dimensional vector from the output of the pre-trained network's last fully connected layer. These deep learning features are then used to train a linear SVM classifier for each of the scene attributes using Liblinear [6]. In Fig.4 we compare our approach to the methods of using single feature GIST, HoG, Self-Similarity, Geometric Color Histogram, and to the combined normalized kernel method in [20]. Our approach outperforms the current state-of-the-art attribute classifier with better accuracy and scalability.

For every image in the city perception database, we also use the pre-trained convolutional network to extract features. Fig. 5 shows images with 4 scene

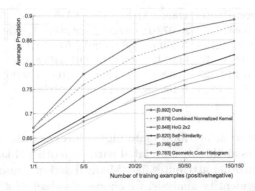

Fig. 4. Average precision (AP) averaged over all the scene attributes for different features. Our deep learning feature classifier is more accurate than the other individual feature classifiers and the combined kernel classifier used in [20].

attributes detected by our scene attribute classifiers from 3 cities Boston, Hong Kong, and Barcelona. Images are ranked according to the SVM confidence. We can see that these scene attributes sufficiently describe the semantics of the image content.

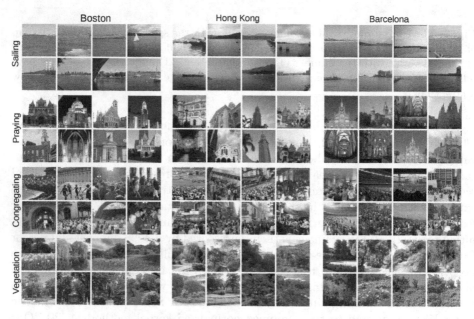

Fig. 5. Images detected with four scene attributes from Boston, Hong Kong, and Barcelona. Images are ranked according to their SVM confidences.

Table 1. The number of images detected with city attribute in 5 cities

	Green	Water	Trans.	Arch.	Ver.	Ath.	Soc.	Total Images
London	53,306	15,865	25,072	12,662	38,253	6,311	11,405	209,264
Boston	5,856	2,735	3,059	1,488	6,291	618	1,142	26,288
Hong Kong	47,708	18,878	14,914	2,066	21,690	1,346	8,354	152,147
Shanghai	8,373	1,623	5,368	862	8,252	509	1,569	35,722
Barcelona	25,831	6,825	9,160	6,810	24,334	2,338	6,093	114,867

We further merge scene attributes into higher level city attributes. Given that some scene attributes are highly correlated with each other (like 'Vegetation' and 'Farming') and some other attributes like 'Medical activity' and 'Rubber' are not relevant to the city identity analysis, we choose a subset of 42 scene attributes that are most relevant to represent city form and function, and combine them into the 7 city attributes commonly used in urban study and city ranking [27,26]: **Green space, Water coverage, Transportation, Architecture, Vertical** building, **Athletic activity**, and **Social activity** (see the lists of selected scene attributes contained in each city attribute in the supplementary materials). Thus, each of the city attribute classifier is modeled as an ensemble of SVMs: One image is detected with that city attribute if any of the constituent scene attributes is detected, while the response of the city attribute is calibrated across the SVMs using logistic regression. We apply the city attribute classifiers to all the images in the City Perception Database. Table 1 shows the number of detected images on each city attribute across 5 cities. These numbers vary across city attributes due to the difference in the scenic spots, tourist places, or the urban characteristics of the cities. Note that one image might be detected with multiple attributes.

2.3   Spatial Analysis of City Attributes

Fig.6 shows the images detected with each of the 7 city attributes on a map. We can see that different city attributes are unequally distributed on map. This makes

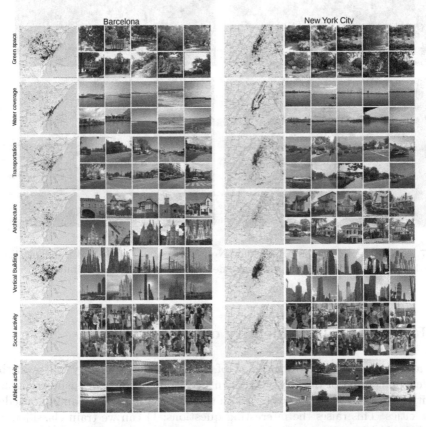

Fig. 6. Spatial distribution of city attributes and the top ranked images classified with each city attribute in Barcelona and New York

sense, given that cities vary in structure and location of popular regions. For example, images with water coverage lie close to the coast line, rivers, or canals of the city, and images with social activities lie in the downtown areas of the city. Note that the images detected by city attribute classifiers have more visual variations to the result of the scene attribute classifiers.

Fig.7 shows the city perception maps for Barcelona, New York City, Amsterdam, and Bangkok, which visualize the spatial distribution of the 7 city attributes in different colors. The city perception map exhibits the visitors' and inhabitants' own experience and perception of the cities, while it reflects the spatial popularity of places in the city across attributes.

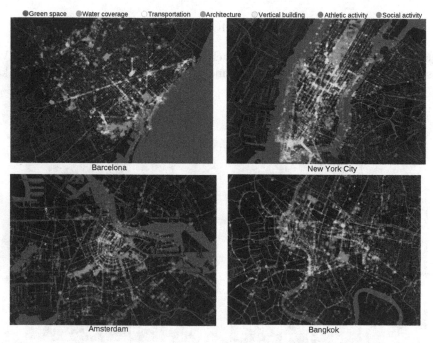

Fig. 7. City perception map of Barcelona, New York, Amsterdam, and Bangkok. Each colored dot represents a geo-tagged image detected with one city attribute.

3   Recognizing City Identity of Images

City identity emerges in every aspect of daily life and implicitly exists in the people's perception of the city. As shown in Fig. 1, people can easily recognize the city identity of these photos based on their former experience and knowledge of the cities. This raises the interesting questions: 1) can we train classifiers to recognize the city identity of images? 2) what are the images with high city identity values, *i.e.*, the representative images of the city?

In this section, we formulate the city identity recognition as a discriminative classification task: Given some images randomly sampled from different cities, we hope to train a classifier that could predict which city the newly given images come from. The challenge of the task lies in the wide variety of the image contents across cities. Here we show that city identity actually could be recognized on different city attributes, while the misclassification rate in the city identity recognition experiment could be used to measure the similarity between cities.

3.1 Attribute-Based City Identity Recognition

As shown in Table 1 and Figure 6, images of each cities with different city attribute are detected. We are more curious about which images are unique in one city as well as discriminative across other cities on some city attribute. Thus we conduct the discriminative classification of all the 21 cities: For each of the 7 city attribute, 500 images with that city attribute are randomly sampled from each city as the train set, while all the remaining images are included in the test set. A linear SVM classifier is trained and tested for each of the 7 city attributes respectively. Here the train set size 500 is empirically determined, as we assume such a number of images contain enough information about the city identity.

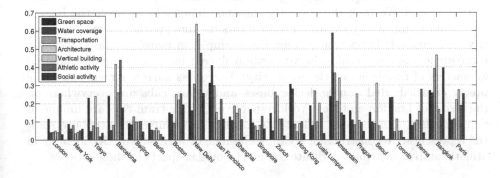

Fig. 8. The accuracies of city identity recogition on each city attribute

Figure 8 plots the accuracies of city identity recognition on each city attribute. Figure 9 illustrates the confusion matrices of city identity recognition on architecture and green space. The performance of city identity recognition is not very high due to the large variety of image contents, but the trained linear SVM classifier actually has good enough discriminative ability compared to the random chance. Meanwhile, we can see that the recognition accuracy varies across both cities and city attributes. It is related to the uniqueness of one city on that city attribute. For example, New Delhi and Bangkok have high accuracy in architecture attribute, since they have unique architectures compared to all the other cities selected in the City Perception Database. Interestingly, the misclassification rate in the city identity recognition actually reflects the similarity of two cities, since there are a high number of indistinguishable images from the two cities. In our case, Paris, Vienna, and Prague are all similar to Barcelona in architecture attribute. This observation leads to our data-driven similarity of cities in Section 3.2.

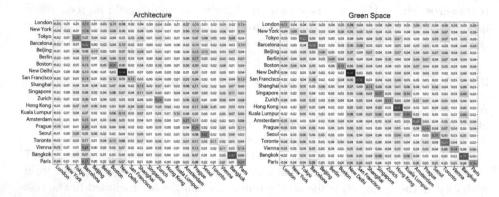

Fig. 9. Confusion matrices of city identity recogntion for architecture attribute and green space attribute

The SVM confidence of an image actually indicates the city identity value of that image. We rank the correctly classified images to discover the images representing salient city identity. Fig.10 shows the images with salient city identity on 5 city attributes respectively. For example, in transportation attribute, there are lots of canal cruises in Amsterdam since it has more than one hundred kilometers of canals across the whole city; Tokyo has narrow streets since it is pretty crowded; Red double decker buses and yellow cabs are everywhere on the street of London and New York respectively, while tram cars are unique in San Francisco. Images with salient city identity in architecture attribute show the representative construction styles, while images with salient city identity in athletic activity attribute indicate the most popular sports in these cities.

3.2 Data-Driven Visual Similarity between Cities

How similar or different are two cities? Intuitively we feel that Paris is more similar to London than to Singapore, while Tokyo is more similar to Beijing than to Boston. Measuring the similarity of cities is still an open question [25,21].

Here we use a data-driven similarity metric between two cities based on the misclassification rate of the city identity recognition. We assume that if two cities are visually similar to each other, the misclassification rate in the city identity recognition task should be high across all the city attributes. Thus we can use the pairwise misclassification rates averaged over all 7 city attributes as a similarity measure. The misclassification rate on each city attribute is computed from the city identity recognition repeated on every pairs of cities, which is the sum of the rate of misclassifying images of city A as city B and the rate of misclassifying images of city B as city A.

Fig. 10. Images with high city identity values on 4 city attributes

Fig.11A plots the similarity network of all the 21 cities in our database. The thickness of the edges indicates the averaged pairwise misclassification rate (for better visualization we remove weak edges). Nodes with the same color are those that belong to the same group, clustered by the community detection algorithm [17]. Cities in one group are closely connected with each others: they are grouped based on their located continents-Europe, North America, or Asia. In Fig.11B we scatter our data-driven similarity with the geodesic distances between the geographical centers of the cities. The correlation coefficient r is -0.57 ($p <$ 0.01).

Our result validates that the geographical distance between cities plays an important role in determining the similarity of cities. Indeed, historically there were more trade and cultural exchanges between spatially-neighboring cities, so they would share similar elements in their form and culture. Besides, there are some outliers detected in our result, such as New Delhi and New York. This is because the culture of New Delhi is quite different from other cities in our database, while New York is a metropolis which mixes the cultures from all over the world. Our data-driven similarity metric between cities is useful for the study of urban sociology and city history.

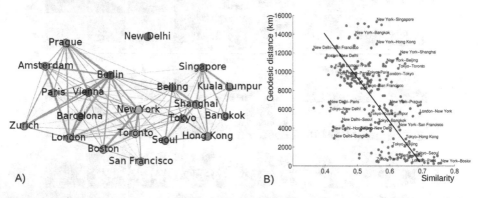

Fig. 11. A) Similarity graph of cities. The nodes indicate cities, the thickness of the edges indicates the similarity computed from the misclassification rate of the city identity recognition. Nodes with the same color belong to the same cluster. B) The scatter of the data-driven similarity over geodesic distance of cities. Each point indicates one pair of cities. Some representative labels of points are plotted. There is high negative correlation between the geodesic distance of a pair of cities and their visual similarity.

4   Further Application in Urban Planning

Estimating people's perceptions of a city from a massive collection of geo-tagged images offers a new method for urban studies and planning. Our data-driven approach could help assess and guide urban form construction.

Following the seminal work of Kevin Lynch [15], our data-driven analysis of images taken by people in a city relates the subjective perception of people with

Table 2. The correlation between the results of geo-tagged image analysis and the urban design indicators for the city of Boston. **: P-value<0.01.

Indicators	Building height	Openness rate	Sidewalk density	Block size	H/W
Image number	0.156**	-0.101**	0.241**	-0.076**	0.112**
Attribute diversity	0.098**	-0.061**	0.296**	-0.092**	0.080**
City identity value	0.070**	0.029	0.235**	-0.092**	0.065**

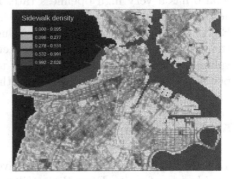

Fig. 12. The map of attribute diversity and the map of sidewalk density in Boston. Color indicates the value intensity.

the urban construction. City identity has been described along various urban dimensions, which additionally allows us to think about urban design in various terms. Here we propose to quantify the correlation between our geo-tagged image analysis and urban construction, using a set of quantitative indicators provided by MassGIS and Boston(Mass.) Department of Innovation and Technology [3] :building height and density, openness rate, sidewalk density, block size, and the ratio of street height and width, available for the city of Boston.

First, we segment the city into 50m×50m connected but non-overlapping spatial cells, so that city regions are quantified by hundreds of cells. For each cell, we represent the people's perception of this cell as the number of images inside, the attribute diversity (the number of the different city attributes in the cell), and the dominant city identity value. Then we calculate the Pearson correlation to see how people's perceptions are relevant to those urban design measurements.

The result of the statistical analysis can be found in Table 2. Most of the urban design indicators are significantly correlated with people's perception of the city. For example, sidewalk density is positively correlated with the attribute diversity (0.296). This means that a place with more space of sidewalk is likely to provide more views of people while it allows people to move between areas more easily. Similar results are found for building height and the ratio of height and width of streets. Regarding the negative correlation, it shows that when block size grows

---

[3] http://www.cityofboston.gov/DoIT/
    http://www.mass.gov/

the place becomes less friendly to the pedestrians. Therefore it has a negative impact on the people's perception of the city. Openness rate, which refers to the percentage of open space in a cell, is a more complex indicator. On the one hand, the positive coefficient between openness rate and city identity value suggests that a larger open space would have higher city identity value. On the other hand, the negative coefficient of the image number and attribute diversity indicates that such a place is less diverse and crowded. For example, Boston common is one of the Boston's well-known public center with a salient city identity, and it also has a very high openness rate. However, because visitors are scattered across the large park, the geo-tagged images won't look quite spatially dense. Fig.12 plots the attribute diversity value and the sidewalk density of Boston in the city maps. This comparison between urban form and city identity provides valuable reference and instructions for urban planners because they incorporate people's subjective preference toward the built environment.

5   Conclusion

This work introduced a novel data-driven approach to understand what makes the identity of a city. From the attribute analysis of many geo-tagged images of cities, we found that the identity of a city could be represented and expressed in various urban dimensions, such as green space, architecture, transportation, and activity. Using the attribute representation of images tailored to describe the form and function of cities, we identified images with salient city identity and measured the similarity between cities. Further applications in the urban planning were discussed.

Our work suggests a fruitful direction of computer vision research in the domain of urban computation. In the future work, we plan to study how a city identity develops over time based on the time-stamps of the geo-tagged images. Meanwhile, by collecting additional urban measurements, such as the distribution of the crime rates and the cleanliness of neighborhoods, we hope to more faithfully identify what makes a city distinctive and suggest how to optimize the urban planning of a specific city, or a cluster of cities, to take into account the people's needs and expectations.

Acknowledgments. We thank Zoya Bylinskii, Christopher Dean, Scott Hu, and the reviewers for insightful suggestions. This work is partly funded by NSF grant 1016862 to A.O, and Google Research Awards to A.O and A.T.

References

1. Branson, S., Wah, C., Schroff, F., Babenko, B., Welinder, P., Perona, P., Belongie, S.: Visual recognition with humans in the loop. In: Daniilidis, K., Maragos, P., Paragios, N. (eds.) ECCV 2010, Part IV. LNCS, vol. 6314, pp. 438–451. Springer, Heidelberg (2010)

2. Chen, D.M., Baatz, G., Koser, K., Tsai, S.S., Vedantham, R., Pylvanainen, T., Roimela, K., Chen, X., Bach, J., Pollefeys, M., et al.: City-scale landmark identification on mobile devices. In: Proc. CVPR (2011)
3. Crandall, D.J., Backstrom, L., Huttenlocher, D., Kleinberg, J.: Mapping the world's photos. In: Proceedings of the 18th International Conference on World wide web (2009)
4. Doersch, C., Singh, S., Gupta, A., Sivic, J., Efros, A.A.: What makes paris look like paris? ACM Transactions on Graphics (TOG) (2012)
5. Donahue, J., Jia, Y., Vinyals, O., Hoffman, J., Zhang, N., Tzeng, E., Darrell, T.: Decaf: A deep convolutional activation feature for generic visual recognition. arXiv preprint arXiv:1310.1531 (2013)
6. Fan, R.E., Chang, K.W., Hsieh, C.J., Wang, X.R., Lin, C.J.: Liblinear: A library for large linear classification. The Journal of Machine Learning Research (2008)
7. Hays, J., Efros, A.A.: Im2gps: estimating geographic information from a single image. In: Proc. CVPR (2008)
8. Khosla, A., An, B., Lim, J.J., Torralba, A.: Looking beyond the visible scene. In: Proc. CVPR (2014)
9. Kisilevich, S., Krstajic, M., Keim, D., Andrienko, N., Andrienko, G.: Event-based analysis of people's activities and behavior using flickr and panoramio geotagged photo collections. In: 2010 14th International Conference on Information Visualisation, IV (2010)
10. Krizhevsky, A., Sutskever, I., Hinton, G.E.: Imagenet classification with deep convolutional neural networks. In: Advances in Neural Information Processing Systems (2012)
11. Lee, Y.J., Efros, A.A., Hebert, M.: Style-aware mid-level representation for discovering visual connections in space and time. In: Proc. ICCV (2013)
12. Li, X., Wu, C., Zach, C., Lazebnik, S., Frahm, J.-M.: Modeling and recognition of landmark image collections using iconic scene graphs. In: Forsyth, D., Torr, P., Zisserman, A. (eds.) ECCV 2008, Part I. LNCS, vol. 5302, pp. 427–440. Springer, Heidelberg (2008)
13. Li, Y., Crandall, D.J., Huttenlocher, D.P.: Landmark classification in large-scale image collections. In: Proc. ICCV (2009)
14. Lin, T.Y., Belongie, S., Hays, J.: Cross-view image geolocalization. In: Proc. CVPR (2013)
15. Lynch, K.: The image of the city. MIT Press (1960)
16. Nasar, J.L.: The evaluative image of the city. Sage Publications Thousand Oaks, CA (1998)
17. Newman, M.E.: Modularity and community structure in networks. Proceedings of the National Academy of Sciences (2006)
18. Oliva, A., Torralba, A.: Modeling the shape of the scene: A holistic representation of the spatial envelope. Int'l Journal of Computer Vision (2001)
19. Parikh, D., Grauman, K.: Relative attributes. In: Proc. ICCV (2011)
20. Patterson, G., Hays, J.: Sun attribute database: Discovering, annotating, and recognizing scene attributes. In: Proc. CVPR (2012)
21. Preoţiuc-Pietro, D., Cranshaw, J., Yano, T.: Exploring venue-based city-to-city similarity measures. In: Proceedings of the 2nd ACM SIGKDD International Workshop on Urban Computing (2013)
22. Proshansky, H.M., Fabian, A.K., Kaminoff, R.: Place-identity: Physical world socialization of the self. Journal of Environmental Psychology (1983)
23. Ripley, B.D.: Spatial statistics, vol. 575. John Wiley & Sons (2005)

24. Salesses, P., Schechtner, K., Hidalgo, C.A.: The collaborative image of the city: mapping the inequality of urban perception. PloS one (2013)
25. Seth, R., Covell, M., Ravichandran, D., Sivakumar, D., Baluja, S.: A tale of two (similar) cities: Inferring city similarity through geo-spatial query log analysis. In: Proceedings of the International Conference on Knowledge Discovery and Information Retrieval (2011)
26. Unit, E.I.: Best cities ranking and report. In: The Economist (2012)
27. Unit, E.I.: Global liveability ranking and report. In: The Economist (2013)
28. Xiao, J., Hays, J., Ehinger, K.A., Oliva, A., Torralba, A.: Sun database: Large-scale scene recognition from abbey to zoo. In: Proc. CVPR (2010)
29. Zhang, H., Korayem, M., Crandall, D.J., LeBuhn, G.: Mining photo-sharing websites to study ecological phenomena. In: Proceedings of the 21st International Conference on World Wide Web (2012)
30. Zheng, Y.T., Zhao, M., Song, Y., Adam, H., Buddemeier, U., Bissacco, A., Brucher, F., Chua, T.S., Neven, H.: Tour the world: building a web-scale landmark recognition engine. In: Proc. CVPR (2009)

A Fast and Simple Algorithm
for Producing Candidate Regions

Boyan Bonev and Alan L. Yuille

University of California, Los Angeles, CA, USA
bonev@ucla.edu, yuille@stat.ucla.edu

Abstract. This paper addresses the task of producing candidate regions for detecting objects (e.g., car, cat) and background regions (e.g., sky, water). We describe a simple and rapid algorithm which generates a set of candidate regions $\mathcal{C_R}$ by combining up to three "selected-segments". These are obtained by a hierarchical merging algorithm which seeks to identify segments corresponding to roughly homogeneous regions, followed by a selection stage which removes most of the segments, yielding a small subset of selected-segments S. The hierarchical merging makes a novel use of the PageRank algorithm. The selection stage also uses a new criterion based on entropy gain with non-parametric estimation of the segments' entropy. We evaluate on a new labeling of the Pascal VOC 2010 set where all pixels are labeled with one of 57 class labels. We show that most of the 57 objects and background regions can be largely covered by three of the selected-segments. We present a detailed per-object comparison on the task of proposing candidate regions with several state-of-the-art methods. Our performance is comparable to the best performing method in terms of coverage but is simpler and faster, and needs to output half the number of candidate regions, which is critical for a subsequent stage (e.g, classification).

Keywords: Hierarchical grouping, segments selection, candidate regions.

1 Introduction

The goal of this paper is to propose a fast and simple way to generate a set $\mathcal{C_R}$ of *candidate regions* which can correspond to objects and background regions (e.g., sky and water) in images, in contrast to methods which only focus on foreground objects [2]. The output of our method is illustrated in figure (1a) which shows candidate regions for car, person, building, and background classes, like ground, grass, building. The candidate regions are obtained combining one to three of a set of *selected-segments*, shown in different colors. Observe that the candidate region for the person contains segments for the head, torso and legs. By contrast, the candidate region for the car contains segments for the car body, the lights, and the window.

There has been recent work on detecting candidate regions for objects. The Ultrametric Contour Map (UCM) algorithm has been extended to perform this task [4]. Other methods include the highly successful Constrained Parametric Min-Cuts (CPMC) [7], Selective Search [22], and the Segmentation by Weighted Aggregation (SWA) algorithm [13] and its variants [3,23] (the SWA family of algorithms output salient segments

D. Fleet et al. (Eds.): ECCV 2014, Part III, LNCS 8691, pp. 535–549, 2014.

which can be thought of as candidate regions). The detection of candidate regions can be followed by a classification stage, for example see [4,7].

In this paper, we specify a fast and simple method for obtaining candidate regions $\mathcal{C}_\mathcal{R}$ for *both objects and background regions*. We start by constructing a hierarchy of segments $\mathcal{S}_\mathcal{H}$, see figure (1b), using a hierarchical merging algorithm. A novel aspect of this grouping algorithm is the use of a PageRank [12] based criterion to select the order of segments to merge. This enables the algorithm to rapidly merge background segments (e.g., the sky) into large segments while maintaining small segments corresponding to birds or airplanes. This segment merging process results in segments which have roughly homogeneous image properties, except at the highest levels where objects and background are merged. Next, we use a selection criterion which aims to remove segments which are subparts of larger homogeneous regions and yield a subset of "selected-segments" $\mathcal{S}$. To do this we use a novel entropy gain criterion which involves introducing a non-parametric method for estimating the entropy of image segments. Our method is fast and runs in 4s per image in a Matlab implementation.

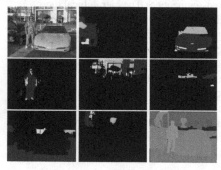

(a) Examples of candidate regions for objects and background regions. Left-to-right and top-to-bottom: image, top three selected-segments for left car, right car, person, building, grass, ground, trees, and ground truth. Most objects are covered well by two to three selected-segments.

(b) Multiple levels in a hierarchy. Segments with a good coverage of objects or parts may happen at different levels. 80% to 90% of the segments can be discarded because they go across boundaries of objects or because they don't cover a large area of an object.

Fig. 1. (a) Examples of candidate regions composed by three selected-segments; (b) Hierarchy of segments

To evaluate our method we study its performance on a dataset with 57 labels for objects and background regions. This is the Pascal VOC 2010 dataset where we have assigned every pixel one of 57 labels. We demonstrate that three segments are typically sufficient to provide good coverage of most objects and background regions. The coverage given by the subset of selected-segments is only 0.2% lower. Next we test the effectiveness of small combinations of our selected-segments (one to three segments) to cover objects and background regions (where coverage is measured by intersection over union). We report good results which are roughly similar to the evaluation of the candidate regions provided by [4]. Our method has the advantage of being simple, fast, and based on two novel ingredients.

This paper is organized as follows. In section 2 we discuss our use of PageRank and non-parametric entropy, which are the most novel aspects of our method. Section 3 describes how we generate the hierarchy of segments and how we select a smaller set of selected-segments from the hierarchy. Our next contribution is in section 4, where we present an analysis of why we need combinations of up to three selected-segments (subsection 4.2). Based on that we generate candidate regions in subsection 4.3 and we test on 57 classes our candidate regions and present a comparison with [4].

1.1 Related Work

Our work has been inspired by previous work on detecting candidate regions. This includes a variety of methods which first construct a hierarchy of segments and then use a procedure to select important, or in our words "selected"-segments. An early attempt [19] which outputs $10,000$ candidates per image, analyzes the importance of spatial support for the segments. A successful recent example is based on the UCM hierarchical algorithm [5,4], which is based on gPb [18]. This method is particularly relevant because it outputs candidate regions for objects and background regions. It uses a combination of three segments output by the UCM algorithm but they do not describe their motivation for choosing this number nor do they give a detailed description of how they select segments and obtain their candidate regions (but they kindly supplied us with these regions for our experiments).

We perform an analysis on the number of segments which cover a foreground or background class. We have not found a similar attempt in the literature. However, our analysis is consistent with [5,4] where the authors make 3-combinations to improve the coverage of their candidate regions. In that work they do not elaborate on the reason for choosing $k = 3$ and they do not specify how they select their segments. Here we experimentally show that 3 is adequate for both foreground and background classes. In our comparison to the candidate regions of [4], the coverage we obtain is slightly lower by using nearly half the number of candidates. This simplifies the task of any further high-level task on top of our candidate regions C_R. Also, our method is two orders of magnitude faster. This is mainly because their method is based on the output of gPb. In this paper, we do not address the task of classifying the segments – unlike [5,4].

Related hierarchical grouping methods include the SWA algorithm [13] and a recent variant [3]. This method has also been extended to video segmentation [23]. After the grouping, it uses a local saliency measure, based on large affinity within the segment and small affinity across its boundaries, to detect salient segments. These methods however, tend not to do a further step of grouping the segments into combinations (as done in [5,4]) and they have been mostly evaluated for finding segments which cover foreground objects, see [3]. A related method which has been also evaluated on covering objects is [22]. There is also related work by [11]. We should also mention hierarchical segmentation which has been used to learn models of objects [21]. But although these approaches have some commonalities with ours they differ in goals and methods (like PageRank or the entropy-based criterion).

Selective Search [22] is a fast method (4s as our method) which gives a very high recall, 98%, on bounding boxes (2,100 candidate boxes). However it is not optimized for proposing candidate masks. It groups an initial set of segments given by [11]. They group them based on appearance properties (color, texture), the size and compactness of the segments.

The CPMC method outputs a set of foreground segments [7]. This method is very successful but restricts itself to objects and does not attempt to find segments for background regions. It proceeds in several stages. The first stage uses repeated applications of a max-flow algorithm to output a set of foregrounds segments based on groupings of an edge map provided by gPb. This set of segments is pruned by non-maximal suppression. The second stage ranks these segments using cues trained on the Pascal VOC dataset. The first stage of this algorithm is most similar to ours (i.e. it uses only low level cues). Their method is one to two orders of magnitude slower than ours, which makes it inapplicable to large scale datasets like ImageNet [9].

A key element of our approach is the use of an entropy gain criterion for selecting segments. This includes using a non-parametric multivariate entropy estimator which is due to [14,20,15]. This estimator has been applied to estimate the entropy of natural images by Chandler and Field [8] but is not widely used in vision. A different non-parametric entropy estimator has been used for model-selection in clustering, including an example of color segmentation [6]. In [16] entropy rate is used for segmentation but the purpose is different: they quantify the stochastic process over the graph, favoring formation of compact and homogeneous clusters. [17] describes a method for segmenting data by encoding criteria. The idea of good encoding relates to our entropy criterion for selecting segments. But our goal is to detect maximal homogeneous segments which are used for later processing and not to segment data.

2   PageRank and Selection by Entropy Gain Criterion

The method in this paper first constructs a hierarchy of segments and then selects a subset of selected-segments. From these we construct candidate regions C_R which are combinations of up to three selected-segments $\in S$. Our method contains two novel and simple ingredients. The first is the use of the PageRank algorithm to create the hierarchy S_H by grouping segments. The second is the selection of segments based on an entropy gain criterion using a non-parametric estimate of the entropy of the segments.

2.1   Grouping Segments by the PageRank Algorithm

Our approach groups only a fraction of the segments at each hierarchy level S_l. In that way it allows large homogeneous areas to grow "faster", coexisting with small segments. The PageRank algorithm [12] is used to determine which of the segments are grouped at each level. Its use is motivated by the desire to start by merging those segments which have similar statistics to their neighbors. PageRank has a straightforward application in our framework because we define an asymmetric dissimilarity measure between the segments, see section (3.1) for details.

PageRank is illustrated in figure (2)-right. It plays a key role in ensuring that our segments take *global properties* of the image into account when merging segments

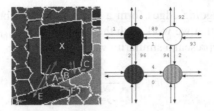

Fig. 2. Left: Asymmetric dissimilarity function. For X, the most similar are B and E (2nd neighbor) because they don't modify a lot the statistics of X. However, X is not the most similar for B and E, from their perspective other merges are preferable. Right: The PageRank algorithm prioritizes merging segments which are very similar to their neighbors. In this example (not related to the left one), the white node (representing a segment) has highest ranking and so is selected first for merging. The edge weights denote (asymmetric) similarity between the segments.

to construct the hierarchy. At each level l of the hierarchy, it selects which segments should be allowed to merge, by taking into account the whole *directed* graph, where the nodes are the segments in S_l and the weights of the directed edges are given by the asymmetric dissimilarity, which we define in (3). In particular, this strategy also allows some segments to grow "faster", that is, the segments S_l of a level l may have different sizes. In that way l is not directly related to the size of the segments (as in [13]), as the appearance also determines the size of the segments. In figure (3a)-right it can be seen that small salient areas can "survive" together with large segments covering homogeneous areas. This is an advantage when searching for region candidates for objects of different sizes and with large background regions.

(a) (a) PageRank output: at each level we merge first the highest rank (whitest) nodes. Note that the "salient" regions have lower rank, while the segments covering homogeneous areas tend to have higher ranks.

(b) (b) The effect of PageRank. Top: original image. Left: best segment without PageRank. Right: best segment using PageRank.

Fig. 3. (a) PageRank output at different levels of the hierarchy; (b) Example of the effect of PageRank.

More formally, PageRank quantifies the importance of each segment (i.e. graph node) after a sequence of probabilistic transitions over the graph. These probabilistic transitions are encoded by a stochastic matrix. At level l, W_l is a stochastic matrix of size N_l where each element is given by the similarity from node i to j, normalized by rows so that the outgoing edges form a probability distribution, $\forall i$, $\sum_{j}^{N_l} w_{ij} = 1$, $i, j \in [1, N_l]$. Given that we work with the dissimilarity $\Delta_{i|j}$ further defined in (3), we need to invert it to represent a similarity value. We define

$$ w_{ij} = \frac{\Delta_{i|j}^{-1}}{\sum_{j=1}^{N_l} \Delta_{i|j}^{-1}}. $$

PageRank returns a ranking of the nodes and we select those nodes with the highest ranks for merging. The merging order does not determine to which of its neighbors a node is merged: for this we use $\Delta_{i|j}$ as explained in section 3.1.

2.2 Non-parametric Entropy and the Entropy Gain Criterion

After constructing the segment hierarchy $S_{\mathcal{H}}$ we need a criterion to obtain the set of selected-segments S. This criterion should ideally select segments which are roughly homogeneous and are as large as possible. We use the entropy of each segment as a measure of its homogeneity. Now suppose that two segments are combined in the hierarchy to form a larger "parent" segment. We compute the difference between the entropy of the parent segment and the entropy of its two children. If the difference is small, then we do not select any of the two segments because we consider them to be subparts of a larger homogeneous region. If the difference is big, then we select the two child segments because we cannot grow them further. This is illustrated in figure (4)-top where segments A and B can be merged (because the entropy gain is small) but where segment C cannot be merged with A or B because the entropy gain would be too big.

We emphasize that the selected-segments can overlap. This is illustrated in figure (4)-bottom where the segments at small scales correspond to windows and are selected individually. The wall of the house (without the windows) is also a selected-segment. Finally the whole house is another selected-segment because at this scale the windows form a semi-regular texture pattern.

This criterion is intuitive but requires a method for computing the entropy of a segment. This is challenging because we do not have a parametric probability distribution for the segment variables from which to calculate the entropy (our data is poorly fit by standard distributions like Gaussians) and, even if we did, for small segments we may not have enough measurements to estimate the distribution. Instead we use a non-parametric method [14,20,15] which has been previously used to measure the entropy of natural images [8]. The power of this method is the ability to estimate entropy in a multivariate way without assuming any kind of independence among the different dimensions of the vector of statistics. It is applicable to small samples because it bypasses the density estimation, working directly on distances between samples.

The estimator of the entropy from n samples $\{x_1, ..., x_n\}$ in p-dimensional space is given by:

$$ H_k^n(f) = \frac{p}{n} \sum_{i=1}^{n} \log R_{i,k,n} + \log \frac{\pi^{p/2}}{\Gamma(\frac{p}{2}+1)} - \frac{\Gamma'(k)}{\Gamma(k)} + \log n, \qquad (1) $$

where $R_{i,k,n}$ is the Euclidean distance between x_i and its kth nearest neighbor in the set $\{x_1, ..., x_n\}$, and $\Gamma(.)$ is the Gamma function.

Fig. 4. Top: Entropy gain: When segments A and B are merged, the increase of entropy is not as big as if they were merged with C. The entropy is calculated from the small (first-level) segments which are shown in the figure. Bottom: Selected-segments at different scales. The walls of the house (left panel). Each of the windows (center panel). The whole house (right panel).

This non-parametric estimator is asymptotically unbiased and consistent [20,15]. It can be derived in three steps. Suppose the unknown probability density function is $f(x)$. The first step estimates its entropy $-\int f(x) \log f(x) dx$ by the normalized sum $\frac{1}{N} \sum_{i=1}^{n} \log f(x_i)$ of the logarithm of the probability density $f(.)$ evaluated at a random sample $x_1, ..., x_n$ of points. The second step estimates $f(x_i)$ by a k- nearest neighbor method by

$$f(x_i) \approx k/n\Gamma(p/2+1)\frac{1}{\pi^{p/2}R_{i,k,n}^p},$$

where $R_{i,k,n}^p$ is the Euclidean distance between x_i and its kth nearest neighbor in the set $\{x_1, ..., x_n\}$. The third step makes an additive correction to this estimator to ensure that it is statistically unbiased, see Theorems 8,9 in [20]. The key intuition behind this method is that the nearest neighbors of random samples can be used to give a local estimate of the probability density (step 2).

The estimator can be applied to image segments by setting the samples x_i to be the appearance features (e.g., color and texture) calculated in the lowest-level segments within the segment (i.e. those at the bottom of the segment hierarchy). See section (3.2) for more details. This method has been only used once in vision, to our knowledge, by Chandler and Field [8] to estimate the entropy of natural images.

3 Method

Our method has two stages. The first constructs a hierarchy of segments, as described in section (3.1). The second uses an information gain criterion to obtain a subset of selected-segments. The characteristics of both stages is that they are simple and fast.

The ingredients are simple image features, an asymmetric similarity measure including an edge term, the PageRank algorithm, and the entropy gain criterion for selection.

3.1   Constructing the Segmentation Hierarchy

The algorithm starts with a basic set of small segments S_1 which are produced by an over-segmentation method. In this work we use the SLIC algorithm described in [1] because of its simplicity, its speed, and because it allows segments with irregular shape. Then we build a segmentation hierarchy $S_H = S_1 \cup S_2 \cup \cdots \cup S_L$ of L levels by merging segments as follows.

Each segment is described by an *appearance vector*

$$V = (\overline{\mu}, \overline{\sigma}, c_x, c_y, w, h), \tag{2}$$

where $\overline{\mu}, \overline{\sigma}$ are the mean and the standard deviation of the Lab color space components and the first and second derivatives on the l channel, $(l, a, b, \nabla_x, \nabla_y, \nabla_x^2, \nabla_y^2)$. Here (c_x, c_y, w, h) are the centroid of the segment and the dimensions of its bounding box. These appearance vectors are designed so that they can be computed efficiently recursively for new segments composed by merging.

We define an asymmetric dissimilarity function $\Delta_{i|j}^A$ between segments at the same level which are 1st or 2nd-order neighbors. The appearance term, see figure (2)-left, is defined to be

$$\Delta_{i|j}^A = ||V_i - V_{i \cup j}||_2.$$

This is the change in the appearance vector of region i caused by merging it with region j. This function is asymmetric – i.e. $\Delta_{i|j}^A \neq \Delta_{j|i}^A$. This terms will encourage merging neighboring regions which have similar appearance vectors. The asymmetry has the meaning that after merging i and j, the statistics of i may be modified in a different degree than the statistics of j. Intuitively, each segment has its own preference for merging or not to a neighbor, and it is based on minimizing the change of appearance.

The appearance dissimilarity function is modified by an edge-term ($E_{i,j} \in [0,1]$) that represents the amount of edge-ness on the boundary between two adjacent regions. This edge term is computed only once. Any fast edge detector can be used. We obtained good results using the Sobel detector and obtained slight improvements (1.7%) when we switched to the Structured Forests method [10] (used for the experiments here). The intuition for this edge modulation is that we penalize the similarity between adjacent regions if there is an edge between them. We do not introduce an edge-term between segments in the 2nd-order neighborhood (because we want to allow this type of merging to jump between regions) and instead we pay a fixed penalty of size 1 (which is the maximum value the edge term can take).

This gives an asymmetric dissimilarity function $\Delta_{i|j}$:

$$\Delta_{i|j} = E_{i,j} + \Delta_{i|j}^A, \text{ if } i, j \text{ are } 1-\text{neighbors},$$

$$\tag{3}$$

$$\Delta_{i|j} = 1 + \Delta_{i|j}^A, \quad \text{ if } i, j \text{ are } 2-\text{neighbors}.$$

Then we use the PageRank algorithm [12] to rank the need of pairing between segments (i, j) based on this dissimilarity function. We allow the top-ranked 30% segments to merge, unless they violate the condition $\Delta_{i|j} > 0.9\Delta_{j|i}$. The intuition is that this ranking encourages merging between segments which are most similar, but that we reject merges in situations where the dissimilarity function between two regions is too asymmetric. After these merges, on the next level of the hierarchy, we re-compute the PageRank algorithm and repeat the process. See ranking examples in figure (3a). Finally, the last level $\mathcal{S}_L$ contains a single segment with the whole image.

Our algorithm does not have an explicit mechanism for handling textures. However it usually merges textures into a single segment. In the case of textures which are finer than the size the first level $\mathcal{S}_1$ segments, the texture characteristics are captured by the mean and standard deviation of the segments and they are likely to be merged. In the case of very coarse textures several big and disconnected segments may be formed.

3.2   Obtaining Selected-Segments

The next stage of our method requires obtaining a set $\mathcal{S}$ of selected segments which are roughly homogeneous but are as large as possible. This is particularly challenging because the sizes of objects and background stuff varies considerably and so we need to select segments at different scales. Also in some cases, see figure (4)-bottom, we need selected-segments that are overlapping and represent structure at different scale (e.g., the windows at one scale, the whole building at another).

The total number of segments $|\mathcal{S}_{\mathcal{H}}|$ produced by our algorithm largely depends on the number of segments of the initial over-segmentation, $|\mathcal{S}_1|$. In this work we set $|\mathcal{S}_1| \approx 600$ which results in $L \approx 35$ levels in the hierarchy with an average total of $|\mathcal{S}_{\mathcal{H}}| \approx 1200$ segments. We estimate that only 5% to 10% of the segments are really needed with which to form candidate regions (by small groups). We propose an entropy gain criterion to select this set $\mathcal{S} \subseteq \mathcal{S}_{\mathcal{H}}$ of segments. The criterion is required to obtain good candidate regions for both object and background regions.

More precisely, we establish a threshold D for the entropy increase d after merging two segments $s_i, s_j \in \mathcal{S}_l$ with area sizes a_i, a_j into a new one $s_m = s_i \cup s_j \in \mathcal{S}_{l+1}$ at the next level $l + 1$. We define the entropy gain as:

$$d = H(s_m) - \{H(s_i) + H(s_j)\}. \tag{4}$$

Here $H(s)$ is the multivariate entropy of the appearance vectors V' of the first level segments $s_f \in \mathcal{S}_1$ which compose the segment s, that is, $\bigcup s_f = s$. Similarly to (2), the appearance vector is $V = (\overline{\mu}, \overline{\sigma})$, where $\overline{\mu}, \overline{\sigma}$ are the mean and the standard deviation of $(l, a, b, \nabla_x, \nabla_y, \nabla_x^2, \nabla_y^2)$. The non-parametric estimation of $H(\cdot)$ was described in section (2.2).

The entropy gain d is not always positive, but we have experimentally observed that it usually is, in natural images. In very homogeneous areas or repeating patterns, d can be negative.

The selection criterion is as follows. For smooth increases $d < D$ we do not select the segments. For increases $d \geq D$ we select the two segments because at the next level they are merged into a more heterogeneous segment. See an example of a selected-segment in figure (5)-third image. Note that we use the entropy value as a threshold for

Fig. 5. Left-to-right: Original image; a segment that is too small for the region it could cover; a selected-segment that covers a large homogeneous area, a segment that covers a still larger but heterogeneous area

checking whether a segment maintains a certain amount of homogeneity. But it is not used for deciding to which segment to merge, as for this purpose we use the appearance vectors of the segments, which provide richer information.

We fix a threshold D such that the amount of selected-segments is approximately $|\mathcal{S}| \approx 0.1 |\mathcal{S}_{\mathcal{H}}|$. We reduce the set of segments from 1200 to 116 on average. This causes a minimal loss: 0.2% less of IoU with respect to not applying any selection criterion. The loss occurs more often on small objects than on large ones.

4 Experiments

4.1 The Dataset

In our experiments we perform analysis on the PASCAL VOC 2010 detection set. There are 57 classes among which 15 are background and the rest are foreground objects. See the list of class labels in figure (6). The 57-class dataset was constructed by hand-labeling the images so that every pixel is assigned to one of 57 object classes or to a default class (this ground truth is being prepared for publication and will be made available if this paper is accepted). The labeling was done by supervised students (i.e, not Mechanical turk).

The objects are placed in a rough taxonomy of four classes.

– Natural objects: bird, cat, cow, dog, flower, horse, mouse, person, sheep.
– Large homogeneous regions: grass, ground, mountain, rock, sky, water, snow, tree, wood, wall.
– Man-made (indoor): bag, clothes, tv monitor, computer, keyboard, bed, book, bottle, cup, plate, food, cabinet, shelves, chair, sofa, table, dining table, ceiling, door, floor, light, potted plant.
– Man-made (outdoor): aeroplane, train, truck, bicycle, motorbike, boat, car, bus, bench, building, fence, road, sidewalk, track, sign, window.

There is also a "default background" class for pixels which cannot be assigned to any of these 57 categories. The number of pixels assigned to this class is negligible and we ignore this class for the results presented here.

4.2 Best Segments Analysis

We first investigate how many of our segments are needed to cover an object or background region, where coverage is the region-based intersection over union (IoU). Most

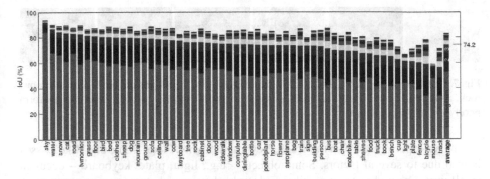

Fig. 6. Overall coverage of the best segments for each object class. Red, black, and blue shows the average proportion of the object covered by the first, second, and third best segments respectively. Observe that the amount of coverage by the first segment ranges from 35 percent (for track and bike" to almost 90 percent for sky. The proportion covered by the first three segments is typically between 70 and 75 percent with a few outliers (e.g., track and sky).

objects consist of several roughly homogeneous regions (e.g., the face, the shirt, and the trousers of a man can each be roughly homogeneous but the complete man is not). Hence, to get good coverage of an object we need to combine several segments.

The coverage by our segments is illustrated in figure (6). This displays the proportion of the object that is covered (IoU) as a function of the number of segments (from one to ten). In this experiment we do not propose selected-segments but we test them all with the ground truth to quantify the optimal performance that could be achieved for the provided set of segments $S_{\mathcal{H}}$. The segments used for this analysis do not overlap, even if belonging to different level S_l. To evaluate if a segment is covering a part of an object we require that at least 80% of it has to be within the ground-truth shape of the object. We use the combination of segments which give optimal coverage for the given segmentation hierarchies.

The results show that our segments have good performance for many object classes in the sense that three segments give over eighty percent of coverage (on average). In particular, good performance is obtained for: (I) All natural objects except for mouse and person (bird, cat, cow, dog, horse, sheep, flower). (II) All large homogeneous regions (grass, ground, mountain, rock, sky, water, snow, tree, wood, wall). (III) A subset of the man-made indoor objects – bag, bed, ceiling, computer, door, sofa, TV monitor, (IV) A subset of the man-made outdoor – airplane, sign, window. The good performance categories have fairly homogeneous appearances and they are typically of medium to large size in the images (e.g., the mouse has worse performance mainly because it tends to appear in small sizes).

Performance is medium quality on object classes such as food, mouse, truck, building, person, potted plant, boat, train, table, book, bench, dinner table, motorbike, car, bus. This is due to several different factors. Some objects – e.g., truck, building, person, boat, and train – have a large variety of image appearance. Other objects – e.g., table, dinner table – are frequently partially occluded. Other objects – e.g., plotted plant and book – are often small and poorly lit.

Fig. 7. Left-to-right and top-to-bottom: Original image, top three segments for bike, wall, snow, rock, and ground truth. Note that the segments are good even for object classes that perform poorly overall (e.g., bike).

The weak performance on the Track, Keyboard, Lights, Plate, Bottle and Bike classes is also due to several factors. Some objects – e.g., light, plate, keyboard – occur in small sizes. Other objects – e.g., bikes and track – have very heterogeneous appearance. Others, like bottle, are both small and often poorly lit.

Figs. (1a, 7) show typical examples of our results. Note that some objects may be described well by a single segment. Others are often well-described by three segments (e.g., person, car). Even some objects in the weak performance class – e.g.. bike – are sometimes covered fairly well by a small number of segments.

4.3 Segment Combinations as Candidate Regions

In this section we evaluate the coverage of objects by our selected-segments set $\mathcal{S} \subseteq \mathcal{S}_{\mathcal{H}}$ (sel-segs) and by combinations of them (CR combs). From the results of our previous section we conclude that three segments are sufficient to give good coverage. Hence we allow combinations of up to three selected-segments. We obtain an average of 116^1 selected-segments per image after selection and from these we make 721 combinations. This number is the average number of candidate region proposals that we output per image. We generate the candidates by combining neighbors from different levels of the hierarchy, with a maximum difference of 5 levels. Big selected-segments (more than 15,000 pixels) are only combined with selected-segments that are no more than five times smaller. We suppress repeated or too similar proposals.

We evaluate the generated candidate regions with the ground truth on our dataset. We compare to three state-of-the-art methods. In [4], the segment combinations generated provide an average of 1,322 candidate regions for each image. These are generated by taking combinations of the 150 segments (on average) that their hierarchical segmentation approach outputs for each image. Their method is more sophisticated than ours and we observe that they tend to get larger and less homogeneous segments than we do. The use of gPb makes their method significantly slower than ours (but it also focuses on image segmentation, which we do not attempt). In table (1) we refer to their segments as UCM-combs and to our candidate regions as CR-combs.

Another method we compare to is the Constrained Parametric Min-Cuts (CPMC) [7]. Their method is designed for foreground objects, which explains its better performance on foreground objects. Their overall performance on the 57 classes is lower than our performance, both for our 721 candidate regions (CR-combs), and for our 155 selected-segments (sel-segs). We show the latter for a fair comparison with CPMC's 150

---

[1] For the sel-segs set in table (1) we relax our selection criterion to obtain a set of 155 selected-segments. This enables us to compare with CPMC [7] who output a set of similar size.

Table 1. Region-based IoU (in %) comparison. CPMC [7], UCM [4], Sel. Search [22], our selected-segments, and our CR – candidate regions. The last four columns show in bold the two best performances. The 20 Pascal VOC classes are marked with (*). Foreground classes are in italic script, background classes are normal script.

	sky	water	road	*bed*	grass	*cat**	mountain	*tv**	floor	*clothes*	wall
CPMC	65.1	65.4	56.3	65.4	56.5	85.5	55.2	76.8	54.5	58.5	51.7
UCM-combs	90.4	83.8	82.4	81.6	79.3	84.4	75.7	84.5	76.7	76.0	75.2
Sel. search	88.9	77.7	73.4	66.5	74.5	68.7	72.5	65.1	69.2	67.8	64.4
Our sel-segs	86.2	70.6	73.4	57.6	65.2	62.6	67.8	59.0	68.0	63.8	65.2
Our CR combs	90.4	83.2	81.0	79.4	78.1	78.1	76.7	76.7	76.5	75.7	74.5
	*sofa**	rock	*dog**	ground	tree	*bird**	*train**	*plane**	*sheep**	*car**	*cow**
CPMC	64.2	61.1	82.6	55.0	54.5	74.8	78.2	78.6	73.7	72.1	79.9
UCM-combs	76.4	75.6	80.7	76.5	76.5	76.9	75.7	78.4	74.7	73.8	79.4
Sel. search	70.0	66.0	68.9	67.2	68.8	67.3	59.9	63.5	64.6	62.0	60.4
Our sel-segs	64.6	57.3	58.9	63.2	59.2	63.2	53.6	59.0	59.6	55.4	56.5
Our CR combs	74.4	73.7	73.6	73.6	73.5	72.2	72.0	72.0	71.7	71.5	71.1
	bus*	cabinet	snow	sidewalk	building	*bottle**	*horse**	wood	window	pc	door
CPMC	78.9	54.9	60.0	53.0	51.6	74.9	77.5	49.4	50.9	70.7	40.0
UCM-combs	74.7	75.0	71.9	81.0	72.2	78.7	78.1	75.1	70.3	72.1	68.2
Sel. search	58.1	63.0	66.1	71.9	62.8	60.6	61.6	70.6	62.4	54.8	65.3
Our sel-segs	51.3	57.9	58.1	65.8	56.6	57.7	57.4	60.5	58.2	52.1	58.9
Our CR combs	71.1	71.0	70.7	70.6	70.5	69.7	69.6	69.2	69.1	67.6	67.2
	flower	keyboard	d. table*	truck	motorbike*	boat*	shelves	person*	pot. plant*	chair*	ceiling
CPMC	51.0	46.8	62.2	61.8	74.2	71.2	52.6	67.6	63.9	51.7	22.4
UCM-combs	64.2	75.0	73.5	70.4	69.5	70.4	65.5	73.3	73.1	71.3	57.0
Sel. search	65.8	73.1	60.8	64.5	60.4	66.3	63.3	56.9	54.6	56.9	61.2
Our sel-segs	53.7	61.6	52.6	52.9	54.3	51.1	56.7	51.7	54.4	49.1	53.3
Our CR combs	67.1	66.5	66.2	66.2	66.2	66.1	65.6	64.5	64.5	63.5	61.9
	table	book	fence	bag	bench	bicycle*	food	track	plate	sign	cup
CPMC	48.9	36.3	42.3	53.2	36.5	64.4	44.9	42.3	44.5	24.6	40.9
UCM-combs	64.1	67.5	61.3	72.3	63.3	63.3	67.1	54.5	57.2	44.6	65.7
Sel. search	52.6	62.8	53.4	58.5	46.7	48.6	67.2	49.4	51.3	58.9	56.6
Our sel-segs	52.4	49.5	49.1	51.6	44.3	40.8	47.4	44.0	40.5	40.5	45.9
Our CR combs	61.4	59.9	57.8	56.3	56.2	55.0	52.9	50.9	46.2	44.5	44.3
	light	*mouse*	**all IoU**	recall	# cands.	time					
CPMC	8.3	12.6	59.6	57.6%	150	250s					
UCM-combs	27.8	52.3	**77.0**	**80.0%**	1322	850s					
Sel. search	38.9	56.8	67.8	66.1%	2100	**4s**					
Our sel-segs	40.8	31.3	62.4	55.6%	**155**	**4s**					
Our CR combs	37.6	26.8	**74.0**	**70.3%**	721	**4s**					

candidates. It is interesting that CPMC is much better on the 20 Pascal VOC objects, marked with (*) in table (1). However, our sel-segs and CR-combs are better than CPMC on most of the 20 newly labeled foreground classes (e.g, bench, book, sign, etc), as well as on the 17 background classes. This suggests that CPMC may be overtuned for those 20 classes, degrading its performance for all other foreground classes.

Finally, we also compare to the Selective Search [22] method because it is competitive in terms of speed. It is optimized for bounding box candidates and performs better on this task: 89.7% box-based IoU and 95.7% box-based recall, compared to 89.5% box-based IoU and 90.9% box-based recall of our method. The recall criterion is the one [22] used: an object is found if its IoU is larger than 50%. However, our method outperforms theirs on the region candidates task (74.0% compared to 67.8% IoU), with less than half the number of proposals. See table (1) for detailed per-class region-based IoU and recall.

The 57-class evaluation is performed on the intersection of our labeled dataset (VOC 2010 detection trainval) and the set of segments provided by [4] (VOC 2011 segmentation trainval), which makes a total of 1288 images. The results are shown in table (1). The objects are sorted by the performance of our CR method. Our performance is lower than [4] but comparable: 74% IoU versus 77% for [4]. But we achieve it with nearly half the number of combinations – 721 compared to 1,322 – and with a simpler and faster algorithm (4s per image in Matlab[2]).

5 Conclusions and Future Work

We propose a novel and simple method for obtaining candidate regions for objects and background regions. The algorithm is based on simple image cues and is very fast, making it applicable to large-scale datasets (e.g., ImageNet).

Our approach has two novelties. Firstly, using the PageRank guiding the hierarchical grouping, which enables global properties of the image to be respected. Secondly, the use of the entropy gain criterion to select maximal homogeneous image segments. The selected-segments form an intermediate-level representation which can be used as a precursor for object detection and classification.

Experiments show that it gives good results on a novel labeling of PASCAL VOC dataset (providing labels for 57 object classes). Firstly, we show that typically one to three segments cover a large part of the object. Secondly, we compare the performance of our candidate regions to the state-of-the-art methods, the best-performing of which is based on UCM. Our performance is comparable to theirs but is obtained using roughly half the number of candidates, by an algorithm which is two orders of magnitude faster. The smaller number of segment combinations is an advantage for a subsequent object classification stage.

It is surprising that such a simple method gives such good results. We plan future work in two directions. Firstly, to see if we can reduce the number of our selected-segments even further by exploring variants of our method including the use of other low-level cues and selection criteria. Secondly, we will start training classifiers on the candidate regions to detect objects and background regions.

Acknowledgements. This work is partially supported by NSF award CCF-1317376, by ONR N00014-12-1-0883 and by NVidia Corp.

References

1. Achanta, R., Shaji, A., Smith, K., Lucchi, A., Fua, P., Susstrunk, S.: SLIC superpixels compared to state-of-the-art superpixel methods. TPAMI 34(11), 2274–2282 (2012)
2. Alexe, B., Deselaers, T., Ferrari, V.: Measuring the objectness of image windows. TPAMI 34(11), 2189–2202 (2012)
3. Alpert, S., Galun, M., Brandt, A., Basri, R.: Image segmentation by probabilistic bottom-up aggregation and cue integration. TPAMI 34(2), 315–327 (2012)
4. Arbelaez, P., Hariharan, B., Gu, C., Gupta, S., Malik, J.: Semantic segmentation using regions and parts. In: CVPR (2012)

---

[2] Download the Matlab code at http://www.dccia.ua.es/~boyan/cr.html

5. Arbelaez, P., Maire, M., Fowlkes, C., Malik, J.: Contour detection and hierarchical image segmentation. TPAMI 33(5), 898–916 (2011)
6. Benavent, A.P., Ruiz, F.E., Saez, J.M.: Learning Gaussian Mixture Models With Entropy-Based Criteria. TNN 20(11), 1756–1771 (2009)
7. Carreira, J., Sminchisescu, C.: Cpmc: Automatic object segmentation using constrained parametric min-cuts. TPAMI 34(7), 1312–1328 (2012)
8. Chandler, D.M., Field, D.J.: Estimates of the information content and dimensionality of natural scenes from proximity distributions. J. Opt. Soc. Am. A 24(4), 922–941 (2007)
9. Deng, J., Dong, W., Socher, R., Li, L.J., Li, K., Fei-Fei, L.: ImageNet: A Large-Scale Hierarchical Image Database. In: CVPR (2009)
10. Dollár, P., Zitnick, C.L.: Structured forests for fast edge detection. In: International Conference on Computer Vision, ICCV (2013)
11. Felzenszwalb, P.F., Huttenlocher, D.P.: Efficient graph-based image segmentation. IJCV 59(2), 167–181 (2004)
12. Franceschet, M.: Pagerank: standing on the shoulders of giants. Commun. ACM 54(6), 92–101 (2011)
13. Galun, M., Sharon, E., Basri, R., Brandt, A.: Texture segmentation by multiscale aggregation of filter responses and shape elements. In: ICCV 2003, p. 716 (2003)
14. Kozachenko, L.F., Leonenko, N.N.: Sample estimate of the entropy of a random vector. Probl. Inf. Transm. 23(1), 95–101 (1987)
15. Leonenko, N., Pronzato, L., Savani, V.: A class of Rényi information estimators for multidimensional densities. Ann. Statist. 36(5), 2153–5182 (2008)
16. Liu, M.Y., Tuzel, O., Ramalingam, S., Chellappa, R.: Entropy rate superpixel segmentation. In: CVPR, pp. 2097–2104 (2011)
17. Ma, Y., Derksen, H., Hong, W., Wright, J.: Segmentation of multivariate mixed data via lossy coding and compression. TPAMI 29(9) (2007)
18. Maire, M., Arbelaez, P., Fowlkes, C.C., Malik, J.: Using contours to detect and localize junctions in natural images. In: CVPR (2008)
19. Malisiewicz, T., Efros, A.A.: Improving spatial support for objects via multiple segmentations. In: BMVC (2007)
20. Singh, H., Misra, N., Hnizdo, V., Fedorowicz, A., Demchuk, E.: Nearest neighbor estimates of entropy. American J. of Math. and Mgmt. Sci. 23(3-4), 301–321 (2003)
21. Todorovic, S., Ahuja, N.: Region-based hierarchical image matching. IJCV 78(1), 47–66 (2008)
22. Uijlings, J.R.R., van de Sande, K.E.A., Gevers, T., Smeulders, A.W.M.: Selective search for object recognition. International Journal of Computer Vision 104(2), 154–171 (2013)
23. Xu, C., Xiong, C., Corso, J.J.: Streaming hierarchical video segmentation. In: Fitzgibbon, A., Lazebnik, S., Perona, P., Sato, Y., Schmid, C. (eds.) ECCV 2012, Part VI. LNCS, vol. 7577, pp. 626–639. Springer, Heidelberg (2012)

Closed-Form Approximate CRF Training
for Scalable Image Segmentation

Alexander Kolesnikov[1], Matthieu Guillaumin[2],
Vittorio Ferrari[3], and Christoph H. Lampert[1]

[1] IST Austria
[2] ETH Zürich, Switzerland
[3] University of Edinburgh, UK

Abstract. We present LS-CRF, a new method for training cyclic Conditional Random Fields (CRFs) from large datasets that is inspired by classical closed-form expressions for the maximum likelihood parameters of a generative graphical model with tree topology. Training a CRF with LS-CRF requires only solving a set of independent regression problems, each of which can be solved efficiently in closed form or by an iterative solver. This makes LS-CRF orders of magnitude faster than classical CRF training based on probabilistic inference, and at the same time more flexible and easier to implement than other approximate techniques, such as pseudolikelihood or piecewise training. We apply LS-CRF to the task of semantic image segmentation, showing that it achieves on par accuracy to other training techniques at higher speed, thereby allowing efficient CRF training from very large training sets. For example, training a linearly parameterized pairwise CRF on 150,000 images requires less than one hour on a modern workstation.

1   Introduction

Many areas of computer vision research have recently made a transition from datasets with a few thousand images to much larger datasets with millions of images. One area that is relatively untouched by this trend is *semantic image segmentation*, i.e. the task of assigning a semantic label, such as *grass* or *building* to every pixel in an image. There are few aspects that hold back the field: a lack of large-scale image segmentation datasets, because manually creating their annotation is tedious and costly, and a lack of learning techniques for structured prediction models that scale to truly large amounts of training data. In this work, we make two contributions that address both problems:

- a method for CRFs training that is *scalable* (training sets can be 100,000 images or larger), *flexible* (allowing for linear or nonlinear predictors), and *easy to implement* (only a few lines of code are required for the linear variant),

- two new *large scale datasets* [1] (over 180,000 training images) for image segmentation, assembled from ImageNet [8] and PASCAL VOC [11] datasets and augmented with semi-automatically created figure-ground annotations.

---

[1] Available online at http://pub.ist.ac.at/~akolesnikov/HDSeg

D. Fleet et al. (Eds.): ECCV 2014, Part III, LNCS 8691, pp. 550–565, 2014.

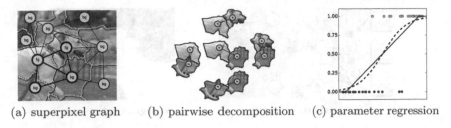

(a) superpixel graph   (b) pairwise decomposition   (c) parameter regression

Fig. 1. Schematic illustration of LS-CRF for image segmentation – training phase: (a) we are given images with predefined graph structure (here based on superpixels) and per-node annotation (here: **fg/bg**), (b) we form training subproblems from all edges in the graph (shown for bold subgraph), (c) for each label combination, we train a linear (solid line) or nonlinear (dashed line) regressor to predict the label combination's conditional probability

We call the new method LS-CRF, where the LS stands both for *least squares* and for *large scale*. It can in principle be used for any pairwise discrete-valued CRFs, but in particular it is suitable for the classes of CRFs that occur in computer vision applications, such as image segmentation, where 1) the CRF (i.e. its underlying graph) is cyclic, 2) all variables are of the same "type", e.g. pixels or superpixels, 3) each variable takes values in a rather small label set, and 4) many training examples are available.

Figures 1 and 2 illustrate LS-CRF for semantic image segmentation. A formal definition and justification are given in Section 2. Our contribution lies in the steps 1(b), 1(c) and 2(a), which we explain in detail in Section 2. The main idea is to decompose the joint learning problem into smaller, tractable subproblems and learn their parameters by independent least-squares regression tasks. For a new image, the output of the regressors provide values for the energy tables for all pairwise terms. This induces a (conditional) probability distribution over the label set, from which we infer a segmentation, for example by maximum-a-posteriori (MAP) prediction.

Compared to existing methods, LS-CRF has several advantages: in contrast to generic maximum likelihood training for CRFs, no step of joint probabilistic inference (i.e. computing marginals over the training data) is required during training. Instead, the training is formulated as solving a collection of subproblems, which can be solved efficiently and even in parallel. This makes training scalable even to large datasets. In our experiments, training with over 150,000 images takes less than one hour on a modern workstation. In contrast to related techniques, such as pseudolikelihood or piecewise training, a closed-form solution for the optimal parameters is available for the case of a linear parameterization and squared loss, which can be solved in just a few lines of code. However, LS-CRF is not limited to linear parameterizations. It also allows efficient learning of nonlinear, even non-parametric, energy functions. In our experiments, we demonstrate this by learning a CRF with an energy function based on gradient boosted decision trees.

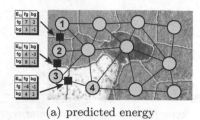   

(a) predicted energy   (b) segmentation result

Fig. 2. Schematic illustration of LS-CRF for image segmentation – prediction phase: (a) for a new image we use the regressors to predict an energy table for each pairwise term (visualized on three edges between four nodes), (b) The energy function defines a probability distribution which yields a segmentation (here: by MAP prediction)

The two new datasets that we introduce, *HorseSeg* and *DogSeg*, are described in Section 5. They are meant to facilitate experiments in two setups that reflect recent trends in computer vision research: large-scale learning, and learning with weakly annotated data. In combination the datasets consist of over 180,000 images that were taken from the PASCAL VOC and the ImageNet dataset. For the test images we provide manually created segmentation masks, thereby allowing for an unbiased evaluation. The training images come with three different levels of annotation: all training images have a class label, some training images have object bounding boxes, few training images have manually created per-pixel segmentations. In this form, the datasets can be used to evaluate segmentation algorithms based on semi-supervised or weakly supervised learning.

In addition, for each training image we provide a segmentation mask created automatically using the *segmentation transfer* method [18]. With this annotation, the datasets can serve as a benchmark for the efficiency of large scale learning methods, or to analyze the stability of learning algorithms to annotation noise.

2   Closed-Form Training of Conditional Random Fields

In this section we formally introduce LS-CRF training and justify its construction from classical results about probabilistic inference and estimation theory. We highlight the similarities and differences of LS-CRF to previous methods for CRF learning and discuss possible extensions.

2.1   Conditional Random Fields

We follow the standard notation for the probabilistic learning of discrete conditional random fields (CRFs). See, e.g., the tutorial [24] for an introduction in the context of computer vision. To facilitate the discussion, we refer to the objects of interest in the context of image segmentation, but note that all steps are also applicable for training CRFs for other tasks.

We denote input images by $x \in \mathcal{X}$, and outputs (segmentations) by $y \in \mathcal{Y}$. Any y is a collection of interacting parts, $y = (y_1, \ldots, y_m)$, where each part y_s for $s = 1, \ldots, m$ takes a value in a finite label set, $\mathcal{L} = \{1, \ldots, r\}$. Every y has a graph, $G = (\mathcal{V}, \mathcal{E})$, associated with it. The vertex set, $\mathcal{V} = \{1, \ldots, m\}$, reflects the parts, and the edge set, $\mathcal{E} \subset \mathcal{V} \times \mathcal{V}$, contains an edge for every directly interacting pair of parts. For example, in image segmentation the edge $\mathcal{E}$ typically contains all pairs of adjacent pixels or superpixels.

A CRF models a conditional distribution of outputs given inputs by

$$p(y|x; w) = \exp(-E(x, y; w))/Z(x; w), \qquad (1)$$

where $E(x, y; w)$ is an *energy function* with parameter w, and the normalizing constant $Z(x; w) = \sum_{y \in \mathcal{Y}} \exp(-E(x, y; w))$ is called the *partition function*. Most popular for computer vision applications are energy functions consisting of *unary* and *pairwise* terms.

$$E(x, y; w) = \sum_{s \in \mathcal{V}} \sum_{j \in \mathcal{L}} \theta_{s;j} [\![y_s = j]\!] + \sum_{(s,t) \in \mathcal{E}} \sum_{(j,k) \in \mathcal{L} \times \mathcal{L}} \theta_{st;jk} [\![y_s = j \wedge y_t = k]\!], \quad (2)$$

where $[\![P]\!] = 1$ if the predicate P is true, and 0 otherwise. The coefficients are functions of a subset of the input x and parameters w. Writing lower indices to indicate which parts of the input and parameter vector to use, we set $\theta_{s;j} = \log g(x_s, w_j)$ and $\theta_{st;jk} = \log f(x_{st}, w_{jk})$. Different choices of g and f result in model of different complexity and expressive power.

Given a training set, $\{(x^1, y^1), \ldots, (x^n, y^n)\}$, the goal of *CRF learning* is to identify the parameters maximizing the *conditional likelihood* (CL) of the data, or equivalently, that minimizes the negative logarithm of this quantity, i.e.

$$w = \operatorname{argmin}_{\bar{w}} \ell_{CL}(\bar{w}), \quad \text{with} \quad \ell_{CL}(\bar{w}) = \sum_{i=1}^{n} E(x^i, y^i; \bar{w}) + \log Z(x^i; \bar{w}). \quad (3)$$

Unfortunately, computing expression (3) exactly is computationally infeasible (more exactly, $\#P$-hard [6]), even for small n, unless the underlying graphs are cycle-free. Consequently, all currently used methods for CRF training on cyclic graphs, as they occur in image segmentation tasks, aim only for approximate solutions. Ultimately, their performance on real data determines their usefulness. We discuss successful previous techniques in Section 3.

2.2   Least Squares CRF Training (LS-CRF)

To introduce LS-CRF, we assume an energy function in *canonical form*, i.e. the energy function contains exactly one term for each maximal clique of the underlying graph and no terms for smaller cliques. For pairwise models in which each part occurs in at least one edge this means that the energy has only pairwise terms. Note that we do not lose any expressive power by this: for every energy function with unary and pairwise terms there is an energy function with only pairwise terms that has identical values for all labelings.

Algorithm 1. LS-CRF – Training

---
input training data: $(x^i, y^i, G^i)_{i=1,\ldots,n}$,

    x^i: images, y^i: ground truth annotation, $G^i = (\mathcal{V}^i, \mathcal{E}^i)$: graphs,

input regularization parameter: $\lambda \geq 0$,

  1: set $\phi_{st}^i \leftarrow \phi(x_{st}^i) \in \mathbb{R}^D$ // edge feature vector for all $i = 1, \ldots, n$, and $(s, t) \in \mathcal{E}^i$

  2: **for** $j, k \in \mathcal{L} \times \mathcal{L}$ **do**

  3:     set $\mu_{st;jk}^i \leftarrow [\![y_s^i = j \wedge y_t^i = k]\!]$ for all $i = 1, \ldots, n$, and $(s, t) \in \mathcal{E}^i$

  4:     form training set $\mathcal{S}_{jk} = \bigcup_{i \in I} \bigcup_{(s,t) \in \mathcal{E}^i} \{(\phi_{st}^i, \mu_{st;jk}^i)\}$

  5:     learn w_{jk} from $\mathcal{S}_{jk}$ by regularized least squares regression

         $w_{jk} \leftarrow \mathrm{argmin}_{\bar{w}_{jk}} \sum_{(\phi,\mu) \in \mathcal{S}_{jk}} \|f(\phi, \bar{w}_{jk}) - \mu\|^2 + \lambda \|\bar{w}_{jk}\|^2$

  6: **end for**

output parameter vector $w = (w_{jk})_{(j,k) \in \mathcal{L} \times \mathcal{L}}$.

Algorithm 2. LS-CRF – Prediction

---
input image x, graph $G = (V, \mathcal{E})$,

input weight vector $w = (w_{jk})_{(j,k) \in \mathcal{L} \times \mathcal{L}}$,

  1: $\phi_{st} \leftarrow \phi(x_{st}, w_{jk}) \in \mathbb{R}^D$ // edge feature vector for all $(s, t) \in \mathcal{E}$

  2: **for** $j, k \in \mathcal{L} \times \mathcal{L}$ **do**

  3:    $\theta_{st;jk} = \log f_{jk}(\phi_{st})$ for all $(s, t) \in \mathcal{E}$

  4: **end for**

  5: $E(x, y; w) = \sum_{(s,t) \in \mathcal{E}, (j,k) \in \mathcal{L} \times \mathcal{L}} \theta_{st;jk} [\![y_s = j \wedge y_t = k]\!]$

output energy function $E(x, y; w)$

Algorithm 1 shows the training phase of our method in pseudocode. The main step is solving multiple independent regression problems in line 5. For each label combination, $(j, k) \in \mathcal{L} \times \mathcal{L}$, we form a training set, $\mathcal{S}_{jk} = \{(\phi^1, \mu^1), \ldots, (\phi^N, \mu^N)\}$, by merging of all pairs $(\phi_{st}^i, \mu_{st;jk}^i)$, where ϕ_{st}^i is a feature vector reflecting the visual information in the parts x_s and x_t, and $\mu_{st;jk}^i$ is an indicator whether the edge (s, t) in the training example x^i was labeled with the current label combination (j, k) or not. Note that the resulting number of samples N will be much larger than the number of training images n, since every training image contributes many edges.

We obtain w_{jk} by solving the regularized least squares regression problem

$$w_{jk} = \mathrm{argmin}_{\bar{w}_{jk}} \sum_{(\phi,\mu) \in \mathcal{S}_{jk}} \|f_{jk}(\phi, \bar{w}_{jk}) - \mu\|^2 + \lambda \|\bar{w}_{jk}\|^2, \qquad (4)$$

where $\lambda \geq 0$ is a regularization parameter. In case of a linear parameterization, $f(\phi, w) = \langle w, \phi \rangle$, Equation (4) has a closed-form solution,

$$w_{jk} = (\Phi \Phi^\top + \lambda I)^{-1} \Phi \mu, \qquad (5)$$

where $\Phi = (\phi^1 | \ldots | \phi^N)$ is the feature matrix and $\mu = (\mu^1, \ldots, \mu^N)^\top$ is the vector of outputs. Computing w_{jk} requires solving a linear system of size $D \times D$ for D-dimensional feature representation, which is possible efficiently even for D in the order of thousands. Since only matrix operations are required, Equation (5) can also be solved easily on a GPU.

To fully train a CRF, one solves one instance of Equation (5) for each label combination (j, k). Only the target vector μ differs between these, so compared to a naive loop we obtain a substantial speedup by precomputing an LU-factorization and then solving the individual problems by backwards substitution.

When the number of training examples is too large for Φ to fit into memory, the computation of $\Phi\Phi^\top$ can become the computational bottleneck. In this case, the use of iterative least-squares solvers instead of the closed-form expression is advisable, for example LBFGS [7], or plain stochastic gradient descent [5].

Algorithm 2 shows how the result of LS-CRF training is used to predict labelings for new images. We use the trained regression functions, f_{jk}, to predict the values of the pairwise terms of an energy function $E(x, y; w)$. As for any CRF, the resulting energy induces a conditional probability distribution over all possible labelings, from which we can predict an output labeling. In this work we rely on MAP prediction, i.e. $y^* = \mathrm{argmax}_{y \in \mathcal{Y}}\, p(y|x; w)$.

2.3 Extensions

Several extensions of the above procedure are possible. For example, pairwise terms of different types can be learned (e.g. vertical versus horizontal edges), by forming individual learning problems for each of them. A particular advantage of LS-CRF is that the main learning step, Equation (4), is not limited to the situation of linearly parameterized energies. This allows increasing the expressive power of the model by training nonlinear predictors when necessary, e.g. for low-dimensional feature spaces. It is also possible to use different loss functions than the squared loss. To illustrate this we also report on experiments using gradient boosted decision trees [13] and logistic loss in Section 5.

2.4 Motivation and Analysis

Like all tractable techniques for the training of cyclic CRFs, LS-CRF does not solve the exact CRF training problem but an approximation to it. In this section, we justify this approximation based on two observation: the fact that one can overcome the intractability of CRF training by constructing bounds to the partition function that decompose into smaller parts, and a classical result how to estimate the optimal parameter for tree-shaped generative probability distributions from samples.

The first aspect LS-CRF shares with other approximate training methods: for any CRFs with an energy function consisting only of pairwise terms the following inequality holds

$$\log Z(x; \theta) = \log \sum_{y \in \mathcal{Y}} \exp(-E(x, y; w)) \leq \sum_{(s,t) \in \mathcal{E}} \log \sum_{(y_s, y_t) \in \mathcal{L} \times \mathcal{L}} \exp(-E_{st}(x, y; w)), \quad (6)$$

where $E_{st}(x, y; \theta) = \sum_{(j,k) \in \mathcal{L} \times \mathcal{L}} \theta_{st;jk} [\![y_s = j \wedge y_t = k]\!]$ is the term of the energy function corresponding to the edge (s, t). This relation has been observed, for example, in [29], where it is used to motivate *piecewise training*: one replaces the $\log Z$ term in the original log-likelihood function (Equation (3)) by its upper bound and performs gradient descent optimization on the resulting approximate objective. This allows for faster training, since the right hand side of (6) decomposes additively over the edge set.

LS-CRF goes one step further, as it estimates the parameters of the decomposed model not by gradient descent on the decomposed approximate conditional likelihood, but by a direct regression between the input features and suitably chosen output values. To show the justification of this procedure, we rely on the classical, but rarely used, result that there exists a closed-form expression for estimating the parameter of a probability distribution (not conditional) with tree-shaped graph structure from samples (see [33, page 150]).

We assume the same situation as Equation 2, except that there is no dependence on x, so $\theta_{s;j}$ and $\theta_{st;jk}$ are constants. Given samples $y^1, \ldots, y^n$ from $p(y; \theta)$, an elementary calculation shows that $\hat{\theta}_{s;j} = \log \hat{\mu}_{s;j}$ and $\hat{\theta}_{st;jk} = \log \frac{\hat{\mu}_{st;jk}}{\hat{\mu}_{s;j}\hat{\mu}_{t;k}}$ are consistent estimators of the optimal $\theta_{s;j}$ and $\theta_{st;jk}$, where $\hat{\mu}_{s;j} = \frac{1}{T}\sum_{i=1}^{n}[\![y_s^i = j]\!]$ and $\hat{\mu}_{st;jk} = \frac{1}{T}\sum_{i=1}^{n}[\![y_s^i = j \wedge y_t^i = k]\!]$ are the empirical unary and pairwise marginals over the training set.

For LS-CRF we generalize the above closed-form expression to a technique for estimating the parameters of a conditional distribution, i.e. a CRF. The samples we observe, $\{(x^1, y^1), (x^2, y^2), \ldots, (x^n, y^n)\}$, are now pairs of inputs and outputs. In particular, no input repeats and for each input only one output is available. Therefore, the empirical marginals are just indicators which labels and label pairs occurred: $\hat{\mu}_{s;j}(x^i) = [\![y_s^i = j]\!]$, and $\hat{\mu}_{st;jk}(x^i) = [\![y_s^i = j \wedge y_t^i = k]\!]$. Nevertheless, we know that these values are i.i.d. samples from the conditional distributions $p(y_s = j|x)$ and $p(y_s = j, y_t = k|x)$, respectively. We can learn predictors $f_{s;j}(x) \approx p(y_s = j|x)$ and $f_{st;jk}(x) \approx p(y_s = j, y_t = k|x)$, and obtain parameter estimates $\hat{\theta}_{s;j}(x) = \log f_{s;j}$ and $\hat{\theta}_{st;jk} = \log \frac{f_{st;jk}}{f_{s;j}(x)f_{t;k}}$ that generalize from the observed samples to unseen data. Algorithm 1 implements the step of learning the pairwise predictor, $f_{st;jk}$, which we'll see below is sufficient for us.

For tree-shaped models, the learned predictors provide a consistent estimator of the conditional distribution, as long as the underlying regression technique is consistent. For cyclic models, we do not have this guarantees. However, we can apply the above construction for each edge (which is loop-free) of the decomposed representation. This yields a partial energy

$$
\begin{aligned}
E_{st}(x; \hat{\theta}_{st}) &= \sum_j \hat{\theta}_{s;j}[\![y_s = j]\!] + \sum_{j,k} \hat{\theta}_{st;jk}[\![y_s = j \wedge y_t = k]\!] + \sum_k \hat{\theta}_{t;k}[\![y_t = k]\!] \\
&= \sum_{j,k} (\hat{\theta}_{s;j} + \hat{\theta}_{st;jk} + \hat{\theta}_{t;k})[\![y_s = j \wedge y_t = k]\!] \\
&= \sum_{j,k} (\log f_{st;jk})[\![y_s = j \wedge y_t = k]\!],
\end{aligned}
\tag{7}
$$

which reflects how Algorithm 2 constructs the energy function. It also shows that only estimates for the pairwise terms are required, not for the unary ones.

3   Related Work

Probabilistic CRF training aims at maximizing the conditional likelihood of the training data. However, doing so requires probabilistic inference as a subroutine, and this is provably intractable for cyclic models [6]. Consequently, all practical methods rely on approximations. The simplest idea is to use approximate inference methods during the optimization. This can lead to unstable behavior of the optimization process or even divergence [9]. This is also not scalable, since even approximate probabilistic inference is computationally demanding.

The empirically most successful techniques form a tractable approximation to the conditional likelihood and then solve for its optimum, in particular pseudolikelihood (PL) [4] and piecewise (PW) training [29]. LS-CRF is related to PW training in that it also relies on a per-edge decomposition, but it differs in how it estimates the parameters. In particular, it supports non-linear and even non-parametric estimates of the energy function. To our knowledge this feature is only shared by *decision tree fields (DTFs)* [25], which differ, however, in other aspects. In particular, they are trained by a PL approximation.

Structured support vector machines (SSVMs) [32] have been proposed as a alternative to CRFs, based not on probabilistic reasoning but on the maximum margin principle. Like CRFs, exact SSVMs training is intractable for almost all cyclic models, since it requires repeated runs of MAP prediction during training. Similarly to CRFs, it has been observed that training with approximate MAP can lead to a drop in prediction quality [12]. In contrast to CRFs, so far few decomposition-based techniques exists for SSVMs. Prominent examples are [10,21,23], which introduce a scheme of alternating between two steps: solving independent subproblems and updating Lagrange multipliers to enforce consistency between the solutions of the subproblems. However many iterations may be required until convergence, and experience in a large-scale setting is so far missing. Another example is pseudo-max [28], which replaces the SSVM objective with a tractable approximation inspired by the PL method.

In computer vision it is common to use hybrid techniques (e.g. [14,26,27]): first, ordinary classifiers, e.g. SVMs or random forests, are trained to predict unary features. Afterwards, a CRF or SSVM is run using the outputs of the classifiers as features or drop-in replacements for the unary terms. This does not avoid training a CRF altogether, though, it only reduces the number of parameters that need to be learned.

4   Implementation

Implementing LS-CRF is straight-forward, since it only requires solving multiple regression problems. Several efficient software packages are readily available for this task. In our experiments with linear regression, we use the *Vowpal Wabbit* package[2] (LBFGS optimization, learning rate 0.5, no explicit regularization), clamping the predictions to the interval $[10^{-9}, 1]$. Vowpal Wabbit is particularly

---

[2] http://hunch.net/~vw/

suitable for large scale learning, since it supports a variety of infrastructures, from single CPUs to compute clusters. As nonlinear regressors we train gradient boosted regression trees using the *MatrixNet* package [31] with default parameters (500 oblivious trees, depth 6, learning rate 0.1).

We also implement several baselines: to study the impact of pairwise terms in the energy function, we train CRFs with only unary terms using the same regression methods as LS-CRF. We also implemented CRF training by piecewise training using Vowpal Wabbit, and by pseudolikelihood using the *grante* library[3]. In the unary-only case, both of these techniques are equivalent to logistic regression, for which we again use Vowpal Wabbit.

In addition, we implement two baselines that require global inference during training: a standard maximum-likelihood CRF trained by gradient descent with approximate gradients obtained by TRW belief propagation, and a structured SVM with approximate subgradients based on MAP prediction using MQPBO+TRWS (see below). Note that convergence for the latter two methods cannot be ensured, see our discussion in Section 5.1. Implementation and model selection is also more involved for these methods, so we suspect that improvements in terms of speed and convergence would be possible.

At test time, we create segmentations of the test images by MAP prediction. For this, we apply MQPBO [19] followed by TRWS [20], both from the *OpenGM2* library [2]. We observed that this combination is very efficient and usually yield close to optimal results.

5   Experimental Evaluation

Our focus in this work lies on large-scale semantic image segmentation, where a semantic label should be assigned to each pixel or superpixel in an image. In the case of *multi-class semantic segmentation*, these labels correspond to semantic classes, such as *road, car* or *person*. The number of labels, r, is typically between 5 and 20 in this case. A case of special interest is *figure–ground segmentation*, where $r = 2$ and the labels indicate *foreground (fg)* and *background (bg)*.

In Section 5.1 we report on experiments on the relatively small *Stanford background* dataset. The reason is that many techniques are applicable in this setup, so we can compare LS-CRF to previous techniques. In Section 5.2 we report on experiments on the *DogSeg* and *HorseSeg* datasets. These two datasets that we introduce in this work are by far larger than existing ones and show how LS-CRF allows scaling CRF training to very large datasets, and how the quality of semi-automatically generated annotation influences the segmentation quality.

5.1   Small Scale Experiments – *Stanford Background* Dataset

The *Stanford background* dataset [16], consists of 715 natural images with manually created ground truth annotation. We represent each image by a graph of

---

[3] http://www.nowozin.net/sebastian/grante/
[4] Note that *grante* is not multi-threaded, so PL runtimes are higher than necessary.

Table 1. Result of LS-CRF (top table), baselines (middle table; LR=logistic regression, PL=pseudolikelihood, PW=piecewise, ML=maximum likelihood, MM=maximum margin) and CRF-like approaches from the literature (bottom table) on the *Stanford background* dataset. Standard deviations are computed over 5 splits of the dataset. Since absolute results are hardly comparable between different publications due to different features used, we also report the absolute and relative improvement from pairwise terms (u→p) where possible.

	Accuracy				Training Time	
	unary	pairwise	u→p (abs)	u→p (rel)	unary	pairwise
LS-CRF linear	70.3 ± 1.0	73.4 ± 1.1	**3.1**	**4.4%**	66s	216s
LS-CRF nonlinear	70.9 ± 1.1	73.3 ± 1.1	**2.4**	**3.4%**	15m	150m
LR	70.4 ± 0.8	–	–	–	45s	—
PL	—	71.0 ± 1.1	**0.6**	**0.9%**	—	2356s[4]
PW	—	72.9 ± 0.9	**2.5**	**3.6%**	—	340s
ML	—	(see text)	–	–	—	>3 hours
MM	–	(see text)	–	–	—	>3 hours
Gould *et al.* [16]	–	74.3	–	–		
Gould, Zhang [17]	–	73.4-73.9	–	–		
Lempitsky *et al.* [22]	–	75.0-81.1	–	–		
Gould [15]	73.0	78.6	**5.6**	**7.7%**		
Tighe, Lazebnik [30]	76.9	77.5	**0.6**	**0.8%**		

SLIC superpixels [1] with an edge for any touching pair of superpixels. For each superpixel, s, we compute of feature vector, ϕ_s, by concatenating of the following base features: average RGB color in s (3-dimensional), center of s in relative image coordinates (2-dim.), rootSIFT descriptor [3] at the center of s (128-dim.), predicted per-label probabilities (8-dim.), where the last vector consists of the outputs of per-label training boosted tree classifiers on a subset of the training data. For each edge (s, t) we define a feature representation by concatenating the features of the contributing superpixels, $\phi_{st} = [\phi_s, \phi_t]$.

Table 1 summarizes the results on the Stanford Background dataset in numeric form. For segmentation examples, please see the supplemental material. We compare following setups: LS-CRF (unary-only or pairwise energies) with linear or nonlinear parameterization, pseudolikelihood (PL), piecewise training (PW), approximate maximum likelihood (ML) training. We also include an SSVM with approximate maximum margin (MM) training. Note, that PL, PW and ML all reduce to logistic regression (LR) when used with only unary terms.

We also report results for related methods (pairwise cyclic CRF) from the literature. In general, it is problematic to compare between results from different segmentation papers on an absolute scale, as the choice of representation and image features has a large impact. This is visible also in Table 1 by large differences already between models with only unary terms. A more robust measure is the increase a method achieves between unary and pairwise energies, which we also report for all methods where data for both cases is available.

Overall, the results show that for learning a segmentation model with only unary terms, the squared loss objective of LS-CRF achieves comparable result to the usual probabilistic loss (i.e. logistic regression). Including pairwise terms into the model improves the segmentation accuracy in all cases. The increase from LS-CRF is comparable to what other methods achieve, including results from

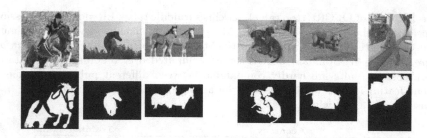

Fig. 3. Example images and segmentation masks from the *HorseSeg* (left) and *DogSeg* (right) datasets. For each dataset we illustrate: manually created annotation (left), annotation from bound boxes (middle) and annotation from per-image labels (right). Annotation from bounding boxes is typically rather accurate, the quality of annotation from per-image class labels varies substantially.

the literature, with the exception of pseudolikelihood training, which was less beneficial in this case. In terms of runtime, LS-CRF was the fastest method for training models with pairwise terms. For unary-only models, logistic regression training is slightly faster.

The nonlinear and the linear versions of LS-CRF achieve comparable performance on the Stanford background dataset, likely because the amount of training data per label or label pair is small, so the additional flexibility of a nonlinear decision function is not required.

ML and MM training are two special cases, as they require joint probabilistic inference or MAP prediction during training. We used TRW for approximate marginal inference, and MQPBO+TRWS for approximate MAP and stopped training after three hours. The results obtained were 64.8 ± 1.4 (lower than unary-only) and 72.5 ± 0.8 (lower than LS-CRF) for ML and MM, respectively. Since there is no fundamental reason why exact training should perform worse than approximate one, we do not believe that these numbers are representative for either of the methods. Better performance might be achievable with better approximate inference techniques and at the expense of longer training times.

5.2   Large Scale Experiments – *HorseSeg* and *DogSeg* Datasets

Our main interest lies on the scalable learning regime, where one hundred thousand or more images are available for training. To analyze this situation we make a second contribution of this paper besides LS-CRF: a new benchmark for large-scale CRF training in the form of two figure–ground image segmentation datasets, *HorseSeg* with 25,078 images and *DogSeg* with 156,368 images, which are available online at http://pub.ist.ac.at/~akolesnikov/HDSeg. The images for both datasets were collected from the ImageNet dataset [8] and the *trainval* part of PASCAL VOC2012 [11]. As test set, we use 241 horse images and 306 dog images, which were annotated manually with figure-ground segmentations. Note, that part of these images were annotated via Amazon Mechanical Turks and can contain a small amount of noise.

All images from the PASCAL dataset have manually created ground truth annotation as well. The remaining images from ImageNet have manual annotation of two different detail levels: each image has a class label, and approximately one quarter of all images also have annotation in form of a manually specified object bounding box. As such, the dataset provides a natural benchmark for weakly supervised or semi-supervised image segmentation in a large scale regime.

To facilitate experiments on large-scale supervised training, we also provide semi-automatically created figure-ground annotation for all images of the two datasets, based on the following procedure. For the images with bounding box annotation (6,044 of the *horse* images and 42,763 of the *dog* images), we apply the *segmentation transfer* method of [18] to the bounding box region. A visual inspection of the output (see Figure 3) shows that the resulting segmentations are of high accuracy, so using them as a proxy for manual annotation seems justified. For the remaining images only a per-image class label is known. To these images we apply the unconstrained segmentation transfer, which also yields figure–ground segmentation mask, but of mixed quality (see Figure 3). One aspect we study in our experimental evaluation is in how far the quality of image segmentation methods can be improved by adding such semi-automatically generated annotation to the training data.

Note that even though part of the training annotation is generated algorithmically, the evaluation is performed with respect to manually created ground truth, so the evaluation procedure is not biased towards the label transfer method.

For our experiments on *HorseSeg* and *DogSeg* we use the same feature representation as for the Stanford dataset, except that we add the output of per-pixel classifiers for foreground and background as two additional dimensions. The questions we would like to answer are: *1) can we scale CRF training to truly large datasets?* and *2) what is the effect of relying on semi-automatically generated annotation for this task?*

We study these questions in three sets of experiments using different subsets of the training data: (a) only images with manually created annotation, (b) images with annotation created manually or by segmentation transfer using bounding box information, (c) all training images. In each case we train CRFs with pairwise terms using the linear and nonlinear variants of LS-CRF, and we compare their segmentation performance to models with only unary terms (which is always computationally feasible). In situation (a), we use the feature vectors of all available superpixels to train the unary-only models, and all neighboring superpixel pairs to train LS-CRF with pairwise terms. In the larger setup, (b) and (c), we reduce the redundancy in the data by using only 25% of all superpixels for the unary-only models, sampled in a class-balanced way. For pairwise models, we record the ratio of pairs with *same label* versus with *different label*. Preserving this ratio, we sample 10% of all superpixels pairs, in a way that combinations with both *foreground* and both *background* are equally likely, and also *foreground/background* and *background/foreground* transitions are equally likely. The percentages are chosen such that the training problems in both situations are of comparable size. On the *DogSeg* dataset, they consists of approximately

Table 2. Results of LS-CRF for figure-ground segmentation on different subsets of the *HorseSeg* and *DogSeg* datasets. Top table: training time (in minutes), bottom row: segmentation accuracy (per-class average in %). Row indicate which subset of the training data was used; manual: only images with manually created annotation, bbox: additionally all images with annotation created automatically from bounding boxes, all: additionally all images with annotation created from per-image class labels.

a) **Training time**	linear/unary	linear/pairwise	nonlinear/unary	nonlinear/pairwise
HorseSeg - manual (147 images)	<1m	<1m	<1m	1.5m
HorseSeg - bbox (6K images)	<1m	<1m	9m	32m
HorseSeg - all (25K images)	1m	2m	88m	354m
DogSeg - manual (249 images)	2.5m	2.5m	<1m	2m
DogSeg - bbox (43K images)	7m	14m	110m	348m
DogSeg - all (156K images)	20m	46m	519m	668m

b) **Accuracy**	linear/unary	linear/pairwise	nonlinear/unary	nonlinear/pairwise
HorseSeg - manual (147 images)	81.4	82.2	81.6	83.8
HorseSeg - bbox (6K images)	82.0	83.6	83.6	86.4
HorseSeg - all (25K images)	81.4	82.5	83.3	84.5
DogSeg - manual (249 images)	77.8	78.5	79.1	80.8
DogSeg - bbox (43K images)	78.5	80.9	81.2	83.8
DogSeg - all (156K images)	78.1	80.0	80.2	82.2

90K data points for situation (a), 3.5M data points for (b), and 13M data points for (c), except the pairwise/nonlinear case, where we use only 6.5M data points for memory reasons. On the *HorseSeg*, the number are roughly half as big for (a), and one sixth for (b) and (c).

The first result is that we can answer question 1) in the positive. Table 2a) lists the approximate training time on a 12 core workstation with enabled hyper-threading, not including the overhead from feature extraction. The table shows that training linear LS-CRF is highly efficient, requiring less than one hour even for the largest dataset. The use of pairwise terms instead of just unaries only incurs a modest slowdown. For comparison, even if probabilistic inference were possible within less than one second per image, training a CRF by ordinary maximum likelihood learning on this dataset would take days or weeks. Training nonlinear predictors is computationally more expensive, but still feasible.

Figure 4 illustrates some segmentation result. More images are provided in the supplemental material. Table 2b) shows a quantitative evaluation of the segmentation accuracy of the different setups. The results allow us to make several observations that we believe will be relevant to other researchers in the area. First, it has been reported previously that pairwise terms have only a minor beneficial effect for image segmentation tasks (e.g. [14]). Our experiments confirm this observation when a linear representation is used and the number of training examples is small. However, when a large training set was used, the difference between unary-only and pairwise models increases.

Second, the use of nonlinear predictors consistently improved the segmentation quality, even though this comes at a significant cost in training time. This can be a useful insight also for other CRF training methods, which rely predominantly on linearly parameterized energy functions.

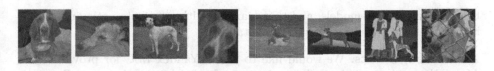

Fig. 4. Example segmentations by LS-CRF for the *DogSeg* dataset

Third, we see a substantial improvement of the segmentation quality when increasing the number of training images by adding images that had their annotation created automatically from bounding boxes information. This indicates that segmentation transfer followed by large-scale CRF learning could be a promising way for leveraging large amounts of images for training even without manually labelling them with pixelwise segmentations. Adding also images with annotation created just from per-image class labels still improves results over not using additional images, but decreases the quality compared to the situation when only images with bounding box information were used. This observation suggests that a tradeoff between the number of training examples (i.e. data collection) and the quality of annotations (i.e. labeling effort) is necessary. We plan to study this aspect in future work.

As a first step in this direction, we performed additional experiments in which we measure how useful the annotated annotation is by itself. For the *HorseSeg* dataset, we trained using exclusively the images with annotation from bounding boxes, or on images with annotation from per-image labels, i.e. we did not use the images with manually created annotation during training. This resulting per-class accuracies are 82.0 (unary) and 83.9 (pairwise) for the bounding box case, and 81.1 (unary) and 82.8 (pairwise) for the per-image case. Comparing this to the values 81.4 (unary) and 82.2 (pairwise) from Table 2b), we see that the generated segmentations do contain useful information. Even training only on images with segmentations inferred from their class label yields comparable results to training on the (much smaller) set of manually annotated images.

6 Summary

In this work we make two main contributions: 1) we present LS-CRF a new technique for inference-free CRF training that scales to very large training sets. Because of its simplicity and flexibility, we believe it has the potential to become a standard tool for training cyclic CRFs. Moreover, in future work we plan to consider approximations other then separable bound (6), for example, the Bethe approximation [33]. 2) we introduce two new benchmark datasets consisting of over 180,000 images and segmentation masks. It is meant to facilitate research on large-scale CRF training and in particular on image segmentation, which so far is held back by the lack of suitably large-scale datasets.

From our experimental evaluation we obtain first insights in this direction: we saw that the positive effect of pairwise terms increased with the size of the training set, that training CRFs with nonlinear energies is feasible and results in better segmentation models, and that learning with semi-automatic annotation is practical and useful for image segmentation.

Acknowledgements. We would like to thank Yandex LLC for providing the *MatrixNet* package. This work was in parts funded by the European Research Council under the European Unions Seventh Framework Programme (FP7/2007-2013)/ERC grant agreement no 308036.

References

1. Achanta, R., Shaji, A., Smith, K., Lucchi, A., Fua, P., Süsstrunk, S.: SLIC super-pixels compared to state-of-the-art superpixel methods. PAMI 34(11) (2012)
2. Andres, B., Beier, T., Kappes, J.H.: OpenGM: A C++ library for discrete graphical models. ArXiv e-prints 1206.0111 (2012), http://arxiv.org/abs/1206.0111
3. Arandjelović, R., Zisserman, A.: Three things everyone should know to improve object retrieval. In: CVPR (2012)
4. Besag, J.: Statistical analysis of non-lattice data. The Statistician (1975)
5. Bottou, L., Bousquet, O.: The tradeoffs of large scale learning. In: NIPS (2007)
6. Bulatov, A., Grohe, M.: The complexity of partition functions. Theoretical Computer Science 348(2) (2005)
7. Byrd, R.H., Lu, P., Nocedal, J., Zhu, C.: A limited memory algorithm for bound constrained optimization. SIAM Journal on Scientific Computing (SISC) 16(5), 1190–1208 (1995)
8. Deng, J., Dong, W., Socher, R., Li, L.J., Li, K., Fei-Fei, L.: ImageNet: A large-scale hierarchical image database. In: CVPR (2009)
9. Domke, J.: Learning graphical model parameters with approximate marginals inference. PAMI (2013)
10. Domke, J.: Structured learning via logistic regression. In: NIPS (2013)
11. Everingham, M., van Gool, L., Williams, C., Winn, J., Zisserman, A.: The Pascal visual object classes (VOC) challenge. IJCV 88(2) (2010)
12. Finley, T., Joachims, T.: Training structural SVMs when exact inference is intractable. In: ICML (2008)
13. Friedman, J.H.: Greedy function approximation: a gradient boosting machine. Annals of Statistics (2001)
14. Fulkerson, B., Vedaldi, A., Soatto, S.: Class segmentation and object localization with superpixel neighborhoods. In: ICCV (2009)
15. Gould, S.: Multiclass pixel labeling with non-local matching constraints. In: CVPR, pp. 2783–2790 (2012)
16. Gould, S., Fulton, R., Koller, D.: Decomposing a scene into geometric and semantically consistent regions. In: ICCV (2009)
17. Gould, S., Zhang, Y.: PATCHMATCHGRAPH: Building a graph of dense patch correspondences for label transfer. In: Fitzgibbon, A., Lazebnik, S., Perona, P., Sato, Y., Schmid, C. (eds.) ECCV 2012, Part V. LNCS, vol. 7576, pp. 439–452. Springer, Heidelberg (2012)
18. Guillaumin, M., Kuettel, D., Ferrari, V.: ImageNet Auto-annotation with Segmentation Propagation. IJCV (2014)
19. Kohli, P., Shekhovtsov, A., Rother, C., Kolmogorov, V., Torr, P.: On partial optimality in multi-label MRFs. In: ICML (2008)

20. Kolmogorov, V.: Convergent tree-reweighted message passing for energy minimization. PAMI 28(10) (2006)
21. Komodakis, N.: Efficient training for pairwise or higher order CRFs via dual decomposition. In: CVPR, pp. 1841–1848 (2011)
22. Lempitsky, V.S., Vedaldi, A., Zisserman, A.: A pylon model for semantic segmentation. NIPS 24, 1485–1493 (2011)
23. Meshi, O., Sontag, D., Jaakkola, T., Globerson, A.: Learning efficiently with approximate inference via dual losses (2010)
24. Nowozin, S., Lampert, C.H.: Structured learning and prediction in computer vision. Foundations and Trends in Computer Graphics and Vision 6 (2011)
25. Nowozin, S., Rother, C., Bagon, S., Sharp, T., Yao, B., Kohli, P.: Decision tree fields. In: ICCV (2011)
26. Schroff, F., Criminisi, A., Zisserman, A.: Object class segmentation using random forests. In: BMVC (2008)
27. Shotton, J., Winn, J., Rother, C., Criminisi, A.: Textonboost for image understanding: Multi-class object recognition and segmentation by jointly modeling texture, layout, and context. IJCV 81(1) (2009)
28. Sontag, D., Meshi, O., Globerson, A., Jaakkola, T.S.: More data means less inference: A pseudo-max approach to structured learning. In: NIPS (2010)
29. Sutton, C., McCallum, A.: Piecewise training of undirected models. In: UAI (2005)
30. Tighe, J., Lazebnik, S.: SuperParsing: Scalable nonparametric image parsing with superpixels. In: Daniilidis, K., Maragos, P., Paragios, N. (eds.) ECCV 2010, Part V. LNCS, vol. 6315, pp. 352–365. Springer, Heidelberg (2010)
31. Trofimov, I., Kornetova, A., Topinskiy, V.: Using boosted trees for click-through rate prediction for sponsored search. In: International Workshop on Data Mining for Online Advertising and Internet Economy (2012)
32. Tsochantaridis, I., Joachims, T., Hofmann, T., Altun, Y.: Large margin methods for structured and interdependent output variables. JMLR 6 (2005)
33. Wainwright, M.J., Jordan, M.I.: Graphical models, exponential families, and variational inference. Foundations and Trends in Machine Learning (2008)

A Graph Theoretic Approach for Object Shape Representation in Compositional Hierarchies Using a Hybrid Generative-Descriptive Model

Umit Rusen Aktas*, Mete Ozay*, Aleš Leonardis, and Jeremy L. Wyatt

School of Computer Science, The University of Birmingham, Edgbaston,
Birmingham, B15 2TT, UK
{u.aktas,m.ozay,a.Leonardis,j.l.wyatt}@cs.bham.ac.uk

Abstract. A graph theoretic approach is proposed for object shape representation in a hierarchical compositional architecture called Compositional Hierarchy of Parts (CHOP). In the proposed approach, vocabulary learning is performed using a hybrid generative-descriptive model. First, statistical relationships between parts are learned using a *Minimum Conditional Entropy Clustering* algorithm. Then, selection of *descriptive* parts is defined as a frequent subgraph discovery problem, and solved using a Minimum Description Length (MDL) principle. Finally, part compositions are constructed using learned statistical relationships between parts and their description lengths. Shape representation and computational complexity properties of the proposed approach and algorithms are examined using six benchmark two-dimensional shape image datasets. Experiments show that CHOP can employ part shareability and indexing mechanisms for fast inference of part compositions using learned shape vocabularies. Additionally, CHOP provides better shape retrieval performance than the state-of-the-art shape retrieval methods.

1 Introduction

Hierarchical compositional architectures have been studied in the literature as representations for object detection [7], categorization [10,19,21] and parsing [25]. A detailed review of the recent works is given in [26].

In this paper, we propose a graph theoretic approach for object shape representation in a hierarchical compositional architecture, called Compositional Hierarchy of Parts (CHOP), using a hybrid generative-descriptive model. Unlike hierarchical compositional architectures studied in the literature, CHOP enables us to measure and employ generative and descriptive properties of parts for the inference of part compositions in a graph theoretic framework considering part shareability, indexing and matching mechanisms. We learn a compositional vocabulary of shape parts considering not just their statistical relationships but also their *shape description* properties to generate object shapes. In addition, we take advantage of integrated models for utilization of part shareability in

---

* The first and second author contributed equally.

D. Fleet et al. (Eds.): ECCV 2014, Part III, LNCS 8691, pp. 566–581, 2014.

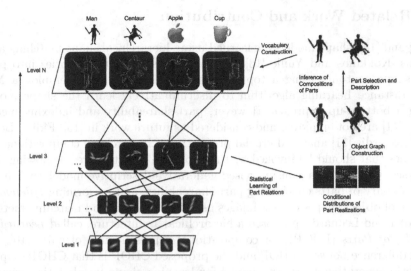

Fig. 1. The information flow of Compositional Hierarchy of Parts (CHOP)

order to construct *dense* representations of shapes in learned vocabularies for fast indexing and matching.

A diagram expressing the information flow in CHOP is given in Fig. 1. At the first layer $l = 1$ of CHOP, we extract Gabor features from a given set of images. We define parts as random graphs and represent part realizations as the instances of random graphs observed on in some dataset. At each consecutive layer, $l \geq 1$, we first learn the statistical relationships between parts using a *Minimum Conditional Entropy Clustering* (MCEC) algorithm [16] measuring conditional distributions of part realizations. For this purpose, we compute the statistical relationship between two parts by measuring the amount of information needed to describe a part realization R_i of a part P_i given the part realization R_j of another part P_j, for all parts represented in a learned vocabulary, and for all realizations observed on images. Using the learned statistical relationships, we represent compositions of object parts as object graphs. Second we define the *contribution* of a part P_i to the representation of a shape by measuring the *conditional description length* of the compositional representation of the shape given the part P_i, using the Minimum Description Length (MDL) principle. In order to select the parts which represent compositional shapes with minimum description lengths, we solve a frequent subgraph discovery problem. Then, part compositions are inferred considering learned statistical relationships between parts and their description lengths. Finally, the inferred part compositions are used to construct shape vocabularies. The steps are recursively employed until no more compositions are inferred.

The paper is organised as follows. Related work and the contributions of the paper is summarized in the next section. The proposed Compositional Hierarchy of Parts (CHOP) algorithm is given in Section 3. Experimental analyses are given in Section 4, and Section 5 concludes the paper.

2 Related Work and Contribution

In [8] and [15], shape models are learned using hierarchical shape matching algorithms. Kokkinos and Yuille [13] first decompose object categories into parts and shape contours using a top-down approach. Then, they employ a Multiple Instance Learning algorithm to discriminatively learn the shape models using a bottom-up approach. However, part-shareability and indexing mechanisms [11] are not employed and considered as future work in [13]. Fidler, Boben and Leonardis [11] analyzed crucial properties of hierarchical compositional approaches that should be invoked by the proposed architectures. Following their analyses, we develop an unsupervised generative-descriptive model for learning a vocabulary of parts considering part-shareability, and performing *efficient* inference of object shapes on test images using an indexing and matching method.

Fidler and Leonardis proposed a hierarchical architecture, called *Learned Hierarchy of Parts* (LHOP), for compositional representation of parts [10]. The main difference between LHOP and the proposed CHOP is that CHOP employs a hybrid generative-descriptive model for learning shape vocabularies using information theoretic methods in a graph theoretic framework. Specifically, CHOP first learns statistical relationships between varying number of parts, i.e. compositions of K-parts instead of the two-part compositions called (duplets) used in LHOP [10,11]. Second, shape descriptive properties of parts are integrated with their statistical properties for inference of part compositions. In addition, the number of layers in the hierarchy are not pre-defined but determined in CHOP according to the statistical properties of the data.

MDL models have been employed for statistical shape analysis [5,24], specifically to achieve compactness, specificity and generalization ability properties of shape models [5] and segmentation algorithms [6]. We employ MDL for the discovery of compositions of shape parts considering the statistical relationships between the parts, recursively in a hierarchical architecture. Hybrid generative-descriptive models have been used in [12] by employing Markov Random Fields and component analysis algorithms to construct descriptive and generative models, respectively. Although their proposed approach is hierarchical, they do not learn compositional vocabularies of parts for shape representation.

Although our primary motivation is constructing a hierarchical compositional model for shape representation, we also examined the proposed algorithms for shape retrieval in the Experiments section. For this purpose, we compare the similarity between shapes using discriminative information about shape structures extracted from a learned vocabulary of parts and their realizations. Theoretical and experimental results of [20,22,23] on spectral properties of isomorphic graphs show that the eigenvalues of the adjacency matrices of two isomorphic graphs are ordered in an interval, and therefore provide useful information for discrimination of graphs. Assuming that shapes of the objects belonging to a category are represented (*approximately*) by isomorphic graphs, we can obtain discriminative information about the shape structures by analyzing spectral properties of the part realizations detected on the shapes.

Our contributions in this work are threefold:

1. We introduce a graph theoretic approach to represent objects and parts in compositional hierarchies. Unlike other hierarchical methods [7,13,25], CHOP learns shape vocabularies using a hybrid generative-descriptive model within a graph-based hierarchical compositional framework. The proposed approach uses graph theoretic tools to analyze, measure and employ geometric and statistical properties of parts to infer part compositions.
2. Two information theoretic methods are employed in the proposed CHOP algorithm to learn the statistical properties of parts, and construct compositions of parts. First we learn the relationship between parts using MCEC [16]. Then, we select and infer compositions of parts according to their shape description properties defined by an MDL model.
3. CHOP employs a hybrid generative-descriptive model for hierarchical compositional representation of shapes. The proposed model differs from frequency-based approaches in that the part selection process is driven by the MDL principle, which effectively selects parts that are both frequently observed and provide *descriptive* information for the representation of shapes.

3   Compositional Hierarchy of Parts

In this section, we give the descriptions of the algorithms employed in CHOP in its training and testing phases. In the next section, we first describe the preprocessing algorithms that are used in both training and testing. Next, we introduce the vocabulary learning algorithms in Section 3.2. Then, we describe the inference algorithms performed on the test images in Section 3.3.

3.1   Preprocessing

Given a set of images $S = \{s_n, y_n\}_{n=1}^N$, where $y_n \in \mathbb{Z}^+$ is the category label of an image s_n, we first extract a set of Gabor features $F_n = \{f_{nm}(\mathbf{x}_{nm}) \in \mathbb{R}\}_{m=1}^M$ from each image s_n using Gabor filters employed at location $\mathbf{x}_{nm}$ in s_n at Θ orientations [10]. Then, we construct a set of Gabor features $F = \bigcup\limits_{n=1}^N F_n$. In this work, we compute the Gabor features at $\Theta = 6$ different orientations. In order to remove the redundancy of Gabor features, we perform non-maxima suppression. In this step, a Gabor feature with the Gabor response value $f_{nm}(\mathbf{x}_{nm})$ is removed from F_n if $f_{nm}(\mathbf{x}_{nm}) < f_{na}(\mathbf{x}_{na})$, for all Gabor features extracted at $\mathbf{x}_{na} \in \aleph(\mathbf{x}_{nm})$, where $\aleph(\mathbf{x}_{nm})$ is a set of image positions of the Gabor features that reside in the neighborhood of $\mathbf{x}_{nm}$ defined by Euclidean distance in $\mathbb{R}^2$. Finally, we obtain a set of suppressed Gabor features $\hat{F}_n \subset F_n$ and $\hat{F} = \bigcup\limits_{n=1}^N \hat{F}_n$.

3.2   Learning a Vocabulary of Parts

Given a set of training images S^{tr}, we first learn the statistical properties of parts using their realizations on images at a layer l. Then, we infer the compositions of parts at layer $l + 1$ by minimizing the description length of the object descriptions defined as *Object Graphs*. In order to remove the redundancy of the compositions, we employ a *local inhibition* process that was suggested in [10]. Statistical learning of part structures, inference of compositions and local inhibition processes are performed by constructing compositions of parts at each layer, recursively, and the details are given in the following subsections.

Definition 1 (Parts and Part Realizations).
The ith part constructed at the lth layer $\mathcal{P}_i^l = (\mathcal{G}_i^l, \mathcal{Y}_i^l)$ is a tuple consisting of a directed random graph $\mathcal{G}_i^l = (\mathcal{V}_i^l, \mathcal{E}_i^l)$, where $\mathcal{V}_i^l$ is a set of nodes and $\mathcal{E}_i^l$ is a set of edges, and $\mathcal{Y}_i^l \in \mathbb{Z}^+$ is a random variable which represents the identity number or label of the part. The realization $R_i^l(s_n) = (G_i^l(s_n), Y_i^l(s_n))$ of $\mathcal{P}_i^l$ is defined by 1) $Y_i^l(s_n)$ which is the realization of $\mathcal{Y}_i^l$ representing the label of the part realization on an image (s_n), and 2) the directed graph $G_i^l(s_n) = \{V_i^l(s_n), E_i^l(s_n)\}$ which is an instance of the random graph $\mathcal{G}_i^l$ computed on a training image $(s_n) \in S^{tr}$, where $V_i^l(s_n)$ is a set of nodes and $E_i^l(s_n)$ is a set of edges of $G_i^l(s_n)$, $\forall n = 1, 2, \ldots, N_{tr}$.

At the first layer $l = 1$, each node of $\mathcal{V}_i^1$ is a part label $\mathcal{Y}_i^1 \in \mathcal{V}_i^1$ taking values from the set $\{1, 2, \ldots, \Theta\}$, and $\mathcal{E}_i^1 = \varnothing$. Similarly, $E_i^1(s_n) = \varnothing$, and each node of $V_i^1(s_n)$ is defined as a Gabor feature $f_{na}^i(\mathbf{x}_{na}) \in \hat{F}_n^{tr}$ observed in the image $s_n \in S^{tr}$ at the image location $\mathbf{x}_{na}$, i.e. the ath realization of $\mathcal{P}_i^l$ observed in $s_n \in S^{tr}$ at $\mathbf{x}_{na}$, $\forall n = 1, 2, \ldots, N_{tr}$. In the consecutive layers, the parts and part realizations are defined recursively by employing layer-wise mappings $\Psi_{l,l+1}$ defined as

$$\Psi_{l,l+1} : (\mathcal{P}^l, R^l, \mathbb{G}_l) \to (\mathcal{P}^{l+1}, R^{l+1}), \forall l = 1, 2, \ldots, L, \tag{1}$$

where $\mathcal{P}^l = \{\mathcal{P}_i^l\}_{i=1}^{A_l}$, $R^l = \{R_i^l(s_n) : s_n \in S^{tr}\}_{i=1}^{B_l}$, $\mathcal{P}^{l+1} = \{\mathcal{P}_j^{l+1}\}_{j=1}^{A_{l+1}}$, $R^{l+1} = \{R_j^{l+1}(s_n) : s_n \in S^{tr}\}_{j=1}^{B_{l+1}}$ and $\mathbb{G}_l$ is an object graph which is defined next. □

In the rest of this section, we will use $R_j^l(s_n) \triangleq R_j^l$, $\forall j = 1, 2, \ldots, B_l$, $\forall l = 1, 2, \ldots, L$, $\forall s_n \in S^{tr}$, for the sake of simplicity in the notation.

Definition 2 (Receptive and Object Graph).
A receptive graph of a part realization R_i^l is a star-shaped graph $RG_i^l = (V_i^l, E_i^l)$, which is induced from a receptive field centered at the root node R_i^l. A directed edge $e_{ab} \in E_i^l$ is defined as

$$e_{ab} = \begin{cases} (a^l, b^l, \phi_{ab}^l), & \text{if } \mathbf{x}_{nb} \in \aleph(\mathbf{x}_{na}), a = i \\ \varnothing, & otherwise \end{cases}, \tag{2}$$

where $\aleph(\mathbf{x}_{na})$ is the set of part realizations that reside in a neighborhood of a part realization R_a^l in an image s_n, $\forall R_a^l, R_b^l \in V_i^l, b \neq i$ and $\forall s_n \in S^{tr}$. ϕ_{ab}^l defines the statistical relationship between R_a^l and R_b^l, as explained in the next subsection.

The structure of part realizations observed at the lth layer on the training set S^{tr} is described using a directed graph $\mathbb{G}_l = (\mathbb{V}_l, \mathbb{E}_l)$, called an object graph, where $\mathbb{V}_l = \bigcup_i V_i^l$ is a set of nodes, and $\mathbb{E}_l = \bigcup_i E_i^l$ is a set of edges, where V_i and E_i is the set of nodes and edges of a receptive graph RG_i, $\forall i$, respectively. □

Learning of Statistical Relationships between Parts and Part Realizations. We compute the *conditional* distributions $P_{\mathcal{P}_i^l}(R_a^l | \mathcal{P}_j^l = R_b^l)$ for each $i = Y_a^l$ and $j = Y_b^l$ between all possible pairs of parts $(\mathcal{P}_i^l, \mathcal{P}_j^l)$ using S^{tr} at the lth layer. However, we select a set of modes $\mathcal{M}^l = \{M_{ij} : i = 1, 2, \ldots, B_l, j = 1, 2, \ldots, B_l\}$, where $M_{ij} = \{M_{ijk}\}_{k=1}^K$ of these distributions instead of detecting a single mode. For this purpose, we define the mode computation problem as a *Minimum Conditional Entropy Clustering* problem [16] as

$$Z_{ijk} := \arg\min_{\pi_k \in C} H(\pi_k, R_a^l | R_b^l), \tag{3}$$

$$H(\pi_k, R_a^l | R_b^l) = - \sum_{\forall \mathbf{x}_{na}^l \in \aleph(\mathbf{x}_{nb}^l)} \sum_{k=1}^K P(\pi_k, R_a^l | R_b^l) \log P(\pi_k, R_a^l | R_b^l). \tag{4}$$

The first summation is over all part realizations R_a^l that reside in a neighborhood of all R_b^l such that $\mathbf{x}_{na}^l \in \aleph(\mathbf{x}_{nb}^l)$, for all $i = Y_a^l$ and $j = Y_b^l$, C is a set of cluster ids, $K = |C|$ is the number of clusters, $\pi_k \in C$ is a cluster label, and $P(\pi_k, R_a^l | R_b^l) \triangleq P_{\mathcal{P}_i^l}(\pi_k, R_a^l | \mathcal{P}_j^l = R_b^l)$.

The pairwise statistical relationship between two part realizations R_a^l and R_b^l is represented as $M_{ijk} = (i, j, \mathbf{c}_{ijk}, Z_{ijk})$, where $\mathbf{c}_{ijk}$ is the center position of the kth cluster. In the construction of an object graph $\mathbb{G}_l$ at the lth layer, we compute $\phi_{ab}^l = (\mathbf{c}_{ijk}, \hat{k})$, $\forall a, b$ as $\hat{k} = \arg\min_{k \in C} \|\mathbf{d}_{ab} - \mathbf{c}_{ijk}\|_2$, where $\|\cdot\|_2$ is the Euclidean distance, $i = Y_a^l$ and $j = Y_b^l$, $\mathbf{d}_{ab} = \mathbf{x}_{na} - \mathbf{x}_{nb}$, $\mathbf{x}_{na}$ and $\mathbf{x}_{nb}$ are the positions of R_a^l and R_j^l in an image s_n, respectively.

Inference of Compositions of Parts Using MDL. Given a set of parts $\mathcal{P}^l$, a set of part realizations $\mathcal{R}^l$, and an object graph $\mathbb{G}_l$ at the lth layer, we infer compositions of parts at the $(l+1)^{st}$ layer by computing a mapping $\Psi_{l,l+1}$ in (1). In this mapping, we search for a structure which *best describes* the structure of parts $\mathcal{P}^l$ as the compositions constructed at the $(l+1)^{st}$ layer by minimizing the length of description of $\mathcal{P}^l$. In the inference process, we search a set of graphs $\mathcal{G}^{l+1} = \{\mathcal{G}_j^{l+1}\}_{j=1}^{A_{l+1}}$ which minimizes the description length of $\mathbb{G}_l$ as

$$\mathcal{G}^{l+1} = \arg\min_{\mathcal{G}_j^{l+1}} value(\mathcal{G}_j^{l+1}, \mathbb{G}_l), \tag{5}$$

where

$$value(\mathcal{G}_j^{l+1}, \mathbb{G}_l) = \frac{DL(\mathcal{G}_j^{l+1}) + DL(\mathbb{G}_l | \mathcal{G}_j^{l+1})}{DL(\mathbb{G}_l)}. \tag{6}$$

is the compression value of an object graph $\mathbb{G}_l$ given a subgraph $\mathcal{G}_j^{l+1}$ of a receptive graph RG_j^l, $\forall j = 1, 2, \ldots, B_l$. Description length DL of a graph G is calculated using the number of bits to represent node labels, edge labels and adjacency matrix, as explained in [3]. The inference process consists of two steps:

1. **Enumeration:** In the graph enumeration step, candidate graphs $\mathcal{G}^{l+1}$ are generated from $\mathbb{G}_l$. However, each $\mathcal{G}_j^{l+1} \in \mathbb{G}_l$ is required to include nodes

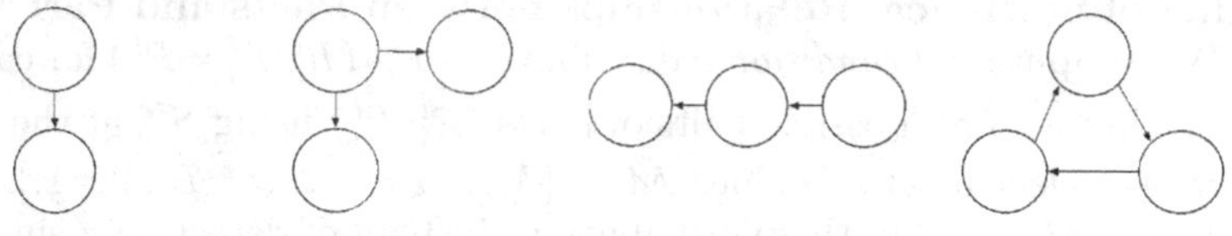

(a) $\mathcal{G}_1^{l+1}$ (Valid)   (b) $\mathcal{G}_2^{l+1}$ (Valid)   (c) $\mathcal{G}_3^{l+1}$ (Invalid)   (d) $\mathcal{G}_4^{l+1}$ (Invalid)

Fig. 2. Valid and invalid candidates

Input : $\mathbb{G}_l = (\mathbb{V}_l, \mathbb{E}_l)$: Object graph, *beam*, *numBest*, *bestPartSize*.
Output: Parts $\mathcal{P}^{l+1}$, realizations $\mathcal{R}^{l+1}$.
1 *parentList* := *null*; *childList* := *null*; *bestPartList* := *null*;
   where *childList*,*bestPartList* are priority queues ordered by MDL scores.
2 Initialize *parentList* with frequent single node parts;
3 **while** *parentList is not empty* **do**
4   Extend parts in *parentList* in all possible ways into *childList*;
5   Evaluate parts in *childList* using (6);
6   Trim *childList* to *beam* top parts;
7   Merge elements of *childList* and *bestPartList* into *bestPartList*;
8   *parentList* := *null*;
9   Swap *parentList* and *childList*;
   end
10 Trim *bestPartList* to *maxBest* top parts;
11 $\mathcal{P}^{l+1}$:= *bestPartList*;
12 $\mathcal{R}^{l+1}$:= *bestPartList*.getInstances();

Algorithm 1: Inference of new Compositions

$\mathcal{V}_j^{l+1}$ and edges $\mathcal{E}_j^{l+1}$ from only one receptive graph RG_i^l, $\forall i$. This selective candidate generation procedure enforces $\mathcal{G}_j^{l+1}$ to represent an area around its centre node. Examples of valid and invalid candidates are illustrated in Fig. 2. $\mathcal{G}_1^{l+1}$ and $\mathcal{G}_2^{l+1}$ are valid structures since each graph is inferred from a single receptive graph, e.g. RG_1^l and RG_2^l, respectively. Invalid graphs $\mathcal{G}_3^{l+1}$ and $\mathcal{G}_4^{l+1}$ are not enumerated since their nodes/edges are inferred from multiple receptive graphs.

2. **Evaluation:** Once we obtain $\mathcal{G}^{l+1}$ by solving (5) with $\mathcal{G}^{l+1}$ subject to constraints provided in the previous step, we compute a set of graph instances of part realizations $G^{l+1} = \{G_i^{l+1}\}_{i=1}^{B_{l+1}}$ such that $G_i^{l+1} \in iso(\mathcal{G}_j^{l+1})$ and $G_i^{l+1} \subseteq \mathbb{G}_l$, where $iso(\mathcal{G}_j^{l+1})$ is a set of all subgraphs that are isomorphic to $\mathcal{G}_j^{l+1}$. This problem is defined as a subgraph isomorphism problem [4], which is NP-complete. In this work, the proposed graph structures are acyclic and star-shaped, enabling us to solve (5) in P-time. In order to obtain two sets of subgraphs $\mathcal{G}^{l+1}$ and G^{l+1} by solving (5), we have implemented a simplified version of the substructure discovery system, SUBDUE [4] which is employed in a restricted search space. The discovery algorithm is explained in

Algorithm 1. The key difference between the original SUBDUE and our implementation is that in Step **4**, *childList* contains only star-shaped graphs, which are extended from *parentList* by single nodes. The parameters *beam*, *numBest*, *bestPartSize* are used to prune the search space.

The label of a part $\mathcal{P}_j^{l+1}$ is defined according to its compression value $\mu_j^{l+1} \triangleq value(\mathcal{G}_j^{l+1}, \mathbb{G}_l)$ computed in (6). We sort compression values in ascending order, and assign the part label to the index of the compression value of the part.

After sets of graphs and part labels are obtained at the $(l+1)^{st}$ layer, we construct a set of parts $\mathcal{P}^{l+1} = \{\mathcal{P}_i^{l+1}\}_{i=1}^{A_{l+1}}$, where $\mathcal{P}_i^{l+1} = (\mathcal{G}_i^{l+1}, \mathcal{Y}_i^{l+1})$. We call $\mathcal{P}^{l+1}$ a set of *compositions* of the parts from $\mathcal{P}^l$, constructed at the $(l+1)^{st}$ layer. Similarly, we extract a set of part realizations $\hat{R}^{l+1} = \{R_j^{l+1}\}_{j=1}^{B_{l+1}}$, where $R_j^{l+1} = (G_j^{l+1}, Y_j^{l+1})$. In order to remove the redundancy in $\hat{R}^{l+1}$, we perform local inhibition as in [10] and obtain a new set of part realizations $R^{l+1} \subseteq \hat{R}^{l+1}$.

Incremental Construction of the Vocabulary

Definition 3 (Vocabulary). *A tuple $\Omega_l = (\mathcal{P}^l, \mathcal{M}^l)$ is the vocabulary constructed at the lth layer using the training set S^{tr}. The vocabulary of a CHOP with L layers is defined as the set $\Omega = \{\Omega_l : l = 1, 2, \ldots, L\}$.* □

We construct Ω of CHOP incrementally as described in the pseudo-code of the vocabulary learning algorithm given in Algorithm 2. In the first step of the algorithm, we extract a set of Gabor features $F_n = \{f_{nm}(\mathbf{x}_{nm})\}_{m=1}^{M}$ from each image $s_n \in S^{tr}$ using Gabor filters employed at location $\mathbf{x}_{nm}$ in s_n at Θ orientations. Then, we perform local inhibition of Gabor features using non-maxima suppression to construct a set of suppressed Gabor features $\hat{F}_n \subset F_n$ as described in Section 3.1 in the second step. Next, we initialize the variable l which defines the layer index, and we construct parts $\mathcal{P}^1$ and part realizations R^1 at the first layer as described in Definition 1.

In steps **5 – 11**, we incrementally construct the vocabulary of the CHOP. In step **5**, we compute the sets of modes $\mathcal{M}^l$ by learning statistical relationships between part realizations as described in Section 3.2. In the sixth step, we construct an object graph $\mathbb{G}_l$ using $\mathcal{M}^l$ as explained in Definition 2, and we construct the vocabulary $\Omega_l = (\mathcal{P}^l, \mathcal{M}^l)$ at the lth layer in step **7**. Next, we infer part graphs that will be constructed at the next layer $\mathcal{G}^{l+1}$ by computing the mapping $\Psi_{l,l+1}$. For this purpose, we solve (5) using our graph mining implementation to obtain a set of parts $\mathcal{P}^{l+1}$ and a set of part realizations R^{l+1} as explained in Section 3.2. We increment l in step **10**, and subsample the positions of part realizations R_i^l by a factor of σ, $\forall n, R_i^l$ in step **11**, which effectively increases the area of the receptive fields through upper layers. We iterate the steps **5 – 11** while a non-empty part graph $\mathcal{G}_l^l$ is either obtained from the training images at the first layer, or inferred from Ω_{l-1}, R^{l-1} and $\mathbb{G}_{l-1}$ at $l > 1$, i.e. $\mathcal{G}^l \neq \varnothing$, $\forall l \geq 1$. As the output of the algorithm, we obtain the vocabulary of CHOP, $\Omega = \{\Omega_l : l = 1, 2, \ldots, L\}$.

Input :
- $S^{tr} = \{s_n\}_{n=1}^N$: Training dataset,
- Θ: The number of different orientations of Gabor features,
- σ: Subsampling ratio.

Output: Vocabulary Ω.

1 Extract a set of Gabor features $F^{tr} = \bigcup\limits_{n=1}^N F_n^{tr}$, where $F_n^{tr} = \{f_{nm}(\mathbf{x}_{nm})\}_{m=1}^M$ from each image $s_n \in S^{tr}$;

2 Construct a set of suppressed Gabor features $\hat{F}^{tr} \subset F^{tr}$ (see Section 3.1);

3 $l := 1$;

4 Construct $\mathcal{P}^1$ and R^1 (see Definition 1);

   while $\mathcal{G}^l \neq \varnothing$ **do**

5   Compute the sets of modes $\mathcal{M}^l$ (see Section 3.2);

6   Construct $\mathbb{G}_l$ using $\mathcal{M}^l$ (see Definition 2);

7   Construct $\Omega_l = (\mathcal{P}^l, \mathcal{M}^l)$;

8   Infer part graphs $\mathcal{G}^{l+1}$ by solving (5) (see Section 3.2);

9   Construct $\mathcal{P}^{l+1}$ and R^{l+1} (see Section 3.2);

10      $l := l + 1$;

11   Subsample the positions of part realizations R_i^l by a factor of σ, $\forall n, R_i^l$;

   end

12 $\Omega = \{\Omega_t : t = 1, 2, \ldots, l - 1\}$;

Algorithm 2: The vocabulary learning algorithm of Compositional Hierarchy of Parts

3.3   Inference of Object Shapes on Test Images

In the testing phase, we infer shapes of objects on test images $s_n \in S^{te}$ using the learned vocabulary of parts Ω. We incrementally construct a set of inference graphs $\mathcal{T}(s_n) = \{\mathcal{T}_l(s_n)\}_{l=1}^L$ of a given test image $s_n \in S^{te}$ using the learned vocabulary $\Omega = \{\Omega_l\}_{l=1}^L$. At each lth layer, we construct a set of part realizations $R^l(s_n) = \left\{R_i^l(s_n) = \left(G_i^l(s_n), Y_i^l(s_n)\right)\right\}_{i=1}^{B'_l}$ and an object graph $\mathbb{G}_l = (\mathbb{V}_l, \mathbb{E}_l)$ of s_n, $\forall l = 1, 2, \ldots, L$. Algorithm 3 explains the inference algorithm for test images. The test image is processed in the same manner as in vocabulary learning (steps $1 - 5$). In step **6**, isomorphisms of part graph descriptions $\mathcal{G}^{l+1}$ obtained from Ω_{l+1} are searched in $\mathbb{G}_l$ in P-time (see Section 3.2). Part realizations R^{l+1} of the new object graph $\mathbb{G}_{l+1}$ are extracted from G^{l+1} in step **7**. The discovery process continues until no new realizations are found.

At the first layer $l = 1$, the nodes of the instance graph $G_i^1(s_n)$ of a part realization $R_i^1(s_n)$ represent the Gabor features $f_{na}^i(\mathbf{x}_{na}) \in \hat{F}_n^{te}$ observed in the image $s_n \in S^{te}$ at an image location $\mathbf{x}_{na}$ as described in Section 3.2. In order to infer the graph instances and compositions of part realizations in the following layers $1 < l \leq L$, we employ a graph matching algorithm that constructs $G_i^{l+1}(s_n) = \{H(\mathcal{P}^{l+1}) : H(\mathcal{P}^{l+1}) \subseteq \mathbb{G}_l\}$ which is a set of subgraph isomorphisms $H(\mathcal{P}^{l+1})$ of part graphs $\mathcal{G}^{l+1}$ in $\mathcal{P}^{l+1}$, computed in $\mathbb{G}_l$.

Input :
- s: Test image,
- Ω: Vocabulary,
- Θ: The number of different orientations of Gabor features,
- σ: Subsampling ratio.

Output: Inference graph $\mathcal{T}(s)$.

1 Extract a set of Gabor features $F = \{f_m(\mathbf{x}_m)\}_{m=1}^{M}$ from image s;
2 Construct a set of suppressed Gabor features $\hat{F} \subset F$ (see Section 3.1);
3 $l := 1$;
4 Construct R^1 from $\hat{F}$ (see Definition 1);

  while $\Omega_{l+1} \neq \varnothing \wedge R^l \neq \varnothing$ **do**

5 | Construct $\mathbb{G}_l$ using $\mathcal{M}^l$ in Ω_l;
6 | Find graph instances of part realizations $G^{l+1} = \{G_j^{l+1}\}_{j=1}^{B'_{l+1}}$ such that $G_j^{l+1} \in iso(\mathcal{G}^{l+1})$ and $G_j^{l+1} \subseteq \mathbb{G}_l$ (see Section 3.2, **Evaluation**);
7 | Construct R^{l+1} from G^{l+1} (see Section 3.2);
8 | $l := l + 1$;
9 | Subsample the positions of part realizations R_i^l by a factor of σ, $\forall R_i^l$;

  end

10 $\mathcal{T}(s) = \{\mathbb{G}_t : t = 1, 2, \ldots, l - 1\}$;

Algorithm 3: Object shape inference algorithm for test images

---

4 Experiments

We examine our proposed approach and algorithms on six benchmark object shape datasets, which are namely the Washington image dataset (Washington) [1], the MPEG-7 Core Experiment CE-Shape 1 dataset [14], the ETHZ Shape Classes dataset [9], 40 sample articulated Tools dataset (Tools-40) [17], 35 sample multi-class Tools dataset (Tools-35) [2] and the Myth dataset [2]. In the experiments, we used $\Theta = 6$ different orientations of Gabor features with the same Gabor kernel parameters implemented in [10]. We used a subsampling ratio of $\sigma = 0.5$. A Matlab implementation of CHOP is available here[1]. Additional analyses related to part shareability and qualitative results are given in the Supplementary Material.

4.1 Analysis of Generative and Descriptive Properties

We analyze the relationship between the number of classes, views, objects, and vocabulary size, average MDL values and test inference time in three different setups, respectively. Vocabulary size and test inference time analyses provide information about the part shareability and generative shape representation behavior of our algorithm. We examine the variations of the average MDL values under different test sets. In order to get a more descriptive estimate of MDL values, we use 10 best parts constructed at each layer of CHOP. While a vocabulary

---

[1] https://github.com/rusen/CHOP.git

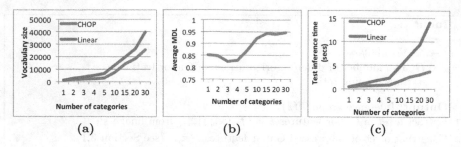

Fig. 3. Analyses with different number of categories. (Best viewed in colour).

layer may contain thousands of parts, most of the parts constructed with the lowest MDL scores belong to a single object in the model, and therefore exhibit no shareability.

The inference time of CHOP is calculated by averaging running times of the inference algorithm which is employed on test images.

Analyses with Different Number of Categories. In this section we use the first 30 categories of the MPEG-7 Core Experiment CE-Shape 1 dataset [14]. We randomly select 5 images from each category to construct training sets.

The vocabulary size grows sub-linearly as shown with the blue line in Fig. 3.a. The higher part shareability observed in the first layers of CHOP is considered as the main contributing factor which affects the vocabulary size. We observe a sub-linear growth of the number of parts as the number of categories increases, which affects the test image inference time as shown in Fig. 3.c. This is observed because the inference process requires searching every composition in the vocabulary within the graph representation of a test image. The efficient indexing mechanism implemented in CHOP speeds up the testing time, and the average test time is calculated as 0.5-3 seconds depending on the number of categories. Average MDL values tend to increase after a boost at around 3-4 categories (lower is better), and converge at 15 categories. The inter-class appearance differences allow for a limited amount of shareability between categories.

4.2 Analyses with Different Number of Objects

In order to analyze the effect of increasing number of images to the proposed performance measures, we use 30 samples belonging to the "Apple Logos" class in ETHZ Shape Classes dataset [9] for training. Compared to the results obtained in the previous section, we observe that average MDL values increase gradually as the number of objects increase in Fig. 4.b. Additionally, the growth rate of the vocabulary size observed in Fig. 4.a is less than the one depicted in Fig. 3.a.

4.3 Analyses with Different Number of Views

In the third set of experiments, we use a subset of Washington image dataset [1] consisting of images captured at different views of the same object. Multiple

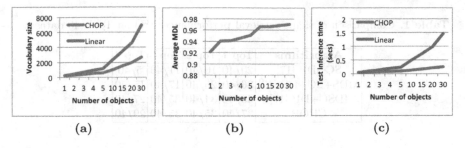

Fig. 4. Analyses with different number of objects. (Best viewed in colour).

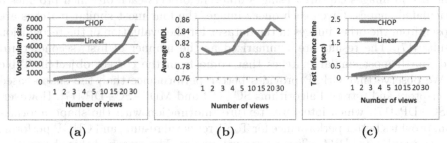

Fig. 5. Analyses with different number of views. (Best viewed in colour).

view images of a cup are used as the training data. Due to the fairly symmetrical nature of a cup except for its textures and handle, the shareability of the parts in the vocabulary remains consistent as the training image set grows. Interestingly, we observe a local maximum at around 15 views in Fig. 5.b. Depending on the inhibition and part selection (SUBDUE) parameters, less frequently observed yet valuable parts may be discarded by the algorithm in mid-layers.

4.4 Shape Retrieval Experiments

Following the results of [20,22,23], we employ eigenvalues of adjacency matrices of edge weighted graphs computed using object graphs of shapes as shape descriptors. For this purpose, we first define edge weights $e_{ab} \in E_l$ of an edge weighted graph $W_l = (V_l, E_l)$ of an object graph $\mathbb{G}_l = (\mathbb{V}_l, \mathbb{E}_l)$ as

$$e_{ab} = \begin{cases} \pi_k, & \text{if } \text{R}_a^l \text{ is connected to } \text{R}_b^l, \quad \forall R_a^l, R_b^l \in \mathbb{V}_l \\ 0, & otherwise \end{cases}, \quad (7)$$

where π_k is the cluster index which minimizes the conditional entropy (4) in (3). Then, we compute the weighted adjacency matrix of W_l and use the eigenvalues as shape descriptors. We compute the distance between two shapes as the Euclidean distance between their shape descriptors.

In the first set of experiments, we compare the retrieval performances of CHOP and the state-of-the-art shape classification algorithms which use inner-distance (ID) measures to compute shape descriptors which are robust to articulation [17]. The experiments are performed on Tools-40 dataset [17] which

Table 1. Comparison of shape retrieval performances (%) on Tools-40 dataset

Algorithms	Top 1	Top 2	Top 3	Top 4
SC+DP [17]	20/40	10/40	11/40	5/40
MDS+SC+DP [17]	36/40	26/40	17/40	15/40
IDSC+DP [17]	40/40	34/40	35/40	27/40
CHOP	37/40	35/40	35/40	29/40

contains 40 images captured using 8 different objects each of which provides 5 articulated shapes. Given each query image, the four most similar matches are chosen from the other images in the dataset for the evaluation of the recognition results [17]. The results are summarized as the number of first, second, third and fourth most similar matches that come from the correct object in Table 1. We observe that CHOP provides better performance than the shape-based descriptors and retrieval algorithms SC+DP and MDS+SC+DP [17]. However, IDSC+DP [17], which integrates texture information with the shape information, provides better performance for Top 1 retrieval results, and CHOP performs better than IDSC+DP for Top 4 retrieval results. The reason of this observation is that texture of shape structures provides discriminative information about shape categories. Therefore, the objects which have the most similar textures are closer to each other than the other objects as observed in Top 1 retrieval results. On the other hand, texture information may dominate the shape information and may lead to overfitting as observed in Top 4 retrieval results (see Table 1).

In the second set of experiments, we use Myth and Tools-35 datasets in order to analyze the performance of the shape retrieval algorithms [18] and CHOP, considering part shareability and category-wise articulation. In the Myth dataset, there are three categories, namely Centaur, Horse and Man, and 5 different images belonging to 5 different objects in each category. Shapes observed in images differ by articulation and additional parts, e.g. the shapes of objects belonging to Centaur and Man categories share the upper part of the man body, and the shapes of objects belonging to Centaur and Horse categories share the lower part of the horse body. In the Tools-35 dataset, there are 35 shapes belonging to 4 categories which are split as 10 scissors, 15 pliers, 5 pincers, 5 knives. Each object belonging to a category differs by an articulation. Performance values are calculated using a Bullseye test as suggested in [18] to compare the performances of CHOP and other shape retrieval algorithms Contour-ID [18] and Contour-HF [18]. In the Bullseye test, five most similar candidates for each query image are considered [18]. Experimental results given in Table 2 show that CHOP outperforms Contour-ID and Contour-HF [18] which employ distributions of descriptor values calculated at shape contours as shape features that are invariant to articulations and deformations in local part structures. However, part shareability and articulation properties of shapes may provide discriminative information about shape structures, especially on the images in the Myth dataset.

Table 2. Comparison of shape retrieval performances (%) on Myth and Tools-35

Datasets	Contour-ID [18]	Contour-HF [18]	CHOP
Tools-35	84.57	84.57	87.86
Myth	77.33	90.67	93.33

5   Conclusion

We have proposed a graph theoretic approach for object shape representation in a hierarchical compositional architecture called Compositional Hierarchy of Parts (CHOP). Two information theoretic algorithms are used for learning a vocabulary of compositional parts employing a hybrid generative-descriptive model. First, statistical relationships between parts are learned using the MCEC algorithm. Then, part selection problem is defined as a frequent subgraph discovery problem, and solved using an MDL principle. Part compositions are inferred considering both learned statistical relationships between parts and their description lengths at each layer of CHOP.

The proposed approach and algorithms are examined using six benchmark shape datasets consisting of different images of an object captured at different viewpoints, and images of objects belonging to different categories. The results show that CHOP can use part shareability property in the construction of *compact* vocabularies and inference trees efficiently. For instance, we observe that the running time of CHOP to perform inference on test images is approximately 0.5-3 seconds for an image. Additionally, we can construct compositional shape representations which provide part realizations that completely cover the shapes on the images. Finally, we compared shape retrieval performances of CHOP and the state-of-the-art retrieval algorithms on three benchmark datasets. The results show that CHOP outperforms the evaluated algorithms using part shareability and fast inference of descriptive part compositions.

In the future work, we will employ discriminative learning for pose estimation and categorization of shapes. In addition, online and incremental learning will be implemented considering the results obtained from the analyses on part shareability performed in this work.

Acknowledgement. This work was supported in part by the European Commission project PaCMan EU FP7-ICT, 600918. The authors would also like to thank Sebastian Zurek for helpful discussions.

References

1. Bo, L., Lai, K., Ren, X., Fox, D.: Object recognition with hierarchical kernel descriptors. In: Proceedings of the 2011 IEEE Conference on Computer Vision and Pattern Recognition, CVPR 2011, pp. 1729–1736. IEEE Computer Society, Washington, DC (2011)

2. Bronstein, A.M., Bronstein, M.M., Bruckstein, A.M., Kimmel, R.: Analysis of two-dimensional non-rigid shapes. Int. J. Comput. Vision 78(1), 67–88 (2008)
3. Cook, D.J., Holder, L.B.: Substructure discovery using minimum description length and background knowledge. J. Artif. Int. Res. 1(1), 231–255 (1994), http://dl.acm.org/citation.cfm?id=1618595.1618605
4. Cook, D.J., Holder, L.B.: Mining Graph Data. John Wiley & Sons (2006)
5. Davies, R.H., Twining, C.J., Cootes, T.F., Waterton, J.C., Taylor, C.J.: A minimum description length approach to statistical shape modeling. IEEE Trans. Med. Imag. 21(5), 525–537 (2002)
6. Delong, A., Gorelick, L., Veksler, O., Boykov, Y.: Minimizing energies with hierarchical costs. Int. J. Comput. Vision 100(1), 38–58 (2012)
7. Felzenszwalb, P., Girshick, R., McAllester, D., Ramanan, D.: Object detection with discriminatively trained part-based models. IEEE Trans. Pattern Anal. Mach. Intell. 32(9), 1627–1645 (2010)
8. Felzenszwalb, P., Schwartz, J.: Hierarchical matching of deformable shapes. In: Proceedings of the 2007 IEEE Computer Society Conference on Computer Vision and Pattern Recognition, pp. 1–8 (June 2007)
9. Ferrari, V., Tuytelaars, T., Van Gool, L.: Object detection by contour segment networks. In: Leonardis, A., Bischof, H., Pinz, A. (eds.) ECCV 2006. LNCS, vol. 3953, pp. 14–28. Springer, Heidelberg (2006)
10. Fidler, S., Leonardis, A.: Towards scalable representations of object categories: Learning a hierarchy of parts. In: Proceedings of the 2007 IEEE Computer Society Conference on Computer Vision and Pattern Recognition, CVPR 2007, pp. 1–8 (June 2007)
11. Fidler, S., Boben, M., Leonardis, A.: Learning hierarchical compositional representations of object structure. In: Dickinson, S.J., Leonardis, A., Schiele, B., Tarr, M.J. (eds.) Object categorization computer and human perspectives, pp. 196–215. Cambridge University Press, Cambridge (2009)
12. Guo, C.-E., Zhu, S.-C., Wu, Y.N.: Modeling visual patterns by integrating descriptive and generative methods. Int. J. Comput. Vision 53(1), 5–29 (2003)
13. Kokkinos, I., Yuille, A.: Inference and learning with hierarchical shape models. Int. J. Comput. Vis. 93(2), 201–225 (2011)
14. Latecki, L., Lakamper, R., Eckhardt, T.: Shape descriptors for non-rigid shapes with a single closed contour. In: Proceedings of the 2000 IEEE Computer Society Conference on Computer Vision and Pattern Recognition, vol. 1, pp. 424–429 (June 2000)
15. Levinshtein, A., Sminchisescu, C., Dickinson, S.J.: Learning hierarchical shape models from examples. In: Rangarajan, A., Vemuri, B.C., Yuille, A.L. (eds.) EMMCVPR 2005. LNCS, vol. 3757, pp. 251–267. Springer, Heidelberg (2005)
16. Li, H., Zhang, K., Jiang, T.: Minimum entropy clustering and applications to gene expression analysis. In: Proceedings of the 2004 IEEE Computational Systems Bioinformatics Conference, CSB 2004, pp. 142–151. IEEE Computer Society, Washington, DC (2004)
17. Ling, H., Jacobs, D.: Shape classification using the inner-distance. IEEE Trans. Pattern Anal. Mach. Intell. 29(2), 286–299 (2007)
18. Nanni, L., Brahnam, S., Lumini, A.: Local phase quantization descriptor for improving shape retrieval/classification. Pattern Recogn. Lett. 33(16), 2254–2260 (2012)
19. Ommer, B., Buhmann, J.M.: Learning the compositional nature of visual object categories for recognition. IEEE Trans. Pattern Anal. Mach. Intell. 32(3), 501–516 (2010)

20. Raviv, D., Kimmel, R., Bruckstein, A.M.: Graph isomorphisms and automorphisms via spectral signatures. IEEE Trans. Pattern Anal. Mach. Intell. 35(8), 1985–1993 (2013)
21. Salakhutdinov, R., Tenenbaum, J.B., Torralba, A.: Learning with hierarchical-deep models. IEEE Trans. Pattern Anal. Mach. Intell. 35(8), 1958–1971 (2013)
22. Shokoufandeh, A., Macrini, D., Dickinson, S., Siddiqi, K., Zucker, S.W.: Indexing hierarchical structures using graph spectra. IEEE Trans. Pattern Anal. Mach. Intell. 27(7), 1125–1140 (2005)
23. Siddiqi, K., Shokoufandeh, A., Dickinson, S.J., Zucker, S.W.: Shock graphs and shape matching. Int. J. Comput. Vision 35(1), 13–32 (1999)
24. Torsello, A., Hancock, E.R.: Learning shape-classes using a mixture of tree-unions. IEEE Trans. Pattern Anal. Mach. Intell. 28(6), 954–967 (2006)
25. Zhu, A.L., Chen, Y., Yuille: Learning a hierarchical deformable template for rapid deformable object parsing. IEEE Trans. Pattern Anal. Mach. Intell. 32(6), 1029–1043 (2010)
26. Zhu, L.L., Chen, Y., Yuille, A.: Recursive compositional models for vision: Description and review of recent work. J. Math. Imaging Vis. 41(1-2), 122–146 (2011)

Finding Approximate Convex Shapes
in RGBD Images

Hao Jiang

Computer Science Department, Boston College, USA

Abstract. We propose a novel method to find approximate convex 3D
shapes from single RGBD images. Convex shapes are more general than
cuboids, cylinders, cones and spheres. Many real-world objects are near-
convex and every non-convex object can be represented using convex
parts. By finding approximate convex shapes in RGBD images, we extract important structures of a scene. From a large set of candidates
generated from over-segmented superpixels we globally optimize the selection of these candidates so that they are mostly convex, have small
intersection, have a small number and mostly cover the scene. The optimization is formulated as a two-stage linear optimization and efficiently
solved using a branch and bound method which is guaranteed to give the
global optimal solution. Our experiments on thousands of RGBD images
show that our method is fast, robust against clutter and is more accurate
than competing methods.

1 Introduction

Finding 3D structures from RGBD images is an important computer vision task.
Instead of finding shape primitives such as planes, cuboids, spheres or cylinders,
we extract shapes that are roughly convex from a single RGBD image. A RGBD
image provides the information of a scene surface from a specific view. Each
point on the surface has not only x, y and z coordinates but also a RGB color.
The motivation to extract approximate convex structures in RGBD images is
that most objects in both indoor and outdoor environments are roughly convex
and all complex objects can be modeled as the composition of a set of convex
shapes. By finding approximate convex shapes from RGBD images, we extract
important structures of a scene. Fig. 1 illustrates finding approximate convex
shapes in single RGBD images using the proposed method. As shown in the
figure, we find a set of near-convex shapes, each corresponding to a set of 3D
points in the point cloud of a RGBD image.

Finding approximate convex shapes in RGBD images is different from approximate convex decomposition [5,10] of mesh graphics models. Previous convex
decomposition methods have been mainly used to simplify complex 3D graphics
objects into approximate convex parts for easier collision control in animation.
These convex decomposition algorithms usually require the input 3D mesh models to be noise free and represent a complete object scan, which has no inter-
or intra-object occlusion and reveals the look of the object from each different

D. Fleet et al. (Eds.): ECCV 2014, Part III, LNCS 8691, pp. 582–596, 2014.

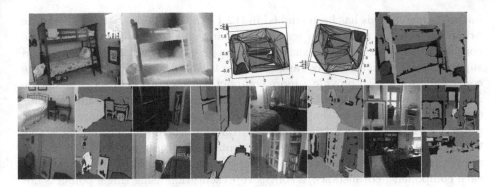

Fig. 1. Finding approximate convex shapes in single RGBD images. Row one shows a color image, its depth map, the convex hulls of the found shapes in two different views and the masks of the shapes on the image plane from the proposed method. Rows 2-3 show more example results of the proposed method (each result is a pair of color image and the approximate convex shape map).

view point. In this paper, we tackle the problem of finding approximate convex structures from a single view of the scene. There are usually heavy occlusions and data is missing in different places. The 3D point cloud is also quite noisy. This makes the problem of finding convex shapes in RGBD images challenging. Another difference of our shape finding task to previous pure geometric data decomposition is that apart from geometry structure we also have color information which helps disambiguate some object level boundaries. Moreover, instead of decomposing a 3D point cloud into roughly convex parts, our task is to find the approximate convex shapes and these shapes are not necessarily completely disjoint. This enables us to build a more efficient method that directly works on shape selection and is able to use shape proposals from different methods. To our knowledge, finding roughly convex shapes in RGBD images has not been attempted before.

In this paper we propose a global optimization method to find the approximate convex shapes in RGBD images by using surface patch candidates (3D superpixels). These candidates can be obtained from different methods by using both color and 3D shape information. The optimization selects shapes from the large set of candidates so that the overall convex fitting error is small, shapes have small overlaps, there is a small number of shapes and the extracted shapes mostly cover the RGBD image. We formulate the optimization problem as a two-stage mixed integer linear program. We find the globally optimal solution using a branch and bound method. Experiments show that our proposed method is more accurate than competing methods and at the same time is more efficient.

1.1   Related Methods

Finding geometric primitives such as planes, spheres, cones, cylinders [1,2] in a point cloud has been intensively studied. Representing objects in RGBD or stereo images using cuboids has been studied in [12,17,18]. Methods that use geometric primitives tend to represent a scene with many small components if the scene contains objects with complex shapes. In [3], a greedy method is proposed to find superquadratics in clutter-free range data. In this paper, we detect approximate convex shapes, which provide a more compact representation of scene structure in cluttered RGBD images. Compared to shape models such as planes, cuboids etc., approximate convex shape model is more general and has more grouping power. With properly constructed energy function, the optimal grouping is able to give near-object level shapes or small number of object parts. When finding approximate convex shapes, we do not simply judge the result by the convexity of each component. For instance, a convex representation using single points is not desirable because it is not a minimum number representation. We are interested in the representation that satisfies overall low local concavity, small intersection, max-covering and min-number constraints. Convexity is one soft constraint in the formulation. Such a setting enables our method to group 3D object regions even with holes or other types of non-convexity.

The proposed method is related to approximate convex decomposition. Different methods have been proposed to decompose a 2D shape or a 3D mesh object to approximate convex components. Delaunay triangulation is a simple method of convex shape decomposition. However, decomposing a polyhedron into minimum number of convex components is NP-Hard [4]. A quadratic bound exists for an approximation algorithm [4]. Fortunately, exact convex decomposition is often not necessary and also not desirable in computer vision applications because very few objects are perfectly convex. A fast greedy merging method has been proposed in [5] for approximate convex decomposition. In [9], methods of finding good concavity cuts are proposed and as an extension in [10], a dynamic programming method is further used to optimize the cuts for the decomposition. Other global optimization methods have also been used in [8,6,7] to optimize these cuts with different extra constraints. These previous methods have been mostly targeted at graphics applications on clean 3D models. In computer vision, their application is mostly limited to 2D shape representation. Different from the previous shape decomposition approach, in this paper, we directly optimize the selection of a set of approximate convex shapes in RGBD images. Ideally, these shapes should represent whole objects that are roughly convex or the convex parts of concave objects. Finding convex objects is different from previous decomposition approaches: we allow small overlaps between shapes due to noisy observations. To our knowledge, there is no previous works that tackle convex object finding in RGBD images. We propose a fast and reliable solution.

Point cloud segmentation is also related to the proposed method. These methods either cluster the points using the affinity of point color and 3D coordinates or rely on semantic classifiers to categorize each point into an object class [13,14,15]. Object supporting relations are further estimated in [11]. A method that uses object bounding box spatial and supporting relations for object region segmentation in stereo images has been proposed in [12]. Different from these previous methods, the proposed method is more about shape finding than segmentation and we allow small overlaps between shape detections. Our method also does not need to recognize the surface point classes in shape detection.

In summary, the contribution of the paper includes: we tackle the new problem of convex shape finding in RGBD images; we propose a new method to extract a set of roughly convex shape candidates from RGBD images; and, we propose a novel two-stage linear optimization method to find approximate convex shapes.

2   Methods

2.1   Overview

Our proposed method first extracts 3D shape candidates. There is no restriction that in these 3D shape candidates there is a disjoint set to partition the scene. We thus can use different candidate generation approaches to increase the success rate of shape detection. In this paper, to illustrate the concept, we use two low-complexity superpixel merging procedures to generate the candidates. Region proposals from other methods can be included to further improve the performance. Each shape candidate is represented as a 3D superpixel on the surface of a scene. Our goal is to select a subset of shape candidates that best describe the RGBD data and satisfy the geometrical constraints.

In more details, let $\mathbf{x}$ be the indicator vector of these shape candidates. Each binary element in the vector $\mathbf{x}$ indicates whether the corresponding shape candidate is selected. We try to optimize the following energy function.

$$\min_{\mathbf{x}}\{U(\mathbf{x}) + \alpha N(\mathbf{x}) + \beta I(\mathbf{x}) - \lambda P(\mathbf{x})\}$$

s.t. $\mathbf{x}$ is a valid shape candidate selection.   (1)

Here $U(.)$ quantifies the costs of the selected candidates. This is a unary term. $U(.)$ measures the concavity of the shapes. By minimizing $U(.)$, the optimization tends to select roughly convex candidates. Term $N(.)$ penalizes the number of selected candidates; we try to select a small number of candidates to represent the scene. $I(.)$ is the intersection term that quantifies the intersection volume between the convex hulls of neighboring shapes and the intersection area of their projections on the image plane. Term $P(.)$ encourages the selected shapes to spread out and cover a large area of the 3D scene surface. Term P is critical; without it, the optimization gives a trivial all zero solution. P is a high order term that couples everything together. Constants α, β and λ control the weight among the terms. By optimizing the above energy function, we select an optimal set of shape candidates so that they are roughly convex, have little 2D and 3D intersection, have a small number and cover a large region of the 3D scene surface. In fact, our optimization contains two stages, each having slightly different objective function and constraints. The first stage is used to deal with the shapes whose convexity is within a range and the second stage is used to handle the rest of the shapes. The optimization contains high order term and is hard to solve directly. Naive exhaustive search is infeasible because we have a large set of candidates. In the following, we study how the formulation can be linearized and how we can solve the problem using an efficient branch and bound method.

2.2 Candidate Extraction

We first find a set of approximate convex shape candidates from the RGBD images. The candidates are essentially composed of a group of 3D points in the original point cloud. We use several different methods to generate these candidates to increase the chance that we include all the approximate convex shapes. Note that we do not require that these candidates all have high quality. The important factor is that the good ones are hopefully included in the candidate set if we generate enough candidate shapes. Through optimization, we make a more accurate final decision. We partition the 3D point clouds into over-segmented superpixels using both the geometry and color information. By merging these 3D superpixels iteratively using the convexity constraints, we generate a set of candidate approximate convex shapes.

The over-segmented superpixels are preferably small planar patches. We use two different approaches to generate these superpixels. The first one is a modification of the graph based segmentation method [16]. Instead of using color alone, we use both color and depth when computing the affinity of neighboring pixels. The x, y and z maps of a RGBD image are normalized to range [0,1]. The color image's three channels are also in the range [0,1]. The distance between two points is defined as the summation of the point and the color distance. With the combined distance, we obtain the superpixels using the graph based segmentation method [16]. Apart from the superpixels generated using the above method, we also use a k-means method to generate over-segmented patches. Each image pixel corresponds to a vector $(n_x, n_y, n_z, d, \bar{z})$, where (n_x, n_y, n_z) is the normalized normal vector of the 3D scene surface at point (x, y, z). Here $d = x n_x + y n_y + z n_z$, the signed distance of the plane passing (x, y, z) with normal (n_x, n_y, n_z) to the origin. $\bar{z}$ is the normalized z in range [0,1]. The k-means clustering on the 5D vectors generates K clusters, e.g. $K = 20$. Note that the number of clusters is different from the number of generated superpixels. Since a cluster from k-means may contain multiple disconnected components, the effective superpixels after we extract connected components are many more than the number of clusters. An example in Fig.3 (c,d) shows the superpixels generated using these two approaches. As shown in the figure, over-segmented superpixels are able to capture the object boundaries quite well. The k-means method essentially clusters image pixels into flat 3D patches. The graph segmentation method uses both the color and the geometric information in the clustering. These over-segmented image patches are usually not able to yield masks for heterogeneous large targets. We therefore successively merge the superpixels to generate more shape candidates. If properly implemented, the merging procedure has a high chance to capture these bigger convex structures.

The merging procedure is built on top of the concavity measurement. Different from a complete mesh model, our mesh model is an incomplete surface that has a "front" side and a "back" side. A 3D superpixel is roughly convex if the shape extrudes towards the front, otherwise it is roughly concave. We define the front and back side of the surface using a ray starting from the camera center: (0,0,0) in the camera coordinate system. The segment of the ray from (0,0,0) to a point

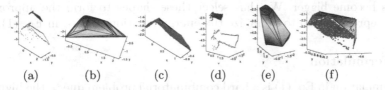

(a)   (b)   (c)   (d)   (e)   (f)

Fig. 2. (a): 3D point set with pushed-away boundaries. Here boundary points are scaled by two. (b): The convex hull. (c): The 3D points on the shape with the frontal hull. (d)-(f) show another concave shape example of measuring the concavity.

in the 3D point cloud is the front and the rest part of the ray is the back of the surface. Note that the seemingly simple way of defining the front and back using an orthographic projection is wrong; there is no guarantee that a ray parallel to the optical axis would have only a single intersection point with the scene surface.

The convexity measurement is obtained as follows. We first extend the boundary points of a 3D superpixel further away from the camera projection center (0,0,0). This can be easily implemented by multiplying a large scaling factor, e.g. 10, to the x, y and z of these boundary points. We then compute a 3D convex hull of this modified 3D superpixel. The next step is to remove the 3D triangles on the convex hull with at least one vertex on the modified boundary points. By removing these patches, we are left with an frontal hull of the 3D superpixel. Fig. 2 shows the procedure. As shown in Fig. 2, if a 3D superpixel is roughly convex, the mean distance of the points to the frontal hull is small; otherwise as shown in Fig. 2 (f), the mean distance of the points to the frontal hull is large. The mean distance of points to the frontal hull is thus used as the measurement of the convexity/concavity of a 3D superpixel. Apart from the 3D concavity, we also measure the concavity of the projected 2D superpixel on the image plane. The 2D concavity is defined as $1 - N_f/N_c$, where N_f is the number of foreground pixels on the 2D superpixel and N_c is the number of pixels on the convex hull of the 2D superpixel. Both of the two measurements are used in the final shape selection.

With the 3D concavity measurement, we successively merge the neighboring superpixels. Two 3D superpixels are deemed as neighbors if their minimum 3D point distance is less than some threshold. In the merging procedure, two neighboring 3D superpixels that have the smallest concavity if combined is merged into a single superpixel. This procedure continues until there is only one superpixel left or all the superpixels are isolated. The shape candidates are composed of the 3D superpixels from the two partition methods and the new superpixels generated in the merging procedure. Since there is no sub-optimal condition for either of the merging process, we cannot just set a stopping criterion and get the optimal set of convex shapes using the simple merging procedure. Even though there is no optimal guarantee, there is still a high chance that the good convex shapes that should appear in the final shape selection exist in the merging procedure. In fact, there is no guarantee that the concavity score increases as the patches become bigger. We thus select these shapes to form the approximate convex representation to minimize the energy function defined in Eq. (1).

2.3   Formulation

The formulation in Eq. (1) is a hard combinatorial problem due to the high order term that couples the candidate selection. Here we propose a two-stage linear formulation that can be efficiently solved using a branch and bound method. In the following, we show how each term can be linearized. Recall that we use a vector of binary variables $(x_1, x_2, ..., x_n)$ to indicate the selection of each candidate shape, where n is the number of 3D shape candidates.

Unary Term. Let $u_i = a g_i N_i + b h_i + c g_i$, where a, b and c are constant coefficients, g_i and h_i are the 3D concavity and 2D concavity and N_i is the number of points in the shape candidate i. Recall that g_i is the average distance of the points on the 3D superpixel to the frontal hull; $g_i N_i$ is the total distance of the points to the frontal hull. We define the overall convexity term as $\sum_{i=1..n} u_i x_i$. When we minimize the unary term, we minimize the total distance of the points on the selected candidates to the local frontal hull, and the selected shapes also should have small concavity individually in both 2D and 3D.

We deal with the shape candidates with concavity higher than some threshold differently from those with lower concavity. Essentially, we want to assign the shape candidates whose concavity is within the range first and then determine the selection of the rest of the candidates. Due to camera distortion, large flat shape candidates such as wall and floor often appear curved (concave shaped) when they are far away from camera. These shape candidates may have large concavity measurement in RGBD images. When this happens, a single stage optimization has a hard time to balance the local shape cost and the global constraint costs no matter how we set the parameters in the energy function. We thus use a two-stage optimization to alleviate this problem. At the first stage optimization u_i is defined above, and at the second stage we only use $g_i N_i$ in the unary term.

Binary Term. A physically feasible selection of 3D shape candidates should have small intersection to each other. Here we use the 3D convex hull intersections of these candidates to quantify how the 3D shapes interact to each other at the first stage of optimization. The intersection of two convex hulls is another convex hull. We represent the convex hull as a polytope: a convex hull can be represented as the intersection of a set of half spaces (the space on one side of a plane). Computing the exact intersection of two polytopes has high computational complexity. Since we only need a ratio to measure the intersection, we obtain the intersection ratio using the following space quantization method. We discretized the 3D finite visible volume in the camera frame of the RGBD image. Let $\{A_i w \leq b_i, i \in I_p\}$ represent the polytope of shape candidate p and $\{A_i w \leq b_i, i \in I_q\}$ the polytope of candidate q. Then the 3D convex hull intersection ratio $r_{p,q} = \sum_{w \in V} s((\cap_{i \in I_p}(A_i w \leq b_i)) \cap (\cap_{i \in I_q}(A_i w \leq b_i)))/\sum_{w \in V} s((\cap_{i \in I_p}(A_i w \leq b_i)) \cup (\cap_{i \in I_q}(A_i w \leq b_i)))$, where V contains all the discretized voxel centers; $s(X) = 1$ if X is true and otherwise 0. The intersection constraint can be formulated as the following binary energy term $\sum_{\{p,q\} \in \mathcal{N}} r_{p,q} x_p x_q$, where $\mathcal{N}$ is the set of all neighboring 3D superpixels. We define two 3D superpixels are neighbors if their minimum point distance is less than a threshold. The intersection term is quadratic. We use a linear programming trick to linearize it. Since the assignment variable x is binary, we let $y_{p,q} = x_p x_q$ with the constraint that $y_{p,q} \geq 0$, $y_{p,q} \geq x_p + x_q - 1$, $y_{p,q} \leq x_p$, $y_{p,q} \leq x_q$. It is easy to verify that $y_{p,q}$ is 1 if and only if x_p and x_q are both 1, and otherwise 0. Therefore, by introducing the auxiliary variable $y_{p,q}$ the intersection term can be converted to linear term $\sum_{\{p,q\} \in \mathcal{N}} r_{p,q} y_{p,q}$ with the constraints on y. We also require that the intersection does not exceed some hard threshold R, i.e., $y_{p,q} = 0$ if $r_{p,q} > R$.

The 3D convex hull intersection constraint is only used at the first stage of optimization. At the second stage, we use the intersection ratio of the projected 2D superpixels on the image plane, $r_{p,q} = l_{p,q} = \mathcal{A}(S_p \cap S_q)/\mathcal{A}(S_p \cup S_q)$, where $\mathcal{A}(.)$ is the area of a region and S_p and S_q are the projected 2D superpixel regions of the 3D shapes on the image plane.

Global Term. It is not enough to use the above unary and binary terms alone. Since all the coefficients in the unary and binary terms are positive, zero vector is a trivial solution. We need a global term to enforce that enough shapes should be selected. We cannot constrain the number of the selection because in most of the cases this number is unknown. A natural choice is to enforce that the set of chosen shape candidates should cover most of the image plane if projected. This in fact is equivalent to let the shapes cover as much of the 3D points as possible since each 3D point corresponds to a single 2D pixel in the image. Note that the seemingly simpler constraint that each point of the image should belong to a selected shape is not always feasible. The max-covering constraint is necessary.

The problem size would be too big if we model the covering term at the point level. Instead, we quantize the image plane into small rectangle patches. For 480×640 images, 20×20 tile is sufficient. A shape candidate covers a tile if the projection of the shape candidate on the image plane has an intersection with the tile. We introduce auxiliary variable z_k to indicate whether tile k is covered: $z_k = 1$ if tile k is covered by at least one shape candidate. The tile covering variable z is related to the candidate selection variable x by: $\sum_{i \in \mathcal{F}_k} x_i \geq z_k$, $0 \leq z_k \leq 1$, where $\mathcal{F}_k$ is the set of shape candidates that cover tile k. To encourage max-covering, we just need to maximize the overall covering $\sum_{k \in \mathcal{T}} z_k$, where $\mathcal{T}$ contains indexes of all the small tiles. In fact, we do not have to constrain z to be binary. We can verify that if at least one selected shape candidate covers tile k, z_k has to be 1 to maximize the covering term; if all the shape candidates that cover tile k are not selected, z_k has to be 0. $\sum_{k \in \mathcal{T}} z_k$ indeed quantifies the amount of covering.

Number Term. By enforcing the max-covering term, we avoid the trivial zero solution problem. However, there is still a bias for the algorithm to select many small shape candidates. Notice that since we multiply the number of points to concavity, we in fact tend to select many small shape candidates to represent the whole scene and this may result in a smaller overall point distance to the local frontal hulls. The other two terms in the convexity term can relieve the problem a little bit. Along with these two terms, we explicitly introduce another number term $\sum_i x_i$ to the objective function to penalize the selection of a large number of shape candidates. By adjusting the weight of this term, we are able to select a relatively small number of large shape candidates to explain the whole scene.

The complete two-stage linear formulation is as follows. At the first stage, we optimize:

$$\min \sum_i (ag_i N_i + bh_i + cg_i + \alpha)x_i + \beta \sum_{\{p,q\}\in\mathcal{N}} r_{p,q}y_{p,q} - \lambda \sum_{k\in\mathcal{T}} z_k$$

$$\text{s.t. } y_{p,q} \geq 0, \ y_{p,q} \geq x_p + x_q - 1, \ y_{p,q} \leq x_p, \ y_{p,q} \leq x_q, \ \forall\{p,q\} \in \mathcal{N}$$

$$y_{p,q} = 0, \text{ if } r_{p,q} > R$$

$$\sum_{i\in\mathcal{F}_k} x_i \geq z_k, \ 0 \leq z_k \leq 1, \ \forall k \in \mathcal{T}$$

$$x_i = 0, \text{ if } g_i > G \text{ or } h_i > H, \ x_i = 0 \text{ or } 1$$

where G and H are thresholds for the 3D and 2D concavity. The first stage of optimization determines the dominant approximate convex shapes. If we just use this optimization, some large shapes that are not convex enough due to the camera distortion will be left unlabeled. The second stage optimization relaxes the labeling criterion. It assumes the labels on the shape candidates that are labeled 1 at stage one fixed but only tries to label the rest of the candidates. The second stage uses a more relaxed 2D intersection measurement and removes the range constraints on x.

$$\min \sum_i (a'g_i N_i + \alpha')x_i + \beta' \sum_{\{p,q\}\in\mathcal{N}} l_{p,q}y_{p,q} - \lambda' \sum_{k\in\mathcal{T}} z_k$$

s.t. constraints on y and z are the same as stage one

$x_i = 1$ if they are labeled as 1 at the first stage, x_i is binary variable

Parameters Training. There are quite a few parameters that need to be determined in the objective function and constraints. The hard constraint parameters G and H can be directly obtained from the training data. They are set such that they are the upper bounds of g_i and h_i for all the positive training data. The intersection bound R is set to 0.5. To obtain the parameters $a, b, c, \alpha, \beta, \lambda$ in the objective function, we optimize a linear program. The idea is that we need to select a set of parameters such that the objective value is less than that of the sub-optimal shape candidate selection. We solve the following linear program to obtain a good set of parameters.

$$\min_{a,b,c,\alpha,\beta,\lambda} M \sum_{j=1}^{J} (a\xi_a^j + b\xi_b^j + c\xi_c^j + \alpha\xi_\alpha^j + \beta\xi_\beta^j - \lambda\xi_\lambda^j) -$$

$$\sum_{j=1}^{J} \sum_{m=1}^{M} (a\phi_a^{j,m} + b\phi_b^{j,m} + c\phi_c^{j,m} + \alpha\phi_\alpha^{j,m} + \beta\phi_\beta^{j,m} - \lambda\phi_\lambda^{j,m})$$

s.t. $a, b, c, \alpha, \beta, \lambda, \geq 0$, $a + b + c + \alpha + \beta + \lambda = 1$.

Here ξ are the coefficients of $a, b, c, \alpha, \beta, \gamma$ in objective function for ground truth data; we have J RGBD images with ground truth approximate convex shape selections. ϕ are the corresponding coefficients in the objective function using randomly generated shape candidate selections in RGBD images; random labeling is repeated M times for each RGBD image. By optimizing the above energy function, we select a set of parameters that give low objectives on the ground truth labeling and high values on the negative samples. Note that we need to optimize the coefficients for both the first stage and second stage linear formulation. We sequentially find these coefficients for stage one and then stage two. The linear program can be solved efficiently using the simplex method or the interior-point Method.

2.4   Optimization

By converting the shape candidate selection into a linear formulation, we can efficiently solve the optimization using a branch and bound procedure. Our formulation is a mixed integer linear program, in which x is binary and the rest of the variables are floating point variables. We first solve the linear program by discarding the integral constraints. If all x are integral, we obtain the global optimal solution. Otherwise, we select x_i that is closest to 0.5 and generate two branches: left branch with $x_i = 0$ and right branch with $x_i = 1$. From the floating point solution of the linear program, we obtain the first guess of the all integer solution for x by rounding x to the closest integer. Other variables' value can be obtained from x. If $x_i = 0.5$ a random selection of 0 or 1 is used to break the tie. Using this first guess, we obtain the first upper bound of the objective function. For each branch, we re-solve the linear program and obtain a lower bound for each branch. If the lower branch is greater than the current upper bound, the branch is pruned. If there is still floating point x, we keep the current branch active. We use the rounding method to re-estimate the upper bound. If the estimated upper bound is lower than the current one, we update the upper bound. Among all the active branches, we choose the one with the lowest lower bound and branch on the most ambiguous x variable. This procedure continues until the lowest lower bound of active branches equals the current upper bound or some pre-defined tolerance gap is achieved. In this paper, the ratio of the tolerance gap to the upper bound is set to be 10^{-6}. For a typical problem with the number of shape candidates around 500. The branch and bound procedure is surprisingly fast: it takes one or two seconds to converge to the global optimal solution for each stage of the candidate selection.

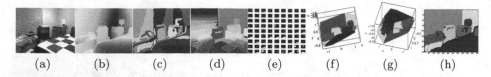

(a)   (b)   (c)   (d)   (e)   (f)   (g)   (h)

Fig. 3. An example. (a): Color image. (b): The aligned depth map. (c): Superpixels from k-means. (d): Superpixels from graph method [16] using both the color and depth image. (e): Sample candidate masks. (f, g): The convex shapes from the proposed method in two different view points. (h): The masks of the shapes on the image plane.

3   Experiments

Fig. 3 shows an example about how the proposed method works in finding approximate convex shapes in a RGBD image. The test image is from NYU RGBD dataset [11] and we captured our 100 sample images using Kinect sensor for parameter training. The parameters are fixed in all the following tests. The proposed method first converts the RGBD image into a color point cloud. As shown in Fig. 3, two over-segmented superpixel maps are extracted using both the color and depth maps. The two maps contain 82 and 162 candidates respectively. The superpixels are then merged successively based on their convexity from the view point to generate a total of 486 candidate shape masks. The optimal set of shape candidates is then chosen using the proposed two-stage linear method. The first stage optimization has 44192 rows (constraints) and 15209 columns (variables). The relaxed linear programs takes 973 steps to converge. The search tree branch and bound only takes one more step since the linear program gives a tight lower bound. The first stage optimization takes 1.3 seconds in a 2.8GHz machine. The second stage optimization has 59463 rows and 20565 columns; it takes just one step to find the global optimum. The convex hulls of these shapes and the shape masks on the image plane are shown in Fig. 3. Our proposed method reliably finds the approximate convex shapes in RGBD images. It is also efficient. The whole procedure takes few seconds.

We further compare the proposed method with HACD (Hierarchical Approximate Convex Decompose) [5], a greedy approach that successively merges regions until some concavity tolerance is reached. HACD is a typical implementation of approximate convex decomposition. HACD is open-source and has been shown to work very well on different graphical mesh models. Its concavity measurement makes it also suitable for finding convex objects on a surface that is a single view of the scene. We adjust the parameters for HACD to achieve the best results. Fig. 4 shows the comparison results of the proposed method against HACD. HACD makes quite a few mistakes in convex decomposition of RGBD meshes: many large objects such as a table and a floor have been split into parts and some convex parts are not separated out. Our proposed method greatly improves the results. In terms of computational complexity, our method is also hundreds of times faster than HACD.

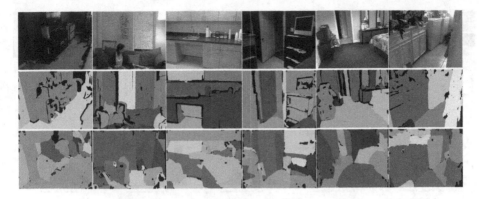

Fig. 4. Comparison between the proposed method and HACD [5]. Row 1: Color images. Row 2: Near-convex 3D shapes found by the proposed method. We show the projections of these shapes to the image plane. Row 3: Near-convex shapes found by HACD [5].

Beyond qualitative results, we further quantify the results by comparing against the ground truth. The original object region ground truth labeling in the NYU dataset [11] is not quite suitable because it contains many non-convex shapes and the labeling often decomposes objects into plane surfaces instead of the convex parts we are most interested in. We labeled 538 images in the NYU dataset and 1471 approximate convex shapes in these images. Some samples of the ground truth shape masks on the images are shown in Fig. 5. With the ground truth labeling, we quantify the performance of different convex shape finding methods using matching score distributions and detection curves. For each ground truth convex shape mask, we go through all the convex shapes found by different methods and if the overlap between the ground truth mask and the shape mask detected is above a threshold we have a successful detection. The overlap between two masks is defined as the ratio of the intersection mask area to the union mask area. Fig. 5 shows the overlap score distributions and the detection curves of the proposed method and HACD. Two criteria are used: one is the per-object overlap score distribution and detection rate, and the other one is the per-frame overlap score distribution and detection rate. The per-frame mask matching score is defined as the average overlap score for all the ground truth objects in an image. If the per-frame overlap score is above a threshold, we deem the frame correctly processed. For better performance, overlap score distribution should have large portion of the curve focused on the right and small tail on the left; the better detection curve gives higher detection rate for each fixed region overlap threshold. Our proposed method gives significantly better results in both the per-object and per-frame test cases than HACD. We also test using just the first stage of the optimization in our method. As shown in Fig. 5, the proposed two-stage approach gives much better result than the one-stage method.

Our method belongs to the class of methods that are based on region proposals. We further compare the proposed method with other methods that are based

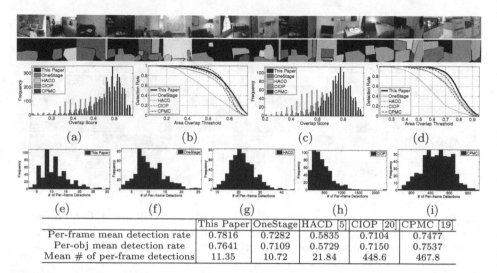

Fig. 5. Row one and two show sample ground truth labeling of approximate convex objects in the RGBD images from the NYU RGBD dataset [11]. OneStage is the method that uses only the first stage optimization of the proposed method. (a): Per-object shape matching score distribution. (b): Per-object detection rate. (c): Mean shape matching score per-frame distribution. (d): Per-frame detection rate. (e)-(i): The per-frame detection number histograms of different methods.

on the region candidates using category independent object proposals (CIOP) [20] or CPMC [19]. These methods' detection rate limit is set by the region candidate proposals. We compare the proposed method with the limit detection rates of competing methods using shape candidates generated from [20] or [19]: if proposal candidate matches the ground truth we deem it is a successful detection. For fair comparison, we modified the code of CIOP and CPMC to use both color image and the depth image for more reliable proposal generation in RGBD images. The per-object and per-frame comparisons of the overlap score distributions and the detection rates are shown in Fig. 5. The per-object detection rate limit of CPMC based methods is a bit higher than the proposed method if the threshold is lower than 0.75. However, the detection rate with threshold greater than 0.75 is what we really care about. Our method gives better results in all the other test cases. The average detection rate of the proposed method is also the highest as shown in Fig. 5.

We have applied the proposed method to find approximate convex objects in all the 1449 RGBD images in the NYU dataset. Fig. 6 shows sample results. Our method reliably detects approximate convex targets in cluttered RGBD images. Failure cases are due to holes and noisy depth data on some object surfaces. The unreliable and noisy data may confuse the convexity estimation and causes missing the true candidate proposal. By further improving the region proposal generation against noise or using sensors with low noise we are able to further improve the results.

Fig. 6. Random sample results of the proposed methods on the NYU RGBD dataset
[11]. Odd columns show the color images and even columns show the approximate
convex object regions projected to the image plane. Our proposed method reliably
detects approximate convex objects in cluttered RGBD images.

4   Conclusion

Finding approximate convex shapes in RGBD images is a new task. In this
paper, we propose a novel global method to tackle the problem. We formulate the
optimization into a two-stage mixed integer program that selects the shapes from
a large set of candidates. An efficient branch and bound method is applied to
solve the two-stage optimization. Our evaluation results on thousands of RGBD
images show that the proposed method is reliable, fast and more accurate than
the competing methods.

Acknowledgment. This research is supported by the U.S. NSF funding 1018641.

References

1. Schnabel, R., Wessel, R., Wahl, R., Klein, R.: Shape Recognition in 3D Point-
   Clouds. In: WSCG 2008 (2008)
2. Li, Y., Wu, X., Chrysathou, T., Sharf, A., Cohen-Or, D., Mitra, N.J.: GlobFit: Consistently Fitting Primitives by Discovering Global Relations. In: ACM SIGGRAPH
   (2011)
3. Leonardis, A., Jaklic, A., Solina, F.: Superquadrics for Segmenting and Modeling
   Range Data. TPAMI 19(11) (1997)

4. Chazelle, B.: Convex Partitions of Polyhedra: A Lower Bound and Worst-Case Optimal Algorithm. SIAM J. Comput. 13, 488–507 (1984)
5. Mamou, K., Ghorbel, F.: A Simple and Efficient Approach for 3D Mesh Approximate Convex Decomposition. In: ICIP (2009)
6. Ma, C., Dong, Z., Jiang, T., Wang, Y., Gao, W.: A Method of Perceptual-based Shape Decomposition. In: ICCV (2013)
7. Ren, Z., Yuan, J., Li, C., Liu, W.: Minimum Near-Convex Decomposition for Robust Shape Representation. In: ICCV (2011)
8. Liu, H., Liu, W., Latecki, L.J.: Convex Shape Decomposition. In: CVPR (2010)
9. Lien, J.M., Amato, N.M.: Approximate Convex Decomposition of Polyhedra. In: ACM Symposium on Solid and Physical Modeling (2007)
10. Ghosh, M., Amato, N.M., Lu, Y., Lien, J.M.: Fast Approximate Convex Decomposition Using Relative Concavity. Computer-Aided Design archive 45(2) (2013)
11. Silberman, N., Hoiem, D., Kohli, P., Fergus, R.: Indoor Segmentation and Support Inference from RGBD Images. In: Fitzgibbon, A., Lazebnik, S., Perona, P., Sato, Y., Schmid, C. (eds.) ECCV 2012, Part V. LNCS, vol. 7576, pp. 746–760. Springer, Heidelberg (2012)
12. Bleyer, M., Rhemann, C., Rother, C.: Extracting 3D Scene-Consistent Object Proposals and Depth from Stereo Images. In: Fitzgibbon, A., Lazebnik, S., Perona, P., Sato, Y., Schmid, C. (eds.) ECCV 2012, Part V. LNCS, vol. 7576, pp. 467–481. Springer, Heidelberg (2012)
13. Koppula, H.S., Anand, A., Joachims, T., Saxena, A.: Semantic Labeling of 3D Point Clouds for Indoor Scenes. In: NIPS 2011 (2011)
14. Silberman, N., Fergus, R.: Indoor Scene Segmentation Using a Structured Light Sensor. In: ICCV Workshop on 3D Representation and Recognition (2011)
15. Gupta, S., Arbelaez, P., Malik, J.: Perceptual Organization and Recognition of Indoor Scenes from RGB-D Images. In: CVPR 2013 (2013)
16. Felzenszwalb, P.F., Huttenlocher, D.P.: Efficient Graph-Based Image Segmentation. IJCV 59(2) (2004)
17. Jiang, H., Xiao, J.: A Linear Approach to Matching Cuboids in RGBD Images. In: CVPR 2013 (2013)
18. Lin, D., Fidler, S., Urtasun, R.: Holistic Scene Understanding for 3D Object Detection with RGBD Cameras. In: ICCV 2013 (2013)
19. Carreira, J., Sminchisescu, C.: Constrained Parametric Min-Cuts for Automatic Object Segmentation. In: CVPR 2010 (2010)
20. Endres, I., Hoiem, D.: Category Independent Object Proposals. In: Daniilidis, K., Maragos, P., Paragios, N. (eds.) ECCV 2010, Part V. LNCS, vol. 6315, pp. 575–588. Springer, Heidelberg (2010)

ShapeForest: Building Constrained Statistical Shape Models with Decision Trees

Saša Grbić, Joshua K.Y. Swee, and Razvan Ionasec

Siemens Corporation, Corporate Technology, Princeton NJ, USA

Abstract. Constrained local models (CLM) are frequently used to locate points on deformable objects. They usually consist of feature response images, defining the local update of object points and a shape prior used to regularize the final shape. Due to the complex shape variation within an object class this is a challenging problem. However in many segmentation tasks a simpler object representation is available in form of sparse landmarks which can be reliably detected from images. In this work we propose ShapeForest, a novel shape representation which is able to model complex shape variation, preserves local shape information and incorporates prior knowledge during shape space inference. Based on a sparse landmark representation associated with each shape the ShapeForest, trained using decision trees and geometric features, selects a subset of relevant shapes to construct an instance specific parametric shape model. Hereby the ShapeForest learns the association between the geometric features and shape variability. During testing, based on the estimated sparse landmark representation a constrained shape space is constructed and used for shape initialization and regularization during the iterative shape refinement within the CLM framework. We demonstrate the effectiveness of our approach on a set of medical segmentation problems where our database contains complex morphological and pathological variations of several anatomical structures.

1 Introduction

The ability to delineate deformable objects from images is critical for many computer vision tasks. In most cases low-level information based on the local image appearance is combined with high-level information based on a shape model to estimate the final object in the image. The low-level information can be noisy due to missing or incomplete image gradients. Thus the shape model is used to regularize the results. The success of these approaches is highly dependent on the way shape priors are modeled, how the low-level information is computed from the images and what optimization approach is utilized to fit the shape model to the low-level information. One of the first approaches was the Active Contour Model proposed by Kass et al. [13]. Hereby, the shape prior is represented as a general regularity term during the optimization, assuming that the shape should deform like a thin plate. Further, more object-specific shape priors

D. Fleet et al. (Eds.): ECCV 2014, Part III, LNCS 8691, pp. 597–612, 2014.

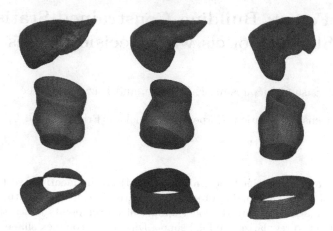

Fig. 1. Examples of complex variation observed among shapes within an object class for the liver (top row), the AV (middle row) and the LVOT (bottom row)

became prevalent, where the shape priors are learned from a set of training samples, such as Active Shape Models (ASM) [2]. Many extensions of this method were proposed within the last decade.

In current literature, shape models confront major challenges. First, shape variations are usually complex and therefore difficult to model using standard linear parametric models. Figure 1 illustrates the complex shape variation within our medical data set, showing three examples of the liver (top row), the aortic valve – AV (middle row) and the left ventricle outflow tract – LVOT (bottom row). Second, shape variation is often local. Shape models should be able to preserve local shape detail in the training data even if it is not statistically significant. Third, even though the final shape consists of hundreds or thousands of vertices a lower level representation using a small number of sparse landmarks associated with each shape is often available. These points define salient locations in the image and are located on or around the object of interest. These landmarks can be robustly detected using object detection algorithms. Shape models should exploit this information during shape alignment and refinement. r

In this paper we introduce a novel constrained statistical shape model, the ShapeForest, which addresses the main challenges presented above in an unified framework. Based on a set of sparse landmarks, which we assume can be detected reliably in the images, we infer an instance specific statistical shape model used for shape initialization and during the iterative shape refinement. We use randomized decision trees to learn the shape-manifold based on geometric features defined by the sparse landmark representation. During testing a subset of shapes is selected and used to construct a constrained parametric statistical shape model. We show that this approach can approximate accurately the shape variation compared to the classical statistical shape model and other multi-modal shape representations. We demonstrate the performance of the ShapeForest in a range of medical image segmentation problems – the aortic valve, the left ventricle outflow tract, and the liver. In addition we show the effects of different choices for the training parameters.

2   Related Work

There is a wide range of literature on matching statistical shape models to images starting with Active Shape Models [2]. Hereby an iterative approach is pursued with an alternating strategy. First an update for each point is found in a small neighborhood of the current shape estimate with a suitably trained detector. Then the shape model parameters are adjusted to match the updated shape points. Active Appearance Models [3] align both models of shape and texture using an efficient parameter update schema. Pictorial structures define a collection of parts arranged in a deformable geometric configuration representing an object model [9]. Each part has an Active Appearance Model representation and the deformable geometric configuration is represented as spring-like connections between pairs of parts. An efficient method was introduced to fit the pictorial structure to an image. Constrained Local Models (CLM) [16,6,15] compute response images, measuring the fit of a specific shape point throughout the whole image. Based on the response images a shape model is matched to the data, estimating the best overall combination of points based on geometric criteria.

In the context of shape modeling, extensions to the classical SSM have been proposed to model multi-modal distributions within the shape prior. A simple extension is to use a mixture of Gaussian to represent the shape model [4]. Manifold learning can also be used to represent the non-linear shape prior [8,18,14]. A data-base guided approach was proposed in [11] whereby a nearest-neighborhood search is used to find the closest shape based on a data-base of shapes. However in most cases the number of clusters is defined a priori.

Another difficulty with SSM is the inability to preserve local details of the input shape when such details are present in the training data but not statistically significant. As PCA performs eigenanalysis and extracts eigenvectors with the largest eigenvalues the discarded eigenvectors are statistically insignificant, but they may contain important local details. Some relevant work can alleviate this problem. Sparse PCA obtains sparser modes and produces near-orthogonal components [17,19]. Thus each mode only affects locally clustered landmarks and captures more detail information. However in most sparse methods the number of training samples used for the sparse shape representation, especially with shapes which contain large number of vertices, is limited as it increases significantly the computational complexity. Some other methods divide the shape model into several independently modeled parts [7], such as the hierarchical approach. Since the smaller parts exhibit less variation, they can be captured with fewer training samples than the variations for the full shape.

Most existing shape segmentation methods pursue a hierarchical estimation approach. Based on lower level information such as a set of sparse landmarks a shape model is initialized and refined to fit the image data. These landmarks represent salient, corner-like structures in the images and are located either on the shape or in close proximity. In our medical imaging domain the problem is further simplified as only one occurrence of each landmark can appear in an image. Given a large database of landmark annotations, state-of-the art detection algorithms can be trained to detect those points reliably. A sliding window approach using discriminative classifiers with descriptive image features is often used in such settings [20]. Regression based approaches could also be utilized to detected the landmarks by exploiting the spatial correlation of image features and landmark positions [10,5]. In our work we assume this workflow as given.

Our method automatically selects a subset of relevant shapes from the training data for a new instance based on geometric features extracted from the detected landmarks. Thus there is no need to define a priori the number of clusters within our database of shapes. In addition the ShapeForest will learn a distance function between the landmarks and the remaining shape variation. Our approach is more robust compared to an Euclidean distance norm in the feature space as it discards non-informative and noisy features. The ShapeForest will select the most relevant geometric features to minimize the variance within the remaining subset of shapes. Thus the shapes that are selected will share geometric properties such as local geometric detail.

3   Shape Modeling

Given a population of n instances of a shape $S = \{s_1, s_2, ..., s_n\}$ that have been aligned to a common coordinate system using Generalized Procrustes Analysis (GPA) and share point correspondences, each aligned shape instance s_n can be represented as a set of k points $s_n = \{s_n^{x1}, s_n^{y1}, s_n^{z1}, ..., s_n^{xk}, s_n^{yk}, s_n^{zk}\}$. S can be viewed as a point cloud in $3k$-dimensional space. A generative shape model, represented as a linear Gaussian parametric model, can be constructed by computing the Principal Component Analysis (PCA) on S. Later each shape s_u can be approximated using the following linear model:

$$s_u = T(\bar{s} + Pb) \tag{1}$$

Here, $\bar{s}$ is the mean of all shapes in S after GPA, Pb is the linear uni-modal Gaussian parametric model with the eigenvectors P that represent the main modes of variation in S and the coefficients b, and T is a global transformation that maps $\bar{s}$ to the coordinate system of s_u. Hereafter we will refer to this model as the *global SSM* or *gSSM* [12].

The ShapeForest instead identifies a subset of shape instances $\hat{S}$ within S that share similar geometric characteristics based on geometric features extracted from an image I. The subset of shapes $\hat{S}$ is later used to generate a constrained version of the global SSM:

$$s_u = T(\hat{s} + \hat{P}\hat{b}) \tag{2}$$

where $\hat{s}$ is the mean shape computed from a subset of shape instances $\hat{S} \subseteq S$ after GPA, and $\hat{P}\hat{b}$ represents the corresponding modes of variation. We will later refer to this shape model as the *constrained SSM* or *cSSM*.

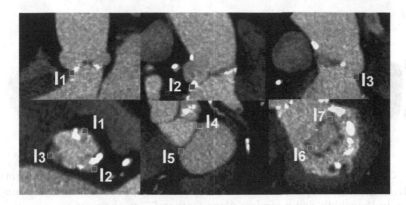

Fig. 2. Sparse Landmark representation $L = \{l_1, l_2, l_3, l_4, l_5, l_6, l_7\}$ for the left ventricle outflow tract (LVOT) in a 3D CT image. Each landmark represents a salient location in the image.

3.1 Landmarks

To select $\hat{S}$ we use geometric features derived from m sparse landmarks L which are detected from the image I. Each landmark corresponds to a salient anatomical point in the image I and can be easily identified and reliably detected using standard object detection algorithms. Landmarks do not need to lie on the shape itself but can also be in close proximity to it. It is important to note that $m \ll k$. Figure 2 illustrates seven sparse landmarks associated with a shape (LVOT). Here, 5 landmarks lie directly on the shape itself, while the remaining 2 represent nearby stable points.

3.2 Geometric Features

From the identified m landmarks L, we compute two simple geometric features: *distance* features and *random plane* features. As the variability of the landmarks is strongly correlated with the shape points, these features are powerful to characterize the morphological and geometric properties of individual shapes.

Given a set of m landmarks associated with a shape, distance features (f_{dist}) are generated for each unique pair of landmarks (p, q) as the Euclidean distance between landmarks p and q:

$$f_{dist}(p, q) = \sqrt{\sum_{i \in \{x,y,z\}} (p^i - q^i)^2} \tag{3}$$

By comparison, random plane features (f_{rp}) are generated for each individual landmark p as the shortest distance between landmark p and a randomly generated plane:

$$f_{rp}(p) = \frac{ap^x + bp^y + cp^z + d}{\sqrt{a^2 + b^2 + c^2}} \; ; \; ax + by + cz + d = 0 \tag{4}$$

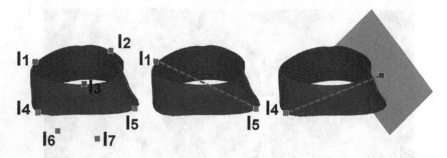

Fig. 3. Geometric features computed based on the sparse landmark representation $L = \{l_1, l_2, l_3, l_4, l_5, l_6, l_7\}$ for the LVOT (left). An example of a distance feature f_{dist} is shown in the middle and a random plane feature f_{rp} on the right.

Distance and random plane features are illustrated in Figure 3. Here, the left diagram shows distance feature $(f_{dist}(l_1, l_5))$, which calculates the Euclidean distance between landmarks l_1 and l_5 associated with the shape. The right diagram shows random plane feature $(f_{rp}(l_4))$, which calculates the shortest distance between landmark l_4 associated with the shape, and a randomly selected plane.

In practice, f_{dist} and f_{rp} were found to be highly complementary when utilized within the ShapeForest, with optimal results produced where given m landmarks, the combined feature set $\{f_{dist} \cup f_{rp}\}$ was computed for each shape s, resulting in a feature set size of $(m^2 - m)/2 + m$ unique features.

3.3   ShapeForest

Spatial features are used in the ShapeForest to obtain a subset of shapes $\hat{S}$ and compute the corresponding constrained SSM. The ShapeForest itself is constructed as a forest of un-pruned decision trees, similar to Breiman's random forest ensemble classifier [1]. At each tree, each non-leaf node contains a feature $f_\theta \in \{f_{dist} \cup f_{rp}\}$ and threshold value τ, with both leaf and non-leaf nodes further containing a subset of shapes $S_t \in S$. Thus the ShapeForest learns the distance function between the geometric features and the shape variance, clustering shape instances with similar shape characteristics in the leaf nodes. A set of m landmarks $\bar{L} = \{l_1, l_2, ..., l_m\}$ that is the *GPA aligned mean* of sparse landmarks associated with each shape in S_t is additionally kept at each node in order to facilitate an optional Shape Selection Optimization step as detailed in Section 3.3.

Training. During training, a subset of shapes $S_t = \{s_1, s_2, ..., s_v\}$ is randomly sampled for each tree, taken from a population of training shapes. Corresponding sets of $LM_t = \{L_1 \cup L_2 \cup ... \cup L_v\}$ are obtained, where each L_v is the set of sparse landmarks associated with shape s_v in S_t, and spatial features are computed using these landmarks as in Section 3.2. S_t and LM_t are placed at root nodes in their respective trees, and the following training algorithm is executed for every tree in the ShapeForest:

1. For each feature type $f_\theta \in \{f_{dist} \cup f_{rp}\}$, construct a set of splitting candidates $\phi = (f_\theta, \tau)$, where each τ represents one of a number of threshold values, equally spaced between $\min(f_\theta(LM_t))$ and $\max(f_\theta(LM_t))$.
2. For each ϕ, partition the set of shapes at the current node S_t into left and right subsets:

$$S_l(\phi) = \{s_v | s_v \in S_t \wedge f_\theta(L_v) \le \tau\} \tag{5}$$

$$S_r(\phi) = \{s_v | s_v \in S_t \wedge f_\theta(L_v) > \tau\} \tag{6}$$

Using GPA, align shapes within subsets S_t, $S_l(\phi)$ and $S_r(\phi)$ to produce aligned sets S_t^a, $S_l^a(\phi)$ and $S_r^a(\phi)$.
3. For each ϕ, compute the information gain $I(S_t, \phi)$ achieved from splitting S_t into $S_l(\phi)$ and $S_r(\phi)$ as:

$$I(S_t, \phi) \quad = \quad \sum_{s \in S_t^a} \log(\delta(s)) \quad - \sum_{i \in \{l, r\}} \left(\sum_{s \in S_i^a(\phi)} \log(\delta(s)) \right) \tag{7}$$

Here, $\delta(s) = s - \bar{s}$ is the deviation of aligned shape s from the mean shape $\bar{s}$ that is calculated from the set of shapes s belongs to (S_t^a, $S_l^a(\phi)$ or $S_r^a(\phi)$), similar to as in [2].
4. Find ϕ^*, the splitting candidate that produces the largest information gain:

$$\phi^* = \operatorname*{argmax}_{\phi} I(S_t, \phi) \tag{8}$$

5. If $I(S_t, \phi^*)$ is greater or equal to a minimum splitting criteria and tree is not at maximum depth, split the node into children, letting $S_t = S_l(\phi^*)$ at the left node and $S_t = S_r(\phi^*)$ at the right node. Update LM_t at each child node accordingly. Finally, save at current node S_t, f_θ and τ from ϕ^*, and $\bar{L}$ as the GPA-aligned mean of landmarks that are associated with each shape in S_t.
6. Repeat steps 1 to 5 of the algorithm at each child node until each tree is fully grown.

cSSM Construction and Tree Aggregation. When presented with a set of sparse landmarks L_u that are associated with a shape, the ShapeForest first computes the feature values for L_u, $f_\theta(L_u) \in \{f_{dist}(L_u) \cup f_{rp}(L_u)\}$. Each individual decision tree is then traversed from their root node through the evaluation of $f_\theta(L_u)$ against τ at each node, branching left or right based on the outcome of this comparison, until a leaf node is reached.

To construct the constrained SSM, the sets of shapes S_t found at the leaf nodes traversed to are returned from every decision tree and aggregated. A shape-frequency histogram is constructed, with the most frequently occurring shapes found across all trees used to set $\hat{S}$ and calculate $\hat{s}$ and $\hat{P}\hat{b}$ of the constrained SSM.

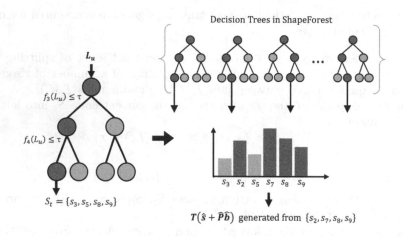

Fig. 4. Example of ShapeForest training and constrained SSM inference

Figure 4 summarizes this process of tree traversal and aggregation described above, showing how a subset of the most frequently occurring shapes (in this case, $\{s_2, s_7, s_8, s_9\}$ can be selected to construct a constrained SSM given the landmarks L.

Shape Selection Optimization (SSO). An optional shape selection optimization step can be applied to all trees in the ShapeForest. This step attempts to utilize the spatial correlation between L_u (the set of sparse landmarks associated with an original shape) and $\bar{L}$ (the set of GPA-aligned mean landmarks stored at a node) to improve node selection after tree traversal, augmenting the set of shapes selection used to construct the constrained SSM.

Selection improvement results in the following algorithm being executed at each tree prior to tree aggregation, starting from selected leaf nodes:

1. At the current node, use GPA to align L_u and $\bar{L}$ and compute corresponding aligned sets L_u^a and $\bar{L}^a$. Calculate $\delta_c(L_u^a) = \delta(L_u^a) - \delta(\bar{L}^a)$, the deviation between both set of landmarks.
2. Repeat Step 1, but using $\bar{L}$ obtained from the current node's' parent to calculate $\delta_p(L_u^a) = \delta(L_u^a) - \delta(\bar{L}^a)$
3. Calculate $\Delta = \delta_c(L_u^a) - \delta_p(L_u^a)$ as the difference in deviation between L_u and mean landmarks at the current node after alignment, and L_u and mean landmarks at the parent node after alignment. If Δ is greater or equal to a pre-set minimum required value, traverse upwards to the parent node.
4. Repeat Steps 1 to 3 until Δ is less than the pre-set value, or current node is root node.

4   Experiments

To evaluate the ShapeForest, a series of experimental tests were performed. First, in Section 4.2, we evaluated the ability of the ShapeForest to represent complex shape variations. Hereby we compare the ability of the ShapeForest to reconstruct new shapes. Second, in Section 4.3, we integrate the ShapeForest in a standard hierarchical shape segmentation approach (CLM) and compare it with other approaches.

For each experiment, three-fold cross validation experiments were performed. Unless otherwise noted, 100 decision trees of depth 20, each containing 30% of overall training data, were used to construct the ShapeForest, with the top 30% most frequently occurring shapes used to generate each constrained SSM. Where shape selection optimization was used, the Δ threshold was set to 0.

4.1   Datasets

Three data sets were used for our quantitative experiments, each consisting of 3D images containing a specific human anatomy – the left ventricle outflow tract or LVOT (283 shapes), the aortic valve root or AV (633 shapes), and the liver (372 shapes). Each element within each data set contained a three dimensional CT image, a manually annotated shape model s and sparse landmarks set L associated with each shape. Figure 1 illustrates examples of liver shapes (top), AV shapes (middle) and LVOT shapes (bottom).

4.2   Reconstruction Error Evaluation

First we evaluate the ability of the ShapeForest to construct constrained SSMs that can accurately reconstruct new shapes. Given a SSM, the reconstruction error for an unseen shape s_u is computed as follows:

1. Calculate s_u^a as s_u after GPA-alignment with the mean shape defined by the SSM.
2. Project s_u^a onto the subspace defined by the SSM. Calculate s_r as the reconstruction of s_u^a in the SSM subspace using PCA coefficients that correspond to *90%* of total variability within the parametric model.
3. Align s_r and s_u using GPA and calculate the reconstruction error as the sum of Euclidean distances between corresponding points in s_r and s_u.

Table 1 summarizes mean reconstruction error results of constrained SSMs produced by the ShapeForest when compared against both the global SSM as well as a multi-modal parametric shape modeling approach, based on methods discussed in [4]. In this alternative approach, the shape model is represented as a mixture of Gaussian parametric models generated by the K-Means clustering of shapes based on their associated landmarks (represented in the table as MixModel2 and MixModel5 depending on the number of mixture components

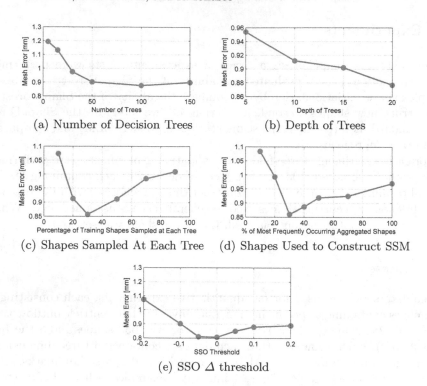

(a) Number of Decision Trees   (b) Depth of Trees

(c) Shapes Sampled At Each Tree   (d) Shapes Used to Construct SSM

(e) SSO Δ threshold

Fig. 5. Effects on segmentation performance of the ShapeForest based on different parameter selection for the LVOT anatomy

used). These experiments show the ShapeForest to consistently be able to reconstruct shapes with a lower error than both the global SSM and the multi-modal parametric shape modeling approach.

In addition we evaluated the ability of the ShapeForest to approximate the shape manifold with respect to both reconstruction accuracy and specificity for the AV anatomy. The reconstruction accuracy is measured for several instances of shape variability as mentioned in the previous paragraph. The specificity is measuring the ability of the SSM to synthesize realistic shapes, similar to shapes from the ground-truth database. Hereby we synthesize 150 shapes by randomly sampling the shape space coefficients b of the corresponding eigenvectors P within ± 2 times the standard deviation. For the specificity evaluation we measure the distance between the synthetically generated shapes and the closest shape from the ground truth database. Hereby we compared the cSSM+SSO with the gSSM for several percentage of preserved variance in the statistical shape models (see Figure 6). Our proposed method (cSSM+SSO) has better reconstruction accuracy compared to the gSSM with improved or similar specificity for 80%, 90%, 95% and 95% of preserved shape variance. For 99% preserved shape variance the cSSM+SSO reconstruction is in similar rage (cSSM+SSO has 1.39% lower reconstruction accuracy) however the specificity improvement using cSSM+SSO is 18.6%.

Table 1. Comparison of reconstruction accuracy of our proposed constrained SSM (and cSSM+SSO) trained with ShapeForest, the global SSM and the Gaussian mixture SSM. The error measurements are computed as the mean Euclidean distance (in millimeters) between the reconstructed shape and the ground-truth test shape. During reconstruction *90%* of total variability within the parametric model was used for each SSM approach.

	gSSM	cSSM	**cSSM+SSO**	MixModel2	MixModel5
LVOT Dataset Error	0.84	0.75	**0.71**	0.81	0.80
AV Dataset Error	0.78	0.66	**0.63**	0.71	0.74
Liver Dataset Error	3.27	3.15	**3.11**	3.32	3.46

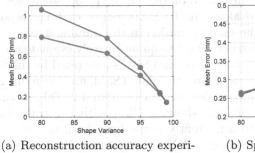

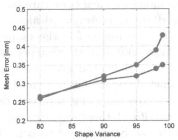

(a) Reconstruction accuracy experiment

(b) Specificity experiment

Fig. 6. Reconstruction experiment for the AV anatomy showing the reconstruction accuracy and specificity for both gSSM (blue) and our proposed method, the cSSM+SSO (red)

4.3 Shape Segmentation Evaluation

To examine the performance of the constrained SSMs produced by the Shape-Forest, we integrated the cSSM into a hierarchical CLM workflow to segment surface shapes from 3D CT images, as illustrated in Figure 7. We apply the same workflow to segment the AV, LVOT and the liver.

Based on a large set of annotations, we train a position detector for each of the landmarks L independently. We use a discriminative learning approach (Probabilistic Boosting Tree) trained with Haar-like features [20] to delineate the points in the images. Based on the landmarks the constrained SSM is constructed using the ShapeForest. For the Gaussian mixture model the cluster (representing an unique Gaussian parametric model) was selected based on the Euclidean distance of the aligned detected landmarks L to the cluster mean landmark model.

Based on the detected landmarks and one of the shape space representations an initial shape model is fitted to the image data. Hereby we use the Powell optimization consecutively to estimate the coefficients for the first 5 largest

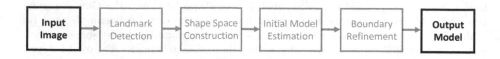

Fig. 7. Hierarchical shape segmentation workflow

eigenvectors. Starting with the largest eigenvector the best value is found to match accurately the landmarks L in the images. Hereby no image information is used to fit the model. Finally an iterative CLM method is applied to locally refine the initialized shape. The feature response images are computed with the probabilistic boosting tree and steerable features. Iteratively the current shape is adjusted along its local curvature based on the feature response images. Later the updated shape is projected along the basis vectors of each corresponding shape space, covering 99% of the shape variation in the training data.

Using this workflow, tests were performed to quantitatively evaluate the accuracy of shape models produced with constrained SSM's generated by the Shape-Forest against shape models produced with the global SSM, and the multi-modal parametric shape modeling approach described in Section 4.2. Table 2 summarizes the results of these experiments, showing CLM with constrained SSMs produced by the ShapeForest to consistently outperform both the global SSM and the multi-modal parametric shape model in each data set. For the LVOT and AV data set the mixture model improved the accuracy compared to the global SSM. However it failed for the liver data as the parametric model assignment based on the Euclidean distance between landmarks was inadequate in many cases. Execution overhead as a result of utilizing constrained SSMs was minimal (< 0.02 second per segmented shape) across all data sets.

Figure 8 shows examples of shapes which are used to construct the global SSM (left column) and the constrained SSM (middle and left column) for the LVOT, AV and the liver. It demonstrates how the ShapeForest clusters shapes with similar geometric properties, preserving local detail in the selected shape population. Parametric models inferred by the ShapeForest approximate more accurately the variation for a new instance, compared to parametric models build from the complete shape population.

4.4 Effect of ShapeForest Parameters

To examine the influence of the ShapeForest parameter selection used for constrained SSM construction, experiments were performed within the CLM segmentation framework for the LVOT data set. Using the parameters in the experiments as described in Section 4.3 with no SSO applied as a baseline, each of the five primary parameters that control constrained SSM construction in the ShapeForest were varied. Results of these experiments are summarized in Figure 5.

Table 2. Comparison of segmentation accuracy of our proposed constrained SSM (and cSSM+SSO) trained with ShapeForest, the global SSM and the Gaussian mixture SSM. The error measurements are computed as the mean Euclidean distance (in millimeters) between the segmented shape and the manually annotated ground-truth shape. *99%* of total variability within the parametric model was used for each SSM approach.

Method	Dataset	Shapes	Landm	Error in Initial Model				Error in Final Model			
				Mean	STD	Median	Improv	Mean	STD	Median	Improv
gSSM	LVOT	283	7	1.65	0.61	1.51	–	1.02	0.41	0.89	–
cSSM	LVOT	283	7	1.32	0.59	1.26	+19.69%	0.84	0.33	0.79	+17.64%
cSSM+SSO	LVOT	283	7	1.29	0.56	1.23	+21.81%	0.81	0.25	0.78	+20.58%
MixModel2	LVOT	283	7	1.51	0.53	1.46	+8.4%	0.88	0.33	0.80	+13.7%
MixModel5	LVOT	283	7	1.50	0.51	1.38	+9.1%	0.87	0.31	0.76	+14.7%
MixModel10	LVOT	283	7	2.73	1.19	2.42	-65.5%	1.82	1.48	1.32	-78.4%
gSSM	AV	633	13	0.99	0.50	0.85	–	0.83	0.20	0.82	–
cSSM	AV	633	13	0.80	0.38	0.79	+19.19%	0.69	0.29	0.63	+16.87%
cSSM+SSO	AV	633	13	0.78	0.32	0.62	+21.21%	0.66	0.19	0.61	+20.48%
MixModel2	AV	633	13	0.85	0.15	0.84	+14.1%	0.76	0.21	0.70	+8.4%
MixModel5	AV	633	13	0.93	0.19	0.91	+10.0%	0.78	0.24	0.75	+6.0%
MixModel10	AV	633	13	1.25	0.64	1.08	-26.3%	0.88	0.20	0.87	-6.0%
gSSM	Liver	372	20	3.99	0.95	3.82	–	2.85	0.92	2.68	–
cSSM	Liver	372	20	3.42	1.19	3.37	+14.28%	2.29	0.90	2.16	+19.64%
cSSM+SSO	Liver	372	20	3.34	1.29	2.86	+16.29%	2.20	0.76	2.16	+22.8%
MixModel2	Liver	372	20	4.05	0.99	3.89	-1.5%	2.88	1.23	2.67	-1.0%
MixModel5	Liver	372	20	4.44	1.28	4.37	-11.2%	3.54	1.54	3.31	-24.2%
MixModel10	Liver	372	20	4.82	1.26	4.94	-20.1%	4.13	1.41	4.16	-44.9%

Number of Decision Trees: The effect of increasing the number of decision trees used in the ShapeForest has on segmentation accuracy is shown in Figure 5(a). Here, increasing the number of trees decreased the mean error progressively, until reaching a plateau once the number of trees had been increased to 100. Increasing the number of trees beyond this point had negligible impact on segmentation accuracy while considerably increasing the memory requirements of the ShapeForest.

Depth of Decision Trees: The effect of increasing the depth of each decision trees is shown in Figure 5(b). A progressive decrease in mean error was noted as depth was increased, with optimal results found when trees were left to grow completely unbounded. Utilizing deeper decision trees increases the memory requirements of the ShapeForest considerably, although contributes only minimal additional overhead to execution time.

Sampled Data at Each Decision Tree: The degree that the amount training data used to construct each decision tree can affect mean error is shown in Figure 5(c), with optimal values observed when 30% of all training data is randomly sampled at each tree. Sampling a small amount of data resulted in trees that shared an insufficient amount of shapes to accurately obtain a set of frequently occurring shapes, while sampling a large amount of data resulted in individual trees being too similar to each other, minimizing the benefit gained from random sampling.

Percentage of Shapes used in SSM Construction: Figure 5(d) shows the effects of increasing the percentage of frequently occurring shapes used to construct the constrained SSM, based on the shape frequency histogram computed based on the aggregation of the results of all decision trees in the ShapeForest. Taking the top 30% most frequently occurring shapes produced the lowest error.

Shape Selection Optimization: Usage of the optimal SSO step was found to be able to improve the accuracy of shape detection, as shown in Figure 5(e), with optimal values found in the range of −0.05 to +0.05. Progressively lower values caused each tree to move back to their root node, with progressively higher values preventing any traversal upwards from the selected leaf node.

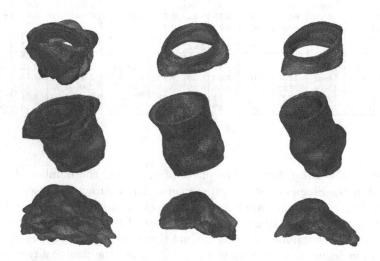

Fig. 8. Aligned Shapes using GPA for the global SSM (left) and inferred shapes with ShapeForest used to compute the constrained (mid, right) SSMs for the LVOT (top), AV (mid) and Liver (bottom) anatomy

5   Conclusion

In this paper we have presented ShapeForest, a novel shape model representation trained with decision trees and geometric features. It enables modeling of complex shape variation, preserves local detail in the training data and incorporates lower-level information in form of sparse landmarks during shape space learning and shape inference. Quantitative experiments on three separate medical data sets have shown that the usage of the constrained statistical shape model produced by the ShapeForest leads to substantial improvement in shape modeling and shape segmentation when incorporated in a Constrained Local Model framework.

References

1. Breiman, L.: Random forests. Machine Learning 45(1), 5–32 (2001)
2. Cootes, T.F., Taylor, C.J., Cooper, D.H., Graham, J.: Active shape models-their training and application. Computer Vision and Image Understanding 61(1), 38–59 (1995)
3. Cootes, T.F., Edwards, G.J., Taylor, C.J.: Active appearance models. IEEE Transactions on Pattern Analysis and Machine Intelligence 23(6), 681–685 (2001)
4. Cootes, T.F., Taylor, C.J.: A mixture model for representing shape variation. Image and Vision Computing 17(8), 567–573 (1999)
5. Criminisi, A., Robertson, D., Konukoglu, E., Shotton, J., Pathak, S., White, S., Siddiqui, K.: Regression forests for efficient anatomy detection and localization in computed tomography scans. Medical Image Analysis (2013)
6. Cristinacce, D., Cootes, T.: Automatic feature localisation with constrained local models. Pattern Recognition 41(10), 3054–3067 (2008)
7. Davatzikos, C., Tao, X., Shen, D.: Hierarchical active shape models, using the wavelet transform. IEEE Transactions on Medical Imaging 22(3), 414–423 (2003)
8. Etyngier, P., Segonne, F., Keriven, R.: Shape priors using manifold learning techniques. In: IEEE 11th International Conference on Computer Vision, ICCV 2007, pp. 1–8. IEEE (2007)
9. Felzenszwalb, P.F., Huttenlocher, D.P.: Pictorial structures for object recognition. International Journal of Computer Vision 61(1), 55–79 (2005)
10. Gall, J., Lempitsky, V.: Class-specific hough forests for object detection. In: Decision Forests for Computer Vision and Medical Image Analysis, pp. 143–157. Springer (2013)
11. Georgescu, B., Zhou, X.S., Comaniciu, D., Gupta, A.: Database-guided segmentation of anatomical structures with complex appearance. In: IEEE Computer Society Conference on Computer Vision and Pattern Recognition, CVPR 2005, vol. 2, pp. 429–436. IEEE (2005)
12. Grbic, S., Ionasec, R., Vitanovski, D., Voigt, I., Wang, Y., Georgescu, B., Comaniciu, D.: Complete valvular heart apparatus model from 4d cardiac ct. Medical Image Analysis 16(5), 1003–1014 (2012)
13. Kass, M., Witkin, A., Terzopoulos, D.: Snakes: Active contour models. International Journal of Computer Vision 1(4), 321–331 (1988)
14. Rodola, E., Bulo, S.R., Windheuser, T., Vestner, M., Cremers, D.: Dense non-rigid shape correspondence using random forests (2014)
15. Saragih, J., Goecke, R.: A nonlinear discriminative approach to aam fitting. In: IEEE 11th International Conference on Computer Vision, ICCV 2007, pp. 1–8. IEEE (2007)
16. Saragih, J.M., Lucey, S., Cohn, J.F.: Deformable model fitting with a mixture of local experts. In: 2009 IEEE 12th International Conference on Computer Vision, pp. 2248–2255. IEEE (2009)
17. Sjostrand, K., Rostrup, E., Ryberg, C., Larsen, R., Studholme, C., Baezner, H., Ferro, J., Fazekas, F., Pantoni, L., Inzitari, D., et al.: Sparse decomposition and modeling of anatomical shape variation. IEEE Transactions on Medical Imaging 26(12), 1625–1635 (2007)
18. Yang, L., Georgescu, B., Zheng, Y., Meer, P., Comaniciu, D.: 3d ultrasound tracking of the left ventricle using one-step forward prediction and data fusion of collaborative trackers. In: IEEE Conference on Computer Vision and Pattern Recognition, CVPR 2008, pp. 1–8. IEEE (2008)

19. Zhang, S., Zhan, Y., Dewan, M., Huang, J., Metaxas, D.N., Zhou, X.S.: Sparse shape composition: A new framework for shape prior modeling. In: 2011 IEEE Conference on Computer Vision and Pattern Recognition (CVPR), pp. 1025–1032. IEEE (2011)
20. Zheng, Y., Georgescu, B., Ling, H., Zhou, S.K., Scheuering, M., Comaniciu, D.: Constrained marginal space learning for efficient 3d anatomical structure detection in medical images. In: IEEE Conference on Computer Vision and Pattern Recognition, CVPR 2009, pp. 194–201. IEEE (2009)

Optimizing Ranking Measures for Compact Binary Code Learning

Guosheng Lin[1], Chunhua Shen[1,*], and Jianxin Wu[2]

[1] University of Adelaide, Australia
chunhua.shen@adelaide.edu.au
[2] Nanjing University, China

Abstract. Hashing has proven a valuable tool for large-scale information retrieval. Despite much success, existing hashing methods optimize over simple objectives such as the reconstruction error or graph Laplacian related loss functions, instead of the performance evaluation criteria of interest—multivariate performance measures such as the AUC and NDCG. Here we present a general framework (termed StructHash) that allows one to directly optimize multivariate performance measures. The resulting optimization problem can involve exponentially or infinitely many variables and constraints, which is more challenging than standard structured output learning. To solve the StructHash optimization problem, we use a combination of column generation and cutting-plane techniques. We demonstrate the generality of StructHash by applying it to ranking prediction and image retrieval, and show that it outperforms a few state-of-the-art hashing methods.

1 Introduction

The ever increasing volumes of imagery available, and the benefits reaped through the interrogation of large image datasets, have increased enthusiasm for large-scale approaches to vision. One of the simplest, and most effective means of improving the scale and efficiency of an application has been to use hashing to pre-process the data [10,24,14,20,16,13].

Depending on applications, specific measures are used to evaluate the performance of the generated hash codes. For example, information retrieval and ranking criteria [17] such as the Area Under the ROC Curve (AUC) [7], Normalized Discounted Cumulative Gain (NDCG) [6], Precision-at-K, Precision-Recall and Mean Average Precision (mAP) have been widely adopted to evaluate the success of hashing methods. However, to date, most hashing methods are usually learned by optimizing simple errors such as the reconstruction error (e.g., binary reconstruction embedding hashing [10]) or the graph Laplacian related loss [26,16,24]. These hashing methods construct a set of hash functions that map the original high-dimensional data into a much smaller binary space, typically with the goal of preserving neighbourhood relations. The resulting compact

---

* Corresponding author.

D. Fleet et al. (Eds.): ECCV 2014, Part III, LNCS 8691, pp. 613–627, 2014.

binary encoding enables fast similarity computation between data points by using the Hamming distance, which can be carried out by rapid, often hardware-supported, bit-wise operations. Furthermore, compact binary codes are much more efficient for large-scale data storage.

To our knowledge, none of the existing hashing methods has tried to learn hash codes that *directly* optimize a multivariate performance criterion. In this work, we seek to reduce the discrepancy between existing learning criteria and the evaluation criteria (such as retrieval quality measures).

The proposed framework accommodates various complex multivariate measures. By observing that the hash codes learning problem is essentially an information retrieval problem, various ranking loss functions can and should be applied, rather than merely pairwise distance comparisons. This framework also allows to introduce more general definitions of "similarity" to hashing beyond existing ones.

In summary, our main contributions are as follows.

1. We propose a flexible binary hash codes learning framework that directly optimizes complex multivariate measures. This framework, *for the first time*, exploits the gains made in structured output learning for the purposes of hashing. Our hashing method, labelled as StructHash, is able to directly optimize various multivariate evaluation criteria, such as information retrieval measures (e.g., AUC and NDCG [6]).
2. To facilitate StructHash, we combine column generation and cutting-plane methods in order to efficiently solve the resulting optimization problem, which may involve exponentially or even infinitely many variables and constraints.
3. Applied to ranking prediction for image retrieval, the proposed method demonstrates state-of-the-art performance on hash function learning.

2   Related Work

One of the best known *data-independent* hashing methods is locality sensitive hashing (LSH) [3], which uses random projection to generate binary codes. Recently, a number of *data-dependent* hashing methods have been proposed. For example, spectral hashing (SPH) [24] aims to preserve the neighbourhood relation by optimizing the Laplacian affinity. Anchor graph hashing (AGH) [16] makes the original SPH much more scalable. Examples of supervised or semi-supervised hashing methods include binary reconstruction embedding (BRE) [10], which aims to minimize the expected distances; and the semi-supervised sequential projection learning hashing (SPLH) [22], which enforces the smoothness of similar data points and the separability of dissimilar data points.

To obtain a richer representation, kernelized LSH [11] was proposed, which randomly samples training data as support vectors, and randomly draws the dual coefficients from a Gaussian distribution. Liu et al. extended Kulis and Grauman's work to kernelized supervised hashing (KSH) [15] by learning the dual coefficients instead. Lin et al. [13] employed ensembles of decision trees as the hash functions. Nonetheless, all of these methods do not directly optimize the multivariate performance measures of interest. We formulate hash codes learning as a structured output learning problem, in order to directly optimize a wide variety of evaluation measures.

This work is primarily inspired by recent advances in learning to rank such as the metric learning method in [17], which directly optimizes several different ranking measures. We aim to learn hash functions, which leads to a very different learning task preventing directly applying techniques in [17]. We are also inspired by the recent column generation based hashing method, column generation hashing (CGH) [12], which iteratively learns hash functions using column generation. However, their method optimizes the conventional classification-related loss, which is much simpler than the multivariate loss that we are interested in here. Moreover, the optimization of CGH relies on all triplet constraints while our method is able to use much less number of constraints without sacrificing the performance.

Our framework is built upon the structured SVM [21], which has been applied to many applications for complex structured output prediction, e.g., image segmentation, action recognition and so on.

Notation. Let $\{(\boldsymbol{x}_i; \boldsymbol{y}_i)\}$, $i = 1, 2 \cdots$, denote a set of input-output pairs. The discriminative function for structured output prediction is[1] $F(\boldsymbol{x}, \boldsymbol{y}) : \mathcal{X} \times \mathcal{Y} \mapsto \mathbb{R}$, which measures the compatibility of the input and output pair $(\boldsymbol{x}, \boldsymbol{y})$. Given a query $\boldsymbol{x}_i$, we use $\mathcal{X}_i^+$ and $\mathcal{X}_i^-$ to denote the subsets of relevant and irrelevant data points in the training data. Given two data points: $\boldsymbol{x}_i$ and $\boldsymbol{x}_j$, $\boldsymbol{x}_i \prec_{\boldsymbol{y}} \boldsymbol{x}_j$ ($\boldsymbol{x}_i \succ_{\boldsymbol{y}} \boldsymbol{x}_j$) means that $\boldsymbol{x}_i$ is placed before (after) $\boldsymbol{x}_j$ in the ranking $\boldsymbol{y}$.

2.1 Structured SVM

First we provide a brief overview of structured SVM. Structured SVM enforces that the score of the "correct" model $\boldsymbol{y}''$ should be larger than all other "incorrect" model $\boldsymbol{y}$, $\forall \boldsymbol{y} \neq \boldsymbol{y}''$, which writes:

$$\forall \boldsymbol{y} \in \mathcal{Y}: \quad \boldsymbol{w}^{\top}[\psi(\boldsymbol{x}, \boldsymbol{y}'') - \psi(\boldsymbol{x}, \boldsymbol{y})] \geq \Delta(\boldsymbol{y}, \boldsymbol{y}'') - \xi. \tag{1}$$

Here ξ is a slack variable (soft margin) corresponding to the hinge loss. $\psi(\boldsymbol{x}, \boldsymbol{y})$ is a vector-valued joint feature mapping. It plays a key role in structured learning and specifies the relationship between an input $\boldsymbol{x}$ and output $\boldsymbol{y}$. $\boldsymbol{w}$ is the model parameter. The label loss $\Delta(\boldsymbol{y}, \boldsymbol{y}'') \in \mathbb{R}$ measures the discrepancy of the predicted $\boldsymbol{y}$ and the true label $\boldsymbol{y}''$. A typical assumption is that $\Delta(\boldsymbol{y}, \boldsymbol{y}) = 0, \Delta(\boldsymbol{y}, \boldsymbol{y}'') > 0$ for any $\boldsymbol{y} \neq \boldsymbol{y}''$, and $\Delta(\boldsymbol{y}, \boldsymbol{y}'')$ is upper bounded. The prediction $\boldsymbol{y}^*$ of an input $\boldsymbol{x}$ is achieved by

$$\boldsymbol{y}^* = \operatorname*{argmax}_{\boldsymbol{y}} F(\boldsymbol{x}, \boldsymbol{y}) = \boldsymbol{w}^{\top} \psi(\boldsymbol{x}, \boldsymbol{y}). \tag{2}$$

---

[1] To be precise, the prediction function should be written as $F(\boldsymbol{x}, \boldsymbol{y}; \boldsymbol{w})$ because it is parameterized by $\boldsymbol{w}$. For simplicity, we omit $\boldsymbol{w}$.

Optimization for the Model Parameter w. For structured problems, the size of the output $|\mathcal{Y}|$ is typically very large or infinite. Considering all possible constraints in (1) is generally intractable. The cutting-plane method [9] is commonly employed, which allows to maintain a small working-set of constraints and obtain an approximate solution of the original problem up to a pre-set precision. To speed up, the 1-slack reformulation is proposed [8]. Nonetheless the cutting-plane method needs to find the most violated label (equivalent to an inference problem)

$$\underset{y \in \mathcal{Y}}{\operatorname{argmax}} \ w^{\top} \psi(x, y) + \Delta(y, y''). \tag{3}$$

Structured SVM typically requires: 1) a well-designed feature representation $\psi(\cdot, \cdot)$; 2) an appropriate label loss $\Delta(\cdot, \cdot)$; 3) solving inference problems (2) and (3) efficiently.

Ranking Prediction with Structured Output. In a retrieval system, given a test data point x, the goal is to predict a ranking of data points in the database. For a "correct" ranking, relevant data points are expected to be placed in front of irrelevant data points. A ranking output is denoted by y. Let us introduce a symbol $y_{jk} = 1$ if $x_j \prec_y x_k$ and $y_{jk} = -1$ if $x_j \succ_y x_k$. The ranking can be evaluated by various measures such as AUC, NDCG, mAP. These evaluation measures can be optimized directly as label losss Δ [7,17]. Here $\psi(x, y)$ can be defined as:

$$\psi(x_i, y) = \sum_{x_j \in \mathcal{X}_i^+} \sum_{x_k \in \mathcal{X}_i^-} y_{jk} \left[\frac{\phi(x_i, x_j) - \phi(x_i, x_k)}{|\mathcal{X}_i^+| \cdot |\mathcal{X}_i^-|} \right]. \tag{4}$$

$\mathcal{X}_i^+$ and $\mathcal{X}_i^-$ are the sets of relevant and irrelevant neighbours of data point x_i respectively. Here $|\cdot|$ is the set size. The feature map $\phi(x_i, x_j)$ captures the relation between a query x_i and point x_j.

We have briefly reviewed how to optimize ranking criteria using structured prediction. Now we review some basic concepts of hashing before introducing our framework.

2.2   Learning-Based Hashing

Given a set of training data x_i, $(i = 1, 2, \dots)$, the task is to learn a set of hash functions $[h_1(x), h_2(x), \dots, h_\ell(x)]$. Each hash function maps the input into a binary bit $\{0, 1\}$. So with the learned functions, an input x is mapped into a binary code of length ℓ. We use $\widetilde{x} \in \{0, 1\}^\ell$ to denote the hashed values of x i.e.,

$$\widetilde{x} = [h_1(x) \dots, h_\ell(x)]^{\top}. \tag{5}$$

Suppose that we are given the supervision information as a set of triplets: $\{(x_i, x_j, x_k)\}(i = 1, 2, \dots)$, in which x_j is an relevant (similar) data point of

x_i (i.e., $x_j \in \mathcal{X}_i^+$) and x_k is an irrelevant (dissimilar) neighbor of x_i (i.e., $x_k \in \mathcal{X}_i^-$). These triplets encode the relative similarity information. After applying the hashing, the distance of two hash codes (of length ℓ) can be calculated using the weighted hamming distance:

$$d_{\mathsf{hm}}(x_i, x_j) = w^\top |\tilde{x}_i - \tilde{x}_j|, \tag{6}$$

where $w > 0$ is a non-negative vector, which can be learned. Such weighted hamming distance is used in CGH [12] and multi-dimension spectral hashing [23]. It is expected that after hashing, the distance between relevant data points should be smaller than the distance between irrelevant data points. That is

$$d_{\mathsf{hm}}(x_i, x_j) \leq d_{\mathsf{hm}}(x_i, x_k),$$

for $x_j \in \mathcal{X}_i^+, x_k \in \mathcal{X}_i^-, \forall i = 1, 2, \cdots$. One can then define the margin $\rho = d_{\mathsf{hm}}(x_i, x_k) - d_{\mathsf{hm}}(x_i, x_j)$. It is then possible to plug this margin into the large-margin learning framework to optimize for the parameter w as well as the hash functions, as shown in [12].

3   The Proposed StructHash Algorithm

For the time being, let us assume that we have already learned all the hashing functions. In other words, *given a data point x, we assume that we have access to its corresponding hashed values $\tilde{x}$, as defined in* (5). Later we will show how this mapping can be explicitly learned using column generation. Now let us focus on how to optimize for the weight w. When the weighted hamming distance is used, we aim to learn an optimal weight w defined in (6). Distances are calculated in the learned space and ranked accordingly. A natural choice for the vector-valued mapping function ϕ in Equ. (4) is

$$\phi(x_i, x_j) = -|\tilde{x}_i - \tilde{x}_j|. \tag{7}$$

Note that we have flipped the sign, which preserves the ordering in the standard structured SVM. Due to this change of sign, sorting the data by ascending $d_{\mathsf{hm}}(x_i, x_j)$ is equivalent to sorting by descending $w^\top \phi(x_i, x_j) = -w^\top |\tilde{x}_i - \tilde{x}_j|$.

The loss function $\Delta(\cdot, \cdot)$ depends on the metric, which we will discuss in detail in the next section. For ease of exposition, let us define

$$\delta\psi_i(y) = \psi(x_i, y_i) - \psi(x_i, y), \tag{8}$$

with $\psi(x_i, y)$ defined in (4). We consider the following problem,

$$\min_{w \geq 0, \xi \geq 0} \|w\|_1 + \frac{C}{m} \sum_{i=1}^{m} \xi_i \tag{9a}$$

$$\text{s.t.: } \forall i = 1, \ldots, m \text{ and } \forall y \in \mathcal{Y}:$$

$$w^\top \delta\psi_i(y) \geq \Delta(y_i, y) - \xi_i. \tag{9b}$$

Unlike standard structured SVM, here we use the ℓ_1 regularisation (instead of ℓ_2) and enforce that w to be non-negative. This is aligned with boosting methods [2,18], and enables us to learn hash functions efficiently.

Algorithm 1. StructHash: Column generation for hash function learning

---

1: **Input:** training examples $(\boldsymbol{x}_1; \boldsymbol{y}_1), (\boldsymbol{x}_2; \boldsymbol{y}_2), \cdots$; parameter C; the maximum iteration number (bit length ℓ).

2: **Initialise:** working set of hashing functions $\mathcal{W}_{\mathrm{H}} \leftarrow \emptyset$; initialise $\lambda_{(\boldsymbol{c},\boldsymbol{y})} = C/m$ by randomly picking m pairs of $(\boldsymbol{c}, \boldsymbol{y})$ and the rest is set to 0.

3: **Repeat**

4:   − Find a new hashing function $h^*(\cdot)$ by solving Equ. (15).

5:   − add h^* into the working set of hashing functions: $\mathcal{W}_{\mathrm{H}}$.

6:   − Solve the structured SVM problem (9) or the equivalent (10) using cutting-plane as discussed in Sec. 3.1.

7: **Until** the maximum iteration is reached.

8: **Output:** Learned hash functions and $\boldsymbol{w}$.

3.1   Learning Weights $\boldsymbol{w}$ via Cutting-Plane

Here we show how to learn $\boldsymbol{w}$. Inspired by [8], we first derive the 1-slack formulation of the original m-slack formulation (9):

$$\min_{\boldsymbol{w} \geq 0, \xi \geq 0} \quad \|\boldsymbol{w}\|_1 + C\xi \tag{10a}$$

$$\text{s.t.:} \ \forall \boldsymbol{c} \in \{0,1\}^m \text{ and } \forall \boldsymbol{y} \in \mathcal{Y}, i = 1, \cdots, m :$$

$$\frac{1}{m} \boldsymbol{w}^\top \left[\sum_{i=1}^m \boldsymbol{c}_i \cdot \delta\psi_i(\boldsymbol{y}) \right] \geq \frac{1}{m} \sum_{i=1}^m \boldsymbol{c}_i \Delta(\boldsymbol{y}_i, \boldsymbol{y}) - \xi. \tag{10b}$$

Here $\boldsymbol{c}$ enumerates all possible $\boldsymbol{c} \in \{0,1\}^m$. As in [8], cutting-plane methods can be used to solve the 1-slack primal problem (10) efficiently. Specifically, we need to solve a maximization for every $\boldsymbol{x}_i$ in each cutting-plane iteration to find the most violated constraint of (10b), given a solution $\boldsymbol{w}$:

$$\boldsymbol{y}_i^* = \underset{\boldsymbol{y}}{\operatorname{argmax}} \ \Delta(\boldsymbol{y}_i, \boldsymbol{y}) - \boldsymbol{w}^\top \delta\psi_i(\boldsymbol{y}). \tag{11}$$

We now know how to efficiently learn $\boldsymbol{w}$ using cutting-plane methods. However, it remains unclear how to learn hash functions (or features). Thus far, we have taken for granted that the hashed values $\tilde{\boldsymbol{x}}$ (or $h(\cdot)$) are given. We would like to learn the hash functions and $\boldsymbol{w}$ in a single optimization framework. Next we show how this is possible using the column generation technique from boosting.

3.2   Learning Hash Functions Using Column Generation

Note that the dimension of $\boldsymbol{w}$ is the same as the dimension of $\tilde{\boldsymbol{x}}$ (and of $\phi(\cdot, \cdot)$, see Equ. (7)), which is the number of hash bits by the definition (5). If we were able to access all hash functions, it may be possible to select a subset of them and learn the corresponding $\boldsymbol{w}$ due to the sparsity introduced by the ℓ_1 regularization in (9). Unfortunately, the number of possible hash functions can be infinitely large. In this case it is in general infeasible to solve the optimization problem exactly.

Column generation [2] can be used to approximately solve the problem by adding variables iteratively into the master optimization problems. Column generation was originally invented to solve extremely large-scale linear programming problem, which mainly works on the dual problem. The basic concept of column generation is to add one constraint at a time to the dual problem until an optimal solution is identified. Columns[2] are generated and added to the problem iteratively to approach the optimality. In the primal problem, column generation solves the problem on a subset of primal variables ($\boldsymbol{w}$ in our case), which corresponds to a subset of constraints in the dual. This strategy has been widely employed to learn weak learners in boosting [18,2,19].

To learn hash functions via column generation, we derive the dual problem of the above 1-slack optimization, which is,

$$\max_{\lambda \geq 0} \sum_{c,y} \lambda_{(c,y)} \sum_{i=1}^{m} c_i \Delta(\boldsymbol{y}_i, \boldsymbol{y}) \tag{12a}$$

$$\text{s.t.:} \quad \frac{1}{m} \sum_{c,y} \lambda_{(c,y)} \left[\sum_{i=1}^{m} c_i \cdot \delta\psi_i(\boldsymbol{y}) \right] \leq 1, \tag{12b}$$

$$0 \leq \sum_{c,y} \lambda_{(c,y)} \leq C. \tag{12c}$$

We denote by $\lambda_{(c,y)}$ the 1-slack dual variable associated with one constraint in (10b). Note that (12b) is a set of constraints because $\delta\psi(\cdot)$ is a vector of the same dimension as $\phi(\cdot,\cdot)$ as well as $\tilde{\boldsymbol{x}}$, which can be infinitely large. One dimension in the vector $\delta\psi(\cdot)$ corresponds to one constraint in (12b). Finding the most violated constraint in the dual form (12) of the 1-slack formulation for generating one hash function is to maximise the l.h.s. of (12b).

The calculation of $\delta\psi(\cdot)$ in (8) can be simplified as follows. Because of the subtraction of $\psi(\cdot)$ (defined in (4)), only those incorrect ranking pairs will appear in the calculation. Recall that the true ranking is $\boldsymbol{y}_i$ for $\boldsymbol{x}_i$. We define $\mathcal{S}_i(\boldsymbol{y})$ as a set of incorrectly ranked pairs: $(j,k) \in \mathcal{S}_i(\boldsymbol{y})$, in which the incorrectly ranked pair (j,k) means that the true ranking is $\boldsymbol{x}_j \prec_{\boldsymbol{y}_i} \boldsymbol{x}_k$ but $\boldsymbol{x}_j \succ_{\boldsymbol{y}} \boldsymbol{x}_k$. So we have

$$\delta\psi_i(\boldsymbol{y}) = \frac{2}{|\mathcal{X}_i^+||\mathcal{X}_i^-|} \sum_{(j,k)\in\mathcal{S}_i(\boldsymbol{y})} [\phi(\boldsymbol{x}_i, \boldsymbol{x}_j) - \phi(\boldsymbol{x}_i, \boldsymbol{x}_k)]$$

$$= \frac{2}{|\mathcal{X}_i^+||\mathcal{X}_i^-|} \sum_{(j,k)\in\mathcal{S}_i(\boldsymbol{y})} (|\tilde{\boldsymbol{x}}_i - \tilde{\boldsymbol{x}}_k| - |\tilde{\boldsymbol{x}}_i - \tilde{\boldsymbol{x}}_j|). \tag{13}$$

---

[2] A column is a variable in the primal and a corresponding constraint in the dual.

With the above equations and the definition of $\tilde{x}$ in (5), the most violated constraint in (12b) can be found by solving the following problem:

$$h^*(\cdot) = \underset{h(\cdot)}{\operatorname{argmax}} \sum_{c,y} \lambda_{(c,y)} \sum_i \frac{2c_i}{|\mathcal{X}_i^+||\mathcal{X}_i^-|} \cdot$$
$$\sum_{(j,k) \in \mathcal{S}_i(y)} (|h(x_i) - h(x_k)| - |h(x_i) - h(x_j)|). \qquad (14)$$

By exchanging the order of summations, the above optimization can be further written in a compact form:

$$h^*(\cdot) = \underset{h(\cdot)}{\operatorname{argmax}} \sum_{i,y} \sum_{(j,k) \in \mathcal{S}_i(y)} \mu_{(i,y)} (|h(x_i) - h(x_k)| - |h(x_i) - h(x_j)|), \qquad (15)$$

$$\text{where,} \quad \mu_{(i,y)} = \frac{2}{|\mathcal{X}_i^+||\mathcal{X}_i^-|} \sum_c \lambda_{(c,y)} c_i. \qquad (16)$$

The objective in the above optimization is a summation of weighted triplet (i, j, k) ranking scores, in which $\mu_{(i,y)}$ is the triplet weighting value. Solving the above optimization provides the best hash function for the current solution w. Once a hash function is generated, we learn w using cutting-plane in Sec. 3.1. The column generation procedure for hash function learning is summarised in Algorithm 1.

The form of hash function $h(\cdot)$ can be any function that outputs a binary value. For a decision stump as the hash function, usually we can exhaustively enumerate all possibility and find the globally best one. However globally solving (15) is generally difficult. In most of our experiments, we use the linear perceptron hash function with the output in $\{0, 1\}$:

$$h(x) = 0.5(\operatorname{sign}(v^\top x + b) + 1). \qquad (17)$$

The non-smooth function $\operatorname{sign}(\cdot)$ here brings the difficulty for optimization. Similar to [12], we replace the $\operatorname{sign}(\cdot)$ function by a smooth sigmoid function, and then locally solve the above optimization (15) (e.g., LBFGS [27]) for learning the parameters of a hash function. We can apply a few heuristics to initialize for solving (15). For example, similar to LSH, we can generate a set of random projection planes and then choose the best one that maximizes the objective in (15) as the initialization. We can also train a decision stump by searching a best dimension and threshold to maximize the objective on the quantized data. Alternatively, one can employ the spectral relaxation method [16] which drops the $\operatorname{sign}(\cdot)$ function and solves a generalized eigenvalue problem to obtain an initial point. In our experiments, we use the spectral relaxation method for initialization.

Next, we discuss some widely-used information retrieval evaluation criteria, and show how they can be seamlessly incorporated into StructHash.

4   Ranking Measures

Here we discuss a few ranking measures for loss functions, including AUC, NDCG, Precision-at-K, and mAP. Following [17], we define the loss function over two rankings $\Delta \in [0\ 1]$ as:

$$\Delta(\boldsymbol{y}, \boldsymbol{y}') = 1 - \text{score}(\boldsymbol{y}, \boldsymbol{y}'). \tag{18}$$

Here $\boldsymbol{y}'$ is the ground truth ranking and $\boldsymbol{y}$ is the prediction. We define $\mathcal{X}_{\boldsymbol{y}'}^+$ and $\mathcal{X}_{\boldsymbol{y}'}^-$ as the indexes of relevant and irrelevant neighbours respectively in the ground truth ranking $\boldsymbol{y}'$.

AUC. The area under the ROC curve is to evaluate the performance of correct ordering of data pairs, which can be computed by counting the proportion of correctly ordered data pairs:

$$\text{score}_{\text{AUC}}(\boldsymbol{y}, \boldsymbol{y}') = \frac{1}{|\mathcal{X}_{\boldsymbol{y}'}^+ || \mathcal{X}_{\boldsymbol{y}'}^-|} \sum_{i \in \mathcal{X}_{\boldsymbol{y}'}^+} \sum_{j \in \mathcal{X}_{\boldsymbol{y}'}^-} \delta(i \prec_{\boldsymbol{y}} j). \tag{19}$$

$\delta(\cdot) \in \{0, 1\}$ is the indicator function. For using this AUC loss, the maximization inference in (11) can be solved efficiently by sorting the distances of data pairs, as described in [7]. Note that the loss of a wrongly ordered pair is not related to their positions in the ranking list, thus AUC is a position insensitive measure.

Precision-at-K. Precision-at-K is to evaluate the quality of top-K retrieved examples in a ranking. It is computed by counting the number of relevant data points within top-K positions and divided by K:

$$\text{score}_{\text{P@K}}(\boldsymbol{y}, \boldsymbol{y}'') = \frac{1}{K} \sum_{i=1}^{K} \delta(\boldsymbol{y}(i) \in \mathcal{X}_{\boldsymbol{y}''}^+). \tag{20}$$

Here $\boldsymbol{y}(i)$ is the example index on the i-th position of a ranking $\boldsymbol{y}$; $\delta(\cdot)$ is an indicator. An algorithm for solving the inference in (11) is proposed in [7].

NDCG. Normalized Discounted Cumulative Gain [6] is to measure the ranking quality of the first K returned neighbours. A similar measure is Precision-at-K which is the proportion of top-K relevant neighbours. NDCG is a position-sensitive measure which considers the positions of the top-K relevant neighbours. Compared to the position-insensitive measure: AUC, NDCG assigns different importances on the ranking positions, which is a more favorable measure for a general notion of a "good" ranking in real-world applications. In NDCG, each position of the ranking is assigned a score in a decreasing way. NDCG can be computed by accumulating the scores of top-K relevant neighbours:

$$\text{score}_{\text{NDCG}}(\boldsymbol{y}, \boldsymbol{y}') = \frac{1}{\sum_{i=1}^{K} S(i)} \sum_{i=1}^{K} S(i)\delta(\boldsymbol{y}(i) \in \mathcal{X}_{\boldsymbol{y}'}^+). \tag{21}$$

Here $\boldsymbol{y}(i)$ is the example index on the i-th position of a ranking $\boldsymbol{y}$. $S(i)$ is the score assigned to the i-th position of a ranking. $S(1) = 1$, $S(i) = 0$ for $i > k$ and

Table 1. Results using NDCG measure (64 bits). We compare our StructHash using AUC (StructH-A) and NDCG (StructH-N) loss functions with other supervised and un-supervised methods. Our method using NDCG loss performs the best in most cases.

Dataset	StructH-N	StructH-A	CGH	SPLH	STHs	BREs	ITQ	SPHER	MDSH	AGH	LSH
				NDCG ($K = 100$)							
STL10	**0.435**	0.374	0.375	0.404	0.214	0.289	0.337	0.318	0.313	0.310	0.228
USPS	**0.905**	0.893	0.900	0.816	0.688	0.777	0.804	0.762	0.735	0.741	0.668
MNIST	0.851	0.798	**0.867**	0.804	0.594	0.805	0.856	0.806	0.100	0.793	0.561
CIFAR	0.335	0.259	0.258	**0.357**	0.178	0.273	0.314	0.297	0.283	0.286	0.168
ISOLET	**0.881**	0.839	0.866	0.629	0.766	0.483	0.623	0.518	0.538	0.536	0.404

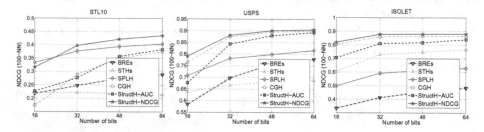

Fig. 1. NDCG results on 3 datasets. Our StructHash performs the best.

$S(i) = 1/\log_2(i)$ for other cases. A dynamic programming algorithm is proposed in [1] for solving the maximization inference in (11).

mAP. Mean average precision (mAP) is the averaged precision-at-K scores over all positions of relevant data points in a ranking, which is computed as:

$$\text{score}_{\text{mAP}}(\boldsymbol{y}, \boldsymbol{y}') = \frac{1}{|\mathcal{X}_{\boldsymbol{y}'}^+|} \sum_{i=1}^{|\mathcal{X}_{\boldsymbol{y}'}^+|+|\mathcal{X}_{\boldsymbol{y}'}^-|} \delta(\boldsymbol{y}(i) \in \mathcal{X}_{\boldsymbol{y}'}^+)\text{score}_{\text{P@K}(K=i)}(\boldsymbol{y}, \boldsymbol{y}'). \quad (22)$$

For using this mAP loss, an efficient algorithm for solving the inference in (11) is proposed in [25].

5   Experiments

Our method is in the category of supervised method for learning compact binary codes. Thus we mainly compare with 4 supervised methods: column generation hashing (CGH) [12],supervised binary reconstructive embeddings (BREs) [10], supervised self-taught hashing (STHs) [26], semi-supervised sequential projection learning hashing (SPLH) [22].

For comparison, we also run some unsupervised methods: locality-sensitive hashing (LSH) [3], anchor graph hashing (AGH) [16], spherical hashing (SPHER) [5], multi-dimension spectral hashing (MDSH) [23], and iterative quantization (ITQ) [4]. We carefully follow the original authors' instruction for parameter setting. For SPLH, the regularization parameter is picked from 0.01 to 1. We use the hierarchical variant of AGH. The bandwidth parameters of Gaussian affinity

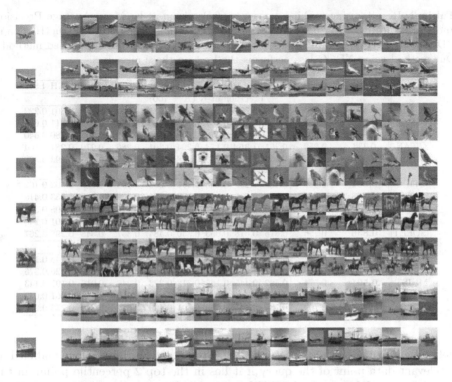

Fig. 2. Some ranking examples of our method. The first column shows query images, and the rest are retrieved images. False predictions are marked by red boxes.

in MDSH is set as $\sigma = t\bar{d}$. Here $\bar{d}$ is the average Euclidean distance of top 100 nearest neighbours and t is picked from 0.01 to 50. For supervised training of our StructHash and CGH, we use 50 relevant and 50 irrelevant examples to construct similarity information for each data point.

We use 9 datasets for evaluation, including one UCI dataset: ISOLET, 4 image datasets: CIFAR10[3], STL10[4], MNIST, USPS, and another 4 large image datasets: Tiny-580K [4], Flickr-1M[5], SIFT-1M [22] and GIST-1M[6]. CIFAR10 is a subset of the 80-million tiny images and STL10 is a subset of Image-Net. Tiny-580K consists of 580,000 tiny images. Flick-1M dataset consists of 1 million thumbnail images. SIFT-1M and GIST-1M datasets contain 1 million SIFT and GIST features respectively.

We follow a common setting in many supervised methods [10,15,12] for hashing evaluation. For multi-class datasets, we use class labels to define the relevant and irrelevant semantic neighbours by label agreement. For large datasets: Flickr-1M, SIFT-1M, GIST-1M and Tiny-580K, the semantic ground truth is

---

[3] http://www.cs.toronto.edu/~kriz/cifar.html
[4] http://www.stanford.edu/~acoates/stl10/
[5] http://press.liacs.nl/mirflickr/
[6] http://corpus-texmex.irisa.fr/

Table 2. Results using ranking measures of Precision-at-K, Mean Average Precision and Precision-Recall (64 bits). We compare our method using AUC (StructH-A) and NDCG (StructH-N) loss functions with other supervised and un-supervised methods. Our method using NDCG loss performs the best on these measures.

Dataset	StructH-N	StructH-A	CGH	SPLH	STHs	BREs	ITQ	SPHER	MDSH	AGH	LSH
			Precision-at-K ($K = 100$)								
STL10	**0.431**	0.376	0.376	0.396	0.208	0.279	0.325	0.303	0.298	0.301	0.222
USPS	**0.903**	0.894	0.898	0.805	0.667	0.755	0.780	0.730	0.698	0.711	0.637
MNIST	0.849	0.807	**0.862**	0.797	0.579	0.790	0.842	0.788	0.100	0.780	0.540
CIFAR	0.336	0.259	0.261	**0.354**	0.174	0.264	0.301	0.286	0.270	0.281	0.164
ISOLET	**0.875**	0.844	0.859	0.604	0.755	0.448	0.589	0.477	0.493	0.493	0.370
			Mean Average Precision (mAP)								
STL10	**0.331**	0.326	0.322	0.299	0.155	0.211	0.233	0.193	0.178	0.162	0.162
USPS	**0.868**	0.851	0.848	0.689	0.456	0.582	0.566	0.451	0.405	0.333	0.418
MNIST	**0.802**	0.790	0.789	0.684	0.397	0.558	0.585	0.510	0.119	0.505	0.343
CIFAR	0.294	**0.300**	0.298	0.289	0.147	0.204	0.215	0.204	0.181	0.201	0.149
ISOLET	**0.836**	0.796	0.815	0.518	0.653	0.340	0.484	0.357	0.348	0.298	0.267
			Precision-Recall								
STL10	**0.267**	0.248	0.248	0.246	0.130	0.181	0.200	0.174	0.164	0.145	0.138
USPS	**0.776**	0.760	0.760	0.609	0.401	0.520	0.508	0.424	0.379	0.326	0.375
MNIST	**0.591**	0.574	0.582	0.445	0.165	0.313	0.323	0.246	0.018	0.197	0.143
CIFAR	0.105	0.093	0.091	**0.110**	0.042	0.066	0.074	0.069	0.064	0.061	0.042
ISOLET	**0.759**	0.709	0.737	0.445	0.563	0.301	0.429	0.321	0.320	0.275	0.238

defined according to the ℓ_2 distance [22]. Specifically, a data point is labeled as a relevant data point of the query if it lies in the top 2 percentile points in the whole dataset. We generated GIST features for all image datasets except MNIST and USPS. we randomly select 2000 examples for testing queries, and the rest is used as database. We sample 2000 examples from the database as training data for learning models. For large datasets, we use 5000 examples for training. To evaluate the performance of compact bits, the maximum bit length is set to 64, as similar to the evaluation settings in other supervised hashing methods [10,12].

We report the result of the NDCG measure in Table 1. We compare our StructHash using AUC and NDCG loss functions with other supervised and un-supervised methods. Our method using NDCG loss function performs the best in most cases. We also report the result of other common measures in Table 2, including the result of Precision-at-K, Mean Average Precision (mAP) and Precision-Recall. Precision-at-K is the proportion of true relevant data points in the returned top-K results. The Precision-Recall curve measures the overall performance in all positions of the prediction ranking, which is computed by varying the number of nearest neighbours. It shows that our method generally performs better than other methods on these evaluation measures. As described before, compared to the AUC measure which is position insensitive, the NDCG measure assigns different importance on ranking positions, which is closely related to many other position sensitive ranking measures (e.g., mAP). As expected, the result shows that on the Precision-at-K, mAP and Precision-recall measures, optimizing the position sensitive NDCG loss performs better than the AUC loss. The triplet loss based method CGH actually helps to reduce the AUC loss. This may explain the reason that our method, which aims to reduce the NDCG loss,

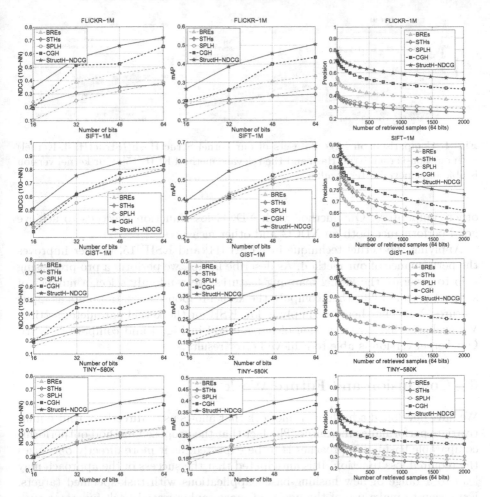

Fig. 3. Results on 4 large datasests: Flickr-1M (1 million Flickr images), Sift-1M (1 million SIFT features), Gist-1M (1 million GIST features) and Tiny580K (580, 000 Tiny image dataset). We compare with several supervised methods. The results of 3 measures (NDCG, mAP and precision of top-K neighbours) are show here. Our StructHash outperforms others in most cases.

is able to outperform CGH in these measures. We also plot the NDCG results on several datasets in Fig. 1 by varying the number of bits. Some retrieval examples are shown in Fig. 2.

We further evaluate our method on 4 large-scale datasets (Flickr-1M, SIFT-1M, GIST-1M and Tiny-580K). The results of NDCG, mAP and the precision of top-K neighbours are shown in Fig. 3. The NDCG and mAP results are shown by varying the number of bits. The precision of top-K neighbours is shown by varying the number of retrieved examples. In most cases, our method outperforms

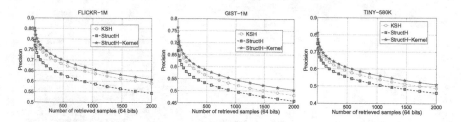

Fig. 4. Comparison on large datasets of our kernel StructHash (StructHash-Kernel) with our non-kernel StructHash and the relevant method KSH [15]. Our kernel version is able to achieve better results.

other competitors. Our method with NDCG loss function succeeds to achieve good performance both on NDCG and other measures.

Applying the kernel technique in KLSH [11] and KSH [15] further improves the performance of our method. As describe in [15], we perform a pre-processing step to generate the kernel mapping features: we randomly select a number of support vectors (300) then compute the kernel response on data points as input features. Note that here we simply follow KSH for the kernel parameter setting. We evaluate this kernel version of our method in Fig. 4 and compare to KSH. Our kernel version is able to achieve better results.

6   Conclusion and Future Work

We have developed a hashing framework that allows us to directly optimize multivariate performance measures. The fact that the proposed method outperforms comparable hashing approaches is to be expected, as it more directly optimizes the required loss function. It is anticipated that the success of the approach may lead to a range of new hashing-based applications with task-specified targets. Extension to make use of the power of more sophisticated hash functions such as kernel functions or decision trees is of future work.

References

1. Chakrabarti, S., Khanna, R., Sawant, U., Bhattacharyya, C.: Structured learning for non-smooth ranking losses. In: Proc. ACM Knowledge Discovery & Data Mining (2008)
2. Demiriz, A., Bennett, K.P., Shawe-Taylor, J.: Linear programming boosting via column generation. Mach. Learn. (2002)
3. Gionis, A., Indyk, P., Motwani, R.: Similarity search in high dimensions via hashing. In: Proc. Int. Conf. Very Large Data Bases (1999)
4. Gong, Y., Lazebnik, S., Gordo, A., Perronnin, F.: Iterative quantization: A procrustean approach to learning binary codes for large-scale image retrieval. IEEE Trans. Patt. Anal. & Mach. Intelli. (2012)
5. Heo, J., Lee, Y., He, J., Chang, S., Yoon, S.: Spherical hashing. In: Proc. Int. Conf. Comp. Vis. & Patt. Recogn. (2012)

6. Järvelin, K., Kekäläinen, J.: IR evaluation methods for retrieving highly relevant documents. In: Proc. ACM Conf. SIGIR (2000)
7. Joachims, T.: A support vector method for multivariate performance measures. In: Proc. Int. Conf. Mach. Learn. (2005)
8. Joachims, T.: Training linear SVMs in linear time. In: Proc. ACM Knowledge Discovery & Data Mining (2006)
9. Kelley Jr., J.E.: The cutting-plane method for solving convex programs. J. Society for Industrial & Applied Math. (1960)
10. Kulis, B., Darrell, T.: Learning to hash with binary reconstructive embeddings. Proc. Adv. Neural Info. Process. Syst. (2009)
11. Kulis, B., Grauman, K.: Kernelized locality-sensitive hashing. IEEE Trans. Patt. Anal. & Mach. Intelli. (2012)
12. Li, X., Lin, G., Shen, C., van den Hengel, A., Dick, A.: Learning hash functions using column generation. In: Proc. Int. Conf. Mach. Learn. (2013)
13. Lin, G., Shen, C., Shi, Q., van den Hengel, A., Suter, D.: Fast supervised hashing with decision trees for high-dimensional data. In: Proc. Int. Conf. Comp. Vis. & Patt. Recogn. Columbus, Ohio, USA (2014), https://bitbucket.org/chhshen/fasthash/src
14. Lin, G., Shen, C., Suter, D., van den Hengel, A.: A general two-step approach to learning-based hashing. In: Proc. Int. Conf. Comp. Vis., Sydney, Australia (2013)
15. Liu, W., Wang, J., Ji, R., Jiang, Y., Chang, S.: Supervised hashing with kernels. In: Proc. Int. Conf. Comp. Vis. & Patt. Recogn. (2012)
16. Liu, W., Wang, J., Kumar, S., Chang, S.F.: Hashing with graphs. In: Proc. Int. Conf. Mach. Learn. (2011)
17. McFee, B., Lanckriet, G.: Metric learning to rank. In: Proc. Int. Conf. Mach. Learn. (2010)
18. Shen, C., Li, H.: On the dual formulation of boosting algorithms. IEEE Trans. Patt. Anal. & Mach. Intelli. (2010)
19. Shen, C., Lin, G., van den Hengel, A.: StructBoost: Boosting methods for predicting structured output variables. IEEE Trans. Patt. Anal. & Mach. Intelli. (2014)
20. Shen, F., Shen, C., Shi, Q., van den Hengel, A., Tang, Z.: Inductive hashing on manifolds. In: Proc. Int. Conf. Comp. Vis. & Patt. Recogn., Oregon, USA (2013)
21. Tsochantaridis, I., Hofmann, T., Joachims, T., Altun, Y.: Support vector machine learning for interdependent and structured output spaces. In: Proc. Int. Conf. Mach. Learn. (2004)
22. Wang, J., Kumar, S., Chang, S.: Semi-supervised hashing for large scale search. IEEE Trans. Patt. Anal. & Mach. Intelli. (2012)
23. Weiss, Y., Fergus, R., Torralba, A.: Multidimensional spectral hashing. In: Proc. Eur. Conf. Comp. Vis. (2012)
24. Weiss, Y., Torralba, A., Fergus, R.: Spectral hashing. In: Proc. Adv. Neural Info. Process. Syst. (2008)
25. Yue, Y., Finley, T., Radlinski, F., Joachims, T.: A support vector method for optimizing average precision. In: Proc. ACM Conf. SIGIR (2007)
26. Zhang, D., Wang, J., Cai, D., Lu, J.: Extensions to self-taught hashing: Kernelisation and supervision. In: Proc. ACM Conf. SIGIR Workshop (2010)
27. Zhu, C., Byrd, R.H., Lu, P., Nocedal, J.: Algorithm 778: L-BFGS-B: Fortran subroutines for large-scale bound-constrained optimization. ACM T. Math. Softw. (1997)

Exploiting Low-Rank Structure from Latent Domains for Domain Generalization

Zheng Xu, Wen Li, Li Niu, and Dong Xu

School of Computer Engineering, Nanyang Technological University, Singapore

Abstract. In this paper, we propose a new approach for domain generalization by exploiting the low-rank structure from multiple latent source domains. Motivated by the recent work on exemplar-SVMs, we aim to train a set of exemplar classifiers with each classifier learnt by using only one positive training sample and all negative training samples. While positive samples may come from multiple latent domains, for the positive samples within the same latent domain, their likelihoods from each exemplar classifier are expected to be similar to each other. Based on this assumption, we formulate a new optimization problem by introducing the nuclear-norm based regularizer on the likelihood matrix to the objective function of exemplar-SVMs. We further extend Domain Adaptation Machine (DAM) to learn an optimal target classifier for domain adaptation. The comprehensive experiments for object recognition and action recognition demonstrate the effectiveness of our approach for domain generalization and domain adaptation.

Keywords: Latent domains, domain generalization, domain adaptation, exemplar-SVMs.

1   Introduction

Domain adaptation techniques, which aim to reduce the domain distribution mismatch when the training and testing samples come from different domains, have been successfully used for a broad range of vision applications such as object recognition and video event recognition [23,17,16,10,11,12,6,7,24]. As a related research problem, domain generalization differs from domain adaptation because it assumes the target domain samples are not available during the training process. Without focusing on the generalization ability on the specific target domain, domain generalization techniques aim to better classify testing data from any unseen target domain [26,22]. Please refer to Section 2 for a brief review of existing domain adaptation and domain generalization techniques.

For visual recognition, most existing domain adaptation methods treat each dataset as one domain [23,17,16,10,11,12,6,7,24]. However, the recent works show the images or videos in one dataset may come from multiple hidden domains[20,15]. In [20], Hofffman et al. proposed a constrained clustering method to discover the latent domains and also extended [23] for multi-domain adaptation by learning multiple transformation matrices. In [15], Gong et al. partitioned

D. Fleet et al. (Eds.): ECCV 2014, Part III, LNCS 8691, pp. 628–643, 2014.

the training samples from one domain into multiple domains by simultaneously maximizing distinctiveness and learnability. However, it is a non-trivial task to discover the characteristic latent domains by explicitly partitioning the training samples into multiple clusters because many factors (*e.g.*, pose and illumination) overlap and interact in images and videos in complex ways [15].

In this work, we propose a new approach for domain generalization by explicitly exploiting the intrinsic structure of positive samples from multiple latent domains without partitioning the training samples into multiple clusters/domains. Our work builds up the recent ensemble learning method exemplar-SVMs, in which we aim to train a set of exemplar classifiers with each classifier learnt by using one positive training sample and all negative training samples. While positive samples may come from multiple latent domains characterized by different factors, for the positive samples captured under similar conditions (*e.g.*, frontal-view poses), their likelihoods from each exemplar classifier are expected to be similar to each other. Using the likelihoods from all the exemplar classifiers as the feature of each positive sample, we assume the likelihood matrix consisting of the features of all positive samples should be low-rank in the ideal case. Based on this assumption, we formulate a new objective function by introducing a nuclear norm based regularizer on the likelihood matrix into the objective function of exemplar-SVMs in order to learn a set of more robust exemplar classifiers for domain generalization and domain adaptation.

To solve the new optimization problem, we further introduce an intermediate variable $\mathbf{F}$ modelling the ideal likelihood matrix, and arrive at a relaxed objective function. Specifically, we minimize the objective function of exemplar-SVMs and the nuclear norm of the ideal likelihood matrix $\mathbf{F}$ as well as the approximation error between $\mathbf{F}$ and the likelihood matrix. Then, we develop an alternating optimization algorithm to iteratively solve the ideal likelihood matrix $\mathbf{F}$ and learn the exemplar classifiers.

During the testing process, we can directly use the whole or a selected set of learnt exemplar classifiers for the domain generalization task when the target domain samples are not available during the training process. For domain adaptation, we propose an effective method to re-weight the selected set of exemplar classifiers based on the Maximum Mean Discrepancy (MMD) criterion, and we further extend the Domain Adaptation Machine (DAM) method to learn an optimal target classifier. We conduct comprehensive experiments for object recognition and human activity recognition using two datasets and the results clearly demonstrate the effectiveness of our approach for domain generalization and domain adaptation.

2   Related Work

Domain adaptation methods can be roughly categorized into feature based approaches and classifier based approaches. The feature based approaches aim to learn domain invariant features for domain adaptation. Kulis *et al.* [23] proposed a distance metric learning method to reduce domain distribution mismatch by learning asymmetric nonlinear transformation. Gopalan *et al.* [17] and Gong *et al.* [16] proposed two domain adaptation methods by interpolating intermediate domains. To reduce the distribution mismatch, some recent approaches learnt a domain invariant subspace [2] or aligned two subspaces from both domains [14].

Classifier based approaches directly learn the classifiers for domain adaptation, among which SVM based approaches are the most popular ones. Huang *et al.* [21] proposed a domain adaptation approach by re-weighting the source domain samples and then learning a weighted SVM classifier with the learnt weights. Duan *et al.* [10] proposed a new method called Adaptive MKL based on multiple kernel learning (MKL) [32], and a multi-domain adaptation method by selecting the most relevant source domains [13]. The work in [3] developed an approach to iteratively learn the SVM classifier by labeling the unlabeled target samples and simultaneously removing some labeled samples in the source domain.

There are a few works specifically designed for domain generalization. To enhance the domain generalization ability, Muandet *et al.* proposed to learn new domain invariant feature representations [26]. Given multiple source datasets/domains, Khosla *et al.* [22] proposed an SVM based approach, in which the learnt weight vectors that are common to all datasets can be used for domain generalization.

Our work is more related to the recent works for discovering latent domains [20,15]. In [20], a clustering based approach is proposed to divide the source domain into different latent domains. In [15], the MMD criterion is used to partition the source domain into distinctive latent domains. However, their methods need to decide the number of latent domains beforehand. In contrast, our method exploits the low-rank structure from latent domains without requiring the number of latent domains. Moreover, we directly learn the exemplar classifiers without partitioning the data into clusters/domains.

Our work builds up the recent work on exemplar-SVMs [25]. In contrast to [25], we introduce a nuclear norm based regularizer on the likelihood matrix in order to exploit the low-rank structure from latent domains for domain generalization. In multi-task learning, the nuclear norm based regularizer is also introduced to enforce the related tasks share similar weight vectors when learning the classifiers for multiple tasks [1,5]. However, their works assume the training and testing samples come from the same distribution without considering the domain generalization or domain adaptation tasks. Moreover, our regularizer is on the likelihood matrix such that we can better exploit the structure of positive samples from multiple latent domains.

3 Low-Rank Exemplar-SVMs

In this section, we introduce the formulation of our low rank exemplar-SVMs as well as the optimization algorithm. For ease of representation, in the remainder of this paper, we use a lowercase/uppercase letter in boldface to represent a vector/matrix. The transpose of a vector/matrix is denoted by using the superscript $'$. $\mathbf{A} = [a_{ij}] \in \mathbb{R}^{m \times n}$ defines a matrix $\mathbf{A}$ with a_{ij} being its (i, j)-th element for $i = 1, \ldots, m$ and $j = 1, \ldots, n$. The element-wise product between two matrices $\mathbf{A} = [a_{ij}] \in \mathbb{R}^{m \times n}$ and $\mathbf{B} = [b_{ij}] \in \mathbb{R}^{m \times n}$ is defined as $\mathbf{C} = \mathbf{A} \circ \mathbf{B}$, where $\mathbf{C} = [c_{ij}] \in \mathbb{R}^{m \times n}$ and $c_{ij} = a_{ij} b_{ij}$.

3.1 Formulation

In the exemplar-SVMs model, each exemplar classifier is learnt by using one positive training sample and all the negative training samples. Let $\mathcal{S} = \mathcal{S}^+ \cup \mathcal{S}^-$ denote the set of training samples, in which $\mathcal{S}^+ = \{\mathbf{s}_1^+, \ldots, \mathbf{s}_n^+\}$ is the set of positive training samples, and $\mathcal{S}^- = \{\mathbf{s}_1^-, \ldots, \mathbf{s}_m^-\}$ is the set of negative training samples. Each training sample $\mathbf{s}^+$ or $\mathbf{s}^-$ is a d-dimensional column vector, $i.e.$, $\mathbf{s}^+, \mathbf{s}^- \in \mathbb{R}^d$. In this work, we use the logistic regression function for prediction. Given any sample $\mathbf{t} \in \mathbb{R}^d$, the prediction function can be written as:

$$p(\mathbf{t}|\mathbf{w}_i) = \frac{1}{1 + \exp(-\mathbf{w}_i'\mathbf{t})}, \tag{1}$$

where $\mathbf{w}_i \in \mathbb{R}^d$ is the weight vector in the i-th exemplar classifier trained by using the positive training sample $\mathbf{s}_i^+$ and all negative training samples[1]. By defining a weight matrix $\mathbf{W} = [\mathbf{w}_1, \ldots, \mathbf{w}_n] \in \mathbb{R}^{d \times n}$, we formulate the learning problem as follows,

$$\min_{\mathbf{W}} J(\mathbf{W}) = \min_{\mathbf{W}} \|\mathbf{W}\|_F^2 + C_1 \sum_{i=1}^{n} l(\mathbf{w}_i, \mathbf{s}_i^+) + C_2 \sum_{i=1}^{n} \sum_{j=1}^{m} l(\mathbf{w}_i, \mathbf{s}_j^-), \tag{2}$$

where $\| \cdot \|_F$ is the Frobenius norm of a matrix, C_1 and C_2 are the tradeoff parameters analogous to C in SVM, and $l(\mathbf{w}, \mathbf{s})$ is the logistic loss, which is defined as:

$$l(\mathbf{w}_i, \mathbf{s}_i^+) = \log(1 + \exp(-\mathbf{w}_i'\mathbf{s}_i^+)), \tag{3}$$
$$l(\mathbf{w}_i, \mathbf{s}_j^-) = \log(1 + \exp(\mathbf{w}_i'\mathbf{s}_j^-)). \tag{4}$$

Now we consider how to discover the latent domains in the training data. Intuitively, if there are multiple latent domains in the training data, the positive training samples should also come from several latent domains. For the positive samples captured under similar conditions ($e.g.$, frontal-view poses), their likelihoods from each exemplar classifier are expected to be similar to each other. Using the likelihoods from all the exemplar classifiers as the feature of each positive sample, we assume the likelihood matrix consisting of the likelihoods of all positive samples should be low-rank in the ideal case. Formally, we denote the likelihood matrix as $\mathbf{G}(\mathbf{W}) = [g_{ij}] \in \mathbb{R}^{n \times n}$, where each $g_{ij} = p(\mathbf{s}_i^+|\mathbf{w}_j)$ is the likelihood of the i-th positive training sample by using the j-th exemplar classifier. To exploit those latent domains, we thus enforce the prediction matrix

---

[1] Although we do not explicitly use the bias term in the prediction, in our experiments we append 1 to the feature vector of each training sample.

$\mathbf{G}(\mathbf{W})$ to be low-rank when we learn those exemplar-SVMs, namely, we arrive at the following objective function,

$$\min_{\mathbf{W}} J(\mathbf{W}) + \lambda \|\mathbf{G}(\mathbf{W})\|_*, \tag{5}$$

where we use the nuclear norm based regularizer $\|\mathbf{G}(\mathbf{W})\|_*$ to approximate the rank of $\mathbf{G}(\mathbf{W})$. It has been shown that the nuclear norm is the best convex approximation of the rank function over the unit ball of matrices [27]. However, it is a nontrivial task to solve the problem in (5), because the last term is a nuclear norm based regularizer on the likelihood matrix $\mathbf{G}(\mathbf{W})$ and $\mathbf{G}(\mathbf{W})$ is a non-linear term w.r.t. $\mathbf{W}$.

To solve the optimization problem in (5), we introduce an intermediate matrix $\mathbf{F} \in \mathbb{R}^{n \times n}$ to model the ideal $\mathbf{G}(\mathbf{W})$ such that we can decompose the last term in (5) into two parts: on one hand, we expect the intermediate matrix $\mathbf{F}$ should be low-rank as we discussed above; on the other hand, we enforce the likelihood matrix $\mathbf{G}(\mathbf{W})$ to be close to the intermediate matrix $\mathbf{F}$. Therefore, we reformulate the objective function as follows,

$$\min_{\mathbf{W},\mathbf{F}} J(\mathbf{W}) + \lambda_1 \|\mathbf{F}\|_* + \lambda_2 \|\mathbf{F} - \mathbf{G}(\mathbf{W})\|_F^2, \tag{6}$$

which can be solved by alternatingly optimizing two subproblems w.r.t. $\mathbf{W}$ and $\mathbf{F}$. Specifically, the optimization problem w.r.t. $\mathbf{W}$ does not contain the nuclear norm based regularizer, which makes the optimization much easier. Also, the nuclear norm based regularizer only depends on the intermediate matrix $\mathbf{F}$ rather than a non-linear term w.r.t. $\mathbf{W}$ (i.e., the likelihood matrix $\mathbf{G}(\mathbf{W})$) as in (5), thus the optimization problem w.r.t. $\mathbf{F}$ can be readily solved by using the Singular Value Threshold (SVT) method [4] (see Section 3.2 for the details).

Discussions: To better understand our proposed approach, in Figure 1, we show an example of the learnt likelihood matrix $\mathbf{G}(\mathbf{W})$ from the "check watch" category in the IXMAS multi-view dataset by using Cam 0 and Cam 1 as the source domain. After using the nuclear norm based regularizer, we observe the block diagonal property of the likelihood matrix $\mathbf{G}(\mathbf{W})$ in Figure 1(a). In Figure 1(b), we also display some frames from the videos corresponding to the two blocks with large values in $\mathbf{G}(\mathbf{W})$. We observe that the videos sharing higher values in the matrix $\mathbf{G}(\mathbf{W})$ are also visually similar to each other. For example, the first two rows in Figure 1(b) are the videos from similar poses. More interestingly, we also observe our algorithm can group similar videos from different views in one block (e.g., the last three rows in Figure 1(b) are the videos from the same actor), which demonstrates it is beneficial to exploit the latent source domains by using our approach.

3.2   Optimization

In this section, we discuss how to optimize the problem in (6). We optimize (6) by iteratively updating $\mathbf{W}$ and $\mathbf{F}$. The two subproblems w.r.t. $\mathbf{W}$ and $\mathbf{F}$ are described in detail as follows.

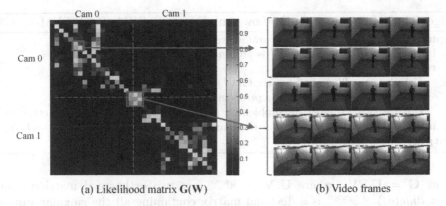

(a) Likelihood matrix $\mathbf{G}(\mathbf{W})$ (b) Video frames

Fig. 1. An illustration of the likelihood matrix $\mathbf{G}(\mathbf{W})$, where we observe the block diagonal property of $\mathbf{G}(\mathbf{W})$ in (a). The frames from the videos corresponding to the two blocks with large values in $\mathbf{G}(\mathbf{W})$ are also visually similar to each other in (b).

Update $\mathbf{W}$: When $\mathbf{F}$ is fixed, the subproblem w.r.t. $\mathbf{W}$ can be written as,

$$\min_{\mathbf{W}} J(\mathbf{W}) + \lambda_2 \|\mathbf{G}(\mathbf{W}) - \mathbf{F}\|_F^2, \tag{7}$$

where the matrix $\mathbf{F}$ is obtained at the k-th iteration, and $\mathbf{G}(\mathbf{W})$ is defined as in Section 3.1. We optimize the above subproblem by using the gradient descent technique. Let us respectively define $\mathbf{S}_1 = [\mathbf{s}_1^+, \ldots, \mathbf{s}_n^+] \in \mathbb{R}^{d \times n}$ and $\mathbf{S}_2 = [\mathbf{s}_1^-, \ldots, \mathbf{s}_m^-] \in \mathbb{R}^{d \times m}$ as the data matrices of positive and negative training samples, and also denote $H(\mathbf{W}) = \|\mathbf{G}(\mathbf{W}) - \mathbf{F}\|_F^2$. Then, the gradients of the two terms in (7) can be derived as follows,

$$\frac{\partial J(\mathbf{W})}{\partial \mathbf{W}} = 2\mathbf{W} + C_1 \mathbf{S}_1 (\mathbf{P}_1 - \mathbf{I}) + C_2 \mathbf{S}_2 \mathbf{P}_2, \tag{8}$$

$$\frac{\partial H(\mathbf{W})}{\partial \mathbf{W}} = 2\mathbf{S}_1 \left(\mathbf{G}(\mathbf{W}) \circ (\mathbf{1}\mathbf{1}' - \mathbf{G}(\mathbf{W})) \circ (\mathbf{G}(\mathbf{W}) - \mathbf{F}) \right), \tag{9}$$

where $\mathbf{P}_1 = diag\left(p(\mathbf{s}_i^+|\mathbf{w}_i)\right) \in \mathbb{R}^{n \times n}$ is a diagonal matrix with each diagonal entry being the prediction on one positive sample by using its corresponding exemplar classifier, $\mathbf{P}_2 = [p(\mathbf{s}_i^-|\mathbf{w}_j)] \in \mathbb{R}^{m \times n}$ is the prediction matrix on all negative training samples by using all exemplar classifiers, $\mathbf{I} \in \mathbb{R}^{n \times n}$ is an identity matrix, and $\mathbf{1} \in \mathbb{R}^n$ is a vector with all entries being 1.

Update $\mathbf{F}$: When $\mathbf{W}$ is fixed, we can calculate the matrix $\mathbf{G} = \mathbf{G}(\mathbf{W})$ at first, then the subproblem w.r.t. $\mathbf{F}$ becomes,

$$\min_{\mathbf{F}} \lambda_1 \|\mathbf{F}\|_* + \lambda_2 \|\mathbf{F} - \mathbf{G}\|_F^2, \tag{10}$$

which can be readily solved by using the singular value thresholding (SVT) method [4,31]. Specifically, let us denote the singular value decomposition of

---

Algorithm 1. Optimization for Low-rank Exemplar-SVMs (LRE-SVMs)

Input: Training data $\mathcal{S}$, and the parameters $C_1, C_2, \lambda_1, \lambda_2$.
1. Initialize $\mathbf{W} \leftarrow \mathbf{W}^0$, where $\mathbf{W}^0$ is obtained by solving (2).
2. **repeat**
3.   Calculate the likelihood matrix $\mathbf{G}(\mathbf{W})$ based on the current $\mathbf{W}$.
4.   Solve for $\mathbf{F}$ by optimizing the problem in (10) with the SVT method.
5.   Update $\mathbf{W}$ by solving the problem in (7) with the gradient descent method.
6. **until** The objective converges or the maximum number of iterations is reached.
Output: The weight matrix $\mathbf{W}$.

$\mathbf{G}$ as $\mathbf{G} = \mathbf{U}\boldsymbol{\Sigma}\mathbf{V}'$, where $\mathbf{U}, \mathbf{V} \in \mathbb{R}^{n \times n}$ are two orthogonal matrices, and $\boldsymbol{\Sigma} = diag(\sigma_i) \in \mathbb{R}^{n \times n}$ is a diagonal matrix containing all the singular values. The singular value thresholding operator on $\mathbf{G}$ can be represented as $\mathbf{U}\mathcal{D}(\boldsymbol{\Sigma})\mathbf{V}'$, where $\mathcal{D}(\boldsymbol{\Sigma}) = diag((\sigma_i - \frac{\lambda_1}{2\lambda_2})_+)$, and $(\cdot)_+$ is a thresholding operator by assigning the negative elements to be zeros.

Algorithm: We summarize the optimization procedure in Algorithm 1 and name our method as *Low-rank Exemplar-SVMs (LRE-SVMs)*. Specifically, we first initialize the weight matrix $\mathbf{W}$ as $\mathbf{W}^0$, where $\mathbf{W}^0$ is obtained by solving the traditional exemplar-SVMs formulation in (2). Then we calculate the prediction matrix $\mathbf{G}(\mathbf{W})$ by applying the learnt classifiers on all positive samples. Next, we obtain the matrix $\mathbf{F}$ by solving the problem in (10) with the SVT method. After that, we use the gradient descent method to update the weight matrix $\mathbf{W}$. The above steps are repeated until the objective converges.

4   Ensemble Exemplar Classifiers

After training the low-rank exemplar-SVMs as described in Section 3.1, we obtain n exemplar classifiers. To predict the test data, we discuss how to effectively use those learnt classifiers in two situations. One is the domain generalization scenario, where the target domain samples are not available during the training process. And the other one is the domain adaptation scenario, where we have unlabeled data in the target domain during the training process.

4.1   Domain Generalization

In the domain generalization scenario, we have no prior information about the target domain. A simple way is to equally fuse those n exemplar classifiers. Given any test sample $\mathbf{t}$, the prediction $p(\mathbf{t}|\mathbf{W})$ can be calculated as,

$$p(\mathbf{t}|\mathbf{W}) = \frac{1}{n} \sum_{i=1}^{n} p(\mathbf{t}|\mathbf{w}_i), \tag{11}$$

where $p(\mathbf{t}|\mathbf{w}_i)$ is the prediction from the i-th exemplar classifier.

Recall the training samples may come from several latent domains, a better way is to only use the exemplar classifiers in the latent domain which the test data likely belongs to. As mentioned before, on one hand, an exemplar classifier tends to output relatively higher prediction scores for the positive samples from the same latent domain, and relatively lower prediction scores for the positive samples from different latent domains; on the other hand, all exemplar classifiers are expected to output low prediction scores for the negative samples. Therefore, given the test sample $\mathbf{t}$ during the test process, it is beneficial to fuse only the exemplar classifiers that output higher predictions, such that we output a higher prediction score if $\mathbf{t}$ is positive, and a low prediction score if $\mathbf{t}$ is negative. Let us define $\mathcal{T}(\mathbf{t}) = \{\, i \mid p(\mathbf{t}|\mathbf{w}_i)$ is one of the top K prediction scores for $i = 1, \ldots, n\}$ as the set of the indices of those selected exemplar classifiers, then the prediction on this test sample can be obtained as,

$$p(\mathbf{t}|\mathbf{W}) = \frac{1}{K} \sum_{i:i\in\mathcal{T}(\mathbf{t})} p(\mathbf{t}|\mathbf{w}_i), \tag{12}$$

where K is the predefined number of exemplar classifiers that output high prediction scores for the test sample $\mathbf{t}$.

4.2   Domain Adaptation

When we have unlabeled data in the target domain during the training process, we can further assign different weights to the learnt exemplar classifiers to better fuse the exemplar classifiers for predicting the test data from the target domain. Intuitively, when the training data of one exemplar classifier is closer to the target domain, we should assign a higher weight to this classifier and vice versa. Let us denote the target domain samples as $\{\mathbf{t}_1, \ldots, \mathbf{t}_u\}$, where u is the number of samples in the target domain. Based on the Maximum Mean Discrepancy (MMD) criterion [18], we define the distance between the training data of one exemplar classifier and the target domain as follows,

$$d_i = \|\frac{1}{n+m} \left(n\phi(s_i^+) + \sum_{j=1}^{m} \phi(s_j^-) \right) - \frac{1}{u} \sum_{j=1}^{u} \phi(\mathbf{t}_j)\|^2, \tag{13}$$

where $\phi(\cdot)$ is a nonlinear feature mapping function induced by the Gaussian kernel. We assign a higher weight n to the positive sample s_i^+ when calculating the mean of source domain samples, since we only use one positive sample for training the exemplar classifier at each time. In other words, we duplicate the positive sample $\mathbf{s}_i^+$ for n times and then combine the duplicated positive samples with all the negative samples to calculate the distance with the target domain.

With the above distance, we then obtain the weight for each exemplar classifier by using the RBF function as $v_i = \exp(-d_i/\sigma)$, where σ is the bandwidth parameter, and is set to be the median value of all distances. Then, the prediction on a test sample $\mathbf{t}$ can be obtained as,

$$p(\mathbf{t}|\mathbf{W}) = \sum_{i:i\in\mathcal{T}(\mathbf{t})} \tilde{v}_i p(\mathbf{t}|\mathbf{w}_i), \tag{14}$$

where $\mathcal{T}(\mathbf{t})$ is defined as in Section 4.1, and $\tilde{v}_i = v_i / \sum_{i:i\in\mathcal{T}(\mathbf{t})} v_i$.

One potential drawback with the above ensemble method is that we need to perform the predictions for n times, and then fuse the top K prediction scores. Inspired by Domain Adaptation Machine [13], we propose to learn a single target classifier on the target domain by leveraging the predictions from the exemplar classifiers. Specifically, let us denote the target classifier as $f(\mathbf{t}) = \tilde{\mathbf{w}}'\phi(\mathbf{t}) + b$. We formulate our learning problem as follows,

$$\min_{\tilde{\mathbf{w}}, b, \xi_i, \xi_i^*, \mathbf{f}} \frac{1}{2}\|\tilde{\mathbf{w}}\|^2 + C\sum_{i=1}^{u}(\xi_i + \xi_i^*) + \frac{\lambda}{2}\Omega(\mathbf{f}), \tag{15}$$

$$\text{s.t.} \quad \tilde{\mathbf{w}}'\phi(\mathbf{t}_i) + b - f_i \le \epsilon + \xi_i, \quad \xi_i \ge 0, \tag{16}$$

$$f_i - \tilde{\mathbf{w}}'\phi(\mathbf{t}_i) - b \le \epsilon + \xi_i^*, \quad \xi_i^* \ge 0, \tag{17}$$

where $\mathbf{f} = [f_1, \ldots, f_u]'$ is an intermediate variable, λ and C are the tradeoff parameters, ξ_i and ξ_i^* are the slack variables in the ϵ-insensitive loss similarly as in SVR, and ϵ is a predefined small positive value in the ϵ-insensitive loss. The regularizer $\Omega(\mathbf{f})$ is a smoothness function defined as follows,

$$\Omega(\mathbf{f}) = \sum_{j=1}^{u} \sum_{i:i\in\mathcal{T}(\mathbf{t}_j)} \tilde{v}_i \left(f_j - p(\mathbf{t}_j|\mathbf{w}_i)\right)^2, \tag{18}$$

where we enforce each intermediate variable f_j to be similar to the prediction scores of the selected exemplar classifiers in $\mathcal{T}(\mathbf{t}_j)$ for the target sample $\mathbf{t}_j$. In the above problem, we use the ϵ-insensitive loss to enforce the prediction score from target classifier $f(\mathbf{t}_j) = \tilde{\mathbf{w}}'\phi(\mathbf{t}_j) + b$ to be close to the intermediate variable f_j. At the same time, we also use a smoothness regularizer to enforce the intermediate variable f_j to be close to the prediction scores of the selected exemplar classifiers in $\mathcal{T}(\mathbf{t}_j)$ for the target sample $\mathbf{t}_j$. Intuitively, when $\tilde{v}_i$ is large, we enforce the intermediate variable f_j to be closer to $p(\mathbf{t}_j|\mathbf{w}_i)$, and vice versa. Recall the weight $\tilde{v}_i$ models the importance of the i-th exemplar classifier for predicting the target sample, we expect the learnt classifier $f(\mathbf{t})$ performs well for predicting the target domain samples.

By introducing the dual variables $\boldsymbol{\alpha} = [\alpha_1, \ldots, \alpha_u]'$ and $\boldsymbol{\alpha}^* = [\alpha_1^*, \ldots, \alpha_u^*]'$ for the constraints in (16) and (17), we arrive at its dual form as follows,

$$\min_{\boldsymbol{\alpha}, \boldsymbol{\alpha}^*} \frac{1}{2}(\boldsymbol{\alpha} - \boldsymbol{\alpha}^*)\tilde{\mathbf{K}}(\boldsymbol{\alpha} - \boldsymbol{\alpha}^*) + \mathbf{p}'(\boldsymbol{\alpha} - \boldsymbol{\alpha}^*) + \epsilon \mathbf{1}_u'(\boldsymbol{\alpha} + \boldsymbol{\alpha}^*), \tag{19}$$

$$\text{s.t.} \quad \mathbf{1}'\boldsymbol{\alpha} = \mathbf{1}'\boldsymbol{\alpha}^*, 0 \le \boldsymbol{\alpha}, \boldsymbol{\alpha}^* \le C\mathbf{1}, \tag{20}$$

where $\tilde{\mathbf{K}} = \mathbf{K} + \frac{1}{\lambda}\mathbf{I} \in \mathbb{R}^{u\times u}$ with $\mathbf{K}$ being the kernel matrix of the target domain samples, $\mathbf{p} = [p(\mathbf{t}_1|\mathbf{W}), \ldots, p(\mathbf{t}_u|\mathbf{W})]'$ with each entry $p(\mathbf{t}_j|\mathbf{W})$ defined in (14) being the "virtual label" for the target sample $\mathbf{t}_j$ as in DAM [13]. In DAM [13], the virtual labels of all the target samples are obtained by fusing the same set of source classifiers. In contrast, we use the predictions from different selected exemplar classifiers to obtain the virtual labels of different target samples. Therefore, DAM can be treated as a special case of our work by using the same classifiers for all test samples in (15).

5   Experiments

In this section, we evaluate our low-rank exemplar-SVMs (LRE-SVMs) approach for domain generalization and domain adaptation, respectively.

5.1   Experimental Setup

Following the work in [15], we use the Office-Caltech dataset [28,16] for visual object recognition and the IXMAS dataset [30] for multi-view action recognition.

Office-Caltech [28,16] dataset contains the images from four domains denoted by A, C, D, and W, in which the images are from Amazon, Caltech-256, and two more datasets captured with digital SLR camera and webcam, respectively. The ten common categories among the 4 domains are utilized in our evaluation. We extract the DeCAF$_6$ feature [9] for the images in the Office-Caltech dataset, which has achieved promising results in visual recognition.

IXMAS dataset [30] contains the videos from eleven actions captured by five cameras (Cam 0, Cam 1, ..., Cam 4) from different viewpoints. Each of the eleven actions is performed three times by twelve actors. To exclude the irregularly performed actions, we keep the first five actions (check watch, cross arms, scratch head, sit down, get up) performed by six actors (*Alba, Andreas, Daniel, Hedlena, Julien, Nicolas*), as suggested in [15]. We extract the dense trajectories features [29] from the videos, and use K-means clustering to build a codebook with $1,000$ clusters for each of the five descriptors (*i.e.*, trajectory, HOG, HOF, MBHx, MBHy). The bag-of-words features are then concatenated to a $5,000$ dimensional feature for each video sequence.

Following [15], we treat the images from different sources in the Office-Caltech dataset as different domains, and treat the videos from different viewpoints in the IXMAS dataset as different domains, respectively. In our experiments, we mix several domains as the source domain for training the classifiers and use the remaining domains as the target domain for testing. For the domain generalization task, the samples from the target domain are not available during the training process. For the domain adaptation task, the unlabeled samples from the target domain can be used to reduce the domain distribution mismatch in the training process.

We compare our low-rank exemplar-SVMs with several state-of-the-art unsupervised domain adaptation methods, as well as the methods specifically proposed for discovering the latent domains. Note that our approach does not require domain labels for both domain generalization and domain adaptation tasks.

5.2   Domain Generalization

We first evaluate our low-rank exemplar-SVMs (LRE-SVMs) for domain generalization. We compare our proposed method with the domain generalization method by undoing dataset bias (Undo-Bias) in [22], and the latent domain discovering methods [20,15]. We additionally report the results from the discriminative sub-categorization(Sub-C) method [19], as it can also be applied to

Table 1. Recognition accuracies (%) of different methods for domain generalization. Our LRE-SVMs approach does not require domain labels or target domain data during the training process. The best results are denoted in boldface.

Source	A,C	D,W	C,D,W	Cam 0,1	Cam 2,3,4	Cam 0,1,2,3
Target	D,W	A,C	A	Cam 2,3,4	Cam 0,1	Cam 4
SVM	82.68	76.06	90.73	71.70	63.83	56.61
Sub-C [19]	82.61	78.65	90.75	78.11	76.90	64.04
Undo-Bias [22]	80.49	69.98	90.98	69.03	60.56	56.84
[20](Ensemble)	79.23	68.06	80.75	71.55	51.02	49.70
[20](Match)	71.26	61.42	72.03	63.81	60.04	48.91
[15](Ensemble)	84.01	77.11	91.65	75.04	68.98	57.64
[15](Match)	80.63	76.52	90.84	71.59	60.73	55.37
E-SVMs	82.73	80.85	91.47	76.86	68.04	72.98
LRE-SVMs	**84.59**	**81.17**	**91.87**	**79.96**	**80.15**	**74.97**

our application. As the Undo-Bias method [22] requires the domain label information, we provide the groundtruth domain labels to train the classifier for this method. For all other methods, we mix multiple domains as the source domain for training the classifiers.

For the latent domain discovering methods [20,15], after partitioning the source domain data into different domains using their methods, we train an SVM classifier on each domain, and then fuse those classifiers for predicting the test samples. We employ two strategies to fuse the learnt classifiers as suggested in [15], which are referred to as the *ensemble* strategy and the *match* strategy, respectively. The ensemble strategy is to re-weight the decision values from different SVM classifiers by using the domain probabilities learnt with the method in [20]. In the match strategy, we first select the most relevant domain based on the MMD criterion, and then use the SVM classifier from this domain to predict the test samples.

Moreover, we also report the results from the baseline SVM method, which is trained by using all training samples in the source domain. The results from exemplar-SVMs (E-SVMs) are also reported, which is a special case of our proposed LRE-SVMs, and we also use the method in (12) to fuse the selected top K exemplar classifiers for the prediction. For our method, we empirically fix $K = 5$, and $C_1 = 10C_2$ for all our experiments. We set the parameters $C_2 = 0.01$, $\lambda_1 = 100$, and $\lambda_2 = 1000$ on the Office-Caltech dataset, and $C_2 = 1$ and $\lambda_1 = \lambda_2 = 10$ on the IXMAS datast. For baseline methods, we choose the optimal parameters according to their recognition accuracies on the test dataset.

The experimental results on two datasets are summarized in Table 1. We observe that the Sub-C method is comparable or better than the SVM method. The results of Undo-Bias are worse than SVM in most cases even after providing the ground-truth domain labels. One possible explanation is that there are many factors (*e.g.*, pose and illumination) interacting in images and videos in complex ways [15], so even the ground truth domain labels may not be the optimal ones for learning classifiers for domain generalization, which is also one of our motivations for this work.

For the two latent domain discovering method [20,15], the recently published method by Gong *et al.* [15] achieves quite competitive results when using the ensemble strategy (*i.e.*, [15](Ensemble) in Table 1). It achieves better results on all six cases when compared with SVM, which demonstrates it is beneficial to discover latent domains in the source domain. However, the method in [20] is not as effective as [15]. We also observe the match strategy generally achieves worse results than the ensemble strategy for those latent domain discovering methods, although the target domain information is used to select the most relevant discovered source domain in the testing process.

Our proposed LRE-SVMs method achieves the best results in all six cases on two datasets, which clearly demonstrates the effectiveness of our method by exploiting the low-rank structure in the source domain for domain generalization. We also observe that our special case (*i.e.*, the exemplar-SVMs (E-SVMs) method) also achieves better results than SVM. Note we also apply the prediction method using (12) for E-SVMs. By selecting the most relevant classifiers, we combine a subset of exemplar classifiers for predicting each test sample, leading to good results. By further exploiting the low-rank structure in the source domain, we implicitly employ the information from latent domains in our LRE-SVMs. In this way, the selected top K exemplar classifiers are more likely from the same latent domain that the test sample belongs to. Thus, our LRE-SVMs method outperforms its special case E-SVMs in all six cases for domain generalization.

5.3   Domain Adaptation

In this section, we further compare our proposed method with the baselines for the domain adaptation task, in which the unlabeled samples from the target domain are available in the training process. For domain adaptation, we adopt the approach proposed in Section 4.2 to fuse the exemplar classifiers learnt by using our LRE-SVMs method, and we refer to our approach for domain adaptation as *LRE-SVMs-DA*. We take the IXMAS multiview action recognition dataset as an example to report the results.

We first investigate the state-of-the-art unsupervised domain adaptation methods, including Kernel Mean Matching (KMM) [21], Sampling Geodesic Flow (SGF) [17], Geodesic Flow Kernel (GFK) [16], Selective Transfer Machine(STM) [8], Domain Invariant Projection (DIP) [2], and Subspace Alignment (SA) [14]. For all those methods, we combine the videos captured from multiple cameras to form one combined source domain, and use the remaining samples as the target domain. Then we apply all the methods for domain adaptation. For the feature-based approaches (*i.e.*, SGF, GFK, DIP and SA), we train an SVM classifier after obtaining the domain invariant features/kernels with those methods. We also select the best parameters for those baseline methods according to the test results.

Table 2. Recognition accuracies (%) of different methods for domain adaptation. The best results are denoted in boldface.

	Source	Cam 0,1	Cam 2,3,4	Cam 0,1,2,3
	Target	Cam 2,3,4	Cam 0,1	Cam 4
	SVM	71.70	63.83	56.61
	KMM	73.92	42.22	52.57
	SGF	60.37	69.04	28.66
	GFK	64.87	55.53	42.16
	STM	68.69	70.53	51.05
	DIP	65.20	70.03	62.92
	SA	73.35	77.92	49.59
GFK (latent)	[20] (Match)	61.33	58.77	46.62
	[20] (Ensemble)	65.32	55.01	42.09
	[15] (Match)	65.32	64.43	47.22
	[15] (Ensemble)	69.12	68.87	51.30
SA (latent)	[20] (Match)	58.49	56.27	55.87
	[20] (Ensemble)	63.01	62.05	62.69
	[15] (Match)	66.27	67.00	63.01
	[15] (Ensemble)	71.04	76.64	72.26
DAM (latent)	[20]	77.92	76.99	53.76
	[15]	77.32	73.94	62.47
LRE-SVMs-DA		**81.79**	**82.43**	**75.26**

The results of those baseline methods are reported in Table 2. We also include the baseline SVM method trained by using all the source domain samples for the comparison. The cross-view action recognition is a challenging task. As a result, most unsupervised domain adaptation methods cannot achieve promising results on this dataset, and they are worse than SVM in many cases. The recently proposed method SA [14] and DIP [2] achieves relatively better results, which are better than SVM on two out of three cases.

We further investigate the latent domain discovering methods [20,15]. We use their methods to divide the source domain into several latent domains. Then, we follow [15] to perform the GFK [16] method between each discovered latent domain and the target domain to learn a new kernel for reducing the domain distribution mismatch, and train SVM classifiers using the learnt kernels. Then we also use the two strategies (i.e., ensemble and match) to fuse the SVM classifiers learnt from different latent domains. Moreover, as the SA method achieves better results than GFK on the combined source domain, we further use the SA method to replace the GFK method for reducing the domain distribution mismatch between each latent domain and the target domain. The other steps are as the same as those when using the GFK method. We report the results using latent domain discovering methods [20,15] combined with GFK and SA in Table 2, which are denoted as *GFK(latent)* and *SA(latent)*, respectively. As our method is also related to the DAM method [13], we also report the results of the

DAM method by treating the discovered latent domains with [20,15] as multiple source domains, which is referred to as *DAM(latent)*.

From Table 2, we observe GFK(latent) using the latent domains discovered by [15] is generally better when compared with GFK(latent) using the latent domains discovered by [20]. By using the latent domains discovered by [15], the results of GFK(latent) using both match and ensemble strategies are better than those of GFK on the combined source domain. However, most results from GFK(latent) are still worse than SVM, possibly because the GFK method cannot effectively handle the domain distribution mismatch between each discovered latent domain and the target domain. When using the SA method to replace GFK, we observe the results from SA(latent) in all three cases are improved when compared with their corresponding results from GFK(latent) by using the latent domains discovered by [15]. Moreover, we also observe DAM(latent) outperforms SVM in all cases or most cases when using the latent source domains discovered by [15] or [20].

Our method achieves the best results in all three cases, which again demonstrates the effectiveness of our proposed LRE-SVMs-DA for exploiting the low-rank structure in the source domain. Moreover, our method LRE-SVMs-DA outperforms LRE-SVMs on three cases (see Table 1). Note LRE-SVMs does not use the target domain unlabeled samples during the training process. The results further demonstrate the effectiveness of our domain adaptation approach LRE-SVMs-DA for coping with the domain distribution mismatch in the domain adaptation task.

6   Conclusions

In this paper, we have proposed a new method called Low-rank Exemplar-SVMs (LRE-SVMs) for domain generalization by exploiting the low-rank structure of positive training samples from multiple latent source domains. Based on the recent work on exemplar-SVMs, we propose to exploit the low-rank structure in the source domain by introducing a nuclear-norm based regularizer on the likelihood matrix consisting of the likelihoods of all positive samples from all exemplar classifiers. To further handle the domain distribution mismatch between the training and test data, we further develop an effective method to re-weight the selected set of exemplar classifiers based on the Maximum Mean Discrepancy (MMD) criterion, and extend the Domain Adaptation Machine (DAM) method to learn a better target classifier. The comprehensive experiments have demonstrated the effectiveness of our approach for domain generalization and domain adaptation.

Acknowledgement. This work is supported by the Singapore MoE Tier 2 Grant (ARC42/13).

References

1. Argyriou, A., Evgeniou, T., Pontil, M.: Multi-task feature learning. NIPS (2007)
2. Baktashmotlagh, M., Harandi, M., Brian Lovell, M.S.: Unsupervised domain adaptation by domain invariant projection. In: ICCV (2013)

3. Bruzzone, L., Marconcini, M.: Domain adaptation problems: A DASVM classification technique and a circular validation strategy. T-PAMI 32(5), 770–787 (2010)
4. Cai, J., Cands, E.J., Shen, Z.: A singular value thresholding algorithm for matrix completion. SIAM Journal on Optimization 20(4), 1956–1982 (2010)
5. Chen, J., Zhou, J., Ye, J.: Integrating low-rank and group-sparse structures for robust multi-task learning. In: SIGKDD (2011)
6. Chen, L., Duan, L., Xu, D.: Event recognition in videos by learning from heterogeneous web sources. In: CVPR, pp. 2666–2673 (2013)
7. Chen, L., Li, W., Xu, D.: Recognizing RGB images by learning from RGB-D data. In: CVPR, pp. 1418–1425 (2014)
8. Chu, W.S., la Torre, F.D., Cohn, J.F.: Selective transfer machine for personalized facial action unit detection. In: CVPR (2013)
9. Donahue, J., Jia, Y., Vinyals, O., Hoffman, J., Zhang, N., Tzeng, E., Darrell, T.: DeCAF: A deep convolutional activation feature for generic visual recognition. In: ICML (2014)
10. Duan, L., Xu, D., Tsang, I.W., Luo, J.: Visual event recognition in videos by learning from web data. T-PAMI 34(9), 1667–1680 (2012)
11. Duan, L., Tsang, I.W., Xu, D.: Domain transfer multiple kernel learning. T-PAMI 34(3), 465–479 (2012)
12. Duan, L., Xu, D., Chang, S.F.: Exploiting web images for event recognition in consumer videos: A multiple source domain adaptation approach. In: CVPR, pp. 1338–1345 (2012)
13. Duan, L., Xu, D., Tsang, I.W.: Domain adaptation from multiple sources: A domain-dependent regularization approach. T-NNLS 23(3), 504–518 (2012)
14. Fernando, B., Habrard, A., Sebban, M., Tuytelaars, T.: Unsupervised visual domain adaptation using subspace alignment. In: ICCV (2013)
15. Gong, B., Grauman, K., Sha, F.: Reshaping visual datasets for domain adaptation. In: NIPS (2013)
16. Gong, B., Shi, Y., Sha, F., Grauman, K.: Geodesic flow kernel for unsupervised domain adaptation. In: CVPR (2012)
17. Gopalan, R., Li, R., Chellappa, R.: Domain adaptation for object recognition: An unsupervised approach. In: ICCV (2011)
18. Gretton, A., Gorgwardt, K.M., Rasch, M.J., Schölkopf, B., Smola, A.: A kernel two-sample test. JMLR 23, 723–773 (2012)
19. Hoai, M., Zisserman, A.: Discriminative sub-categorization. In: CVPR (2013)
20. Hoffman, J., Kulis, B., Darrell, T., Saenko, K.: Discovering latent domains for multisource domain adaptation. In: Fitzgibbon, A., Lazebnik, S., Perona, P., Sato, Y., Schmid, C. (eds.) ECCV 2012, Part II. LNCS, vol. 7573, pp. 702–715. Springer, Heidelberg (2012)
21. Huang, J., Smola, A., Gretton, A., Borgwardt, K., Scholkopf, B.: Correcting sample selection bias by unlabeled data. In: NIPS (2007)
22. Khosla, A., Zhou, T., Malisiewicz, T., Efros, A.A., Torralba, A.: Undoing the damage of dataset bias. In: Fitzgibbon, A., Lazebnik, S., Perona, P., Sato, Y., Schmid, C. (eds.) ECCV 2012, Part I. LNCS, vol. 7572, pp. 158–171. Springer, Heidelberg (2012)
23. Kulis, B., Saenko, K., Darrell, T.: What you saw is not what you get: Domain adaptation using asymmetric kernel transforms. In: CVPR (2011)
24. Li, W., Duan, L., Xu, D., Tsang, I.W.: Learning with augmented features for supervised and semi-supervised heterogeneous domain adaptation. T-PAMI 36(6), 1134–1148 (2014)

25. Malisiewicz, T., Gupta, A., Efros, A.A.: Ensemble of exemplar-SVMs for object detection and beyond. In: ICCV (2011)
26. Muandet, K., Balduzzi, D., Schölkopf, B.: Domain generalization via invariant feature representation. In: ICML (2013)
27. Recht, B., Fazel, M., Parrilo, P.A.: Guaranteed minimum rank solutions to linear matrix equations via nuclear norm minimization. SIAM Review 52(3), 471–501 (2010)
28. Saenko, K., Kulis, B., Fritz, M., Darrell, T.: Adapting visual category models to new domains. In: Daniilidis, K., Maragos, P., Paragios, N. (eds.) ECCV 2010, Part IV. LNCS, vol. 6314, pp. 213–226. Springer, Heidelberg (2010)
29. Wang, H., Kläser, A., Schmid, C., Liu, C.L.: Dense trajectories and motion boundary descriptors for action recognition. International Journal of Computer Vision 103(1), 60–79 (2013)
30. Weinland, D., Boyer, E., Ronfard, R.: Action recognition from arbitrary views using 3d exemplars. In: ICCV (2007)
31. Xiao, S., Tan, M., Xu, D.: Weighted block-sparse low rank representation for face clustering in videos. In: ECCV (2014)
32. Xu, X., Tsang, I.W., Xu, D.: Soft margin multiple kernel learning. T-NN 24(5), 749–761 (2013)

Sparse Additive Subspace Clustering

Xiao-Tong Yuan[1,2] and Ping Li[2]

[1] S-mart Lab, Nanjing University of Information Science and Technology
Nanjing, 210044, China
[2] Department of Statistics and Biostatistics, Department of Computer Science
Rutgers University, Piscataway, New Jersey, 08854, USA
xtyuan@nuist.edu.cn, pingli@stat.rutgers.edu

Abstract. In this paper, we introduce and investigate a sparse additive model for subspace clustering problems. Our approach, named **SASC** (**S**parse **A**dditive **S**ubspace **C**lustering), is essentially a functional extension of the Sparse Subspace Clustering (SSC) of Elhamifar & Vidal [7] to the additive nonparametric setting. To make our model computationally tractable, we express SASC in terms of a finite set of basis functions, and thus the formulated model can be estimated via solving a sequence of grouped Lasso optimization problems. We provide theoretical guarantees on the subspace recovery performance of our model. Empirical results on synthetic and real data demonstrate the effectiveness of SASC for clustering noisy data points into their original subspaces.

1 Introduction

This paper deals with the problem of subspace clustering which assumes that a collection of data points lie near a union of unknown linear subspaces and aims to fit these data points to their original subspaces. This is an unsupervised learning problem in that we do not know in advance to which subspace these data points belong. It is thus of interest to simultaneously cluster the data points into multiple subspaces and uncover the low-dimensional structure of each subspace. Subspace clustering has been widely applied in numerous scientific and engineering domains, including computer vision [30,35], data mining [20,1], networks analysis [8,10], switched system identification in control [2,16] and computational biology [17,11]. In many such applications, the lower dimensional representations are characterized by multiple low-dimensional manifolds which can be well approximated by subspaces with only slightly higher dimensions than those of the underlying manifolds. For example, in a video sequence, geometric argument shows that trajectories of same rigid-body motion lie on a subspace of dimension 4 [25]. The partitions of observed trajectories correspond to different rigid objects and thus are useful for understanding the scene dynamics. The task of finding these partitions serves as a standard application of subspace clustering which is known as multi-body motion segmentation [30] in computer vision.

1.1 Problem Setup and Motivation

Assume that the underlying K subspaces $\{S_k\}_{k=1}^K$ of $\mathbb{R}^p$ have unknown dimensions $\{d_k\}_{k=1}^K$ respectively. Let $\mathcal{Y} \subset \mathbb{R}^p$ be a given data set of cardinality n which

D. Fleet et al. (Eds.): ECCV 2014, Part III, LNCS 8691, pp. 644–659, 2014.

may be partitioned as $\mathcal{Y} = \bigcup_{k=1}^{K} \mathcal{Y}_k$ with each $\mathcal{Y}_k$ being a collection of n_k vectors that are distributed around subspace S_k. The task of subspace clustering is to approximately segment the point points in $\mathcal{Y}$ into their respective underlying subspaces. Due to the presence of noise, it is usually assumed in real applications that each observation $\boldsymbol{y} = [y^{(1)}, ..., y^{(p)}]^{\top} \in \mathcal{Y}$ is generated from the following superposition stochastic model [24]:

$$\boldsymbol{y} = \boldsymbol{x} + \boldsymbol{e},$$

where $\boldsymbol{x}$ is a sample belonging to one of the subspaces and $\boldsymbol{e}$ is a random perturbation term with a bounded Euclidean norm. For noiseless samples, it is intuitive to assume that these points are distributed uniformly at random on each subspace. The state-of-the-art robust subspace clustering algorithms take advantage of the so-called self-expressiveness property of linear subspaces, i.e., each noiseless data point from one of the subspaces can be reconstructed by a combination of the other noiseless data points from the same subspace. Formally, the self-expressiveness model is defined as:

Definition 1 (Self-Expressiveness (SE) property [7]). *For each data point* $\boldsymbol{x}_i$, *there exist coefficients* $\{\theta_{ij}\}$ *such that* $\boldsymbol{x}_i = \sum_{j \neq i} \theta_{ij} \boldsymbol{x}_j$.

Note that the coefficients $\{\theta_{ij}\}$ are sparse as we assume that the subspace S_k has d_k-dimensionality. Ideally, it is expected that the non-zero coefficients are from those points belonging to the same subspace as $\boldsymbol{x}_i$, and thus the joint parameter matrix $\boldsymbol{\Theta} = (\theta_{ij}) \in \mathbb{R}^{n \times n}$ has block diagonal structure with blocks corresponding to clusters. Since $\boldsymbol{y}_i = \boldsymbol{x}_i + \boldsymbol{e}_i$, the SE property of clean data leads to the following noisy linear representation model for the noisy observations:

$$\boldsymbol{y}_i = \sum_{j \neq i} \theta_{ij} \boldsymbol{y}_j + \boldsymbol{z}_i, \tag{1}$$

where the perturbation term $\boldsymbol{z}_i = \boldsymbol{e}_i - \sum_{j \neq i} \theta_{ij} \boldsymbol{e}_j$. Inspired by this intuitive property, Elhamifar & Vidal [7] introduced the **SSC** (Sparse Subspace Clustering) approach using sparse reconstruction coefficients as similarity measures; the sparse coefficients are obtained by reconstructing each sample $\boldsymbol{y}_i$ using all the rest samples $\{\boldsymbol{y}_j\}_{j \neq i}$, while regularizing the coefficient vector by ℓ_1-norm to promote sparsity. Hence SSC amounts to solving a sequence of ℓ_1-minimization problems (for noiseless data) or Lasso problems (for noisy data) which are computationally tractable and statistically efficient in high dimensional setting [24][23]. The task of clustering is then finalized by applying a spectral clustering method [18] to a symmetric affinity matrix constructed from these representation coefficients.

While SSC has strong theoretical guarantees and impressive practical performances, it essentially fits the data with a high dimensional linear regression model in (1). Unfortunately, due to the presence of distortion beyond random additive perturbation, real-world observations often do not conform exactly to such a linear model assumption.

1.2 Our Contribution

In this paper, we relax the strong linear model assumption made by SSC and investigate a novel class of nonparametric subspace clustering models called SASC (Sparse Additive Subspace Clustering). We assume that for each observed data point y_i, there exists a potentially nonlinear transformation f_i such that the transformed data point $\{f_i(y_i)\}$ obeys the noisy SE model in (1). This problem setup is more challenging than SSC in the sense that the transformations $\{f_i\}$, subspaces $\{S_k\}$ and random noises are all unknown. Indeed, SSC is a special case of SASC when $f_i(a) = a$. Our method combines the ideas from SSC and SpAM which is a sparse additive model for nonparametric regression tasks [22]. To make our model computationally tractable, we follow SpAM to project the unknown f_i onto a functional subspace with a known basis (e.g., the truncated Fourier basis). While the two methods share some common principles, there are two fundamental differences between SASC and SpAM: i) obviously the problem setups are different; ii) as the regressors are dependent on noisy data, we need to deal with noisy design matrix which was not addressed by SpAM.

We provide some theoretical guarantees on the subspace recovery capability of our model. Since there are no "true" parameters to compare the solution against, a subspace clustering algorithm succeeds if each data point is represented by those data points belonging to the same subspace. Therefore, it is desirable that the output representation coefficients matrix has block diagonal structure (under proper arrangement of data). We conduct a deterministic sparsity recovery analysis for our model followed by a stochastic extension. Our results show that under mild conditions, the underlying diagonal block structure of the representation matrix can be efficiently recovered with high probability. We test the numerical performance of our model on simulated and real data. The experimental results show that in many cases our model significantly outperforms the state-of-the-art methods in in terms of clustering accuracy.

1.3 Notation and Outline

Notation. We denote scalars by lower case letters (e.g., x and a), and vectors/matrices by bold face letters (e.g. x and A). The Euclidean norm of a vector x is denoted by $\|x\|$. Given a disjoint group structure G over a vector x, we use the notation x_g as the tuple formed by the components of x belonging to group $g \in G$. We define $\|x\|_{G,2} = \sum_{g \in G} \|x_g\|$ and $\|x\|_{G,\infty} = \max_{g \in G} \|x_g\|$. With this notation, we extend the signum function as $\mathrm{sgn}(x_g) = x_g/\|x_g\|$ in which we adopt the convention that $\mathrm{sgn}(0)$ can be taken to be any vector with norm less than or equal to one. Also, given a disjoint group structure G over the rows of a matrix A, we denote $\|A\|_{G,\infty} = \max_i \|A_{i,\cdot}\|_{G,2}$ where $A_{i,\cdot}$ is the i-th row of A. For $T \subseteq G$, we define $T^c = G \setminus T$. The element-wise infinity norm of a matrix A is denoted by $\|A\|_{\infty,\infty}$ and the row-wise infinity norm by $\|A\|_\infty$.

Outline. The remainder of this paper is organized as follows: Some prior works are briefly reviewed in §2. We introduce in §3 the sparse additive subspace clustering model along with statistical analysis. Monte-Carlo simulations and real data experiments are presented in §4. Finally, we conclude this paper in §5.

2 Prior Work

In the last decade, various algorithms have been proposed for subspace clustering. A vast body of these algorithms are contributed by researchers in computer vision to address problems such as multi-body motion segmentation, face clustering and image compression. Among them, several representative algorithms include factorization based methods [6], algebraic methods such as Generalized Principal Component Analysis (GPCA) [29] and Local Subspace Affinity (LSA) [34], sparsity/low-rank induced methods such as Sparse Subspace Clustering (SSC) [7] and Low Rank Representation (LRR) [12,19], to name a few. Some other well-known methods include K-plane [3] and Spectral Curvature Clustering (SCC) [4]. For a comprehensive review and comparison of subspace clustering algorithms, we refer the interested readers to the tutorial [28] and references there in.

In the current investigation, we are particularly interested in a popular class of subspace clustering methods which are built upon the SE property as defined in Definition 1. Inspired by this intuitive property, Elhamifar & Vidal [7] introduced the SSC approach using sparse reconstruction coefficients as similarity measures. An identical framework was independently considered by Cheng et al. [5] to construct ℓ_1-graph for subspace learning and semi-supervised image analysis. In order to further capture the global structures of data, Liu et al. [12] proposed LRR to compute the reconstruction collaboratively by penalizing the nuclear norm of the joint representation matrix. They also provided a robust version to resist random perturbation and element-wise sparse outliers. More recently, Lu et al. [15] proposed a unified convex optimization framework for SE based subspace clustering of which SSC and LRR can be taken as special cases. Most existing SE based subspace clustering methods are restricted to linear or affine models. There is a recent trend to extend SE models to nonlinear manifolds. For example, Patel et al. [21] proposed Non-Linear Latent Space SSC (NLS3C) as a nonlinear extension of SSC via kernel embedding. Our work advances in this line of research.

Theoretical justification of SSC has received significant interests from computer vision researchers as well as statisticians. It is shown in [7] that when subspaces are disjoint, i.e. they are not overlapping, the block structure of affinity matrix can be exactly recovered. Similar block structure guarantees were established for LRR and LSR (Least Square Regression) [15]. When data is noise free, Soltanolkotabi & Candès[23] provided a geometric functional analysis for SSC which broadens the scope of the results significantly to the case where subspaces are allowed to be overlapping. Under the circumstances of corrupted data, Wang & Xu[32] and Soltanolkotabi et al. [24] independently showed that high statistical efficiency could still be achieved by SSC when the underlying subspaces are well separated and the noise level does not exceed certain geometric gap.

As nonparametric extensions of linear models, additive models [9] assume that the nonlinear multivariate regression function admits an additive combination of univariate functions, one for each covariate. In high dimensional analysis, progress has been made on additive models by imposing various sparsity-inducing

functional penalties [22,36]. More recently, the idea of component-wise nonparametric extensions has been investigated in Gaussian graphical models learning
[14,13,33]. Our approach shares some spirits with these methods in the sense that
we model for each data point a nonlinear transformation.

3   Sparse Additive Subspace Clustering (SASC)

In this section, we propose the SASC (Sparse Additive Subspace Clustering)
method. We first introduce in §3.1 an additive self-expressive model as a non-
parametric extension of the SE model (1). Then we investigate the related parameter estimation and clustering issues in §3.2. Finally, we provide some sparse
recovery guarantees on SASC in §3.3.

3.1   Additive Self-Expressive Model

Our method follows the same problem setup as discussed in §1.1. We further assume that there exist n univariate functions $\{f_i(\cdot)\}_{i=1}^n$ such that the transformed
data points $\{f_i(\boldsymbol{y}_i)\}_{i=1}^n$ obey the following superposition model:

$$f_i(\boldsymbol{y}_i) = \boldsymbol{x}_i + \boldsymbol{e}_i,$$

where $f_i(\boldsymbol{y}_i) = [f_i(y_i^{(1)}), ..., f_i(y_i^{(p)})]^\top$ and $\boldsymbol{e}_i$'s are random noises. From the SE
property of the clean data points$\{\boldsymbol{x}_i\}$,

$$f_i(\boldsymbol{y}_i) = \sum_{j \neq i} \theta_{ij} f_j(\boldsymbol{y}_j) + \boldsymbol{z}_i. \tag{2}$$

Clearly, this is a nonparametric extension of the noisy linear model (1). It depends on $\{f_i\}$ as well as the coefficient matrix $\boldsymbol{\Theta}$, all of which are unknown in
advance and need to be estimated from data. In this paper, we assume $f_i \not\equiv 0$
to avoid degeneration.

Remark 1. One may compare the additive self-expressive model in (2) with the
SpAM model for sparse nonparametric regression [22]. Given a random response
y and a fixed regressor $\boldsymbol{x} = (x_j)$, SpAM considers the additive regression model
$y = \sum_j f_j(x_j) + \varepsilon$ in which f_j's are unknown. Although the basic ideas are
similar, the model in (2) is more general than SpAM as its response $f_i(\boldsymbol{y}_i)$ is
also nonparametric. Moreover, the regressors $\{f_j(\boldsymbol{y}_j)\}_{j \neq i}$ in (2) are random.
Such differences contrast our method to SpAM.

Remark 2. It is noteworthy that Patel *et al.* [21] recently proposed NLS3C as a
kernel extension of SSC to nonlinear manifolds. Without imposing latent space
assumption, NLS3C essentially considers the following linear model in a extended
feature space $\mathcal{F}$:

$$\phi(\boldsymbol{y}_i) = \sum_{j \neq i} \theta_{ij} \phi(\boldsymbol{y}_j) + \boldsymbol{z}_i,$$

where $\phi(\cdot)$ is a feature map from $\mathbb{R}^p$ to $\mathcal{F}$. By using standard kernel trick, NLS3C can be formulated as an ℓ_1-regularized kernel regression problem. Although sharing some similar elements, our model in (2) is apparently different from the above NLS3C model in two aspects: (i) NLS3C uses an arbitrary feature map ϕ over all the data points for nonlinear embedding while our model allows different nonlinear functions $\{f_i\}$ to be applied to different data points $\{y_i\}$, without embedding; and (ii) the kernel matrix appeared in NLS3C is typically user specified while in our model the univariate functions f_i are unknown and as we will see shortly that they can be learned in a data-driven manner.

Identifiability. In the nonparametric SE model (2), since both the coefficients θ_{ij} and the functions f_i are all unknown, there might be different interpretations of the same data which lead to different segmentations. For instance, as an extreme example, one could pick f_i identically equal to a constant. This would put all the points in a single cluster, independently from their original distribution. Thus, in general, the model (2) is unidentifiable.

To make this model tractable, we need to impose certain restrictions on the space from which the functions f_i are drawn. To this end, we propose to express $\{f_i(y_i)\}$ appeared in (2) in terms of basis functions. For each data point y_i, we denote $\{\psi_{i\ell}(\cdot), \ell = 1, 2, ...\}$ as a set of uniformly bounded, orthonormal functional bases with respect to proper Lebesgue measure. We consider

$$f_i(y_i) = \sum_{\ell=1}^{q} \alpha_{i\ell}\psi_{i\ell}(y_i), \tag{3}$$

where q is the truncation order parameter. It is well-known that for sufficiently large q, the above defined f_i can accurately approximate the function $\tilde{f}_i(y_i) = \sum_{\ell=0}^{\infty} \alpha_{i\ell}\psi_{i\ell}(y_i)$ defined in terms of infinity basis. Therefore, in this paper we will only pursue the truncated formulation (3) which is more of practical interests. For the sake of identifiability, we assume that $\alpha_{i\ell} \neq 0$ for all pairs (i, ℓ). By combining (2) and (3), we obtain

$$\psi_{i\ell}(y_i) = -\sum_{t\neq\ell} \alpha_{it}/\alpha_{i\ell}\psi_{it}(y_i) + \sum_{j\neq i} \theta_{ij} \sum_{t=1}^{q} \alpha_{jt}/\alpha_{i\ell}\psi_{jt}(y_j) + \varepsilon_{i\ell}. \tag{4}$$

Obviously, this is a linear model with respect to the data image under the (known) basis functions and thus is generally identifiable. Next, we will show how to use such a linear model for nonlinear subspace clustering.

Re-Parametrization. One issue with the linear model (4) is that its parameters $\alpha_{i\ell}$ and θ_{ij} are coupled which complicates the optimization and analysis. To address this challenge, we introduce the following re-parametrization scheme:

$$\beta_{it}^{i\ell} := \alpha_{it}/\alpha_{i\ell}, \text{ for } t \neq \ell \quad ; \quad \beta_{jt}^{i\ell} := \theta_{ij}\alpha_{jt}/\alpha_{i\ell}, \text{ for } j \neq i.$$

Then, for each pair $(i, \ell) \in \{1, ..., n\} \times \{1, ..., q\}$, we arrive at the following Additive Self-Expressive (ASE) model:

$$\psi_{i\ell}(\boldsymbol{y}_i) = \sum_{t \neq \ell} \beta_{it}^{i\ell} \psi_{it}(\boldsymbol{y}_i) + \sum_{j \neq i} \sum_{t=1}^{q} \beta_{jt}^{i\ell} \psi_{jt}(\boldsymbol{y}_j) + \varepsilon_{i\ell}, \tag{5}$$

where $\{\beta_{it}^{i\ell}, t = 1, ..., \ell - 1, \ell + 1, ..., q\}$ and $\{\beta_{jt}^{i\ell}, j \neq i, t = 1, ..., q\}$ are unknown parameters to be estimated.

Remark 3. Note that the introduced re-parametrization is not invertible, and thus it is hopeless to recover the parameters θ_{ij} and $\alpha_{i\ell}$ (i.e., f_i) of the original model in (4) from those of the ASE model in (5). Fortunately, for the purpose of subspace clustering, what really matters in (4) is the sparse pattern of the parameters θ_{ij} rather than their exact values and the values of $\alpha_{i\ell}$. Since we have assumed $\alpha_{i\ell} \neq 0$, it is immediately known that $\beta_{jt}^{i\ell} = 0$ if and only if $\theta_{ij} = 0$. That is, the sparse pattern of coefficients θ_{ij} is encoded in the group sparse structure of $\beta_{jt}^{i\ell}$. One interesting implication of this observation is that we may hopefully estimate the sparse pattern of the original model in (4) via estimating that of the re-parameterized model in (5). As we will see shortly that an appealing merit of expression (5) is that it suggests a convex solver which eases the consequent optimization and analysis. Therefore, in the following analysis, we choose to use expression (5) for sparse pattern discover, even though its parameters cannot be readily used to estimate the nonlinear functions $\{f_i\}$.

As discussed in Remark 3, it is expected that the parameters $\{\beta_{jt}^{i\ell}, j \neq i, t = 1, ..., q\}$ exhibit group-level sparsity in terms of the groups defined over the q bases. In the next subsection, we will propose to use grouped Lasso programming to estimate these parameters.

3.2   Parameter Estimation and Clustering

Let us abbreviate $\psi_{i\ell} = \psi_{i\ell}(\boldsymbol{y}_i)$, $\boldsymbol{\Psi}_i = [\psi_{i1}, ..., \psi_{iq}]$ and $\boldsymbol{\Psi} = [\boldsymbol{\Psi}_1, \boldsymbol{\Psi}_2, ..., \boldsymbol{\Psi}_n]$. With obvious notations $\boldsymbol{\beta}_i = [\beta_{i1}, ..., \beta_{iq}]^{\top}$ and $\boldsymbol{\beta} = [\boldsymbol{\beta}_1^{\top}, ..., \boldsymbol{\beta}_n^{\top}]^{\top}$. Based on these notations, we naturally define a group structure as $G = \{1, 2, ..., n\}$, i.e., the elements inside each $\boldsymbol{\beta}_i$ form a group. In order to estimate ASE model (5) at a given pair of (i, ℓ), we consider a grouped lasso estimator which is defined as the solution to the following convex optimization problem:

$$\hat{\boldsymbol{\beta}}^{i\ell} = \arg \min_{\boldsymbol{\beta}} \frac{1}{2p} \|\psi_{i\ell} - \boldsymbol{\Psi}\boldsymbol{\beta}\|^2 + \lambda \|\boldsymbol{\beta}\|_{G,2} \quad \text{subject to } \beta_{i\ell} = 0, \tag{6}$$

where $\lambda > 0$ is the regularization strength parameter and the constraint $\beta_{i\ell} = 0$ is imposed to leave out trivial solutions. The above grouped Lasso estimator is strongly convex, and thus admits a unique global minimizer. In this paper, we use a standard proximal gradient descent algorithm [27] to find the optimal solution $\hat{\boldsymbol{\beta}}^{i\ell}$. After recovering $\hat{\boldsymbol{\beta}}^{i\ell}$ for each index pair (i, ℓ), we define a similarity matrix $\boldsymbol{W} = (w_{ij})$ in which $w_{ij} = \sqrt{\sum_{\ell=1}^{q} \sum_{t=1}^{q} (\beta_{jt}^{i\ell})^2}$ and set the affinity matrix to be

$C = |W| + |W|^\top$. Then we construct clusters by applying spectral clustering algorithms (e.g., [18] as conventionally used in literature) to the affinity matrix C. A high level summary of our SASC method is described in Algorithm 1.

Algorithm 1. Sparse Additive Subspace Clustering (SASC)

Input : A collection of data vectors $\mathcal{Y} = \{y_i \in \mathbb{R}^p\}_{i=1}^n$ and a set of pre-fixed functional bases $\{\psi_{i\ell}(\cdot), i = 1, ..., n, \ell = 1, ..., q\}$.

1. Compute $\psi_{i\ell} = \psi_{i\ell}(y_i)$ and set $\Psi_i = [\psi_{i1}, ..., \psi_{iq}]$, $\Psi = [\Psi_1, \Psi_2, ..., \Psi_n]$.

2. **for** $(i, \ell) \in \{i = 1, 2, ...n\} \times \{1, ..., q\}$ **do**

  | Estimate the minimizer $\hat{\beta}^{i\ell}$ of the grouped Lasso programming (6).

end

3. Construct the n-by-n similarity matrix W with entry (i, j) defined as $w_{ij} = \sqrt{\sum_{\ell=1}^q \sum_{t=1}^q (\beta_{jt}^{i\ell})^2}$. Form the affinity matrix by $C = |W| + |W|^\top$.

4. Let $\gamma_1 \geq \gamma_2 \geq ... \geq \gamma_n$ be the sorted eigenvalues of the normalized Laplacian matrix of C. Estimate the number of clusters as

$$\hat{K} = n - \underset{i=1,...,n-1}{\arg\max} (\gamma_i - \gamma_{i+1}).$$

5. Apply a spectral clustering method to the affinity matrix C to produce $\hat{K}$ disjoint clusters $\{\mathcal{Y}_k\}_{k=1}^{\hat{K}}$ of the data.

Output: Constructed Clusters $\{\mathcal{Y}_k\}_{k=1}^{\hat{K}}$ of $\mathcal{Y}$.

3.3 Theoretical Analysis

This subsection is devoted to analyzing the sparse recovery performance of SASC. We are particularly interested in the conditions under which the grouped Lasso estimator (6) may reliably select out points sharing the same underlying subspace as y_i over those not. In other words, the hope is that whenever $\hat{\beta}_j^{i\ell} \neq 0$, y_i and y_j belong to the same subspace. This is formally defined as the following concept of additive subspace detection property:

Definition 2 (Additive Subspace Detection Property). *Let W be the constructed similarity matrix of Step 3 of Algorithm 1. We say the additive subspace detection property holds if (1) for all (i, j) obeying $w_{ij} \neq 0$, x_i and x_j belong to the same subspace; (2) for all i, the entries $\{w_{ij}\}_{j \neq i}$ are not all zero.*

This property ensures that the weight matrix W has a block diagonal structure with each block representing a subspace cluster, and thus the affinity matrix C. In the subsequent subsections, we will provide some sufficient conditions under which the additive subspace detection property holds for Algorithm 1. We start with a deterministic analysis and then extend the results to stochastic settings.

A Deterministic Analysis. Let us consider the ASE model in (5) as a deterministic model. Without loss of generality, we assume that the columns of Ψ are arranged as $\Psi = [\Psi_{T_1}, ..., \Psi_{T_K}]$ in which the sub-matrix Ψ_{T_k} contains those columns associated with $\mathcal{Y}^{(k)}$ from the subspace S_k. Let $\bar{\beta}^{i\ell}$ be the true parameter vector for the ASE model in (5), i.e.,

$$\psi_{i\ell}(\boldsymbol{y}_i) = \sum_{t \neq \ell} \bar{\beta}_{it}^{i\ell} \psi_{it}(\boldsymbol{y}_i) + \sum_{j \neq i} \sum_{t=1}^{q} \bar{\beta}_{jt}^{i\ell} \psi_{jt}(\boldsymbol{y}_j) + \varepsilon_{i\ell}.$$

The following is our deterministic result on the additive subspace detection property of SASC.

Theorem 1. *Assume that there exists a universal constant $\delta \in (0,1)$ such that for any $k \in \{1, ..., K\}$, $\|(\boldsymbol{\Psi}_{T_k}^\top \boldsymbol{\Psi}_{T_k})^{-1}\boldsymbol{\Psi}_{T_k}^\top \boldsymbol{\Psi}_{T_k^c}\|_{T_k^c, \infty} \leq 1 - \delta$. If for any $\boldsymbol{y}_i \in \mathcal{Y}^{(k)}$, the regularization parameter λ satisfies the following two conditions*

(i) $\forall \ell \in \{1, ..., q\}$,

$$\lambda > \frac{\left\| \boldsymbol{\Psi}_{T_k^c}^\top \psi_{i\ell} - \boldsymbol{\Psi}_{T_k^c}^\top \boldsymbol{\Psi}_{T_k} (\boldsymbol{\Psi}_{T_k}^\top \boldsymbol{\Psi}_{T_k})^{-1} \boldsymbol{\Psi}_{T_k}^\top \psi_{i\ell} \right\|_{T_k^c, \infty}}{p\delta},$$

(ii) $\exists \ell \in \{1, ..., q\}, \boldsymbol{y}_j \in \mathcal{Y}^{(k)}, t \in \{1, ..., q\}$ such that

$$\lambda < \frac{|\bar{\beta}_{jt}^{i\ell}|}{\left\| \left(\frac{1}{p}\boldsymbol{\Psi}_{T_k}^\top \boldsymbol{\Psi}_{T_k}\right)^{-1} \right\|_{T_k, \infty}} - \left\| \frac{1}{p}\boldsymbol{\Psi}_{T_k}^\top (\psi_{i\ell} - \boldsymbol{\Psi}\bar{\beta}^{i\ell}) \right\|_{T_k, \infty},$$

then the additive subspace detection property holds.

A proof of this result is provided in Appendix A.

Remark 4. The constant $\delta \in (0,1)$ in the theorem is known as *incoherence parameter* in compressive sensing literature [31]. The main message this theorem conveys is that if the K subspaces respectively spanned by the basis $\{\boldsymbol{\Psi}_{T_k}\}_{k=1}^K$ are weakly correlated to each other, and the regularization parameter λ is well bounded from both sides, then the additive subspace detection property holds. Concerning the compatibility between the condition (i) and condition (ii), if the residual term $\psi_\ell^i - \boldsymbol{\Psi}\bar{\beta}^{i\ell}$ is well bounded and $\min_{jt} |\bar{\beta}_{j,t}^{i\ell}|$ is sufficiently large, then these two conditions are compatible. This point will be made more explicit in the following statistical analysis

A Statistical Analysis. We further consider the ASE model (5) as a stochastic model in which the design $\boldsymbol{\Psi}$ and the noise ε are both random. In this setting, we assume that the $\|\boldsymbol{\Psi}\|_{\infty,\infty} \leq c$ (which is reasonable as the basis functionals $\{\psi_{i\ell}(\cdot)\}$ are assumed to be uniformly bounded) and the noise levels are bounded by σ. The following is our main result on such a stochastic model.

Theorem 2. *Assume that there exist two universal constants $\delta \in (0,1)$ and $l > 0$ such that for any $k \in \{1, ..., K\}$, $\left\| \mathbb{E}[(\boldsymbol{\Psi}_{T_k}^\top \boldsymbol{\Psi}_{T_k})^{-1}\boldsymbol{\Psi}_{T_k}^\top \boldsymbol{\Psi}_{T_k^c}] \right\|_{T_k^c, \infty} \leq 1 - 2\delta$ and $\max_k \{\|\mathbb{E}[(\frac{1}{p}\boldsymbol{\Psi}_{T_k}^\top \boldsymbol{\Psi}_{T_k})^{-1}]\|_{T_k, \infty}\} \leq 0.5l$. If p is sufficiently large and for any $\boldsymbol{y}_i \in \mathcal{Y}^{(k)}$ the regularization parameter λ satisfies the following two conditions* *(i)* $\forall \ell \in \{1, ..., q\}$,

$$\lambda > \frac{c\sigma}{\delta}\sqrt{\frac{n}{p\eta}},$$

(ii) $\exists \ell \in \{1, ..., q\}, y_j \in \mathcal{Y}^{(k)}, t \in \{1, ..., q\}$ *such that*

$$\lambda < \frac{|\bar{\beta}_{jt}^{i\ell}|}{l} - c\sigma\sqrt{\frac{n}{p\eta}},$$

then the additive subspace detection property holds with probability at least $1 - n\eta$.

A proof of this theorem is provided in Appendix B.

Remark 5. Clearly, when $|\bar{\beta}_{jt}^{i\ell}| > (1 + 1/\delta)lc\sigma\sqrt{n/(p\eta)}$, the conditions (i) and (ii) are compatible, i.e., the feasible interval of regularization parameter λ is not empty. In this theorem, the dependence of the bounds on p and n is by no means optimal. Indeed, we use the relatively loose Chebyshev's inequality throughout the derivation to bound the concentration behavior. The reason that the much tighter Chernoff's inequality is not directly applicable here is that the entries of each basis vector $\psi_{i\ell}$ are dependent to each other when $p \geq d_k$. Although it is still possible to obtain sharper bounds using Chernoff's inequality with stronger assumptions and more involved analysis, we choose not to pursue in that direction for the sake of presentation clarity. Moreover, in the high dimensional settings where $p \gg n$, the bounds stated in Theorem 2 are still meaningful.

4   Experiments

We evaluate the performance of SASC for robust subspace clustering on synthetic and real data sets. We first investigate subspace detection performance using Monte-Carlo simulation, and then we apply our method to a motion segmentation benchmark data set.

4.1   Monte-Carlo Simulation

This is a proof-of-concept experiment. The purpose of this experiment is to confirm that when the observed data points from each subspace are contaminated by a highly nonlinear transformation, our approach can be significantly superior to existing subspace clustering models for inferring.

Simulated Data. In our simulation study, we generate 5 overlapping subspaces $\{\mathcal{S}_k\}_{k=1}^5 \subset \mathbb{R}^{1000}$ whose bases $\{U_k\}_{k=1}^5$ are generated by $U_{k+1} = RU_k$, $1 \leq k \leq 4$, where R represents a random rotation matrix and U_1 a random orthogonal matrix of dimensions 1000×50. Thus each subspace has a dimension of 50. 20 data vectors are sampled from each subspace by $X^{(k)} = U_k D_k$, $1 \leq k \leq 5$ with D_k being a 50×20 matrix whose entries are i.i.d. standard Gaussian variables. The observed samples are generated as $Y^{(k)} = f^{-1}(X^{(k)} + \varepsilon^{(k)})$ where f is a smooth invertible function and $\varepsilon^{(k)}$ is Gaussian noise. We consider two transformations: (i) the polynomial transform: $f(a) = (x - 0.2)^3$; and (ii) the logarithm transform: $f(a) = -\log a$. Note that f is unknown to our algorithm. For the former transformation, we fit the data to ASE model (5) with polynomial basis, and Fourier basis for the latter.

Comparison of Models and Evaluation Criterion. We compare the performance of our estimator to two representative SE based subspace clustering methods: SSC [7] and LRR [12]. Since the subspace information of the data is available, we measure the performance by *Detection Precision* of the top k links on the constructed graph (corresponding to the top $2k$ entries in the affinity matrix C). A link is regarded as *true* if and only if it connects two data points belonging to the same subspace. Also, we use the clustering accuracy as a measurement to evaluate the overall clustering performance.

Results. Figure 1 shows the subspace link detection precision curves on the simulated data. From these curves we can see that SASC is significantly better than SSC and LRR. The clustering accuracies of the considered methods are listed in Table 1. It can be seen that SASC succeeds while SSC and LRR perform poorly on these two synthetic data sets. This result makes sense as SASC explicitly models the underlying nonlinear perturbations which are not addressed by SSC and LRR. Concerning the running time, SASC is slightly slower than SSC because it needs to decompose each data point into the combination of multiple basis and then apply grouped Lasso programming on these extracted basis.

4.2 Motion Segmentation Data

We further evaluate SASC on Hopkins 155 motion dataset [26] which is a benchmark for subspace clustering study. This data set consists of 120 sequences of

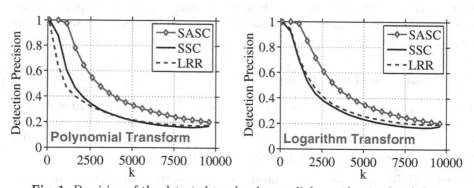

Fig. 1. Precision of the detected top k subspace links on the simulated data

Table 1. Clustering accuracies on the simulated data

Methods	SASC	SSC	LRR
Poly. Trans. $f(a) = (a - 0.2)^3$	**1.00**	0.58	0.36
Log. Trans. $f(a) = -\log a$	**1.00**	0.91	0.72

two motions and 35 sequences of three motions (a motion corresponding to a subspace). Each sequence is a sole segmentation task and so there are 155 subspace segmentation tasks totally. On average, each sequence of two motions has $N = 266$ point trajectories and $F = 30$ frames, while each sequence of three motions has $N = 398$ point trajectories and $F = 29$ frames. We compare the performance of SASC with SSC and LRR which are two representative state-of-the-art subspace clustering algorithms on this data. We follow the experimental protocol in [7] to apply the considered algorithms on the original $2F$-dimensional trajectories and on the $4n$-dimensional subspace (n is the number of subspaces) extracted by PCA. In this experiment, we implement SASC with Fourier basis.

Table 2(a) lists the mean and median clustering errors of the considered methods on the original $2F$-dimensional data points. It can be clearly seen from this table that SASC performs favorably. Table 2(b) lists the clustering errors of the considered methods on the $4n$-dimensional data points obtained by applying PCA. In this setting, SASC achieves the lowest clustering errors on two motion sequences and all sequences, while SCC is the best on three motion sequences. Overall, the observation is that SASC performs the best in most cases. This group of results reveal that the motion trajectories in Hopkins 155 might be contaminated by nonlinear distortions that can be robustly captured by SASC.

Table 2. Hopkins 155: Mean and median clustering errors (%) of the three considered algorithms

(a) $2F$-dimensional data points

Methods	2 Motions		3 Motions		All	
	Mean	Med.	Mean	Med.	Mean	Med.
SASC	**0.90**	0	**3.33**	0.60	**1.45**	0
SSC	1.52	0	4.40	**0.56**	2.18	0
LRR	2.13	0	4.03	1.43	2.56	0

(b) $4n$-dimensional data points by PCA

Methods	2 Motions		3 Motions		All	
	Mean	Med.	Mean	Med.	Mean	Med.
SASC	**0.91**	0	4.46	0.81	**1.71**	0
SSC	1.83	0	**4.40**	**0.56**	2.41	0
LRR	3.41	0	4.86	1.47	3.74	0

5   Conclusions

In this paper, we proposed SASC as a novel nonparametric subspace clustering method. The main idea is to assume that there exists an unknown function for each data point such that the elementwise transformed data point lies near a subspace. This assumption allows us to capture complex perturbations beyond additive random noises in the observed data. In order to make our model computationally tractable, we project the unknown univariate mapping functions onto proper truncated functional spaces. Based on the self-expressiveness property of the clean data, SASC can be formulated as a sequence of nonparametric additive models whose parameters can be estimated via grouped Lasso programming. Statistical analysis shows that under mild conditions, with high probability, SASC is able to successfully recover the underlying subspace structure. Experimental results show that SASC is consistently better than or comparable to the best state-of-the-art methods in clustering accuracy, at a cost of only slightly increased computational time.

Acknowledgements. Xiao-Tong Yuan is supported by NSFJP-BK20141003, NSFJP-BK2012045, NSFC-61272223, ONR-N00014-13-1-0764, and AFOSR-FA9550-13-1-0137. Ping Li is supported by ONR-N00014-13-1-0764, AFOSR-FA9550-13-1-0137, NSF III 1360971, and NSF BIGDATA 1419210.

A   Proof of Theorem 1

We need a technical lemma before proving the theorem. Given a response $z \in \mathbb{R}^p$ and a design matrix $\boldsymbol{\Psi} \in \mathbb{R}^{p \times n}$, let us consider the following general grouped Lasso estimator associated with a disjoint group structure G over the parameters:

$$\hat{\boldsymbol{\beta}} = \arg\min_{\boldsymbol{\beta}} \frac{1}{2p} \|z - \boldsymbol{\Psi}\boldsymbol{\beta}\|^2 + \lambda\|\boldsymbol{\beta}\|_{G,2}. \tag{7}$$

Lemma 1. *Let $T \subseteq G$ be a subset of the groups. Assume that there exists a universal constant $\delta \in (0,1)$ such that $\|(\boldsymbol{\Psi}_T^\top \boldsymbol{\Psi}_T)^{-1}\boldsymbol{\Psi}_T^\top \boldsymbol{\Psi}_{T^c}\|_{T^c,\infty} \leq 1 - \delta$. If the regularization parameter λ satisfies*

$$\lambda > \frac{\|\boldsymbol{\Psi}_{T^c}^\top z - \boldsymbol{\Psi}_{T^c}^\top \boldsymbol{\Psi}_T (\boldsymbol{\Psi}_T^\top \boldsymbol{\Psi}_T)^{-1}\boldsymbol{\Psi}_T^\top z\|_{T^c,\infty}}{p\delta},$$

then

(a) any optimal solution

$$\hat{\boldsymbol{\beta}} = \arg\min_{\boldsymbol{\beta}} \frac{1}{2p} \|z - \boldsymbol{\Psi}\boldsymbol{\beta}\|^2 + \lambda\|\boldsymbol{\beta}\|_{G,2}$$

must satisfy $\hat{\boldsymbol{\beta}}_{T^c} = \mathbf{0}$.

(b) Moreover, for any $\bar{\boldsymbol{\beta}}$ satisfying $\bar{\boldsymbol{\beta}}_{T^c} = \mathbf{0}$, the element-wise estimation error is bounded by

$$\|\hat{\boldsymbol{\beta}} - \bar{\boldsymbol{\beta}}\|_\infty \leq \left\|\left(\frac{1}{p}\boldsymbol{\Psi}_T^\top \boldsymbol{\Psi}_T\right)^{-1}\right\|_{T,\infty} \left(\left\|\frac{1}{p}\boldsymbol{\Psi}_T^\top(z - \boldsymbol{\Psi}\bar{\boldsymbol{\beta}})\right\|_{T,\infty} + \lambda\right).$$

A proof of this lemma is given in the supplementary material. We are now in the position to prove Theorem 1.

Proof (of Theorem 1). Let us consider a fixed data point $y_i \in \mathcal{Y}^{(k)}$. From the condition (i) and the part (a) of Lemma 1 we know that $\forall \ell \in \{1, ..., q\}$, $\hat{\beta}_{T_k^c}^{i\ell} = \mathbf{0}$. From the condition (ii) and the part (b) of Lemma 1 we obtain that $\exists \ell \in \{1, ..., q\}, y_j \in \mathcal{Y}^{(k)}, t \in \{1, ..., q\}$, such that $\hat{\beta}_{jt}^{i\ell} \neq \mathbf{0}$. Combining these two results and from the construction of W we get that $w_{ij} = 0$ whenever $y_j \notin \mathcal{Y}^{(k)}$, and $\exists y_j \in \mathcal{Y}^{(k)}, j \neq i$ such that $w_{ij} \neq 0$. This verifies the additive subspace detection property.

B   Proof of Theorem 2

We start with a technical lemma needed in the proof. Let us consider the following stochastic model

$$z = \Psi\bar{\beta} + \varepsilon,$$

where the design Ψ is random and $\varepsilon = [\varepsilon_1, ..., \varepsilon_p]$ are p i.i.d. Gaussian noise with zero mean and variance σ^2.

The following lemma is a statistical extension of Lemma 1.

Lemma 2. *Let $T \subseteq G$ be a subset of the groups. Assume that there exists a constant $\delta \in (0,1)$ and a constant $l > 0$ such that*

$$\left\| \mathbb{E}[(\Psi_T^\top \Psi_T)^{-1}\Psi_T^\top \Psi_{T^c}] \right\|_{T^c,\infty} \leq 1 - 2\delta, \quad \left\| \mathbb{E}\left[\left(\frac{1}{p}\Psi_T^\top \Psi_T \right)^{-1} \right] \right\|_{T,\infty} \leq 0.5l.$$

If p is sufficiently large and the regularization parameter λ satisfies

$$\lambda > \frac{c\sigma}{\delta}\sqrt{\frac{n}{p\eta}},$$

then with probability at least $1 - \eta$

(a) any optimal solution

$$\hat{\beta} = \arg\min_{\beta} \frac{1}{2}\|z - \Psi\beta\|^2 + \lambda\|\beta\|_{G,2}$$

must satisfy $\hat{\beta}_{T^c} = 0$.

(b) Moreover, for any $\bar{\beta}$ satisfying $\bar{\beta}_{T^c} = 0$, then the element-wise estimation error is bounded by

$$\|\hat{\beta} - \bar{\beta}\|_\infty \leq \|(\Psi_T^\top \Psi_T)^{-1}\|_{T,\infty}(\|\Psi_T^\top(z - \Psi\bar{\beta})\|_{T,\infty} + \lambda).$$

A proof of this lemma is provided in the supplementary material. Now we prove Theorem 2.

Proof (of Theorem 2). Let us consider a fixed data point $y_i \in \mathcal{Y}^{(k)}$. From the condition (i) and the part (a) of Lemma 2 we know that $\forall \ell \in \{1, ..., q\}$, $\hat{\beta}_{T_k^c}^{i\ell} = 0$ holds with probability at least $1 - \eta$. It is easy to check that with probability at least $1 - \eta$

$$\left\| \frac{1}{p}\Psi_{T_k}^\top(\psi_\ell^i - \Psi\bar{\beta}^{i\ell}) \right\|_{T_k,\infty} = \left\| \frac{1}{p}\Psi_{T_k}^\top \varepsilon_\ell^i \right\|_{T_k,\infty} \leq c\sigma\sqrt{\frac{n}{p\eta}}.$$

When p is sufficiently large, from the condition (ii) and the part (b) of Lemma 2 we obtain that $\exists \ell \in \{1, ..., q\}$, $y_j \in \mathcal{Y}^{(k)}$, $t \in \{1, ..., q\}$, such that $\hat{\beta}_{jt}^{i\ell} \neq 0$ holds with probability $1 - \eta$. Combining these two results and from the construction of W we get that $w_{ij} = 0$ whenever $y_j \notin \mathcal{Y}^{(k)}$, and $\exists y_j \in \mathcal{Y}^{(k)}$, $j \neq i$ such that $w_{ij} \neq 0$ holds with probability $1 - \eta$. By union of probability, we know that the additive subspace detection property holds with probability at least $1 - n\eta$. This proves the claim.

References

1. Agrawal, R., Gehrke, J., Gunopulos, D., Raghavan, P.: Automatic subspace clustering of high dimensional data for data mining applications. In: Proceedings of the 1998 ACM SIGMOD International Conference on Management of Data (SIGMOD 1998), pp. 94–105 (1998)
2. Bako, L.: Identification of switched linear systems via sparse optimization. Automatica 47(4), 668–677 (2011)
3. Bradley, P.S., Mangasarian, O.L.: K-plane clustering. Journal of Global Optimization 16(1), 23–32 (2000)
4. Chen, G., Lerman, G.: Spectral curvature clustering (scc). International Journal of Computer Vision 81(3), 317–330 (2009)
5. Cheng, B., Yang, J., Yan, S., Fu, Y., Huang, T.: Learning with ℓ_1-graph for image analysis. IEEE Transactions on Image Processing 19(4), 858–866 (2010)
6. Costeira, J., Kanade, T.: A multibody factorization method for independently moving objects. International Journal of Computer Vision 29(3), 159–179 (1998)
7. Elhamifar, E., Vidal, R.: Sparse subspace clustering: Algorithm, theory, and applications. IEEE Transactions on Pattern Analysis And Machine Intelligence 35(11), 2765–2781 (2013)
8. Eriksson, B., Balzano, L., Nowak, R.: High-rank matrix completion. In: Proceedings of the 15th International Conference on Artificial Intelligence and Statistics (AISTATS 2012), pp. 373–381 (2012)
9. Hastie, T., Tibshirani, R.: Generalized Additive Models. Chapman & Hall/CRC (1990)
10. Jalali, A., Chen, Y., Sanghavi, S., Xu, H.: Clustering partially observed graphs via convex optimization. In: Proceedings of the Twenty-Eighth International Conference on Machine Learning (ICML 2011). ACM (2011)
11. Kriegel, H.P., Kröger, P., Zimek, A.: Clustering high-dimensional data: A survey on subspace clustering, pattern-based clustering, and correlation clustering. ACM Transactions on Knowledge Discovery from Data (TKDD) 3, 1–58 (2009)
12. Liu, G., Lin, Z., Yan, S., Sun, J., Yu, Y., Ma, Y.: Robust recovery of subspace structures by low-rank representation. Transactions on Pattern Analysis and Machine Intelligence 35(1), 171–184 (2013)
13. Liu, H., Han, F., Yuan, M., Lafferty, J., Wasserman, L.: High dimensional semiparametric gaussian copula graphical models. The Annals of Statistics 40(4), 2293–2326 (2012)
14. Liu, H., Lafferty, J., Wasserman, L.: The nonparanormal: Semiparametric estimation of high dimensional undirected graphs. Journal of Machine Learning Research 10, 2295–2328 (2009)
15. Lu, C.-Y., Min, H., Zhao, Z.-Q., Zhu, L., Huang, D.-S., Yan, S.: Robust and efficient subspace segmentation via least squares regression. In: Fitzgibbon, A., Lazebnik, S., Perona, P., Sato, Y., Schmid, C. (eds.) ECCV 2012, Part VII. LNCS, vol. 7578, pp. 347–360. Springer, Heidelberg (2012)
16. Ma, Y., Vidal, R.: Identification of deterministic switched arx systems via identification of algebraic varieties. In: Morari, M., Thiele, L. (eds.) HSCC 2005. LNCS, vol. 3414, pp. 449–465. Springer, Heidelberg (2005)
17. McWilliams, B., Montana, G.: Subspace clustering of high-dimensional data: A predictive approach. Data Mining and Knowledge Discovery 28(3), 736–772 (2014)
18. Ng, A.Y., Jordan, M.I., Weiss, Y.: On spectral clustering: Analysis and an algorithm. In: Proceedings of the 16th Annual Conference on Neural Information Processing Systems, NIPS 2002 (2002)

19. Ni, Y., Sun, J., Yuan, X.T., Yan, S., Cheong, L.F.: Robust low-rank subspace segmentation with semidefinite guarantees. In: Proceedings of the Workshop on Optimization Based Methods for Emerging Data Mining Problems (OEDM 2010 in conjunction with ICDM 2010) (2010)
20. Parsons, L., Haque, E., Liu, H.: Subspace clustering for high dimensional data: A review. ACM SIGKDD Explorations Newsletter 6(1), 90–105 (2004)
21. Patel, V., Nguyen, H., Vidal, R.: Latent space sparse subspace clustering. In: Proceedings of IEEE International Conference on Computer Vision, ICCV 2013 (2013)
22. Ravikumar, P., Lafferty, J., Liu, H., Wasserman, L.: Sparse additive models. Journal of the Royal Statistical Society: Series B (Statistical Methodology) (JRSSB) 71(5), 1009–1030 (2009)
23. Soltanolkotabi, M., Candès, E.J.: A geometric analysis of subspace clustering with outliers. The Annals of Statistics 40(4), 2195–2238 (2012)
24. Soltanolkotabi, M., Elhamifar, E., Candès, E.J.: Robust subspace clustering. The Annals of Statistics (to appear, 2014)
25. Tomasi, C., Kanade, T.: Shape and motion from image streams under orthography: A factorization method. International Journal of Computer Vision 9(2), 137–154 (1992)
26. Tron, R., Vidal, R.: A benchmark for the comparison of 3-d motion segmentation algorithms. In: Proceedings of IEEE International Conference on Computer Vision and Pattern Recognition, CVPR 2007 (2007)
27. Tseng, P.: On accelerated proximal gradient methods for convex-concave optimization. Submitted to SIAM Journal of Optimization (2008)
28. Vidal, R.: Subspace clustering. IEEE Signal Processing Magazine 28(3), 52–68 (2011)
29. Vidal, R., Ma, Y., Sastry, S.: Generalized principal component analysis (gpca). Transactions on Pattern Analysis and Machine Intelligence 27(12), 1945–1959 (2005)
30. Vidal, R., Tron, R., Hartley, R.: Multiframe motion segmentation with missing data using power factorization and gpca. International Journal of Computer Vision 79, 85–105 (2008)
31. Wainwright, M.J.: Sharp thresholds for high-dimensional and noisy sparsity recovery using ℓ_1-constrained quadratic programming (lasso). IEEE Transactions on Information Theory 55(5), 2183–2202 (2009)
32. Wang, Y., Xu, H.: Noisy sparse subspace clustering. In: Proceedings of the 30 th International Conference on Machine Learning (ICML 2013), pp. 849–856 (2013)
33. Xue, L., Zou, H.: Regularized rank-based estimation of high-dimensional nonparanormal graphical models. The Annals of Statistics 40(5), 2541–2571 (2012)
34. Yan, J., Pollefeys, M.: A general framework for motion segmentation: Independent, articulated, rigid, non-rigid, degenerate and non-degenerate. In: Leonardis, A., Bischof, H., Pinz, A. (eds.) ECCV 2006. LNCS, vol. 3954, pp. 94–106. Springer, Heidelberg (2006)
35. Yang, A., Wright, J., Ma, Y., Sastry, S.: Unsupervised segmentation of natural images via lossy data compression. Computer Vision and Image Understanding 110, 212–225 (2008)
36. Yin, Y., Chen, X., Xing, E.: Group sparse additive models. In: Proceedings of the 29th International Conference on Machine Learning, ICML 2012 (2012)

Boosting VLAD with Supervised Dictionary Learning and High-Order Statistics

Xiaojiang Peng[1,4,3,*], Limin Wang[2,3,*], Yu Qiao[3], and Qiang Peng[1]

[1] Southwest Jiaotong University, Chengdu, China
[2] Department of Information Engineering, The Chinese University of Hong Kong, Hong Kong, China
[3] Shenzhen Key Lab of CVPR, Shenzhen Institutes of Advanced Technology, CAS, Shenzhen, China
[4] Hengyang Normal University, Hengyang, China

Abstract. Recent studies show that aggregating local descriptors into super vector yields effective representation for retrieval and classification tasks. A popular method along this line is vector of locally aggregated descriptors (VLAD), which aggregates the residuals between descriptors and visual words. However, original VLAD ignores high-order statistics of local descriptors and its dictionary may not be optimal for classification tasks. In this paper, we address these problems by utilizing high-order statistics of local descriptors and peforming supervised dictionary learning. The main contributions are twofold. Firstly, we propose a high-order VLAD (H-VLAD) for visual recognition, which leverages two kinds of high-order statistics in the VLAD-like framework, namely diagonal covariance and skewness. These high-order statistics provide complementary information for VLAD and allow for efficient computation. Secondly, to further boost the performance of H-VLAD, we design a supervised dictionary learning algorithm to discriminatively refine the dictionary, which can be also extended for other super vector based encoding methods. We examine the effectiveness of our methods in image-based object categorization and video-based action recognition. Extensive experiments on PASCAL VOC 2007, HMDB51, and UCF101 datasets exhibit that our method achieves the state-of-the-art performance on both tasks.

1 Introduction

Effective representation of image and video is crucial for visual recognition such as object recognition and action recognition. One popular representation is Bag of Visual Words (BoVW) model with local descriptors [5,36,22]. Approaches along this line include vector quantization (VQ) [27], sparse coding (SC) [39], soft-assignment (SA) [19], locality-constrained linear coding (LLC) [34], Fisher vector (FV) [23], and vector of locally aggregated descriptors (VLAD) [12]. These methods start from extracting local low-level descriptors (e.g., SIFT [20] or HOG, HOF, MBH [32]), then learn a codebook or dictionary from training set, encode descriptors to new vectors, and finally aggregate them to a global vector. After normalization, these vectors are used to train a classifier for visual classification.

---

* Indicates equal contribution.

D. Fleet et al. (Eds.): ECCV 2014, Part III, LNCS 8691, pp. 660–674, 2014.

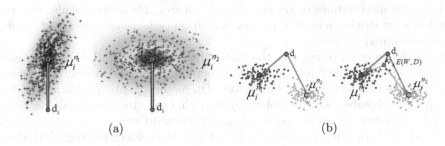

(a)   (b)

Fig. 1. The illustration of VLAD problem and dictionary refining process. (a) The descriptors ("+") assigned to word $\mathbf{d}_i$ in the n_1-th and n_2-th samples from different classes share the same mean. It results in two similar VLAD representations. However, the discrimination is preserved when incorporating high-order statistics of the assigned descriptors. (b) For the dictionary, our supervised learning method tunes the dictionary to minimize the classification error E and achieves better cosine-like similarity measure.

Recent study works show that super vector based encoding methods provide successful representations for visual recognition [5,36,22]. VLAD [12] is a kind of efficient super vector encoding method. For VLAD, it trains a codebook in the feature space using K-means. Each block of VLAD can be viewed as the difference between the mean of the descriptors assigned to the visual word and the word itself. VLAD can be efficiently computed and its effectiveness has been verified in several tasks, such as instance retrieval [12,1], scene recognition [8], and action recognition [11]. However, there are still two main issues about VLAD representation:

- It ignores the high order information of the descriptor distribution. As illustrated in Fig. 1 (a), the descriptors assigned to word $\mathbf{d}_i$ in the n_1-th and n_2-th samples share the same means. This results in two similar aggregated vectors by original VLAD method. However, the distributions of the two sets of descriptors are obviously different.
- The dictionary is another important issue for VLAD [1]. The similarity between two VLAD vectors is more sensitive to the visual words. As illustrated in the Fig. 1 (b), the two VLAD blocks, generated by $\mathbf{d}_i$ for the n_1-th and n_2-th samples are deemed to be similar due to the acute angle between them. But in practice, the two sets of descriptors may come from different categories, and their similarity is desired to be not large.

To address this issues, we introduce two important methods to boost the representation capacity of VLAD. Firstly, we leverage two high-order statistics in the VLAD-like framework, including diagonal covariance and skewness, to construct a high-order version of VLAD (H-VLAD). The covariance of descriptors reflects the distribution shape which is beneficial for classification. We utilize the residuals between the diagonal covariance from clusters and that from assigned descriptors to enhance the original VLAD. Mean and covariance are sufficient to describe a pure Gaussion distribution [9]. However, as shown in [13], there always exist heavy tails for the distributions of gradient-based features. Therefore, we also test the third-order statistics, namely skewness, which capture the asymmetry of the descriptors around the mean.

Secondly, in order to enhance the discriminative power of VLAD, we propose a supervised dictionary learning (SDL) method. The VLAD with supervised dictionary are called S-VLAD. Our novel SDL method jointly optimizes the dictionary and classifier, which is solved by updating the visual words and learning model alternately. A slight update of the visual word will revise the similarity at the desired direction as shown in Fig. 1 (b). It is worth **noting that** there are plenty of research works on SDL for traditional encoding methods [3,30], but to our best knowledge, we are the first to introduce SDL for VLAD encoding, which is independent with the recent work of Deep Fisher Kernel [29], where the GMM parameters are discriminatively tuned in Fisher Vector framework.

The main contributions of this paper can be summarized as follows: (i) we extend VLAD with high-order statistics while keeping both high performance and high extraction speed (Section 3). (ii) we are the first to explore supervised dictionary learning for VLAD and verify its effectiveness (Section 4). (iii) Our method obtains the state-of-the-art performance on several challenging benchmarks including PASCAL VOC 2007, HMDB51 and UCF101 datasets for object and action recognition (Section 5).

2   Related Works

Super Vector Based Encoding Method. Bag of Visual Words (BoVW) [5,36] model with local descriptors has become a popular method for visual recognition and super vector based encoding methods [40,12,23] have obtained the state-of-the-art performance in several tasks. Super vector based encoding methods yield very high dimensional representations by aggregating high order statistics and typical methods include Super Vector Coding (SVC) [40], Vector of Locally Aggregated Descriptors [12], and Fisher Vector [23]. SVC assumed to learn a smooth nonlinear function $f(x)$ defined on a high dimensional space and derive a good coding scheme $\phi(x)$ to approximate $f(x)$ in a linear form $\omega^\top \phi(x)$. The resulting super vector coding $\phi(x)$ can be viewed as a super vector aggregating zero order and first order statistics. FV [23] was derived from Fisher Kernel [10] by representing the sample using the parameter gradient vector of log likelihood. In practice, FV aggregates not only the first order statistics, but also the second order statistics. Thus, its performance is usually better than VLAD, where only the first order statistics is kept. The idea of augmenting VLAD with high order information is inspired by these super vector encoding methods. However, this augmenting method shares two advantages: (i) it is able to bridge the performance gap between VLAD and FV; (ii) it also shares the high speed of VLAD.

Supervised Feature Learning. Feature learning (or deep learning) [2] has become more popular in computer vision community. Among them, the discriminatively trained deep convolutional neural networks (CNN) [18] have recently achieved impressive state-of-the-art results over a number of areas, including object recognition [16] and action recognition [26]. One of the main advantages of CNN is that it is able to supervised learn the network parameters according to specific task from a large dataset. The idea of supervised learning has been extended to traditional methods, such as sparse coding [3], soft assignment [30]. These methods mainly resorted to jointly optimize the dictionary and classifiers. However, they did not deal with super vector based encoding methods. The latest paper [29] designed an end-to-end learning method to discriminatively tune the GMM parameters for Fisher vector. Our work of supervised dictionary learning for VLAD is independent with them and we obtains much better results on the PASCAL VOC 2007 dataset.

3   Augmenting VLAD with High Order Statistics

In this section, we first review the original VLAD computation and its corresponding normalization operation. We then introduce adding high-order statistics in VLAD computation framework.

3.1   VLAD Review

VLAD is proposed by Jégou *et al.* in [12]. Similar to standard BoVW, a dictionary $\mathbf{D} = [\mathbf{d}_1, \mathbf{d}_2, \cdots, \mathbf{d}_K] \in \mathcal{R}^{d \times K}$ is first learned by K-means from training samples. Let $\mathbf{X} = [\mathbf{x}_1, ... \mathbf{x}_N] \in \mathcal{R}^{d \times N}$ denote a set of local descriptors from a video V. For each codeword $\mathbf{d}_k$, a vector $\mathbf{v}_k$ is yielded by aggregating the differences between the assigned descriptors and codeword $\mathbf{d}_k$:

$$\mathbf{v}_k = \sum_{\mathbf{x}_j : NN(\mathbf{x}_j)=k} (\mathbf{x}_j - \mathbf{d}_k), \tag{1}$$

where $NN(\mathbf{x}_j)$ denotes that the nearest neighborhood of $\mathbf{x}_j$ in $\mathbf{D}$. The VLAD representation is the concatenation of all the d-dimensional vectors $\mathbf{v}_k$ and is therefore a Kd-dimensional vector. The representative capacity of VLAD can be enhanced by pre-processing the local features with PCA-Whitening [6,22], and performing intra-normalization on the final representation [1]. Thus, the final representation of VLAD is expressed as follows:

$$\psi(\mathbf{X}, \mathbf{D}) = \left[\frac{\mathbf{v}_1}{||\mathbf{v}_1||_2}; ...; \frac{\mathbf{v}_i}{||\mathbf{v}_i||_2}; ...; \frac{\mathbf{v}_K}{||\mathbf{v}_K||_2} \right]. \tag{2}$$

3.2   High-Order VLAD

This section introduce a simple yet effective method to augment original VLAD, which is motivated by the fact that VLAD will lose discriminative capacity in two cases. The first case is as shown in Fig. 1(a) that it would yield the same VLAD representation when the two sets of assigned descriptors share the same mean. We call this problem as *"share-means"*. Another one is that those zero aggregated vectors are ambiguous, because of both the facts that no descriptor is assigned to the codeword and that the mean of assigned features is equal to the codeword. We call this problem as *"evil-zeros"*. In order to solve these problems, we propose a higher-order VLAD (H-VLAD), which makes use of two high-order statistics in the VLAD-like framework, including diagonal covariance and skewness. The technical details are as follows.

The original version of VLAD defined in Equation (1) can be rewritten as:

$$\mathbf{v}_k = N_k \left(\frac{1}{N_k} \sum_{j=1}^{N_k} \mathbf{x}_j - \mathbf{d}_k \right) = N_k (\mathbf{m}_k - \mathbf{d}_k), \tag{3}$$

where N_k is the number of descriptors assigned to codeword $\mathbf{d}_k$, which can be omitted when the intra-normalization is used, and $\mathbf{m}_k$ is the mean of these descriptors assigned to codeword $\mathbf{d}_k$. Thus, the original VLAD can be interpreted as the difference between the mean of descriptors and codeword. Similarly, using covariance, we formulate the second-order super vector as follows:

$$\mathbf{v}_k^c = \hat{\sigma}_k^2 - \sigma_k^2 = \frac{1}{N_k} \sum_{j=1}^{N_k} (\mathbf{x}_j - \mathbf{m}_k)^2 - \sigma_k^2, \tag{4}$$

where the square of a vector is element-wise one and σ_k^2 is the diagonal elements of covariance matrix of the k-th cluster.

As for standard Gaussian distribution, the first and second statistical information is sufficient to determine the distribution. However, low-level descriptors (e.g., SIFT) are not usually Gaussian distribution in reality [13]. Therefore, we also employ the third-order statistics (skewness) to exploit extra complementary information. Skewness is a measure of the asymmetry of the data around the sample mean. We formulate third-order super vector as follows,

$$\mathbf{v}_k^s = \hat{\gamma}_k - \gamma_k = \frac{\frac{1}{N_k} \sum_{j=1}^{N_k} (\mathbf{x}_j - \mathbf{m}_k)^3}{\left(\frac{1}{N_k} \sum_{j=1}^{N_k} (\mathbf{x}_j - \mathbf{m}_k)^2 \right)^{\frac{3}{2}}} - \gamma_k, \tag{5}$$

where the power of a vector is also the element-wise one. The γ_k is the skewness of k-th cluster.

After intra-normalization separately, these two extra vectors are concatenated to the original VLAD to form a longer representation which is *the final representation of our H-VLAD*. Note that the statistics in Equation (3,4,5) can be quickly computed using Matlab toolbox. The H-VLAD requires no soft weight computation and contains higher statistical information compared with FV.

4   Supervised Dictionary Learning for VLAD

In this section, we first discuss the importance of dictionary for VLAD. Then, we formulate the supervised dictionary learning method for VLAD, and finally extend it to the spatial pyramid situation.

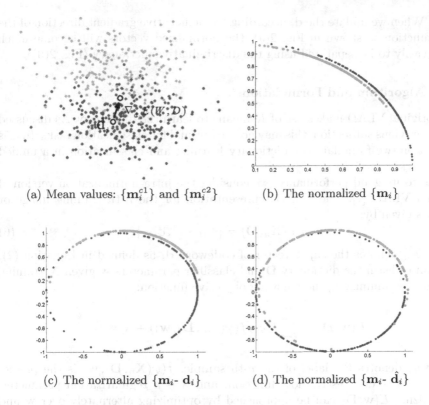

(a) Mean values: $\{\mathbf{m}_i^{c1}\}$ and $\{\mathbf{m}_i^{c2}\}$ (b) The normalized $\{\mathbf{m}_i\}$

(c) The normalized $\{\mathbf{m}_i\text{-}\mathbf{d}_i\}$ (d) The normalized $\{\mathbf{m}_i\text{-}\hat{\mathbf{d}}_i\}$

Fig. 2. Graphical interpretation of the importance of subtraction operation and a good dictionary. Two sets of mean values $\{\mathbf{m}_i^{c1}\}$ and $\{\mathbf{m}_i^{c2}\}$ from class $c1$ and $c2$ (a) are normalized by L2-norm and distribute in the 1st quadrant of a standard circle (b). After minus a particular anchor $\mathbf{d}_i$ (e.g., learned by K-means), they embed in the whole circle (c). An optimized anchor make the two sets of $\mathbf{m}_i$ more separate (d). Note that we make a micro shift to the points in (b), (c) and (d) for better visualization.

4.1   Importance of Dictionary

The dictionary plays an important role of subtractor in original VLAD. As illustrated in Fig. 2(a), two sets of VLAD blocks $\mathbf{m}_i^{c1}$ and $\mathbf{m}_i^{c2}$ defined in Equation (3) are from class $c1$ and $c2$ and scattered in a high-dimensional space. The separability of $\{\mathbf{m}_i^{c1}\}$ and $\{\mathbf{m}_i^{c2}\}$ determines the performance of final discriminative classifier. After normalization, all the vectors are projected to the 1st quadrant of a unit circle due to the positive property of descriptors (e.g., SIFT, HOG, etc) as shown in Fig.2(b). A linear classifier will produce a large error since almost half of samples overlap in this case. As for original VLAD, both sets of $\mathbf{m}_i^{c1}$ and $\mathbf{m}_i^{c2}$ will subtract an anchor vector $\mathbf{d}_i$ (the cluster center from K-means), then the normalized vectors will project to the whole unit circle, which make the samples more easily be separated (Fig. 2(c)). Since $\mathbf{d}_i$ affects the distribution of normalized vectors, we may find an optimized one to minimize the classification error. When we update the $\mathbf{d}_i$ according to the negative gradient direction of the cost function as shown in Fig. 2(a), the normalized vectors will become much more easily to be separated using the discriminative dictionary (Fig. 2(d)).

4.2   Algorithm and Formulation

The original VLAD makes use of K-means to learn the dictionary. As discussed in the previous subsection, this may not be optimal for classification tasks. In this subsection, we formulate the dictionary learning and classification in a unified framework.

Due to its good performance, we consider the intra-normalization version of original VLAD [1]. The VLAD representation for the n-th training image or video is given by:

$$\phi_n = \psi(\mathbf{X}_n, \mathbf{D}) = [\phi_{n1}, \cdots, \phi_{nK}], \tag{6}$$

where ϕ_{ni} denotes the super vector of codeword $\mathbf{d}_i$ as defined in Equation (2). We aim to learn the dictionary $\mathbf{D}$ and classifier parameters $\mathbf{w}$ given N training samples by minimizing the following objective function:

$$E(\mathbf{w}, \mathbf{D}) = \sum_{n=1}^{N} \ell(y_n, f(\psi(\mathbf{X}_n, \mathbf{D}), \mathbf{w})) + \lambda ||\mathbf{w}||_2^2 \tag{7}$$

where y_n denotes the label of the n-th sample, $f(\psi(\mathbf{X}_n, \mathbf{D}), \mathbf{w})$ is the prediction model, ℓ denotes the loss function, and λ is a regularization parameter. Minimizing $E(\mathbf{w}, \mathbf{D})$ can be approached by optimizing alternately over $\mathbf{w}$ and $\mathbf{D}$. We utilize logistic regression and softmax activation function for binary and multi-class classification, respectively. This is because the performance of them are similar to that of linear SVMs but their cost functions are differentiable [3].

Consider the binary classification problem first, where $y_n \in \{0, 1\}$ and $f_n = \sigma(\mathbf{w}^T \phi_n)$. The σ denotes the sigmoid function $\sigma(x) = 1/(1 + \exp(-x))$. With cross-entropy loss, the cost function E is given by:

$$E = -\sum_{n=1}^{N} \{y_n \ln f_n + (1 - y_n)\ln(1 - f_n)\} + \lambda ||\mathbf{w}||_2^2. \tag{8}$$

The gradient of E over $\mathbf{w}$ is:

$$\nabla_{\mathbf{w}} E = \sum_{n=1}^{N} (f_n - y_n)\phi_n + 2\lambda \mathbf{w}. \tag{9}$$

Given dictionary $\mathbf{D}$, we can use gradient descent method to find optimal $\mathbf{w}$. Given the model $\mathbf{w}$, in order to optimize E over $\mathbf{D}$, we apply the chain rule to compute the gradient as follows:

$$\nabla_{\mathbf{d}_i} E = \sum_{n=1}^{N} \frac{\partial \ell}{\partial f_n} \frac{\partial f_n}{\partial \phi_n} \frac{\partial \phi_n}{\partial \mathbf{d}_i}. \tag{10}$$

The computational processes of the first two gradients in the right side are similar with that of $\nabla_{\mathbf{w}} E$. The key problem is reduced to compute the gradient of the VLAD representation ϕ_n over $\mathbf{d}_i$. Ignoring the effect of $\mathbf{m}_i$ (we set a small learning rate to meet this condition in practice), we can compute the gradient as follows:

$$\frac{\partial \phi_n}{\partial \mathbf{d}_i} = \left[\mathbf{0}, \cdots, \frac{\partial \phi_{ni}}{\partial \mathbf{d}_i}, \cdots, \mathbf{0} \right], \tag{11}$$

$$\frac{\partial \phi_{ni}}{\partial \mathbf{v}_{ni}} = \frac{1}{\|\mathbf{v}_{ni}\|_2} (\mathbf{I} - \phi_{ni} \phi_{ni}^{\top}), \tag{12}$$

$$\frac{\partial \mathbf{v}_{ni}}{\partial \mathbf{d}_i} = -N_{ni} \mathbf{I}, \tag{13}$$

where $\mathbf{I} \in \mathcal{R}^{d \times d}$ is a unit matrix. Therefore, the gradient of E over $\mathbf{d}_i$ is given by:

$$\nabla_{\mathbf{d}_i} E = -\sum_{n=1}^{N} (f_n - y_n) \frac{N_{ni}(\mathbf{I} - \phi_{ni} \phi_{ni}^{\top})}{\|\mathbf{v}_{ni}\|_2} \mathbf{w}_{(i)}, \tag{14}$$

where $\mathbf{w}_{(i)}$ is the i-th block of $\mathbf{w}$ with the same size of $\mathbf{d}_i$.

As for multi-class problem, y_n and f_n are C dimensional vectors and the activation function is $f_{nc} = \exp(\mathbf{w}_c \phi_n) / \Sigma_{j=1}^{C} \exp(\mathbf{w}_j \phi_n)$. Using cross-entropy loss, the cost function with regularization is defined by:

$$E = -\sum_{n=1}^{N} \sum_{c=1}^{C} y_{nc} \ln f_{nc} + \lambda \|\mathbf{w}\|_2^2. \tag{15}$$

Applying the chain rule to compute the gradient of E over $\mathbf{d}_i$, we obtain:

$$\nabla_{\mathbf{d}_i} E = \sum_{n=1}^{N} \sum_{c=1}^{C} \frac{\partial \ell}{\partial f_{nc}} \frac{\partial f_{nc}}{\partial \phi_n} \frac{\partial \phi_n}{\partial \mathbf{d}_i} \tag{16}$$

$$= -\sum_{n=1}^{N} \frac{N_{ni}(\mathbf{I} - \phi_{ni} \phi_{ni}^{\top})}{\|\mathbf{v}_{ni}\|_2} \sum_{c=1}^{C} (f_{nc} - y_{nc}) \mathbf{w}_{(i)c}.$$

We summarize our supervised dictionary learning method for both binary and multi-class classification in Algorithm 1. The dictionary $\mathbf{D}$ is usually initialized by K-means from a subset of local descriptors.

Supervised Dictionary Learning with Spatial Pyramid. Spatial pyramid (SPM) is usually beneficial to image classification. Here we present the supervised dictionary learning method with spatial pyramid. Suppose M cells are used for the n-th sample, then the final VLAD representation with SPM is $\Phi_n = [\phi_n^1, ..., \phi_n^M]$. The predict model is then changed to $f(\Phi_n, \mathbf{w}) = \sigma(\sum_m \mathbf{w}^m \phi_n^m)$. Then, for the binary case, the gradient of E over $\mathbf{D}$ can be written as follows:

Algorithm 1. Supervised Dictionary Learning Algorithm for VLAD

Input : Local descriptors and labels in training data: $\{(\mathbf{X}_n, y_n)\}$. Parameters:
$\quad\quad$ K, $\lambda, \lambda_d, \lambda_w$

Output: Dictionary: $\mathbf{D}$, Predict Model: $\mathbf{w}$

Initialization: $\mathbf{D}^0 \leftarrow$ init by K-means, $\mathbf{w} \leftarrow$ randomly select from normal distribution;

0. Compute VLAD using $\mathbf{D}^0$
while $t < T$ *and* $\delta > \epsilon$ **do**
$\quad$| 1. Update $\mathbf{D}$ fix $\mathbf{w}$: $\mathbf{D}^t \leftarrow \mathbf{D}^{t-1} - \lambda_d \nabla_{\mathbf{d}_i} E$;
$\quad$| 2. Recompute VLAD using $\mathbf{D}^t$;
$\quad$| 3. Optimize $\mathbf{w}$ fix $\mathbf{D}$: $\arg\min_{\mathbf{w}} E$;
$\quad$| 4. $\delta \leftarrow$ error(t) - error(t-1);
end

$$\nabla_{\mathbf{d}_i} E = \sum_{n=1}^{N} \frac{\partial \ell}{\partial f_n} \sum_{m=1}^{M} \frac{\partial f_n}{\partial \phi_n^m} \frac{\partial \phi_n^m}{\partial \mathbf{d}_i}. \tag{17}$$

$$= -\sum_{n=1}^{N}(f_n - y_n) \sum_{m=1}^{M} \frac{N_{ni}^m (\mathbf{I} - \phi_{ni}^m \phi_{ni}^{m\top})}{\|\mathbf{v}_{ni}^m\|_2} \mathbf{w}_{(i)}^m,$$

where N_{ni}^m denotes the number of descriptors assigned to word $\mathbf{d}_i$ at the m-th cell in n-th sample. Similar with Algorithm 1, the desired dictionary and the model with spatial pyramid can be optimized alternately.

5   Experiments

We verify the effectiveness of our proposed method on two recognition tasks, namely visual object categorization (PASCAL VOC2007 [7]) and human action recognition (HMDB51 [17] and UCF101 [28]). In this section, we first conduct extensive experiments on PASCAL VOC 2007 to evaluate the performance of our H-VLAD and S-VLAD. And then we apply them to video-based action recognition with a large number of classes.

5.1   Evaluation on Object Classification

Our first and most extensive experiments are conducted on the well-known PAS-CAL VOC2007 dataset [7]. This challenge is known as one of the most difficult image classification tasks due to significant variations both in appearances and poses even with occlusions. It consists of about 10,000 images with 20 different object categories. There are 5,011 training images (train+val sets) and 4,952 test images. The performance is evaluated by the standard PASCAL protocol which computes average precision (AP) based on the precision-recall curve. We also report the mean of AP (mAP) over 20 categories.

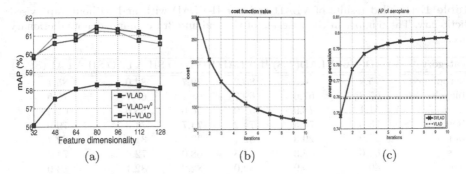

Fig. 3. (a) Performance of the VLAD and our H-VLAD with various local feature dimensionality on PASCAL VOC2007 without SPM. (b) The training cost curve for the supervised learning process. (c) The test accuracy curve of class aeroplane in the supervised learning process.

Implementation Details. We densely extract local SIFT descriptors with a spatial stride of 4 pixels at 9 scales, and the width of SIFT spatial bins is fixed as 8 pixels, which are the default parameters setting in the VLFeat toolbox [31], version 0.9.17. We learn dictionary from a subset of 256k SIFT descriptors. All descriptors are whitened after PCA processing. The regularized factor λ is fixed to 0.01, and the learning rates for D and w (λ_d and λ_w) are set to 0.001 and 0.01, respectively. To ensure the effective estimation, we compute high-order statistics only when N_i is larger than a threshold which is set to d (the same size as the dimension of feature) empirically. For all the encoding methods, the long vectors are post-processed by "power+intra" normalization. Note that during supervised dictionary learning process, no power-normalization is performed due to the gradient computation. As for SPM, we divide the image in $1 \times 1, 2 \times 2, 3 \times 1$ grids.

H-VLAD. Fig.3(a) illustrates the mAPs of VLAD, VLAD with the 2nd-order statistics, and H-VLAD (VLAD with 2nd and 3rd order statistics). The dictionary size are all fixed to 256 as common setting. All the approaches perform better when feature dimensionality increases, while reach the upper bounds at the dimension of 80. Adding the 2nd-order statistics boosts the performance (by 2.4%–3.8%) of original VLAD as expected. We find the result obtained by the single 2nd-order statistics (v^c) is inferior to that of VLAD by 1.5%–3.5% when testing them separately. We argue that the locations of the means from local descriptors are more discriminative than the distribution shapes of descriptors, and the distribution shapes contain complementary information to the mean of distribution, which is beneficial for classification. We also find the result from only usage of 3rd-order statistics is inferior to that of 2nd-order. Our H-VLAD is superior to the others when the dimensions are larger than 80. This indicates the skewness can provide complementary information to the 1st and 2nd statistics.

For fair comparison, we extend the dimension of VLAD to the same as that of H-VLAD by increasing dictionary size. The first three columns in Table 1 show the detailed results for each category in VOC2007 dataset. From the 2nd

Table 1. Detailed results of VLAD and our H-VLAD with and without supervised dictionary. The number in the brackets of the 2nd and 3rd columns denote dictionary size.

category	VLAD(256)	VLAD(768)	H–VLAD	S–VLAD	SH–VLAD	SH–VLAD(SPM)
aeroplane	75.9	76.5	80.3	79.7	84.0	85.1
bicycle	65.8	67.6	69.7	68.7	69.7	70.5
bird	51.1	48.9	55.9	50.6	55.6	61.5
boat	73.6	74.5	74.2	74.7	74.3	79.9
bottle	28.9	29.3	32.1	32.8	31.1	*32.1*
bus	63.6	62.3	64.8	68.0	72.4	74.0
car	80.3	79.9	82.0	82.2	82.1	83.0
cat	59.3	59.7	61.5	60.3	62.9	66.6
chair	52.1	55.6	53.6	53.2	54.5	57.9
cow	44.0	46.7	49.4	47.9	50.7	53.6
diningtable	50.5	49.2	55.5	53.2	59.5	61.1
dog	42.9	45.9	44.4	45.3	44.3	48.3
horse	78.8	79.6	81.0	81.3	81.9	83.7
motorbike	62.4	62.3	65.4	67.7	68.9	69.4
person	85.0	84.8	86.6	86.4	86.7	87.3
pottedplant	26.1	26.8	32.1	31.2	33.1	36.6
sheep	46.1	46.0	46.2	48.2	49.2	51.8
sofa	49.6	51.1	53.6	54.2	57.8	57.9
train	76.3	74.9	80.2	78.8	84.6	85.3
tvmonitor	52.8	54.2	55.2	54.3	57.9	58.9
mAP	58.3	58.8	61.2	60.9	63.1	65.2

column of Table 1, it is clear that the performance improvement is very limited from increasing dictionary size and our H-VLAD is also superior to VLAD with the same dimension.

Supervised Dictionary. We evaluate the impact of dictionary on VLAD and our S-VLAD algorithm by fixing the PCA dimensionality as 80. First, we test the performance of three random dictionaries (randomly selected SIFT descriptors) and the mAPs are [51.0%, 50.9%, 50.0%]. This result verifies the importance of a good dictionary. Then, we initialize the supervised dictionary by K-means with the size fixed to 256 and learn a supervised dictionary with logistic function. Fig. 3(b) and (c) illustrates the optimization process of S-VLAD for class "aeroplane". We plot the cost function value and AP for each iteration. As expected, the AP increases and the cost function value decreases during iteration. The improvement is limited when the iteration reaches 8. Therefore, we fix the iterations to 8 for all the categories.

The last three columns in Table 1 show the results of all the categories by using supervised dictionary for VLAD. The notation "SH-VLAD" denotes the combination of H-VLAD and S-VLAD. We only conduct supervised dictionary learning for VLAD in current implementation. The supervised dictionary for both VLAD and H-VLAD can improve the performance, and the improvements are 2.6% and 1.9% for VLAD and H-VLAD, respectively. The performance becomes even better when performing the proposed SH-VLAD with spatial pyramid scheme (the last column).

5.2   Application to Action Recognition

With the observation in VOC2007, we also perform experiments on the HMDB51 and UCF101 action datasets. The HMDB51 dataset [17] consists 51 action categories with 6,766 manually annotated clips which are extracted from a variety of sources ranging from digitized movies to YouTube. We follow the experimental settings in [17] and report the mean average accuracy over all classes. The UCF101 dataset [28] has been the largest action recognition dataset so far, and exhibits the highest diversity in terms of actions, with the presence of large variations in camera motion, object appearance and pose, object scale, viewpoint, cluttered background, illumination conditions and so on. It contains 13,320 videos collected from YouTube and includes total number of 101 action classes. We perform evaluation on three train/test splits [1] and report the mean average accuracy over all classes.

For both datasets, we densely extract improved trajectories using the code from Wang [33]. Each trajectory is described by HOG, HOF, and MBH descriptors. We reduce the descriptor dimensions by a factor of two using PCA+Whiten pre-processing. We use soft-max function in Algorithm 1 to learn dictionaries for each type of descriptor. All the super vectors are consistently normalized using the same strategy as VOC2007. To combine different features, we concatenate their final representations. A linear *one-vs-all* SVM with C=100 is used for classification.

Table 2 compares our methods with VLAD and the improved FV [23] on HMDB51 and UCF101 action datasets. For each individual type of features, our H–VLAD outperforms VLAD with a large margin on both datasets, and achieves very similar results as FV. This indicates the importance of high-order information. Supervised dictionaries are beneficial to recognition for all types of feature. Our SH–VLAD obtains best results on both datasets with a slight better than that of FV. Besides, we also present the time costs of VLAD, H–VLAD, and FV in Table 2. We implement these encoding methods in Matlab without any parallel processing and use KD-Tree to search the nearest neighbor for VLAD and H–VALD. We randomly select 10 videos, and compute the average cost per video for encoding all types of feature. Note that the dictionary does not affect the time cost in test phase. From Table 2, it is clear that the cost of our H–VLAD is very close to that of original VLAD, but largely lower than that of FV.

5.3   Comparison and Discussion

Table 3 compares our best results to several recently published results in the literature on each dataset. Our method outperforms these previously reported results on all datasets. As for VOC2007 dataset, the most similar performance

---

[1] http://crcv.ucf.edu/ICCV13-Action-Workshop/

Table 2. Performance and computational cost of VLAD, S–VLAD, H–VLAD, SH–VLAD, and FV on HMDB51 and UCF101 action datasets. Note that the time costs of VLAD and H–VLAD are largely less than that of FV.

| | HMDB51 | | | | | UCF101 | | | | |
	VLAD	H–VLAD	S–VLAD	SH–VLAD	FV	VLAD	H–VLAD	S–VLAD	SH–VLAD	FV
HOG	35.9	42.1	37.5	45.1	42.7	67.5	73.3	68.9	74.1	73.1
HOF	46.7	49.0	47.9	50.7	50.8	75.2	76.8	76.4	78.3	77.3
MBHx	38.4	43.0	44.4	44.1	44.3	70.2	76.0	74.6	76.6	75.1
MBHy	43.2	47.9	48.5	50.0	49.0	73.6	78.1	76.9	78.6	77.6
Combined	55.5	58.3	57.1	59.8	58.5	84.8	86.5	85.9	87.7	86.7
Time (s)	2.63	3.38	–	–.	57.21	–	–	–	–	–

Table 3. Comparison of our results to the state of the arts

| VOC 2007 | | HMDB51 | | UCF101 | |
Methods	mAP	Methods	Accuracy	Methods	Accuracy
winner (2007)	59.4%	iDT+FV[33] (2013)	57.2%	winner [14] (2013)	85.9%
[5] (2011)	61.7%	[35] (2013)	42.1%	[4] (2014)	83.5%
[24] (2012)	57.2%	[32] (2013)	46.6%	[37] (2014)	84.2%
[15] (2013)	62.2%	[25] (2013)	47.6%		
[38] (2013)	64.1%	[21] (2013)	52.1%		
Our result	**65.2%**	Our result	**59.8%**	Our result	**87.7%**

with ours comes from [38]. They applied a layered model to PHOG and SIFT features to obtain a desired mid-level representation, and learned this representation in a *supervised* way. Compared with [38], our approach only use SIFT descriptors and is simpler, but achieves better performance. This should be partly ascribed to high-dimensional representations we used. For the HMDB51 and UCF101 datasets, our approach improve the state-of-the-art performance (57.2% and 85.9%) [33] by 2.6% and 1.8%, respectively, which may be because of the supervised dictionary.

6   Conclusion

This paper first proposes to enhance the VLAD representation by aggregating high-order information of local descriptors, which is called H–VLAD. The covariance and skewness are demonstrated to be complementary with the original VLAD in our experiments. We then discuss the importance of a good dictionary and propose the supervised dictionary learning method for VLAD, which we refer to S–VLAD. Adding supervised dictionary can further boost the performance of VLAD. Theoretically, our supervised dictionary learning method can be easily extended for other super vector based methods. We verify the effectiveness of our method for the tasks of object and action recognition. We conduct experiments on three challenging benchmarks: PASCAL 2007, HMDB51, and UCF101, and conclude that our method achieves the state-of-the-art performance.

Acknowledgements. This work is partly supported by Natural Science Foundation of China (91320101, 61036008, 60972111), Shenzhen Basic Research Program (JC201005270350A, JCYJ20120903092050890, JCYJ201 20617114614438), 100 Talents Program of CAS, Guangdong Innovative Research Team Program (201001D0104648280), and Jiangxiao Peng is supported by the construct program of the key discipline in Hunan province. Yu Qiao is the corresponding author.

References

1. Arandjelovic, R., Zisserman, A.: All about VLAD. In: CVPR (2013)
2. Bengio, Y., Courville, A.C., Vincent, P.: Representation learning: A review and new perspectives. TPAMI 35(8) (2013)
3. Boureau, Y.L., Bach, F., LeCun, Y., Ponce, J.: Learning mid-level features for recognition. In: CVPR (2010)
4. Cai, Z., Wang, L., Peng, X., Qiao, Y.: Multi-view super vector for action recognition. In: CVPR (2014)
5. Chatfield, K., Lempitsky, V.S., Vedaldi, A., Zisserman, A.: The devil is in the details: An evaluation of recent feature encoding methods. In: BMVC (2011)
6. Delhumeau, J., Gosselin, P.H., Jégou, H., Pérez, P., et al.: Revisiting the vlad image representation. In: ACM MM (2013)
7. Everingham, M., Van Gool, L., Williams, C.K.I., Winn, J., Zisserman, A.: The PASCAL Visual Object Classes Challenge 2007 (VOC 2007) Results (2007)
8. Gong, Y., Wang, L., Guo, R., Lazebnik, S.: Multi-scale orderless pooling of deep convolutional activation features. CoRR abs/1403.1840 (2014)
9. Hogg, R.V., Craig, A.: Introduction to mathematical statistics (1994)
10. Jaakkola, T., Haussler, D., et al.: Exploiting generative models in discriminative classifiers. In: NIPS (1999)
11. Jain, M., Jégou, H., Bouthemy, P.: Better exploiting motion for better action recognition. In: CVPR (2013)
12. Jégou, H., Perronnin, F., Douze, M., Schmid, C., et al.: Aggregating local image descriptors into compact codes. TPAMI (2012)
13. Jia, Y., Darrell, T.: Heavy-tailed distances for gradient based image descriptors. In: NIPS (2011)
14. Jiang, Y.G., Liu, J., Roshan Zamir, A., Laptev, I., Piccardi, M., Shah, M., Sukthankar, R.: THUMOS challenge: Action recognition with a large number of classes (2013), http://crcv.ucf.edu/ICCV13-Action-Workshop/
15. Kobayashi, T.: BoF meets HOG: Feature extraction based on histograms of oriented pdf gradients for image classification. In: CVPR (2013)
16. Krizhevsky, A., Sutskever, I., Hinton, G.E.: Imagenet classification with deep convolutional neural networks. In: NIPS (2012)
17. Kuehne, H., Jhuang, H., Garrote, E., Poggio, T., Serre, T.: HMDB: A large video database for human motion recognition. In: ICCV (2011)
18. LeCun, Y., Bottou, L., Bengio, Y., Haffner, P.: Gradient-based learning applied to document recognition. Proceedings of the IEEE 86(11) (1998)
19. Liu, L., Wang, L., Liu, X.: In defense of soft-assignment coding. In: ICCV (2011)
20. Lowe, D.G.: Distinctive image features from scale-invariant keypoints. IJCV (2004)
21. Mihir, J., Jegou, H., Bouthemy, P.: Better exploiting motion for better action recognition. In: CVPR (2013)

22. Peng, X., Wang, L., Wang, X., Qiao, Y.: Bag of visual words and fusion methods for action recognition: Comprehensive study and good practice. CoRR abs/1405.4506 (2014)

23. Perronnin, F., Sánchez, J., Mensink, T.: Improving the fisher kernel for large-scale image classification. In: Daniilidis, K., Maragos, P., Paragios, N. (eds.) ECCV 2010, Part IV. LNCS, vol. 6314, pp. 143–156. Springer, Heidelberg (2010)

24. Russakovsky, O., Lin, Y., Yu, K., Fei-Fei, L.: Object-centric spatial pooling for image classification. In: Fitzgibbon, A., Lazebnik, S., Perona, P., Sato, Y., Schmid, C. (eds.) ECCV 2012, Part II. LNCS, vol. 7573, pp. 1–15. Springer, Heidelberg (2012)

25. Shi, F., Petriu, E., Laganiere, R.: Sampling strategies for real-time action recognition. In: CVPR (2013)

26. Simonyan, K., Zisserman, A.: Two-stream convolutional networks for action recognition in videos. CoRR abs/1406.2199 (2014)

27. Sivic, J., Zisserman, A.: Video google: A text retrieval approach to object matching in videos. In: ICCV (2003)

28. Soomro, K., Zamir, A.R., Shah, M.: UCF101: A dataset of 101 human actions classes from videos in the wild. ArXiv:1212.0402 (2012)

29. Sydorov, V., Sakurada, M., Lampert, C.H.: Deep fisher kernels - end to end learning of the fisher kernel gmm parameters. In: CVPR (2014)

30. Tariq, U., Yang, J., Huang, T.S.: Maximum margin gmm learning for facial expression recognition. In: FG Workshops (2013)

31. Vedaldi, A., Fulkerson, B.: VLFeat: An open and portable library of computer vision algorithms (2008)

32. Wang, H., Kläser, A., Schmid, C., Liu, C.L.: Dense trajectories and motion boundary descriptors for action recognition. IJCV (2013)

33. Wang, H., Schmid, C., et al.: Action recognition with improved trajectories. In: ICCV (2013)

34. Wang, J., Yang, J., Yu, K., Lv, F., Huang, T., Gong, Y.: Locality-constrained linear coding for image classification. In: CVPR (2010)

35. Wang, L., Qiao, Y., Tang, X.: Motionlets: Mid-level 3D parts for human motion recognition. In: CVPR (2013)

36. Wang, X., Wang, L., Qiao, Y.: A comparative study of encoding, pooling and normalization methods for action recognition. In: ACCV (2012)

37. Wu, J., Zhang, Y., Lin, W.: Towards good practices for action video encoding. In: CVPR (2014)

38. Wu, R., Yu, Y., Wang, W.: Scale: Supervised and cascaded laplacian eigenmaps for visual object recognition based on nearest neighbors. In: CVPR (2013)

39. Yang, J., Yu, K., Gong, Y., Huang, T.: Linear spatial pyramid matching using sparse coding for image classification. In: CVPR (2009)

40. Zhou, X., Yu, K., Zhang, T., Huang, T.S.: Image classification using super-vector coding of local image descriptors. In: Daniilidis, K., Maragos, P., Paragios, N. (eds.) ECCV 2010, Part V. LNCS, vol. 6315, pp. 141–154. Springer, Heidelberg (2010)

Recognizing Complex Events in Videos by Learning Key Static-Dynamic Evidences

Kuan-Ting Lai[1,2], Dong Liu[3], Ming-Syan Chen[1,2], and Shih-Fu Chang[3]

[1] Graduate Institute of Electrical Engineering, National Taiwan University, Taiwan
[2] Research Center for IT Innovation, Academia Sinica, Taiwan
[3] Department of Electrical Engineering, Columbia University, USA
{ktlai,mschen}@arbor.ee.ntu.edu.tw, {dongliu,sfchang}@ee.columbia.edu

Abstract. Complex events consist of various human interactions with different objects in diverse environments. The evidences needed to recognize events may occur in short time periods with variable lengths and can happen anywhere in a video. This fact prevents conventional machine learning algorithms from effectively recognizing the events. In this paper, we propose a novel method that can automatically identify the key evidences in videos for detecting complex events. Both static instances (objects) and dynamic instances (actions) are considered by sampling frames and temporal segments respectively. To compare the characteristic power of heterogeneous instances, we embed static and dynamic instances into a multiple instance learning framework via instance similarity measures, and cast the problem as an Evidence Selective Ranking (ESR) process. We impose ℓ_1 norm to select key evidences while using the Infinite Push Loss Function to enforce positive videos to have higher detection scores than negative videos. The Alternating Direction Method of Multipliers (ADMM) algorithm is used to solve the optimization problem. Experiments on large-scale video datasets show that our method can improve the detection accuracy while providing the unique capability in discovering key evidences of each complex event.

Keywords: Video Event Detection, Infinite Push, Key Evidence Selection, ADMM.

1 Introduction

Recognizing complex multimedia event in videos is becoming increasingly important in the field of computer vision. In 2010, the TREC Video Retrieval Evaluation (TRECVID) [15] Multimedia Event Detection (MED) evaluation task defined a wide range of complex events, and spurred broad research interests in the computer vision community. These complex events include "attempting board trick", "landing a fish", "changing a vehicle tire", and "flash mob gathering", to name a few. In contrast to the human activity videos in action recognition [19], which mainly focus on a single person's simple motions in the 5 to 10 seconds short video clips, the complex event videos consist of various interactions of human actions and objects in different scenes, and may last from

D. Fleet et al. (Eds.): ECCV 2014, Part III, LNCS 8691, pp. 675–688, 2014.
© Springer International Publishing Switzerland 2014

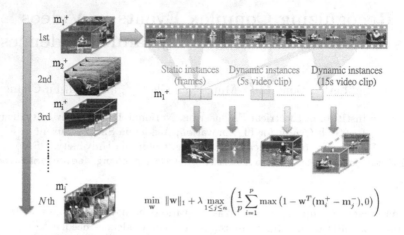

Fig. 1. The proposed Evidence Selective Ranking (ESR) framework. The static/dynamic instances of variable lengths are first extracted from a video, and mapped to a pre-learnt static/dynamic instance codebook via maximum similarity measure (instance embedding). The heterogeneous embedded vectors are then concatenated and trained by Infinite Push loss function with ℓ_1 norm to select the key evidences while enforcing positive videos to have higher detection scores.

several minutes to even an hour. Therefore, it is challenging to develop robust event detection models that can precisely capture the essential information in event videos.

Although many algorithms have been proposed to recognize complex events [8], the most popular method is still aggregating the raw audio/visual/motion features extracted from the videos into different variants of Bag-of-Words (BoW) histogram, and then feed it into sophisticated statistical learning models for event modeling. However, the main issue with this strategy is that it treats different components of a long event video as equally important, and ignores the fact that an event video may contain significant amount of background components that have no direct association with the target event. In fact, a complex event can usually be recognized by spotting a few key static and/or dynamic evidences [2]. For example, a "wedding ceremony" video can be correctly detected by successfully identifying several static frames containing *bride* and *groom*, while a "attempting bike trick" video can be detected by spotting some dynamic short segments containing the activity of *jumping with a bike*.

This motivates us to develop a method that is able to identify the key static-dynamic evidences in event videos and leverage them for improving the overall performance of event detection. Nevertheless, this is a nontrivial task due to the following reasons. First, given a complex event video, there are large amounts of frames and video segments that can be potential evidences, and the characteristic power of heterogeneous instances cannot be directly compared. To address those issues, we employ the instance embedding method [4] to map different kinds of instances into pre-learnt instance codebooks and concatenate the

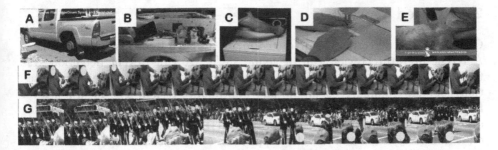

Fig. 2. Some of the top key event evidences selected by our method. (A) to (E) are static instances, while (F), (G) are dynamic instances with 15 and 10 seconds length. (A) is changing a tire; (B), (C) are fixing an appliance; (D) is sewing project; (E), (F) are grooming animals; (G) is parade.

embedded vectors. Specifically, given an event video set, we first sample frames from each video as static instances and short video segments at varied length as the dynamic instances. The static and dynamic instances are then clustered respectively to form the static and dynamic instance codebooks. Finally, we map all static/dynamic instances in a video onto the static/dynamic instance codebook, in which the value of each static/dynamic codeword is determined by the maximal similarity between all static/dynamic instances and the codeword. In this way, we end up with a compact heterogeneous instance representation that comprehensively encodes static and dynamic instances in each video.

Second, even after we have a compact instance representation, we need to investigate novel solutions that can select most distinctive evidences (positive instances) from videos and effectively utilize the information to detect complex events. Indeed, the video event detection task can be seen as a ranking process that aims at assigning higher detection scores to positive videos than negative videos. This inspires us to formulate event detection problem as an Evidence Selective Ranking (ESR) procedure, which discovers the key static-dynamic evidences in event videos while directly enforcing positive videos to have the highest scores in the detection results. Specifically, a ℓ_1-norm is first imposed to induce sparsity on the heterogeneous instance representation and determine a subset of dimensions. To ensure that the positive videos have the highest detection scores, we use $\ell_{1,\infty}$ infinite push loss to maximize the number of positive videos having higher detection scores than the negative videos. With this evidence selective ranking process, we can identify the key static-dynamic evidences while pushing the positive videos to rank at higher positions in the ranking list of detection result. Figure 1 illustrates the framework of our proposed method.

In the following sections, we will demonstrate experimentally that the proposed ESR method can achieve significant performance gains over various video event detection benchmarks. We will also show that our method is able to reveal the key static-dynamic evidences for identifying a video event (see Figure 2).

2 Related Work

Complex event detection has attracted many research interests in recent years. A recent literature review can be found in [8]. A video event detection system usually consists of the following procedures: feature extraction, quantization/pooling, training/recognition, and multimodal fusion. The local low-level features include static features, spatio-temporal features and audio features. Recently the Dense Trajectory based Features (DTF) [24] achieved great results on action recognition and is widely applied in event detection system. In terms of training/recognition approaches, the current methods can be roughly categorized into large margin based methods, graphical models, and knowledge based techniques. The commonly used method is baesd on large margin framework with kernel techniques. Most previous methods represent video as an aggregated global feature vector and train the event model with SVM [8,12,20]. However, as aforementioned, these approaches treat all evidences in videos as equally important and cannot effectively leverage the key evidences to improve the detection performance. To alleviate the above issue, some existing works exploited the short segments in event videos to improve event detection performance. Cao *et al.* [3] proposed a scene aligned pooling method for video representation. The basic assumption in this method is that a video clip is often composed of segments of different scenes, and this motivates the authors to perform video feature pooling within the individual scenes. However, the main focus of this work is to obtain a robust video feature pooling result, and cannot judiciously select the key evidences in event videos as our method does. Similarly, Li *et al* [10] proposed a Dynamic Pooling method for event detection, in which an event video is decomposed into short segments, and the most informative segments for detecting this event are identified through latent variable inference and used for video feature pooling. Differently, our method focuses on selecting the most informative evidences in videos, which goes beyond feature pooling procedure and achieves better performance than the method in [10] (see Table 2).

One available solution for learning key evidences in videos is Multiple Instance Learning (MIL). Initially MIL was introduced to solve drug design problem [5]. The labels are given to bags (drugs) instead of to the instances (molecules) inside. A bag is labeled as positive if at least one of its instance is positive, or negative if all its instances are negatives. This assumption works well for drug design because only one molecule form works for a drug. But in computer vision applications, the positive and negative bags may share some visual cues in common, and the above assumption is typically not true. In contrary, our method based on instance embedding [4,6] does not make any assumption on the instances in videos, and directly chooses any number of the most useful instances for event modeling.

Methodologically, our method adopts learning-to-rank algorithm to perform video event detection. One classic large-margin ranking algorithm that can be applied is Ranking SVM [9]. However, it focuses on optimizing pairwise ranking accuracy without considering the entire ranking list. Newly developed ranking algorithms, such as p-norm push [18] and Infinite Push [16], put emphasis on optimizing the accuracy at the top of the rank list, which is more suitable for event detection. Inspired by the Infinite Push ranking [1], which is the generalization bound of l_p norm push, we utilize the infinite push model to ensure a good ranking in the video detection results.

3   Evidence Selective Ranking for Video Event Detection

3.1   Compact Heterogeneous Instance Representation

Suppose there is an event video collection $\mathcal{X} = \{X_i\}_{i=1}^N$ with N videos, where $X_i = \{S_i \bigcup D_i\}$ is a video consisting of a static instance subset $S_i = \{\mathbf{s}_{i1}, \ldots, \mathbf{s}_{i,n_i}\}$ with n_i static frames and a dynamic instance subset $D_i = \{\mathbf{d}_{i1}, \mathbf{d}_{i2}, \ldots, \mathbf{d}_{i,m_i}\}$ with m_i dynamic segments. Here $\mathbf{s}_{ij} \in \mathbb{R}^{k_s}$ and $\mathbf{d}_{ij} \in \mathbb{R}^{k_d}$ are respectively the feature vector of the j-th static and dynamic instance of video X_i with k_s and k_d being the feature dimensionality. Furthermore, we collect all frames and segments into a static instance set $S = \{S_i\}_{i=1}^N$ and a dynamic instance set $\mathcal{D} = \{D_i\}_{i=1}^N$.

We first construct codebooks for the static and dynamic instance set respectively. Specifically, we perform K-means clustering to partition S and $\mathcal{D}$ into G_s and G_d clusters, and treat each cluster center as one codeword. We define $\mathcal{V}_s = \{\mathbf{c}_1^s, \ldots, \mathbf{c}_{G_s}^s\}$ and $\mathcal{V}_d = \{\mathbf{c}_1^d, \ldots, \mathbf{c}_{G_d}^d\}$ as the static and dynamic codebooks, where $\mathbf{c}_i^s \in \mathbb{R}^{k_s}$ ($\mathbf{c}_i^d \in \mathbb{R}^{k_d}$) is the i-th codeword in static (dynamic) codebook.

Next, the static and dynamic instances in a video are mapped onto their respective codebooks to generate the heterogeneous instance representation. In this work, we apply a similarity embedding method in [4] to effectively encode multiple instances in a video onto each codeword. Given the static instance set S_i of video X_i, its encoding value on the l-th static codeword $\mathbf{c}_l^s$ is defined as:

$$s(S_i, \mathbf{c}_l^s) = \max_{1 \leq j \leq n_i} \exp\left(-\frac{d(\mathbf{s}_{ij}, \mathbf{c}_l^s)}{\sigma}\right), \tag{1}$$

where $d(\mathbf{s}_{ij}, \mathbf{c}_l^s)$ is the χ^2 distance function which measures the distance between an instance $\mathbf{s}_{ij}$ and codeword $\mathbf{c}_l^s$. σ is the radius parameter of the Gaussian function, which is set as the mean value of all pairwise distances among the static instances. The encoding value of the dynamic instance set D_i of video X_i can be calculated in a similar way. In the end, video X_i is encoded as a compact static-dynamic instance vector $\mathbf{m}_i \in \mathbb{R}^{G_s + G_d}$:

$$\mathbf{m}_i = [s(S_i, \mathbf{c}_1^s), \ldots, s(S_i, \mathbf{c}_{G_s}^s), s(D_i, \mathbf{c}_1^d), \ldots, s(D_i, \mathbf{c}_{G_d}^d)]^\top. \tag{2}$$

In the heterogeneous instance representation, each codeword in static/dynamic codebook characterizes a consistent static/dynamic pattern. When mapping the static/dynamic instances in a video onto one codeword, we use the maximum similarity to choose the most similar instance to generate the encoding value. This essentially measures the maximal coherence between the instances in a video and one pattern in the entire video set, and thus achieves robust heterogeneous instance representation.

3.2   Evidence Selective Ranking

Given an event category, assume we have a labeled training video set $\{\mathbf{m}_i, y_i\}_{i=1}^{V}$ with V videos, in which $\mathbf{m}_i$ is the static-dynamic evidence vector of the i-th video, and $y_i \in \{0, 1\}$ is the event label. To ease the following presentation, we partition all labeled training videos into a positive subset $\mathcal{P} = \{\mathbf{m}_i^+\}_{i=1}^{p}$ and a negative subset $\mathcal{N} = \{\mathbf{m}_i^-\}_{i=1}^{n}$, where $\mathbf{m}_i^+$ and $\mathbf{m}_i^-$ denote the evidence vector of a positive video and a negative video. p and n are respectively the total number of positive and negative training videos.

We want to learn an event detection function $f(\mathbf{m}) = \mathbf{w}^\top \mathbf{m}$, where $\mathbf{w} \in \mathbb{R}^{G_s+G_k}$ is the parameter vector. Our evidence selective ranking based event detection method is formulated as follows:

$$\min_{\mathbf{w}} \quad \|\mathbf{w}\|_1 + \lambda \ell(\mathcal{P}, \mathcal{N}; \mathbf{w}), \tag{3}$$

where λ is a tradeoff parameter among the two terms. The first term is a ℓ_1 norm induced sparse regularization on the heterogeneous instance representation that explicitly selects a subset of codeword dimensions. Such selected dimensions can be used to identify the key evidences in each event video. Specifically, given a selected dimension, the corresponding key evidence in a video is actually the instance that has been used to generate the encoding value on this dimension (i.e., the one which has maximal similarity with the corresponding codeword of this given dimension).

The second term is a ranking loss function, which is used to penalize a mis-ranked pair in which the negative video has higher detection score than the positive one. In principle, we can instantiate this loss with any loss function in the learning-to-rank algorithms. In this work, we choose the recently introduced Infinite Push loss function as the loss function in our model due to its outstanding performance [1]. The objective of Infinite Push is to maximize the number of positive videos on the absolute top positions of the entire video rank list, without paying too much attention about getting an accurate ranking order among other parts of the list, which perfectly matches the goal of video event detection.

To design the Infinite Push loss function, the authors notice that maximizing positive videos at top is equivalent to minimize the number of positive videos scored lower than the highest-scored negative video. Furthermore, the number of positive videos scored lower than the highest-scored negative video is equivalent to the largest number of positive training videos scored lower than any negative video, which is a fraction of the total number of positive videos p and can be defined as:

$$\ell(\mathcal{P}, \mathcal{N}; \mathbf{w}) = \max_{1 \leq j \leq n} \left(\frac{1}{p} \sum_{i=1}^{p} I_{\mathbf{w}^T \mathbf{m}_i^+ < \mathbf{w}^T \mathbf{m}_j^-} \right), \tag{4}$$

where $I_{(\cdot)}$ is the indicator function which is 1 if the argument is true or 0 otherwise. Directly optimizing Eq. (4) is infeasible due to its discrete nature. Therefore, it is relaxed into a convex upper bound as below:

$$\ell(\mathcal{P}, \mathcal{N}; \mathbf{w}) = \max_{1 \leq j \leq n} \left(\frac{1}{p} \sum_{i=1}^{p} \max\left(1 - \mathbf{w}^\top (\mathbf{m}_i^+ - \mathbf{m}_j^-), 0\right) \right), \tag{5}$$

Based on the above definition, the objective function can be rewritten as:

$$\min_{\mathbf{w}} \ \|\mathbf{w}\|_1 + \lambda \max_{1 \le j \le n} \left(\frac{1}{p} \sum_{i=1}^{p} \max \left(1 - \mathbf{w}^T(\mathbf{m}_i^+ - \mathbf{m}_j^-), 0 \right) \right), \tag{6}$$

The above objective function is actually the sparse support vector Infinite Push recently proposed in [17], which is convex and thus can achieve global optimum. In the next subsection, we will elaborate on the optimization procedure.

3.3 Optimization Procedure

We directly adopt the Alternating Direction Method of Multipliers (ADMM) iterative optimization procedure in [17] to solve the optimization problem. The objective function is first rewritten as the following linearly-constrained problem:

$$\min_{\mathbf{w},\{a_{ij}\}} \ \|\mathbf{w}\|_1 + \lambda \max_{1 \le j \le n} \left(\frac{1}{p} \sum_{i=1}^{p} \max(a_{ij}, 0) \right), \tag{7}$$

$$\text{s.t.,} \quad a_{i,j} = 1 - \mathbf{w}^\top(\mathbf{m}_i^+ - \mathbf{m}_j^-).$$

By defining matrix $\mathbf{M}$ whose rows are of the form $(\mathbf{m}_i^+ - \mathbf{m}_j^-)^\top$, vector $\mathbf{a}$ composing of all α_{ij}'s and function $g(\mathbf{a}) = \lambda \max_j(\frac{1}{p} \sum_i \max(a_{ij}, 0))$, the optimization can be rewritten as :

$$\min_{\mathbf{w},\mathbf{a}} \ \|\mathbf{w}\|_1 + g(\mathbf{a}), \tag{8}$$

$$\text{s.t.,} \quad \mathbf{Mw} + \mathbf{a} - 1 = 0.$$

The augmented Lagrangian of the above problem is:

$$\mathcal{L}(\mathbf{w}, \mathbf{a}, \delta, \mu) = \|\mathbf{w}\|_1 + g(\mathbf{a}) + \delta^\top(\mathbf{Mw} + \mathbf{a} - 1) + \frac{\mu}{2}\|\mathbf{Mw} + \mathbf{a} - 1\|^2, \tag{9}$$

where δ is a vector of Lagrangian multipliers for the equality constraint, and μ is a parameter of quadratic penalty setting as 10^{-4} according to the suggestion in ADMM procedure. The formula can be rearranged as:

$$\mathcal{L}(\mathbf{w}, \mathbf{a}, \gamma) = \|\mathbf{w}\|_1 + g(\mathbf{a}) + \frac{\mu}{2}\|\mathbf{Mw} + \mathbf{a} - 1 + \gamma\|^2, \tag{10}$$

where $\gamma = \frac{\delta}{\mu}$. Finally, the problem can be solved alternatively at iteration k the following subproblems:

$$\mathbf{w}^{k+1} = \arg\min_{w} \mathcal{L}(\mathbf{w}, \mathbf{a}^k, \gamma^k), \tag{11}$$

$$\mathbf{a}^{k+1} = \arg\min_{a} \mathcal{L}(\mathbf{w}^{k+1}, \mathbf{a}, \gamma^k), \tag{12}$$

$$\gamma^{k+1} = \gamma^k + \mathbf{Mw} + \mathbf{a} - 1. \tag{13}$$

In particular, subproblem in Eq. (11) can be solved as a standard Lasso problem. Subproblem in Eq. (12) can be solved by first decoupling $\mathbf{a}$ into $\mathbf{a}^+$ and $\mathbf{a}^-$, and then solving them by Block Coordinate Descent as introduced in [17]. ADMM has a fast convergence rate of $O(1/t)$, where t is the iteration number. The running time of ESR will be reported in our experiments.

4   Experiments

In this section, we will evaluate the effectiveness of our Evidence Selective Ranking (ESR) method over the currently largest video datasets: TRECVID Multimedia Event Detection (MED) 2011 and 2012. In MED evaluation tasks, the test events of each year include events from pervious years. There are 15 events in MED 2011 and 25 events in MED 2012, which are listed in Table 1. We compare our ESR method with (1) Static instance (ST-inst) only. (2) Dynamic instances (Dyn-inst) only. (3) MILES [4], which is based on instance embedding and ℓ_1 SVM feature selection. We train an event model with a binary SVM classifier after the features are selected, and (4) The state-of-the-art event detection methods.

To generate the static instances, we extract frames from each video every 2 seconds and scale them down to 320×240 pixels. Then the SIFT features [11] are extracted by dense SIFT function in VLFeat library [23] with a 10-pixel step. Finally, each frame is represented as a $5,000$-dimensional SIFT BoW. The dynamic instances are generated by applying the sliding window approach to each video clip. We consider 5 kinds of video segments with different lengths as all dynamic instances in a video, in which we adopt 3, 5, 10, 15, 20 seconds sliding windows with 2, 3, 7, 10, 15 seconds overlapping to extract segments. For static and each of the 5 dynamic instances, the Yael K-means library [7] is used to learn a codebook with $5,000$ codewords. The final static-dynamic video instance vector is the concatenation of all encoding values over all 6 kinds of codebooks, which has $30,000$ feature dimensions in total.

To evaluate the performance of each method, the Average Precision (AP) is employed as the evaluation metric. Regarding the parameter setting, we use

Table 1. The 25 events defined in TRECVID MED 2011 and 2012

ID	MED 2011 Events	ID	MED 2012 Events
1	Attempting board trick	16	Attempting bike trick
2	Feeding animals	17	Cleaning appliance
3	Landing a fish	18	Dog show
4	Wedding ceremony	19	Give directions to location
5	Woodworking project	20	Marriage proposal
6	Birthday party	21	Renovating a home
7	Changing a tire	22	Rock climbing
8	Flash mob gathering	23	Town hall meeting
9	Getting vehicle unstuck	24	Win race without a vehicle
10	Grooming animal	25	Work on metal craft project
11	Making sandwich		
12	Parade		
13	Parkour		
14	Repairing appliance		
15	Work on sewing project		

3-fold cross-validation and vary the value of parameter $\lambda = \{0.1, 1, 10\}$ in the objective function to determine the appropriate parameter for each method.

4.1 Experiment on TRECVID MED 2011

The official MED 2011 dataset consists of three data splits: Event Collection (EC), the development collection (DEVT) and test collection (DEVO). The EC set contains $2,680$ training videos over 15 events. The DEVT set includes $10,403$ videos and is provided for participants to validate their systems. The DEVO set containing $32,061$ test videos is used to evaluate final performance. In MED 2011, the length of the videos ranges from several seconds to one hour. In this experiment, we follow these official data splits, in which we use EC and DEVT set to train/validate and use DEVO set to test. Notice that DEVO set does not include any videos of Event 1 to Event 5, so only test results of Event 6 to Event 15 are reported. Empirically we can achieve satisfactory results within only 5 iterations, so we set the max iterations of our ESR to 5 to save running time. The average running time of ESR for each MED11 event on a single Intel Xeon 2.67GHz core is around one hour.

Figure 4 and Table 2 show the performance of different methods in comparison, in which Table 2 mainly quotes the state-of-the-art results in literature. These results are from the recent proposed methods including DMS [13], VD-HMM [21], dynamic pooling with segment-pairs (SPP) [10] and multiple kernel latent SVM (MKL-KLSVM) [22], each of which follows the same setting of the official MED 11 data splits.

Table 2. The APs of different methods on TRECVID MED11 DEVO dataset

Event Name (006 - 015)	DMS [13]	VD-HMM [21]	SPP [10]	MKL-KLSVM[22]	MILES (SVM-$l1$)	Our Method
Birthday party	2.25%	4.38%	6.08%	6.24%	5.08%	**7.45%**
Change a vehicle tire	0.76%	0.92%	3.96%	**24.62%**	9.50%	14.44%
Flash mob gathering	8.30%	15.29%	35.28%	37.46%	33.77%	**40.87%**
Get a vehicle. unstuck	1.95%	2.04%	8.45%	**15.72%**	7.38%	7.72%
Groom an animal	0.74%	0.74%	**3.05%**	2.09%	1.76%	1.83%
Make a sandwich	1.48%	0.84%	4.95%	**7.65%**	3.13%	4.86%
Parade	2.65%	4.03%	8.95%	12.01%	14.34%	**17.69%**
Parkour	2.05%	3.04%	24.62%	10.96%	20.14%	**25.3%**
Repair an appliance	4.39%	10.88%	19.81%	**32.67%**	25.81%	31.75%
Work on sewing project	0.61%	5.48%	6.53%	7.49%	4.66%	**8.34%**
mean AP	2.52%	4.77%	12.27%	15.69%	12.56%	**16.02%**

From the results, we have the following observations: (1) The proposed ESR method produces better results than all other methods in comparison, which demonstrates its effectiveness in the task of video event detection. (2) The ESR method performs significantly better than the single instance based methods, and (3) Our ESR method shows performance improvement over MILES method that detects videos based on SVM classifier instead of the infinite push ranking model. This verifies the benefits of introducing ranking model to event detection task. Notice that some new proposed technique like Fisher vector can be adopted in our framework and further improve the recognition accuracy [14].

As mentioned, one advantage of our method is that it is capable of locating the selected key evidences in each video for further visualization and analysis. Recall that, although the instances in a video are embedded into instance codebook space, the selected instances can be located simply by searching the instances with maximum similarities to the instance codebook in a video. Using this method, Figure 3 shows three of top evidences with the largest weights in the videos of some exemplary events, in which the static evidence is represented as a frame and the dynamic evidence is represented as a sequence of successive frames in the selected key segment. As can be seen, for "flash mob gathering" and "parade", the most distinctive event evidences are dynamic instances; for "change vehicle tire", "fix an appliance", and "sewing project", the selected event evidences are mainly static frames. These selected evidences are interpretable for human and useful for analyzing event videos.

To study the influences of the length of the video segments, we generate video segments with length of 3, 5, 10, 15 and 20, and use each kind of segments as dynamic instances to run our ESR method. We compare these results with our proposal that mixes segments of different lengths together, and the results can be shown in Figure 5. From the results, we can see that when there is only one fixed length dynamic instance for evidence selection, the 3-second and 5-second short video segments achieve best results on most events. However, using mixed length segments as dynamic instances always generates better performance than others, which confirms the soundness of our proposed dynamic evidence generation strategy.

In Figure 6, we further plot the proportions of each kind of evidences (both static and dynamic) selected from training videos of each MED11 event. As shown, event "flash mob gathering", "getting vehicle unstuck", and "grooming animals" have higher proportion of dynamic evidences, while "birthday party", "changing a tire" and "working on sewing project" have selected more static evidences. The evidence proportion distributions are intuitive to human and further show the advantages of our method.

4.2   TRECVID MED 2012

The MED12 dataset contains 25 complex events as shown in Table 1, which includes 15 events in MED11. The total training videos of the 25 events is 5, 816 videos. We choose two thirds of the data as training set (3, 878 videos) and use the rest as test set (1, 938 videos). In this experiment, we follow the same setting as we did in MED11. The APs of MED12 events are shown in Figure 7. The average running time of ESR is similar to MED11 events since the dimensions of heterogenous instance vectors are the same. Once again, the experiment results confirm the effectiveness of our proposed event detection method.

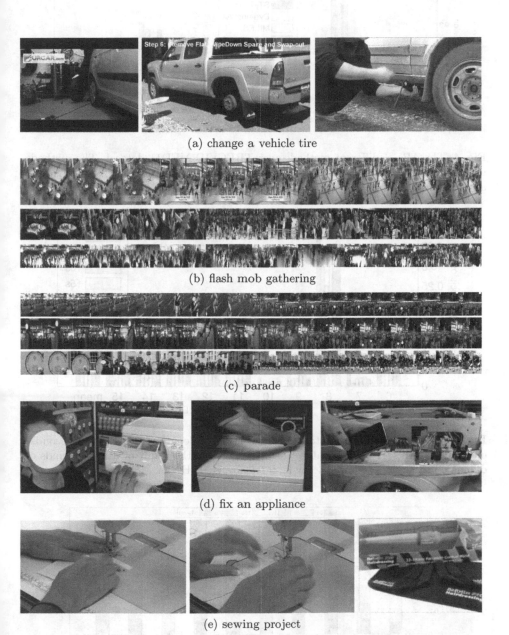

(a) change a vehicle tire

(b) flash mob gathering

(c) parade

(d) fix an appliance

(e) sewing project

Fig. 3. The top static/dynamic evidences selected for identifying target events

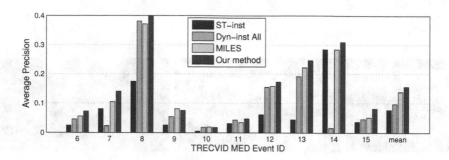

Fig. 4. The APs of different methods over TRECVID MED11 dataset. The methods in comparison include static instance only (ST-inst), all dynamic instances (Dyn-inst all), MILES with ℓ_1 SVM based feature selection and our ESR method.

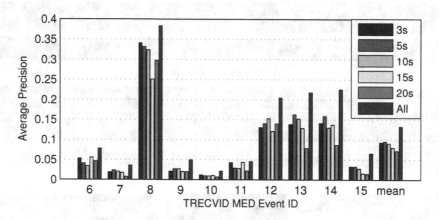

Fig. 5. The APs of dynamic instances with varied time lengths (3, 5, 7, 15, 20 seconds) on TRCVID MED11 DEVO dataset. "All" represents the result of using all kinds of dynamic instances. The applied low-level feature is MBH [25].

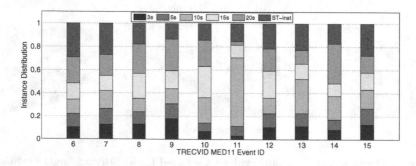

Fig. 6. The distribution of selected key evidences for MED11 events. The region in red represents the proportion of static instance (ST-inst), while others represent dynamic instance with different time length.

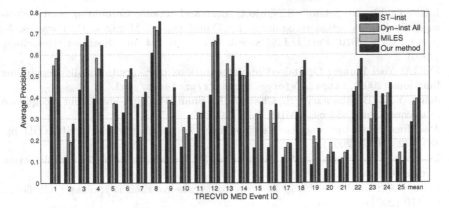

Fig. 7. The APs of different methods over TRECVID MED12 dataset. The methods in comparison include static instance only (ST-inst), all dynamic instances (Dyn-inst all), MILES with ℓ_1 SVM based feature selection and our ESR method.

5   Conclusion

We have proposed a novel event detection method by selecting key static-dynamic evidences from video content. To represent the static and dynamic evidences in videos, we encode the static frames and dynamic video segments into a compact heterogeneous instance representation through codebook generation and similarity mapping. Then a novel Infinite Push Ranking algorithm with ℓ_1-norm regularization is applied to simultaneously select the most useful evidences and rank positive videos at the top positions in the event detection rank list. Furthermore, the evidences discovered in our framework are interpretable for human, which can facilitate deep analysis of the complex events. The experimental results on large video dataset are promising and verify the effectiveness of our method.

References

1. Agarwal, S.: The infinite push: A new support vector ranking algorithm that directly optimizes accuracy at the absolute top of the list. In: SDM, pp. 839–850. Society for Industrial and Applied Mathematics (2011)
2. Bhattacharya, S., Yu, F.X., Chang, S.F.: Minimally needed evidence for complex event recognition in unconstrained videos. In: ICMR (2014)
3. Cao, L., Mu, Y., Natsev, A., Chang, S.-F., Hua, G., Smith, J.R.: Scene aligned pooling for complex video recognition. In: Fitzgibbon, A., Lazebnik, S., Perona, P., Sato, Y., Schmid, C. (eds.) ECCV 2012, Part II. LNCS, vol. 7573, pp. 688–701. Springer, Heidelberg (2012)
4. Chen, Y., Bi, J., Wang, J.Z.: Miles: Multiple-instance learning via embedded instance selection. PAMI 28(12), 1931–1947 (2006)
5. Dietterich, T.G., Lathrop, R.H., Lozano-Pérez, T.: Solving the multiple instance problem with axis-parallel rectangles. Artificial Intelligence 89(1), 31–71 (1997)

6. Ikizler-Cinbis, N., Sclaroff, S.: Object, scene and actions: Combining multiple features for human action recognition. In: Daniilidis, K., Maragos, P., Paragios, N. (eds.) ECCV 2010, Part I. LNCS, vol. 6311, pp. 494–507. Springer, Heidelberg (2010)

7. INRIA: Yael library: Optimized implementations of computationally demanding functions (2009), https://gforge.inria.fr/projects/yael/

8. Jiang, Y.G., Bhattacharya, S., Chang, S.F., Shah, M.: High-level event recognition in unconstrained videos. IJMIR, 1–29 (2012)

9. Joachims, T.: Optimizing search engines using clickthrough data. In: SIGKDD, pp. 133–142. ACM (2002)

10. Li, W., Yu, Q., Divakaran, A., Vasconcelos, N.: Dynamic pooling for complex event recognition. In: ICCV (2013)

11. Lowe, D.G.: Distinctive image features from scale-invariant keypoints. IJCV 60(2), 91–110 (2004)

12. Natarajan, P., Wu, S., Vitaladevuni, S., Zhuang, X., Tsakalidis, S., Park, U., Prasad, R.: Multimodal feature fusion for robust event detection in web videos. In: CVPR (2012)

13. Niebles, J.C., Chen, C.-W., Fei-Fei, L.: Modeling temporal structure of decomposable motion segments for activity classification. In: Daniilidis, K., Maragos, P., Paragios, N. (eds.) ECCV 2010, Part II. LNCS, vol. 6312, pp. 392–405. Springer, Heidelberg (2010)

14. Oneata, D., Verbeek, J., Schmid, C.: Action and event recognition with fisher vectors on a compact feature set. In: ICCV, pp. 1817–1824 (2013)

15. Over, P., Awad, G., Michel, M., Fiscus, J., Sanders, G., Kraaij, W., Smeaton, A.F., Quenot, G.: Trecvid 2013 – an overview of the goals, tasks, data, evaluation mechanisms and metrics. In: Proceedings of TRECVID 2013. NIST (2013)

16. Quattoni, A., Carreras, X., Collins, M., Darrell, T.: An efficient projection for $l_{1,\infty}$, infinity regularization. In: ICML (2009)

17. Rakotomamonjy, A.: Sparse support vector infinite push. In: ICML (2012)

18. Rudin, C.: The p-norm push: A simple convex ranking algorithm that concentrates at the top of the list. JMLR 10, 2233–2271 (2009)

19. Soomro, K., Zamir, A.R., Shah, M.: Ucf101: A dataset of 101 human actions classes from videos in the wild. CRCV-TR-12-01 (2012)

20. Tamrakar, A., Ali, S., Yu, Q., Liu, J., Javed, O., Divakaran, A., Cheng, H., Sawhney, H.: Evaluation of low-level features and their combinations for complex event detection in open source videos. In: CVPR (2012)

21. Tang, K., Fei-Fei, L., Koller, D.: Learning latent temporal structure for complex event detection. In: CVPR (2012)

22. Vahdat, A., Cannons, K., Mori, G., Oh, S., Kim, I.: Compositional models for video event detection: A multiple kernel learning latent variable approach. In: ICCV, pp. 1185–1192 (2013)

23. Vedaldi, A., Fulkerson, B.: Vlfeat: An open and portable library of computer vision algorithms (2008), http://www.vlfeat.org/

24. Wang, H., Klaser, A., Schmid, C., Liu, C.L.: Action recognition by dense trajectories. In: CVPR (2011)

25. Wang, H., Kläser, A., Schmid, C., Liu, C.L.: Dense trajectories and motion boundary descriptors for action recognition. IJCV, 1–20 (2013)

A Hierarchical Representation for Future Action Prediction

Tian Lan, Tsung-Chuan Chen, and Silvio Savarese

Stanford University, USA

Abstract. We consider inferring the future actions of people from a still image or a short video clip. Predicting future actions before they are actually executed is a critical ingredient for enabling us to effectively interact with other humans on a daily basis. However, challenges are two fold: First, we need to capture the subtle details inherent in human movements that may imply a future action; second, predictions usually should be carried out as quickly as possible in the social world, when limited prior observations are available.

In this paper, we propose *hierarchical movemes* - a new representation to describe human movements at multiple levels of granularities, ranging from atomic movements (e.g. an open arm) to coarser movements that cover a larger temporal extent. We develop a max-margin learning framework for future action prediction, integrating a collection of moveme detectors in a hierarchical way. We validate our method on two publicly available datasets and show that it achieves very promising performance.

1 Introduction

Every day, humans are faced with numerous situations in which they must predict what actions other people are about to do in the near future. These predictions are a critical ingredient for enabling us to effectively interact with other humans on a daily basis. Consider the example shown in Fig. 1. When presented with a short video clip or even a static image, we can easily predict what is going to happen in the near future (e.g. the man and the woman are about to hug). The ability of the human visual system to predict future actions is possibly thanks to years of previous observations of interactions among humans.

Predicting the action of a person before it is actually executed has a wide range of applications in autonomous robots, surveillance and health care. For autonomous navigation, in order for an agent to safely and effectively operate alongside humans, it is important for it to predict what people are about to do next. This ability can enable the robot to plan ahead for reactive responses or to avoid potential accidents. For example, if an autonomous agent observes a person that is losing balance, then it is highly probable that s/he would fall. If the vehicle can predict it, then it would stop and thus avoid an accident.

In this paper, we consider the problem of future action prediction in natural (non-staged) scenarios. Given a large collection of training videos containing

D. Fleet et al. (Eds.): ECCV 2014, Part III, LNCS 8691, pp. 689–704, 2014.

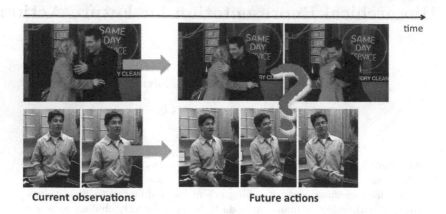

Current observations   **Future actions**

Fig. 1. Future action prediction. Given a static image or a short video clip (left), our goal is to infer the actions (as well as a sequence of movements) that are going to happen in the near future. The key contribution of this paper is to unveil the subtle details behind these movements and make correct action predictions.

human actions in the real world (e.g. TV series), we learn how human behaviors tend to evolve dynamically in a short period of time. Our goal is to infer the action that a person is going to perform next, from the observation of a short video clip or even a single frame.

Compared to the well-studied human action recognition, there are two characteristics of future action prediction: First, predicting future actions requires identifying the fine-grained details inherent to the current observations that would lead to a future action. For example, seeing a person with open arms indicates that s/he is probably going to hug. Second, it is often the case that future action prediction must be carried out with only the short-term observations of people in a short video clip or even a static image. It is important for an autonomous robot to react to the environments (e.g. a person appearing unexpectedly) as quickly as possible.

This paper introduces a new representation called *hierarchical movemes*, which is able to capture the typical structure of human movements before an action is executed. The term *"moveme"* was first introduced in the early work of Bregler [1], which is used to represent the atomic component of human movements, such as reaching and grabbing [1,5]. We generalize the notion of "movemes" to capturing human movements at multiple levels of semantic and temporal granularity, ranging from an atomic motion with consistent viewpoints lasting a few frames, to larger motion segments covering more than one atomic motion. In the extreme case, we have "movemes" depicting all possible movements prior to an action. An example of hierarchical movemes representation is shown in Fig. 2. Given a new image or a short video clip, we infer the action that is going to happen using this hierarchical representation. In this paper, we focus on modeling human movements before the action is actually executed.

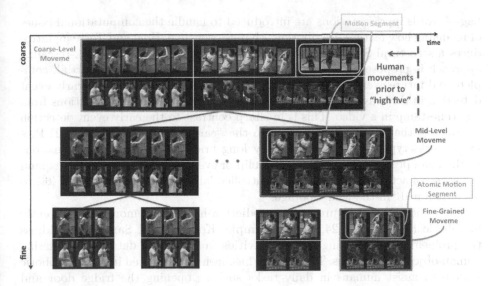

Fig. 2. An illustration of the *hierarchical movemes* representation. In this example, the structure of human movements prior to "high five" is represented, from coarse to fine. At the top level, movemes (*coarse-level movemes*) capture generic viewpoint and pose characteristics of the future action we wish to predict (i.e. that take place before the action we want to predict). At the second level, movemes (*mid-level movemes*) capture viewpoint-specific but pose-generic characteristics of the future action. At the lower level, movemes (*fine-grained movemes*) capture viewpoint-specific AND pose-specific characteristics of the future action.

However, the representation is general and can be applied to recognizing observed actions with complex structures.

2   Previous Work

Human action recognition is an extremely important research area in computer vision, and has grown dramatically in the last decade. Recent research has stepped past recognizing simple human actions, such as walking and standing in constrained settings [19], and gradually moved towards understanding complex actions in realistic video and still images collected from movies [11], TV shows [14], sport games [10], internet [28], etc. These scenarios typically include background clutter, occlusions, viewpoint changes, etc and have imposed significant challenges on action recognition. In the video domain, bag-of-features representations of local space-time features [22] have achieved impressive results. In the image domain, the contextual information such as attributes [28], objects [27] and poses [25,23] are jointly modeled with actions.

Recent research in early event detection has attempted to expand the spectrum of human action recognition to actions in the future. Ryoo [18] addresses the problem of early recognition of unfinished activities. Two variants of the bag-of-words representations are introduced to handle the computational issues of modeling how feature distributions change over time. Hoai and Torre [6] introduces a structural SVM framework for early event detection. A slack-rescaling approach is proposed to constrain the monotonicity among past, partial, complete and future event. Our work differs from previous literatures on early event detection in three aspects: 1) Our method is able to predict future actions from any timestamp in a video. This is in sharp contrast to the early event detection approaches that constrain the input to the "early stage of an action". 2) Previous works typically require relatively long prior observations of actions, our method can predict from a short video clip or even a static image. 3) We expand the scope of action prediction from controlled lab settings (as in [18] and [6]) to unconstrained "in-the-wild" footage.

The importance of future action prediction has been demonstrated recently in robotic applications [24,9]. For example, Koppula and Saxena [9] address the problem of anticipating future activities from RGB-D data by considering human-object interactions. The method has been implemented into a real robotic system to assist humans in daily tasks such as opening the fridge door and refilling water glasses.

Predicting the future exists in other domains of computer vision. Most of the works are focused on predicting (or forecasting) the future trajectories of pedestrians [15,7]. There are also literatures on predicting motion from still images [29]. Our work is philosophically similar to these, but we focus on predicting motion patterns associated to semantically meaningful actions..

We highlight the main contributions of our paper. 1) We consider predicting future actions from still images or short video clips in unconstrained data. There is a body of work [18,6] that considers early action prediction from stream videos in constrained settings. This paper is the first that attempts to predict future actions from a single frame in the challenging real-world scenarios. 2) We introduce a novel representation called *hierarchical movemes* to capture multiple levels of granularities in human movements. 3) We develop a max-margin learning framework that jointly learns the appearance models of different movemes, as well as their relations. We demonstrate experimentally that this framework is effective in future action prediction.

3   Hierarchical Movemes - A New Representation for Actions in the Future

Modeling human actions is a very challenging problem in that: 1) Humans are highly articulated objects; 2) Actions can be described at different levels of semantic granularities, ranging from higher level actions, such as handshaking and talking, to finer grained motions, such as reaching and grabbing. Traditional action recognition methods usually focus on recognizing the higher level action classes. In action prediction, however, critical clues are usually hidden in finer grained motions. For example, an open arm usually implies hugging, but "open arm" is not necessarily an important class for action recognition.

In this paper, we propose a new representation called *hierarchical movemes* for future action prediction. The hierarchy depicts human movements at multiple levels of granularities from coarse to fine. An example of hierarchical moveme representation is shown in Fig. 2. We start by describing the procedure of constructing the hierarchy.

3.1 Hierarchy Construction

During training, we assume that we are given a collection of videos annotated with bounding boxes around the true locations of the people in each frame, tracks associated with each person across frames, action and viewpoint labels for each frame. We use the tracks associated with each person in the training videos to construct the hierarchy. We truncate the tracks that contain an action of interest (e.g. handshake, hug, kiss), such that the last frame of each track is right before the starting point of the action we want to predict. This allows our learning algorithm to only focus on modeling people's movements before actions are executed. See Fig. 3 for an example.

Track 1
Future action: handshake
Pose: face right

Action starts

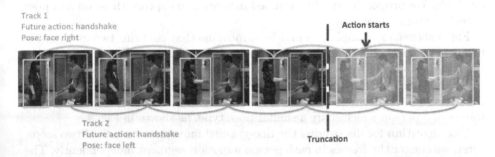

Track 2
Future action: handshake
Pose: face left

Truncation

Fig. 3. Example of annotations for training [14]. Annotations include bounding boxes around the true locations of the people in each frame, tracks associated with each person across frames, action and viewpoint labels for each frame. We truncate the tracks associated with each person, such that the last frame of each track is right before the starting point of the action we want to predict. We define the starting point of an action according to the annotation of the dataset [14]. For example, persons are labeled as "handshake" when their hands touch each other.

We construct a 3-layer "moveme" hierarchy to capture human movements at different levels of semantic and temporal granularity. An example hierarchy is shown in Fig. 2. At the top level, movemes (which we call *coarse-level movemes*) capture generic viewpoint and pose characteristics of the future action we wish to predict (using frames that take place before the action we want to predict). For example, in Fig. 2, this layer captures a collection of generic human movements that lead to the action "high five" in the near future. At the second level, movemes (which we call *mid-level movemes*) capture viewpoint-specific but pose-generic characteristics of the future action. For example, Fig. 2 shows two movemes in the second layer that are associated to movements observed from the "right" viewpoint, the other from the "left" respectively. At the lower level, movemes (which we call *fine-grained movemes*) capture viewpoint-specific and pose-specific characteristics of the future action. For example, in Fig. 2, the second fine-grained moveme in the third layer represents movements observed from the right and correspond to a pose configuration where arms are raised.

In training, the labels (including actions and viewpoints) for the coarse-level and mid-level movemes are given, while the fine-grained movemes are automatically discovered from the training data. In the following, we will introduce how to discover the fine-grained movemes via discriminative temporal clustering. An overview of the clustering process is shown in Fig. 4.

Fine-Grained Moveme Discovery. Given "mid-level movemes" that correspond to movements of people with consistent viewpoints, our goal is to partition the examples in each mid-level moveme into multiple "fine-grained movemes", each corresponding to a specific human pose type (e.g. raise hand, reach, etc.). The intuition is that, though consistent in viewpoint, the mid-level movemes still cannot capture the level of details that are typically important for inferring the future actions, particularly when only a single frame or a short video clip is available. We propose to use fine-grained movemes to capture these human pose types (or atomic motions).

Fig. 4 shows an example of a mid-level moveme that contains two motion segments of persons with the same viewpoint, before the starting point of the action (high five). To avoid the confusion of terminology, we will use "motion segment" to denote the track associated with a person truncated at the starting point of the action we wish to predict, and "atomic motion segment" for the consecutive frames of a person which share a similar pose type, as shown in Fig. 4.

Our algorithm for discovering the fine-grained movemes consists of two steps: First, we cluster the frames in each person's motion segment independently. The goal is to find the atomic motion segments of each person which share a similar pose type. Second, we merge the different person's atomic motion segments that correspond to the same pose type into a fine-grained moveme. In this way, a fine-grained moveme contains multiple persons with consistent atomic motions (pose type). These two steps are explained in details below.

STEP 1. We develop a discriminative temporal clustering based method for finding the atomic motion segments for each person independently. Given all of the frames in a person's track prior to the action we want to predict, we cluster them based on appearance. These clusters will correspond to certain pose types. Every frame of the person is represented by a rigid HOG template. Instead of using the high-dimensional HOG representation for clustering, we train an exemplar SVM [13,20] for each person example, and use the detection score of each example to create a $K \times K$ similarity matrix. The (i, j) entry in the similarity matrix is the detection score of running the i-th detector on the j-th example. Once we have the similarity matrix, we cluster the frames of the person using a recently proposed temporal clustering algorithm [4]. We use a dynamic time warping (DTW) kernel

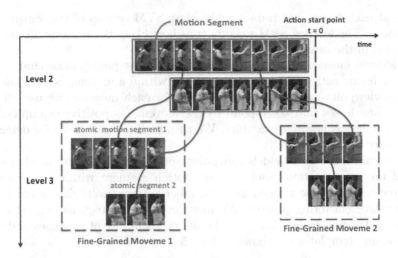

Fig. 4. Discovering fine-grained movemes. The figure illustrates how to discover the fine-grained movemes from the mid-level movemes. First, we cluster the frames in each person's motion segment to find the atomic motion segment of each person, which share a similar pose type. Then we merge the different person's atomic motion segments that correspond to the same pose type into a fine-grained moveme.

to achieve the invariance of temporal order, i.e. each cluster contains the atomic segment of the person with consecutive frames with the same order of the original sequence, as shown in Fig. 4.

STEP 2. The second step of our algorithm is to merge the atomic motion segments that correspond to the same pose type into a fine-grained moveme. For example, in Fig. 4, each of the discovered atomic motion segments correspond to a pose type of the human movement. Both of the atomic motion segments in the bottom left of Fig. 4 correspond to the first pose type, while the ones in the bottom right correspond to the second pose type. Atomic motion segments corresponding to the same pose type are merged into a fine-grained moveme. Thus each fine-grained moveme represents a particular pose type (e.g. raise hand, reach, etc.). We consider at most 3 pose types for each motion segment.

3.2 Learning a Collection of Moveme Classifiers

Given a hierarchy of movemes, we learn a classifier for each moveme in the hierarchy. Our goal is to predict future actions based on a single frame or a short video clip. Thus for each moveme, we learn two classifiers, based on appearance (HOG) and motion cues (HOF and MBH [22]), respectively. When the input is a single frame, we only consider classifiers trained with appearance features, while the input is a video clip, we consider both.

A coarse-level moveme models generic pose and viewpoint characteristics of certain action that is about to take place. Each motion segment within a moveme is associated to the same future action label. We compute feature descriptors for persons at each frame and train a multi-class SVM on top of the feature representations. The learned SVM weights tells how likely the person will perform each action in the near future.

A mid-level moveme models viewpoint-specific but pose-generic characteristics of the future action. Each motion segment within a moveme is associated to the same viewpoint and future action label. For each moveme, we use all person bounding boxes that correspond to the moveme as positive examples, and random patches as negative examples. We then train a linear SVM for detecting the presence of the moveme.

A fine-grained moveme models viewpoint-specific and pose-specific characteristics of the future action. Each atomic motion segment within a moveme is associated with the fine-grained moveme label automatically discovered in the discriminative clustering process. We use the same strategy as defined above for training the fine-grained moveme classifiers. Examples of movemes and their corresponding templates are shown in Fig. 5.

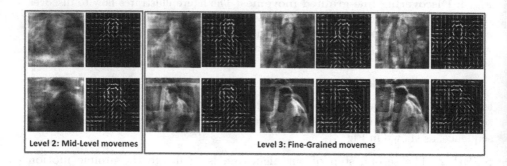

Level 2: Mid-Level movemes   Level 3: Fine-Grained movemes

Fig. 5. Averaged images and moveme templates. We visualize the learned templates of the mid-level movemes and the fine-grained movemes in the hierarchy for hug (first row) and handshake (second row). For each template, we show the images averaged over all examples that belong to the same moveme.

4   Model

We introduce a model that is able to combine information across different movemes in a structured hierarchical way. It performs future action prediction and explicitly models the relations between movemes in different layers. Moreover, the model implicitly performs viewpoint prediction and temporal localization of the input frame (or short video clip) w.r.t. the start point of the action.

4.1   Model Formulation

The input to our learning module is a set of N video frames and short clips of persons. Each person example X is associated with labels corresponding to one branch of the movemes hierarchy: $Y = \{y_i\}_{i=1}^{L}$, where L is the total number of levels of the hierarchy (we set it to 3) and y_i is the index of the corresponding moveme at level i. For example, y_1 corresponds to the future action label, y_2 corresponds to the label of a future action with a particular viewpoint (e.g. handshake while facing to left) and y_3 corresponds to the fine-grained moveme label that is automatically discovered by our clustering algorithm.

Our scoring function for labeling an example X with movemes Y is written as:

$$\Phi(X, Y) = \sum_{i=1}^{L} \alpha_{y_i}^{\top} \phi(X, y_i) + \sum_{i=1}^{L-1} \beta_{y_i, y_{i+1}}^{\top} \psi(y_i, y_j) \tag{1}$$

Unary model $\alpha_{y_i}^{\top} \phi(X, y_i)$: This potential function captures the compatibility between the example X and the moveme y_i. We use $\phi(X, y_i)$ to denote response of running the moveme classifier of y_i on the person example X. If X corresponds to a person track over a short clip, then we take the max response of the moveme classifier over all frames on the track. To learn biases between different movemes, we append a constant 1 to the end of each response.

Pairwise model $\beta_{y_i, y_{i+1}}^{\top} \psi(y_i, y_j)$: This potential function captures the compatibility between a pair of movemes located across different levels of the hierarchy. We write $\psi(y_i, y_j) = 1$ if the movemes y_i and y_j are connected by an edge in the hierarchy, and $-\infty$ otherwise. This means we exclude the co-occurrence of certain pairs of movemes: e.g. a person can not be described by movemes corresponds to the prior observation of different actions at the same time. Here $\beta_{y_i, y_{i+1}}$ is a model parameter that favors certain pair of movemes to be chosen for a person.

4.2   Inference

For an example X that corresponds to a person in a single frame or over a short video clip, our inference corresponds to solving the following optimization problem: $Y = \arg\max_{y_i : i=1,\ldots,L} \Phi(X, Y)$. For the example X, the inference is on a chain structure where we jointly infer moveme labels at all levels together. This is a simple exact inference and we solve it using Belief Propagation. The moveme at the top layer of the hierarchy y_1 corresponds to the future action label of the person. Our inference procedure also returns other more detailed predictions of the person (e.g. viewpoint, temporal state) through movemes at the other layers of the hierarchy (latent variables in our model) $\{y_i\}_{i=2}^{L}$.

4.3   Learning

Given a collection of training examples in the form of $\{X^n, Y^n\}_{n=1}^{N}$, we learn the model parameters θ that tend to correctly predict the future action labels. We formulate this as follows:

$$\min_{\theta, \xi \geq 0} \frac{1}{2} ||\theta||^2 + C \sum_n \xi_n$$
$$\theta^{\top} \Phi(X^n, Y^n) - \theta^{\top} \Phi(X^n, Y^*) \geq \Delta(y_1^n, y_1^*, t) - \xi_n, \forall n, \tag{2}$$

where $\Delta\ (y_1^n, y_1^*, t)$ is a loss function measuring the cost incurred by predicting y_1^* when the ground truth is y_1^n. Since our goal is to predict the future action labels, we only penalize the incorrect predictions of the future action label, rather than movemes in other layers of the hierarchy. A standard loss function of Structural SVM is the $0 - 1$ loss which equally penalizes all incorrect predictions at any time prior to the future action. However, this is inadequate for the task of future action prediction, since prediction from a frame at a long time before the start point of an action is obviously more difficult than from those at a few frames before the action is happening. If we treated them equally in training, then the learned decision boundaries might become unreliable.

Here we introduce a new loss function that depends on the temporal distance to the future action: $\Delta\ (y_1^n, y_1^*, t) = 1 - \mu t$ if $y_1 \neq y_i^*$, and 0 otherwise. If the example is in a sequence that does not contain any action of interest, we simply use the $0 - 1$ loss. Here $t \in (0, T]$ is the temporal distance to the starting point of the action we wish to predict, and $t = 0$ corresponds to the first frame of the action, T is the maximum number of frames before the action that we consider. $\mu \in (0, 1/T]$ is a tunable parameter. In this case, incorrect prediction from frames longer before the action is happening receives less penalties.

The optimization problem of Eq. 2 is convex and many well-tuned solvers can be applied to solve this problem. Here we use the bundle optimization solver in [2].

5   Experiments

Our goal is to test the performance of the proposed method on future action prediction in the challenging real world scenarios. At that end, we choose a very challenging dataset collected from TV shows [14], which include actions that we typically perform at a daily basis. We show that our method significantly outperforms baselines in future action prediction when the input is only a single frame or a short video clip.

The proposed method is generic and will not lose the discriminative power in classifying videos containing activities at relatively early stage or even the fully observed activities. We also evaluate our method on the UT-Interaction benchmark dataset [18]. We show that our method achieves state-of-the-art performance in early activity prediction.

Implementation Details. In all experiments, the penalty parameter C of the Structured SVM objective (Eq. 2) is set to 1 for both our method and the baselines. The codebook size for the dense trajectory descriptors [22] is set to 2000 for TV Interaction dataset and 800 for UT Interaction dataset.

5.1   TV Human Interaction Dataset

This dataset consists of 300 video clips collected from over 20 different TV shows. It contains five action classes: handshake, high five, hug, kiss and none. The class "none" represents all other more general actions such as walking and standing.

Annotations are provided for every frame of the videos, including the upper body bounding boxes, discrete head orientations and action labels for each person.

We use the training/testing split provided along with the dataset. For training, we sample a collection of frames and short clips from all of the videos in the training set, which contains more than 25,000 person examples. This ensures that the system has "seen" a large number of videos on human actions before making a prediction. In testing, the experiments were conducted with different settings on the lengths of the input video clips as well as their temporal distances to the start point of the action we wish to predict (see below for details). In the most challenging scenario, we predict future actions from a static video frame.

Baselines. We compare our method agains the following baselines: 1) SIFT flow [12]. Given a testing image, it first finds the nearest neighbor from the training data using the SIFT flow algorithm, which matches densely sampled SIFT features between the two images, while preserving spatial discontinuities. The future action label of the matched training image is directly transferred to the testing image. 2) Dense flow [22]. We apply one of the state-of-the-art action recognition methods for future action prediction. The model is trained with video clips containing fully executed actions and tested for future action prediction. A linear SVM is used. 3) Our model with only the top most layer ("1-Layer"). 4) Our model with the top two layers ("2-Layer").

Results. We evaluate the performances when the input is a single image or a short video clip of four different lengths $(1, 3, 5, 7$ frames$)$. All of the videos in this dataset have the same frame rate of 24 fps. Thus the longest video clip we provide at testing (7 frames) is less than 0.3 s, making the problem of future action prediction very challenging. Note that the input clip of length 1 denotes that we use a single frame as input, but with both shape and motion features.

We only use the shape feature (HOG) to represent the person when the input is a single image, and use both shape (HOG) and motion features (the dense trajectory descriptors [22]) when the input is a video clip. We set the trajectory length to 5 frames. Note that for each frame, the trajectories are computed using the feature points sampled from the five-frame temporal segment before the current frame. This guarantees that we don't have access to any *future* information in feature computation.

In order to test the methods' ability in predicting future actions at different stages, we measure the performances with 5 different temporal stage settings, from -20 to 0, with a step size of 5. The numbers denote the temporal distance (in frames) from the input image to the start point of the action. For example, the methods' performances at a temporal stage -20 describe the classification accuracies given all of the testing frames within 20 frames before the start point of the action we wish to predict. The temporal stage of 0 indicates all testing images are taken within 5 frames after the start point of the action, making the problem a conventional action classification problem. The comparative results are shown in Fig. 6. Our method outperforms all of the baselines at all different temporal settings. It is interesting to see that there is a notable performance increase of our

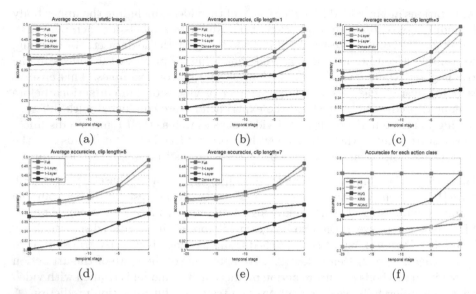

(a)   (b)   (c)

(d)   (e)   (f)

Fig. 6. Future action prediction accuracies. We evaluate performances when a static frame (a) or a short video clip (b)-(e) is available. The X axis corresponds to the temporal stages of the input frames, while the Y axis corresponds to the mean-per class accuracies. The red curve denotes our method, green for using the first two layers of the moveme hierarchy, blue for using the first layer, black for Dense flow [22] and magenta for SIFT flow [12]. (f) shows the accuracies for each action class given a single frame using the full model. HS and HF denote handshake and high five respectively.

Fig. 7. Future action prediction visualizations. We show predictions of our method at different temporal stages before the action is executed (in yellow). For example, $t = -15$ in the first image denotes that the image is taken 15 frames before the action (handshake) starts. Correct predictions are shown in green and incorrect predictions in red. The last row shows examples of failure.

full model as well as the 2-Layer moveme model, starting from 10 (around 0.5 s) before the action is executed. This is because the fine-grained appearance and motion that characterize the actions tend to appear around 10 frames before the action starts. This can be verified by the visualization of our predictions shown in Fig. 7[1].

5.2   UT Interaction Dataset

The proposed hierarchical moveme representation is generic and captures the "multi-modality" nature of human movements. Thus its application domain is not limited to future action prediction, but also other aspects of human activity understanding, such as early action prediction and action recognition.

We validate the proposed method on the UT-Interaction benchmark dataset [17]. The dataset contains a total of 120 videos of 6 classes of human interactions (e.g. handshake, hug and kick). In order for a fair comparison with other reported numbers on this dataset, we follow the experiment settings as in [18]: we evaluate the proposed method on both Set #1 and Set #2 of UT-Interaction (segmented version), and use leave-one-sequence-out cross validation for measuring the performances. We run the person detector and tracker provided by [21] to obtain person tracks in the video sequences.

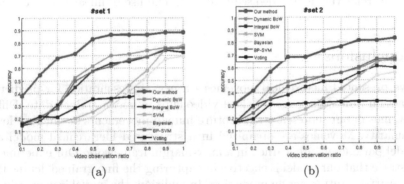

(a)   (b)

Fig. 8. Early action prediction accuracies. The comparisons of the proposed model and all other methods (reported in [18]) on the UT-Interaction dataset.

Fig. 8 compares our model with existing methods on early activity prediction. Following [18], we tested our full model using 10 different observation ratios. Our method significantly outperforms all other methods on both # Set 1 and # Set 2 of UT-Interaction. Table 1 compares results of our method with leading approaches on the UT-Interaction dataset. Our method achieves state-of-the-art in terms of predicting activities at a relatively early stage, accessing only the first 50% of the testing video. An average classification accuracy of 83.1% is achieved, which is nearly 10% better than the current best result [16] on this benchmark.

---

[1] More visualizations are available at our website
http://cs.stanford.edu/$\sim$taranlan.

Table 1. Performance comparisons on UT Interaction # 1. Table compares classification accuracies of our approach and the previous approaches; leading approach is in **bold**. The second and third columns report the accuracies using the first half and the entire video, respectively. Our method achieves state-of-the-art in recognition at an early stage when only the first half of the video is available, and outperforms the current best result [16] by nearly 10%.

Methods	Accuracy w. half videos	Accuracy w. full videos
Our model	**83.1%**	88.4%
Ryoo [18] (Avg.)	61.8%	76.7%
Ryoo [18] (Best)	70%	85%
Cuboid+SVMs [3] (Avg.)	25.3%	78%
Cuboid+SVMs [3] (Best)	31.7%	85%
BP+SVM [18] (Avg.)	57.7%	75.9%
BP+SVM [18] (Best)	65%	83.3%
Raptis & Sigal [16]	73.3%	93.3%
Yao et al. [26]	-	88%
Vahdat et al. [21]	-	93.3%
Zhang et al. [30]	-	**95%**
Kong et al. [8]	-	88.3

For action recognition, our number is slightly lower than state of the art [30], we think it is for two reasons: 1) our method is designed for prediction from a single frame or short video clip, so we don't model the temporal relations across frames over relatively long video sequences. 2) The use of linear versus complex kernels.

6   Conclusions

We have presented hierarchical movemes - a new representation for predicting future action from still images or short video clips in unconstrained data. Different movemes in our representation capture human movements at different levels of granularity. Movemes are organized in a structured hierarchical model and the model parameters are learned in a max-margin framework. Our experiments demonstrate that our model is effective in capturing the fine-grained details that are necessary for future action prediction. In addition, the model is generally applicable to other aspects of human activity understanding: the proposed model outperforms multiple state-of-the-art methods in early action prediction on a benchmark dataset.

Acknowledgments. We acknowledge the support from a Ford-Stanford Innovation Alliance Award and the ONR award N00014-13-1-0761.

References

1. Bregler, C.: Learning and recognizing human dynamics in video sequences. In: CVPR (1997)
2. Do, T.M.T., Artieres, T.: Large margin training for hidden markov models with partially observed states. In: ICML (2009)

3. Dollár, P., Rabaud, V., Cottrell, G., Belongie, S.: Behavior recognition via sparse spatio-temporal features. In: ICCV 2005 Workshop on Visual Surveillance and Performance Evaluation of Tracking and Surveillance (2005)
4. Zhou, F., De la Torre, F., Hodgins, J.K.: Hierarchical aligned cluster analysis for temporal clustering of human motion. PAMI (2013)
5. Fanti, C.: Towards Automatic Discovery of Human Movemes. Ph.D. thesis, California Institute of Technology (2008)
6. Hoai, M., De la Torre, F.: Max-margin early event detectors. In: Proceedings of IEEE Conference on Computer Vision and Pattern Recognition (2012)
7. Kitani, K.M., Ziebart, B.D., Bagnell, D., Hebert, M.: Activity forecasting. In: European Conference on Computer Vision (2012)
8. Kong, Y., Jia, Y., Fu, Y.: Learning human interaction by interactive phrases. In: Fitzgibbon, A., Lazebnik, S., Perona, P., Sato, Y., Schmid, C. (eds.) ECCV 2012, Part I. LNCS, vol. 7572, pp. 300–313. Springer, Heidelberg (2012)
9. Koppula, H.S., Saxena, A.: Anticipating human activities using object affordances for reactive robotic response. In: Robotics: Science and Systems, RSS (2013)
10. Lan, T., Sigal, L., Mori, G.: Social roles in hierarchical models for human activity recognition. In: Computer Vision and Pattern Recognition, CVPR (2012)
11. Laptev, I., Marszalek, M., Schmid, C., Rozenfeld, B.: Learning realistic human actions from movies. In: IEEE Computer Society Conference on Computer Vision and Pattern Recognition (2008)
12. Liu, C., Yuen, J., Torralba, A., Sivic, J., Freeman, W.T.: SIFT flow: Dense correspondence across different scenes. In: European Conference on Computer Vision (2008)
13. Malisiewicz, T., Gupta, A., Efros, A.A.: Ensemble of exemplar-SVMs for object detection and beyond. In: IEEE International Conference on Computer Vision (2011)
14. Patron-Perez, A., Marszalek, M., Reid, I., Zisserman, A.: Structured learning of human interactions in tv shows. PAMI (2013)
15. Pellegrini, S., Ess, A., Schindler, K., Gool, L.J.V.: You'll never walk alone: Modeling social behavior for multi-target tracking. In: ICCV (2009)
16. Raptis, M., Sigal, L.: Poselet key-framing: A model for human activity recognition. In: Proceedings of the IEEE Conference on Computer Vision and Pattern Recognition, CVPR (2013)
17. Ryoo, M., Aggarwal, J.: Spatio-temporal relationship match: Video structure comparison for recognition of complex human activities. In: ICCV (2009)
18. Ryoo, M.S.: Human activity prediction: Early recognition of ongoing activities from streaming videos. In: IEEE International Conference on Computer Vision (2011)
19. Schuldt, C., Laptev, I., Caputo, B.: Recognizing human actions: A local SVM approach. In: IEEE International Conference on Pattern Recognition, vol. 3, pp. 32–36 (2004)
20. Singh, S., Gupta, A., Efros, A.A.: Unsupervised discovery of mid-level discriminative patches. In: Fitzgibbon, A., Lazebnik, S., Perona, P., Sato, Y., Schmid, C. (eds.) ECCV 2012, Part II. LNCS, vol. 7573, pp. 73–86. Springer, Heidelberg (2012)
21. Vahdat, A., Gao, B., Ranjbar, M., Mori, G.: A discriminative key pose sequence model for recognizing human interactions. In: VS (2010)
22. Wang, H., Schmid, C.: Action recognition with improved trajectories. In: IEEE International Conference on Computer Vision (2013)
23. Wang, Y., Tran, D., Liao, Z., Forsyth, D.: Discriminative hierarchical part-based models for human parsing and action recognition. JMLR (2012)

24. Wang, Z., Deisenroth, M., Amor, H.B., Vogt, D., Scholkopf, B.: Probabilistic modeling of human movements for intention inference. In: Robotics: Science and Systems, RSS (2013)
25. Yang, W., Wang, Y., Mori, G.: Recognizing human actions from still images with latent poses. In: IEEE Computer Society Conference on Computer Vision and Pattern Recognition (2010)
26. Yao, A., Gall, J., Gool, L.V.: A hough transform-based voting framework for action recognition. In: CVPR (2010)
27. Yao, B., Fei-Fei, L.: Modeling mutual context of object and human pose in human-object interaction activities. In: IEEE Computer Society Conference on Computer Vision and Pattern Recognition (2010)
28. Yao, B., Jiang, X., Khosla, A., Lin, A.L., Guibas, L., Fei-Fei, L.: Human action recognition by learning bases of action attributes and parts. In: IEEE International Conference on Computer Vision (2011)
29. Yuen, J., Torralba, A.: A data-driven approach for event prediction. In: European Conference on Computer Vision (2010)
30. Zhang, Y., Liu, X., Chang, M.-C., Ge, W., Chen, T.: Spatio-temporal phrases for activity recognition. In: Fitzgibbon, A., Lazebnik, S., Perona, P., Sato, Y., Schmid, C. (eds.) ECCV 2012, Part III. LNCS, vol. 7574, pp. 707–721. Springer, Heidelberg (2012)

Continuous Learning of Human Activity Models Using Deep Nets*

Mahmudul Hasan and Amit K. Roy-Chowdhury

University of California, Riverside, USA

Abstract. Learning activity models continuously from streaming videos is an immensely important problem in video surveillance, video indexing, etc. Most of the research on human activity recognition has mainly focused on learning a static model considering that all the training instances are labeled and present in advance, while in streaming videos new instances continuously arrive and are not labeled. In this work, we propose a continuous human activity learning framework from streaming videos by intricately tying together deep networks and active learning. This allows us to automatically select the most suitable features and to take the advantage of incoming unlabeled instances to improve the existing model incrementally. Given the segmented activities from streaming videos, we learn features in an unsupervised manner using deep networks and use active learning to reduce the amount of manual labeling of classes. We conduct rigorous experiments on four challenging human activity datasets to demonstrate the effectiveness of our framework for learning human activity models continuously.

Keywords: Continuous Learning, Active Learning, Deep Learning, Action Recognition.

1 Introduction

Recognizing human activities in videos is a widely studied problem in computer vision due to its numerous practical applications. It is still a difficult problem due to large intra class variance, scarcity of labeled instances, and concept drift in dynamic environments. In the activity recognition problem dealing with surveillance or streaming videos, it may be necessary to learn the activity models incrementally because all the training instances might not be labeled and available in advance (Fig. 1). Current activity recognition approaches [29] do not perform well in these scenarios because they are based on a setting which assumes that all the training instances are labeled and available beforehand. Moreover, most of these approaches use hand engineered features. Such manually chosen features may not be the best for all application domains and requires to be done separately for each application. Thus, there is a need to develop methods for

---

* This work was supported in part by ONR grant N00014-12-1-1026 and NSF grant IIS-1316934. Mahmudul Hasan is with Dept. of Computer Science and Amit K. Roy-Chowdhury is with Dept. of Electrical Engineering at UCR.

D. Fleet et al. (Eds.): ECCV 2014, Part III, LNCS 8691, pp. 705–720, 2014.
© Springer International Publishing Switzerland 2014

activity classification that can work with streaming videos by taking the advantage of newly arriving training instances, and where the features can be learned automatically.

Fig. 1. A sequence of VIRAT [26] streaming video, where new unlabeled activities are continuously arriving. These new activities can be exploited to incrementally improve current activity recognition model.

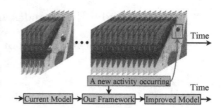

Since the emergence of deep learning [11], it has received huge attention because of its well founded theory and excellent generalized performance in many applications of computer vision such as image denoising [40], scene understanding [5], object detection [14], activity recognition [1,12,16,38], etc. Deep learning based techniques such as autoencoder, stacking, and convolution have been used for unsupervised learning of meaningful hierarchical features [16], which in many cases outperform hand-engineered local features such as SIFT [21] and HOG [7]. In the context of above discussion, we pose an important question in this paper: *Can deep learning be leveraged upon for continuous learning of activity models from streaming videos?*

The ability of deep sparse autoencoder to learn hierarchical sparse features from unlabeled data makes it a perfect tool for continuous learning of activity models. This is because sparse autoencoder has the ability to incrementally update [42] and fine tune [11] its parameters upon the availability of new instances. In the long run, concept drift may occur in streaming videos, which means that the definition of a particular activity class may change over time. Current activity recognition approaches often have problems dealing with these situations because the models are learned a priori. We can overcome this problem by incorporating the above properties of deep learning, whereby it is possible to update the sparse autoencoder parameters to reflect changes to the dynamic environments.

As new instances arrive, it would be unrealistic to have a human to manually label all the instances. In addition to deep learning, active learning can also be leveraged upon to learn activity models continuously from unlabeled streaming instances and to reduce the amount of manual labeling. In active learning [35], the learner asks queries about unlabeled instances to a teacher, who labels only instances that are assumed to be the most informative for training and require least possible cost. The purpose of the learner is to achieve a certain level of accuracy with least amount of manual labeling.

1.1 Overview and Main Contributions

In this work, we propose a novel framework *for continuous learning of activity models from streaming videos by intricately tying together deep learning and*

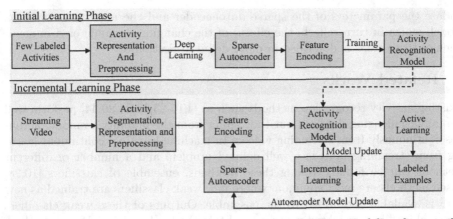

Fig. 2. This figure illustraes our proposed continuous activity modeling framework. Inital learning phase is comprised of learning primary models for sparse autoencoder and activity recognition with few labeled activities, which is followed by the incremental learning phase.

active learning. The goal is threefold: a) to automatically learn the best set of features for each activity class in an unsupervised manner, b) to reduce the amount of manual labeling of the unlabeled incoming instances, and c) to retain already learned information without storing all the previously seen data and continuously improve the existing activity models. Detailed overview of our proposed framework is illustrated in Fig. 2.

At first, we segment and localize the activities in streaming videos using a motion segmentation based algorithm. We collect STIP [15] features from the activity segments, which is a universal set of features, from where we will automatically learn the most effective features. Then, we compute a single feature vector for each activity using the STIP features by a technique based on spatio-temporal pyramid and average pooling. Our method has two phases: initial learning phase and incremental learning phase. During the initial learning phase, with smaller amount of labeled and unlabeled instances in hand, we learn a sparse autoencoder. Then, we encode features for the labeled instances using the sparse autoencoder and train a prior activity model. In this work, we propose to use a multinomial logistic regression or softmax classifier. Note that *the prior model is not assumed to be comprehensive* with regard to covering all activity classes or in modeling the variations within the class. It is only used as a starting point for the continuous learning of activity models.

We start incremental learning with the above mentioned prior model and prior sparse autoencoder and update it during each run of incremental training. When a newly segmented activity arrives, we encode features using the prior sparse autoencoder. We compute the probability score and gradient length of this particular instance. With this information, we employ active learning to decide whether to label this instance manually or not. After getting the label, we store the instances into a buffer. When the buffer is full, we incrementally update the parameters of the sparse autoencoder and the activity recognition model, which in turn reflects the effects of the changing dynamic environment. Each of these steps is described in more detail in Section 3.

2 Related Works

Existing activity recognition methods such as [4,15,23,23,24,29,44] perform well in many challenging datasets but they suffer from the inability to model activities continuously from streaming videos. In machine learning, continuous learning from streaming data is a well defined problem and a number of different methods can be found. Among these methods, ensemble of classifiers [10,28] based methods are most common, where new weak classifiers are trained as new data is available and added to the ensemble. Outputs of these weak classifiers are combined in a weighted manner to obtain the final decision. However, these approaches are unrealistic in many scenarios since the number of weak classifiers increases with time.

A few methods can be found in the literature on incremental activity modeling. In [31], an incremental action recognition method was proposed based on a feature tree, which grows in size when additional training instances become available. In [23], an incremental activity learning framework was proposed based on human tracks. However, these methods are infeasible for continuous learning from streaming videos because [31] requires to store all the seen training instances in the form of a feature tree, while [23] requires the annotation of human body in the initial frame of an action clip. The method proposed in [9] is based on active learning and boosted SVM classifiers. They always train a set of new weak classifiers for newly arrived instances with hand-engineered features, which is inefficient for continuous learning in dynamic environments.

Active learning has been successfully used in speech recognition, information retrieval, and document classification [35]. Some recent works used active learning in several computer vision related applications such as streaming data [22], image segmentation [2], image and object classification [18], and video recognition [39]. Even though they continuously update the classifiers, they require the storage of all training instances. As mentioned in Section 1, deep learning based human activity recognition approaches have shown promising performances [1,12,16,38]. In [16], independent subspace analysis was combined with deep learning techniques such as stacking and convolution. In [1], [12], and [38] 3D convolutional network was used to automatically learn spatio-temporal features from video. However, none of these methods have the ability to continuously learn activity models from streaming videos.

3 Methodology

3.1 Initial Activity Representation

We segment activities from the streaming videos as follows. At first, we detect motion regions using an adaptive background subtraction algorithm [45]. We detect moving persons around these motion regions using [8]. We use these detected persons to initialize the tracking method developed in [37], which gives us local trajectories of the moving persons. We collect STIP features [15] only for these motion regions. We segment these motion regions into activity segments using the method described in [3] with STIP histograms as the model observation.

As in [11], raw pixels would be an effective initial feature representation for learning unsupervised hierarchical features if the number of pixels is small. However, a typical activity segment has overwhelming number of pixels, which makes it unrealistic to use directly for training a neural network. For example, in KTH [32] a representative activity segment consists of $375 - 500$ frames with a resolution of 160×120 pixels. Hence, the total number of pixels is around 7.2×10^6 to 9.6×10^6. These numbers are even higher for more challenging datasets. Even though some works used 2D [14] or 3D [38] convolutional network to find a compact representation, these networks are computationally expensive and infeasible to use in continuous learning from streaming videos due to huge number of tweakable hyper-parameters and trainable parameters.

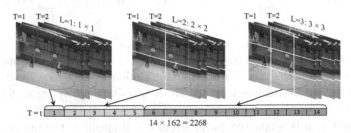

Fig. 3. Initial activity representation ($T = 2, L = 3$). Red dots are STIPs.

In order to find a compact and efficient representation of the activity segments, we use spatio-temporal pyramid and average pooling based technique on the extracted STIP features similar to [43] (see Fig. 3). Let, $G = \{g_1, \ldots, g_n\}$ be the set of extracted STIP features, T and L be the number of temporal and spatial levels respectively, and $G_c^{t,l}$ be the set of STIP features belonging to cube c at $T = t$ and $L = l$. Hence, average pooling gives us the feature $f_c^{t,l} = \text{Avg}\left(G_c^{t,l}\right)$, which is a vector of size 162 (HoG+HoF). Subsequently, we get the initial feature representation x by concatenating these pooled features from lower level to higher level as, $x = \{f_c^{t,l}, t = 1, \ldots, T, l = 1, \ldots, L, c = 1, \ldots, L^2\}$.

Preprocessing: We preprocess this initial feature set before applying it to the next levels such as training or feature encoding by the sparse autoencoder. The main goal is two fold: to make the features less correlated and to make them have similar variance. We use the method known as ZCA whitening described in [6]. Let $X = \{x^1, \ldots, x^m\}$ be the set of feature vectors and Σ be the feature covariance. Σ can be written as $\Sigma = E[XX^T] = VDV^T$. Hence, ZCA whitening uses the transform $P = VD^{-1/2}V^T$ to compute the whitened feature vector $X = PX$.

3.2   Sparse Autoencoder

In order to learn features automatically from unsupervised data, we use a single layer sparse autoencoder ($\mathcal{A}_W$), which is essentially a neural network with one input, one hidden, and one output layer. It has been used in many areas to learn features automatically from unsupervised data [11]. A simple sparse autoencoder is shown in Fig. 4(b), where the input feature vector size is n and the number of neurons in the hidden layer is k. In response to a feature vector $x^i \in \mathcal{R}^n$, the activation of the hidden layer and the output of the network are $h(x^i) = f(W^1 x^i + b^1)$ and $\hat{x}^i = f(W^2 h(x^i) + b^2)$ respectively, where $h(x^i) \in \mathcal{R}^k$, $f(z) = 1/(1 + exp(-z))$ is the sigmoid function, $W^1 \in k \times n$ and $W^2 \in n \times k$ are weight matrices, $b^1 \in \mathcal{R}^k$ and $b^2 \in \mathcal{R}^n$ are bias vectors, and $\hat{x}^i \in \mathcal{R}^n$. Given a set of training instances $X = \{x^1, \ldots, x^m\}$, the goal is to find the optimal values of $W = [W^1, W^2, b^1, b^2]$ so that the reconstruction error is minimized, which turns into the following optimization problem:

$$\arg\min_W J_a(W) = \frac{1}{2m} \sum_{i=1}^m \|x^i - \hat{x}^i\|^2 + \lambda \left(\|[W^1, W^2]\|^2 \right) + \beta \sum_{j=1}^k \Psi(\rho\|\hat{\rho}_j), \quad (1)$$

where, $\sum_{i=1}^m \|x^i - \hat{x}^i\|^2$ is the reconstruction error and $\lambda \left(\|W^1\|^2 + \|W^2\|^2 \right)$ is the regularization term. In order to obtain sparse feature representation, we would like to constrain the neurons in the hidden layer to be inactive most of the time. It can be achieved by adding a sparsity penalty term, $\Psi(\rho\|\hat{\rho}_j) = \rho \log \frac{\rho}{\hat{\rho}_j} + (1 - \rho) \log \frac{1-\rho}{1-\hat{\rho}_j}$, where $\hat{\rho}_j = \frac{1}{m} \sum_{i=1}^m h_j(x^i)$ is the average activation of hidden unit j, ρ is a sparsity parameter, which specifies the desired level of sparsity, and β is the weight of the sparsity penalty term [17]. If the number of hidden units k is less than the number of input units n, then the network is forced to learn a compressed and sparse representation of the input. This network can be trained using gradient descent and backpropagation algorithm as described in Fig. 4(a). Gradients of the Equation 1 can be found in [25]. After training, encoded features ($\tilde{x}^i$) are obtained by taking the output from the hidden layer.

Fine Tuning the Sparse Autoencoder: Fine tuning is a common strategy in deep learning. The goal is to fine tune the parameters of the sparse autoencoder upon the availability of labeled instances, which improves performance significantly. Even though, above two networks- sparse autoencoder and softmax classifier- are trained independently, during fine tuning they are considered as a single network as shown in Fig. 4(c). The weights are updated using backpropagation algorithm as shown in Fig. 4(a). The only exception is that weights are initialized with the previously trained weights.

3.3   Activity Model

We use multinomial logistic regression as the activity classification model $\mathcal{H}_\theta$, which is known as the softmax regression in neural network literature. In a multinomial logistic regression model, the probability that x^i belongs to class j

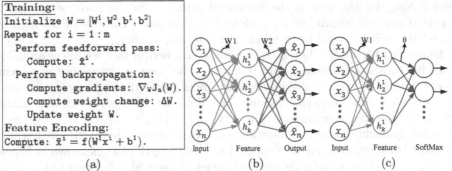

Fig. 4. (a) Training sparse autoencoder using backpropagation algorithm. (b) A single layer sparse autoencoder with one hidden layer. (c) Fine tuning is performed by stacking softmax at the end of sparse autoencoder.

is written as $\mathcal{H}_\theta(x^i) = p(y^i = j|x^i; \theta) = \frac{\exp(\theta_j^T x^i)}{\sum_{l=1}^{c} \exp(\theta_l^T x^i)}$, where, for $j \in \{1, \ldots, c\}$ is the set of class labels, θ_j^T is the weight vector corresponding to class j, and the superscript T denotes transpose operation. The output of the model or prediction is taken as, $y_{pred} = \arg\max_j P(y^i = j|x^i, \theta)$. Given a set of labeled training instances $X = \{(x^1, y^1), \ldots, (x^m, y^m)\}$, the weight matrix $\theta \in c \times k$ is obtained by solving the convex optimization problem as shown in Equation 2. It is solved using gradient descent method, which provides a globally optimal solution.

$$\arg\min_\theta J_s(\theta) = -\frac{1}{m} \sum_{i=1}^{m} \sum_{j=1}^{c} 1\{y^i = j\} \log p\left(y^i = j|x^i; \theta\right). \tag{2}$$

3.4 Active Learning

As discussed in Section 1, active learning can be used to reduce the amount of manual labeling during learning from streaming data. Based on the type of teacher available, the active learning systems are classified into two categories: strong teacher and weak teacher. Strong teachers are mainly humans, who generally provides correct and unambiguous class labels. But they are assumed to have a significant cost. On the other hand, weak teachers generally provide more tentative labels. They are assumed to be classification algorithms, which make errors but perform above the accuracy of random guess. Our proposed framework provides the opportunity to take advantages of both kind of teachers. Given a pool of unlabeled instances $U = \{x^1, \ldots, x^p\}$, an activity model $\mathcal{H}_\theta$, and the corresponding cost function $J_s(\theta)$, we select a teacher as follows.

Teacher Selection: When the pool of unlabeled activities U are presented to the system, current activity model $\mathcal{H}_\theta$ is applied on them, which generates a set of tentative decisions $Y = \{y^1, \ldots, y^p\}$ with probabilities $P = \{p(y^1|x^1, \theta), \ldots, (y^p|x^p, \theta)\}$. Now, we invoke the weak teacher when the tentative decision y^i has higher probability. That means, if $p(y^i = j|x, \theta)$ is greater than a threshold δ, the unlabeled activity is labeled using the label y^i from the current activity model. Now, for the rest of the unlabeled activities in the pool, we compute expected gradient length [36] for each activity. We select those with the highest expected gradient length to be labeled by a strong teacher.

Expected Gradient Length: The main idea here is that we select an unlabeled instance as a training sample if it brings the greatest change in the current model. Since, we train our classification model with gradient descent, we add the unlabeled instance to the training set if it creates the greatest change in the gradient of the objective function, $\nabla_{\theta_j} J_s(\theta) = -x^i \left[1\{y^i = j\} - p\left(y^i = j|x^i; \theta\right) \right]$. However, gradient change computation requires the knowledge of the label, which we don't have. So, we compute expected gradient length of x^i as shown in Equation 3. Given the pool of unlabeled activities U, we add a fraction (α) of U to the set of training activities as shown in Equation 4.

$$\Phi(x^i) = \sum_{j=1}^{c} p(y^i = j|x^i) \|\nabla_{\theta_j} J_s(\theta)\| \tag{3}$$

$$U^* = \underset{X \subseteq U \cap (|X|/|U|) = \alpha}{\arg \max} \sum_{x \in X} \Phi(x) \tag{4}$$

3.5 Incremental Learning

We train the sparse autoencoder and softmax classifier using gradient descent method, which can be done using two modes: batch mode and online mode. In batch mode, weight changes are computed over all the accumulated instances and then, they are updated. On the contrary, in online mode, weight changes are computed for each training instances one at a time and then, they are updated one by one [42]. The second mode is more appropriate for incrementally learning the weights as new training instances arrive from the streaming videos. However, the approach we use for incrementally learning the weights is known as mini-batch training in literature [33]. Here, weight changes are accumulated over some number, u, of instances before actually updating the weights, in which $1 < u < N$. N is the total number of training instances. Mini-batch incremental training is shown in Fig. 5(a).

However, performance of the above mentioned method deteriorates if the newly arrived training instances contain noise. To deal with this situation, we propose two more incremental learning scenarios based on the availability of memory: Infinite Buffer and Fixed Buffer. In infinite buffer approach, all the training instances that arrived so far are stored in the memory and all of them are used to incrementally train the network. On the other hand, in fixed buffer approach, there are limited memory to store training instances. So, we select a number of diverse training instances from the set to be stored in the memory. Suppose, we want to select K_c most diverse instances from available N_c instances of class c. If N_c is greater than K_c, we divide the N_c instances into K_c clusters and select one instance randomly from each cluster. The algorithm for selecting most diverse instances are shown in Fig. 5(b).

The overall algorithm for continuous learning of activity models with deep nets is presented in Algorithm 1.

	Repeat for each class c.
Initialize the weights.	Available instances: N_c.
Repeat the following steps:	Available memory spaces: K_c
If u training instances available:	If $K_c < N_c$:
Process u training instances.	Use kmean clustering algo. to
Compute gradients.	compute K_c clusters from N_c.
Update the weights.	Assign N_c inst. to K_c clusters.
Else	Store one instance per cluster.
Wait for stream data to arrive	Else
	Store all of the N_c instances.
(a)	(b)

Fig. 5. (a) Mini-batch training algorithm. (b) Most diverse instances selection algorithm.

Algorithm 1. Continuous Learning of Activity Models

Data: $\mathcal{V}$: Continuous Streaming Video.
Result: Activity Recognition Model $\mathcal{H}_\theta$, Sparse Autoencoder Model
    $\mathcal{A_W}$, Labeled Activities $[(x_{t_0+i}, y_{t_0+i})|i = 1, \ldots]$.
Parameters: Feature design parameters: T, L, and k, Training
parameters: $\beta, \rho,$ and λ, and Experiment design parameters: $K_c,$ and α.
Step 0: Learn the prior sparse autoencoder $\mathcal{A_W}$ and the prior
activity model $\mathcal{H}_\theta$ using fewer training data available. (Fig. 4(a))
Step 1: Segment the video $\mathcal{V}$ at timestamp $(t_0 + i)$ to get an
unlabeled activity segment, x_i (Sec. 3.1).
Step 2: Apply the current model $\mathcal{H}_\theta$ on x_i. Based on the condition
met, get a label y^i for x^i and put (x^i, y^i) in the buffer $\mathcal{U}$ (Sec.
3.4)
Step 3: If $\mathcal{U}$ is full, goto step 4 for incremental learning,
otherwise goto step 1.
Step 4: Update the model parameters W and θ (Fig. 5(a)).
Step 5: goto step 1 for next batch of training instances.

---

4 Experiments

We conduct rigorous experiments on four different datasets to verify the effectiveness of our framework. First two datasets are KTH [34] and UCF11 [19]. Here, we assume that activity segmentation is already given and we send the activity segments as the unlabeled instances to our continuous activity learning framework sequentially. We perform the other two experiments on VIRAT ground human activity dataset [26] and TRECVID [27], where we have to segment the activities from the streaming videos.

Objective: The main objective of the experiments is to analyze the performance of our proposed framework in learning activity models continuously from streaming videos. In ideal case, we would like to see that the performance is increasing smoothly as new instances are presented to the system and ultimately, it converges to the performance of one time exhaustive learning approaches which assumes that all the examples are labeled and presented beforehand. Based on the use of active learning and the size of buffer, we conduct our experiments in the following four different scenarios.

1. Active learning and fixed buffer (A1F1): This is the most realistic case, where we use active learning to reduce the amount of manual labeling of the incoming instances. We also assume that we have limited memory to store labeled training instances. So we have to select most diverse instances as discussed in the algorithm presented in Fig 5(b). We only use the training instances stored in this fixed buffer to incrementally update the parameters of sparse autoencoder $\mathcal{A}_W$ and activity model $\mathcal{H}_\theta$.

2. Active learning and infinite buffer (A1F0): Here, we use active learning to reduce the amount of manual labeling but we assume that we have infinite memory. We store all the labeled training instances and use all of them to incrementally update the parameters of sparse autoencoder $\mathcal{A}_W$ and activity model $\mathcal{H}_\theta$.

3. No active learning and fixed buffer (A0F1): Here, we do not use active learning and we assume that all the incoming instances are manually labeled. We have limited memory and we select the most diverse instances to store. We only use the training instances stored in this fixed buffer to incrementally update the parameters of sparse autoencoder $\mathcal{A}_W$ and activity model $\mathcal{H}_\theta$.

4. No active learning and infinite buffer (A0F0): This is the least realistic case, where we assume that all the incoming instances are manually labeled and we have infinite memory to store all of them. We use all the instances arrived so far to incrementally update the parameters of sparse autoencoder $\mathcal{A}_W$ and activity model $\mathcal{H}_\theta$. The performance of this, when the entire video is seen, should approach that of the batch methods in the existing literature, and can be used to compare our results with the state-of-the-art.

We maintain following conventions during all experiments:

1. Depending upon the sequence in which the data is presented to the learning module, each run of continuous learning on same dataset shows significant variance in accuracy. So, we take the mean of multiple runs of the results and then, report it in this paper.

2. We perform five fold cross validation. Three folds are used as the training set, one fold as the validation set, and one fold as the testing set. Instances in the training set are fed to the framework sequentially.

Fig. 6(a, c, e, g) show performances over all activities on KTH, UCF11, VIRAT, and TRECVID respectively. The x-axis shows the amount of training instances presented so far and the y-axis shows the accuracy. We compute this accuracy by dividing the number of correct classifications by the total number of instances presented to the classifier. On the other hand Fig. 6(b, d, f, h) show activity-wise performances on these datasets. Each group of stacked bar shows performances of an activity class. Each group contains four bars corresponding to A1F1, A1F0, A0F1, and A0F0 respectively from left to right. Each bar has four or less stacks. Each stack represents the performance increment of the improved activity model as a new batch of instances presented to the framework.

A missing stack means no performance improvement occurs during that step. More results are available in the supplementary material.

KTH Human Action Dataset: KTH [34] dataset consists of six actions such as *boxing, handclapping, handwaving, jogging, running, and walking*. These actions are performed by 25 subjects in four different scenarios such as outdoors, scale variation, different clothes, and indoors with lighting variation. There are totally 599 video clips with the resolution of 160×120 pixels. Detailed results of the experiments on KTH dataset are presented in Fig. 6(a-b). Fig. 6(a) shows the accuracies over all activities. As expected, A0F0 performs better than other three test cases. The most constrained case A1F1 also performs well by keeping it very close to A0F0. Performance of A0F1 is worst because it has fixed buffer size and might has to get rid of some informative instances as it does not use active learning. Performance of A1F0 is similar to A1F1, though it has infinite buffer. The reason behind this is that selection of diverse instances has less impact on results than the active learning. However, the most important point is that all the performances are asymptotically increasing as new instances are presented to the framework. Fig. 6(b) shows activity-wise performances. It is evident that, as new instances are arriving, our framework improves performance of each of the activity model. When all the instances are seen, our models A0F0 and A1F1 have achieved 96.6% and 94.1% accuracy respectively, which is very competitive with other works such as spatio-temporal feature based methods: 92.1% (HoF) [41] and 91.8% (HoG/HoF) [41]; active learning based method: 96.3% [20]; deep learning based methods: 93.9% (ICA) [16], 90.2% (3DCNN) [12] and 94.39% (3DCNN) [1]; and incremental learning based methods: 96.1% [23] and 90.3% [31].

UCF11 Human Action Dataset: We perform the second experiment on more challenging UCF11 dataset [19], which consists of eleven actions such as *basketball, biking, diving, golf_swing, horse_riding, soccer_juggling, swing, tennis_swing, trampoline_jumping, volleyball_spiking, and walking*. These actions are performed by 25 subjects under different scenarios and illumination conditions. There are totally 1600 video clips with the resolution of 320×240 pixels. Detailed results of the experiments on UCF11 dataset are presented in Fig. 6(c-d), where it is evident that performance is asymptotically increasing as new instances are presented to the system. Plots show similar trends like KTH but the gaps are widen. The reason is that UCF11 is more complex dataset than KTH and it requires more instances for A1F1 to achieve performance closer to A0F0. When all the instances are seen, our models A0F0 and A1F1 have achieved 59.73% and 49.52% accuracies respectively, which is very competitive with the spatio-temporal feature based method in [30] (59.89%).

VIRAT Dataset: VIRAT Ground dataset [26] is a state-of-the-art human activity dataset with many challenging characteristics. It is consists of 11 activities such as *person loading an object (PLV), person unloading an object (PUV), person opening a vehicle trunk, (POV), person closing a vehicle trunk (PCV), person getting into a vehicle (PGiV), person getting out of a vehicle (PGoV), person gesturing (PG), person carrying an object (PO), person running (PR), person entering a facility (PEF), and person exiting a facility (PXF)*. Videos

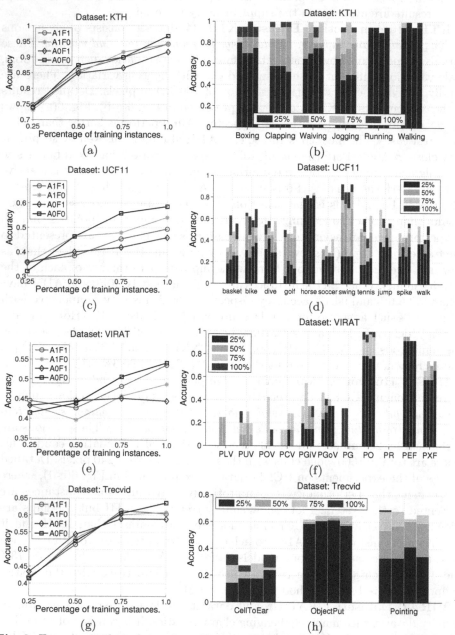

Fig. 6. Experimental results on four datasets- KTH, UCF11, VIRAT, and TRECVID (top to bottom row). Left plots show performances averaged over all activity classes, whereas right plots show the activity-wise performances. Each group in the right plots, contains four bars corresponding to A1F1, A1F0, A0F1, and A0F0 respectively from left to right. Plots are best viewable in color.

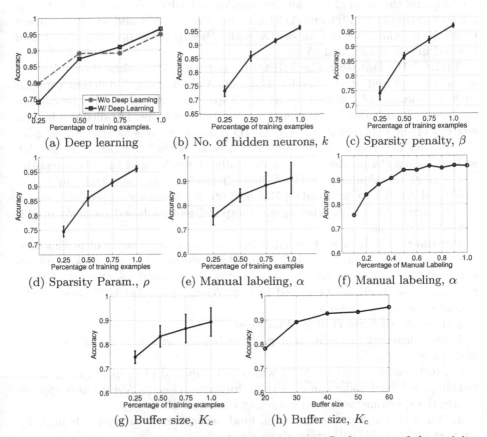

(a) Deep learning   (b) No. of hidden neurons, k (c) Sparsity penalty, β

(d) Sparsity Param., ρ (e) Manual labeling, α (f) Manual labeling, α

(g) Buffer size, K_c (h) Buffer size, K_c

Fig. 7. Plot (a) shows the benefit of using deep learning. Performance of the activity model that does not use deep learning is better initially, but as more instances are presented to the framework deep learning based method outperform other method by a margin of 1.7%. It demonstrates the ability of our framework in concept drift. Plots (b-h) show the sensitivity analysis of different parameters on KTH. (b) k is varied from 100 to 1500 with 100 increment. (c) β is varied from 0.5 to 5 with 0.5 increment (d) ρ is varied from 0.05 to 0.5 with 0.05 increment. In each of these cases, we show the mean and the variance of the accuracies for each incremental training epoch. Performance variation is significant initially but reduced later as more instances are presented to the system. (e) and (f) show the effect of the amount of manual labeling. Performance variation is large as expected. However, it is interesting that with around 50%-60% manual labeling our framework can achieve performance close to 100% manual labeling. (g) and (h) show the effect of buffer size K_c, which has significant effect on the performance. Performance increases with buffer size as expected. K_c is varied from 20 to 60 instances per class with 10 instances increment.

are 2 to 15 minutes long and 1920×1080 pixel resolution. Detailed results of the experiments on this dataset are presented in Fig. 6(e-f). The performance is increasing and the trend of the plots are similar to UCF11. When all the instances are seen, our models A0F0 and A1F1 have achieved 54.20% and 53.66% accuracy respectively, which is very competitive with other spatio-temporal feature based method in [13] (52.3% and 55.4%).

TRECVID Dataset: The TRECVID dataset [27] consists of over 100 hrs of videos captured at the London Gatwick Airport using 5 different cameras with a resolution of 720×576 pixel at 25 fps. The videos recorded by camera number 4 are excluded as few events occurred in this scene. Detailed results and analysis of the experiments on TRECVID dataset are presented in Fig. 6(g-h). We conduct experiments on recognizing three activities: *CellToEar*, *ObjectPut*, and, *Pointing*. Performance is asymptotically increasing and the characteristics of the plots are similar to KTH. When all the instances are seen, our model A0F0 and A1F1 have achieved 63.75% and 60.56% accuracy respectively, which is very competitive with other spatio-temporal feature based methods in [12] (60.56% and 62.69%).

Parameter Values and Sensitivity: We have three types of parameters, newly feature selection (T, L, and k), model training (β, rho, and λ), and experiment design parameters (K_c and α). Sensitivity analysis of most of these parameters on KTH are presented in Fig. 7(b-h). Fig. 7(a) is illustrating the benefit of using deep learning.

Summary of Experiment Analysis:

1. Deep learning has significant positive impact on learning activity models continuously (Fig. 7(a)).

2. Most realistic method A1F1 which is comprised of deep learning, active learning, and fixed buffer can achieve performance close to A0F0 which approximates the batch methods in the existing literature (Fig. 6).

3. When all the instances are seen, final accuracies of our methods in A1F1 are very competitive with state-of-the-art works.

5 Conclusion

In this work, we proposed a novel framework for learning human activity models continuously from streaming videos. Most of the research works on human activity recognition assumes that all the training instances are labeled and available beforehand. These works don't take the advantage of newly incoming instances. Our proposed framework improves the current activity models by taking the advantage of new unlabeled instances and intricately trying together deep networks and active learning. Rigorous experimental analysis on four challenging datasets proved the robustness of our framework. In future, we will incorporate context as the feature in our framework to learn more complex activity models. We will also investigate how to learn new unseen activity classes.

References

1. Baccouche, M., Mamalet, F., Wolf, C., Garcia, C., Baskurt, A.: Sequential deep learning for human action recognition. In: Human Behavior Understanding (2011)
2. Buhmann, J.M., Vezhnevets, A., Ferrari, V.: Active learning for semantic segmentation with expected change. In: CVPR (2012)
3. Chaudhry, R., Ravichandran, A., Hager, G., Vidal, R.: Histograms of oriented optical flow and binet-cauchy kernels on nonlinear dynamical systems for the recognition of human actions. In: CVPR (2009)
4. Choi, W., Shahid, K., Savarese, S.: Learning context for collective activity recognition. In: CVPR (2011)
5. Farabet, C., Camille Couprie, L.N., LeCun, Y.: Learning hierarchical features for scene labeling. PAMI (2013)
6. Coates, A., Ng, A.Y.: Selecting receptive fields in deep networks. In: NIPS (2011)
7. Dalal, N., Triggs, B.: Histograms of oriented gradients for human detection. In: CVPR (2005)
8. Felzenszwalb, P.F., Girshic, R.B., McAllester, D.: Discriminatively trained deformable part models, release 4,
   http://people.cs.uchicago.edu/pff/latent-release4/
9. Hasan, M., Roy-Chowdhury, A.: Incremental activity modeling and recognition in streaming videos. In: CVPR (2014)
10. He, H., Chen, S., Li, K., Xu, X.: Incremental learning from stream data. IEEE TNN 22(12), 1901–1914 (2011)
11. Hinton, G.E.: Learning multiple layers of representation. Trends in Cognitive Sciences (2007)
12. Ji, S., Xu, W., Yang, M., Yu, K.: 3d convolutional neural networks for human action recognition. PAMI (2013)
13. Jiang, Y.G., Ngo, C.W., Yang, J.: Towards optimal bag-of-features for object categorization and semantic video retrieval. In: ACM-CIVR (2007)
14. Krizhevsky, A., Sutskever, I., Hinton, G.E.: Imagenet classification with deep convolutional neural networks. In: NIPS (2012)
15. Laptev, I.: On space-time interest points. IJCV (2005)
16. Le, Q., Zou, W., Yeung, S., Ng, A.: Learning hierarchical invariant spatio-temporal features for action recognition with independent subspace analysis. In: CVPR (2011)
17. Lee, H., Ekanadham, C., Ng, A.Y.: Sparse deep belief net model for visual area v2. In: NIPS (2007)
18. Li, X., Guo, Y.: Adaptive active learning for image classication. In: CVPR (2013)
19. Liu, J., Luo, J., Shah, M.: Recognizing realistic actions from videos "in the wild". In: CVPR (2009)
20. Liu, X., Zhang, J.: Active learning for human action recognition with gaussian processes. In: ICIP (2011)
21. Lowe, D.: Object recognition from local scale-invariant features. In: ICCV (1999)
22. Loy, C.C., Hospedales, T.M., Xiang, T., Gong, S.: Stream-based joint exploration-exploitation active learning. In: CVPR (2012)
23. Minhas, R., Mohammed, A., Wu, Q.: Incremental learning in human action recognition based on snippets. IEEE TCSVT (2012)
24. Nayak, N., Zhu, Y., Roy-Chowdhury, A.: Exploiting spatio-temporal scene structure for wide-area activity analysis in unconstrained environments. IEEE TIFS 8(10) (2013)

25. Ng, A.: (2013),
    http://deeplearning.stanford.edu/wiki/index.php/UFLDL_Tutorial
26. Oh, S., Hoogs, A., et al.: A large-scale benchmark dataset for event recognition in surveillance video. In: CVPR (2011)
27. Over, P., Awad, G., Michel, M., Fiscus, J., et al.: An overview of the goals, tasks, data, evaluation mechanisms, and metrics. In: TRECVID (2012)
28. Polikar, R., Upda, L., Upda, S., Honavar, V.: Learn++: An incremental learning algorithm for supervised neural networks. IEEE TSMC Part:C 31(4) (2001)
29. Poppe, R.: A survey on vision-based human action recognition. Image and Vision Computing (2010)
30. Reddy, K.K., Shah, M.: Recognizing 50 human action categories of web videos. MVAP (2012)
31. Reddy, K., Liu, J., Shah, M.: Incremental action recognition using feature-tree. In: ICCV (2009)
32. Sarawagi, S., Cohen, W.W.: Semi-markov conditional random fields for information extraction. In: NIPS (2004)
33. Sarle, W.S.: (2002), ftp://ftp.sas.com/pub/neural/faq2.html
34. Schuldt, C., Laptev, I., Caputo, B.: Recognizing human actions: A local svm approach. In: ICPR (2004)
35. Settles, B.: Active learning. Morgan & Claypool (2012)
36. Settles, B., Craven, M., Ray, S.: Multiple-instance active learning. In: NIPS (2008)
37. Song, B., Jeng, T., Staudt, E., Roy-Chowdury, A.: A stochastic graph evolution framework for robust multi-target tracking. In: ECCV (2010)
38. Taylor, G., Fergus, R., LeCun, Y., Bregler, C.: Convolutional learning of spatio-temporal features. In: ECCV (2010)
39. Vijayanarasimhan, S., Jain, P., Grauman, K.: Far-sighted active learning on a budget for image and video recognition. In: CVPR (2010)
40. Vincent, P., Larochelle, H., Lajoie, I., Bengio, Y., Manzagol, P.A.: Stacked denoising autoencoders: Learning useful representations in a deep network with a local denoising criterion. Journal of Machine Learning Research (2010)
41. Wang, H., Ullah, M.M., Klaser, A., Laptev, I., Schmid, C.: Evaluation of local spatio-temporal features for action recognition. In: BMVC (2009)
42. Wilsona, D.R., Martinezb, T.R.: The general inefficiency of batch training for gradient descent learning. Neural Networks (2003)
43. Yang, J., Yu, K., Gong, Y., Huang, T.: Linear spatial pyramid matching using sparse coding for image classification. In: CVPR (2009)
44. Zhu, Y., Nayak, N.M., Roy-Chowdhury, A.K.: Context-aware modeling and recognition of activities in video. In: CVPR (2013)
45. Zivkovic, Z.: Improved adaptive gaussian mixture model for background subtraction. In: ICPR (2004)

DaMN – Discriminative and Mutually Nearest: Exploiting Pairwise Category Proximity for Video Action Recognition

Rui Hou[1], Amir Roshan Zamir[1], Rahul Sukthankar[2], and Mubarak Shah[1]

[1] Center for Research in Computer Vision at UCF, Orlando, USA
[2] Google Research, Mountain View, USA
http://crcv.ucf.edu/projects/DaMN/

Abstract. We propose a method for learning discriminative category-level features and demonstrate state-of-the-art results on large-scale action recognition in video. The key observation is that one-vs-rest classifiers, which are ubiquitously employed for this task, face challenges in separating very similar categories (such as running vs. jogging). Our proposed method automatically identifies such pairs of categories using a criterion of mutual pairwise proximity in the (kernelized) feature space, using a category-level similarity matrix where each entry corresponds to the one-vs-one SVM margin for pairs of categories. We then exploit the observation that while splitting such "Siamese Twin" categories may be difficult, separating them from the remaining categories in a two-vs-rest framework is not. This enables us to augment one-vs-rest classifiers with a judicious selection of "two-vs-rest" classifier outputs, formed from such discriminative and mutually nearest (DaMN) pairs. By combining one-vs-rest and two-vs-rest features in a principled probabilistic manner, we achieve state-of-the-art results on the UCF101 and HMDB51 datasets. More importantly, the same DaMN features, when treated as a mid-level representation also outperform existing methods in knowledge transfer experiments, both cross-dataset from UCF101 to HMDB51 and to new categories with limited training data (one-shot and few-shot learning). Finally, we study the generality of the proposed approach by applying DaMN to other classification tasks; our experiments show that DaMN outperforms related approaches in direct comparisons, not only on video action recognition but also on their original image dataset tasks.

1 Introduction

Attributes are mid-level visual concepts, such as "smiling", "brittle", or "quick" that are typically employed to characterize categories at a semantic level. In recent years, attributes have been successfully applied to a variety of computer vision problems including face verification [11], image retrieval [30], action recognition [15], image-to-text generation [1]. Category-level attributes are popular not only because they can represent the shared semantic properties of visual classes but because they can leverage information from known categories to enable existing classifiers to generalize to novel categories for which there exists limited training data.

D. Fleet et al. (Eds.): ECCV 2014, Part III, LNCS 8691, pp. 721–736, 2014.

Ideally, attributes should capture human-interpretable semantic characteristics that can be reliably recognized by machines from visual data. However, the focus on human-interpretation means that developing attribute classifiers typically demands a labor-intensive process involving manual selection of attribute labels and collection of suitable training data by domain experts (e.g., [12]).

Our stance is that while human interpretability of attributes is obviously desirable, it should be treated as a secondary goal. Thus, we seek fully automated methods that learn discriminative category-level features to serve as useful mid-level representations, directly from data.

We propose DaMN, a method for automatically constructing category-level features for multi-class problems based on combining one-vs-one, one-vs-rest and two-vs-rest classifiers in a principled manner. The key intuition behind DaMN is that similar activities (e.g., jogging vs. running) are often poorly represented by one-vs-rest classifiers. Rather than requiring methods to accurately split such "Siamese Twin" categories, we choose to augment one-vs-rest classifiers with a *judicious selection* of two-vs-rest classifiers that keep the strongly related categories together. The challenge is how best to identify such categories and then how to combine information from the different classifiers in a principled manner. Figure 1 (left) illustrates examples of category pairs identified as closely related by DaMN; the complete grouping of DaMN pairs extracted for UCF101 is shown in Figure 1 (right). It is important to note that the DaMN category pairs are (by construction) similar in kernel space and generally well separated from the remaining categories. By contrast, the manually constructed category-attribute matrix for UCF101 is not as amenable to machine classification despite having human-interpretable names [14]. Such experiences drive us to explore the idea of data-driven category features as an alternative to human selected attributes, with the hope that such features can still offer the benefits (such as cross-dataset generalization and one-shot learning) of traditional attributes.

We are not the first to propose such a data-driven approach. For instance, Farhadi et al. suggested searching for attributes by examining random splits of the data [5] and Bergamo & Torresani recently proposed Meta-class [2], an approach for identifying related image categories based on misclassification errors on a validation set. Although we are the first to apply such approaches for video action recognition, we do not claim this as a significant contribution of our work.

More importantly, our experiments on UCF101 and HMDB51 confirm that these automatically learned features significantly improve classification performance and are also effective vehicles for knowledge transfer to novel categories.

Our paper's contributions can be summarized as follows.

1. We propose a novel, general-purpose, fully automated algorithm that generates discriminative category-level features directly from data. Unlike earlier work, DaMN trains from all of the available data (no random test/train splits nor validation sets).

2. We evaluate DaMN on large-scale video action recognition tasks and show that: a) the proposed category-level features outperform the manually generated category-level attributes provided in the UCF101 dataset; b) DaMN is a strong choice for a mid-level action representation, enabling us to obtain the highest-reported results on the UCF101 dataset.

3. We show that DaMN outperforms existing methods on knowledge transfer, both across dataset and to novel categories with limited training data.

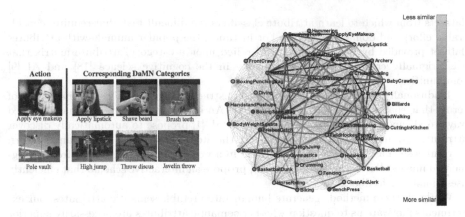

Fig. 1. Left: Examples of DaMN category pairs automatically discovered in UCF101. For the actions shown on the left, three sample mutually nearest categories are shown on the right. Explicitly representing such category-level information enables improved action recognition accuracy. **Right:** Visualization of the extracted pairwise category similarity (Section 3.1) for UCF101. To manage visual clutter, only the first 43 categories are shown, with edges shaded according to the pairwise similarity between the respective classes. We see that DaMN identifies meaningful semantic groups, such as *weightlifting*, *bat-and-ball sports*, and *face-centered actions*. Also note the presence of singleton categories.

4. While our focus is on video action recognition, the proposed method can also be applied to other problems and we show DaMN's superiority on the Animals-with-Attributes [12] dataset.

The remainder of the paper is structured as follows. Section 2 presents an overview of related work. Section 3 details the proposed method of generating DaMN category-level features. Section 4 describes video action recognition experiments on UCF101, knowledge transfer to HMDB51, one-shot learning and a study on semantic attributes vs. data driven category-level features. We also present results on image datasets, consider extensions beyond second-order relationships and provide a brief analysis of DaMN's computational complexity. Section 5 concludes and outlines promising directions for future work.

2   Related Work

This section reviews a representative subset of the related work in this area and details the key differences between the proposed approach and current efforts to directly learn discriminative attributes or category-level features from data.

2.1   Semantic Attributes

The majority of research on attributes focuses on how semantic attributes can better solve a diverse set of computer vision problems [1,4,8,11,15,30] or enable new applications [12,19]. Generally, specifying these semantic attributes and generating suitable datasets from which to learn attribute classifiers is a difficult task that requires considerable effort and domain expertise. For instance, the popular animals-with-attributes dataset provided by Lampert et al. [12] relied upon a category/attribute matrix that was originally created by domain experts in the cognitive science [18] and AI [9] communities.

Traditionally, semantic attributes are constructed by manually selecting a set of terms that characterize the concept [15, 28]. An important line of work has explored ways to alleviate this human burden. Berg et al. [1] propose to automatically discover attributes by mining text and images on the web. Ferrari and Zisserman [7] learn attributes such as "striped" and "spotted" in a weakly supervised scheme from unsegmented images. Parikh and Grauman [20] propose an interactive scheme that efficiently uses annotator feedback.

While all these methods generate human-interpretable semantic attributes, our experiments motivate us to question whether semantic attributes are necessarily superior to those learned directly from low-level features. The recently released large-scale action recognition dataset, UCF101 [22] has been augmented by a set of category-level attributes, generated using human rater judgments, for the ICCV'13 THUMOS contest on Action Recognition [14]. Section 4 discusses that even though the THUMOS semantic attributes encode an additional source of information from human raters, they are significantly outperformed by the automatically learned DaMN features.

2.2   Data-Driven Category-Level Features

Category-level features (sometimes termed *data-driven attributes*) are mid-level representations that are typically learned from low-level features without manual supervision. Their main drawbacks are that: 1) the distinctions found in the feature space may not correspond in any obvious way to a semantic difference that is visible to humans; 2) unlike the attributes described in Section 2.1, which incorporate additional domain knowledge from human raters, it is unclear whether data-driven features should be expected to glean anything from the low-level features that a state-of-the-art classifier employing the same features would fail to extract.

Farhadi et al. [5] discover promising attributes by considering large numbers of random splits of the data. Wang & Mori [26] propose a discriminatively trained joint model for categories and their visual attributes in images. Liu et al. [16] combine a set of manually specified attributes with data-driven attributes for action recognition. Yang and Shah [27] propose the use of data-driven concepts for event detection in video. Mensink et al. [17] propose an efficient method for generalizing to new categories in image classification by extending the nearest class mean (NCM) classifier that is reminiscent of category-level features. Our work is related to that of Yu et al. [29], which independently proposes a principled approach to learning category-level attributes from data by formulating the similarity between two categories based on one-vs-one SVM margins. However, DaMN differs from [29] in several key respects. First, our features are real-valued while theirs (like most attributes in previous work) are binary. Second, our method centers on identifying pairs of strongly-connected categories (mutual near neighbors) while theirs is set up as a Rayleigh quotient optimization problem and solved using a greedy algorithm. Third, their application is in image classification while we are primarily interested in action recognition with a large number of classes. Nonetheless, we show in direct comparisons that DaMN outperforms [29] using their experimental methodology on image datasets.

At a high level, the work most closely related to DaMN is Bergamo & Torresani's Meta-Class features, which also seek to group categories in a data-driven manner in order to improve upon one-vs-rest classifiers. The fundamental difference is in how the two algorithms determine which categories to group: meta-class trains an auxiliary SVM classifier and treats the classification error (computed over a validation set) as a proxy for the similarity between two categories. By contrast, DaMN directly formulates principled measures for this category-level distance, such as the pairwise (one-vs-one) SVM margin. The latter is an improvement both in terms of theory and is experimentally validated in direct comparisons on several datasets.

2.3 Knowledge Transfer

Category-level features and attributes are well suited to vision tasks that require trained classifiers to generalize to novel categories for which there exists limited training data. This is because an classifier trained to recognize an attribute such as "furry" from cats and dogs is likely to generalize to recognizing other furry mammals. Attribute-driven knowledge transfer has been successfully demonstrated both in the one-shot [12] and zero-shot [19, 21] context. In the action recognition domain, Liu et al. [15] explore attribute-driven generalization for novel actions using manually specified action attributes.

Our approach for generalizing to novel categories is purely data-driven. At a high level, our approach to one-shot learning is related to the use of one-vs-rest classifiers or classemes [23] by which novel categories can be described; DaMN features can be viewed as augmenting one-vs-rest with the most useful subset of potential two-categories-vs-rest classifiers. Our experiments (Section 4) confirm that our DaMN category-level features are significantly superior to existing approaches in both cross-dataset and novel category generalization scenarios.

3 Proposed Approach: DaMN

Figure 2 (right) provides a visual overview of the DaMN process, detailed further in this section. Action recognition in video is typically formulated as a classification problem where the goal is to assign a category label $y \in \mathcal{Y}$ to each video clip $v \in \mathcal{V}$. Although our proposed method also works with more complex feature families, let us simplify the following discussion by assuming that the given video v is represented by some feature $\mathbf{x}_v \in \mathbb{R}^d$.

Let $n = |\mathcal{Y}|$ denote the number of categories and $\mathcal{F}$ the set of category-level features that describe how categories are related. The size of this set, $m = |\mathcal{F}|$; $m = n$ in the case of one-vs-rest classifiers, and $m > n$ for DaMN — with the number of two-vs-rest classifiers given by $m - n$. In general, the category-level relationships can be expressed by a binary-valued matrix $\mathbf{B} \in \mathbb{B}^{n \times m}$. The ith row of $\mathbf{B}$ contains the features for category y_i while the jth column of the matrix denotes the categories that share a given category-level feature. Each column is associated with a classifier, $f_j(\mathbf{x}_v)$ (such as a kernel SVM), trained either one-vs-rest or two-vs-rest, that operates on a given instance (video clip) v.

Our goal is to automatically identify the set of suitable features $\mathcal{F}$, train their associated classifiers $f(.)$ using the available training data and use the instance-level predictions to classify novel videos. In the additional task of one-shot learning, we use the same category-level features with an expanded set of categories, $\mathcal{Y}'$, for each of which we are given only a single exemplar.

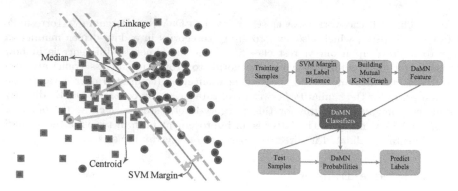

Fig. 2. **Left:** Illustration of different category-level distance metrics. The illustration uses a linear kernel only to simplify visualization; all of these, except for centroid, are actually performed in kernel space. **Right:** Overview of the DaMN Learning/Prediction Process.

3.1   Pairwise Category Similarity

We train one-vs-one SVM classifiers for every pair of categories to compute the category-level similarity. We propose a natural generalization from the instance-level similarity, typically expressed through some kernel function $K(.,.)$ that compares their respective low-level feature representation (e.g., using χ^2 for bag-of-words features) typically used in action recognition to category-level similarity as the margin of a one-vs-one SVM trained to discriminate the two categories, expressed in the dual form as

$$d_{y_i,y_j} = \sum_{\forall(p,q)\in y_i \cup y_j} \alpha_p \alpha_q (-1)^{I[c(p)\neq c(q)]} K(\mathbf{x}_p,\mathbf{x}_q) \tag{1}$$

where p and q are all pairs of instances from the union of the two categories, α their non-negative weights (> 0 only for support vectors), $c(.)$ is a function that returns the category of the given instance and $I[.]$ denotes the indicator function whose value is 1 when its argument is true and 0 otherwise. Figure 1 (right) visualizes the similarity values computed using this metric for UCF101; to manage visual clutter, we show only the first 43 categories, with edges shaded according to the pairwise similarity between respective categories. Note that even though there are $\binom{n}{2}$ such classifiers, they are quick to train since each classifier uses only a tiny subset of the training data — a fact exploited by one-vs-one multi-class SVMs.

Given similarities between categories (at the feature level), we seek to identify pairs of categories that are close. For this, we construct a mutual k-nearest neighbor (kNN) graph over categories. A mutual kNN graph is similar to the popular kNN graph except that nodes p and q are connected if and only if p lists q as among its k closest neighbors and q also lists p among its k closest neighbors. Let $G = (V, E)$ be a graph with n nodes, V, corresponding to the category labels y and weights given by:

$$w_{pq} = \begin{cases} 0 & y_p \text{ and } y_q \text{ are not mutual } k\text{NN}, \\ d_{y_p,y_q} & \text{otherwise.} \end{cases} \tag{2}$$

Unlike a k-nearest neighbor graph, where every node has degree k, a mutual kNN graph exhibits much sparser connectivity.

3.2 Constructing the DaMN Category-Level Feature Matrix

The DaMN category-level feature matrix is composed of two parts: 1) features to separate each category individually (identical to one-vs-rest); 2) pair classifiers designed to separate mutually proximate pairs of categories from the remaining classes. Among the $\binom{n}{2}$ possible category pairs, DaMN selects only those that are mutually proximate ($w_{pq} > 0$) as additional features.

Thus, $\mathbf{B}$ is an $n \times m$ matrix composed of two portions: an $n \times n$ identity matrix corresponding to the one-vs-rest classifiers augmented by additional columns for the selected category pairs. Each of the additional columns c in the second block is associated with a category pair (p, q) and the entries of the new column are given by:

$$B_{ic} = \begin{cases} 1 & \text{if } i = p \text{ or } i = q \\ 0 & \text{otherwise.} \end{cases} \tag{3}$$

3.3 Training Category-Level Feature Classifiers

Each column in $\mathbf{B}$ defines a partition over labels that is used to split the training set into positives (those instances whose labels possess the given feature) and negatives (instances lacking the feature). We learn a χ^2 kernel SVM using this data split to predict the new feature.

Since the first n columns of $\mathbf{B}$ have a single non-zero entry, they correspond to training regular one-vs-rest SVMs. The remaining $m - n$ columns have two non-zero entries and require training a set of somewhat unusual two-category-vs-rest SVMs to separate similar category pairs from the other classes.

3.4 Predicting Categories

Given a video v from the test set, we extract its low-level features x_v and pass it through the trained bank of DaMN classifiers, both one-vs-rest and two-vs-rest. We also have a set of one-vs-one classifiers to distinguish between the two categories in one DaMN pair. For the given video v, let $P(y_i)$ denote the probabilistic score returned by the one-vs-rest classifier of category y_i, and $P(y_i \oplus y_j)$ represent the score computed by the two-vs-rest classifier of the DaMN pair (y_i, y_j). Also, let $P(y_i | y_i \oplus y_j)$ denote the score returned by the one-vs-one classifier which distinguishes between the categories y_i and y_j. All of the SVM classifier scores are Platt-scaled to provide probabilistic values.

We now compute a score that quantifies the match between v and each candidate category y_i by combining the traditional one-vs-rest score with those two-vs-rest scores that involve y_i, weighted by a one-vs-one classifier between y_i and the other class in the DaMN pair. All of these individual probabilities are then combined to obtain the final score for category y_i:

$$T_{y_i} = \frac{P(y_i) + \sum_{\{j : (y_i, y_j) \in \text{DaMN}\}} P(y_i \oplus y_j) \times P(y_i | y_i \oplus y_j)}{\sum_{c=1}^{m} B_{ic}}. \tag{4}$$

The argument of the summation in the numerator is equivalent to the following probabilistic rule for finding the probability of event a: $P(a) = P(a \cup b) \times P(a | a \cup b)$. The set $\{j : (y_i, y_j) \in \text{DaMN}\}$ represents the DaMN pairs that involve the category y_i. Since there are several of such pairs, the score T_{y_i} is defined as the mean of the scores acquired from all of those pairs as well as the score of the one-vs-rest classifier (i.e., $P(y_i)$). Therefore, the denominator of Eq. 4 is equal to the total number of DaMN pairs that involve category y_i plus one (to count for its one-vs-rest classifier).

Since, as seen in Figure 1 (right), some categories participate in many more DaMN pairs than others, the final score for such categories involves more terms. At the other extreme are categories that do not show up in any DaMN pair, for which only the one-vs-rest score is used; this situation corresponds to a highly distinctive category, which is easily discriminated from others (as evidenced by a high margin in kernel space). An intuitive illustration is that when computing a score for v with respect to the category *running*, we should focus on DaMN features generated by pairs like *jogging-running* or *walking-running* rather than those seeded by *makeup-shaving*.

Finally, we assign the test video to the category with the highest match score:

$$\hat{y} = \arg\max_{y \in \mathcal{Y}} (T_y). \tag{5}$$

3.5 Knowledge Transfer to Novel Categories

This section details how DaMN features enable generalization to novel categories through knowledge transfer. Consider the scenario where m features have been generated using abundant training data from n categories, resulting in an $m \times n$ binary matrix and an $n \times n$ adjacency matrix describing the weighted mutual kNN graph. We are now presented with n' novel categories, each containing only a few instances. The goal is to classify instances in the test set generated from all $n + n'$ categories (both existing and novel).

We proceed as follows. First, for each new label y', we determine its similarity to the known categories $\mathcal{Y}$ using the small amount of new data and Equation 1. Note that while the data from novel categories may be insufficient to enable accurate training of one-vs-rest classifiers, it is sufficient to provide a rough estimate of similarity between the new category and existing categories. From such rough estimate, we determine the k categories that are most similar to y' and synthesize a new row for the matrix $\mathbf{B}$ for the novel category from the rows of similar categories:

$$B_{y'j} = \sum_{y \in k\text{NN}(y')} B_{yj}, \tag{6}$$

where $\sum$ is treated as the OR operator since $\mathbf{B}$ is a binary-valued matrix and kNN(.) returns the k categories most similar to the novel category.

At test time, we obtain scores from the bank of existing DaMN feature classifiers and determine the most likely category using Equations 4 and 5. Note that for the novel categories, Equation 4 employs the synthesized values in the matrix.

4 Experiments

Our experimental methodology focuses on clarity, thoroughness and reproducibility rather than tuning our system to squeeze the best possible results. Even under these conditions, as detailed below, DaMN generates the best classification results to date on both the UCF101 and HMDB51 datasets.

All of our experiments are conducted on the two latest publicly available action recognition datasets, UCF101 [22] and HMDB51 [10], which contain YouTube videos

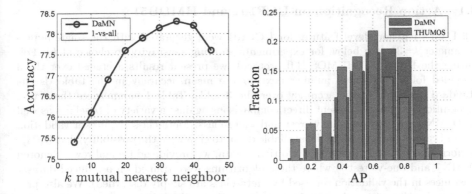

Fig. 3. Left: DaMN is tuned using a single hyper-parameter, k. Accuracy on UCF101 with DTF (late fusion) as k is varied. DaMN outperforms the strongest baseline for $k>15$ and even at its worst, DaMN outperforms all remaining methods. **Right:** Histogram showing the fraction of classifiers that achieve a given AP on UCF101. DaMN features can be detected more reliably than the manually prescribed attributes provided by THUMOS.

from 101 and 51 categories, respectively. For UCF101 experiments, we closely follow the protocol specified in the ICCV'13 THUMOS action recognition challenge [14], for which test/train splits, manually generated category-level semantic attributes and baseline results are provided.

We restrict ourselves to low-level features for which open source code is available, and select the Dense Trajectory Features (DTF) [25] and Improved Dense Trajectory Features (I-DTF) [24] based on their state-of-the-art results reported in recent competitions. DTF consists of four descriptors: histogram-of-gradients (HOG), histogram-of-flow (HOF), motion-based histograms (MBH) and trajectories. The descriptors are traditionally combined using early fusion (concatenation) but we also present results using the individual component descriptors and late fusion (using equally weighted combination of SVMs). For each descriptor, we generate a 4000-word codebook and build a standard bag-of-words representation for each video by aggregating bin counts over the entire clip.

For classification, we employ the popular LIBSVM [3] implementation of support vector machines with $C=1$ and the χ^2 kernel, since our features are histograms. Because DaMN already employs one-vs-one SVMs for determining category proximity, results from multi-class one-vs-one SVMs serve as a natural baseline. Following Yu et al. [29], we also train 101 one-vs-rest SVM classifiers to serve as a stronger baseline[1].

Implementing DaMN is straightforward, but we provide open-source code to enable the research community to easily duplicate our experiments and to employ DaMN in other domains.

---

[1] Others (e.g., the majority of the submissions to ICCV'13 THUMOS Challenge [14]) report that one-vs-rest SVMs consistently outperform multi-class one-vs-one SVMs for reasons that are not clearly understood; an observation that merits further study.

4.1   Action Recognition on UCF101 and HMDB51

All DaMN category-level features for UCF101 were generated with the single hyper-parameter $k=35$ (see below for experiments showing sensitivity to choice of k). Following the ICCV'13 THUMOS [14] protocol, we present results averaged over the 3 provided folds. The small number next to the mean accuracy in the tables is the standard deviation of the accuracy over the 3 folds. Table 1 summarizes the action recognition results. We present direct comparisons against a variety of baselines as well as DaMN's competitors, one-vs-rest and meta-class. Meta-class requires a validation set and cannot train on all of the available data; to eliminate the possibility that DaMN performs better solely due to the additional data, we provide additional rows (denoted DaMN$^-$ and one-vs-rest$^-$) where these algorithms were trained on a reduced dataset (instances in the validation set used by Meta-class are simply discarded). We also provide two baselines from the THUMOS contest: 1) the THUMOS contest baseline using STIP [13] + bag-of-words + χ^2 kernel SVM, and 2) a baseline computed using the manually generated THUMOS semantic attributes for UCF101. For the latter baseline, we employ the same methodology as DaMN to ensure a fair direct comparison. We make the following observations.

First, we note that switching from STIP to DTF features alone generates a large improvement over the THUMOS baseline and combining DTF components using late fusion (LF) is generally better than with the early fusion (EF) originally employed by the DTF authors. These are consistent with the results reported by many groups at the ICCV THUMOS workshop and are not claimed as a contribution. We simply note that STIP features are no longer a strong baseline for future work in this area.

Second, we observe that the manually generated THUMOS semantic features are outperformed by all of the methods. This drives a more detailed investigation (see Section 4.2).

Third, we note that the DaMN features in conjunction with *any* of the component features (either individual of fused) provides a consistent boost over both one-vs-rest or meta-class, regardless of experimental condition. In particular, DaMN outperforms meta-class even after discarding a portion of the data (which meta-class employs for estimating category-level similarity). Interestingly, meta-class outperforms one-vs-rest only when one-vs-rest is not given access to the full data (one-vs-rest$^-$); this demonstrates that, unlike DaMN, meta-class makes inefficient use of the available data and is not a recommended technique unless there is an abundance of training data. This additional training data boosts DaMN's accuracy by a further 6% in the late-fused DTF condition (DaMN vs. DaMN$^-$), which convincingly shows the benefits of the proposed approach over previous methods.

As discussed in Section 3, DaMN only employs a single hyper-parameter. Figure 3 (left) shows how UCF101 classification accuracy varies with k using the DTF features (late fusion). We observe that DaMN is better than the strongest baseline after $k=15$ and peaks on UCF101 around $k=35$. Even the worst instance of DaMN ($k=5$) is better than all of the remaining methods.

Table 2 shows action recognition results on HMDB51 using its standard splits [10]. The selected parameters for DaMN and the baselines for this dataset were the same as for UCF101. DaMN achieves state-of-the-art results on HMDB51, outperforming the recent results [24] that employ one-vs-rest SVM on Improved DTF features.

Table 1. UCF101 Results. DaMN consistently boosts results across all features. DaMN achieves the best reported results on UCF101 using I-DTF.

	I-DTF [24]	DTF (LF)	DTF (EF)	MBH	HOG	HOF	Traj.
DaMN	**87.00**±1.1	**78.33**±1.7	**75.93**±1.8	**73.25**±1.3	**57.60**±0.6	**57.42**±2.1	**55.18**±1.6
1-vs-rest	85.90±1.2	75.88±2.4	74.60±2.5	71.32±2.9	56.94±2.3	56.08±3.1	53.72±1.6
1-vs-1	79.12±1.9	69.25±3.3	68.32±3.6	66.00±2.4	51.40±3.2	51.80±2.3	48.63±1.1
DaMN⁻	**80.03**±0.4	**71.82**±1.4	**70.04**±1.5	**66.73**±1.1	**51.63**±0.7	**49.83**±1.9	**49.74**±1.5
Meta-class	78.65±0.6	69.71±1.8	68.32±1.4	60.07±2.3	44.15±2.6	44.98±0.8	43.91±1.0
1-vs-rest⁻	78.54±0.6	67.84±1.9	66.91±2.1	62.34±2.2	43.71±1.6	44.93±1.4	43.71±1.3
Semantic	58.99	50.19	49.73	51.56	32.68	43.77	33.85
THUMOS [14] baseline (STIP + BOW + χ^2 SVM): 43.9%							

Table 2. HMDB51 Results. DaMN achieves the best reported results on this dataset.

	DaMN	1-vs-rest	Meta-class
I-DTF	**57.88**±0.46	57.01±1.44	57.36±0.24

4.2 DaMN vs. THUMOS Semantic Attributes

To be of practical use, attributes need to be semantic as well as machine-detectable. The THUMOS attributes clearly capture the first criterion, since they were developed by human raters. However, since they are category-level there is a danger that the attributes envisioned by the raters may not actually be visible (or reliably detectable) in a given instance from that category.

The accuracy of an attribute classifier captures the reliability with which the given attribute can be recognized in data. Figure 3 (right) plots histograms of accuracy for THUMOS and DaMN classifiers and Table 3 (left) summarizes some key statistics.

Table 4 examines a natural question: how do different choices for the category-level distances illustrated in Figure 2 (left) impact DaMN's performance? We briefly describe the choices. Given the set of distances $\{d_{ij} : i \in I, j \in J\}$ for kernel distances between instances in categories I and J, *linkage* is defined as the minimum distance; *median* is the median distance between pairs; *average* is the mean over the distances in this set; and *centroid* is the distance between the centroids of each category (in feature space). *SVM Margin* is the margin for an one-vs-one SVM trained on instances from each category. We see that the SVM Margin is better for almost all features, is robust to outliers and is thus the default choice for DaMN in this paper.

We observe that the DaMN classifiers are more reliable than the THUMOS ones. The DaMN features were designed to identify pairs of categories that are mutually close (i.e., share an attribute) and to separate them from the remaining categories. As confirmed by these statistics, such a data-driven strategy enables very accurate recognition of attributes. Fortuitously, as shown in Figures 1 (left) and 1 (right), the selected pairs are also usually (but not always) meaningful to humans. Our results confirm that any price that we may pay in terms of human interpretability is more than offset by the gains we observe in recognition accuracy, both at the attribute and the category level.

In the remaining experiments, we evaluate how well DaMN enables knowledge transfer, both within and across datasets.

Table 3. Left: Performance vs. THUMOS semantic attributes. **Right**: Marginal benefits obtained by adding three-vs-rest classifiers to DaMN.

	mAP	StD	Min	Max		DTF (LF)	DTF (EF)	MBH	HOG	HOF	Traj.
THUMOS	0.53	0.19	0.07	99.08	pairs	**78.33**	75.93	**73.25**	**57.60**	**57.42**	55.18
DaMN	**0.64**	0.18	0.12	95.74	triples	77.88	**76.30**	73.04	57.51	57.20	**55.28**

Table 4. Empirical evaluation of different category-level distance metrics (in the feature space projected using χ^2 kernel)

	DTF (LF)	MBH	HOG	HOF	Traj.
SVM Margin	**78.33**±1.7	**73.25**±1.3	**57.60**±0.6	57.42±2.1	**55.18**±1.6
Average	77.59±1.6	72.84±1.7	57.41±0.8	57.20±1.6	53.82±0.7
Linkage (Min)	77.38±1.8	72.66±1.1	57.12±0.3	57.05±1.8	55.03±1.4
Median	77.79±1.7	72.97±1.5	57.49±0.8	**57.50**±1.7	54.81±1.7
Centroid	77.22±1.9	72.64±1.5	57.49±0.8	57.00±2.0	54.60±1.6

4.3   Cross-Dataset Generalization to HMDB51

The focus of this experiment is to see how well the DaMN category-level features learned on UCF101 enable us to perform action recognition on a subset of 12 HMDB51 categories with no additional training. Since the category names are different and UCF101 categories more fine-grained, we roughly align them as shown in Table 5.

We follow the same experimental settings as in Section 4.1 but use just the MBH feature rather than late fusion for simplicity. We perform experiments using 3-fold cross-validation, with each run training on two folds of UCF101 and testing on the third fold of HMDB51. Table 5 shows results averaged over these three folds. We see that DaMN achieves an overall higher accuracy than both one-vs-rest and meta-class on cross-dataset generalization.

4.4   Generalization Performance with Limited Training Data

A popular use for attributes and category-level features is that they enable generalization to novel classes for which we have small amounts of training data; an extreme case of this is one-shot learning, where only a single exemplar is provided for each novel category [6].

For this experiment, we randomly select 10 categories to serve as "novel" and treat the remaining 91 as "known". Results are averaged on the three folds specified by THUMOS. We learn DaMN features (k=30) and train semantic and classeme (one-vs-rest) classifiers using the data from two folds of the known classes; we test on the entire third fold of the novel categories. As in cross-dataset scenario, all classifiers use the MBH feature rather than late fusion for simplicity.

We vary the number of training instances per novel category from 1 to 18, while ensuring that all three methods are given identical data. Figure 4 (left) summarizes the results (averaged over three folds). As in the UCF101 action recognition experiments (Section 4.1), the semantic attributes perform very poorly and DaMN does the best, outperforming both meta-class and one-vs-rest in every trial.

The difference between DaMN and the next best is much greater in this experiment, often more than 20%. This demonstrates that the information captured in DaMN generalizes much better across classes.

Table 5. Cross-Dataset Generalization: UCF101 → HMDB51

HMDB51 label	UCF101 IDs	DaMN	1-vs-rest	Meta-class
Brush hair	13	**57.78**	40.00	54.44
Climb	74 & 75	74.44	**83.33**	75.56
Dive	26	**77.78**	57.78	70.00
Golf	33	**66.67**	**66.67**	68.89
Handstand	30	43.33	**45.56**	41.11
Pullup	70	58.89	**68.89**	56.67
Punch	17 & 18	**81.11**	80.00	72.22
Pushup	72	**62.22**	56.67	54.44
Ride bike	11	72.22	**73.33**	67.78
Shoot ball	8	22.22	25.56	**30.00**
Shoot bow	3	**38.89**	36.67	**43.33**
Throw	7	**57.78**	**57.78**	54.44
Average		**59.44**±0.7	57.69±0.8	54.44±1.1

4.5 Extending DaMN to Image Datasets

Although DaMN was primarily developed for applications in action recognition, we recognize that the algorithm can be applied to any classification task. In order to demonstrate the generality of our method, we present a direct comparison against Yu et al.'s recently published method [29] for eliciting category-level attributes on the Animals with Attributes images dataset [12].

Figure 4 (right) shows the accuracy of DaMN, one-vs-rest and Yu et al. [29] using the experimental methodology and data splits prescribed in [29]. We see that one-vs-rest and Yu et al. perform similarly, but both are consistently outperformed by DaMN.

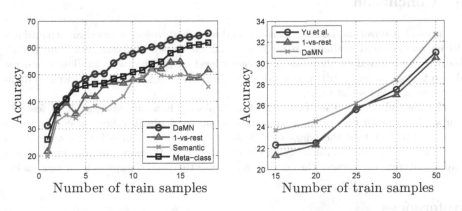

Fig. 4. Left: Knowledge transfer to novel categories with limited data (1 to 18 instances per category). DaMN consistently outperforms one-vs-rest, meta-class and THUMOS semantic attributes. **Right:** Generalization of DaMN to image datasets. DaMN outperforms one-vs-rest and Yu et al. [29] on the Animals with Attributes dataset.

4.6   Extending DaMN Beyond Pairs

Just as DaMN improves over one-vs-rest by judiciously mining suitable two-vs-rest classifiers, it is natural to explore whether one can obtain additional benefits by considering higher-level information, such as cliques consisting of 3 (or more) mutually near categories. Table 3 (right) shows that the improvements are marginal. We believe that this is due to several reasons: 1) there are relatively few such higher-order category groupings; 2) many of the relationships are already captured by the DaMN features since a triplet of similar categories also generates three two-vs-rest pairs; 3) the additional complexity of discriminating within the higher-order grouping of categories may not be merited, whereas the one-vs-one classifiers used to differentiate within the pair were already trained during the DaMN pair selection process. For these reasons, we do not extend DaMN beyond pair categories.

4.7   Computational Complexity

While DaMN may seem to be prohibitively more expensive in terms of computation than the popular one-vs-rest classifiers employed in the action recognition community, we show that training these additional classifiers is both computationally manageable and worthwhile since they generate such consistent (if small) improvements in mAP and classification accuracy. In the interests of space, we briefly summarize wall-clock times for the UCF-101 experiments. Total time for one-vs-one SVM training: 10.14s; one-vs-one SVM testing: 1682.72s; total one-vs-rest and two-vs-rest SVM training: 2752.74s; one-vs-rest and two-vs-rest testing: 2546.51s. For each descriptor type in DTF, DaMN employs ∼800 one-vs-one SVMs, ∼800 two-vs-rest SVMs and 101 one-vs-rest SVMs. Training time for the two-vs-rest classifiers is similar to the one-vs-rest since they have the same number of training instances, but with different labels.

5   Conclusion

We present a novel method for learning mid-level features in a discriminative, data-driven manner and evaluate on large-scale action recognition datasets. The DaMN features are selected on the basis of category-level mutual pairwise similarity and are shown to convincingly outperform existing approaches, both semantic as well as data-driven on a broad set of tasks.

The natural direction for future work is exploring how our category-level features can apply to problems outside action recognition (and possibly beyond computer vision). We believe that the image classification experiments where DaMN outperform recent approaches are a promising sign in this direction. We hope that our open source implementation encourages the community to use the DaMN approach on new tasks.

References

1. Berg, T.L., Berg, A.C., Shih, J.: Automatic attribute discovery and characterization from noisy web data. In: Daniilidis, K., Maragos, P., Paragios, N. (eds.) ECCV 2010, Part I. LNCS, vol. 6311, pp. 663–676. Springer, Heidelberg (2010)
2. Bergamo, A., Torresani, L.: Meta-class features for large-scale object categorization on a budget. In: Computer Vision and Pattern Recognition (2012)

3. Chang, C.C., Lin, C.J.: LIBSVM: A library for support vector machines. ACM Transactions on Intelligent Systems and Technology 2(3) (2011), software available at http://www.csie.ntu.edu.tw/~cjlin/libsvm

4. Duan, K., Parikh, D., Crandall, D., Grauman, K.: Discovering localized attributes for fine-grained recognition. In: Computer Vision and Pattern Recognition (2012)

5. Farhadi, A., Endres, I., Hoeim, D., Forsyth, D.: Describing objects by their attributes. In: Computer Vision and Pattern Recognition, pp. 1778–1785 (2009)

6. Fei-Fei, L., Fergus, R., Perona, P.: One-shot learning of object categories. IEEE Transactions on Pattern Analysis and Machine Intelligence 28(4), 594–611 (2006)

7. Ferrari, V., Zisserman, A.: Learning visual attributes. In: NIPS (2007)

8. Jain, A., Gupta, A., Rodriguez, M., Davis, L.: Representing videos using mid-level discriminative patches. In: Computer Vision and Pattern Recognition (2013)

9. Kemp, C., Tenenbaum, J.B., Griffiths, T.L., Yamada, T., Ueda, N.: Learning systems of concepts with an infinite relational model. In: AAAI (2006)

10. Kuehne, H., Jhuang, H., Garrote, E., Poggio, T., Serre, T.: HMDB: A large video database for human motion recognition. In: International Conference on Computer Vision (2011)

11. Kumar, N., Berg, A.C., Belhumeur, P.N., Nayar, S.K.: Attribute and simile classifiers for face verification. In: International Conference on Computer Vision (2009)

12. Lampert, C., Nickisch, H., Harmeling, S.: Learning to detect unseen object classes by between-class attribute transfer. In: Computer Vision and Pattern Recognition (2009)

13. Laptev, I., Marszałek, M., Schmid, C., Rozenfeld, B.: Learning realistic human actions from movies. In: Computer Vision and Pattern Recognition (2008)

14. Laptev, I., Piccardi, M., Shah, M., Sukthankar, R., Jiang, Y.G., Liu, J., Roshan Zamir, A.: THUMOS: ICCV 2013 workshop on action recognition with a large number of classes (2013)

15. Liu, J., Kuipers, B., Savarese, S.: Recognizing human actions by attributes. In: Computer Vision and Pattern Recognition, pp. 3337–3344 (2011)

16. Liu, J., Luo, J., Shah, M.: Recognizing realistic actions from videos "in the wild". In: Computer Vision and Pattern Recognition (2009)

17. Mensink, T., Verbeek, J., Perronin, F., Csurka, G.: Distance-based image classification: Generalizing to new classes at near-zero cost. IEEE Transactions on Pattern Analysis and Machine Intelligence 35(11) (2013)

18. Osherson, D.N., Stern, J., Wilkie, O., Stob, M., Smith, E.E.: Default probability. Cognitive Science 15(2) (1991)

19. Palatucci, M., Pomerleau, D., Hinton, G., Mitchell, T.: Zero-shot learning with semantic output codes. In: NIPS (2009)

20. Parikh, D., Grauman, K.: Interactively building a discriminative vocabulary of nameable attributes. In: Computer Vision and Pattern Recognition, pp. 1681–1688 (2011)

21. Rohrbach, M., Stark, M., Schiele, B.: Zero-shot learning in a large-scale setting. In: Computer Vision and Pattern Recognition (2011)

22. Soomro, K., Zamir, A.R., Shah, M.: UCF101: A dataset of 101 human action classes from videos in the wild. Tech. Rep. CRCV-TR-12-01, UCF Center for Research in Computer Vision (November 2012)

23. Torresani, L., Szummer, M., Fitzgibbon, A.: Efficient object category recognition using classemes. In: Daniilidis, K., Maragos, P., Paragios, N. (eds.) ECCV 2010, Part I. LNCS, vol. 6311, pp. 776–789. Springer, Heidelberg (2010)

24. Wang, H., Schmid, C.: Action recognition with improved trajectories. In: International Conference on Computer Vision (2013)

25. Wang, H., Kläser, A., Schmid, C., Liu, C.L.: Action Recognition by Dense Trajectories. In: Computer Vision and Pattern Recognition, pp. 3169–3176 (2011), http://hal.inria.fr/inria-00583818/en
26. Wang, Y., Mori, G.: A discriminative latent model of object classes and attributes. In: Daniilidis, K., Maragos, P., Paragios, N. (eds.) ECCV 2010, Part V. LNCS, vol. 6315, pp. 155–168. Springer, Heidelberg (2010)
27. Yang, Y., Shah, M.: Complex events detection using data-driven concepts. In: Fitzgibbon, A., Lazebnik, S., Perona, P., Sato, Y., Schmid, C. (eds.) ECCV 2012, Part III. LNCS, vol. 7574, pp. 722–735. Springer, Heidelberg (2012)
28. Yao, B., Jiang, X., Khosla, A., Lin, A.L., Guibas, L.J., Fei-Fei, L.: Action recognition by learning bases of action attributes and parts. In: International Conference on Computer Vision (2011)
29. Yu, F., Cao, L., Feris, R., Smith, J., Chang, S.F.: Designing category-level attributes for discriminative visual recognition. In: Computer Vision and Pattern Recognition (2013)
30. Yu, F.X.: Weak attributes for large-scale image retrieval. In: Computer Vision and Pattern Recognition, pp. 2949–2956 (2012)

Spatio-temporal Object Detection Proposals

Dan Oneata, Jerome Revaud, Jakob Verbeek, and Cordelia Schmid

Inria*

Abstract. Spatio-temporal detection of actions and events in video is a challenging problem. Besides the difficulties related to recognition, a major challenge for detection in video is the size of the search space defined by spatio-temporal tubes formed by sequences of bounding boxes along the frames. Recently methods that generate unsupervised detection proposals have proven to be very effective for object detection in still images. These methods open the possibility to use strong but computationally expensive features since only a relatively small number of detection hypotheses need to be assessed. In this paper we make two contributions towards exploiting detection proposals for spatio-temporal detection problems. First, we extend a recent 2D object proposal method, to produce spatio-temporal proposals by a randomized supervoxel merging process. We introduce spatial, temporal, and spatio-temporal pairwise supervoxel features that are used to guide the merging process. Second, we propose a new efficient supervoxel method. We experimentally evaluate our detection proposals, in combination with our new supervoxel method as well as existing ones. This evaluation shows that our supervoxels lead to more accurate proposals when compared to using existing state-of-the-art supervoxel methods.

1 Introduction

Detection of human actions and activities is one of the most important and challenging problems in automatic video analysis. Recently there has been considerable progress in the recognition of human actions and events in challenging uncontrolled datasets such as HMDB [21], Hollywood2 [27], and TrecVid MED [30]. There are two main driving factors behind this progress. The first is the use of well engineered optical-flow based features computed along dense feature trajectories, see *e.g.* [19,42]. The second important factor is the use of state-of-the-art local feature pooling methods, such as the Fisher vector [28,36]. This progress, however, concerns the problem of classification of complete videos (as for TrecVid MED), or classification of clips that are well cropped around the actions of interest (as for HMDB and Hollywood2). The spatio-temporal detection problem is a more challenging one, since in each frame of the video we need to estimate a bounding box of the action of interest, which together form a spatio-temporal tube that locates the action in space and time.

Whereas sliding window search is still viable for temporal action localization, see *e.g.* [11,15,29], it becomes computationally prohibitive when searching in the much

---

* LEAR team, Inria Grenoble Rhône-Alpes, Laboratoire Jean Kuntzmann, CNRS, Univ. Grenoble Alpes, France.

D. Fleet et al. (Eds.): ECCV 2014, Part III, LNCS 8691, pp. 737–752, 2014.
© Springer International Publishing Switzerland 2014

larger space of spatio-temporal tubes. Efficient search methods for spatio-temporal action localization have been proposed in the past, exploiting additivity structures of bag-of-word representations and linear classifiers, $e.g.$ using branch-and-bound search or dynamic programming [38,48]. These methods, however, do not apply when the representation is non-additive, as is the case for the Fisher vector representation used in recent state-of-the-art action classification methods, due to its non-linear power and ℓ_2 normalizations. Some recent work partially addresses this issue using efficient implementations [23,40] or approximate normalizations [29]. A more general technique to tackle this issue, which has recently surfaced in the 2D object recognition literature, is the use of generic class independent detection proposals [2,12,26,39]. These methods produce image-dependent but unsupervised and class-independent tentative object bounding boxes, which are then assessed by the detector. This enables the use of more computationally expensive features, that would be too expensive to use in sliding window approaches. Recent state-of-the-art object detectors based on this approach use various representations, $e.g.$ Fisher vectors [8], max-pooling regionlets [42], and convolutional networks [17].

In this paper we explore how we can generate video tube proposals for spatio-temporal action detection. We build on the recent approach of Manen et $al.$ [26] that uses a randomized superpixel merging procedure to obtain object proposals. Our first contribution is to extend their approach to the spatio-temporal domain, using supervoxels as the units that will be merged into video tube proposals. We introduce spatial, temporal and spatio-temporal pairwise supervoxel features that are used to learn a classifier that guides the random merging process. Our second contribution is a new hierarchical supervoxel method that starts with hierarchical clustering of per-frame extracted superpixels. We experimentally evaluate our detection proposals, in combination with our new supervoxel method as well as existing ones. This evaluation shows that our supervoxels lead to more accurate proposals when compared to using existing state-of-the-art supervoxel methods.

Below, we first review related work in more detail in Section 2. Then, in Section 3 we present our supervoxel method, and in Section 4 our tube proposal method. In Section 5 we present our experimental evaluation results, and we conclude in Section 6.

2   Related Work

In this section we discuss the most relevant related work on supervoxels, and efficient detection methods based on object proposals and other techniques.

2.1   Supervoxel Methods

Instead of a complete survey of supervoxel methods, we concentrate here on the approaches most related to our work. The recent evaluation by Xu and Corso [45] compares five different methods [9,13,14,18,32] to segment videos into supervoxels. They identify GBH [18] and SWA [9] as the most effective supervoxel methods according to several generic and application independent criteria. SWA is a hierarchical segmentation method that solves normalized cuts at each level. At the finest levels, it defines similarities from voxel intensity differences, while at higher levels it uses aggregate features which are computed over regions merged at earlier levels. GBH is a hierarchical extension of the graph-based method of Felzenszwalb and Huttenlocher [13]. A streaming version of GBH was introduced in [47], which performs similar to GBH, but at a fraction of the cost by using overlapping temporal windows of the video to optimize the segmentation. GBH, similar to SWA, also uses aggregate features (such as color histograms) to define similarities once an initial segmentation is performed based on intensity differences.

While SWA and GBH directly work on the 3D space-time voxel graph, the recent VideoSEEDS approach of Van den Bergh et al. [41] shows that supervoxels of similar quality can be obtained by propagating 2D superpixels computed over individual frames in a streaming manner. In our own work we take a similar approach, in which we take per-frame SLIC superpixels [1] as the starting point, and merge them spatially and temporally to form supervoxels. The advantage of starting from per-frame superpixels is that the graphs that are used to form larger supervoxels are much smaller than those based on individual voxels. The superpixels themselves are also efficient to obtain since they are extracted independently across frames.

Since objects can appear at different scales, a single segmentation of a video into supervoxels does typically not succeed in accurately capturing all objects and either leads to under or over segmentation. Xu et al. [46] recently proposed a supervoxel hierarchy flattening approach that selects a slice through such a hierarchy that can maximize a variety of unsupervised or supervised criteria. In this manner the segmentation scale can be locally adapted to the content. Our work is related, in the sense that we also aim to use (hierarchical) supervoxel segmentation to find regions that correspond to objects. Unlike Xu et al. [46], however, we do not restrict ourselves to finding a single segmentation of the video, and instead allow for overlap between different detection hypotheses.

2.2 Object Proposals for Detection in Video

Several spatio-temporal action detection approaches have been developed based on ideas originally developed for efficient object detection in still images. Yuan et al. [48] proposed an efficient branch-and-bound search method to locate actions in space-time cuboids based on efficient subwindow search [22]. Search over space-time cuboids is, however, not desirable since the accuracy of the spatial localization will be compromised as the object of interest undergoes large motion. Tran and Yuan [38] proposed an efficient method for spatio-temporal action detection, which is based on dynamic programming to search over the space of tubes that connect still-image bounding boxes that are scored prior to the spatio-temporal search. Building the trellis, however, is computationally expensive since it requires per frame a sliding-window based scoring of all considered bounding boxes across different scales and aspect ratios if the tube size is allowed to vary over time. Moreover, the efficiency of such approaches relies on the additive structure of the score for a video cuboid or tube. This prevents the use of state-of-the-art feature pooling techniques that involve non-additive elements, including max-pooling [42], power and ℓ_2 normalization for Fisher vector representations [28] or second-order pooling [6].

Recently, several authors have proposed efficient implementations [23,40] and approximate normalizations [29] to efficiently use Fisher vector representations with non-linear normaliztions. A technique that is more general and applies to arbitrary representations, is the use of generic class-independent proposals [2,12,26,39], which have recently surfaced in the context of 2D object localization. These methods rely on low-level segmentation cues to generate in the order of several hundreds to thousands of object proposals per image, which cover most of the objects. Once the detection problem is reduced to assessing a relatively modest number of object hypotheses, we can use stronger representations that would otherwise have been prohibitively costly if employed in a sliding window detector, see the recent state-of-the-art results in e.g. [8,17,43]. Here we just discuss two of the most effective object proposal methods. Uijlings et al. [39] generate proposals by performing a hierarchical clustering of superpixels. Each node in the segmentation hierarchy produces a proposal given by the bounding box of the merged superpixels. The approach of Manen et al. [26] similarly agglomerates superpixels, but does so in a randomized manner. In Section 4 we show how this technique can be adapted for space-time detection proposals based on supervoxel segmentation.

Van den Bergh et al. [41] proposed a video objectness method based on tracking windows that align well with supervoxel boundaries. The tracking is based on the evolution of the supervoxels inside the tracked window. Unlike [26,39] and our work, however, their method is inherently dependent on the scale of the supervoxels that produce the boundaries which define the objectness measure.

In parallel to our work, Jain et al. [20] developed an extension of the hierarchical clustering method of Uijlings et al. [39] to the video domain to obtain object proposals. The most notable difference with our work is that they compute their initial supervoxels from an "independent motion evidence" map. This map estimates for each pixel in each frame the likelihood that its motion is different from the dominant motion. While this approach is effective to segment out objects that are in motion w.r.t. the background, it does not provide a mechanism to recover objects that are static in the scene. Furthermore, estimating the dominant motion is often error prone in real world videos.

Finally, several recent methods address the related but different problem of motion segmentation in video [25,31,49]. Their goal is to produce a pixel-wise segmentation of the dominant moving object in videos. Unlike the methods discussed above, they produce a single estimate of the dominant object, which is assumed to be at least partially in motion. Both [25] and [49] are based on linking still-image object proposals from [12]. They refine the window-based solution using a pixel-wise MRF. Papazoglou and Ferrari [31] proposed a method using motion boundaries to estimate the outline of the object of interest, and refine these estimates using an object appearance model. Instead of relying on object proposal bounding boxes per frame, they rely on per-frame superpixel segmentation as the base units over which the energy function is defined. In our experiments we compare to the results of [31] on the YouTube Objects dataset.

3   Hierarchical Supervoxels by Spatio-temporal Merging

Our supervoxel approach starts from superpixels as basic building blocks, and aggregates spatially and temporally connected superpixels using hierarchical clustering.

Fig. 1. Illustration of our supervoxel construction. From left to right: video frame, detected edges, flow boundaries, superpixels, and hierarchical clustering result at the level with eight supervoxels.

In Section 3.1 we detail the superpixel graph construction and the definition of the edge costs. Then, in Section 3.2 we present the hierarchical clustering approach which includes a novel penalty term that prevents merging physically disconnected objects.

3.1 Construction of the Superpixel Graph

We use SLIC [1] to independently segment each video frame into N superpixels. SLIC superpixels have been shown to accurately follow occlusion boundaries [24], and are efficient to extract. For each superpixel n, we compute its mean color $\mu(n)$ in Lab space, a color histogram $h_{col}(n)$ using ten bins per channel, and a flow histogram $h_{flow}(n)$ that uses nine orientation bins. We construct a graph $\mathcal{G} = (\mathcal{S}, \mathcal{E})$, where $\mathcal{S}$ is the set of superpixels, and $\mathcal{E}$ is the set of edges between them. In Section 5.1 we detail how we set the parameters of the graph weights using a small set of training images.

Spatial Neighbor Connections. Spatial connection edges are created per frame for each pair of neighboring superpixels n and m, and their weight $w^{sp}(n, m)$ is given by the weighted sum of distances based on several cues that we detail below:

$$w^{sp}(n, m) = \alpha_\mu d_\mu(n, m) + \alpha_{col} d_{col}(n, m) + \alpha_{flow} d_{flow}(n, m)$$
$$+ \alpha_{mb} d_{mb}(n, m) + \alpha_{edge} d_{edge}(n, m), \tag{1}$$

where $d_\mu(n, m) = \min(\|\mu(n) - \mu(m)\|, 30)$ is the robust thresholded-distance between the color means [33], $d_{col}(n, m)$ and $d_{flow}(n, m)$ are chi-squared distances between the color and flow histograms. In our implementation we use the LDOF optical flow method of Brox and Malik [5].

The last two terms, $d_{mb}(n, m)$ and $d_{edge}(n, m)$, are geodesic distances between the superpixels centroids, efficiently computed using the distance transform [44]. We use the norm of the gradient of the flow and the output of the recent structured edge detector [10] respectively, to define their geodesic pixel-wise cost. In practice, it means that if two superpixels are separated by an edge —either image-based or motion-based— the distance between them will increase proportionally to the edge strength. See Figure 1 for an illustration of these two distance terms.

Second-Order Spatial Connections. We also add second-order spatial edges to connect neighbors of neighbors. The rationale behind this setting is to be robust to small occlusions. Imagine, e.g., the case of a lamp post in front of a tree: we would like the two parts of the tree to be connected together before they are merged with the lamp post. In this case we drop the geodesic distances, since they are affected by occlusions, and add a constant penalty $\alpha_{2\text{hop}}$ instead:

$$w^{2\text{hop}}(n, m) = \alpha_\mu d_\mu(n, m) + \alpha_{\text{col}} d_{\text{col}}(n, m) + \alpha_{\text{flow}} d_{\text{flow}}(n, m) + \alpha_{2\text{hop}}. \qquad (2)$$

Whenever a second-order neighbor can be reached through an intermediate neighbor k with a smaller distance, i.e. when $w^{\text{sp}}(n, k) + w^{\text{sp}}(k, m) \leq w^{2\text{hop}}(n, m)$, we remove the second-order edge between n and m. This avoids spurious connections between physically disconnected regions, and also significantly reduces the number of edges in the graph.

Temporal Neighbor Connections. Temporal connections are naturally introduced using optical flow. We connect each superpixel with its neighbor in the next frame indicated by the flow. Because the flow is sometimes noisy, we enforce a one-to-one correspondence in the temporal connectivity. More precisely, for each superpixel at frame t, we compute its best match match in frame $t + 1$ according to flow and pixel-wise color difference. We run this procedure in the opposite temporal direction as well, and keep only reciprocal connections. For two temporally connected superpixels n and m, we set the edge weight to:

$$w^t(n, m) = \alpha_\mu^t d_\mu(n, m) + \alpha_{\text{col}}^t d_{\text{col}}(n, m) + \alpha_{\text{flow}}^t d_{\text{flow}}(n, m). \qquad (3)$$

This is similar to the spatial edge weight, but excludes the motion and contour boundaries as we do not have a temporal counterpart for them.

3.2 Hierarchical Clustering

Once the superpixel graph $\mathcal{G} = (\mathcal{S}, \mathcal{E})$ is constructed, we run a hierarchical clustering with average linkage [3]. For two clusters $A \subset \mathcal{S}$ and $B \subset \mathcal{S}$, we denote the set of edges connecting them as $\mathcal{B}(A, B) = \{(n, m) \mid n \in A, m \in B, (n, m) \in \mathcal{E}\}$. By construction, $\mathcal{B}(A, B)$ only contains edges at the boundary between A and B, or slightly deeper for the second-order connections. We define the distance between A and B as

$$w(A, B) = \frac{1}{|\mathcal{B}(A, B)|} \sum_{(n,m) \in \mathcal{B}(A,B)} w(n, m). \qquad (4)$$

This corresponds to measuring the distance between two clusters as the average edge weight along their common boundary. Because the graph is sparse, the clustering can be computed efficiently: if the number of connections per superpixel is independent of the number of superpixels —as is the case in practice— the complexity is linear in the number of superpixels.

While such a clustering approach gives good results for image segmentation [3], its temporal extension tends to group clusters corresponding to different physical objects that are only accidentally connected in a small number of frames, see Figure 2.

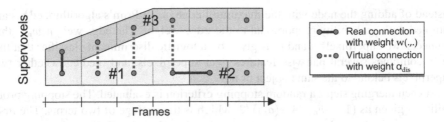

Fig. 2. Illustration of several supervoxels (SV) during the hierarchical clustering. While SV#1 and SV#2 can be merged without penalty, merging SV#1 and SV#3 will trigger a penalty α_{dis} in the form of a virtual edge added in all frames where both are present but not in contact.

We propose a simple solution to solve this issue. We add a penalty α_{dis} acting as a virtual edge for each frame where the two clusters are present but not in contact:

$$\tilde{w}(A, B) = \frac{c(A, B)w(A, B) + s(A, B)\alpha_{dis}}{c(A, B) + s(A, B)}, \qquad (5)$$

where $c(A, B)$ is the number of frames where A and B are connected by direct or second-order spatial connections, and $s(A, B)$ is the number of frames where both are present but not connected. In practice, we set α_{dis} to the cost of the last merge of a hierarchical clustering performed preliminarily without temporal penalty, which corresponds to the weight of the hardest merge.

For an illustration of the supervoxel clustering process see the two right-most panels of Figure 1 which show the SLIC superpixels, and the hierarchical clustering result obtained from them.

The overall complexity of our method is linear in the number of frames. In practice, about 99% of the computational cost is devoted to computing LDOF optical flow [5]. Concretely, for a video of 55 frames with resolution 400×720 pixels, computing the flow with LDOF takes 13.8 minutes (about 15s/fr), computing the SLIC superpixels 9.7s, computing superpixels connection weights 7.8s, and performing hierarchical clustering 1.7s (all times are given for a single core @3.6GHz). Our method can benefit from the existing GPU implementation of LDOF [37], as well as a trivial parallelization over frames for the per-frame feature pipeline to compute SLIC, edges, and flow.

4 Spatio-temporal Object Detection Proposals

In this section we describe how to produce spatio-temporal object detection proposals based on a given supervoxel segmentation.

4.1 Randomized Supervoxel Agglomeration

We extend the region growing method of Manen *et al.* [26], which is a randomized form of Prim's maximum spanning tree algorithm. It starts from a random seed superpixel, and iteratively adds nodes that are connected to the ones that are already selected.

Instead of adding the node with the maximum edge, as in Prim's algorithm, edges are sampled with probability proportional to the edge weight. The edge weight w_{nm} that connects two superpixels n and m is given by a logistic discriminant classifier that linearly combines several pairwise features over superpixels, and predicts whether two superpixels belong to the same object or not.

At each merging step t a random stopping criterion is evaluated. The stopping probability is given as $(1 - w_{nm} + s(a_t))/2$, which is the average of two terms. The first, $(1 - w_{mn})$, is the probability (as given by the classifier) that the sampled edge connects superpixels that belong to different objects. This term avoids growing the proposal across object boundaries. The second term, $s(a_t)$ gives the fraction of objects in the training dataset that is smaller than the size a_t of the current proposal. This term ensures that the size distribution of the proposals roughly reflects the size distribution of objects on the training set. The sampling process can be repeated to produce a desired number of detection proposals.

To apply this method for spatio-temporal proposals, we consider a graph over the supervoxels, with connections between all supervoxels that are connected by a regular 3D 6-connected graph over the individual voxels. To ensure that we sample proposals that last for the full video duration, we continue the merging process as long as the full duration of the video is not covered, and use the stopping criterion only after that point. Once a merged set of supervoxels is obtained, we produce a space-time tube by taking in each frame the bounding box of the selected supervoxels in that frame.

4.2   Learning Supervoxel Similarities

We train a logistic discriminant model to map a collection of pairwise features to a confidence value that two supervoxels should be merged. To this end we generate a training set of supervoxel pairs from a collection of training videos. Each supervoxel is labeled as positive if it is contained for at least 60% inside a ground truth object, and negative otherwise. We then collect pairs of neighboring supervoxels that are either both positive, which leads to a positive pair, or for which one is positive and the other is negative, which leads to a negative pair. Neighboring supervoxel pairs that are both negative are not used for training.

We use eight different pairwise features between supervoxels, and list them below.

1. **Color feature.** We use the chi-squared distance between supervoxel color histograms $f_{\text{color}}(n, m) = d_{\chi^2}(h_{\text{col}}(n), h_{\text{col}}(m))$. We use the same color histogram as used for our supervoxels, *i.e.* using ten bins per channel in the Lab space.
2. **Flow feature.** We measure chi-squared distances between histograms of optical flow $f_{\text{flow}}(n, m) = d_{\chi^2}(h_{\text{flow}}(n), h_{\text{flow}}(m))$. Here we also use the same histograms as before, *i.e.* using LDOF [5] and nine orientation bins.
3. **Size feature.** The size feature favors merging small supervoxels first, and is defined as the sum of the volumes of the two supervoxels: $f_{\text{size}}(n, m) = a_n + a_m$. The volumes a_n and a_m are normalized by dividing over the volume of the full video.
4. **Fill feature.** The fill feature that favors merging supervoxels that form a compact region, and measures to which degree the two supervoxels fill their bounding box: $f_{\text{fill}}(n, m) = (a_n + a_m)/b_{nm}$, where b_{nm} is the volume of the 3D bounding box of the two supervoxels, again normalized by the video volume.

5. **Spatial size feature.** This feature only considers the spatial extent of the supervoxels, and not their duration: $f_{\text{size2D}}(n, m) = \frac{1}{|t_m \cup t_n|} \sum_{t \in (t_m \cup t_n)} a_n^t + a_m^t$, where t_n is a set of frames in which supervoxel n exists, while a_n^t denotes the area of the supervoxel in frame t, normalized by the frame area.

6. **Spatial fill feature.** Similarly, the fill feature can be made duration invariant by averaging over time: $f_{\text{fill2D}}(n, m) = \frac{1}{|t_m \cup t_n|} \sum_{t \in (t_m \cup t_n)} (a_n^t + a_m^t)/b_{nm}^t$, where b_{nm}^t gives the area of the bounding box in frame t.

7. **Temporal size feature.** In analogy to the spatial size feature, we also consider the joint duration $f_{\text{duration}}(n, m) = |t_m \cup t_n|/T$, where T is the duration of the video.

8. **Temporal overlap feature.** We measure to what extent the supervoxels last over the same period of time by intersection over union: $f_{\text{overlap}} = |t_m \cap t_n|/|t_m \cup t_n|$.

The color (1), size (3) and fill (4) features are similar to those used by [26,39] for still-image object detection proposals. Besides these features, we also include features based on optical flow, as well as size and fill features that consider separately the spatial and temporal extent of the supervoxels (2, 5, 6, 7, 8). We do not include the motion boundary and edge features of Section 3, since these are not defined for neighboring supervoxels that have no temporal overlap.

In our experiments we use the same set of eight features regardless of the underlying supervoxel segmentation, but we do train specific weights for each segmentation to account for their different characteristics.

5 Experimental Evaluation Results

Before presenting our experimental results, we first briefly describe the experimental setup, datasets, and evaluation protocols in Section 5.1. We then evaluate our supervoxel algorithm in Section 5.2, and our spatio-temporal detection proposals in Section 5.3.

5.1 Experimental Setup

Supervoxel Segmentation. We evaluate our supervoxel method on the Xiph.org benchmark of Chen et al. [7], using the following two of the evaluation measures proposed in [45]. The *3D segmentation accuracy* averages over all ground truth segments g the following accuracy: the volume of g covered by supervoxels that have more than 50% of their volume inside g, divided by the volume of g. The *3D undersegmentation error* averages the following error over all ground truth segments: the total volume of supervoxels that intersect g minus the volume of g, divided by the volume of g.

Spatio-temporal Detection Proposals. The first dataset we use is UCF Sports [35], which consists of 150 videos of 10 sports: diving, golf, kicking, lifting, horse riding, running, skating, swinging, high bar, and walking. We use five videos of each class for training our supervoxel similarities, and to select other hyperparameters such as the granularity of the base segmentation level. The remaining 100 videos are used for testing. Since the original ground-truth data is not very precise, we re-annotated the objects more accurately every 20 frames. These annotations, as well as the train-test division, are all publicly available on our project webpage.[1]

The second dataset we consider is the YouTube Objects dataset [34]. It contains a total of 1407 video shots divided over ten object categories. Each video contains one dominant object, for which a bounding box annotation is available in only one frame.

Similar to the 2D object proposal evaluation in [39], we measure performance using the best average overlap (BAO) of proposals with ground truth actions and objects. The BAO of a ground truth object v is given by the proposal p in the set of proposals P_v for v that maximizes the average overlap with the ground truth bounding boxes across all annotated frames. More formally:

$$\mathrm{BAO}(v) = \max_{p \in P_v} \frac{1}{|T_v|} \sum_{t \in T_v} \mathrm{Overlap}(p_t, b_v^t), \qquad (6)$$

where T_v is the set of frames for object v with ground-truth annotation, and b_v^t denotes the bounding box of v in frame t, and p^t is the bounding box of the proposal in that frame. We measure the per-frame overlap in the usual intersection-over-union sense.

Based on the BAO we compute the mean BAO (mBAO) across all ground truth actions/objects. We also consider the correct localization (CorLoc) rate, as in [31], which measures the fraction of objects for which the BAO is above 50%.

5.2 Experimental Evaluation of Supervoxel Segmentation

Setting of Supervoxel Parameters. For our supervoxel method we set the number of SLIC superpixels to $N = 1,000$ per frame. We set the parameters of the hierarchical superpixel merging weights using a 9D grid search over their values, and evaluate the performance using a subset of 10 videos from the UCF Sports training set. For a given set of parameters, we generate the segmentation hierarchy, and for each node n in the hierarchy we evaluate the precision and recall w.r.t. the ground-truth object bounding box in all annotated frames. Precision $p(n)$ is defined as the fraction of the supervoxel that is inside the ground-truth box, and recall $r(n)$ the fraction of the ground-truth box that is inside the supervoxel. We then compute the maximum score of the product of recall and precision $F(n) = p(n)r(n)$ across all supervoxels in the hierarchy, and take the average of $\max_n F(n)$ across all annotated frames in all videos. In experiments on the Xiph.org benchmark we do not use boundary features, since the resolution of 240×160 of the videos in this data set is too small to obtain accurate boundary estimates.

Supervoxel Segmentation Evaluation Results. We compare our approach to GBH [18] and SWA [9], as well as the GB [13], Nyström [14], and meanshift [32] methods as evaluated in [45]. We used the publicly available implementation in LIBSVX.[2] For GBH we also used the online processing service which also uses optical flow features that are not included in the SVX implementation.[3] For our own method we also evaluate the effect of the penalty term α_{dis} that penalizes spatially distant supervoxel clusters.

---

[1] See http://lear.inrialpes.fr/~oneata/3Dproposals.
[2] See http://www.cse.buffalo.edu/~jcorso/r/supervoxels.
[3] See http://www.cc.gatech.edu/cpl/projects/videosegmentation.

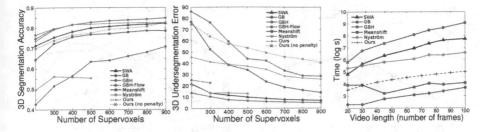

Fig. 3. Comparison of our and state-of-the-art supervoxel methods on the Xiph.org benchmark

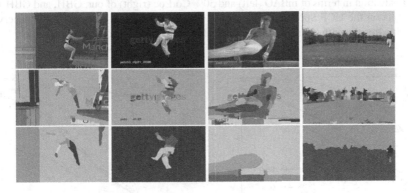

Fig. 4. Supervoxel comparison on videos of UCF Sports: video frames (top), GBH-Flow (middle), ours (bottom). For each video both methods are set to produce the same number of supervoxels.

The evaluation results are presented in Figure 3. In terms of segmentation accuracy (left) our method is comparable to the best methods: GBH and GBH-Flow. For the undersegmentation error (middle) our method gives significantly worse results than the best results obtained with GBH. The discrepancy of the evaluation results across these measures is due to the fact that our method tends to produce larger supervoxels, as well as many tiny supervoxels that consist of single isolated superpixels. Figure 4 illustrates this in comparison to GBH-Flow, where both methods are set to produce the same number of supervoxels for each video. Our method seems to produce less supervoxels due to isolated superpixels, which constitute more than 50% of the supervoxels. The undersegmentation error suffers from this, since a large supervoxel that overlaps a ground truth segment by a small fraction can deteriorate the error significantly.

Our method improves in both evaluation measures with the addition of the penalty term α_{dis} for spatially disconnected components, demonstrating its effectiveness. We therefore include it in all further experiments.

We compare the run times of the different supervoxel methods in the right panel of Figure 3. We do not include the GBH-Flow method here, since we ran it over the online service which does not allow us to evaluate its run time. As compared to GBH, the top performing method, our method runs one to two orders of magnitudes faster; and compared to the fastest method, GB, it is only about 4 times slower.

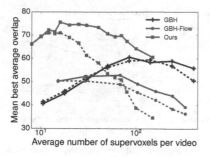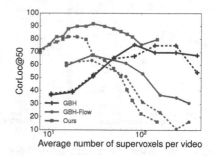

Fig. 5. Evaluation in terms of mBAO (left) and 50% CorLoc (right) of our, GBH, and GBH-Flow supervoxels on the UCF Sport train set, using 1,000 proposals as a function of the supervoxel granularity. Results with (solid) and without (dashed) full-duration constraint are shown.

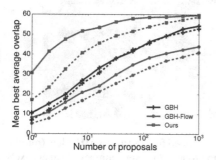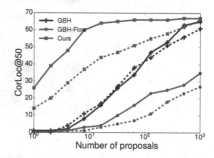

Fig. 6. UCF Sport testset performance against the number of proposals for our, GBH, and GBH-Flow supervoxels. Results with (solid) and without (dashed) full-duration constraint are shown.

5.3 Evaluation of Spatio-tempoal Dection Proposals

Video Tube Proposals for UCF Sports. In our first experiment we consider the performance using supervoxels from GBH, GBH-Flow, and our method with different granularities, i.e. different numbers of extracted supervoxels. In Figure 5 we compare the performance on the training set of the UCF Sports dataset. We consider the performance using 1,000 proposals for different granularities. The results show that our supervoxels lead to substantially better proposals. Moreover, using our supervoxels, a smaller number of supervoxels leads to optimal results. This means that the random proposal sampling is performed on a smaller graph which improves its efficiency. The full-duration temporal constraint, which accepts proposals only if they span the full duration of the video, improves results for all methods. It is particularly important for our supervoxels when using finer segmentations, probably because it helps to deal with very short supervoxels that are frequent in our approach. Based on these results we choose for each supervoxel method the optimal granularity, which will be used on the test set.

The results for the UCF Sports test set are given in Figure 6. For both evaluation measures, we need far fewer proposals for a given level of performance using our supervoxels, as compared to using GBH or GBH-Flow supervoxels. Also in this case the

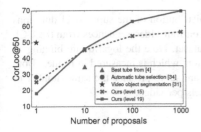

Fig. 7. Performance on the YouTube Objects dataset (50% CorLoc), as a function of the number of proposals. We show results for two levels of our supervoxel hierarchy (depicted as lines) and compare to other related methods (depicted as points). Level 15 (brown, dashed line) was the best performing one on the UCF Sports train set, while level 19 (red, solid line) was the best one tested on the YouTube Objects dataset.

full-duration temporal constraint benefits the performance, particularly so when generating few proposals using our supervoxels.

Video Tube Proposals for YouTube Objects. We now evaluate our approach on the YouTube Objects dataset, and compare our results to the video object segmentation method of [31], and weakly supervised learning method of Prest *et al.* [34]. The video object segmentation approach of [31] is unsupervised, and only outputs a single segmentation per shot. Prest *et al.* [34] used the method of Brox and Malik [4] to output coherent motion segments, to which they fit spatio-temporal tubes. This leads to between 3 and 15 tubes per shot. They then use a weakly supervised training to automatically select the tube corresponding to the object of interest, exploiting class labels given at the video level. We report their results, and the result for the best tube among the proposals from [4].

Figure 7 compares the aforementioned methods to ours when using between one and 1,000 proposals. When using 10 proposals, comparable to the number produced by [4], we obtain with 46.1% CorLoc, a result that is more than 10% points above the 34.8% of [4]. As compared to the video object segmentation method of [31], our method is about 5% worse when using 10 proposals, but eventually we recover more objects when more proposals are used.

5.4 Discussion

In our experiments we have found that the supervoxel evaluation measures of [45] are not directly indicative of the performance of these methods when used to generate spatio-temporal detection proposals (which is the goal of this paper). In its hierarchical clustering process our method quickly agglomerates large segments for objects, while also retaining a set of small fragments. In contrast, other methods such as GBH steadily produce larger segments from smaller ones, which leads to more homogeneously sized supervoxels. See Figure 4 for an example of our and GBH supervoxels at a given frame, and Figure 8 for the distribution of supervoxel durations. It seems that our more heterogeneous size distribution is advantageous for proposal generation, since good proposals can be made by merging a few large supervoxels. For spatio-temporal over-segmentation as measured by the supervoxel benchmark metrics, however, this unbalanced size distribution is sub-optimal since it is more likely to be imprecise at the object boundaries.

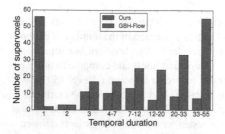

Fig. 8. Distribution of the supervoxel durations obtained on four video sequences from the UCF Sports dataset. Note the logarithmic binning of the duration, which is measured in frames. Both methods are set to produce the same number of supervoxels per video.

Recent supervoxel evaluation metrics proposed by Galasso *et al.* [16], which also assess temporal consistency and hierarchies, might be more related to the properties that are important for proposal generation.

6 Conclusion

In this paper we made two contributions. First, we have presented a new supervoxel method, that performs a hierarchical clustering of superpixels in a graph with spatial and temporal connections. Experimental results demonstrate that our supervoxel method is efficient, and leads to state-of-the-art 3D segmentation accuracy. Its 3D undersegmentation error is worse than that of competing state-of-the-art methods. This is probably due to the fact that our method yields supervoxels with a more heterogeneous size and duration distribution as compared to other methods. This seems to be detrimental for the undersegmentation error, but advantageous for proposal generation.

Second, we have adapted the randomized Prim 2D object proposal method to the spatio-temporal domain. To this end we have introduced a set of new pairwise supervoxel features, which are used to learn a similarity measure that favors grouping supervoxels that belong to the same physical object. Our experimental evaluation demonstrates that using our supervoxels leads to significantly better proposals than using existing state-of-the-art supervoxel methods. In future work we will integrate and evaluate the spatio-temporal proposals in a full detection system.

In our work we used optical flow as a cue to derive similarity in both the supervoxel stage and the proposal generation stage. Recent related approaches [20,31] used optical flow also to focus the proposal generation on areas where flow indicates the presence of objects moving against their background. While such an approach is clearly effective in cases where the object of interest undergoes significant motion as a whole, it is less clear whether it is still effective in cases where only part of the object is in motion. For example, consider a case where we want to detect a person that is drinking: if the person is seated, most of the body will be static and only the arm, hand, and cup in motion might be segmented out. In future work we plan to investigate this issue.

Acknowledgements. This work was supported by the European integrated project AXES and the ERC advanced grant ALLEGRO.

References

1. Achanta, R., Shaji, A., Smith, K., Lucchi, A., Fua, P., Süsstrunk, S.: SLIC superpixels compared to state-of-the-art superpixel methods. PAMI 34(11), 2274–2282 (2012)
2. Alexe, B., Deselares, T., Ferrari, V.: Measuring the objectness of image windows. PAMI 34(11), 2189–2202 (2012)
3. Arbeláez, P., Maire, M., Fowlkes, C., Malik, J.: Contour detection and hierarchical image segmentation. PAMI 33(5), 898–916 (2011)
4. Brox, T., Malik, J.: Object segmentation by long term analysis of point trajectories. In: Daniilidis, K., Maragos, P., Paragios, N. (eds.) ECCV 2010, Part V. LNCS, vol. 6315, pp. 282–295. Springer, Heidelberg (2010)
5. Brox, T., Malik, J.: Large displacement optical flow: Descriptor matching in variational motion estimation. PAMI (2011)
6. Carreira, J., Caseiro, R., Batista, J., Sminchisescu, C.: Semantic segmentation with second-order pooling. In: Fitzgibbon, A., Lazebnik, S., Perona, P., Sato, Y., Schmid, C. (eds.) ECCV 2012, Part VII. LNCS, vol. 7578, pp. 430–443. Springer, Heidelberg (2012)
7. Chen, A., Corso, J.: Propagating multi-class pixel labels throughout video frames. In: Proceedings of Western New York Image Processing Workshop (2010)
8. Cinbis, R., Verbeek, J., Schmid, C.: Segmentation driven object detection with Fisher vectors. In: ICCV (2013)
9. Corso, J., Sharon, E., Dube, S., El-Saden, S., Sinha, U., Yuille, A.: Efficient multilevel brain tumor segmentation with integrated Bayesian model classification. IEEE Trans. Med. Imaging 27(5), 629–640 (2008)
10. Dollár, P., Zitnick, C.: Structured forests for fast edge detection. In: ICCV (2013)
11. Duchenne, O., Laptev, I., Sivic, J., Bach, F., Ponce, J.: Automatic annotation of human actions in video. In: ICCV (2009)
12. Endres, I., Hoiem, D.: Category independent object proposals. In: Daniilidis, K., Maragos, P., Paragios, N. (eds.) ECCV 2010, Part V. LNCS, vol. 6315, pp. 575–588. Springer, Heidelberg (2010)
13. Felzenszwalb, P., Huttenlocher, D.: Efficient graph-based image segmentation. IJCV 59(2), 167–181 (2004)
14. Fowlkes, C., Belongie, S., Chung, F., Malik, J.: Spectral grouping using the nyström method. PAMI 26(2), 214–225 (2004)
15. Gaidon, A., Harchaoui, Z., Schmid, C.: Actom sequence models for efficient action detection. In: CVPR (2011)
16. Galasso, F., Nagaraja, N., Cardenas, T., Brox, T., Schiele, B.: A unified video segmentation benchmark: Annotation, metrics and analysis. In: ICCV (2013)
17. Girshick, R., Donahue, J., Darrell, T., Malik, J.: Rich feature hierarchies for accurate object detection and semantic segmentation. In: CVPR (2014)
18. Grundmann, M., Kwatra, V., Han, M., Essa, I.: Efficient hierarchical graph-based video segmentation. In: CVPR (2010)
19. Jain, M., Jégou, H., Bouthemy, P.: Better exploiting motion for better action recognition. In: CVPR (2013)
20. Jain, M., van Gemert, J., Bouthemy, P., Jégou, H., Snoek, C.: Action localization with tubelets from motion. In: CVPR (2014)
21. Kuehne, H., Jhuang, H., Garrote, E., Poggio, T., Serre, T.: HMDB: A large video database for human motion recognition. In: ICCV (2011)
22. Lampert, C., Blaschko, M., Hofmann, T.: Efficient subwindow search: a branch and bound framework for object localization. PAMI 31(12), 2129–2142 (2009)

23. Li, Z., Gavves, E., van de Sande, K., Snoek, C., Smeulders, A.: Codemaps, segment classify and search objects locally. In: ICCV (2013)
24. Lu, J., Yang, H., Min, D., Do, M.: Patch match filter: Efficient edge-aware filtering meets randomized search for fast correspondence field estimation. In: CVPR (2013)
25. Ma, T., Latecki, L.: Maximum weight cliques with mutex constraints for video object segmentation. In: CVPR (2012)
26. Manén, S., Guillaumin, M., Gool, L.V.: Prime object proposals with randomized Prim's algorithm. In: ICCV (2013)
27. Marszalek, M., Laptev, I., Schmid, C.: Actions in context. In: CVPR (2009)
28. Oneata, D., Verbeek, J., Schmid, C.: Action and event recognition with Fisher vectors on a compact feature set. In: ICCV (2013)
29. Oneata, D., Verbeek, J., Schmid, C.: Efficient action localization with approximately normalized Fisher vectors. In: CVPR (2014)
30. Over, P., Awad, G., Michel, M., Fiscus, J., Sanders, G., Shaw, B., Kraaij, W., Smeaton, A., Quénot, G.: TRECVID 2012 – an overview of the goals, tasks, data, evaluation mechanisms and metrics. In: Proceedings of TRECVID (2012)
31. Papazoglou, A., Ferrari, V.: Fast object segmentation in unconstrained video. In: ICCV (2013)
32. Paris, S., Durand, F.: A topological approach to hierarchical segmentation using mean shift. In: CVPR (2007)
33. Pele, O., Werman, M.: Fast and robust earth mover's distances. In: ICCV (2009)
34. Prest, A., Leistner, C., Civera, J., Schmid, C., Ferrari, V.: Learning object class detectors from weakly annotated video. In: CVPR (2012)
35. Rodriguez, M., Ahmed, J., Shah, M.: Action MACH: a spatio-temporal maximum average correlation height filter for action recognition. In: CVPR (2008)
36. Sánchez, J., Perronnin, F., Mensink, T., Verbeek, J.: Image classification with the Fisher vector: Theory and practice. IJCV 105(3), 222–245 (2013)
37. Sundaram, N., Brox, T., Keutzer, K.: Dense point trajectories by gpu-accelerated large displacement optical flow. In: Daniilidis, K., Maragos, P., Paragios, N. (eds.) ECCV 2010, Part I. LNCS, vol. 6311, pp. 438–451. Springer, Heidelberg (2010)
38. Tran, D., Yuan, J.: Optimal spatio-temporal path discovery for video event detection. In: CVPR (2011)
39. Uijlings, J., van de Sande, K., Gevers, T., Smeulders, A.: Selective search for object recognition. IJCV 104(2), 154–171 (2013)
40. van de Sande, K., Snoek, C., Smeulders, A.: Fisher and VLAD with FLAIR. In: CVPR (2014)
41. Van den Bergh, M., Roig, G., Boix, X., Manen, S., Gool, L.V.: Online video SEEDS for temporal window objectness. In: ICCV (2013)
42. Wang, H., Schmid, C.: Action recognition with improved trajectories. In: ICCV (2013)
43. Wang, X., Yang, M., Zhu, S., Lin, Y.: Regionlets for generic object detection. In: ICCV (2013)
44. Weber, O., Devir, Y., Bronstein, A., Bronstein, M., Kimmel, R.: Parallel algorithms for approximation of distance maps on parametric surfaces. ACM Trans. Graph. (2008)
45. Xu, C., Corso, J.: Evaluation of super-voxel methods for early video processing. In: CVPR (2012)
46. Xu, C., Whitt, S., Corso, J.: Flattening supervoxel hierarchies by the uniform entropy slice. In: ICCV (2013)
47. Xu, C., Xiong, C., Corso, J.J.: Streaming hierarchical video segmentation. In: Fitzgibbon, A., Lazebnik, S., Perona, P., Sato, Y., Schmid, C. (eds.) ECCV 2012, Part VI. LNCS, vol. 7577, pp. 626–639. Springer, Heidelberg (2012)
48. Yuan, J., Liu, Z., Wu, Y.: Discriminative subvolume search for efficient action detection. In: CVPR (2009)
49. Zhang, D., Javed, O., Shah, M.: Video object segmentation through spatially accurate and temporally dense extraction of primary object regions. In: CVPR (2013)

Depth-of-Field and Coded Aperture Imaging on XSlit Lens

Jinwei Ye, Yu Ji, Wei Yang, and Jingyi Yu

University of Delaware, Newark, DE 19716, USA

Abstract. Recent coded aperture imaging systems have shown great success in scene reconstruction, extended depth-of-field and light field imaging. By far nearly all solutions are built on top of commodity cameras equipped with a single spherical lens. In this paper, we explore coded aperture solutions on a special non-centric lens called the crossed-slit (XSlit) lens. An XSlit lens uses a relay of two orthogonal cylindrical lenses, each coupled with a slit-shaped aperture. Through ray geometry analysis, we first show that the XSlit lens produces a different and potentially advantageous depth-of-field than the regular spherical lens. We then present a coded aperture strategy that individually encodes each slit aperture, one with broadband code and the other with high depth discrepancy code, for scene recovery. Synthetic and real experiments validate our theory and demonstrate the advantages of XSlit coded aperture solutions over the spherical lens ones.

1 Introduction

Recent advances in computational imaging and photography have enabled many new solutions to tackle traditionally challenging computer vision problems. A notable class of solutions is coded computational photography: by strategically blocking light over time [11], space [5,14], and wavelength [1], etc. These solutions can facilitate scene reconstruction as well as preserve image quality. For example, coded aperture, which is initially developed in astronomy or X-ray imaging, has been extended onto commodity cameras. The coded pattern correlates the frequency characteristics of defocus blurs with scene depth to enable reliable deconvolution and depth estimation.

By far nearly all coded aperture systems are built on top of commodity cameras equipped with a spherical thin lens and circular aperture. Spherical lenses can effectively emulate pinhole projection when the aperture is small. This model also facilitates easy analysis of the depth-of-field in terms of aperture size and object distance. To implement coded aperture, it is common practice to replace the circular aperture with the desired coded patterns. Earlier approaches insert printed masks [5,14,21] between the lens and the sensor whereas more recent solutions replace the mask with programmable Liquid Crystal on Silicon (LCoS) to enable dynamic aperture encoding [7]. Tremendous efforts have been focused on developing reliable coding schemes and deconvolution algorithms. In contrast, very little research has been conducted from the perspective of the lens.

D. Fleet et al. (Eds.): ECCV 2014, Part III, LNCS 8691, pp. 753–766, 2014.

In this paper, we explore coded aperture imaging on a special non-centric lens called the crossed-slit (XSlit) lens. Geometrically, an XSlit lens aims to collect rays that simultaneously pass through two oblique slits in 3D space. Its imaging model is non-centric and the acquired images are multi-perspective [18]. Comprehensive studies have been focused on studying XSlit imaging property [23], geometry [9,10], and its applications in image-based rendering [12,19]. The theoretical foundations have recently led to the constructing real anamorphic or XSlit lenses. Yuan et al.[20] developed an XSlit anamorphot and derived the first-order monochromatic aberration. Ye et al.[15] constructed a portable version of the anamorphot by using a relay of two orthogonal cylindrical lenses, each coupled with a (rectangular) slit-shaped aperture. They have further demonstrated using the XSlit lens in Manhattan scene recovery [15] and stereo matching [16].

This paper makes the first attempt to implement coded aperture on an XSlit lens. Clearly, the first question is whether XSlit coded aperture would bring any benefits to the regular spherical lens based solutions. We hence first conduct a ray geometry analysis to study the depth-of-field (DoF) in the XSlit lens. We show that, with the same light throughput, the XSlit lens can produce a different and potentially advantageous DoF than the spherical lens. Specifically, for each XSlit lens, we introduce its throughput equivalent spherical lens (TESL) with a square aperture. We show that the XSlit blur kernels are 2D rectangularly-shaped where the shape is depth-dependent. However, compared with its TESL's square kernels, they are generally smaller in one dimension and remain the same in the other.

Based on our analysis, we further present a strategy to separately encode each slit aperture for scene reconstruction. Developing coded patterns is a dilemma: an ideal pattern will have to have two conflicting properties, i.e., reliable deconvolution vs. high depth discrepancy. The former requires the aperture pattern to be broadband to ensure robust deconvolution whereas the latter requires the code to contain many zero crossings in the frequency domain to distinguish different depth layers. Our strategy is to encode the smaller dimension to the TESL's using broadband codes and the other using high depth discrepancy codes. Synthetic and real experiments demonstrate that our XSlit coded aperture outperforms its TESL's in reliability and accuracy.

2   XSlit vs. Spherical Lenses in Depth-of-Field

We first compare depth-of-field produced by an XSlit lens vs. the traditional spherical lens. We adopt the XSlit lens model in [15] that uses a relay of two cylindrical lenses. For simplicity, we focus our analysis on Parallel Orthogonal XSlit (POXSlit) lenses where the cylindrical axis of the second lens is orthogonal to the first. The general case (when the two slits are not orthogonal) follows a similar derivation and can be found in the supplementary material.

We start with explaining our notation and lens/aperture settings. We assume the two orthogonal cylindrical lenses lie at $z = l_1$ and $z = l_2$ ($l_1 > l_2$) with focal lengths f_1 and f_2, respectively. Further, we assume the cylindrical axis of first lens is horizontal and the one of the second is vertical, as shown in Fig. 1. The simplest apertures are rectangular-shaped apertures of width w_1 and w_2 on the two lenses respectively. Same as the spherical lens, we can define the f-number of the lenses as $N_i = f_i/w_i$, $i = 1, 2$.

2.1   Cylindrical Lens Transform

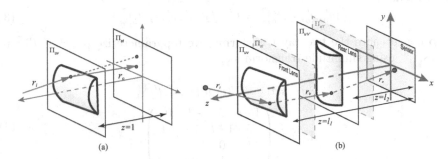

(a)   (b)

Fig. 1. (a)Ray transformation through a single cylindrical lens; (b) Ray transformation through an XSlit lens

To conduct a DoF analysis, we first study how rays are transformed through the XSlit lens. We start with a single cylindrical lens transform and then concatenate the transforms of two lenses. In the language of ray geometry[17], we set out to derive the cylindrical lens operator (CLO), analogous to the spherical lens operator [8,3].

To parameterize rays, we adopt the two-plane parametrization [6]. Each ray is parameterized by its intersections with two parallel planes Π_{uv} and Π_{st}. We place the cylindrical lens on Π_{uv}. Given an incident ray $r_i = [s_i, t_i, u_i, v_i]^\top$ emitted from the scene towards the lens, the CLO maps r_i to an exit ray $r_o = [s_o, t_o, u_o, v_o]^\top$, leaving the lens towards the sensor. When the cylindrical lens is horizontal, it leaves the u component of the ray unaltered and focuses only the v component; when the lens is vertical, it only focuses the u component. By applying the thin-lens law and similitude relationship, we have the horizontal and vertical CLO as

$$[u_o, v_o, s_o, t_o]^\top = C(f)[u_i, v_i, s_i, t_i]^\top$$

$$\text{horizontal: } C_h(f) = \begin{pmatrix} 1 & 0 & 0 & 0 \\ 0 & 1 & 0 & 0 \\ 0 & 0 & 1 & 0 \\ 0 & -1/f & 0 & 1 \end{pmatrix}; \text{ vertical: } C_v(f) = \begin{pmatrix} 1 & 0 & 0 & 0 \\ 0 & 1 & 0 & 0 \\ -1/f & 0 & 1 & 0 \\ 0 & 0 & 0 & 1 \end{pmatrix}$$

(1)

where f is the focal length of the cylindrical lens.

Next we study the concatenation of two cylindrical lenses and derive the XSlit lens operator (XSLO). Specifically, we can trace along an incident ray r_i through the horizontal lens, map it to r_b incident the vertical lens, and compute the final exit ray r_o reaching (incident to) the sensor. By simply applying the horizontal CLO (Eqn. (1)), we have

$$[u_b, v_b, s_b, t_b]^\top = C_h(f_1)[u_i, v_i, s_i, t_i]^\top \tag{2}$$

To reuse CLO on the second lens, we represent r_b and r_o under a new 2PP $u'v's't'$, where $\Pi_{u'v'}$ is the lens plane of the second lens. By applying the vertical CLO, we have

$$[u'_o, v'_o, s'_o, t'_o]^\top = C_v(f_2)[u'_b, v'_b, s'_b, t'_b]^\top \tag{3}$$

To concatenate the two ray transforms, we reparameterize $[u', v', s', t']^\top$ to $[u, v, s, t]^\top$ using similitude transform as

$$[u, v, s, t]^\top = L(l)[u', v', s', t']^\top$$

$$L(l) = \begin{pmatrix} 1+l & 0 & -l & 0 \\ 0 & 1+l & 0 & -l \\ l & 0 & 1-l & 0 \\ 0 & l & 0 & 1-l \end{pmatrix} \tag{4}$$

where $l = l_1 - l_2$ is the separation between two cylindrical lenses. A similar 2PP reparameterization has been used in previous work for correlating in-lens light fields to out-of-lens ones [8].

Finally, by applying $L^{-1}(l)$ on Eqn. (2) and substituting r_b into Eqn. (3), we have the XSlit Lens Operator (XSLO): $S(f_1, f_2, l)$ as

$$\begin{aligned} [u_o, v_o, s_o, t_o]^\top &= L(l)C_v(f_2)L^{-1}(l)C_h(f_1)[u_i, v_i, s_i, t_i]^\top \\ &= S(f_1, f_2, l)[u_i, v_i, s_i, t_i]^\top \end{aligned} \tag{5}$$

For the more general case where the two cylindrical lenses are not orthogonal, we need to consider their angle and the derivation can be found in the supplementary material.

2.2   Aperture Operator

Same as the spherical lens, a wide aperture can introduce defocus blurs and reduce the DoF. We therefore analyze defocus blurs under the regular shaped slit apertures with width w_1 and w_2. We introduce the two aperture operators: A_1 for the horizontal lens and A_2 for the vertical lens. Notice they are parameterized in v and u' on their lens planes respectively.

$$A_1(v) = \begin{cases} 1 & |v| \leq w_1/2 \\ 0 & else \end{cases} \quad \text{and} \quad A_2(u') = \begin{cases} 1 & |u'| \leq w_2/2 \\ 0 & else \end{cases} \tag{6}$$

Since only rays that passing through both apertures can reach the sensor, we can derive the closed-form point spread function (PSF) in the XSlit lens as follows. Consider a scene point $\dot{P}$ at depth z, we map all rays originating from $\dot{P}$

to pixels. Without loss of generosity, we assume $\dot{P}$ is on the z-axis. The incident rays r_i originated from $\dot{P}$ can be written as:

$$r_i = [u_i, v_i, (\frac{z - l_1 + 1}{z - l_1})u_i, (\frac{z - l_1 + 1}{z - l_1})v_i]^\top \tag{7}$$

By applying XSLO on r_i, we compute the exit ray r_o as

$$r_o = [\frac{\xi}{f_2 z - l_1 f_2}u_i, v_i, \frac{\xi - z + l_2 + f_2}{f_2 z - l_1 f_2}u_i, (\frac{z - l_1 + 1}{z - l_1})v_i]^\top \tag{8}$$

where $\xi = l_1 z - l_2 z - l_1 l_2 + l_2^2 - l_1 f_2 + f_2 z$.

The incident rays are constrained by the two apertures (Eqn. (6)):

$$|u_i| \le \frac{w_2(z - l_1)}{2(z - l_2)} , \ |v_i| \le w_1/2 \tag{9}$$

Substituting Eqn. (8) into Eqn. (9), we can map the aperture constraint onto r_o:

$$|u_o| \le \frac{w_2 \xi}{2(f_2 z - f_2 l_2)}, \ |v_o| \le w_1/2 \tag{10}$$

Since the sensor is the xy-plane at $z = 0$, we can directly obtain the PSF from r_o by mapping Eqn. (10) onto the xy-plane:

$$\text{PSF}(x, y) = \begin{cases} 1 & |x| \le \frac{w_2}{2}(\frac{z}{z - l_2} - \frac{l_2}{f_2}) \text{ and } |y| \le \frac{w_1}{2}(\frac{z}{z - l_1} - \frac{l_1}{f_1}) \\ 0 & else \end{cases} \tag{11}$$

The XSlit PSF is non-isotropic and its shape is depth dependent as shown in Fig. 2.

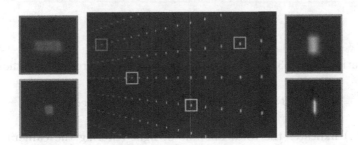

Fig. 2. Captured XSlit PSFs at different depths. We use an XSlit camera with focal length 50mm & 50mm to capture a 32×24 dot-array projected on a slanted screen (ranging from 15cm to 36cm w.r.t.the camera). The XSlit PSFs vary both in shape and scale w.r.t.depth.

2.3   Throughput Equivalent Spherical Lens

One of the most interesting questions regarding the XSlit lens is: is it better than the regular spherical thin lens? We therefore compare the XSlit PSF with the spherical thin lens PSF. For fairness, we need to ensure that the two types

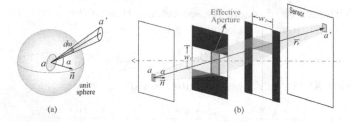

Fig. 3. Light throughput analysis on the XSlit lens. (a) Measure the flux from a to a' using solid angle $d\omega$. (b) Measuring the light enters the camera through the XSlit lens using the effective aperture.

of lenses have the same light throughput. We thus further conduct a radiometry analysis. Specifically, for every XSlit lens, we find its dual *throughput equivalent spherical lens (TESL)*.

Consider a thin pencil of light emanating from a small surface element a of an object at depth z. Assume the radiance of a is B, the light energy (flux) radiated per second from a to the another surface element a' is given by the Lambert's law:

$$d\Phi = B \cdot a \cos \alpha d\omega \tag{12}$$

where α is the angle between a's normal and the line connecting a and a'; $d\omega$ is the solid angle subtended by a' at a, as shown in Fig. 3(a).

By Eqn. (6), the area of effective aperture is $\frac{z-l_1}{z-l_2}w_1w_2$. The project area of the effective aperture as seen by a can be computed as $\frac{z-l_1}{z-l_2}w_1w_2 \cos \alpha$. By mapping the project area onto the unit sphere, we obtain the solid angle

$$\omega = \frac{z-l_1}{z-l_2}w_1w_2 \cos^3 \alpha \tag{13}$$

Substituting Eqn. (13) into Eqn. (12), we have the flux received at the effective aperture

$$\Phi = B \cdot a \cos \alpha \omega = B \cdot a \frac{w_1w_2}{(z-l_1)(z-l_2)} \cos^4 \alpha \tag{14}$$

Eqn. (14) indicates the total amount of light entering the camera. We can further map Φ to irradiance (flux per area) received at sensor. We have the imaged area of a as $a' = \frac{l_1l_2a}{(z-l_1)(z-l_2)}$ by using similar triangles. Dividing Φ by a', we have the irradiance received at sensor:

$$E_{\text{XSlit}} = \frac{\Phi}{a'} = B\frac{w_1w_2}{l_1l_2} \cos^4 \alpha \tag{15}$$

Since the lens-to-scene distance is much larger than the lens-to-sensor distance, we can approximate l_i/w_i using f_i/w_i. Therefore, we rewrite Eqn. (15) in terms of f-numbers

$$E_{\text{XSlit}} = BN_1N_2 \cos^4 \alpha \tag{16}$$

Recall that, for a spherical lens with focal length f_p and f-number N_p, the irradiance can be computed as:

$$E_{\text{spherical}} = BN_p^2 \cos^4 \alpha \qquad (17)$$

By Eqn. (16) and Eqn. (17), given a XSlit lens with f-numbers N_1 and N_2, its TESL will have f-number $N_p = \sqrt{N_1 N_2}$.

2.4   Depth-of-Field Comparisons

Now that we have derived the TESL of an XSlit lens, we can compare their DoFs. It is very important to note that, different from the spherical lens, if the two cylindrical lenses in an XSlit lens have identical focus length, it is not practical to focus the two lenses at the same depth (the only in-focus depth is $z = l_1 + l_2$, which is too close to the front horizontal lens at $z = l_1$). We therefore focus the two lenses at two different depths. At the first glance, this focus setting may appear highly undesirable as no 3D point can be clearly focused in the image. A deeper analysis as follows, however, reveals that it has several advantages.

Recall that the front lens is horizontal thus producing vertical blurs and the rear lens (closer to the sensor) is vertical resulting in horizontal blurs. By Eqn. (11), the horizontal and vertical PSF scales are:

$$b_v = (\frac{z}{z - l_1} - \frac{l_1}{f_1})w_1 \quad \text{and} \quad b_h = (\frac{z}{z - l_2} - \frac{l_2}{f_2})w_2 \qquad (18)$$

We assume that the TESL coincides with the the front lens. Recall that the spherical lens' PSF is uniform. Therefore, the spherical PSF scale b is always identical to the vertical scale of XSlit PSF ($b = b_v$). Given the lens parameters and focused depth, we can plot the curves of PSF scales vs. scene depth, as shown in Fig. 4(b). The red curve corresponds to b_v and the green one corresponds to b_h. Assume z_{front} refers to the depth that the front lens focuses at, z_{rear} refers to the one that the rear lens focuses at, and z_{inter} between z_{front} and z_{rear} refers to the depth the two curves intersect.

At z_{front}, the TESL has zero PSF whereas the XSlit lens has only zero vertical scale but appear defocused horizontally. This is a major disadvantage of the XSlit, i.e., no point in the scene can be clearly focused either horizontally or vertically when using the same focal length for each cylindrical lens.

Let us consider an important depth z_{inter} where the two curves intersects. Before z_{inter}, the XSlit performs worse, i.e., it incurs more horizontal blur than the TESL ($b_h > b_v = b$). Although this is undesirable, this range is much smaller than the complete scene range in a typical scene. Therefore, under the same setup, only a small range of depth exhibits worse PSF in XSlit than in the pinhole lens while majority depths in XSlit will appear much clearly focused.

The key advantage of the XSlit is that after z_{inter} the horizontal scale of the XSlit PSF is always smaller than the spherical lens one ($b_h < b_v = b$). One can explain this phenomena by either algebraic reasoning or geometry/optics reasoning. Algebraically, since the two lenses focuses at different scene depth,

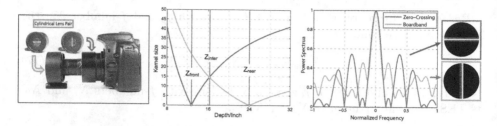

Fig. 4. (a) XSlit camera prototype; (b) XSlit PSF scales vs. depth; (c) The power Spectra of our selected coded apertures

b_h and b_v map to two different curves. The two curves will intersect somewhere between z_{front} and z_{rear}, after which b_h will always be smaller than b_v. From the geometric optics perspective, we can also reason this phenomena. The rear lens focuses farther away than the front lens. Since the two lenses have an identical focal length, after depth z_{rear}, the rear lens will incur smaller defocus blur because the relative depth of the corresponding point to its focal plane is larger than to front one.

3   XSlit Coded Aperture Imaging

The analysis above indicates that the XSlit lens have a different and potentially advantageous DoF than its TESL. In this section, we exploit the special property of XSlit DoF and implement a coded aperture system for scene recovery.

Depth recovering using coded aperture has been thoroughly explored on spherical lenses in the past decade [5,14,7,22,13]. The basis idea is to analyze the coded pattern and defocused images to recover scene depth and produce an all-focus image. However, designing the code is a dilemma. To discriminate depth, the aperture pattern should have zero-crossings in the frequency domain to purposely introduce variations among blurry images in terms of depths [5]. However, to ensure robust deconvolution, the aperture pattern should be broadband, i.e., its frequency profile should have few zero-crossings [14].

When only a single coded aperture is used on the spherical lens, one can potentially combine the two types of codes through multiplexing, e.g., horizontally using the broadband and vertically using the high depth discrepancy ones. Recall that the DoF analysis shows that compared with its TESL, the XSlit lens (under the focus configuration as discussed in Section 2.4) exhibits less horizontal blurs and approximately the same vertical blurs under the same light throughput. Our strategy hence is to encode the first cylindrical lens (the horizontal one) using the high discrepancy kernel and the vertical lens with a broadband one. We choose this strategy to remain the same depth discrepancy as its TESL (since they have identical vertical blur scale) whereas the other dimension is less blurred to provide more robust deconvolution. If we switch the coding scheme (i.e., the first with broadband pattern and the second with high depth discrepancy one), although the all-focus image can be more easily restored, the depth discriminative ability is compromised.

3.1 Code Selection

Next we discuss how to choose the appropriate coded pattern for each cylindrical lens. Assume the vertical pattern is $K_v(x)$ and the horizontal pattern is $K_h(y)$, the overall blur kernel is therefore $K(x,y) = K_v(x) \cdot K_v(y)$ where x and y are further constrained by the close-form PSF (Eqn. (11)). For each 1D pattern, we choose from a series of randomly sampled 13-bit codes. Since the vertical code K_v is required to be broadband, we select the one with the maximum min-value in the frequency domain.

Then we fix K_v and find the optimal K_h. Assume the blur kernel at depth i is $K^i = K_v^i \cdot K_h^i$. To have better depth discrepancy, we want to maximize the distance between blurry image distributions caused by kernels at different depths, i.e., K^i and K^j ($i \neq j$). We use the commonly used Kullback-Leibler (KL) divergence to measure the distance between two blurry image distributions

$$D(P^i(y), P^j(y)) = \int_y P^i(y)(\log P^i(y) - \log P^j(y))dy \qquad (19)$$

where P^i and P^j are the blurry image distribution for K^i and K^j respectively and we use the hyper-Laplacian distribution of natural images for computing them [5,4].

Finally, we use "1010010011111" as the vertical code and "110011110011" as the horizontal code in our implementation. The power spectra of the selected codes are plotted in Fig. 4(c).

3.2 Depth Estimation

To estimate depth, we first precompute the corresponding point spread function (PSF) for each layer using the coded pattern and the closed-form PSF derived in Section 2. Once we acquire the image, we check which PSF yields to the optimal results. Specifically, we conduct deconvolution using PSFs of different depth layers: when the scale is larger than the actual one, the result will exhibit strong ringing artifacts; when the scale is smaller than the actual one, the image would appear less sharp but still without ringing. We use Gabor filter to detect ringing in the deconvolved image, i.e., greater responses correspond to more severe ringing. A Gabor filter is a Gaussian kernel function modulated by a sinusoidal plane wave and can be written as

$$G_{\lambda,\theta}(x,y) = \exp(-\frac{x'^2 + \gamma y'^2}{2\sigma^2}) \cos(2\pi \frac{x'}{\lambda}) \qquad (20)$$

$$x' = x\cos\theta - y\sin\theta, \; y' = x\sin\theta - y\cos\theta$$

where λ is the wavelength (reciprocal of the spatial frequency), θ is the orientation of the filter, γ is aspect ratio, and σ is the standard deviation of Gaussian.

We use Gabor filters with $\theta = 0°$ and $90°$ for ringing detection. We define the response of a Gabor filter G_θ as

$$R_\theta(x, y) = \iint I(x, y)G_\theta(x - u, y - v)dudv \tag{21}$$

We sum up the horizontal and vertical Gabor responses on each deconvolved image and thus the one with smallest value corresponds to the optimal depth. We discretize the scene to N depth layers and reuse the graph-cut algorithm [2] for assigned depth labels. We use the Gabor response as the penalty term for building the graph. Therefore, the energy function E of assigning a depth label d_i to a pixel p is formulated as

$$E(d_i) = \alpha \cdot \sum_{p \in P} E_d(p, d_i(p)) + \sum_{p_1, p_2 \in N} E_s(p_1(d_i), p_2(d_j)) \tag{22}$$

where P represents all pixels in the image; N represents the pixel neighborhood; $E_d(p, d_i(p))$ is the Gabor response as the data term; E_s is the smooth term; and the non-negative coefficient α balances the data term and the smooth term.

To recover all-focus image, since our blur kernel only compromises 1D scene information, we simply reuse the modified Wienner deconvolution using natural image priors [21] which is much faster than the Iteratively Reweighted Least Squares (IRLS) deconvolution [5] that can handle kernels with many zero-crossings.

4   Experiments

We validate our DoF analysis and coded aperture imaging model on real XSlit lenses as shown in Fig. 4(a). We follow the same design as [15] to construct the XSlit lens using a relay of two cylindrical lenses with focal length 50mm. We use a 50mm spherical lens as its TESL. We use the camera body of Canon 60D. For all experiments, we use ISO 100 and shutter speed 1/100s.

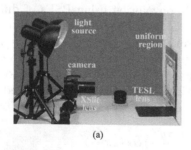
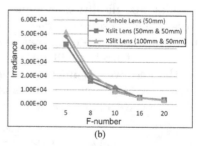

(a)   (b)

Fig. 5. Light throughput comparison between the XSlit lens and its TESL. (a) Experimental setup; (b) The irradiance vs. f-number curve for the three lenses.

Throughput. Given a specific f-number, e.g., $f/10$ (i.e., with both slit aperture widths 5mm), we can compute the aperture size of its TESL by dividing the f-number with the focal length (in this case, a square aperture of 5mm×5mm). We further construct the second XSlit lens where the two cylindrical lenses have different focal lengths (the first of 100mm and the second of 50mm). By the definition of f-number in Section 2, for the second XSlit lens to have the same throughput as the first and its TESL, we need to double the aperture width of the 100mm lens (e.g., in this example 10mm). In our experiments, we compare the throughput of all three lenses with $f/5$, $f/8$, $f/10$, $f/16$ and $f/20$.

We use all three lenses to capture a uniform white diffuse surface under the same lighting condition, as shown in Fig. 5(a). We use the averaged intensity value of the linearly tone-mapped raw image from the camera as irradiance measure. Fig. 5(b) plots irradiance vs. f-number curves of all three lenses. Our results are consistent with the throughput analysis: as far as the XSlit lenses and the TESL have the same f-number, they have equivalent light throughput.

Notice though that when the aperture size gets too big (e.g., $f/5$), the XSlit lenses exhibit strong vignetting.

Depth-of-Field. Next we valid our DoF analysis of the XSlit lens vs. its TESL. We construct a scene that consists of three objects lying at depth 38cm, 50cm and 63cm w.r.t.the camera. For the XSlit lens, the front lens focuses at 40cm and the rear lens at 45cm whereas its TESL focuses at 40cm. The image captured by the XSlit and its TESL are shown in Fig. 6(a) and (b) respectively. Our analysis predicts that the PSF of the XSlit should be narrow in the horizontal direction than the TESL for objects lying far away. Notice that layer 2 and layer 3 have depth greater than z_{inter} and in the acquired images, they appear less horizontally blurred in the XSlit image than the TESL one, which is consistent with our prediction. Furthermore, the vertical blur scales are approximately the same in both the XSlit and its TESL. The XSlit hence improves the depth-of-field for objects at depth greater than z_{inter}, e.g., the texts in layer 3 appear clearer in the XSlit image than in its TESL's.

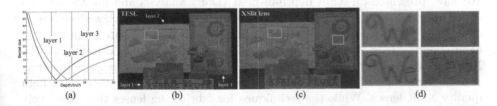

Fig. 6. DoF comparison between the XSlit lens and its TESL. (a) PSF scale vs. depth curve; (b) and (c) are the images captured by the TESL and XSlit lens respectively; (d) shows close-up views in (b) and (c).

Coded Aperture Imaging. Next, we demonstrate coded aperture imaging on the XSlit lens for scene reconstruction. Same as existing solutions, we first conduct experiments on synthetic data to compare the performance of XSlit coded aperture vs. its TESL's. We construct a simple scene with three depth layers at 20cm, 40cm and 80cm. The XSlit lens focuses at 16cm and 24cm. The TESL's focal plane coincides with the front focal plane of the XSlit. For the TESL, we use the optimal coded pattern presented [5] which is expected to have high depth discrepancy. For our XSlit lens, we use the codes described in Section 3.1.

Fig. 7 shows the recovered depth map and all-focus image using the two lenses. For image deconvolution, we apply IRLS (first column) and Wiener filters (the other two columns). Coded aperture result on the TESL using the optimal code [5] produces a high quality depth map although the recovered all-focus image exhibits ring artifacts near occlusion boundaries due to zero-crossings in the frequency domain, as discussed in Section 3.1. Our XSlit coded aperture solution is able to reduce the ringing artifacts thanks to smaller horizontal PSFs and special coding schemes and its recovered depth map is comparable to the TESL's.

Finally, we use our XSlit lens to acquire real scenes. We printed the coded pattern on clear masks and insert them on the aperture plane of each cylindrical lens. The scene consists of three cards at depth 50cm, 80cm, and 100cm respectively. The front lens is focused at 30cm and the rear lens at 60cm. We use the same code as in the synthetic case and apply graph-cut based depth estimation. In particular, we discretize depth to 10 labels ranging from 30cm to 120cm. We segment the captured defocus blurred image into 10×10 patches, compute the Gabor response for each depth layer, and find the optimal depth labeling. Our XSlit coded aperture imaging is able to recover satisfactory depth maps and all-focus images as shown in Fig. 8. The blocky effect in our depth output is partially due to the large window sizes.

5   Discussions and Future Work

We have presented an XSlit depth-of-field (DoF) analysis and an XSlit-based coded aperture imaging solution. Despite being highly theoretical, we have show-cased that an XSlit lens is potentially advantageous than its throughput equivalent spherical lens: when the two types of lenses have a similar throughput, the XSlit lens will exhibit better DoF and hence can benefit coded aperture imaging. A major limitation of our approach though is the challenges in constructing high quality XSlit lenses. While the techniques for fabricating lenses that effectively emulate spherical thin lenses have matured in the past century, relatively little work has focused on designing high quality cylindrical lenses and let alone XSlit lenses. In fact, our self-constructed XSlit exhibits high distortions, poor anti-reflection, and strong vignetting. It is our important future work to work with optical engineers to fabricate a larger scale XSlit lens for experimenting our coded aperture scheme.

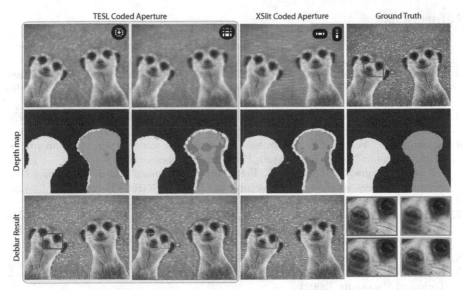

Fig. 7. Coded aperture result on a synthetic scene. We compare our XSlit coded aperture and its TESL with two different coded patterns: on the left we use the coding scheme in [5] and on the right we use the coding scheme that is a combination of the XSlit codes.

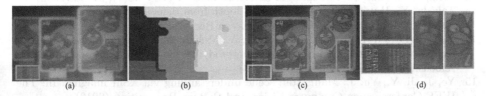

Fig. 8. Coded aperture result on a real scene. (a) The captured defocused image using the proposed XSlit coded aperture scheme; (b) Our recovered depth map; (c) Our recovered all-focus image; (d) Close-up views in (a) and (c).

Another future direction we plan to explore is scene-dependent coded aperture designs. A natural scene often contains patterns that exhibit strong directional features, e.g., a scene can contain mostly horizontal features and few vertical ones. We therefore can potentially encode the vertical and horizontal slit apertures differently to simultaneously account for depth estimation and defocus compensation. Finally, our analysis shows that XSlit defocus blurs different significantly from the ones of spherical lenses: the PSFs vary both in size and shape at different depths. In particular, the shape of the kernel can help validate depth hypothesis in scene recovery. In the future, we plan to explore reliable solutions to integrate this useful depth cue into scene recovery.

Acknowledgements. This project was supported by the National Science Foundation under grants IIS-CAREER-0845268.

References

1. Arguello, H., Arce, G.R.: Code aperture optimization for spectrally agile compressive imaging. J. Opt. Soc. Am. A 28(11), 2400–2413 (2011)
2. Boykov, Y., Veksler, O., Zabih, R.: Efficient approximate energy minimization via graph cuts. IEEE Transactions on Pattern Analysis and Machine Intelligence 20(12), 1222–1239 (2001)
3. Ding, Y., Xiao, J., Yu, J.: A theory of multi-perspective defocusing. In: The IEEE Conference on Computer Vision and Pattern Recognition (2011)
4. Krishnan, D., Fergus, R.: Fast image deconvolution using hyper-laplacian priors. In: Advances in Neural Information Processing Systems (2009)
5. Levin, A., Fergus, R., Durand, F., Freeman, W.T.: Image and depth from a conventional camera with a coded aperture. In: ACM SIGGRAPH (2007)
6. Levoy, M., Hanrahan, P.: Light field rendering. In: ACM SIGGRAPH (1996)
7. Nagahara, H., Zhou, C., Watanabe, T., Ishiguro, H., Nayar, S.K.: Programmable aperture camera using LCoS. In: Daniilidis, K., Maragos, P., Paragios, N. (eds.) ECCV 2010, Part VI. LNCS, vol. 6316, pp. 337–350. Springer, Heidelberg (2010)
8. Ng, R.: Fourier slice photography. In: ACM SIGGRAPH (2005)
9. Pajdla, T.: Geometry of two-slit camera. Tech. Rep. CTU-CMP-2002-02, Czech Technical University (2002)
10. Ponce, J.: What is a camera? In: The IEEE Conference on Computer Vision and Pattern Recognition (2009)
11. Raskar, R., Agrawal, A., Tumblin, J.: Coded exposure photography: Motion deblurring using fluttered shutter. In: ACM SIGGRAPH (2006)
12. Seitz, S.M., Kim, J.: The space of all stereo images. IJCV 48(1), 21–38 (2002)
13. Takeda, Y., Hiura, S., Sato, K.: Fusing depth from defocus and stereo with coded apertures. In: Computer Vision and Pattern Recognition (2013)
14. Veeraraghavan, A., Raskar, R., Agrawal, A., Mohan, A., Tumblin, J.: Dappled photography: Mask enhanced cameras for heterodyned light fields and coded aperture refocusing. In: ACM SIGGRAPH (2007)
15. Ye, J., Ji, Y., Yu, J.: Manhattan scene understanding via XSlit imaging. In: The IEEE Conference on Computer Vision and Pattern Recognition (2013)
16. Ye, J., Ji, Y., Yu, J.: A rotational stereo model based on XSlit imaging. In: The IEEE International Conference on Computer Vision (2013)
17. Ye, J., Yu, J.: Ray geometry in non-pinhole cameras: A survey. The Visual Computer 30(1), 93–112 (2014)
18. Yu, J., McMillan, L., Sturm, P.: Multi-perspective modelling, rendering and imaging. Eurographics 29(1), 227–246 (2010)
19. Yu, J., Ding, Y., Mcmillan, L.: Multiperspective modeling and rendering using general linear cameras. Communications in Information & Systems 7(4), 359–384 (2007)
20. Yuan, S., Sasian, J.: Aberrations of anamorphic optical systems. ii. primary aberration theory for cylindrical anamorphic systems. Appl. Opt. 48(15), 2836–2841 (2009)
21. Zhou, C., Nayar, S.K.: What are Good Apertures for Defocus Deblurring? In: IEEE International Conference on Computational Photography (2009)
22. Zhou, C., Lin, S., Nayar, S.: Coded Aperture Pairs for Depth from Defocus and Defocus Deblurring. IJCV 93(1), 53 (2011)
23. Zomet, A., Feldman, D., Peleg, S., Weinshall, D.: Mosaicing new views: The crossed-slits projection. IEEE Transactions on Pattern Analysis and Machine Intelligence 25(6), 741–754 (2003)

Refraction Wiggles for Measuring Fluid Depth and Velocity from Video

Tianfan Xue[1], Michael Rubinstein[2,1], Neal Wadhwa[1], Anat Levin[3],
Fredo Durand[1], and William T. Freeman[1]

[1] MIT CSAIL, USA
[2] Microsoft Research, USA
[3] Weizmann Institute, Israel

Abstract. We present principled algorithms for measuring the velocity and 3D location of refractive fluids, such as hot air or gas, from natural videos with textured backgrounds. Our main observation is that intensity variations related to movements of refractive fluid elements, as observed by one or more video cameras, are consistent over small space-time volumes. We call these intensity variations "refraction wiggles", and use them as features for tracking and stereo fusion to recover the fluid motion and depth from video sequences. We give algorithms for 1) measuring the (2D, projected) motion of refractive fluids in monocular videos, and 2) recovering the 3D position of points on the fluid from stereo cameras. Unlike pixel intensities, wiggles can be extremely subtle and cannot be known with the same level of confidence for all pixels, depending on factors such as background texture and physical properties of the fluid. We thus carefully model uncertainty in our algorithms for robust estimation of fluid motion and depth. We show results on controlled sequences, synthetic simulations, and natural videos. Different from previous approaches for measuring refractive flow, our methods operate directly on videos captured with ordinary cameras, do not require auxiliary sensors, light sources or designed backgrounds, and can correctly detect the motion and location of refractive fluids even when they are invisible to the naked eye.

1 Introduction

Measuring and visualizing the flow of air and fluids has great importance in many areas of science and technology, such as aeronautical engineering, combustion research, and ballistics. Multiple techniques have been proposed for this purpose, such as sound tomography, Doppler LIDAR and Schlieren photography, but they either rely on complicated and expensive setups or are limited to in-lab use. Our goal is to make the process of measuring and localizing refractive fluids cheaper, more accessible, and applicable in natural settings.

In this paper, we develop passive, markerless techniques to measure the velocity and depth of air flow using natural video sequences. Our techniques are based on visual cues produced by the bending of light rays as they travel through air of differing densities. Such deflections are exploited in various air measurement techniques, described below in related work. As the air moves, small changes in the refractive properties appear as small visual distortions (motions) of the background, similar to the shimmering effect experienced when viewing objects across hot asphalt or through exhaust gases. We call

D. Fleet et al. (Eds.): ECCV 2014, Part III, LNCS 8691, pp. 767–782, 2014.

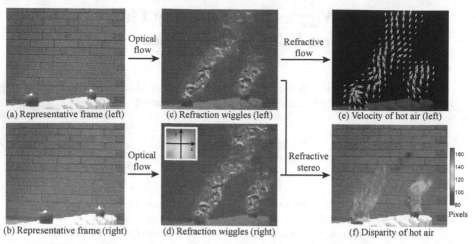

Fig. 1. Measuring the velocity and depth of imperceptible candle plumes from standard videos. The heat rising from two burning candles (a, b) cause small distortions of the background due to light rays refracting as they travel from the background to the camera passing through the hot air. Methods such as synthetic Schlieren imaging (c, d) are able to *visualize* those small disturbances and reveal the heat plume, but are unable to *measure* its actual motion. We show that, under reasonable conditions, the refraction patterns (observed motions) move coherently with the refracting fluid, allowing to accurately measure the 2D motion of the flow from a monocular video (e), and the depth of the flow from a stereo sequence (f). The full sequence and results are available in the supplementary material.

such motions *"refraction wiggles"*, and show they can be tracked using regular video cameras to infer information about the velocity and depth of a refractive fluid layer. However, wiggles are related to the fluid motion in nontrivial ways, and have to be processed by appropriate algorithms.

More specifically, measuring refractive flow from video poses two main challenges. First, since the air or fluid elements are transparent, they cannot be observed directly by a camera, and the position of intensity texture features is not directly related to the 3D position of the fluid elements. We therefore cannot apply standard motion analysis and 3D reconstruction techniques directly to the intensity measurements. Our main observation in this paper is that such techniques are still applicable, but in a *different feature space*. Specifically, while *intensity* features result from a background layer and their location is not directly related to the fluid layer, *motion* features (wiggles) correspond to the 3D positions and motion of points on the transparent fluid surface. The movement of those wiggles between consecutive frames (i.e. the motion of the observed motions) is an indicator of the motion of the transparent fluid, and the disparity of these motion features between viewpoints is a good cue for the depth of the fluid surface.

Following this observation, we derive algorithms for the following two tasks: 1) tracking the movement of refractive fluids in a single video, and 2) recovering the 3D position of points on the fluid surface from stereo sequences. Both these algorithms are based on the *refractive constancy* assumption (analogous to the brightness constancy assumption of ordinary motion analysis): that intensity variations over time (the wiggles) are explained by the motion of a constant, non-uniform refractive field. This distortion is measured by computing the wiggle features in an input video, and then using those features to estimate the motion and depth of the fluid, by matching them across frames and viewpoints. In this paper, we focus on estimating the fluid motion and depth from stationary cameras, assuming a single, thin refractive layer between the camera and the background.

The second challenge in measuring refractive flow from video is that the distortion of the background caused by the refraction is typically very small (on the order of 0.1 pixels) and therefore hard to detect. The motion features have to be extracted carefully to overcome inherent noise in the video, and to properly deal with regions in the background that are not sufficiently textured, in which the extracted motions are less reliable. To address these issues, we develop probabilistic refractive flow and stereo algorithms that maintain estimates of the uncertainty in the optical flow, the refractive flow, and the fluid depth.

The proposed algorithms have several advantages over previous work: (1) a simple setup that can be used outdoors or indoors, (2) they can be used to visualize and measure air flow and 3D location directly from regular videos, and (3) they maintain estimates of uncertainty. To our knowledge, we are the first to provide a complete pipeline that measures the motions and reconstructs the 3D location of refractive flow directly from videos taken in natural settings.

All the videos and results presented in this paper, together with additional supplementary material, are available on: http://people.csail.mit.edu/tfxue/proj/fluidflow/.

2 Related Work

Techniques to visualize and measure fluid flow can be divided into two categories: those that introduce tracers (dye, smoke or particles) into the fluid, and those that detect the refraction of light rays through the fluid, where variations in index of refraction serve as tracers.

In tracer-based methods, the fluid motion is measured by tracking particles introduced into the fluid, a technique called particle image velocimetry (PIV). Traditional PIV algorithms are based on correlating the particles between image patches [1]. Recently, optical flow algorithms were used with PIV images [19,20], and different regularization terms were proposed to adapt the optical flow methods to track fluids rather than solid objects [13].

In tracer-free methods, Schlieren photography is a technique to visualize fluid flow that exploits changes in the refractive index of a fluid. It works by using a carefully aligned optical setup to amplify deflections of light rays due to refraction [21,22,24,25]. To measure the velocity of the fluid, researchers have proposed Schlieren PIV [14,5], in which the motion of a fluid is recovered by tracking vortices in Schlieren photographs using PIV correlation techniques. These methods still require the optical setup for Schlieren photography, which can be expensive and hard to deploy outside a lab.

The initial stage of our approach is most similar to a technique called Background Oriented Schlieren (BOS, a.k.a Synthetic Schlieren) [6,8,10,12,15,18]. The optical setup in Schlieren photography is replaced by optical flow calculations on a video of a fluid in front of an in-focus textured background. The refraction due to the fluid motion is recovered by computing optical flow between each frame of the video and an undistorted reference frame. Most previous BOS techniques focus on visualizing, not measuring, the fluid flow, and produce visualizations of the flow similar to the results shown in Fig. 1(c,d). Atcheson et al. use BOS tomography to recover the volumetric 3D shape of air flow [6]. However, their technique requires a camera array that covers 180° of the air flow of the interest, making the whole system difficult to use outdoors. To the best of our knowledge, ours is the simplest camera-based system–only requiring stereo video–that can measure the motion and 3D location of air flow.

While artificial backgrounds are often used when performing BOS [6], Hargather et al. [12] showed that natural backgrounds, such as a forest, are sufficiently textured for BOS, allowing for the visualization of large-scale air flows around planes and boats. To address the fact that the background must be in focus, Wetzstein et al. [28] introduced light field BOS imaging in which the textured background is replaced by a light field probe. However, this comes at the cost of having to build a light field probe as large as the flow of interest.

Another limitation of the aforementioned BOS algorithms is that they require a reference frame, which has no air flow in front of it. To avoid having to capture such a reference frame, Raffel et al. proposed background-oriented stereoscopic Schlieren (BOSS) [17] , where images captured by one camera serve as reference frames for the other camera. It is important to note that BOSS uses stereo setup for a different purpose than our proposed refractive stereo algorithm: the acquisition of a background image, not depth. BOSS uses stereo to achieve a reference-frame-free capture while we use it for depth recovery. Moreover, an important weakness of all of these BOS algorithms is that they require a background that has a strong texture. While texture also helps our algorithms, the probabilistic framework we propose also allows for more general backgrounds.

Complementary to the visualization of BOS, several methods have been developed to recover quantitative information about a scene from refraction. Several authors have shown that it is possible to recover the shape of the surface of an air-water interface by filming a textured background underneath it [9,16,30]. Alterman et al. [4] proposed to recover refraction location and strength from multiple cameras using tomography. Tian et al. [27] showed that atmospheric turbulence provides a depth cue as larger deflections due to refraction typically correspond to greater depths. Wetzstein et al. [29] proposed to recover the shape of a refractive solid object from light field distortions. Alterman et al. [2,3] showed that it is possible to locate a moving object through refractive atmospheric turbulence or a water interface.

3   Refraction Wiggles and Refractive Constancy

Gradients in the refractive properties of air (such as temperature and shape) introduce visual distortions of the background, and changes in the refractive properties over time show up as minute motions in videos. In general, several factors may introduce such changes in refractive properties. For example, the refractive object may be stationary but change in shape or temperature. In this paper, however, we attribute those changes to non-uniform refractive flow elements *moving* over some short time interval $[t, t + \Delta t]$. We assume that for a small enough Δt, a refractive object maintains its shape and temperature, such that the observed motions in the video are caused mostly by the motion of the object (and the object having a non-uniform surface, thus introducing

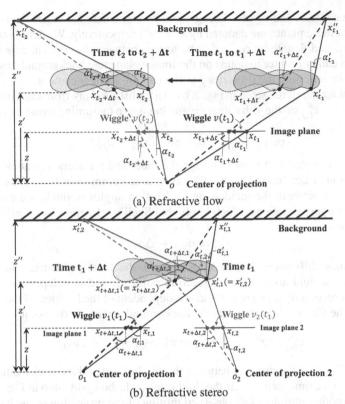

(a) Refractive flow

(b) Refractive stereo

Fig. 2. Refractive distortions (wiggles) in a single view (a) and multiple views (b). A single, thin refractive layer is moving between one or more video cameras and a background. As the refractive fluid moves between time t_i (solid lines) and time $t_i + \Delta t$ (dashed lines), changes in the refractive patterns move points on the background (shown in blue and red) to different positions on the image plane, generating the observed *"wiggles"* (red and blue arrows). The direction of the wiggles on the image plane can be arbitrary, but they are *consistent* over short time durations and between close viewpoints as the fluid moves (see text). By tracking the wiggles over time we can recover the projected 2D fluid motion (a), and by stereo-fusing the wiggles between different views, we can recover the fluid's depth (b). **Note:** as discussed in the text, wiggle constancy holds if the refraction, the motion of the object and the baseline between the cameras are small. In these illustrations we exaggerated all these quantities for clarity.

variation in the refractive layer). While this is an assumption, we found it to hold well in practice as long as the video frame-rate is high enough, depending on the velocity of the flow being captured (more details in the experimental section below). In this section, we establish the relation between those observed motions in one or more cameras and the motion and depth of refractive fluids in a visual scene.

To understand the basic setup, consider Fig. 2. A video camera, or multiple video cameras, are observing a static background through a refractive fluid layer (such as hot air). In this paper, we assume that the cameras are stationary, and that a single, thin and moving refractive layer exists between the camera and the background. We use the notation $x_{t,j}$ for points on the j'th camera sensor plane at time t, $x'_{t,j}$ for points on the (locally planar) fluid, and $x''_{t,j}$ for background points, where t denotes the time index. The depths of these planes are denoted by z, z', z'', respectively. We denote the camera centers by o_j, and denote by $\alpha_{t,j}, \alpha'_{t,j}$ the angles between the optical axis to the ray from the j'th camera center to points on the image plane and background, respectively. For brevity, we will omit the subscript j in the case of a single camera.

Now consider the stereo setup in Fig. 2(b). An undistorted ray from the camera center o_j to points $x_{t,j}, x'_{t,j}$ on the j'th camera plane has angle (assuming small $\alpha_{t,j}$, such that $\tan \alpha_{t,j} \approx \alpha_{t,j}$)

$$\alpha_{t,j} = (x_{t,j} - o_j)/z = (x'_{t,j} - o_j)/z'. \tag{1}$$

This ray is distorted as it passes through the fluid, and transfers into angle $\alpha'_{t,j}$. The exact distortion is determined by Snell's law. As is common in the optics literature, if the difference between the incident and refraction angles is small, we can use first order paraxial approximations, which imply that Snell's refraction law is effectively an additive constant,

$$\alpha'_{t,j} \approx \alpha_{t,j} + \Delta\alpha_t, \tag{2}$$

where the angle difference $\Delta\alpha_t$ depends only on the local geometric and refractive properties of the fluid around the intersection point x'_t, and is independent of the incoming ray direction $\alpha'_{t,j}$, and in particular independent of the location of the observing camera o_j. The distorted ray then hits the background surface at the point

$$x''_{t,j} = x'_{t,j} + \zeta \cdot \alpha'_{t,j} = x'_{t,j} + \zeta(\alpha_{t,j} + \Delta\alpha_t) \tag{3}$$

where $\zeta = z'' - z'$ is the distance between the fluid object and the background.

At a successive time step $t + \Delta t$ the fluid moves (dashed gray blob in Fig. 2(b)). We assume this motion introduces an observed motion of the projection of the background point $x''_{t,j}$ on the image plane, from point $x_{t,j}$ to point $x_{t+\Delta t,j}$. We call that motion a *"refraction wiggle"*, or *"wiggle"* for short. The geometry of the fluid can be complex and predicting the exact path of the light ray mathematically is not straightforward. Nevertheless, We define as $x'_{t+\Delta t,j}$ the point at which a ray connecting $x''_{t,j}$ to the camera center o_j intersects and refracts at the fluid layer.

Let us now fix a point $\bar{x}'_t = x'_{t,j}$ on the fluid surface, and refer to the image $x_{t,j}$ of that same physical point in all cameras. The rays from each camera to that point have different angles $\alpha'_{t,j}$, and as a result they intersect the background layer at different points $x''_{t,j}$. Thus, the texture intensity observed by each camera at the points $x_{t,j}$ can be arbitrarily different. Therefore, we cannot match intensities between the cameras if we wish to match features on the fluid layer and recover their depth. However, we observe that the wiggles correspond to features on the fluid layer rather than on the background, which allows us to stereo-fuse them to estimate the fluid depth. For this we need to show that despite the fact that, without loss of generality, $x''_{t,1} \neq x''_{t,2}$, the two points are refracted at time $t + \Delta t$ via the same fluid point $x'_{t+\Delta t,1} = x'_{t+\Delta t,2}$. To see that, we use Eq. (3) to express

$$x'_{t+\Delta t,j} - x'_{t,j} = -\zeta(\alpha_{t+\Delta t,j} - \alpha_{t,j}) - \zeta(\Delta\alpha_{t+\Delta t} - \Delta\alpha_t), \tag{4}$$

and from Eq. (1), we have

$$\alpha_{t+\Delta t,j} - \alpha_{t,j} = (x'_{t+\Delta t,j} - x'_{t,j})/z'. \tag{5}$$

Plugging Eq. (5) in Eq. (4) we thus have

$$x'_{t+\Delta t,j} - x'_{t,j} = c \cdot (\Delta\alpha_{t+\Delta t} - \Delta\alpha_t), \tag{6}$$

where $c = -(z'' - z')z'/z''$. Therefore, since the terms on the RHS of Eq. (6) are all camera-independent (under our setup and assumptions), if $x'_{t,1} = x'_{t,2} = \bar{x}'_t$, we conclude that $x'_{t+\Delta t,1} = x'_{t+\Delta t,2}$ and the wiggles in both cameras are equal.

This *refraction constancy* can be shown similarly for the monocular case (Fig. 2(a)). That is, if the fluid object is moving at constant velocity over a short spatio-temporal window, then the observed refraction wiggles move coherently with the fluid object between consecutive frames. This stands in contrast to the fact that the observed motions themselves (the wiggles) are *unrelated* to the actual fluid motion, and in fact can point in opposite directions (Fig. 1, Fig. 4). We refer the interested reader to our supplementary material for the derivation, as well as for a more detailed version of the derivation we gave here. Also note that in Eq. (1) and Eq. (3) we assumed the viewing angle α is small to simplify the derivation, however refraction constancy is not restricted by the viewing angle (not to be confused with $\Delta\alpha$, which does need to be small). In the supplementary material we give the derivation without making this assumption.

The practical implication of the observations we made in this section is that **if we wish to match the projection of a point on the fluid object across frames or viewpoints, we can match the observed wiggle features**. That is, while the position of *intensity texture* features is unrelated to the fluid 3D structures, the position of *wiggle* features respect features on the fluid surface, and can serve as an input feature for optical flow and stereo matching algorithms. In the following sections we will use this to derive optical flow and stereo algorithms for tracking and localizing refractive fluids.

4 Refractive Flow

The goal of fluid motion estimation is to recover the projected 2D velocity, $\mathbf{u}(x, y, t)$, of a refractive fluid object from an observed image sequence, $I(x, y, t)$ (Fig. 2(a)). As discussed in the previous section, the wiggle features $\mathbf{v}(x, y, t)$, not the image intensities $I(x, y, t)$, move with the refractive object. Thus, there are two steps in estimating the fluid's motion: 1) computing the wiggle features $\mathbf{v}(x, y, t)$ from an input image sequence $I(x, y, t)$, and 2) estimating the fluid motion $\mathbf{u}(x, y, t)$ from the wiggle features $\mathbf{v}(x, y, t)$. We will now discuss each of these steps in turn.

Computing wiggle features. We use optical flow to compute the wiggles $\mathbf{v}(x, y, t)$ from an input image sequence. Recall the *brightness constancy* assumption in optical flow is that any changes in pixel intensities, I, are assumed to be caused by a translation $\mathbf{v} = (v_x, v_y)$ over spatial horizontal or vertical positions, x and y, of the image intensities, where v_x and v_y are the x and y components of the velocity, respectively. That is,

$$I(x, y, t + dt) = I(x - v_x dt, y - v_y dt, t). \tag{7}$$

Based on this brightness constancy equation, a traditional way to calculate the motion vector v is to minimize the following optical flow equation [7]:

$$\tilde{\mathbf{v}} = \arg\min_{\mathbf{u}} \sum_{\mathbf{x}} \alpha_1 \left\| \frac{\partial I}{\partial x} v_x + \frac{\partial I}{\partial y} v_y + \frac{\partial I}{\partial t} \right\|^2 + \alpha_2 \left(\left\| \frac{\partial \mathbf{v}}{\partial x} \right\|^2 + \left\| \frac{\partial \mathbf{v}}{\partial y} \right\|^2 \right), \tag{8}$$

where α_1 and α_2 are weights for the data and smoothness terms, respectively.

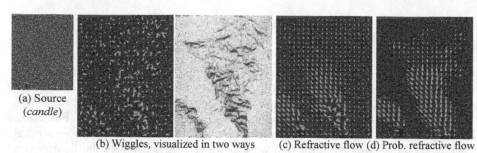

(a) Source
(*candle*)

(b) Wiggles, visualized in two ways   (c) Refractive flow (d) Prob. refractive flow

Fig. 3. Example result of our refractive flow algorithm (single view) on a sequence of burning candles. Wiggle features (b) are extracted from the input video (a). Notice how the directions of the wiggles (observed motions) are arbitrary and inconsistent with the air flow direction (the right visualization in (b) uses the same wiggle color coding as in Fig. 1). (c) and (d) show refractive flows calculated by two algorithms, refractive flow and probabilistic refractive flow, respectively.

Estimating fluid motion. Let u_x and u_y be the x and y components of the fluid's velocity as seen in the image. Following Section 3, we thus define the *refractive constancy* equation for a single view sequence as

$$\mathbf{v}(x, y, t + \Delta t) = \mathbf{v}(x - u_x \Delta t, y - u_y \Delta t, t). \tag{9}$$

Notice that refractive constancy has the exact same form as brightness constancy (Eq. 7), except that the features are the wiggles, $\mathbf{v}$, rather than the image intensities, I. This implies that running an optical flow algorithm on the wiggle features $\mathbf{v}$ (i.e. the motion of the motion features), will yield the fluid motion $\mathbf{u}$.

Formally, we calculate the fluid motion $\mathbf{u}$ by minimizing the following equation:

$$\tilde{\mathbf{u}} = \arg \min_{\mathbf{u}} \sum_{\mathbf{x}} \beta_1 \left\| \frac{\partial \tilde{\mathbf{v}}}{\partial x} u_x + \frac{\partial \tilde{\mathbf{v}}}{\partial y} u_y + \frac{\partial \tilde{\mathbf{v}}}{\partial t} \right\|^2 + \beta_2 \left(\left\| \frac{\partial \mathbf{u}}{\partial x} \right\|^2 + \left\| \frac{\partial \mathbf{u}}{\partial y} \right\|^2 \right). \tag{10}$$

This is similar to the Horn-Schunck optical flow formulation, except that we use L_2-norm for regularization, as opposed to robust penalty functions such as L_1-norm traditionally used by optical flow methods. This is because fluid objects, especially hot air or gas, do not have clear and sharp boundaries like solid objects. We use a multi-scale iterative algorithm to solve Eq. 10, as is common in the optical flow literature.

Fig. 3 demonstrates a result of this refractive flow algorithm, when applied to a video of burning candles. First, wiggle features (Fig. 3(b)) are extracted from the input video (Fig. 3(a)). Since wiggle features move coherently with the air flow, the algorithm correctly estimates the motion of the thermal plume rising from the candle. Notice that the observed motions (wiggles) have arbitrary directions, yet the estimated refractive flow is much more coherent.

Such processing is very sensitive to noise, however, as can be seen in Fig. 3(b) (the noise is more obvious in an enlarged image). The problem is even more severe for less textured backgrounds. This motivates the probabilistic formulation, which we will now describe.

4.1   Probabilistic Refractive Flow

We seek to estimate both the refractive flow, and its uncertainty. Consider a background that is smooth in the x direction and textured in the y direction. Due to the aperture problem [11], the flow in the x direction may be dominated by noise, while the optical flow in the y direction can be clean. Knowing the uncertainty in the flow allows uncertain estimates to be down-weighted, increasing the robustness of the algorithm.

To find the variance of the optical flow, let us reformulate Eq. (8) as a posterior distribution:

$$P(\mathbf{v}|I) = \exp\left(-\sum_{\mathbf{x}} \alpha_1 \left\|\frac{\partial I}{\partial x}v_x + \frac{\partial I}{\partial y}v_y + \frac{\partial I}{\partial t}\right\|^2 + \alpha_2 \left\|\frac{\partial \mathbf{v}}{\partial x}\right\|^2 + \alpha_2 \left\|\frac{\partial \mathbf{v}}{\partial y}\right\|^2\right). \quad (11)$$

Here, $P(\mathbf{v}|I)$ is a Gaussian distribution, and the mean of $P(\mathbf{v}|I)$ is equal to the solution of the original optical flow equation (8). With this formulation, we can also calculate the variance of the optical flow (the wiggle features). Please refer to the supplementary material for the detailed calculation. Let $\tilde{\mathbf{v}}$ and Σ_v be the mean and covariance, respectively, of the wiggle features computed from Eq. (11).

Then, with the variance of the wiggle features, we can reweight the fluid flow equation as follows:

$$\tilde{\mathbf{u}} = \arg\min_{\mathbf{u}} \sum_{\mathbf{x}} \beta_1 \left\|\frac{\partial \tilde{\mathbf{v}}}{\partial x}u_x + \frac{\partial \tilde{\mathbf{v}}}{\partial y}u_y + \frac{\partial \tilde{\mathbf{v}}}{\partial t}\right\|^2_{\Sigma_v} + \beta_2 \left(\left\|\frac{\partial \mathbf{u}}{\partial x}\right\|^2 + \left\|\frac{\partial \mathbf{u}}{\partial y}\right\|^2\right) + \beta_3\|\mathbf{u}\|^2, \quad (12)$$

where $\|\mathbf{x}\|^2_{\Sigma} = \mathbf{x}^{\mathsf{T}}\Sigma^{-1}\mathbf{x}$ is the squared Mahalanobis distance. In this formulation, the data term is reweighted by the variance of the optical flow to robustly estimate the fluid motion: wiggle features with less certainty, such as motions measured in regions of low-contrast, or of flat or one-dimensional structure, will have lower weight in the fluid flow equation. To increase the robustness, we also penalize the magnitude of $\mathbf{u}$ to avoid estimating spurious large flows. Including the uncertainty information leads to more accurate estimation of the fluid motion, as shown in Fig. 3(d).

In practice, calculating the covariance matrix precisely for each pixel is computationally intractable, as we need to compute the marginal probability distribution for each optical flow vector. To avoid this calculation, we concatenate all the optical flow vectors into a single vector and compute its covariance. See the supplementary material for the details. Also, notice that the fluid flow equation (12) still has a quadratic form, so we can model the posterior distribution of the fluid flow $\mathbf{u}$ as a Gaussian distribution, and compute its variance. This variance serves as a confidence measure in the estimated fluid motion.

5   Refractive Stereo

The goal of fluid depth estimation is to recover the depth $z'(x, y)$ of a refractive fluid object from a stereo sequence $I_L(x, y, t)$ and $I_R(x, y, t)$ (Fig. 2(b)). Following Section 3, we can find the depth of the fluid object by stereo-matching the refraction wiggles from the left and right views. Therefore, we first use the algorithm discussed in the previous section to calculate the mean and variance of the optical flows in the left and right views, $\mathbf{v}_L \sim N(\tilde{\mathbf{v}}_L, \Sigma_L)$ and $\mathbf{v}_R \sim N(\tilde{\mathbf{v}}_R, \Sigma_R)$, respectively. We then use a discrete Markov Random Field (MRF), commonly used in the stereo literature [23], to regularize the depth estimates.

Formally, let x_L and x_R be the projection of a point on the fluid object onto the left and right image plane, respectively, and define disparity as $d = x_L - x_R$. We first solve the disparity map by minimizing the objective function

$$\tilde{\mathbf{d}} = \min_{\mathbf{d}} \sum_{x,y} f(\mathbf{v}_R(x,y), \mathbf{v}_L(x + \mathbf{d}(x,y), y)) + \alpha \left(\left\| \frac{\partial \mathbf{d}}{\partial x} \right\|^2 + \left\| \frac{\partial \mathbf{d}}{\partial y} \right\|^2 \right), \quad (13)$$

where $f(\mathbf{v}_R, \mathbf{v}_L)$ is the data term based on the observed wiggles $\mathbf{v}_R$ and $\mathbf{v}_L$, and the last two terms regularize the disparity field. We found that using the L_2-norm for regularization generates better results overall, better explaining the fuzzy boundaries of fluid refractive objects (similar to what we observed for estimating the optical flow in Section 4).

As with the refractive flow, we weigh the data term by the variance of the optical flow to make the depth estimation robust to points in a scene where the extracted wiggles are not as reliable. To achieve this, we define the data term, $f(\mathbf{v}_R, \mathbf{v}_L)$, as the log of the covariance between the two optical flows from the left and right views,

$$f(\tilde{\mathbf{v}}_R, \tilde{\mathbf{v}}_L) = \log cov(\mathbf{v}_R, \mathbf{v}_L) = \frac{1}{2} \log |\Sigma_L + \Sigma_R| + \frac{1}{2} \|\overline{\mathbf{v}}_R - \overline{\mathbf{v}}_L\|^2_{\Sigma_L + \Sigma_R}, \quad (14)$$

where $\|\overline{\mathbf{v}}_R - \overline{\mathbf{v}}_L\|^2_{\Sigma_L + \Sigma_R} = (\overline{\mathbf{v}}_R - \overline{\mathbf{v}}_L)^{\mathsf{T}} (\Sigma_L + \Sigma_R)^{-1} (\overline{\mathbf{v}}_R - \overline{\mathbf{v}}_L)$. This data term will assign a higher penalty to inconsistencies in the wiggle matching where the wiggles are more reliable, and a lower penalty where the wiggles are less reliable (typically where the background is less textured and the optical flow is noisy). The choice of the log of the covariance as the data term is not arbitrary. It is the log of the conditional marginal distribution of $\mathbf{v}_L$ and $\mathbf{v}_R$, given that $\mathbf{v}_L$ and $\mathbf{v}_R$ match. See the supplementary material for a detailed derivation.

With calibrated cameras, we can then compute the depth map, $z'(x,y)$, from the disparity map, $d(x,y)$.

6 Experiments

We show several examples of measuring and localizing hot air radiating from several heat sources, such as people, fans, and heating vents. **Please refer to the supplementary materials for the full sequences and results.**

All the videos were recorded in raw format to avoid compression artifacts. To deal with small camera motions or background motions, we subtracted the mean flow for each frame from the optical flow result. For each sequence we captured, we first applied a temporal Gaussian blur to the input sequence to increase SNR. For fast-moving flow, we recorded high-speed videos using a Phantom v10 high-speed camera. In some of the indoor high-speed sequences that required additional lighting, we used a temporal band-stop filter to remove intensity variations from the lighting due to AC power.

6.1 Refractive Flow

Qualitative Results. In Fig. 4 we show several results of refractive flow analysis from a single camera.

We first tested our algorithm in a controlled setting, using a textured background. In *hand*, we took a 30fps video of a person's hand after he held a cup of hot water. The algorithm was able to recover heat radiating upward from the hand. In *hairdryers*, we took a 1000fps high-speed video of two hairdryers placed in opposite directions

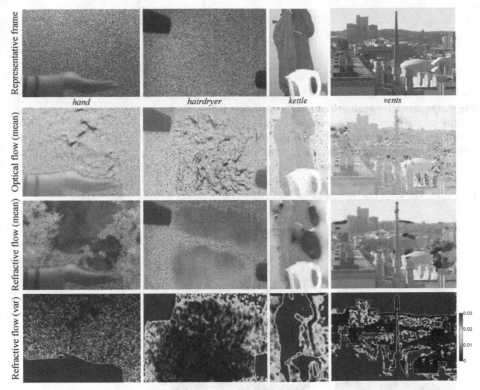

Fig. 4. Refractive flow results. First row: sample frames from the input videos. Second row: the mean of the optical flow for the same representative frames (using the colormap shown in Fig. 1), overlayed on the input images. Third row: the mean of the refractive flow, weighted by the variance. Fourth row: the variance of the estimated refractive flow (the square root of the determinant of the covariance matrix for each pixel). For this visualization, variance values above 0.03 were clipped. The full videos are available in the accompanying material.

(the two dark shapes in the top left and bottom right are the front ends of the hairdryers), and our algorithm detected two opposite streams of hot air flows.

kettle and *vents* demonstrate the result on videos with more natural backgrounds. In *vents* (700fps), the background is very challenging for traditional Background Oriented Schlieren algorithms (BOS), as some parts of the background are very smooth or contain edges in one direction, such as the sky, the top of the dome, and the boundary of the buildings or chimneys. BOS algorithms rely on the motion calculated from input videos, similar to the wiggle features shown in the second row of Fig. 4, which is very noisy due to the insufficiently textured background. In contrast, the fluid flow (third row of Fig. 4) clearly shows several flows of hot air coming out from heating vents. By modeling the variance of wiggles in the probabilistic refractive flow (bottom row of Fig. 4), most of noise in the motion is suppressed.

Quantitative Evaluation. To quantitatively evaluate the fluid velocity recovered by the proposed algorithm, we tested it on simulated sequences with precise ground truth. We generated a set of realistic simulations of dynamic refracting fluid using Stable

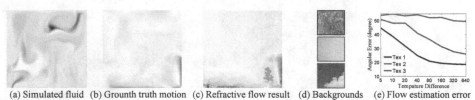

(a) Simulated fluid (b) Grounth truth motion (c) Refractive flow result (d) Backgrounds (e) Flow estimation error

Fig. 5. Quantitative evaluation of refractive flow using synthetic sequences. Simulated fluid density (a) and velocity field (b) were generated by Stable Fluids [26], a physics-based fluid flow simulation technique, and rendered on top of three different textures (d). The recovered velocity field from one of the simulations in which the fluid was at 320° Celsius (c) is similar to the ground truth velocity field (b). Quantitative evaluation is given in (e). As expected, larger temperature-related index of refraction differences between the fluid and the background give better flow estimates. The error also increases for backgrounds that do not contain much texture.

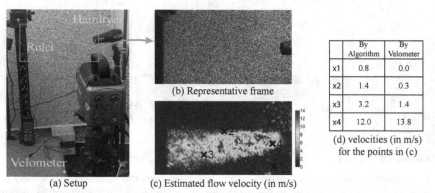

(a) Setup   (c) Estimated flow velocity (in m/s)

(b) Representative frame

	By Algorithm	By Velometer
x1	0.8	0.0
x2	1.4	0.3
x3	3.2	1.4
x4	12.0	13.8

(d) velocities (in m/s) for the points in (c)

Fig. 6. Quantitative evaluation of refractive flow using a controlled experiment. (a) The experiment setup. (b) A representative frame from the captured video. (c) The mean velocity of the hot air blown by the hairdryer, as computed by our algorithm, in m/s. (d) Numerical comparison of our estimated velocities with velocities measured using a velometer, for the four points marked $x_1 - x_4$ in (c).

Fluids [26], a physics-based fluid flow simulation technique, resulting in fluid densities and (2D) ground truth velocities at each pixel over time (Fig. 5(a-b)). We then used the simulated densities to render refraction patterns over several types of background textures with varying spatial smoothness (Fig. 5(d)). To render realistic refractions, we assumed the simulated flow is at a constant distance between the camera and background, with thickness depending linearly on its density (given by the simulation). For a given scene temperature (we used 20° Celsius) and a temperature of the fluid, we can compute exactly the amount of refraction at every point in the image. We then apply our algorithm to the refraction sequences. The angular error of the recovered fluid motion at different temperature is shown in (e). All the sequences and results are available in the supplemental material.

To further demonstrate that the magnitude of the motion computed by the refractive flow algorithm is correct, we also performed a controlled experiment shown in Fig. 6. We use a velocimeter to measure the velocity of hot air blown from a hairdryer, and compare it with the velocities extracted by the algorithm. To convert the velocity on the image plane to the velocity in the real world, we set the hairdryer parallel to the imaging plane and put a ruler on the same plane of the hairdryer. We measured the velocity of the flow at four different locations as shown in Fig. 6(c). Although our estimated flow does not match the velocimeter flow exactly, it is highly correlated, and we believe the agreement is accurate to within the experimental uncertainties.

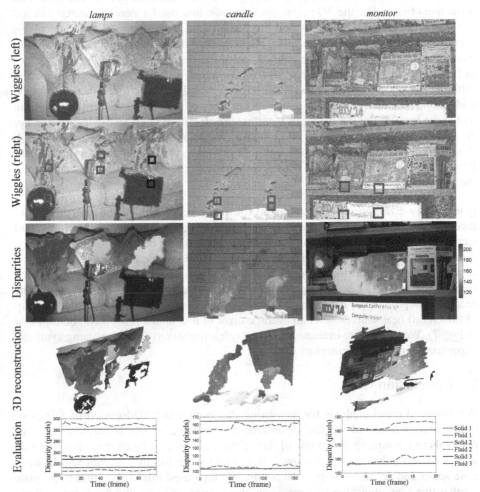

Fig. 7. Refractive stereo results. First and second rows: representative frames from the input videos. The observed wiggles are overlayed on the input frames using the same color coding as in Fig. 1. Third row: the estimated disparity maps (weighted by the confidence of the disparity) of the fluid object. Forth row: 3D reconstruction of the scene, where standard stereo is used for solid objects (and the background), and refractive stereo is used for air flows (the depth was scaled for this visualization). Bottom row: Comparison of our estimated refractive flow disparities, with the disparities of the (solid) heat sources that generated them as computed with a standard stereo algorithm, for the points marked as rectangles on the frames in the second row.

6.2 Refractive Stereo

Qualitative Results. We captured several stereo sequences using our own stereo rig, comprised of two Point Grey Grasshopper 3 cameras recording at 50fps. The two cameras are synchronized via Genlock and global shutter is used to avoid temporal misalignment. All videos were captured in 16-bit grayscale.

Several results are shown in Fig. 7. The third row in Fig. 7 shows the disparity map of air flow as estimated by our refractive stereo algorithm, and the forth row shows a 3D reconstruction of the scene according to the estimated depths of the solid and refractive objects. For the 3D reconstructions, we first used a standard stereo method to reconstruct the (solid) objects and the background, and then rendered fluid pixels according to their depth as estimated by our refractive stereo algorithm, colored by their disparities (and weighted by the confidence of the disparity). In *candle*, two plumes of hot airs at different depth are recovered. In *lamps*, three lights were positioned at different distances from the camera: the left one was the closest to the camera and the middle one was the furthest. The disparities of three plumes recovered by the algorithm match the locations of the lights. In *monitor*, the algorithm recovers the location of hot air radiating from the center top of a monitor. We intentionally tilted the monitor such that its right side was closer to the camera to introduce variation in the depth of the air flow. The algorithm successfully detects this gradual change in disparities, as shown in the right column of Fig. 7.

Quantitative Evaluation. We compared the recovered depths of the refractive fluid layers with that of the heat sources generating them, as computed using a standard stereo algorithm (since the depth of the actual heat sources, being solid objects, can be estimated well using existing stereo techniques). More specifically, we picked a region on the heat source and picked another region of hot air right above the heat source (second row in Fig. 7), and compared the average disparities in these two regions. The recovered depth map of the (refractive) hot air matched well the recovered depth map of the (solid) heat sources, with an average error of less than a few pixels (bottom row in Fig. 7). We show more evaluations of our refractive stereo algorithm using synthetic experiments in the supplementary material.

7   Conclusion

We proposed novel methods for measuring the motion and 3D location of refractive fluids directly from videos. The algorithms are based on wiggle features, which corresponds to the minute distortions of the background caused by changes in refraction as refractive fluids move. We showed that wiggles are locally constant within short time spans and across close-by viewpoints. We then used this observation to propose a refractive flow algorithm that measures the motion of refractive fluids by tracking wiggle features across frames, and a refractive stereo algorithm that measures the depth of the fluids by matching wiggle features across different views. We further proposed a probabilistic formulation to improve the robustness of the algorithms by modeling the variance of the observed wiggle signals. This allows the algorithms to better handle noise and more natural backgrounds. We demonstrated results on realistic, physics-based fluid simulations, and recovered flow patterns from controlled and natural monocular and stereo sequences. These results provide promising evidence that refractive fluids can be analyzed in natural settings, which can make fluid flow measurement cheaper and more accessible.

Acknowledgements We thank the ECCV reviewers for their comments. Tianfan Xue was supported by Shell International Exploration & Production Inc. and Motion Sensing Wi-Fi Sensor Networks Co. under Grant No. 6925133. Neal Wadhwa was supported by the NSF Graduate Research Fellowship Program under Grant No. 1122374. Part of this work was done when Michael Rubinstein was a student at MIT, supported by the Microsoft Research PhD Fellowship.

References

1. Adrian, R.J., Westerweel, J.: Particle image velocimetry. Cambridge University Press (2011)
2. Alterman, M., Schechner, Y.Y., Perona, P., Shamir, J.: Detecting motion through dynamic refraction. IEEE Trans. Pattern Anal. Mach. Intell. 35(1), 245–251 (2013)
3. Alterman, M., Schechner, Y.Y., Swirski, Y.: Triangulation in random refractive distortions. In: 2013 IEEE International Conference on Computational Photography (ICCP), pp. 1–10. IEEE (2013)
4. Alterman, M., Schechner, Y.Y., Vo, M., Narasimhan, S.G.: Passive tomography of turbulence strength. In: Fleet, D., Pajdla, T., Schiele, B., Tuytelaars, T. (eds.) ECCV 2014, Part IV. LNCS, vol. 8692, pp. 47–60. Springer, Heidelberg (2014)
5. Arnaud, E., Mémin, É., Sosa, R., Artana, G.: A fluid motion estimator for schlieren image velocimetry. In: Leonardis, A., Bischof, H., Pinz, A. (eds.) ECCV 2006, Part I. LNCS, vol. 3951, pp. 198–210. Springer, Heidelberg (2006)
6. Atcheson, B., Ihrke, I., Heidrich, W., Tevs, A., Bradley, D., Magnor, M., Seidel, H.P.: Time-resolved 3D capture of non-stationary gas flows. ACM Trans. Graph. 27(5), 132:1–132:9 (2008)
7. Baker, S., Scharstein, D., Lewis, J., Roth, S., Black, M., Szeliski, R.: A database and evaluation methodology for optical flow. International Journal of Computer Vision 92(1), 1–31 (2011)
8. Dalziel, S.B., Hughes, G.O., Sutherland, B.R.: Whole-field density measurements by "synthetic schlieren". Experiments in Fluids 28(4), 322–335 (2000)
9. Ding, Y., Li, F., Ji, Y., Yu, J.: Dynamic fluid surface acquisition using a camera array. In: 2011 IEEE International Conference on Computer Vision (ICCV), pp. 2478–2485 (2011)
10. Elsinga, G., van Oudheusden, B., Scarano, F., Watt, D.: Assessment and application of quantitative schlieren methods: Calibrated color schlieren and background oriented schlieren. Experiments in Fluids 36(2), 309–325 (2004)
11. Fleet, D., Weiss, Y.: Optical flow estimation. In: Handbook of Mathematical Models in Computer Vision, pp. 237–257. Springer, US (2006)
12. Hargather, M.J., Settles, G.S.: Natural-background-oriented schlieren imaging. Experiments in Fluids 48(1), 59–68 (2010)
13. Has, P., Herzet, C., Mmin, E., Heitz, D., Mininni, P.D.: Bayesian estimation of turbulent motion. IEEE Trans. Pattern Anal. Mach. Intell. 35(6), 1343–1356 (2013)
14. Jonassen, D.R., Settles, G.S., Tronosky, M.D.: Schlieren "PIV" for turbulent flows. Optics and Lasers in Engineering 44(3-4), 190–207 (2006)
15. Meier, G.: Computerized background-oriented schlieren. Experiments in Fluids 33(1), 181–187 (2002)
16. Morris, N.J., Kutulakos, K.N.: Dynamic refraction stereo. In: 2005 IEEE International Conference on Computer Vision (ICCV), vol. 2, pp. 1573–1580 (2005)

17. Raffel, M., Tung, C., Richard, H., Yu, Y., Meier, G.: Background oriented stereoscopic schlieren (BOSS) for full scale helicopter vortex characterization. In: Proc. of International Symposium on Flow Visualization (2000)
18. Richard, H., Raffel, M.: Principle and applications of the background oriented schlieren (BOS) method. Measurement Science and Technology 12(9), 1576 (2001)
19. Ruhnau, P., Kohlberger, T., Schnörr, C., Nobach, H.: Variational optical flow estimation for particle image velocimetry. Experiments in Fluids 38(1), 21–32 (2005)
20. Ruhnau, P., Schnörr, C.: Optical stokes flow estimation: An imaging-based control approach. Experiments in Fluids 42(1), 61–78 (2007)
21. Ruhnau, P., Stahl, A., Schnörr, C.: On-line variational estimation of dynamical fluid flows with physics-based spatio-temporal regularization. In: Franke, K., Müller, K.-R., Nickolay, B., Schäfer, R. (eds.) DAGM 2006. LNCS, vol. 4174, pp. 444–454. Springer, Heidelberg (2006)
22. Schardin, H.: Die schlierenverfahren und ihre anwendungen. In: Ergebnisse der Exakten Naturwissenschaften, pp. 303–439. Springer (1942)
23. Scharstein, D., Szeliski, R.: A taxonomy and evaluation of dense two-frame stereo correspondence algorithms. International Journal of Computer Vision 47(1-3), 7–42 (2002)
24. Settles, G.S.: Schlieren and shadowgraph techniques: visualizing phenomena in transparent media, vol. 2. Springer, Berlin (2001)
25. Settles, G.S.: The penn state full-scale schlieren system. In: Proc. of International Symposium on Flow Visualization (2004)
26. Stam, J.: Stable fluids. In: Proceedings of the 26th Annual Conference on Computer Graphics and Interactive Techniques, SIGGRAPH 1999, pp. 121–128. ACM Press/Addison-Wesley Publishing Co., New York (1999)
27. Tian, Y., Narasimhan, S., Vannevel, A.: Depth from optical turbulence. In: 2012 IEEE Conference on Computer Vision and Pattern Recognition (CVPR), pp. 246–253. IEEE (June 2012)
28. Wetzstein, G., Raskar, R., Heidrich, W.: Hand-held schlieren photography with light field probes. In: 2011 IEEE International Conference on Computational Photography (ICCP), pp. 1–8 (April 2011)
29. Wetzstein, G., Roodnick, D., Heidrich, W., Raskar, R.: Refractive shape from light field distortion. In: 2011 IEEE International Conference on Computer Vision (ICCV), pp. 1180–1186 (2011)
30. Ye, J., Ji, Y., Li, F., Yu, J.: Angular domain reconstruction of dynamic 3d fluid surfaces. In: 2012 IEEE Conference on Computer Vision and Pattern Recognition (CVPR), pp. 310–317 (2012)

Blind Deblurring Using Internal Patch Recurrence

Tomer Michaeli and Michal Irani

Dept. of Computer Science and Applied Mathematics
Weizmann Institute of Science, Israel

Abstract. Recurrence of small image patches across different scales of a natural image has been previously used for solving ill-posed problems (*e.g.,* super-resolution from a single image). In this paper we show how this multi-scale property can also be used for "blind-deblurring", namely, removal of an unknown blur from a blurry image. While patches repeat 'as is' across scales in a *sharp* natural image, this cross-scale recurrence significantly diminishes in blurry images. We exploit these *deviations from ideal patch recurrence* as a cue for recovering the underlying (unknown) blur kernel. More specifically, we look for the blur kernel k, such that if its effect is *"undone"* (if the blurry image is deconvolved with k), the patch similarity across scales of the image will be maximized. We report extensive experimental evaluations, which indicate that our approach compares favorably to state-of-the-art blind deblurring methods, and in particular, is more robust than them.

Keywords: Blind deblurring, blind deconvolution, blur kernel estimation, internal patch recurrence, fractal property, statistics of natural images.

1   Introduction

Photos often come out blurry due to camera shake, defocus or low-grade optics. Undoing this undesired effect has attracted significant research efforts over the last decade. In cases in which the blur is uniform (same across the entire image), the blurry image y is often modeled as having been obtained from the desired sharp image x as

$$y = k * x + n, \tag{1}$$

where $*$ denotes convolution, k is some blur kernel and n is noise.

Since both the blur k and the sharp image x are unknown, and since many different pairs of x and k may result in the same blurry image y, blind deblurring heavily relies on the availability of prior knowledge on x. Most existing algorithms rely, either explicitly or implicitly, on the fact that images contain enough step edges. This assumption is formulated in various ways. Some studies assume simple parametric probability models, which promote sparsity of image gradients [5,17,12,13,10]. Others assume a parametric form for the spectrum of the image [8], which decays polynomially with frequency (corresponding to the Fourier transform of step edges). Finally, many approaches employ heuristic methods for detecting and/or enhancing edges in the blurry image. These range from setting a threshold on the image gradients [9] to shock and bilateral filtering [1,19,2].

D. Fleet et al. (Eds.): ECCV 2014, Part III, LNCS 8691, pp. 783–798, 2014.

Gradient priors model interactions between *pairs* of pixels. In recent years, the advantage of using priors over larger neighborhoods (patches) has been recognized. Patch priors model more complex structures and dependencies in larger neighborhoods. Such priors have led to state-of-the-art results in various inverse problems [16] including *non-blind* deblurring [3,22,4] (namely, deblurring with a *known* blur kernel). Recently, Sun *et al.* [18] used a patch prior learned from an external collection of sharp natural images for *blind* deblurring (*unknown* blur kernel). This resulted in a significant improvement in performance over all the previous blind deblurring methods [13,10,1,19,2].

In this paper, we present an approach for blind-deblurring, which is based on the *internal patch recurrence* property within a single natural image. It was empirically shown by [7,20] that almost any small image patch in a natural image (5×5 or 7×7) re-appears "as is" (without shrinking the patch) in smaller scaled-down versions of the image (Fig. 1(a)). This observation was successfully used for various *non-blind* inverse problems (where the degradation process is known), including single-image super-resolution [7,6] and image-denoising [21].

The cross-scale recurrence property was also recently used in [14] for *blind* Super-Resolution (SR). While, superficially, blind-deblurring can be thought of as a special case of blind-SR with a magnification factor $\alpha = 1$, there is a conceptual difference between the two. The goal in blind-SR [14] is to recover an α-times larger image, whose blur is α-times narrower than in the input image (thus imitating an optical zoom-in). Consequently, as opposed to blind-deblurring, the optimal SR blur kernel k_{SR} is *not* the point spread function (PSF) of the camera. Rather, as shown in [14], it is given in the Fourier domain by the following PSF ratio: $K_{\mathrm{SR}}(\omega) = \mathcal{PSF}(\omega)/\mathcal{PSF}(\omega/\alpha)$, where α is the SR magnification factor. Thus, for a magnification factor $\alpha = 1$, the optimal SR blur kernel of [14] reduces to $K_{SR}(\omega) \equiv 1$, namely, a *delta function* in the spatial domain. This is *regardless of the blur in the input image*. Therefore, the blind-SR algorithm of [14] cannot be used for blind deblurring. Put differently, in blind-deblurring we seek to recover the PSF, and not the *ratio* between two PSFs as in blind-SR. Nevertheless, we show that the cross-scale patch recurrence property can still serve as a strong prior for blind-deblurring, but requires a different strategy.

Our approach is conceptually simple. While patches repeat across scales in a *sharp* natural image (Fig. 1(a)), this cross-scale recurrence significantly diminishes in blurry images (Fig. 1(b)). We exploit these *deviations from ideal patch recurrence* as a cue for recovering the underlying (unknown) blur kernel. This is done by seeking a blur kernel k, such that if its effect is *undone* (if y is deconvolved by k), the patch similarity across scales will be maximized. Moreover, while the blur is strong in the original scale, the blur decreases at coarser scales of the image. Thus, sharper image patches "naturally emerge" in coarser scales of the blurry image (*e.g.,* Fig. 1(b)). The patches in coarser image scales can thus serve as a good patch prior (sharper examples) for deblurring the input scale. This allows recovery of the unknown blur kernel. We show that blind deblurring based on the internal patch recurrence prior compares favorably to all previous blind-deblurring approaches. We further show that this is a very stable prior, in the sense that it rarely diverges on any input image (unlike other priors).

The rest of this paper is organized as follows. Section 2 provides an overview of our approach and explains the intuition underlying the optimization process. Section 3 is

(a) **Patch recurrence across scales in a sharp image:**

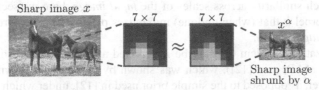

Sharp image x 7×7 7×7 x^α

$\approx$

Sharp image
shrunk by α

(b) **In a blurry image, cross-scale patch recurrence deminishes:**

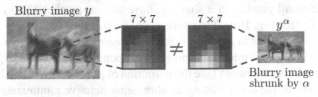

Blurry image y 7×7 7×7 y^α

$\neq$

Blurry image
shrunk by α

Fig. 1. *The cross-scale patch recurrence is strong in sharp images and weak in blurry images.*
(a) Small patches (*e.g.,* 5×5, 7×7) tend to recur across scales in an "ideal" (sharp) natural image x. Namely, if we down-scale x by a factor of α, then for most patches in x, there exist almost identical patches in the down-scaled image x^α. (b) In contrast, in a blurry image $y = x * k$, this is no longer true. The similarity between patches in y and in its down-scaled version y^α is significantly reduced. Patches in the down-scaled version y^α tend to be α-times sharper than their corresponding patches in y. Thus, down-scaling generates a pool of sharper patches, which can be used as a prior for removing the blur in y.

devoted to an in-depth explanation of our algorithm. Finally, in Section 4, we demonstrate and compare the performance of our algorithm to other state-of-the art methods.

2 Overview of the Approach

We start with a high-level overview of our approach, focusing on the intuition behind the proposed method. We defer the detailed definitions and derivations to Section 3.

While patches repeat across scales in a *sharp* natural image under *ideal* downscaling (Fig. 1(a)), this cross-scale recurrence significantly diminishes in blurry images (Fig. 1(b)). We thus seek a blur kernel k, such that if its effect is *undone* (if y is deconvolved by k), the patch similarity across scales will be maximized. More specifically, we look for an image $\hat{x}$ and a blur kernel $\hat{k}$ such that on the one hand, $\hat{x}$ satisfies the patch recurrence property (namely, strong similarity between patches across scales of $\hat{x}$), and, on the other hand, $\hat{k} * \hat{x}$ is close to the blurry image y. This is done by solving the optimization problem

$$\arg\min_{\hat{x},\hat{k}} \underbrace{\|y - \hat{k} * \hat{x}\|^2}_{\text{data term}} + \lambda_1 \underbrace{\rho(\hat{x}, \hat{x}^\alpha)}_{\text{image prior}} + \lambda_2 \underbrace{\|\hat{k}\|^2}_{\substack{\text{kernel} \\ \text{prior}}}, \tag{2}$$

where $\hat{x}^\alpha$ is an α-times smaller version of $\hat{x}$. The second term $\rho(\hat{x}, \hat{x}^\alpha)$ measures the degree of *dissimilarity* between patches in $\hat{x}$ and their Nearest Neighbor patches (NNs) in $\hat{x}^\alpha$. The third term is a regularizer on the kernel k.

Note that as opposed to blind-SR [14], where the optimal SR kernel is the one which maximizes patch similarity across scales of the *input image*, here we seek a different kernel – the kernel k that (when undone) maximizes patch similarity across scales of the *unknown output image*.

Our optimization problem (2) may be interpreted as a joint MAP estimation of x and k (coined $\text{MAP}_{x,k}$ in [12]), which was shown by [12] to lead to wrong (trivial) results. However, as opposed to the simple prior used in [12], under which the $\text{MAP}_{x,k}$ strategy indeed favors blurry reconstructions, our prior $\rho(\hat{x}, \hat{x}^\alpha)$ avoids such solutions. This is because small patches in a sharp $\hat{x}$, have similar patches (NNs) in its down-scaled version $\hat{x}^\alpha$ (see Fig. 1(a)). Therefore, for a sharp $\hat{x}$, the penalty $\rho(\hat{x}, \hat{x}^\alpha)$ is small. On the other hand, patches in a blurry $\hat{x}$, are *less similar* to patches in its down-scaled $\hat{x}^\alpha$ (Fig. 1(b)). Therefore, for a blurry image $\hat{x}$, the penalty $\rho(\hat{x}, \hat{x}^\alpha)$ is large.

The objective (2) is not convex (see the definition of $\rho(\hat{x}, \hat{x}^\alpha)$ in Sec. 3.2), and has no closed-form solution. We solve it using an alternating iterative minimization procedure comprising of three steps in each iteration, as described in Algorithm 1 below. The iterative process is initialized with the blur kernel $\hat{k}$ being a delta function, and $\hat{x}$ is initially the blurry input image y.

Input: Blurry image y
Output: Blur kernel $\hat{k}$
Initialize $\hat{k} = \delta$ and $\hat{x} = y$;
for $t = 1, \ldots, T$ **do**
    1. **Image Prior Update**: Down-scale image $\hat{x}$ by a factor of α to obtain $\hat{x}^\alpha$ (Sec. 3.1).
    2. **Deblurring**: Minimize (2) w.r.t $\hat{x}$, holding $\hat{k}$ and $\hat{x}^\alpha$ fixed (Sec. 3.2).
    3. **Kernel Update**: Minimize (2) w.r.t $\hat{k}$, holding $\hat{x}$ and $\hat{x}^\alpha$ fixed (Sec. 3.3).
end

Algorithm 1. Kernel estimation

At first sight, our iterative approach may seem similar to other methods, such as [1,19,18], which iterate between an x-step (updating $\hat{x}$ with $\hat{k}$ fixed) and a k-step (updating $\hat{k}$ with $\hat{x}$ fixed). However, close inspection reveals that our x-step is fundamentally different. Rather than using a *fixed generic* prior on natural images, we use an *evolving image-specific* prior based on patches extracted from the down-scaled (sharper) version of the previous image extimate $\hat{x}$. Since our estimate $\hat{x}$ gets sharper from iteration to iteration, *the prior also changes from iteration to iteration*.

Step 1: The purpose of Step 1 of the algorithm is to produce an image $\hat{x}^\alpha$, which serves as *a pool of sharper patches*. Intuitively, if we shrink a blurry image $\hat{x}$ by a factor of α, then the result $\hat{x}^\alpha$ contains α-times less the amount of blur. For example, if we scale-down $\hat{x}$ by a factor of $\alpha = 2$, then an edge smeared over 10 pixels in $\hat{x}$ would appear smeared over only 5 pixels in $\hat{x}^\alpha$. However, the image $\hat{x}^\alpha$ is also α-times smaller. In Section 3.1 we prove that, despite the fact that $\hat{x}^\alpha$ is smaller, the pool of small patches (*e.g.*, 5×5) extracted from $\hat{x}^\alpha$ is roughly *the same* as the pool of small patches extracted from the larger image $\hat{x}$, only α-times sharper. This is due to the recurrence of small patterns at various sizes in the *continuous* scene (see Section 3.1).

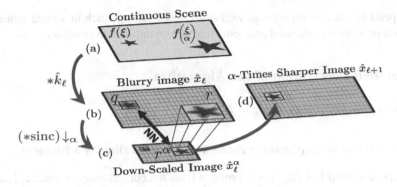

Fig. 2. *Enforcing the cross-scale patch prior in each iteration.* (a) A small pattern recurs in the continuous scene at multiple sizes (*blur stars*). (b) At the ℓ-th iteration, the image estimate $\hat{x}_\ell$ corresponds to the convolution of the scene with the kernel estimate $\hat{k}_\ell$. Thus the two patterns in the scene appear as two blurry patches q and r in the image $\hat{x}_\ell$. (c) In the down-scaled version $\hat{x}_\ell^\alpha$, the child patch of r contains the same structure as the patch q in $\hat{x}_\ell$, only α-times sharper. (d) We construct a sharper image $\hat{x}_{\ell+1}$ such that each of its patches is constrained to be similar to its sharper version in $\hat{x}_\ell^\alpha$ (*e.g.*, the new version of q in $\hat{x}_{\ell+1}$ should be similar to the sharper patch r^α in $\hat{x}_\ell^\alpha$).

Step 2:   Step 1 resulted in an image $\hat{x}^\alpha$, which provides a pool of patches that are α-times sharper than those in the image estimate $\hat{x}$. These patches are used in Step 2 as examples for how patches in $\hat{x}$ should look like if we were to sharpen them by a factor of α. To construct a new α-times sharper $\hat{x}$, we minimize (2) with respect to $\hat{x}$ while holding $\hat{k}$ and $\hat{x}^\alpha$ fixed. Disregarding the last term in (2), which does not depend on $\hat{x}$, this amounts to solving

$$\arg\min_{\hat{x}} \|y - \hat{k} * \hat{x}\|^2 + \lambda_1 \rho(\hat{x}, \hat{x}^\alpha). \tag{3}$$

This is in fact the deblurring of y by the current kernel estimate $\hat{k}$, where the prior is represented by the patches in $\hat{x}^\alpha$. In practice, this step tries to assemble a new sharper $\hat{x}$ from the sharper patches in $\hat{x}^\alpha$, as shown in Fig. 2(d). For example, in the *first* iteration (in which $\hat{k} = \delta$), this process results in an image $\hat{x}$, which is close to y, but at the same time its patches are similar to the α-times sharper patches in $\hat{x}^\alpha$. Therefore, intuitively, the image $\hat{x}_1$ recovered in the first iteration contains α-times less the amount of blur than y. At the second iteration, the image $\hat{x}_2$ is α-times sharper than $\hat{x}_1$, and thus α^2-times sharper than y. The image $\hat{x}_\ell$ at the ℓ-th iteration is α^ℓ times sharper than y, and intuitively tends to x for large ℓ.

Step 3:   Finally, we update the kernel estimate $\hat{k}$, by computing the blur between the current deblurred estimate $\hat{x}$ and the input image y. Thus, in the ℓ-th iteration, we recover the kernel $\hat{k}_\ell$ such that $y = \hat{k}_\ell * \hat{x}_\ell$. Since for large enough ℓ, $\hat{x}_\ell$ converges to x, the kernel estimate $\hat{k}_\ell$ converges to k. This is the final output of our algorithm.

To speed up the convergence, as well as to avoid getting stuck in a local minimum, the above process is performed coarse-to-fine in a pyramid data structure.

3   Detailed Description of the Algorithm

We now explain in detail each step of Alg. 1.

3.1   Step 1: Generating Sharper Patches by Down-Scaling by a Factor α

The purpose of Step 1 of Alg. 1 is to produce from the current image estimate, $\hat{x}$, a pool of patches that are less blurry. We now formally explain why shrinking a *blurry* image y by a factor of α, generates an α-times smaller image y^{α}, which contains *approximately the same pool of patches* as in (the larger) image y, only α-times sharper.

Glasner *et al.* [7] showed that most patches in a *sharp* natural image, recur multiple times in its scaled-down version[1]. As further noted in [14], the source of this patch recurrence is the repetitions of small patterns at various sizes in the *continuous scene*. Consider a small pattern $f(\xi)$ in the continuous scene which recurs elsewhere as $f(\xi/\alpha)$, *i.e.*, α times larger (represented by blue stars in Fig 2(a)). Ignoring sampling issues for the moment, these two patterns are convolved with the blur of the camera $k(\xi)$, and appear in the observed image as the patches q and r (Fig. 2(b)):

$$q(\xi) = k(\xi) * f(\xi), \quad r(\xi) = k(\xi) * f\left(\frac{\xi}{\alpha}\right). \tag{4}$$

Now, if we shrink the blurry image by a factor of α, then the patch r becomes

$$r^{\alpha}(\xi) = r(\alpha\xi) = \alpha \cdot k(\alpha\xi) * f(\xi). \tag{5}$$

In other words, $r^{\alpha}(\xi)$ corresponds to the same continuous structure, $f(\xi)$, but convolved with the α-times narrower kernel $\alpha \cdot k(\alpha\xi)$, rather than with $k(\xi)$. This implies that the patch r^{α} in the smaller image is exactly an α-times sharper version of the patch q in the original blurry image, as visualized in Fig 2(c).

The above shows that shrinking an image by a factor of α produces a pool of patches *of the same size* that are α-times sharper. In Step 2 of the algorithm we use this pool of sharper patches as a nonparametric prior for the purpose of sharpening the blurry image by a factor of α (see Sec. 3.2). Thus, at the first iteration of the algorithm, we recover an image of the scene blurred with the narrower kernel $\alpha \cdot k(\alpha\xi)$. In the second iteration, we further reduce the blur to $\alpha^2 \cdot k(\alpha^2\xi)$, and so on. As visualized in Fig. 3(a) by the red solid curves, the residual blur in the sequence of recovered images becomes narrower and narrower and eventually converges to $\lim_{\ell \to \infty} \alpha^{\ell} \cdot k(\alpha^{\ell}\xi) = \delta(\xi)$.

However, the analysis so far assumed *continuous* signals, whereas in practice we work with discrete images. Had the image $\hat{x}_{\ell}$ recovered in the ℓ-th iteration corresponded to point-wise samples of $\alpha^{\ell} \cdot k(\alpha^{\ell}\xi) * f(\xi)$, we would eventually tend to

---

[1] For example, according to [7], approximately 90% of the 5×5 patches in a *sharp* natural image, recur "as is" 10 or more times in the image scaled-down to 3/4 of the size ($\alpha = 4/3$).

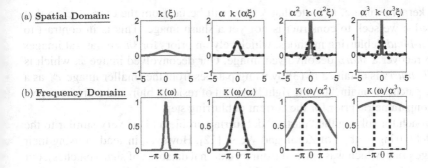

Fig. 3. *The residual blur in repeated sharpening iterations.* Continuous-domain sharpening (*solid red curve*) tends in the spatial domain (a) to $\lim_{\ell \to \infty} \alpha^{\ell} \cdot k(\alpha^{\ell}\xi) = \delta(\xi)$ and in the frequency domain (b) to $\lim_{\ell \to \infty} K(\omega/\alpha^{\ell}) = K(0) = 1$. Aliasing-aware sharpening (*dashed black curve*) tends in the spatial domain (a) to $\mathrm{sinc}(\xi)$ and in the frequency domain (b) to $\mathrm{rect}(\omega)$.

point-wise samples of the continuous $f(\xi)$, which would cause aliasing effects. Indeed, as shown in Fig. 3(b) by the red solid curves, the Fourier transform of $\alpha^{\ell} \cdot k(\alpha^{\ell}\xi)$, which is $K(\omega/\alpha^{\ell})$, converges to[2] $\lim_{\ell \to \infty} K(\omega/\alpha^{\ell}) = K(0) = 1$ for all ω. Therefore, eventually, all frequencies are retained prior to sampling.

To avoid undesired aliasing effects, we want the recovered $\hat{x}_{\ell}$ to correspond to samples of the continuous scene $f(\xi)$ convolved with the *band-limited* blur kernel $K(\omega/\alpha^{\ell}) \cdot$ $\mathrm{rect}(\omega)$, where $\mathrm{rect}(\omega) = 1$ for $|\omega| < \pi$ (the Nyquist frequency[3]) and is zero elsewhere. The logic here is to shrink the blur in the spatial domain (expand it in the frequency domain), but not beyond the Nyquist frequency π (*i.e.*, zero all frequencies above π). Indeed, as illustrated in Fig. 3(b) by the black dashed curves, the function $K(\omega/\alpha^{\ell}) \cdot \mathrm{rect}(\omega)$ tends to $K(0) \cdot \mathrm{rect}(\omega) = \mathrm{rect}(\omega)$, as ℓ tends to infinity. Therefore, in this case, $\hat{x}_{\ell}$ converges to samples of the continuous scene convolved with the ideal low-pass filter $\mathrm{sinc}(\xi)$. This is illustrated in Fig. 3(a) by the black dashed curves.

To summarize, the down-scaling operation we perform on the blurry image $\hat{x}_{\ell}$ should be done so that patches in the resulting $\hat{x}_{\ell}^{\alpha}$ are discrete versions of the continuous scene blurred with $K(\omega/\alpha^{\ell}) \cdot \mathrm{rect}(\omega)$. In the Supplementary Material, as well as in www.wisdom.weizmann.ac.il/~vision/BlindDeblur.html, we provide a proof that if the camera blur $K(\omega)$ is bandlimited to π (so that the blurry image y does not suffer from aliasing), then down-sampling with a sinc kernel leads exactly to the desired result. Therefore, in Step 1 of the algorithm, the down-scaling is performed using a sinc kernel.

3.2 Step 2: Deblurring Using Internal Patch Recurrence

In Step 2 of the algorithm we minimize (2) with respect to $\hat{x}$ while holding $\hat{k}$ and $\hat{x}^{\alpha}$ fixed, which corresponds to solving Eq. (3). This step is in effect a deblurring of y by

---

[2] We assume that $\int k(\xi)d\xi = 1$, which implies that in the frequency domain, $K(0) = 1$.

[3] Assuming that the sampling period is 1, the Nyquist frequency is π.

the current kernel estimate, $\hat{k}$. Note that $\hat{k}$ may still be far from the correct k, so that the deblurred $\hat{x}$ we seek to construct is not yet a sharp image. This is in contrast to standard *non-blind* deblurring methods, which rely on priors for *sharp* natural images and seek to recover a *sharp* deconvolved image. Our deconvolved image $\hat{x}$, which is still *partially blurry* is obtained in (3) by using patches from the smaller image $\hat{x}^\alpha$ as a prior. These patches contain "just the right" amount of residual blur, and therefore serve as a good nonparametric prior for the current deblurring step.

Our approach for solving the "partial" deblurring problem (3) is very similar to the non-blind deblurring method of Zoran and Weiss [22]. However, instead of using their natural image prior (which was learned from an external database of sharp patches), our prior is learned from the patches in $\hat{x}^\alpha$. Problem (3) can be written in vector form as

$$\arg\min_{\hat{x}} \|y - \hat{K}\hat{x}\|^2 + \lambda_1 \rho(\hat{x}, \hat{x}^\alpha), \tag{6}$$

where $\hat{K}$ is a matrix that corresponds to convolution with $\hat{k}$. We start by giving a formal definition of the function $\rho(\hat{x}, \hat{x}^\alpha)$. As in [22], we define $\rho(\hat{x}, \hat{x}^\alpha)$ as minus the *expected log likelihood* (EPLL) of patches in $\hat{x}$. Namely, $\rho(\hat{x}, \hat{x}^\alpha) = -\sum_j \log p(Q_j\hat{x})$, where Q_j is a matrix that extracts the j-th patch from $\hat{x}$. However, as opposed to [22], here we learn the probability $p(Q_j\hat{x})$ from the patches in $\hat{x}^\alpha$. Specifically, letting R_i denote the matrix which extracts the i-th patch from $\hat{x}^\alpha$, we approximate $p(Q_j\hat{x})$ using nonparametric density kernel estimation as

$$p(Q_j\hat{x}) = c \sum_i \exp\left\{-\frac{1}{2h^2}\|Q_j\hat{x} - R_i\hat{x}^\alpha\|^2\right\}, \tag{7}$$

where h is a bandwidth parameter and c is a constant independent of $\hat{x}$. This results in the prior term

$$\rho(\hat{x}, \hat{x}^\alpha) = -\sum_j \log\left(\sum_i \exp\left\{-\frac{1}{2h^2}\|Q_j\hat{x} - R_i\hat{x}^\alpha\|^2\right\}\right). \tag{8}$$

Having defined $\rho(\hat{x}, \hat{x}^\alpha)$, we now proceed to derive an algorithm for minimizing the objective (6). In Appendix B, we show that substituting (8) into (6) and setting the gradient to zero, leads to the requirement that

$$\left(\hat{K}^T\hat{K} + \beta I\right)\hat{x} = \hat{K}^T y + \beta z. \tag{9}$$

Here, I is the identity matrix and $\beta = \lambda_1 M^2/h^2$, where M is the patch size. z is an image constructed by replacing each patch in $\hat{x}$ by a weighted average of its nearest neighbor (NN) patches in $\hat{x}^\alpha$ (for full expressions see Appendix B). Equation (9) cannot be solved in closed form since z depends nonlinearly on $\hat{x}$. Instead, we alternate a few times between solving for $\hat{x}$ (using (9)) and for z (using (14)–(16) in Appendix B).

What this process boils down to is the following: In the first phase, we replace each patch in the current image $\hat{x}$ by a weighted average of its NNs (using L_2 distance) from the (sharper) image $\hat{x}^{\alpha}$ (see Fig. 2(d)). This phase actually enforces our prior, which is that patches in the recovered image should be similar to patches in $\hat{x}^{\alpha}$. The resulting image z, however, does not necessarily conform to the data fidelity term, which requires that when the reconstruction is blurred with $\hat{k}$, it should be similar to y. Thus, in the second phase, we plug z back into (9) and update $\hat{x}$. We then repeat the NN search for the patches in the updated $\hat{x}$, generate an updated z, etc. Alternating these phases a few times, leads to an image $\hat{x}$ which satisfies both requirements. Namely, the patches of $\hat{x}$ are similar to those in $\hat{x}^{\alpha}$, *and* its blurry version $\hat{x} * \hat{k}$ resembles y.

3.3   Step 3: Kernel Update

Step 3 in Alg. 1 corresponds to updating the kernel $\hat{k}$, given the current estimate of the image $\hat{x}$. Disregarding the second term in (2), which does not depend on $\hat{k}$, and requiring that the kernel entries be nonnegative, our optimization problem can be written in vector form as

$$\arg\min_{\hat{k} \geq 0} \|y - \hat{X}\hat{k}\|^2 + \lambda_2 \|\hat{k}\|^2, \tag{10}$$

where $\hat{X}$ is a matrix that corresponds to convolution with our current image estimate $\hat{x}$.

As explained above, the residual blur in the ℓ-th iteration, is intuitively $K(\omega/\alpha^{\ell})$ in the Fourier domain. Consequently, the kernel recovered in the ℓ-th iteration, should approximately correspond to $K(\omega)/K(\omega/\alpha^{\ell})$. For large ℓ, we have that $K(\omega/\alpha^{\ell}) \approx 1$ and the recovered kernel becomes close to the correct $K(\omega)$. However, for small ℓ, the kernel $K(\omega)/K(\omega/\alpha^{\ell})$ may still be very different from $K(\omega)$ and, in particular, it can have negative values in the spatial domain. Consequently, we impose the nonnegativity constraint in (10) only during the last few iterations of Algorithm 1.

3.4   Implementation Details

To speed up the convergence of the algorithm we work in a coarse-to-fine manner. That is, we apply Alg. 1 on each of the levels of an image pyramid constructed from the blurry input image y. The recovered $\hat{x}$ and $\hat{k}$ at each pyramid level are interpolated to constitute an initial guess for the next pyramid level. The pyramid is constructed with scale-gaps of $\alpha = 4/3$ using down-scaling with a sinc. The number of pyramid levels is chosen such that, at the coarsest level, the blur is smaller than the size of the patches used in the deblurring stage (5×5 patches in our implementation). Additional speed up is obtained by using the fast approximate NN search of [15] in the deblurring step, working with a single NN per patch.

For computational efficiency, we solve the large linear system of equations (9) in the Fourier domain. Specifically, it is easy to verify that the matrix $\hat{K}^T$ appearing in (9) corresponds to convolution with a mirrored version of $\hat{k}$, which is equivalent to multiplication by $K^*(\omega)$ in the frequency domain. It thus follows that solving for $\hat{x}$ while fixing z can be implemented as

$$\hat{X}(\omega) = \frac{\hat{K}^*(\omega)Y(\omega) + \beta Z(\omega)}{|\hat{K}(\omega)|^2 + \beta}. \tag{11}$$

Blurry Input   Levin *et al.*   Xu&Jia   Sun *et al.*   Ours

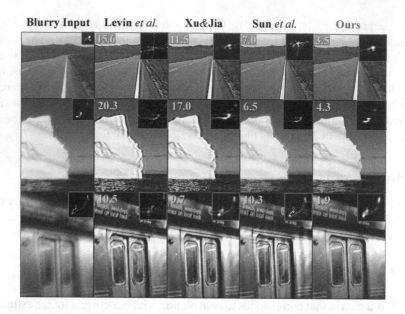

Fig. 4. *Example deblurring results.* The left column shows the blurry input image and the ground-truth blur kernel. The other columns show the deblurring results obtained with the kernels estimated by each of the tested methods. The recovered kernel is shown at the top-right corner of each recovered image. The number on each image is its error ratio r. Please <u>zoom-in</u> on screen to see the differences (see www.wisdom.weizmann.ac.il/~vision/BlindDeblur.html for full sized images and more results).

We use FFTs with proper padding to avoid undesired border effects. This formulation is about 50 times faster than *e.g.*, using conjugate gradients to solve this least-squares problem, as done in [22].

In our current implementation we apply 8 iterations of Alg. 1 per pyramid level. We enforce the nonnegativity constraint in (10) starting from the 5th iteration. For gray-values in the range $[0, 255]$, we use $\beta = 0.4$ in the deblurring step (9) and $\lambda_2 = 7.5^2$ in the kernel update step (10).

4   Experiments

We tested our algorithm on the large database introduced by Sun *et al.* [18]. This database comprises 640 large natural images of diverse scenes (typically 1024×768), which were obtained by synthetically blurring 80 high-quality images with the 8 blur kernels from [12] and adding 1% white Gaussian noise. The kernels range in size from 13×13 to 27×27. We present qualitative and quantitative comparisons to the blind deblurring algorithms of [1,19,13,2,10,18]. Specifically, we follow the protocol of [18], which used the kernel recovered by each method[4] to perform deblurring with the

---

[4] For [18], we report results with the "natural" patch prior, which performs slightly better than their "synthetic" patch prior. For all other algorithms, we used the results posted by [18] (see their paper for additional details).

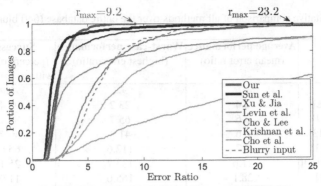

Fig. 5. Cumulative distribution of error ratios

state-of-the-art non-blind deblurring method of [22]. Since the blur kernel can only be recovered up to a global translation, we align the deblurred image with the ground-truth image in order to compute the error. Following the setting of Sun *et al.* [18], we do not assume that the size of the kernel is known and thus always recover a 51×51 kernel.[5]

We measure the quality of a recovered blur kernel $\hat{k}$, using the *error ratio* measure (proposed in [12] and commonly used by others):

$$r = \frac{\|x - \hat{x}_{\hat{k}}\|^2}{\|x - \hat{x}_k\|^2}, \tag{12}$$

where $\hat{x}_{\hat{k}}$ corresponds to deblurring with the recovered kernel $\hat{k}$, and $\hat{x}_k$ corresponds to deblurring with the ground-truth kernel k. The smaller r is, the better the reconstruction. In principle, if $r = 1$, we achieve "ground-truth performance" (*i.e.,* performance of nonblind deblurring with the ground-truth kernel). However, we empirically observe that the deblurring results are still visually pleasing for error-ratios $r \leq 5$, when using the non-blind deblurring of [22] (see Appendix A for a more detailed explanation).

Fig. 4 shows a few visual examples of the kernel estimates, the deblurring results, and their corresponding error ratios r, obtained by us and by the best competing methods [13,19,18] on several images from the database of [18] (all deblurred using the method of [22]). Complex textures with strong edges, such as the sea in the second row, are better represented by the internal image-specific patch prior, than by any of the other more generic priors (please zoom-in on screen to see fine image details). For example, it seems that the sea regions do not conform to the assumption of sparsity of image gradients of Levin *et al.*[13], and that patches within them do not find good NNs in the external patch prior of Sun *et al.*[18]. The sea region, therefore, distracts most blind deblurring methods, and leads to inaccurate kernel estimates. In contrast, the sea is self-similar within the image, at least across small scale-gaps. Therefore, the internal patch recurrence prior used by our method manages to produce more accurate kernel estimates in such difficult cases.

---

[5] When we provide our algorithm the correct kernel size, our results significantly improve.

Table 1. Quantitative comparison of all methods over the entire database (640 blurry images)

	Average performance (mean error ratio)	Worst-case performance (highest error-ratio)	Success rate (percent of images with error ratio < 5)
Our	2.6	9.2	95.9%
Sun et al.[18]	**2.4**	23.2	93.4%
Xu & Jia [19]	3.6	65.7	86.1%
Levin et al.[13]	6.6	41.2	46.7%
Cho & Lee [1]	8.7	112.6	65.6%
Krishnan et al.[10]	11.6	133.7	25.1%
Cho et al.[2]	28.1	165.6	11.9%

The graph in Fig. 5 shows the cumulative distribution of error-ratios over the entire database. The statistics indicate that our algorithm and the algorithm of Sun et al.[18], which are the only patch-based methods, outperform all other approaches by a large gap. The method of [18] is slightly more accurate than ours at very low error ratios. Nevertheless, empirical inspection shows that the visual differences between results with error-ratios smaller than 3 (when using the deblurring of [22]) are often indistinguishable. As can be seen, our method is *more robust* than all competing approaches, in the sense that it rarely fails to recover the kernel with reasonable accuracy (low r_{max}). In fact, as we show in Fig. 6, even our *worst* result over the entire database (namely, the recovered image with the highest error-ratio, $r_{max} = 9.2$), is still slightly better than the input blurry image, both visually and in terms of error. In contrast, the worst results of the other methods obtain high errors and are significantly worse than the blurry inputs.

Table 1 further compares the performance of the various blind deblurring methods using three quantitative measures: (i) the *average performance*, (ii) the *worst-case performance*, and (iii) the *success rate*. The *average performance* corresponds to the mean of the error-ratios attained for all images in the database[6]. As can be seen, our average error-ratio is close to that of Sun et al.[18] and lower than the rest of the competing methods. Interestingly, only three methods attain an *average* error-ratio smaller than 5 (which can be considered as a threshold for good deblurring; see Appendix A): our method, Sun et al. [18], Xu and Jia [19]. This suggests that the visual quality of the remaining methods [1,13,2,10] is unsatisfactory on average.

The *worst-case performance* is the highest error-ratio over the entire database. It measures the robustness of the methods. As can be seen in Table 1, our method is *more robust* than all competing approaches, in the sense that it rarely fails to recover the kernel with reasonable accuracy.

The *success rate* is the percent of images which obtained good-quality deblurring (*i.e.*, an error ratio below 5). As can be seen in Table 1, our method attains an error ratio larger than 5 only 4.1% of the times, which correspond to 26 out of the 640 images in the database. The worst of these 26 'failure cases' can be seen in Fig. 6.

---

[6] Note that the geometric mean used by Sun et al.[18] is not sensitive to a small number of severe failures, which is why we prefer the standard (arithmetic) mean.

Blurry Input Image   Recovered Image   Blurry Input Image   Recovered Image

Fig. 6. *Worst results.* For each algorithm, the result with the highest error-ratio is shown along with the recovered kernel and the corresponding error-ratio (number in yellow). The number in blue is the ratio between the error of the deblurred (output) image and the error of the blurry (input) image. Values below and above 1 indicate, respectively, improvement or degradation in quality. As can be seen, our worst-case result is still better than the blurry input image while the worst-case results of the competing methods are significantly worse than their input images. See www.wisdom.weizmann.ac.il/~vision/BlindDeblur.html for full sized images.

5 Summary

In this paper we presented a blind deblurring method, which uses *internal* patch recurrence as a cue for estimation of the blur kernel. Our key observation is that patch recurrence across scales is strong in sharp images, but weak in blurry images. We seek a blur kernel k, such that if *"undone"* (if the blurry image is deconvolved with k), the patch similarity across scales will be maximized. Extensive empirical evaluations confirm that the internal patch recurrence property is a strong prior for image deblurring, and exhibits higher robustness than other priors. We attribute this to the fact that each image uses *its own image-specific* patch prior.

Acknowledgments. Thanks to Shahar Kovalski, Yuval Bahat and Maria Zontak. Funded in part by the Israel Science Foundation, Israel Ministry of Science, Citigroup Foundation and a Viterbi Fellowship (Technion).

A What Is "Good" Blind Deblurring?

The error-ratio measure r in Eq. (12) depends on the type of *non-blind* deblurring method used. We use the state-of-the-art non-blind deblurring method of [22] (which was also the setting used in [18]). We empirically observe that images recovered with an error-ratio smaller than 5 are usually visually pleasing, while error-ratios above 5 are often associated with distracting artifacts. Levin *et al.* [13] reported a threshold of 3 between good and bad visual results. However, their error ratios were computed with the non-blind deblurring of [11]. Using a simulation study (see the Supplementary Material and www.wisdom.weizmann.ac.il/~vision/BlindDeblur.html for details), we computed the best linear fit between the two types of error ratios, and found that an error ratio of 3 with [11] indeed corresponds to an error-ratio of approximately 5 with [22]. Thus, based on our observations and those of Levin *et al.* [13], we regard 5 as a threshold for good-quality deblurring when using the non-blind deblurring of [22].

B Derivation of Equation (9)

Assuming the patches are $M \times M$, substituting (8) into (6) and setting the gradient to zero, leads to the requirement that

$$\left(\hat{K}^T \hat{K} + \beta \frac{1}{M^2} \sum_j Q_j^T Q_j \right) \hat{x} = \hat{K}^T y + \beta z, \tag{13}$$

were $\beta = \lambda_1 M^2 / h^2$ and

$$z = \frac{1}{M^2} \sum_j Q_j^T z_j, \tag{14}$$

with

$$z_j = \sum_i w_{i,j} R_i \hat{x}^\alpha \tag{15}$$

and

$$w_{i,j} = \frac{\exp\left\{ -\frac{1}{2h^2} \|Q_j \hat{x} - R_i \hat{x}^\alpha\|^2 \right\}}{\sum_m \exp\left\{ -\frac{1}{2h^2} \|Q_j \hat{x} - R_m \hat{x}^\alpha\|^2 \right\}}. \tag{16}$$

It is easy to verify that, up to border effects, multiplying a column-stacked image by $\sum_j Q_j^T Q_j$ is equivalent to multiplying all pixels of the image by M^2, or, in other words, that $\sum_j Q_j^T Q_j = M^2 I$. Substituting this term into (13) leads to (9).

Note that z_j in (15) can be interpreted as an approximation of the patch $Q_j \hat{x}$, which uses the patches $\{R_i \hat{x}^\alpha\}$ from the small image $\hat{x}^\alpha$ as examples. In practice, most of the weights $w_{i,j}$ are very small, so that each patch in $\hat{x}$ is actually approximated by a very small number of its NNs in $\hat{x}^\alpha$ (for efficiency, we often use only a single NN – see Section 3.4). The matrix Q_j^T takes a patch and places it at location j in an image. Therefore, the image z in (14) can be thought of as an approximation of the image $\hat{x}$, where the prior is learned from the patches in $\hat{x}^\alpha$.

References

1. Cho, S., Lee, S.: Fast motion deblurring. ACM Transactions on Graphics (TOG) 28, 145 (2009)
2. Cho, T.S., Paris, S., Horn, B.K., Freeman, W.T.: Blur kernel estimation using the Radon transform. In: IEEE Conference on Computer Vision and Pattern Recognition (CVPR), pp. 241–248 (2011)
3. Dabov, K., Foi, A., Katkovnik, V., Egiazarian, K.: Image restoration by sparse 3D transform-domain collaborative filtering. In: SPIE Electronic Imaging, vol. 6812
4. Danielyan, A., Katkovnik, V., Egiazarian, K.: BM3D frames and variational image deblurring. IEEE Transactions on Image Processing 21(4), 1715–1728 (2012)
5. Fergus, R., Singh, B., Hertzmann, A., Roweis, S.T., Freeman, W.T.: Removing camera shake from a single photograph. ACM Transactions on Graphics (TOG) 25, 787–794 (2006)
6. Freedman, G., Fattal, R.: Image and video upscaling from local self-examples. ACM Transactions on Graphics (TOG) 30(2), 12 (2011)
7. Glasner, D., Bagon, S., Irani, M.: Super-resolution from a single image. In: IEEE International Conference on Computer Vision (ICCV) (2009)
8. Goldstein, A., Fattal, R.: Blur-kernel estimation from spectral irregularities. In: Fitzgibbon, A., Lazebnik, S., Perona, P., Sato, Y., Schmid, C. (eds.) ECCV 2012, Part V. LNCS, vol. 7576, pp. 622–635. Springer, Heidelberg (2012)
9. Joshi, N., Szeliski, R., Kriegman, D.: PSF estimation using sharp edge prediction. In: IEEE Conference on Computer Vision and Pattern Recognition (CVPR), pp. 1–8 (2008)
10. Krishnan, D., Tay, T., Fergus, R.: Blind deconvolution using a normalized sparsity measure. In: IEEE Conference on Computer Vision and Pattern Recognition (CVPR), pp. 233–240 (2011)
11. Levin, A., Fergus, R., Durand, F., Freeman, W.T.: Image and depth from a conventional camera with a coded aperture. ACM Transactions on Graphics (TOG) 26(3), 70 (2007)
12. Levin, A., Weiss, Y., Durand, F., Freeman, W.T.: Understanding and evaluating blind deconvolution algorithms. In: IEEE Conference on Computer Vision and Pattern Recognition (CVPR), pp. 1964–1971 (2009)
13. Levin, A., Weiss, Y., Durand, F., Freeman, W.T.: Efficient marginal likelihood optimization in blind deconvolution. In: IEEE Conference on Computer Vision and Pattern Recognition (CVPR), pp. 2657–2664 (2011)
14. Michaeli, T., Irani, M.: Nonparametric blind super-resolution. In: IEEE International Conference on Computer Vision (ICCV) (December 2013)
15. Olonetsky, I., Avidan, S.: TreeCANN–K-D tree coherence approximate nearest neighbor algorithm. In: Fitzgibbon, A., Lazebnik, S., Perona, P., Sato, Y., Schmid, C. (eds.) ECCV 2012, Part IV. LNCS, vol. 7575, pp. 602–615. Springer, Heidelberg (2012)
16. Roth, S., Black, M.J.: Fields of experts. International Journal of Computer Vision 82(2), 205–229 (2009)
17. Shan, Q., Jia, J., Agarwala, A.: High-quality motion deblurring from a single image. ACM Transactions on Graphics (TOG) 27, 73 (2008)
18. Sun, L., Cho, S., Wang, J., Hays, J.: Edge-based blur kernel estimation using patch priors. In: IEEE International Conference on Computational Photography (ICCP), pp. 1–8 (2013)
19. Xu, L., Jia, J.: Two-phase kernel estimation for robust motion deblurring. In: Daniilidis, K., Maragos, P., Paragios, N. (eds.) ECCV 2010, Part I. LNCS, vol. 6311, pp. 157–170. Springer, Heidelberg (2010)

20. Zontak, M., Irani, M.: Internal statistics of a single natural image. In: IEEE Conference on Computer Vision and Pattern Recognition, CVPR (2011)
21. Zontak, M., Mosseri, I., Irani, M.: Separating signal from noise using patch recurrence across scales. In: IEEE Conference on Computer Vision and Pattern Recognition (CVPR), pp. 1195–1202 (2013)
22. Zoran, D., Weiss, Y.: From learning models of natural image patches to whole image restoration. In: IEEE International Conference on Computer Vision (ICCV), pp. 479–486 (2011)

Crisp Boundary Detection Using Pointwise Mutual Information

Phillip Isola, Daniel Zoran, Dilip Krishnan, and Edward H. Adelson

Massachusetts Institute of Technology, USA
{phillipi,danielz,dilipkay,eadelson}@mit.edu

Abstract. Detecting boundaries between semantically meaningful objects in visual scenes is an important component of many vision algorithms. In this paper, we propose a novel method for detecting such boundaries based on a simple underlying principle: pixels belonging to the same object exhibit higher statistical dependencies than pixels belonging to different objects. We show how to derive an affinity measure based on this principle using pointwise mutual information, and we show that this measure is indeed a good predictor of whether or not two pixels reside on the same object. Using this affinity with spectral clustering, we can find object boundaries in the image – achieving state-of-the-art results on the BSDS500 dataset. Our method produces pixel-level accurate boundaries while requiring minimal feature engineering.

Keywords: Edge/Contour Detection, Segmentation.

1 Introduction

Semantically meaningful contour extraction has long been a central goal of computer vision. Such contours mark the boundary between physically separate objects and provide important cues for low- and high-level understanding of scene content. Object boundary cues have been used to aid in segmentation [1,2,3], object detection and recognition [4,5], and recovery of intrinsic scene properties such as shape, reflectance, and illumination [6]. While there is no exact definition of the "objectness" of entities in a scene, datasets such as the BSDS500 segmentation dataset [1] provide a number of examples of human drawn contours, which serve as a good objective guide for the development of boundary detection algorithms. In light of the ill-posed nature of this problem, many different approaches to boundary detection have been developed [1,7,8,9].

As a motivation for our approach, first consider the photo on the left in Figure 1. In this image, the coral in the foreground exhibits a repeating pattern of white and gray stripes. We would like to group this entire pattern as part of a single object. One way to do so is to notice that white-next-to-gray co-occurs suspiciously often. If these colors were part of distinct objects, it would be quite unlikely to see them appear right next to each other so often. On the other hand, examine the blue coral in the background. Here, the coral's color is similar to the color of the water behind the coral. While the change in color is subtle along

D. Fleet et al. (Eds.): ECCV 2014, Part III, LNCS 8691, pp. 799–814, 2014.
© Springer International Publishing Switzerland 2014

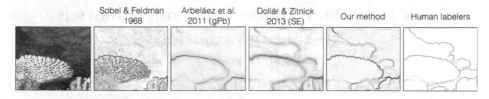

Fig. 1. Our method suppresses edges in highly textured regions such as the coral in the foreground. Here, white and gray pixels repeatedly occur next to each other. This pattern shows up as a suspicious coincidence in the image's statistics, and our method infers that these colors must therefore be part of the same object. Conversely, pixel pairs that straddle the coral/background edges are relatively rare and our model assigns these pairs low affinity. From left to right: Input image; Contours recovered by the Sobel operator [10]; Contours recovered by Dollár & Zitnick 2013 [8]; Contours recovered by Arbeláez et al. (gPb) [1]; Our recovered contours; Contours labeled by humans [1]. Sobel boundaries are crisp but poorly match human drawn contours. More recent detectors are more accurate but blurry. Our method recovers boundaries that are both crisp and accurate.

this border, it is in fact a rather unusual sort of change – it only occurs on the narrow border where coral pixels abut with background water pixels. Pixel pairs that straddle an object border tend to have a rare combination of colors.

These observations motivate the basic assumption underlying our method, which is that the statistical association between pixels *within* objects is high, whereas for pixels residing on different objects the statistical association is low. We will use this property to detect boundaries in natural images.

One of the challenges in accurate boundary detection is the seemingly inherent contradiction between the "correctness" of an edge (distinguishing between boundary and non-boundary edges) and "crispness" of the boundary (precisely localizing the boundary). The leading boundary detectors tend to use relatively large neighborhoods when building their features, even the most local ones. This results in edges which, correct as they may be, are inherently blurry. Because our method works on surprisingly simple features (namely pixel color values and very local variance information) we can achieve both accurate *and* crisp contours. Figure 1 shows this appealing properties of contours extracted using our method. The contours we get are highly detailed (as along the top of the coral in the foreground) and at the same time we are able to learn the local statistical regularities and suppress textural regions (such as the interior of the coral).

It may appear that there is a chicken and egg problem. To gather statistics within objects, we need to already have the object segmentation. This problem can be bypassed, however. We find that natural objects produce probability density functions (PDFs) that are well clustered. We can discover those clusters, and fit them by kernel density estimation, without explicitly identifying objects. This lets us distinguish common pixel pairs (arising within objects) from rare ones (arising at boundaries).

In this paper, we only look at highly localized features – pixel colors and color variance in 3x3 windows. It is clear, then, that we cannot derive long feature vectors with sophisticated spatial and chromatic computations. How can we hope to get good performance? It turns out that there is much more information in the PDFs than one might at first imagine. By exploiting this information we can succeed.

Our main contribution is a simple, principled and unsupervised approach to contour detection. Our algorithm is competitive with other, heavily engineered methods. Unlike these previous methods, we use extremely local features, mostly at the pixel level, which allow us to find crisp and highly localized edges, thus outperforming other methods significantly when more exact edge localization is required. Finally, our method is unsupervised and is able to adapt to each given image independently. The resulting algorithm achieves state-of-the-art results on the BSDS500 segmentation dataset.

The rest of this paper is organized as follows: we start by presenting related work, followed by a detailed description of our model. We then proceed to model validation, showing that the assumptions we make truly hold for natural images and ground truth contours. Then, we compare our method to current state-of-the-art boundary detection methods. Finally, we will discuss the implications and future directions for this work.

2   Related Work

Contour/boundary detection and edge detection are classical problems in computer vision, and there is an immense literature on these topics. It is out of scope for this paper to give a full survey on the topic, so only a small relevant subset of works will be reviewed here.

The early approaches to contour detection relied on local measurements with linear filters. Classical examples are the Sobel [11], Roberts [12], Prewitt [13] and Canny [14] edge detectors, which all use local derivative filters of fixed scale and only a few orientations. Such detectors tend to overemphasize small, unimportant edges and lead to noisy contour maps which are hard to use for subsequent higher-level processing. The key challenge is to reduce gradients due to repeated or stochastic textures, without losing edges due to object boundaries.

As a result, over the years, larger (non-local) neighborhoods, multiple scales and orientations, and multiple feature types have been incorporated into contour detectors. In fact, all top-performing methods in recent years fall into this category. Martin et al. [15] define linear operators for a number of cues such as intensity, color and texture. The resulting features are fed into a regression classifier that predicts edge strength; this is the popular Pb metric which gives, for each pixel in the image the probability of a contour at that point. Dollár et al. [16] use supervised learning, along with a large number of features and multiple scales to learn edge prediction. The features are collected in local patches in the image.

Recently, Lim et al. [7] have used random forest based learning on image patches to achieve state-of-the-art results. Their key idea is to use a dictionary of human generated contours, called Sketch Tokens, as features for contours within a patch. The use of random forests makes inference fast. Dollár and Zitnick [8] also use random forests, but they further combine it with structured prediction to provide real-time edge detection. Ren and Bo [17] use sparse coding and oriented gradients to learn dictionaries of contour patches. They achieve excellent contour detection results on BSDS500.

The above methods all use patch-level measurements to create contour maps, with non-overlapping patches making independent decisions. This often leads to noisy and broken contours which are less likely to be useful for further processing for object recognition or image segmentation. Global methods utilize local measurements and embed them into a a framework which minimizes a global cost over all disjoint pairs of patches. Early methods in this line of work include that of Shashua and Ullman [18] and Elder and Zucker [19]. The paper of Shashua and Ullman used a simple dynamic programming approach to compute closed, smooth contours from local, disjoint edge fragments.

These globalization approaches tend to be fragile. More modern methods include a Conditional Random Field (CRF) presented in [20], which builds a probabilistic model for the completion problem, and uses loopy belief propagation to infer the closed contours. The highly successful gPb method of Arbeláez et al. [1] embeds the local Pb measure into a spectral clustering framework [21,22]. The resulting algorithm gives long, connected contours higher probability than short, disjoint contours.

The rarity of boundary patches has been studied in the literature before, e.g. [23]. We measure rarity based on pointwise mutual information [24] (PMI). PMI gives us a value per patch that allows us to build a pixel-level affinity matrix. This local affinity matrix is then embedded in a spectral clustering framework [1] to provide global contour information. PMI underlies many experiments in computational linguistics [25,26] to learn word associations (pairs of words that are likely to occur together), and recently has been used for improving image categorization [27]. Other information-theoretic takes on segmentation have been previously explored, e.g., [28]. However, to the best of our knowledge, PMI has never been used for contour extraction or image segmentation.

3   Information Theoretic Affinity

Consider the zebra in Figure 2. In this image, black stripes repeatedly occur next to white stripes. To a human eye, the stripes are grouped as a coherent object – the zebra. As discussed above, this intuitive grouping shows up in the image statistics: black and white pixels commonly co-occur next to one another, while white-green combinations are rarer, suggesting a possible object boundary where a white stripe meets the green background.

In this section, we describe a formal measure of the *affinity* between neighboring image features, based on statistical association. We denote a generic pair of neighboring features by random variables A and B, and investigate the joint distribution over pairings $\{A, B\}$.

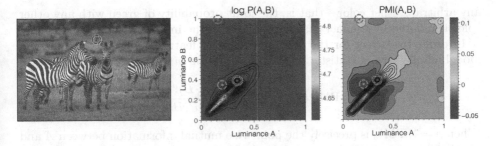

Fig. 2. Our algorithm works by reasoning about the pointwise mutual information (PMI) between neighboring image features. Middle column: Joint distribution of the luminance values of pairs of nearby pixels. Right column: PMI between the luminance values of neighboring pixels in this zebra image. In the left image, the blue circle indicates a smooth region of the image where all points are on the same object. The green circle a region that contains an object boundary. The red circle shows a region with a strong luminance edge that nonetheless does not indicate an object boundary. Luminance pairs chosen from within each circle are plotted where they fall in the joint distribution and PMI functions.

Let $p(A, B; d)$ be the joint probability of features A and B occurring at a Euclidean distance of d pixels apart. We define $P(A, B)$ by computing probabilities over multiple distances:

$$P(A, B) = \frac{1}{Z} \sum_{d=d_0}^{\infty} w(d)p(A, B; d), \tag{1}$$

where w is a weighting function which decays monotonically with distance d (Gaussian in our implementation), and Z is a normalization constant. We take the marginals of this distribution to get $P(A)$ and $P(B)$.

In order to pick out object boundaries, a first guess might be that affinity should be measured with joint probability $P(A, B)$. After all, features that always occur together probably should be grouped together. For the zebra image in Figure 2, the joint distribution over luminance values of nearby pixels is shown in the middle column. Overlaid on the zebra image are three sets of pixel pairs in the colored circles. These pairs correspond to pairs $\{A, B\}$ in our model. The pair of pixels in the blue circle are both on the same object and the joint probability of their colors – green next to green – is high. The pair in the bright green circle straddles an object boundary and the joint probability of the colors of this pair – black next to green – is correspondingly low.

Now consider the pair in the red circle. There is no physical object boundary on the edge of this zebra stripe. However, the joint probability is actually lower for this pair than for the pair in the green circle, where an object boundary did in fact exist. This demonstrates a shortcoming of using joint probability as a measure of affinity. Because there are simply more green pixels in the image than white pixels, there are more chances for green accidentally show up next to any arbitrary other color – that is, the joint probability of green with any other color is inflated by the fact that most pixels in the image are green.

In order to correct for the baseline rarity of features A and B, we instead model affinity with a statistic related to *pointwise mutual information*:

$$\mathrm{PMI}_\rho(A, B) = \log \frac{P(A, B)^\rho}{P(A)P(B)}. \tag{2}$$

When $\rho = 1$, PMI_ρ is precisely the pointwise mutual information between A and B [24]. This quantity is the log of the ratio between the observed joint probability of $\{A, B\}$ in the image and the probability of this tuple were the two features independent. Equivalently, the ratio can be written as $\frac{P(A|B)}{P(A)}$, that is, how much more likely is observing A given that we saw B in the same local region, compared to the base rate of observing A in the image. When $\rho = 2$, we have a stronger condition: in that case the ratio in the log becomes $P(A|B)P(B|A)$. That is, observing A should imply that B will be nearby and vice versa. As it is unclear a priori which setting of ρ would lead to the best segmentation results, we instead treat ρ as a free parameter and select its value to optimize performance on a training set of images (see Section 4).

In the right column of Figure 2, we see the pointwise mutual information over features A and B. This metric appropriately corrects for the baseline rarities of white and black pixels versus gray and green pixels. As a result, the pixel pair between the stripes (red circle), is rated as more strongly mutually informative than the pixel pair that straddles the boundary (green circle). In Section 6.1 we empirically validate that PMI_ρ is indeed predictive of whether or not two points are on the same object.

4　Learning the Affinity Function

In this section we describe how we model $P(A, B)$, from which we can derive $\mathrm{PMI}_\rho(A, B)$. The pipeline for this learning is depicted in Figure 3(a) and (b). For each image on which we wish to measure affinities, we learn $P(A, B)$ specific to that image itself. Extensions of our approach could learn $P(A, B)$ from any type of dataset: videos, photo collections, images of a specific object class, etc. However, we find that modeling $P(A, B)$ with respect to the internal statistics of each test image is an effective approach for unsupervised boundary detection. The utility of internal image statistics has been previously demonstrated in the context of super-resolution and denoising [29] as well as saliency prediction [30].

Because natural images are piecewise smooth, the empirical distribution $P(A, B)$ for most images will be dominated by the diagonal $A \approx B$ (as in Figure 2). However, we are interested in the low probability, off-diagonal regions of the PDF. These off diagonal regions are where we find changes, including both repetitive, textural changes and object boundaries. In order to suppress texture while still detecting subtle object boundaries, we need a model that is able to capture the low probability regions of $P(A, B)$.

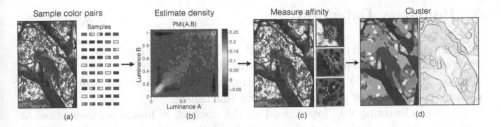

Fig. 3. Boundary detection pipeline: (a) Sample color pairs within the image. Red-blue dots represent pixel pair samples. (b) Estimate joint density P(A,B) and from this get PMI(A,B). (c) Measure affinity between each pair of pixels using PMI. Here we show the affinity between the center pixel in each patch and all neighboring pixels (hotter colors indicate greater affinity). Notice that there is low affinity across object boundaries but high affinity within textural regions. (d) Group pixels based on affinity (spectral clustering) to get segments and boundaries.

We use a nonparametric kernel density estimator [31] since it has high capacity without requiring an increase in feature dimensionality. We also experimented with a Gaussian Mixture Model but were unable to achieve the same performance as kernel density estimators.

Kernel density estimation places a kernel of probability density around every sample point. We need to specify on the form of the kernel and the number of samples. We used Epanechnikov kernels (i.e. truncated quadratics) owing to their computational efficiency and their optimality properties [32], and we place kernels at 10000 sample points per image. Samples are drawn uniformly at random from all locations in the image. First a random position x in the image is sampled. Then features A and B are sampled from image locations around x, such that A and B are d pixels apart. The sampling is done with weighting function $w(d)$, which is monotonically decreasing and gives maximum weight to $d = 2$. The vast majority of samples pairs $\{A, B\}$ are within distance $d = 4$ pixels of each other.

Epanechnikov kernels have one free parameter per feature dimension: the bandwidth of the kernel in that dimension. We select the bandwidth for each dimension through leave-one-out cross-validation to maximize the data likelihood. Specifically, we compute the likelihood of each sample given a kernel density model built from all the remaining samples. As a further detail, we bound the bandwidth to fall in the range $[0.01, 0.1]$ (with features scaled between $[0, 1]$) – this helps prevent overfitting to imperceptible details in the image, such as jpeg artifacts in a blank sky. To speed up evaluation of the kernel density model, we use the kd-tree implementation of Ihler and Mandel [33]. In addition, we smooth our calculation of PMI_ρ slightly by adding a small regularization constant to the numerator and denominator of Eq. 2.

Our model has one other free parameter, ρ. We choose ρ by selecting the value that gives the best performance on a training set of images completely independent of the test set, finding $\rho = 1.25$ to perform best.

5   Boundary Detection

Armed with an affinity function to tell us how pixels should be grouped in an image, the next step is to use this affinity function for boundary detection (Figure 3 (c) and (d)). Spectral clustering methods are ideally suited in our present case since they operate on affinity functions.

Spectral clustering was introduced in the context of image segmentation as a way to approximately solve the Normalized Cuts objective [34]. Normalized Cuts segments an image so as to maximize within segment affinity and minimize between segment affinity. To detect boundaries, we apply a spectral clustering using our affinity function, following the current state-of-the-art solution to this problem, gPb [1].

As input to spectral clustering, we require an affinity matrix, $\mathbf{W}$. We get this from our affinity function PMI_ρ as follows. Let i and j be indices into image pixels. At each pixel, we define a feature vector $\mathbf{f}$. Then, we define:

$$\mathbf{W}_{i,j} = e^{\mathrm{PMI}_\rho(\mathbf{f}_i, \mathbf{f}_j)} \tag{3}$$

The exponentiated values give us better performance than the raw PMI_ρ values. Since our model for feature pairings was learned on nearby pixels, we only evaluate the affinity matrix for pixels within a radius of 5 pixels from one another. Remaining affinities are set to 0.

In order to reduce model complexity, we make the simplifying assumption that different types of features are independent of one another. If we have M subsets of features, this implies that,

$$\mathbf{W}_{i,j} = e^{\sum_{k=1}^{M} \mathrm{PMI}_\rho(\mathbf{f}_i^k, \mathbf{f}_j^k)} \tag{4}$$

In our experiments, we use two feature sets: pixel color (in L*a*b* space) and the diagonal of the RGB color covariance matrix in a 3x3 window around each pixel. Thus for each pixel we have two feature vectors of dimension 3 each. Each feature vector is decorrelated using a basis computed over the entire image (one basis for color and one basis for variance).

Given $\mathbf{W}$, we compute boundaries by following the method of [1]: first we compute the generalized eigenvectors of the system $(\mathbf{D} - \mathbf{W})\mathbf{v} = \lambda \mathbf{D} \mathbf{v}$, where $\mathbf{D}_{i,i} = \sum_{j \neq i} \mathbf{W}_{i,j}$. Then we take an oriented spatial derivative over the first N eigenvectors with smallest eigenvalue ($N = 100$ in our experiments). This procedure gives a continuous-valued edge map for each of 8 derivative orientations. We then suppress boundaries that align with image borders and are within a few pixels of the image border. As a final post-processing step we apply the Oriented Watershed Transform (OWT) and create an Ultrametric Contour Map (UCM) [1], which we use as our final contour maps for evaluation.

In addition to the above approach, we also consider a multiscale variant. To incorporate multiscale information, we build an affinity matrix at three different image scales (subsampling the image by half in each dimension for each subsequent scale). To combine the information across scales, we use the multigrid,

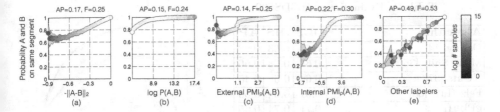

Fig. 4. Here we show the probability that two nearby pixels are on the same object segment as a function of various cues based on the pixel colors A and B. From left to right the cues are: (a) color difference, (b) color co-occurrence probability based on internal image statistics, (c) PMI based on external image statistics, (d) PMI based on internal image statistics, and (e) theoretical upper bound using the average labeling of $N-1$ human labelers to predict the Nth. Color represents number of samples that make up each datapoint. Shaded error bars show three times standard error of the mean. Performance is quantified by treating each cue as a binary classifier (with variable threshold) and measuring AP and maximum F-measure for this classifier (sweeping over threshold).

multiscale angular embedding algorithm of [35]. This algorithm solves the spectral clustering problem while enforcing that the edges at one scale are blurred versions of the edges at the next scale up.

6   Experiments

In this section, we present the results of a number of experiments. We first show that PMI is effective in detecting object boundaries. Then we show benchmarking results on the BSDS500 dataset. Finally, we show some segmentation results that are derived using our boundary detections.

6.1   Is PMI_ρ Informative about Object Boundaries?

Given just two pixels in an image, how well can we determine if they span an object boundary? In this section, we analyze several possible cues based on a pair of pixels, and show that PMI_ρ is more effective than alternatives.

Consider two nearby pixels with colors A and B. In Figure 4 we plot the probability that a random human labeler will consider the two pixels as lying on the same object segment as a function of various cues based on A and B.

To measure this probability, we sampled 20000 nearby pairs of pixels per image in the BSDS500 training set, using the same sampling scheme as in Section 4. For each pair of pixels, we also sample a random labeler from the set of human labelers for that image. The pixel pair is considered to lie on the same object segment if that labeler has placed them on the same segment.

A first idea is to use color difference $\|A - B\|_2$ to decide if the two pixels span a boundary (Figure 4(a); note that we use decorrelated L*a*b* color space with

Table 1. Evaluation on BSDS500

Algorithm	ODS	OIS	AP
Canny [14]	0.60	0.63	0.58
Mean Shift [36]	0.64	0.68	0.56
NCuts [37]	0.64	0.68	0.45
Felz-Hutt [38]	0.61	0.64	0.56
gPb [1]	0.71	0.74	0.65
gPb-owt-ucm [1]	0.73	0.76	0.73
SCG [9]	**0.74**	0.76	0.77
Sketch Tokens [7]	0.73	0.75	0.78
SE [8]	**0.74**	0.76	0.78
Our method – SS, color only	0.72	0.75	0.77
Our method – SS	0.73	0.76	**0.79**
Our method – MS	**0.74**	**0.77**	0.78

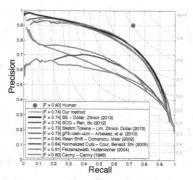

Fig. 5. Precision-recall curve on BSDS500. Figure copied from [8] with our results added.

values normalized between 0 and 1). Color difference has long been used as a cue for boundary detection and unsurprisingly it is predictive of whether or not A and B lie on the same segment.

Beyond using pixel color difference, boundary detectors have improved over time by reasoning over larger and larger image regions. But is there anything more we can squeeze out of just two pixels?

Since boundaries are rare events, we may next try $\log P(A, B)$. As shown in Figure 4(b), rarer color combinations are indeed more likely to span a boundary. However, $\log P(A, B)$ is still a poor predictor.

Can we do better if we use PMI? In Figure 4(c) and (d) we show that, yes, $\mathrm{PMI}_\rho(A, B)$ (with $\rho = 1.25$) is quite predictive of whether or not A and B lie on the same object. Further, comparing Figure 4(c) and (d), we find that it is important that the statistics for PMI_ρ be adapted to the test image itself. Figure 4(c) shows the result when the distribution $P(A, B)$ is learned over the entire BSDS500 training set. These *external* statistics are poorly suited for modeling individual images. On the other hand, when we learn $P(A, B)$ based on color co-occurrences *internal* to an image, PMI_ρ is much more predictive of the boundaries in that image (Figure 4(d)).

6.2 Benchmarks

We run experiments on three versions of our algorithm: single scale using only pixel colors as features (labeled as *SS, color only*), single scale using both color and color variance features (*SS*), and multiscale with both color and variance features (*MS*). Where possible, we compare against the top performing previous contour detectors. We choose the Structured Edges (SE) detector [8] and gPb-owt-ucm detector [1] to compare against more extensively. These two methods currently achieve state-of-the-art results. SE is representative of the supervised learning approach to edge detection, and gPb-owt-ucm is representative of affinity-based approaches, which is also the category into which our algorithm falls.

BSDS500: The Berkeley Segmentation Dataset [39,1] has been frequently used as a benchmark for contour detection algorithms. This dataset is split into 200 training images, 100 validation images, and 200 test images. Although our algorithm requires no extensive training, we did tune our parameters (in particular ρ) to optimize performance on the validation set. In Table 1 and Figure 5, we report our performance on the test set. ODS refers to the F-measure at the optimal threshold across the entire dataset. OIS refers to the per-image best F-measure. AP stands for area under the precision-recall curve. On each of these popular metrics, we match or outperform the state-of-the-art. It is also notable that our *SS, color only* method gets results close to the state-of-the-art, as this method only uses *pixel pair colors* for its features. We believe that this result is noteworthy as it shows that with carefully designed nonlinear methods, it is possible to achieve excellent results without using high-dimensional feature spaces and extensive engineering.

In Figure 8 we show example detections by our algorithm on the BSDS500 test set. These results are with our *MS* version with $\rho = 1.25$. We note that our results have fewer boundaries due to texture, and crisper boundary localization. Further examples can be seen in the supplementary materials.

High Resolution Edges: One of the striking features of our algorithm is the high resolution of its results. Consider the white object in Figure 6. Here our algorithm is able to precisely match the jagged contours of this object, whereas gPb-owt-ucm incurs much more smoothing. As discussed in the introduction, good boundary detections should be both "correct" (detecting real object boundaries) and "crisp" (precisely localized along the object's contour). The standard BSDS500 metrics do not distinguish between these two criteria.

However, the benchmark metrics do include a parameter, r, related to crispness. A detected edge can be r pixels away from a ground truth edge and still be considered a correct detection. The standard benchmark code uses $r = 4.3$ pixels for BSDS500 images. Clearly, this default setting of r cannot distinguish whether or not an algorithm is capturing details above a certain spatial frequency. Varying r dramatically affects performance (Figure 7). In order to benchmark on the task of detecting "crisp" contours, we evaluate our algorithm on three settings of r: r_0, $r_0/2$, and $r_0/4$, where $r_0 = 4.3$ pixels, the default setting.

In Figure 7, we plot our results and compare against SE (with non-maximal suppression) and gPb-owt-ucm. While all three methods perform similarly at $r = r_0$, our method increasingly outperforms the others when r is small. This quantitatively demonstrates that our method is matching crisp, high resolution contours better than other state-of-the-art approaches.

Speed: Recently several edge detectors have been proposed that optimize speed while also achieving good results [8,7]. The current implementation of our method is not competitive with these fast edge detectors in terms of speed. To achieve our *MS* results above, our highly unoptimized algorithm takes around 15 minutes per image on a single core of an Intel Core i7 processor.

However, we can tune the parameters of our algorithm for speed at some cost to resolution. Doing so, we can match our state-of-the-art results (ODS=0.74,

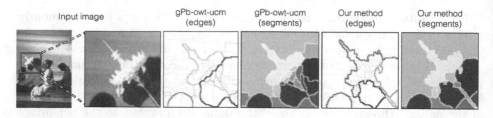

Fig. 6. Here we show a zoomed in region of an image. Notice that our method preserves the high frequency contour variation while gPb-owt-ucm does not.

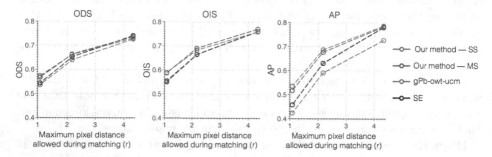

Fig. 7. Performance as a function of the maximum pixel distance allowed during matching between detected boundaries and ground truth edges (referred to as r in the text). When r is large, boundaries can be loosely matched and all methods do well. When r is small, boundaries must be precisely localized, and this is where our method most outperforms the others.

OIS=0.77 AP=0.80 on BSDS500 using the standard $r = 4.3$) in about 30 seconds per image (again on a single core of an i7 processor). The tradeoff is that the resulting boundary maps are not as well localized (at $r = 1.075$, this method falls to ODS=0.52, OIS=0.53, AP=0.43, which is well below our full resolution results in Figure 7). The speed up comes from 1) downsampling each image by half and running our SS algorithm, 2) approximating $\text{PMI}_\rho(A, B)$ using a random forest prior to evaluation of $\mathbf{W}$, and 3) using a fixed kernel bandwidth rather than adapting it to each test image. Code for both fast and high resolution variants of our algorithm will be available at http://web.mit.edu/phillipi/crisp_boundaries.

6.3   Segmentation

Segmentation is a complementary problem to edge detection. In fact, our edge detector automatically also gives us a segmentation map, since this is a byproduct of producing an Ultrametric Contour Map [1]. This ability sets our approach, along with gPb-owt-ucm, apart from many supervised edge detectors such as SE, for which a segmentation map is not a direct byproduct. In Figure 9, we compare results of segmentations with our contours to those of gPb contours. Notice that in the coral image, our method recovers the precise shape of the bottom, reddish

Input image   gPb   SE   Our method   Human labelers

Fig. 8. Contour detection results for a few images in the BSDS500 test set, comparing our method to gPb [1] and SE [8]. In general, we suppress texture edges better (such as on the fish in the first row), and recover crisper contours (such as the leaves in upper-right of the fifth row). Note that here we show each method without edge-thinning (that is, we leave out non-maximal suppression in the case of SE, and we leave out OWT-UCM in the case of gPb and our method).

Input image	gPb-owt-ucm (edges)	gPb-owt-ucm (segments)	Our method (edges)	Our method (segments)

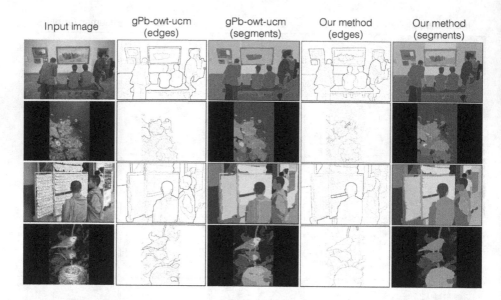

Fig. 9. Example segmentations for a few images in the BSDS500 test set, comparing the results of running OWT-UCM segmentation on our contours and those of gPb [1].

coral, while gPb-owt-ucm misses some major features of the contour. Similarly, in the bird image, our method captures the beak of the top bird, whereas gPb-owt-ucm smooths it away.

7   Discussion

In this paper, we have presented an intuitive and principled method for contour detection which achieves state-of-the-art results. We have shown that, contrary to recent trends, it is possible to achieve excellent boundary detection results using very local information and low-dimensional feature spaces. This is achieved through the use of a novel statistical framework based on pointwise mutual information.

In future work, we plan to extend the learning to videos or multiple images. This could be used to build statistical model of specific objects. Such a model would have direct applications in object detection and recognition.

Acknowledgements. We thank Joseph Lim, Zoya Bylinskii, and Bill Freeman for helpful discussions. This work is supported by NSF award 1212849 Reconstructive Recognition, and by Shell Research. P. Isola is supported by an NSF graduate research fellowship.

References

1. Arbeláez, P., Maire, M., Fowlkes, C., Malik, J.: Contour detection and hierarchical image segmentation. IEEE Trans. Pattern Anal. Mach. Intell. 33(5), 898–916 (2011)
2. Arbeláez, P., Hariharan, B., Gu, C., Gupta, S., Bourdev, L., Malik, J.: Semantic segmentation using regions and parts. In: 2012 IEEE Conference on Computer Vision and Pattern Recognition (CVPR), pp. 3378–3385. IEEE (2012)
3. Levin, A., Weiss, Y.: Learning to combine bottom-up and top-down segmentation. In: Leonardis, A., Bischof, H., Pinz, A. (eds.) ECCV 2006. LNCS, vol. 3954, pp. 581–594. Springer, Heidelberg (2006)
4. Shotton, J., Blake, A., Cipolla, R.: Contour-based learning for object detection. In: Tenth IEEE International Conference on Computer Vision, ICCV 2005, vol. 1, pp. 503–510. IEEE (2005)
5. Opelt, A., Pinz, A., Zisserman, A.: A boundary-fragment-model for object detection. In: Leonardis, A., Bischof, H., Pinz, A. (eds.) ECCV 2006. LNCS, vol. 3952, pp. 575–588. Springer, Heidelberg (2006)
6. Barron, J., Malik, J.: Shape, illumination, and reflectance from shading. Technical report, Berkeley Tech. Report (2013)
7. Lim, J.J., Zitnick, C.L., Dollár, P.: Sketch tokens: A learned mid-level representation for contour and object detection. In: CVPR, pp. 3158–3165 (2013)
8. Dollár, P., Zitnick, C.: Structured Forests for Fast Edge Detection. In: ICCV (2013)
9. Xiaofeng, R., Bo, L.: Discriminatively trained sparse code gradients for contour detection. In: NIPS, pp. 593–601 (2012)
10. Sobel, I., Feldman, G.: A 3x3 isotropic gradient operator for image processing (1968)
11. Duda, R.O., Hart, P.E., et al.: Pattern classification and scene analysis, vol. 3. Wiley, New York (1973)
12. Roberts, L.G.: Machine Perception of Three-Dimensional Solids. PhD thesis, Massachusetts Institute of Technology (1963)
13. Prewitt, J.M.: Object enhancement and extraction. Picture Processing and Psychopictorics 10(1), 15–19 (1970)
14. Canny, J.: A computational approach to edge detection. IEEE Transactions on Pattern Analysis and Machine Intelligence (6), 679–698 (1986)
15. Martin, D.R., Fowlkes, C.C., Malik, J.: Learning to detect natural image boundaries using local brightness, color, and texture cues. IEEE Transactions on Pattern Analysis and Machine Intelligence 26(5), 530–549 (2004)
16. Dollár, P., Tu, Z., Belongie, S.: Supervised learning of edges and object boundaries. In: 2006 IEEE Computer Society Conference on Computer Vision and Pattern Recognition, vol. 2, pp. 1964–1971. IEEE (2006)
17. Ren, X., Bo, L.: Discriminatively trained sparse code gradients for contour detection. In: NIPS (2012)
18. Sha'ashua, A., Ullman, S.: Structural saliency: The detection of globally salient structures using a locally connected network. In: ICCV (1988)
19. Elder, J.H., Zucker, S.W.: Computing contour closure. In: Buxton, B.F., Cipolla, R. (eds.) ECCV 1996. LNCS, vol. 1064, pp. 399–412. Springer, Heidelberg (1996)
20. Ren, X., Fowlkes, C.C., Malik, J.: Scale-invariant contour completion using conditional random fields. In: Tenth IEEE International Conference on Computer Vision, ICCV 2005, vol. 2, pp. 1214–1221. IEEE (2005)
21. Shi, J., Malik, J.: Normalized cuts and image segmentation. IEEE Transactions on Pattern Analysis and Machine Intelligence 22(8), 888–905 (2000)

22. Malik, J., Belongie, S., Leung, T., Shi, J.: Contour and texture analysis for image segmentation. International Journal of Computer Vision 43(1), 7–27 (2001)
23. Zoran, D., Weiss, Y.: Natural images, gaussian mixtures and dead leaves. In: NIPS (2012)
24. Fano, R.M.: Transmission of information: A statistical theory of communications. American Journal of Physics 29, 793–794 (1961)
25. Church, K.W., Hanks, P.: Word association norms, mutual information, and lexicography. Computational Linguistics 16(1), 22–29 (1990)
26. Chambers, N., Jurafsky, D.: Unsupervised learning of narrative event chains. In: ACL, pp. 789–797 (2008)
27. Bengio, S., Dean, J., Erhan, D., Ie, E., Le, Q., Rabinovich, A., Shlens, J., Singer, Y.: Using web co-occurrence statistics for improving image categorization. ArXiv preprint ArXiv:1312.5697 (2013)
28. Mobahi, H., Rao, S., Yang, A., Sastry, S., Ma, Y.: Segmentation of natural images by texture and boundary compression. International Journal of Computer Vision 95, 86–98 (2011)
29. Zontak, M., Irani, M.: Internal Statistics of a Single Natural Image. In: CVPR (2011)
30. Margolin, R., Tal, A., Zelnik-Manor, L.: What makes a patch distinct? In: 2013 IEEE Conference on Computer Vision and Pattern Recognition (CVPR), pp. 1139–1146. IEEE (2013)
31. Parzen, E., et al.: On estimation of a probability density function and mode. Annals of Mathematical Statistics 33(3), 1065–1076 (1962)
32. Epanechnikov, V.A.: Non-parametric estimation of a multivariate probability density. Theory of Probability & its Applications 14(1), 153–158 (1969)
33. Ihler, A., Mandel, M.: http://www.ics.uci.edu/~ihler/code/kde.html
34. Shi, J., Malik, J.: Normalized cuts and image segmentation. PAMI 22(8), 888–905 (2000)
35. Maire, M., Yu, S.X.: Progressive Multigrid Eigensolvers for Multiscale Spectral Segmentation. In: ICCV (2013)
36. Comaniciu, D., Meer, P.: Mean shift: A robust approach toward feature space analysis. IEEE Transactions on Pattern Analysis and Machine Intelligence 24(5), 603–619 (2002)
37. Cour, T., Benezit, F., Shi, J.: Spectral segmentation with multiscale graph decomposition. In: CVPR (2005)
38. Felzenszwalb, P.F., Huttenlocher, D.P.: Efficient graph-based image segmentation. International Journal of Computer Vision 59(2), 167–181 (2004)
39. Martin, D., Fowlkes, C., Tal, D.: A database of human segmented natural images and its application to evaluating segmentation algorithms and measuring ecological statistics. In: ICCV (2001)

Rolling Guidance Filter

Qi Zhang[1], Xiaoyong Shen[1], Li Xu[2], and Jiaya Jia[1]

[1] The Chinese University of Hong Kong, Hong Kong
[2] Image & Visual Computing Lab, Lenovo R&T, Hong Kong
http://www.cse.cuhk.edu.hk/leojia/projects/rollguidance

Abstract. Images contain many levels of important structures and edges. Compared to masses of research to make filters edge preserving, finding scale-aware local operations was seldom addressed in a practical way, albeit similarly vital in image processing and computer vision. We propose a new framework to filter images with the complete control of detail smoothing under a scale measure. It is based on a rolling guidance implemented in an iterative manner that converges quickly. Our method is simple in implementation, easy to understand, fully extensible to accommodate various data operations, and fast to produce results. Our implementation achieves realtime performance and produces artifact-free results in separating different scale structures. This filter also introduces several inspiring properties different from previous edge-preserving ones.

Keywords: Image filter, scale-aware processing, edge preserving.

1 Introduction

To smooth images while preserving different levels of structures, filter techniques were broadly studied. They are popular in visual processing and are sometimes must-perform operations to remove detrimental or unwanted content. Among all filters, edge-aware ones form a major stream. They include representatives of anisotropic diffusion [20], bilateral filter (BF) [26], guided filter (GF) [13], geodesic filters [7,11], weighted median filters [18,34], to name a few. These filters and their variations pursue similar goals to preserve high-contrast edges and remove low-contrast or graduate changes.

Strong edges, measured as large discrepancy between local pixel values, contain important image information. This explains the popularity of these approaches. Meanwhile, we note other than magnitude, another measure that is similarly essential in solving many computer vision problems, including invariant feature construction, data compression, object classification, segmentations, and motion analysis, is about the scale of images/objects/regions.

Natural scenes are composed of objects in different sizes and contain structures of various scales, which deliver diverse information to human. Small structures, usually referred to as details, represent content classified as texture, small objects, and noise, while large scale information generally encodes boundaries, slow spatial color transition, and flat regions. The latter tells more about how

D. Fleet et al. (Eds.): ECCV 2014, Part III, LNCS 8691, pp. 815–830, 2014.

Fig. 1. Examples of high-contrast details in natural images. As explained, edge-aware filters aim to maintain them due to the large magnitude of edges.

objects are arranged in the scene. Separation of structures with respect to their scales is an important process that has been discussed in many areas, such as segmentation [3], object detection [10], and saliency detection [31].

To date, incorporating scales in filter design remains a hard problem. Edge-aware methods can hardly separate structure from details because edge strength and object scale are completely different concepts. Several examples are shown in Fig. 1 where magnitudes of gradients in detail/texture regions are high enough to let edge-aware filters preserve them by nature.

Aiming to handle texture, Subr et al. [25] suppressed high-contrast oscillation by averaging local extrema manifolds and Xu et al. [30] used a global optimization method to remove texture. Karacan et al. [14] computed patch-based weighted average using region covariance with the similar objective to remove texture. These methods involve relatively heavy computation due to the need to employ patch-based filtering or solve large linear systems. They also cannot be easily changed to the filter form for realtime and spatially varying operations.

The iterated nonlocal means proposed by Brox and Cremers [5] for noise removal is also related to our approach. But there exist a few essential differences on both objectives and frameworks (detailed later in Section 2). We note the major challenge to propose a scale-aware filter is twofold.

1. it is not clear yet what is the optimal way to define scale in images regarding local pixel information for filter design because structures may not be with obvious boundaries and they are generally irregularly shaped.
2. Spatial color variation in different scales is unavoidably mixed and overlapped, making their separation very difficult.

We address these problems by proposing an effective scale-aware filter that can remove different levels of details in any input natural images. This algorithm is amazingly easy to implement, efficient, and low-cost in computation. Online processing can be achieved even on a single CPU core. Existing techniques for accelerating edge-aware filters can also be adopted to speed up ours. Our major technical contribution is as follows.

1. We introduce a scale measure following scale space theory. This definition brings the breakthrough to control the level of details during filtering.
2. We propose a new rolling guidance method to automatically refine edges that can be preserved in order to preserve large-scale structures optimally.

In addition, our filtering framework is general and can be extended or modified for different special applications. We show our experimental results and applications in Section 5. More are provided in our project website.

2   Related Work

We review popular and related image filters proposed in recent years and discuss the important difference.

Edge-Aware Filter. Edge-aware filters are developed in different strategies. But the pursuit is to similarly preserve only high-contrast edges. Technically, average- and optimization-based methods are most widely employed.

Average-based filters include anisotropic diffusion [20], bilateral filter [26,8,19,6,32,33], guided filter [13], and geodesic filters [7,11]. This category basically defines different types of affinity between neighboring pixel pairs by considering intensity/color difference. It smoothes images through weighted average. Large and small affinities are defined for low- and high-contrast regions respectively. A variant is *joint/cross* filtering [21,16,13,11]. They are to smooth an image using guidance when defining the pixel affinity.

Optimization-based methods include total variation (TV) [23], weighted least squares (WLS) [9], and L_0 gradient minimization [29]. These methods restore images by optimizing global functions containing terms defined in L_1 norm, weighted L_2 norm or L_0 norm. All these approaches are not easily accelerated in the form of filter due to the need to solve large linear systems.

Mode/Median Filters. Mode and median filters can remove high-contrast details. This class mainly includes mode filter [27,15], median filter [28,15], and weighted median filter [18,34]. These filters compute mode or (weighted) median rather than average in local patches, which inevitably result in higher computational costs. They can perfectly remove salt&pepper noise. But for fast-oscillating signals, local mode and median still produce oscillating results. Thus they cannot optimally remove details in images.

Iterated Nonlocal Means. The iterated nonlocal means (INM) proposed by Brox and Cremers [5] is the most related work to ours. There are several major differences nevertheless. First, we aim at scale-aware smoothing while the method of [5] is for texture preserving during noise removal. Second, algorithmically we use iterations to recover blurred edges, while INM adopts fixed point iterations for optimizing a global function. Third, initialization and weight definition are set differently in these two methods.

Fig. 2. Illustration of scales. As the Gaussian kernel gets larger, more and more structures disappear.

Texture Smoothing. Texture is one type of small-scale oscillations locally. The specialty is on its repeated identical or similar patterns. Subr et al. [25] smoothed texture by averaging two manifolds generated from local minimum and maximum. Xu et al. [30] optimized a global function with relative total variation (RTV) regularization. RTV protects structural edges. This method needs to solve a linear system.

Karacan et al. [14] adopted a weighted-average strategy with the covariance of patch features. It leverages the repetition property of texture and is also time-consuming for pixel affinity computation. Recently, Bao et al. [4] combined bilateral weight with a tree weight defined on a minimum spanning tree. Su et al. [24] combined low-pass filter, edge-preserving filter and L_0 edge correction to achieve the similar goal.

These texture smoothing methods basically make use of the texture repetition property. They are different by nature from the *scale-aware filters* defined in this paper. Our goal is to separate out details, even without repetitive patterns. Only the scale metric is used in our method.

3   Problem Definition and Analysis

We first define the structure scale as *the smallest Gaussian standard deviation σ_s* such that when this σ_s deviation Gaussian is applied to an image, corresponding structure disappears. We denote the convolution process with the input image I and Gaussian $g_v(x, y)$ of variance $v = \sigma_s^2$ as

$$L_v = g_v * I, \tag{1}$$

where $g_v(x, y) = \frac{1}{\sqrt{2\pi v}} \exp(-\frac{x^2+y^2}{2v})$ and $*$ denotes convolution. L_v is the result at scale v. In scale-space theory [17], v is referred to as the *scale parameter*. When the image structure scale is smaller than $\sqrt{v}$ (i.e., σ_s), it will be completely removed in L_v, as claimed in [17]. An illustration is given in Fig. 2. When applying Gaussians with varying σ_s to the image, structures are suppressed differently according to their sizes.

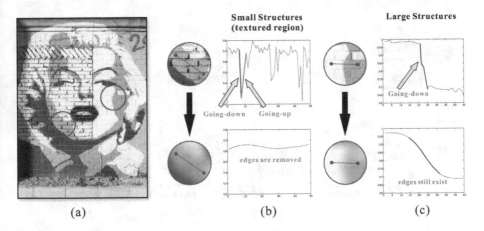

Fig. 3. Comparison of small- and large-structure results after Gaussian filtering. (a) Input image. (b)-(c) 1D signals of pixel values in two lines. The upper signals are the input and the lower ones are results of Gaussian filtering.

Note this definition of scales may not correspond to the actual size or radius of a pattern because the latter is hard to measure given the complexity of image structures. But it tells the relative information. If a structure gets larger, its scale according to our definition must increase, and vice versa.

Now that Gaussian filter sizes determine structure scales, is it possible to directly use Gaussian for scale-aware filtering? The answer is obviously negative because Gaussian filter blurs all edges no matter they are strong or weak. In what follows, we propose a new framework based on this scale definition to retain a level of structures according to their original appearance.

3.1 Our Observation

Gaussian filtering produces blurred images. We analyze result difference on small and large structures. On the one hand, edges of structures with scales below the smoothing scale are completely removed according to the Gaussian average mechanism. On the other hand, large-scale structures are blurred instead of eliminated. To understand the effects, we use the example in Fig. 3. The close-ups in (b) are the 1D signals in a textured region, which originally contain many fast changes with edges going upwards and downwards. When applying Gaussian filter, average of the edges removes nearly all texture patterns. For the large-scale intensity variation shown in Fig. 3(c), Gaussian filter only blurs it and the edge can still be found.

This observation corresponds to an intriguing fact – that is, when edges of small structures are removed by Gaussian filtering, visually there is no clue to manifest they ever exist in the input by only inspecting the result. Contrarily, by watching blurred large-scale structures that are filtered in the same way, one can still be aware of their existence without referring to the input image.

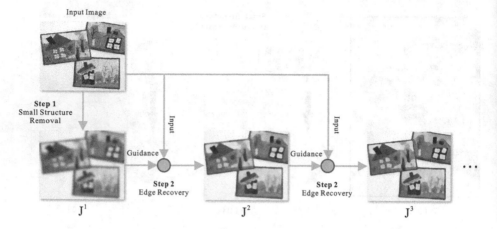

Fig. 4. Flow chart of our method. It contains two steps respectively for small structure removal (Section 4.1) and edge recovery (Section 4.2). Step 2 is an iterative process. The final result is obtained in 3–5 iterations.

We note this finding is the key to developing the rolling-guidance filter scheme. It enlists the power of distinguishing between structures in terms of scales without needing to know the exact form (or model) of texture, details, or noise.

4   Our Method

Our method is composed of two main steps, i.e., small structure removal and edge recovery. We explain them in what follows along with a general and simple modification of our rolling guidance framework in Section 4.3. We also discuss the difference between our work and similar techniques in Section 4.4 and show its variants in Section 4.5. Fig. 4 illustrates the work flow.

4.1   Small Structure Removal

The first step is to remove small structures. As aforementioned, Gaussian filter is related to our structure scale determination. We express this operator in a weighted average form, which takes the input image I and outputs image G. Letting p and q index pixel coordinates in the image and σ_s denote the standard deviation, we write the filter as

$$G(p) = \frac{1}{K_p} \sum_{q \in N(p)} \exp\left(- \frac{||p-q||^2}{2\sigma_s^2} \right) I(q), \tag{2}$$

where $K_p = \sum_{q \in N(p)} \exp(-\frac{||p-q||^2}{2\sigma_s^2})$ is for normalization and $N(p)$ is the set of neighboring pixels of p. This filter completely removes structures whose scale is smaller than σ_s as claimed in the scale space theory. It is implemented efficiently by separating kernels in perpendicular directions. Approximation by box filter is also feasible.

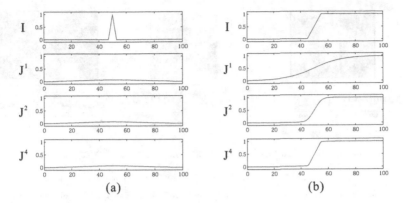

Fig. 5. 1D signal examples and their results in rolling guidance. (a) One small structure. (b) One edge of a large structure.

4.2 Edge Recovery

The iterative edge recovery step forms the major contribution in our method. In this process, an image J is iteratively updated. We denote J^{t+1} as the result in the t-th iteration. Initially, J^1 is set as G in Eq. (2), which is the output of Gaussian filtering. The value of J^{t+1} in the t-th iteration is obtained in a joint bilateral filtering form given the input I and the value in previous iteration J^t:

$$J^{t+1}(p) = \frac{1}{K_p} \sum_{q \in N(p)} \exp\left(-\frac{\|p-q\|^2}{2\sigma_s^2} - \frac{\|J^t(p) - J^t(q)\|^2}{2\sigma_r^2}\right) I(q), \qquad (3)$$

where

$$K_p = \sum_{q \in N(p)} \exp\left(-\frac{\|p-q\|^2}{2\sigma_s^2} - \frac{\|J^t(p) - J^t(q)\|^2}{2\sigma_r^2}\right)$$

for normalization. I is the same input image used in Eq. (2). σ_s and σ_r control the spatial and range weights respectively.

This expression can be understood as a filter that smoothes the input I guided by the structure of J^t. This process is different by nature from how previous methods employ joint bilateral filter – we iteratively change the guidance image in passes. It yields illuminating effects, explained below. We name this iterative operation *rolling guidance*.

To demonstrate how it works, we show simple 1D examples in Fig. 5 where one small structure and one edge of a large structure are presented. The four rows show inputs and J^t obtained by rolling guidance respectively. Since this process uses J^t to compute the affinity between pixels, it makes resulting structures similar to J^t. Put differently, it yields structure transform from J to I.

Small Structure. In the first example (Fig. 5(a)), since the edges of the small structure are completely removed in J^1 by Gaussian filter, J^1 is mostly flat.

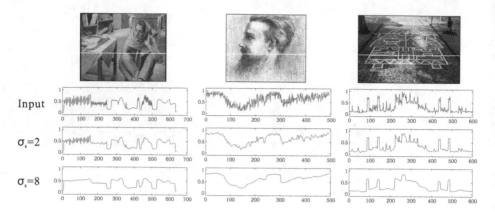

Fig. 6. 1D examples from real images. The curves are inputs and filtering results under different σ_s. Large-scale edges and changes are preserved well.

In Eq. (3), the term $\|J^t(p) - J^t(q)\|$ is almost zero for any (p, q) pairs, which makes the joint bilateral filter behave like a Gaussian filter due to the inoperative range weight. Therefore, the output J^2 remains flat. All following iterations cannot add the detail back.

Large Structure. In the second example (Fig. 5(b)), we show how rolling guidance processes a large scale edge. In the first iteration, J^1 is blurred and I is sharp. Since each-iteration process takes weighted average on I, result J^2 is smoother than, or at most with similar sharpness as I. It is also guaranteed to be sharper than J^1 because J^2 is smoothed weaker than J^1 due to the involvement of range weights. Notice that the range weight is no longer inoperative as in the small structure case. Now the order of smoothness can be expressed as

$$I \leq J^2 < J^1.$$

In following iterations, following the same analysis, sharpness of J^{t+1} is always between I and J^t since more range difference is involved in computing the weight and less averaging is preformed around the edge. It is conclusive that the sharpness is restored gradually and eventually goes back to original degree in the input, as shown in the bottom of Fig. 5(b).

Fig. 5 sheds light on understanding the new property of our scale-aware filter. It not only optimally preserves large scale edges, but also smoothes texture and other details. There is no need in prior to know how the structures are formed. As long as they are kept, even partially, after Gaussian smoothing, our method can recover the large-scale shape with nice edge preserving. Whether an edge is preserved or not is not dependent of its magnitude, marking the inherent difference to other edge-preserving filters.

By changing the value of σ_s, this framework can be used to remove structures in different scales. Fig. 6 shows the 1D examples from real images. Structures of

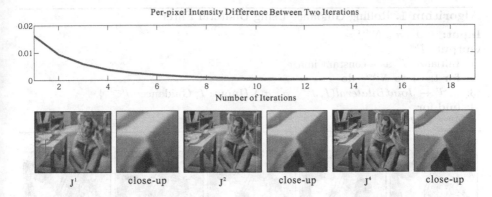

Fig. 7. Plot of difference between input and output images in iterations. The difference of two successive iterations reduces monotonically and the result is guaranteed not an all-constant image. We use $\sigma_s = 4$ and $\sigma_r = 0.1$ for this example. Please view them in the original resolutions to compare all details.

different scales are removed gradually while faithfully preserving necessary edges when σ_s grows.

Convergence. Another fascinating property is that the rolling guidance iterations converge rapidly. We plot difference between J^t and J^{t+1} from all iterations in Fig. 7. For most average-based filters, such as Gaussian filter, bilateral filter [26], domain-transform filter [11], and guided filter [13], if they are performed repeatedly, the result of any image is eventually a constant-value one as all pixels are averaged to the same intensity. Unlike these filters, the rolling guidance procedure converges to a meaningful image faithful to the input no matter how many iterations are performed, which is worth further theoretical study. Empirically, We have tested this filter on thousands of images and failed it on *none* of them. Therefore, it is a filter with very attractive and unique features.

4.3 Combination of the Two Steps

In our framework, steps described in Sections 4.1 and 4.2 can be combined into one, by starting rolling guidance simply from a constant-value image. In Eq. (3), if we set all values in J^t to a constant C, i.e., $\forall p, J^t(p) = C$, it updates to

$$J^{t+1}(p) = \frac{1}{K_p} \sum_{q \in N(p)} \exp\left(-\frac{\|p - q\|^2}{2\sigma_s^2}\right) I(q). \tag{4}$$

The form in Eq. (4) is exactly the same as Eq. (2). Therefore, we save one step by starting rolling guidance from J^0, where $\forall p, J^0(p) = C$. Correspondingly, the step to evolve from J^0 to J^1 is exactly the one explained in Section 4.1; later iterations correspond to the step in Section 4.2. This modification makes our algorithm even more general and easier to understand. Algorithm 1 depicts our final scale-aware filter construction.

Algorithm 1. Rolling Guidance Using Bilateral Filter

Input: I, σ_s, σ_r, N^{iter}
Output: I^{new}
1: Initialize J^0 as a constant image
2: **for** t:= 1 **to** N^{iter} **do**
3:     $J^t \leftarrow JointBilateral(I, J^{t-1}, \sigma_s, \sigma_r)$ {Input: I; Guidance: J^{t-1} }
4: **end for**
5: $I^{\text{new}} \leftarrow J^{N^{\text{iter}}}$

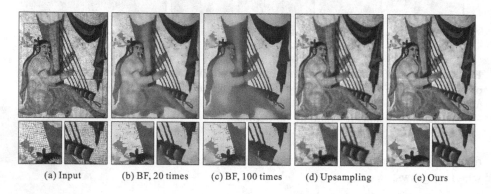

(a) Input   (b) BF, 20 times   (c) BF, 100 times   (d) Upsampling   (e) Ours

Fig. 8. Comparison with other techniques. (a) Input image. (b) Successively performing bilateral filter for 20 times with $\sigma_s = 3$ and $\sigma_r = 0.1$. (c) Successively performing bilateral filter for 100 times with the same parameters. (d) Joint bilateral upsampling. Downsampling is with Gaussian filter with $\sigma_s = 3$ and upsampling is with $\sigma_s = 3$ and $\sigma_r = 0.1$. (e) Our result with the same parameters in 5 iterations.

4.4   Comparison with other Techniques

In this section, we compare our method with other related ones and clarify their inherent difference.

Successively Performed Bilateral Filtering. When successively applying bilateral filtering or other average-based edge-aware filters, a general expression becomes

$$J^0 = I, \quad J^{t+1} = f(J^t), \tag{5}$$

where J^0 is the initial image, J^t is the result in the t-th iteration, and $f(\cdot)$ is the filter. This process has two fundamental differences to ours.

First, successively performing edge-aware filters does not remove small-scale structures. Instead, they could over-smooth large-scale ones. One example is shown in Fig. 8(b)-(c). Second, average-based filters do not converge as ours as discussed above. A final blurred image is obviously not what we want in scale-aware filtering.

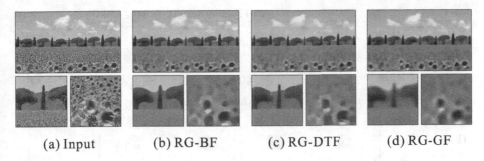

| (a) Input | (b) RG-BF | (c) RG-DTF | (d) RG-GF |

Fig. 9. Results when setting the rolling guidance as bilateral filter (b), domain-transform filter (c), and guided filter (d). The parameters are as follows. (b) ($\sigma_s = 5, \sigma_r = 0.1$); ($\sigma_s = 2.8, \sigma_r = 0.1$); ($\sigma_s = 4, \sigma_r = 0.1$). (c) ($\sigma_s = 10, \sigma_r = 0.1$); ($\sigma_s = 6, \sigma_r = 0.1$); ($\sigma_s = 6, \sigma_r = 0.1$). (d) ($r = 6, \epsilon = 0.003$); ($r = 3, \epsilon = 0.0012$); ($r = 3, \epsilon = 0.0036$).

Joint Bilateral Upsampling. Similarly denoting input image as I and output as J, this technique can be expressed as

$$J(p) = \frac{1}{K_p} \sum_{q \in N(p)} \exp\left(-\frac{||p - q||^2}{2\sigma_s^2} - \frac{||I(p) - I(q)||^2}{2\sigma_r^2}\right) M(q_\downarrow), \qquad (6)$$

where M is a downsampled image and $p_\downarrow$ is the corresponding coordinate of p in M. If we set M as a downsampled input image $I_\downarrow$, the formulation changes to

$$J(p) = \frac{1}{K_p} \sum_{q \in N(p)} \exp\left(-\frac{||p - q||^2}{2\sigma_s^2} - \frac{||I(p) - I(q)||^2}{2\sigma_r^2}\right) I_\downarrow(q_\downarrow), \qquad (7)$$

which seems similar to our algorithm.

In fact, the difference between these processes can be understood in three major aspects. (1) Joint bilateral upsampling uses the clear image as guidance. Contrarily, our method uses a blurry image to guide filtering. (2) Joint bilateral upsampling does not remove small-scale structures because the guidance image already contains many of them, as illustrated in Fig. 8(d). (3) It is not an iterative process. If conducted successively, joint bilateral upsampling results in a very blurry image like the case of bilateral filter.

4.5   Extensible Rolling Guidance Design

Our rolling guidance is a general framework with the freedom to use almost all types of joint filters. Our method allows for iteratively replacing the guidance image with the filtering result in previous pass. It is thus not restricted to joint bilateral filter. Average-based joint filters, such as domain-transform [11], guided filter [13], and recursive bilateral filter [32], all can be employed in our framework.

In Fig. 9, we compare results generated using bilateral filter, domain-transform filter, and guided filter as the rolling guidance. They generate similar scale-aware

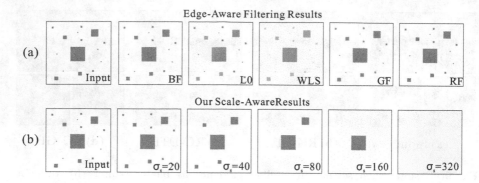

Fig. 10. (a) Edge-aware filtering results on the image composed of squares in different sizes. We apply bilateral filter [26] ($\sigma_s = 40$, $\sigma_r = 0.1$), L_0 filter [29] ($\lambda = 1000$), WLS filter [9] ($\lambda = 5$, $\alpha = 1.2$), guided filter [13] ($\epsilon = 0.01$, $r = 20$), and recursive filter [11] ($\sigma_s = 10$, $\sigma_r = 0.1$). (b) Our results under different σ_s. σ_r is set to 0.1. 4 iterations are used. The recursive filter [11] is used in rolling guidance.

results although, when applying alone, they are edge-preserving. Difference can be observed as well among the results. In particular, applying bilateral filter guidance creates smoothly curved edges, as shown in Fig. 9(b). Domain-transform filter guidance, on the contrary, generates many horizontal and vertical edges as shown in (c), since it performs filtering by scanning the image in these directions. Finally, guided filter as guidance produces smoother results as shown in (d). It is in accordance with the explanation provided in the original paper [13].

The generality of this rolling guidance framework makes it extensible in many ways to suit various applications and scenarios. It also provides loads of possibilities for further approximation and acceleration when replacing the bilateral filter by others.

5   Experiments

We conduct experiments to more extensively evaluate this filter. Besides Fig. 6, we show another interesting example in Fig. 10 to exhibit the unique property of rolling guidance filter. The input image contains a few square patterns in different scales. Results of edge-aware filters are shown in (a). They do not remove even the smallest scale square because all edges are with high contrast. Our results are shown in (b) using different σ_s. Squares are progressively removed according to their scales in an ascending order. More results of our scale-aware filter on natural images are shown in Fig. 11.

Our experiments are conducted on a PC with an Intel i7 3.4GHz CPU and 8GB memory. Only a single thread is used without involving any SIMD instructions. Since acceleration of edge-aware filtering was well studied, many tools are available [8,19,28,22,33,32,2,1,11,12,13]. They can be used directly in our framework to accelerate rolling guidance. Our implementation is easy with only several

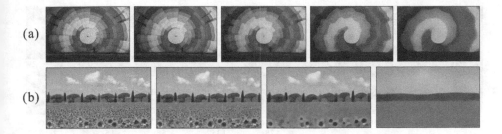

Fig. 11. Scale-aware filtering results on natural images

Table 1. Running time comparison. "s/Mp" stands for "seconds per mega-pixel". Our method uses 4 iterations. The first iteration uses fast Gaussian filter.

Algorithms	Grayscale Image (s/Mp)	Color Image (s/Mp)
Local Extrema [25]	95	–
RTV [30]	14	35
Zhang et al. [34]	5	16
Covariance M2 [14]	198	614
Ours with BF [33]	0.2	–
Ours with BF [1]	–	2
Ours with GF [13]	0.12	0.8
Ours with DTF [11]	**0.05**	0.15

lines of code based on Algorithm 1. In Table 1, we tabulate running time of implementing our method using different rolling guidance options (Section 4.5). It also lists time of running related texture smoothing methods. Our implementation is 10-100 times faster than the previous fastest method [34]. The implementation with DTF [11] achieves realtime performance even for one-megapixel images.

Applications. Due to the useful scale-aware property and fast speed, our filter profits a variety of applications, including detail enhancement, tone-mapping, denoising, edge extraction, de-halftoning, JPEG artifact removal, multi-scale structure decomposition, segmentation, saliency detection, optical flow, and stereo matching.

We show results of texture smoothing and virtual contour restoration in this section. More applications can be found on our project website. Texture on the object surface is generally of small scale structures. Our algorithm can painlessly remove them in different levels. Meanwhile, global color variation and main edges can be preserved. Our implementation is much faster than all other texture smoothing tools. Results and comparisons are provided in Fig. 12.

In natural images, not all contrast that human perceive can be expressed in form of large gradients. Virtual edges are thus common and correspond to large-scale image information possibly useful for segmentation. Our algorithm can restore these originally nonexistent edges reflecting large scale contrast, as shown in Fig. 13.

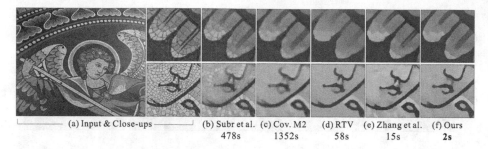

(a) Input & Close-ups   (b) Subr et al.   (c) Cov. M2   (d) RTV   (e) Zhang et al.   (f) Ours
478s   1352s   58s   15s   **2s**

Fig. 12. Texture smoothing results and close-ups. (b)-(e) are results of [25], [14], [30], and [34] respectively. Parameters are (b) $k = 5$, (c) $\sigma = 0.3$, $k = 9$, (d) $\lambda = 0.015$, $\sigma = 5$, (e) $r = 3$, $\sigma_r = 0.3$, 10 iterations, (f) $\sigma_s = 5$, $\sigma_r = 0.1$.

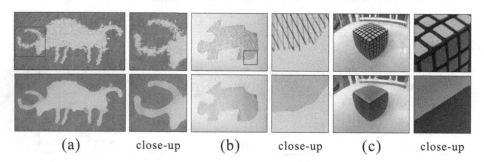

(a)   close-up   (b)   close-up   (c)   close-up

Fig. 13. Virtual contour restoration. Large contrast naturally forms region boundaries in human perception. Our filter can simulate this process.

6 Concluding Remarks

We have presented a new type of filter for scale-aware operations. It is the first in its kind to remove small-scale structures while preserving other content, parallel in terms of importance to previous edge-preserving filters. This framework is simple to implement, greatly extensible to accommodate various tools for rolling guidance, and yields decent performance. Our future work will be to apply it to more applications.

Acknowledgements. The work described in this paper was supported by a grant from the Research Grants Council of the Hong Kong Special Administrative Region (Project No. 412911).

References

1. Adams, A., Baek, J., Davis, M.A.: Fast high-dimensional filtering using the permutohedral lattice. Comput. Graph. Forum 29(2), 753–762 (2010)
2. Adams, A., Gelfand, N., Dolson, J., Levoy, M.: Gaussian kd-trees for fast high-dimensional filtering. ACM Transactions on Graphics (TOG) 28(3), 21 (2009)

3. Arbelaez, P., Maire, M., Fowlkes, C., Malik, J.: Contour detection and hierarchical image segmentation. IEEE Transactions on Pattern Analysis and Machine Intelligence 33(5), 898–916 (2011)
4. Bao, L., Song, Y., Yang, Q., Yuan, H., Wang, G.: Tree filtering: Efficient structure-preserving smoothing with a minimum spanning tree. IEEE Transactions on Image Processing 23(2), 555–569 (2014)
5. Brox, T., Cremers, D.: Iterated nonlocal means for texture restoration. In: Sgallari, F., Murli, A., Paragios, N. (eds.) SSVM 2007. LNCS, vol. 4485, pp. 13–24. Springer, Heidelberg (2007)
6. Chen, J., Paris, S., Durand, F.: Real-time edge-aware image processing with the bilateral grid. ACM Trans. Graph. 26(3), 103 (2007)
7. Criminisi, A., Sharp, T., Rother, C., Perez, P.: Geodesic image and video editing. ACM Trans. Graph. 29(5), 134 (2010)
8. Durand, F., Dorsey, J.: Fast bilateral filtering for the display of high-dynamic-range images. ACM Transactions on Graphics (TOG) 21(3), 257–266 (2002)
9. Farbman, Z., Fattal, R., Lischinski, D., Szeliski, R.: Edge-preserving decompositions for multi-scale tone and detail manipulation. ACM Trans. Graph. 27(3) (2008)
10. Felzenszwalb, P.F., Girshick, R.B., McAllester, D., Ramanan, D.: Object detection with discriminatively trained part-based models. IEEE Transactions on Pattern Analysis and Machine Intelligence 32(9), 1627–1645 (2010)
11. Gastal, E.S., Oliveira, M.M.: Domain transform for edge-aware image and video processing. ACM Transactions on Graphics (TOG) 30(4), 69 (2011)
12. Gastal, E.S., Oliveira, M.M.: Adaptive manifolds for real-time high-dimensional filtering. ACM Transactions on Graphics (TOG) 31(4), 33 (2012)
13. He, K., Sun, J., Tang, X.: Guided image filtering. In: Daniilidis, K., Maragos, P., Paragios, N. (eds.) ECCV 2010, Part I. LNCS, vol. 6311, pp. 1–14. Springer, Heidelberg (2010)
14. Karacan, L., Erdem, E., Erdem, A.: Structure-preserving image smoothing via region covariances. ACM Transactions on Graphics (TOG) 32(6), 176 (2013)
15. Kass, M., Solomon, J.: Smoothed local histogram filters. ACM Transactions on Graphics (TOG) 29(4), 100 (2010)
16. Kopf, J., Cohen, M.F., Lischinski, D., Uyttendaele, M.: Joint bilateral upsampling. ACM Trans. Graph. 26(3), 96 (2007)
17. Lindeberg, T.: Scale-space theory: A basic tool for analyzing structures at different scales. Journal of Applied Statistics 21(1-2), 225–270 (1994)
18. Ma, Z., He, K., Wei, Y., Sun, J., Wu, E.: Constant time weighted median filtering for stereo matching and beyond. In: IEEE ICCV (2013)
19. Paris, S., Durand, F.: A fast approximation of the bilateral filter using a signal processing approach. In: Leonardis, A., Bischof, H., Pinz, A. (eds.) ECCV 2006. LNCS, vol. 3954, pp. 568–580. Springer, Heidelberg (2006)
20. Perona, P., Malik, J.: Scale-space and edge detection using anisotropic diffusion. IEEE Transactions on Pattern Analysis and Machine Intelligence 12(7), 629–639 (1990)
21. Petschnigg, G., Szeliski, R., Agrawala, M., Cohen, M., Hoppe, H., Toyama, K.: Digital photography with flash and no-flash image pairs. ACM Transactions on Graphics (TOG) 23(3), 664–672 (2004)
22. Porikli, F.: Constant time o (1) bilateral filtering. In: IEEE Conference on Computer Vision and Pattern Recognition (CVPR), pp. 1–8 (2008)
23. Rudin, L.I., Osher, S., Fatemi, E.: Nonlinear total variation based noise removal algorithms. Physica D: Nonlinear Phenomena 60(1), 259–268 (1992)

24. Su, Z., Luo, X., Deng, Z., Liang, Y., Ji, Z.: Edge-preserving texture suppression filter based on joint filtering schemes. IEEE Transactions on Multimedia 15(3), 535–548 (2013)
25. Subr, K., Soler, C., Durand, F.: Edge-preserving multiscale image decomposition based on local extrema. ACM Transactions on Graphics (TOG) 28(5), 147 (2009)
26. Tomasi, C., Manduchi, R.: Bilateral filtering for gray and color images. In: International Conference on Computer Vision (ICCV), pp. 839–846. IEEE (1998)
27. van de Weijer, J., Van den Boomgaard, R.: Local mode filtering. In: IEEE Conference on Computer Vision and Pattern Recognition (CVPR), vol. 2, pp. II–428 (2001)
28. Weiss, B.: Fast median and bilateral filtering. ACM Trans. Graph. 25(3), 519–526 (2006)
29. Xu, L., Lu, C., Xu, Y., Jia, J.: Image smoothing via l 0 gradient minimization. ACM Transactions on Graphics (TOG) 30(6), 174 (2011)
30. Xu, L., Yan, Q., Xia, Y., Jia, J.: Structure extraction from texture via relative total variation. ACM Transactions on Graphics (TOG) 31(6), 139 (2012)
31. Yan, Q., Xu, L., Shi, J., Jia, J.: Hierarchical saliency detection. In: IEEE Conference on Computer Vision and Pattern Recognition (CVPR), pp. 1155–1162 (2013)
32. Yang, Q.: Recursive bilateral filtering. In: Fitzgibbon, A., Lazebnik, S., Perona, P., Sato, Y., Schmid, C. (eds.) ECCV 2012, Part I. LNCS, vol. 7572, pp. 399–413. Springer, Heidelberg (2012)
33. Yang, Q., Tan, K.H., Ahuja, N.: Real-time o(1) bilateral filtering. In: IEEE Conference on Computer Vision and Pattern Recognition (CVPR), pp. 557–564 (2009)
34. Zhang, Q., Xu, L., Jia, J.: 100+ times faster weighted median filter. In: IEEE Conference on Computer Vision and Pattern Recognition, CVPR (2014)

Physically Grounded Spatio-temporal Object Affordances

Hema S. Koppula and Ashutosh Saxena

Department of Computer Science, Cornell University, USA
{hema,asaxena}@cs.cornell.edu

Abstract. Objects in human environments support various functionalities which govern how people interact with their environments in order to perform tasks. In this work, we discuss how to represent and learn a functional understanding of an environment in terms of object affordances. Such an understanding is useful for many applications such as activity detection and assistive robotics. Starting with a semantic notion of affordances, we present a generative model that takes a given environment and human intention into account, and *grounds* the affordances in the form of spatial locations on the object and temporal trajectories in the 3D environment. The probabilistic model also allows uncertainties and variations in the grounded affordances. We apply our approach on RGB-D videos from Cornell Activity Dataset, where we first show that we can successfully ground the affordances, and we then show that learning such affordances improves performance in the labeling tasks.

Keywords: Object Affordances, 3D Object Models, Functional Representation of Environment, Generative Graphical Model, Trajectory Modeling, Human Activity Detection, RGBD Videos.

1 Introduction

Functional understanding of an environment through object affordances is important for many applications in computer vision. For example, reasoning about the interactions with objects helps in activity detection [28,43,18], understanding the spatial and structural relationships between objects improves object detection [16] and retrieval [8], and understanding what actions are supported by the objects in an environment is essential for many robotic applications [17,30]. Our goal is to learn a rich functional representation of the environment in terms of object affordances from RGB-D videos of people interacting with their surrounding environment.

The definition of 'affordance' had been hotly debated first in philosophy [9,33,32], and then in psychology (e.g., [4]). While the intuitions behind all these debates were similar, the interpretations vary from purely symbolic and abstract [9] to more physically-grounded meanings [32]. Recent works in computer vision have revisited these aspects. For example, the symbolic notion of affordances can be interpreted as an object attribute labeling problem [25,36,7,3,42], and more

D. Fleet et al. (Eds.): ECCV 2014, Part III, LNCS 8691, pp. 831–847, 2014.

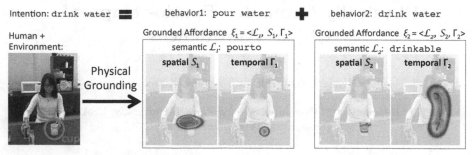

Fig. 1. Grounded affordance for an object cup. Given an intention I of a human H in an environment E, our approach outputs the sequence of physically-grounded affordances ξ_k for the objects in the scene. In this figure, we show the affordance of a cup for the intention of **drinking water**. The grounded affordances comprise semantic affordances $\mathcal{L}_k$, 3D spatial affordances S_k and 3D temporal trajectories Γ_k. Due to noise and uncertainty in the agent's behavior, several groundings are valid, and therefore our approach outputs a *belief* over the possible groundings. In this figure, the belief is represented by heatmaps for the spatial and temporal affordances.

recently, physical aspects have been explored in [10,12,16], where they model the functionality-based spatial interactions of humans with their environments. For example, Grabner et al. [10] uses the interactions between a sitting human pose and the environment to identify *sittable* regions, Delaitre et al. [5] observed people to extract semantic and geometric affordances for large furniture-like objects, and Jiang, Koppula and Saxena [16] uses the spatial affordances of objects with respect to possible human poses for the task of labeling objects. These works only consider the spatial aspect of static affordances.

In contrast, affordances are often dynamic, have a temporal motion aspect, and they vary depending on the environment and the intention of the human. Consider the cup in Fig. 1, where in order to **drink water** the affordance is **pour-to** for it to receive water, and then it is **drinkable** for transferring water into the human's mouth. The actual 3D coordinates of the interactions with the object and the object's 3D trajectory would vary depending on the geometry of the environment. Furthermore, if the intent of the human was to hurt someone, the cup could also be used as a projectile to throw at someone! Capturing these dynamic and temporal aspects of affordances is necessary in many applications. For example, assistive robots need to reason about 'what can be done with objects?' as well as 'how?' for planning their actions [23,22].

In this work, we take a unified view where we focus on grounding the affordances into a given environment for a human intention. As illustrated in Fig. 1, by grounding we mean outputting the semantic affordances, the 3D location of interaction on the object ('spatial affordances'), as well as object's motion trajectory ('temporal affordances'). Multiple groundings are valid because of noise and uncertainty in the agent's behavior. We therefore model this uncertainty using a generative probabilistic model for the semantic, spatial and temporal groundings of the affordances. Our generative model is based on a conditional mixture of density functions, where the density functions are discrete (for semantic affordances), product of Gaussians and von Mises (for spatial affordances), and parameterized Gaussian Processes (for the temporal affordances). We train the parameters of our model from the training data comprising RGB-D videos, and test on hold-out test data.

We present extensive evaluation of our proposed affordance learning framework on RGB-D videos form the Cornell Activity Dataset – where we introduce a new affordance dataset consisting of semantic activities along with spatio-temporal motions for several objects. We show that our generative model can reconstruct these trajectories well. We also show that our approach can improve the affordance and activity detection performance on the CAD-120 dataset [23]. The contributions of this paper are as follows:

- We present a representation for affordances that consist of semantic, 3D spatial and *temporal trajectory* components. Our work thus extends previous works that considered only semantic or spatial affordances.
- Our grounding of affordances into spatial and temporal belief maps is context-dependent on the environment and the intention of the agent.
- Our generative probabilistic approach models the uncertainty and variations in the grounded affordances.
- We contribute a new affordance dataset, on which we show that we can predict grounded affordances well. We also show improvement in the labeling performance on an existing RGB-D activity dataset.

2 Related Work

J.J. Gibson [9] described the concept of affordance as the "Action possibilities in the environment in relation to the action capabilities of an actor". The term *affordances* was later appropriated by D. Norman [33] as the *"perceived action possibilities"*. This makes the concept also depend on the actor's goals, plans, values, beliefs, and past experiences. There are other definitions which narrow down the meaning of affordances, for example, *physical affordances* [32] which are perceived only from the physical structure of objects.

Symbolic Affordances. There have been many attempts in the computer vision and robotics literature to reason about object functionality (e.g., sit-table, drinkable, etc.) instead of object identities (e.g., chairs, mugs, etc.). Most works take a recognition based approach where they first estimate physical attributes/parts and then jointly reasoned about them to come up with an object hypothesis [38]. Some works predict affordance-based or function-based object attributes. For example, [19] consider newspapers and books as *readable* and books and hammers as *hammerable*. Such interpretation was also used in several other works [25,36,7]. These works are the first step for a functional understanding of the scene. Our work, in contrast, is focussed on grounding these symbolic affordances.

Scene Understanding: Geometry, Humans and Objects. Physical aspects of affordances have been recently explored in [10,12,5,16]. For example, interactions between a sitting human pose and the environment are used to identify *sittable* regions [10], semantic and geometric affordances of large objects such as furniture are extracted by observing people [5,12], and spatial affordances of objects with respect to possible human poses are used for placing and labeling objects [17,16]. Another notable work is [11], where they looked at how humans manipulate objects for the purpose of recognizing them. These works use particular interpretations of affordances suited to the specific application. In particular, they consider the spatial aspect of static affordances only. In contrast, we consider temporal affordances and infer a belief over the physically grounded affordances. Koppula and Saxena [22] proposed generation of possible future object trajectories for anticipating future activities, where they represent object trajectories as Bézier curves and estimate the parameters from data. However, the Bézier curves can only model limited types of object trajectories. We build upon these ideas and propose a generative probabilistic model which provides a generic framework for modeling various types of affordances and also show that it performs better than [22] for predicting future object trajectories.

Robotics Planning: Navigation and Manipulation. Most of the work in robotics community has focused on predicting opportunities for interaction with an object either by using visual cues [39,14,2] or through observation of the effects of exploratory behaviors [31,35,13]. For instance, Sun et al. [39] proposed a probabilistic graphical model that leverages visual object categorization for learning affordances and Hermans et al. [14] proposed the use of physical and visual attributes as a mid-level representation for affordance prediction. Aldoma et al. [2] proposed a method to find affordances which depends solely on the objects of interest and their position and orientation in the scene. There is some recent work in interpreting human actions and interaction with objects [26,1,20] in context of learning to perform actions from demonstrations. Lopes et al. [26] use context from objects in terms of possible grasp affordances to focus the attention of their recognition system. This work is specific to robotic grasping task. Affordances (i.e., prediction of the object's reaction to robot's touch) have also been used in planning (e.g., [27,41]). Jain et al. [15] used object affordances for planning user-preferred motion trajectories for mobile manipulators. Misra et al. [29] learned the relation between language and robotic actions. Pandey et al. [34] proposed mightability maps and taskability graphs that capture affordances such as reachability and visibility. However, they manually define affordances in terms of kinematic and dynamic constraints. Recently, Koppula et al. [23,21] show that human-actor based affordances are essential for robots working in human spaces in order for them to interact with objects in a human-desirable way. They applied it to look-ahead reactive planning for robots. These works in robotics planning are complementary to ours.

3 Affordance Representation and Grounding

Previous formalizations of affordance in literature (e.g., [37]) include defining relation instances of the form $\mathcal{A} = \langle \text{effect}, (\text{object}, \text{behavior}) \rangle$, which state that there exists a potential to generate a certain *effect* by applying the *behavior* on an *object*. Here, the *object* refers to the state of the environment as perceived by an agent. For example, the lift-ability affordance implies that a *lift behavior* applied to an *object*, say a stone, results in the *lifted effect*, i.e., the stone will be perceived as elevated compared to its previous position. Here, one needs to provide a physical-grounding to each of these elements ⟨effect, ⟨object, behavior⟩⟩. We define one such physical-grounding of these elements for a given agent, intention and the environment.

For physically grounding an affordance we consider the following context: 1) the agent H, which takes into account the physical capability of agent to perform a behavior, for example, a *sittable* object might be too small for the person to perform the *sit* behavior, 2) the intention I of the agent, which determines which affordance of the object is of relevance, for example, the agent wants to *sit* in a chair vs *move* a chair, 3) the environment E, which takes into account the physical constraints to perform a behavior in a particular situation, for example, an object might not be *liftable* if there is another object blocking it from above. This gives us a generic grounded representation ξ of the affordances $\mathcal{A}$ as:

$$\mathcal{G}(\mathcal{A}|H, E, I) = \xi$$
$$\mathcal{G}(\langle \text{effect}, \langle \text{object}, \text{behavior} \rangle \rangle | H, E, I) = \langle \mathcal{L}, \mathcal{S}, \Gamma \rangle \tag{1}$$

where the symbols denote the following:
  $\mathcal{L}$ semantic affordance label, e.g., *pourable*, etc.
  $\mathcal{S}$ spatial distribution of the affordance
  Γ motion trajectory, 6-dof location/orientation over time

For example, when an object has the *liftable* affordance, the physical grounding of the behavior and its effect are specified by the spatial distribution $\mathcal{S}$ on the object indicating where to hold the object and a vertical motion trajectory Γ for lifting the object, and for the *sittable* affordance, the behavior and its effect are specified by the spatial distribution over the objects indicating where a person can sit on it and a stationary trajectory for the object.

Note that for more complex intentions such as *drinking coffee*, an object can have a sequence of affordances, for example, a cup is first *reachable*, then *movable* and *drinkable*, and finally *placeable*. We denote the sequence with the corresponding symbols in bold $\mathcal{A}$, and denote the kth element in the sequence with a subscripted symbol $\mathcal{A}_k$.

4 Probabilistic Model for Physically Grounding the Affordances

Our goal is to infer the grounding $\xi = \langle \mathcal{L}, \mathcal{S}, \Gamma \rangle$, given the context (H, E, I). In order to model the variations in the grounding, we formulate the grounding inference problem as a probabilistic model $P(\xi|H, E, I)$, where the probability indicates how likely a particular grounding ξ is. During inference time (e.g., for use in some application), one can use the full belief or compute the most likely grounding as: $\xi^* = \arg\max_\xi P(\xi|H, E, I)$.

In detail, we assume the following: (i) the environment, not including the object of interest and the human, is static; and (ii) there is only one active affordance at a given instant of time for a given object. Each intention can have multiple sequential sub-goals and hence the object can have multiple active affordances in the given sequence of frames.

The relationship between the components of the grounded affordance ξ can be viewed as a graphical model shown in Fig. 2. The kth semantic affordance $\mathcal{L}_k$ depends on human pose H, the environment E and parameters Θ_L, for a given intention I. The spatial affordance $\mathcal{S}_k$ depends on the human pose H_k, the environment E_k, the active semantic affordance $\mathcal{L}_k$ and parameters Θ_S. The parameters for the affordance motion trajectory Γ_k are denoted by θ_Γ and depend on the semantic affordance $\mathcal{L}_k$ as well as the human pose H_k and the environment E_k, as shown by the directed edges. Following the independencies in the graphical model, the joint distribution of all the variables can be written as:

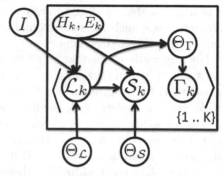

Fig. 2. Our graphical model: For a given intention I, human H and environment E, our model generates the grounded affordance $\langle \mathcal{L}, \mathcal{S}, \Gamma \rangle$. Θ's are the parameters and $k = 1, \ldots, K$ indicates the affordance sequence.

$$P(\langle \mathcal{L}, \mathcal{S}, \Gamma \rangle, \Theta_\Gamma | I, H, E, \Theta_L, \Theta_S) = \prod_{k=1}^{K} \underbrace{P(\mathcal{L}_k | I, H_k, E_k, \Theta_L)}_{\text{Semantic Affordance}}$$

$$\underbrace{P(\mathcal{S}_k | \mathcal{L}_k, H_k, E_k, \Theta_S)}_{\text{Spatial Affordance}} \underbrace{P(\Gamma_k | \Theta_\Gamma) P(\Theta_\Gamma | \mathcal{L}_k, H_k, E_k)}_{\text{Temporal Affordance}} \quad (2)$$

We discretize the time to align with frames of the video and consider the set of time-steps (video frames) corresponding to one intention as one instance of data. Therefore, at each time-step we have the 3D coordinates corresponding to the human, objects and the environment from the video frames. We now describe the conditional distributions and their parameters in more detail.

Semantic Affordance. Each semantic affordance variable $\mathcal{L}_k$ can take a value from $\{1..M\}$, where M is the total number of class labels. We model the probability that the object has an active affordance $l \in \{1..M\}$ given the observations, environment E_k, human poses H_k and the intention I, as a discrete distribution generated from the training data based on the object's current position with respect to the human in the scene (e.g., in contact with hand). For example, if the human is holding the object and intention is to drink water, then the affordances *drinkable* and *pour-to* have equal probability, with all others being 0.

Spatial Affordance. We model the spatial affordance as a potential function which gives high scores to the contact points for the given semantic affordance label. The relative location and orientation of these contact points with respect to the object depends on the activity as well as the human pose. For example, these contact points are usually on the top of the object, say a box, for opening it compared to the sides of the box when moving it (see Fig. 3). Also, which sides of

For the object cereal-box (left), Right-top shows the spatial affordance for openable *and Right-bottom for* movable.

For the object microwave (left), Right-top shows the spatial affordance for openable *and Right-bottom for* movable.

Fig. 3. Learned Spatial Affordance Distributions. For the objects in an environment, we show the spatial distribution heat map (red indicates high probability).

the box would be held depends on the relative orientation of the box with respect to the human. Therefore, for the scoring function to capture these properties we consider the following potentials – distance potentials for modeling the distance between the contact points and the skeleton joints, normalized distance and height of contact points with respect to the object, and angular potentials for modeling the orientation of the contact points with respect to the object and human. The general form of this distribution for a semantic affordance label l given the observations is $P(S_k | \cdots) = \prod_i \psi_{dist_i} \prod_j \psi_{ori_j}$, where ψ_{dist_i} is the ith distance potential and ψ_{ori_j} is the jth relative angular potential. We model each distance potential with a Gaussian distribution and each relative angular potential with a von Mises distribution.

We find the parameters of the affordance potential functions from the training data using maximum likelihood estimation. Since the potential function is a product of the various components, the parameters of each distribution can be estimated separately. In detail, the mean and variance of the Gaussian distribution have closed form solutions, and we numerically estimate the mean and concentration parameter of the von Mises distribution.

Temporal Affordance. We model the object motion trajectory Γ_k as a Gaussian Process with mean trajectory $\mu(\cdot)$ and covariance function $\Sigma(\cdot, \cdot)$ as shown in Eq. (3). The mean trajectory $\mu(\cdot)$, defines the general shape of the trajectory, for example, a circular trajectory for the *stirrer* affordance. The deviation from the mean trajectory is modeled by the covariance function $\Sigma(\cdot, \cdot)$. The mean and covariance functions are parametrized by Θ_Γ.

$$P(\Gamma_k | \Theta_\Gamma) \sim \mathcal{GP}(\mu(\cdot; \Theta_\Gamma), \Sigma(\cdot, \cdot; \Theta_\Gamma)) \qquad (3)$$

The form of the parametrization and the trajectory generation process is explained in more detail in Section 4.1. These parameters depend on the semantic affordance $\mathcal{L}_k$, human poses H_k and the environment E_k, i.e., certain trajectories are more likely for a given semantic affordance, human pose and environment than others. We model this probability $P(\Theta_\Gamma | \mathcal{L}_k, H_k, E_k)$ as:

$$P(\Theta_\Gamma | \mathcal{L}_k, H_k, E_k) \propto \exp\left(-w^T \phi(\mathcal{L}_k, H_k, E_k)\right) \qquad (4)$$

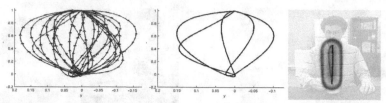

Fig. 4. Illustration of our Trajectory Representation and Generation. Left: The blue lines show the bezier curves fitted to the normalized drinking trajectories from the dataset (the black arrows indicate the direction of motion). Middle: The black lines represent the set of trajectories obtained by clustering the parameters of the drinking trajectories. Right: Drinking activity with predicted trajectory shown in gray and the corresponding probability distribution is shown as the heat map (red corresponds to high probability). The black line denotes the actual ground-truth trajectory.

where w is the weight vector. The features ϕ we consider are the human pose features described in [40] and the relative features of the object w.r.t. the skeleton joints and other objects in the environment, e.g., distance between the object centroid and human joints, distance to the closest object and average distance to all objects in proximity. In the next section, we describe how we represent the mean trajectory function $\mu(\cdot)$, and use it for generating trajectories.

4.1 Trajectory Generation

Objects can follow various types of motion trajectories depending on the active affordance. In this section, we describe the different types of motion trajectories we consider and how we parametrize them to obtain the mean and covariance functions of the Gaussian process. The trajectory types we consider are:

1) Goal-location based trajectories: These trajectories depend on the object's goal location. For example, a cup is moved to the mouth for drinking and moved to a shelf for storing, etc. These trajectories are usually smooth 3D curves.

2) Periodic motion trajectories: These trajectories are characterized by the repetition of certain motions, e.g., a knife is moved up and down multiple times for chopping and a spoon undergoes a periodic circular motion when used to stir.

3) Random motion trajectories: Random trajectories with zig-zag motion are often observed in activities where the goal is not directly related to a particular physical location, for example, cleaning, scrubbing, etc. Even though there might be some repetition/periodic motion in these trajectories owing to their random nature, e.g., scrubbing the same spot over and over again, repetition is not a characteristic property seen in this type of trajectories.

The trajectory types described above cover the majority of the object motions we come across in our daily life. Our framework is generic and other types of trajectories can be included similarly. We now describe how we model each of these trajectory types below.

Goal Based Trajectories. For these trajectories we need to model both the goal location of the object as well as the path taken by the object to reach the

Fig. 5. Distribution over trajectory goal locations. The heatmaps show the distribution over goal locations for *placeability* (left), *pourability* (middle) and *drinkability* (right). The red signifies the most likely goal location for a given affordance.

goal location. Similar to [22], we model these as parametrized cubic equations, in particular Bézier curves, which are often used to generate human hand like motions [6]. Such a cubic Bézier curve (Eq. 5), is parameterized by a set of four points: the start and end point of the trajectory (L_0 and L_3 respectively), and two control points (L_1 and L_2) which define the shape of the curve.

$$B(x) = (1-x)^3 L_0 + 3(1-x)^2 x L_1 + 3(1-x)x^2 L_2 + x^3 L_3, \quad x \in [0,1] \quad (5)$$

We know the current position L_0 of the object, therefore the remaining three control points (L_1, L_2 and L_3) form the trajectory parameters Θ_Γ. Therefore, for the goal based trajectories, the mean trajectory $\mu(\cdot)$ of the Gaussian Process in Eq. 3 is given by Eq. 5 using the estimated parameters.

During learning phase, we first transform and normalize the trajectories in the training data so that all of them have the same start and end points. We estimate the two control points, L_1 and L_2, for each trajectory in the training data. We then cluster these trajectories and obtain a representative set of control points C_l for the affordance class l. Figure 4 shows the trajectories from the training data and those corresponding to the cluster centroids for the *drinking* sub-activity. For a test scenario, we sample the end point L_3 from the distribution over the goal location (as described below) and pair them with the representative set of control points C_l after applying the appropriate inverse transform.

Distribution over goal locations. In order to obtain the probability distribution over the possible goal locations of the object, we define a potential function similar to the one for spatial affordance based on how the object is being interacted with when a particular semantic affordance label is active. We use distance potentials for modeling the distance of the object to skeleton joints and to the other objects in environment and use angular potentials for modeling the orientation with respect to the human pose and other objects in environment, i.e., $P(L_3|\cdots) = \prod_i \psi_{dist_i} \prod_j \psi_{ori_j}$, The parameters are learnt from the training data by maximizing the log likelihood of the goal location for a given active affordance. Figure 5 shows the heatmaps generated for the goal location of the object when its semantic label is *placeable*, *pourable* and *drinkable*.

Periodic Motion Trajectories. For modeling these trajectories, we define two parameterized periodic motion templates – 1) circular and 2) to-and-fro motion. The circular one is used for affordances such as stirring or cycling, and it has four parameters for specifying radius and orientation. The to-and-fro trajectories model the rest of the repetitive motions such as shaking or cutting. These trajectories are parameterized by the curvature, the arc length and the orientation. Similar to the case of the goal-based trajectories, during learning, we compute a representative set of parameters from the training data by clustering and use this basis to represent the trajectories during inference time.

Random Motion Trajectories. These trajectories are the hardest to reconstruct or predict exactly due to their random nature. However, it is easy to generate trajectories which have similar semantic and statistical properties using information from the environment and human poses. For example, for a cleaning action, the goal is to move the cleaner over the object being cleaned. We therefore, generate a trajectory by randomly selecting 3D locations from the target object which are reachable given the human pose and do not result in collisions in the environment. Note that considering the human pose and environment information is important to obtain semantically meaningful activities as shown later in Section 5.1.

4.2   Inference

We focus on the task of inferring the set of physically grounded affordance ξ for the given human intention and environment, i.e., computing the most likely grounding $\xi^* = \arg\max_\xi P(\xi|H, E, I)$. We take a sampling approach for this, where we generate many samples from the learnt conditional distributions and use the sample with the highest likelihood under the joint distribution in Eq. (2) as the final predicted physical grounding of the affordances.

Given (I, H, E), we first sample the semantic affordance labels $\mathcal{L}_k$ from the discrete distribution. We then sample the contact points from the spatial distribution $P(\mathcal{S}_k|\mathcal{L}_k, H_k, E_k, \Theta_\mathcal{S})$. For grounding the motion trajectory, we first sample the trajectory parameters Θ_Γ depending on the type of the motion trajectory associated with the semantic class $\mathcal{L}_k$ as described in Section 4.1. We then construct the mean and covariance functions with these parameters and sample the motion trajectory from the Gaussian process in Eq. (3).

5   Experiments

We first evaluate our approach on the task of generating physically-grounded affordances, and then we apply our approach to the task of labeling activities.

5.1   Generating Physically-Grounded Affordances

We collected a new physically-grounded affordance dataset. It consists of 130 RGBD videos of humans interacting with various objects. There are a total of 4 subjects, **35 object-types** and **17 affordance types**. The activities include {*moving, stirring, pouring, drinking, cutting, eating, cleaning, reading, answering phone, wearing, exercising, hammering, measuring*} and the corresponding affordances are {*movable, stirrable, pourable, pourto, drinkable, cuttable, edible, cleanable, cleaner, readable, hearable, wearable, exercisable, hammer, hammerable, measurer, measurable*}. We use the OpenNI skeleton tracker, to obtain the skeleton poses in these RGBD videos. We obtained the ground-truth object bounding box labels via labeling and SIFT-based tracking using the code given in [23]. The dataset is publicly available (along with open-source code): http://pr.cs.cornell.edu/humanactivities/data.php. We combined our affordance RGB-D videos with those from the CAD-120 dataset [23] and obtain a total of 815 instances for our experiments.

On this combined dataset, we evaluate the affordance prediction task. Here we are given the human intention (or the activity) that is being performed, the initial human pose and environment at the beginning of the activity. We predict the grounded affordances ξ, i.e., the sequence of semantic labels, spatial distribution and the object motion trajectories.

Evaluation Metric. We perform four-fold cross-validation by dividing the data into four folds, with each fold having data belonging to one subject. We train the parameters of our model on three folds and test it on the fourth fold. Specifically, we always test on a *new subject*. We use the following metrics for evaluation:
1) *Spatial Likelihood.* For evaluating the spatial affordances, we compute the likelihood of the observed contact regions under the predicted distribution.
2) *Trajectory Metric.* For evaluating the quality of the predicted temporal affordance, we compute the modified Hausdorff distance (MHD) as a physical measure of the distance between the predicted object motion trajectories and the true object trajectory from the test data.[1]

Baseline Algorithms. We compare our method against the following baselines:
1) *Chance:* It selects a random training instance for the given human intention and uses its affordances as the predictions.
2) *Nearest Neighbor Exemplar:* It first finds an example from the training data which is the most similar to the test sample and uses the affordances from that training sample as the predicted affordances. To find the exemplar, we perform a nearest neighbor search in the feature space for the first frame, using the features described in Section 3.
3) *Koppula et al. [22]:* This method models the goal-based trajectories with Bézier curves (Eq. 5). The L_1 and L_2 parameters are learnt from the trajectories in the training data and the object's target location is modeled using the spatial distribution over goal locations as described in Section 4.1. This method does not model the uncertainty in the trajectories.
4) *Data-driven uniform sampling:* We first compute the set of possible trajectory parameters, Θ_Γ, from the data and then uniformly sample parameters for trajectory generation.
5) *Our model - Estimated Goal:* Our model where we estimate the goal location and sample the rest of the trajectory parameters from a uniform distribution.

---

[1] The MHD metric allows for local time warping by finding the best local point correspondence over a small temporal window. When the temporal window is zero, MHD is same as Euclidean distance between the trajectories. We normalize the distance by the length of the trajectory in order to compare performance across trajectories of different lengths.

Table 1. Temporal Affordance Evaluation. Over 4-fold cross-validation, testing on a new subject in each time, we report the error (in centimeters) in predicting the temporal affordances. In addition to MHD metric (see text), we also report the error in predicting the end-point for goal-based trajectories.

Model	End Point Dist. for Goal-based traj.	Error per Trajectory Type (MHD in cm)			Average Error (MHD in cm)
		Goal-based	Periodic	Random	
Chance	56.4	53.3	67.0	75.4	65.2
Nearest Neighbor (NN)	32.7	32.0	40.3	36.4	36.2
Data-driven uniform sampling	47.7	20.6	34.6	50.8	35.3
Koppula et al. [22]	19.4	11.8	-	29.4	20.6
Our Method - Est. Goal + Str. Line Traj.	19.4	10.8	15.7	19.5	15.3
Our Method - Est. Goal + NN	19.4	9.3	13.5	19.5	14.1
Our Full Method	19.4	**8.9**	**10.3**	**19.5**	**12.9**

6) Our model - Estimated Goal + Straight Line Trajectory: Our model where we predict straight line trajectories to the estimated goal location.

7) Our method - Estimated Goal + Near Neighbor Trajectory: Our model where we estimate the goal location and use the remaining trajectory parameters of the Nearest Neighbor Exemplar described above.

Results. Table 1 shows the results for predicting the temporal affordance. It shows that the baseline methods give quite high error. However, using our estimation method gives significant improvements. Examples of the observed and estimated trajectories for the various affordances can be seen in Fig. 6. We discuss the following aspect of our approach in more detail.

1) Going Beyond Target Locations for Modeling Spatial Affordances. Our model allows learning affordance-dependent interactions with objects. For example, Fig. 3 shows the learnt spatial interaction heatmap for the *openable* and *movable* affordances. This goes beyond the target location prediction proposed by Koppula et al. [22], where they predict the reachable regions on the objects by predicting the target location of the hand joints. In their work, it only helped in anticipating the most likely *reaching trajectory* for a short duration. However, for the purpose of object manipulation, it is desirable that the reached locations on the objects support the intention of the reach, for example, if the intention is to open the object, the reached location should allow for opening the object, and this is captured by our spatial affordance model as can be seen in Fig. 3. We evaluate the spatial affordances by computing the likelihood of the observed contact points under the learnt distributions. We obtain an average likelihood of 0.6 for the observed contact points compared to a likelihood of 3.1×10^{-5} for randomly chosen contact points on the object.

2) How Important is Modeling the Probability Over Possible Trajectories? . As compared to the baselines which select a trajectory (or the corresponding parameters) from the training data, our method achieves a significant reduction in trajectory error metric. This shows the importance of modeling the uncertainties and variations in the temporal affordances that vary with the human intentions as well as with the surrounding environments.

3) Choice of Mean Trajectory Function. Our model reduces the trajectory error metric significantly compared to the baseline methods, even when we approximate the trajectories as straight lines (Table 1-row 5). However, by incorporating the shape of the trajectories into the mean functions (Bézier curves

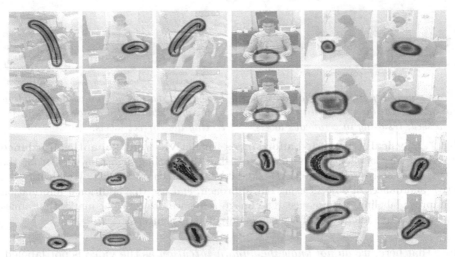

Fig. 6. Learned Temporal Affordance Distributions. The images show the observed trajectories (rows 1 and 3) and the corresponding predicted trajectories (rows 2 and 4) as sampled trajectory points and the distribution as a heatmap. Red signifies higher probability. The affordances in top two rows are (left to right): *placeable*, *pourable*, *wearable*, *readable*, *cleaner* and *cleaner*, and the bottom two rows are: *cutter*, *stirrer*, *hammer*, *shakable*, *exercisable* and *salter*. The trajectory points of the *cleaner* affordance are not shown for clarity.

as mean functions for goal-based trajectories and the curvature parameter for periodic trajectories), we can achieve further reduction in the error metric. Also, as we can see from Fig. 6, goal-based trajectories are easier to estimate as they are more deterministic in nature, but the rest have a large variation in the way the objects are moved, for example in the cleaning or shaking activities. Our approach allows us to cope with these variations in a principled way by using appropriate mean functions to modeling the different trajectory types.

5.2 Activity and Semantic Affordance Labeling

Previous activity labeling approaches [23,22] heavily rely on human poses for temporal segmentation and labeling, which sometimes miss boundaries between sub-activities and result in labeling errors. Koppula et al. [23] show that good temporal segmentation is very important for the labeling task. We show that using additional information in the form of grounded affordances can provide an important cue for temporal segmentations. As can be seen in Fig. 7-right, we identify better transitions between the activities using our method, resulting in better labeling. We do this by finding the active affordance for each object in sampled video frames, and identify where changes in active affordances occur.

The intuition behind this is that a change in the active affordance of an object usually happens with change in the current activity. Therefore, our grounded affordances can be used to identify temporal boundaries with high probability.

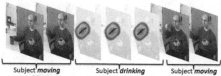

Subject *moving moveable* object   Subject *moving moveable* object   Subject *drinking* from *drinkable* object   Subject *moving moveable* object

When physically-grounded affordances are not considered, the drinkability affordance is missed, resulting in erroneous labels.   Using our spatial and temporal grounding of the drinkability affordance results in detecting the correct labels.

Fig. 7. Physically-grounded affordances for activity and semantic affordance labeling. The labeling results generated using the labeling algorithm of [24] for the *having meal* activity from the CAD-120 dataset is shown on the left. We identify the active affordances of objects using our approach, and use this additional information to improve labeling performance. The image sequence on the right marks the frames where the active affordance of the cup is detected as *drinkable*.

Note that here, *we do not know the human intention* as the video is not labeled. To find the active affordance, we compute the likelihood of the observations under our learned affordance model and take the one which has the highest value. This gives us temporal boundaries in the video based on the active affordances. We evaluated our approach on the CAD-120 dataset [23], which has 4 subjects performing 120 high-level activities and each high-level activity is a sequence of sub-activities. We take the labeling output of [24] and modify it by including the temporal boundaries computed as above. This gives us a new segmentation hypothesis, which we label using the full energy function described in [24].

Table 2 compares the labeling metrics for the various segmentation methods which use uniform length segmentations, heuristic segmentation hypotheses [23], energy function based segmentation [24], and our method of using additional affordance based segments. Our approach im-

Table 2. Activity Detection Results. 4-fold cross validation results on CAD-120 dataset (tested on a new subject).

model	Sub-activity Detection		Object Affordance Detection	
	Accuracy	f1-score	Accuracy	f1-score
chance	10.0	10.0	8.3	8.3
Uniform+Heuristic[23]	68.2	66.3	83.9	69.6
Koppula et al. [24]	70.3	70.2	**85.4**	71.9
Our Method	**70.5**	**71.2**	84.6	**72.6**

proves the f1-scores for semantic affordance labeling as well as activity detection. We observe that our grounded affordance model mainly helps in improving precision and recall values of infrequent classes.

6 Conclusion

Our work extended the affordance-based understanding of objects, where we considered grounding the affordances into a given environment as: the semantic affordances, the spatial locations and the temporal trajectories in the 3D space. We presented a generative probabilistic graphical model for modeling the uncertainty in the grounded affordances. Our model used Gaussian Processes for representing the uncertainty in the trajectories. We then evaluated our approach on predicting the grounded affordances and showed that our approach improves performance on labeling activities.

There are several directions for future work: 1) The space of objects and affordances is significantly richer than what our work have considered—scaling to a larger and richer object and affordance set would be useful; 2) There are many possible applications of our grounded object affordances approach. While we have considered RGB-D activity detection, this approach could be useful in the area of human-robot interaction, as well as in other applications such as 3D scene understanding, robot planning, function-based object retrieval, and so on.

Acknowledgements. We thank Hakim S. and Xingyu X. for their help with the data collection. This work was supported by ARO award W911NF- 12-1-0267, Google PhD Fellowship to Koppula, and NSF Career Award to Saxena.

References

1. Aksoy, E.E., Abramov, A., Dörr, J., Ning, K., Dellen, B., Wörgötter, F.: Learning the semantics of object-action relations by observation. IJRR 30(10), 1229–1249 (2011)
2. Aldoma, A., Tombari, F., Vincze, M.: Supervised learning of hidden and non-hidden 0-order affordances and detection in real scenes. In: ICRA (2012)
3. Anand, A., Koppula, H., Joachims, T., Saxena, A.: Contextually guided semantic labeling and search for 3d point clouds. IJRR (2012)
4. Borghi, A.: Object concepts and action: Extracting affordances from objects parts. In: Acta Psyhologica (2004)
5. Delaitre, V., Fouhey, D.F., Laptev, I., Sivic, J., Gupta, A., Efros, A.A.: Scene semantics from long-term observation of people. In: Fitzgibbon, A., Lazebnik, S., Perona, P., Sato, Y., Schmid, C. (eds.) ECCV 2012, Part VI. LNCS, vol. 7577, pp. 284–298. Springer, Heidelberg (2012)
6. Faraway, J., Reed, M., Wang, J.: Modeling three-dimensional trajectories by using bezier curves with application to hand motion. J. Royal Stats. Soc. Series C-Applied Statistics 56 (2007)
7. Farhadi, A., Endres, I., Hoiem, D., Forsyth, D.: Describing objects by their attributes. In: CVPR (2009)
8. Fisher, M., Savva, M., Hanrahan, P.: Characterizing structural relationships in scenes using graph kernels. In: SIGGRAPH (2011)
9. Gibson, J.J.: The ecological approach to visual perception. Houghton Mifflin (1979)
10. Grabner, H., Gall, J., Van Gool, L.: What makes a chair a chair? In: CVPR (2011)
11. Gupta, A., Davis, L.S.: Objects in action: An approach for combining action understanding and object perception. In: CVPR (2007)
12. Gupta, A., Satkin, S., Efros, A.A., Hebert, M.: From 3d scene geometry to human workspace. In: CVPR (2011)
13. Hermans, T., Rehg, J.M., Bobick, A.: Decoupling behavior, perception, and control for autonomous learning of affordances. In: ICRA (2013)
14. Hermans, T., Rehg, J.M., Bobick, A.: Affordance prediction via learned object attributes. In: ICRA: Workshop on Semantic Perception, Mapping, and Exploration (2011)
15. Jain, A., Wojcik, B., Joachims, T., Saxena, A.: Learning trajectory preferences for manipulators via iterative improvement. In: Neural Information Processing Systems, NIPS (2013)

16. Jiang, Y., Koppula, H., Saxena, A.: Hallucinated humans as the hidden context for labeling 3d scenes. In: CVPR (2013)

17. Jiang, Y., Lim, M., Saxena, A.: Learning object arrangements in 3d scenes using human context. In: ICML (2012)

18. Jiang, Y., Saxena, A.: Modeling high-dimensional humans for activity anticipation using gaussian process latent crfs. In: Robotics: Science and Systems, RSS (2014)

19. Kjellstrom, H., Romero, J., Kragic, D.: Visual object-action recognition: Inferring object affordances from human demonstration. In: CVIU (2011)

20. Konidaris, G., Kuindersma, S., Grupen, R., Barto, A.: Robot learning from demonstration by constructing skill trees. IJRR 31 (2012)

21. Koppula, H., Jain, A., Saxena, A.: Anticipatory planning for human-robot teams. ISER (2014)

22. Koppula, H., Saxena, A.: Anticipating human activities using object affordances for reactive robotic response. In: RSS (2013)

23. Koppula, H.S., Gupta, R., Saxena, A.: Learning human activities and object affordances from rgb-d videos. IJRR 32(8) (2013)

24. Koppula, H.S., Saxena, A.: Learning spatio-temporal structure from rgb-d videos for human activity detection and anticipation. In: ICML (2013)

25. Liu, J., Kuipers, B., Savarese, S.: Recognizing human actions by attributes. In: CVPR (2011)

26. Lopes, M., Santos-Victor, J.: Visual learning by imitation with motor representations. IEEE Trans. Systems, Man, and Cybernetics, Part B: Cybernetics 35(3), 438–449 (2005)

27. Lorken, C., Hertzberg, J.: Grounding planning operators by affordances. In: Int'l Conf. Cog. Sys. (2008)

28. McCandless, T., Grauman, K.: Object-centric spatio-temporal pyramids for egocentric activity recognition. In: British Machine Vision Conference, BMVC (2013)

29. Misra, D.K., Sung, J., Lee, K., Saxena, A.: Tell me dave: Context-sensitive grounding of natural language to mobile manipulation instructions. In: Robotics: Science and Systems, RSS (2014)

30. Montesano, L., Lopes, M., Bernardino, A., Santos-Victor, J.: Learning object affordances: from sensory–motor coordination to imitation. IEEE Trans. Robotics 24(1), 15–26 (2008)

31. Montesano, L., Lopes, M., Bernardino, A., Santos-Victor, J.: Learning object affordances: From sensory–motor coordination to imitation. IEEE Trans. Robotics 24(1), 15–26 (2008)

32. Neisser, U.: Cognition and Reality: Principles and Implications of Cognitive Psychology. W. H. Freeman (1976)

33. Norman: The Psychology of Everyday Things. Basic Books (1988)

34. Pandey, A.K., Alami, R.: Mightability maps: A perceptual level decisional framework for co-operative and competitive human-robot interaction. In: IROS (2010)

35. Ridge, B., Skočaj, D., Leonardis, A.: Unsupervised learning of basic object affordances from object properties. In: Proc. 14th Comp. Vision Winter Work, CVWW (2009)

36. Russakovsky, O., Fei-Fei, L.: Attribute learning in large-scale datasets. In: ECCV Int'l Work. Parts & Attributes (2010)

37. Sahin, E., Cakmak, M., Dogar, M.R., Ugur, E., Ucoluk, G.: To afford or not to afford: A new formalization of affordances toward affordance-based robot control. Adaptive Behavior 15(4) (2007)

38. Stark, M., Lies, P., Zillich, M., Wyatt, J.C., Schiele, B.: Functional object class detection based on learned affordance cues. In: Gasteratos, A., Vincze, M., Tsotsos, J.K. (eds.) ICVS 2008. LNCS, vol. 5008, pp. 435–444. Springer, Heidelberg (2008)
39. Sun, J., Moore, J.L., Bobick, A., Rehg, J.M.: Learning visual object categories for robot affordance prediction. IJRR (2009)
40. Sung, J., Ponce, C., Selman, B., Saxena, A.: Unstructured human activity detection from rgbd images. In: ICRA (2012)
41. Ugur, E., Sachin, E., Oztop, E.: Affordance learning from range data for multi-step planning. In: Epirob (2009)
42. Wu, C., Lenz, I., Saxena, A.: Hierarchical semantic labeling for task-relevant rgb-d perception. In: RSS (2014)
43. Yao, B., Fei-Fei, L.: Modeling mutual context of object and human pose in human-object interaction activities. In: CVPR (2010)

Author Index

Printed in the United States
By Bookmasters